FEDERAL INCOME TAXATION
OF CORPORATIONS AND SHAREHOLDERS

by

BORIS I. BITTKER

Southmayd Professor of Law, Yale University

and

JAMES S. EUSTICE

Professor of Law, New York University

Second Edition

FEDERAL TAX PRESS, INC.

Branford, Conn.

Library of Congress Catalog Card No. 66-25746

PRINTED IN THE UNITED STATES OF AMERICA
FOURTH PRINTING

to

GERALD L. WALLACE
Teacher, Colleague, and Friend

Preface

There have been many statutory, judicial, and administrative developments in the area to which this book is devoted since its publication in 1959. Even so, and despite many friendly and flattering demands from practitioners and teachers for a revised edition, I doubt that I could have summoned up the enthusiasm and energy necessary for the task had I not succeeded in enlisting the collaboration of James S. Eustice. The revision is a true joint product, in which the original text predominates or is submerged depending upon the extent of the post-1959 developments. Although Mr. Eustice's contribution is reflected on every page, his responsibility for Chapter 12 (Corporate Reorganizations) and Chapter 13 (Corporate Tax Attributes: Transfer, Survival, and Multiplication) is especially great.

As in the case of the first edition, I am indebted to several generations of Yale law students for their suggestions, and I have also had the benefit of comments by a number of readers of the first edition. Mr. Eustice and I are also very grateful to Gersham Goldstein, of the University of Cincinnati Law School, for reading the manuscript of this revision and making many helpful comments and suggestions.

B.I.B.

New Haven, Conn.
June, 1966

CONDENSED TABLE OF CONTENTS

TABLE OF CONTENTS

Ch. 9. Complete Liquidations

Ch. 10. Collapsible Corporations

Ch. 11. Corporate Divisions

Ch. 12. Corporate Reorganizations

Part A.   General Considerations

Part B.   Definitions of Reorganization

Ch. 13. Corporate Tax Attributes: Transfer, Survival, and Multiplication

Part A.   General Background and Introduction

Part B.   Carryovers and §381

Part C.   Limitations on Enjoyment of Corporate Tax Attributes

Part D.   Multiple Corporations

Ch. 14. Corporate Elections Under Subchapter S

FEDERAL INCOME TAXATION
OF CORPORATIONS AND SHAREHOLDERS

Chapter One

INTRODUCTORY

Sec. 1.01. The corporate income tax

The federal government has taxed the income of corporations continuously since the Payne-Aldrich Tariff Act of 1909, which ante-dated the adoption of the Sixteenth Amendment by four years. Corporate income was taxed even earlier, by the income tax of 1894, but the Supreme Court held in Pollock v. Farmers' Loan & Trust Co., 158 U.S. 601, 3 AFTR 2602 (1895), that a federal tax on income from real estate and personal property was a "direct" tax that had to be apportioned among the states in proportion to population, under Article I, Section 9, Clause 4 of the Constitution,[1] and that the rest of the taxing scheme (including the tax on corporations) was so inextricably bound up with these unconstitutional portions that the entire statute must fall. Profiting by this experience, the 1909 Act was levied "with respect to the carrying on or doing business" by corporations (as well as joint stock companies, associations, and insurance companies); and this change in approach led the Supreme Court in Flint v. Stone Tracy Co., 220 U.S. 107, 3 AFTR 2834 (1911), to find that what Congress had imposed was not a "direct" tax, but an "excise" or "indirect" tax upon "the exercise of the privilege of doing business in a corporate capacity":

> . . . [T]he tax is imposed not upon the franchises of the corporation irrespective of their use in business, nor upon the property of the corporation, but upon the doing of corporate or insurance

[1] The principal constitutional provisions regarding taxation are:
Article I, Section 8, Clause 1:
The Congress shall have Power To lay and collect Taxes, Duties, Imposts and Excises, to pay the Debts and provide for the common Defence and general Welfare of the United States; but all Duties, Imposts and Excises shall be uniform throughout the United States.
Article I, Section 9, Clause 4:
No Capitation, or other direct, Tax shall be laid, unless in Proportion to the Census or Enumeration herein before directed to be taken.
Amendment XVI:
The Congress shall have power to lay and collect taxes on incomes, from whatever source derived, without apportionment among the several States, and without regard to any census or enumeration.
See also Article I, Section 2, Clause 3, and Article I, Section 7, Clause 1.

business and with respect to the carrying on thereof, in a sum
equivalent to one per centum upon the entire net income over
and above $5,000 received from all sources during the year; that
is, when imposed in this manner it is a tax upon the doing of
business with the advantages which inhere in the peculiarities
of corporate or joint stock organizations of the character described. (220 U.S. at 145-6.)

Since the tax was not a "direct" tax, the Constitution did not require
it to be apportioned according to population. The Court then went
on to hold that corporate activities were subject to federal taxation
even though carried on under a state charter, that the tax was "uniform throughout the United States" as required by the Constitution
even though individual proprietors and partnerships were not taxed,
that the tax was not a "direct" tax merely because it reached income
from municipal bonds and other nontaxable securities, and that various other constitutional objections were equally invalid.

By virtue of Flint v. Stone Tracy Co., the corporate income tax
was well entrenched in the federal fiscal system by 1913, when the
Sixteenth Amendment, empowering Congress "to lay and collect
taxes on incomes, from whatever source derived, without apportionment among the several states, and without regard to any census or
enumeration," was adopted. Because Flint v. Stone Tracy Co. vali-
dated the 1909 measure as a tax on "the exercise of the privilege of
doing business in a corporate capacity," however, it did not explicitly
destroy the protection afforded by Pollock v. Farmers' Loan and Trust
Co. to "passive" income received from real estate or personal property by a corporation that engaged in no other activities.[2] By empowering Congress to reach such income without apportionment, the

---

[2] In Flint v. Stone Tracy Co., the Court held that income from investments
in municipal bonds and other nontaxable securities and in real estate and personal property not used in the business could be taxed:
> It is . . . well settled by the decisions of this court that when the sovereign
> authority has exercised the right to tax a legitimate subject of taxation as
> an exercise of a franchise or privilege, it is no objection that the measure
> of taxation is found in the income produced in part from property which
> of itself considered is non-taxable. Applying that doctrine to this case, the
> measure of taxation being the income of the corporation from all sources,
> as that is but the measure of a privilege tax within the lawful authority
> of Congress to impose, it is no valid objection that this measure includes,
> in part at least, property which as such could not be directly taxed. (220
> U.S. at 165).

The Court did not have any occasion to decide whether income from passive
investments could be taxed if the corporation was a mere holding company,
since such a corporation was not engaged in "doing business" within the meaning of the taxing statute. See Zonne v. Minneapolis Syndicate, 220 U.S. 187, 3
AFTR 2853 (1911); McCoach v. Minehill & Schuylkill Haven R. Co., 228 U.S.
295, 3 AFTR 2872 (1913).

Sixteenth Amendment may have enlarged the federal power to tax corporate income. With this possible exception, however, the federal corporate income tax, unlike the federal income tax on individuals, seems to owe nothing to the Sixteenth Amendment.

The 1909 Act imposed a tax of 1 percent of net income, with an exemption of $5,000 per corporation. Returns were filed for 1909 by about 262,500 corporations, and the aggregate yield of the tax for that year was about $21 million, which represented 2.2 percent of federal revenues. By contrast, the corporate income tax rate is now (1966) 22 percent of the first $25,000 of corporate taxable income and 48 percent of the excess over $25,000.[3] For the fiscal year 1961-2, 1,200,000 corporate returns were filed, reporting an aggregate tax liability of $22.2 billion, which represented about 25 percent of federal revenues.

Under the statutory scheme in force today, every corporation (except insurance companies, regulated investment companies, foreign corporations not engaged in business in the United States, and a few others) is subject to a normal tax of 22 percent of its taxable income and a surtax of 26 percent of taxable income over $25,000. As in the case of individuals, however, the rate of tax on the excess of net long-term capital gain over net short-term capital loss, if any, may not exceed 25 percent. The term "corporation" is defined by §7701(a)(3) to include "associations" and "joint stock companies," so the tax is imposed on some enterprises that do not constitute corporations under state law. With exceptions that will be discussed hereafter, the "taxable income" of a corporation is computed in the same fashion as an individual's taxable income. Thus, the corporation's annual accounting period (calendar year or fiscal year) is employed; the corporation's regular accounting method (cash receipts and disbursements, accrual, completed contract, etc.) is controlling, unless it does not clearly reflect income; the corporation must include in gross income, and may deduct, most of the items that are taxable to or deductible by the individual; and the Internal Revenue Service may reallocate income and deductions among two or more businesses under common control, in order to reflect income accurately, whether they are incorporated or not. Similarly, the grand principles or "doctrines" of income taxation (e.g., no assignment-of-earned-income, substance-over-form, business-purpose, and step-transactions[4]) are

---

[3] The corporate rates were changed by the Revenue Act of 1964 from 30 and 22 percent to 22 and 28 percent for taxable years beginning in 1964 and to 22 and 26 percent for years beginning after Dec. 31, 1964. §11, 1954 Code.

[4] *Infra,* Sec. 1.05.

applicable to corporations as well as to individuals. Finally, most of the administrative provisions of the Internal Revenue Code — governing the filing of returns and payment of tax, assessments, collection, interest on deficiencies and overpayments, penalties, procedure in the Internal Revenue Service, and litigation — are equally applicable to both corporations and individuals.[5]

The 1964 reduction in the normal corporate rate from 30 percent to 22 percent increased the value to the taxpaying corporation of the $25,000 surtax exemption, and thus provided an additional incentive to the conduct of business through "multiple" corporations. Not wishing to rely entirely on the government's other weapons (see generally *infra*, Ch. 13) to combat the tax-motivated use of multiple corporations, Congress enacted §§1561-1563 as an additional safeguard. These provisions require the "component members" of a "controlled group of corporations" (as defined)[6] to divide a single $25,000 surtax exemption between them (either prorata, or as they elect under regulations), unless they elect under §1562 to retain their individual surtax exemptions but to pay an additional tax of 6 percent on the first $25,000 of taxable income. Since the additional tax imposed on electing corporations by §1562 does not eliminate the surtax exemptions but only reduces their potential value by $1,500 per exemption, the election will ordinarily be the preferable alternative. An election under §1562 does not preclude a denial of the surtax exemption under §269 or §1551, but the additional 6 percent tax will be taken into account in computing the deficiency if the exemption is disallowed. For general discussion, see *infra*, Ch. 13.

As will be seen in Chapter 2, where the major deviations between the corporate income tax and the individual income tax are discussed, the most vexing tax problems in the use of the corporation as a method of carrying on business do not arise in determining the corporation's income tax liability. The difficulties arise, rather, because distributed corporate income is taxed to the shareholder while undistributed income is not, because an exchange of stock or securities by the investor may or may not be an appropriate occasion for recognizing gain or loss, and because transactions between a corporation and its shareholders are often not conducted at arm's length. Chapters 3

---

[5] For corporations with estimated tax liabilities exceeding $100,000, 1964 amendments to §6074, §6154, and §6655 provide for a speed-up in current tax payments on a graduated basis from 1964 to 1969.

[6] The term "controlled group of corporations" is elaborately defined by §1563(a); in general, it includes all corporations owned directly or indirectly, to the extent of 80 percent of voting power or total value, by a common parent corporation or one individual, estate or trust. Ownership is determined by the application of the constructive ownership rules of §1563(e).

through 14 of this book are concerned in detail with the ramifications of these problems, but a few words of introduction may be in order.

Sec. 1.02.   Undistributed corporate income

Under the Code, corporate income is taxed to the corporation, and the shareholders are taxed only when, as, and if the corporate earnings are distributed to them.[7] This means that the corporation's undistributed earnings are taxed at the relatively flat, or non-graduated, corporate income tax rates and are not subjected to the more steeply graduated individual income tax rates. The contrast between the corporate and individual rates was sharper before World War II, but even now the marginal rate on individuals ranges from 14 percent to 70 percent, while the corporate rate is 22 percent of the first $25,000 of taxable income and 48 percent of the balance. In more specific terms, the following table compares the tax liability of a corporation with the liability of an unmarried individual receiving the same amount of taxable income.

TABLE I
Tax Burden—Proprietorship vs. Corporation*

Taxable Income	Individual Liability	Corporate Liability
$25,000	$8,530	$5,500
50,000	22,590	17,500
100,000	55,490	41,500
250,000	160,490	113,500
500,000	335,490	233,500

*The tax burden reflected by the table assumes that the corporate earnings are accumulated rather than distributed. The effect of a distribution of the corporate earnings is shown by Table II (*infra*, Sec. 1.03).

This disparity between the relatively flat corporate rates and the graduated individual rates is a constant inducement to the accumu-

---

[7] The government argued in Eisner v. Macomber, 252 U.S. 189, 3 AFTR 3020 (1920), that a shareholder could be taxed, under the Sixteenth Amendment, on his "share in the accumulated profits of the corporation even before division by the declaration of a dividend of any kind." The argument was rejected, "since the Amendment applies to income only, and what is called the stockholder's share in the accumulated profits of the company is capital, not income." 252 U.S. at 219. Whether the Supreme Court would adhere to this view today is problematical, but Congress has not attempted to compel shareholders to report undistributed corporate income (except in the limited instance of foreign personal holding companies and controlled foreign corporations, *infra*, Sec. 6.40 and Sec. 6.51). Optional inclusion of undistributed income, as under Subchapter S (*infra*, Ch. 14) or the "consent dividend" procedure (*infra*, Sec. 6.09) is, of course, something else again.

lation of business or investment income in a corporation, where it will be shielded against a hostile tax collector. As will be seen, however, the tax collector in turn has been armed with statutory weapons to attack undistributed corporate earnings in the more blatant cases of tax avoidance. One weapon is the accumulated earnings tax (*infra*, Ch. 6), imposed by §531 on the undistributed income of a corporation that is formed or availed of for the purpose of avoiding the income tax by accumulating instead of distributing its earnings. Ordinarily this tax is applicable only if the corporation has accumulated its earnings beyond the reasonable needs of its business. The other weapon is the personal holding company tax (*infra*, Ch. 6), imposed by §541 on the undistributed income of a "personal holding company," which, roughly speaking, embraces corporations whose principal function is the collection of dividends, interest, and other passive income, as well as so-called 'incorporated talents" and incorporated country estates and yachts. Relatively few corporations run afoul of either the accumulated earnings tax of §531 or the personal holding company tax of §541, however, and the use of the corporation as a temporary or permanent refuge from the graduated individual income tax rates is one of the principal landmarks of our tax landscape.

Of course, earnings can be accumulated in the corporation only if the shareholders have no immediate need for the funds for living or other personal expenses. Some shareholders are in this happy position, and for them one of the attractions of the corporation may be that business or investment income can be accumulated year after year, with the stock being eventually passed on at death. The heirs may then liquidate the corporation or sell the stock; and, since the stock will have a "stepped-up basis" under §1014 equal to its fair market value on the date of the testator's death, they may receive the corporate assets or their equivalent in sales proceeds at no tax cost. In this event, the corporate earnings will not have been subjected to the individual income tax, either during the original shareholder's life or even thereafter.

If the financial status of the shareholder does not permit such a dramatic exploitation of the corporation's tax avoidance potential, he will have to be content with half-way measures. One possibility—and this is probably typical of most successful closely-held corporations—is to draw down in salary and dividends enough of the earnings to meet living expenses, allowing only the balance to accumulate. Another possibility, as either an alternative or a supplement to the withdrawal of funds in the form of salary or dividends, is the sale of stock, since the profit on the sale is ordinarily taxed as long-term capital gain at the maximum rate of 25 percent. More sophisticated devices that enable the shareholder to realize on the corporate earnings without paying tax at the graduated individual income tax rate are redemptions of stock, partial liquidations, and complete liquidations, all of which on occasion are treated as sales of stock, with the profit being taxed as long-term capital gain. As will be seen later (Chapters 7-10), however, these devices may explode in the shareholder's face if he is not careful. Still another possibility is the accumulation of earnings in the corporation, with the stock being used for intra-family or other gifts; the donees may then hold the stock, reporting dividends on their individual returns at a rate that may be lower than would have been paid by the donor, or sell it, reporting the profit as long-term capital gain.

Sec. 1.03.   Distributed corporate income

Although accumulated corporate income is not subjected to the graduated individual income tax rates, the other face of the coin is that corporate income that is distributed as dividends to the shareholders is taxable as personal income. This characteristic of the federal tax system is the so-called "double taxation" of corporate income. It may be illustrated by an extension of Table I (*supra*, Sec. 1.02), on the assumption that the corporation is entirely owned by one man and that its income, after payment of the corporate tax, is distributed to him in full. The following table compares the "take-home" results of given amounts of income, received as an individual proprietor or as the sole shareholder of a corporation:

TABLE II
Proprietorship vs. Corporation (income distributed)

Taxable Income	Proprietorship (Net after taxes)*	Sole Shareholder-Corporation		
		Distributed**	Tax on Shareholder***	Net after taxes
$25,000	$16,470	$19,500	$5,845	$13,655
50,000	27,410	32,500	12,485	20,015
100,000	44,510	58,500	27,860	30,640
250,000	89,510	136,500	81,040	55,460
500,000	164,510	266,500	172,040	94,460

*Income less individual tax liability (from Table I, *supra*, Sec. 1.02).
**Income less corporate tax liability (from Table I).
***Ignoring the $100 dividend exclusion of §116.

This is not the place for an extended discussion of the equity and economic consequences of imposing independent taxes on the corporation and its shareholders; but surely the real issue is not whether in legal form there are two separate taxes. For many closely-held enterprises, which can choose between the corporation and either the proprietorship or the partnership as a method of doing business, the Code offers an election,[8] and some find it cheaper, rather than more expensive, to follow the "double tax" route. For those that must use the corporation for business reasons, the real issue is not the validity of the label "double taxation," but whether the corporation is taxed more heavily than competing proprietorships and partnerships, without compensating tax or other advantages. And for publicly-held enterprises, the real issue is whether corporate earnings are over-taxed (or under-taxed) in relation to other types of income and the demands of national fiscal policy, problems that in turn pose the unsolved question of whether the corporation income tax is shifted so that its burden does not rest upon the shareholders.[9]

For our purposes, it is sufficient to note that the "double taxation" of corporate income was mitigated to a degree in 1954 by the enactment of §116, providing for the exclusion of the first $50 of dividends received by an individual, and §34, providing that 4 percent of the dividends received by an individual could be credited against his income tax. By the Revenue Act of 1964, the credit was reduced to 2 percent for dividends received during 1964 and repealed for dividends received thereafter; but the exclusion allowed by §116 was simultaneously increased from $50 to $100. See infra, Sec. 5.06. The dividends-received exclusion of §116 is allowed to non-corporate taxpayers only; if the shareholder receiving the dividends is a corporation, it is subject to the special rules governing intra-corporate dividends discussed infra, Sec. 2.25.

Although the dividends-received exclusion granted by §116 to individuals is only a mild palliative, many shareholders, especially in the case of closely-held corporations, are able to adopt measures of self-help to reduce the impact of the separate taxes on the corpora-

[8] The choice was expanded in 1954 by the enactment of §1361 (permitting unincorporated enterprises to elect to be taxed as corporations, infra, Sec. 2.11) and again in 1958 by Subchapter S (permitting some corporations to elect a special form of taxation under which the corporation pays no tax and the earnings are taxed directly to the shareholders, infra, Ch. 14).

See generally Strecker, When Will the Corporate Form Save Taxes? 18 Vand. L. Rev. 1695 (1965).

[9] See Holland, *The Income-Tax Burden on Stockholders* (1958); Goode, *The Corporation Income Tax* (1951); Marberry, On the Burden of the Corporate-Income Tax, 11 Nat'l Tax J. 323 (1958); and Goode, Who Bears the Corporation Income Tax? 32 U. of Chi. L. Rev. 410 (1965).

tion and individual. Since wages and salaries paid by the corporation are deductible as business expenses under §162 in computing its taxable income, any amounts paid to shareholder-employees in this form will avoid the corporate income tax and be taxed only to the recipients. For many closely-held businesses, this may afford a method of withdrawing business profits in large part or even in their entirety, with the result that in these instances the federal income tax liability is about the same as though the enterprise had been conducted as a proprietorship or partnership. Such an arrangement is feasible only to the extent that the compensation paid to the shareholder-employees can be justified as "a reasonable allowance . . . for personal services actually rendered" so as to be deductible under §162; if the compensation is excessive, it will be disallowed as a corporate deduction *pro tanto* (*infra*, Sec. 5.05). Although the possibility of disallowance is always present, especially if earnings fluctuate widely and shareholder salaries are adjusted from year to year to exhaust the earnings, it is common knowledge that many closely-held corporations are able to pay out their entire business earnings, give or take a few dollars, year after year.[10] Other methods by which shareholders may withdraw funds from the corporation in a form that will give rise to a deduction at the corporate level are: interest on loans to the corporation; rent on property leased by the shareholders to the corporation; and royalties on patents owned by the shareholders and used by the corporation under licenses. As with salaries, however, these payments must be justified as bona fide arrangements rather than disguised dividends (*infra*, Sec. 5.05).

Another method of reducing the impact of the separate taxation of corporate income and of distributed dividends is, as mentioned earlier, to realize the corporate profits in the form of long-term capital gain. In its simplest form, this can be done by accumulating earnings in the corporation and then selling the stock. If the profit on selling the stock is equal to the accumulated earnings, the total tax burden will consist of the corporate tax on its income plus the shareholder's tax on his long-term capital gain. This burden is compared with the tax that is imposed on an individual proprietor by Table III, which extends Table I (*supra*, Sec. 1.02) for a ten-year period, assuming

10 For example, of 1,190,000 corporate returns filed for the fiscal year 1961-62, 649,000 corporations reported taxable income within plus or minus $5,000 of breaking even. See U.S. Treas. Dept., *Statistics of Income 1961-62, Corporation Income Tax Returns* 162 (1964). Although these figures do not indicate whether the same corporations remained near the break-even point over several taxable years, it is a reasonable inference that a substantial number were closely-held corporations whose business profits were regularly paid out as salaries to shareholder-employees.

that taxable income and tax rates do not change, that the corporation's income, after taxes, is accumulated during the ten-year period, and that the sole shareholder sells his stock at the end of the period for an amount equal to his original investment plus the accumulation.

TABLE III

Proprietorship vs. Corporation (income accumulated, with sale of stock in tenth year)

Taxable Income (aggregate)	Proprietorship Net after taxes*	Sole Shareholder-Corporation		
		Profit on sale**	Tax (long-term capital gain)	Net after taxes
$250,000	$164,700	$195,000	$48,750	$146,250
500,000	274,100	325,000	81,250	243,750
1,000,000	445,100	585,000	146,250	438,750
2,500,000	895,100	1,365,000	341,250	1,023,750
5,000,000	1,645,100	2,665,000	666,250	1,998,750

*From Table II (*supra*, Sec. 1.03), multiplied by ten.
**Profit: accumulated income (corporation's income less tax liability, from Table I), multiplied by ten.

Although Table III is based on a one-man corporation, the comparison is also of importance for the publicly-held corporation, whose shareholders may prefer to have the corporation accumulate its earnings rather than pay them out because dividends would be taxable at the graduated individual income tax rates, whereas growth in the value of the stock need not be realized until the investor chooses to sell and will then be taxable at the more favorable capital gain rate.

Table III assumes a sale of the stock, which may be a drastic step, especially for the owners of a closely-held business. But, as will be seen, there are other ways to avoid the graduated individual income tax rates by realizing on corporate accumulations at the capital gains rate—although these devices are not as sure-fire as the talk around the country club bar sometimes suggests. One of the most persistent problems in the taxation of corporations and their shareholders, in fact, is the ordinary income-capital gain dichotomy in the field of corporate distributions; and much of this book is devoted to this problem as it applies to stock redemptions (Ch. 7, Part B), partial liquidations (Ch. 7, Part E), complete liquidations (Ch. 9), "collapsible" corporations (Ch. 10), sales and redemptions of preferred stock dividends (Ch. 8), and corporate spin-offs (Ch. 11).

Sec. 1.04.   Exchanges of corporate stock and securities

Another persistent problem in the taxation of corporation and investors is the treatment of exchanges of corporate stock and securities. If stock or securities are sold, the seller is of course taxed on his profit (or may deduct his loss), and ordinarily his gain or loss will be capital gain or loss. If he exchanges stock or securities for other property—*e.g.*, real estate, race horses, or groceries—his gain or loss will be recognized in a similar fashion, since under the Code an exchange or barter of property is ordinarily taxed in the same manner as a sale.

There are, however, a variety of transactions in which the taxpayer's gain or loss goes unrecognized under the Internal Revenue Code, either because it is regarded as inchoate or "unrealized" or because non-recognition is thought to be good economic policy; and many of these "non-recognition transactions" involve corporate stock or securities.[11] An example is the transfer by an individual proprietor of his business assets to a newly-formed corporation in exchange for all of its stock: even if the assets have appreciated or depreciated in value, so that the stock received for the assets is worth more or less than the basis of the assets, the transferor's gain or loss goes unrecognized under §351 (*infra*, Ch. 3). On these facts, it can be plausibly argued that the transferor's gain or loss is too problematical to warrant recognition for tax purposes. Another more controversial example is the exchange of stock of one corporation for the stock of a second corporation into which the first is to be merged; the stock received may be worth ten times (or one-tenth) the basis of the old stock, but the shareholder's gain or loss ordinarily goes unrecognized under §354 (*infra*, Ch. 12). If the two corporations were already under common control, the merger might be regarded

---

[11] When gain or loss goes unrecognized on an exchange, the taxpayer's original basis ordinarily carries over and attaches to the property received by him, so that the "non-recognition" provisions are sometimes called "postponement" provisions on the theory that the unrecognized gain or loss will be taken into account when the new property is sold. Even if this occurs, no allowance is made for the delay in recognizing the gain or loss, and the tax rates or the taxpayer's other income, or both, may be different in the year of sale. Moreover, if the new property is held until death, the postponed gain or loss will be obliterated by §1014, under which the heirs will take the property with a new basis equal to its value at the date of death. The "postponement" theory is also weakened by the fact that the property may be given away, without recognition of gain or loss; if the donee sells it, his tax on the sale may be more or less than the donor would have paid. Finally, if the donee is a charitable institution, the donor will get a charitable deduction under §170 equal to the property's fair market value, Regs. §1.170-1(c), and the donee can sell without tax consequences.

as no more than a change of form, not justifying the recognition of gain or loss, though even here it might be argued that unrealized appreciation or depreciation on property should be taken into account as soon as the owner makes a change in the manner of holding it that will have significant legal consequences, either for taxation or for other matters. But what if the first corporation is a one-man enterprise, owning an office building, and it is merged into a widely-held steel manufacturing firm: should the shareholder's gain or loss go unrecognized when his economic status is so drastically altered? As will be seen in later chapters, a recurring problem in the taxation of the corporation and its shareholders is the determination of when an exchange of stock or securities is a taxable occasion, so that the investor's gain or loss is to be recognized, and when it comes within one of the numerous non-recognition provisions of the Code.

The recognition-nonrecognition dichotomy does not exhaust the possibilities in this area, however; an exchange may also resemble a dividend. For example, if two corporations owned by the same person are merged, and the surviving corporation issues bonds in exchange for the stock of the absorbed corporation, the result may be substantially the same as though one of the corporations had distributed bonds—or even cash—to its shareholder without any merger. If so, it would be appropriate to treat the bonds as a dividend to the extent of their fair market value, a result that would be very different from treating the transaction as either a sale or a non-recognition transaction. Another example of the possibility that an exchange may be treated for tax purposes as a dividend is the redemption of stock by a one-man corporation from its sole shareholder: since he remains in complete control of the corporation despite the redemption of part of his stock, and since the redemption is the functional equivalent of a dividend in virtually all respects, it is ordinarily so treated for tax purposes (*infra*, Ch. 7, Part B).

Sec. 1.05.   The corporation as an entity

Legal philosophers have for centuries disagreed about the "nature" of the corporation, and the courts concurrently have had to decide in concrete cases whether corporations should be treated as entities wholly independent of their shareholders or as groups with a legal status dependent upon the identity and behavior of the shareholders. Judicial decisions have cleaved to no single doctrine, to the disappointment of the philosophers and the despair of text-writers, and the diversity of legal approaches found in other branches of the law is well mirrored in the tax law.[12]

In general, of course, the corporation is treated as an independent taxpaying entity by the Internal Revenue Code, unaffected by either the identity of its shareholders or changes in their composition. A domestic corporation must ordinarily pay the corporate income tax even though its stock is owned entirely by one man, by a tax-exempt organization, or by nonresident aliens beyond United States jurisdiction. Similarly, a corporation's taxable year is not terminated by the fact that some or even all of its stock changes hands, nor does such a shift in ownership ordinarily alter the corporation's basis for its assets, earnings and profits account, method of accounting, or other tax attributes. Moreover, transactions between a corporation and its shareholders ordinarily have the same tax consequences as similar transactions with outsiders.

There are, however, many statutory exceptions to the general principle of treating the corporation as wholly independent of its shareholders.[13] Among these exceptions are:

1. §267, forbidding the deduction of certain losses, expenses, and interest incurred in transactions between a corporation and certain of its shareholders (*infra*, Sec. 2.24). See also §1235(d), §1237(a)(2)(A), and §1239(a)(2).

2. §269, disallowing certain tax benefits if control of a corporation is acquired for the principal purpose of tax avoidance (*infra*, Ch. 13).

3. §401(a)(4), providing that a stock bonus, pension, or profit-sharing plan will qualify for certain tax benefits only if it does not discriminate in favor of, *inter alia*, shareholders.

4. §531, imposing an additional tax on a corporation that is formed or availed of for the purpose of avoiding the income tax on shareholders by accumulating instead of distributing its earnings (*infra*, Ch. 6).

5. §541, imposing an additional tax on personal holding

---

[12] For example, in Hair Industry, Ltd. v. United States, 340 F.2d 510, 15 AFTR 2d 257 (2d Cir. 1965), it was held that a one-man corporation could not refuse to produce records in response to an Internal Revenue Service subpoena on the grounds that its sole shareholder might be incriminated by their contents. To the same effect is Wild v. Brewer, 329 F.2d 924, 13 AFTR 2d 1622 (9th Cir. 1964). Compare U.S. v. Silverstein, 314 F.2d 789, 11 AFTR 2d 1025 (2d Cir. 1963) (real estate "syndicate" not entitled to self incrimination privilege).

[13] Sometimes, but not always, a transaction between a corporation and an affiliate (another corporation or organization under common control) is as vulnerable as though it had occurred between the corporation and its shareholders.

companies, which are defined in part by reference to the number of shareholders (*infra*, Ch. 6).

6. §382, limiting or disallowing the net operating loss carryover in cases where stock ownership shifts in specified ways (*infra*, Ch. 13).

7. §341(e)(5)(A), which for certain purposes treats the corporation's assets as non-capital assets if they would have this character in the hands of a shareholder (*infra*, Ch. 10).

8. §267(c)(1), §318(a)(2)(C), and §544(a)(1), which for certain purposes treat stock owned by a corporation as though it were owned by the corporation's shareholders (and, under §318(a)(3)(C), vice versa).

9. §1501, permitting an "affiliated" group of corporations to file a consolidated return (*infra*, Ch. 13).

The foregoing is by no means an exhaustive catalogue of the statutory provisions that take account of stock ownership in prescribing the tax results of transactions by the corporation, its shareholders, or both. Even though the list could easily be extended, however, these provisions can appropriately be described as exceptions to the statutory principle that the corporation is for tax purposes an independent entity.

It is equally accurate to say that the courts ordinarily take the corporation at face value and do not merge it with its shareholders. There are exceptions in the judicial arena to this generalization, just as in the Code, but the judicial exceptions are less susceptible to classification or even description. One attempt, by Judge Learned Hand, summarizes the leading cases, has itself become a much-quoted restatement, and, at the same time, demonstrates the high level of abstraction that inevitably attends any generalization in this area:

> [The tax] result depends upon whether, in the situation just disclosed, we should recognize transactions of sale or exchange between a corporation and its sole shareholder; and our decision turns upon three decisions of the Supreme Court: Burnet v. Commonwealth Improvement Company, 287 U.S. 415; Higgins v. Smith, 308 U.S. 473, and Moline Properties, Inc. v. Commissioner, 319 U.S. 436, 63 S. Ct. 1132. In the first of these the question was whether, it was proper to tax a corporation for profits upon transactions between itself and a decedent's estate which owned all its shares. The court merely declared that, since a corporation was for most purposes recognized as a separate jural person, and since the situation was not one of the exceptions where the "corporate form" should be "disregarded," it should be taxed upon its gains, regardless of the fact that no living person had gained or lost a cent. When Higgins v. Smith,

supra, was before us (Smith v. Higgins, 2 Cir., 102 F. 2d 456) we assumed that this rule held good in a case where the Commissioner had refused to allow a deduction to the sole shareholder of losses sustained in transactions between him and his corporation. In this we were in error, however, for the Supreme Court held that, although the Treasury might insist upon the separate personality of the corporation when it chose, it might also disregard it, when it chose. It explained Burnet v. Commonwealth Improvement Co., supra, by saying that "a taxpayer is free to adopt such organization of his affairs as he may choose and having elected to do some business as a corporation, he must accept the tax disadvantages. On the other hand, the Government may not be required to acquiesce in the taxpayer's election of that form for doing business which is most advantageous to him. The Government may look at actualities and upon determination that the form employed of doing business or carrying out the tax event is unreal or a sham may sustain or disregard the effect of the fiction as best serves the purposes of the tax statute. ***It is command of income and its benefits which marks the real owner of property." [308 U.S. 473.]

This language we later interpreted as meaning that "the Treasury may take a taxpayer at his word, so to say; when that serves its purpose, it may treat the corporation as a separate person from himself; but that is a rule which works only in the Treasury's own favor; it cannot be used to deplete the revenue." United States v. Morris & Essex R. Co., 2 Cir., 135 F. 2d 711, 713. Again we were wrong; we neglected to observe that the corporate "form" must be "unreal or a sham," before the Treasury may disregard it; we had taken too literally the concluding language that it was the "command of income and its benefits which marks the real owner of property."

This error was made plain in the third decision of the Supreme Court—Moline Properties, Inc. v. Commissioner, 319 U.S. 436. In that case the question was whether the corporation might insist upon the Treasury's including capital gains within the gross income of its sole shareholder, and the court decided that it might not. That was the same situation as existed in Burnet v. Commonwealth Improvement Co., supra. The gloss then put upon Higgins v. Smith, supra, was deliberate and is authoritative: it was that, whatever the purpose of organizing the corporation, "so long as that purpose is the equivalent of business activity or is followed by the carrying on of business by the corporation, the corporation remains a separate taxable entity." 319 U.S. 439. That, as we understand it, is the same interpretation which was placed upon corporate reorganizations in Gregory v. Helvering, 293 U.S. 465, and which has sometimes been understood to contradict the doctrine that the motive to avoid taxation is never, as such, relevant. In fact it does not trench upon that doctrine; it merely declares that to be a separate jural person for purposes of taxation, a corporation must engage in some industrial, commercial, or other activity besides avoiding taxation: in other words, that the term "corporation" will be interpreted to mean a corporation which does some "business" in the ordinary meaning; and that escaping taxation is not "business" in the ordinary meaning. (National Investors Corp. v. Hoey, 144 F. 2d 466, 467-68, 32 AFTR 1219 (2d Cir. 1944).)

One of the difficulties with generalizations—Judge Hand's included —about disregard of the corporate "entity" is that issues are never presented to the courts, and are almost never decided, on the theory that the corporation is to be disregarded for all tax purposes. It is entirely possible, indeed it is likely, that the identity of interest between the corporation and its shareholders will triumph for some purposes and not for others. Thus, Higgins v. Smith, cited by Judge Hand, held that a shareholder could not deduct a loss incurred on a sale of depreciated property to his wholly-owned corporation,[14] but it is far from clear that the government would be entitled to tax income received by the corporation on other property, or even on the property thus transferred, to the shareholder. Similarly, even though a corporation engages in industrial or commercial activity, particular transactions with shareholders may be disregarded or recast for tax purposes, while other transactions with outsiders or even with shareholders are fully honored.[15]

The value of generalizations about corporate entity and taxation is impaired still further by the fact that the broad judicial principles of income taxation are as applicable to corporations and their shareholders as to other taxpayers, so that "disregard of the corporate entity" may be merely a label for a tax result that would be reached as to individuals, estates, trusts, or partnerships by the application of other fundamental principles of income taxation. Conversely, these principles may be employed by the courts in reaching a result that could, alternatively, be regarded as a partial or total disregard of the corporate entity. Applications of these principles will be frequently encountered in later chapters of this book and only a brief mention of them will be made at this point:

1. No assignment of earned income. In the famous case of Lucas v. Earl, 281 U.S. 111, 8 AFTR 10287 (1930), the court held that a husband was taxable on his entire earnings, despite an agreement made with his wife (before the Sixteenth Amendment was adopted)

---

[14] The taxable year in question antedated the enactment of §267(a)(1) (infra, Sec. 2.24).

[15] See infra, Sec. 2.09, and Ch. 13.

that each would have a one-half interest in the other's earnings. The court said that "the statute could tax salaries to those who earned them and provide that the tax could not be escaped by anticipatory arrangements and contracts however skilfully devised to prevent the salary when paid from vesting even for a second in the man who earned it" and that "no distinction can be taken according to the motives leading to the arrangement by which the fruits are attributed to a different tree from that on which they grew." 281 U.S. at 114-115. In Helvering v. Horst, 311 U.S. 112, 24 AFTR 1058 (1940), the same theory was applied to an assignment of investment income. These assignment of income principles apply with equal force to corporate transactions.[16]

　　2. Substance over form. One of the persistent problems of income taxation, as of other branches of the law, is the extent to which legal consequences should turn on the "substance" of a transaction rather than on its form. It is easy to say that substance should control, but in practice form usually has some substantive consequences, so that if two transactions differ in form, they will probably not be identical as to substance. Even so, they may be sufficiently similar to warrant identical tax treatment. Thus, a "loan" by a shareholder to his corporation may be treated as an equity investment (*infra*, Sec. 4.04), a "salary" paid by the corporation to the shareholder may be treated as a dividend (*infra*, Sec. 5.05), and a sale of property by the shareholder may be treated as though made by the corporation (*infra*, Sec. 9.63), or ignored as a "sham," as in National Lead Co. v. Commissioner, 336 F. 2d 134, 14 AFTR 2d 5591 (2d Cir. 1964).

　　3. Business purpose. It is often said that a transaction will not be given effect for tax purposes unless it serves some purpose other than tax avoidance. The leading case in this area is Gregory v. Helvering (*infra*, Sec. 11.02), involving a corporate reorganization, and the theory has had its fullest flowering in this area of tax law; but it is by no means confined in its application to corporate reorganizations or even to the corporate-shareholder relationship.[17]

　　4. Step transactions. A business transaction, like the rest of life,

[16] See generally Lyon and Eustice, Assignment of Income: Fruit and Tree as Irrigated by the P. G. Lake Case, 17 Tax L. Rev. 293, 396 (1962); and Eustice, Contract Rights, Capital Gain, and Assignment of Income—the Ferrer Case, 20 Tax L. Rev. 1, 51 (1964); Johansson v. United States, 336 F. 2d 809, 14 AFTR 2d 5605 (5th Cir. 1964).

[17] For some of the ramifications of this vague doctrine, see Holzman, Ten Years of the Gregory Case, 79 J. Accy. 215 (1945); for its application to corporate reorganizations, see Michaelson, "Business Purpose" and Tax-Free Reorganization, 61 Yale L.J. 14 (1952); Bittker, What Is "Business Purpose" in Reorganizations? 8 N.Y.U. Inst. on Fed. Taxation 134 (1950).

has no sharp beginning or clearly-defined end, but it is necessary in practice to cut it, usually chronologically, into segments for tax purposes. If the segment is too thin, however, the tax results may be unfair to the taxpayer, to the government, or to both. In viewing a dynamic whole, the courts often say that an integrated transaction must not be broken into independent steps or, conversely, that the separate steps must be taken together in attaching tax consequences. The so-called "step transaction" doctrine is often encountered in the taxation of corporations and shareholders, but its scope is much broader.[18]

In enunciating or applying these principles or doctrines, the courts often omit any reference to specific statutory provisions, as though they were laying down a kind of "common law" of income taxation. Sometimes, however, the following statutory provisions are cited, as though they either supported these broad principles or were alternative routes to the same result:

1. §61(a), defining gross income. In Helvering v. Clifford, 309 U.S. 331, 23 AFTR 1077 (1940), the court held that a grantor of a short term trust of which his wife was the beneficiary was taxable on the trust income under §22(a) of the 1939 Code (§61(a) of the 1954 Code) on the ground that the trust effected only "a temporary reallocation of income within an intimate family group" and did not deprive the grantor "of the substance of full enjoyment of all the rights which previously he had in the property." The language of the opinion, though anchored to §61(a), echoes the "no-assignment-of-earned-income" cases, the "substance-over-form" cases, and, though less explicitly, the "business-purpose" cases.[19]

2. §446(b), requiring an accounting method that clearly reflects income. Although the taxpayer's method of accounting is normally controlling in computing taxable income, the government may prescribe another method under §446(b) if the taxpayer has no method or if his method "does not clearly reflect income." For an example of the use of §446(b), which has no special application to corporate taxpayers, see *infra*, Sec. 9.62.

3. §482, permitting the government to reallocate gross income,

---

[18] For applications, see *infra*, Sec. 3.09; and for general discussion, see Paul and Zimet, Step Transactions, *Selected Studies in Federal Taxation* (2d series, 1938), pp. 200-254; Mintz and Plumb, Step Transactions in Corporate Reorganizations, 12 N.Y.U. Inst. on Fed. Tax. 247 (1954).

[19] For an application in the field of corporate taxation, see Advance Machinery Exchange, Inc. v. Commissioner, ¶49,026 P-H TC Memo (1949), affirmed on another ground, 196 F.2d 1006, 41 AFTR 1362 (2d Cir. 1952), cert. denied, 344 U.S. 835 (1952).

See *infra*, Ch. 13, for general discussion of the multiple corporation problem.

deductions, etc. among two or more organizations under common control. When a business enters into transactions with another business controlled by the same interests, appearances may be deceiving. Under §482, the Internal Revenue Service has the power to distribute, apportion, or allocate gross income, deductions, credits, or allowances between or among two or more organizations, trades or businesses which are "owned or controlled directly or indirectly by the same interests," if it determines that such action is necessary to prevent evasion of taxes or to clearly reflect the income of any of the organizations, trades, or businesses. The statute is expressly made applicable whether the enterprises or entities are incorporated or not. The provision has been applied "to circumstances involving an improper manipulation of financial accounts, an improper juggling of the accounts between the related organizations, an improper 'milking' of one business for the benefit of the other, or some similar abuse of proper financial accounting, all made possible by the control of the two businesses by the same interests."[20]

The foregoing judicial principles and statutory provisions, which often overlap in practice, are a useful deterrent to tax avoidance schemes of varying scope and ingenuity. Forcing transactions heavily freighted with tax motives to withstand judicial analysis in the context of these principles, vague and uncertain in application though they may be, is more salutary than uncompromising literalism in applying the statutory system for taxing corporations and shareholders.[21]

Sec. 1.06. Special classes of corporations

Because of their specialized character, the following classes of corporations are outside the scope of this work:

1. Regulated investment companies. Certain investment companies (primarily those registered under the Investment Company Act of 1940), including mutual funds, may elect to be taxed under Subchapter M (§§851-855), under which, in general, the corporation is taxed only on undistributed income, while the shareholders report

---

[20] See *infra,* Sec. 13.32. For more specialized provisions, confined in their application to corporations and their shareholders, see §269, §1551, and §382, *infra,* Ch. 13.

[21] For further discussion, see *infra,* Ch. 13; Cleary, The Corporate Entity in Tax Cases, 1 Tax L. Rev. 3 (1945); Rice, Judicial Techniques in Combating Tax Avoidance, 51 Mich. L. Rev. 1021 (1953); Paul, Restatement of the Law of Tax Avoidance, *Studies in Federal Taxation* (1937), pp. 9-157; Cohen, Taxing the State of Mind, 12 Tax Exec. 200 (1960); and discussion of "dummy" corporations, *infra,* Sec. 2.09.

the distributed income as ordinary income or capital gain, as the case may be. There is an elaborate network of conditions to be satisfied to qualify for the election, of which the salient features are that 90 percent of gross income must be derived from dividends, interest, and gains on the sale of stock or securities and that the corporation's investments must be diversified.[22]

2. Real estate investment trusts. In 1960, Congress enacted §§856-858, providing that certain real estate investment trusts ("REIT") shall be treated as corporations if 90 percent or more of current income is distributed to their beneficiaries. Under a "conduit" principle similar to that applicable to regulated investment companies, the distributed income of a qualifying real estate investment trust is taxed to the distributees but not to the trust itself.[23]

3. Small business investment companies. The Small Business Investment Act of 1958 provides for the creation of corporations to make capital available to small business firms by the purchase of convertible debentures. Under §1243, a loss incurred by a "small business investment company" on such debentures is treated as an ordinary, rather than a capital, loss; see also §243(a)(2), providing that the dividends received deduction (*infra*, Sec. 2.24) for such a company is 100 percent, rather than the usual 85 percent, of dividends received. As to the shareholders of a small business investment company, under §1242 worthless stock gives rise to an ordinary, rather than a capital, loss, and if the loss is not fully used in the year it is incurred, the excess may be carried over under §172 (net operating loss deduction) as though incurred in the shareholder's trade or business.[24]

These provisions apply only to corporations operating under the Small Business Investment Act of 1958, and should not be confused with the more widely applicable provisions of §1244 (*infra*, Sec. 4.09) or Subchapter S (*infra*, Ch. 14), both of which apply to "small business corporations" but use the term in different senses.

4. Banks and trust companies. Subchapter H (§§581-601) provides special rules for certain banks, trust companies, and common trust funds maintained by banks.

5. Insurance companies. Life insurance companies are taxable

---

[22] See Andrews, Guide to the Administration of Regulated Investment Companies, 35 Taxes 662 (1957).

[23] See Grant and Scheifly, Tax Business Planning for the Real Estate Investment Trust, 1963 So. Calif. Tax Inst. 197; articles by Sarner, Roeder, Sexton, Rubin, and Schlitt, 20 N.Y.U. Inst. on Fed. Tax. 609-98 (1962).

[24] See Comment, The Small Business Investment Act of 1958, 47 Cal. L. Rev. 144 (1959).

under the Life Insurance Company Tax Act of 1959 (Code §§801-
820). Other insurance companies are subject to §§821-832; but see
§501(c)(12) and (15) (certain tax-exempt insurance companies)
and §526 (partially tax-exempt shipowners' protection and indemnity
associations). See United States v. Atlas Life Ins. Co., 381 U.S. 233,
15 AFTR 2d 1001 (1965).

6. *Western Hemisphere Trade Corporations.* A special deduction (equal, at 1965 tax rates, to about 29 percent of taxable income)
is granted to a Western Hemisphere Trade Corporation, defined by
§921 as a domestic corporation (a) doing all of its business (except
for incidental purchases) in North, Central, or South America or in
the West Indies, (b) deriving 95 percent or more of its gross income
for the 3-year period preceding the close of the taxable year from
sources without the United States, and (c) deriving 90 percent or
more of its gross income for the same period from the active conduct
of a trade or business.[25]

7. *Possessions Corporations.* For certain domestic corporations,
§931 limits gross income to income from sources within the United
States. To qualify, a corporation must (a) derive 80 percent or more
of its gross income for the 3-year period preceding the close of the
taxable year from sources within a United States possession (Panama
Canal Zone, Guam, American Samoa, Wake and the Midway Islands,
and Puerto Rico) and (b) derive 50 percent or more of its gross income for the same period from the active conduct of a trade or business within a possession.[26]

8. *China Trade Act Corporations.* Corporations organized under
the China Trade Act (42 Stat. 849) are allowed by §§941-943 to
deduct a specified portion of income derived from sources within
Formosa and Hong Kong upon paying a "special dividend" to residents of these areas and residents and citizens of the United States.

9. *Foreign corporations.* Foreign corporations engaged in trade
or business within the United States are taxed under §882, in general,
like domestic corporations, except that (a) gross income includes
only income from sources within the United States, (b) deductions
are allowed only to the extent connected with United States income,
and (c) the foreign tax credit of §901 is not allowed. Other foreign
corporations are taxed under §881 at a flat rate of 30 percent on

[25] See Raskind, The Western Hemisphere Trade Corporation: A Functional Perspective, 16 Vand. L. Rev. 1 (1962).

[26] See Friedman and Silbert, The Interrelationship of Puerto Rican and
United States Income Tax, 21 N.Y.U. Inst. on Fed. Tax. 807 (1963); Novak, A
New Appraisal of Puerto Rico in the Light of Recent Tax Legislation, 19 Tax
L. Rev. 203 (1964).

dividends, some interest, rent, and certain fixed or determinable income from sources within the United States. In addition, these rules may be affected by tax treaties, designed to eliminate double taxation of income from international operations.[27]

In 1962, Congress drastically revised the tax treatment of certain "controlled foreign corporations" and their United States shareholders. These provisions, which may constitute the most complex set of statutory rules in the entire United States Code, are summarized *infra*, Secs. 6.50-6.54 (current taxation of the United States shareholders of such corporations on undistributed foreign income) and Sec. 9.06 (special treatment of the gain realized by the shareholders on selling their stock or liquidating such corporations). "Foreign investment companies" (defined by §1246(b)) were also subjected to new rules in 1962; the United States shareholder's gain on a sale or exchange of the stock of such a company must be reported as ordinary income, rather than as capital gain, to the extent provided by §1246, unless the corporation elects under §1247 to distribute substantially all of its income currently.

Also to be noted are the provisions of §367, requiring *advance* approval by the Treasury that certain non-recognition exchanges involving foreign corporations are not part of a tax avoidance plan. This subject is dealt with in context throughout the succeeding related materials. In addition, various information returns and records are required to be filed by certain foreign corporations and their officers, directors and shareholders; see §§6038, 6046, and 964(c).[28]

On the foreign tax credit, which includes a credit for a domestic corporation in respect of foreign taxes paid by a foreign corporation in which it owns a certain percentage of stock, see §§901-905; see also Owens, *The Foreign Tax Credit* (1961), for an exhaustive study of these provisions which, however, unfortunately antedates the 1962 amendments.

10. Personal service corporations. Under Supplement S of the 1939 Code, a "personal service corporation" could elect to be exempt from the excess profits tax, in which event its shareholders were taxed on the undistributed corporate income. (Subchapter S of the 1954 Code provides for a somewhat similar election, but the rules of eligibility are very different. See *infra*, Ch. 14). Although repealed, these sections are reflected in §312(h) of the 1954 Code, which

---

[27] See generally O'Connor, United States Taxation of Earnings of American-Controlled Foreign Corporations, 42 Taxes 588 (1964); Kalish, Tax Considerations in Organizing for Business Abroad, 44 Taxes 71 (1966).

[28] See Kanter, Congress Expands Information Reporting Requirements for Foreign Corporate Operations, 42 Taxes 84 (1964).

adjusts the earnings and profits of such a corporation to accord with its status under the 1939 Code. The Revenue Acts of 1917-21 also provided special treatment for personal service corporations, reflected in §301(e) of the 1954 Code.

11. Co-operatives. Co-operative organizations are, in general, allowed to exclude from income any "patronage" refunds or dividends allocated to members; and some farmers' organizations (so-called "exempt" cooperatives) are, in addition, permitted by §521 and §1381 to deduct dividends paid on capital stock and amounts allocated to patrons with respect to non-patronage income.[29]

12. Tax-exempt corporations. Section 501(c) grants tax exemption to a number of corporations, primarily non-profit institutions (charitable, educational, and religious organizations; federal instrumentalities; civic leagues; labor unions; social clubs; credit unions; cemetery companies; etc.) and mutual or cooperative organizations that provide economic benefits for their members only (fraternal benefit societies; voluntary employees' associations providing life, sickness, or similar benefits; local teachers' retirement funds; local benevolent life insurance associations; mutual irrigation or telephone companies; etc.). In some instances, the organization must be a corporation to enjoy the tax exemption; in other cases, any legal form (corporation, trust, association, etc.) will qualify if the organization serves the purposes set out in §501(c).

A corporation operated for the primary purpose of carrying on a trade or business for profit (a "feeder" corporation) will not qualify for tax exemption, however, even though its profits are payable to an exempt organization. §502. Moreover, some (but not all) tax-exempt organizations are taxed on their "unrelated business taxable income" by §551, and will lose their tax exemption altogether if they abuse their status by engaging in a "prohibited transaction" (§503) or by unreasonably accumulating, diverting, or jeopardizing their undistributed income (§504).[30]

---

[29] See Asbill, Final Regulations on Co-Ops Offer Some Leeway, 18 J. Tax. 368 (1963); Ravenscroft, The Proposed Limitation on the Patronage Dividend Deduction, 12 Tax L. Rev. 151 (1957); Asbill, Cooperatives: Tax Treatment of Patronage Refunds, 42 Va. L. Rev. 1087 (1956); Murphey, Income Taxation of Exempt Farmers' Cooperatives, 17 Ohio St. L.J. 58 (1956); Couper, The Farmer, The Cooperative, and the Commissioner, 7 Hastings L.J. 143 (1956).

[30] The literature on tax-exempt organizations is far too voluminous to be cited here. The following recent articles, which cite relevant earlier sources, may be helpful: Webster, Effect of Business Activities on Exempt Organizations, 43 Taxes 777 (1965); Comment, Preventing the Operation of Untaxed Business by Tax-Exempt Organizations, 32 U. of Chi. L. Rev. 581 (1965); see also annotated bibliography in Proceedings of A.B.A. Section of Real Property, Probate and Trust Law (Aug. 10-12, 1964), p. 84.

Sec. 1.07.   The corporation vs. the partnership

Although an explication of the tax treatment of partnerships is beyond the scope of this work, a brief comparison of the salient differences for tax purposes between the corporation and the partnership may be helpful.[31]

1. Organization. A partner does not recognize gain or loss on contributing property to a partnership (§721); the basis of the property carries over to the partnership (§723) and it also governs the partner's basis for his interest in the partnership (§722). Substantially identical rules are ordinarily applicable to contributions of property by a shareholder to a corporation, but in unusual circumstances the transfer of property will produce gain or loss to the shareholder (*infra*, Chapter 3).

Organizational expenditures may be amortized over a 5-year period by the corporation (*infra*, Sec. 2.26), but there is no parallel provision for partnerships.

2. Taxability of income. The corporation is taxed on its income (computed after allowance for bona fide salaries, rent, etc., if any, paid to shareholders, *infra*, Sec. 5.05); any amounts distributed to the shareholder as dividends are taxed to him as ordinary income, subject to the dividends received exclusion (*infra*, Sec. 5.06). Undistributed income is not subject to the individual income tax, but it may become subject to the accumulated earnings tax or the personal holding company tax (*infra*, Ch. 6) in the hands of the corporation.

Partnerships are not taxed as such, but each partner is taxed on his share of the firm's income, whether it is distributed to him or not. Under the prevailing conduit theory, the character of such items as ordinary income, capital gains and losses, charitable contributions, tax-exempt interest, etc., carries over to the partner (§702).

3. Deductibility of losses. Corporate losses can be deducted by the corporation itself, subject to the 3-year carryback and 5-year carryforward of net operating losses (§172) and the 5-year carryforward of capital losses (§1212). The shareholder may not avail himself of unused corporate losses, except that he may deduct a loss on worthless stock, ordinarily as a capital loss unless the stock was "Section 1244 stock" (*infra*, Sec. 4.09).

---

[31] As to partnerships that elect under §1361 to be taxed as corporations, see *infra*, Sec. 2.11. For corporations that elect under Subchapter S to be taxed, in the main, as partnerships, see *infra*, Ch. 14. See generally Knapp and Semmel, *Forms of Business Organization and the Federal Tax Laws* (P.L.I., 1962); Axelrad, Choice of Form: Partnership, Corporation, or In-Between, 19 N.Y.U. Inst. on Fed. Tax. 361 (1961).

Partnership losses are deducted directly by the partners. For this reason, it is not uncommon to organize a hazardous enterprise as a partnership, thus allowing the investors to offset its losses against their other income, and to convert to a corporation if and when success is achieved. But §270, imposing a limit on deductions if a trade or business produces a loss of $50,000 or more for each of 5 consecutive years, is applicable to partners, Regs. §1.702-1(a)(8)(ii), but not to corporations (*infra*, Sec. 2.24).

4. Fiscal year. A corporation may select its own taxable year, while a partnership must use the taxable year of its principal partners unless a business purpose for another taxable year is established (§706).

5. Declarations of estimated tax. In filing his declaration of estimated tax, a partner must include his share of partnership income (see Rev. Rul. 55-348, 1955-1 C.B. 132). A corporation must file a declaration of estimated tax only if its tax liability can reasonably be expected to exceed $100,000 (taxable income of about $208,000). It is required to pay gradually increasing portions of this estimated liability in four installments (on Apr., June, Sept., and Dec. 15th, in the case of a calendar year corporation) over the period from 1964-1969; thereafter the entire estimated tax is payable in equal quarterly installments on the above dates. See §§6016, 6074 and 6154.[32]

As to the tax itself, a calendar year individual must file his return on April 15th and pay the balance of the tax at that time; a calendar year corporation must file its return on March 15th, but may elect under §6152 to pay the tax in two equal installments (March 15th and June 15th).

6. Shareholders as employees. Because a shareholder may be an employee of his corporation, he may be included in pension, profit-sharing, stock option, deferred compensation, wage continuation, group life insurance, and employee death benefit plans and arrangements. A partner cannot be an "employee" of his firm for these purposes, even though he may receive a "salary" under §707(c). See *infra*, Sec. 2.01, however, for the use of an "association" in order to obtain these fringe benefits without incorporating, and *infra*, Ch. 14, for use of Subchapter S corporations for this purpose.

7. Income-splitting. Income-splitting within the family through the use of a partnership is affected by §704(e), requiring the donor of an interest in a partnership to receive a reasonable allowance for

---

[32] Changes in the Revenue Act of 1964 provided for the speed-up of current tax payments on a graduated basis from 1964 to 1969. *Supra,* note 5.

his personal services before the donee's distributive share of the firm's income is computed. If shares of a corporation are given to children or other donees, however, the donor may contribute his services to the corporation without receiving compensation, even though this may increase the value of the donee's stock or the amount of dividends paid to him.

8. *Sales.* On selling his stock, the shareholder will realize a capital gain or loss, unless he is a dealer in securities or the corporation is "collapsible" (*infra*, Ch. 10). The sale of a partnership interest similarly produces capital gain or loss, except for amounts received for "unrealized receivables" and substantially appreciated inventory items (§§741 and 751).

9. *Liquidation.* The shareholder ordinarily realizes capital gain or loss on the complete liquidation of a corporation, except for "collapsible" corporations (*infra*, Ch. 10) and liquidations under §332 (*infra*, Sec. 9.40) or §333 (*infra*, Sec. 9.20). Partial liquidations and some stock redemptions also produce capital gain or loss; other stock redemptions are taxed as dividends (*infra*, Ch. 7). The liquidation of a partner's interest ordinarily produces capital gain or loss, recognized as provided in §731, subject to special rules in the case of retiring and deceased partners (§736).

Chapter Two

THE CORPORATION INCOME TAX

Part A. What Is A "Corporation"?

Sec. 2.01. Introductory — "Associations" in general

Section 11(a) of the Code imposes a tax on the taxable income of "every corporation" but does not define the term "corporation." The Code's definitional section, however, provides in §7701(a)(3) that "the term corporation *includes* associations, joint stock companies and insurance companies." Although this "definition" leaves much to be desired in the way of precision, the issue of whether a business organization constitutes a "corporation" for federal tax purposes is not often encountered in practice. When the issue does arise, the definitional problem typically is whether the enterprise is an "association" (to be treated as a corporation), or whether it is some other form of tax entity (*e.g.*, partnership, trust, or proprietorship).

In reaching out to impose corporate tax status on some entities that are not classified as corporations by state law, a practice going as far back as the income tax of 1894 (28 Stat. 556), Congress presumably had in mind the fact that a business entity may resemble a corporation in form and function without having a state charter. See Flint v. Stone Tracy Co., 220 U.S. 107, 146, 151, 3 AFTR 2834 (1911) (sustaining the corporate income tax of 1909 as to joint stock companies on the ground that they share many of the benefits of corporate organization, and referring to the advantages which arise from corporate or quasi-corporate organization); Burk-Waggoner Oil Ass'n v. Hopkins, 269 U.S. 110, 114, 5 AFTR 5663 (1925) ("nothing in the Constitution precludes Congress from taxing as a corporation an association which, although unincorporated, transacts its business as if it were incorporated"). Conversely, the fact that a state has conferred the label of "corporation" on a business organization should not per se control its status for federal tax purposes since this issue is inherently a question of federal, rather than state, law. On the other hand, local law must, of necessity, govern the legal relationships of an organization's associates (a) among themselves, (b) to third persons (*e.g.*, customers, suppliers, creditors and employees), and (c) to the property of the venture, which factors will, in turn, have a significant bearing on the entity's federal tax status. See Regs. §301.7701-1(c).

1. Classification issues and stakes. The question of corporate classification most often arises in the context of whether the profits of a particular organization are subject to the corporate tax of §11(a) (and, as a corollary thereto, whether distribution of those profits to its beneficial owners will be subject to a second round of taxation, as "dividends," under the rules of §§301 and 316, *infra,* Ch. 5). But once "corporate status" is found, it should be noted that *all* the consequences of operating in corporate form will flow from this determination (*i.e.,* the full panoply of tax rules relating to the treatment of corporations and shareholders will govern the organization, operation, liquidation, and reorganization of the enterprise, and the taxability of distributions to its associates). On the other hand, if noncorporate status exists, the tax consequences will be controlled by other applicable Code provisions (*e.g.,* Subchapter J for trusts and beneficiaries, or Subchapter K for partners and partnerships).

Taxpayers may seek to avoid corporate status for reasons in addition to the "double taxation" consequence noted above: thus, "conduit" treatment may be desired in order to "pass-through" current operating losses of the venture to its owners, or to preserve the special tax character of certain items of income or deduction (*e.g.,* tax-exempt interest, long-term capital gain, percentage depletion, and depreciation). To a limited extent, certain corporations now can obtain the benefits of conduit treatment in one form or another (*e.g.,* Subchapter S corporations, *infra,* Ch. 14; mutual funds and real estate investment trusts, *supra,* Sec. 1.06), but the partnership or trust device often provides a simpler method of attaining this goal. Consequently, many real estate, theatrical, and natural resource ventures are organized in partnership form to gain "conduit" benefits for their investors. At the other end of the scale are investors who seek to obtain rather than avoid corporate (or "quasi-corporate") status, so that they can become "employees" of the enterprise and thus obtain the deferred compensation benefits of qualified pension and profit-sharing plans and such employee fringe benefits as the sick pay exclusion, excludible employee death benefits, non-taxable meals and lodging furnished for the "convenience of the employer," and stock option plans. In addition, income-splitting goals are generally easier to accomplish through use of a corporation and a corporation may serve to "shelter" business income from the progressive rates applicable to individuals.

2. *Corporate classification criteria in general.* The leading case in this area is Morrissey v. Commissioner, 296 U.S. 344, 16 AFTR 1274 (1935), holding that the corporate income tax was properly imposed on a trust created to develop certain real estate. In reaching its decision, the Court noted that "it is impossible in the nature of things to translate the statutory concept of 'association' into a particularity of detail that would fix the status of every sort of enterprise or organization which ingenuity may create," and that "the inclusion of associations with corporations [in the statutory definition] implies resemblance; but it is resemblance and not identity." The classification approach employed by the Court in *Morrissey* was a balancing or weighing process, in which the characteristics of the organization under examination were compared with the characteristics of "typical" or "ordinary" corporations. This approach, involving as it does the exercise of judgment on facts that are almost never duplicated, has been characterized by fluidity and confusion, especially in the penumbral zone of "hybrid" entities possessing some, but not all, of the basic corporate indicia.

The principal characteristics of a "corporation," noted by the Court in *Morrissey* and largely codified by Regs. §301.7701-2, are as follows: (a) associates; (b) an objective to carry on a trade or business and divide the profits; (c) continuity of life of the enterprise, notwithstanding the death, disability or withdrawal of its members; (d) centralized management by representatives of the owners; (e) limited liability of the owners; and (f) free transferability of beneficial interests in the organization. Other corporate characteristics, not specifically mentioned by the regulations, include: ownership of property by the entity; the right to do business in the name of the entity; applicability of federal and state laws and regulations to the entity; and various corporate formalities such as stock certificates, articles of incorporation, by-laws, and the like. The regulations, §301.7701-2(a)(3), establish a relatively mechanical criterion that an unincorporated organization shall not be classified as a corporation unless it has *more* of the significant corporate characteristics than non-corporate characteristics (and, for this purpose, all characteristics common to both types of organization being compared must be ignored). The regulations do, however, require an objective to carry on a business for profit as a minimum condition for "corporate" status.[1]

---

[1] Regs. §301.7701-2(a)(2).

The regulations, §301.7701-2, discuss four corporate characteristics in some detail:

1. Continuity of life. This factor is present if the death, disability, or withdrawal of any member of the organization will not cause its dissolution. See Glensder Textile Co., 46 B.T.A. 176 (1942) (Acq.).

2. Centralized management. To satisfy this factor, the exclusive, continuing power to make necessary management decisions must be concentrated in a managerial group (composed of *less* than all the members), who have the authority to act on behalf of the organization independently of its members. What is crucial is the focus of necessary operating authority in the hands of a particular group, unlike the "mutual agency" relationship of a partnership, where each member can bind the organization by his acts.

3. Limited liability. The owners of a corporation typically are liable for its debts (whether created by contract or tort) only to the extent of corporate property. If creditors of the organization may seek satisfaction of their unpaid claims by proceeding against the individual members, this corporate characteristic is not present. This shield against personal liability must arise from the nature of the organization itself, not by means of liability-shifting private agreements.

4. Free transferability of interests. This factor is present if a member is free to assign *all* the attributes of his benefical interest in the organization without the consent of other members. Thus, a member must be free to transfer not only his interest in the profits of the venture, but also his rights to share in its control and assets; and such a transfer must not work a dissolution of the organization under local law. The regulations provide for a form of "modified transferability," however, where the other members have a right of first refusal to purchase such interest at its fair market value. But this type of transferability is entitled to less significance than "free" transferability.

These principles are illustrated by examples in Regs. §301.7701-2(g). Although detailed examination of the decided cases is beyond the scope of this work, the areas in which most of the problems have arisen are discussed hereafter.[2]

---

[2] See generally Lyons, Comments on the New Regulations on Associations, 16 Tax. L. Rev. 441 (1961); Zarky, Unincorporated Associations Taxable as Corporations, 1961 So. Cal. Tax. Inst. 277; Sarner, Associations Taxable as Corporations: A Review and a Look Ahead, 20 N.Y.U. Inst. on Fed. Tax. 609 (1962). For earlier discussions, prior to adoption of the 1960 association regulations, see Smith, Associations Classified as Corporations Under the Internal Revenue Code, 34 Cal. L. Rev. 461 (1946); Driscoll, The Association Problem in Joint Ventures and Limited Partnerships; 17 N.Y.U. Inst. on Fed. Tax. 1067 (1959); and Taubman, *The Joint Venture and Tax Classification* (1957).

3. Unscrambling the eggs on a change of classification. Although there is an abundance of litigation on the proper classification of various business organizations, there is surprising little authority on the problems that arise when an organization is authoritatively classified as a partnership or trust after reporting on the corporate basis for a period of years, or vice versa. If the statue of limitations on the earlier years has not run, the eggs can be unscrambled by the use of amended returns, under which the tax liability of all parties can be recomputed as a prelude to the appropriate additional payments and refunds. If any earlier years are closed by the statute of limitations, however, and if it is not "mitigated" under §§1311-1314 by the assertion of inconsistent positions by either the government or the taxpayers, the errors of the past will go uncorrected. In such a case, the courts may apply an estoppel doctrine to prevent a current benefit from being built on an uncorrectible error.[3]

In the few instances in which the question has been raised, it has been held that a change to the correct method of reporting by an organization that has erroneously reported as a corporation does not constitute its "liquidation."[4]

Sec. 2.02.   Trusts as "associations"

The classification of trusts has been especially troublesome, since by its very nature a trust concentrates title and management in the trustee, and relieves the beneficiaries of personal liability; moreover, trusts often continue in existence despite a beneficiary's death or transfer of his interest. Since many trusts thus automatically partake of certain corporate attributes (or, perhaps more accurately, since corporations and trusts have certain overlapping characteristics),[5] it becomes necessary to search for criteria by which the "strict" or "ordinary" trust (taxable under the trust rules of Subchapter J) can be distinguished from a trust taxable as a corporation.

At this crucial point, the regulations become somewhat vague. Thus, after hinting that an "ordinary" trust is one not created by the beneficiaries, the regulations go on to suggest that an "ordinary" trust can also be created by the beneficiaries themselves and, conversely, that a trust can be an "association" whether created by its

[3] See Alderson v. Healy, — F. Supp. —, 15 AFTR 2d 536 (D. Mont. 1965); Demmon v. United States, 321 F.2d 203, 12 AFTR 2d 5371 (7th Cir. 1963).
[4] Rev. Rul. 63-107, 1963-1 C.B. 71 (change in status due to change in regulations); Rev. Proc. 65-27, 1965-43 I.R.B. 34, Sec. 5.02 (professional service organizations).
[5] See generally Stephens and Freeland, The Federal Tax Meaning of Estates and Trusts, 18 Tax L. Rev. 251 (1963); Lyons, *supra,* note 2, at 447.

beneficiaries or not. They also note the high degree of overlap between trust and corporate characteristics, and come to rest, in the last analysis, on the purpose for which the trust was created: viz., whether the primary objective was to hold, protect and conserve the trust property for beneficiaries under the ordinary rules applied in chancery and probate courts (an "ordinary trust"), or whether it was to carry on a joint business enterprise, as associates, for profit (a "business trust"). Reg. §301.7701-2(a)(2) and §301.7701-4(a). This primacy of the "business objective" factor in distinguishing "ordinary trusts" from "business trusts" taxable as associations is directly traceable to the *Morrissey* case,[6] where the Court emphasized the purpose of "associates" to carry on a joint business enterprise in finding corporate status for a real estate development trust. The trust in *Morrissey* also possessed other corporate characteristics (limited liability, centralized control, continuity of existence, and transferability of interests), but a close reading of the opinion makes clear the Court's heavy reliance on the presence of a "business objective." In determining whether a trust was created for the purpose of carrying on a "business" by "associates," it is the *power* to carry on business activities (ascertained by reference to the governing instrument), rather than the actual exercise of that power, that is crucial.[7] Finally, ascertainment of the "business objective" and "associates" elements may, in large part, be influenced by the presence or absence of certain other corporate characteristics (centralized management, continuity of existence, and transferability of interests).

The difficulty of applying these standards in a given case can be formidable, and it is increased by (a) the growing tendency, in many otherwise "ordinary" trusts, to relieve the trustee of the orthodox restrictions on investments and other practices that the regulations call "the ordinary rules applied in chancery or probate courts," and

---

[6] Morrissey v. Commissioner, 296 U.S. 344, 16 AFTR 1274 (1935).

[7] Thus, in Helvering v. Coleman-Gilbert Associates, 296 U.S. 369, 16 AFTR 1270 (1935), and Swanson v. Commissioner, 296 U.S. 362, 16 AFTR 1268 (1935), companion cases to *Morrissey,* the Court held that trusts for the operation and management of rental real estate were taxable as associations; and in Helvering v. Combs, 296 U.S. 365, 16 AFTR 1272 (1935), a trust to finance and drill an oil well was likewise held taxable as a corporation. See also Mid-Ridge Investment Co. v. United States, 324 F.2d 945, 12 AFTR 2d 5969 (7th Cir. 1963) (rental real estate management trust held taxable as a corporation); and compare Rohman v. United States, 275 F.2d 120, 5 AFTR 2d 871 (9th Cir. 1960) ("passive" holding of rental real estate did not, on facts, make trust an association).

For an illustration of the importance of the stated purpose, compare Sears v. Hassett, 111 F.2d 961, 25 AFTR 23 (1st Cir. 1940) (business objective made Massachusetts real estate trust taxable as a corporation), with Sears v. Hassett, 45 F. Supp. 772, 29 AFTR 1113 (D. Mass. 1942) (same trust held free from corporate tax, apparently after amendment of trust instrument).

(b) the converse fact that trustees of even the most free-wheeling business trust may at times be curbed by a court of equity. Thus the legal restraints on the trustees of what are allegedly two types of trusts ("ordinary" and "business") may coalesce both in theory and practice.

The regulations refer to two other types of trusts that bear special note: certain "investment trusts" (so-called management trusts and fixed-investment trusts); and "liquidating trusts." As to the former, association status will be found, say the regulations, "if there is power under the trust agreement to vary the investment of the certificate holders."[8] "Liquidating trusts," on the other hand, are not treated as associations under the regulations, if the primary purpose of the trust is to liquidate and distribute assets transferred to it and if its activities are reasonably necessary to, and consistent with, this purpose.[9] If the liquidation is unreasonably prolonged, or if the liquidation purpose becomes submerged by the conduct of business activities, however, the liquidation process itself may constitute the conduct of a trade or business for profit and result in association status.[10] (This distinction between "liquidation" and "business" is reminiscent of cases in the capital gain area where courts must

[8] Regs. §301.7701-4(c), citing Commissioner v. North American Bond Trust, 122 F.2d 545, 27 AFTR 892 (2d Cir. 1941), cert. denied, 314 U.S. 701 (1942). In this decision, the court contrasted the facts before it with those of a companion case, Commissioner v. Chase Nat. Bank, 122 F.2d 540, 27 AFTR 887 (2d Cir. 1941), where the trustee had virtually no power to alter the nature of a certificate holder's investment. See also Cleveland Trust Co. v. Commissioner, 115 F.2d 481, 25 AFTR 1020 (6th Cir. 1940), cert. denied, 312 U.S. 704 (1941) (trust created to hold title to real property subject to a long-term lease was not an association, even though beneficial interests were sold to the public, where the trustee was required to pay over the rents periodically to the beneficiaries and, in the event of a sale, was to pay over the proceeds rather than reinvest them); but cf. Main-Hammond Land Trust v. Commissioner, 200 F.2d 308, 42 AFTR 958 (6th Cir. 1952) (held an association on similar facts). See also Royalty Participation Trust, 20 T.C. 466 (1953) (Acq.); Rev. Rul. 61-175, 1961-2 C.B. 128 (investment trust taxable as a strict trust); and Rev. Rul. 64-220, 1964-2 C.B. 335 (passive title-holding land trust taxable as a partnership rather than as an association or a trust).

The cases are collected in Lyons, Comments on the New Regulations on Associations, 16 Tax L. Rev. 441, 449-453 (1961).

[9] Regs. §301.7701-4(d); Rev. Rul. 63-228, 1963-2 C.B. 229 (creditors' liquidating trust not an association).

[10] Compare Helvering v. Washburn, 99 F.2d 478, 21 AFTR 1140 (8th Cir. 1938) (trust to liquidate a large tract of grazing land held not taxable as a corporation on a showing that management activity during the process of liquidation was minimal and that the dominant purpose was to effect a sale rather than manage a business); with Mullendore Trust Co. v. United States, 271 F.2d 748, 4 AFTR 2d 5751 (10th Cir. 1959) (upon termination of a trust taxable as an association, the trustees carried on business during the period of winding up in the interest of a greater yield from the assets—held, an association despite "paramount objective" to liquidate); and United States v. Homecrest Tract, 160 F.2d 150, 35 AFTR 970 (9th Cir. 1947) (liquidation process held a trade or business, and trust taxed as a corporation).

determine whether property was "held for sale to customers in the ordinary course of business," and thus subject to ordinary gain or loss treatment, or whether it was held for investment, so as to be subject to capital treatment.[11] Examples of liquidating trusts include trusts created to liquidate a single parcel of real estate or to effect an expeditious disposal of the assets of an estate or a dissolved corporation. The regulations also treat bondholder's protective committees and voting trusts formed to protect the interests of security holders during insolvency proceedings as liquidating trusts so long as they are not used to "further the control or profitable operation of a going business on a permanent basis."[12]

Sec. 2.03. Partnerships as "associations"

Under the regulations, an organization may be a partnership for local law purposes but an association within the meaning of §7701(a)-(3) if it has more corporate than non-corporate characteristics, Regs. §301.7701-2(a), and §301.7701-3(b); for this purpose, characteristics common to both types of organization (e.g., intent to carry on business as associates) are not considered. But a "business partnership," to be classified as an association, must possess at least three of the following corporate criteria; continuity of existence, centralized management, limited liability, and transferable interests. "Non-business" partnerships, on the other hand, can never be treated as associations under the regulations, since a "business objective" is indispensable to association status.

The regulations also make it plain that partnerships governed by the Uniform Partnership Act and the Uniform Limited Partnership Act, or their local equivalents, can rarely, if ever, be treated as associations. For example, the factors of continuity of life, centralized management, and free transferability of interests will not be present if, under local law, one member has the power to dissolve the organization, notwithstanding provisions to the contrary in the partnership agreement.[13] If local law permits continuity of existence by agreement of the parties, however, the regulations give effect to the agreement even though a member may have the residual power to terminate the firm in breach of the agreement. For the most part, the

---

[11] See generally Mauldin v. Commissioner, 195 F.2d 714, 41 AFTR 1126 (10th Cir. 1952); Pennroad Corp. v. Commissioner, 261 F.2d 325, 2 AFTR 2d 6202 (3rd Cir. 1958), cert. denied, 359 U.S. 958 (1959); but see Greenspon v. Commissioner, 229 F.2d 947, 48 AFTR 979 (8th Cir. 1956).

[12] Regs. §301.7701-4(d).

[13] Regs. §301.7701-2(b), (c), (e), and (g), Examples (2)-(4) and (7); Glensder Textile Co., 46 B.T.A. 176 (1942) (Acq.).

cases appear to have accepted the agreement of the parties as written, without considering its effect under local law; this acceptance of the agreement at face value may result from the failure of the parties to establish that it would fail, as a matter of local law, to achieve its purported ends, or from the theory that continuity of existence is sufficiently attained if a breach of the agreement could result in an action for damages.[14]

As to the factor of centralized management, similar considerations are applicable. The regulations state that concentration of exclusive authority in a management group by agreement of the parties will not satisfy the centralized management requirement if, as a matter of local law, such an agreement would be ineffective against an outsider who had no notice of it. Regs. §301.7701-2(c)(4). Thus, this factor will be absent, say the regulations, if the parties cannot, by contract, limit their mutual agency relationship as to third parties. Whether courts will look beyond the face of the partnership agreement, to determine its effectiveness under local law (as required by the regulations), remains to be seen.

On the question of limited liability, the regulations similarly provide that attempts to limit the liability of a general partner by agreement will not be effective if, under local law, such partners remain liable to third party creditors of the organization. Regs. §301.7701-2(d)(1). This personal liability will be present in the case of a general partnership organized under statutes corresponding to the Uniform Partnership Act. The regulations also state that, in the case of limited partnerships, the personal liability of the general partners negates the corporate characteristic of limited liability, unless the general partners have no substantial assets which could be reached by creditors of the organization and are mere "dummies" acting as agents of the limited partners. Finally, neither the size of the partnership nor the number of limited partners apparently will be significant per se to prevent partnership status. See Regs. §301.7701-3(b)(2), Example (2).

[14] See *e.g.*, Wholesalers Adjustment Co. v. Commissioner, 88 F.2d 156, 19 AFTR 96 (8th Cir. 1937); United States v. Kintner, 216 F.2d 418, 46 AFTR 995 (9th Cir. 1954). In Burke-Waggoner Oil Association v. Hopkins, 269 U.S. 110, 5 AFTR 5663 (1925), the Court held that a Texas joint stock association was taxable as an association even though treated as a partnership under local law.

See Cincinnati Stamping Co., ¶45,258 P-H Memo TC (1945), treating an organization as a corporation despite a theoretical right in each associate to terminate the firm, where exercise of the right would give the remaining associates the right to buy him out for 25 percent of the book value of his interest, which was only a fraction of fair market value. This potential sacrifice of value serves to distinguish the agreement in this case from the more typical partnership buy-sell agreement.

The laws of Pennsylvania and a few other states provide for the creation of "partnership associations," under which *all* partners enjoy limited liability, interests are transferable, and management is centralized in representatives. The regulations provide that such organizations will be taxed as associations if they more nearly resemble a corporation than other types of business entities, a conclusion that seems to follow from their predominantly corporate characteristics.[15]

Sec. 2.04.   Syndicates, joint ventures, etc., as "associations"

A syndicate, pool, joint venture, or other unincorporated group which carries on a business, financial operation, or venture is, under Regs. §301.7701-3(a), taxable as a partnership unless it constitutes a trust, estate or association.[16] To be taxable as an association, however, a syndicate or similar organization must possess not only the characteristics of "associates" and "business objective," but a majority of the other corporate criteria as well (continuity, centralized management, limited liability, and transferability). As a consequence of these requirements, syndicates and joint ventures are rarely treated as associations.[17]

In the oil and gas industry, dispersion of ownership and investment has led to the frequent use of joint arrangements for exploiting mineral resources. The form and effect of these agreements are dictated by the special characteristics of this industry, however, and discussion of them is beyond the scope of this work.[18] One aspect of this problem is worthy of special note; the regulations state that "since associates and an objective to carry on business for joint profit are essential characteristics of all organizations engaged in business for profit . . . the absence of either of these essential characteristics will cause an arrangement among co-owners of property for the development of such property for the *separate* profit of each not to be

---

[15] Regs. §301.7701-3(c); Giant Auto Parts, Ltd., 13 T.C. 307 (1949).

[16] See §761(a) for a statutory endorsement of this definition. The second sentence of §761(a) authorizes the Treasury to exclude certain organizations from the ambit of the partnership provisions, a power that has been exercised by Regs. §1.761-1(a)(2). These regulations, in addition to their principal purpose of limiting the election afforded by §761(a), point the way toward avoiding the status of "association," *i.e.*, an unincorporated group that is so organized and conducted as to qualify for the §761(a) election will, by the same token, not be taxable as a corporation.

[17] For litigated cases concerning syndicates and similar organizations, see Junior Miss Co., 14 T.C. 1 (1950); Bloomfield Ranch v. Commissioner, 167 F.2d 586, 36 AFTR 959 (9th Cir. 1948.).

[18] See Bruen, Federal Income Tax Aspects of Oil and Gas Ventures — A Summary for the Investor, 14 Tax L. Rev. 353, 362-73 (1959); Sneed, More About Associations in the Oil and Gas Industry, 33 Texas L. Rev. 168 (1954).

classified as an association." Regs. §301.7701-2(a)(2). The last portion of this sentence appears to incorporate the Internal Revenue Service's long standing position in I.T. 3930[19] that certain joint operating agreements for the development of mineral properties did not constitute associations because such arrangements were operations for the separate, rather than joint, profit of their members.

Sec. 2.05.　Professional associations and professional corporations

Although most of the "association" litigation concerns unincorporated entities that wish to avoid corporate tax status, occasionally the roles are reversed, with taxpayers seeking to have their organization classified as an association. Foremost among the motives for such corporate yearnings is the desire of the organization's members to participate in the deferred compensation benefits of qualified pension and profit sharing plans, which are restricted to "employees." In most cases, of course, their ambition can be easily satisfied by incorporating under state law; but if local law, professional ethics, or business reasons stand in the way, they may seek to confer enough corporate characteristics on an unincorporated organization to qualify it as an "association" for federal tax purposes. In United States v. Kintner, 216 F. 2d 418, 46 AFTR 995 (9th Cir. 1954), this goal was realized by a group of physicians who reorganized their partnership into an "association," primarily to obtain the tax benefits of a qualified pension plan. Applicable state law prohibited the practice of medicine in corporate form, but the court found that the organization possessed the corporate characteristics of associates, business purpose, continuity of life, and partial limitation of liability (although members' interests were non-transferable), so as to qualify as an association under the *Morrissey* "resemblance" test. The *Kintner* opinion refused to deny association status merely because state law barred the corporate practice of medicine, noting that the classification of an entity for income tax purposes was a question of federal, rather than state, law. The Treasury initially refused to follow the *Kintner* decision, but when the "association" regulations under the 1954 Code were published in 1960, they included an example that

---

[19] 1948-2 C.B. 126. But the failure of co-owners to retain the power to deal separately with their own property interests and the production therefrom could result in a finding of association status. See, for example, United States v. Stierwalt, 287 F2d 855, 7 AFTR 2d 1013 (10th Cir. 1961); and John Provence No. 1 Well v. Commissioner, 321 F.2d 840, 12 AFTR 2d 5059 (3rd Cir. 1963).

was similar to the *Kintner* facts, except that it specified a modified form of transferability for the interests of the members.[20]

The enactment in 1962 of the Self-Employed Individuals Retirement Act reduced somewhat the pressure in this area by permitting self-employed taxpayers, including partners, to create their own deferred compensation plans. This legislation contains restrictions that are not applicable to qualified pension and profit-sharing plans,[21] however, so that "association" status remained an appealing goal for many physicians, lawyers, and other professional taxpayers, especially since the 1962 legislation did nothing to extend to self-employed taxpayers such other tax benefits as the sick pay exclusion of §105, the employee death benefit exclusion of §101(b), etc.

Recognizing these continuing disparities between "employees" and self-employed persons, and finding the *Kintner* route to equality inadequate or, in some states, unavailable, taxpayers have recently turned to their state legislatures for assistance in achieving corporate tax status. Some thirty-five states have responded, in one way or another, to this demand by enacting legislation permitting lawyers, doctors, and other professionals to organize "professional corporations" or "professional associations" for the practice of their specialties. The Treasury, in turn, has amended the "association" regulations to eliminate the *Kintner* example that was promulgated in 1960, and to provide that a "professional service organization" must meet the *Morrissey* criteria to be treated as a corporation, regardless of its local label.[22] Few if any new-style professional organizations will be able to meet the standards of the 1965 regulations, but since they are "interpretative" rather than "legislative" regulations and were issued long after the statutory provision they interpret, they will probably not weigh very heavily when the courts come to cope with the flood of litigated cases that can be anticipated. In the last analysis, therefore, the courts will have to make an independent judgment on the proper classification of these organizations.[23]

[20] Regs. §301.7701-2(g), Example (1) (deleted in 1965); see also, for cases applying the *Kintner* rule, Galt v. United States, 175 F. Supp. 360, 4 AFTR 2d 5224 (N.D. Tex. 1957); and Foreman v. United States, 232 F. Supp. 134, 13 AFTR 2d 1430 (D. Fla. 1964).

[21] See Snyder and Weckstein. Quasi-Corporations, Quasi-Employees and Quasi-Tax Relief for Professional Persons, 48 Corn. L. Q. 613 (1963).

[22] Regs. §301.7701-2(h), promulgated Feb. 2, 1965; see also §301.7701-2(a)-(5), for the effective date of the new provisions; Rev. Proc. 65-27, 1965-43 I.R.B. 34, implementing the new provisions and providing, *inter alia*, that a professional service organization will be treated as a corporation for taxable years ending on or before Dec. 31, 1964 if it filed timely corporate returns for such years; see also Rev. Rul. 66-92, 1966-17 I.R.B. p. 6. See also *infra*, Sec. 6.22, n.77, for a possible personal holding company problem in this area.

[23] For the views of the senior author of this work, see Bittker, Professional

Sec. 2.06.   One-man associations

The *Morrissey* case, *supra*, Sec. 2.01, said that the term "association" as used in §§7701(a)(3) "implies associates," and the regulations similarly seem to proceed on the assumption that a one-man organization cannot be an association. Reg. §301.7701-2(a)(2). This notion might be extracted from the word "association" if it is "viewed as inert language," a canon of construction rejected in another tax case, Bazley v. Commissioner, 331 U.S. 737, 741, 35 AFTR 1190 (1947), but there is nothing else to commend it; one-man corporations are subject to the corporate income tax and there is no good reason for exempting a one-man organization if it possesses enough corporate attributes. Thus, a Massachusetts business trust with a single beneficiary ought to be taxable as an association. See Lombard Trustees, Ltd. v. Commissioner, 136 F. 2d 22, 31 AFTR 90 (9th Cir. 1943). Ordinarily, of course, an enterprise owned beneficially by a single individual will not have such corporate attributes as continuity of existence and centralized management, and several cases holding that one-man enterprises are not associations are best explained on this ground.[24]

Sec. 2.07.   Defectively organized corporations

Organizations that purport to be corporations but have failed to attain *de jure* status under local law have been held taxable as corporations, either on the theory that the term "corporation" includes organizations that are *de facto* corporations under state law,[25] or on the theory that a defectively organized corporation is an "association."[26] If a *de facto* corporation attains *de jure* status during a taxable year, it is probably to be treated as a single taxpayer for the

Associations and Federal Income Taxation: Some Questions and Comments, 17 Tax. L. Rev. 1 (1961). For some of the nearly-unanimous contrary voices, see Snyder and Weckstein, *supra* note 21; Grayck, Professional Associations and the Kintner Regulations: Some Answers, More Questions, and Further Comments, 17 Tax L. Rev. 469 (1962); Ohl, Corporate Practice of Law in New York, 40 Taxes 263 (1962); Anderson, Tax Aspects of Professional Corporations, 1963 So. Cal. Tax. Inst. 309; Scallen, Federal Income Taxation of Professional Associations and Corporations, 49 Minn. L. Rev. 603 (1965); Mow, Professional Associations and Professional Corporations, 16 Southwestern L. J. 462 (1962). See generally, Note, Professional Corporations and Associations, 75 Harv. L. Rev. 776 (1962).

24 A. A. Lewis & Co. v. Commissioner. 301 U.S. 385, 19 AFTR 486 (1937); Knoxville Truck Sales & Service, Inc., 10 T.C. 616 (1948); Coast Carton Co., 10 T.C. 894 (1948).

25 For difficulties in applying the *de facto* theory, see Ballantine, *Corporations* (rev. ed. 1946) 68-100.

26 R. L. Brown Coal & Coke Co., 14 BTA 609 (1928); Soeder v. United

entire period.[27] Use of the "association" theory in cases where the enterprise does not even attain *de facto* status under state law, however, is open to question in that an enterprise that would be treated as an ordinary partnership under state law cannot attain association status for want of the corporate characteristics of continuity of existence, transferability of interests, limited liability and centralized management.[28]

Sec. 2.08. Corporations in the process of winding up

Similar problems of ascertaining corporate identity can occur at the close of an organization's legal life. At what point does the enterprise cease to exist as a corporation and assume another character (*e.g.*, partnership, trust, proprietorship) for federal income tax purposes? On several occasions, an organization that was continued in the guise of a corporation after expiration of its corporate charter was held taxable as an "association."[29] Similarly, a corporation in the process of winding up its affairs prior to liquidation and dissolution continues to be taxable as a "true" corporation until its corporate "existence" terminates.[30]

In order to assure an orderly liquidation, a corporation frequently will convey its assets to trustees (often one or more of its directors), either pursuant to state statutory procedures or other-

States, 142 F.2d 236, 32 AFTR 569 (6th Cir. 1944); Bell, ¶56,291 P-H Memo TC (1956); see also Burleson, ¶53,279 P-H Memo TC (1953).

In Skarda v. Commissioner, 250 F.2d 429, 52 AFTR 1082 (10th Cir. 1957), an enterprise was held to be a corporation (so that its losses were not deductible by the stockholders), although there were no meetings of stockholders, no by-laws were adopted, officers were not formally elected, minute books were not kept, stock was not issued, property was not formally transferred by a predecessor partnership, and the right to do business was forfeited (though later revived) for failure to file an annual report.

As to the "association" rationale if the enterprise is beneficially owned by a single person, see *supra*, Sec. 2.06.

[27] Camp Wolters Land Co. v. Commissioner, 160 F.2d 84, 35 AFTR 873 (5th Cir. 1947) (which also deals with transactions by promoters preceding the attainment of *de facto* status).

[28] See J. W. Frentz, 44 T.C. 485 (1965), where an organization was held not to be in "existence" as a corporation, either *de jure* or *de facto*, at the time it attempted to make an election under Subchapter S, so that the election was invalid.

[29] Coast Carton Co. v. Commissioner, 149 F.2d 739, 33 AFTR 1468 (9th Cir. 1945); Crocker v. Commissioner, 84 F.2d 64, 17 AFTR 1256 (7th Cir. 1936).

[30] See National Metropolitan Bank v. United States, 345 F.2d 823, 15 AFTR 2d 987 (Ct. Cl. 1965) (bank in liquidation held to continue in existence for tax return purposes); and M. H. McDonnell, ¶65,125 P-H Memo TC (1965).

The Service has ruled, however, that a corporation may be dissolved *de facto*, even though it has not dissolved *de jure* under state law, so that a net operating loss sustained after such a *de facto* dissolution could not be carried back to an earlier year. Rev. Rul. 61-191, 1961-2 C.B. 251; see also Regs. §1.6012-2(a)(2) (re corporate "existence"); *infra*, Sec. 9.02 and Secs. 9.60-9.68.

wise.[31] Under the 1939 Code, the regulations stated flatly that sales of property by such trustees were taxable to the corporation and implied that the same was true of other types of income. Regs. 118, §39.22(a)-20. The corresponding regulations under the 1954 Code, Regs. §1.336-1, are less clear: they state that "gain or loss is recognized to a corporation on all sales by it, whether directly or indirectly (as through trustees or receivers)," and further provide in Regs. §1.6012-2(a)(2) that "a corporation does not go out of existence if it is turned over to trustees who continue to operate it." Thus, if the trustees are acting in a representative capacity on behalf of the corporation, their actions will be attributed to the corporation which will be taxed on the income (or will obtain the benefit of deductions) produced thereby.[32] Distinction should be made, however, between a trust whose sole purpose is to dispose of the remaining corporate property in an orderly fashion on behalf of the liquidating corporation and its shareholders, and a trust which does not dispose of the assets expeditiously or engages in a new and unrelated venture; in the latter case, the organization may be separately taxed as an "association" in its own right.[33]

A liquidating or dissolving corporation may distribute its assets in kind to its shareholders, and they may select a trustee, agent, or other representative to hold, manage, or dispose of the assets on their behalf. Such a representative is not a continuation of the corporation, and the status of the enterprise must be determined on its own characteristics;[33a] but the line between a corporate-chosen trustee in dissolution and a shareholder representative is, in practice, not always easily drawn.

Sec. 2.09.   Disregard of the corporate entity — "Dummy" corporations

As noted earlier, *supra*, Sec. 1.05, the mere existence of a corporation will not, of itself, require its recognition as an independent

---

[31] For the effect of this procedure on the corporation's taxable year, see §443(a)(2) and §443(b)(2)(B)(ii); see also Regs. §1.6012-3(b)(4), re filing of returns.

[32] See Hersloff v. United States, 310 F.2d 947, 10 AFTR 2d 6072 (Ct. Cl. 1962), cert. denied, 373 U.S. 923 (1963), for extensive discussion.

The importance of this principle was reduced by the enactment in 1954 of §337, providing that a liquidating corporation shall not recognize gain or loss on certain sales of property during the 12-month period following its adoption of a plan of complete liquidation. See discussion *infra*, Sec. 9.64.

[33] See generally Goodman, ¶46,300 P-H Memo TC (1946) (year 1938 — Issue G); J.W. Wells Lumber Co. Trust A, 44 B.T.A. 551 (1941).

[33a] See Regs. §307.7701-4(d), as to the possible corporate status of certain "liquidating trusts," and *supra*, Sec. 2.02.

taxable entity. Courts have always felt free, where the facts warrant, to determine that an entity was not what it purported to be, or that a transaction was consummated by a taxpayer other than its formal principal; and to invoke in support of their conclusions such vague doctrines as "business purpose," "form versus substance," "sham arrangement," "economic reality," and "step transactions." Many of the decisions in this area have involved artificial arrangements heavily charged with tax avoidance motives; in such instances, it is not surprising that the courts are willing to recast the form of a challenged transaction to prevent violation of the spirit, if not the letter, of the taxing statute.

One aspect of this problem, however, bears special note. A corporation, like an individual, may act as an agent or nominee for another person without becoming taxable on income collected by it on behalf of its principal. Thus, if a corporation is a mere "dummy" or *alter ego* for its shareholders, serving no other function and engaging in no significant business activity, its separate taxable identity may be disregarded. Requests to ignore a corporate entity, or to treat it as a mere "nominee" of the shareholders, have come most often at the behest of the Internal Revenue Service;[34] but taxpayers have also sometimes argued successfully that a corporation should be disregarded for tax purposes, so that its income and deductions could be attributed directly to its shareholders. For example, in Paymer v. Commissioner, 150 F.2d 334, 33 AFTR 1536 (2d Cir. 1945), it was held that a corporation serving as a "passive dummy" to take and hold title to real property, as a blind to deter the creditors of one of its shareholders, was not taxable on the income from the property. Other examples of corporations acting as mere "title-holding vehicles" for the convenience of their shareholders can be found.[35] If the entity has not been completely inert, however, the taxpayer is likely to meet both administrative and judicial resistance when he seeks to disregard the separate existence of his own creature. Thus, it was held in Commissioner v. State-Adams Corp., 283 F.2d 395, 6 AFTR 2d 5752 (2d Cir. 1960), that a corporation engaging in any "business activity," such as mortgaging property, executing leases, collecting rentals, making improvements, maintaining a bank account, or nego-

---

[34] See, for example, Factor v. Commissioner, 281 F.2d 100, 6 AFTR 2d 5028 (9th Cir. 1960), where a shareholder was taxed on the income of his corporation under the "agency" theory, and a fraud penalty was upheld as well; Johansson v. United States, 336 F.2d 809, 14 AFTR 2d 5605 (5th Cir. 1964) (corporate income taxed directly to shareholder who "earned it").

[35] Jackson v. Commissioner, 233 F.2d 289, 49 AFTR 1208 (2d Cir. 1956); John A. Mulligan, 16 T.C. 1489 (1951 (Non-acq.).

tiating sales, could not be regarded as a mere agent or nominee of its shareholders.[36]

As an original proposition, the theory that "business activity" is inconsistent with the status of agent or nominee seems dubious. Agents are often employed to execute leases, collect rents, negotiate sales, and otherwise manage property. The theory finds some support, however, in National Carbide Corp. v. Commissioner, 336 U.S. 422, 37 AFTR 834 (1949), holding that three subsidiary corporations were taxable on income earned in certain business operations although they were obligated by contract to pay over to their common parent all profits in excess of 6 percent of their capital stock (which was nominal in amount). See also Moline Properties, Inc. v. Commissioner, 319 U.S. 436, 30 AFTR 1291 (1943):

> Whether the purpose [of incorporating] be to gain an advantage under the law of the state of incorporation or to avoid or to comply with the demands of creditors or to serve the creator's personal or undisclosed convenience, so long as that purpose is the equivalent of business activity or is followed by the carrying on of business by the corporation, the corporation remains a separate taxable entity. (319 U.S. at 438-9.)

Although these Supreme Court decisions are frequently quoted in support of the theory that "business activity" is inconsistent with an agency relationship between the corporation and its shareholders, they do not fully support this theory. A better explanation of these cases is that the corporation must establish that it is an agent for its shareholders (with respect to the transactions in question) by evidence other than the control which shareholders automatically possess over their corporations. If the corporation merely holds title to property, and the management functions are carried on by the shareholders, it is comparatively easy to infer that the corporation is acting only as an agent or nominee. But if the corporation not only holds title but also manages the property or business operations, there is less reason to draw this inference; and if the shareholders disclaim responsibility for the corporation's activities, they are *ipso facto* rejecting the status of principals. It is significant that the relationship between the corporation and its shareholders has been ambiguous in the litigated cases; and there have been no decided cases in which the corporation was avowedly an agent of the shareholders for such purposes as binding them on contracts, pledging their credit, accepting service of pro-

[36] See also Given v. Commissioner, 238 F.2d 579, 50 AFTR (8th Cir. 1956); Greer v. Commissioner, 334 F.2d 20, 14 AFTR 2d 5154 (5th Cir. 1964).

cess, etc. It is of course possible that the shareholders will be bound by the actions of the corporation even in the absence of an explicit agreement to this effect, and if this can be established in a particular case, the corporation might be regarded as an agent for tax purposes also. But the taxpayer can hardly expect to receive the benefit of the doubt if the relationship has been deliberately left ambiguous, to be clarified only if some tax advantage looms on the horizon.[37]

Sec. 2.10.   Successor corporations

As stated earlier, a corporation's tax attributes are not ordinarily affected by changes in the ownership of its stock or the character of its business activities. *Supra,* Sec. 1.05. The same can be said of changes in its financial structure, such as refinancing operations, recapitalizations, and the like. If the corporation participates in a merger or consolidation or if its assets are acquired by another corporation, however, a myriad of questions arises: Does the taxable year end? Does the basis of property carry over to the resulting corporation? Does it inherit its predecessor's earnings and profits and net operating loss and capital loss carryovers? Must or may new elections be made as to accounting methods, inventory valuation, depreciation, and installment sales? Before the enactment of the 1954 Code, there were explicit statutory provisions regarding the carryover of basis in such transactions, but the transfer of other tax attributes was left obscure by Congress, and some of the cases relied heavily on form in determining whether the "new" corporation was a continuation of the "old" corporation or not.[38] Section 381 was enacted in 1954 to provide a comprehensive set of rules for the preservation of tax attributes, to be "based upon economic realities rather than upon such artificialities as the legal form of the reorganization"[39] Its principles are discussed *infra,* Ch. 13.

---

[37] For more on this problem, see Interstate Transit Lines v. Commissioner, 319 U.S. 590, 30 AFTR 1310 (1943) (parent denied deduction under §162(a) for payment to defray subsidiary's operating deficit for taxable year, although by contract the parent was to receive subsidiary's profits and reimburse it for losses); Fishing Tackle Products Co., 27 T.C. 638 (1957) (allowing a deduction in similar circumstances); Rev. Rul. 56-542, 1956-2 C.B. 327 (treating a "captive mine," held and operated by a corporation, as a joint venture of the shareholders, so that corporation may file a tax return showing neither income nor deductions, but allocating these items to the shareholders in proportion to their interests); Rev. Rul. 59-247, 1959-2 C.B. 14; Cleary, Use of Subsidiary as an Agent after the National Carbide Corporation Case, 8 N.Y.U. Inst. on Fed. Taxation 48 (1950); Comment, Income Tax Status of the Wholly Owned Subsidiary Corporation, 29 Texas L. Rev. 87 (1950).

[38] See *infra,* Sec. 13.02.

[39] S. Rept. No. 1622, 83d Cong., 2d sess., p.52.

The carryover of tax attributes from one corporation to another (either under the pre-1954 case law or under §381 of the 1954 Code) can lead to the acquisition of corporations primarily because of these attributes. Although on occasion any of the items that are preserved for the acquiring corporation may be a valuable prize, the most commonly-sought attribute is a net operating loss carryover; and for some years advertisements for defunct corporations with such carryovers have been sprinkled through the pages of the metropolitan and financial press. As will be seen, however, the Internal Revenue Service is armed with three statutory weapons for attacking such transactions: §269 (applicable to any tax attributes that may underlie an acquisition) and §382(a) and (b) (applicable only to the net operating loss carryover). Attention should also be called to Libson Shops, Inc. v. Koehler, 353 U.S. 382, 51 AFTR 43 (1957), restricting the use of a net operating loss carryover after a statutory merger.[40]

Sec. 2.11.   Unincorporated enterprises electing to be taxed as corporations under §1361

In 1954, Congress enacted §1361, permitting certain unincorporated business enterprises to elect to be taxed as corporations. The stated purpose of §1361 was to permit "the business to select the form or organization which is most suitable to its operations without being influenced by Federal income tax considerations," S. Rep. No. 1622, 83d Cong., 2d Sess., p. 119, but it has been said that §1361 "apparently received its main impetus and perhaps the only reason for its existence from the situation of a particular Georgia partnership."[41] A companion provision, permitting corporations to elect to be taxed as partnerships, was passed in 1954 by the Senate but rejected by the House, H. R. No. 2543, 83d Cong. 2d Sess.; the idea was revived in 1958 and enacted as Subchapter S (§§1371-77), *infra*, Ch. 14. At the same time, the Senate rejected a House attempt to repeal §1361.

---

[40] These matters are considered in detail, *infra*, ch. 13.

[41] Surrey, The Congress and the Tax Lobbyist — How Special Tax Provisions Get Enacted, 70 Harv. L. Rev. 1145, 1149n (1957).

For a general discussion of §1361, see Brown, Unincorporated Business Enterprises Electing to be Taxed as Domestic Corporations — Section 1361, 1955 So. Calif. Tax. Inst. 281.

The many enigmas that result from superimposing a quasi-corporate tax structure on an unincorporated enterprise, the limited importance of the provision, or both, may account for the fact that regulations under §1361 were not issued until 1960. Oblique notice of this delay was taken by §63 of the Technical Amendments Act of 1958, providing that an election may be retroactively revoked on or before the last day of the third month following the month in which the final regulations were published.

The Treasury persisted in its attack on §1361, however, and in 1966 Congress provided that no further elections could be made thereunder, and that all elections already in force will terminate on Jan. 1, 1969. In the meantime, electing enterprises may revoke their elections, under regulations to be prescribed by the Treasury. *The description that follows should be read in the light of these 1966 changes in §1361.*

An election under §1361 makes the enterprise subject to the corporate normal tax and surtax (§11), the accumulated earnings tax (§531), and the alternative capital gains tax (§1201). To elect, the enterprise must satisfy these conditions:

> 1. Ownership must be vested in an individual or in a partnership consisting of not more than 50 individual members;
> 2. No person having more than a 10 percent interest in the profits or capital of the enterprise may have a similar interest in another electing enterprise;
> 3. No owner may be a nonresident alien or foreign partnership; and
> 4. Either (a) capital must be "a material income producing factor,"[42] or (b) 50 percent or more of gross income must be derived from trading as a principal or from buying and selling real property, stock, securities, or commodities for the account of others.[43]

Of these conditions, the fourth is the most restrictive. It "rule[s] out firms engaged in professional services such as the law, accounting, medicine, engineering, and others," S. Rep. No. 1622, 83d Cong., 2 Sess., p. 119, and thus confines the use of §1361 to firms engaged in manufacturing, mercantile, brokerage, and similar activities.[44] Since such firms can almost always incorporate if they wish to be taxed as corporations, §1361 can at best serve a very limited function. Its usefulness is diminished still further by §1361(d), providing that the owners of the electing enterprise are not employees for purposes of

[42] The requirement that capital be a material income producing factor is found also in §704(e) (relating to family partnerships), and the regulations under §1361 are similar to the regulations under §704(e). Regs §1.1361-2(e)(2); Regs. §1.704-1(e)(1)(iv). See also §911(b), relating to the definition of earned income.

[43] Apparently income from trading as a principal, like brokerage income, must come from the types of property listed in §1361(b)(4). The regulations permit both types of income to be combined to meet the 50 percent requirement. Regs. §1.1361-2(e)(1).

[44] On the requirement of §1361(b)(4) that capital be a material income producing factor, see Fred J. Sperapani, 42 T.C. 308 (1964) (capital material in printing business); Howard J. Lewis, 42 T.C. 885 (1964) (capital not material in a health clinic business).

§401(a) (relating to pension and profit-sharing plans), and by §1361(i), providing that certain personal holding company income shall be segregated from operating income and taxed to the owners of the enterprise rather than to the entity. In these respects, the enterprise is not identical for tax purposes with a corporation. See also §1361(c) (not a corporation as to self-employment tax); §1361(m) (not a corporation for purposes of Parts III and IV of Subchapter C, relating to corporate reorganizations, etc.); Regs. §1.1361-3(a)(3)-(5).

An election under §1361 is irrevocable, so long as the enterprise remains unincorporated, unless the electing owners' interest in profits or capital drops to 80 percent or less. In such a case, a new election may be made, but all owners must join in. It should be noted that the conditions of §1361(b), set out above, are not ambulatory, so that a valid election is not destroyed by the later entry of an unqualified owner (unless the original owners' combined interest is reduced to 80 percent or less) or by a change in the nature of the enterprise's income.

If an electing enterprise becomes incorporated, the resulting change in its legal status is to be treated as a liquidation of the original business, with the tax consequences prescribed by §331, §334(a), and, where applicable, §341, according to the regulations.[45]

Part B.   The Corporation Income Tax

Sec. 2.20.   Introductory

The corporate income tax, as imposed by §11 for taxable years beginning in 1965 and thereafter, consists of a normal tax of 22 percent of taxable income and a surtax of 26 percent of that part of taxable income which exceeds $25,000. If the corporation received any partially tax-exempt interest (*infra*, Sec. 2.22), however, it may be deducted in computing taxable income for purposes of the normal tax only. If the corporation incurred an excess of net long-term capital gain over net short-term capital loss, an alternative tax is computed under §1201, with the result that the excess is taxed at not more than 25 percent. Taxable income is defined by §63(a) as gross income

---

[45] Regs. §1.1361-5(b); accord, Wein's Estate v. Commissioner, 330 F.2d 957, 13 AFTR 2d 1207 (3rd Cir. 1964); see also Rev. Rul. 61-41, 1961-1 C.B. 667, holding that the old unincorporated enterprise and the newly created corporation are two separate entities for tax return purposes; Rev. Rul. 66-25, 1966-5 I.R.B. 12.

less the deductions allowed by Chapter 1 of the income tax title of the Internal Revenue Code. The differences between an individual's gross income and a corporation's gross income are discussed in Sec. 2.21 hereof, and the differences in deductions are discussed in Sec. 2.22.

Sec. 2.21.   The corporation's gross income

Gross income is defined by §61(a), which makes no distinction between individuals and corporations. The term gross income is given greater specificity by §§71-77, which lay down more explicit rules for the inclusion of certain receipts, again with no distinction between corporations and individuals,[46] except in so far as some of the items (*e.g.*, alimony) could not be received by a corporation. In the case of the exclusions from gross income that are granted by §§101-119, however, there are a few explicit distinctions between corporations and individuals:

> *1. Income from discharge of indebtedness.* The option granted by §108 to exclude income from the discharge of indebtedness is available to an individual only if the indebtedness was incurred or assumed in connection with property used in his trade or business, but if the taxpayer is a corporation, any indebtedness will qualify.
>
> *2. Lessee's payment of lessor's income taxes.* The exclusion by a lessor of income arising from the payment of its income tax by a lessee is restricted, by §110, to cases where both the lessor and lessee are corporations.
>
> *3. Sports programs for American Red Cross.* Section 114, excluding from gross income the proceeds of a sports program conducted by the taxpayer for the benefit of the American National Red Cross, is available only to corporations. See Sturges, The Legal Status of the Red Cross, 56 Mich. L. Rev. 1, 20-21 (1957). But see Regs. §1.61-2(c) and G.C.M. 27026, 1951-1 C.B. 7, affording a means of excluding the proceeds of an event conducted for the benefit of charity which is not restricted either to corporations or to Red Cross benefits.
>
> *4. Exclusion of dividends received by individuals.* §116's exclusion of dividends received, up to $100 per taxpayer, is limited to individuals. But see §243, permitting corporations to deduct 85 percent of dividends received, discussed *infra*, Sec. 2.25.

---

[46] §74(b), relating to tax-exempt prizes and awards, was probably intended to apply only to individuals, but corporations are not explicitly excluded. The use of the word "his" in §74(b)(1) should not in itself exclude corporations, since "his" is used elsewhere to avoid the more cumbersome form "his, hers, or its" (*e.g.*, §75, §106 and §1221).

5. *Contributions to capital.* §118, providing that contributions to capital are not taxable as income, is restricted by its terms to corporate taxpayers. See further, *infra*, Sec. 3.16.

In addition to the items just described, §§101-119 exclude from gross income a number of items that by their nature could not be received by corporations, *e.g.*, employee death benefits under §101(b), combat pay under §112, scholarships and fellowships under §117, etc.

Sec. 2.22. Deductions

As respects deductions, the principal differences between corporate taxpayers and individuals are these:

1. *Standard deduction.* The optional standard deduction is allowed by §63(b) only to individuals. Corporations must itemize their deductions.

2. *Personal exemptions.* The deductions for personal exemptions ($600 per taxpayer, etc.) are restricted by §151(a) to individuals. A corporation is subject to tax no matter how small its taxable income may be.

3. *Personal deductions.* The personal deductions of §§213-217 (extraordinary medical expenses, child care expenses, alimony, payments to cooperative housing corporations and moving expenses) are explicitly restricted to individual taxpayers.

4. *Shareholder's tax paid by corporation.* Section 164(e) permits a corporation to deduct a tax imposed on a shareholder on his interest as a shareholder, if the corporation pays the tax and is not reimbursed by the shareholder. The taxes in question are imposed by some states on the capital stock of banks and some other corporations.[47]

5. *Deductibility of losses.* Section 165(a) provides that any loss sustained during the taxable year, if not compensated for by insurance or otherwise, may be deducted. In the case of an individual, however, §165(c) goes on to restrict the breadth of §165(a) by allowing the deduction only if the loss was incurred in a trade or business, a transaction entered into for profit, or a casualty. The restrictions of §165(c) are not applicable to corporations, presumably on the theory that all corporate transactions arise in trade or business. On several occasions, however, corporations have been denied deduc-

---

[47] On §164(e), see General Motors Corp. v. United States, 283 F.2d 699, 6 AFTR 2d 5762 (Ct. Cl. 1960); Rev. Rul. 92, 1953-1 C.B. 39; Ferguson v. Fidelity Union Trust Co., 24 F.2d 520, 6 AFTR 7334 (3d Cir. 1928) (deductibility for years preceding enactment of §164(e)).

tions under §162(a) (business expenses) and §167 (depreciation) on the ground that the property in respect of which the items arose was held for the personal convenience of the corporation's shareholders rather than for business purposes, and losses incurred on such property might well be treated as personal rather than corporate items even in the absence of a specific provision.[48] Note also that certain corporate payments for the benefit of its shareholders may constitute non-deductible constructive dividends. See *infra*, Sec. 5.05.

6. *Bad debts.* In the case of bad debts, a taxpayer other than a corporation is confined by §166(d) to a capital loss on "nonbusiness debts." This restriction is not, by its terms, applicable to corporations. In Cooper-Brannan Naval Stores Co., 9 B.T.A. 105 (1927), the court allowed a corporation to deduct an uncollectible loan made to the son-in-law of the principal shareholder, stating "that it is not proper for this Board to go into the question of the motive of petitioner's officers in making the . . . loan . . . nor into the question of whether or not such loan was an *ultra vires* act." Although the Internal Revenue Service has acquiesced in the decision, VII-1 C.B. 7 (1928), it would be perilous to assume that such a transaction could not be regarded as a personal rather than a corporate transaction.

Section 166(f), permitting certain payments by guarantors to be deducted from ordinary income, is restricted to non-corporate taxpayers, presumably on the theory that corporations were already entitled to ordinary deductions in such cases.

7. *Charitable contributions.* The deduction for charitable contributions is computed differently for corporations than for other taxpayers. Under the general rule of §170(a)(1), the contribution must be "paid" within the taxable year, regardless of the taxpayer's mode of accounting; but §170(a)(2) mitigates this requirement as to corporations on the accrual basis. They may elect to treat a contribution as paid during the taxable year if it is authorized by the board of directors during the year and paid within the first 2½ months of the following taxable year. The ceiling on the deduction for charitable contributions is, in the case of individuals, 20 percent of adjusted gross income (increased to 30 percent for certain contributions); but

---

[48] See Greenspon v. Commissioner, 229 F.2d 947, 48 AFTR 979 (8th Cir. 1956) (expenses of maintaining "unique horticultural showplace" at sole shareholder's farm disallowed as business expenses and taxed as constructive dividends to shareholder); Black Dome Corp., ¶46,130 P-H Memo TC (1946) (country estate); Savarona Ship Corp. ¶42,596 P-H Memo TC (1942); International Trading Co. v. Commissioner, 275 F.2d 578, 5 AFTR 2d 970 (7th Cir. 1960); Fleischer, The Tax Treatment of Expenses Incurred in Investigation for a Business or Capital Investment, 14 Tax L. Rev. 567, notes 42, 43, and 111 (1959).

for corporations, the ceiling is 5 percent of taxable income (computed with certain adjustments). Contributions by a corporation in excess of this amount may be carried forward for five years, and deducted (together with any other contributions made in those years) subject to the 5 percent ceiling for those years.

8. Amortizable bond premium. Section 171, relating to the amortization of bond premium, distinguishes between corporations and other taxpayers in two ways. By virtue of §171(d), a bond or other evidence of indebtedness does not qualify for amortization in the hands of the holder unless it was issued by a corporation. Secondly, in the case of partially tax-exempt bonds, amortization is mandatory for corporations but optional for other taxpayers.

9. Net operating loss deduction. There are several differences between corporations and other taxpayers in computing the net operating loss deduction, but they merely reflect other differences in computing taxable income for corporations and other taxpayers. See §172(d)(2)-(6).

10. Expenses for production of income. Section 212 was enacted in 1942 to permit the deduction of so-called "non-business expenses" (expenses paid or incurred for the production of income or for the management, conservation, or maintenance of property held for the production of income), and was enlarged in 1954 to embrace expenses incurred in the determination, collection, or refund of taxes. §212 is restricted to individuals, presumably on the theory that §162(a) covers the same ground for corporations that §162(a) and §212 in combination cover for other taxpayers. Thus, if a corporation engaged in manufacturing holds some securities as an incidental investment, the cost of a safe deposit box, investment advice, bookkeeping, etc. incurred with respect to the securities would be deductible under §162(a) as trade or business expenses, even though an individual proprietor holding such securities would have to resort to §212 as authority for deducting such expenses.[49]

11. Partially tax-exempt interest. Under §242, a corporation may deduct partially tax-exempt interest (interest on federal obligations, if exempt from normal tax under the statute authorizing the issuance of the obligation). This deduction is allowed only in computing the

---

[49] During the 1942 hearings on §212, a taxpayer representative recommended its enlargement to include corporations. Hearings on Revenue Act of 1942, Senate Finance Committee, 77th Cong., 2d Sess., p. 1733. The recommendation was not adopted, probably because it was thought to be unnecessary. At any rate, it has been generally assumed since 1942 that corporation can deduct under §162(a) any expenses that could be deducted under §212 by an individual proprietor or partnership.

corporation's normal tax (22 percent of taxable income), not in computing the surtax (26 percent of taxable income in excess of $25,000). (The deduction must be reduced under §171(a)(3) for the amortizable bond premium for the taxable year, if any.) In the case of individuals, the allowance for partially tax-exempt interest takes the form of a credit under §35(a)(1), but the difference in result is minor (see §36).

12. *Dividends received deduction.* Sections 243-246 permit the corporation to deduct certain dividends received from other corporations. Of these provisions, discussed *infra*, sec. 2.25, the most important is §243, providing for a deduction of 85 percent of dividends received from domestic taxable corporations.

13. *Dividends paid by public utilities on certain preferred stock.* Although dividends paid by a corporation are not normally deductible, §247 grants a limited deduction for dividends paid by public utility corporations on certain perferred stock. This exception to the general rule that dividends are not deductible by the paying corporation was enacted in 1942, in response to testimony that regulatory restrictions on the issuance of debt by public utilities would make expansion to meet war demands difficult, and that a deduction for dividends paid on preferred stock would make it easier to attract equity capital. Hearings on H.R. 7378, House Committee on Ways and Means, 77th Cong., 2d Sess., pp. 200-05, 3330-31 (1942).

14. *Organizational expenditures.* Section 248, discussed *infra*, sec. 2.26, permits a corporation to amortize its organizational expenditures over a period of five years or more.

Sec. 2.23. Special deduction problems arising from corporate-shareholder relationship.

The relationship between corporations and their shareholders often generates questions about the deductibility of expenditures incurred by both groups. The corporation's right to deduct "shareholder-connected" expenditures is governed by the provisions of §162 (ordinary and necessary business expenses), while the shareholder's right to deduct "corporate-connected" outlays is governed by §162 and §212 (investment expenses); but account must also be taken of §262 and §263(a)(1), denying deductions for personal expenses and capital expenditures, respectively. The application of these statutory provisions and of such related doctrines as the "frustration of public policy" rule depends so heavily on principles growing out of noncorporate contexts that a full discussion of this area is beyond the scope of this treatise; but mention may be made of a few categories of corporate-connected and shareholder-connected expenses of special interest.[50]

1. Proxy fight expenses. Expenses incurred for the acquisition of stock in a corporation and the resulting control of its management generally constitute a capital expenditure, to be added to the basis of the acquired stock.[51] Several recent decisions have allowed insurgent shareholders to deduct the expense of soliciting proxies from their fellow-shareholders, however, where their purpose was to alter the business policies of the incumbent directors in order to increase their dividend income or the value of their stock.[52] By the same token, the expenses incurred by a corporation in resisting the insurgents have been held deductible, at least where the management believed in good faith that resistance was in the best interests of all shareholders.[53]

2. Shareholder derivative suit expenses. Payments by corporations or their directors to resist or settle claims arising in shareholder derivative suits for breach of a director's fiduciary duty, have generally been held deductible as an ordinary and necessary outgrowth of the corporation's or director's trade or business, but the possibility of an expenditure that must be capitalized should not be overlooked.

---

[50] Another area of great importance — corporate outlays that constitute constructive distributions to the shareholders — is discussed *infra*, Sec. 5.05.

On the treatment of expenditures by a shareholder to promote the business of his corporation, see Deputy v. du Pont, 308 U.S. 488, 23 AFTR 808 (1940); James M. Rawkins, 20 T.C. 1069 (1953) (deduction denied); Tom C. Connally, ¶61, 312 P-H Memo TC (do.).

[51] See Dwight Williamson, 17 B.T.A. 1112 (1929).

[52] Alleghany Corp., 28 T.C. 298 (1957) (Acq.); Graham v. Commissioner, 326 F.2d 878, 13 AFTR 2d 423 (4th Cir. 1964); Surasky v. United States, 325 F.2d 191, 12 AFTR 2d 6005 (5th Cir. 1963). The Court in *Graham* distinguished J. Raymond Dyer, 36 T.C. 456 (1961), which denied a deduction for expenses of a small shareholder who "crusaded" for a particular point of view; such expenses could not reasonably be expected to affect either dividend income or stock value. The Service has announced that it will follow the result in *Graham* and *Surasky*, but only if the expenses are proximately related to the production of income or to the conservation of income property. Rev. Rul. 64-236, 1964-2 C.B. 64.

See generally, Note, Proxy Fight Expenses: Problems of Tax Deduction, 43 Va. L. Rev. 891 (1957).

[53] Locke Mfg. Co. v. United States, 237 F. Supp. 80, 14 AFTR 2d 6104 (D. Conn. 1964).

For other expenditures growing out of disputes between a corporation and its shareholders, see Smith Hotel Enterprises v. Nelson, 236 F. Supp. 303, 15 AFTR 2d 76 (D. Wis. 1964) (expenses in defending a dissenting shareholder's appraisal suit deductible); Boulder Bldg. Corp. v. United States, 125 F. Supp. 512, 46 AFTR 1225 (W.D. Okla. 1954) (contra); Baltimore Steam Packet Co. v. United States, 180 F. Supp. 347, 5 AFTR 2d 567 (Ct. Cl. 1960) (premium paid on redeeming debentures owned by dissatisfied shareholder held deductible); Heller v. Commissioner, 2 T.C. 371 (1943), aff'd., 147 F. 2d 376, 33 AFTR 681 (9th Cir. 1945) (§212 deduction for litigation expenses incurred by dissenting shareholder in appraisal suit); Five Star Mfg. Co. v. Commissioner, 355 F.2d 724, 17 AFTR 2d 183 (5th Cir. 1966) (purchase of stock).

If the expenditure is incurred by the shareholder rather than by the corporation or the defendant directors, it may be either a deductible expense under §212 or a captial outlay to be added to the basis of his stock under §263(a)(1) and §1016(a)(1) (or partly one and partly the other), depending on the nature of his claim and the outcome of the suit.[54]

3. *Repayment of "insider" profits.* In Rev. Rul. 61-115, 1961-1 C.B. 56, involving a corporate "insider's" repayment of his "short-swing" profits to his corporation under §16(b) of the Securities and Exchange Act of 1934, the Service announced that it would not seek to apply the "frustration of public policy" principle to disallow a deduction by the insider. The ruling does not specify the statutory authority for the deduction itself, but presumably it is either §165(c)-(2) (loss from transaction entered into for profit) or §212 (expense of producing income). In line with Arrowsmith v. Commissioner, 344 U.S. 6, 42 AFTR 649 (1952), the ruling states that the prior related transaction will determine whether the payment is deductible as an ordinary loss or as a capital loss.

4. *Stock issuance expenses.* Expenditures incurred by a corporation in issuing or selling its own stock, whether on organization or pursuant to a stock dividend or recapitalization, are treated as nondeductible capital outlays.[55]

5. *Liquidation and reorganization expenses.* The expense of liquidating a corporation is ordinarily deductible on the liquidating corporation's final return (*infra*, Sec. 9.68), but reorganization expenses usually constitute capital expenditures unless incident to a liquidation or unless they relate to the oragnization of a new corporation so as to qualify for deduction under §248 (*infra*, Sec. 2.26).[56] *Shareholder* expenses incurred in liquidating their corporation are capital in nature and enter into the computation of their gain or loss on the liquidation distribution. But see Commissioner v. Doering, 335 F.2d 738, 14 AFTR 2d 5070 (2d Cir. 1964) (shareholder's ex-

---

[54] See Hochschild v. Commissioner. 161 F.2d 817, 35 AFTR 1373 (2d Cir. 1947) (director's legal fees in successful defense of shareholder derivative suit alleging breach of "corporate opportunity" doctrine); Graham v. Commissioner, 326 F.2d 878, 13 AFTR 2d 423 (4th Cir. 1964) (settlement of suit against director alleging "waste of corporate assets" in reimbursing proxy expenses of insurgents who acquired control of the corporation; Ingalls Iron Works v. Patterson, 158 F. Supp. 627, 1 AFTR 2d 785 (D. Ala. 1958) (corporate reimbusement of shareholder's legal expenses incurred in a derivative suit, held deductible by the corporation); Pennroad Corp., 21 T.C. 1087 (1954); see also Ditmars v. Commissioner, 302 F. 2d 481, 9 AFTR 2d 1269 (2d Cir. 1962) (payments by trustee to settle breach of trust charge, held deductible).

[55] See General Bancshares Corp. v. Commissioner, 326 F.2d 712, 13 AFTR 2d 549 (8th Cir. 1964); *infra*, Sec. 2.26 and Sec. 9.68, n. 108.

[56] See Kingsford Co., 41 T.C. 646 (1964) (Acq.); *infra*, Sec. 9.68.

pense in collecting a contingent corporate claim distributed in liquidation, held deductible).

Sec. 2.24. Non-deductible items

The Code lists in §§261-275 certain items that may not be deducted in computing taxable income. In general, these restrictions are applicable equally to corporations and individuals, but these distinctions may be noted:

1. Disallowed losses. Section 267(a)(1) provides that losses from sales or exchanges of property, directly or indirectly, between certain related persons may not be deducted. (An exception is made for losses in corporate liquidations, see *infra*, Sec. 7.81). The relationships that will cause losses to be disallowed are specified by §267(b); they include (a) an individual and a corporation of which he owns, directly or indirectly, more than 50 percent in value of the outstanding stock; (b) two corporations, if the same individual owns more than 50 percent in value of the outstanding stock of both *and* if one of the corporations was a personal holding company or foreign personal holding company during the taxable year preceding the sale; and (c) a fiduciary of a trust and a corporation, if the trust or a grantor thereof owns, directly or indirectly, more than 50 percent in value of the corporation's outstanding stock. The ownership of stock is to be determined by reference to the constructive ownership rules of §267-(c).

2. Disallowed expenses and interest. Section 267(a)(2) provides that expenses or interest, otherwise deductible under §§162, 163, or 212, may not be deducted in certain cases where the taxpayer and the payee are related persons (as determined by the rules applicable to §267(a)(1), described in the previous paragraph). Although §267-(a)(2) is applicable without discrimination to corporate and individual taxpayers, its main purpose is to prevent a one-man, accrual basis corporation from deducting expenses and interest due to its sole shareholder, if he is on the cash basis and the amounts are not actually or constructively received by him within the taxable year and the first 2½ months of the succeeding taxable year. See Paul, Some Problems Under the New Section 24(c), 32 Taxes 191 (1954); Carroad and Handman, The Nondeductibility of Certain Losses, Expenses and Interest Items, 33 *ibid.* 142 (1955).

3. Limitation on deduction of losses over $50,000 for five successive years. Section 270 provides that if a trade or business conducted by an individual produces a net loss of more than $50,000 in each of five successive years, his tax shall be recomputed so as to disallow the excess deductions. By its terms, §270 applies only to individuals, not to corporations.[57] As to the possibility of avoiding §270 by incorporating the trade or business every fifth year, see §269 (*infra*, Ch. 13).

4. Deduction for capital gains. Taxpayers other than corporations are allowed by §1202 to deduct 50 percent of the excess of net long-term capital gain over net short-term capital loss, with the result that the total tax burden is moderated even for those who gain no advantage from the 25 percent tax ceiling of §1201(b). In the case of a corporation, however, this deduction is not allowed, and the sole concession granted to long-term capital gains is the 25 percent ceiling of §1201(a).

5. Limitation on capital losses. A corporation may deduct its capital losses only from capital gains, under §1211(a); it does not enjoy the privilege, granted to other taxpayers by §1211(b), of applying the excess against ordinary income to the extent of $1,000. Under §1212(a), a corporation is entitled to a 5 year carryover (as a short term capital loss) for the unused portion of its capital losses; while an individual, under §1212(b), is able to carry forward such losses indefinitely.

6. Acquisition of corporation to avoid income taxes. Section 269 provides for the disallowance of deductions, etc., (a) if any person or persons acquire control of a corporation, or (b) if a corporation acquires the property of another corporation, not previously controlled by it, in such a way that the basis of the property carries over from the transferor to the transferee, provided that the principal purpose of the acquisition is avoidance of federal income taxes. For discussion, see *infra*, Ch. 13.

Sec. 2.25.   Dividends received deduction

Dividends received by a corporate taxpayer ordinarily qualify for the deduction provided by §243 (85 percent of dividends received from a domestic corporation subject to federal income taxes), §244

---

[57] The exclusion of corporations from §270 is ironic since §270's enactment was supported by a number of legislators who thought that it would strike at Marshall Field, Jr., the publisher of the controversial New York newspaper PM. Although §270 thus gained a popular name ("the Marshall Field amendment"), it did not apply to Mr. Field, whose publishing was carried on through corporations. Another bit of historical curiosa is that Mr. Field's father had been allowed to deduct his losses in running a racing stable, on the ground that they were incurred in a trade or business; and *these* losses would have been disallowed in part by §270 if it had been in effect for earlier years. Field v. Commissioner, 26 B.T.A. 116 (1932), aff'd. 67 F.2d 876, 13 AFTR 415 (2d Cir. 1933). Although §270 was designed to disallow such losses, the Field horses were evidently overshadowed by the Field newspapers and played no role in the debate.

(60.208 percent, at 1965 rates, of dividends received on certain preferred stock of public utilities), or §245 (85 percent of a specified portion of the dividends received from certain foreign corporations) — all subject to the limitations imposed by §246. Of these provisions, §243 is of principal importance. By permitting the corporate taxpayer to deduct 85 percent of dividends received from other corporations,[58] §243 reduces the effective maximum tax rate on dividends received by a corporation to 7.2 percent, *i.e.*, the corporate tax rate of 48 percent is imposed on only 15 percent of the dividends received. If the corporation's taxable income is below $25,000, the effective tax rate on dividends received by it is only 3.3 percent (22 percent on 15 percent of the dividends received).

From 1917 to 1935, corporations were not taxed on dividends received from other corporations, in order to prevent the multiple taxation of corporate earnings as they passed from one corporation to another, possibly within the same chain of beneficial ownership. The law was revised in 1935, however, to exempt only 85 percent of the dividends received, in order to discourage the use of multiple entities for tax avoidance and as a part of the New Deal program of pressing for the simplification of elaborate corporate structures.[59] The 85 percent rule, adopted in 1935, is still controlling, but the deduction has been refined in several respects since then.

The salient features of §§243-245 are these:

1. Dividends from domestic corporations. Section 243(a)(1) provides generally that 85 percent of the amount received as dividends from a domestic corporation which is subject to federal income taxation may be deducted. The requirement that the paying corporation be subject to income taxation reflects the fact that the purpose of the deduction is to mitigate the multiple taxation of corporate earnings. In harmony with this principle, §243(c)(1) excludes amounts deductible by the paying corporation under §591 (relating to dividends paid by mutual savings banks and domestic building and loan associations, loosely referred to as "interest"), and §243(c)(2) limits the deductibility of certain dividends received from a regulated investment company (*supra*, Sec. 1.06).

---

[58] In the case of a "small business investment company" (*supra*, Sec. 1.06), the deduction is 100 percent of the dividends received, and the limit of §246(b) is inapplicable. §243(a)(2). In the case of certain "electing affiliated groups," the deduction is also 100 percent by virtue of §243(a)(3), enacted in 1964. *Infra*, Sec. 13.31.

[59] The program also included, in the arena of taxation, the former 2 percent surcharge for filing consolidated returns (*infra*, Sec. 13.40) and the nonrecognition of gain or loss on the liquidation of a subsidiary (§332, *infra*, Sec. 9.40).

2. Dividends of "affiliated groups." Section 243(a)(3) was enacted, in 1964, as part of a general revision of the treatment of
"affiliated corporations"; it permits a 100 percent deduction for certain intra-corporate dividends, subject to an election under which all
members of an "affiliated group" of corporations must consent to
divide a single $25,000 surtax exemption, and $100,000 minimum accumulated earnings credit among them. The election must also cover
the exploration expense deduction, and certain other matters set out
in §243(b). The treatment of multiple corporations, and "affiliated
groups" in general, is considered in greater detail, *infra*, Ch. 13.

3. Dividends on public utility preferred stock. Public utility corporations are allowed, by §247, to deduct a portion of dividends paid
by them on certain perferred stock (*supra*, Sec. 2.22). Since (at 1965
rates) 14/48ths of the dividends paid is deductible by the paying
corporation, §244 permits the recipient corporation to take only the
remaining 34/48ths into account in computing its dividends received
deduction. The 85 percent deduction is applied against this residue,
the net result being that 60.208 percent (85/100 x 34/48) of the
entire dividend is deductible.

4. Dividends from certain foreign corporations. Dividends paid
by a foreign corporation qualify for the dividends received deduction
under §245 only if the paying corporation (a) is not a foreign personal
holding company (*infra*, Sec. 6.40), (b) is subject to federal income
taxation, (c) has engaged in business within the United States for
a period of 36 successive months ending with the year in which the
dividends were paid (or for its entire existence, if less than such 36
month period), and (d) has derived 50 percent or more of its gross
income from sources within the United States for the same period. If
the foreign corporation's dividends qualify under these tests, the 85
percent deduction is applied to a portion of the dividends determined
by reference to the ratio of gross income from sources within the
United States to total gross income.[60] By virtue of these complex
limitations, the 85 percent deduction is applicable to dividends paid
by a foreign corporation only to the extent that, roughly speaking,
they reflect income that has been subjected to United States taxation.
Thus, if 60 percent of the foreign corporation's gross income is from
sources within the United States, 60 percent of its dividends will be
eligible, in the hands of a recipient corporation, for the 85 percent
deduction.

---

[60] This computation is made separately for dividends out of current earnings and profits and for dividends out of earnings and profits accumulated during
the 36 month period. See *infra*. Sec. 5.02.

The term "dividend," as used in §§243-245, is defined by §316 (*infra*, Sec. 5.02). Although §§243-245 do not say so explicitly, dividends should not qualify for the dividends received deduction unless they are includible in gross income. For this reason, stock dividends that are excluded from gross income under §305 (*infra*, Sec. 5.61) should not give rise to a dividends received deduction.[61] For the same reason, if a distribution is made in property other than money, the dividends received deduction should be calculated on the property's fair market value or its adjusted basis in the hands of the distributing corporation, whichever is lower, since §301(b) prescribes this method of determining the amount of the distribution (*infra*, Sec. 5.23). The regulations explicitly adopt this position with respect to the dividends received deduction under §243, Regs. §1.243-1(a), but it seems equally applicable to the deduction authorized by §244.[62] Similarly, a distribution in partial or complete liquidation, being treated as the proceeds of a sale of the stock rather than as a dividend (*infra*, Ch. 7), would not qualify for the dividends received deduction; and the same should be true of a stock redemption if it escapes dividend treatment (*infra*, Ch. 7).[63] Likewise, other non-dividend receipts should not be entitled to the dividends received deduction of §243.[64]

Although there are technically three separate dividend received deductions (§243, for dividends paid by domestic corporations; §244, for preferred dividends paid by public utilities; and §245, for dividends paid by certain foreign corporations), they are aggregated by §246 for the purpose of imposing certain limitations:

[61] The Internal Revenue Service takes the position that ordinary income is realized on a sale of stock rights (*infra*, Sec. 5.63), and it was held in Tobacco Products Export Corp., 21 T.C. 625 (1954) (Non-acq.), that the income thus realized qualified for the dividends received credit of the 1939 Code.

[62] As to dividends received from foreign corporations, the statute was amended in 1962 to provide specifically that the amount of a property distribution which qualifies for treatment under §245 is to be determined under the rules of §301(b)(1)(B). §245(b). Other property distributions from foreign corporations are to be taken into account at fair market value. §301(b)(1)(C). If the distribution is only partly under §245, then pro-ration is required in accordance with §301(b)(1)(C)(i) and (ii).

[63] See §331(b); Robert Gage Coal Co., 2 T.C. 488 (1943); Fostorial Glass Co. v. Yoke, 45 F. Supp. 962, 965, 29 AFTR 1115 (N.D.W. Va. 1942).

For a related problem under the "deemed paid" foreign tax credit provision of §902, see Associated Tel. & Tel. Co. v. United States, 306 F. 2d 824, 10 AFTR 2d 5414 (2d Cir. 1962) (distribution in complete liquidation not a "dividend" under §902); Fowler Hosiery Co. v. Commissioner, 301 F. 2d 394, 9 AFTR 2d 1252 (7th Cir. 1962) (same for partial liquidation).

[64] See Liston Zander Credit Co. v. United States, 276 F.2d 417, 5 AFTR 2d 986 (5th Cir. 1960) (alleged "dividends" held to be refunds of insurance premiums paid by the taxpayer, and hence not eligible for the §243 deduction); United States v. Georgia R.R. and Banking Co., 348 F.2d 278, 16 AFTR 2d 5061 (5th Cir. 1965) (§243 deduction belongs to the "beneficial owner" of the stock receiving the dividends).

1. Certain distributing corporations excluded. §246(a) provides that the dividends received deductions of §§243-245 shall not apply to dividends paid by China Trade Act corporations (*supra*, Sec. 1.06), corporations that are exempt from tax under §501 (charitable corporations, federal instrumentalities,[65] mutual telephone companies, etc.) or §521 (farmers' cooperative associations, or corporations under §931 (*supra*, Sec. 1.06). These corporations are disqualified because their earnings are wholly or partially tax-exempt; §246(a) thus buttresses, and in part overlaps, the rules set out in §§243-245.

In the case of corporations under §501, §521, and §931, the disqualification of §246(a) is operative if the forbidden status exists during the year in which the distribution is made or existed in the preceding taxable year.

2. Ceiling on aggregate deduction. Unless the taxpayer corporation has incurred a net operating loss in the taxable year, the aggregate deduction under §§243-245 may not exceed 85 percent of taxable income computed without regard to the deductions under §172 (net operating loss carryover from another year), §§243-245, or §247 (dividends paid on public utility preferred stock).[66]

3. Sales of stock ex-dividend. Before 1958, the dividends received deduction held out to the corporate taxpayer the possibility of buying stock just before a dividend became payable and selling it immediately thereafter, in order to deduct the loss on the sale (presumably equal to the amount of the dividend, assuming no other market fluctuations), while paying income tax on only 15 percent of this amount. A similar manipulative device was the maintenance of both "long" and "short" positions in the stock over the dividend payment date, in order to deduct the amount of the dividend paid to the lender of the "short" stock from ordinary income while reporting only 15 percent of the dividend received on the "long" stock. To close these loopholes, §246-(c) was enacted by the Technical Amendments Act of 1958. This provision denies any deduction under §§243-245 if the stock is not held for more than 15 days (90 days in the case of certain preferred stock), the holding period being so calculated as to prevent avoidance of the restriction. The 1958 amendment also denies the deduction if the taxpayer maintains a "short" position (or is subject to a similar obligation with respect to the dividend), in substantially identical stock or securities. See S. Rep. No. 1983, 85th Cong., 2d Sess., pp. 28-29, 139-140.

---

[65] But see Rev. Rul. 56-510, 1956-2 C.B. 168, holding that dividends paid by the Federal National Mortgage Association ("Fanny May") qualify because, although exempt, it makes payments to the Treasury in lieu of taxes.

[66] For this complex, but rarely encountered restriction, see Graichen, The Net Operating Loss, 16 N.Y.U. Inst. on Fed. Taxation 865, 867 (1958); Hellerstein, Intercorporate Dividends and the Interplay between the Dividends Received Credit and other Provisions, 7 *Ibid.* 547 (1949) (under 1939 Code); Rev. Rul. 56-151, 1956-1 C.B. 382.

Sec. 2.26. Organizational expenditures

Before 1954, a corporation's organizational expenditures, such as legal fees for drafting the charter, by-laws, and stock certificates, could not be deducted when paid or incurred, but were treated as investments to be deducted as a loss on dissolution or, in the unusual case of a corporation of limited duration, to be amortized over the life specified in its charter.[67] For the stated purpose of conforming "tax accounting more closely with general business accounting for these costs,"[68] §248 was enacted in 1954 to permit the corporation to elect to amortize its "organizational expenditures" over a period of 60 months or more from the month in which the corporation begins business. S. Rep. No. 1622, 83d Cong., 2d Sess., p. 37. The regulations state that the date a corporation "begins business" is a question of fact, and that ordinarily it is the date when the corporation "starts the business operation for which it was organized," not the date when it comes into existence. Regs. §1.248-1(a)(3).

The term "organizational expenditures" is defined by §248(b) to mean any expenditure which:

1. is incident to the creation of the corporation;
2. is chargeable to capital account; and
3. is of a character which, if expended incident to the creation of a corporation having limited life, would be amortizable over such life.

The regulations list as "examples" of expenditures that will qualify under §248: "legal services incident to the oragnization of the corporation, such as drafting the corporate charter, by-laws, minutes of organizational meetings, terms of original stock certificates, and the like; necessary accounting services; expenses of temporary directors and of

---

[67] See generally Shellabarger Grain Products Co. v. Commissioner, 146 F.2d 177. 185, 33 AFTR 351 (7th Cir. 1944); Blumberg Brothers Co., 12 B.T.A. 1021 (1928); Hershey Mfg. Co. v. Commissioner, 43 F.2d 298, 9 AFTR 71 (10th Cir. 1930); Weissman, Allowable Deductions on the Formation, Reorganization, and Liquidation of a Corporation, 53 Northwestern Univ. L. Rev. 681 (1959); Note, Certain Tax Aspects of Organization, Reorganization and Liquidation Costs, 10 Stanf. L. Rev. 112 (1957); Weiss, Income Tax Deductions on Corporate Termination, 9 Tax L. Rev. 490 (1954).

For the deductibility of organizational expenditures by a liquidating corporation, see *infra*, Sec. 9.68.

[68] According to Paton, *Accountants' Handbook* (3d ed. 1945), p. 128, however, accountants agree that early amortization of organization costs is "proper," but a "more reasonable view" is to treat these expenses as an asset to be amortized only when the corporation contracts or liquidates. See also American Institute of Accountants, Accounting Research Bulletin No. 43, recommending that certain intangibles (including organization costs) be amortized only if they will not continue to have value during the entire life of the enterprise.

organizational meetings of directors or stockholders; and fees paid to State of incorporation." Regs. §1.248-1(b)(2).

The regulations go on to exclude expenditures connected with issuing or selling stock, such as commissions, professional fees, and printing costs. This exclusion of the expense of raising capital is in harmony with Surety Finance Co. v. Commissioner, 77 F.2d 221, 15 AFTR 1373 (9th Cir. 1935) (endorsed by the Senate Report on the 1954 Code, *supra*, at p. 224), holding that such expenses are the equivalent of selling the stock at a discount and that they do not create an asset that is exhausted over the life of the corporation. Similar expenses in selling securities are also excluded from §248 by the regulations, but they may be amortized over the term of the loan on the theory that they increase the interest expense on the borrowed funds.[69] The regulations also state that expenditures connected with the transfer of assets to a corporation do not qualify for amortization under §248; no examples are given, but presumably the reference is to the cost of title searches, recordation, transportation, etc., which would be added to the basis of the assets themselves, to be depreciated over the life of the assets or offset against the proceeds when the assets are sold. Finally, the regulations state that expenditures connected with a corporation's reorganization, unless "directly incident to the creation of a corporation," do not qualify under §248, echoing a statement in the Senate Report on the 1954 Code, *supra*, at p. 224. Some "reorganizations" include the creation of a new corporation (*e.g.*, some consolidations and transfers to controlled corporations), and this part of the expenses can be amortized under §248.[70]

The election to amortize organizational expenditures under §248 must be made on or before the date for filing the tax return for the taxable year in which the corporation begins business. §248(c). The election must specify an amortization period of 60 months or longer, which must commence with the month in which the taxpayer begins business and may not be altered, and the expenditures are to be deducted ratably over the specified period. The regulations state that an election "shall apply" to all of the corporation's organizational expenditures, thus prohibiting a partial election, but that only expenditures "incurred" before the end of the taxable year in which business begins will qualify. Regs. §1.248-1(a)(2). This statement leaves am-

---

[69] Helvering v. Union Pacific R. Co., 293 U.S. 282, 14 AFTR 705 (1934); Molloy, The Ambiguous Tax Nature of the Various Costs of Borrowing Capital, 11 Tax L. Rev. 363 (1956).

[70] As to the possibility of deducting the balance on a later dissolution of the reorganized corporation, see Weissman, *supra*, n.67 at v. 709; Weiss, *supra* n. 67 at p. 492; Kingsford Co., 41 T.C. 646 (1964) (Acq.).

biguous the status of subsequently incurred organizational expenditures; it may be the position of the Treasury that they are not only outside §248, but also disqualified for deduction on dissolution.

Failing an election, organizational expenditures may be deducted only on dissolution (except for a corporation of limited life), under the judicial rules developed before the enactment of §248. If a corporation that elects under §248 is dissolved before its expenditures have been fully amortized, it should be entitled to deduct the balance at that time, but §248 is silent on this point.

Chapter Three

TRANSFERS OF PROPERTY TO A CORPORATION

Sec. 3.01. Introductory

In general, a corporation does not recognize either gain or loss on issuing its stock (*infra*, Sec. 3.15). As to the shareholder, the acquisition of stock for cash similarly entails no immediate tax consequences: he has made an investment, the gain or loss on which will be reckoned up only when he sells or otherwise disposes of his stock or when, to his chagrin, it becomes worthless. (This is on the assumption that he pays the fair market value for the shares; a "bargain purchase" might constitute compensation for services or other taxable income.)

If the purchaser acquires the stock for property rather than for money, however, he may have to recognize gain or loss on the transaction. The transfer of the property to the corporation in exchange for the stock is a "sale or other disposition" of the property within the meaning of §1001(a), upon which the transferor realizes gain or loss equal to the difference between the adjusted basis of the property given up and the value of the stock received in exchange. By virtue of §1002, the entire amount of this gain or loss is to be recognized by the transferor of the property unless the transaction comes within one of the "non-recognition" provisions of the Code.

Since property is frequently transferred for corporate stock or securities, especially on the organization of a new corporation, the following "non-recognition" provisions relating to such transactions are of great importance:

> 1. §351, providing that no gain or loss shall be recognized if property is transferred to a corporation solely in exchange for its stock or securities, and if the transferor or transferors control the corporation immediately after the exchange.
> 2. §361(a), providing that no gain or loss shall be recognized if a corporation that is a party to a reorganization transfers property to another corporation a party to the reorganization.

This chapter will deal primarily with transfers under §351. This section is of particular importance when individual proprietorships and partnerships are incorporated. It also embraces the transfer of property to a previously organized corporation by its controlling shareholders. Section 361(a), mentioned above, is discussed *infra*, Sec. 12.32. It may be noted at this point, however, that a transfer may qualify under both §351 and §361(a), *e.g.*, when a corporation creates a subsidiary by transferring part of its property for all the stock of the subsidiary and then distribute the subsidiary's stock as described in §368(a)(1)(D).

Whether or not a transaction qualifies under §351 is a question that may arise either at the time the transaction occurs or at some later date. When the transaction occurs, the applicability of §351 is critical because it determines whether the transferor recognizes gain or loss on the transfer. But the applicability of §351 may be put in issue later on, when the transferor sells the stock he received for the transferred property, since his basis for the stock depends upon whether the transaction in which he got it met the conditions of §351. If it did, the basis of the stock is the same as the basis of the property he gave up. §358. If, on the other hand, the exchange was not within §351, the basis of the stock is its "cost" (§1012) — ordinarily the fair market value of the property given up. The corporation's basis for the property transferred to it similarly depends, under §362, upon whether or not the transfer met the requirements of §351. As a result, controversy over the application of §351 to a given transaction may arise decades after the transaction occurred. In Manhattan Building Co., 27 T.C. 1032 (1957) (Acq.), for example, the corporation's gain or loss on the sale of a building in 1945 depended upon whether it acquired the property in 1922 in a transaction qualifying under the predecessor of §351.

Section 351 dates from the Revenue Act of 1921, its announced purpose being to facilitate business re-adjustments. Under previous revenue acts, the creation of even a one-man corporation by the transfer of appreciated or depreciated property for its entire capital stock was an occasion on which gain or loss was recognized by the transferor. Jefferson Livingston, 18 B.T.A. 1184 (1930) (Acq.). Since 1921, however, gain or loss has not been recognized on such a transaction.

The main features of today's §351 may be found in the 1921 provision, although there have been several amendments in the intervening period, most recently in 1954. Before turning to the details of §351, it may be helpful to spend a few moments on its purpose and philosophy.

In recommending the enactment of §351's predecessor in 1921, the Senate Finance Committee pointed out that exchanges of property were ordinarily taxable:

Probably no part of the present income tax law has been productive of so much uncertainty or has more seriously interfered with necessary business re-adjustments. The existing law makes a presumption in favor of taxation. The proposed Act . . . specifies . . . certain classes of exchanges on which no gain or loss is recognized even if the property received in exchange has a readily realizable market value. These classes comprise the cases where . . . an individual or individuals transfer property to a corporation and after such transfer are in control of such corporation.

The preceding amendments [the predecessors of §§351, 354 and 1031], if adopted, will, by removing a source of grave uncertainty and by eliminating many technical constructions which are economically unsound, not only permit business to go forward with the readjustments required by existing conditions but also will considerably increase the revenue by preventing taxpayers from taking colorable losses in wash sales and other fictitious exchanges. (S. Rep. No. 275, 67th Cong., 1st Sess., reprinted in 1939-1 C.B. (Part 2), 181 188-9.)

The basic premise of §351 is that a transfer of appreciated or depreciated property to a corporation that is controlled by the transferor works a change of form only, which should not be an occasion for reckoning up the transferor's gain or loss on the transferred property.[1] See Portland Oil Co. v. Commissioner, 109 F.2d 479, 488, 24 AFTR 225 (1st Cir. 1940), where the Court said:

It is the purpose of [§351] to save the taxpayer from an immediate recognition of a gain, or to intermit the claim of a loss, in certain transactions where gain or loss may have accrued in a constitutional sense, but where in a popular and economic sense there has been a mere change in the form of ownership and the taxpayer has not really "cashed in" on the theoretical gain, or closed out a losing venture.

The premise upon which §351 rests is in general sound, even though for most purposes the controlled corporation is treated as an entity separate from its shareholders. In point of fact, however, the language of §351 goes beyond its purpose and embraces some transfers that arguably ought to be treated as sales because the taxpayer has "cashed in" on his gain, either in whole or in part.

Thus, §351 is not restricted to transfers by a single individual to his one-man corporation; it also embraces transfers by two or more persons to a corporation that they control collectively. If *A* owns a

---

[1] So far as loss is concerned, a taxpayer transferring depreciated property to a controlled corporation is barred from deducting his loss by §267(a)(1) if he owns directly or indirectly more than 50 percent of the transferee's stock; but this provision, which thus overlaps §351 to some extent, was not enacted until 1936. *Supra*, Sec. 2.24; *infra*, note 16.

patent with a cost of $1,000 and a fair market value of $10,000 and
B owns land with a cost of $20,000 and a value of $10,000 and they
transfer their property to a new corporation in exchange for the stock
(each taking one-half), one might argue that the transfer is not merely
a matter of form, and that their economic positions have changed sufficiently so that A's gain ($9,000) and B's loss ($10,000) should be
recognized. But it has long been established that §351 embraces transfers of property by two or more persons who were not previously associated, on the ground that "instead of the transaction having the
effect of terminating or extinguishing the beneficial interests of the
transferors in the transferred property, after the consummation of the
transaction the transferors continue to be beneficially interested in
the transferred property and have dominion over it by virtue of their
control of the new corporate owner of it." American Compress & Warehouse Co. v. Bender, 70 F.2d 655, 657, 13 AFTR 1052 (5th Cir. 1934).

While in many cases, the transferors of property to a controlled
corporation do "continue to be beneficially interested in the transferred property," there are occasions when their interest is so attenu-
ated that the transaction can hardly be regarded as a matter of form
alone. Thus, if 1,000 independent business men, each owning a corner
grocery store, simultaneously transfer their assets to a newly organized corporation, each taking his share of the stock, the economic
status of each man has changed vitally. In the same vein, what of a
transfer of his assets by one corner groceryman for 0.01 percent of the
stock of a newly organized corporation, simultaneously with a transfer
by A. & P. of its assets in exchange for 99.99 percent of the stock?
The language of §351 is broad enough to confer tax-free status on
both of these hypothetical transfers, but the cautious tax advisor
would surely have some qualms about them. The hypothetical 1,000
storekeepers are discarding their roles as small tradesmen in order to
become investors in a widely held corporation, and it would be a triumph of literalism to apply §351 to their transaction. The same can
be said of the corner groceryman who intends to turn his back on
Mrs. Klotz and her complaints about his pork chops in order to devote
his attention to the *Wall Street Journal*. As to A. & P., however, the
transaction does seem to be a change of form rather than of substance,
and the spirit as well as the letter of §351 is applicable.

The availability of §351 as a vehicle for the tax-free diversification of investments by previously unrelated taxpayers came to the
fore with the recent development of the so-called "Centennial Fund"
or "swap-fund" exchange plan. This plan involves the transfer of appreciated securities by a large number of unrelated individuals to a

newly-organized investment company, in exchange for its stock. Each transferor thus unfreezes his investment in the securities of a single corporation by exchanging them for shares of a company with a diversified portfolio, in which his block of securities is only one of many. (A similar plan involves the transfer of appreciated real estate to a real estate investment trust in exchange for beneficial interests therein.) When the "swap-fund" idea first appeared, the Internal Revenue Service ruled in a number of private rulings that the exchange was tax-free under §351 because the transferors owned all of the stock of the transferee corporation immediately after the exchange; but since 1961, the Service has refused to issue rulings when such transactions occur "as a result of solicitations by promoters, brokers, or investment houses." This no-ruling policy was not followed up by an attempt to disallow the tax treatment claimed by participating investors, however, and exchanges of this type have been subsequently effected on the basis of favorable opinions of counsel.[2]

Another weakness in the theory that §351 applies only to changes of form in the taxpayer's investment stems from the fact that it embraces transfers of property for securities, as well as transfers for stock. If the shareholder of a one-man corporation transfers property to it in exchange for bonds of the corporation, it is not unreasonable to say that his economic position has not changed sufficiently to reckon up gain or loss, even though he is now a creditor of his corporation, as well as its sole shareholder. But can the same be said if A and B transfer property to a newly organized corporation, A taking back bonds and B taking all the stock? If this transaction passes muster, what if we vary the facts so that there are fifty transferors, one of whom receives bonds for his property, while all the others take stock only? Nothing in the language of §351 puts these transactions beyond its protection, but for the transferor who receives bonds, the transfer is hard to distinguish from a sale.[3]

---

[2] See generally Chirelstein, Tax Pooling and Tax Postponement — The Capital Exchange Funds, 75 Yale L. J. 183 (1965). For the Service's no-ruling position, see Rev. Proc. 64-31, Sec. 3.10, 1964-2 C.B. 947. This policy also applies to similar transfers of appreciated securities to partnerships, trusts, or other entities. Rev. Proc. 63-20, 1963-2 C.B. 754.

[3] It has been argued that a remark in the Senate Report on the 1954 Code validates a transaction in which A receives bonds and B stock. The passage in question states that "if M and N each owning property having a value of $100 transfer such property to a newly formed corporation X, and M receives all of the stock, such transaction would not be subject to tax under section 351." S. Rep. No. 1622, 83d Cong., 2d sess., p. 264. The context suggests, however, that the example is concerned with a case in which M receives all the stock (and N received nothing), because N is making a gift or paying compensation to M in the amount of $100. We are not told that §351 would be applicable if N had received bonds for his property.

Fortunately for the tax advisor, marginal cases of the types suggested in the two preceding paragraphs rarely arise. If they were of frequent occurrence, moreover, it is likely that §351 would by now have been amended to provide a statutory guide to their solution. In the absence of statutory provisions, one can only point out that the courts have not hesitated to engraft judicial restrictions on the language of other portions of Subchapter C of the Internal Revenue Code (*supra*, Sec. 1.05), and suggest that there is no reason to think that they would not exercise this prerogative under §351 in extreme cases. They might, for example, make use of the "continuity of interest" doctrine, which was created to prevent an undeserving transaction from qualifying as a tax-free corporate reorganization even though it came within the literal terms of the statutory language. For a discussion of this possibility, see *infra*, Sec. 3.04.

So much for the purpose and philosophy of §351. It is now time to turn to its details. The major requirements of the provision are these:

> 1. One or more persons must transfer "property" to a corporation.
> 2. The transfer must be "solely in exchange for stock or securities in such corporation."
> 3. The transferor or transferors must be "in control" of the corporation "immediately after the exchange." The term "control" is defined by §368(c).

If these requirements are met, the transferor or transferors recognize neither gain nor loss on the exchange; the transferee corporation takes over the transferor's basis for the property received by it (§362); and the transferor's basis for the stock or securities received by him is the same as his basis for the property transferred (§358).

Sec. 3.02.   Transfer of "property"

Section 351 provides that gain or loss shall not be recognized if "property" is exchanged solely for stock or securities of a controlled corporation. The term "property" as used in §351 is not defined by statute (the definition in §317(a) being applicable only to Part I of Subchapter C, which does not include §351), but the absence of a definition has not been troublesome in most cases.

Although the term "property" as used in other provisions of the Code does not always embrace money, it does include money under §351. G.C.M. 24415, 1944 C.B. 219; George M. Holstein, 23 T.C. 923 (1955). There is a compelling reason for so construing the term "property" under §351. A newly organized corporation almost always needs cash for working capital, and if §351 did not permit the tax-free transfer of money to such a corporation, it would either lose much of its usefulness or invite evasion in the form of a transfer of cash in an allegedly independent transaction after the other assets had been transferred under §351.

Section 351(a) provides that "stock or securities issued for services shall not be considered as issued in return for property." This provision entered the Code in 1954, though it may have been implicit in earlier years. An exchange is not automatically cast out of §351, however, merely because the corporation issues stock or securities for services. The effect of the 1954 provision, rather, is that a person receiving stock or securities in exchange for services cannot be counted in determining whether the transferors of "property" are in control of the transferee corporation immediately after the exchange. But if the persons who transfer property *are* "in control," their exchange of property for stock or securities qualifies under §351, even though at the same time stock or securities are issued for services to one or more other persons. Moreover, if a person who transfers property in exchange for stock or securities *also* receives stock or securities in exchange for services, his stock (whether received for property or services) is to be counted in determining whether the transferors of "property" have control of the corporation. To illustrate: if A and B transfer property to a newly organized corporation for 78% of its stock and C, as part of the same transaction, receives 22% of the stock for services rendered to the corporation, the transfer does not qualify under §351 because the transferors of property (A and B) have less than 80 percent of the stock and hence do not have "control," as that term is defined by §368(c) for purposes of §351. If, however, A and B received 80 percent or more of the stock, and C 20 percent or less, the exchange would qualify. Moreover, if A and B received 78 percent of the stock for property and C received 22 percent for a combination of services and property, the transfer would qualify (though as to C, the stock received for services would produce taxable income), unless C's transfer of property was only a sham designed to support a claim by A and B for non-recognition of gain or loss. Regs. §1.351-1(a)(1) and (2). Finally, the disqualification of services by §351 probably does not apply to stock or securities issued for property that was, in turn, earned by the performance of services.[4]

Disqualification in §351(a) of stock or securities issued for serv-

---

[4] See Roberts Co., Inc. v. Commissioner, 5 T.C. 1 (1945) (Acq.) (interest in property arising under attorney's contingent fee agreement is "property"); Fahs v. Florida Machine & Foundry Co., 168 F.2d 957, 36 AFTR 1161 (5th Cir. 1948) (claim that the recipient of stock had an equitable interest in the transferred

ices seems to assume that the services were rendered to the corporation. The transaction takes on another complexion if the services were performed for someone else, such as one of the transferors of property. An example is the individual proprietor who incorporates his business, taking part of the stock himself and directing that the rest be issued to an employee as compensation for services performed in years past. Such a transaction is to be treated as though all the stock had been issued first to the proprietor in exchange for the assets of the business, with part of it being used by him to pay his debts. The incorporation would qualify under §351 if the proprietor retained at least 80 percent of the stock, Regs. §1.351-1(b)(1) and (2); and even if he retained less than 80 percent, it might qualify if the loss of "control" (as defined by §368(c)) was not an integral part of the transaction.[5] If the proprietor in such a case is regarded as paying his debt to the employee with stock, as suggested by Regs. §1.351-1(b)(2), Example (1), he will recognize gain or loss on the difference between the amount of the debt and the adjusted basis of the stock. In the alternative, the transaction might be regarded as a transfer of property by the proprietor in exchange for stock and an assumption of his indebtedness by the corporation, followed by a payment of the debt by the corporation. On the tax consequences of such an assumption of the transferor's debt, see *infra*, Sec. 3.06.

In practice, of course, it may be difficult to determine whether stock is issued for services performed in the past for one of the transferors, as an incentive to the future performance of services for the transferee corporation, or both.[6] United States v. Frazell, 335 F.2d 487, 14 AFTR 2d 5378 (5th Cir. 1964), is a graphic example of this difficulty. Here the taxpayer "earned" a contingent 13% interest in the assets of an oil partnership by performing geological services. Shortly before this interest was to vest in the taxpayer, the partnership was terminated and its assets were transferred to a newly created corporation, with the taxpayer receiving 13% of the corporation's stock in exchange for his partnership interest. The court held that the value of the stock was taxable compensation for his prior services to the partnership, although Regs. §1.351-1(a)(1)(i) refers only to services "rendered or to be rendered to or for the benefit of the issuing corporation." Evidently the court did not regard a cash basis tax-

property rejected on the facts, with possible implication that on stronger facts the alleged equitable owner would be a transferor of "property").

[5] See G. & W. H. Corson, Inc., ¶53,242 P-H Memo T.C. (1953); *infra*, Sec. 3.09.

[6] See Herwitz, Allocation of Stock Between Services and Capital in the Organization of a Close Corporation, 75 Harv. L. Rev. 1098 (1962).

payer's claim for compensation rendered to a third person (*i.e.*, the partnership) as "property" under §351, although it also suggested an alternative theory for its result, viz., that the taxpayer's compensation claim vested and became taxable to him prior to the incorporation transfer. Under this theory, the claim would qualify as property in determining whether the exchange was tax-free under §351.

The problem before the court in the *Frazell* case — whether income must be recognized on the incorporation of a going business when previously untaxed rights or claims created by personal services are transferred for stock — is reminiscent of cases in the capital gain area involving such items as industrial know-how, trade names, professional good will, trade secrets, employment contracts, etc. Profit on the sale of such assets has sometimes been denied capital gain status, partly on the ground that the transferred item did not constitute "property" within the meaning of §1221; but since §351 was intended to permit the tax-free incorporation of going businesses, there is less reason to interpret "property" as used in §351 to exclude such commonly-encountered items.[7] The lack of a body of law in this area implies that the administrative practice of the Internal Revenue Service has been in accord with this suggestion. At the same time, however, it must be recognized that in appropriate cases the Service could rightly treat an alleged transfer of "property" as a device, in whole or in part, to compensate the transferor for past services or to convert an "income item" whose sale would produce ordinary income into a block of stock that can qualify as a capital asset on sale.[8]

Sec. 3.03.   "Stock or securities" — Problems of classification

Section 351(a) permits the tax-free transfer of property to a controlled corporation only if the transfer is "solely in exchange for stock or securities" in such corporation. While there have been few decisions construing the term "stock or securities" as used in §351, it has been held that the term has the same meaning here as in §354(a)(1) and §361(a), providing for the nonrecognition of gain or loss on an exchange in the course of a corporate reorganization.[9]

---

[7] For the capital gain area, see the discussion and cases cited in Eustice, Contract Rights, Capital Gain, and Assignment of Income — The Ferrer Case, 20 Tax L. Rev. 1 (1964). See also Rev. Rul. 64-56, 1964-1 C.B. 133 (transfer of industrial know-how qualifies for non-recognition under §351, under certain conditions); Commisioner v. P. G. Lake, Inc., 356 U.S. 260, 1 AFTR 2d 1394 (1958) (transfer of potential income item did not qualify for non-recognition of gain under §1031); *infra*, Sec. 3.17.

[8] On the latter possibility, see also *infra*, Ch. 10.

[9] Lloyd-Smith v. Commissioner, 116 F.2d 642, 644, 26 AFTR 189 (2d Cir. 1941).

As used in the reorganization sections, the term "stock or securities" does not include short-term notes. The reason for this restrictive construction of the term "stock or securities" is that the underlying purpose of the reorganization sections is to permit the tax-free transfer of property only if the transfer is not analogous to a sale. Regs. §1.368-1(b). Where short-term notes are received for the property, courts construing the reorganization sections have held that the transaction is so akin to a sale that any gain realized by the transferor should be recognized to the extent of the value of the short-term notes. In the leading case on this question, Pinellas Ice & Cold Storage Co. v. Commissioner, 287 U.S. 462, 11 AFTR 1112 (1933), the Supreme Court rested its decision partly on the theory that the transaction (a transfer of property for cash and short-term notes) fell entirely outside the intended ambit of the reorganization sections:

> ... to be within the exemption the seller must acquire an interest in the affairs of the purchasing company more definite than that incident to ownership of its short-term purchase-money notes. (287 U.S. at 470.)

Although this was not only an appropriate but also a sufficient ground for its determination, the Court also said that the notes "were not securities within the intendment of the act." 287 U.S. at 468-9. This part of the *Pinellas* opinion has been cogently criticized, Griswold, "Securities" and "Continuity of Interest," 58 Harv. L. Rev. 705 (1945), but it is now so well imbedded in the law that the later decisions in this area have been preoccupied principally with the tantalizing question: How long is too long? And even when the classification of notes as "securities" is said to depend upon an "over-all evaluation of the nature of the debt," the length of time to maturity is regarded as the most important single earmark. Notes with a five year term or less seem to be unable to qualify as "securities," while a term of ten years or more is apparently sufficient to bring them within the statute.[10] It should also be noted that a debt instrument may be found to be a substitute for stock, if the corporation is undercapi-

---

[10] The earlier cases are collected in Camp Wolters Enterprises, Inc. v. Commissioner, 22 T.C. 737, 750-751 (1945), aff'd, 230 F.2d 555, 49 AFTR 283 (5th Cir. 1956), cert. denied, 352 U.S. 826; see Campbell v. Carter Foundation Production Co., 322 F.2d 827, 12 AFTR 2d 5659 (5th Cir. 1963); Harrison v. Commissioner, 235 F.2d 587, 49 AFTR 1767 (8th Cir. 1956) (shareholder's drawing accounts not "securities"); Turner v. Commissioner, 303 F.2d 94, 9 AFTR 2d 1528 (4th Cir. 1962) (unsecured, noninterest bearing demand note not a "security"; later bond indenture substituted therefor was a "security," but was not part of original transaction); Warren H. Brown, 27 T.C. 27 (1956) (10 year installment sale contract not a "security"); J.I. Morgan, Inc., 30 T.C. 881 (1958

talized or if the parties do not intend to treat the obligation as a true debt.[11]

But the fact that short-term notes are not "stock or securities" as those terms are used in §351 does not automatically exclude a transaction from the benefits of §351. For if the transfer otherwise qualifies under §351, *e.g.*, if the transferors exchange property for a combination of stock and short-term notes, the notes will come within the ambit of §351(b). Under this provision, if the transferor of property receives not only "stock or securities" which can be received tax-free under §351(a) (so-called "non-recognition property"), but also "other property or money" (so-called "boot"), his gain on the exchange (if any) will be recognized, but not in an amount in excess of the money plus the fair market value of the other "boot." Thus, assume that *A* transfers property with an adjusted basis of $10,000 and a fair market value of $50,000 to a corporation for all its stock (worth $45,000) plus $5,000 of short-term notes (having a fair market value equal to their face amount). *A's* gain is $40,000 (fair market value of stock and notes received less adjusted basis of property given by him), but it is recognized only to the extent of $5,000, the fair market value of the notes. For more on the tax treatment of "boot," see *infra*, Sec. 3.05.

Most of the turmoil over the meaning of "stock or securities" has concerned debt instruments, and it has generally been assumed that the term "stock" is virtually self-defining. The regulations, however, state that stock rights and stock warrants do not come within the term "stock or securities." Regs. §1.351-1(a)(1), last sentence. The inspiration for this statement may be Helvering v. Southwest Consolidated Corp., 315 U.S. 194, 28 AFTR 573 (1942), holding that warrants are not "voting stock" within the meaning of §368(a)(1)(B),

---

(Acq.) (7 year installment sale contract not a "security"); Truck Terminals Inc. v. Commissioner, 314 F.2d 449, 11 AFTR 2d 901 (9th Cir. 1963) (purported sale of assets by parent to subsidiary held, in substance, a contribution to capital); Gooding Amusement Co. v. Commissioner, 236 F.2d 159, 49 AFTR 1973 (6th Cir. 1956) (5 year notes issued pro rata with stock in a §351 exchange held not a true "debt"); Nassau Lens Co., Inc. v. Commissioner, 308 F.2d 39, 10 AFTR 2d 5581 (2d Cir. 1962); *infra*, note 57; and Goldstein, Corporate Indebtedness to Shareholders: "Thin Capitalization" and Related Problems, 16 Tax L. Rev. 1 (1960); Note, Section 351 Transfers to Controlled Corporations: The Forgotten Term — "Securities," 114 U. of Pa. L. Rev. 314 (1965).

Another problem was injected into the "securities" area by the enactment in 1964 of §483. Requiring that "imputed interest" income be reported on the disposition of property under a contract for deferred payments if the parties have neglected to provide an adequate interest rate, §483 seems to apply to debt securities received in a §351 exchange. See Branda, Imputed Interest And Fictitious Sales Prices: The Unexpected Effects of Section 483, 21 J. of Tax. 194 (1964).

[11] *Infra*, Ch. 4.

relating to corporate reorganizations. Perhaps stock rights and warrants should not be taken into account in determining whether the transferors of property are in "control" of the corporation immediately after the exchange (see *infra*, Sec. 3.09), but if they do have control, there seems to be no good reason for disqualifying a transfer of property for stock rights or warrants or for treating them as "boot." A recent Tax Court case accepts this view.[12]

Sec. 3.04. "Stock or securities" — The "continuity of interest" doctrine

In the *Pinellas* case, *supra*, Sec. 3.03, the Supreme Court said not only that short term notes are not "securities," but also that they do not give the transferor "an interest in the affairs" of the transferee corporation that will qualify under the reorganization provisions. This judicial requirement of a "continuity of interest" was developed more fully in later cases. In LeTulle v. Scofield, 308 U.S. 415, 23 AFTR 789 (1940), for example, it was employed to disqualify a reorganization in which the transferor of property received bonds plus cash, but no stock, from the transferee corporation. The "continuity of interest" doctrine, which is set out in the regulations, Regs. §1.368-1(b), does not derive from any specific language in the reorganization sections. It is instead a doctrine of judicial origin based on what is conceived to be the unstated but fundamental statutory purpose of providing for non-recognition of gain or loss only if the reorganization exchange is distinguishable from a sale. It should be noted that there is a drastic difference between (a) holding that an exchange fails to qualify under §351 because the transferor does not retain a continuing proprietary interest, and (b) holding that some of the instruments received by the transferor do not constitute "stock or securities." In the former case, the entire gain or loss will be recognized; in the latter situation, if the transferor also receives stock evidencing a substantial continuity of interest, gain will be recognized only to the extent of the unqualified instruments (or "boot").

Since the transferors who seek to invoke §351 must be in control of the transferee corporation after the exchange by virtue of owning 80 percent or more of its stock, the "continuity of ownership" doctrine if applicable to §351 transactions would almost invariably be satisfied. This would be true even if the transferors received nothing but bonds or other debt instruments on the exchange itself, since they would have to own 80 percent or more of the stock to meet the con-

---

[12] James C. Hamrick, 43 T.C. 21 (1964) (Acq.); see also *infra*, Sec. 12.31.

trol requirement.[13] But if one transferor receives all of the stock of a newly organized corporation, while the other transferor receives nothing but bonds, it is possible that the government will be able to disqualify the entire transaction under the *Pinellas* and *LeTulle* cases, for want of a continuity of interest.[14]

Sec. 3.05.   "Solely" in exchange — The receipt of "boot"

Section 351 provides that no gain or loss shall be recognized if property is transferred to a controlled corporation "solely" in exchange for stock or securities in such corporation. It has already been pointed out that if the transferor or transferors receive from the controlled corporation not only "stock or securities," but also short-term notes, they are required by §351(b) to recognize their gain (if any) to the extent of the fair market value of the notes. The rule of §351(b) comes into play whenever the exchange would qualify under §351(a) except for the fact that the transferor or transferors have received not only "stock or securities" (so-called "non-recognition property"), but also money or other property (so-called "boot"). At the same time, §351(b) requires the recognition of gain only if gain has been "realized" under §1001. Thus, if a taxpayer transfers property with an adjusted basis of $10,000 and a fair market value of $50,000 to a controlled corporation in exchange for stock worth $30,000, cash of $10,000, and other property with a fair market value of $10,000,[15] his gain under §1001 is $40,000, but only $20,000 of it is recognized under §351(b). The computation is as follows:

1. Amount realized:		
a. Stock		$30,000
b. Cash ("boot")		10,000
c. Other property ("boot")		10,000
d. Total		$50,000
2. Less: adjusted basis of property transferred		10,000
3. Gain realized		$40,000
4. Gain recognized (1b plus 1c, or 3, whichever is less)		$20,000

If the adjusted basis of the property (line 2 above) was $45,000, instead of $10,000, the gain under §1001 would be only $5,000, and

---

[13] For such a case, see Parkland Place Co. v. United States, 355 F.2d 916, 17 AFTR 2d 97 (5th Cir. 1966).

[14] See *supra,* note 3. It can be argued, however, that the transferor who received only stock in the exchange qualifies under §351, on the ground that he retains a continuity of interest through his ownership of the corporation's stock.

[15] For problems in valuing "boot," see *infra*, Sec. 9.03.

only this amount would be recognized under §351(b). If the adjusted basis of the property was more than $50,000, there would be a realized loss under §1001, but by virtue of §351(b)(2), it could not be recognized even though boot was received.[16]

When gain must be recognized because "boot" has been received in a §351 exchange, the character of the asset transferred will ordinarily determine whether the gain is ordinary income or capital gain and, in the latter case, whether it is long-term or short-term gain. Account must also be taken, however, of the following provisions, applicable to special categories of property:

1. §1239, providing that gain recognized on the transfer of depreciable property to a corporation cannot be treated as capital gain if more than 80 percent of the transferee corporation's stock is owned by the transferor, his spouse, and his minor children or grandchildren.[17]

2. §1245, providing for the "recapture" of post-1961 depreciation if gain is recognized on a §351 transfer of certain types of property (other than real property).

3. §1250, providing for the "recapture" of post-1963 depreciation on similar transfers of real property, but only in more limited circumstances.

4. §47(a), providing for recapture of the investment credit allowed by §38 on a premature disposition of the property or if it ceases to be §38 property. Although this provision, unlike those mentioned above, applies whether gain is recognized on the transfer of the property or not, a §351 transfer of a going business will ordinarily come within the exemption of §47(b), covering "a mere change in the form of conducting the trade or business so long as the property is retained in such trade or business as section 38 property and the taxpayer retains a substantial interest in such trade or business."[18]

---

[16] Another barrier to recognition of the loss is §267(a)(1), which disallows losses on sales or exchanges between "related" taxpayers (e.g., an individual and a corporation more than 50 percent owned, actually or constructively, by him). §351(b)(2) and §267(a)(1) overlap in many cases (e.g., where the transferor has 80% control); but §267 may have the broader coverage (as where only 51 percent control is present); or, in other instances, §351(b)(2) may apply to situations not covered by §267 (as where the transferor is a corporation).

[17] In Mitchell v. Commissioner, 300 F.2d 533, 9 AFTR 2d 954 (4th Cir. 1962), the court held Regs. §1.1239-1 invalid in requiring stock owned beneficially by the taxpayer's minor children through a trust to be treated as owned by him in computing the 80 percent stock test of §1239. Accord: Rothenberg v. United States, 350 F.2d 319, 16 AFTR 2d 5591 (10th Cir. 1965).

See Harry Trotz, 43 T.C. 127 (1964), applying §1239 where the taxpayer owned only 79 percent of the stock, but had an option to purchase the other 21 percent, exercisable upon contingencies within his exclusive control.

[18] See S. Rep. No. 1881, 87th Cong., 2d Sess., 1962-3 C.B. 707, 856, citing the incorporation of a going business under §351 as an example of this exception.

Because §351 exchanges seldom involve the receipt of "boot" by the transferors, the Service and the courts have not had to face up to a number of questions in the computation, recognition, and characterization of gain that are not explicitly answered by the statutory provision. These questions grow out of the fact that the property transferred may consist not of a single asset (as assumed in the example above), but of several assets, each with its own adjusted basis, fair market value, status as capital or ordinary, and holding period. Thus, if the property transferred in the example above consisted of two assets, with an adjusted basis of $25,000 each but a fair market value of $5,000 for one and $45,000 for the other, there would be no "realized gain" if their adjusted bases are combined on line 2; but if each asset is taken separately, there would be a realized gain of $20,000 on the first and a realized loss of $20,000 on the second. The realized loss would not be recognized by virtue of §351(b)(2); and the amount of the realized gain to be recognized under §351(b)(1) would depend on the method used to allocate the stock, cash, and other property received among the two assets given up by the transferor. If the consideration received is allocated to the assets according to their relative fair market values, the appreciated asset would account for 9/10ths of the stock, cash, and other property, with the result that the $20,000 of realized gain on this asset would be recognized to the extent of its "share" of the boot ($18,000). Instead of using relative fair market values in allocating the consideration received, it might be allocated according to the adjusted basis of the assets transferred, or relative to the appreciation involved. A "relative basis" allocation has little to commend it; in the foregoing example, it would assume that property with a fair market value of $5,000 accounted for $25,000 of the consideration received. A better case can be made for allocating boot to appreciated property exclusively, up to the amount of the realized gain thereon, on the ground that it is "responsible" for the recognition of gain; if this approach is employed in the example just given, there would be $20,000 of recognized gain on the appreciated property. The example can be complicated further by assuming that some assets are capital assets and some ordinary, that the holding periods of the capital assets vary, that some of the assets are subject to the depreciation "recapture" rules of §1245 or §1250, etc.

In other areas involving similar problems, an asset-by-asset approach has carried the day as against an aggregate approach;[19] and

[19] Williams v. McGowan, 152 F.2d 570, 34 AFTR 615 (2d Cir. 1945); Johnson's Estate, 42 T.C. 441 (1964); U.S. Holding Co., 44 T.C. 323 (1965); Curtis

this seems to imply that each category of consideration received should be separately allocated to the transferred assets by reference to their relative market values. On balance, this seems to involve fewer complexities and anomolies than any other method of allocating the gain to be recognized.

If the exchange agreement explicitly adopts its own method of allocating the consideration to be paid for the transferred property (*e.g.*, assigning stock and securities exclusively to the appreciated property, and boot exclusively to assets on which there is no realized gain), will the agreed allocation be controlling? In view of the non-arm's length character of the average §351 transaction, this does not seem to be a very promising route; but if the allocation serves a business purpose and is free of self-dealing because there are several independent transferors, perhaps it will pass muster.[20] Another possibility in this area is a tax-free §351 exchange of the appreciated property, and a separate sale or exchange of the depreciated property for the boot. If prearranged, however, the two transfers may be amalgamated for tax purposes in the name of the "step transaction" doctrine.

Sec. 3.06.   Assumption of liability

On many §351 exchanges, particularly when a going business is incorporated, the transferee corporation assumes liabilities of the transferor or takes property subject to liabilities. What is the effect of its doing so? For many years it was widely assumed that such a transaction would not require the recognition of gain under §351 or under the analogous reorganization sections. In United States v. Hendler, 303 U.S. 564, 20 AFTR 1041 (1938), however, the Supreme Court held that the assumption and payment by a transferee corporation of a liability of the transferor would constitute "boot" to the transferor, at least in some circumstances, under the reorganization provisions.

Immediately after winning this decision, the Treasury Department recognized that a host of incorporations and reorganizations in the past, thought to be tax-free when consummated, might in fact have been partially taxable because of the assumption of liabilities. Unless

---

v. United States, 336 F.2d 714, 14 AFTR 2d 5685 (6th Cir. 1964); Regs. §1.357-2; but see Sayre v. United States, 163 F. Supp. 495, 1 AFTR 2d 2035 (D. W.Va. 1958), where the Service's attempt to apportion boot on the basis of relative values was rejected in the context of a §1031 exchange.

For discussion, see Sheppard, Depreciation Recapture: Some practical problems in working with Section 1245, 24 J. Tax. 194 (1966).

[20] See Carl L. Danielson, 44 T.C. 549 (1965), and cases there cited.

estoppel or a similar doctrine was applicable,[21] the transferee corporation would be entitled to "step up" its basis for the assets received by it by the amount of gain that should have been recognized on the exchange (*infra*, Sec. 3.10); and such a "stepped-up" basis would impair the revenue by increasing the corporation's depreciation deduction for any depreciable assets received on the exchange and by reducing its gain or increasing its loss on any subsequent disposition of the assets. Similarly, the transferor could step up the basis of the stock or securities received by him on the exchange. It was also perceived that if gain was to be recognized upon a reorganization or incorporation whenever the transferee assumed a liability of the transferor or took property subject to a liability, the usefulness of §351 and similar nonrecognition provisions would be seriously impaired.

The upshot was that the Treasury Department promptly urged Congress to enact legislation that would relinquish the victory it had just won in the *Hendler* case by providing that an assumption of liability by the transferee corporation (or its receipt of property subject to a liability) in an otherwise non-taxable exchange would not constitute "boot" to the transferor. Congress responded in 1939 with the statutory principles that are now, with minor changes, embodied in the "general rule" of §357(a) and the exception of §357(b).[22] Another exception to the general rule, §357(c), was added in 1954.

By virtue of the "general rule" of §357(a), the transferee corporation's assumption of liability or its acquisition of property subject to a liability is not to be treated as money or other property, nor does it prevent the exchange from qualifying under §351. Thus, the incorporation of property or of a going business will ordinarily qualify as a tax-free transaction under §351, even though the corporation assumes, or acquires property subject to, liabilities. The operation of §357(a) may be illustrated by the following example: A transfers property with a basis of $40,000 and a value of $100,000 (but subject to a mortgage of $30,000) to controlled corporation X in exchange for stock worth $70,000 and X's assumption of the mortgage. A's realized gain is $60,000 (value of the X stock plus assumption of A's debt, less A's basis for the property), but his recognized gain is zero, since §357(a) provides that the assumed liability is not to be counted as boot under §351(b). A's basis for his stock will be $10,000 under §358 (property

---

[21] *Infra*, notes 43 and 47.

[22] The *Hendler* victory became completely pyrrhic in 1939, when the tax therein imposed was refunded to the taxpayer by Congress. 53 Stat. 1402.

On §357(a) and (b), see generally Surrey, Assumption of Indebtedness in Tax-Free Exchanges, 50 Yale L. J. 1. (1940).

basis of $40,000 less the assumed liability of $30,000), and X's basis for the property will be $40,000 under §362(a)(1).[23]

While the application of §357 is ordinarily straightforward, there are several problems of interpretation. Thus, if the transferor's liability is *discharged* on the transfer (by payment, or by a novation between the creditor and the corporate transferee), would this event fall outside §357(a) on the ground that the transferee neither assumed the debt nor took property subject to it; and generate taxable boot or cancellation of indebtedness income to the transferor? Since the *Hendler* case itself involved a prompt (and no doubt prearranged) payment of the assumed liabilities by the transferee corporation, §357(a) ought to be construed to cover this situation, as well as a discharge of the liability that is simultaneous with the exchange. Moreover, if the transferor's liability is not discharged by payment or novation at the time of the exchange, and he remains liable(ordinarily in the capacity of a surety), a later payment of the debt by the transferee[24] ought not to be treated as taxable income to the transferor. Otherwise, the utility of §357 would be undermined, and many incorporation transfers would become partially taxable for the same reason that prompted Congress to overrule the *Hendler* decision by enacting §357. Although the statutory language leaves something to be desired in the way of clarity, the courts have been chary about reopening an area which Congress has attempted to put to rest.[25]

Although the principle of §357(a) makes good sense as a general rule, it might tempt the transferor of property under §351 to borrow against the property just before the exchange, with the intention of keeping the borrowed funds and of causing the corporation either to assume the liability or to take the property subject to it. For the transferor, this chain of events could be the equivalent of receiving cash "boot" from the corporation in exchange for unencumbered property; but if the general rule of §357(a) were applicable, the corporation's assumption of the liability or acquisition of the property subject to it would not be treated as "boot." To frustrate transactions of this type, §357(b) carves out an exception to the general rule of §357(a): the assumption or acquisition is to be treated as money received by

---

[23] The basis provisions are discussed *infra*, Sec. 3.10 (transferor's basis) and Sec. 3.11 (transferee's basis).

[24] For the effect on the transferee of paying such liabilities, see *infra*, Sec. 3.11.

[25] See Jewell v. U.S., 330 F.2d 761, 13 AFTR 2d 1258 (9th Cir. 1964); Easson v. Commissioner, 294 F.2d 653, 8 AFTR 2d 5448 (9th Cir. 1961); see also Arthur L. Kniffen, 39 T.C. 553 (1962). In effect, these cases regard the "tax avoidance" and "business purpose" restrictions of §357(b) as the appropriate safeguards against improprieties under §357(a).

the transferor (i.e., as "boot" under §351(b) if "taking into consideration the nature of the liability and the circumstances in the light of which the arrangement for the assumption or acquisition was made, it appears that the principal purpose of the taxpayer . . . was a purpose to avoid Federal income tax on the exchange, or . . . if not such purpose, was not a bona fide business purpose." Although the statute itself speaks only of a "bona fide business purpose," the regulations provide that the income tax returns of the transferor and of the corporation for the year of the exchange must state "the *corporate* business reason" for the assumption of any liability. Regs. §1.351-3(a)(6) and (b)(7). Section 357(b) goes on to tinker, with uncertain effect, with the burden of proof in cases of alleged improper purpose. Section 357(b) was amended in 1954 to provide that if an improper purpose exists with respect to *any* liability, the total amount of *all* liabilities involved in the exchange shall be considered as money received by the taxpayer; according to the Senate Report on the 1954 Code, the amendment was "intended merely to clarify existing law." S. Rep. No. 1622, 83rd Cong., 2d sess., p. 270.

The special provision of §357(b) would probably apply not only to the hypothetical case of a liability created just before the §351 exchange in order to wring some cash out of the transaction, but also to the assumption by a transferee corporation of personal obligations (grocery bills, rent, alimony, etc.) that are not ordinarily taken over in a §351 exchange, unless there was a bona fide business purpose for such unusual action. On the other hand, the general rule of §357(a) rather than the exception of §357(b) should ordinarily be applicable to mortgages placed on business assets in the ordinary course of business, trade obligations, bank loans, customers' deposits, and the like; and this should be true even though at the time of the §351 exchange the transferor is able to pay such obligations himself but chooses instead to have the transferee corporation assume, or take property subject to, them.[26]

---

[26] For cases holding §357(b) applicable to an assumption of liabilities, see Thompson v. Campbell, 353 F.2d 787, 16 AFTR 2d 6002 (5th Cir. 1965); Wheeler v. Campbell, 342 F.2d 837, 15 AFTR 2d 578 (5th Cir. 1965); Bryan v. Commissioner, 281 F.2d 233, 6 AFTR 2d 5191 (4th Cir. 1960); F. W. Drybrough, 42 T.C. 1029 (1964). Section 357(b) was held not applicable in W.H.B. Simpson, 43 T.C. 900 (1965) (desire to avoid future taxes under §531 and §541 not fatal); Easson v. Commissioner, 294 F.2d 653, 8 AFTR 2d 5448 (9th Cir. 1961) (desire for liquidity); Jewell v. Commissioner, 330 F.2d 761, 13 AFTR 2d 1258 (9th Cir. 1964); Stoll's Estate, 38 T.C. 223 (1962) (1939 Code; estate planning); see also Wolf v. Commissioner, 357 F.2d 483, 17 AFTR 2d 601 (9th Cir. 1966) (transfer of stock subject to binding redemption contract not qualified for §351 treatment).

Regs. §1.357-1(c) provides that a tax avoidance motive related to *any* liability assumed in the exchange requires *all* liabilities to be treated as boot; see also

The 1954 Code introduced an additional restriction on the "general rule" of §357(a). Under §357(c), if the liabilities encumbering the transferred property or assumed by the transferee corporation exceed the aggregate adjusted basis of the properties transferred, the excess is to be considered as a gain on the sale or exchange of such property.[27] The effect of §357(c) may be illustrated by the following example: A exchanges property with an adjusted basis of $10,000 and a fair market value of $70,000, subject to a mortgage liability of $30,000, for stock of a controlled corporation worth $40,000 and the transferee's assumption of the mortgage. A's realized gain under §1001 is $60,000 (the value of the stock received plus the liability assumed, less the property's basis); and, under §357(c), he must recognize gain in the amount of $20,000. Since A has so far received a return of $30,000 (the amount of the mortgage liability assumed by the transferee) on an investment of $10,000, his taxable gain of $20,000 under §357(c) corresponds to his economic gain. The balance of A's realized gain ($40,000) will be recognized if the stock is sold for its market value ($40,000), since the basis of the stock will have been reduced to zero to take account of the liability assumed by the corporate transferee under §358(d) (*infra*, Sec. 3.10). Although the example just used to illustrate §357(c) involves a realized gain to the transferor on the §351 exchange, he is taxed on the excess of liabilities-over-basis regardless of the amount of gain realized, and even if none is realized. Thus, his gain on the transaction would be $20,000 even if the value of the

---

Stoll's Estate, supra. It is hard to justify this severity, which makes it worse to cause the corporation to assume the liability in question than to receive cash from the corporation in order to pay the debt; and it is possible that this punitive result accounts for the judicial reluctance to find a tax avoidance motive that is exhibited in several of the cases cited above.

[27] For the contrary rule under the pre-1954 law, see Woodsam Associates, Inc. v. Commissioner, 198 F.2d 357, 42 AFTR 505 (2d Cir. 1952); Easson v. Commissioner, 294 F.2d 653, 8 AFTR 2d 5448 (9th Cir. 1961); see also Simon v. Commissioner, 285 F.2d 422, 6 AFTR 2d 6077 (3rd Cir. 1960) (transfer of property mortgaged in excess of basis shortly before the transfer; held a "bargain sale" by the taxpayer to his corporation); Cooper, Negative Basis, 75 Harv. L. Rev. 1352 (1962).

For a provision similar to §357(c), also enacted in 1954, see §311(c), *infra*, Sec. 5.21; compare similar treatment under the installment sale regulations for liabilities in excess of basis; Regs. §1.453-4(c); Burnet v. S. & L. Bldg. Corp., 288 U.S. 406, 12 AFTR 15 (1933).

The relationship between §357(b) and (c) and contributions of mortgaged property to the corporation's capital remains to be worked out. The *Simon* case, *supra*, involved a "contribution" of property that was mortgaged in excess of its basis; but because the court held that the transaction constituted a sale in substance rather than a contribution to capital, as well as because it occurred in a pre-1954 year, the court did not have to say whether §357(c) can be avoided by transferring excessively-mortgaged property as a contribution to capital rather than in a §351 exchange. See Rev. Rul. 64-155, 1964-1 C.B. 138 (capital contribution treated as §351 transaction).

transferred property was only $25,000 (i.e., $5,000 less than the mortgage). He might argue against this result, on the ground that there is a substantial likelihood of default by the corporation, but the mandate of §357(c) is clear and it is difficult to believe that it would be held unconstitutional.[28]

Gain recognized by virtue of §357(c) must be reported as ordinary income, long term capital gain, or short term capital gain according to the nature and the holding period of the transferred property. The language of §357(c) does not attempt to characterize the *nature* of this gain — it is merely an exception to non-recognition treatment under §351.[29] Similarly, if more than one type of property is transferred, the recognized gain apparently must be allocated among the various classes of assets in proportion to their relative fair market values.[30]

In determining whether §357(c) is applicable, the aggregate amount of the liabilities is compared with the aggregate adjusted basis of the assets transferred. To return to the example in the preceding paragraph, if A had transferred not only property with a basis of $10,000 subject to a mortgage of $30,000, but also unencumbered property with a basis of $10,000, the gain to be reported would be only $10,000 (liability of $30,000 less aggregate basis of $20,000). Regs. §1.357-2(a). Although at first blush it may seem strange that A can reduce his gain by transferring other property along with the mortgaged property, the theory underlying §357(c)'s use of the total basis of all property transferred as the measure of *A's* gain may be that the properties transferred constitute a single investment of $20,000, from which A's total return so far amounts to $30,000. If there are two or more transferors, it would seem appropriate to apply §357(c) on a person by person basis, rather than to aggregate all property transferred by all transferors, but neither §357(c) itself nor the regulations are explicit on this point.[31]

[28] Under §311(c), a comparable provision discussed *infra,* Sec. 5.21, Congress has chosen to limit the transferor's gain to the excess of the property's market value over its basis if the transferee takes subject to, but does not assume, the liability. But see Crane v. Commissioner, 331 U.S. 1, 35 AFTR 776 (1947).

[29] It may be argued that the character of the asset is the controlling factor in determining the nature of the recognized §357(c) gain, precluding resort to the "hotch-pot" rules of §1231 — but it seems relatively clear that Congress merely dealt with the recognition of gain under §357(c), leaving the classification of that gain to other general definitional rules in the Code. The Service assumed this result in Rev. Rul. 60-302, 1960-2 C.B. 223 (holding that §1239 applied to gain recognized under §357(c)), and this conclusion would likewise embrace such provisions as §1245 and §1250.

[30] See discussion *supra,* Sec. 3.05, and Regs. §1.357-2(b).

[31] Although the language of §357(c) ("the total of the adjusted basis of the property transferred pursuant to such exchange") may imply that the total

It is possible for a transfer of property to be subject both to §357(b), because of the transferor's improper purpose, and to §357(c), because liabilities exceed the basis of the transferred property. In this event, §357(b) takes precedence, with the result that the entire amount of liabilities, not just the excess over the property's adjusted basis, is "boot."[32]

Both §357(b) and §357(c) compute the transferor's gain on the assumption that the indebtedness giving rise to the gain will be paid by the transferee corporation. If the transferor is called upon to pay the debt as a result of the transferee's default, his outlay should either be added to the basis of the stock or securities received on the exchange or deducted as a loss. See *infra*, Sec. 3.10.

Sec. 3.07.   "Control" — The 80 percent rule

Section 351 applies only if the transferors of property are "in control" of the corporation, as defined in §368(c), immediately after the exchange. Their "control" need not be acquired through the exchange itself, however; §351 embraces a transfer of property to a corporation already controlled by the transferor, as well as transfers to newly organized corporations.

The term "control" is defined by §368(c) to mean the ownership of (1) at least 80 percent of the total combined voting power of all classes of stock entitled to vote, and (2) at least 80 percent of the total number of shares of all other classes of stock of the corporation. In most cases §368(c) presents no problems of interpretation, either because the corporation issues only one class of stock or because the

---

basis of all properties transferred *by all transferors* is to be employed in determining the gain, an absurd result would be produced thereby. Thus, if A transferred properties with a total basis of $20,000 but subject to a mortgage of $30,000 and B simultaneously transferred unencumbered property with a basis of $7,000, the gain to be recognized under §357(c) — if computed by aggregating A and B — would be $3,000 (mortgage of $30,000 less total basis of $27,000). This result is curious, since A has enjoyed an economic gain of $10,000; and it would be even more curious if the $3,000 gain thus computed were allocated between A and B, since the value of the property transferred by B, and hence the value of the stock or securities received by him, may be less than the adjusted basis of the property transferred by him. An aggregate approach to §357(c) would also produce difficulties in the calculation of the transferors' basis for the stock and securities received by them. Since the language of §357(c) does not unmistakably require A and B to be lumped together, it should be applied person-by-person, so that on the foregoing facts A would recognize $10,000 of gain regardless of the basis of property transferred by other persons.

[32] An interesting problem in the relationship between §357(b) and §357(c) is to be found in W. H. B. Simpson, 43 T.C. 900 (1965), holding that the taxpayer's effort to avoid the effect of §357(c) by keeping the liabilities assumed to an amount just below the basis of the transferred assets did not constitute tax avoidance under §357(b).

transferors receive all stock of all classes. This is fortunate, since there are almost no guides to the meaning of "total combined voting power" or of "stock entitled to vote."[33] The term "stock entitled to vote" presumably does not include stock having merely the power under local law to vote on such extraordinary events as charter amendments, mergers, sales of assets, etc., since in most states all classes of stock have voting power of this character; if they were regarded as "stock entitled to vote," the statutory category of "other classes of stock" would be a vacuum. As to stock with contingent voting rights, such as preferred stock that may vote for directors if dividends are passed for a stated period, Regs. §1.302-3(a)(3) states that such stock is generally not "voting stock" until the specified event occurs, but it may be that "stock entitled to vote," the term employed in §368(c), is not identical with "voting stock," as that term is used in §302 and elsewhere.

Once the "stock entitled to vote" has been identified and segregated, it is necessary to determine whether the transferors of property own 80 percent or more of the "total combined voting power." Presumably this requires a realistic weighting of the stock's right to vote, so that ownership of less than 80 percent of the total market value or the total number of shares may qualify, but difficulties may arise if the shares are not fungible as regards their power to vote. It is usually assumed that the computation of "total combined voting power" is not to take account of shareholders' voting agreements or similar arrangements even though they may alter the balance of power; but the question is not foreclosed by case law or rulings.[34]

If there are "other classes of stock," the transferors to qualify under §351 must own at least 80 percent of the total number of such shares. There is no good reason why the statute should require control of such stock to be ascertained by total number, a test that has no relevance to the policy underlying §351, rather than by market value

---

[33] These phrases are also to be found in §302(b)(2)(B) and §334(b)(2)(B), *infra*, Secs. 7.22 and 9.44. See also §1504(a), relating to consolidated returns, which employs the terms "voting power" and nonvoting stock." *Infra*, Sec. 13.40. For the treatment of warrants, see *supra*, Sec. 3.03.

[34] See Federal Grain Corp., 18 B.T.A. 242 (1929) (holding that control means "ownership" of the voting stock, not actual exercise of the voting rights).

Rev. Rul. 63-226, 1963-2 C.B. 341, held that shareholder restrictive voting agreements (whether by pooling or voting agreement, charter provision, or any other device which gives disproportionate voting rights to shareholders) created "more than one class of stock," which disqualified a corporation from Subchapter S treatment. See *infra*, Ch. 14; Weinstein, Stockholder Agreements and Subchapter S Corporations, 19 Tax L. Rev. 391 (1964). This approach would not be troublesome under §351 if both "classes" are held by the transferors; but if they are not, the class-by-class rule applied by the Internal Revenue Service (*infra*, note 35) might disqualify a given exchange.

(except perhaps to avoid the necessity of an appraisal). Although §368(c) appears to lump all non-voting shares together regardless of class or privileges, the Internal Revenue Service has ruled that "80 percent of the total number of shares of all other classes of stock," as used in §368(c), means 80 percent of the total number of shares of *each class* of stock.[35]

Sec. 3.08.   Two or more transferors

As the language of §351 explicitly recognizes, there will sometimes be more than one transferor of property. In such cases, the transaction will qualify as tax-free under §351 if the transferors *as a group* are in control of the corporation immediately after the exchange. Apparently it is permissible for one transferor to receive voting stock while another transferor receives non-voting stock. As for an exchange in which one transferor receives only common stock, while another transferor receives only bonds, see *supra*, note 3.

When there are two or more transferors, each one will ordinarily as a result of arm's-length bargaining, receive stock or securities with a fair market value equal to that of the assets transferred by him; but on occasion there may be discrepancies between the value of the assets given up and the value of the stock or securities received. Do such variations in value affect the tax consequences of the transaction?

Before 1954, the statute provided for non-recognition of gain or loss in the case of an exchange by two or more persons "only if the amount of the stock and securities received by each is substantially in proportion to his interest in the property prior to the exchange." The policy underlying this requirement, which if violated would lead to the full recognition of gain or loss by all parties to the exchange, was obscure, and there were also uncertainties in its application.[36]

---

[35] Rev. Rul. 59-259, 1959-2 C.B. 115.

[36] See generally Hoffman, The Substantial Proportionment Requirement of [1939 Code] Section 112(b)(5), 5 Tax. L. Rev. 235 (1950). In applying the requirement, the courts vacillated between the so-called "control" test and the "relative value" test. Both are best explained by an illustration. Assume that A, B, and C transfer properties worth $75,000, $20,000, and $5,000 respectively, and that in exchange they receive from the corporation stock or securities worth $77,500, $17,500, and $5,000. Applying the "control test," A gave up 75 percent of the total assets and received 77.5 percent, thus "gaining" 2.5 percent of control ("control" in this sense means merely the percentage of total *value* "controlled," not voting power); B gave up 20 percent and received 17.5 percent, thus "losing" 2.5 percent; and C's "control" was unchanged. Changes as minor as these would be disregarded because the stock or securities received needed to be only "substantially" in proportion to the assets given up. If the "relative value" test is applied to the illustration, however, A would have a "gain" of $2,500 on his 75,000 investment, or 3.33 percent, while B would have a "loss" of $2,500 on his $20,000 investment, or 12.5 percent. The "spread" between A's "gain" and B's "loss" would disqualify the transaction. The leading case up-

The pre-1954 requirement was eliminated by the 1954 Code, the Senate Report on the 1954 Code stating that §351 is to be applied "irrespective of any disproportion of the amount of stock or securities received by [a transferor] as a result of the transfer." S. Rep. No. 1622, 83d Cong., 2d sess., p. 264. The report goes on, however, to say that if the disproportion in value "results in an event taxable under other provisions of this code, your committee intends that such distribution will be taxed in accordance with its true nature." This theme is embodied in the regulations, which provide that "in appropriate cases the transaction may be treated as if the stock and securities had first been received in proportion [to the value of the property transferred] and then some of such stock and securities had been used to make gifts [subject to gift tax under §2501], to pay compensation [taxable as income under §61(a)(1)], or to satisfy obligations of the transferor of any kind." Regs. §1.351-1(b)(1); see also the cross-references in §351(d)(3) and (4). If a transaction is so "realigned," in addition to the tax consequences suggested by the extract from the regulations, the transferor may have to recognize gain or loss on his constructive disposition of the stock or securities and may in some situations be entitled to a deduction under §162(a) (business expenses). A "realignment" of stock may also affect the computation of "control," since the transferors of property may be treated as constructively owning, immediately after the exchange, more shares than are issued to them, at least if their use of shares to make gifts, pay compensation, etc., is not an integral step in the entire transaction.[37]

holding the "control" test is Mather & Co. v. Commissioner, 171 F.2d 864, 37 AFTR 689 (3rd Cir. 1949), cert. denied 337 U.S. 907, and the leading support for the "relative value" test is Bodell v. Commissioner, 154 F.2d 407, 34 AFTR 1107 (1st Cir. 1946); see also Uinta Livestock Corp., 355 F.2d 761, 17 AFTR 2d 245 (10th Cir, 1966) (relative value). Neither test effectively screened out transactions that reflected changes of substance rather than of form, nor did they seem to have any other connection with the policy underlying §351. Moreover, if a transaction failed under whichever test the court thought applicable, all transferors recognized their realized gain or loss. This might mean that a transferor would have a deductible loss because the value of the stock or securities received was less than the adjusted basis of the property transferred by him, although he enjoyed a "gain" as against the other transferors. Finally, all the usual difficulties of valuing assets, especially the intangibles of a going concern, meant that an exchange might turn out to be disproportionate, despite the best efforts of the parties to qualify under §351. For all these reasons, it was not surprising that the substantial proportionment test was eradicated by the 1954 Code.

[37] See *infra*, Sec. 3.09, on the phrase "immediately after the exchange"; also consider the implications of realignment in determing whether stock was issued for services. It may be noted that as originally proposed, the regulations required a realignment of the stock or securities whenever they were disproportionate to the assets transferred, 19 Fed. Reg. 8237, 8268 (1954); the regulations as issued, however, require a realignment only "in appropriate cases." Regs. §1.351-1(b)(1).

Sec. 3.09.   Control "immediately after the exchange"

The statute requires the transferors of property to be in control of the corporation "immediately after the exchange." The regulations say of this requirement:

> The phrase "immediately after the exchange" does not necessarily require simultaneous exchanges by two or more persons, but comprehends a situation where the rights of the parties have been previously defined and the execution of the agreement proceeds with an expedition consistent with orderly procedure. (Regs. §1.351-1(a)(1).)

Under this interpretation, the stockholdings of two or more transferors can be aggregated in determining whether they control the corporation "immediately after the exchange" if their transfers are part of a single transaction. Thus, if A owns all of the stock of a corporation, consisting of 100 shares, and if the corporation is to be expanded by issuing 200 shares to B for property and 200 more shares to C for other property, B and C will be in control of the corporation "immediately after the exchange" (by virtue of owning 400 out of 500 shares, or 80 percent), even though B's exchange is not simultaneous with C's.

There has been litigation in abundance over the requirement that the transferors control the transferee corporation "immediately after the exchange," the principal problem being whether the statute is satisfied if the transferors own 80 percent or more of the stock for a moment, but thereafter dispose of some shares so that they are left with less than the 80 percent required by §351 and §368(c). Such a loss of "control" may occur if the transferors dispose of part of their stock to donees or purchasers, if the corporation issues additional stock to investors or employees, or in some other manner. Section 351(c) provides that in determining control, the fact that a *corporate transferor* distributes stock received in the exchange to its shareholders shall not be taken into account.[38] The Senate Report on the 1954 Code states that this provision, which was enacted in 1954, was added because it was not clear whether such a distribution would prevent application of §351 under existing law. S. Rep. No. 1622, 83d Cong., 2d sess., p. 265. The new provision, unfortunately, does not

---

[38] While a distribution of stock by a corporate transferor will not take the exchange outside of §351, the distribution may be taxable to the distributees as a dividend or otherwise. See Darrell, Corporate Organizations and Reorganizations Under the Internal Revenue Code of 1954, 32 Taxes 1007, 1009-1010 (1954).

shed any light on the meaning of the phrase "immediately after the exchange" in circumstances to which it is not applicable.

At first blush, the statutory phrase "immediately after the exchange" seems to focus upon a point in time, to the exclusion of any requirement that control persist thereafter. And some early decisions held, or expressed the view, that the statute was satisfied if the transferors controlled the corporation momentarily, despite a prompt loss of control by a sale or other disposition of stock as an integral part of the plan of incorporation or even pursuant to a pre-existing contract. See, for example, Portland Oil Co. v. Commissioner, 109 F.2d 479, 24 AFTR 225 (1st Cir. 1940). The tendency today, however, is to hold that momentary control is not sufficient if the transferors agreed beforehand to transfer enough of their stock to lose "control" or if such a transfer is an integral part of the plan of incorporation.

A recent illustration of the current attitude is Manhattan Building Co., 27 T.C. 1032 (1957) (Acq.), which concerned the transfer of certain assets by one Miniger to Electric Auto-Lite Co. in exchange for 250,000 shares of common stock and $3,000,000 in bonds. Miniger had purchased the assets in question with borrowed funds, under an agreement requiring him to transfer the assets to Auto-Lite in exchange for the stock and bonds, to deliver the bonds and 75,000 shares of stock to the lender (a firm of investment bankers), and to turn back 49,000 shares to Auto-Lite as a contribution to capital. The question before the court was whether the predecessor of §351 was applicable to this transaction, under which Miniger owned 100 percent of the stock fleetingly, but less than the requisite 80 percent when the plan was fully consummated:

> This depends upon whether the transfer of assets to Auto-Lite in exchange for its stock and bonds and the transfer of stock and bonds to the underwriters were mutually interdependent transactions. The test is, were the steps taken so interdependent that the legal relations created by one transaction would have been fruitless without a completion of the series. American Bantam Car Co., 11 T.C. 397 (1948) [aff'd. per curiam, 177 F.2d 513, 38 AFTR 820 (3d Cir. 1949)], certiorari denied 339 U.S. 920 (1950). In the present case when the transfer of assets to Auto-Lite occurred on July 17, 1922, Miniger was under a binding contract to deliver the bonds and 75,000 shares of stock to the underwriters and to return 49,000 shares to the corporation. The contract between Miniger and the underwriters shows this clearly. Miniger could not have completed the purchase of the assets without the cash supplied by the underwriters and could not have had the cash except in exchange for the bonds and stock and could not have secured the bonds and stock except for the assets.

After the exchanges Miniger had . . . less than 80 percent, of the voting stock. At no time did he have the right to hold more . . . The 1922 transaction was taxable as the petitioner contends. (27 T.C. at 1042.)

The *American Bantam Car Co.* case, cited in the extract above and often relied on, is also concerned with a loss of "control" by the transferors of property as a result of an underwriting agreement, but in this case the court held that the requirements of §351 were met. The owners of a manufacturing business transferred its assets, with $500 in cash, to a new corporation in exchange for all of the common stock, under a plan calling for a sale of preferred stock by the corporation to the public through underwriters who were to receive, in addition to their underwriting discounts and commissions, certain amounts of the common stock when and if they succeeded in selling the preferred stock to the public. The transfer of the assets to the new corporation for 300,000 shares of common stock occurred on June 3, 1936; five days later, the new corporation executed a contract with the underwriters for the sale of the preferred stock and the shareholders agreed that the underwriters would receive 100,000 shares of their common stock in specified installments as and if the preferred stock was sold; and in October, 1937, the underwriters received 87,900 shares of the common stock for their services. Although the transferors thus held less than 80 percent of the common stock after October, 1937, when the 87,900 shares were transferred to the underwriters, the Tax Court held that the requisite control in the transferors existed in June, 1936 — "immediately after the exchange" — and that the loss of "control" in October, 1937, was not an integral part of the transaction:

> The standard required by the courts to enable them to say that a series of steps are interdependent and thus should be viewed as a single transaction do not exist here. It is true that all the steps may have been contemplated under the same general plan of May 1936; yet the contemplated arrangement for the sale of preferred stock to the public was entirely secondary and supplemental to the principal goal of the plan — to organize the new corporation and exchange its stock for the Austin assets. The understanding with the underwriters for disposing of the preferred stock, however important, was not a *sine qua non* in the general plan, without which no other step would have been taken. While the incorporation and exchange of assets would have been purposeless one without the other, yet both would have been carried out even though the contemplated method of marketing the preferred stock might fail. The very fact that in the contracts

of June 8, 1936, the associates retained the right to cancel the marketing order and, consequently the underwriters' means to own common stock issued to the associates, refutes the proposition that the legal relations resulting from the steps of organizing the corporation and transferring assets to it would have been fruitless without the sale of the preferred stock in the manner contemplated. (11 T.C. at 406-7.)

Although the Tax Court rejected "the proposition that the legal relations resulting from the steps of organizing the corporation and transferring assets to it would have been fruitless without the sale of the preferred stock in the manner contemplated," it is readily apparent from the facts that additional capital was essential and that the incorporation was only the first step in a plan which, if successful, would result in a loss of control. On the other hand, had the capital not been raised "in the manner contemplated," the transferors might have been able to devise some other method, and in that sense the incorporation viewed alone was not necessarily a useless step.

In addition to holding that the underwriting agreement was "not a *sine qua non* in the general plan, without which no other step would have been taken," the Tax Court in the *American Bantam Car Co.* case emphasized that, although there was an informal oral understanding before the exchange occurred, a written agreement was not executed until five days after the exchange. This fact, it thought, distinguished the case before it from other cases in which the transferors would lose control under a contract pre-dating the exchange, so that "at the moment of the exchange the recipient of the stock did not own it, but held it subject to a binding contractual obligation to transfer a portion." (11 T.C. at 406.) Perhaps the convenience of a mechanical rule justifies this stress upon the formal execution of a document, as distinguished from the meeting of the minds; certainly nothing else does. But why should an agreement to sell, even if reduced to writing before an exchange of property, take it wholly outside of §351, rather than merely produce gain or loss on the shares disposed of? The agreement might, of course, be evidence that the loss of control was an integral part of the whole transaction, but this is not necessarily so. For example, two equal partners in a going business form a corporation in order to limit their liability; one of them, in need of funds to discharge debts of a personal nature, agrees in advance of the exchange to sell half of his stock to a third person. If the agreement to sell must be taken into account, the two transferors of property will own only 75 percent of the stock "immediately after the exchange," with the result that both must recognize gain or loss on the exchange, even though one of them may not have even known of the other's commitment to sell part of the stock. In such circumstances, it may be that a contract pre-dating the exchange will not be fatal.

Although the courts have not distinguished between commercial and non-commercial transactions in deciding whether a loss of control after the exchange is fatal, much can be said for treating these situations differently. If the transferors of property receive all of the stock of the transferee corporation and then reduce their ownership below the requisite 80 percent by giving some of the stock to their wives or children, the courts will usually find it possible to apply §351. See, for example, Wilgard Realty Co., Inc. v. Commissioner, 127 F.2d 514, 29 AFTR 325 (2d Cir. 1942), cert. denied, 317 U.S. 655, concerning a transfer of property for all the stock of a newly organized corporation. On the same day that the transferor received the stock, he gave more than 20 percent of it to members of his family. The court held that the transfer of the property to the corporation was a tax-free exchange under §351, not on the narrow ground that the transferor owned the shares of the corporation for an instant, but on a broader ground:

> In the absence of any restriction upon [the transferor's] freedom of action after he acquired the stock, he had "immediately after the exchange" as much control of the [corporation] as if he had not before made up his mind to give away most of his stock and with it consequently his control. And that is equally true whether the transaction is viewed as a whole or as a series of separate steps. . . . Where the recipient of the stock on the exchange has not only the legal title to it "immediately after the exchange" but also the legal right then to determine whether or not to keep it with the control that flows from such ownership, the requirements of the statute are fully satisfied. It is immaterial how soon thereafter he elects to dispose of his stock by gift or otherwise and whether or not such disposition is in accord with a preconceived plan not amounting to a binding obligation. (127 F.2d at 516.)

This case must be contrasted, however, with one in which the facts were nearly identical except that more than 20 percent of the shares were issued directly by the corporation to the transferor's donee. The District Court held that issuing the stock directly to the donee was fatal under §351 and the Court of Appeals affirmed. Fahs v. Florida Machine & Foundry Co., 168 F.2d 957, 36 AFTR 1161 (5th Cir. 1948). It is surprising to find important tax consequences hinging on so trivial a formality. Indeed, one might argue with respect to the extract quoted above from the *Wilgard Realty Co.* case that the requisite control should be found even if the transferor has already bound himself to transfer the shares, and even though the assets were incorporated in order to facilitate the making of the gifts. Otherwise, the taxpayer is given an option that contravenes the policy of §351. If he wishes the transaction to qualify under §351, he can either give the donees an interest in the assets themselves (so that they will be "transferors" of property under §351 when the corporation is organized) or give the stock to the donees in a later, independent transaction. If, on the other hand, the donor wishes to avoid §351 (*e.g.,* to procure a stepped-up basis for the assets and stock), he can follow the procedure of the transferor in the *Florida Machine & Foundry Co.* case. Moreover, the principle of §351 — non-recognition of gain or loss on formal transfers — is as applicable when the transferor and his donees control the corporation as when the transferor alone controls it. For these reasons, neither an obligation to transfer part of the stock nor the fact that the loss of control was an integral part of the entire transaction should be given the weight in gift cases that they have in commercial transactions.

Do the transferors have control "immediately after the exchange" if another person has an option to acquire enough shares, either from the corporation or from the transferors themselves, to terminate their control? In the *American Bantam Car Co.* case, *supra,* the Tax Court relied in part on the fact that the transferors would lose control only if the underwriters sold enough preferred stock to the public to earn the promised common stock. This approach, which looks to the likelihood that the option will be exercised, has much to commend it. The option can be properly disregarded if there is a genuine possibility that it will not be taken up; but if its exercise is a foregone conclusion (*e.g.,* if only a nominal consideration is payable for valuable stock), it may take the transaction outside of §351, unless the option-holder can himself be regarded as a transferor of property to be aggregated with the other transferors in computing control or unless the transfer of property and the option are not integral steps in a single transaction.[39]

---

[39] For more on the meaning of the phrase "immediately after the exchange," see, in addition to the cases cited in the text: May Broadcasting Co. v. United States, 200 F.2d 852, 42 AFTR 1039 (8th Cir. 1953); S. Klein On The Square, Inc. v. Commissioner, 188 F.2d 127, 40 AFTR 369 (2d Cir. 1951), cert. denied, 342 U.S. 824; Mojonnier & Sons, Inc. v. Commissioner, 12 T.C. 837 (1949) (Non-acq.); Maine Steel, Inc. v. United States, 174 F. Supp. 702, 4 AFTR 2d 5127 (D.Me. 1959); Commissioner v. National Bellas Hess, Inc., 220 F.2d 415, 47 AFTR 341 (8th Cir. 1955); Mintz and Plumb, Step Transactions in Corporate Reorganizations, 12 N.Y.U. Inst. on Fed. Taxation 247 (1954).

Sec. 3.10.   The transferor's basis

When gain or loss goes unrecognized at the time of an exchange, the transferor's basis for the property given up is ordinarily preserved and applied to the property received. Section 358 applies this principle to an exchange under §351. In the simplest situation, an exchange under §351 of property solely for stock or securities (so-called "non-recognition property"), §358(a)(1) provides that the basis of the stock or securities received shall be the same as the basis of the property transferred. If several classes of stock or stock and securities are received, §358(b)(1) requires an allocation of the basis of the property transferred among the various classes of stock and securities received on the exchange and the regulations provide that the allocation shall be in proportion to the market values of the stock and securities received. Regs. §1.358-2(b). Thus, if the basis of the transferred property was $5,000, and the transferor received in exchange common stock worth $6,000 and bonds worth $4,000, the basis of the stock would be $3,000 (6,000/10,000 x $5,000) and the basis of the bonds would be $2,000 (4,000/10,000 x $5,000). Assuming no later fluctuations in value, the transferor will realize $3,000 of gain on selling his stock and $2,000 of gain on selling the bonds. This total gain of $5,000, it will be noted, is equal to the gain that went unrecognized on the exchange itself because of §351(a), *viz.*, the difference between the basis of the property transferred and the value of the stock and bonds received in exchange.[40]

Section 358 is also applicable if the transferor received "boot" on the exchange. In this case, §351(b)(1) would have required him to recognize his gain on the exchange (if any was realized, *i.e.*, if the value of what he received exceeded the adjusted basis of the property he gave up) to the extent of the value of the "boot." Section 358(a)(2) provides that the "boot" (except money) shall be given a basis equal to its fair market value. And §358(a)(1) provides that the basis of the "non-recognition property" (*i.e.*, the stock or securities received on the exchange) is the same as the basis of the property given up, minus the money and the fair market value of the "boot" received, plus the gain recognized on the exchange.[41] These principles can be

---

[40] The "substituted basis" rules of §358 are similar to those of §1031, dealing with non-recognition exchanges of "like kind" property.

[41] §358(a)(1)(B)(i), providing for a further upward adjustment if any part of the property received on the exchange was treated as a dividend, is primarily concerned with certain transactions under §306 (*infra*, Ch. 8), according to the Senate Report on the 1954 Code. S. Rep. No. 1622, 83d Cong., 2d sess., p. 271. In unusual circumstances, however, it might be applicable to an exchange under §351. See *infra*, Sec. 3.13.

illustrated by assuming that the transferor of property with an adjusted basis of $4,000 received on the exchange stock and bonds worth $8,000, cash in the amount of $1,500 and other property worth $500. His realized gain of $6,000 (value received of $10,000, less adjusted basis of $4,000) would be recognized under §351(b) to the extent of the "boot," or $2,000. The basis of the "other property" received, under §358(a)(2), would be its fair market value, $500. The basis of the stock and bonds (the "non-recognition property") would be $4,000 (adjusted basis of property given up, $4,000, less cash of $1,500 and other property of $500, plus gain recognized of $2,000), to be allocated between the stock and bonds in proportion to their respective values.[42] The computation is as follows:

1. Amount realized:
   a. Stock and bonds $8,000
   b. Cash 1,500
   c. Other property 500
2. Total $10,000
3. Less: Adjusted basis of transferred property 4,000
4. Gain realized $6,000
5. Gain recognized (1b plus 1c, or 4, whichever is less) $2,000
6. Basis of property received:
   a. Cash —
   b. Other property (fair market value) $ 500
   c. Stock and bonds (line 3, less 1a and 1b, plus 5) $4,000

If the stock and bonds were then sold for their market value ($8,000), the owner would recognize $4,000 of gain, which, added to the $2,000 of gain recognized at the time of the §351 exchange, is equal to his full economic gain of $6,000 (total value of $10,000 received on the exchange less adjusted basis of original property of $4,000).[43]

---

[42] The same result for the non-recognition property can be reached by starting with its fair market value ($8,000) and reducing it by the realized but unrecognized gain ($4,000), or in case of a loss, increasing it by the unrecognized loss.

[43] The reader will have noted that the basis of the property received on the exchange reflects, under §358(a)(1)(B)(ii), the "amount of gain to the taxpayer which was *recognized*" on the §351 exchange. What if the transferor treats an exchange as non-taxable, but later claims a stepped-up basis for the stock and securities received by him on the ground that gain should have been recognized? There is authority by analogy for allowing him to use the stepped-up basis, at least where the failure to recognize gain on the exchange was not fraudulent or otherwise blameworthy, see Margaret S. Bullock, ¶44,406 P-H Memo T.C. (1944); Bennet v. Helvering, 137 F.2d 537, 31 AFTR 441 (2d Cir. 1943); see also Fahs v. Florida Machine & Foundry Co., 168 F.2d 957, 36 AFTR 1161 (5th Cir. 1948), holding that the transferee corporation, whose basis for the transferred assets is also dependent upon whether the exchange was a taxable transaction, is not estopped by the errors of the transferor. But if the transferor

If the transferee corporation assumed a liability of the transferor or took property subject to a liability, §358(d) provides that the amount of the liability shall be treated "as money received" by the transferor upon the exchange. This requirement, which is applicable whether the liability gave rise to income at the time of the exchange under §357(b) or §357(c) or came within the "general rule" of §357(a) (*supra*, Sec. 3.06), has the effect of reducing the basis that would otherwise be allocated under §358(a)(1) to the non-recognition property" by the amount of the liability. Thus, if A transfers property with a cost basis of $50,000 to a corporation for all of its stock plus the assumption of a $30,000 mortgage, A's basis for the stock will be $20,000. If A then sells the stock for $25,000, he will realize $5,000 of gain. Provided the mortgage is discharged in due course, this tax treatment accords with economic reality: A's net investment was $20,000 (the cost of the land less the amount of the mortgage) and he ultimately realized $25,000. If the transferee corporation fails to pay the debt at maturity and A is called upon to pay it, however, A would presumably be entitled to increase the basis of his stock (if he still owns it) by the amount of his outlay or to take a deduction under §165 or §166. There is a possibility that if the stock had been sold by A before he was called upon to pay the debt, his loss on payment would be treated as a capital loss because the sale of the stock was a capital gain transaction.[44]

On selling stock or securities received tax-free under §351(a), the transferor determines his holding period under §1223(1) by including ("tacking") the period during which he held the transferred property, provided the transferred property was either a capital asset or a §1231(b) asset. If the transferred property consisted of a mix-

insists upon a stepped-up basis, the government may assess an additional tax against him for the year of the exchange, nothwithstanding the running of the statute of limitations. §1312(7); Regs. §1.1312-7(c), Example (1)(ii) (which assumes that the transferor is not estopped to claim a stepped-up basis); Burford, Basis of Property After Erroneous Treatment of a Prior Transaction, 12 Tax L. Rev. 365, 370 (1957). Note, however, that §1314(d) prevents an assessment for a pre-1932 taxable year.

Gooding v. United States, 326 F.2d 988, 14 AFTR 2d 5268 (Ct. Cl. 1964), involved the converse of this situation. The taxpayer had erroneously treated the §351 exchange as a partially taxable exchange; following a court determination, involving the corporate transferee, that the exchange was wholly tax-free, the transferor sought under §§1311-1314 to obtain a refund of the tax erroneously paid in the year of the exchange. The court held that §1312(7) applied, although it would seem that a §1311 adjustment should have awaited the outcome of any dispute arising on a sale by the taxpayer of his stock. See §1312(7)(B), and Regs. 1.1312-7(c), Example (5).

See also *infra*, note 47.

[44]See Rees Blow Pipe Mfg. Co., 41 T.C. 598 (1964), reaching a comparable result under §1031 in reliance on Arrowsmith v. Commissioner, 344 U.S. 6, 42 AFTR 649 (1952).

ture of capital assets, §1231(b) assets, and non-capital assets, as in the ordinary case of incorporating a going business, it may be necessary to make an allocation under §1223(1), with the result either that some of the shares or securities received will have a holding period dating from the §351 exchange while others will have longer holding periods, or that each share or security will be divided for holding period purposes.[45]

Can the transferor transfer some assets for stock and others for securities, in order to control the basis or holding period of the stock and securities received? It is doubtful that such an earmarking of the transferred property would succeed, if both transfers were interdependent steps in a single transaction. Section 358 and the regulations promulgated under it seem to contemplate that the aggregate basis of the property transferred will be assigned to the properties received, leaving little room for any "planning" of basis by the foresighted taxpayer, and §1223(1) is no more helpful since its applicability depends upon §358.[46]

Sec. 3.11.   The transferee corporation's basis

Section 362(a) provides that the basis to the transferee corporation of the property received on the exchange shall be the transferor's basis for the property, increased in the amount of gain recognized to the transferor. What if the transferor erroneously recognized (or erroneously failed to recognize) gain on the prior exchange? Does §362 mean *actual* recognition, or should this language be read as meaning "recognizable"? The latter construction has won judicial support, whether the transferor's error was in recognizing or in failing to recognize gain.[47] The assumption of liabilities by the transferee

[45] "Tacking" is provided for by §1223(1) if the property whose holding period is to be determined has, for determining gain or loss on a sale or exchange, "the same basis in whole or in part . . . as the property exchanged." This requirement is readily satisfied if the §351 exchange is wholly tax-free; if boot is received, the stock's basis is determined *by reference to* the basis of the property given up and this may constitute a use of that basis "in part," but if the transferor's gain is wholly recognized on the exchange, this result is more doubtful.

In permitting "tacking" only if the property given up was a capital or §1231 asset (a requirement applicable only to exchanges after March 1, 1954, when this provision was enacted), §1223(1) seems to embrace §1231 assets even if subject to ordinary income treatment by virtue of the depreciation rules of §1245 or §1250. Such an asset can be said to be "described in section 1231," as required by §1223(1).

[46] See Nassau Lens Co. Inc. v. Commissioner, 35 T.C. 268 (1960), rev'd on other grounds, 308 F.2d 39, 10 AFTR 2d 5581 (2d Cir. 1962), suggesting this conclusion; *supra,* Sec. 3.05 (last paragraph).

[47] Erroneous recognition of gain: Truck Terminals, Inc. v. Commissioner, 314 F.2d 449, 11 AFTR 2d 901 (9th Cir. 1963). Erroneous nonrecognition: Fahs

does not enter into the computation of its basis for the transfered property (except in the unusual case in which gain is recognized to the transferor under §357); and since the assumed liabilities are part of its acquisition cost for the assets, it cannot deduct the amounts paid to discharge these liabilities or add them to its inherited tax basis.[48] The transferor's basis may also be subject to special adjustment rules, such as the "lower of cost or value" rule when personal-use property is converted to income or business functions.[49]

Neither the Code nor the regulations state how the carried-over basis is to be allocated by the transferee corporation among the various assets received. For example, if the controlled corporation issues stock in exchange for an asset with an adjusted basis to the transferor of $10,000 and a value of $10,000 and another asset with an adjusted basis of $20,000 and a value of $50,000, is the aggregate basis of $30,000 to be divided between the two assets in proportion to their market values or should the old basis of each asset be preserved intact? In P.A. Birren & Son, Inc. v. Commissioner, 116 F.2d 718, 26 AFTR 197 (7th Cir. 1940), it was held under the predecessor of §362(a) that the transferee corporation steps into the shoes of the transferor, preserving intact the old basis for each asset received on the exchange; see also Gunn v. Commissioner, 25 T.C. 424, 438 (1955) aff'd per curiam, 244 F.2d 408, 51 AFTR 397 (10th Cir. 1957), cert. denied, 355 U.S. 830. This rule, which has the virtue of avoiding an appraisal of the assets at the time of the exchange, will ordinarily be helpful to the taxpayer when a going concern is incorporated. If the transferor's aggregate basis for all the assets of the business had to be allocated by the transferee corporation in proportion to the market values of the various assets, a portion of the total basis, and perhaps

v. Florida Machine & Foundry Co., discussed *supra,* note 43. See also Regs. 1.1312-7(c), Example 1(i), assuming that the transferee corporation is not estopped to claim a stepped-up basis and that this will not open up the statute of limitations as to the transferor.

[48] §362(a)(1) makes no allowance for the liabilities except to the extent that gain was recognized as a result of §357(b) or (c); see also H. Rep. No. 855, 76th Cong., 1st sess., p. 20 (1939) (no change in inherited tax basis when transferee subsequently discharges the liabilities). For cases denying a deduction for the amount paid on the ground that it is part of the transferee's cost of acquiring the property, see Holdcroft Transp. Co. v. Commissioner, 153 F.2d 323, 34 AFTR 860 (8th Cir. 1946); Rodney, Inc. v. Commissioner, 145 F.2d 692, 33 AFTR 115 (2d Cir. 1944); see also Regs. 1.381(c)(16)-1; Magruder v. Supplee, 316 U.S. 394, 29 AFTR 196 (1942). The treatment of post-transfer expenditures by the transferee, such as interest paid on the liabilities, is governed by the normal rules of deductibility; and this would evidently permit a deduction of interest imputed under §483 if liabilities subject to that provision were assumed (or taken subject to) on the transfer.

[49] Regs. §1.167(g)-1; see Au v. Commissioner, 330 F.2d 1008, 13 AFTR 2d 1283 (9th Cir. 1964) (personal car transferred to partnership).

a substantial portion, would usually have to be allocated to good will. This would often be disadvantageous to the transferee corporation because it would reduce the basis of inventory and similar property (which presumably will be sold within a reasonable period) and machinery, equipment and plant (on which depreciation is allowed), while increasing the basis of good will, which will ordinarily not be sold or depreciated. Under the *Birren* case, however, there will be no such re-allocation of basis.

If the §351 exchange was partly taxable because "boot" was received, §362(a) provides that the basis to be assigned to the transferred assets is to be increased by the amount of gain recognized. But neither the Code nor the regulations state how this increase should be allocated among the various assets. One method would be for the corporation to take over the transferor's basis for each asset, under the *Birren* case, increased by the same percentage that the gain recognized bears to the aggregate old basis. Thus, if the total old basis was $25,000 and the gain recognized was $5,000, the basis of each transferred asset would be increased by 20 percent. This method has the advantage of simplicity, since it requires no appraisal of the transferred assets, but it is open to the objection that an asset's increase in basis may bear no relationship to its contribution to the recognition of gain. In the alternative, the gain could be allocated among the assets in proportion to their market values at the time of the exchange or in proportion to their actual increase in value above basis. Both alternatives would require an appraisal, but the latter one would have the merit of assigning the increase in basis to the assets "responsible" for it.

If the corporation disposes of any of the assets transferred to it under §351 in a transaction that produces capital gain or loss, the transferor's holding period can be "tacked" under §1223(2). It may be, moreover, that the transferor's holding period can be "tacked" under §1223(2) even though the property became a capital asset only when it was acquired by the transferee corporation.[50]

Sec. 3.12.   Transfer under §351 vs. "sale"

It is sometimes necessary to determine whether the transfer of property to a controlled corporation qualifies as a transfer under §351 or constitutes, instead, an ordinary sale of the property. If §351

---

[50] See Commissioner v. Gracey, 159 F.2d 324, 35 AFTR 680 (5th Cir. 1947); and note that §1223(2) was not amended in 1954, as was §1223(1), to nullify the *Gracey* rule. For further discussion of "tacking," see *supra,* note 45.

governs, the transfer is either wholly tax-free or taxable to the extent of any "boot" received, but no loss will be recognized. If, on the other hand, the transfer is a sale, the transferor will recognize his gain or loss under §1001 and §1002. For this reason, the owners of property that has declined in value sometimes wish to "sell" it to a corporation controlled by them and deduct their loss without losing control of the property.[51] The transferee corporation's basis for the transferred assets will also be affected by whether the transfer falls under §351 or is a sale; if §351 is applicable, the corporation must carry over the transferor's basis, while if the transaction is a sale, the corporation's basis will be its cost.

Relying on these principles, owners of land that has appreciated in value and that is ripe for a subdivision or other building project sometimes endeavor to "sell" the land to a controlled corporation for subdividing, so that (a) the appreciation will be taxed to them as capital gain (possibly over a period of years, if a §453(b) installment sale is made[52]) and (b) the corporation will start with a higher basis for the land and hence will realize correspondingly less ordinary income from its sales. If successful, this plan permits the business profits ultimately realized by selling the land to outsiders to be divided between the individual (reporting capital gain) and the corporation (reporting ordinary income), whereas a transfer of the land to the corporation under §351 would result in the corporation's realizing the entire profits as ordinary income. A "sale" may also be preferred over a §351 exchange as a means of stepping up the basis of depreciable property: if business equipment or real property with high current market value has a low adjusted basis, the owner may "sell" it to a controlled corporation in order to give the corporation a stepped-up basis for depreciation at the cost to him of a capital gain tax under §1231.[53] In cases of this sort, where the owner of property is seeking to give his corporation a stepped-up basis for assets at the cost of a capital gain tax to himself, an alternative to a "sale" is a transfer of

[51] Even if such a transaction is treated as a sale rather than as a tax-free transfer under §351, the transferors may run afoul of §267, which forbids the deduction of a loss on a sale by an individual to a corporation of which he owns, directly or indirectly, more than 50 percent in value of the outstanding stock. Moreover, the judicial doctrine embodied in Higgins v. Smith, 308 U.S. 473, 23 AFTR 800 (1940) (disallowing a claimed loss on a sale by a shareholder to his one-man corporation), may create a penumbra around §267 in which some losses that are not automatically disallowed by §267 will nevertheless be held non-deductible after a judicial appraisal of all the facts.

[52] When a deferred payment plan is employed, §483 provides for imputing interest, to be taxed as ordinary income, if the sales contract fails to provide for interest or employs an inadequate rate.

[53] See supra, Sec. 3.05, for the possible application of §1239, §1245, and §1250 to sales or other taxable transfers of depreciable property.

the property under §351 in exchange for stock plus cash, short-term notes, or other taxable "boot." The §351 route is not always a feasible alternative, however, since the use of short-term notes or other "boot" may have business disadvantages.[54]

Recognizing that the courts may convert what the parties have called a "sale" into a tax-free §351 exchange in which the transferee corporation must take over the transferor's basis for the property, we turn now to the factual patterns in which the issue usually presents itself.

If property is to be transferred to a controlled corporation solely for stock or securities, it is difficult to see how the parties can avoid §351(a). Section 351 is applicable "if property is transferred to a corporation . . . solely in exchange for stock or securities," and the impact of this language can hardly be avoided by affixing the label "sale" to the transfer. In more naive days, it was sometimes thought that the organizers of a corporation, wishing to deduct a loss on depreciated property, could purchase the corporation's stock for cash and then successfully "sell" the property to it for the cash just paid in, but the quietus was put on such transactions as early as 1932, in *Labrot v. Burnet*, 57 F.2d 413, 10 AFTR 1558 (D.C. Cir. 1932), and the device is not likely to be revived. A contrary construction of §351, moreover, would be indefensible because it would convert §351 into an optional provision, in contravention of the Congressional purpose.[55]

Even if the transaction is cast in the form of a "sale" of property for stock or securities plus cash or other property, its tax consequences should be governed by §351(a) and (b), so that the transferor should recognize gain (but not loss) to the extent of the "boot." The language of §351 is broad enough to embrace the transaction, and a contrary construction would endow the transferor with an option that was not intended by Congress. (As suggested above, if the transferor's purpose is to give the property a stepped-up basis in the hands of the corporation, rather than to enjoy a deductible loss, a transfer under §351 for stock or securities and "boot" may be a satisfactory alterna-

---

[54] See also Rev. Rul. 63-28, 1963-1 C.B. 76, revoking Rev. Rul. 56-303, 1956-2 C.B. 193. The latter ruling had held that a transfer of real estate to a controlled corporation for stock and short-term notes was a partially taxable §351 exchange with boot. The Service now refuses to rule whether obligations issued in a §351 exchange constitute stock, securities, or boot. Rev. Proc. 64-31, 1964-2 C.B. 947.

[55] A caveat must be introduced, however, for the case of a transfer that does not satisfy the "continuity of interest" doctrine; as suggested *supra*, Sec. 3.04, it may be that a transaction will be treated as a sale rather than as a transfer under §351 if the transferor owns no stock in the transferee corporation and receives none on the exchange or if his economic position is otherwise altered so drastically that the underlying assumptions of §351 are not applicable.

tive to a "sale.") Nor should the tax consequences of such a transfer be altered by dividing it into a "sale" of some of the property for cash and a transfer of the balance for stock or securities, if the two steps are integral parts of a single transaction.[56]

If, on the other hand, the property is transferred to a controlled corporation solely for cash or property, the transfer cannot qualify under either §351(a) (which requires that the sole consideration be stock or securities) or §351(b) (which permits the receipt of "boot," but only if the transferor has *also* received stock or securities). Conversely, if the transferor does not have 80 percent control of the transferee corporation (alone, or with other transferors) immediately after the exchange, the transfer will fall outside §351 and gain or loss will be recognized under §1001 and §1002.

Section 351 may be equally inapplicable if the corporation issues no stock or securities, but agrees to pay for the property at a specified time in the future or in installments. See Warren H. Brown, 27 T.C. 27 (1956) (Acq.). This conclusion, though it finds support in the language of §351, allows form to control the tax results of the transaction, since to the parties there may be no economic difference between a controlled corporation's promise to pay and its notes or debentures. Moreover, it was also held in the *Brown* case, that an installment sales contract (under which property was "sold" to a controlled corporation, the sales price to be paid in ten equal annual installments) was not a "security" as that term is used in §351. The court distinguished between an instrument evidencing "a continuing interest in the affairs of the corporation" and one intended "to effect a termination of such a continuing interest," a distinction that will not be easy to apply.[57]

In the foregoing discussion, we have focussed on whether §351 is or is not applicable to a transaction. It would be perilous to assume that a transaction falling outside §351 is *necessarily* a "sale" merely because it bears that label. For example, if property is transferred to a controlled corporation solely for cash, §351 is inapplicable for the

---

[56] See Houck v. Hinds, 215 F.2d 673, 46 AFTR 573 (10th Cir. 1954).

[57] In addition to cases cited *supra,* Sec. 3.03 and note 10, see Arthur F. Brook, ¶64,285 P-H Memo TC (1964); Aqualane Shores Inc. v. Commissioner, 269 F.2d 116, 4 AFTR 2d 5346 (5th Cir. 1959); Foresun, Inc., 41 T.C. 706 (1964); Marsan Realty Corp., ¶63,297 P-H Memo TC (1963); Charles E. Curry, 43 T.C. 667 (1965); Murphy Logging Co. v. United States, 239 F. Supp. 794, 15 AFTR 2d 623 (D. Ore. 1965; Burr Oaks Corp., 43 T.C. 635 (1965).

It should also be noted that a transfer may be treated as a bona fide sale to the extent of the transferred property's fair market value, but a dividend or other distribution to the extent of any excess to be paid above that amount. See Arthur M. Rosenthal, ¶65,254 P-H Memo TC; Crabtree v. Commissioner, 22 T.C. 61 (1954), aff'd per curiam, 221 F.2d 807, 47 AFTR 777 (2d Cir. 1955).

reasons stated above, but the taxpayer may still have to establish that the transfer is a sale rather than a contribution to capital of the property coupled with a distribution of cash.

One more caveat: whenever property is "sold" to a controlled corporation, the taxpayer must be prepared to establish that appearances correspond with reality. The Internal Revenue Service has more than once argued, sometimes with success, that a corporation's promise to pay for property should be disregarded, either because the corporation's capitalization was too "thin" or for some other reason, and that a "sale" should be treated either as a §351 transfer or as a contribution to capital. See *infra*, Sec. 3.16.

Finally, it should be noted that the shoe may be on the other foot: the taxpayer may seek to escape the consequences of a "sale" by arguing that a transaction was "really" a transfer under §351. While he is probably not barred by estoppel from such a reversal, the claim that his own paperwork did not mean what it said may strike the courts as less than sporting.[58]

Sec. 3.13.   Transfer under §351 vs. dividend

The regulations under §351 suggest the possibility that a distribution by a corporation of its stock or securities "in connection with an exchange subject to section 351(a)" may have "the effect of the distribution of a taxable dividend."[59] Although this part of the regulations does not identify the circumstances under which such a distribution might occur, there are at least these possibilities:

> 1. A transfer of property to a controlled corporation in exchange for stock and securities having a value greater than the property transferred. The excess value might be treated as a distribution under §301. See Regs. §1.301-1 (j).
>
> 2. A transfer of property to a controlled corporation in exchange for securities, if the transfer was merely a device, lacking in business purpose, for extracting the securities from the cor-

[58] See Harry F. Shannon, 29 T.C. 702 (1958).

[59] Regs. §1.351-2(d). Section 351(d) does not include a cross-reference to the basic dividend provision, §301, and §301(g)(3) might be read to imply that there is no overlap between §301 and §351. But this would put too much weight on statutory cross-references that were intended simply as convenient guides to the busy practitioner. See §7806(a). In any event, as the examples in the text indicate, the fact that a transfer complies with the the the terms of §351 does not mean that it cannot be accompanied by a §301 distribution. See Darrell, Corporate Organizations and Reorganizations Under the Internal Revenue Code of 1954, 32 Taxes 1007, 1010 (1954).

A surprising theory of the Tax Court, holding that §351 is controlling when it overlaps §301, was evidently rejected on appeal, though implicitly rather than explicitly, in Commissioner v. Haserot, 355 F.2d 200, 17 AFTR 2d 71 (6th Cir. 1965); see *infra*, Sec. 7.31.

poration. The government might assert that a transfer in these circumstances was "really" a contribution to capital, coupled with a distribution of securities taxable under §301.

    3. A reincorporation. See *infra*, Sec. 3.14.

Although Regs. §1.351-2(d), in warning of the possibility that a dividend may occur in conjunction with a §351 exchange, speaks only of a "distribution of stock or securities," it is equally possible that a distribution of money or other property would, in the circumstances described above, be taxed as a dividend under §301, rather than as "boot" under §351(b).

Sec. 3.14. Reincorporations

If a corporation pays a dividend by issuing its bonds or debentures to its shareholders, the distribution, for reasons discussed *infra*, Sec. 5.40, will be taxed about the same as a distribution of property. But if the corporation is liquidated and the stockholders, by prearrangement, then transfer the assets to a newly organized corporation in exchange for stock and bonds or debentures, can they treat the transaction for tax purposes as (a) a liquidation of the old corporation (which is an occasion for recognizing capital gain or loss, or possibly even tax-free, see *infra*, Sec. 9.01), and (b) a tax-free exchange of property for the stock and securities of the new corporation, under §351? If so, they will have accomplished their purpose without realizing the ordinary income that is ordinarily produced by a distribution of securities by a going corporation. It is possible, of course, that the courts would disregard the liquidation of the old corporation and the creation of the new as a sham, giving effect only to the distribution of securities and taxing it as a dividend. Another approach would be to give effect to the liquidation, but to treat the reincorporation as consisting of (a) an exchange of assets for stock, tax-free under §351, and (b) a separable distribution of securities, taxable as a dividend. See Regs. §1.301-1(1). Reincorporations have come to the fore in recent years as tax avoidance devices of burgeoning potentialities, at least in the discussion of tax advisors, and the problem just mentioned is only a small segment of this area, which will be discussed further in conjunction with corporate liquidations and reorganizations. *Infra*, Secs. 9.05 and 12.22.

Sec. 3.15. Corporate gain or loss on issue or sale of stock: §1032

Section 1032, enacted in 1954, provides that a corporation shall not recognize gain or loss "on the receipt of money or other property in

exchange for stock (including treasury stock) of such corporation."
Before 1954, in the absence of a statutory rule, the regulations had
provided that a corporation realized neither gain nor loss on the
original issuance of its stock, even though the subscription or issue
price exceeded, or was less than, the par or stated value of the stock,
but that:

> if a corporation deals in its own shares as it might in the shares
> of another corporation, the resulting gain or loss is to be com-
> puted in the same manner as though the corporation were dealing
> in the shares of another. (Regs. 118, §39.22(a)-15(b).)

As applied, this regulation often resulted in the recognition of
gain or loss on the disposition by a corporation of treasury shares, although no gain or loss would have been recognized if the corporation
had used authorized but unissued shares. Moreover, some courts
held that a corporation had dealt "in its own shares as it might in
the shares of another" in a transaction in which the shares of another
corporation would not have served the same purpose (such as a sale
of shares to employees, as an incentive device). Other courts, however, construed the regulation more narrowly.[60]

In its regulations under §1032, the Treasury has recognized the
intent to depart from the pre-1954 rules by expressly providing that
the corporation will not recognize gain or loss even though it deals in
its own shares as it might in the shares of another corporation. Regs.
§1.1032-1(a). The regulations also provide that §1032 applies to a
transfer of stock as compensation for services, Regs. §1.1032-1(a), although the statutory language refers only to "the receipt of money
or other property" in exchange for the stock.[61] The regulations also
clarify a statutory ambiguity in determining the corporation's basis
for property acquired in exchange for stock. Although §1032(b) refers to §362 as though it were the only provision governing the corporation's basis, the regulations state that §362 is applicable if the
exchange qualifies under §351 (*supra*, Sec. 3.11) or under the reorganization provisions (*infra*, Ch. 12), but that the basis of property

---

[60] The cases are reviewed in Penn-Texas Corp. v. United States, 308 F.2d
575, 10 AFTR 2d 5704 (Ct. Cl. 1962); see also Hercules Powder Co. v. United
States, 337 F.2d 643, 14 AFTR 2d 5783 (Ct. Cl. 1964).

[61] In Commissioner v. Fender Sales, Inc., 338 F.2d 924, 14 AFTR 2d 6076
(9th Cir. 1964), it was held that a corporation realized no income under §1032,
on issuing shares in payment of its debts to shareholders, thus treating the
cancellation of the debts as equivalent to the receipt of money or other property
by the corporation. The same result was reached under the 1939 Code as an
exception to the general principles governing cancellation-of-indebtedness income. See Eustice, Cancellation of Indebtedness and the Federal Income Tax:
A Problem of Creeping Confusion, 14 Tax L. Rev. 225, 238 (1959).

acquired by the corporation in *taxable* exchanges is governed by §1012 (basis of property is "cost"). Thus, if stock is issued to acquire property from an outsider, the basis of the property to the corporation will be its "cost," i.e., the fair market value of the stock given up.

The term "stock" is not defined by §1032, or elsewhere in the Code, and on several occasions the courts have had to say whether a corporation was entitled to the benefit of §1032 on receiving payment for rights embodied in a document of ambiguous character. Thus, Community T.V. Ass'n v. United States, 203 F. Supp. 270, 9 AFTR 2d 1084 (D. Mont. 1962), held that payments for so-called "Class B" stock, which had to be purchased as a condition to the receipt of television services to be furnished by the issuing corporation, did not qualify for exemption under §1032 and thus constituted taxable income to the corporation under §61. The "stock" was redeemable at par and did not entitle the owner to vote, to participate in the profits of the company, or to share in its assets on liquidation until the class A stock had been paid in full. A similar result was reached with respect to fees paid for "membership certificates" in a cooperative organization, even though the holders were entitled to vote and to share in assets on liquidation, because the substance of the transaction was a payment for the privilege of buying goods at a saving, rather than an equity investment in the taxpayer.[62]

The relationship between the nonrecognition of gain or loss on §1032 transactions and certain other statutory provisions is obscure. A recent ruling carries forward the pre-1954 rule that the fair market value of stock issued as compensation for services rendered may be deducted as a business expense if a payment of cash would have given rise to such a deduction, and presumably the same rule would apply to stock issued for property if a cash payment would have been deductible.[63] The ruling seems proper; a deduction does not conflict with §1032's purpose of recognizing neither gain nor loss on the *receipt* of money or property in exchange for stock. The same can be said of an allowance under §248 (amortization of organizational expenses),

---

[62] Affiliated Govt. Employees' Distributing Co. v. Commissioner, 322 F.2d 872, 12 AFTR 2d 5606 (9th Cir. 1963); see also Rev. Rul 61-18, 1961-1 C.B. 5 (excess of amount received over value of stock issued taxed as income to issuing corporation); and note the relationship of the results in the *Community TV Ass'n* and *Affiliated Govt. Employees* cases to Corn Products Refining Co. v. Commissioner, 350 U.S. 46, 47 AFTR 1789 (1955).

[63] Rev. Rul. 62-217, 1962-2 C.B. 59; for the pre-1954 law, see Int'l Freighting Corp. v. Commissioner, 135 F.2d 310, 30 AFTR 1433 (2d Cir. 1943); Montana Power Co. v. United States, 171 F. Supp. 943, 3 AFTR 2d 1108 (Ct. Cl. 1959). See also Hercules Powder Co. v. United States, 180 F. Supp. 363, 5 AFTR 2d 713 (Ct. Cl. 1960) (§265(1), relating to expenses connected with "exempt" income, held inapplicable).

or a deduction when appropriate, for the value of stock issued in payment for the corporation's organizational expenses.[64] If a corporation is to be paid for stock over a period of time, the proposed regulations under §483 indicate that interest will be imputed on the deferred payments if the contract does not stipulate an adequate rate of return;[65] although this approach is debatable, since §483 was enacted to prevent interest income from being received under the guise of capital gain, the language of §483 is sweeping, and the proposed regulation simply makes explicit the interest element that is implicit in the arrangement in any event. The relationship between §1032 and §453 (installment obligations) was explored in a recent case involving an unusual set of facts.[66]

Sec. 3.16.   Contributions to capital

Section 118, providing that gross income shall not include contributions to the corporation's capital, was enacted in 1954 as a restatement of "existing law as developed through administration and court decisions." S. Rep. No. 1622, 83d Cong., 2d sess., p. 190. In the case of pro rata contributions by shareholders, the exclusion from gross income might be regarded as a corollary to §1032 (*supra*, Sec. 3.15), under which the issue of stock does not produce corporate gain or loss. The purpose of §118 was not to confirm existing law with respect to contributions made by shareholders, however, but to give a Congressional blessing to pre-1954 cases holding that certain contributions by non-shareholders were not taxable as income:

> It [§118] deals with cases where a contribution is made to a corporation by a governmental unit, chamber of commerce, or other association of individuals having no proprietary interest in the corporation. In many such cases because the contributor expects to derive indirect benefits, the contribution cannot be called a gift; yet the anticipated future benefits may also be so intangible as to not warrant treating the contribution as a payment for future services. (S. Rep. No. 1622, *supra*, at 18-19.)

It will be noted that §118 takes hold only if the transaction is a "contribution to the capital of the taxpayer," and does not attempt to

---

[64] See Hollywood Baseball Assoc., 42 T.C. 234 (1964) (3d issue); for §248, see *supra*, Sec. 2.26.

[65] See Proposed Regs. §1.483-1(b)(6), Example (6).

[66] Jack Ammann Photogrammetric Engineers, Inc. v. Commissioner, 341 F.2d 466, 15 AFTR 2d 422 (5th Cir. 1965) (corporation issued stock in exchange for its own installment obligations, previously issued in payment for certain assets; held, acquisition and cancellation of its obligations not a disposition of them by it under §453).

define the term "contribution to capital." The regulations distinguish between (a) contributions "by a governmental unit or civic group to induce the corporation to locate its business in a particular community or to expand its operating facilities," which are subject to §118, and (b) payments for goods or services rendered and subsidies paid to induce the corporation to limit its production, to which §118 is inapplicable. Regs. §1.118-1.

The indicia that have been thought relevant in determining whether an amount received by a corporation (whether from a shareholder or from an outsider) is a tax-free contribution to its capital under §118 include: the corporation's need for additional capital; the expectation of ultimate return through an increase in the contributor's equity in the corporation; the intent or purpose of the contribution (i.e., whether the payment is for the benefit of the corporation's capital position, or, instead constitutes consideration for corporate goods or services rendered or to be rendered for the benefit of the payor); whether the contribution is voluntary and pro-rata among the shareholders; and the form of the contribution (a lump sum payment of money or property, as opposed to annual periodic payments in the nature of "dues" or "fees").[66a] Many of the contribution to capital cases have arisen in the context of a forgiveness of corporate indebtedness by shareholder-creditors. The regulations state that a shareholder who gratuitously forgives a debt owed to him by his corporation has made a contribution to capital to the extent of the principal of the debt.[67] But if the cancelled debt was deducted by the corporate debtor (e.g., as interest or as a business expense), the Service sometimes

[66a] See discussion in United Grocers Ltd. v. United States, 186 F. Supp. 724, 6 AFTR 2d 5588 (N.D. Cal. 1960), modified, 188 F. Supp. 735, 7 AFTR 2d 1481 (1961), aff'd, 308 F.2d 634, 10 AFTR 2d 5721 (9th Cir. 1962); see also Edwards v. Cuba Railroad Co., 268 U.S. 628, 5 AFTR 5398 (1925); Detroit Edison Co. v. Commissioner, 319 U.S. 98, 30 AFTR 1096 (1943); Brown Shoe Co., Inc. v. Commissioner, 339 U.S. 583, 39 AFTR 327 (1950); Teleservice Co. v. Commissioner, 254 F.2d 105, 1 AFTR 2d 1249 (3rd Cir. 1958), cert. denied, 357 U.S. 919; Maryland Jockey Club v. United States, 189 F. Supp. 70, 7 AFTR 2d 351 (D. Md. 1960), aff'd per curiam, 292 F.2d 469, 8 AFTR 2d 5037 (4th Cir. 1961); Rev. Rul. 58-555, 1958-2 C.B. 25; supra, note 62.

See generally Sneed, The Criteria of Federal Income Tax Policy, 17 Stanf. L. Rev. 567, 604-613; Freeman and Speiller, Tax Consequences of Subsidies to Induce Business Location, 9 Tax L. Rev. 255 (1954); O'Meara, Contributions to Capital by Non-Shareholders, 3 ibid. 568 (1948); Note, Tax Consequences of Non-Shareholder Contributions to Corporate Capital, 66 Yale L.J. 1085 (1957); Kumler, Contributions and Distributions of Property in Kind to and by Corporations, 33 Taxes 938 (1955).

[67] Regs. §1.61-12(a). Sometimes the taxpayer relies in the alternative on the assertion that there was no indebtedness to cancel, because the advance in question was in fact an equity investment; and secondly, that viewed as a debt, its cancellation was a contribution to capital. See J. A. Maurer, Inc., 30 T.C. 1273 (1958), deciding for the taxpayer on the former ground.

takes the position that the "tax benefit" principle overrides the exemption of §118. Most courts have rejected this argument, however, if the shareholder-creditor intended to make a capital contribution by cancelling the debt.[68] The capital contribution concept is often also invoked in cases involving alleged purchases of property by a corporation from its shareholders, if the arrangement shows an intention to commit the property to the risks of the business, or if the corporation is "thinly" capitalized; here it is ordinarily the government rather than the taxpayer who seeks to characterize the transaction as a contribution to capital.[69]

For many years, the Code has provided that the corporation's basis for property acquired as paid-in surplus or as a contribution to capital shall be the same as the transferor's basis. This rule, now embodied in §362(a)(2) of the Code, is comparable to §362(a)(1), under which property received by the corporation in exchange for stock in a transaction under §351 will retain the transferor's basis. Taken in conjunction, §362(a)(1) and (2) provide for the preservation of basis whether the stockholder gets stock in exchange or not, in recognition of the fact that the receipt of stock will be a matter of indifference if the shareholders' contributions are pro rata. The basis provision of §362 was amended in 1954, however, to reflect the fact that a contribution to a corporation's capital by an *outsider* has the effect of increasing the corporation's net worth, at no tax cost under the pre-1954 cases and the newly drafted §118. An exception to §362(a)(2) was enacted, providing that property (other than money) that is "not contributed by a shareholder as such" shall have a zero basis in the hands of the corporation. If the contribution consists of money, the corporation must reduce the basis of any property acquired within the following 12-month period with the contributed money, and if enough property is not so acquired, the basis of other property held by the corporation must be reduced *pro tanto*.[70] Like §118, §362(c) is ap-

---

[68] See Utilities & Industries Corp., 41 T.C. 888 (1964); Sheraton Plaza Co., 39 T.C. 697 (1963) (Acq.); Commissioner v. Auto Strop Safety Razor Co., 74 F.2d 226, 14 AFTR 828 (2d Cir. 1934); but see Helvering v. Jane Holding Corp., 109 F.2d 933, 24 AFTR 426 (8th Cir. 1940).

Where no tax benefit was received from the earlier deduction of the debt, §111 might be an alternate to §118 as a route to tax immunity in the year of cancellation. And where there was a tax benefit, a taxpayer who anticipates an application of the *Jane Holding Corp.* approach might, if sufficiently foresighted, elect to exclude the amount under §108.

See Eustice, *supra* note 61, at 250-51.

[69] See *supra*, sec. 3.12, and *infra*, ch. 4.

[70] §362(c): Presumably the phrase "not contributed by a shareholder as such" includes a civic "booster" who happens to be a shareholder of the cor-

plicable only if the property or money constitutes a "contribution to capital"; if it is received as payment for goods or services, no adjustment to basis is required. Section 362(c) is evidently also inapplicable to property or money received by a corporation as a gift; if so, the corporation would carry over the donor's basis under §1015.[71]

If the person making the contribution is a shareholder, the contribution will ordinarily be reflected in an increased basis for his stock. See Reg. §1.118-1, stating that voluntary pro rata payments by the shareholders are "in the nature of assessments upon, and represent an additional price paid for" the stock. If the contribution is made in property other than money, however, it is not clear whether the basis of the stock is to be increased by the basis, or the fair market value, of the property. If the contribution is voluntary, it does not produce gain or loss to the shareholder; and in this event, the shareholder should probably be regarded as contributing the basis of the property, rather than its fair market value. If the property is transferred to the corporation in payment of an assessment, however, the shareholder would realize gain or loss on discharging his indebtedness with property; and the basis of his stock should be increased by the fair market value of the property.[72]

Non-shareholder contributions to a corporation's capital might be deductible business expenses, e.g., if the contributor expects to

poration, if his contribution is out of proportion to his proprietary interest in the corporation. But what of a contribution by a major shareholder to a poverty-stricken corporation, if the other shareholders do not contribute proportionately? If the contributor's main interest is in salvaging the value of his stock, the contribution should be regarded as made by a "shareholder as such," subject to §362(a)(2) rather than to §362(c).

For the method of reducing basis under §362(c), see Regs. §1.362-2. The proper basis adjustment on a cancellation of indebtedness is left unclear but it should arguably be treated like money; see Greer v. Commissioner, 230 F.2d 490, 49 AFTR 260 (5th Cir. 1956) (pre-1954 taxable year).

The statutory rule of §362(c) overrules the result in Brown Shoe Co. v. Commissioner, supra, note 66a, as to contributions on or after June 22, 1954.

[71] As to amounts received as payment for goods or services, see supra note 66a; as to gifts, S. Rep. No. 1622, 83d Cong., 2d sess., p. 272; H. Rep. No. 1337, p. A128; Bothin Real Estate Co. v. Commissioner, 90 F.2d 91, 19 AFTR 810 (9th Cir. 1937); Veterans Foundation v. Commissioner, 317 F.2d 456, 11 AFTR 2d 1500 (10th Cir. 1963) (used clothing, etc. donated to taxpayer for sale in thrift stores were contributions to capital with zero basis under §362(c) rather than gifts with carryover basis under §1015); see also Hitchon's Estate, 45 T.C. 96 (1965) (Acq.) (gift by one shareholder to corporation, if intended to benefit other shareholders, entitles them to increase the basis of their shares).

[72] See Edward Mallinckrodt, 38 B.T.A. 960, 969 (1938) (increase by basis of contributed property); Greer v. Commissioner, supra note 70 (increase by fair market value). The latter decision is of doubtful validity; it is difficult to see why a shareholder should obtain a higher basis for his stock investment in a controlled corporation by making a capital contribution of property without taking back additional stock, when the receipt of stock or securities on a §351 transfer would require a carryover of his basis under §358, supra, Sec. 3.10.

derive business benefits from the relocation of industry in his area; and occasionally a shareholder's contribution, especially if not pro rata, can qualify for deduction.[73]

Sec. 3.17. "Mid-stream" transfers of potential income under §351

By providing for the nonrecognition of gain or loss on the transfer of property to a controlled corporation and for a carryover of the transferor's basis, §351 and §358 contemplate as a general principle that the unrecognized gain or loss will be taken into account by the transferee corporation when it disposes of the property received. When a going business is incorporated, however, the transferred assets do not ordinarily consist solely of investment property, but include inventory, accounts receivable, property under contract or earmarked for customers, materials and supplies whose cost was deducted by the transferor on acquisition, work in process, installment obligations, contract rights, and other items that would have generated taxable income to the transferor in the ordinary course of business, possibly within a few days or weeks. Attention has already been called (*supra*, Sec. 3.02) to the possibility that some claims and other items of this character, especially if created by the transferor's personal services, may not constitute "property" within the meaning of §351(a), in which event the transferor's receipt of stock or securities of the controlled corporation in exchange for the item in question will result in taxable income under §61(a) or §§1001 and 1002. Even if the "property" requirement of §351 is fully satisfied, however, the taxpayer must contend with the possibility that its provision for nonrecognition of gain is subordinate in certain cases to such basic doctrines as the assignment of income and tax benefit principles or to the Commissioner's statutory authority under §446(b) and §482 to require an accounting method or an allocation of income and deductions in order to "clearly reflect income." When applicable, these rules require the transferor to take certain items into account in his return, rather than shifting their burden to the transferee corporation. Although these principles should not be permitted to frustrate the Congressional desire to facilitate the incorporation of going businesses by enacting

---

[73] See I.T. 3706, 1945 C.B. 87 (contributions to civic development fund); Simons Brick Co., 14 B.T.A. 878 (1928) (contributions to organization boosting Southern California); Julius C. Miller, 45 B.T.A. 292 (1941) (Acq.) (shareholder allowed to deduct difference between basis of stock surrendered to improve corporation's capital status and the proportionate benefit to his remaining stock); Charles H. Duell, ¶60,248 P-H Memo TC (1960) (accord).

§351's rule of nonrecognition of gain and loss, it is equally unreasonable to assume that §351 transcends all other statutory and judicial principles of tax liability.[74] Because no standards susceptible of extrapolation to other instances have as yet emerged in this burgeoning area, the best that can be done at this point is to mention some of the trouble spots and summarize the results that have been reached:

1. Assignment of income. Despite §351, and in reliance on such cases as Lucas v. Earl, 281 U.S. 111, 8 AFTR 10,287 (1930), and Helvering v. Horst, 311 U.S. 112, 24 AFTR 1058 (1940), a taxpayer transferring a claim for personal services has been taxed when the transferee corporation collected the amount due; a newly-formed corporation's sale of growing crops has been treated as a sale by the transferor who held them until shortly before harvesting; and a shareholder who cancelled his claim for unpaid salary against a controlled corporation in exchange for its stock was held to have disposed of the claim for value.[75] In Thomas W. Briggs, ¶56,086 P-H Memo TC (1956), however, the Tax Court refused to require a cash basis taxpayer to report accounts receivable that were transferred by him as part of a going business to a newly-formed corporation.

2. Clear reflection of income (§446(b) and §482). In Palmer v. Commissioner, 267 F.2d 434, 3 AFTR 2d 1170 (9th Cir. 1959), a taxpayer in the construction business who had been reporting income on the completed contract method of accounting transferred the business

---

[74] The problem in this area has much in common with the problem that the concept of "income in respect of a decedent" (§691) was created to solve. In the §351 area, however, the general principle is that the transferor is relieved of tax liability on condition that his gain be recognized later by the transferee corporation, a carryover of basis being the mode of insuring this result; and the doctrines discussed in the text alter this rule by requiring the transferor to report the item in question. On transfers at death, by contrast, the general principle is the permanent exclusion of gain on transferred property from the tax base, effected by giving the transferee a basis equal to the date-of-death value; and the exception of §691 requires the transferee to report the special items as income. Thus the parallelism is not precise; the disparity can be seen most readily in the tax benefit and "clear reflection of income" cases described in the text, which would not come within the scope of §691.

A similar problem of allocating items between transferor and transferee can arise on the liquidation of a corporation, especially if a going business is transferred to the shareholders; and many of the cases in this area have implications for §351 exchanges. See *infra*, Sec. 9.62.

See generally Arent, Reallocation of Income and Expenses in Connection with Formation And Liquidation of Corporations, 40 Taxes 995 (1962); Lyon & Eustice, Assignment of Income: Fruit and Tree As Irrigated By the P. G. Lake Case, 17 Tax L. Rev. 293, 424 (1962); Eustice, Contract Rights, Capital Gain, and Assignment of Income — The Ferrer Case, 20 Tax L. Rev. 1 (1964); Hickman, Incorporation and Capitalization, 40 Taxes 974 (1962).

[75] Brown v. Commissioner, 115 F.2d 337, 25 AFTR (2d Cir. 1940) (claim for legal fees); Clinton Davidson, 43 B.T.A. 576 (1941) (insurance commissions); Adolph Weinberg, 44 T.C. 233 (1965) (growing crops); Commissioner v. Fender Sales, Inc., 338 F.2d 924, 14 AFTR 2d 6076 (9th Cir. 1964).

to a controlled corporation shortly before the major payment fell due for work largely done before the transfer. The court upheld an adjustment putting him on the percentage of completion accounting method in order to reflect his ratable share of the net income earned before incorporation, thereby allocating a substantial portion of the corporate income back to him. In Rooney v. United States, 305 F.2d 681, 10 AFTR 2d 5110 (9th Cir. 1962), the Commissioner's accounting adjustment took a different form: shareholder deductions were reallocated to the corporation under §482 in order to prevent a distortion of the net income from a farming business which had been incorporated after the costs of raising certain crops had been incurred but before they were harvested and sold.[76]

3. *Tax benefit rule.* In Rev. Rul. 62-128, 1962-2 C.B. 139, the Service took the position that a sole proprietor transferring a business under §351 was required to take his bad debt reserve into income, to the extent that additions to the reserve had been deducted in prior years with tax benefit. Judicial response to this approach, which could affect many other items deducted by the transferor before the §351 exchange, is divided.[77]

4. *Business purpose.* The transfer of stock, on which a large dividend was about to be paid, to a second corporation controlled by the transferors, without any business purpose but in the hope of qualifying the dividend for the dividend-received deduction of §243 (*supra,* Sec. 2.25) was held to be ineffective in Rev. Rul. 60-331, 1960-2 C.B. 189, with the result that the dividend was taxable to the individual transferors. It should also be noted that a transfer of property to a corporation, with no purpose other than to prepare for a sale of the stock in the hope of reporting capital gain thereon, may be disregarded, in which event the transaction will be treated as a direct sale of the property itself (*infra,* Sec. 10.04, note 15).

Aside from these doctrines of vague ambit, which of course sometimes are overlapping routes to the same end, there are also a number

---

[76] See also Commissioner v. Montgomery, 144 F.2d 313, 32 AFTR 1197 (5th Cir. 1944), where the Commissioner lost in an attempt to tax the entire profit on a construction contract to the transferor; unlike the *Palmer* case, cited in the text, this was an attempt to impute the *entire* profit to the transferor.

[77] Schmidt's Estate v. Commissioner, 355 F.2d 111, 17 AFTR 2d 242 (9th Cir. 1966), rejects Rev. Rul. 62-128; the opinion cites but does not discuss West Seattle National Bank v. Commissioner, 288 F.2d 47, 7 AFTR 2d 790 (9th Cir. 1961), a decision of the same court upholding the government's position in a comparable though not identical situation, see *infra,* Sec. 9.62.

In at least one area (the recapture of depreciation deductions that prove in retrospect to have been "excessive"), the existence of statutory solutions (§1245 and §1250) that explicitly limit their applicability to §351 exchanges appears to pre-empt the possibility of a recapture on tax benefit principles.

of statutory provisions which require the transferor of certain types of property to report income on a "disposition" or other transfer. The statute itself may go on to say whether a §351 exchange is to be so treated (as in §1245 and §1250, exempting §351 transfers if wholly tax-free); but sometimes this is left to administrative and judicial construction. An example is §453, relating to installment obligations, under which the regulations and cases hold that a §351 transaction does not constitute a taxable disposition of such assets.[78]

Sec. 3.18.   Transfers under §351 to foreign corporations

Transfers of property to a foreign corporation present special problems in addition to those previously discussed. Section 367 provides that in determining the extent to which gain shall be recognized in a §351 exchange, a foreign corporation shall not be considered a corporation unless prior to the exchange it has been proven to the Treasury that such exchange is not in pursuance of a plan having as one of its principal purposes the avoidance of federal income taxes. Despite the curious language of §367 ("a foreign corporation shall not be considered as a corporation"), its effect is to require recognition of the gain realized by the transferor on the exchange; the transferee does not lose its corporate status in determining such matters as its basis for transferred property, earnings and profits, and existence as a separate taxable entity.[79] In this respect, and in its insistence that "clearance" be obtained from the Internal Revenue Service before the exchange is made, §367 applies not only to §351 transfers, but to most of the tax-free liquidations, reorganizations, and other corporate transactions discussed elsewhere in this work.

In determining whether a transfer to a foreign corporation has a tax avoidance purpose, account must be taken of a variety of factors,

---

[78] Regs. §1.453-9(c)(2); Portland Oil Co. v. Commissioner, 109 F.2d 479, 24 AFTR 225 (1st Cir. 1940); but see Jack Ammann Photogrammetric Engineers, Inc. v. Commissioner, 341 F.2d 466, 15 AFTR 2d 422 (5th Cir. 1965), which strongly implies a contrary result based on Commissioner v. P. G. Lake, Inc., 356 U.S. 260, 1 AFTR 2d 1394 (1958). The latter approach might also be taken toward a transfer of so-called "section 306 stock" in view of its unusual susceptibility to use for tax avoidance (see infra, Sec. 8.02).

See also supra, note 18, to the effect that a §351 transfer of a going business does not trigger a recapture of the investment credit.

See also Ezo Products Co., 37 T.C. 385 (1961) transferee corporation is not the same taxpayer as the transferor, in applying §481, relating to adjustments required on a change in method of accounting; Regs. §1.167(c)-1(a)(6) (similar theory applied, so that "original use" of depreciable transferred property does not commence with transferee.)

[79] See Rev. Rul. 64-158, 1964-1 C.B. 140.

including the statutory provisions relating to foreign source income, since such a transfer will not automatically reduce the enterprise's United States tax liability; moreover, a persuasive business reason may outweigh any tax reduction that will occur. Because of the Service's failure to publish rulings in this area, however, practitioners must glean their information on its views by direct contact with the appropriate office or from other practitioners who have applied for rulings. The Service has often intimated that this unsatisfactory if not inexcusable state of affairs will be remedied by the promulgation of informative rulings or guidelines, but as of this writing (February, 1966), a few rulings have appeared on peripheral legal issues, but none on the criteria used in determining if a plan has "as one of its principal purposes the avoidance of federal income taxes." Thus, whether transfers resulting in a deferral of taxes can be distinguished from those resulting in a permanent reduction is still a murky question. It should be noted that there are no cases on the taxpayer's right to judicial review of an unfavorable ruling; while some remedy may be theoretically available in an aggravated case of arbitrary action, business opportunities are not likely to wait while a new cause of action is being judicially established.

It is usually assumed that Section 367's requirement of clearance *before* the exchange occurs cannot be excused at the taxpayer's behest, no matter how persuasive an excuse he offers for his failure to apply for a ruling. This may be too dogmatic a conclusion, but it is a good working hypothesis; and it argues for wariness in any transfer of appreciated property to a foreign corporation, since what is thought to be outside the ambit of §367 (e.g., a contribution to capital) will result in the recognition of gain if it turns out to be a §351 exchange.[79a] If the taxpayer deliberately refrains from requesting a ruling in order to achieve a taxable transaction with a concomitant step-up in basis, however, he may find that §367 is a one-way street. The Service has so ruled, on the ground that §367 was enacted solely to close a tax loophole.[80]

Since §367 applies only to realized gains, a transfer of depreciated property to a foreign corporation will not generate a deductible loss under §351 whether a §367 ruling is obtained or not. Moreover, if the transferor realizes both gains and losses on the transfer, his failure to obtain a favorable ruling under §367 would no doubt require his gains to be recognized under §367 while his losses went unrecognized under

---

[79a] See Rev. Rul. 64-155, 1964-1 C.B. 138.
[80] Rev. Rul. 64-177, 1964-1 C.B. 141.

§351.[81] Section 367 applies to §351 transfers only if the *transferee* is a foreign corporation; a transfer of property *by* a foreign corporation to a domestic one needs no clearance to qualify under §351.[82] Similarly, if the property transferred under §351 consists of the stock or securities of a foreign corporation, §367 seems inapplicable if the transferee is a domestic corporation.[83]

[81] See Commissioner v. Whitney, 169 F.2d 562, 37 AFTR 211 (2d Cir., 1948), where netting of nonrecognizable losses against recognizable gains was prevented in an analogous situation, and *supra,* sec. 3.05.

[82] See Rev. Rul. 55-45, 1955-1 C.B. 34.

[83] On the special reporting rules applicable to transactions with foreign corporations, see *supra,* Sec. 1.06.

See also §1491 (excise tax on transfer of appreciated securities to a foreign corporation as paid-in surplus or contribution to capital).

For §367, see generally McDonald, Section 367 — A Modern Day Janus, 64 Col. L. Rev. 1012 (1964); Ross, The Impact of The Revenue Act of 1962 On Reorganizations And Other Rearrangements Involving Foreign Corporations, 22 N.Y.U. Inst. on Fed. Taxation 761 (1964); Rapp, Section 367 Rulings: How the IRS Regards Exchanges With Foreign Corporations, 13 J. Tax 344 (1960); Kumler, Problems in Formation and Liquidation of Foreign Corporations, 1959 So. Calif. Tax Inst. 299; Whitehill, Foreign Corporate Exchanges, 36 Taxes 622 (1958).

Chapter Four

THE CORPORATION'S CAPITAL STRUCTURE

Sec. 4.01. Introductory

The organizers of a corporation normally have freedom, within the limits imposed by state law and business needs, to create a capital structure of stock alone (including different classes of stock, such as common and preferred), or to use a combination of stock and debt. Their choice is not impaired by the fact that the assets to be transferred to the corporation consist of property or a going business, rather than money, nor does it matter that the organization of the corporation is tax-free under §351(a), partly taxable under §351(b), or wholly outside of §351.[1]

If the corporation must acquire cash or property from outsiders, the choice between stock or debt investment will be governed primarily by non-tax pressures, though in some cases the tax consequences may play an important role. The organizers will have a freer hand in deciding what is to be issued for the assets which they themselves are furnishing to the corporation, and here the federal income tax consequences may be the controlling, if not the sole, influence. In any event, they will ordinarily want to consider some debt in the initial capital structure for tax reasons, especially since much can be accomplished with ease at the time of organization that if attempted later will have adverse consequences. Thus, preferred stock and bonds can ordinarily be issued at incorporation on a tax-free basis; but a later distribution of such instruments may require them to be treated as "section 306 stock" or a dividend, respectively.[2]

The principal factors to be considered in the choice between debt and stock capital are as follows:

1. The corporation will obtain a deduction under §163(a) for interest paid on indebtedness (*pro tanto* avoiding the "double tax" on corporate profits), whereas dividends paid on stock are not deductible. But interest is taxable in full to the recipient (regardless of corporate earnings and profits), while dividends are entitled to the $100 exclusion of §116 for individual shareholders,

---

[1] See *supra*, Ch. 3.
[2] For "section 306 stock," see *infra*, Ch. 8; for taxability of a distribution of bonds to shareholders, see *infra*, Sec. 5.40.

and the 85% dividends received deduction of §243 for corporate shareholders.

2. Payment of debt at maturity may constitute a "reasonable business need" under §533(a) which will justify an accumulation of earnings and profits and thus help to avoid the penalty tax imposed by §531; the redemption of stock, however, is less likely to qualify as a "reasonable need of the business." See *infra*, Sec. 6.07.

3. Payment of principal on the debt will ordinarily be a tax-free recovery of basis to the creditor (or will produce capital gain under §1232 if collections exceed the adjusted basis of the debt); whereas the redemption of stock is often taxed as a dividend to the redeemed shareholders. See *infra*, Ch. 7.

4. Debt (and to a lesser degree, preferred stock) may be transferred within the family, to outsiders, or donated to charity without diluting the insiders' control of the corporation.

5. If the holder's investment becomes worthless, capital loss treatment is the usual result for both debt and stock security holders. Losses from worthless stock are governed by §165(g)(1), which provides for "constructive sale" treatment on the last day of the year; a worthless debt, if evidenced by an instrument having interest coupons attached or in registered form, is governed by the same provision. Other worthless debts are treated as short term capital losses under §166(d) if they are held by individuals and constitute "non-business debts," and as ordinary losses under §166(a) otherwise.

An important exception to capital loss treatment, available only for "section 1244 stock" of a so-called small business corporation, is discussed *infra*, Sec. 4.10.

6. Common stock, preferred stock, and debt instruments which are "securities" may be received without recognition of gain on the transfer of property to a controlled corporation under §351; non-security debt instruments, however, may be taxable as "boot" under §351(b) (with a corresponding basis increase to the corporate transferee). See Chapter 3, *supra*.

The foregoing factors may serve to stimulate the excessive use of debt instead of equity investment in the corporate capital structure, thereby increasing fixed annual charges and helping to bring on insolvency, with consequent economic dislocation and losses both to the enterprise itself and to the national economy. In addition, the effort to stave off bankruptcy may lead the management to skimp on maintenance and repairs and to adopt other short-sighted business practices. For these reasons, most students of corporate financial policy since the 1930's have applauded the efforts of the SEC, state regulatory commissions, and bankruptcy courts to scale down fixed charges, and have criticized the tax incentives to the use of debt that even these supervisory agencies find it impossible to disregard. Less attention, however, has been given to the other side of the coin: the possibility that the opportunity to "trade on a thin equity" may attract speculative investment by shareholders, with favorable consequences for the national economy that, in the long run, may outweigh the dangers of excessive debt.[3]

It is not possible to segregate for measurement the effect of the Internal Revenue Code on corporate financial structures, but it is common knowledge that closely-held corporations often use debt instead of stock primarily for tax reasons. Since the debt in such cases is usually owed to the shareholders pro rata, however, the fixed charges will not ordinarily precipitate bankruptcy proceedings or encourage unwise management policies; the shareholders will usually subordinate or extend their claims rather than insist on payment (a fact that has led several courts to find that a capital contribution was intended rather than a loan).[4] But it is possible that the shareholder-creditors' dual role will lead to unfair competition with outside creditors.

In the case of publicly-held corporations, the use of debt is less frequently traceable to the Internal Revenue Code; but there have been some striking instances in recent years of corporations that, upon emerging from bankruptcy proceedings with a "sound" financial structure of common and preferred stock, have issued income or even fixed interest debentures to replace their preferred stock, primarily to take advantage of the interest deduction.[5] Since the debt of such corporations is almost never held pro rata by shareholders, they are not likely to have trouble in classifying it as bona fide debt unless "hybrid" securities are used.[6]

The use of debt obligations to obtain a corporate interest deduction for payments to investors should be considered as one of several ways of accomplishing the same objective. Instead of transferring assets to the corporation for debt instruments, for example, the shareholders can lease them, thus entitling the corporation to a deduction for rent under §162(a)(3) if the arrangement is bona fide and the rent is reasonable. Other standard techniques for avoiding or miti-

[3] See Groves, *Postwar Taxation and Economic Progress* 31-35 (1946); Goode, *The Corporation Income Tax* 136-8 (1951); Lent, Bond Interest Deduction and the Federal Corporation Income Tax, 2 Nat. Tax J. 131 (1949); Donaldson, *Corporate Debt Capacity* (1961).

[4] *Infra*, Sec. 4.04.

[5] See Silberman, How Much Can Business Borrow? *Fortune* (June, 1956) p. 131; Donaldson, *supra*, note 3; Molloy, Federal Income Tax Aspects of New Trends in Railroad Corporate Finance, 12 Tax L. Rev. 113 (1957); Comment, Bond-Income Bonds-Rights of Bond-holders and Deductibility of Interest for Federal Income Tax Purposes, 56 Mich. L. Rev. 1334 (1958).

[6] *Infra*, Sec. 4.03.

gating the statutory pattern of double taxation of corporate profits are the payment of salaries to shareholder-employees for their services and elections under Subchapter S (*infra*, Ch. 14).

Sec. 4.02.   Stock vs. debt — Major litigation areas

The shareholders of a closely-held corporation often cast part of their investment in the form of "debt" for tax rather than business reasons. Because the courts have upheld the government's refusal to accept the form of the instrument as controlling, there has been a vast amount of litigation over the proper classification of disputed instruments.[7] Most of the cases arise on one or more of three occasions: (1) on the receipt of the purported debt obligation in exchange for property (raising the issue of recognition of gain or loss to the transferor and basis to the transferee where the transaction, as is typically the case, occurs in the context of an incorporation under §351);[8] (2) during the term of the obligation, when "interest" is paid or accrued and deducted by the corporation; and (3) at maturity of the obligation, when it is collected by the holder or written off as worthless (see *infra*, Sec. 4.07). This is by no means an exhaustive list of the times when classification may be required; and it should also be noted that

---

[7] See generally Goldstein, Corporate Indebtedness to Shareholders: "Thin Capitalization" and Related Problems, 16 Tax L. Rev. 1 (1960); Weyher and Weithorn, Capital Structure of New Corporations, 16 N.Y.U. Inst. on Fed. Tax. 277 (1958); Pennell, Tax Planning at the Time of Incorporation, 35 Taxes 927 (1957); Hellerstein, Planning the Corporation, 1958 Tulane Tax Inst. 416, 427ff; Bittker, Thin Capitalization: Some Current Questions, 34 Taxes 830 (1956), reprinted with minor revisions in 10 U. Fla. L. Rev. 25 (1957); Caplin, The Caloric Count of a Thin Incorporation, 17 N.Y.U. Inst. on Fed. Tax. 771 (1959); Rockler, Transfers to Controlled Corporations: Considerations of Thinness and Multiplicity, 39 Taxes 1078 (1961); Hickman, Incorporation and Capitalization, 40 Taxes 974, 983 (1962); Stutsman, Debt Financing Upon Incorporation, 1960 So. Cal. Tax Inst. 211 (1960); Note, Thin Capitalization and Tax Avoidance, 55 Col. L. Rev. 1054 (1955); Schlesinger, Acceptable Capital Structures: How Thin is Too Thin? 5 U. Fla. L. Rev. 355 (1952); Schlesinger, "Thin" Incorporations: Income Tax Advantages and Pitfalls, 61 Harv. L. Rev. 50 (1947); Semmel, Loan Versus Investment — Inadequate Capitalization, 5 Tax L. Rev. 424 (1950); Levitan, How to Reduce the Amount of Equity Capital Invested in Controlled Corporations, 21 J. Tax. 214 (1964).

For an analysis of the litigated cases, comparing the facts in each case in tabular form, see Prentice-Hall, *1966 Federal Tax Service*, ¶13,096.

The House version of the 1954 Code attempted to specify by definition precisely what instruments would qualify for certain tax privileges. But the Senate dropped these definitions, stating (S. Rep. No. 1622, 83d Cong., 2d Sess., p. 42):

> Your committee believes that any attempt to write into the statute precise definitions which will classify for tax purposes the many types of corporate stocks and securities will be frustrated by the numerous characteristics of an interchangeable nature which can be given to these instruments.

[8] *Supra*, Sec. 3.03 and 3.12.

an unexpected classification may have serious side effects (e.g., if purported "debt" is found to be a second class of stock, the corporation's election under Subchapter S will be ineffective, see *infra*, Sec. 14.02). Although both the corporation and its shareholders ordinarily prefer "debt" classification, while the government usually seeks to classify a disputed instrument as "stock," the roles may be reversed; and both taxpayers and government may take inconsistent positions in different years, depending on the context in which the issue arises.[9]

Because the proper classification of a disputed instrument is ordinarily treated as a question of fact under vague standards that ultimately refer to the "intent" of the parties and the "substance" of the transaction, predictions of results in this area are bound to be hazardous, and the Internal Revenue Service will not usually issue advance rulings.[10] Moreover, when a case is litigated, the trial court's conclusion is not easily upset. Finally, it should be noted that in litigated cases, classification has been treated as an all-or-nothing question, so that instruments have not been fragmented into part-equity and part-debt. There is nothing to forbid this approach, however, but it may be more appealing as a method of settling a case at the administrative level than as a judicial resolution of the dispute.

Sec. 4.03.   Stock vs. debt — Formal characteristics; hybrid securities

In an effort to exploit the tax advantages of debt without being burdened by its non-tax restrictions (e.g., impairment of future borrowing capacity), taxpayers have often experimented with unusual instruments. Although form is not controlling,[11] a failure to endow the

---

[9] See §§1311-1314, mitigating the statute of limitations for certain inconsistent position cases; see also *supra,* Sec. 3.10, n. 43.

[10] See Lyon, Federal Income Taxation, 1957 Ann. Survey Am. L. 123, 142:
   One might say this is one of those areas of the tax law where the virtues of vagueness exceed its vices; that courts must look to all the facts and circumstances of each case to see what is really "intended" or what has "substantial economic reality": and that it is salutory to tell taxpayers only that there is a danger zone which they enter at their peril.
   For the Service's "no ruling" policy, see Rev. Proc. 64-31, Sec. 3.01 (2) and (10) (a), 1964-2 C.B. 947.

[11] Although the cases in this area have ordinarily involved instruments labelled "debt," there have been a few decisions in which the issuing corporation has sought to deduct as "interest" its payments on "preferred stock" which had the legal indicia, though not the label. of debentures or bonds. The deduction was allowed in United States v. Title Guarantee & Trust Co., 133 F.2d 990, 30 AFTR 1008 (6th Cir. 1943); Choctaw Inc., ¶53,397 P-H Memo TC (1953); and Bowersock Mills & Power Co. v. Commissioner. 172 F.2d 904, 37 AFTR 960 (10th Cir. 1949). In the *Title Guarantee* case, the misleading label was employed to avoid recognition of debt in the issuer's balance sheet; in *Choctaw,* it was

instrument with enough indicia of debt may be a threshold barrier for the taxpayer who seeks to deduct interest or qualify for some other tax benefit. A debt instrument ordinarily contains an unconditional obligation, to pay a principal sum certain, on or before a fixed maturity date not unreasonably far in the future, with interest payable in all events and not later than maturity. In addition, the obligation is ordinarily not subordinated in priority to general creditors,[12] and does not entitle the holder to voting rights, except possibly on default. Conversely, the indicia that may require the instrument to be treated as equity (whether common stock, preferred stock, or a contribution to capital is often left unclear by the courts) are: an excessively far-off maturity date, or no maturity date; "interest" contingent on earnings, or discretionary with corporate directors; subordination of interest or principal (or both) to the claims of general creditors; voting rights or the right to participate in management; and restrictions on assignability.

In the leading case on "hybrid" securities — instruments that look like preferred stock to creditors but will, it is hoped, pass muster as debt for tax purposes — the Supreme Court was faced with claims by two corporations that "interest" paid by them on such securities was deductible. The Tax Court had upheld the deduction in one case and denied it in the other, although there were strong similarities between the instruments. The Supreme Court, finding that they "embody elements of obligations and elements of stock," held (a) that "[t]here is no one characteristic, not even exclusion from management, which can be said to be decisive in the determination of whether the obligations are risk investments in the corporation or debts"; and (b) that the Tax Court's determination in such matters, as the initial trier of fact, was conclusive.[13] The scope of appellate review of Tax Court de-

---

apparently intended to give corporate investors an opportunity to claim the dividends received deduction under §243; while in the *Bowersock* case, the label was used to enable the company to obtain bank credit.

Milwaukee & Suburban Transport Corp. v. Commissioner, 283 F.2d 279, 6 AFTR 2d 5719 (7th Cir. 1960), holding that certain instruments could not be treated as debt for federal income tax purposes, gave some weight to the fact that they had been represented as preferred stock to a regulatory commission.

[12] Even if subordination is not explicitly required by the agreement, it may be judicially imposed in the event of corporate insolvency if the debt is held by the controlling shareholders. under the so-called "Deep Rock" doctrine. See Taylor v. Standard Gas & Electric Co., 306 U.S. 307 (1939): Baker and Cary, *Cases and Materials on Corporations* (3d ed. 1958) 390-400. Several cases have recognized the relevance of this doctrine to the tax question: Janeway v. Commissioner, 147 F.2d 602, 33 AFTR 718 (2d Cir. 1945); Kraft Foods Co. v. Commissioner, 232 F.2d 118, 49 AFTR (2d Cir. 1956); Jewell Ridge Coal Corp. v. Commissioner, 318 F.2d 695, 11 AFTR 2d 1663 (4th Cir. 1963).

[13] John Kelley Co. v. Commissioner, 326 U.S. 521, 34 AFTR 314 (1946).

cisions was subsequently enlarged by the enactment of §7482,[14] but the trial court's characterization of hybrid securities is not likely to be upset on appeal.

Sec. 4.04. Stock vs. debt — Classification of non-hybrid securities

Though hybrid securities were frequently encountered at one time, they are no longer fashionable, possibly because of their uncertain tax status; and most current litigation deals with obligations which are clearly debt on their face — *i.e.*, fixed maturity date, fixed interest payments, no voting rights, and no subordination to general creditors. Despite occasional suggestions that judicial analysis should not go beyond the four corners of the instrument,[15] however, it is well established that the formal terms are not decisive. On the other hand, no alternative standards can be distilled from the cases, which commonly refer to such general principles as "intent of the parties," the "psychology" of an outside lender, "substance over form," "business purpose," "tax avoidance," and the like. Perhaps these judicial ruminations can be summarized, without disrespect or loss of clarity, by saying that they come down to a standard that becomes instinctive with the experienced lawyer in this, as in many other areas: the "pig" theory, so named after the Wall Street adage that "You can make money being a bull, and you can make money being a bear; but you can't make money being a pig."[16] The themes that occur most frequently in the decided cases are these:

1. Pro rata holding of stock and debt. Although it is not fatal per se to debt classification, the fact that debt is owned in proportion to stockholdings tends to poison the atmosphere and to invite special scrutiny by the courts.[17] Conversely, a substantial disproportion in holdings of debt and stock will aid in establishing that the "debt" is what it purports to be — but in determining this disproportion, family solidarity is usually taken into account.[18] Although the debt of a pub-

---

[14] See Rice, Law, Fact, and Taxes: Review of Tax Court Decisions under Section 1141 of the [1939] Internal Revenue Code, 51 Col. L. Rev. 439 (1951).

[15] See Gloucester Ice & Cold Storage Co. v. Commissioner, 297 F.2d 183, 9 AFTR 2d 514 (1st Cir. 1962), Caplin, The Caloric Count of a Thin Incorporation, 17 N.Y.U. Inst. on Fed Tax. 771, 812 (1959).

[16] See Lyon, Federal Income Taxation, 36 N.Y.U. L. Rev. 642, 643 (1961).

[17] Gilbert v. Commissioner, 248 F.2d 399, 52 AFTR 634 (2d Cir. 1957); Gooding Amusement Co. v. Commissioner, 236 F.2d 159, 49 AFTR 1973 (6th Cir. 1956), cert. denied, 352 U.S. 1031 (1957); P.M. Finance Corp. v. Commissioner, 302 F.2d 786, 9 AFTR 2d 1454 (3rd Cir. 1962); Wilbur Security Co. v. Commissioner, 279 F.2d 657, 5 AFTR 2d 1553 (9th Cir. 1960).

[18] Disproportionate holdings of stock and debt were helpful to the taxpayers in Leach Corp., 30 T.C. 563 (1958) (Acq.); and in Charles E. Curry, 43 T.C.

licly-held corporation is rarely held by its shareholders in proportion to their stock, the inter-company debt of such corporations may have a pro rata character (e.g., the debt of a subsidiary to its parent) and have to run the gauntlet of judicial inspection.[19]

2. *Excessive debt-equity ratio ("thin capitalization")*. Some corporations are so unconcerned with their credit standing that they can issue seemingly orthodox debt securities in an amount which overwhelms the equity investment, e.g., bonds in the amount of $99,000 plus common stock, against assets valued at $100,000. Here the problem is whether the bonds, although containing iron clad indicia of debt, may be treated as the equivalent of stock for tax purposes, because anyone purchasing such instruments would regard himself, in light of the corporation's trivial equity, as a stockholder or potential stockholder.

In the *John Kelley* case (*supra*, note 13), the Supreme Court made this statement:

> As material amounts of capital were invested in stock, we need not consider the effect of extreme situations such as nominal stock investments and an obviously excessive debt structure. (326 U.S. at 526).

This dictum started the courts on a search for proper debt-equity ratios, generating a number of decisions holding that the corporation's "equity" was too "thin" to support the purported "debt" superstructure.[20] In computing the ratio of debt to equity, the use of market values of the assets (including goodwill), rather than par or book value, seems well established,[21] and "outside" debt is generally counted, especially if guaranteed by the stockholders; but there are many unresolved questions in this area. As to the ratio itself, the courts have not laid down any mathematical formula, recognizing that

---

667 (1965), but see Merlo Builders, Inc., ¶64,030 P-H Memo TC (advances treated as equity even though made by an unrelated person who was not a shareholder). Family solidarity minimized the significance of disproportionate holdings in the *P.M. Finance* and *Wilbur Security* cases, *supra*, note 17.

[19] Such debt was upheld in Kraft Foods Co. v. Commissioner, *supra*, note 12; Toledo Blade Co. v. Commissioner, 11 T.C. 1079 (1948), aff'd per curiam, 180 F.2d 357, 39 AFTR 7 (6th Cir. 1950), cert. denied, 340 U.S. 811 (1950); but see American-La France-Foamite Corp. v. Commissioner. 284 F.2d 723, 6 AFTR 2d 6056 (2d Cir. 1960) ("advances" by a parent to its 51% subsidiary treated as capital contributions).

[20] E.g., Dobkin v. Commissioner, 15 T.C. 31 (1950), aff'd per curiam, 192 F.2d 392, 41 AFTR 356 (2d Cir. 1951). Compare the bankruptcy cases subordinating stockholder debt to the claims of "outside" creditors when the corporation is inadequately capitalized, *supra* note 12.

[21] Kraft Foods Co. v. Commissioner, *supra* note 12; Gooding Amusement Co. v. Commissioner, *supra* note 17, Sheldon Tauber, 24 T.C. 179 (1955); Miller's Estate v. Commissioner, 239 F.2d 729, 50 AFTR 1210 (9th Cir. 1956).

what is excessive in one industry may be normal in another and that corporations vary in their financial requirements even in the same industry. It is usually assumed, however, that a ratio of debt to equity that does not exceed 3 to 1 is likely to withstand attack. A less favorable ratio is likely to invite attention, but there is a growing judicial tendency to regard even an "excessive" ratio as no more than a factor to be considered, rather than as an independent test of the purported debt's validity, and there are a few cases in which it is regarded as virtually irrelevant.[22]

3. Debt issued for "essential" assets. Courts have sometimes suggested or held that "debt" is not bona fide if issued to shareholders in exchange for "essential" assets (e.g., machinery, plant, equipment, etc.) needed to get the business under way, at least in the absence of a business purpose for issuing such debt. The leading exponent of this view is Schnitzer v. Commissioner, 13 T.C. 43 (1949), aff'd per curiam, 183 F.2d 70, 39 AFTR 636 (9th Cir. 1950), cert. denied, 340 U.S. 911 (1951); but the Tax Court found other infirmities in the instruments as well, so it is not clear whether the inability of the corporation to function without the assets for which such debt was issued controlled the decision. Conversely, if a corporation shows that it could have operated without the assets represented by the debt, a favorable inference has been drawn.[23] Since loans from outsiders would be honored as such even if used to purchase "essential" assets, however, a similar use of shareholder advances is not a satisfactory reason for treating them as equity investments.

4. "Intent" to create a creditor-debtor relationship. On occasion, the Tax Court has come close to holding that loans by a shareholder to his corporation cannot be bona fide because he can never be as authentic a Shylock as an outside lender. In Gooding Amusement Co. v. Commissioner, 23 T.C. 408 (1954), for example, the Tax Court held that notes issued by a corporation to its shareholders did not create a debtor-creditor relationship, although they were normal both in form and amount, because the dominant shareholder (who, with his family, owned all the notes and, at the outset, all the stock) had no

> intention at the time of issuance of the notes ever to enforce payment of his notes, especially if to do so would either impair the

[22] See Gloucester Ice & Cold Storage Co. v. Commissioner, *supra* note 15; Rowan v. United States. 219 F.2d 51, 49 AFTR 2d 1636 (5th Cir. 1955); Byerlite Corp. v. Williams, 286 F.2d 285, 6 AFTR 2d 6069 (6th Cir. 1960).

[23] Morgan v. Commissioner, 30 T.C. 881 (1958), rev'd on other issues, 272 F.2d 936, 5 AFTR 2d 318 (9th Cir. 1959).

credit rating of the corporation, cause it to borrow from other sources the funds necessary to meet the payments, or bring about its dissolution. (23 T.C. at 418-19.)

Although the judgment in this case was affirmed on the ground that "the findings of fact of the Tax Court are supported by substantial evidence and are not clearly erroneous" (*supra*, note 17), the "finding of fact" that the shareholder did not "intend" to enforce the notes more nearly resembles an irrebuttable presumption or inference drawn from the shareholder-corporation relationship, rather than a conclusion based on evidence.

On the whole, however, the appellate courts have adopted a more traditional view of the intent necessary to uphold the validity of shareholder debt. Thus, in the *Gilbert* case (*supra*, note 17), the Second Circuit said that in determining whether there was a reasonable expectation of repayment on the part of the lenders, resort should be had to such objective criteria as the ratio of debt to equity, pro rata holdings of debt and stock, use of the borrowed funds, whether outside investors would have made such an advance on similar terms, and conduct generally consistent with that of a creditor. The question thus boils down to whether the loan was so "risky" that it should be regarded as venture capital. Although this standard — "substantial economic reality," as phrased in a later decision of the Second Circuit[24] — does not lend itself to mechanical application, it is as good a generalization as can be devised for this area.[25]

Sec. 4.05.   Stock vs. debt — Capital asset status

To the investor, stock or debt instruments will almost always be "capital assets" as defined by §1221, so that gain or loss on a sale or exchange will be capital gain or loss under §1222. This is generally also true for debt claims that are not evidenced by a written instrument, e.g., open account claims. Thus, classification as debt or stock occupies a minor role in this area. The principal exceptions to capital asset status for such items are:

1. Dealers in securities, who hold stock or debt instruments primarily for sale to customers in the ordinary course of business within the meaning of §1221(1); but by complying with §1236,

[24] Nassau Lens, Inc. v. Commissioner, 308 F.2d 39, 10 AFTR 2d 5581 (2d Cir. 1962).
[25] See *supra,* note 16.

even dealers may hold securities in a segregated investment account, and thus qualify them for capital gain or loss treatment.[26]

2. §1221(4), which excludes from the category of capital assets accounts or notes receivable acquired in the ordinary course of trade or business for services rendered or from the sale of stock in trade, etc.[27]

3. Bonds or other evidences of corporate debt issued after 1954 at a discount or purchased with interest coupons detached, which are governed by the special rules of §1232(a)(2) and §1232(c) (*infra*, Sec. 4.06).

4. Stock in a "collapsible corporation," governed by the special rules of §341 (*infra*, Ch. 10).

5. "Section 306 stock," governed by the special rules of §306 (*infra*, Ch. 8).

6. Stock or debt acquired and held as an integral part of a regular business transaction, under the still uncertain criteria of Corn Products Refining Co. v. Commissioner, 350 U.S. 46, 47 AFTR 1789 (1955), and Commissioner v. Bagley & Sewall Co., 221 F.2d 944, 47 AFTR 790 (2d Cir. 1955). Here the "business function" of the security flavors the character of ultimate gain or loss with ordinary income status, despite such property's literal qualification as a capital asset under §1221.[28]

7. Stocks, securities, and debt claims that are flavored with an ordinary income character by assignment of income principles.[29]

8. Losses on "section 1244 stock" of a so-called "small business corporation" are specially treated (see *infra*, Sec. 4.09)

Sec. 4.06.   Stock vs. debt — Repayment of "loan," redemption of "stock," or dividend?

As indicated earlier (*supra*, Sec. 4.02), it is often necessary to determine whether a taxpayer's investment in a corporation constitutes a "loan" or "equity," in order to decide the tax consequences of

---

[26] See Van Suetendael v. Commissioner, ¶44,305 P-H Memo TC (1944), aff'd per curiam, 152 F.2d 654, 34 AFTR 638 (2d Cir. 1945); Frank v. Commissioner, 321 F.2d 143, 12 AFTR 2d 5362 (8th Cir. 1963); Nielsen v. United States, 333 F.2d 615, 14 AFTR 2d 5052 (6th Cir. 1964).

[27] See Burbank Liquidating Corp., 39 T.C. 999 (1963); Merchants Acceptance Co., ¶64,149 P-H Memo TC (1964). For capital gain or loss treatment under the law prior to 1954, see City Stores Co. v. United States, 225 F. Supp. 867, 13 AFTR 2d 672 (E.D. Pa. 1964).

[28] See Troxell and Noall, Judicial Erosion of the Concept of Securities as Capital Assets, 19 Tax L. Rev. 185 (1964); Electrical Fittings Corp. 33 T.C. 1026 (1960); John V. Grier & Co. v. United States, 328 F.2d 163, 13 AFTR 2d 745 (7th Cir. 1964); Weather-Seal, Inc., ¶63,102 P-H Memo TC (1963); Tulane Hardwood Lumber Co., 24 T.C. 1146 (1955).

[29] See Eustice, Contract Rights, Capital Gain and Assignment of Income — The Ferrer Case, 20 Tax L. Rev. 1 (1964); Lyon and Eustice, Assignment of Income; Fruit and Tree as Irrigated by the P.G. Lake Case, 17 Tax L. Rev. 293 (1962).

amounts paid to him by the corporation to liquidate or discharge the investment.

In the case of a debtor-creditor relationship, if bonds or other evidences of indebtedness are surrendered, retirement of the debt will be treated as an "exchange" under §1232(a)(1), with capital gain or loss treatment to the creditor if his claim is a capital asset.[30] The purpose of sale treatment for corporate bond retirements is to avoid unwarranted discrimination between a bond sold by the holder just prior to maturity and one held until retirement.[31] The general rule of §1232(a) is qualified if the creditor's gain is attributable to "original issue discount" on an instrument issued after 1954 and held for more than 6 months, §1232(a)(2), or if an instrument is purchased after the interest coupons have been detached, §1232(c). Both provisions are designed to separate the "disguised interest" component of the creditor's gain from the "true" capital gain component, and they are applicable to gain realized on a true sale or exchange, as well as to gain arising from a §1232(a) exchange on retirement.[32] If the debt that is discharged by the payment in question is not evidenced by a written instrument (e.g., an open account indebtedness), §1232 does not

[30] For capital asset status, see *supra*, Sec. 4.05. Of course, gain or loss is realized only if the amount realized on repayment exceeds or falls short of the taxpayer's basis for the debt.

[31] But the parallel between retirements and sales is not complete: (a) §1232(a) applies only to corporate "evidences of indebtedness," not to open accounts or individual debtor obligations; (b) if the instrument was issued before 1955, §1232(a)(1) applies only if it was issued with interest coupons or in registered form, or was in such form on March 1, 1954 (see Gerard v. Helvering, 120 F.2d 235, 27 AFTR 420 (2d Cir. 1941), for the meaning of "in registered form," and Driscoll v. Commissioner, 37 T.C. 52 (1961), rev'd, 306 F.2d 35, 10 AFTR 2d 5307 (7th Cir. 1962), on the possibility of registering or deregistering at will); and (c) §1232(a) applies only to amounts received on the "retirement" of an instrument, so that a creditor who is paid in a transaction which does not constitute a "retirement," may be subject to ordinary gain or loss treatment, although a sale would have produced a capital gain or loss.

On the meaning of "retirement" under §1232, see McClain v. Commissioner, 311 U.S. 527, 24 AFTR 1087 (1941), holding that the term retirement is broader than, and includes. the term redemption.

[32] Section 1232 was amended in 1958 to block transactions whereby the corporate debtor would issue long term obligations intending to "call" the debt substantially in advance of maturity, thus inflating the denominator of the ordinary gain fraction and reducing "discount income." For a decision anticipating this provision, see V. David Leavin, 37 T.C. 766 (1962); but cf. Ted Bolnick, 44 T.C. 245 (1965), finding capital gain with respect to unearned issue discount.

See also Dixon v. United States, 381 U.S. 68, 15 AFTR 2d 842 (1965) (original issue discount on pre-1954 obligations taxed as ordinary income); and, for other problems in the application of §1232 to discount obligations. Zafft, Discount Bonds — Ordinary Income or Capital Gain? 11 Tax L. Rev. 51 (1955); Lyon and Eustice, *supra* note 29, at 358.

The applicability of §483 to obligations received in exchange for property should be borne in mind, since it requires interest income to be imputed if the obligations do not provide for interest or stipulate an inadequate rate of interest.

apply, and case law principles will operate to deny sale or exchange treatment for the mere "collection" of a claim.[33]

If the amounts received by the taxpayer are in redemption of stock (including purported debt that is treated as stock), the transaction runs a substantial risk of being taxed as a dividend, under §302. As is pointed out in the discussion of this provision (*infra*, Ch. 7), however, redemptions are sometimes treated as sales or exchanges giving rise to capital gain or loss, primarily in the following circumstances:

1. A redemption of all of the stock of one or more shareholders. §302(b)(3).

2. A non-pro rata redemption, as measured by the rules of §302(b)(2).

3. A redemption that is "not essentially equivalent to a dividend." §302(b)(1).

4. A redemption of stock included in the gross estate of a decedent, to pay death taxes and funeral and administrative expenses. §303.

5. A redemption that constitutes a "partial liquidation" (reflecting a contraction of the corporation's business) under §346.

The repayment of a contribution to capital (including purported debt that is treated as a contribution to capital), however, may be unable to qualify under any of these exceptions, since the taxpayer will have no "stock" to be redeemed; with the result that the payment will be treated as a distribution under §301, and taxed as a dividend under §316 to the extent of earnings and profits.

One of the principal reasons for issuing debt securities at the time of incorporation is to set the stage for future extraction of corporate earnings tax-free or, if the repayment exceeds the taxpayer's adjusted basis for the obligations, at the capital gain rate. Because §1232 is more lenient than §302, as the discussion above indicates, such a "springing" or "floating" bail-out of corporate earnings can be accomplished more easily with debt securities than with stock. On the other hand, if debt instruments are not issued to the investor when the corporation is organized but are distributed to him at a later time (without an additional investment on his part), the distribution itself may be a taxable dividend to him (*infra*, Sec. 5.40). By contrast, a distribution of preferred stock by a profitable corporation can ordinarily be *received* tax-free (*infra*, Sec. 5.61), but its later redemption will ordinarily be taxed as a dividend under §306 (*infra*, Ch. 8).

---

[33] Fairbanks v. United States. 306 U.S. 436, 22 AFTR 300 (1939); Ogilvie v. Commissioner, 216 F.2d 748, 46 AFTR 1089 (6th Cir. 1954).

Sec. 4.07.   Stock vs. debt — Character of investor's loss on sale or worthlessness

The tax consequences of investment losses are governed by a variety of complex statutory provisions and judicial doctrines, the precise inter-relationship of which remains unclear at best. In general, the amount and timing of a loss deduction is a function of three elements: adjusted basis, amount realized (if any), and the event which causes the loss to be "sustained" (i.e., sale, partial collection, or total worthlessness). The character of the loss (as capital or ordinary) is controlled in turn by the following considerations: (1) capital asset status of the property (*supra*, Sec. 4.05); (2) existence of a sale or exchange (actual or constructive); (3) form of the investment (i.e., stock, "security," or non-security debt claim); (4) relationship of the loss to the taxpayer's business, if any; (5) taxpayer's holding period for the property; and (6) whether the taxpayer is an individual or a corporation. As will be seen, the investor's loss may be treated as an ordinary loss, a long-term capital loss, a short-term capital loss, or an unrecognized loss, depending on the way these elements are combined in a particular case. The principal combinations are the following:

1. Noncorporate taxpayers — loss on stock. The losses of an individual or other noncorporate shareholder, whether arising from the sale, redemption, liquidation, or total worthlessness of his equity investment, normally receive long-term capital loss treatment if the stock is a "capital asset"[34] and has been held for more than six months. This parity of tax treatment, regardless of the event in which the loss is realized, is the result of a policy choice by Congress. Thus, §165(g)(1) (the worthless security loss provision) creates an artificial "sale" for stock that becomes totally worthless in the hands of the taxpayer. The reason for this provision (enacted in 1938) is that a sale of the stock just before its value disappears would create a capital loss (unless the sale is for a nominal amount and hence can be disregarded as a "sham"); and there is no good reason to treat the taxpayer differently if he holds the stock a little longer until its value completely evaporates.[35] Similarly, a liquidation is treated as the

[34] On the capital asset status of stock, see *supra*, Sec. 4.05.

[35] Section 165(g)(1) provides that the sale will be deemed to occur on the last day of the taxable year (presumably because of difficulties in pinpointing the exact day of worthlessness), thus ordinarily creating a long term holding period even if the time between the purchase of the stock and the corporation's failure is less than six months. Had the taxpayer been able to sell the stock just before it became worthless, his loss would have been short term.

Section 165(g)(1) comes into play, however, only if the security "becomes worthless during the taxable year," and thus does not preclude the government from arguing that the taxpayer's deduction is premature or should have been

equivalent of a sale or exchange of the stock by §331 (*infra,* Sec. 9.03), so that the shareholder will be entitled to a capital loss if he receives less for his stock than its adjusted basis. This will also be true of a redemption, unless it is treated as the equivalent of a dividend under §302 (*infra,* Ch. 7).

Special rules applicable to losses on "section 1244 stock" are discussed *infra,* Sec. 4.09.

2. Noncorporate taxpayers — loss on debt evidenced by corporate "security." If an individual or other noncorporate taxpayer's debt claim against the corporation is evidenced by a "security" that has been held for more than six months, a loss from sale, retirement, or worthlessness will be a long-term capital loss.[36]

3. Noncorporate taxpayers — loss on debt not evidenced by "security" — capital loss treatment for worthless "nonbusiness debts." If the individual or other noncorporate creditor's claim against the corporation is not evidenced by "a bond, debenture, note, or certificate, or other evidence of indebtedness . . . with interest coupons or in registered form," a loss on worthlessness[37] is not governed by §165 (g)(1) (worthless securities), but by §166 (bad debts). This fact is of particular importance to investors in closely held corporations, since their advances are frequently open account loans or are evidenced merely by simple promissory notes. Although the general rule of §166(a) allows an ordinary loss deduction for worthless debts, this principle is subject to an important exception: by virtue of §166(d), an individual or other noncorporate taxpayer is confined to a short-term capital loss if the uncollectible claim is a "nonbusiness debt." Moreover, §166(a) permits a claim that is partially worthless to be written off pro tanto even though the balance retains some value;

---

taken in an earlier year. (An extended statute of limitations, §6511(d)(1), offers some protection against an attempt by the government to assign the loss to a year on which the statute has run.) To avoid an argument over the year of worthlessness, the taxpayer may be well advised to sell the security, if a bona fide buyer can be found. See generally Boehm v. Commissioner, 326 U.S. 387, 34 AFTR 10 (1945); and De Loss v. Commissioner, 28 F.2d 803, 7 AFTR 8228 (2d Cir. 1928).

[36] See §§1221 and 1222 for sales; §§1221 and 1232 for retirement; and §§1221 and 165(g)(1) for worthlessness. In each case, of course, the loss must satisfy such general provisions as §165(c)(2) ("transaction entered into for profit") and §267 (losses between related persons) to qualify for a deduction of any kind. If the security has been held for less than six months, a sale or retirement for less than its adjusted basis will generate a short-term capital loss, while a loss on worthlessness will be treated by §165(g)(1) as occurring on the last day of the taxable year and will thus ordinarily be a long-term capital loss; the same phenomenon as to stock has been noted, *supra* note 35.

[37] The treatment of a loss on the sale of such a claim depends on whether it is a capital asset or not (*supra,* Sec. 4.05).

debts subject to §166(d), however, cannot be deducted in installments but only when the unpaid balance is wholly uncollectible.

Section 166(d) was enacted in 1942, its stated purpose being to combat the practice of deducting, as bad debts, "loans" to friends and relatives which were intended as gifts. Because of the difficulty in determining whether such a loan was bona fide, the Treasury recommended that the taxpayer be limited to a capital loss.[38] The language employed by §166(d) was broader than would have been necessary to achieve this purpose, however, and the courts have given it its full sweep, partly because they have perceived another purpose for the legislation. This, said the Supreme Court in the *Putnam* case, is "to put nonbusiness investments in the form of loans on a footing with other nonbusiness investments," viz., to confine the creditor to a capital loss whether his worthless investment took the form of open account advances, bonds, or shares of stock.[39]

The term "nonbusiness debt" is defined in §166(d)(2) by indirection; it means a debt other than one (a) created or acquired in connection with a trade or business of the taxpayer, or (b) the loss from the worthlessness of which is incurred in the taxpayer's trade or business.[40] Because of the imprecision in the definition of "nonbusiness debt," and because open account advances by investors to closely-held corporations often turn sour, there have been scores of cases on the status of particular loans under this provision. The typical pattern involves a shareholder who owns all the stock of a corporation, either by himself or with his family, and who provides additional funds as loans in the early stages of the corporation's life. If the corporation fails, the government usually insists that the debt is a nonbusiness debt, resulting from an investment rather than a trade or business of the shareholder-creditor.[41]

---

[38] H.R. Rep. No. 2333, 77th Cong., 2nd Sess. (1942), reprinted in 1942-2 C.B. 372, 408-09; in an analogous area, losses on sales between related parties, the statutory remedy was disallowance of the deduction, §267(a)(1).

[39] Putnam v. Commissioner, 352 U.S. 82, 50 AFTR 502 (1956). If this was one of the purposes of the 1942 legislation, Congress neglected to say so: and it failed to establish complete parity, since §166(d)(1) establishes short-term capital loss treatment, while worthless securities (including stock) usually give rise to long-term capital losses.

[40] The latter part of the definition dates from 1942; the former part was aded in 1954 to overrule Regs. 118, §39.23(k)-6(c), holding that a debt that arose in the taxpayer's business was a nonbusiness debt if he was no longer in business when it became worthless. Section 166(d)(2)(A) was further amended in 1958 to preclude the argument that the former language ("in connection with *a* taxpayer's business") embraced a debt created or acquired in connection with a trade or business of someone other than *the* taxpayer.

[41] This argument is often coupled with an alternative argument: that the advance was a contribution to capital, deductible only as a capital loss when the stock became worthless. See *supra*, Sec. 4.04.

Taxpayer hopes for ordinary deduction treatment in this area suffered a serious blow in the *Whipple* case, where the Supreme Court denied business debt status to loans to the taxpayer's controlled corporation (which was one of a number of companies through which he conducted various business activities).[42] The Court was not persuaded by the fact that the taxpayer devoted all of his time to the business of his corporate enterprises, holding that this did not establish a "business" distinct from that of a shareholder attempting to increase the return on his investments. A series of later shareholder-investor cases indicates that short-term capital loss treatment under §166(d) will be the rule,[43] and that taxpayers will be able to qualify for ordinary loss deductions only if the loan arises (a) in a business of money-lending; (b) in a business of organizing, promoting, financing, and selling corporate enterprises; (c) in an effort to protect or advance the taxpayer's business of working as an employee for the debtor; or (d) in some other commercial relationship with the debtor that can be characterized as a business rather than an investment.[44]

[42] Whipple v. Commissioner, 373 U.S. 193, 11 AFTR 2d 1454 (1963).

[43] For a nearly unbroken string of post-*Whipple* cases denying business bad debt treatment, see Louis Schwartz, ¶64.247 P-H Memo TC (1964); Eugene H. Rietzke, 40 T.C. 443 (1963); Sol Gelfond, ¶64.242 P-H Memo TC (1964); Weddle v. Commissioner, 325 F.2d 849, 12 AFTR 2d 6103 (2d Cir. 1963); United States v. Byck, 325 F.2d 551, 13 AFTR 2d 303 (5th Cir. 1963); Samuel J. Grauman, ¶64.226 P-H Memo TC (1964); James J. Brahms, ¶64.238 P-H Memo TC (1964); and Est. of Ira A. Campbell, ¶64.053 P-H Memo TC (1964).

[44] For the "promoter" or "money lender" escape from §166(d), see Henry E. Sage, 15 T.C. 299 (1950); Vincent C. Campbell, 11 T.C. 510 (1948) (Acq.); Giblin v. Commissioner, 227 F.2d 692, 48 AFTR 478 (5th Cir. 1955); Commissioner v. Stokes' Estate, 200 F.2d 637, 42 AFTR 1011 (3rd Cir. 1953). *Whipple* disapproved of these decisions to the extent they found business status for one who serves his own corporations in order to create future investment income (i.e., dividends, etc.) through those enterprises, rather than to generate profit on their sale. But see Ralph Biernbaum, ¶63,210 P-H Memo TC (1963), where a taxpayer satisfied the "promoter" test.

For the effect of employee status, see Trent v. Commissioner, 291 F.2d 669, 7 AFTR 2d 1599 (2d Cir. 1961). The Court in *Whipple* noted that this exception would play a limited role in the case of controlling shareholder-employees, a fact on which the Second Circut subsequently relied to find investor status in Weddle v. Commissioner, *supra* note 43. See Note, Shareholder-Creditor Bad Debts under Section 166 of the Internal Revenue Code, 75 Harv. L. Rev. 589 (1962); Comment, Loss on Employee's Loan to Corporation Deductible as Business Bad Debt, 37 N.Y.U. L. Rev. 143 (1962); Waterman, Aspects of the Bad Debt-Loss Dichotomy, 18 Tax L. Rev. 121 (1962).

For other business possibilities, note that there was a remand in the *Whipple* case itself to consider the impact of the taxpayer's status as a landlord of property rented to the corporation to which loans were made; see also Maloney v. Spencer, 172 F.2d 638, 37 AFTR 907 (9th Cir. 1949) (shareholder was in the business of acquiring, owning, expanding and leasing plants to his corporate debtor); J. T. Dorminey, 26 T.C. 940 (1956) (loans to a corporation formed to facilitate the acquisition of necessary business supplies); Estate of Lawrence M. Weil, 29 T.C. 366 (1957) (Acq.) (loans to a corporate sales agent of a business operated by the taxpayer as an individual proprietorship); Tony Martin, 25 T.C. 94 (1955) (Acq.) (loan by an entertainer to a corporation

4. Corporate taxpayers — investment losses. Although the tax consequences of investment losses incurred by corporations are not free of some ambiguities, the pattern is less complex than for individual investors:

a. Worthless bad debts, if not evidenced by "securities" within the meaning of §165(g)(2)(C), are deductible as ordinary losses under §166(a); the "nonbusiness debt" rules of §166(d) (discussed *supra*) do not apply to corporations.[45]

b. Worthless "securities" (including shares of stock as well as debt claims) give rise to a capital loss as of the last day of the taxable year in which they become worthless by virtue of §165 (g)(1). The term "security" is defined for this purpose by §165 (g)(2)(C); it does not include stock, bonds, notes, etc., when issued by an "affiliated corporation," as defined in §165(g)(3).

c. Worthless securities of an "affiliated corporation" (owned by the taxpayer to the extent of at least 95 percent of each class of stock,[46] and 90 percent or more of whose gross receipts consist of operating income as distinguished from dividends, royalties, and similar "passive" income) give rise to an ordinary loss deduction by virtue of §165(g)(3). (Because the stock ownership rule of §165(g)(3)(A) speaks of "direct ownership, Regs. §1.165-5(i), Example (1), limit its application to "first tier" subsidiaries). The purpose of this exception to §165(g)(1) is to approximate roughly the treatment that would have been accorded to the loss if it had been incurred directly by the taxpayer parent. If the subsidiary was engaged primarily in investment or trading activities, however, its worthless securities will produce a capital loss under §165(g)(1), conforming to the tax result that would have followed if the parent had carried on such operations in its own right. The affiliation percentage of §165(g)(3) evidently stems from the 95 percent control required to fi'e consolidated returns when this provision was enacted in 1942; it was not changed when the consolidated return requirement was reduced in 1954 to 80 percent (*infra*, Sec. 13.40).

d. Special rules apply to losses incurred on the liquidation of subsidiaries (*infra*, Secs. 9.41 and 9.42).

---

formed to produce a picture in order to re-establish the taxpayer's reputation); Wilfred J. Funk, 35 T.C. 42 (1960) (loan by an author-shareholder to a publishing corporation formed to furnish an outlet for his writing); but see United States v. Keeler, 308 F.2d 424, 10 AFTR 2d 5641 (9th Cir. 1962).

[45] This virtual certainty of ordinary deduction treatment for corporate-held debts which turn sour adds fuel to the "stock versus debt" controversy over the status of such advances. See American-LaFrance-Foamite Corp. v. Commissioner, *supra* note 19, and Jewell Ridge Coal Corp. v. Commissioner, *supra* note 12, classifying advances as capital contributions; cf. Byerlite Corp. v. Williams, *supra* note 22 (advances to a wholly-owned subsidiary treated as debts).

[46] See Hunter Manufacturing Corp., 21 T.C. 424 (1954), disregarding a tax-motivated purchase of stock to acquire the requisite 95 percent control under §165(g)(3).

Sec. 4.08.   Outside loans guaranteed by shareholders

As indicated *supra*, Sec. 4.07, when a loan made by an individual shareholder to his corporation becomes worthless, he is ordinarily confined to a capital loss by §165(g)(1) (if his debt is evidenced by a "security") or by §166(d)(1) (if his debt is not evidenced by a "security," but is a "nonbusiness debt"). He will be able to deduct the loss from ordinary income as a bad debt under §166(a) only if he can establish that it is not a "nonbusiness debt," and this phrase has been so construed by the courts as to bar a deduction under §166-(a) in most cases.

What if the corporation borrows the funds it requires from a bank or other outside lender on notes endorsed by its shareholders, and they pay off the loan upon the corporation's failure? At one time, it appeared that this technique would assure a deduction from ordinary income for the shareholder who had to make good on a defaulted loan, since several courts of appeals held that payment on the guarantee (if not reimbursed by the corporation) gave rise to a loss on a "transaction entered into for profit" under §§165(a) and (c)(2), rather than to a bad debt that might be subject to the restriction of §166(d). In 1956, however, the Supreme Court pointed out that the guarantor, on paying the corporation's debt to the bank, is subrogated to the bank's claim against the corporation, and it concluded from this principle of private law that "the loss sustained by the guarantor unable to recover from the debtor is by its very nature a loss from the worthlessness of a debt."[47] This holding, treating the guarantor's loss as a bad debt, relegates him to a short-term capital

---

[47] Putnam v. Commissioner, *supra* note 39; the earlier cases are cited in note 5 of the Court's opinion. See Regs. §1.166-8(b) and (c), Example (4); Rev. Rul. 60-48, 1960-1 C.B. 112; Brown, Putnam v. Commissioner — The Reimbursable Outlay Under the Tax Law, 6 Buffalo L. Rev. 283 (1957).

In Nelson v. Commissioner, 281 F.2d 1, 6 AFTR 2d 5150 (5th Cir. 1960), the *Putnam* decision was applied to the interest (as well as the principal) of a corporate loan guaranteed by a shareholder, so that his payment of interest on the loan gave rise to a non-business bad debt deduction, rather than to an interest deduction; the court also rejected, on the facts, the taxpayer's argument that he was the primary obligor on the note rather than a guarantor.

The *Putnam* doctrine is ordinarily disadvantageous to the taxpayer, since it usually requires his loss to be deducted as a capital loss rather than an ordinary one. If the guarantee is given as an accommodation to a relative or friend, however, *Putnam* may be helpful; this is because bad debts are deductible even though they arise out of a personal context, while a "loss" incurred by an individual can be deducted only if it meets the standards of §165(c)(2) or (3) and will be nondeductible if its motivation is wholly personal. But see E. J. Ellisberg, *infra*, note 50.

It should be noted that §166(f), permitting an individual taxpayer who guarantees the debts of another individual to deduct his loss as an ordinary loss in certain circumstances, does not apply to guarantees of corporate obligations.

loss if the debt is a "nonbusiness debt" under §166(d). Just as in the case of a direct loan to the corporation, therefore, the guarantor can now ordinarily deduct his loss from ordinary income under §166(a) only if he can escape the "nonbusiness debt" label of §166(d). There remain, however, some subtle distinctions in the law of suretyship that may in special circumstances enable the taxpayer who has acted as guarantor to bring himself within the ambit of §165(a) and (c)(2).[48]

The use of loans guaranteed by shareholders has also been suggested as a method of avoiding the "thin capitalization" problem.[49] The theory is that if the corporation is organized with a minimum of equity capital and borrows whatever funds it may need from a bank or other outside lender on notes endorsed by its shareholders, the interest paid to the lender will be deductible under §163 and the repayment of the borrowed funds at maturity will not constitute a dividend to the shareholders. This recommendation of guaranteed loans as a solution to the problems of the thin corporation underestimates the perspicacity of the courts. Just as a "bond" is not necessarily a bond, so a "lender" is not necessarily a lender; and a "guarantor" is not necessarily a guarantor. *In form* the bank may have lent money to the corporation upon the guaranty of the shareholders; but *in substance*, the bank may have made the loan to the shareholders, who in turn passed the funds on to the corporation as — perish the thought — a capital contribution. If the transaction is recast in this fashion, the payments by the corporation to the bank (whether labeled "interest" or "repayment of loan") would serve to discharge obligations of the shareholders to the bank and thus would be disguised dividends (*infra*, Sec. 5.05), while if the corporation became insolvent the shareholders would suffer capital losses under §165(g), rather than short-term capital losses under §166(d) as interpreted in the *Putnam* case (*supra*, note 47). For a recent decision to this effect, see Murphy Logging Co. v. United States, 239 F.Supp. 794, 15 AFTR 2d 623 (D. Ore. 1965), where the court held that a bank loan to a newly created corporation, which was guaran-

---

[48] See Eugene H. Rietzke, 40 T.C. 443 (1963) (ordinary loss allowed because no subrogation rights arose from part payment under guaranty); Commissioner v. Condit, 333 F.2d 585, 14 AFTR 2d 5001 (10th Cir. 1964) (shareholder's payment to his co-investor under an agreement to share equally the losses of their corporate venture, held deductible as an ordinary loss rather than a nonbusiness bad debt); Mankoff, Deduction of Indemnity Losses Under Section 165, 50 A.B.A.J. 782 (1964). But compare United States v. Keeler, 308 F.2d 424, 10 AFTR 5641 (9th Cir. 1962), where payments to indemnify capital losses of fellow shareholders were deductible only as capital losses.

[49] *Supra*, Sec. 4.04.

teed by the shareholders and the proceeds of which were simultaneously used to "purchase" certain basic assets from the incorporators, constituted, in substance, a loan to the shareholders followed by a capital contribution of the assets to the corporation. As a result, the corporation took a carryover basis for the contributed assets and later payments by the corporation on the debt were held to constitute constructive dividends to the shareholders.[50]

Sec. 4.09. Loss on "section 1244 stock"

The preceding several sections of this chapter have shown that when an investment in a corporation becomes worthless the investor's loss is usually treated as a capital loss, rather than as an ordinary loss. If the investment is evidenced by stock or securities, capital loss treatment is dictated by §165(g); if an open account loan or

---

[50] For an earlier case holding that a guaranteed loan was not what it purported to be, see E. J. Ellisberg, 9 T.C. 463 (1947), refusing to allow a fond father to deduct a loss arising from a guaranty of his son's bank loan. On the ground that there was "no reasonable expectation" when the father guaranteed his son's debt that the son would pay the bank or reimburse his father, the court held that "the transaction in question is equivalent to one in which a father borrowed money from a bank and, in effect, made a gift of the proceeds to his son."

In the *Ellisberg* case, to be sure, the endorser's veil was pierced only after the court found that the son, who was the ostensible borrower, "was without resources and was likely never to have any." When a corporation borrows funds on notes endorsed by its shareholders, the expectation of the parties is that the corporation will be successful enough to pay off the borrowed funds itself. But this is equally true when the shareholders make "loans" directly to a thin corporation; the intent to have the corporation pay off the "loans" is, in such instances, regarded as no more than an intent to have the corporation pay dividends. So with guaranteed loans. An intention to repay them out of corporate profits does not make them "loans" by the bank to the corporation. They can — in appropriate circumstances — be regarded as loans by the bank to the shareholders, the proceeds of which are used by the shareholders to make capital contributions to the corporation; the intention to apply corporate profits to their repayment can be regarded as no more than an intention to pay disguised dividends when, as, and if the corporation's financial condition permits. See the penultimate sentence of Putnam v. Commissioner, 352 U.S. 82, at 92-93, 50 ATFR 502 at 507: "There is no real or economic difference between the loss of an investment made in the form of a direct loan to a corporation and one made indirectly in the form of a guaranteed bank loan." To this, one may add that there is no real or economic difference between a direct "loan" that must be treated as a contribution to capital because the corporation's equity is too "thin" and a loan made indirectly by endorsing the corporation's notes. But see Fors Farms, Inc. v. United States, 17 AFTR 2d 222 (W.D. Wash. 1965) (bank loan treated as corporate obligation though shareholders signed as coprincipals).

See also Note, New Thin Incorporation Threat: Repayment of Guaranteed Bank Loans Treated as Dividends, 23 J. Tax. 197 (1965); Bittker, Thin Capitalization: Some Current Questions, 34 Taxes 830, 834-5 (1956); reprinted with minor revisions in 10 U. Fla. L. Rev. 25, 35-7 (1957); Holzman, The Current Trend in Guaranty Cases: An Impetus to Thin-Incorporation? 11 Tax L. Rev. 29, 47-8 (1955).

a promissory note is used, and the investor is not a corporation, he is ordinarily restricted to a capital loss by §166(d), relating to "nonbusiness debts." In contrast to this capital loss treatment of most investments in a corporation, an individual proprietor or a partner who participates in a losing venture usually is entitled to deduct the expenses and losses incurred in the business from any outside income he may be receiving. For this reason, investors in speculative enterprises sometimes operate in partnership form for the early years when the risk of loss is greatest, and incorporate only after success seems likely.

In 1958, Congress made two important changes in the Code, both of which reduce this disparity between corporations on the one hand and proprietorships and partnerships on the other. Subchapter S (*infra*, Ch. 14) permits certain corporations to elect to be exempt from the corporation income tax, under a system by which the corporation's undistributed income or net operating loss, as the case may be, is passed through to the shareholders and reported on their individual tax returns. As a result, the shareholders of an electing corporation will enjoy a deduction from ordinary income, rather than a capital loss, if the corporation's ventures fail. The other 1958 change is §1244, under which an individual's loss on "section 1244 stock" may be deducted from ordinary income to a limited extent.[51]

The announced purpose of §1244 is to "encourage the flow of new funds into small business" and to place shareholders in small corporations "on a more nearly equal basis with . . . proprietors and partners." H.R. Rep. No. 2198, 85th Cong., 1st Sess., reprinted in 1959-2 C.B. 709, 711. Under §1244, which is applicable only to individuals (excluding trusts and estates as well as corporations), a loss on "section 1244 stock" issued to an individual or to a partnership which would otherwise constitute a capital loss is treated as an ordinary loss. For any taxable year, however, the aggregate amount which may be treated as an ordinary loss under §1244 is $50,000 (husband and wife filing a joint return) or $25,000 (other taxpayers). (If the

---

[51] Under §1244(a), any loss on "section 1244 stock" that would otherwise "be treated as a loss from the sale or exchange of a capital asset" qualifies for transformation into ordinary loss. Though there is some shilly-shallying in the committee reports in describing the transactions to which §1244 applies — H.R. Rep. No. 2198, 85th Cong., 2d Sess. p. 4 (1958) ("sale or exchange"), *ibid* p. 8 ("losses on the sale, exchange or worthlessness"), and H.R. Rep. No. 2632, 85th Cong., 2d Sess. p. 43 (1958) ("sales and other dispositions") — Regs. §1.1244(a) 1(a) provides that §1244 covers a loss on a sale or exchange, "including a transaction treated as a sale or exchange, such as worthlessness." This statement presumably embraces losses on complete and partial liquidations and on stock redemptions, as well as losses incurred when the stock is sold or becomes worthless.

loss exceeds these limits, the excess will remain subject to the other provisions of the Code, *i.e.*, it will ordinarily be a capital loss.) The concession thus granted to losses on "section 1244 stock" is available only if both the stock and the issuing corporation meet certain conditions. There are many uncertainties in §1244, some arising from concepts new to the Internal Revenue Code, but they are largely peripheral difficulties; and many closely-held corporations will not be troubled by them. Moreover, it should be noted that a failure to qualify under §1244 will ordinarily leave the taxpayer where he was before its enactment (viz., with a capital loss), without producing any new travails for him.

The conditions and limitations of §1244 are as follows:

1. The taxpayer. Section 1244 applies only to individual taxpayers, §1244(d)(4) explicitly disqualifying trusts and estates. Moreover, the stock must have been "issued" to the individual claiming the loss or to a partnership, with the result that vendees, donees, and other transferees of "section 1244 stock" do not qualify.[52] The term "issued" is evidently intended to restrict the benefits of §1244 to individuals who invested funds or property in the corporation, so that transferees are disqualifed, but it should embrace a sale of treasury stock by the corporation as well as an original issue of stock.[53]

2. The corporation. To qualify under §1244, the stock must have been issued by a domestic corporation meeting these conditions:

(a) When the plan to offer the stock was adopted,[54] the corpora-

---

[52] Under Regs. §1.1244(a)-1(b)(2) and the example at §1.1244(a)-1(c)(2), this disqualification extends even to stock issued to a partnership if it was distributed before the loss was sustained, although the statute itself seems to require only (a) that the loss be sustained by an individual and (b) that the stock have been issued either to him or to a partnership. (The regulations are based on a statement in the Conference Report, H.R. Rep. No. 2632, *supra* note 51, at p. 43.) If the stock was issued to a partnership and distributed pro rata to persons who were partners when the stock was issued, this position is hard to reconcile with either the letter or the spirit of §1244(a). It could upset a bona fide attempt to create "Section 1244 stock" on the incorporation of a partnership business; such as where the stock is issued directly to the transferor partnership entity, which then proceeds to hold it for a period of time before finally liquidating and distributing the stock pro rata to the partners.
Regs. §1.1244(a)-1(b)(2) also provide that a partner can qualify under §1244 only if he was a partner when the partnership acquired the §1244 stock.
See generally Moore and Sorlien, Adventures in Subchapter S and Section 1244, 14 Tax L. Rev. 453 (1959); Nicholson, Section 1244 stock, 38 Taxes 303 (1960); Bledsoe and Beck, Two Problems Under Section 1244: Real Estate Investments and Partners as Stockholders, 16 J. Tax. 7 (1962).
[53] But see Firestone Tire & Rubber Co., 2 T.C. 827 (1943).
[54] Regs. §1.1244(c)-1(c) provide that the stock must be issued pursuant to a "written plan." For problems which arise in determining what is a "plan" and when it is "adopted," see *infra*, Sec. 9.64; Rev. Rul. 66-67, 1966-12 I.R.B. 9 (minutes of directors' meeting as "plan").

tion must have been a "small business corporation." This term is defined by reference to two requirements:

1. Under §1244(c)(2)(A), the aggregate amount which may be offered under the plan, plus the aggregate amount of money and other property (taken at adjusted basis for determining gain as of the time received, reduced by liabilities which were assumed or to which the property was subject) received by the corporation after June 30, 1958, for stock, as contributions to capital, and as paid-in surplus, must not exceed $500,000. The "aggregate amount which may be offered under the plan" is probably the offering price of the stock, though the House Report refers only to "aggregate dollar amount of stock."[55] Purported "debt" that should be regarded as stock or as a contribution to capital under the principles discussed *supra*, Sec. 4.04, would presumably be changed against the $500,000 limit.

2. Under §1244(c)(2)(B), the aggregate amount which may be offered under the plan, plus the "equity capital" of the corporation on the date of the adoption of the plan, must not exceed $1,000,000. "Equity capital" is the sum of the corporation's money and other property (at adjusted basis for determining gain), less indebtedness to persons other than shareholders. It will be noted that indebtedness to shareholders is treated as "equity capital" in computing the $1,000,000, limit even if it would be treated as bona fide debt for other purposes.

(b) In addition to being "a small business corporation" *when the plan to offer the stock was adopted*, the corporation must meet the the test of §1244(c)(1)(E) *when the loss was sustained*. Therefore, it cannot be said with certainty when stock is issued that it will qualify for §1244 treatment. For the 5 taxable years immediately preceding the year when the loss was sustained (or for a specified shorter period if the corporation was not in existence for this 5-year period), the corporation must have derived more than 50 percent of its aggregate "gross receipts" from sources other than royalties, rents, dividends, interest, annuities, and sales or exchanges of stock or securities. This restriction is evidently designed to prevent a shareholder from enjoying a deduction from ordinary income under §1244 if the corporation was primarily engaged in investment activities which, if carried on in his individual capacity, would have produced capital losses. The forbidden sources of income are similar to those that may convert a corporation into a personal holding company (*infra*, Sec. 6.21). The "gross receipts" limitation is not applicable to a corpora-

---

[55] H.R. Rep. No. 2198, *supra* note 51. The regulations clarify this point by a melding of both the statute and House Report; they make their calculations with "the aggregate dollar amount to be paid for stock which may be offered under the plan," Regs. §1.1244(c)-2(b).

tion whose deductions for the specified period, other than deductions under §172 (net operating loss carryover), §242 (partially tax-exempt interest), and §§243-245 (dividends received), exceeded its gross income.

3. The stock. To qualify under section 1244, the stock must be "common" stock.[56] The regulations provide that "common stock" may be either voting or nonvoting, and that for purposes of section 1244, neither securities convertible into common stock nor common stock convertible into other securities shall be treated as common stock.[57] Presumably stock with a preference in the distribution of earnings or assets on liquidation is not "common stock," but the status of "Class B common" having a secondary preference (e.g., $5 per share to Class A common, then $5 per share to Class B common, with both classes participating in any distributions thereafter) is uncertain.

The stock must have been issued under a plan adopted by the corporation after June 30, 1958, to offer such stock for a period specified in the plan and ending not later than two years after the plan was adopted. It is also essential that "no portion of a prior offering was outstanding" when the plan was adopted, but the regulations suggest that a prior offering may be withdrawn.[58] The concept of an "offering" is new to the Internal Revenue Code, and the extent to which the meaning it has accumulated under the Securities Act of 1933 can be carried over, is unclear.[59] If after the plan to offer "section 1244 stock" is adopted, a "subsequent offering of stock has been made by the corporation" (including an offering of preferred or some other unqualified stock), stock subsequently issued under the prior plan will not qualify (§1244(c)(1), last sentence), and stock issued under the later plan will also be disqualified because it was adopted while a portion of the prior offering was outstanding. The subsequent offering will not, however, retroactively disqualify any stock issued under the prior plan before the subsequent offering was made.[60]

---

[56] For other uses of the term "common stock," see §302(b)(2)(C) (*infra,* Sec. 7.22) and §306(C)(1) (*infra,* Sec. 8.03).

[57] Regs. §1.1244(c)-1(b). For an insight into the tax problems which arise from the convertibility of stocks or bonds, see Fleischer and Cary, The Taxation of Convertible Bonds and Stock, 74 Harv. L. Rev. 473 (1961).

[58] A prior offering of either preferred or common stock will tend to disqualify the inchoate §1244 plan, Regs. §1.1244(c)-1(e).

Regs. §1.1244(c)-1(e) provide that an offer is outstanding unless and until it is withdrawn by affirmative action prior to the time the plan required under §1244 is adopted. See also Regs. §1.1244(c)-1(h)(2), which provide, in reference to a subsequent offering, that a corporation may withdraw a plan and adopt a new plan to issue stock.

[59] See Loss, *Securities Regulation* (2d ed. 1961, 1962 Supp.), Ch. 3, Sec. C-2.

[60] Regs. §1.1244(c)-1(h).

A final restriction, §1244(c)(1)(D), provides that stock can qualify only if it was issued for money or other property, to the exclusion of stock issued for services, securities, or other stock. This limitation, in turn, is subject to a possible exception: the Treasury is given authority by §1244(d)(2) to provide by regulation that common stock received in exchange for "section 1244 stock" in a reorganization under §368(a)(1)(F) (mere change in identity, form, or place of organization) or whose basis is determined by reference to the taxpayer's basis for qualified stock will itself qualify. Exercising this authority, the Treasury has provided in Regs. §1.1244 (d)-3 that common stock received as a stock dividend or in a recapitalization will qualify if received with respect to "section 1244 stock."

4. Limitations on amount to be deducted. Section 1244(b) provides that the aggregate amount treated by the taxpayer as an ordinary loss for any taxable year shall not exceed $25,000 or (in the case of husband and wife filing a joint return) $50,000.[61] If the ordinary loss component ($25,000 or $50,000, as the case may be) cannot be employed in the taxable year in which the loss is sustained, it becomes part of the taxpayer's net operating loss by virtue of §1244(d)(3). If the net operating loss is then carried to a taxable year in which the taxpayer is using his full allowance ($25,000 or $50,000) because of a loss on *other* "section 1244 stock," it is not clear whether the net operating loss carryover is to be employed in full without regard to its origin in §1244. If part or all of the net operating loss carryover is to be disallowed because it stems from a §1244 loss in another year, the taxpayer may be worse off than if his loss had been treated as a capital loss (subject to the capital loss carryover of §1212) from the outset. It seems more likely that taxpayer's loss on "section 1244 stock" — up to the amount of $25,000 or $50,000 for the year of loss — is to be deductible either in the year of loss or within the 8-year carryback-carryover period of §172, without diminution by reason of his §1244 losses in other years.

In computing the taxpayer's loss on the sale or exchange of stock, the adjusted basis of the stock is ordinarily compared with the amount realized. Under §1244(d)(1)(A), however, the adjusted basis of the stock must be reduced in computing the amount of loss for purposes of §1244, if (a) the stock was received in exchange for property, (b) the basis of the stock is determined by reference to the

---

[61] The $50,000 limit applies to joint returns even though the loss may have been sustained by only one of the spouses, Regs. §1.1244(b)-1. This regulation also provides that in the case of a partnership, the limitation shall be determined separately as to each partner.

taxpayer's basis for the property, and (c) the adjusted basis of the property (for determining loss) immediately before the exchange exceeded its fair market value. In the absence of such a protective restriction, a taxpayer holding a depreciated capital asset could transfer it to a controlled corporation under §351 and then sell the stock (which under §358 would have the same basis as the property) in order to enjoy an ordinary loss under §1244. It should be noted that the loss on the sale of the stock in such a case would not be disallowed; It would simply be excluded from §1244, with the result that the shareholder would be relegated to a capital loss. A second limitation is provided by §1244(d)(1)(B), under which any increase in the basis of "section 1244 stock" (through contributions to capital or otherwise) is excluded in computing the loss under §1244. By virtue of this provision, a loss will qualify under §1244 only to the extent of the money or property paid for the stock when it was originally acquired by the taxpayer from the corporation. The purpose of §1244(d)(1)(B) is not given in the committee reports; it may have been designed to prevent an evasion of the dollar limits of §1244(c)(2) by an offer of stock up to the full amount permitted, to be followed by contributions to capital of additional assets.

Chapter Five

DIVIDENDS AND OTHER NON-LIQUIDATING DISTRIBUTIONS

Part A.   Distributions in Cash

Sec. 5.01.   Introductory

We have already seen (*supra*, Sec. 1.05) that the corporation is a separate taxable entity under the Internal Revenue Code, so that corporate income is taxed to the corporation and dividends paid by the corporation are taxable to the shareholders. In this Chapter, we shall examine in more detail the taxation of corporate distributions, a wonderfully complex subject.

A framework for the taxation of corporate distributions is provided by §301(a), §301(c), and §316. By virtue of these provisions, a corporate distribution is a "dividend" that must be included in the recipient's gross income under §301(c)(1) and §61(a)(7) if, and to the extent that, it comes out of earnings and profits of the corporation accumulated after February 28, 1913 or out of earnings and profits of the taxable year. Most distributions of most corporations fall well within this category of taxable "dividends" and hence are taxed as ordinary income to the shareholder.[1] To the extent that a distribution by a corporation is not covered by current or post-1913 earnings and profits, however, it is treated by §301(c)(2) as a return of capital to the shareholder, to be applied against and in reduction of the adjusted basis of his stock. If the distribution exceeds the adjusted basis of the stock, the excess is ordinarily taxed as capital gain, with an exception of minor importance for distributions out of increase in the value of corporate property accrued before March 1, 1913. §301(c)(3)(A) and (B).

If we assume a corporation newly organized for cash, the reason for gearing the taxability of its distributions to its record of earnings and profits is clear enough. Until the corporation has engaged in profitable operations, any distribution to its original stockholders is

---

[1] If the shareholder is an individual, the dividends ordinarily are eligible for the $100 dividends received exclusion of §116 (*infra*, Sec. 5.06). If the shareholder is a corporation, the 85 percent dividends received deduction of §§243-246 ordinarily is applicable (*supra*, Sec. 2.25).

a return of their investment rather than income. Once the corporation has realized profits, on the other hand, its distributions may *pro tanto* be fairly regarded as income to the stockholders.

The equity of §§316 and 301(c) is far less clear if we assume that after a period of corporate profits the stock changes hands and that before additional earnings arise (the next day, if you will) there is a distribution to the new stockholder. Has not *he* received a return of *his* capital? The economist might say that a distribution in these circumstances ought to be regarded as a return of capital, but §§301(c) and 316 of the Internal Revenue Code are inescapable, so that to the extent of his share of the corporation's earnings and profits, the surprised stockholder has realized income. This "miracle of income without gain" — the phrase is from Powell, Income From Corporate Dividends, 35 Harv. L. Rev. 363 (1922) — long ago was attested by the Supreme Court in United States v. Phellis, 257 U.S. 156, 3 AFTR 3123 (1921):

> Where, as in this case, the dividend constitutes a distribution of profits accumulated during an extended period and bears a large proportion to the par value of the stock, if an investor happened to buy stock shortly before the dividend, paying a price enhanced by an estimate of the capital plus the surplus of the company, and after distribution of the surplus, with corresponding reduction in the intrinsic and market value of the shares, he were called upon to pay a tax upon the dividend received, it might look in his case like a tax upon his capital. But it is only apparently so. In buying at a price that reflected the accumulated profits, he of course acquired as a part of the valuable rights purchased the prospect of a dividend from the accumulations — bought "dividend on," as the phrase goes — and necessarily took subject to the burden of the income tax proper to be assessed against him by reason of the dividend if and when made. He simply stepped into the shoes, in this as in other respects, of the stockholder whose shares he acquired, and presumably the prospect of a dividend influenced the price paid, and was discounted by the prospect of an income tax to be paid thereon. (257 U.S. at 171-2.)

In point of fact, however, the purchaser of stock must bid against many other potential buyers, who would be affected in varying degrees by the income tax on a dividend and some of whom may be tax-exempt organizations, so that the price could rarely if ever be accurately "discounted by the prospect of an income tax to be paid" on dividends that may be declared immediately after the stock is purchased. Moreover, the distribution will be a "dividend" under §316 only if it is paid from the corporation's earnings and profits, and since the calculation of earnings and profits may be a complex operation (*infra*, Sec. 5.03), the purchaser would often not know the proper discount to apply (except possibly in the case of a closely-held corporation) even if he were so foresighted as to anticipate the problem.

Just as the concept of earnings and profits may be unfair to a shareholder who buys stock before a corporate distribution, so on occasion it may with equal irrationality shower him with riches. If the corporation into which he buys is a deficit corporation, distributions by the corporation may be treated as wholly or partly tax-free returns of capital to the shareholder even though they reflect earnings by the corporation after he buys his stock. This bonanza can occur if the corporation has neither post-1913 nor current earnings and profits, and if (to reverse the "discount" theory of the *Phellis* case) the shareholder did not pay a premium when he bought his shares for the tax advantage lurking in the corporation's deficit.

Despite these shortcomings, the existing system of relating the tax status of corporate distributions to the corporation's earnings and profits is responsive to the felt need for a method of protecting returns of capital from the tax on dividends; and while a better response to this need could no doubt be devised, Congress has shown no disposition to depart from the present method.[2]

Before turning to the details of the general rule set out above, under which a distribution by a corporation is a "dividend" if it comes out of current or post-1913 earnings and profits and a return of capital to the extent of any excess, it should be noted that special rules are provided for certain categories of distributions, among which are:

    1. Distributions in kind, i.e., property other than money (*infra*, Sec. 5.20).

    2. Distributions of the corporation's own obligations (*infra*, Sec. 5.40).

    3. Distributions of the corporation's own stock or of rights to purchase its stock (*infra*, Sec. 5.60).

---

[2] Without attempting to work out the details, one approach would be to treat all receipts from the corporation as taxable income, and to compute the shareholder's gain or loss on his capital investment when he sells or otherwise disposes of his shares or when they become worthless. Another method of taxing the shareholder would be to apply all distributions against basis until his cost was recouped, taxing all subsequent distributions or receipts as ordinary income, capital gain, or a combination thereof.

See Andrews, "Out of Its Earnings and Profits:" Some Reflections on the Taxation of Dividends, 69 Harv. L. Rev. 1403 (1956); Cohen, Surrey, Tarleau, and Warren, A Technical Revision of the Federal Income Tax Treatment of Corporate Distributions to Shareholders, 52 Col. L. Rev. 1, 6-9 (1952).

4. Distributions in redemption of stock, including partial liquidations (*infra*, Ch. 7) and complete liquidations (*infra*, Ch. 9).

5. Distributions in corporate reorganizations and similar transactions (*infra*, Ch. 11 and 12).

Sec. 5.02. "Dividend" — A term of art

Under §301(c), a distribution is includible in the shareholder's gross income to the extent that it is a "dividend," as defined in §316; the balance of the distribution, if any, is a return of capital under §301(c)(2) and (3). The term "dividend" as defined for income tax purposes by §316(a) does not correspond to the term "dividend" under state law, with the result that a corporate distribution may be a "dividend" under §316(a), although it impairs capital or is otherwise unlawful under state law.[3] Conversely, it is possible for a distribution to constitute a lawful "dividend" under state law without qualifying as a "dividend" under §316(a).

The definition of "dividend" in §316 is two-edged: a distribution by a corporation to its shareholders is a "dividend" if it is made (1) out of earnings and profits accumulated after February 28, 1913, or (2) out of earnings and profits of the taxable year. "Earnings and profits" is a term of art that will be examined in detail *infra*, Sec. 5.03; but it must be pointed out here that it is *not* identical with "earned surplus" nor is it represented by a bank account or other specific corporate assets: a distribution is "out of" earnings and profits if the corporation operated profitably in the period under consideration, and no "tracing" or "earmarking" of funds or assets is required.

The first part of §316(a), providing that a distribution is a "dividend" if it comes from earnings and profits accumulated since February 28, 1913, looks to the financial success of the corporation over the long haul. If the corporation has operated profitably since 1913 (or since organization, if it was incorporated after 1913), distributions will be taxed to the shareholders as "dividends." The exemption of earnings and profits accumulated before February 28, 1913 (the date of the first federal income tax imposed after the adoption of

---

[3] See Rudick (*infra*, note 9, at 866): ". . . what the distributing corporation may call a dividend, or what the state law may call a dividend, or even what the recipient thinks of without question as a dividend, is not necessarily a 'dividend' for federal income tax purposes." On state law, see Kreidmann, Dividends — Changing Patterns, 57 Col. L. Rev. 372 (1957).

If the distribution is a "dividend" for federal tax purposes, it will ordinarily be taxable to the stockholder under the "claim of right" doctrine, notwithstanding his potential liability to creditors under state law. United States v. Lesoine, 203 F.2d 123, 43 AFTR 643 (9th Cir. 1953); but see Knight Newspapers, Inc. v. Commissioner, 143 F.2d 1007, 32 AFTR 1111 (6th Cir. 1944).

the Sixteenth Amendment) is a matter of legislative grace, rather than constitutional right. It affects only corporations organized before 1913 and their successors; and since even a corporation that belongs to this select group is likely to keep its distributions to shareholders well within its current or recent earnings and profits, the complicated network of law built on the 1913 benchmark is of interest to very few shareholders.[4]

The second part of §316(a) provides that a distribution is a "dividend" if it comes from earnings and profits of the taxable year.[5] Since most distributions are made by corporations that are currently profitable, §316(a)(2) often makes it unnecessary to compute the corporation's post-1913 accumulated earnings and profits. This makes for simplicity, but it also means that a distribution may be a taxable "dividend" even though the corporation has a deficit; if the concept of earnings and profits serves any useful purpose, it is partly undermined by §316(a)(2). For the original shareholders of a corporation, there is no economic difference between a distribution before the corporation has had any earnings, which is not a "dividend" under either §316(a)(1) or §316(a)(2), and a distribution after it has suffered a loss; but the latter is a "dividend" under §316(a)(2) if there are current earnings, even though they are insufficient to repair the deficit. For shareholders who acquire their stock after the deficit but before the earnings, §316(a)(2) is more defensible, to be sure; but here §316(a)(2) does not go far enough, since its impact can be avoided if the distribution can be postponed until a year in which the corporation has no earnings and profits.

[4] See Lynch v. Hornby, 247 U.S. 339, 3 AFTR 2992 (1918); see also Helvering v. Canfield, 291 U.S. 163, 13 AFTR 857 (1934), holding that pre-1913 earnings and profits may be wiped out by post-1913 losses and need not be restored from later earnings.
The Treasury Department has made several assaults on the immunity of pre-1913 earnings and profits, but has not been able to persuade Congress to repeal it. See House Ways and Means Committee, 77th Cong., 2d sess., Hearings On Revenue Revision of 1942, pp. 1691ff; H.R. Rep. No. 2319, 81st Cong., 2d Sess., reprinted in 1950-2 C.B. 380, 418-19.
[5] §316(a)(2) has a curious ancestry. It was enacted in 1936 as a relief measure when the undistributed profits tax was in effect. That tax was imposed on the undistributed part of corporate income, computed by deducting "dividends" from total income. Unless a deficit corporation could treat distributions out of current earnings as "dividends" for this purpose, it would be unable to avoid the undistributed profits tax no matter how large its distributions to stockholders were. To enable such corporations to obtain a credit for distributions out of current earnings, §316(a)(2) was enacted. Apparently no thought was given to the effect of the new subsection apart from the undistributed profits tax; and it was left intact when the undistributed profits tax was repealed in 1939. Its impact can sometimes be avoided by postponing the distribution until the next year. If the corporation has no earnings in that year and still has a deficit, the distribution will be receivable tax-free since it will fall under neither §316(a)(1) nor §316(a)(2).

If the corporation has neither post-1913 accumulated earnings and profits nor current earnings and profits, a distribution cannot be a "dividend." It is, instead, subject to §301(c)(2) and (3). Under §301(c)(2), the distribution is applied against and reduces the adjusted basis of the shareholder's stock. If the distribution is greater than the adjusted basis of the stock, the excess is subject to §301(c)-(3). In this event, it will be treated as gain from the sale or exchange of property (and thus as capital gain if the stock is a capital asset), unless it is out of a pre-1913 increase in the value of the corporation's property, in which event it will enjoy an exemption from tax.[6]

The second sentence of §316(a) lays down an irrebutable presumption that every distribution is out of earnings and profits to the extent thereof, and that it comes from the most recently accumulated earnings and profits. This prevents "earmarking" a distribution to control its tax status; e.g., a corporation having current earnings and profits, post-1913 accumulated earnings and profits, and pre-1913 accumulated earnings and profits, cannot make a distribution from the pre-1913 earnings and profits until the current and post-1913 earnings and profits have been exhausted.[7] After its current, post-1913, and pre-1913 earnings and profits have been exhausted, however, the corporation may be able to earmark a distribution so as to qualify it for the exemption conferred by §301(c)(3)(B) (pre-1913 increase in value) and thus protect its shareholders against a capital gain tax under §301(c)(3)(A). For an example of the foregoing principles, see Regs. §1.301-1(f), Example (1).

In determining whether a distribution is out of earnings and profits of the taxable year, §316(a)(2) provides that the earnings and profits for the year are to be computed as of the close of the taxable year without diminution by reason of distributions during the year. This means that a distribution will be a "dividend" if the corporation has earnings and profits at the end of the taxable year, even though it had none when the distribution occurred; contrariwise, a distribution that appeared to be a "dividend" when made may turn out to be a return of capital because the corporation has no earnings and profits at the

---

[6] See Higginson v. United States, 81 F. Supp. 254, 37 AFTR 766 (Ct. Cl. 1948), modified, 101 F. Supp. 763, 41 AFTR 567 (Ct. Cl. 1952); Ernest E. Blauvelt, 4 T.C. 10 (1944) (Acq.); Commissioner v. Gross, 236 F.2d 612, 50 AFTR 68 (2d Cir. 1956).

For the special rules governing a "collapsible" corporation's distributions in excess of basis, see infra, Ch. 10.

[7] Earmarking was permissible in 1916-17, and the effects of an exercise of the privilege in those years linger on in Regs. §1.312-6(e).

end of the year. If the distributions for the year exceed in amount both the earnings and profits of the taxable year and the post-1913 accumulated earnings and profits, the regulations prescribe a method of allocating the two categories of earnings and profits to the various distributions in order to ascertain the "dividend" component of each one.

The above principles may be illustrated by the following examples (in which it is assumed that the X Co. has only individual shareholders, and that all parties are on the cash basis calendar year method of accounting):

1. X Co. has a deficit of $20,000 in its earnings and profits at the beginning of 1965, has earnings and profits of $10,000 during 1965, and distributes $10,000 to its shareholders on July 1, 1965. Under §316(a)(2), the 1965 distribution is a taxable "dividend," notwithstanding X Co.'s deficit.

2. If X Co. waited until 1966 to make this distribution, and if it had no current earnings and profits for 1966, however, the distribution would be treated as a return of capital under §301(c)(2) and (3) since X Co.'s 1965 earnings and profits would be absorbed by its deficit, leaving no accumulated earnings to support dividend treatment in 1966.

3. X Co. has accumulated earnings and profits of $15,000 on Jan. 1, 1965, has earnings and profits of $10,000 during 1965, and distributes $20,000 to its shareholders in April and $20,000 in September of 1965. Current earnings and profits are allocated pro rata among current distributions, while the balance of these distributions is deemed to come from the most recently accumulated earnings in chronological order. Thus, Regs. §1.316-2(b) and (c) provide that the April distribution is a dividend in its entirety ($5,000 coming from current earnings and $15,000 from accumulated earnings), while only $5,000 of the September distribution is a dividend ($5,000 from current earnings, the accumulated earnings having been exhausted by the April distribution).[8]

4. X Co. has accumulated earnings of $20,000 at the start of 1965, incurs a current operating deficit of $16,000 in 1965, and distributes $20,000 to its shareholders in July 1, 1965. The regulations suggest that the current deficit is prorated throughout the year if it cannot specifically be allocated to a part of the year. If the deficit is prorated, accumulated earnings at the date of the distribution would be reduced by $8,000 (one-half of the deficit) to $12,000, and the distribution would be a dividend to this extent; but if the deficit can be traced and allocated in full to the

---

[8] These dividend "source" rules have significance only where there are changes of stock ownership during the year of distribution. Thus, in the text example, the April shareholders would be taxed differently from the September shareholders, although the two distributions were equal in amount.

first half of 1965, accumulated earnings would be reduced by $16,000, and the dividend portion of the distribution would be $4,000.[8a]

Sec. 5.03.   Earnings and profits

It is a curious fact that the Internal Revenue Code, ordinarily so prodigal in the use of words, nowhere defines the term "earnings and profits," although it has no counterpart in the field of corporation law.[9] The phrase entered the federal tax law in 1916, but until 1940 it was given meaning solely by judicial and administrative construction. In 1940, the effect of a few transactions upon a corporation's "earnings and profits," was prescribed by statute, and Congress has intervened several times since then, but a comprehensive definition is still lacking.[10] To compute a corporation's earnings and profits is often no

---

[8a] Regs. §1.316-2(b), last sentence. See also The Steel Improvement & Forge Co. v. Commissioner, 36 T.C. 265 (1961), rev'd other grounds, 314 F. 2d 96, 11 AFTR 2d 953 (6th Cir. 1963), for similar implications in a related area. A third possibility would be to ignore the effect of current losses on current distributions, thus resulting in a $20,000 dividend since the entire distribution would be covered by accumulated earnings at the *start* of 1965. This view would restrict the accumulated earnings account to the results of years *prior* to the current year of the distribution, an approach which may be symmetrical with the "nimble dividend" rule of §316(a)(2) but which seems to violate both the spirit and purpose of §316(a)(1) (note also that this provision merely speaks of earnings accumulated *after* 1913). Another approach would be to compute the accumulated profits figure as of the end of 1965 (taking account of the current year's losses at this point), and then allocate the current distributions in chronological order against that amount ($4,000).

[9] There are two landmark articles on earnings and profits, both outdated at certain points but still useful: Rudick, "Dividends" and "Earnings or Profits" Under the Income Tax Law: Corporate Non-Liquidating Distributions, 89 U. Pa L. Rev. 865 (1941); Paul, Ascertainment of "Earnings or Profits" for the Purpose of Determining Taxability of Corporate Distributions, 51 Harv. L. Rev. 40 (1937), reprinted with revisions in Paul, Selected Problems in Federal Taxation (2d series, 1938) 149. The Rudick article is supplemented by Albrecht, "Dividends" and "Earnings or Profits," 7 Tax. L. Rev. 157 (1952); see also Emmanuel, Earnings and Profits: An Accounting Concept? 4 Tax L. Rev. 494 (1949).

More recent articles on the subject are Andrews, *supra* note 2; Katcher, What is Meant by Earnings and Profits, 18 N.Y.U. Inst. on Fed. Tax. 235 (1960); Benesh, Internal Revenue Service Procedures For Determinations of Accumulated Earnings and Profits, 15 Tax Exec. 125 (1963); Zarky and Biblin, The Role of Earnings and Profits in the Tax Law, 1966 So. Calif. Tax Inst. 145. See Rev. Proc. 65-10, 1965-1 C.B. 738, for guidelines in determining earnings and profits.

[10] Because corporations ordinarily keep their distributions well under current earnings and profits, it is rarely necessary to ascertain the corporation's earnings and profits with precision, and many questions in the computation of earnings and profits are unanswered for want of litigation. This lamentable obscurity was dispelled to some degree by litigation under the excess profits taxes of World War II and the Korean War, because the corporation's liability depended in part upon its invested capital, which included earnings and profits, thus requiring an accurate determination of the earnings and profits account for some corporations. A number of recent cases in this field stem from fraud investigations: shareholders diverting corporate income in large amounts (e.g.,

simple task, especially if it has gone through a series of corporate reorganizations or other adjustments. It may be necessary to go back many years to decide how a transaction should have been treated under a now interred statute because of its effect upon earnings and profits.[11]

The computation of "earnings and profits" is not appreciably simplified when we find that, in all probability, the term had little or no meaning to the Congress that invented it. As already mentioned, the phrase first appeared in the Revenue Act of 1916. The Revenue Act of 1913 had taxed "dividends" *simpliciter,* and by failing to define the term Congress apparently intended to adopt its meaning in common parlance. The Treasury was quick to give it the broadest possible meaning, including among other things distributions from corporate surplus accumulated before the adoption of the Sixteenth Amendment. This construction was upheld by the Supreme Court in Lynch v. Hornby, 247 U.S. 339, 3 AFTR 2992 (1918):

> Hence we construe the provision of the act that "the net income of a taxable person shall include gains, profits, and income derived from *** interest, rent, dividends, *** or gains or profits and income derived from any source whatever" as including . . . all dividends declared and paid in the ordinary course of business by a corporation to its stockholders after the taking effect of the act (March 1, 1913), whether from current earnings, or from the accumulated surplus made up of past earnings or increase in value of corporate assets, notwithstanding, it accrued to the corporation in whole or in part prior to March 1, 1913. In short, the word "dividends" was employed in the act as descriptive of one kind of gain to the individual stockholder; dividends being treated as the tangible and recurrent returns upon his stock, analogous to the interest and rent received upon other forms of invested capital. (247 U.S. at 344.)

by pocketing the proceeds of cash sales) have litigated the question whether their fraudulent diversions constituted dividend income under §301(c)(1), returns of capital under §301(c)(2), or capital gain under §301(c)(3)(A). *Infra,* Sec. 5.04.

The status of the corporation's earnings and profits account may have to be determined in applying various other provisions of the Code; e.g., §531 (accumulated earnings tax); §333 (one-month liquidations); §1371 (Subchapter S corporations); §951 (controlled foreign corporations); §902 (deemed paid foreign tax credit); §1248 (stock of a controlled foreign corporation).

[11] Because there is no statute of limitations on the effect of prior transactions on accumulated earnings and profits, the permanent retention of corporate records is advisable.

See Jacob M. Kaplan, 43 T.C. 580 (1965), and Alderson v. Healy, ... F. Supp. ...., 15 AFTR 2d 536 (D. Mont. 1965), for the application of estoppel principles to bar taxpayers from adopting an inconsistent position on the effect of prior transactions on earnings and profits.

In the meantime, however, Congress had expressly provided in the Revenue Act of 1916 that:

> the term "dividends" as used in this title shall be held to mean any distribution made or ordered to be made by a corporation . . . out of its earnings or profits accrued since March first, nineteen hundred and thirteen . . . (39 Stat. 757 (1916).)

It seems reasonably clear that the term "earnings or profits" crept into the federal income tax law by accident when Congress was establishing March 1, 1913 as a dividing line between taxable distributions and non-taxable distributions. In the first regulations issued under the 1916 Act, the Treasury Department seemingly regarded "earnings and profits" as identical with surplus."[12] It was inevitable, however, that the existence of a corporate surplus could not serve to differentiate between taxable and non-taxable distributions, unless the surplus was first "adjusted" almost beyond recognition. For example, a distribution of common stock by a corporation having only common stock outstanding decreases its surplus, although it does not subject the stockholders to tax (infra, Sec. 5.61); if surplus were the criterion of taxability, a corporation could sweep its surplus account clean by a tax-free stock dividend, and then distribute cash free of tax. (This might be done even if the distribution of cash would be improper under local law, since in practice and often even by their terms state dividend statutes penalize the stockholders or directors only if creditors are injured by the distribution.) Another defect in using corporate surplus as a criterion of taxability is that is can be reduced by reserves for "contingencies"; if these were taken into account, the floodgates would be opened to a stream of tax-free cash distributions for as long as the corporation's directors could conjure up "contingencies" that would warrant the creation of reserves. It is not surprising, therefore, that surplus has been rejected as a criterion and that the term "earnings and profits" has acquired a meaning more in keeping with its function.

When we search for the meaning of "earnings and profits," then, we are in reality asking how a corporate transaction *should* affect the stockholder who receives a distribution of cash or property from the corporation after the transaction has occurred. To take a simple illustration, assume that during the first year of a corporation's life it earns $10,000, pays a federal income tax of $3,000, and distributes $8,000 to its shareholders. Ignoring other facts, it would probably be agreed that $7,000 should be taxed to the shareholders as a dividend

---

[12] Regs. 33 (revised), Arts. 106-7 (1918).

and that the remaining $1,000 should be treated by them as a return of capital.

Not all problems in the computation of earnings and profits, however, are solved so easily. Suppose, in the example just given, the corporation's business earnings amounted to $10,000 but that in addition it had received $500 of tax-exempt interest on state and municipal bonds. Should the $8,000 distribution to the stockholders be treated as a dividend to the extent of $7,500, with only $500 being treated as a return of capital? Or should the bond interest be excluded from earnings and profits as well as from taxable income? One might argue that the interest, which would not have been taxed to the shareholders had they held the bonds in their personal capacities, should not become taxable as income to them merely because it was filtered through the corporate entity; despite this argument, the regulations have long taken the position that tax-exempt bond interest increases earnings and profits, presumably on the theory that the corporation's capital is not invaded by a distribution of such income. Regs. §1.312-6(b). On the same theory, apparently, the regulations provide that depletion on mines and oil and gas wells must be based on cost (or on March 1, 1913 value) in computing earnings and profits, even though percentage depletion is used in computing taxable income. Regs. §1.312-6 (c). Thus, if the corporation's earnings are $10,000 computed with the benefit of percentage depletion, but would have been $10,500 had depletion been based on cost, and if federal income taxes are $3,000, the corporation's earnings and profits are $7,500; and a distribution of $8,000 would be a "dividend" to the extent of $7,500 and a return of capital to the extent of only $500. Would the result in any of the foregoing cases be altered if the corporation had created a revaluation surplus or deficit by writing the value of its assets up or down to correspond with changes in their market value? Although one might argue for taking such adjustments into account in computing earnings and profits, since the market value rather than the cost of the corporation's assets is what realistically determines whether a distribution invades its capital or not, it is quite clear that appreciation or depreciation in value that has not been "realized" in the income tax sense does not affect earnings and profits.[13] A contrary rule would require the Treasury to appraise the assets with each distribution or, at least, with each revaluation by the directors.

[13] Elton Hoyt, 2d, 34 B.T.A. 1011 (1936); see also Commissioner v. Gross, 236 F. 2d 612, 50 AFTR 68 (2d Cir. 1956). Unrealized depreciation will affect earnings and profits, however, when reflected in the valuation of the corporation's inventory by a write-down from cost to market.

It should be apparent by now that a corporation's accumulated earnings and profits are not necessarily equal to its surplus (despite occasional loose use of the terms, even in tax cases, as interchangeable) nor are they equal to total taxable income. There is, however, a distinct relationship between all three; starting with taxable income, for example, one can derive both earnings and profits and surplus by going through the corporation's books and records and adjusting for items and transactions that are treated one way in computing taxable income and another way in computing either earnings and profits or surplus. By a similar process, with surplus as a starting point, one can derive taxable income and earnings and profits; and with earnings and profits as a base, taxable income and surplus can be computed. Indeed, the corporation income tax return contains a schedule on which the taxpayer reconciles his taxable net income with the increase or decrease in surplus for the taxable year. In a similar manner, the increase or decrease in earnings and profits for the same year could be computed.

Although earnings and profits can be derived by adjustments to surplus, it is more common to start with taxable income, and to the extent that the Internal Revenue Code and regulations define earnings and profits, both ordinarily take taxable income as the point of departure. The regulations state, for example, that "the amount of the earnings and profits in any case will be dependent upon the method of accounting properly employed in computing taxable income," so that if the corporation computes taxable income on the cash receipts or disbursements basis, it may not use the accrual method for computing earnings and profits.[14] Without endeavoring to provide a comprehensive account of the computation of earnings and profits, it may be said that the adjustments to convert taxable income into earnings and profits fall into three categories:

1. *Certain items excluded from taxable income must be included in computing earnings and profits.* Regs. §1.312-6(b) states that:

> Among the items entering into the computation of corporate earnings and profits for a particular period are all income exempted by statute, income not taxable by the Federal Government under the Constitution, as well as all items includible in gross income under section 61 or corresponding provisions of prior revenue acts.

---

[14] Regs. §1.312-6(a). Accounting matters are treated in more detail, *infra*, Sec. 5.04.

In referring to "income not taxable by the Federal Government under the Constitution," the regulations no doubt mean interest on state and municipal obligations (though the constitutional immunity of such interest is far from clear), and the quoted extract is followed by an explicit statement that such interest is taxable when distributed to shareholders as dividends. The reference in the regulations to "all income exempted by statute" is ambiguous; taken in its broadest sense, it would require all income items excluded from gross income by Part III of Subchapter B to be included in earnings and profits.[15] Although authority is scant, the leading commentators have agreed with the regulations in including in earnings and profits the proceeds of life insurance exempt from taxable income under §101(a), interest on federal, state, and municipal obligations exempt under §103, and compensation for injuries or sickness exempt under §104(a). On the other hand, the commentators have thought that contributions to capital, gifts, and bequests received by a corporation should be excluded from "earnings and profits" as well as from taxable income, partly on the theory that gifts and bequests cannot be "earned" and are not thought of as "profits", and partly on the theory that such gratuitous receipts are not income at all.[16]

There are, however, a number of "realized" income items that are "exempted" from income by statute only in the limited sense that income is recognized not at the outset of a transaction but at a later time (either through lower depreciation deductions or when the pro-

---

[15] Of the items in Part III, the following might be received by a corporation: life insurance proceeds under §101(a); gifts and bequests under §102; interest on certain governmental obligations under §103; compensation for injuries or sickness under §104, see Castner Garage, Ltd., 43 B.T.A. 1 (1940) (Acq.); income from discharge of indebtedness under §108; the value of a lessee's improvements on the lessor's property under §109; income taxes paid by a lessee corporation under §110; recovery exclusions under §111; the proceeds of certain sports programs under §114 (but if included in earnings and profits, §114 proceeds would presumably be offset by a charitable contribution, even if in excess of the 5 percent limit of §170); capital contributions under §118; and most of the items referred to by §122.

[16] Rudick, *supra* note 9, at 882; Albrecht, *supra* note 9, at 186; Paul, *supra* note 9, at 49. Rev. Rul. 54-230. 1954-1 C.B. 114, states that the excess of life insurance proceeds (from a policy insuring the life of a stockholder) over the aggregate premiums paid is includible in earnings and profits. (Although the Supreme Court in United States v. Supplee-Biddle Hardware Co., 265 U.S. 189, 4 AFTR 3989 (1924), reserved the question whether life insurance proceeds constitute income in the constitutional sense, the ruling seems correct in assuming that the answer would be affirmative, if it arose today.) This would be appropriate if the premiums had not been deducted from earnings and profits, but not otherwise. See *infra*, Sec. 5.03, suggesting that earnings and profits should be reduced by the excess of premiums paid but disallowed under §264 over the cash surrender value of the policy. As to bequests, A. J. Diebold, ¶53,052 P-H Memo TC (1953), holds that they constitute contributions to capital and do not increase earnings and profits.

perty eventually is sold). Since 1940, the Code has provided in what is now §312(f)(1)[17] that such gains and losses do not enter into earnings and profits until they are "recognized"; thus, as to these items, the corporation's earnings and profits and its taxable income are computed in a similar manner. Nonrecognition transactions within the purview of §312(f)(1) include: §1031 ("like kind" exchanges); §1033 (replacements of involuntarily converted property); §351 (transfers to a controlled corporation, see *supra*, Ch. 3); §361 (reorganization transfers, see *infra*, Ch. 12); and §1091 ("wash sale" losses). In all of these transactions, unrecognized gain or loss is deferred through the operation of "substituted basis" rules, and it seems appropriate to carry through this deferral policy in the earnings and profits account as well.[18] In line with this approach, courts have extended the principle of §312(f)(1) to transactions which are so similar in character to nonrecognition exchanges as to justify nonrecognition treatment in computing earnings and profits. An example is income from a bargain discharge of the corporation's indebtedness where the corporation exercises its option, under §108, to exclude such income when realized. Since the basis of its assets must be reduced under §1017, the income will be reflected in taxable income when the assets are depreciated or sold; and it has been held that earnings and profits are to be increased not when the debt is cancelled, but only subsequently.[19]

---

[17] The Supreme Court, in Commissioner v. Wheeler, 324 U.S. 542, 33 AFTR 595 (1945), held that Congress had merely codified existing law on this question. *Wheeler* involved property acquired by the corporate transferee in a tax-free §351 exchange.

[18] Although §312(f)(1) is primarily concerned with realized gains that will be recognized at a later date, its language is broad enough to exclude gains on the sale of treasury shares from earnings and profits, since these gains are not recognized by virtue of §1032 (*supra*, Sec. 3.15). See Sprouse, Accounting for Treasury Stock Transactions; Prevailing Practices and New Statutory Provisions, 59 Col. L. Rev. 882 (1959); United National Corp. v. Commissioner, 143 F. 2d 580, 32 AFTR 1026 (9th Cir. 1944) (gain on retirement of preferred stock did not increase earnings and profits).

[19] Bangor & Aroostook R. Co. v. Commissioner, 193 F. 2d 827, 41 AFTR 648 (1st Cir. 1951), cert. denied, 343 U.S. 934 (1952); Alabama By-Products Corp. v. United States, 137 F. Supp. 252, 48 AFTR 1153 (N.D. Ala. 1955), aff'd per curiam, 228 F.2d 958, 52 AFTR 342 (5th Cir. 1956); see also Commissioner v. Wheeler, *supra* note 17; Leon R. Meyer, 46 T.C. No. 8 (1966) (cancellation of debt under Chapter XI of Bankruptcy Act).

If the corporate debtor does not elect to exclude its cancellation of indebtedness income under §108 and §1017, its earnings and profits should be increased by the gain on debt cancellation, unless it qualifies for one of the non-statutory exceptions to cancellation of indebtedness income. See Annis V. N. Schweppe, 8 T.C. 1224 (1947), aff'd per curiam, 168 F.2d 284, 36 AFTR 1037 (9th Cir. 1948); but see Liberty Mirror Works, 3 T.C. 1018 (1944), implying that an *American Dental* "gift" cancellation increases earnings and profits. See generally Eustice, Cancellation of Indebtedness and the Federal Income Tax: A Problem of Creeping Confusion, 14 Tax L. Rev. 225 (1959).

The effect on earnings and profits of non-taxable contributions to capital (*supra*, Sec. 3.16) is less clear, but it would seem that they should be treated as nonrecognition transactions by analogy to the principles of §312(f)(1) since the basis rules of §362 require the transferee to carry over the transferor's basis for the property or, in the case of nonshareholder capital contributions, to use a zero basis.[20] Similarly, a lessor corporation ought not to be required to increase earnings and profits by the value of improvements made by its lessee when §109 is applicable; taxable income, and hence earnings and profits, will be greater in later years because the basis of the property will not reflect the lessee's improvements. These rules can be reconciled with Regs. §1.312-6(b) by reading the reference to income "exempted by statute" as embracing items that are permanently excluded from income, but not items whose taxable recognition is merely postponed.[21]

On the other hand, Regs. §1.312-6(b) probably requires an amount excluded from taxable income by virtue of the "recovery exclusion" of §111 to be included in earnings and profits if a deduction of the item giving rise to the recovery exclusion served to reduce earnings and profits in an earlier year.[22] Similarly, if depreciation in excess of the amount allowable under §167 was deducted by the taxpayer, earnings and profits should be adjusted upward when the property is sold, even though the taxpayer is able to take advantage of §1016(a)(2)(B) in computing taxable income because the excess deductions were of no tax benefit.

2. Certain items deducted in computing taxable income may not be deducted in computing earnings and profits. This category, as described by Rudick (*supra*, note 9, at 885), consists of "artificially created deductions, or credits which are allowed for purposes of computing taxable net income, but which do not represent actual expenses or expenditures, *i.e.*, there is no outlay by the corporation for the deductions or credits represented by such items." As already mentioned, in computing earnings and profits, depletion must be based on cost, even though percentage depletion is employed in computing taxable income. Dividends received from another corporation must be in-

---

[20] See Annis V.N. Schweppe, *supra* note 19.

[21] Compare the cases involving the deductibility under §265 of expenses attributable to nonrecognized gain: Commissioner v. McDonald, 320 F.2d 109, 12 AFTR 2d 5162 (5th Cir. 1963); Commissioner v. Universal Leaf Tobacco Co., 318 F.2d 658, 11 AFTR 2d 1614 (4th Cir. 1963).

[22] The Service so ruled in Rev. Rul. 58-546, 1958-2 C. B. 143; but see the doubtful contrary result in Lasater's Estate v. Scofield, 74 F. Supp. 458, 36 AFTR 370 (W.D. Tex. 1947).

cluded in full in computing the recipient corporation's earnings and profits, without regard to the 85 percent deduction allowed by §243 in computing taxable income. The net operating loss deduction of §172 cannot be used to reduce earnings and profits, since it is simply a carryback or carryover of losses that reduced earnings and profits in the year they occurred. The same is true of the capital loss carryover of §1212.

3. *Certain items that cannot be deducted in computing taxable income may be deducted in computing earnings and profits.* This category, as described by Rudick (*supra,* note 9 at 887), "consists of expenses and losses which are not allowed as deductions in computing taxable net income, but which clearly deplete the income available for distribution to the stockholders." They must be deducted in computing earnings and profits to prevent distributions of the corporation's capital from being taxed as "dividends" to the stockholders. Among the items that require such a downward adjustment of earnings and profits are the following:

1. Dividend distributions in prior years (note that under §316(a)(2), current distributions do not reduce current earnings and profits; and that under §312(a), distributions cannot create a deficit in current or accumulated earnings and profits).
2. Federal income taxes (net of such credits as the investment credit of §38 and the foreign tax credit of §33).[23]
3. Expenses and interest incurred in earning tax-exempt interest, even though non-deductible under §265.
4. "Excess" charitable contributions, i.e., amounts not deductible in computing taxable income because of the 5 percent ceiling of §170(b)(2).[24]
5. Premiums on term life insurance disallowed in computing taxable income by §264.[25]

[23] Rev. Rul. 63-63, 1963-1 C.B. 10, ruled that the investment credit must be applied against the tax liability in computing earnings and profits, and that earnings and profits may not be reduced by the adjustment to basis required by §48(g) before its repeal in 1964. Foreign taxes, however, should serve to reduce earnings and profits even though claimed as a credit in computing the corporation's tax liability, since they represent an actual expenditure of funds.

[24] See Jacob M. Kaplan, 43 T.C. 580, 599 (1965).

[25] The practice with respect to premiums paid for ordinary life policies is evidently to reduce earnings and profits by the excess of the premiums paid over the increase in the policy's cash surrender value; see the stipulated computation of earnings and profits in Sidney Stark, 29 T.C. 122 (1957) (Non-Acq.). It is at least arguable that the premiums should be deductible in full from earnings and profits on the ground that the increase in the policy's cash surrender value is unrealized appreciation (see *supra,* note 13); but the contrary view is more harmonious with the fact that earnings and profits are not reduced by investment outlays.

To the extent that the premiums have been deducted in computing earn-

6. The excess of capital losses over capital gains, non-deduct-ible by virtue of §1211.[26]

7. Losses, expenses, and interest incurred in transactions with controlling shareholders, non-deductible under §267.[27]

Earnings and profits should probably also be adjusted for certain other corporate outlays that are not deductible in computing taxable income, such as lobbying expenses and political contributions;[28] there is little reason to think that Congress would have wanted such items to be disregarded in determining whether a distribution to stock-holders came out of earnings or capital. More doubtful, however, is the proper treatment of expenses that are disallowed in computing taxable income on grounds of public policy, such as fines, bribes, over-ceiling price and wage payments, and the like, as well as contributions to organizations engaged in "prohibited transactions" or subversive activities, see §170(h)). Although these items might be classed with penalties for federal income tax fraud, which have long been allowed by the Internal Revenue Service itself as deductions in computing earnings and profits,[29] the "frustration of public policy" doctrine might be applied to a computation of earnings and profits, as well as to the computation of taxable income.[30]

In addition to the foregoing adjustments, the calculation of earn-ings and profits must take account of a great variety of financial trans-actions that may occur only occasionally in the life of any one cor-poration. Among these transactions, most of which are discussed else-where, are the following:

---

ings and profits, Rev. Rul. 54-230, 1954-1 C.B. 114, is overly generous in includ-ing only the excess of the proceeds over the premiums in earnings and profits; possibly it is based on the unstated assumption that the premiums were not deducted from earnings and profits when paid.

[26] Regs. §1.312-7(b)(1).

[27] Regs. §1.312-7(b)(1).

[28] Cammarano v. United States, 358 U.S. 498, 3 AFTR 2d 697 (1959); see also the limited deduction for lobbying expenses in §162(e), added in 1962.

[29] Rev. Rul. 57-332, 1957-2 C.B. 231; but see Bernstein v. United States, 234 F.2d 475, 49 AFTR 1457 (5th Cir. 1956), cert. denied, 352 U.S. 915 (1956), suggesting a contrary result. See also infra, Sec. 5.04.

[30] Tank Truck Rentals, Inc. v. Commissioner, 356 U.S. 30, 1 AFTR 2d 1154 (1958) (overweight fines not deductible as ordinary and necessary busi-ness expenses under §162); Hoover Motor Express Co., Inc. v. United States, 356 U.S. 38, 1 AFTR 2d 1157 (1958) (same); but see Commissioner v. Sulli-van, 356 U.S. 27, 1 AFTR 2d 1158 (1958) (wages, rent, etc., paid by an illegal business deductible under §162); Tellier v. Commissioner, — U.S., —, 17 AFTR 2d 633 (1966). These cases might be distinguished as resting on the "ordinary and necessary" requirement of §162; but Tank Truck Rentals and Hoover Motor Express were hostile to any tax concession that might reduce the "sting" of a fine for violating state or federal law. The Sullivan case, on the other hand, suggests that earnings and profits should be reduced by cor-porate expenditures, in order to achieve a result in accord with economic reality so far as the shareholder is concerned.

1. The receipt by a corporation of tax-free distributions from other corporations, such as stock dividends (*infra*, Sec. 5.61), non-dividend distributions of cash and property (*supra*, Sec. 5.02), etc.

2. Distributions by a corporation of property (*infra*, Sec. 5.24), its own stock (*infra*, Sec. 5.61), and its own obligations (*infra*, Sec. 5.40).

3. Distributions by a corporation in partial liquidation or in redemption of its stock (*infra*, Sec. 7.85).

4. Distributions by a corporation which is obligated on a loan made, guaranteed, or insured by the United States (or its agencies or instrumentalities), if the amount of the loan exceeds the adjusted basis of the property constituting security for the loan.[31]

5. An election under Subchapter S (*infra*, Ch. 14).

6. Mergers, consolidations, liquidations, transfers of property, spin-offs, and other transactions by which one corporation succeeds to the assets and tax attributes of another corporation (*supra*, Sec. 2.10; *infra*, Ch. 13).

Sec. 5.04. Tax accounting principles in computing earnings and profits and dividend income

Although ordinary tax accounting principles are applicable at many points in the computation of earnings and profits, there are a number of divergencies; and there are also some special rules governing the time when a shareholder is required to take dividends into account in computing his taxable income.

1. Accounting for earnings and profits. Regs. §1.312-6(a) provides generally that the method of accounting used in computing earnings and profits is to follow that used for determining the corporation's taxable income. Thus, if the corporation computes taxable income on the cash basis method of accounting, it cannot use the accrual method for computing earnings and profits. In addition, this requirement of accounting consistency probably applies to such special items as: the depreciation method selected under §167(b); inventory methods; the treatment of bad debts under §166; reporting of installment sales profits under §453; reporting of income from long term contracts under Regs. §1.451-3; the special deductions for circulation expenses (§173), research and experimental expenses (§174), soil and water conservation expenses (§175), and trade mark and trade name expenses (§177); amortization of organizational expenses under §248; and other items that are specially treated in computing taxable income.

---

[31] §312(j); see Commissioner v. Gross, 236 F.2d 612, 50 AFTR 68 (2d Cir. 1956); Alexander, Some Earnings and Profits Aspects of the Internal Revenue Code of 1954, 7 Hastings L. J. 285, 297-300 (1956).

Similarly, items such as reserves for future expenses, even if proper under non-tax accounting principles, should not reduce earnings and profits if not deductible for tax purposes; conversely, if an advance receipt is includible in taxable income, it likewise should be reflected in earnings and profits even though non-tax accounting practice would sanction deferral.[32] As to certain items that are not taken into account in computing taxable income (e.g., federal income taxes and fraud penalties), however, variations from tax accounting principles have been permitted in the determination of earnings and profits. Thus, cash basis corporations have been allowed to accrue federal taxes and fraud penalties in computing earnings and profits;[33] and accrual basis corporations have been allowed to accrue contested tax deficiencies for the year to which the tax related and fraud penalties for the year in which the fraudulent return was filed, although in computing taxable income, disputed liabilities are normally deductible only when the contest is settled.[34] These departures from normal tax accounting principles add to the complexity of this area, without making any offsetting contribution to rationality.

2. *Accounting for dividends.* The time when a distribution must be taken into account is important for two purposes: to fix the time when earnings and profits must be measured in order to determine whether it is a taxable dividend; and to determine the year in which it must be reported by the recipient. In Rev. Rul. 62-131, 1962-2 C.B. 94, the Service ruled that the date of payment, rather than the date of declaration, is controlling in determing whether a distribution comes out of earnings and profits.[35] Similarly, Regs. §1.301-1(b) pro-

---

[32] See Corinne S. Koshland, 33 B.T.A. 634 (1935) (depreciation); Benjamin Siegel, 29 B.T.A. 1289 (1934) (bad debts); Regs. §1.312-6(a) (installment sales); Commissioner v. South Texas Lumber Co., 333 U.S. 496, 36 AFTR 604 (1948) (ditto); I.T. 3543, 1942-1 C.B. 111 (amortization of emergency facilities); Paulina du Pont Dean, 9 T.C. 256 (1947) (reserves); Neptune Meter Co. v. Price, 98 F.2d 76, 21 AFTR 659 (2d Cir. 1938) (reserves).

[33] Demmon v. United States, 321 F.2d 203, 12 AFTR 2d 5371 (7th Cir. 1963); Thompson v. United States, 214 F.Supp. 97, 11 AFTR 2d 446 (N.D. Ohio 1962); contra, Helvering v. Alworth Trust, 136 F.2d 812, 31 AFTR 230 (8th Cir. 1943); Paulina du Pont Dean, 9 T.C. 256 (1947); Newark Amusement Corp., ¶60,137 P-H Memo TC (1960).

[34] See Demmon v. United States and Thompson v. United States, *supra*, note 33; Rev. Rul 57-332, 1957-2 C.B. 231; but see Bernstein v. United States, 234 F.2d 475, 49 AFTR 1457 (5th Cir. 1956); see also Sidney Stark, 29 T.C. 122 (1957) (Non-acq.) (interest on contested tax liabilities accrues year by year); Fairmont Park Raceway, Inc., ¶62,014 P-H Memo TC (1962) (ditto).

Section 461(f), added in 1964 to overrule United States v. Consolidated Edison Co., 366 U.S. 380, 7 AFTR 2d 1451 (1961), relates only to the accrual of contested *deductible* taxes, and hence would seem inapplicable to this area.

[35] See also Mason v. Routzahn, 275 U.S. 175, 6 AFTR 7072 (1927); *supra*, Sec. 5.02 (re allocation of earnings and profits when they are less than the corporation's distributions); but see Commissioner v. Goldwyn, 175 F.2d 641,

vides that if property other than money is distributed as a dividend, its fair market value (and hence its dividend status) is determined as of the date of the distribution, even if this is different from the date on which the distribution is includible in the recipient's gross income.

In determining the proper time for including distributions in the recipient's gross income, five points in time might in theory be relevant: (1) the declaration date; (2) the record date; (3) the date on which the distribution is payable; (4) the date on which the corporation is willing and able to pay; and (5) the date the distribution is received by the shareholders. The Service's position on this question is set out in Regs. §1.301-1(b), providing that distributions are includible in gross income "when the cash or other property is unqualifiedly made subject to [the shareholders'] demands." This language appears to eliminate the first two of the five possible dates, and probably the third as well, so that a choice must be made between the fourth and fifth. Elsewhere in the regulations, it is provided that year-end dividends, paid by checks mailed in December but received by the shareholders in January, are not constructively received in the earlier year.[36] Despite this acceptance of the fifth possible date (actual receipt) as controlling in the case of year-end distributions, however, the doctrine of constructive receipt (the fourth date, in the foregoing scheme) is applied if the shareholder deliberately turns his back on a distribution that he could have for the asking.[37] It has been held that these rules apply equally to accrual basis taxpayers, so that they are placed on a cash basis for distributions, even though they acquire a claim against the payor corporation under local law on the declaration or record date.[38]

[38] AFTR 97 (9th Cir. 1949), holding that a prior year's dividend reduced accumulated earnings and profits at the time of its declaration rather than when paid to the recipient. This failure to apply a uniform rule for determining the effect of earnings on distributions and of distributions on earnings is criticized by Albrecht, *supra*, note 9, at 173-176.

[36] Regs. §1.451-2(b), evidently based on Avery v. Commissioner, 292 U.S. 210, 13 AFTR 1168 (1934); see also Rev. Rul. 64-290, 1964-2 C.B. 465, and Rev. Rul. 65-23, 1965-1 C.B. 520, relating to the reporting of distributions by the paying corporation under §6042(a), and pointing out the distinction between the year for determining the taxable status of distributions and the year they are to be included in the recipient's income.

[37] See Aramo-Stiftung v. Commissioner, 172 F.2d 896, 37 AFTR 958 (2d Cir. 1949); A. D. Saenger, Inc. v. Commissioner, 84 F.2d 23, 17 AFTR 1245 (5th Cir. 1936), cert. denied, 299 U.S. 577; Brundage v. United States, 275 F.2d 424, 5 AFTR 2d 740 (7th Cir. 1960); but see Commissioner v. Fox, 218 F.2d 347, 46 AFTR 1459 (3d Cir. 1954).

[38] See Commissioner v. American Light & Traction Co., 156 F.2d 398, 34 AFTR 1544 (7th Cir. 1946); and note that Regs. §1.301-1(b) makes no reference to the shareholder's accounting method, and that §301, §116, and §243 all speak of distributions or dividends "received" by the shareholder, implying that there is to be no distinction between cash and accrual basis taxpayers.

Sec. 5.05.   Constructive distributions

The rules of §301(c) (under which corporate distributions are to be treated as "dividends" or returns of capital, depending on the amount of the corporation's current and post-1913 earnings and profits) come into play only if a corporation makes distribution to a shareholder "with respect to its stock." According to Regs. §1.301-1(c), §301 "is not applicable to an amount paid by a corporation to a shareholder unless the amount is paid to the shareholder in his capacity as such." Thus, if a corporation transfers property to a shareholder who is also a creditor of the corporation in satisfaction of his claim, the transaction is not governed by §301; other examples would include payments to a shareholder-employee as compensation for services, to a shareholder-vendor as payment for property, and to a shareholder-lessor as rent for the use of property.[39] Even if such transfers are regarded as "distributions,"[40] they are not made to a shareholder "with respect to [his] stock," as required by §301(a), and hence their tax consequences are governed by other sections of the Internal Revenue Code.

A distribution to a shareholder in his capacity as such, however, is subject to §301 even though not declared in a formal fashion. Instances of "constructive" or "disguised" distributions are commonly encountered in the context of closely-held corporations whose dealings with their shareholders are, more often than not, characterized by informality. Although publicly-held corporations rarely engage in this practice, some railroad and public utility corporations are parties to leases requiring the lessee to pay a fixed annual amount directly to their shareholders, an arrangement that is equivalent to a payment of rent to the lessor, coupled with a distribution by the lessor to its shareholders.[41]

Informal distributions can assume many forms; a transfer need not constitute a distribution under state law to be treated as such for federal income tax purposes, nor need all shareholders participate, though disproportionate transfers are less vulnerable than pro rata

---

[39] See example in S. Rep. No. 1622, 83d Cong., 2d Sess., p. 231 (1954); see also Commissioner v. Fender Sales, Inc., 338 F.2d 924, 14 AFTR 2d 6076 (9th Cir. 1964).

[40] The label seems inappropriate if the consideration received by the corporation is equal to the value of the amount paid by it, despite Palmer v. Commissioner, 302 U.S. 63, 19 AFTR 1201 (1937) ("a sale of corporate assets to stockholders is, in a literal sense, a distribution of its property").

[41] See United States v. Joliet & Chicago R. Co., 315 U.S. 44, 28 AFTR 215 (1942); Commissioner v. Western Union Telegraph Co., 141 F.2d 774, 32 AFTR 492 (2d Cir. 1944).

ones.[42] An economic benefit may constitute a constructive distribution, even though no money or property is transferred to the shareholder; but this possibility is clouded by the countervailing principles that a shareholder and his corporation are separate taxable entities and that not every corporate action which is beneficial to the shareholder will generate taxable income to him. The characterization of an amount received by a shareholder, directly or indirectly, from his corporation may be important in determining (a) whether the corporation may deduct it, (b) whether it reduces the corporation's current earnings and profits in computing taxability of current distributions or merely reduces the earnings available for future distributions, (c) whether the recipient must treat it as ordinary gross income under §61(a) or may treat it in whole or in part as a return of capital under §301(c), and (d) whether the recipient is entitled to the dividends received exclusion of §116 or intercorporate dividends received deduction of §243. These classification difficulties can become acute in the case of payments which might in appropriate cases be treated as compensation to shareholder-employees (such as reimbursed shareholder expenses, travel and entertainment expenses, diversions of corporate income, and rent-free use of corporate property), rather than distributions. Some of the most frequently-encountered transactions that may be treated as constructive or disguised distributions by a corporation to its shareholders are the following:[43]

1. Corporate "loans" to shareholders. If corporate funds are "loaned" to a shareholder but there is no intent to create a bona fide creditor-debtor relationship, the withdrawals may be treated as constructive or disguised distributions. The intent of the parties is to be gleaned from an examination of all the facts, but the use of interest-bearing notes and a history of actual payments on account of principal and interest create a favorable climate; on the other hand, open ac-

[42] Chism's Estate v. Commissioner, 322 F.2d 956, 12 AFTR 2d 5300 (9th Cir. 1963) (state law adjudication not controlling); Lengsfield v. Commissioner, 241 F.2d 508, 50 AFTR 1683 (5th Cir. 1957) (disproportionate distribution); see also Paramount-Richards Theatres, Inc. v. Commissioner, 153 F.2d 602, 34 AFTR 931 (5th Cir. 1946); Lester E. Dellinger, 32 T.C. 1178 (1959). See also Ernest H. Berger, 37 T.C. 1026 (1962), holding that shareholders could not deduct amounts repaid to their corporation ("excessive" salaries) on the theory that the payments were improper under local law.

[43] In the discussion that follows, the term "constructive dividend" is often used. Although the constructive or disguised distribution area is not limited to distributions that constitute "dividends," the same principles being applicable to constructive non-dividend distributions, the litigated cases have ordinarily involved corporations with accumulated or current earnings and profits.

Constructive distributions are usually received by the shareholder himself, but a transfer by the corporation to relatives of the shareholder may

count "loans" with no provision for interest and no ascertainable maturity date are quite vulnerable.[44] Withdrawals that constitute genuine loans when made are not necesarily immune in perpetuity, however, since it may be found in a later year that the corporation has forgiven the debt, an action that constitutes a constructive distribution.[45]

2. *Corporate payments on "loans" by shareholders.* As pointed out earlier (*supra*, Sec. 4.06), if an alleged loan by a shareholder to his corporation is found to be an equity investment in the nature of stock or a contribution to capital, payments of "interest" or "principal" by the corporation will be treated as distributions to him, comparable to dividends or distributions in redemption of his stock.

3. *Corporate payments for shareholder benefit.* This category of informal distributions ranges from borderline expenditures (e.g., for travel and entertainment), where an allocation between the shareholder and the corporation may be in order, to the blatant payment of personal expenses in an aura of fraud. The underlying principle is found in the landmark decision in Old Colony Trust Co. v. Commissioner, 279 U.S. 716, 7 AFTR 8875 (1929), holding that an employee realized income when his legal obligations were discharged

qualify for this status and be taxed to him. And in George W. Knipe, ¶65,131 P-H Memo T.C. (1965), payments (not warranted by business relations) by one corporation to another corporation under common control were taxed as constructive dividends to the shareholders of the payee corporation. This decision seems to be the first in which such payments were treated as constructive dividends, and it raises the possibility of similar treatment where income is reallocated among controlled corporations pursuant to §482; but see Helvering v. Gordon, 87 F.2d 663, 18 AFTR 791 (8th Cir. 1937) (transfer of funds from one controlled corporation to another taxed to shareholder of latter in year of *distribution* rather than in earlier year of transfer).

See generally Comment, Disguised Dividends: A Comprehensive Survey, 3 U.C.L.A. Rev. 207 (1956); Toll, Constructive Dividends, 1951 So. Cal. Tax Inst. 211; Anthony, The Involuntary Dividend: A Constant Hazard to the Tax Planner, 16 J. Tax. 194 (1962).

[44] Jacob M. Kaplan, *supra* note 24; Chism's Estate v. Commissioner, *supra* note 42; Oyster Shell Products Corp. v. Commissioner, 313 F.2d 449, 11 AFTR 2d 777 (2d Cir. 1963); Roschuni v. Commissioner, 29 T.C. 1193 (1958), aff'd per curiam, 271 F.2d 267, 4 AFTR 2d 5759 (5th Cir. 1959); William C. Baird, 25 T.C. 387 (1955); Gurtman v. United States, 237 F. Supp. 533, 15 AFTR 2d 186 (D. N.J. 1965); A. J. Cohen, ¶63,234 P-H Memo TC (1963); Commissioner v. Makransky, 321 F.2d 598, 12 AFTR 2d 5097 (3d Cir. 1963).

See generally Werner, Stockholder Withdrawals — Loans or Dividends?, 10 Tax L. Rev. 569 (1955).

[45] See Regs. §1.301-1(m); Shephard v. Commissioner, 340 F.2d 27, 15 AFTR 2d 123 (6th Cir. 1965); Eustice, *supra* note 19.

If the government relies on an alleged forgiveness as the crucial event, the taxpayer may counter by asserting that the original withdrawal was a constructive distribution, even though he did not report it as such, especially if the statute of limitations has run on that year. Such inconsistencies may be prevented or remedied by the equitable doctrines of estoppel or recoupment or by application of §§1311-1314.

by his employer. The basic issue is whether the corporate expenditure was incurred primarily to benefit the corporation's trade or business, or primarily for the personal benefit of the stockholders. In cases of the latter type, the Service in former years was often content with disallowing deductions at the corporate level, but increasingly its practice has been to couple this disallowance with an assessment against the shareholder on a constructive distribution theory.[46] The line between shareholder benefit and corporate benefit is not always clear, however, because some expenditures embody both elements; and an indirect benefit to the shareholder should not by itself be treated as a distribution to him.[47]

A capital outlay or other investment by the corporation is not ordinarily treated as a constructive distribution to its shareholders; the transaction changes the character of the assets held by the corporation (usually from cash to property) without affecting its net worth or bringing the shareholder any closer to personal enjoyment of the enterprise's earnings. In two areas, however, the benefits indirectly derived by a shareholder from a corporate investment have sometimes led the courts to regard it as a constructive distribution. The redemption by a corporation of the shares of one or more shareholders may be treated as a distribution to the remaining shareholders if they are thereby relieved of a personal liability to pay for the shares; this troublesome subject is discussed *infra*, Sec. 7.25. Similarly, when a corporation pays the premiums on key-man life insurance policies owned by its shareholders, the economic benefit to them amounts to a constructive distribution.[48]

---

[46] See American Properties, Inc., v. Commissioner, 28 T.C. 1100 (1957), aff'd per curiam, 262 F.2d 150, 2 AFTR 2d 6292 (9th Cir. 1958) (expenses of speed boats, paid by a one-man corporation; not deductible by corporation and taxable as disguised dividends to shareholder); Greenspon v. Commissioner, 229 F.2d 947, 48 AFTR 979 (8th Cir. 1956) (corporation's payments for erecting and maintaining "a unique horticultural show place" at stockholder's farm disallowed and taxed as constructive dividends); Sachs v. Commissioner, 277 F.2d 879, 5 AFTR 2d 1291 (8th Cir. 1960) (corporate payment of fine imposed on stockholder-president for filing a fraudulent corporate return taxed as constructive dividend); Jaeger Motor Car Co. v. Commissioner, 284 F.2d 127, 6 AFTR 2d 5874 (7th Cir. 1960) (corporate improvements to property leased from its controlling stockholder); Challenge Mfg. Co., 37 T.C. 650 (1962) (controlling shareholder's personal expenses).

[47] E.g., payments by the corporation to discharge its debts, where the shareholder is secondarily liable (but see *infra*, Sec. 7.25) and corporate contributions to a charity whose purposes are favored by the shareholder (see T.I.R. 457, 1963-11 I.R.B. 27, stating that such contributions will not ordinarily be treated as constructive distributions even if exceeding the 5 percent limit on corporate deductions).

[48] See Prunier v. Commissioner, 248 F.2d 818, 52 AFTR 693 (1st Cir. 1957), where the court went to some lengths to find that the corporation was the equitable owner and beneficiary of the policies; see also Casale v. Commis-

4. Bargain purchases or rentals of corporate property by share-holders. The regulations state that a sale of property by a corporation to its shareholders for less than fair market value is a "distribution" under §301; thus, if a corporation sells property worth $100 to its shareholders for $60, the bargain "spread" of $40 will be treated as a distribution under §301.[49] This rule does not apply, however, to bargain sales by a corporation of its own shares, including distributions of stock rights, for reasons discussed *infra*, Sec. 5.61.

The tax treatment of an option to buy corporate property at its then fair market value, if the option has a value when issued or if there is a "spread" when it is exercised, is not clear. In Palmer v. Commissioner, 302 U.S. 63, 19 AFTR 1201 (1937), the Court held that the distribution of option rights to shareholders entitling them to purchase corporate assets at their then market value did not constitute a taxable distribution, even though the options had a present market value. In addition, the Court held that the shareholders did not realize income on the spread between value and purchase price at the date of exercise of the options; an increase in value after the option was issued, said the Court, did not convert a sale "at market" into a taxable distribution.[50] The *Palmer* principle is not applicable if the option price is less than the property's fair market value when the

sioner, 247 F.2d 440, 52 AFTR 122 (2d Cir. 1957); Sanders v. Fox, 253 F.2d 855, 1 AFTR 2d 1382 (10th Cir. 1958); Rev. Rul. 59-184, 1959-1 C.B. 65 (acquiescing in *Prunier* and *Casale*). The principle of these cases was applied in Edward D. Lacey, 41 T.C. 329 (1963) (Acq.), where the shareholder's estate was the beneficiary of policies owned by the corporation; notwithstanding the Service's acquiescence, cautious advisers are not likely to use the case as a pattern in planning future transactions. See also Paramount-Richards Theaters, Inc. v. Commissioner, 153 F.2d 602, 34 AFTR 931 (5th Cir. 1946) (policies owned by shareholders; held, constructive distribution).

As to the treatment of a shareholder-beneficiary of policies owned by the corporation, see Ducros v. Commissioner, 272 F.2d 49, 4 AFTR 2d 5856 (6th Cir. 1959) (payment exempt under §101(a) rather than a constructive dividend), which will not be followed by the Service, Rev. Rul. 61-134, 1961-2 C.B. 250; see also Charles J. Thornley, 41 T.C. 145 (1963); Storey v. United States, 305 F.2d 733, 10 AFTR 5301 (6th Cir. 1962).

See generally Goldstein, Tax Aspects of Corporate Business Use of Life Insurance, 18 Tax L. Rev. 133 (1963); Sneed, A Defense of the Tax Court's Result in Prunier and Casale, 43 Cornell L.Q. 339 (1958); Smith, Recent Developments in The Field of Corporate Business Purchase Agreements, 14 Tax L. Rev. 413 (1959); Note, The Use of Life Insurance To Fund Agreements Providing For Disposition of A Business at Death, 71 Harv. L. Rev. 687 (1958).

[49] Regs. §1.301-1(j); for examples, see Timberlake v. Commissioner, 132 F.2d 259, 30 AFTR 583 (4th Cir. 1942); Lester E. Dellinger, 32 T.C. 1178 (1959); Lacy v. Commissioner, 341 F.2d 54, 15 AFTR 286 (10th Cir. 1965).

The example in the text assumes that the shareholder is an individual; for the special rules governing distributions of property by one corporation to another, see Regs. §1.301-1(j), discussed *infra,* Sec. 5.23.

[50] See also Robert Lehman, 25 T.C. (1955); Oscar E. Baan, 45 T.C. 71 (1965).

option is issued; and it may also be destined for re-examination in the light of later Supreme Court decisions in the employee stock option area, treating the spread at the time an option is exercised as a taxable occasion.[51]

Like a bargain purchase, a bargain lease of corporate property by a shareholder is a constructive distribution to the extent of the spread between the property's fair rental value and the amount paid by the shareholder.[52] Rather than estimate the rental value of such property, however, the Service may treat the corporation's depreciation charges and maintenance expenses as a constructive distribution to the extent they exceed the rent paid by the shareholder.[53] Where the shareholder-use of corporate property takes the form of an interest-free loan to him of corporate funds, the case for a constructive distribution (equal to interest at a fair rate) is equally persuasive, but as a practical matter the income thus imputed to the shareholder would almost always be offset by an interest deduction under §163; and the only case in point cited this as its reason for holding that there was no distribution.[54]

5. Excessive payments by corporation on purchasing or leasing shareholder's property. This category of constructive distributions is the converse of the preceding one; here the shareholders are receiving too much from the corporation on a sale or lease of *their* property rather than paying too little for *its* property. In either event, the crucial test is whether the parties arrived at arm's length terms in

[51] Choate v. Commissioner, 129 F.2d 684, 29 AFTR 965 (2d Cir. 1942); for employee stock options, see Commissioner v. LoBue, 351 U.S. 243, 49 AFTR 832 (1956), and Regs. §1.421-6.

[52] Rev. Rul. 58-1, 1958-1 C.B. 173; 58th St. Plaza Theatre, Inc. v. Commissioner, 195 F.2d 724, 41 AFTR 1130 (2d Cir. 1952), cert. denied, 344 U.S. 820 (lease to shareholder's wife).

[53] Lash v. Commissioner, ¶56,087 P-H Memo TC, aff'd per curiam, 245 F.2d 20, 51 AFTR 492 (1st Cir. 1957); Challenge Mfg. Co., 37 T.C. 650 (1962); Dean v. Commissioner, 187 F.2d 1019, 40 AFTR 352 (3d Cir. 1951) (citing §61(a) rather than §301); see also International Trading Co. v. Commissioner, 275 F.2d 578, 5 AFTR 2d 970 (7th Cir. 1960), limiting the corporation's deduction for expenses attributable to property rented to its shareholders (at a fair rental) to the rental income on the ground that the excess expenses were not ordinary and necessary under §162; J. Simpson Dean, 9 T.C. 256 (1947), aff'd on other grounds in Dean v. Commissioner, *supra* (rent-free use of corporation's riding horses not a constructive distribution because exercising them was beneficial to corporation); Peacock v. Commissioner, 256 F.2d 160, 1 AFTR 2d 1931 (5th Cir. 1958) (difference between fair rental value and rent paid was intended as tax-free gift by corporation to shareholder).

[54] J. Simpson Dean, 35 T.C. 1083 (1961) (5 judges dissenting); it should be noted that an offsetting deduction under §163 would not be available if the shareholder elected the optional standard deduction or if the imputed interest was non-deductible under §265(2); Rev. Rul. 64-328, 1964-2 C.B. 11 (revoking earlier ruling treating "split-dollar" insurance plan as a tax-free no-interest loan by employer to employee).

their purported sale, lease, or license transaction; if not, the arrangement will be treated as a device for the payment of an informal dividend.[55] Some cases in this area involve the added feature of a distribution in kind of corporate property to the shareholders, followed by a lease-back to the distributing corporation, in the hope of generating a corporate rental expense deduction under §162. The courts have not hesitated to find a lack of business reality in these transactions, treating the "rental" payments as constructive dividends; but the fact that the lessor and lessee are related does not per se produce this result if the transaction otherwise comports with reasonable economic standards.[56]

6. *Excessive salaries paid to the shareholders or their relatives.* Under §162(a), the corporation is entitled to deduct "a reasonable allowance for salaries or other compensation for personal services actually rendered." If no services are rendered, a purported salary may be treated as a constructive distribution under §301 to the stockholder who received it or whose relative or donee received it. It is often assumed that if services are rendered but the compensation paid is excessive, the excess should be treated as a constructive distribution under §301; and this has been the formula used in most excessive compensation cases involving shareholder-employees of closed corporations. It is arguable, however, that a payment might exceed what is "reasonable" under §162(a) without thereby becoming a distribution under §301, and that the entire amount is taxable to the recipient as compensation rather than as a dividend distribution (thus eliminating the need for corporate earnings and profits to support an inclusion in gross income to the recipient).[57] This approach may be particularly

---

[55] Crabtree v. Commissioner, 22 T.C. 61 (1954), aff'd per curiam, 221 F.2d 807, 47 AFTR 777 (2d Cir. 1955) (contingent selling price a disguised dividend); Goldstein v. Commissioner, 298 F.2d 562, 9 AFTR 2d 752 (9th Cir. 1962) (excessive selling price a disguised dividend); A. A. Emmerson, 44 T.C. 86 (1965); but see George J. Staab, 20 T.C. 834 (1953) (bona fide sale). For disallowance of rents and royalties at the corporate level in such transactions, see Potter Electric Signal & Mfg. Co. v. Commissioner, 286 F.2d 200, 7 AFTR 2d 511 (8th Cir. 1961); Stanwick's Inc. v. Commissioner, 15 T.C. 556 (1951), aff'd per curiam, 190 F.2d 84, 40 AFTR 842 (4th Cir. 1951); Byers v. Commissioner, 199 F.2d 273, 42 AFTR 687 (8th Cir. 1952); but see Ransom W. Chase, ¶65,202 P-H Memo TC (1965) (license of shareholder-owned patents to controlled corporation upheld, with discussion of effect of tax motive).

[56] See Armston Co., Inc. v. Commissioner, 188 F.2d 531, 40 AFTR 460 (5th Cir. 1951); Ingle Coal Corp. v. Commissioner, 174 F.2d 569, 37 AFTR 1485 (7th Cir. 1949) (denying corporate deductions); but see Alden B. Oakes, 44 T.C. 524 (1965) (deductions allowed). See generally Oliver, Income Tax Aspects of Gifts and Leasebacks of Business Property in Trust, 51 Corn. L.Q. 21 (1965).

[57] For the "constructive distribution" rationale, see Regs. §1.162-8; J. Warren Leach, 21 T.C. 70 (1953); Quarrier Diner, Inc., ¶63,069 P-H Memo T.C. (1963). For assessments predicated on §61(a) rather §301, see Sterno

apt where the excessive compensation payments are not proportional to stockholdings. On this theory, an alleged salary might be allocated among a combination of the following three categories: (a) compensation, deductible by the corporation under §162 and taxable to the recipient as compensation; (b) unreasonable compensation, not deductible by the corporation under §162 but taxable to the recipient as compensation; and (c) distributions disguised as compensation, not deductible by the corporation and taxable to the shareholder (who is not necessarily the recipient) only under §301.

A gratuitous payment by a corporation to the widow of a deceased stockholder may, in appropriate cases, be treated as a distribution under §301. While most of the widow-payment litigation has focused on claims that the receipt was a tax-free gift under §102, some courts have found such payments to be disguised distributions, particularly if the widow owned a substantial stock interest in the corporation, either directly or as beneficiary of her husband's estate.[58]

7. *Unlawful diversion of corporate income by shareholder.* Fraudulent devices by which shareholders intercepted payments by customers before they reached the corporate treasury, collected kick-backs from suppliers, etc., have often been treated as constructive distributions; but the courts have sometimes relied on §61(a) rather than §301 in order to uphold deficiencies assessed against the shareholders

---

Sales Corp. v. United States, 345 F.2d 552, 15 AFTR 2d 979 (Ct. Cl. 1965); Bone v. United States, 46 F.2d 1010, 9 AFTR 856 (M.D. Ga. 1931).

It has been shown that originally the phrase here involved — "including a reasonable allowance for salaries or other compensation for personal services actually rendered" — was intended not as a *limitation* on §162(a)'s blanket allowance of "all ordinary and necessary business expenses," but rather as an authorization to deduct an additional allowance for services where the salary *actually* paid or incurred therefor was inadequate. Griswold, New Light on "A Reasonable Allowance for Salaries," 59 Harv. L. Rev. 286 (1945). The contrary belief, that the phrase was intended to restrict rather than to enlarge what would otherwise be deductible as a business expense, however, is apparently imbedded beyond correction. See Waits, Inc. v. Commissioner, ¶47,003 P-H Memo T.C.; and note that the 1954 Code re-enacted the phrase after innumerable cases had interpreted it as a limitation on the deduction of business expenses.

See generally Brodsky, What Constitutes Reasonable Compensation: Contingent Plans; Factors in Proving Reasonableness of Compensation, 19 N.Y.U. Inst. on Fed. Tax. 169 (1961).

[58] See Barbourville Brick Co., 37 T.C. 7 (1961); Lengsfield v. Commissioner, 241 F.2d 508, 50 AFTR 1683 (5th Cir. 1957); and Schner-Block Co., Inc. v. Commissioner, 329 F.2d 875, 13 AFTR 2d 1081 (2d Cir. 1964). The cases are collected in Rubber Associates, Inc. v. Commissioner, 335 F.2d 75, 14 AFTR 2d 5260 (6th Cir. 1964). See also Montgomery Engineering Co. v. United States, 230 F. Supp. 838, 13 AFTR 2d 1747 (D.N.J. 1964), where the widow owned no stock in the corporation, but the payment was held to be a constructive dividend to an unrelated controlling stockholder who caused the corporation to make the payment because he felt a moral obligation to correct an injustice which he felt had been done to the widow by her deceased husband.

without regard to the corporation's earnings and profits account.[59] When Commissioner v. Wilcox, 327 U.S. 404, 34 AFTR 811 (1946), holding that embezzled funds were not taxable to the embezzler, was in force, the government sought to avoid this decision in unlawful diversion cases by proceeding on a constructive distribution theory under §301. With the overruling of *Wilcox* by James v. United States, 366 U.S. 313, 7 AFTR 2d 1361 (1961), this strategy became unnecessary; and an assessment under §61(a) became preferable from the government's point of view because taxability then does not turn on the corporation's earnings and profits account. Despite the authority upholding this approach, much can be said for the contrary view that an unlawful diversion of corporate funds is a constructive distribution pure and simple.

Sec. 5.06.　Dividends received exclusion and credit for individuals

Bowing to the "double taxation" argument (*supra*, Sec. 1.03), Congress in 1954 enacted §116 and §34, providing for relief at the shareholder level in the form of a dividends received exclusion of $50 per taxable year and a credit of 4 per cent of dividends received above the amount excluded. (Only noncorporate taxpayers qualified for these allowances; corporations were entitled to deduct a portion, ordinarily 85 percent, of dividends received under §§243-246, *supra*, Sec. 2.25.) These provisions were the most controversial aspect of the 1954 Code revisions;[60] and the 4 percent credit allowed by §34 survived only until 1964, when it was reduced to 2 percent for dividends received in 1964 and repealed for dividends received thereafter. There was a concomitant 1964 change in the exclusion, however, by which it was increased to $100.

In computing the exclusion under §116, the taxpayer excludes from gross income the first $100 of dividends received during the taxable year; on a joint return, the total exclusion will be $200 if each spouse has at least $100 of dividend income. Thus, if each receives $250 of dividends, $200 is excluded and $300 included in gross income. If the husband receives $150 of dividends and the wife only $50, the amount excluded is $150 ($100 for the husband and $50 for the wife)

---

[59] See DiZenzo v. Commissioner, 348 F.2d 122, 16 AFTR 2d 5107 (2d Cir. 1965), which cites and discusses the earlier cases; Schmidt, *Legal and Accounting Handbook of Federal Tax Fraud*, pp.282-286 (1963). If the diversion is treated as a constructive distribution, the earnings and profits account must be adjusted to reflect the deficiencies, penalties, and interest for which the corporation is liable. See *supra*, Sec. 5.04.

[60] For the policy issues, see Smith, Two Years of Republican Tax Policy: An Economic Appraisal, 8 Nat. Tax J. 2 (1955); Shoup, The Dividend Exclusion and Credit in the Revenue Code of 1954, *ibid.* 136.

and the amount included is $50. Under Regs. §1.116-1(c), the dividends on stock held in a tenancy in common or by the entirety are to be treated as received by each tenant in accordance with his rights under local law, and dividends on community property stock are considered as received one-half by each spouse. The exclusion is available only to "individuals" (excluding certain nonresident aliens); special rules govern dividends received by a partnership, trust or estate.[61]

Dividends qualify for the exclusion of §116 only if paid by a domestic corporation. Moreover, since §116 was enacted to mitigate the "double taxation" of corporate earnings, dividends paid by the following corporations, all of which receive certain tax concessions at the corporate level, do not qualify for further relief at the shareholder level:

1. Mutual savings banks and domestic building and loan corporations, if the "dividend" (often called "interest") is deductible by the corporation under §591 (amounts paid to depositors and holders of withdrawable accounts).

2. Regulated investment companies (supra, Sec. 1.06), except as provided in §854(b).

3. Corporations that have elected to be taxed under Subchapter S (infra, ch. 14), to the extent the dividends are out of earnings and profits of the taxable year under §316(a)(2).

4. Corporations that, for the year of distribution or the preceding year, are exempt from tax under §501 or §521 or are entitled to the special treatment accorded to "Possessions Corporations" (supra, Sec. 1.06).

5. China Trade Act corporations (supra, Sec. 1.06).

6. So-called dividends that are refunds of amounts paid by the taxpayer, such as "dividends" received by the owner of an insurance policy as a partial refund of premiums paid by him.

Sec. 5.07. Assignments of dividend income

On a gift, sale, or other transfer of stock, it is often necessary to determine whether dividend income on the transferred shares is to be reported by the transferor or transferee. This question can be answered only in the context of broad assignment-of-income principles, an area that is beyond the scope of this work;[62] and little more can be

---

[61] If stock is owned by a partnership, each partner takes into account his "distributive share" of the dividends received, see §702 and § 704. If dividends received by an estate or trust are allocable to the beneficiaries, each beneficiary includes his share in computing the exclusion on his individual return; the estate or trust is entitled to the exclusion not allocable to the beneficiaries. See §642(a), §652(b), and §662(b).

[62] See generally Lyon and Eustice, Assignment of Income: Fruit and Tree as Irrigated by the P. G. Lake Case, 17 Tax L. Rev. 293, 362 (1962); Eustice,

done here than to suggest some of the issues and possible solutions.

So far as gifts are concerned, it is well established that the assignment of the right to receive a future dividend, without an accompanying transfer of the underlying stock, will not shift taxability of the dividends to the donee.[63] If the stock itself is transferred, however, the record date is the relevant cut-off point for assignment of income purposes (i.e., if the gift occurs after the record date, the donor is taxable on the assigned dividend income; but if the gift precedes this date, the dividend income is taxed to the donee).[64] Controlling shareholders sometimes waive their dividend rights for a period of time to strengthen the corporation's financial position; although this action is not likely to be treated as a constructive assignment of dividend income to the non-waiving minority shareholders if it serves a bona fide business purpose, it is vulnerable if the beneficiaries of the waiver are members of the controlling shareholder's family.[65]

An attempt to convert anticipated dividend income into capital gain by selling the right to receive the dividend after the record date

Contract Rights, Capital Gain and Assignment of Income: The Ferrer Case, 20 Tax L. Rev. 1 (1965); Rice, Judicial Trends in Gratuitous Assignments to Avoid Federal Income Taxes, 64 Yale L.J. 991 (1955).

[63] Regs. §1.61-9(c); Margaret G. Dunham, 35 T.C. 705 (1961); Overton v. Commissioner, 162 F.2d 155, 35 AFTR 1427 (2d Cir. 1947) (assignment of stock whose only effect was, or was thought to be, a shifting of dividend income to taxpayers' wives ignored as a sham); Choate v. Commissioner, 129 F.2d 684, 29 AFTR 965 (2d Cir. 1942) (assignment of stock rights taxable to donor when exercised by donee). If the stock is transferred in trust, however, the dividend income will not be taxed to the grantor if the statutory rules of §§671-678 do not so require, even though ownership of the stock may revert to him at some future date. Moreover, a transfer of the right to dividends for a long period of years (e.g., more than 10 years) may be effective, on the ground that the transfer is comparable to a long-term trust. See generally Helvering v. Horst, 311 U.S. 112, 24 AFTR 1058 (1940); Rev. Rul. 55-38, 1955-1 C.B. 389.

For the converse (where the stock is transferred but the right to the dividends is reserved), see Willard S. Heminway, 44 T.C. 96 (1965), holding that a transfer of stock with a reservation of dividend income by the transferor for life did not shift taxability on the dividends to transferee; United States v. Georgia R.R. & Banking Co., 348 F.2d 278, 16 AFTR 2d 5061 (5th Cir. 1965) (lessee of stock taxable on dividends).

[64] Transfers after record date: I.T. 4007, 1950-1 C.B. 11; Lillian M. Newman, 1 T.C. 921 (1943); but cf. Machette v. Helvering, 81 F.2d 73, 17 AFTR 186 (2d Cir. 1936). Transfers before record date: Bishop v. Shaughnessy, 195 F.2d 683, 41 AFTR 1116 (2d Cir. 1952) (gift of preferred stock with dividend arrearages); Smith's Estate v. Commissioner, 292 F.2d 478, 8 AFTR 2d 5040 (3d Cir. 1961) (contra, but on unusual facts); Rev. Rul. 60-331, 1960-2 C.B. 198 (ditto). See generally, Cutler, Dividend Arrearages, 37 Taxes 309 (1959).

See also Estate of Putnam v. Commissioner, 324 U.S. 393, 33 AFTR 599 (1945), holding that §691 ("income in respect of decedent") does not apply to dividends declared on stock owned by a taxpayer if he dies before the record date. Rev. Rul. 64-308, 1964-2 C.B. 176, is to the same effect for constructive dividends on stock in a Subchapter S corporation (infra, Ch. 14).

[65] See Rev. Rul. 65-256, 1965-46 I.R.B. p. 27, citing earlier rulings; cf. Hodgkins' Estate, ¶65,225 P-H Memo TC (1965); XIX ABA Tax Section Bulletin, p. 134 (Jan., 1966).

but before the payment date was rejected in Estate of Rhodes v. Commissioner, 131 F.2d 50, 30 AFTR 220 (6th Cir. 1942). A sale of stock "dividend-on," however, generally produces capital gain or loss to the seller.[66] This approach, which differs from the practice of requiring a seller of a bond to report the interest accrued to the date of sale under Regs. §1.61-7(d), seems largely a matter of administrative convenience; and it would not prevent the Service, in an extreme case, from invoking assignment-of-income principles to require part of the proceeds from a sale of stock just before the record date to be allocated to dividend arrears or even to dividends about to vest in the record owner.[67] Identification of the proper taxpayer is often troublesome in the case of a bootstrap sale of corporate stock, where dividends are credited against the purchase price. The Regulations, §1.61-9(c), provide that such dividends are taxable to the purchaser even though he is not the legal owner of the stock and does not receive the dividends, if the seller retains legal title to the stock solely to secure payment. In such case, the full sales proceeds, including the portion defrayed by the dividends, will enter into the calculation of the seller's capital gain or loss.[68]

Part B.   Distributions in Kind

Sec. 5.20.   Introductory

When a corporation distributes cash to its shareholders, the tax consequences to both the recipient and his corporation can be easily determined if the corporation's earnings and profits are known. The distribution is a "dividend" to the extent of the corporation's current and accumulated post-1913 earnings and profits; the balance, if any, is applied against and reduces the adjusted basis of the shareholder's stock under §301(c)(2); and any excess is subject to §301(c)(3). The shareholder, having received cash, has no problem of basis. As to the corporation, the distribution itself is not a taxable event; and its earnings and profits are reduced to the extent that the distribution is a "dividend" to the shareholders.

---

[66] Regs. §1.61-9(c); Eugenia R. Jemison, 28 B.T.A. 514 (1933); Stanley D. Beard, 4 T.C. 756 (1945). The same principle governs the transfer of stock with dividend arrearages. See Cutler, *supra* note 64, at 320.

[67] Brundage v. United States, 275 F.2d 424, 5 AFTR 2d 740 (7th Cir. 1960), cert. denied, 364 U.S. 831 (1961).

[68] See O'Brien Co. v. Commissioner, 301 F.2d 813, 9 AFTR 2d 1217 (3rd Cir. 1962); Steel Improvement and Forge Co. v. Commissioner, 314 F.2d 96, 11 AFTR 2d 953 (6th Cir. 1963); DeGuire v. Higgins, 159 F.2d 921, 35 AFTR 868 (2d Cir. 1947); Grayck, Taxing Income That is Applied Against the Purchase Price, 12 Tax L. Rev. 381 (1957).

When we turn from a corporate distribution of cash to a distribution in kind,[69] however, the problems quickly proliferate. Does the mere distribution of appreciated property create corporate income or earnings and profits? Does the distribution of depreciated property produce a corporate loss? If the distribution itself does not produce corporate gain or loss, is a prompt sale of appreciated or depreciated property by the distributees to be treated as a corporate transaction, so that the gain or loss will be imputed to the corporation? Does a distribution of property come "out of" current or post-1913 earnings and profits (so as to constitute a "dividend") if the earnings and profits exceed the adjusted basis of the property but are less than its fair market value? Are the corporation's earnings and profits to be reduced by the fair market value of the distributed property, or by its adjusted basis? What is the basis of the distributed property in the hands of the shareholders?

Before the 1954 Code was enacted, these questions engaged the attention of the most acute commentators on the federal income tax. Their answers were far from unanimous, and the judicial opinions were usually unsatisfactory. Many of the disputed issues have been settled by the 1954 Code, however, and the status of pre-1954 distributions will be discussed hereafter only as background to the new rules.[70]

Sec. 5.21.   Corporate income or loss on distribution of property

Before 1954, the Treasury on a number of occasions advanced the theory that a corporation, on distributing appreciated property to its shareholders, realized taxable income just as though it had sold the property for its fair market value or used it to satisfy an obligation in that amount. The courts consistently rejected the Treasury's argument, usually with a citation to General Utilities & Operating Co. v. Helvering, 296 U.S. 200, 16 AFTR 1126 (1935). In fact, although the government had argued for the recognition of taxable income upon a

---

[69] The term "distribution in kind" is used here to mean a distribution of property other than money or the distributing corporation's own stock or obligations.

[70] See generally Scott, Taxation of Corporate Distributions in Kind, 12 Stan. L. Rev. 529 (1960); Mintz and Plumb, Dividends in Kind — The Thunderbolt and the New Look, 10 Tax L. Rev. 41 (1954), and their Postscript, ibid., 405 (discussing both pre- and post-1954 law); Tritt, Corporate Distributions of Property, 1957 So. Cal. Tax Inst. 69; Alexander, supra note 31; Raum, Dividends in Kind — Their Tax Aspects, 63 Harv. L. Rev. 593 (1950); Block, Non-Liquidating Corporate Distributions: Effect on Income and Earnings and Profits, 17 N.Y.U. Inst. on Fed. Tax 267 (1959); North, Corporate Distributions of Appreciated Property — A Comment on Policy; 36 Nebr. L. Rev. 528 (1957); Johnson, Corporation and Stockholder — Dividends in Kind, 1 Tax L. Rev. 86 (1945); Wallace, A Dissent, ibid., 93.

distribution of appreciated property in the *General Utilities & Operating Co.* case, the Supreme Court did not find it necessary to pass on this issue;[71] but even though the question was not foreclosed by that case, the result reached by the lower courts was endorsed, at least for the future, by the enactment in 1954 of §311(a)(2).

Section 311(a)(2) provides, with four exceptions, that "no gain or loss shall be recognized to a corporation on the distribution, with respect to its stock, of . . . property." The provision is applicable, it will be noted, only if the corporation makes a distribution "with respect to its stock." The regulations state:

> Section 311 does not apply to transactions between a corporation and a shareholder in his capacity as debtor, creditor, employee, or vendee, where the fact that such debtor, creditor, employee, or vendee is a shareholder is incidental to the transaction. (Regs. §1.311-1(e)(1).)

Thus, if the corporation sells property to one of its shareholders in the ordinary course of business, the corporation's gain or loss will be recognized in the usual manner, since the fact that the buyer is a shareholder is incidental to the transaction. Gain or loss would also be recognized by a corporation that used property to pay compensation to an employee who happened also to be a shareholder or to discharge a debt held by a shareholder.[72]

---

[71] The government's argument on this point was as follows:
. . . In making it [the appreciation] available to its own stockholders the corporation is realizing the appreciation, and nothing more is necessary. It is our view that the addition to surplus on account of the increased value and the distribution of this increased value in satisfaction of the company's general liability to its stockholders, are the evidence that the gain has been realized, for it is incomprehensible how a corporation can distribute to its stockholders something which it has not itself received . . . It is clear that petitioner used the increased value for a corporate purpose, and was thereby enabled to pay its stockholders $1,071,426.25. Thus was petitioner serving the principal end for which it was organized — to earn profits which it would distribute to its stockholders — and we submit that in so justifying the hopes of its organizers this economic entity, called a corporation, truly derived an economic gain. (Respondent's brief, pp. 18, 25.)
The Supreme Court refused to consider this issue, which was not raised below; the only government argument it noticed was that the corporation's dividend resolution created an indebtedness to the shareholders, which was satisfied by the use of appreciated property. It has been argued that in rejecting this argument, the Court must have assumed *a fortiori* that the mere distribution of the appreciated property was not a taxable event; but there is a big difference beween answering a question and assuming an answer in the absence of timely argument.
For the pre-1954 cases mentioned in the text, see Molloy, Some Tax Aspects of Corporate Distributions in Kind, 6 Tax L. Rev. 57, 60, n. 20 (1950).
[72] Northern Coal & Dock Co., 12 T.C. 42 (1949) (Acq.); see also the Senate Report on the 1954 Code, which states:

Before 1954, there were several cases in which a corporation realized gain or loss on the distribution of appreciated or depreciated property to its shareholders, because the resolution authorizing the distribution created an obligation in terms of money. In Bacon-McMillan Veneer Co., 20 B.T.A. 556 (1930), for example, the dividend resolution provided for a "fifty per cent dividend" (evidently 50 percent of the stock's par value), "payable in Liberty Loan Bonds in denominations of $1,000.00 each, at their market value this date," with odd amounts to be paid in cash. The court held that the corporation, on using the bonds to defray the indebtedness created by the dividend resolution, realized income in an amount equal to the excess of the fair market value of the bonds over their adjusted basis:

> The resolution provided that a 50 percent dividend be declared. A 50 per cent dividend is a definite amount. It created an obligation of the corporation to its stockholders. Then when that obligation was satisfied by the distribution of the Liberty bonds owned by the [corporation], we have a realization of a gain through disposition thereof. When the dividend of 50 percent was declared the corporation could not satisfy the legal demands of the stockholders by delivering to them bonds less than that value. The corporation discharged its obligations to its stockholders by giving them the bonds which here had a value in excess of the cost. We think that this is a realization of gain in every substantial sense of the word.[73]

The status of these cases is not entirely clear under the 1954 Code. It is at least arguable that the distribution is made to the shareholder "with respect to his stock" (so as to invoke the non-recognition rule of §311(a)), even though he is also a creditor of the corporation. But it is by no means clear that the pre-1954 cases were to be overruled by the enactment of §311(a), and these cases might be preserved on the ground that it is not the distribution, but the satisfaction of the debt, that produces gain or loss. The issue can ordinarily be avoided, if the property has appreciated in value, by a divided resolution referring only to the property, since, if there is no indebtedness measurable

---

Your committee does not intend, however, through [§311(a)(2)] to alter existing law in the case of distributions of property, which has appreciated or depreciated in value, where such distributions are made . . . to shareholders in a capacity other than that of a shareholder. For example, distribution of property made to a shareholder in his capacity as a creditor of the distributing corporation is not within the rule of [§311(a)]. (S. Rep. No. 1622, 83d Cong., 2d Sess. p. 247.)

[73] 20 B.T.A. at 559; see also Callanan Road Improvement Co., 12 B.T.A. 1109 (1928) (Acq.) (loss on distribution of depreciated property); Mintz and Plumb, *supra* note 70, at 44, n. 15, and 53-54.

in dollars, the *Bacon-McMillan Veneer Co.* rationale is inapplicable.[74] If the property has depreciated in value, on the other hand, the corporation may find it feasible to realize a deductible loss by selling the property and distributing only the proceeds to its shareholders.

A major uncertainty in the scope of §311(a) was created by the statement in the Senate Report on the 1954 Code (S. Rep. No. 1622, 83d Cong., 2d Sess., p. 247) that "your committee does not intend to change existing law with respect to attribution of income of shareholders to their corporation as exemplified for example in the case of *Commissioner* v. *First State Bank of Stratford* [168 F.2d 1004, 36 AFTR 1183 (5th Cir. 1948), cert. denied 335 U.S. 867]." That case was concerned with the tax consequences of a distribution by a bank to its shareholders of certain notes that it had written off as worthless in earlier years. Despite the write-offs, the notes were thought at the time of distribution to be collectible in part. They were endorsed by the bank (without recourse) to one of its employees, who proceeded to make collections on them as though they were still owned by the bank, except that the proceeds were deposited in a special account for the benefit of the shareholders. The court held that the collections were income to the bank, but the basis of the opinion is far from clear. One thought running through it is that the bank's enjoyment of a tax benefit from writing the notes off as worthless carried with it an obligation to report any later recoveries as taxable income. But the court also suggested that the bank was taxable on the broader theory that the distribution itself was an anticipatory assignment of income, comparable to the gift of bond coupons in Helvering v. Horst, 311 U.S. 112, 24 AFTR 1058 (1940):

> Even though the bank never received the money, it derived money's worth from the disposition of the notes which it used in place of money in procuring a satisfaction that was procurable only by the expenditure of money or money's worth. The enjoyment of the economic benefit was realized as completely as it would have been if the bank had collected the notes in dollars and cents and paid the money as a dividend to its shareholders . . .

[74] See Natural Gasoline Corp. v. Commissioner, 219 F.2d 682, 46 AFTR 1748 (10th Cir. 1955) (ambiguous resolution construed as property distribution); General Utilities & Operating Co. v. Helvering, *supra*.

The narrow statutory ground of Rev. Rul. 55-410, 1955-1 C.B. 297 (holding that the satisfaction of a charitable pledge, made in a dollar amount, with appreciated or depreciated property does not produce gain or loss), distinguishes it from the dividend resolution cases, but its spirit is hostile to the recognition of gain or loss.

> The acquisition of profits for its shareholders was the purpose of its creation. The collection of interest on loans was a principal source of its income. The payment of dividends to its shareholders was the enjoyment of its income. A body corporate can be said to enjoy its income in no other way. Like the "life-rendering pelican," it feeds its shareholders upon dividends (168 F.2d at 1009.)

This portion of the opinion seems to mean that the corporation must recognize income on the distribution of any property with a value greater than its basis, at least if the shareholders sell the property or otherwise realize income from it. Moreover, the court's reasoning comes perilously close to the argument of the government in the *General Utilities & Operating Co.* case, that a distribution of appreciated property is itself a taxable realization by the corporation of the increase in value, even if the property is not thereafter sold by the shareholders.[75]

Since the Senate Report, quoted above, states that the *Stratford Bank* case is only an "example" of the existing law which is left undisturbed by §311(a), we must cope with the possibility that there are other examples of the "attribution of income of shareholders to their corporation." The *Court Holding Co.* case, 324 U.S. 331, 33 AFTR 593 (1945), is a classic example of this doctrine; there a corporation was about to sell an appreciated apartment house, but the corporate negotiations were called off at the last minute in favor of a distribution of the property in complete liquidation of the corporation, followed by a sale of the property by the shareholders. The Supreme Court upheld the Tax Court's determination that the corporation was taxable on the profit from the sale of the property, although the sale was in form made by the shareholders:

> A sale by one person [the corporation] cannot be transformed for tax purposes into a sale by another by using the latter as a conduit through which to pass title . . . [T]he executed sale was in substance the sale of the corporation. (324 U.S. at 334.)

Nothing in §311(a), providing that the corporation shall not recognize gain or loss on the "distribution" of property, undercuts the theory of the *Court Holding Co.* case, under which income is attributed to the

---

[75] *Supra*, note 71. See generally Lyon and Eustice, Assignment of Income: Fruit and Tree as Irrigated by the P. G. Lake Case, 17 Tax L. Rev. 293, 396 (1962); Eustice, Contract Rights, Capital Gain, and Assignment of Income — the Ferrer Case, 20 Tax L. Rev. 1, 54 (1964).

corporation not because of the distribution, but because of a factual determination that the sale by the shareholders "was in substance the sale of the corporation."[76]

Another example of pre-1954 law on the attribution of shareholder income to the corporation that may have survived the enactment of §311(a) is United States v. Lynch, 192 F.2d 718, 41 AFTR 407 (9th Cir. 1951), cert. denied, 343 U.S. 934 (1952), requiring a corporation to report income realized by its shareholders on the sale of fruit that had been distributed to them as a dividend in kind. The fruit was part of the corporation's inventory; after the distribution, the corporation proceeded to market the fruit in its customary manner, except that it acted on behalf of its shareholders rather than on its own account. The court said:

> The dividend in question was not the kind of a distribution contemplated by the statute, . . . and must be ignored for tax purposes. Distribution of corporate inventory with the expectation of immediate sale by the shareholders pointedly suggests a transaction outside the range of normal commercially-motivated and justifiable corporate activity, yet we have here a stronger case, because the sale was to be made by utilizing the corporation's facilities in the ordinary course of its business; the shareholders did not engage in a separate and independent business in which the apples were to be used. (192 F.2d at 720).

The court in the *Lynch* case relied heavily on Commissioner v. Transport Trading & Terminal Corp. 176 F.2d 570, 38 AFTR 365 (2d Cir. 1949), cert. denied, 338 U.S. 955 (1950), where the Court of Appeals for the Second Circuit indicated that it might go so far as to attribute the profit on a sale to the corporation even if there had been no corporate negotiations or use of corporate selling facilities and even if non-inventory property was involved, merely because the distribution served no non-tax function and was made in the expectation that the distributee would sell the distributed property immediately after receiving it.

It seems likely, then, that in preserving "existing law with respect to attribution of income of shareholders to their corporation," the

---

[76] As will be seen (*infra*, Sec. 9.63), the *Court Holding Co.* doctrine has been somewhat limited by United States v. Cumberland Public Service Co., 338 U.S. 451, 38 AFTR 978 (1950), and §337 of the 1954 Code (*infra*, Sec. 9.64) made it inapplicable to certain sales in conjunction with a complete liquidation; but its heart is otherwise intact, unimpaired by the enactment of §311(a). See General Guaranty Mortgage Co., Inc. v. Tomlinson, 335 F.2d 518, 14 AFTR 2d 5324 (5th Cir. 1964), applying the *Court Holding Co.* principle to tax a distributing corporation on proceeds collected by its sole shareholder on the prearranged termination of an exclusive service contract.

1954 Code requires the corporation to report not only the kind of income involved in the *Stratford Bank* case, *i.e.* the proceeds of property with a zero basis, the cost of which was previously written off with tax benefit. The corporation can probably also be taxed under the *Court Holding Co.* doctrine, where a corporate transaction is called off at the last minute; under the *Lynch* case, where inventory property is distributed and corporate facilities are thereafter employed to market the property in the usual manner;[77] and possibly also under the *Transport & Trading Corp.* theory, where a sale by the distributee is expected and the distribution serves no non-tax purpose.[78]

The foregoing discussion has centered on the attribution of taxable gain to the corporation. If the property has depreciated in value, and is sold by the distributees for less than its adjusted basis to the corporation, can the corporation claim a loss on the ground that there was "really" a sale by it? Although there appear to be no cases in point, the *Court Holding Co.* case might be applied in appropriate circumstances, unless the courts are prepared to hold that the taxpayers must stand by the form of their transaction even if the government is not bound by it. Ordinarily the shareholders would seek to avoid the issue by having the corporation sell any depreciated property in its own name. Such a transaction in its turn might be attacked by the government with still another variation on the *Court Holding Co.* theme: if a plan to distribute depreciated property was "called off" at the last moment after the shareholders had arranged for a sale, a pur-

---

[77] Section 311(b), providing that the excess of non-LIFO value over LIFO value is taxable to the corporation at the time of distribution, does not stand in the way of attributing income to the corporation on a later sale of the property by the shareholders. The profit at that time would be calculated on the non-LIFO value. Since the Senate Report refers to the "attribution of income," however, it is not clear whether a loss could be claimed by the corporation if the sales price were less than the non-LIFO value.

[78] In the liquidation area, the *Cumberland Public Service Co.* case, cited *supra*, note 76, and discussed *infra*, Sec. 9.63, conflicts with the spirit of the *Transport & Trading Corp.* case, since the former honors a liquidating distribution for the sole purpose of enabling the distributees to sell the property. But it is less clear that the same respect would be paid to a tax-motivated distribution by a going concern; there is a hint to this effect in the Court's statement in *Cumberland* that "[t]he corporate tax is thus aimed primarily at the profits of a going concern." 338 U.S. at 455. Moreover, a liquidation, whatever its motivation, has non-tax consequences that do not flow from a non-liquidating distribution.

See ABCD Lands, Inc., 41 T.C. 840 (1964), where the Tax Court blended and expanded the principles of *Lynch* and *Transport Trading* to tax a corporation which distributed crop share rents to its shareholders with the "expectation" that the crops would be sold by the shareholders immediately after the dividend distribution; but see Rev. Rul. 57-490, 1957-2 C.B. 231 (corporation distributing inventoried crops as a dividend in kind to its shareholders protected by §311(a)).

ported sale by the corporation followed by a distribution of the proceeds might be regarded as "in substance" a distribution of the property itself coupled with a sale by the shareholders. Viewed as a shareholder transaction, the sale would not give rise to a deduction by the corporation.

To the general rule of §311(a) that the corporation shall not recognize gain or loss on the distribution of property with respect to its stock, there are these statutory exceptions:

1. LIFO inventory. On a distribution of LIFO inventory, §311(b) requires the distributing corporation to recognize gain to the extent (if any) that the LIFO value is less than the basis determined by a non-LIFO method. (Ordinarily this would be FIFO, although the taxpayer apparently has some range for choice, since §311(b)(1)(A) speaks merely of "a" method authorized by §471.) The difference between the LIFO and non-LIFO values is thus belatedly taken into income.

2. Liability in excess of basis. On a distribution of property that is subject to a liability, or in connection with the distribution of which the shareholder assumes a liability, §311(c) requires the corporation to recognize gain to the extent that the liability exceeds the adjusted basis of the property. (If the liability is not assumed, the gain to be recognized by the corporation may not exceed the excess of the value of the property over its adjusted basis.) In effect, the distribution is treated as a sale of the property for the amount of the liability, with the proceeds being applied to satisfy the liability for which the corporation is now only secondarily liable. The statute does not expressly so state, but presumably if the liability is not paid by the shareholder or satisfied by the property by which it is secured, the corporation on paying will have a deductible loss or bad debt.[79]

3. Installment obligations. On a distribution of installment obligations, §§311(a) and 453(d) require the corporation to recognize gain or loss to the extent of the difference between the basis of the obligation and its fair market value at the time of distribution.

4. Depreciable property. On a distribution of appreciated "section 1245 property," the depreciation "recapture" rules of §1245 will override §311(a)(2) and cause recognition of gain to the distributing corporation to the extent of prior depreciation deductions taken with respect to such property. Similar, though less stringent, treatment applies to dividend distributions of real estate covered by §1250.

5. Investment credit property. A comparable adjustment

---

[79] However, the excess of the property's value over the amount of the liability thereon (i.e., the net equity value) is protected by the nonrecognition rule of §311(a). See the somewhat analogous treatment of liabilities in excess of basis by §357(c), *supra*, Sec. 3.06.

must be made in the event of a distribution that constitutes an "early disposition" of "section 38 property" (property giving rise to an investment credit under §38), but the adjustment takes the form of an increase in the tax itself, rather than an addition to taxable income. See §47(a)(1).

Sec. 5.22.   Taxability of distribution to individual distributees

The tax on the recipient of a distribution in kind depends, by virtue of a 1954 change in the Internal Revenue Code, upon whether the recipient is a corporation or an individual (including estates, trusts, and other non-corporate taxpayers).

To take first the case of noncorporate distributee, if the value of the distributed property is fully covered by the corporation's current or post-1913 earnings and profits, the distribution is a taxable "dividend" to the extent of its fair market value, under §§301(b)(1)(A), 301(c), and 316.[80] If the value of the distributed property exceeds the corporation's current and post-1913 earnings and profits, however, the regulations state that the distribution is a "dividend" only to the extent of the earnings and profits. Regs. §1.316-1(a)(2). The balance would reduce the basis of the distributee's stock under §301(c)(2), with any excess over basis being subject to §301(c)(3). The regulations illustrate the principle that the distribution is a "dividend" only to the extent of the corporation's earnings and profits in the following way:

[80] §301(b)(1)(A) provides that, in case of a noncorporate distributee, the "amount" of a distribution in kind is its fair market value, adjusted under §301(b)(2) for liabilities assumed by the shareholder or to which the distributed property is subject. By virtue of §301(b)(3), fair market value is to be determined "as of the date of the distribution." This date may differ from the date when the distribution is includible in gross income, according to Regs. §1.301-1(b). (But query whether, if the date of inclusion in gross income *precedes* the date of distribution and the property increases in value between the two dates, the higher value can be included in computing income on the earlier date.) Note also that a distribution may become a "dividend" by virtue of earnings and profits arising during the taxable year but after the date of distribution. §316(a)(2).

These principles are subject to an exception in the case of distributions of stock in compliance with anti-trust decrees, under §1111, the so-called Du Pont tax relief provision, enacted in 1962 to govern the distribution of General Motors stock by Du Pont under an anti-trust decree. The legislation and committee reports are reprinted in 1962-1 C.B. 370 and 375; see also Hearings on Tax Aspects of Du Pont Divestiture, Senate Finance Committee, 89th Cong., 1st Sess. (March 17 and 24, 1965). In general, the mechanics of this relief are as follows: (1) the distribution is treated as a return of capital under §301-(c)(2) and (3) to noncorporate shareholders, §1111(a); (2) "general" corporate shareholders follow the normal dividend in kind rules with respect to such distribution, §1111(b); and (3) "specially treated corporate shareholders," who were parties to the antitrust proceedings, are taxed on the fair market value of the distributed stock, §301(f)(2), and determine their basis for such stock under the special rules of §301(f)(3).

Example. X and Y, individuals, each own one-half of the stock of Corporation A which has earnings and profits of $10,000. Corporation A distributes property having a basis of $6,000 and a fair market value of $16,000 to its shareholders, each shareholder receiving property with a basis of $3,000 and with a fair market value of $8,000 in a distribution to which section 301 applies. The amount taxable to each shareholder as a dividend under section 301(c) is $5,000. (Regs. §1.316-1(a)(3), Example.)

The issue that is so calmly resolved by this example was heatedly debated under both the 1939 and 1954 Codes; and the debate is not yet over. Even a recapitulation of the debate under the 1939 Code would be too lengthy, so we must content ourselves here with saying that the two principal competing views were: (a) That a shareholder could never be required to report more dividend income than his pro rata share of the corporation's earnings and profits, as in the above example from the 1954 regulations; and (b) that a distribution of appreciated property was taxable to the extent of its fair market value, if its adjusted basis was fully covered by earnings and profits, so that in the example given the shareholders should each recognize $8,000 of dividend income. A third, and bolder, thesis was that a distribution was a "dividend" to the shareholders unless it impaired the corporation's capital, so that the appreciation in value of the distributed property was taxable even if the corporation had *no* earnings and profits.[81] As might be expected when the views of acute commentators are so divergent, neither side could find more than tenuous support in the 1939 Code, and for some time the judicial decisions were meager both in number and in persuasive power. After the House of Representatives had passed its version of the 1954 Code, however, the Courts of Appeals for the Second and Third Circuits decided the *Hirshon* and *Godley* cases (involving different shareholders of the same corpora-

---

[81] The first view was espoused by Molloy, *supra* note 71, at 69-70; the second by the government, see Mintz and Plumb, *supra* note 70, at 58-9; and the "captial impairment" theory, by Raum, *supra* note 70, at 613. A variation on the "capital impairment" theory is that the appreciation in value does not come from either earnings and profits or capital, and is taxable under the catch-all phraseology of §22(a) of the 1939 Code (now, with revisions in language, §61 of the 1954 Code); this argument was fully advanced by the government and rejected by the court in Harry H. Cloutier, 24 T.C. 1006, 1015 (1955) (Acq.); see also Commissioner v. Gross, 236 F.2d 612, 50 AFTR 68 (2d Cir. 1956). A fourth theory, which virtually all commentators found too bizarre for acceptance, was that the distribution was fully taxable if the property had been purchased "with" earnings and profits (i.e., purchased when the corporation's earnings and profits were equal to or exceeded the purchase price), without regard to the earnings and profits account at the time of distribution. See Commissioner v. Wakefield, 139 F.2d 280, 31 AFTR 1056 (6th Cir. 1943).

tion) and held (under the 1939 Code) that the full fair market value
of appreciated property was taxable to the shareholders if the corporation's earnings and profits were sufficient to cover the adjusted
basis of the property. The theory of these cases is not free from doubt,
but apparently the judges started with the proposition that earnings
and profits should be reduced by the adjusted basis of the distributed
property, and inferred therefrom (a) that, so far as the corporation
was concerned, the distribution was a "dividend" in its entirety if its
adjusted basis was covered by earnings and profits, and (b) that the
term "dividend" should mean the same thing to the distributees as to
the distributing corporation.[82]

The language of the 1954 Code is not quite the same as the 1939
Code, on which the *Hirshon* and *Godley* cases rest, and it has been in-
geniously argued that the 1954 changes destroy the basis of those
cases;[83] but if the draftsmen really intended a change, they could
hardly have concealed their purpose more successfully. Despite the
similarities between the two statutes, however, the House and Senate
Reports on the 1954 Code both express the view (contrary to the
result in *Hirshon* and *Godley*) that the shareholders realize dividend
income on the distribution of appreciated property only to the extent
of the corporation's earnings and profits. Although it is difficult to
find a satisfactory basis for these committee statements, the statute

---

[82] Commissioner v. Hirshon Trust, 213 F.2d 523, 45 AFTR 1608 (2d Cir.
1954), cert. denied, 348 U.S. 861; Commissioner v. Godley's Estate, 213 F.2d
529, 45 AFTR 1614 (3d Cir. 1954), cert. denied, 348 U.S. 862. The Tax Court,
after exhaustively reviewing the legislative history of the 1939 Code in the light
of these cases, however, adhered to its earlier view that the distribution can be
a "dividend" only to the extent of the corporation's earnings and profits.
Harry H. Cloutier, *supra,* note 81.

It is debatable whether the courts in *Hirshon* and *Godley* accepted the full-
blown capital impairment theory; it would require the appreciation in value
to be taxed as a "dividend" to the shareholders whether the corporation had
earnings and profits or not, and at points both courts relied upon a construction of the statute that would permit the appreciation to be taxed in full only
if the property's adjusted basis was covered by earnings and profits. If so,
the corporation in the *Hirshon* and *Godley* cases could have *reduced* its shareholders' taxable income by *increasing* its distribution. It distributed about $2
million in cash and property worth about $9 million when its earnings and
profits amounted to about $5.7 million. The distribution was held to be a
"dividend" to the extent of $11 million. By distributing $5.7 million in cash
(instead of $2 million), the corporation could have wiped its earnings and
profits account clean, so that (on the foregoing hypothesis), a later distribution
of the property would have been a return of capital. By increasing its distribution from $11 million to $14.7 million, then, the corporation would have
reduced its shareholders' dividend income from $11 to $5.7 million.

[83] Mintz and Plumb, *supra,* note 70. As they say (at 72, n. 154), it is hard
"to find the change on the face of the statute, except by some close semantic
reasoning."

is sufficiently ambiguous to tolerate them, and the validity of the regulations quoted earlier in this section, if attacked, will probably be upheld.[84]

In the example above, the corporation's earnings and profits exceed the adjusted basis of the property. If the earnings and profits were only $5,000 (instead of $10,000), each shareholder would have dividend income of only $2,500, and would treat the remaining $5,500 of his distribution as a return of capital.

If the corporate distribution consists of depreciated property, the governing principles are the same: to the extent of the earnings and profits, the fair market value of the property is a dividend; the balance, if any, is a return of capital, subject to §§301(c)(2) and (3).

The distributee's basis for the distributed property is its fair market value, determined as of the date of the distribution. §301(d)(1) (*supra*, note 80). If the shareholder assumes (or takes the distributed property subject to) a liability of the distributing corporation, the "amount" of the distribution is reduced pro tanto (but not below zero) by §301(b)(2). This will affect the amount to be taken into income by the shareholder, but not his basis for the property, which remains its fair market value under §301(d)(1).

Sec. 5.23. Taxability of distribution to corporate distributees

The status of distributions in kind to corporate distributees is complicated by §301(b)(1)(B), which provides that the "amount" of a distribution to such a distributee is the property's fair market value (determined as of the time of the distribution) or its adjusted basis

---

[84] Committee reports: H.R. Rep. No. 1337, 83d Cong., 2d Sess., p. A94; S. Rep. No. 1622, p. 248. The author has elsewhere suggested that the committee reports may have been based on a misapprehension of the *Hirshon* and *Godley* cases. Bittker, Stock Dividends, Distributions in Kind, Redemptions and Liquidations Under the 1954 Code, 1955 So. Calif. Tax Inst. 349, 366-7. The Treasury's proposed regulations adhered to the result in *Hirshon* and *Godley,* despite the position of the committee reports. Proposed Regs. §1.316-1(a)(2) and (3), 19 Fed. Reg. 8253 (Dec. 11, 1954). In their final form, however, the regulations accepted the theory of the committee reports. Regs. §1.316-1(a) (2) and (3).

As to pre-1954 law, the Senate Report on the 1954 Code disclaims "any implication . . . with respect to the effects of a distribution of property on earnings and profits and on the shareholders under the 1939 Code." *Supra.* at 248.

In 1956, Congress retroactively amended the 1939 Code to provide, in general, that a distribution of appreciated property was a "dividend" only to the extent of earnings and profits, thus applying the 1954 rule (as set out in the regulations) to pre-1954 years and rejecting the contrary rule of the *Hirshon Trust* and *Godley* cases. §115(n), 1939 Code. See S. Rep. No. 1941, 84th Cong.. 2d Sess., in 1956-2 C.B. 1227.

in the hands of the distributing corporation, whichever is the lesser.[85] The corporate distributee's basis for the distributed property similarly is the lower of the property's value or its adjusted basis (increased by certain recognized gain) in the hands of the distributing corporation. §301(d)(2). Having determined the "amount" of the distribution under §301(b), the distributee corporation must report the part which is covered by earnings and profits as a dividend, and the balance, if any, as a capital distribution subject to the rules of §301(c)(2) and (3).

The purpose of this rather elaborate system for taxing distributions in kind to corporate distributees may be illustrated by an example. Assume that X (the distributing corporation) is wholly owned by A, another corporation. X, having earnings and profits of $100,000, distributes property to A with a value of $100,000 and an adjusted basis in its hands of $10,000. Were it not for §301(b)(1)(B), A would have $100,000 of dividend income on receipt of the property; but, by virtue of the 85 percent deduction for inter-corporate dividends provided by §243 (*supra*, Sec. 2.25), only $15,000 would be subject to tax. Thus, at trivial tax cost, A could obtain a $100,000 stepped-up basis for computing depreciation and gain or loss on the distributed property.[86] The "lower of value or basis" rule of §301(b)(1)(B) avoids this result, with its attendant possibilities for manipulation, by providing that the "amount" of the distribution to A is only $10,000, the property's adjusted basis to X; similarly, §301(d)(2) provides that A's basis for the property will be $10,000, its basis in the hands of

---

[85] The distributing corporation's basis is increased by any gain recognized by it under §311(b) (LIFO inventory), §311(c) (liabilities in excess of basis), or §1245 and §1250 (depreciation recapture rules). See *supra*, Sec. 5.21. It is not clear why §301(b)(1)(B) does not provide a similar adjustment for gain recognized by the distributing corporation under §§311(a) and 453(d) (distribution of installment obligations). This omission is especially puzzling in view of the upward adjustment for §§1245 and 1250 gain recognized by the distributing corporation. Perhaps the adjusted basis of distributed installment obligations is simultaneously stepped-up at the corporate level because of the recognized gain on their distribution, but this result is by no means clear.

If the distributee assumes (or takes the distributed property subject to) a liability of the distributing corporation, the "amount" of the distribution is reduced accordingly, under §301(b)(2).

[86] Another statutory approach to this problem was in effect from 1950 to 1954; §26(b) of the 1939 Code limited the dividends received credit to 85 percent of the distributing corporation's basis for the property; see H.R. No. 2319, 81st Cong., 2d Sess., reprinted in 1950-2 C.B. 380. See ABA Section of Taxation, 1962 Program and Committee Reports, p. 50, for another approach.

Section 301(b)(1)(B) is made inapplicable to certain distributions of property by foreign corporations by §301(b)(1)(C); if the dividends received deduction of §245 (*supra*, Sec. 2.25) is inapplicable to the distribution, the amount to be taken into account is the property's fair market value, and this becomes its basis by virtue of §301(d)(3).

X.[87] If X was required to recognize $5,000 of gain on the distribution (e.g., because of §1245), then the "amount" of A's §301 distribution, and its basis for the distributed property, would be increased by the recognized gain to $15,000.

If a corporation has both corporate and noncorporate shareholders, its choice of property for distribution may affect the tax liability of the shareholders. Assume that X Corporation owns two parcels of property, each worth $50,000, but with adjusted basis of $10,000 and $90,000 respectively. Assume also that X has $100,000 of earnings and profits and is owned equally by A, another corporation, and B, an individual. If the first parcel is distributed to A, its dividend income and basis for the property will be $10,000. If the second parcel is distributed to A, however, it will have dividend income, and a basis, of $50,000. For B, the choice is immaterial; the distribution of either parcel to him will result in dividend income, and a basis, of $50,000. X Corporation, therefore, can benefit A by distributing either the low or high basis property to it (depending upon whether the added tax cost to A of receiving the high basis property is outweighed by the attainment of a stepped-up basis), without prejudice to B, the individual shareholder. The Commissioner might assert, however, that "in reality," X distributed a 50 percent interest in each parcel to A and B, and that A and B thereafter rearranged their interests. If the distribution is realigned in this fashion, the taxability of the distribution would be altered, and it is also possible that this constructive exchange between A and B would be a taxable event, unless it could be brought within a non-recognition provision, such as §1031(a).

Another problem caused by the existence of both corporate and noncorporate shareholders concerns the proper method for allocating earnings and profits between these two types of stockholders when the amount of the §301(b) distribution exceeds available earnings and profits. To illustrate: if, in the above example, X Corporation's earnings and profits were only $30,000, and the low basis property was distributed to the corporate shareholder A, it is not clear whether A's "dividend" income would be $10,000 or $5,000. If X's earnings are allocated ratably between the two shareholders in proportion to their

---

[87] The rule has another consequence, possibly unintended but none the less important. In the case of transfers of property from a subsidiary corporation to its parent (e.g., from a manufacturing corporation to a parent sales corporation), at the property's cost or above, there is no need to compute the property's fair market value as the first step in determining whether the excess of its value over the price paid was a taxable dividend or the result of a bona fide bargain sale (see *supra*, notes 39 and 40).

stock ownership rights, then A's "ratable share" of X's earnings would be $15,000; thus the amount of its §301(b) distribution ($10,000) would be fully covered by earnings and profits for dividend status purposes. If, however, the earnings are allocated in proportion to the relative *amounts* of the distribution as computed under §301(b), one sixth ($10,000 : $60,000) of earnings and profits would be allocated to A's distribution, resulting in a $5,000 dividend.[88]

Sec. 5.24   Distributions in kind — Effect on earnings and profits

The corporation's earnings and profits account must be adjusted to reflect a distribution in kind. But the mechanics of this process, found in §312 of the Code, may prove difficult and elusive in application. Also, many of these rules represent legislative compromises which reflect conflicting alternatives of tax doctrine and policy, a factor which does little to foster symmetry. The discussion herein will consider three categories of earnings and profits adjustments for distributions in kind:

1. The general rule of §312(a). This provision states that earnings and profits shall be decreased by the adjusted basis of the distributed property. Thus, if X Corporation, with earnings and profits of $15,000, distributes property with an adjusted basis of $5,000 and a value of $10,000 to A, an individual and its sole stockholder, A's dividend income will be $10,000, but X's earnings and profits will be reduced by only $5,000 (leaving $10,000 of earnings and profits for future distribution). A cash distribution of $15,000 in a subsequent taxable year (when X has no current earnings and profits), therefore, would result in $10,000 of dividend income to A plus a $5,000 reduction in basis for his stock. The tax consequences of these two distributions would be drastically altered if their order were reversed. An initial distribution of $15,000 in cash would constitute a dividend to A in the amount of $15,000 and wipe X's earnings and profits account clean. A distribution of the property in a later taxable year, therefore, would not be a "dividend" to any extent; instead, it would result in a $10,000 reduction in the basis of A's stock.

Timing is also critical if the distributed property is worth less than its adjusted basis. If the adjusted basis of the distributed pro-

[88] The latter approach was adopted by the Internal Revenue Service in an unpublished ruling relating to the Du Pont divestiture of General Motors stock (*supra,* note 80); see letter ruling, May 9, 1958, in Prentice-Hall Federal Tax Service, ¶54,944. Note that §316(a), unlike §356(a)(2) and some other provisions of the Code, does not speak of the shareholder's "ratable share" of earnings and profits, but only of a distribution that is "out of" earnings and profits.

perty in the first example above had been $15,000 (instead of $5,000), earnings and profits would be reduced by $15,000 on a distribution of the property, even though A's dividend amounted to only $10,000 (the value of the distributed property). Thus, a dividend in kind worth only $10,000 would sweep the earnings and profits account clean, so that a distribution of $15,000 in cash, in a subsequent taxable year, would be applied to reduce the basis of A's stock, rather than taxed as a dividend. Had the cash been distributed before the property, however, A would have had $15,000 of dividend income and a $10,000 stock basis reduction from the two distributions.

A further complexity is introduced if the corporation distributes both cash and property in the same taxable year. Here, it is necessary to know both the amount of post-1913 accumulated profits (against which distributions are charged in chronological order), and the amount of current earnings and profits (which, under §316(a)(2), are computed as of the close of the taxable year without reduction for current distributions, and which, under Regs. §1.316-2(b) and (c), are apportioned among all *cash* distributions in that year). See *supra*, Sec. 5.02. It is not clear whether current earnings and profits are apportioned among current property distributions, or among current cash and property distributions, in determining the status of such distributions. (The issue would be important if some shareholders received cash and others property, or if there were changes in the ownership of stock during the year.) The regulations speak only of cash distributions in this context, but it is difficult to see why the same approach should not be applicable to property distributions as well. The language of §316(a)(2) does not purport to distinguish qualitatively between cash and property distributions, and it is doubtful that the courts would do so if such a case were presented.

2. *Certain inventory assets.* A special rule is provided by §312(b)-(1) to govern earnings and profits if the corporation distributes "inventory assets" with a fair market value in excess of their adjusted basis. The term "inventory assets" is defined to mean not only stock in trade and other property properly includible in inventory, but also certain "unrealized receivables or fees." On a distribution of such assets, the corporation must (a) increase earnings and profits by the excess of their fair market value over their adjusted basis, and (b) decrease earnings and profits (but not below zero) by their fair market value.[89]

---

[89] The regulations do not state whether fair market value is to be computed at retail, what adjustments if any are to be made for anticipated selling costs, etc. For an analogous problem of determining "value," see Regs. §1.170-1(c)

Congress has not been willing to require the distributing corporation to recognize taxable income on the distribution of appreciated assets (except to the limited extent noted *supra*, Sec. 5.21); but, on the other hand, it was not willing to give "inventory assets" the same treatment as other property, whose distribution produces neither taxable income nor earnings and profits. In effect, Congress has compromised by putting inventory assets in an intermediate category, where a distribution will produce earnings and profits but not corporate taxable income.[90] This treatment attempts to insure that the corporation will have enough earnings and profits to cover the appreciation in value of distributed inventory assets, so that noncorporate distributees will have to report at least this amount as dividend income. The shareholders of a corporation, therefore, will be unable to get a "cheap" stepped-up basis for distributed inventory assets, even if the corporation has no earnings and profits when the distribution is made; the distribution itself will create enough current earnings and profits to cover the appreciation in value, and noncorporate shareholders ordinarily will have to report dividend income *pro tanto* rather than apply the entire distribution in reduction of the basis of their stock.[91]

(1), dealing with charitable contributions of inventory items. For an application of §312(b), see Lester E. Dellinger, 32 T.C. 1178 (1959).

[90] But if the distribution consists of LIFO inventory, both §311(b) and §312(b) may be applicable, so that the distribution will produce (a) taxable income, and hence earnings and profits, on the excess of FIFO value over LIFO value, and (b) earnings and profits, but not taxable income, on the excess of fair market value over FIFO value. See Regs. §1.312-4, Example (3), for an illustration of the interaction between §311(b) and §312(b); the example makes clear that there will not be a double increase in the distributing corporation's earnings and profits (as a literal reading of the statutory language might suggest) on a distribution of LIFO inventory covered by both §311(b) and §312(b).

[91] The adjustments of §312(b) must be made even if the distributees are corporations, despite the fact that corporate distributees are denied a stepped-up basis by virtue of §301(d)(2) (*supra*, Sec. 5.23).

Section 312(b) does not guarantee that the distribution of inventory assets will produce a taxable dividend, since the increase in current earnings and profits may be offset by a current operating loss; and there may be no post-1913 accumulated earnings and profits.

The operation of §312(b)(1) can be illustrated by these two examples, involving a distribution by X Corporation to A, an individual who owns all of X's stock, of inventory assets with an adjusted basis of $10,000 and a fair market value of $50,000:

1. X has neither accumulated earnings nor a deficit at the start of the year, and breaks even on current operations. The amount of A's "dividend" is $40,000, under §316(a)(2), due to the increase in current earnings and profits provided by §312(b)(1)(A); the remaining $10,000 is a return of capital under §301(c)(2) and (3).

2. If X had an accumulated deficit of $20,000 at the start of the year, the tax results to A would be the same; and the $20,000 accumulated

It should not be forgotten that income realized in form by the distributees of inventory assets may be imputed to the corporation, e.g., if they promptly sell the assets in accordance with a prearranged plan or with the aid of corporate facilities. The relationship of the earnings and profits adjustments required by §312(b) at the time *of the distribution* to the earnings and profits that are created by a later sale or other disposition imputed to the corporation is not illuminated by either the Code or the regulations. It is surprising that the problem was left in such obscurity, since sales by the shareholders of inventory property or collections by them of "unrealized receivables or fees" would often — perhaps ordinarily — be imputed to the corporation on the principles discussed *supra*, Sec. 5.21. Certainly the appreciation in value of such assets should not be reflected in earnings and profits more than once. Since §312(b) requires an adjustment to earnings and profits at the time of the distribution, any later realization of taxable income should affect earnings and profits only to the extent that the appreciation has not already been taken into account.

3. Other adjustments. In addition to the above adjustments, earnings and profits will be affected by distributions of certain types of specially treated assets, such as encumbered property, installment obligations, or depreciable property. The statute, in §312(c), is at best opaque, providing merely that "proper adjustment" shall be made to earnings and profits if the distributee assumes or takes subject to liabilities, or if gain is recognized by the distributing corporation under §§311(b), 311(c), 1245(a) or 1250. Similarly, there is a circular quality to the rule as stated in Regs. §1.312-3:

> The amount of any reduction in earnings and profits described in §312(a) or (b) shall be (a) reduced by the amount of any liability to which the property distributed was subject and by the amount of any other liability of the corporation assumed by the shareholder in connection with such distribution, and (b) increased by the amount of gain recognized to the corporation under §311(b) or (c), or under §1245(a).

Obviously, reasonable men may disagree as to what this means, but Regs. §1.312-4, Example (2), seems to indicate that the distributing corporation ends up with an increase in its earnings and profits after a distribution of property with a liability in excess of basis or of section 1245 assets.[92]

---

deficit would carry forward, unchanged, to the next taxable year, since the reduction in earnings and profits provided by §312(b)(1)(B) applies to current earnings to the extent thereof.

[92] The distribution of "inventory assets," on the other hand, is subject to the special treatment of §312(b), providing that earnings and profits are to be

To illustrate: X Corporation, with no current or accumulated earnings and profits, distributes nondepreciable real estate (adjusted basis $20,000; fair market value, $100,000; subject to a mortgage lien of $70,000) to its sole individual shareholder, A, who takes subject to the liability. It is clear that the amount of A's distribution is $30,000 under §301(b)(2) and that X recognizes taxable gain of $50,000 on the distribution under §311(c); in addition, X's earnings and profits would be increased by the amount of this gain so that A would have dividend income of $30,000. The status of X's earnings and profits account after the distribution is unclear: viz., does it stay at $50,000, reflecting merely the increase caused by §311(c) gain; or is it reduced to zero on the theory that the gain was distributed by X to A? It would seem that the former is the proper result, since if X had made a bargain sale of the property to A for $70,000 (the amount of the mortgage lien), A would realize $30,000 of dividend income, but there would seem to be no justification for a reduction in earnings and profits under §312(a)(3).[93]

Other distributions (e.g., taxable stock dividends, redemptions, spin-offs, corporate reorganizations, etc.) may require an adjustment to the distributing corporation's earnings and profits; in general, the appropriate adjustment is discussed in connection with the basic rules governing the transaction itself in subsequent chapters of this book.

Part C.   Distributions of Corporation's Own Obligations

Sec. 5.40.   Distributions of corporation's own obligations

In lieu of distributing cash or property, the corporation may make a distribution to its shareholders of its own obligations, ordinarily (but not necessarily) evidenced by notes, bonds, debentures, or other securities. The Internal Revenue Code appears to assume that such a distribution will have the same tax consequences as a distribution of other types of property, but the regulations depart from this assumption at certain points in the interest of simplicity.

In the case of a noncorporate distributee, it is reasonably clear

---

reduced by the *value* of the inventory assets (to the extent of earnings and profits). See Regs. §1.312-4, Example (3). As to a distribution of installment obligations, see §311(a) and §453(d) (*supra*, Sec. 5.23).

[93] A different approach might be adopted if the gain is created on a distribution of §1245 property, on the ground that the gain recognized counterbalances excessive depreciation deductions taken previously, so that the adjusted basis of the property should be stepped up (in computing the downward adjustment to earnings and profits) to reflect the recapture of depreciation. Similarly, it could be persuasively argued that the basis of installment obligations should be stepped up to reflect the gain recognized on their distribution.

that the distribution of a corporation's own obligations is a distribution of "property" under §301(b)(1)(A), even though the Code is not explicit on this point,[94] so that the "amount" of the distribution is the fair market value of the obligations. It follows from this and from §§301(c)(1) and 316 that the distribution is a "dividend" to the extent of current and post-1913 earnings and profits, and that any excess is to be treated as a return of capital under §§301(c)(2) and (3). And, under §301(d)(1), the basis of the distributed obligations in the hands of the distributee is their fair market value. In these respects, there is no difference between a distribution of the corporation's own obligations and a distribution of other types of property, *supra*, Sec. 5.22.

It will be recalled, however, that if the distributee is another corporation, the "amount" of a distribution of property is either the property's fair market value or its adjusted basis in the hands of the distributing corporation, whichever is the lesser. *Supra*, Sec. 5.23. Although the Code itself does not state that a distribution of the corporation's own obligations is to be treated differently, the regulations provide that the fair market value of the obligations is controlling, thus confining the operation of §301(b)(1)(B) to distributions of property other than the corporation's own obligations or stock. See Regs. §1.301-1(d). In most instances, of course, the letter of §301(b)(1)(B) could not be applied to the corporation's own obligations, because they would have no adjusted basis; but it is possible for a corporation to issue securities and reacquire them, and in this event, they might possibly be regarded as having an adjusted basis that could be controlling under §301(b)(1)(B) if they were later distributed to shareholders. Despite this possibility, the regulations under §301(b) ignore the adjusted basis of the obligations.[95] Similarly, §301(d)(2) provides that the basis to a corporate distributee of "property" is its fair market value or its adjusted basis in the hands of the distributing cor-

---

[94] Both §301(b), regarding the "amount" of a distribution, and §301(d), prescribing the basis of distributed property, speak of "property," without explicitly mentioning the distributing corporation's own obligations. Section 317(a), defining "property," is equally laconic, and the regulations under §317(a) state that the term "property" includes "indebtedness *to* the corporation," but say nothing about indebtedness *of* the corporation. Despite these unsatisfactory gaps, a distribution of the corporation's own obligations almost certainly is to be treated as a distribution of "property," and the regulations under §301 so assume. See also §312(a), which explicitly includes the corporation's own obligations within the term "property."

[95] The regulations do not explicitly negate the significance of the adjusted basis of the corporation's own obligations in laying down the tax consequences of a bargain sale of "property" to a corporate distributee, Regs. §1.301-1(j), but the omission is probably a mere oversight.

poration, whichever is the lesser, but the regulations confine this provision to distributions of property other than the corporation's own obligations, and provide that the basis of such obligations is their fair market value.[96]

Although the *fair market value* of the corporation's obligations controls both the "amount" of the distribution and the basis of the obligations, as just indicated, §312(a)(2) provides that the distributing corporation's earnings and profits are to be reduced by the *principal amount* of the obligations. In many cases, these amounts will be identical. If the obligations are worth less than their face amount, however, the discrepancy between the distribution's impact on the shareholders and its effect on the distributing corporation's earnings and profits recognizes that the corporation's assets will eventually be reduced by the principal amount of the obligations, at least in the normal case where they are paid in full, and that the shareholders (if they still hold the obligations at maturity) will recognize income equal to the difference between the fair market value of the obligations at distribution, which is their adjusted basis under §301(d), and their principal amount.[97] Perhaps it would have been theoretically more accurate to charge earnings and profits at distribution with the fair market value of the obligations, treating the difference between the fair market value and the face amount as debt discount, and reducing earnings and profits in an appropriate amount each year; but this refinement would hardly have been worth the added complication of such a procedure.

Part D.   Distributions of Stock and Stock Rights

Sec. 5.60.   Introductory

The provisions of the 1954 Code relating to stock dividends are the outgrowth of a long history of confusion and conflict that cannot be ignored in the interpretation of the new statute.[98] The Revenue

---

[96] Regs. §1.301-1(h)(2)(i). See Denver & Rio Grande Western R. R. Co. v. United States, 318 F.2d 922, 11 AFTR 2d 1600 (Ct. Cl. 1963), involving a distribution of obligations of an unusual type to a corporate shareholder.

[97] The shareholder would realize capital gain under §1232(a)(1) if the obligation was evidenced by a security, unless its fair market value at the time of distribution was regarded as the "issue price" so as to bring into play the requirement of §1232(a)(2) that "original issue discount" be taxed as ordinary income. See *supra*, Sec. 4.06.

[98] This portion of the text is concerned with distributions by a corporation of its own shares, or of rights to acquire its own shares. The distribution of shares of *another* corporation is treated as a distribution in kind governed by the principles discussed *supra*, Sec. 5.22ff.

Act of 1913 said nothing about stock dividends and an attempt by the Treasury to tax such dividends under the catch-all language of what is now §61(a), 1954 Code, was rejected by the Supreme Court in Towne v. Eisner, 245 U.S. 418, 3 AFTR 2959 (1918), on the ground that a stock dividend did not constitute "income" as that term was used in the statute. The Revenue Act of 1916, however, explicitly provided that a "stock dividend shall be considered income, to the amount of its cash value." But in Eisner v. Macomber, 252 U.S. 189, 3 AFTR 3020 (1920), the most celebrated case in the annals of federal income taxation, the Supreme Court held that the distribution of common stock by a corporation having only common stock outstanding could not be constitutionally taxed as income to the shareholders:

> We are clear that not only does a stock dividend really take nothing from the property of the corporation and add nothing to that of the shareholder, but that the antecedent accumulation of profits evidenced thereby, while indicating that the shareholder is the richer because of an increase of his capital, at the same time shows he has not realized or received any income in the transaction.
>
> It is said that a stockholder may sell the new shares acquired in the stock dividend; and so he may, if he can find a buyer. It is equally true that if he does sell, and in doing so realizes a profit, such profit, like any other, is income, and so far as it may have arisen since the 16th Amendment is taxable by Congress without apportionment. The same would be true were he to sell some of his original shares at a profit. But if a shareholder sells dividend stock he necessarily disposes of a part of his capital interest, just as if he should sell a part of his old stock, either before or after the dividend. What he retains no longer entitles him to the same proportion of future dividends as before the sale. His part in the control of the company likewise is diminished. Thus, if one holding $60,000 out of a total $100,000 of the capital stock of a corporation should receive in common with other stockholders a 50 per cent stock dividend, and should sell his part, he thereby would be reduced from a majority to a minority stockholder, having six-fifteenths instead of six-tenths of the total stock outstanding. A corresponding and proportionate decrease in capital interest and in voting power would befall a minority holder should he sell dividend stock; it being in the nature of things impossible for one to dispose of any part of such an issue without a proportionate disturbance of the distribution of the entire capital stock, and a like diminution of the seller's comparative voting power — that "right preservative of rights" in the control of a corporation. Yet, without selling, the shareholder, unless possessed of other resources, has not the wherewithal to pay an income tax upon the dividend stock. Nothing could more clearly show that to tax a

stock dividend is to tax a capital increase, and not income, than this demonstration that in the nature of things it requires conversion of capital in order to pay the tax. . . . (252 U.S. at 212-13).

Mr. Justice Holmes, with whom Mr. Justice Day concurred, dissented, saying:

> I think that the word "incomes" in the Sixteenth Amendment should be read in "a sense most obvious to the common understanding at the time of its adoption." . . . The known purpose of this Amendment was to get rid of nice questions as to what might be direct taxes, and I cannot doubt that most people not lawyers would suppose when they voted for it that they put a question like the present to rest. I am of opinion that the Amendment justifies the tax. (252 U.S. at 219-20.)

Mr. Justice Brandeis, with whom Mr. Justice Clarke concurred, dissented in a more elaborate opinion. The opinions in *Eisner* v. *Macomber* have been acutely and amply criticized, and there is no need to paraphrase here the views of the commentators.[99]

Although the constitutional theory of *Eisner* v. *Macomber* has few defenders today, its practical importance to corporate practice and to the collection of revenue has been exaggerated. Had the case gone the other way, stock splits would probably have been employed as a substitute for stock dividends, coupled if necessary with periodic increases in par value or in stated capital; and if a method of taxing stock splits had been developed, fractional shares could have been used to serve the principal functions of stock dividends without adverse tax consequences.

In response to *Eisner* v. *Macomber*, Congress provided in the Revenue Act of 1921 (42 Stat. 228) that a "stock dividend shall not be subject to tax." Immunity was thus granted by statute to all stock dividends, whether the dividend shares were common or preferred and without regard to the number of classes of stock outstanding, although in *Eisner* v. *Macomber* the Supreme Court had passed only on a dividend of common on common by a corporation having no other class outstanding.

---

[99] Among many, see Powell, Stock Dividends, Direct Taxes, and the Sixteenth Amendment, 20 Col. L. Rev. 536 (1920); Eustice Seligman, Implications and Effects of the Stock Dividend Decision, 21 *ibid.* 313 (1921); E.R.A. Seligman, *Studies in Public Finance* 99-123 (1925); Magill, *Taxable Income* 31 (rev. ed. 1945); Lowndes, The Taxation of Stock Dividends and Stock Rights, 96 U. Pa. L. Rev. 147 (1947); Rottschaefer, Present Taxable Status of Stock Dividends in Federal Law, 28 Minn. L. Rev. 106 and 163 (1944).

The 1921 statute said nothing about the basis of shares received as a stock dividend, but the Treasury's regulations required the adjusted basis of the old stock to be allocated between the old shares and the dividend shares in proportion to their respective market values at the time of distribution. The Treasury's requirement that the basis of the old shares be divided between the old shares and the dividend shares was successfully challenged by a taxpayer in Koshland v. Helvering, 298 U.S. 441, 17 AFTR 1213 (1936), concerning a corporation having both common and non-voting preferred stock outstanding, which distributed common stock as a dividend on its preferred but not on its common. A preferred shareholder asserted that she was entitled to compute the gain on a sale of her original shares by using her full adjusted basis, without allocating any of that basis to the common stock received as a dividend. The Supreme Court held that Eisner v. Macomber did not apply to a stock dividend that "gives the stockholder an interest different from that which his former stock holdings represented," 298 U.S. at 446, that the dividend in the *Koshland* case could have been taxed as income to the shareholder when she received it, and that the failure of Congress to tax the dividend shares on distribution did not authorize the Treasury to allocate part of the basis of the old shares to the dividend shares. The Court thus agreed with the taxpayer that the old shares retained their full basis for computing gain or loss on their disposition.[100]

---

[100] Besides making clear that Eisner v. Macomber did not immunize all stock dividends from tax, the *Koshland* case opened up the possibility of an escape from taxation by taxpayers who had accepted the benefit of the basis regulation by allocating part of their original basis to the dividend shares on selling such shares; it was possible that they could now claim the full original basis on selling the original shares.

Not long after deciding the *Koshland* case, the Supreme Court held in Helvering v. Gowran, 302 U.S. 238, 19 AFTR 1226 (1937), that under the 1921-36 revenue acts the basis of dividend shares was zero, since they had cost the shareholders nothing and were not taxed as income on receipt. This determination opened up the possibility — the converse of the possible escape from taxation under the *Koshland* case — that a taxpayer who had complied with the invalidated regulation on selling his original shares (by allocating part of his basis to the retained dividend shares) would have to use a zero basis on selling the dividend shares, and thus would not recoup his original investment tax-free. (Section 1311, which now opens up the earlier year despite the running of the statute of limitations, in certain cases where either the taxpayer or the government adopts inconsistent positions, was not enacted until 1938.)

But in 1939, Congress enacted §113(a)(19) of the 1939 Code, the predecessor of §307(a) of the 1954 Code, adopting the allocation rules applied under the invalidated Treasury regulations, and also providing for situations in which income on the sale of either the original or dividend shares had been computed in a fashion inconsistent with the old regulations. Alvord and Biegel, Basis Provisions for Stock Dividends under the 1939 Revenue Act, 49 Yale L. J. 841 (1940).

In response to the *Koshland* case, Congress provided in §115(f)-(1) of the Revenue Act of 1936 that:

> A distribution made by a corporation to its shareholders in its stock or in rights to acquire its stock shall not be treated as a dividend to the extent that it does not constitute income to the shareholder within the meaning of the Sixteenth Amendment of the Constitution.

Did this section tender the Supreme Court an opportunity to re-examine Eisner v. Macomber or did it take that case as its starting point? In Helvering v. Griffiths, 318 U.S. 371, 30 AFTR 403 (1943), a majority of the Court held that Congress did not intend to invite a reconsideration of Eisner v. Macomber; the minority saw such an invitation, however, and expressed the view that Eisner v. Macomber should be overruled. As §115 (f) (1) of the 1939 Code was interpreted by the majority, then, "the tax status of a [pre-1954] stock dividend . . . turns in effect on what would have been unconstitutional under Eisner v. Macomber if Eisner v. Macomber had been correct in its premise that a constitutional issue is present."[101]

Just what stock dividends could be taxed under §115(f)(1) of the 1939 Code, as thus construed, was veiled in obscurity. In Strassburger v. Commissioner, 318 U.S. 604, 30 AFTR 1087 (1943), the Supreme Court held (by a 5-3 vote), that a distribution of a newly created issue of non-voting cumulative preferred stock by a corporation that had only common stock outstanding was not taxable. All of the common stock was owned by the taxpayer. The Court said:

> While the petitioner . . . received a dividend in preferred stock, the distribution brought about no change whatever in his interest in the corporation. Both before and after the event he owned exactly the same interest in the net value of the corporation as before. At both times he owned it all and retained all the incidents of ownership he had enjoyed before. (318 U.S. at 607.)

In Helvering v. Sprouse, decided at the same time as the *Strassburger* case, the Court held that a distribution of non-voting common stock by a corporation having both voting and non-voting common outstanding was also non-taxable. The non-voting common was distributed to the holders of both the voting and the non-voting common; the taxpayer, before the stock dividend, owned only voting

[101] Cohen, Surrey, Tarleau, and Warren, A Technical Revision of the Federal Income Tax Treatment of Corporate Distributions to Shareholders, 52 Col. L. Rev. 1, 9-10 (1952).

common. The government argued that the distribution came within the rule of the *Koshland* case that "where a stock dividend gives the stockholder an interest different from that which his former stock holdings represented he receives income." But the Court (5-3) held:

> We think *Koshland* v. *Helvering* . . . distinguishable. That was a case where there were both preferred and common stockholders, and where a dividend in common was paid on the preferred. We held, in the circumstances there disclosed, that the dividend was income, but we did not hold that any change whatsover in the character of the shares issued as dividends resulted in the receipt of income. On the contrary, the decision was that, to render the dividend taxable as income, there must be a change brought about by the issue of shares as a dividend whereby the proportional interest of the stockholder after the distribution was essentially different from his former interest. (318 U.S. at 607-8.)

With the *Strassburger* and *Sprouse* cases as their guides, the lower courts struggled with but did not solve the problem of separating taxable stock dividends from non-taxable ones.[102]

These decisions left so much uncertainty in the taxation of stock dividends under the 1939 Code that the draftsmen of the 1954 Code essayed a new approach to the problem. The cases just cited are of continuing importance, however, because pre-1954 law governs the basis of the original and dividend shares (and the earnings and profits of the distributing corporation) if the stock dividend was distributed before June 22, 1954. See §§307(c), 312(d)(2), 391, and 1052(c).

Sec. 5.61   Non-taxable stock dividends under the 1954 Code

Section 305(a) of the 1954 Code lays down the general rule that "gross income does not include the amount of any distribution made by a corporation to its shareholders, with respect to the stock of such corporation, in its stock or in rights to acquire its stock." Concerned as it is with distributions by a corporation "with respect to [its] stock," §305 has no effect on transfers of stock to creditors, vendors, employees, etc., who happen to be shareholders as well.[103] Moreover, §305 is limited to distributions of the corporation's *own* stock; dis-

---

[102] See, e.g., Tourtelot v. Commissioner, 189 F.2d 167, 40 AFTR 668 (7th Cir. 1951); Wiegand v. Commissioner, 194 F.2d 479, 41 AFTR 721 (3d Cir. 1952); Schmitt v. Commissioner, 208 F.2d 819, 45 AFTR 37 (3d Cir. 1954); John A. Messer, 20 T.C. 264 (1953); Pizitz v. Patterson, 183 F. Supp. 901, 6 AFTR 2d 5050 (D. Ala. 1960).

[103] See §305(c)(3); and note the interpretations of virtually identical

tributions by a corporation of the stock of another corporation are treated as distributions of money or other property, to which §305 has no application. Finally, §305 is concerned with distributions of "stock" or of rights to acquire "stock." Debt instruments (or instruments that purport to be stock but on analysis are found to be evidences of indebtedness, *supra*, Sec. 4.02), are not subject to §305. The regulations, however, provide that §305 applies to treasury stock and to rights to acquire treasury stock, as well as to unissued stock.

Upon receiving a distribution of stock that is exempt from tax under §305(a), the shareholder is required by §307(a) to allocate the basis of the old stock between the old and the new stock under regulations to be prescribed. Pursuant to §307(a), the Treasury requires an allocation of basis in proportion to the fair market values of the old and new stock on the date of distribution. Regs. §1.307-1. The holding period of the new stock, for determining whether capital gain or loss on a sale or exchange is long-term or short-term, includes the period for which the shareholder held the old stock, by virtue of §1223(5). Ordinarily, therefore, the shareholder will report any gain or loss recognized on a sale, redemption, or other disposition of his dividend shares as long-term capital gain or loss. If the dividend shares are "section 306 stock" (primarily preferred stock distributed as a tax-free dividend by a corporation having earnings and profits), however, the taxpayer may realize ordinary income on their disposition, under rules discussed *infra*, Ch. 8.

The distributing corporation does not reduce its earnings and profits when it makes a non-taxable distribution of its stock, §312(d)-(1)(B);[104] and the recipient, if a corporation, does not increase its earnings and profits on receiving such a distribution, §312(f)(2).

The statutory exceptions to the general rule of §305(a) are discussed in the next section.

---

language in §301(a) and §311(a), found in Regs. §1.301-1(c) and §1.311-1(e), *supra*, Sec. 5.05 (notes 39-40) and Sec. 5.21 (note 72).

For decisions taxing shareholders on the receipt of stock in a non-shareholder capacity, see Commissioner v. Fender Sales, Inc., 338 F.2d 924, 14 AFTR 2d 6076 (9th Cir. 1964) (stock received in cancellation of claims for salary by two 50 per cent shareholders); James C. Hamrick, 43 T.C. 21 (1965) (release of cause of action against other shareholders and the corporation); but see DeLoss E. Daggitt, 23 T.C. 31 (1954), and Joy Mfg. Co. v. Commissioner, 230 F.2d 740, 49 AFTR 326 (3d Cir. 1956), which are contra, for pre-1954 taxable years. See Note, Application of Eisner v. Macomber to Pro Rata Stock Distributions in Payment of Salaries: An Opportunity for Tax Manipulation, 64 Yale L.J. 929 (1955).

[104] The expense of issuing a stock dividend cannot be deducted under §162; see *supra*, Sec. 2.23, note 55. This rule, which seems applicable whether the stock dividend is taxable to the recipients or not, would also preclude a reduction in earnings and profits to reflect the expense.

Sec. 5.62.   Taxable stock dividends

There are two exceptions to the general rule of §305(a) that stock dividends are receivable tax-free:

1. Optional distributions.   Section 305(b)(2) provides that §305(a) is inapplicable if the distribution is payable, at the election of any of the shareholders, either in stock or in property. The Senate Report on the 1954 Code states that this provision "continues the rule of . . . existing law that where a shareholder has an election to take a dividend in stock or in cash, the election to take a stock dividend will not prevent the stock being subject to tax." S. Rep. No. 1622, 83d Cong., 2d Sess., p.44. The corresponding provision of the 1939 Code, however, provided explicitly that if *any* of the shareholders had such an option, "the distribution shall constitute a taxable dividend in the hands of all shareholders, regardless of the medium in which paid." §115(f)(2), 1939 Code. Despite the reference in the Senate Report to "existing law," the language of the 1954 Code does not state as clearly as did the 1939 Code that if any shareholder has an option to take cash or other property, all shareholders realize income. The regulations, however, state that an option in one shareholder is fatal to all.[105]

If the shareholders have an election to take money or other property in lieu of stock, §305(b)(2) is applicable whether the option is exercised before or after the distribution is declared. Regs. §1.305-2. Plainly, §305(b)(2) would become a dead letter unless it embraced options granted to the shareholder and exercised before the declaration, as well as those that arise and are exercised after the declaration. But how far back of the declaration was §305(b)(2) intended to reach? An amendment to the regulations, proposed in 1956 and still pending (March, 1966), provides that if a corporation has two classes of common stock outstanding, one class being entitled to dividends in stock only while the other is entitled to dividends in cash, the shareholder who owns shares of the former class has an option, within the meaning of §305(b)(2), since a choice arises from the mere existence of the two classes of stock.   If the shareholder could freely convert one class into the other, much could be said for

---

[105] Regs. §1.305-2(a). If Eisner v. Macomber can still be regarded as valid, however, it could be argued that a stock dividend exempt under that decision cannot be taxed to its recipient simply because some *other* shareholder has an option to take cash or other property. See Bittker, *supra* note 84, at 350-351; Lester Lumber Co., Inc., 14 T.C. 255, 261 (1950), stating that corporate law requires all stockholders to be treated alike, so that the corporation may not offer cash to a limited group of stockholders and require the others to accept a stock dividend.

the theory of the proposed regulation. As applied to non-convertible shares, it is rather drastic. Even if the two classes of stock are identical except for their dividend rights, and are equal in value, the shareholder owning shares entitled to stock dividends only does not have an option to take cash currently, except by selling his stock (at the cost of taxes and brokerage commissions) and buying shares of the other class; and neither this power nor his original decision to buy one class rather than the other seems to be the type of "election" to which §305(b)(2) was intended to refer.[106]

2. *Preferred arrears.* The second exception to the nontaxability of stock dividends is §305(b)(1), providing that a distribution "in discharge of preference dividends" for the corporation's current or preceding taxable year shall be treated as a §301 distribution. The House version of the 1954 Code contained a similar exception, but it applied more broadly to *any* distribution in discharge of preference dividends, whether currently owing or in arrears. The provision as enacted "limits the taxability to stock dividends distributed in lieu of dividends on preferred stock which are in effect currently owing." Senate Report on 1954 Code, S. Rep. No. 1622, 83d Cong., 2d Sess., 44 (1954). If a distribution of stock is made to clear up arrears in preference dividends for a number of years, the portion attributable to the earlier years would be exempt from tax under §305(a); only the portion of the distribution that is allocable to the arrears for the current and preceding taxable years would be taxed under §305(b)-(1). Even this mild measure can be avoided, however, if the arrears are cleared up by a bona fide recapitalization of the corporation.[107]

The Code does not define "preference dividends" as that term is used in §305(b)(1). The Senate Report on the 1954 Code refers to "dividends on preferred stock." S. Rep. No. 1622, 83d Cong., 2d Sess., 44 (1954). Does this include so-called "Class A" common stock, *i.e.*, nonvoting stock with a dividend claim of a fixed amount which must be paid ahead of any dividends on Class B common and a right to participate in further dividends after a secondary "preference" of the Class B common stock has been satisfied? Under §312(b) of the House version of the 1954 Code, apparently neither Class A nor

---

[106] The proposed amendment may be found in 21 Fed. Reg. 5104; see also T.D. 6476, 1960-2 C.B. 111, stating that it "will be given further consideration before final action is taken thereon." The long delay in acting on the proposal suggests a lack of confidence in its theory. See: IRS Attempts to Stop 2-Classes-of-Common Tax-Saving Plan; Legality Questioned, 5 J. Tax. 178 (1956); Rev. Rul. 65-256, 1965-46 I.R.B. 27 (receipt of non-dividend stock in statutory merger will not cause dividend income to the holder when distributions are made on other stock).

[107] *Infra*, Sec. 12.16; Regs. §1.368-2(e)(5).

Class B would have been "participating stock," with the result that a stock distribution in discharge of their preference arrears would have been taxable. The Senate revised the House version, however, and the reference in the Senate Report to "dividends on preferred stock" appears to exclude the Class B stock and to leave ambiguous the status of Class A.[108]

When stock dividends are subject to either §305(b)(1) or §305(b)(2), the distribution is to be treated as a distribution of property to which §301 applies. In a "taxable election" transaction under §305(b)(2), the amount of the distribution depends upon whether the shareholder takes the stock or rights in the distributing corporation, or chooses to take other property instead. In the former case, Regs. §1.305-2(c) and §1.301-1(d) provide that the fair market value of the stock or rights is the amount of the §301 distribution, whether the distributee is an individual or a corporation.[109] In this respect, taxable stock dividends are treated like distributions by a corporation of its own obligations (supra, Sec. 5.23, notes 95 and 96). The distributing corporation's charge to earnings and profits for such distributions is, under Regs. §1.312-1(d), the fair market value of the stock or rights. Similarly, the basis of the distributed stock or rights in the hands of the shareholders, individual or corporate, is fair market value under §301(d)(1). The holding period of stock or rights received in a taxable distribution commences with the date of acquisition; there is no provision in §1223 for "tacking" in this case.

If, however, a shareholder exercises his election to receive money or other property in lieu of stock or stock rights, Regs. §1.305-2(c) provide that the normal dividend rules govern taxability of the distribution; i.e., if property other than money is received, corporate distributees use the lower of value or basis principle of §301(b)(1)-(B) in measuring the amount of their distribution, the basis of the property is determined under §301(d)(2), and the charge to earnings and profits is governed by the rules discussed supra, Sec. 5.24; individual distributees, on the other hand, use the value of the property as the amount of their §301 distribution and as its basis. If the "elected property" consists of obligations of the distributing corporation, the principles discussed supra, Sec. 5.40, presumably would apply, although the regulations are not specific on this point.

---

[108] But see Bittker, supra note 84, at 354-4; see also §565(f).

[109] For a corporate distributee of property, the amount of the distribution is ordinarily the property's fair market value (supra, Sec. 5.23). Ordinarily the distributing corporation would not have a basis for its own stock, but it might distribute treasury stock. Both §317(b) and §1032 can be cited in support of the Treasury's decision to disregard basis in the case of a distribution of stock; see Bittker, supra note 84, at 354-355.

Sec. 5.63.   Stock rights

Section 305 lumps together distributions of stock rights and distributions of the stock itself, providing that a distribution by a corporation of "rights to acquire its stock" is not includible in the shareholder's gross income, unless (a) the distribution is made in discharge of preference dividends for the corporation's current or preceding taxable year, or (b) the distribution is, at the election of any of the shareholders, payable either in stock rights or in property. Even though §305 does not discriminate between stock and stock rights, however, a distribution of rights presents certain peculiar problems.[110]

In the case of a nontaxable distribution of rights, basis is to be allocated under §307. The "general rule" prescribed by §307(a) and the regulations issued thereunder is an allocation of basis between the old stock and the stock rights in proportion to their fair market values as of the date of distribution. Regs. §1.307-1(a) and (b). The regulations also state that basis is to be allocated only if the rights are exercised (in which case the amount allocated to the rights is added to the cost of the stock acquired by exercising the rights) or sold (in which case the amount allocated to the rights is used in determining the shareholder's gain or loss on the sale). Regs. §1.307-1(a) and (b). The effect of this limitation is that the shareholder realizes no loss if he allows the rights to expire without exercise or sale.

The rule of allocation is subject to an exception. Section 307(b) provides that if the fair market value of the rights is less than 15 percent of the fair market value of the old stock at the time of distribution, the basis of the rights shall be zero unless the shareholder elects to allocate basis under the method of allocation provided by §307(a). (The method of making an election is set out in Regs §1.307-2.) The purpose of §307(b) is to avoid the necessity for trifling basis adjustments on a distribution of rights of little value; unless the shareholder elects to allocate his basis, he uses a zero basis for the rights whether they are exercised (in which case the basis of the new stock is its actual cost) or sold (in which case the entire proceeds of sale will be taxable gain), leaving the basis of the old stock intact.

If the shareholder sells his rights, §1223(5) permits the holding period of the underlying shares to be "tacked" on in determining the holding period of the rights if their basis "is determined under sec-

---

[110] See generally, Comment, Taxation of Stock Rights, 51 Calif. L. Rev. 146 (1963); Whiteside, Income Tax Consequences of Distributions of Stock Rights to Shareholders, 66 Yale L.J. 1016 (1957).

tion 307"; this embraces rights with a zero basis under §307(b), as well as rights with an allocated basis under §307(a). Rev. Rul. 56-572, 1956-2 C.B. 182.

When a distribution of rights is taxable, because the shareholders have an option to take property instead of rights or because the distribution discharges arrears in preference dividends for the corporation's current or preceding taxable year, §305(b) provides that "the distribution shall be treated as a distribution of property to which section 301 applies." Under the 1939 Code, the rules relating to receipt, exercise, sale, and lapse of taxable rights were in a state of great confusion; and it is not entirely clear whether we are free of this legacy. The confusion resulted from Choate v. Commissioner, 129 F.2d 684, 29 AFTR 965 (2d Cir. 1942), which in turn rested upon Palmer v. Commissioner, 302 U.S. 63, 19 AFTR 1201 (1937), holding (a) that a distribution of rights was not taxable (even though a distribution of the stock subject to the rights would have been taxable) in the absence of a corporate intention to distribute earnings (ordinarily evidenced by the existence of a substantial "spread" between option price and fair market value of the stock at the time of distribution); and (b) that even when such a corporate intent was manifest, income was realized only upon exercise or sale of the rights, not upon issuance.[111]

The pre-1954 rules for taxable rights rested on a reading of the 1939 Code, however, and it may be that they have been swept away by the 1954 Code. Under §305(b), stock rights are taxable only if issued in discharge of preference dividends for the corporation's current or preceding taxable year or if the shareholders can elect to receive property instead of the rights; and it would not be unreasonable to take the new statute at face value in these narrow circumstances: viz., that the distribution "shall be treated as a distribution of property to which section 301 applies," with the result that the distribution itself would be taxable (assuming adequate earnings and profits) to the extent of the fair market value of the rights, whether they are subsequently sold, exercised, or allowed to lapse. On this theory, a lapse of the rights would give rise to a deductible loss, unless all shareholders allowed their rights to lapse so that their economic relationships to the corporation and to each other were unchanged.

[111] See Oscar E. Baan, 45 T.C. 71 (1965), for a recent application of these principles; see also Gibson v. Commissioner, 133 F.2d 308, 30 AFTR 767 (2d Cir. 1943); Tobacco Products Export Corp., 21 T.C. 625 (1954) (Non-Acq.); G.C.M. 25063, 1947-1 C.B. 45; Whiteside, supra, note 110, at 1018-22.

Chapter Six

ACCUMULATED EARNINGS AND UNDISTRIBUTED INCOME

Part A. The Accumulated Earnings Tax

Sec. 6.01. Introductory

The disparity between the steeply graduated tax on the income of individuals and the more modest, relatively flat rate on corporations has for many years tempted taxpayers to use the corporation as a shield against the individual income tax. To illustrate: a married couple with taxable income of $500,000 will incur a tax liability of about $320,000 (1965 rates), leaving $180,000 of spendable income, but if a corporation is interposed between the individuals and the $500,000 of taxable income, the corporate tax burden will be about $235,000, leaving $265,000 after taxes — almost 50 percent more than would be left after the individual income tax. To be sure, the corporate after-tax income is not immediately available for personal consumption, but this may not be critical: the sole shareholder of the corporation may be satisfied to accumulate the income in the corporation for ultimate transfer at his death, to sell the stock (reporting the accumulated income as long-term capital gain), or to exchange it for the marketable stock of a publicly-held corporation in a tax-free merger. The reader should not be surprised to learn, however, that the game just described is not without its perils. The principal obstacle to be surmounted is the accumulated earnings tax of §531, to be described in Part A of this chapter. Subsidiary perils are the penalty taxes on personal holding companies (*infra*, Part B); and the special treatment of shareholders of foreign personal holding companies, controlled foreign corporations, and collapsible corporations (*infra*, Parts C and D, and Ch. 10).

The accumulated earnings tax of §531 can trace its lineage to the Revenue Act of 1913 (38 Stat. 166), which provided that if a corporation was "formed or fraudulently availed of" for the purpose of escaping the individual income tax by permitting gains and profits to accumulate in the corporation, each shareholder's ratable share of the corporate income was taxable to him whether distributed or not. The fact that the corporation was "a mere holding company" or that its accumulations were "beyond the reasonable needs of the business" was *prima facie* evidence of "a fraudulent purpose to escape [the individual income] tax." The term "fraudulently" was dropped in 1916, and doubts about the constitutionality of taxing the shareholders on undistributed corporate income, engendered by Eisner v. Macomber (*supra*, Sec. 5.60), led the Congress in 1921 to abandon this mechanism in favor of a tax on the offending corporation itself. The constitutionality of the revised tax was upheld, against a variety of objections, in Helvering v. National Grocery Co., 304 U.S. 282, 20 AFTR 1269 (1938).[1]

Since 1921, there have been only minor changes in the accumulated earnings tax, primarily those enacted in 1954. The principal features of the tax as presently constituted are:

    1. The tax is imposed on "every corporation [except personal holding companies, foreign personal holding companies, and tax exempt corporations] formed or availed of for the purpose of avoiding the income tax with respect to its shareholders . . . by permitting earnings and profits to accumulate instead of being divided or distributed." §532.

    2. The fact that the corporation is "a mere holding or investment company" is *prima facie* evidence of the purpose to avoid the income tax on its shareholders. §533(b).

    3. The fact that earnings and profits are allowed to accumulate "beyond the reasonable needs of the business" is determinative of the purpose to avoid income tax on its shareholders, unless the corporation proves to the contrary by the preponderance of the evidence. The term "reasonable needs of the business" includes the "reasonably anticipated needs of the business." If a notice of deficiency is based on an alleged unreasonable accumulation, the burden of proof in any Tax Court proceeding depends in part upon whether the taxpayer has been so notified by the government and has submitted an answering counter statement with regard to this question §§533(a), 537, 534.

    4. When applicable, the tax is levied at the rate of 27-1/2 percent of the first $100,000 of "accumulated taxable income" and at the rate of 38-1/2 percent of any "accumulated taxable

---

[1] In its opinion, the Court said "Kohl [sole shareholder of the corporate taxpayer], the sole owner of the business, could not by conducting it as a corporation, prevent Congress, if it chose to do so, from laying on him individually the tax on the year's profits," citing the 1913 act referred to in the text, and thus suggested that the 1921 change, laying the tax on the corporation, was an unnecessary precaution by Congress, at least as to a one-man or other closely-held corporation.

income" above $100,000. The term "accumulated taxable income" means the corporation's taxable income for the year in question (with certain adjustments), minus the sum of (a) the dividends paid deduction of §561 (primarily, dividends paid during the taxable year), and (b) an "accumulated earnings credit" (permitting a corporation, unless barred by §1551 or §269, to accumulate at least $100,000 during its lifetime). §§531, 535.

Before analyzing the accumulated earnings tax in detail, several general points should be noted. The basic purpose of §§531-537 is to discourage the use of a corporation as an accumulation vehicle to shelter its individual stockholders from the personal income tax rates. The Congressional approach to this problem is a rule phrased in terms of the evil which the statute is designed to prevent, viz., "unreasonable" accumulations of corporate earnings *for the purpose of* avoiding personal income taxation at the shareholder level. Thus, liability for the tax turns on the state of mind or intent of the corporation, primarily a question of fact; and this essentially factual nature of §531 cases gives special weight to the trial court's decision and is an important consideration in litigation strategy. Since each case depends on its own facts, moreover, the decided cases, although numerous, are not very useful as precedents.[2]

The corporate penalty tax on unreasonable accumulations is not popular with the business community, involving as it does a hindsight verdict on management's business judgment. On the whole, however, the courts are sensitive to this problem, and exercise restraint in over-ruling corporate dividend and accumulation policies in cases where reasonable men could differ.[3] But as long as substantial differ-

---

[2] The discussion of cases that follows, therefore, is selective rather than comprehensive. For a complete tabular analysis of cases under §531, see Prentice-Hall, 1966 Federal Tax Service, ¶4056.

See generally Weithorn, What Constitutes a Reasonable Accumulation? 17 N.Y.U. Inst. on Fed. Tax. 299 (1959); Altman, Corporate Accumulation of Earnings, 36 Taxes 933 (1958); Panel discussion, Corporate Accumulations: How To Meet The Problems of Section 531, 23 N.Y.U. Inst. on Fed. Tax. 745 (1965); Cuddihy, Accumulated Earnings and Personal Holding Company Taxes, 21 *ibid.* 401 (1963); Cohen, Taxing The State of Mind, 12 Tax Exec. 200 (1960); and Kendall, Business Factors In Justifying Accumulation of Earnings Under Section 531, 1959 So. Cal. Tax. Inst. 225.

Earlier works of continuing interest are: Cary, Accumulations Beyond the Reasonable Needs of the Business: The Dilemma of Section 102(c), 60 Harv. L. Rev. 1282 (1947); Rudick, Section 102 and Personal Holding Company Provisions of the Internal Revenue Code, 49 Yale L.J. 171 (1939); for the 1954 changes, see Cohen, Phillips, Surrey, Tarleau, and Warren, The Internal Revenue Code of 1954: Carry-overs and the Accumulated Earnings Tax, 10 Tax L. Rev. 277, 299-306 (1955); Hall, Revision of the Internal Revenue Code and Section 102, 8 Nat'l Tax J. 275 (1955); Rudick, Effect of The Corporate Income Tax on Management Policies, 2 How. L.J. 232, 238-253 (1956) (policy issues).

[3] For discussion, see John P. Scripps Newspapers, 44 T.C. 453 (1965). It is

ences in the corporate and individual tax rates persist, the need for some form of protection against excessive corporate accumulations will continue. The pressure was reduced somewhat in 1964, when the top individual rate bracket was lowered to 70 percent, but for some taxpayers it may still be more profitable to deliberately absorb a §531 tax than to distribute the corporate earnings as a dividend. In this situation, the shareholders have everything to gain and nothing to lose by causing their corporation to accumulate its earnings rather than pay dividends, especially since the §531 liability may not have to be paid until after years of administrative discussion and litigation. (Although a corporation might confess liability for the §531 tax on filing its return, there is no formal procedure for such a self-assessment.) Quite aside from these exceptional cases, it is often a good gamble to refrain from paying dividends; the corporation may win its §531 case, or be able to settle it on terms that leave the shareholders in a better position than if the corporate earnings had been distributed.

Sec. 6.02.   The forbidden purpose: §532

Section 532(a) imposes the accumulated earnings tax on any corporation that is formed or availed of for the purpose of avoiding the income tax on its shareholders by permitting its earnings and profits to accumulate instead of being distributed. Tax liability thus depends on the taxpayer's intent or state of mind with respect to its accumulations. The major features of this test, which is difficult to apply in practice, are:

1. Corporations subject to tax. Since personal holding companies and the United States shareholders of foreign personal holding companies are subject to special penalty taxes on undistributed income (*infra*, Parts B and C of this Chapter), corporations of these types are exempted from the accumulated earnings tax of §531, as are tax-exempt corporations, §532(b). An accumulation for the purpose of sheltering a *corporate* shareholder against income tax is within the literal scope of §532(a); but since tax avoidance is nominal in this instance (because of the 85 percent deduction for intercorporate dividends allowed by §243, *supra*, Sec. 2.25), it would be difficult to establish the forbidden purpose.

often alleged that revenue agents threaten to assert §531 deficiencies as a weapon to obtain agreement on other deficiencies. It is inherent in such charges that they are easily made and easily denied, but nearly impossible to substantiate or disprove.

Attention has therefore focused on accumulations for the purpose of shielding *individual* shareholders against income tax, and the regulations explicitly require avoidance of the "individual income tax."[4] The tax can be imposed, however, if the purpose is to avoid income tax on the shareholders of another corporation; e.g., when the accumulating corporation's stock is owned by a second corporation, and the purpose of the subsidiary's accumulation is to protect the individual shareholders of the parent corporation against the tax they would have to pay if the subsidiary distributed its earnings to the parent corporation and it in turn paid dividends to its shareholders.[5]

The accumulated earnings tax seems limited, as a practical matter, to closely held corporations in view of the requirement of §532(a) that the corporation be availed of to avoid taxes with respect to its shareholders. Thus, publicly held corporations have little to fear from §531 if management is independent and not under the domination of a few large stockholders, and if individual stockholdings are sufficiently diffused so that no single group can exercise effective control over corporate dividend policy. Moreover, the threat of stockholder pressure, including possible law suits, if the corporation improperly accumulates its surplus probably constitutes a greater incentive for such corporate managements to declare dividends than §531 itself.[6] Congress noted this in 1954, when the House version of the 1954 Code specially exempted corporations with more than 1500 shareholders from §531 liability if no more than 10 percent of the stock was held by one family. The proposal was rejected by the Senate, partly because large corporations often would be unable to prove their right to the exemption because their records would not disclose how much stock was owned by any one family, and partly because "this tax is not now in practice applied to publicly held corporations . . ." S. Rep. No. 1622, 83rd Cong., 2d Sess. 69 (1954). The only reported

---

[4] Regs. §1.532-1(a)(1). Before 1954, avoidance of "surtax" was required, but with the amalgamation of the normal tax and the surtax in the 1954 Code, this requirement was eliminated.

[5] Regs. §1.532-1(a)(2). For the history of this provision, see Mead Corporation v. Commissioner, 116 F.2d 187, 26 AFTR 1 (3d Cir. 1940). For applications, see United States v. McNally Pittsburgh Mfg. Co., 329 F.2d 273, 15 AFTR 2d 484 (10th Cir. 1965); Hedberg-Freidheim Contracting Co. v. Commissioner, 251 F.2d 839, 1 AFTR 2d 840 (8th Cir. 1958).

[6] These suits may take the form of an action to compel payment of dividends, e.g., Dodge v. Ford Motor Co., 204 Mich. 459, 170 N.W. 668 (Mich. 1919); and Kales v. Woodworth, 32 F.2d 37, 7 AFTR 8668 (6th Cir. 1929); or a shareholder's derivative action on behalf of the corporation to recover from the directors the amount of any §531 tax paid. See Mahler v. Trico Products Corp., 296 N.Y. 902, 72 N.E. 2d 622 (N.Y. 1947); Note, Derivative Actions Arising From Payment of Penalty Taxes Under Section 102, 49 Col. L. Rev. 394 (1949).

instance of the §531 tax being imposed on a publicly held corporation is the *Trico Products* litigation. There, however, six shareholders controlled about two thirds of the shares, so that the courts were able to determine that the accumulations were motivated by the individual interests of this group. A stockholder's derivative action against the directors, who were also the principal shareholders, was settled by their personal payment of almost $2.5 million to the corporation for subjecting it to the §531 penalty.[7]

Thus, a common denominator in all §531 cases is concentration of ownership and control of the corporation in a small group of stockholders. Even if the corporation is closely held, however, special facts may show that it was not availed of for the prohibited purpose. For example, the existence of a substantial minority stock interest that would have objected to an unreasonable accumulation of earnings might negate a tax avoidance purpose for the accumulation; or the improper purpose might be rebutted by evidence that the shareholders were deadlocked on policy decisions.[8] Although the statute does not identify the person or persons whose purpose is crucial, presumably it refers to those who control the corporation, through stock ownership or otherwise; unless the person with a tax avoidance state of mind can exercise control over the corporate dividend policy, his purpose hardly meets the statutory requirement.[9]

2. Tax avoidance purpose — general. The language of §532(a) could be interpreted to impose the penalty tax whenever the prohibited purpose exists, whether it is successfully consummated or not. However, courts may well hesitate to adopt this draconic construction of §531, and may require instead a showing of actual, rather than hoped-for, avoidance of shareholder income taxes. Thus, if the

---

[7] Trico Products Corp. v. Commissioner, 137 F.2d 424, 31 AFTR 394 (2d Cir. 1943), cert. denied, 320 U.S. 799; Trico Products Corp. v. McGowan, 169 F.2d 343, 37 AFTR 176 (2d Cir. 1948), cert denied, 335 U.S. 899 (1948); Mahler v. Trico Products Corp., *supra* note 6.

[8] For cases involving a minority stock interest, see Carolina Rubber Hose Co., ¶65,229 P-H Memo TC; Mountain State Steel Foundries, Inc. v. Commissioner, 284 F.2d 737, 6 AFTR 2d 5910 (4th Cir. 1960); and Ted Bates & Co., ¶65,251 P-H Memo TC. For shareholder deadlocks, compare Casey v. Commissioner, 267 F.2d 26, 3 AFTR 2d 1440 (2d Cir. 1959), with Hedberg-Freidheim Contracting Co. v. Commissioner, *supra* note 5.

[9] See the *Trico Products Corp.* cases, *supra* note 7; Casey v. Commissioner, *supra* note 8; and Pelton Steel Casting Co. v. Commissioner, 251 F.2d 278, 1 AFTR 2d 542 (7th Cir. 1958), cert. denied, 356 U.S. 958, stating that "the corporation's intent will be considered to be that of those responsible for its acts." See also Regs. §1.341-2(a)(2) (*infra,* Sec. 10.04), for a similar problem under the collapsible corporation provisions; Alvord v. Commissioner, 277 F.2d 713, 5 AFTR 2d 1438 (4th Cir. 1960) (foreign personal holding company tax not imposed for years in which the United States, as the result of a tax assessment, prevented distribution of corporate income).

corporation is formed for the purpose of tax avoidance, but abandons its plans, or if the directors accumulate for the purpose of shielding shareholders against tax but their action turns out to be a *brutem fulmen* because the shareholders are in fact tax-exempt, or if for some other reason the forbidden purpose fails to achieve its intended result, it is unlikely that the tax will be asserted or upheld.[10] Even if reduction of shareholders' income tax liability is not indispensable, however, it can obviously be extremely important to the government's case: here, as elsewhere in the law, a purpose can be inferred from the results. Hence, it is common practice in §531 cases for courts to consider, as evidence of the forbidden purpose, the tax effect that a dividend distribution would have had on the shareholders. On the other hand, courts have been quick to point out that the mere fact that shareholders would have paid more taxes if the earnings had been distributed as dividends rather than accumulated is not fatal on the question of tax avoidance.[11]

Several courts have been faced with the question of whether an honest, though mistaken, belief that accumulations were necessary for a purpose other than shareholder tax avoidance will protect the corporation from the penalty tax of §531. In a concurring opinion in Casey v. Commissioner, 267 F.2d 26, 3 AFTR 2d 1440 (2d Cir. 1959), Judge Learned Hand expressed the view that it should:

> I believe that the statute meant to set up as a test of "reasonable needs" only the corporation's honest belief that the existing accumulation was no greater than was reasonably necessary. Section 532(a) was a penal statute, designed to defeat any plan to evade the shareholders' taxes, and there can be no doubt that

---

[10] In Helvering v. National Grocery Co., *supra* note 1, the taxpayer argued that the tax was unconstitutional because, *inter alia,* "the liability is laid upon the mere purpose to prevent imposition of the surtaxes, not upon the accomplishment of that purpose." If the court accepted this construction of the statute, it was only for the purpose of argument; the facts were far more favorable to the government. The same may be said of other cases, such as DeMille v. Commissioner, 31 B.T.A. 1161 (1935), aff'd, 90 F.2d 12 (9th Cir. 1937), cert. denied, 302 U.S. 713, to the extent that they imply that liability can be imposed if the forbidden purpose exists but is not achieved.

[11] See Trico Products Corp., 46 B.T.A. 346, 364-5 (1942) (findings re additional income taxes that would have been paid by the shareholders had the corporation distributed its earnings); Apollo Industries, Inc., 44 T.C. 1 (1965) (limited importance of offsetting capital gains on a later sale of corporation's stock), reversed on other grounds, 358 F.2d 867, 17 AFTR 2d 517 (1st Cir. 1966); see also R. Gsell & Co., Inc. v. Commissioner, 294 F. 2d 321, 8 AFTR 2d 5507 (2d Cir. 1961) (shareholder liability not conclusive); Commissioner v. Young Motor Co., Inc., 316 F.2d 267, 11 AFTR 2d 1361 (1st Cir. 1963) (ditto); Florida Iron & Metal Co., ¶42,408 P-H Memo TC (tax not imposed because accumulation resulted from bookkeeper's mistake, unknown to the directors, in understating earnings).

it presupposes some deliberate purpose to do so and is not satisfied by proving that the corporation was mistaken in its estimate of its future "needs."[12]

Accordingly, it would seem that a corporation should not be liable for the accumulated earnings tax if it accumulates for reasons other than the forbidden purpose of §532(a), and this should be true even though the directors may have accumulated earnings out of caprice, spite, miserliness, or stupidity rather than for good business reasons. Consequently, if dividends are withheld to freeze out a minority shareholder or because of the controlling person's obsessive fear of future economic collapse, for example, rather than for the purpose of sheltering stockholders against income tax, the conditions of §532 are not satisfied, and the tax should not be imposed.[13]

A final aspect of the forbidden purpose issue should be noted at this point: i.e., must tax avoidance be the *primary* or *dominant* purpose for accumulation, or is the statute satisfied if it is merely *one* of the determining purposes thereof? The decided cases on this question are in conflict. In the *Young Motor Co.* case, the court held that tax avoidance must be "the" purpose, not merely "a" purpose; but other decisions apply a less rigorous standard, holding that the prohibited purpose need only be *one* of the determining purposes for the failure to distribute earnings.[14] Whatever the test, it seems relatively clear that tax avoidance need not be the *sole* purpose for the tax to apply; on the other hand, such a purpose should be more than a mere *incidental* reason for the accumulation in order to impose the penalty tax.

3. Factors evidencing the prohibited purpose. The regulations, Regs. §1.533-1(a)(2), provide that the following facts, among others, are to be considered in determining whether the tax avoidance purpose was present: (a) dealings between the corporation and its shareholders, including loans to shareholders and expenditures of corporate

---

[12] 267 F2d 26, at 32. See also Duke Laboratories, Inc. v. United States, 337 F.2d 280, 14 AFTR 2d 5797 (2d Cir. 1964), where the government conceded that a corporation's honest belief that its earnings were not excessive, though mistaken, may exempt it from liability under §532(a); Bremerton Sun Publ. Co., 44 T.C. 566 (1965).

[13] But see Smoot Sand & Gravel Corp. v. Commissioner, 274 F.2d 495, 5 AFTR 2d 626 (4th Cir. 1960) ("reasonable" purpose required).

[14] Young Motor Co. v. Commissioner, 281 F.2d 488, 6 AFTR 2d 5350 (1st Cir. 1960); but see World Publishing Co. v. United States, 169 F.2d 186, 37 AFTR 150 (10th Cir. 1948), cert. denied, 335 U.S. 911; Barrow Mfg. Co., Inc. v. Commissioner, 294 F.2d 79, 8 AFTR 2d 5330 (5th Cir. 1961); Duke Laboratories, Inc. v. United States, *supra* note 12; see also Malat v. Riddell, 383 U.S. 569, 17 AFTR 2d 604 (1966).

funds for the personal benefit of the shareholders; (b) investments of undistributed earnings in assets having no reasonable connection with the corporation's business; and (c) the corporation's dividend history. It should be noted that these factors are not controlling on the tax avoidance issue; rather they are merely evidence of whether the accumulation was for the prohibited purpose. Thus, corporations have escaped the penalty tax of §531, despite poor dividend records, unrelated investments, and loans to shareholders, on establishing that the purpose of the accumulation was not to avoid shareholder tax; conversely, corporations with good dividend records and with no loans to shareholders or unrelated investments, have nevertheless been held subject to the tax where the prohibited purpose existed.

Corporate loans to, or expenditures on behalf of, shareholders tend to show that the corporation has the capacity to distribute these funds as dividends; if there is a pattern of such transactions, it is but a short step to the conclusion that the loan is a substitute for a dividend, showing that corporate earnings were unreasonably diverted from corporate business needs.[15] A similar inference may arise if the corporation has invested its funds for purposes which are not reasonably related to its business. Such unrelated investments may evidence not only the liquidity and dividend-paying capacity of the corporation, but the forbidden purpose as well, since the diversion of corporate funds to uses not connected with its business supports an inference that the failure to distribute such funds as dividends was for the purpose of avoiding shareholder taxes. Here again, however, these adverse inferences may be rebutted by additional evidence.[16] Finally, the corporation's dividend and earnings history is relevant to the question of whether funds were accumulated for the prohibited purpose. A failure to distribute dividends (or, in the case of an owner-managed business, to pay substantial salaries to shareholder-officers)

---

[15] See generally, Oyster Shell Products Corp., Inc. v. Commissioner, 313 F.2d 449, 11 AFTR 2d 777 (2d Cir. 1963); see also Nemours Corp., 38 T.C. 585 (1962); Bardahl Manufacturing Corp., ¶65,200 P-H Memo TC (some loans showed tax avoidance purpose; others were bona fide and hence did not constitute unreasonable diversion of corporate funds); Vuono-Lione, Inc., ¶65,096 P-H Memo TC (tax not imposed despite loans to shareholders); Sterling Distributors, Inc. v. United States, 313 F. 2d 803, 11 AFTR 2d 767 (5th Cir. 1963) (same); James M. Pierce Corp., 38 T.C. 643 (1962) (same).

Of course, if the loans to shareholders are found to be constructive distributions under the principles discussed *supra*, Sec. 5.05, liability under §531 will be avoided *pro tanto*, but at the cost of tax assessments at the shareholder level.

[16] Compare Smith, Inc. v. Commissioner, 292 F.2d 470, 8 AFTR 2d 5119 (9th Cir. 1961), with Sandy Estate Co., 43 T.C. 361 (1964).

For discussion of what constitutes "the" business of the taxpayer, and the relationship of its investments to that business, see *infra*, Sec. 6.06.

suggests that earnings may have been accumulated to avoid shareholder taxes. A good dividend or salary record, on the other hand,
suggests that accumulations were not for the prohibited purpose.[17] An
important aspect of the corporation's dividend record is its legal and
financial ability to distribute earnings and profits to its shareholders.
If a distribution would illegally impair the corporation's capital under
local law or violate a bona fide loan agreement, a failure to distribute
earnings and profits should not, absent special facts, generate liability
under §531.[18]

At one time, revenue agents were instructed to give "close attention" in auditing returns to corporations failing to distribute at least
70 percent of their earnings as taxable dividends. In 1959, however,
this administrative rule of thumb was confined to pre-1954 years; the
change was prompted, no doubt, by a statement in the Senate Finance Committee Report on the 1954 Code that, "Some of the standards informally employed in the past, such as the distribution of 70
percent of earnings, have been erroneous or irrelevant."[19] A by-prod-
uct of the 1959 change was abandonment of the corollary of the 70
percent principle, under which corporations distributing more than
this percentage of earnings were ordinarily not subjected to §531
scrutiny.

*4. Relation of "tax avoidance purpose" to "reasonable needs of
the business" question.* Although §532, imposing the tax on corporations formed or availed of for the forbidden purpose, must be taken
in conjunction with §533(a) (relating to accumulations beyond the
reasonable needs of the business) and §533(b) (relating to "mere"
holding or investment companies), it is important to note that §533
is a mere procedural buttress to §532, and that the latter is the operative provision of the statute. The ultimate question, in other words,
is not whether the corporation had business needs for the accumulation, but whether it was formed or availed of for the prohibited purpose. Many cases, however, have been presented and decided as

[17] Once more, it must be noted that no one factor is conclusive. See generally Bremerton Sun Publishing Co., 44 T.C. 566 (1965); Henry Van Hummell,
Inc., ¶64,290 P-H Memo TC.

[18] Note, however, the consent dividend procedure of §§561 and 565 (*infra,*
Sec. 6.09), which avoids the necessity of an actual distribution. A self-imposed
restriction (e.g., a freezing of surplus by the distribution of a tax-free stock
dividend) should not serve as an excuse in a §531 case (see *infra,* Sec. 6.05);
see also R. L. Blaffer & Co. v. Commissioner, 103 F.2d 487, 22 AFTR 1083 (5th
Cir. 1939) (statutory prohibition against distribution of dividends did not justify an investment company's accumulation); Trico Securities Corp., 41 B.T.A.
306 (1940) (Non-Acq.) (loan agreement restriction).

[19] S. Rep. No. 1622, 83d Cong., 2d sess. 69 (1954); T.D. 6378, 1959-1 C.B.
680.

though an accumulation necessarily stems *either* from a purpose to provide for the reasonable needs of the business *or* from a purpose to reduce shareholders' taxes. This false dichotomy probably arises from §533(a), which provides that the fact that earnings are permitted to accumulate beyond the reasonable needs of the business shall be "determinative" of the purpose to avoid shareholder income taxes unless the corporation shall prove to the contrary by a preponderance of the evidence.[20] By virtue of this provision, most of the cases have been won or lost on the battleground of reasonable business needs.

Thus, where business needs for the accumulation have been established, the government has ordinarily conceded or achieved defeat, despite the theoretical possibility that the accumulation was in fact motivated by a tax avoidance purpose rather than by business needs.[21] Conversely, when an accumulation has been found to be unreasonable, taxpayers have rarely succeeded in rebutting the inference that tax avoidance was the motive for the accumulation.[22]

Sec. 6.03.   "Reasonable needs of the business" — In general

As stated above, although a corporation is subject to the penalty tax only if formed or availed of for a tax avoidance purpose, the issue

---

[20] Before 1954, the corporation's burden was to prove to the contrary by a "clear" preponderance of the evidence.

[21] See R. Gsell & Co. v. Commissioner, *supra* note 11, to the effect that a finding of business needs "amounts to a finding favorable to the taxpayer on the most persuasive fact which would show that the corporation was not availed of for the purpose of preventing the imposition of a surtax upon its shareholders"; see also, to the same effect, Electric Regulator Corp. v. Commissioner, 336 F.2d 339, 14 AFTR 2d 5447 (2d Cir. 1964).

The possibility mentioned in the text, never very substantial, was diminished still further by the enactment in 1954 of §535(c)(1), providing a credit in computing the §531 tax of such current earnings "as are retained" for business needs (*infra,* Sec. 6.09); although this language does not explicitly exclude a government claim that current earnings were retained for tax avoidance rather than to meet a business need, it was held in John P. Scripps Newspapers, *supra* note 3, that a showing of business needs made it unnecessary to consider whether the corporation was availed of for the forbidden purpose. See also Vuono-Lione, Inc., *supra* note 15; Freedom Newspapers, Inc., ¶65,248 P-H Memo TC.

For the pre-1954 confusion in this area, compare World Publishing Co. v. United States, *supra* note 14 ("the tax may be imposed even though the accumulation is not unreasonably large"); with Smoot Sand & Gravel Corp. v. Commissioner, *supra* note 13 ("To the extent surplus has been translated into plant expansion, increased receivables, enlarged inventories, or other assets related to its business, the corporation may accumulate surplus with impunity").

[22] Ted Bates & Co., Inc., *supra* note 8; I.A. Dress Co., Inc. v. Commissioner, 273 F.2d 543, 5 AFTR 2d 429 (2d Cir. 1960); Bremerton Sun Publ. Co., *supra* note 17 (burden carried by taxpayer); Duke Laboratories, Inc. v. United States, *supra* note 12 (same, in jury case).

that is ordinarily most bitterly contested is whether its earnings have accumulated "beyond the reasonable needs of the business." This is because §533(a) provides that such an accumulation is determinative of the proscribed purpose unless the corporation, by the preponderance of the evidence, proves to the contrary. Moreover, the phrase "reasonable needs of the business" became doubly important in 1954, because the accumulated earnings credit enacted then (*infra*, Sec. 6.09) includes an allowance for current earnings retained for such needs. The phrase itself came into the tax law in 1913, but Congress has never undertaken to provide a statutory definition, and for many years the regulations said only that working capital, additions to plant, and sinking fund obligations were reasonable business needs. The regulations under the 1954 Code are somewhat more detailed, providing in Regs. §1.537-2(b) for five grounds which may justify an accumulation.

Before we turn to these and other business needs, several preliminary points should be noted. It is frequently stated that the existence of reasonable business needs is, in the first instance, a matter for the officers and directors of the corporation, and that courts should be hesitant to substitute their judgment and attribute a tax avoidance motive unless the facts and circumstances clearly warrant the conclusion that the accumulation was unreasonable and for the prohibited purpose.[23] In determining whether current earnings were accumulated for reasonable business purposes, the regulations (and most courts) require a determination of whether *prior* accumulations were, in fact, sufficient to meet the taxpayer's current needs, Regs. §1.535-3(b)(ii). In making this determination, it is necessary to examine the character of the corporation's assets, since earnings used for the expansion of business plant and equipment, inventories, or accounts receivable cannot be readily distributed to the shareholders, no matter how large the corporation's earned surplus may be.[24] The "business needs" issue, therefore, invites a thorough analysis of the corporation's business and financial status, including (a) its balance sheet position (i.e., the size, character, and relationship of its various asset, liability, and surplus accounts); (b) its profit and loss statements; (c) its liquidity and cash flow positions; (d) the type of business; (e) the economic conditions prevailing in the taxpayer's business; and (f) any other relevant facts (e.g., technology, abnormal

---

[23] See, e.g., John P. Scripps Newspapers, *supra* note 3; Electric Regulator Corp. v. Commissioner, *supra* note 21.

[24] See Smoot Sand & Gravel Corp. v. Commissioner, *supra* note 21; Electric Regulator Corp. v. Commissioner, *supra* note 21; John P. Scripps Newspaper, *supra* note 3.

industry risks, industry cycles, etc.). In addition, it is usually necessary to go behind the formal books and records of the taxpayer to its contracts, correspondence, and business policies in preparing a defense based on reasonable business needs. Accountants, business analysts, investment bankers, and loan officers are often used as expert witnesses in this open-ended pursuit of evidence bearing on the reasonableness of the corporation's accumulations.

Turning now to the specific grounds that are most frequently encountered in "business needs" cases, the following are listed in Regs. §1.537-2(b):

1. Bona fide expansion of business or replacement of plant. These are probably the most commonly asserted grounds for accumulating earnings and profits. The decisions are clear that financing replacements and expansion by reinvesting retained earnings, rather than by selling additional stock or borrowing, does not give rise to an adverse inference.[25] If earnings are immediately translated into an expansion of the taxpayer's business or replacement of its plant and equipment, the accumulation will not ordinarily be challenged by the government: but, as is more often the case, where expansion or replacement needs will arise at some time in the future, the Service may claim that present accumulations for these purposes are not justified. This problem is complicated by §537 (enacted in 1954), which provides that the phrase "reasonable needs of the business" includes "reasonably anticipated needs" (*infra*, Sec. 6.04). Another difficult problem is whether earnings are being accumulated to expand or diversify "the" business of the taxpayer, or, instead, are being diverted to an unrelated business or investment purpose. For discussion, see *infra*, Sec. 6.06. Several decisions have considered the relationship between depreciation reserves and accumulations of surplus to finance replacement of plant and equipment. Since depreciation deductions are current charges against earnings, an additional reserve for the purpose of replacing plant or equipment will have to be justified by proof of the inadequacy of the taxpayer's depreciation reserves (e.g., because replacement costs will exceed the reserves); otherwise, there would be, in effect, a double accumulation for replacing the same equipment or plant.[26]

----

[25] See, for example, John P. Scripps Newspapers, *supra* note 3; Electric Regulator Corp. v. Commissioner, *supra* note 21; Duke Laboratories, Inc. v. United States, *supra* note 12. But see *infra*, Sec. 6.05.

[26] See Smoot Sand & Gravel Corp. v. Commissioner, *supra* note 21; Henry Van Hummell, Inc., *supra* note 17; see also Ted Bates & Co., Inc., *supra* note 8, extending this principle to promotional expenses normally deducted by the taxpayer as incurred.

2. Acquisition of a business enterprise through purchasing stock or assets. This ground for an accumulation is stated without qualification by Regs. §1.537-2(b)(2), so as to suggest that diversification, however unrelated to the taxpayer's existing line of business, will constitute a reasonable business need. See also Regs. §1.537-3(a), stating that "the business" of a corporation is not merely that which it has previously carried on but includes, in general, any line of business which it may undertake." Despite these statements, an accumulation to embark on a radically new venture may be perilous. See discussion *infra*, Sec. 6.06.

3. Retirement of bona fide business indebtedness. An accumulation for the purpose of retiring bona fide business indebtedness (especially debt held by non-stockholder creditors) has long been recognized as a reasonable business need. Debt held by shareholders, on the other hand, may be another matter; some courts have exhibited less tolerance for accumulations to retire this type of obligation.[27] To the extent that shareholder-held indebtedness qualifies, there is yet another inducement to the use of "thin" corporations (*supra*, Sec. 4.02).

4. Working capital for inventories, etc. This ground for accumulating earnings, often associated with business expansion, is concerned with an essentially revolving fund of liquid assets to finance the recurring operations of a business during its typical operating cycle. If relied on, this justification for accumulating earnings must be supported by an analysis of the corporation's cash flow, which in turn is a function of operating expenses, cost of goods sold, inventory size, rate of inventory turnover, credit policies, accounts receivable, collection rates, availability of credit, and other relevant matters.[28] As an aid in determining whether a corporation's working capital is sufficient to meet its needs, courts have sometimes resorted to certain rules of thumb, e.g., that a ratio of current assets to current liabilities in the neighborhood of 2 1/2 to 1 is reasonable; or that an accumulation of earnings to meet operating expenses for at least one year is

---

[27] E.g., Smoot Sand & Gravel Corp. v. Commissioner, *supra* note 21; see also the caveat, *infra*, Sec. 6.05.

[28] See Smoot Sand & Gravel Corp. v. Commissioner, 241 F.2d 197, 50 AFTR 1612 (4th Cir. 1957); John P. Scripps Newspapers, *supra* note 3; Sandy Estate Co., *supra* note 16; Bardahl Manufacturing Corp., *supra* note 15; Vuono-Lione, Inc., *supra* note 15; Henry Van Hummell, Inc., *supra* note 17; Apollo Industries, Inc., *supra* note 11; R. Gsell & Co., Inc. v. Commissioner, *supra* note 11; The Kirlin Co., ¶64,260 P-H Memo TC; and Ted Bates & Co., Inc., *supra* note 8; Sears Oil Co., Inc. v. Commissioner, —— F.2d ——, 17 AFTR 2d 833 (2d Cir. 1966) (need to analyze inventory requirements of business).

justified.[29] Since business needs may differ widely, however, these are little more than guidelines in the interest of administrative convenience.

5. *Investments or loans to suppliers or customers.* The regulations were amended in 1959 to state that investments or loans to suppliers or customers, if necessary to maintain the business of the corporation, are reasonable business needs. Such investments and loans have not played an important role in the litigated cases, but in a few industries, it may be essential to accumulate earnings for this purpose.

6. *Other grounds for accumulations.* Aside from the grounds mentioned in Regs. §1.537-2(b), which is expressly stated to be a non-exclusive list, accumulations may be justified by a range of business needs that is as diversified as the character of modern business itself. Among the reasons for accumulating earnings that have received a sympathetic judicial response (though the taxpayer was not always successful in establishing that its accumulation was in fact so motivated) are the following: the need to meet competition; the need to finance pension or profit sharing plans for employees; reserves for various business risks and contingencies, such as self-insurance against casualties, potential liability from litigation, and unsettled industrial conditions, including threatened strikes or fear of depression; possible loss of principal customer and need to move plant to new location; self-insurance for key personnel; and special surety bonding needs in the taxpayer's business.[30]

Having set out some of the grounds that may constitute reasonable business needs, the regulations go on to list some indications that earnings are being accumulated beyond the reasonable needs of the business. See Regs. §1.537-2(c), referring to: (a) loans to shareholders and the expenditure of corporate funds for the personal benefit of shareholders; (b) loans to relatives or friends of shareholders, or to other persons if the loans have no reasonable relation to the

[29] See Bremerton Sun Publishing Co., *supra* note 17, and cases cited therein; for an extended analysis of working capital requirements, see Apollo Industries, Inc. v. Commissioner, *supra* note 11.

[30] John P. Scripps Newspapers, *supra* note 3 (meeting competition); Bremerton Sun Publ. Co., *supra* note 17 (pension plan); Smoot Sand & Gravel Corp. v. Commissioner, *supra* note 28 (reserves against risks); Casey v. Commissioner, *supra* note 8 (litigation); Smokeless Fuel Co., ¶43,425 P-H Memo TC (threat of strikes); L. R. Teeple Co., 47 B.T.A. 270 (1942) (loss of customer; moving location); Bradford-Robinson Printing Co. v. United States, 1 AFTR 2d 1278 (D. Colo. 1957) (self-insurance); Vuono-Lione, Inc., *supra* note 15 (surety bond requirements).

For more comprehensive compilations, see *supra* note 2; on accumulations to redeem stock, see *infra* Sec. 6.07.

conduct of its business; (c) loans to another corporation, the business of which is not that of the taxpayer corporation (see *infra*, Sec. 6.06), if both corporations are under common control; (d) investments in properties or securities that are unrelated to the corporation's business (see *infra*, Sec. 6.06); and (e) retention of earnings to provide against "unrealistic hazards."[31] It should be noted that the foregoing transactions are not necessarily inconsistent with an accumulation for business needs — thus, funds that will be required for working capital or expansion might be properly temporarily invested in marketable securities or lent to shareholders — nor do they establish that the corporation's purpose is to shield shareholders against the individual income tax. They serve as signals to the government, however, and may bring on a searching inquiry as to the corporation's reasons for accumulating its earnings.

Sec. 6.04.   "Reasonable needs of the business" — Anticipated needs

Section 537, providing that the term "reasonable needs of the business" includes "the reasonably anticipated needs of the business," was enacted in 1954. According to the Senate Report on the 1954 Code:

> It is intended that this provision will make clear that there is no requirement that the accumulated earnings and profits be invested immediately in the business so long as there is an indication that future needs of the business require such accumulation. In any case where there exists a definite plan for the investment of earnings and profits, such corporation need not necessarily consummate these plans in a relatively short period after the close of the taxable year. However, where the future needs of the business are uncertain or vague, or the plans for the future use of the accumulations are indefinite, the amendment does not prevent application of the accumulated earnings tax. (S. Rep. No. 1622, 83d Cong., 2d sess., p. 318).

The Senate Report also states (p. 69) that §537 will eliminate "the so-called immediacy test, under which there must be an immediate need for the funds in order to justify the retention of earnings." Of the pre-1954 litigated cases, the most frequently cited examples of the "immediacy test" are World Publishing Co. v. United States, 169

---

[31] The unreasonableness of such an accumulation is self-evident; the more interesting and relevant question is whether it negates, rather than establishes, the tax avoidance purpose required by §531. See *supra* Sec. 6.02.

F.2d 186, 37 AFTR 150 (10th Cir. 1948), cert. denied 335 U.S. 911, and KOMA, Inc. v. Commissioner, 189 F.2d 390, 40 AFTR 712 (10th Cir. 1951), but in both of these cases the taxpayer's plans for expansion could not have been carried out for an uncertain period of time, and it is doubtful that §537 would have made any difference in the result.[32] It should also be noted that §537 does not repudiate the theory of the *World Publishing Co.* case that the reasonableness of an accumulation for expenditures that cannot be made until a later year is dependent, in part, on whether the corporation is likely to enjoy substantial earnings during the waiting period.

The regulations state that the corporation's plans, in order to constitute a reasonably anticipated business need, must be specific, definite, and feasible. As a practical aid to demonstrating the "concreteness" of such plans, book entries (e.g., specific reserve accounts) may be helpful, although courts have been quick to note that they are not controlling.[33] Where the future business needs are uncertain or vague, or the plans for future use of an accumulation are inchoate and nebulous, suggesting an afterthought on the part of the taxpayer, the tax has ordinarily been imposed, since the needs for the accumulation were not reasonable anticipated.[34] The regulations, Regs. §1.537-1(b)(2), provide that subsequent events will not vitiate an accumulation if all the elements of reasonable anticipation are present at the close of the accumulation year. Thus, it has been held that current accumulations for future needs were reasonable when made, even though the plans are abandoned at a later date, or where a long delay was justified.[35] But an unexplained delay in carrying out the plans or an indefinite postponement may be considered in determining whether the taxpayer actually intended to carry out its alleged plans. The regulations also note that if the plans are not consummated, this fact may be considered in determining the reasonableness of *subsequent* accumulations.

[32] See also Frank H. Ayres & Son, ¶54,278 P-H Memo TC ("immediate need" is a label used in cases where there was an unreasonable accumulation of earnings either because the need or plan of the corporation was so vague, tentative or indefinite that it did not justify the accumulation or . . . for some reason the contemplated expenditures could not be made during the period under review or in the ascertainable future").

[33] See Smoot Sand and Gravel Corp. v. Commissioner, *supra* note 28; Ted Bates & Co., Inc., *supra* note 8.

[34] See American Metal Products Corp. v. Commissioner, 287 F.2d 860, 7 AFTR 2d 1005 (8th Cir. 1961); I.A. Dress Co., Inc. v. Commissioner, *supra* note 22; Dixie, Inc. v. Commissioner, 277 F.2d 526, 5 AFTR 2d 1239 (2d Cir. 1960); Barrow Mfg. Co., Inc. v. Commissioner, *supra* note 14.

[35] Sterling Distributors, Inc. v. United States, *supra* note 15; Carolina Rubber Hose Co., ¶65,229 P-H Memo TC.

Sec. 6.05.   "Reasonable needs of the business" — Methods
of financing

The "reasonable needs of the business" can be satisfied, in many
cases, either with equity capital or with borrowed funds. Despite this
fact, the cases under §533 have almost invariably assumed that working capital, replacement of plant, and expansion will be financed in
full with retained earnings and not with borrowed funds. Similarly,
it has usually been assumed that funds to pay off indebtedness at
maturity, or perhaps even earlier, constitute a business need, even
though the debt might be refinanced if the corporation chose. In
Helvering v. Chicago Stock Yards Co., 318 U.S. 693, 30 AFTR 1091
(1943), however, the Supreme Court suggested that an accumulation
to pay off debt that could be refinanced might be unreasonable. If so,
debt held pro rata by stockholders would seem to be especially vulnerable.[36]

Even if an accumulation to pay off corporate indebtedness or to
purchase property without resorting to borrowing is found to be
beyond the reasonable needs of the business, thus bringing §533(a)
into play, the corporation might still rebut the existence of a tax
avoidance purpose by showing that the directors' excessive caution or
childhood training in thrift was the sole motivation for the accumulation. Such a defense is easily advanced but less easily proved, however, so the status of equity financing under §533(a) remains exceedingly important.

A related problem arises from the fact that earnings do not
necessarily have to be retained by a corporation with business needs
for funds, since it could pay a dividend and the stockholders could
reinvest the amounts thus received by them. This possibility was also
suggested in the *Chicago Stock Yards Co.* case, *supra* at 701-2; but
the suggestion has not been picked up for use in later cases, for the
reason that, if rigorously applied, it would always prevent the use of
retained earnings for business needs if the shareholder's after-tax
receipts would be sufficient to meet them if reinvested.[37] One aspect

[36] Cases that assume or hold that business needs may be properly financed
by retained earnings rather than outside funds are: Duke Laboratories, Inc. v.
United States, *supra* note 12; Electric Regulator Corp. v. Commissioner, *supra*
note 21; John J. Scripps Newspapers, *supra* note 3; Gazette Telegraph Co. v.
Commissioner, 19 T.C. 692 (1953) (Acq.), aff'd, 209 F.2d 926, 45 AFTR 267
(10th Cir. 1954); but see Nemours Corp., 38 T.C. 585 (1962).

For the vulnerability of shareholder-held debt, see Smoot Sand & Gravel
Corp. v. Commissioner, *supra* note 28.

[37] See discussion in Smoot Sand & Gravel Corp. v. Commissioner, *supra*
note 28.

The consent dividend procedure of §565 (*infra*, Sec. 6.09) amounts to a

of internal financing that bears special note is the effect of stock dividends. Under §312(d), the distribution of a non-taxable stock dividend has no effect on earnings and profits; hence, the fact that surplus has been capitalized by a stock dividend should not be relevant in determining whether earnings have been unreasonably accumulated for purposes of the §531 tax. The contrary holding in Harry A. Koch Co. v. Vinal, 228 F. Supp. 782, 13 AFTR 2d 1241 (D.C. Neb. 1964), was not appealed by the Service, but it will not be followed as a precedent, Rev. Rul. 65-68, 1965-1 C.B. 246, and few tax advisers are likely to rely on it.

Sec. 6.06. "Reasonable needs of the business" — What is "the" business?

Section 533 (a) speaks of the reasonable needs of "the" business, and the regulations contain the sweeping statement that the business of a corporation "is not merely that which it has previously carried on but includes, in general, any line of business which it may undertake." Regs. §1.537-3(a). This statement, as well as the cases, validates an accumulation of earnings and profits to finance natural growth, including both vertical and horizontal integration.[38] If a single corporation is engaged in two entirely separate businesses, their needs can probably be considered in the aggregate, so that the earnings of one enterprise may be accumulated to feed the other. This seems to follow *a fortiori* from cases allowing a corporation to accumulate earnings to finance a subsidiary engaged in an unrelated business.[39]

The reference in the regulations to "any line of business which [the corporation] may undertake" appears to endorse an accumulation to finance any business that the corporation's charter permits it to enter, a sweeping suggestion in these days of omnibus charters and relaxed charter amendment rules. In this connection, it should be

constructive distribution coupled with a reinvestment; as a mode of financing business needs, it is open to the same objection as an actual distribution followed by a reinvestment.

[38] See, for example, Ted Bates & Co., Inc., *supra* note 8 (extension of business operations to Europe); Metal Office Furniture Co., ¶52,313 P-H Memo TC (new line of merchandise); Lion Clothing Co., 8 T.C. 1181 (1947) (Acq.) (department store buying out leased department); Defiance Lumber Co., ¶53,246 P-H Memo TC (lumber manufacturer buying retail outlet); Smoot Sand & Gravel Corp. v. Commissioner, *supra* note 28 (possible entrance into ready-mix concrete business by sand and gravel company; but found, in latter proceeding cited *supra* note 13, not to be a "reasonable" possibility); Freedom Newspapers, Inc., ¶65,248 P-H Memo TC (accumulation to build up newspaper chain); Lane Drug Co., ¶44,131 P-H Memo TC (retail drug chain).

[39] See Sandy Estate Co., *supra* note 16 (one corporation, two businesses); Lannom Mfg. Co., ¶52,043 P-H Memo TC (1952); see also Latchis Theatres of Keene, Inc. v. Commissioner, 214 F.2d 834, 837, 45 AFTR 1836 (1st Cir. 1954).

noted that for many years the regulations qualified the statement just quoted with the warning that "a radical change of business when a considerable surplus has been accumulated may afford evidence of a purpose to avoid the surtax." Regs. 118, §39.102-3(b). This statement has been dropped from the 1954 regulations.

Against this ambiguous background, we must assess the provisions in the regulations that an accumulation "[t]o acquire a business enterprise through purchasing stock or assets" is permissible and that the business of a corporation "is not merely that which it has previously carried on but includes, in general, any line of business which it may undertake." Regs. §§1.537-2(b)(2) and 1.537-3(a). Let us assume that a corporation engaged in publishing a newspaper in New York City accumulates its earnings and profits primarily for the purpose of acquiring a cement factory in Colorado. If we take at face value the statement in Regs. §1.537-3(a) that the business of the corporation is "not merely that which it has previously carried on but includes, in general, any line of business which it may undertake," the accumulation is within the corporation's business needs and cannot be regarded as an investment in properties "unrelated to the activities of the business." Regs. §1.537-2(c)(4). The statutory presumption of §533(a) would then be inapplicable. Without relying on §533(a), however, the government might argue that the radical change in the character of the corporation's activities was evidence of a purpose to avoid tax on its shareholders, and that if on all the evidence the tax was applicable, the accumulated earnings credit of §535(c)(1) would immunize the accumulation only to the extent that it was required to purchase the cement factory, leaving any residue subject to tax.

Although the regulations do not bring the distinction to the fore, it seems essential that "business" be differentiated from "investment" in determining if an accumulation is beyond the reasonable needs of "the" business. If our New York City newspaper publisher accumulated its earnings and profits in order to purchase oil royalties or mining claims, intending to hold them as investments, §533(a) would presumably be brought into play just as it would by an accumulation to purchase marketable securities or to increase idle cash balances. As to an accumulation to acquire rental real estate (apartment houses, etc.), the relevant line may be that which is drawn under §355, between rental property held for investment and that which is held as part of an active conduct of a trade or business (*infra*, Sec. 11.04); although §533(a) does not speak of "active conduct" of the business, as does §355, this concept seems implicit in the statutory purpose.[40]

What if a corporation accumulates its earnings and profits for investment in another corporation (in the form of a contribution to capital, a purchase of stock, or a loan evidenced by securities or on open account)? According to the regulations, the business of the second corporation "may be considered in substance, although not in legal form, the business of the first corporation," if the second corporation is "a mere instrumentality" of the first. Reg. §1.537-3(b). This relationship may be established, according to the regulations, if the first corporation owns at least 80 percent of the second corporation's voting stock; if less than this amount is owned, "the particular circumstances of the case" will determine whether the first corporation is accumulating for a business of its own or not. The 80 percent benchmark is not to be found in the Code; it derives from a congressional committee report on the 1954 Code, where it is expressed as "the opinion" of the committee. H. Rep. No. 1337, 83d Cong., 2d Sess., 53; see also S. Rep. No. 1622, *ibid.*, 70. The regulations also echo the committee reports in stating that the first corporation's business does not include the business of a second corporation if the latter is a personal holding company, an investment company, or a corporation not engaged in the active conduct of a trade or business. Although the subsidiary may thus be regarded as an extension of the parent corporation in some circumstances, presumably the parent may accumulate to finance the subsidiary's activities only if the subsidiary's own resources are insufficient.[41]

The regulations focus on accumulations by parent corporations for the business needs of their subsidiaries, and say nothing about the propriety of an accumulation by a "brother" corporation to meet the business needs of a "sister" corporation. See, however, Regs. §1.537-2(c)(3), stating that loans to another corporation under common control with the taxpayer may evidence an unreasonable accumulation, if the business of the borrowing corporation "is not that of the taxpayer corporation."[42]

[40] See Henry Van Hummell, Inc., *supra* note 17; Kerr-Cochran, Inc. v. Commissioner, 253 F.2d 121, 1 AFTR 2d 1109 (8th Cir. 1958); Jacob Sincoff, Inc. v. Commissioner, 20 T.C. 288, 292 (1953), aff'd 209 F.2d 569, 45 AFTR 175 (2d Cir. 1953); Smith, Inc., v. Commissioner, 292 F.2d 470, 8 AFTR 2d 5119 (9th Cir. 1961).

[41] See Olin Corporation v. Commissioner, 42 B.T.A. 1203, 1216 (1940), aff'd 128 F.2d 185, 29 AFTR 492 (7th Cir. 1942); Automotive Rebuilding Co., Inc. ¶58,197 P-H Memo TC (1958).

[42] See Latchis Theatres of Keene, Inc. v. Commissioner, *supra* note 39; Factories Investment Corp. v. Commissioner, 328 F.2d 721, 13 AFTR 2d 880

Sec. 6.07.   "Reasonable needs of the business" — Stock redemptions

In a number of recent cases, the courts have had to pass on the applicability of §531 to accumulations of earnings and profits for the purpose of redeeming the corporation's stock or to provide for business needs after the corporate assets were depleted by a redemption. As will be seen (*infra*, Ch. 7), a pro rata redemption of stock from all shareholders is ordinarily taxable as a dividend to the extent of the corporation's earnings and profits. An accumulation of earnings to effect such a redemption, therefore, is no different than an accumulation of current earnings to pay dividends in later years; unless the distribution is delayed for an unreasonable period or is designed to give the shareholders the benefit of an anticipated lower effective tax rate when payment is made, the accumulation seems to raise no §531 problem. A redemption that is not pro rata, however, can be treated as a sale by the shareholder of the redeemed stock, with the result that the difference between the amount received by him and the adjusted basis of his stock will constitute capital gain or loss (*infra*, Ch. 7); and a few pro rata redemptions receive similar treatment. Although such a transaction transfers corporate assets to the shareholder, its capital gain (or loss) consequences differentiate it from the kind of taxable distribution that §531 is intended to encourage; and this may lead the Internal Revenue Service to assert that the accumulation was a way of avoiding the income tax on the shareholders,[43] was not for the reasonable needs of the business, or both.

A redemption of the stock of one or more shareholders is fre-

---

(2d Cir. 1964) (relation of taxpayer's accumulations to business of corporation under common ownership; accumulation to assist tenant); Fine Realty, Inc. v. U.S., 209 F. Supp. 286, 10 AFTR 2d 5751 (D. Minn. 1962) (multiple real estate development corporations); John P. Scripps Newspapers, *supra* note 3; Bremerton Sun Publishing Co., *supra* note 17 (loans to "sister" corporations, engaged in the same line of business as the taxpayer, did not constitute "unrelated investments").

See generally, Altman, Corporate Accumulation of Earnings, *supra* note 2, at 949-958.

[43] To the extent of his gain, of course, the shareholder whose stock is redeemed pays an income tax, though at the capital gain rate. Although this suggests that the corporation has not been availed of "for the purpose of avoiding the income tax with respect to its shareholders" within the meaning of §532(a), the Service would no doubt respond that the income tax has been "avoided" to the extent of the shareholder's adjusted basis for his stock, as well as by the shareholders whose stock is not redeemed; moreover, the concept of "avoidance" may encompass a rate lower than that imposed on ordinary income, in view of §531's function. See Apollo Industries, Inc., 44 T.C. 1 (1965) (accumulation not excused by possibility of future tax at capital gain rate), reversed on another ground, *supra* note 11.

quently employed as a method of shifting partial or complete control of the corporation to the remaining shareholders, without depleting their personal funds in the process. An accumulation of corporate earnings for this purpose hardly seems to provide for "the reasonable needs of the business" within the meaning of §533(a); but there are several cases in which a business nexus has been found, usually because the shareholders who were brought out constituted a dissenting minority or because the remaining shareholders were key employees whose increased proprietary interest was regarded as helpful to the corporation's business. Because the importance of the redemption to the corporation's business activities is often tenuous or debatable, however, while the success of the remaining shareholders in achieving an increase in their proportional control is ordinarily obvious, some courts have viewed with less tolerance the accumulation of corporate earnings to effect a non pro rata redemption; and the unsettled state of the law suggests caution in relying on the pro-taxpayer decisions, especially if the contemplated redemption is not likely to occur until a distant future date.[44]

If the redemption is not an unavoidable response to a business problem, but is required by a shareholder agreement to retire the shares of any party thereto upon his death or retirement, it seems even more vulnerable. The retention of shares after retirement (or their transfer to a deceased shareholder's heirs) does not necessarily threaten any harm to the business; and the dominant motive for such agreements is usually the desire of active shareholder-employees to keep others from sharing in the earning capacity of the business and in its management, neither of which possibilities automatically endangers "the business." In a particular case, of course, a shareholder's death or retirement may create the kind of business danger

---

[44] See Dill Mfg. Co., 39 B.T.A. 1023 (1939) (redemption of 49 percent interest justified); Gazette Publ. Co. v. Self. 103 F. Supp. 779, 41 AFTR 1033 (D. Ark. 1952) (same, where 25 percent minority threatened sale to outsiders); Pelton Steel Casting Co. v. Commissioner, 251 F.2d 278, 1 AFTR 2d 542 (7th Cir. 1958), cert. denied, 356 U.S. 958 (§531 applied to accumulation to redeem 80 percent interest); Ted Bates & Co., ¶65,251 P-H Memo TC (redemption to permit sale of stock to key executives; §531 tax held inapplicable) KOMA, Inc. v. Commissioner, 189 F.2d 390, 40 AFTR 712 (10th Cir. 1951) (stock retired for non-corporate reason); see also Penn Needle Art Co., ¶58,099 P-H Memo TC (tax inapplicable where accumulation for other business purposes was used to redeem stock of 50 percent shareholder to end a serious and unexpected dispute); Hedberg-Friedheim Contracting Co. v. Commissioner, supra note 5 (shareholder deadlock; §531 tax upheld); Five Star Mfg. Co. v. Commissioner, 355 F.2d 724, 17 AFTR 2d 183 (5th Cir. 1966) (payment for dissenting shareholder's stock deductible as business expense).

See generally, Herwitz, Stock Redemptions and the Accumulated Earnings Tax, 74 Harv. L. Rev. 866 (1961); Altman, supra note 2, at 941-949.

that has led some courts to regard a redemption as a reasonable need of the business; but it is a long step from this possibility to the conclusion that accumulating earnings to eliminate such hypothetical dangers is always responsive to an actual or "reasonably anticipated" need of the business. (Moreover, an *option*, rather than an *obligation*, to retire the shares of retiring or deceased stockholders would usually protect the corporation adequately; it could then accumulate or not, according to its business judgment from time to time; and if insurance policies were procured, the proceeds could be retained or paid out, depending on the circumstances.) Although some authorities believe that the issue will be decided in the corporation's favor, especially if its obligation is funded by life insurance, the question can hardly be regarded as settled.[44a]

Whatever may be the status of the redemption itself, subsequent accumulations to meet business needs (e.g., expansion, etc.) are less vulnerable, even though they would not have been necessary if the corporate assets had not been depleted by the redemption. In such a case, the pre-redemption accumulations might have been improper; but the government's failure to attack them does not mean that the post-redemption accumulations exceed the reasonable needs of the business. The status of post-redemption accumulations to pay off a debt incurred to finance the redemption itself is more debatable; if the

---

[44a] See Goldstein, Tax Aspects of Corporate Business Use of Life Insurance, 18 Tax L. Rev. 133, 207ff (1963); Polasky, Planning for the Disposition of a Substantial Interest in a Closely Held Business (Part III), 46 Iowa L. Rev. 516 (1961); Note, The Use of Life Insurance to Fund Agreements Providing for Disposition of a Business Interest at Death, 71 Harv. L. Rev. 687 (1958); Herwitz, *supra* note 44. Emeloid Co., Inc. v. Commissioner, 189 F.2d 230, 40 AFTR 674 (3d Cir. 1951), which is often quoted for its statement that "key man insurance" is essential to a closely-held business, involved a limited question, viz., whether funds borrowed to purchase single-premium life insurance policies to finance a corporation's obligation under a stock-retirement agreement constituted "borrowed invested capital" for excess profits tax purposes under a regulation requiring the debt to be "incurred for business reasons and not merely to increase the excess profits credit." It should be noted, moreover, that an accumulation of corporate earnings in connection with key man insurance policies whose proceeds *will be retained by the corporation* is much more easily defended than an accumulation for policies whose proceeds must be used to redeem stock. On the other hand, if the corporation's obligation to redeem stock under a shareholder agreement is funded with low-cost insurance, the resulting accumulation of earnings and profits may be quite small until the proceeds are collected.

The use of life insurance in conjunction with stock retirement plans raises a number of collateral questions, e.g., the effect on the corporation's taxable income and earnings and profits of paying the premiums and, later, receiving the proceeds (see §264 re non-deductibility of premiums; *supra*, Sec. 5.03, re effect on earnings and profits; §101, re receipt of proceeds by beneficiary), and the possibility that a payment of premiums will be treated as a constructive distribution by the corporation (*supra*, Sec. 5.05). For further discussion, see articles cited *supra*.

discharge of such a debt is treated as a bona fide business need, corporations contemplating a redemption could side-step the risk of a pre-redemption accumulation by redeeming first and accumulating later.[45]

Sec. 6.08.   Presumptions and burden of proof problems

Under procedural principles generally applicable to income tax litigation, the Commissioner's determination of additional tax liability is presumptively correct; the burden of proving the determination wrong by a preponderance of the evidence, together with the corresponding burden of going forward with the evidence, is on the taxpayer. Thus, the taxpayer ordinarily is the moving party in civil tax litigation, and bears the risk of non-persuasion if the evidence is in equipoise.

1. *Statutory presumption re "business needs."* In addition to this presumption of correctness in favor of the government, §533(a) provides that the fact that earnings are permitted to accumulate beyond the reasonable needs of the business shall be determinative of the forbidden purpose to avoid shareholder taxes, unless the taxpayer corporation proves to the contrary by a preponderance of the evidence (*supra* note 20). The regulations state that the presumption created by §533(a) adds "still more weight" to the Commissioner's determination of a §531 tax liability, Regs. §1.533-1(b); and in practice, the taxpayer's last clear chance to prove that the unreasonable accumulation was not motivated by a desire to avoid shareholder taxes is rarely availed of.[46]

2. *Burden of proof in Tax Court cases: §534.* In 1954, Congress enacted §534, providing a method by which the taxpayer can switch to the Commissioner the burden in certain Tax Court proceedings of proving that its accumulations were unreasonable. Briefly stated, §534 provides that if a notice of deficiency is based in whole or in part on an allegation that earnings were permitted to accumulate beyond the reasonable needs of the business, the burden of proof shall be on the government unless, before the notice of deficiency is mailed to the taxpayer, it is notified that the proposed deficiency includes an accumulated earnings tax. If the corporation is given such a notification, it may submit a statement of the grounds on which it relies to establish that the accumulation is not beyond the reasonable needs

---

[45] But "Redeem Now, Pay Later" was upheld as a corporate way of life in Mountain State Steel Foundries, Inc. v. Commissioner, 284 F.2d 737, 6 AFTR 2d 5910 (4th Cir. 1960).

[46] *Supra* note 22.

of the business, together with facts sufficient to show the basis thereof; and the government then has the burden of proof with respect to the grounds set out in the statement.[47] To be effective in shifting the burden of proof, the taxpayer's "section 534 statement" must constitute more than mere notice of an intent to prove the reasonableness of the accumulation; rather, the taxpayer must show its hand by stating with clarity and specificity the grounds on which it will rely to prove reasonable business needs, and by setting out the facts (not the evidence, but more than conclusions of law) that, if proven, support the alleged business needs for the accumulation.[48]

The importance of §534 in practice is not easily assessed. Since the Tax Court has steadfastly refused to rule in advance of trial on the sufficiency of §534 statements, an attorney would need an abnormally strong nervous system to risk his client's entire case on a test of strength over the burden of proof issue. As a result, taxpayers ordinarily put in all available evidence on the reasonableness and purpose of their accumulations rather than remain at parade rest in the hope that the government's case will be inadequate. Thus §534 may shift the burden of persuasion, but it is not likely to alter the burden of going forward with the evidence. In a number of cases, the Tax Court has refrained from passing on the adequacy of a taxpayer's §534 statement because it found "on the whole record" that the accumulation exceeded the reasonable needs of the business; and this practice elicited a recent admonition by the Court of Appeals for the Second Circuit that "in close cases the determination of who has the burden of proof on the unreasonable accumulations issue must be resolved."[49] If the issue is resolved in the taxpayer's favor, the

---

[47] Section 534 was enacted in response to complaints of unfairness in administration of the accumulated earnings tax, especially because of the difficulty and expense of proving that an accumulation was for the corporation's business needs. See Casey v. Commissioner, *supra* note 8 ("Congress did not want the tax authorities to be second-guessing the responsible managers of corporations as to whether and to what extent profits should be distributed or retained, unless the taxing authorities were in a position to prove that their position was correct"); H.R. Rep. No. 1337, 83d Cong., 2d Sess. 52 (1954); S. Rep. No. 1622, 83d Cong., 2d Sess. 68 (1954).

As enacted, §534 embraced only 1954 Code years, but in 1955, it was amended to apply to 1939 Code years for cases tried on the merits thereafter.

[48] For decisions on the adequacy of the taxpayer's §534 statement, see Factories Investment Co. v. Commissioner, 39 T.C. 908 (1963), aff'd, 328 F.2d 721, 13 AFTR 2d 880 (2d Cir. 1964); Bremerton Sun Publishing Co., *supra* note 17; I.A. Dress Co., Inc. v. Commissioner, *supra* note 22; Dixie, Inc. v. Commissioner, *supra* note 34; Commissioner v. Young Motor Co., Inc., *supra* note 11.

[49] R. Gsell & Co. v. Commissioner, *supra* note 11; Holzman, Burden of Proof in Accumulated Earnings Tax Cases and Its Development In the Second Circuit Court of Appeals, 11 Buff. L. Rev. 328 (1962); Wagman, Taxation of Accumulated Earnings and Profits: A Procedural Wrangle, 37 Taxes 573 (1959).

determination may be controlling in computing the accumulated earnings credit of §535(c)(1) as well as under §533(a), though this question has not yet been answered by the courts.[49a]

3. Presumption applicable to holding and invesment companies. Section 533(b) provides that the fact that a corporation is "a mere holding or investment company" shall be prima facie evidence of the purpose to avoid the income tax on its shareholders. The regulations state that a "holding company" is a corporation "having practically no activities except holding property and collecting the income therefrom or investing therein" and that an "investment company" is a corporation whose activities consist substantially of buying and selling stock, securities, real estate, or other investment property "so that the income is derived not only from the investment yield but also from profits upon market fluctuations."[50] As in the case of a business corporation that has accumulated beyond its reasonable needs, a holding or investment company may refute, with appropriate evidence, the inference that its accumulations were motivated by the purpose to avoid tax on its shareholders.

Section 533(b) must be considered in conjunction with §532(b)-(1) and (2), exempting personal holding companies (*infra*, Sec. 6.20) and foreign personal holding companies (*infra*, Sec. 6.40) from the accumulated earnings tax. These exemptions are not animated by charity; rather, they reflect the fact that the undistributed income of personal holding companies and of foreign personal holding companies is subject to a special system of taxation, whether the accumulation was motivated by a tax avoidance purpose or not. Because most closely-held holding or investment companies are exempt from the accumulated earnings tax by virtue of §532(a)(1) and (2), there are few targets left for §533(b). Moreover, although by its terms it is applicable to any holding or investment company, whether closely-held or not, §533(b) is not regarded as a threat by publicly-held companies, which can usually rebut the existence of a tax avoidance purpose. A publicly-held corporation might be uneasy about §533(b), however, if it deliberately appealed to upper-bracket shareholders with an announced investment policy of accumulating its investment income.

[49a] Without discussing the question, the Tax Court may have assumed that the statement could have this double effect in John P. Scripps Newspapers, *supra* note 3.

[50] Regs. §1.533-1(c). The regulations assume that every holding or investment company is automatically a "mere" holding or investment company within the meaning of §533(b); but see Industrial Bankers Securities Corp. v. Higgins, 104 F.2d 177, 181, 23 AFTR 34 (2d Cir. 1939).

Sec. 6.09.   Computation of accumulated earnings tax

The accumulated earnings tax is imposed by §531 on the corporation's "accumulated taxable income," the rate being 27½ percent of the first $100,000 of accumulated taxable income and 38½ percent of any accumulated taxable income over $100,000. The tax is imposed in addition to the regular corporate income tax. Despite this fact, in extreme cases the shareholders may find it advisable to accumulate earnings in the corporation, subject to both the corporate income tax and the accumulated earnings tax, rather than receive the earnings as dividends. And, even in less extreme cases, the uncertainties in §531 may lead the shareholder to gamble on an accumulation in the hope that the corporation will either escape scot-free or be able to compromise its potential §531 liability.

As stated, the taxable base is the corporation's "accumulated taxable income" for the year or years in question. (The tax is imposed on the accumulated taxable income of the year or years for which the forbidden purpose is found, not the entire accumulation of earlier years; but the latter may be relevant on the tax avoidance or reasonable business needs issues.) The term "accumulated taxable income" is defined by §535 to mean the corporation's taxable income, with certain adjustments, minus the sum of (a) the dividends paid deduction of §561, and (b) the accumulated earnings credit of §535(c). In more detail, the computation of "accumulated taxable income" is as follows:

1. Adjustments to taxable income. The corporation's taxable income, defined by §63(a), is subjected to certain adjustments, primarily for the purpose of deriving an amount that corresponds more closely to economic reality and thus measures more accurately the corporation's dividend-paying capacity for the year. Thus, taxable income is reduced by corporate income taxes accrued by the corporation during the taxable year, charitable contributions disallowed by the 5 percent limitation of §170(b)(2), and capital losses disallowed by §1211(a). Conversely, the net operating loss deduction, capital loss carryover, and 85 percent dividends received deduction are disallowed. The excess of net long-term captial gain over net short-term capital loss (adjusted for taxes attributable to this excess) is eliminated from taxable income, and a few other adjustments of a minor nature are also made.[51]

---

[51] These adjustments resemble, but are not identical with, those required to convert taxable income to earnings and profits (*supra,* Sec. 5.03); see Ted Bates & Co., *supra* note 8. Sitrick, The Computation of Earnings and Profits for

2. *Dividends paid deduction.* Taxable income, as thus adjusted, is then reduced by the dividends paid deduction of §561. This deduction is the sum of two amounts:

(a) *Dividends paid during the taxable year.* This amount must obviously be taken into account in computing the accumulated earnings tax, which is fundamentally a tax on undisturbed income. The term "dividend" means a distribution from current earnings and profits or from post-1913 accumulated earnings and profits, as under §316 (*supra*, Sec. 5.02), so that, in general, the corporation gets a deduction in computing its accumulated earnings tax only if the shareholder must report the distribution as ordinary income. There is an exception for amounts distributed in liquidation, however, which permits the corporation to deduct some distributions that may be treated by the shareholder as capital gain or even as a return of capital.[52] Because of the difficulty of determining a corporation's undistributed income with exactitude before the taxable year comes to a close, §563(a) provides that the dividends paid deduction for a particular year shall include dividends paid within the first 2½ months of the following year.

(b) *"Consent dividends" for the taxable year.* The "consent dividend" procedure, found in §565, permits the shareholders of a corporation to agree to treat a specified portion of the corporation's earnings and profits as a dividend, even though no actual distribution is made. This enables a corporation that has earnings and profits but does not wish to make an actual distribution to avoid possible liability for the accumulated earnings tax. The "consent dividend" is treated as though it had been distributed to the shareholders in money on the last day of the corporation's taxable year and had been turned back by them to the corporation as a contribution to capital.

3. *Accumulated earnings credit.* The final step in the computation of "accumulated taxable income" is to deduct the "accumulated earnings credit" of §535(c). This credit was created by the 1954 Code to permit small companies to accumulate a minimum amount

Purposes of the Accumulated Earnings Tax, 20 Tax L. Rev. 733 (1965), argues that the §531 penalty itself should be applied to reduce earnings and profits of the year in which the deficiency notice is issued, a theory that seems to place undue emphasis on the timing of the 90-day letter.

[52] Amounts distributed in liquidation (including partial liquidations and some stock redemptions) qualify for the dividends paid deduction of §561 (if the distribution is pro rata among the shareholders) to the extent "properly chargeable to earnings and profits." §562(b)(1)(A). (For similar language, see §312(e), *infra,* Sec. 7.85). Moreover. if a complete liquidation occurs within 24 months after the adoption of a plan of liquidation, all pro rata distributions during this period constitute "dividends" to the extent of the liquidating corporation's *current* earnings for the year of such distribution. §562(b)(1)(B). Hence, a liquidating corporation can obtain as many as three taxable years of immunity from §531 by carefully timing its distributions.

of earnings and profits (originally set at $60,000, but increased to $100,000 in 1958), free of any risk that the accumulation will be found unreasonable, as well as to exempt, in the case of operating companies, such portion of the taxable year's accumulation as is retained for any reasonable business needs. The $100,000 minimum must be adjusted to reflect any accumulations carried forward from prior years, since it is an overall allowance for the corporation's entire life. Thus, in the case of a "mere holding or investment company," the credit is the amount, if any, by which $100,000 exceeds the accumulated earnings and profits at the close of the preceding taxable year. In the case of other corporations, the credit is either (a) the amount just described, or (b) an amount equal to such part of the earnings and profits for the taxable year as is retained for the reasonable needs of the business (adjusted if the corporation had an excess of net long-term capital gain over net short-term capital loss), whichever is greater.[53] The credit is not allowed in certain circumstances if the corporation is formed or acquired for a tax avoidance purpose; and the number of credits allowed to the members of an affiliated group of corporations is sometimes limited (*infra*, Secs. 13.31 and 13.33).

Part B.   Personal Holding Companies

Sec. 6.20.   Introductory

Since 1934, the Internal Revenue Code has imposed a special tax on the undistributed income of so-called "personal holding companies" — corporations controlled by a limited number of shareholders and deriving a large percentage of their income from specified sources. Personal holding companies were singled out for this punishment after extensive investigations in 1934 and again in 1937 led Congress to conclude that they were vehicles by which their shareholders could avoid the graduated income tax imposed on individuals, and that the traditional weapon against such a use of the corporation, the accumulated earnings tax of §531, could be avoided if the forbidden purpose was not detected or proved. Three of the most common devices were:

    1. "Incorporated pocket books." An individual would organize a corporation to hold his investment securities, so that the dividends and interest received would be taxed at the rela-

---

[53] On the retention of current earninigs for business needs, see *supra* note 21; for illustrative computations of the credit, see Regs. §1.535-3(b)(3).

tively flat and low corporate rate, rather than at the more steeply graduated individual rate.

2. *"Incorporated talents."* A motion picture actor (or other highly compensated person) would organize a corporation and agree to work for it for a relatively modest salary. The corporation would then "contract out" his services at their fair value, so that the difference between the amount received by it and the amount paid would be taxed only at the corporate rate.[54]

3. *Incorporated yachts, country estates, etc.* In its simplest form, this device consisted of transferring a yacht, country estate, or similar property to a corporation, together with income-producing property, in the hope that the corporation could deduct the operating expenses and depreciation on the yacht, etc., from the income yielded by the other property. Another version, more modest but also more sophisticated, depended on proof that the yacht could not be rented to an outsider for as much as its operating expenses and depreciation. The corporation would then charter the yacht to its sole shareholder for this "arm's-length" amount, and he would transfer to the corporation enough income-producing property to make up the "deficit" between the rent received by the corporation and the operating expenses and depreciation. In either form, the arrangement was dependent on establishing that the corporation's expenses in operating the yacht were "ordinary and necessary" business expenses; but the second version offered a greater hope of success.

Although these devices were not fool-proof, the Treasury in 1934 and 1937 asked for more explicit legislation, and Congress responded with a tax on the undistributed income of any corporation meeting certain mechanical standards of stock ownership and income. The 1934 law was extensively revised in 1937; from then until 1964, changes were largely confined to matters of detail, but in 1964 there was another comprehensive revision and tightening of these provisions.

As revised in 1964, the personal holding company tax (§§541-547) has the following characteristics, discussed in more detail hereafter:

1. *Definition of "personal holding company."* To qualify as a personal holding company, a corporation must meet both an income test and a stock ownership test, *viz.*, at least 60 percent

---

[54] See Commissioner v. Laughton, 113 F.2d 103, 25 AFTR 340 (9th Cir. 1940), holding that the validity of such a device (apart from the personal holding company provisions) depended on "whether [Charles] Laughton's hiring of himself to his wholly-owned corporation for a salary substantially less than the compensation for which the corporation supplied his services as its employee to various motion picture producers, constituted, in effect, a single transaction by Laughton in which he received indirectly the larger sum paid by the producers." See also Fontaine Fox, 37 B.T.A. 271 (1938).

of its "adjusted ordinary gross income" must be "personal holding company income" (primarily passive investment income,
plus personal service income in the case of "incorporated talents,"
infra, Sec. 6.21); and more than 50 percent of its stock (by
value) must be owned — directly or indirectly, actually or constructively — by 5 or fewer individuals (*infra*, Sec. 6.23).

Certain corporations are exempt from the personal holding
company category — primarily tax-exempt corporations, banks,
life insurance companies, surety companies, certain finance companies, foreign personal holding companies, and certain foreign
corporations (*infra*, Sec. 6.24).

2. *Tax rate and base*. The tax is imposed on the corporation's "undistributed personal holding company income." In some
instances this phrase means the corporation's taxable income,
less its federal income tax and any dividends paid by it, but
usually a number of other adjustments are required to convert
"taxable income" into "undistributed personal holding company
income" (*infra*, Sec. 6.25). The tax rate is 70 percent of undistributed personal holding company income.

3. *Deficiency dividend procedure*. Because the prime purpose of the personal holding company tax is not to raise revenue
but to force such corporations to distribute earnings to their
shareholders (in whose hands the distributed earnings will be
subject to the graduated income tax), and in recognition of
the tax's virtually confiscatory rate, the Internal Revenue Code
provides a *locus poenitentiae* in the form of the "deficiency dividend" procedure. Briefly stated, this procedure permits the corporation, after its liability for a personal holding company tax
has been established, to make a dividend distribution to its
shareholders and to take this distribution into account in retroactive reduction of its tax liability. In effect, the shareholders
will be taxed currently by virtue of the distribution, and the
corporation will thereby become entitled to a partial or complete
refund of its personal holding company tax. The corporation's
liability for interest on the personal holding company tax is not
eliminated, however, nor is its liability for penalties, additions
for late filing or negligence, etc.

4. *Collateral consequences*. Personal holding companies are
not subject to the accumulated earnings tax of §531 — for whatever comfort this may confer. In the event that property (other
than money) is distributed to the shareholders of a personal
holding company in complete liquidation, §6162 permits the
Internal Revenue Service to extend the time for paying the
capital gains tax under §331(a)(1) (*infra*, Sec. 9.01) for a
period of five years on a showing of hardship. Section 267(a)(1),
denying the deduction of losses incurred on sales or exchanges
between related taxpayers (*supra*, Sec. 2.24), applies to transactions between two corporations under common control, if one
is a personal holding company.

5. *Special liquidation rules*. The Revenue Act of 1964 pro-

vided favorable liquidation treatment for certain corporations which became personal holding companies because of the 1964 changes (*infra*, Sec. 6.26).

The personal holding company tax is not a major revenue factor in the taxation of corporations and shareholders, with respect to either the number of personal holding company returns filed,[55] or the amount of penalty taxes actually paid. This may be due to the fact that many of the "incorporated pocketbooks" at which the personal holding company provisions were aimed by Congress, either operate under the scrutiny of attorneys and accountants who see to it that substantially all their income is distributed, or have been liquidated or sold by their shareholders.[56] In other instances, however, the practices that led to the enactment of the tax in 1934 and 1937 may be pursued in more sophisticated form, since personal holding company status can be avoided if care is taken to arrange a corporation's affairs so as to fall outside the definitional rules of thumb. Today's equivalent of the 1930-model personal holding company, in other words, may be satisfactorily disguised as a manufacturing or mercantile company, whose only risk in this area is the possible application of §531 (*supra*, Sec. 6.01) to its undistributed income.

Moreover, there is some reason to believe that at least part of the revenue raised by the personal holding company is contributed by

---

[55] Personal holding companies are required to file Schedule PH with their regular corporate income tax return, Form 1120. If the schedule is not filed, the statute of limitations on assessment of the personal holding company tax is extended from the usual 3 years to 6 years. §6501(f). Before 1954, a separate return was required, and a failure to file (except for reasonable cause) resulted in a 25 percent addition to the personal holding company tax. O'Sullivan Rubber Co. v. Commissioner, 120 F.2d 845, 27 AFTR 529 (2d Cir. 1941); Haywood Lumber & Mining Co. v. Commissioner, 178 F.2d 769, 38 AFTR 1223 (2d Cir. 1950).

[56] In exceptional cases, the shareholders of a personal holding company may be better off, on balance, if the corporation accumulates its income and pays the penalty tax than if it makes distributions to them. See Nemours Corporation, 38 T.C. 585, 593 (1962).

Personal holding companies of the "classic" variety sometimes merge into publicly-held investment companies, on a tax-free basis, so that the shareholders receive shares in these diversified companies in exchange for their personal holding company stock. See In the matter of Massachusetts Investors Trust, SEC Investment Company Act Release No. 2882 (May 20, 1959); In the matter of One William Street Fund, Inc., *ibid.* No. 2894 (July 2, 1959). The Service no longer issues advance rulings on whether the reorganization provisions apply to such transactions if the shareholders "achieve substantially wider diversification of the investment assets underlying their stock holdings." Rev. Proc. 62-32, 1962-2 C.B. 527, 530; Rev. Proc. 64-31, 1964-2 C.B. 947. The theory of the Service may be that, because of the diversification, there is no continuity of business enterprise (*infra*, Sec. 12.19); and in some cases, it may take the position that the personal holding company was not engaged in a "business" for purposes of the reorganization provisions.

corporations that have become personal holding companies only by accident, so to speak. One litigated case involved a closely-held manufacturing corporation that was in the process of liquidation. Its assets had been sold on credit, and more than 80 percent of its income in the taxable year consisted of interest on the sales price. The tax was held applicable:

> But, urges the petitioner, the personal holding company surtax was enacted to remedy the evil of the "incorporated pocketbook," deliberately created to reduce the personal taxes of those who created them, and therefore, to impose the tax upon a corporation in petitioner's position is a perversion of the Congressional purpose . . . It is, however, abundantly clear that Congress, in correcting an evil, is not narrowly confined to the specific instances which suggested the remedy . . . In enacting the very section being applied here, Congress was attempting to foreclose the defense available under [the accumulated earnings tax] that the accumulation of profits was responsive to a legitimate business need.[57]

Thus, the fact that a corporation does not have a Wall Street address or that its assets do not consist of inherited wealth does not immunize it against personal holding company tax liability; and the risk of accidental exposure was increased by the 1964 changes. As a consequence, these provisions are of wider interest than many attorneys realize.[58]

Sec. 6.21. Personal holding company income: The 60 percent income test

For a corporation to be classified as a personal holding company, both the stock ownership test of §542(a)(2) (*infra*, Sec. 6.23) and the "tainted income" test of §542(a)(1) must be satisfied. Because almost all closely-held corpoations (as well as some others) meet the

---

[57] O'Sullivan Rubber Co. v. Commissioner, 120 F.2d 845, 847-8, 27 AFTR 529 (2d Cir. 1941); 320 East 47th Street Corp. v. Commissioner, 243 F.2d 894, 51 AFTR 200 (2d Cir. 1957) (interest on a condemnation award held personal holding company income; but see the 1964 change in §543(b)(2)(C); McKinley Corp. of Ohio, 36 T.C. 1182 (1961).

[58] See Lubin, Personal Holding Companies and the Revenue Act of 1964, 63 Mich. L. Rev. 421 (1965); Shapiro, Personal Holding Companies Under the 1964 Revenue Act, 1965 So. Cal. Tax. Inst. 187; Lubick, Personal Holding Companies — Yesterday, Today and Tomorrow, 42 Taxes 855 (1964). For pre-1954 discussions, see Greenfield, Personal Holding Company Dangers and How To Meet Them, 13 N.Y.U. Inst. on Fed. Tax. 823 (1955); Cleary, Personal Holding Company Pitfalls, 11 *ibid.* 467 (1953); Klooster, Tax Advantages and Hazards In Operating as a Personal Holding Company, 8 J. Tax. 101 (1958); Jansen, Personal Holding Companies, 1958 Tulane Tax Inst. 482. For the early history of these provisions, see Rudick, Section 102 and Personal Holding Company Provisions of the Internal Revenue Code, 49 Yale L.J. 171 (1939); Paul, The Background of the Revenue Act of 1937, 5 U. of Chi. L. Rev. 41 (1937).

stock ownership test, the income requirement is ordinarily the acid test of personal holding company status.[59] This requirement is that at least 60 percent of the corporation's "adjusted ordinary gross income" for a taxable year constitute "personal holding company income."[60] "Adjusted ordinary gross income" was adopted in 1964 as the relevant measuring rod in an attempt to distinguish more precisely than prior law between the corporation's active business income and its passive investment income. Certain categories of income, such as rents, royalties, and interest, could in many cases be either active or passive depending on the circumstances; the adjusted ordinary gross income definition was designed to effect a more realistic classification of these items.

Briefly stated, "adjusted ordinary gross income" is defined by §543(b) to mean gross income less gains from the sale or other disposition of capital assets or §1231(b) assets;[61] and less depreciation, taxes, interest, and rent incurred in connection with certain rental income and mineral royalties. The latter adjustments are designed to determine whether these specially-treated activities are significant elements in the corporation's economic function or merely tax avoidance operations to disguise the importance of its personal holding company income.[62] Aside from these adjustments, however, the cor-

---

[59] For corporations filing a consolidated return, adjusted ordinary gross income and personal holding company income are ordinarily computed on a consolidated basis, thus eliminating intra-group dividends and interest. See §542(b); Regs. §1.1502-30(a) and (b)(4). Strict mechanical tests must be satisfied, however, to qualify for this treatment.

[60] Before the 1964 revision, §542 required that 80 percent of the corporation's gross income consist of personal holding company income.

[61] Because capital gains are excluded from "adjusted ordinary gross income," they now constitute a neutral category of income, counting neither for nor against the taxpayer when the 60 percent test is applied. This category evidently embraces income that is treated as capital gain under such provisions as §§301(c)(3), 302, 331, 1232(a), 1234, and 1241, as well as §1231 gains regardless of the outcome of the §1231 hotchpot. On the other hand, gain on the sale of a capital asset is included in "adjusted ordinary gross income" if it is taxed as ordinary income under such provisions as §§1245, 1250, 1239, 1246, and 1232(a)(2). See H.R. Rep. No. 749, 88th Cong., 2d sess., reprinted, 1964-1 C.B. (Part 2) 125, 347.

[62] Under prior law, highly-mortgaged rental property could be used to shelter personal holding company income regardless of its profitability, because the corporation's *gross income* was crucial. By looking to "adjusted ordinary gross income," the 1964 changes greatly reduce the usefulness of such rental property in this area. But high-gross-low-net *operating* businesses (e.g., bowling alleys, telephone answering services, automatic laundries, etc.) remain available even under the 1964 amendments, though the reduction of the percentage benchmark from 80 to 60 percent means that $100 of gross operating income will shelter only about $150 of tainted income (i.e., total gross income of $250; tainted income must be less than $150), whereas before 1964, it would shelter almost $400 (i.e., total gross income of $500; tainted income had to be less than $400).

poration's gross income is of primary importance under §542; and it should be noted that a bona fide manufacturing or mercantile corporation whose cost of goods sold in a given year approaches its gross receipts from sales, so that there is little or no gross operating income, may become a personal holding company if it receives any dividends, interest, or other personal holding company items. Note also that the corporate tax return itself does not contain an entry for "gross income," and §61, which purports to define this term, may include certain penumbral receipts not readily apparent on its face. Similarly, the line between expenditures that enter into the computation of gross income, and those that are deductible only in computing taxable income is not always clear.[63]

Sec. 6.22. "Personal holding company income": §543(a)

In applying the 60 percent test of §542(a)(1) (*supra*, Sec. 6.21), the following items of "adjusted ordinary gross income" are taken into account by §543(a), which defines personal holding company income:

1. *Dividends, interest, royalties, and annuities.* Dividends are included in personal holding company income whether they come within the normal rule of §316,[64] or attain that status by reason of such special rules as §1248 (sale of stock of controlled foreign corporation), §78 (gross-up of foreign tax paid by foreign subsidiary), or §551 (undistributed foreign personal holding company income).

The term "interest" is defined by Regs. §1.543-1(b)(2) as "any amounts, includible in gross income, received for the use of money loaned." Aside from the troublesome subject of original issue discount,[65] this definition is not ordinarily difficult to apply.[66] It should

---

[63] See Levine, Gross Income In The Personal Holding Company, 9 Tax L. Rev. 453 (1954).

For purposes of the extended statute of limitations, applicable if the taxpayer omits more than 25 percent of gross income, the term "gross income" is given a meaning virtually equivalent to gross receipts by §6501(e)(1)(A)(i) of the 1954 Code, but no comparable change was made in 1954 in the personal holding company provisions. For §6501, see Richards, The Extended Statute of Limitations on Assessment, 12 Tax L. Rev. 297 (1957).

[64] See *supra*, Sec. 5.02. Constructive distributions seen clearly embraced by §543(a)(1), see McKinley Corp. of Ohio, *supra* note 57; but cf. Fredbro Corp. v. Commissioner, 315 F.2d 784, 11 AFTR 2d 1216 (2d Cir. 1963).

[65] Compare Regs. §1.61-8(c), stating that original issue discount is interest, except as otherwise provided by law, with §1232(a)(2), providing that gain attributable to such discount "shall be considered as gain from the sale or exchange of property which is not a capital asset." See also United States v. Midland-Ross Corp., 381 U.S. 54, 15 AFTR 2d 836 (1965), equating original issue discount income with stated interest income; Jaglom v. Commissioner, 303 F.2d 847, 9 AFTR 2d 1686 (2d Cir. 1962) (allocation between principal and interest required where bonds with defaulted interest were purchased and

be noted that the "imputed interest" provisions of §483, enacted in 1964, will generate interest income where none would have existed under prior law. Two types of interest were excluded from adjusted ordinary gross income, and hence from personal holding company income, by the enactment in 1964 of §543(b)(2)(C): interest on condemnation awards, judgments and tax refund claims; and interest earned by certain dealers in United States securities. Moreover, interest that constitutes "rent" is treated as such under §543(a)(2) rather than as interest under §543(a)(1); and some finance companies and other commercial lenders whose income consists largely of interest are exempted from the personal holding company provisions (*infra*, Sec. 6.24).

"Royalties," as the term is used in §543(a)(1), generally include periodic receipts from licenses to use various kinds of intangible property right (such as patents, trademarks, trade names, franchises, good will, or technical know-how). Mineral, oil, and gas royalties are specially treated, as described *infra*, and so are copyright royalties. In some circumstances, moreover, royalties constitute "rents"[67] and are subject to the special rules of §543(a)(2) (*infra*). The principal classification problem concerns transactions in which it is not clear whether the transferor of property has granted a license on which it is receiving royalty payments, or has sold the property and is receiving installment payments on the sale price.[68] Another troublesome area is the agreement that combines a license of property with an undertaking by the licensor to perform services, so that the payments received must be allocated between "royalties" and compensation for services.[69]

2. *Rents.* Under pre-1964 law, rents were treated as personal

---

resold "flat"); Lubin v. Commissioner, 335 F.2d 209, 14 AFTR 2d 5341 (2d Cir. 1964).

[66] See Western Credit Co., Inc. v. Commissioner, 325 F.2d 1022, 13 AFTR 2d 431 (9th Cir. 1963) ("contract charges" imposed by lender held to be "interest"); Gunderson Bros. Engineering Corp., 42 T.C. 419 (1964) (finance charges treated as interest).

[67] See I.T. 3401, 1940-2 C.B. 166, where "delay rentals" under an oil and gas lease were held to constitute rents rather than royalties; Rev. Rul. 54-284, 1954-2 C.B. 275 (compensation from distribution and exhibition of films produced by taxpayer constituted rents; but note §543(a)(5), enacted in 1964).

[68] See Du Pont & Co. v. United States, 288 F.2d 904, 7 AFTR 2d 1107 (Ct. Cl. 1961) (disclosure of information held a license); Dairy Queen of Oklahoma, Inc. v. Commissioner, 250 F.2d 503, 52 AFTR 1092 (10th Cir. 1958) (sub-franchise agreement held a sale); T.E. Moberg v. Commissioner, 310 F.2d 782, 10 AFTR 2d 5974 (9th Cir. 1962); Rev. Rul 64-56, 1964-1 C.B. 133 (transfer of know-how).

[69] Portable Industries, Inc., 24 T.C. 571 (1964) (Acq.); Rev. Rul. 64-56, *supra* note 68; *infra*, Sec. 14.03 (re income from rents, royalties, and services).

holding company income unless they constituted 50 percent or more of the corporation's gross income. This was a compromise between the theory that rents were the kind of passive investment income that should not escape the graduated individual income tax by being accumulated in a corporation, and the theory that *bona fide* real estate operating corporations should not be subject to the penalty tax. In practice, however, the pre-1964 rule offered a convenient device for sheltering other forms of personal holding company income from the tax, since $100 of gross rental income could shield up to $100 of portfolio investment income. The attractiveness of real estate as a shelter from personal holding company status was further enhanced by the modest equity investment needed to acquire heavily mortgaged real estate generating large amounts of gross rent.

The 1964 revision of the personal company provisions attacked this problem (as pointed out *supra*, Sec. 6.21) by taking only the taxpayer's "adjusted income" from rents and mineral royalties, rather than its gross receipts from these sources, into account in computing "adjusted ordinary gross income." The corporation's "adjusted income" from rents is personal holding company income, unless (a) it constitutes 50 percent or more of the corporation's adjusted ordinary gross income and (b) dividends for the taxable year equal or exceed the amount (if any) by which its non-rent personal holding company income for that year exceeds 10 percent of its ordinary gross income. Thus, a corporation engaged predominantly in rental activities may escape personal holding company status, but if its non-rental personal holding company income is substantial, it must make taxable distributions thereof. The effect of the 1964 changes can be seen in this example:

> A corporation with gross income of $60,000 from rents and $40,000 from dividends would not have been a personal holding company under prior law; if the specially-treated deductions attributable to the rental property amounted to $30,000, however, it would fail the new 50 percent test of §543(a)(2)(A), since its "adjusted income" from rents ($30,000) is less than 50 percent of adjusted ordinary gross income ($70,000). If its specially-treated deductions were only $20,000, its "adjusted income" from rents would be $40,000 — 50 percent of its adjusted gross income ($80,000), and it would satisfy the 50 percent test of §543-(a)(2)(A). It would not satisfy the 10 percent test of §543(a)-(2)(B), however, unless it distributed at least $30,000, viz., the excess of dividend income ($40,000) over 10 percent of its ordinary gross income ($100,000). Only if its gross rental income were $360,000 or more could it avoid paying a dividend and at the same time avoid personal holding company status.

The term "rents" as used in §543(a)(2) excludes: (a) amounts that constitute personal holding company income by virtue of §543-(a)(6) (compensation for use of corporate property by a shareholder); (b) copyright royalties, as defined in §543(a)(4); and (c) produced film rents, as defined in §543(a)(5)(B). Interest on the sales price of real property sold to customers in the ordinary course of business, however, is treated as rent by §543(b)(3), in order to permit real estate dealers receiving interest on purchase money mortgages to avoid personal holding company status.[70]

3. Mineral, oil, and gas royalties. Under prior law, mineral, oil, and gas royalties were treated as personal holding company income, unless (a) they constituted 50 percent or more of the corporation's gross income, and (b) the corporation's business deductions under §162, other than compensation for the personal services of its shareholders, were at least 15 percent of its gross income. As revised in 1964, §543(a)(3) modifies these tests by providing that: (a) the 50 percent rule applies to the ratio of "adjusted royalty income" (*supra*, Sec. 6.21) to adjusted ordinary gross income; (b) other personal holding company income cannot exceed 10 percent of the corporation's ordinary gross income; and (c) depreciation, interest, and other business deductions that are specifically allowable under sections other than §162 are not to be counted in computing the 15 percent business expense rule.

The 15 percent business expense test is designed to separate operating companies from holding companies by demanding a minimum level of business activity; but the statute does not expressly require that these expenses be related to the production of royalty income. The 10 percent test, like that for rents, ensures that mineral royalties can not be used to shelter an excessive amount of other passive income. Finally, although income from working interests in oil and gas properties is not treated as personal holding company income, it must be adjusted under §543(b)(2)(B) in computing adjusted ordinary gross income (*supra*, Sec. 6.21), thereby making it more difficult to use this kind of income to avoid personal holding company status.

Mineral royalties are now defined by §543(b)(4) to include income from production payments and overriding royalties, thus overruling a questionable decision under prior law that this term did not include receipts from reserved production payments.[71]

4. Copyright royalties. Copyright royalties constitute personal

---

[70] For prior law, see W.G.S. Operating Co., Inc., ¶43,002 P-H Memo TC.
[71] United States v. 525 Co., 342 F.2d 759, 15 AFTR 2d 592 (5th Cir. 1965).

holding company income under §543(a)(4), but publishers and other active business firms are exempted by virtue of rules similar to those applicable to rental income and mineral royalties. To qualify for the exemption, the corporation's copyright royalties (except for shareholder-created works) must constitute 50 percent or more of its ordinary gross income; its other personal holding company income must not exceed 10 percent of its ordinary gross income; and its §162 deductions allocable to its copright royalties (other than for personal services rendered by shareholders and certain other items) must meet a complex test designed to insure a substantial level of business activity.[72]

5. *Produced film rents.* Produced film rents (defined as amounts derived from film properties acquired before substantial completion of production) are subject under §543(a)(5) to the treatment formerly accorded to rents, viz., such amounts are personal holding company income unless they constitute 50 percent or more of the corporation's ordinary gross income. This test is relatively easy to satisfy, and should protect most bona fide film production companies. Income from film properties acquired after substantial completion of production, however, is treated as copyright royalty income, and is subject to the more stringent rules of §543(a)(4).

6. *Compensation for use of corporate property by shareholders.* Compensation for the use of corporate property constitutes personal holding company income if the person entitled to use it owns (directly, indirectly, or constructively) 25 percent or more of the corporation's stock at any time during the taxable year. This provision, now found in §543(a)(6), was enacted to reach the rent paid by shareholders for the use of incorporated yachts, country estates, and similar property. Taken by itself, however, §543(a)(6) would not have put an end to the practice of incorporating yachts and country homes in order to offset an operating loss against the corporation's investment income, since the corporation, though a personal holding company, would have no income and hence no undistributed income on which the penalty tax could be levied. But §543(a)(6) must be examined in conjunction with §545(b)(8), which closes the gap by providing that in computing the corporation's "undistributed personal holding company income," deductions for expenses and depreciation allocable to corporate property shall be allowed only to the extent of the rent or other compensation received for the use of the property,

---

[72] See Cohen, Personal Holding Companies — Entertainment Industries, 1962 So. Calif. Tax Inst. 651.

unless the Internal Revenue Service is satisfied (a) that the rent was the highest obtainable (or, if none was received, that none was obtainable), (b) that the property was held in the course of a business carried on bona fide for profit, and (c) either that the property was necessary to the conduct of the business or that its operation could reasonably be expected to yield a profit.[73] Applied to an incorporated yacht rented from a corporation by its sole shareholder, §543(a)(6) would require the rent to be treated as personal holding company income, and §543(a)(1) would have the same effect on the corporation's income from dividends and interest. Assuming no other income, the corporation would be a personal holding company. Under §545(b)-(8), its deductions for expenses and depreciation incurred in operating the yacht would be limited to the amount of the rent, and the excess (or "loss") could not be applied against the dividend and interest income. If not distributed, therefore, these items would be subject to the personal holding company tax.

As stated earlier, the function contemplated for §543(a)(6) was to "taint" rent received by the corporation for yachts, country estates, and similar property used by an individual owning 25 percent or more of its stock. By its terms, however, §543(a)(6) reaches rent for *any* property of the corporation, if such a shareholder is entitled to its use. In Hatfried, Inc. v. Commissioner, 162 F.2d 628, 35 AFTR 1496 (3d Cir. 1947), the court refused to restrict the broad statutory language and held that rent received by a corporation from its sole shareholder for the use of a hotel operated by her as a bona fide business enterprise was personal holding company income. Under the *Hatfried, Inc.* case, many real estate corporations would be personal holding companies, though used primarily to avoid personal liability on mortgages or for convenience in financing the purchase of property, with no thought of tax avoidance. In 1954, however the second sentence of §543(a)(6) was enacted, providing that §543(a)(6) will apply only if the corporation has personal holding company income — other than rent — in excess of 10 percent of its ordinary gross

[73] Although §545(b)(8) was enacted primarily to limit the corporation's deductions for maintenance and depreciation on incorporated yachts, estates, and similar property used by the shareholders, it is more broadly applicable to all corporate property, whether used by shareholders or not. See Wilson Bros. & Co. v. Commissioner, 170 F.2d 423, 37 AFTR 532 (9th Cir. 1948), cert. denied, 336 U.S. 909 (cargo vessels). Indeed, the language of §545(b)(8)(A) seems to forbid any deduction for maintenance or depreciation on corporate business property used by the corporation in the course of its own business activity, unless the corporation shows that no rent was "obtainable" (i.e., that the property could not have been rented out). But literalism should not be carried this far, not even to penalize the despised personal holding company.

income.[74] If the corporation has this much income from other tainted sources, however, §543(a)(6) is applicable even to property used by the shareholder in a *bona fide* business (as in the *Hatfried, Inc.* case). Conversely, in the absence of other personal holding company income in the amount specified by the 1954 amendment, not even the rent from incorporated yachts and estates will fall afoul of §543(a)(6).

Section 543(a)(6) is applicable to amounts received as compensation for the use of corporate property, under the circumstances stated, regardless of designation, and whether paid by the shareholder himself or not. Thus, rent received by a lessor corporation from a lessee corporation can be included if the property is subleased by the lessee to an individual owning more than 25 percent in value of the lessor's stock.[75]

7. Personal service contracts. Amounts received under a "personal service contract" constitute personal holding company income if (a) the individual who is to perform the services is designated (by name or by description) in the contract or can be so designated by some person other than the corporation, and (b) the designated person owns (directly, indirectly, or constructively) 25 percent or more (by value) of the corporation's stock at some time during the taxable year. Amounts received from the sale or other disposition of such a contract are also included in personal holding company income. This type of income is included in order to reach actors, producers, and other flamboyant "incorporated talents."[76] Section 543-

---

[74] More precisely, the corporation is not subject to §543(a)(6) unless its personal holding company income, computed without regard to §543(a)(6) (shareholder-used property) and §543(a)(2) (other rents, including certain interest receipts), exceeds the stated percentage.

Prior to the enactment of the 1954 Code, Congress had enacted a palliative to the rule of Hatfried, Inc. v. Commissioner, restricted to rent for property used by the shareholder in the operation of a bona fide commercial, industrial, or mining enterprise, 64 Stat. 947; 69 *ibid.* 4. This legislation was of a temporary character and does not apply to taxable years governed by the 1954 Code, for which the second sentence of §543(a)(6) provides relief. See Medical-Surgical Group, Inc., 33 T.C. 888 (1960).

[75] See 320 East 47th St. Corp. v. Commissioner, 243 F.2d 894, 51 AFTR 200 (2d Cir. 1957) (property leased to second corporation under common control with lessor corporation); Minnesota Mortuaries, Inc., 4 T.C. 280 (1944) (Non-Acq.) (contra); Randolph Products Co. v. Manning, 176 F.2d 190, 38 AFTR 281 (3d Cir. 1949) (lease to partnership of which shareholder was a member); American Valve Co. v. United States, 137 F. Supp. 249, 48 AFTR 1150 (S.D.N.Y. 1956) (same).

[76] "Incorporated talents" in the entertainment world were a prime target of the original provisions (*supra*, Sec. 6.20 and note 54). For an illustration, see Regs. §1.543-1(b)(8), Example (1).

Although gain on the sale of a personal service contract is included by §543(a)(7), this provision can operate only if the gain is taxable as ordinary income. If capital gain is generated by the sale, it will be excluded from "ordinary gross income" and hence from "adjusted ordinary gross income" by

(a) (7) is equally applicable, however, to corporations performing engineering, financial, or technical services of a more sober nature, though such corporations ordinarily are safe because they, rather than the other contracting party, designate the person or persons to perform the services. Although §543(a)(7) may have been drafted on the implicit assumption that the shareholder would not be designated in the contract unless his talents were of a special or unique character, so that the services contracted for could not have been supplied with equal skill by a non-shareholder employee of the corporation, no such requirement is explicit; and evidence that a designated shareholder's talents were not unique seems irrelevant to the operation of §543(a)(7). On the other hand, even if the 25 percent shareholder's skills are unique, it has been held that the compensation does not come within §543(a)(7) merely because of an expectation, not embodied in the contract, that he will perform the services.[77]

If the contract designates a 25 percent shareholder to perform services, but contemplates that other employees will assist or work with him, does all, none, or part of the compensation received by the corporation for their joint services fall under §543(a)(7)? Several early cases held that the entire amount was within, or outside, the statutory provision, depending on whether the services of the other employees were incidental or important.[78] The Treasury accepted the no-allocation principle for menial or incidental services by non-shareholder employees, but amended the Regulations in 1958 to provide for an allocation if their services are "important and essential." It has been held that this does not permit an allocation unless the contract explicitly "requires" the performance of important services by other employees.[79]

§543(b)(1), and, by virtue of §543 (a), from "personal holding company income." But capital gain on the sale of a personal service contract is not easily achieved; see Eustice, Contract Rights, Capital Gain, and Assignment of Income — The Ferrer Case, 20 Tax L. Rev. 1 (1964).

[77] S. O. Claggett, 44 T.C. 503 (1965). Before too much reliance is placed on this decision, it should be noted that §543(a)(7) does not require the contract to be in writing. This issue will come acutely to the fore if the new-style professional service corporations are recognized as corporate entities (supra, Sec. 2.05), since the organization's clients will ordinarily expect the principal shareholders to perform the services.

If the contract designates the person to perform the service only by description, not by name, it may be more difficult to apply the description to the shareholder if his skills are not unique.

[78] General Management Corp. v. Commissioner, 135 F.2d 882, 31 AFTR 80 (7th Cir. 1943), cert. denied, 320 U.S. 757 (services of auxiliary employees compared to "the trowel of the mason, the plane of the carpenter, the nurse assisting the physician"); Allen Machinery Corp., 31 T.C. 441 (1958).

[79] Regs. §1.543-1(b)(8)(ii) and (iii), Example (2); Kurt Frings Agency, Inc., 42 T.C. 472 (1964). See also Portable Industries, Inc., supra note 69 (allocation between royalties and compensation for services).

8. Income from estates and trusts. If the corporation is a beneficiary of a trust or estate, amounts includible in its income by virtue of the provisions of Subchapter J are treated as personal holding company income.

Sec. 6.23.   Definition of "personal holding company": Stock ownership

As stated earlier, a corporation is a "personal holding company" if both its stock ownership and its gross income meet certain mechanical tests. The stock ownership test is met if, at any time during the last half of the taxable year, more than 50 percent in value of the corporation's outstanding stock is owned, directly or indirectly, by or for not more than 5 individuals.[80] The term "individual" presumably has the same meaning as in §1 of the Code, except that §542-(a)(2) has provided, since 1954, that some tax-exempt organizations and trusts are to be treated as individuals, evidently on the theory that they may be dominated by the other shareholders of the corporation.

If *all* of the corporation's outstanding stock is owned by fewer than 10 individuals, the stock ownership requirement of §542(a)(2) will automatically be satisfied, since more than 50 percent of the stock will necessarily be owned by 5 individuals or fewer. If the stock is more widely dispersed, however, or if some of it is owned by corporations, trusts, estates or other entities, a closer examination of the facts will be required, since the ownership of stock is to be determined by the constructive ownership rules of §544. The principal features of these constructive ownership rules[81] are:

> 1. Stock owned by corporations, partnerships, estates, or trusts is attributed proportionately to the shareholders, partners, or beneficiaries of these entities.
> 2. An individual is considered as owning the stock owned by his brothers, sisters, spouse, ancestors, and lineal descendants.

---

[80] "Hybrid" securities and the debt of "thin" corporations may be treated as stock for this purpose, at least to make the corporation a personal holding company. Query, however, whether the corporation may escape this status by impeaching its own debt instrument. See Washmont Corp. v. Hendricksen, 137 F.2d 306, 31 AFTR 390 (9th Cir. 1943).

See Coshocton Securities Co., 26 T.C. 935 (1956), holding that the taxpayer was a personal holding company by reason of its stock ownership and gross income, althought it could not have determined this fact for itself because some of its stock was owned by another corporation that would not have disclosed its beneficial ownership.

[81] For a more detailed discussion, see Ringel, Surrey, and Warren, Attribution of Stock Ownership in the Internal Revenue Code, 72 Harv. L. Rev. 209 (1958); see also *infra*, Sec. 7.21.

3. A member of a partnership is considered as owning the stock owned by his partners.

4. A person having an option to acquire stock is considered as owning the stock itself.

5. Certain securities convertible into stock are treated as outstanding stock.

Sec. 6.24. Definition of "personal holding company": Exemptions

Certain categories of corporations are not subject to the personal holding company provisions:

1. Corporations exempt from tax under Subchapter F (§501 and following). §542(c)(1).

2. Banks (as defined by §581), building and loan associations, surety companies, and life insurance companies. §§542-(c)(2)-(4).

3. Certain licensed personal finance companies, regulated small loan companies, loan or investment companies, and finance companies engaged in purchasing or discounting accounts or making secured loans. §§542(c)(6) and (d). These exceptions, applicable to companies whose income would ordinarily be personal holding company income under §543(a)(1) (interest), are hedged about by an intricate network of restrictions, which defy summary and are, in any event, not of general interest.[82]

4. Foreign personal holding companies (*infra,* Sec. 6.40), §542(c)(5); and other foreign corporations if gross income from United States sources is less than 50 percent of total gross income and all stock outstanding during the last half of the taxable year is owned by nonresident alien individuals directly or through other foreign corporations, §542(c)(7).[83]

5. Small business investment companies (*supra,* Sec. 1.06), unless a shareholder owns an interest of 5 percent or more in a concern to which the investment company has advanced funds. §542(c)(8).

Sec. 6.25. Computation of personal holding company tax

If the corporation is found to be a personal holding company, a tax (in addition to the regular corporate income tax) is imposed by §541 at the rate of 70 percent of the "undistributed personal holding company income." In the interest of brevity (and on the theory that any corporation that finds itself subject to this tax will have ample

[82] See Roberts and Kaster, Commercial Finance Companies and the Personal Holding Company Exception, 42 Taxes 638 (1964).

[83] See Alexander, Foreign Personal Holding Companies and Foreign Corporations That Are Personal Holding Companies, 67 Yale L.J. 1173 (1958).

leisure to work out the details of the computation), only the high-lights of the computation will be set out here. There are three steps in computing the taxable base ("undistributed personal holding company income"):

1. Adjustments to taxable income. The corporation's taxable income is adjusted in the manner prescribed by §545(b). These adjustments transform taxable income into an amount that more closely resembles the corporation's net economic gain for the year: thus, federal income taxes are deducted; the 85 percent dividends received deduction of §243 is eliminated; the deduction for charitable contributions is not limited to 5 percent of taxable income but is increased to the 20-30 percent limit applicable to individuals; the excess of net long-term capital gain over net short-term capital loss (less the taxes allocable thereto) is eliminated from taxable income (so that, in effect, the corporation may accumulate long-term capital gains); the limitation on business expenses and depreciation of §545(b)(8) is applied (*supra*, note 73); and certain other adjustments are made.

2. Special deduction for pre-1964 corporations. Corporations that in one of their two taxable years immediately preceding enactment of the Revenue Act of 1964 (Feb. 26, 1964) were not personal holding companies, but that would have been personal holding companies if the 1964 amendments had been applicable to that year, are permitted a special deduction in computing undistributed personal holding company income for amounts paid or set aside to amortize certain "qualified indebtedness" (generally, debt incurred before 1964). §545(c).

3. Dividends paid deduction. From taxable income as thus adjusted, there is deducted the dividends paid deduction of §561. This deduction is the sum of (a) the dividends paid during the taxable year,[84] (b) the consent dividends for the taxable year as provided in §565, and (c) the dividend carryover of §564. Items (a) and (b) were described *supra*, §6.09, in conjunction with the accumulated earnings tax. Item (c) is the excess of dividends paid during the two preceding taxable years over the corporation's taxable income, as adjusted under §545, for those years.

---

[84] The term "dividend" is defined by §562, which looks primarily to the standard definition of §316(a) (*supra*, Sec. 5.02) as modified by §316(b)(2)(A), providing that certain distributions by personal holding companies are taxable to the shareholders as dividends notwithstanding an absence of earnings and profits. §316(b)(2)(A) was intended as a relief measure; before its enactment, a personal holding company might be unable to make a "dividend" distribution of its personal holding company income because it had no earnings and profits. Thus, §316(b)(2)(A) is similar in its purpose and effect to §316(a)(2) (*supra*, Sec. 5.02). See Morris Investment Corp. v. Commissioner, 156 F.2d 748, 35 AFTR 32 (3d Cir. 1946), cert. denied 329 U.S. 788; H. Rept. No. 2333, 77th Cong., 2d sess., reprinted in 1942-2 C.B. 372, 473.

The Revenue Act of 1964 made important changes in the dividends paid deduction for liquidating distributions by personal holding companies. Under prior law, personal holding companies were entitled to the benefits of what is now §562(b)(1), *viz.*, pro rata distributions in liquidation (including, for this purpose, §302 redemptions), and distributions within a 24-month period following adoption of a plan of complete liquidation, qualified as dividends paid in computing the corporation's personal holding tax liability, even if the distribution was a capital gain or loss transaction at the shareholder level. Section 562(b)(1) remains applicable in computing the accumulated earnings tax (*supra*, Sec. 6.09), but personal holding companies may now get a dividend paid deduction for such liquidating distributions only when permitted by §562(b)(2), viz., only in the case of certain distributions in complete liquidations, and then only if the distributee is another corporation. Liquidating distributions to non-corporate shareholders can qualify for the dividends paid deduction only if the corporation designates them as "dividends" under §316(b)(2)(B), in which event they must be so treated by the recipients.[85]

Since the personal holding company tax is imposed on the corporation's *undistributed* personal holding company income, it is often said that a personal holding company can ward off liability for this tax by distributing its entire income for the taxable year. This general rule is not precise enough as a guide to action, however; what is required is not a distribution of the corporation's taxable income, earnings and profits, or economic gains, but a distribution of such an amount as will leave behind no "undistributed personal holding company income." Thus, a corporation with a substantial amount of taxable income may not need to make any distribution, if it has a §564 dividend carryover that will eliminate its personal holding company income for the year; on the other hand, a corporation with little taxable income may find it necessary to make a substantial distribution because its taxable income reflects a dividends received deduction under §243 that is not allowed in computing undistributed personal holding company income.

After a corporation's liability for a personal holding company tax has been determined, it has a final opportunity to mitigate or elimin-

---

[85] See Friedman, Liquidation of Corporations Becoming Domestic Personal Holding Companies Under the Revenue Act of 1964, 20 Tax L. Rev. 435 (1965); Feder. Relieving the Impact of the Revenue Act of 1964 on "New" Personal Holding Companies, 23 N.Y.U. Inst. on Fed. Taxation 723 (1965); McClennen, Relief Provisions for Personal Holding Companies in the Act of 1964, 1965 So. Calif. Tax Inst. 213.

ate its tax liability. The opportunity is created by the deficiency dividend procedure of §547, described *supra*, Sec. 6.20. As stated there,
liability for interest or penalties is not eliminated by a deficiency
dividend distribution.

Sec. 6.26. Liquidation of pre-1964 corporations

In tightening up the personal holding company provisions by the
Revenue Act of 1964, Congress provided special relief for any corporation that was not a personal holding company in one of its two taxable
years immediately preceding Feb. 26, 1964 (when the 1964 Act was
enacted), but that would have been such a company if the amendments had been applicable in that year. Such "would have been" personal holding companies are entitled to a special deduction for
payments or accumulations on account of "qualified indebtedness"
(*supra*, Sec. 6.25); and they are also made eligible for favorable treatment if they liquidate before 1966 or 1967, or, in some cases, before a
prescribed later date.[86]

Part C.   Foreign Personal Holding Companies

Sec. 6.40.   Introductory

The foreign personal holding company provisions (§§551-558)
were enacted in 1937, after a congressional investigation brought to
light the formation of a number of "incorporated pocket books" in
the Bahama Islands, Panama, and Canada by citizens of the United
States. Dividends, interest, and other types of investment income
were thus realized by U.S.-owned corporations domiciled in countries
with low or no income taxes; and the corporations might also be
employed to avoid United States taxes on the sale of the income-producing property, to create deductions for their U.S. affiliates or shareholders, and for more esoteric manipulations.

For jurisdictional and administrative reasons, Congress decided
to close this set of tax loopholes by taxing the United States shareholders of foreign personal holding companies on their proportionate
shares of the corporation's undistributed income, rather than by imposing a penalty tax on the corporation itself. The constitutionality
of this procedure was assumed in Eder v. Commissioner, 138 F.2d 27,
31 AFTR 627 (2d Cir. 1943).[87]

---

[86] For discussions of these relief provisions, see *supra* note 85; *infra*, Sec.
9.24. Experience with other temporary legislation in this area (*infra*, Sec. 9.20)
suggests that the pressure to extend the deadline for §333(g) may be irresistible.

Sec. 6.41.   Foreign personal holding companies

The term "foreign personal holding company" is defined by §552 to mean any foreign corporation (except tax-exempt corporations and certain foreign banking corporations), if it meets the following two conditions:

1. Gross income. At least 60 percent (50 percent in some instances) of its gross income for the taxable year is "foreign personal holding company income." This term (whose scope is similar to "personal holding company income under pre-1964 law) is defined by §553 to include the following categories of income: (a) dividends, interest, and royalties; (b) the excess of gains over losses from sales of stocks, securities, and commodity future contracts; (c) income from an estate or trust, or from the sale of an interest therein; (d) income from certain personal service contracts; (e) compensation for the use of corporate property by a 25 percent shareholder; and (f) rents, if they constitute less than 50 percent of gross income.

In keeping with the purpose of the foreign personal holding company provisions, "gross income" is defined by §555(a) for this purpose as including foreign source income, as well as income from domestic sources.

2. Stock ownership. At any time during the taxable year, more than 50 percent in value of the corporation's outstanding stock is owned, directly or indirectly, by not more than five individuals who are citizens or residents of the United States. Section 554 applies constructive ownership rules which are virtually identical to those for domestic personal holding companies.[88]

By virtue of §542(c)(5), the foreign personal holding company provisions take precedence over the personal holding company provisions, but a foreign corporation that is not a foreign personal holding company may be caught up in the meshes of the personal holding company provisions (unless immunized by §542(c)(7), *supra*, Sec.

---

[87] See also Helvering v. National Grocery Co., *supra* note 1, regarding the power of Congress to tax undistributed corporate income to the shareholder; Alvord v. Commissioner, 277 F.2d 713, 5 AFTR 2d 1438 (4th Cir. 1960), holding that the foreign personal holding company tax could not be imposed on the majority shareholder of a foreign personal holding company for years in which the United States, as the result of a tax assessment, prevented the distribution of its income.

See generally, Alexander, *supra* note 83; for background, see Paul *supra* note 58, at 49-56, and Rudick, *supra* note 58, at 207-213.

[88] *Supra*, Sec. 6.23; but see Estate of Nettie Miller, 43 T.C. 760 (1965), holding (a) that stock owned by foreigners was not attributable to their brother, a U.S. citizen, so as to make the corporation a foreign personal holding company, when the brother was not himself a shareholder; and (b) that certain "bearer warrants" (with voting and dividend rights) were "stock."

6.24), or it may be subject to the accumulated earnings tax of §531.

Once it is determined that a corporation is a foreign personal holding company, each United States shareholder is required by §551(b) to include in gross income the amount he would have received as a dividend if his share of the corporation's "undistributed foreign personal holding company income" had been distributed to him. "Undistributed foreign personal holding company income" is defined by §556 as taxable income, with certain adjustments, less the dividends paid deduction of §561.[89] Because the United States shareholder is taxed on undistributed income, he is permitted to increase the basis of his stock, as though the constructive dividend had been reinvested in the corporation as a contribution to capital.

Foreign personal holding companies are also subject to §1014(b)-(5) (basis of stock not stepped-up on stockholder's death, except to reflect the estate tax paid thereon, under §1022, enacted in 1964) and to §267(b)(3) (certain transactions between two corporations under common control do not give rise to deductions, if one is a foreign personal holding company).

Part D.   Controlled Foreign Corporations

Sec. 6.50.   Introductory

Under §§881-882, foreign corporations are taxed on their income from United States sources only, and a foreign corporation not engaged in trade or business here is taxed on such income only to the extent that it is derived from dividends, interest, and other "fixed or determinable annual or periodical" sources.[90] Because the "foreign source" income of a foreign corporation is not subject to United States taxation (while domestic corporations are taxed on their world-wide income), American corporations and individuals frequently find it advantageous to segregate their foreign business activities in a foreign corporation, especially if the country in which the operations are conducted taxes business income at a lower rate than the United States. In this way, no United States tax need be paid until

---

[89] *Supra,* Sec. 6.25; under §562(b) as amended in 1964, liquidating distributions by a foreign personal holding company do not qualify for this deduction.

[90] The "source" rules are prescribed by §§861-864; these definitions make no special reference to foreign corporations, and are controlling in other areas as well, e.g., §904 (limit on foreign tax credit), §911 (exclusion of income earned abroad), and §871 (nonresident aliens). See Dailey, The Concept of the Source of Income, 15 Tax L. Rev. 415 (1960).

See also *supra,* Sec. 1.06.

the foreign corporation's earnings are "repatriated" in the form of dividends or a liquidating distribution to its American shareholders, or until they sell their stock. At that time, the shareholders report their receipts or profit as dividend income or capital gain, as the case may be.[91] If dividends are received by a domestic corporation owning at least 10 percent of the voting stock of the foreign corporation, it is entitled to a foreign tax credit for its share of the subsidiary's foreign income taxes as a "deemed paid" or "derivative" credit under §902(a).[92]

When the foreign corporation and its American parent (or its American shareholders, if it is not a wholly-owned subsidiary) are engaged in several aspects of a single enterprise — e.g., if the foreign corporation is a sales subsidiary of a United States manufacturer — their inter-company transactions take on a special importance because the foreign corporation's share of the enterprise's world-wide income is not taxed by the United States until repatriation. In recent years, the Internal Revenue Service has manifested a much greater interest in these arrangements than previously, recognizing that the "deferral" of United States tax on earnings that are segregated in the foreign corporation may continue for many years, and bids fair to become permanent in some instances. In demanding that the foreign corporation and its domestic parent adopt an arm's-length pattern for their inter-company transactions, the Service relies primarily on §482 (reallocation of income, deductions, etc., among related taxpayers), but it can also call upon assignment of income principles, "form vs. substance," the "step transaction" doctrine, and §446(b) (account-

---

[91] The shareholder's gain on a sale or liquidation of a corporation may be taxable as ordinary income, under rules enacted in 1962, if it is a "foreign investment company" (*supra*, Sec. 1.06) or a "controlled foreign corporation" (*infra*, Sec. 9.06).

[92] Under §902(b), the "deemed paid" credit also includes foreign income taxes paid by a foreign sub-subsidiary, if 50 percent or more of its voting stock is owned by the first-tier foreign subsidiary.

The structure of the foreign tax credit was changed in 1962 by the enactment of §78, requiring a corporation claiming a "deemed paid" credit to treat the amount credited as a constructive dividend, unless the subsidiary is a "less developed country corporation" (*infra*, Sec. 6.52). The effect of this "gross-up" is to increase the parent corporation's gross income; but this disadvantage is mitigated by the fact that the credit is not limited by the rule of American Chicle Co. v. United States, 316 U.S. 450 (1942). See Stone, U.S. Taxation of Profits Withdrawn from Foreign Corporations Under the Revenue Act of 1962, 5 Inst. on Private Investments Abroad (Southwest Legal Foundation), p. 85 (1963).

For an exhaustive study of the deemed paid credit, see Owens, The Foreign Tax Credit, 91-194 (1961) (written before the 1962 changes); see also Schoenfeld, Some Definitional Problems in the Deemed Paid Foreign Tax Credit of Section 902: "Dividends" and "Accumulated Profits," 18 Tax L. Rev. 401 (1963).

ing method must "clearly reflect income") as sources of authority.[93]

In 1961, the Treasury asked Congress to provide detailed rules for the allocation of income and expenses arising in foreign operations, and the House version of the Revenue Act of 1962 amended §482 accordingly; but this change was eliminated in conference, with a statement that the Treasury "should explore the possibility of developing and promulgating regulations under [§482, as it exists] which would provide additional guidelines and formulas for the allocation of income and deductions in cases involving foreign income."[94] As of this writing (April, 1966), the first installment of proposed regulations pursuant to this legislative direction has been issued, and others are expected. Pending final regulations, the Internal Revenue Service has announced that a domestic parent whose income has been increased under §482 can receive an appropriate payment from the subsidiary without paying an additional federal income tax, provided the terms of the original transaction were not part of a tax avoidance plan. It has also announced, but as to pre-1963 taxable years only, that it will not require interest, royalties, or other charges to be imputed to the foreign subsidiary in certain circumstances; that no allocation under §482 will be required if the foreign subsidiary paid out at least 90 percent of its earnings as dividends to its domestic parent; and that deficiencies assessed under §482 can be reduced by any foreign income taxes actually paid by the subsidiary that would not have been payable if the terms of the transaction itself had been in accord with the §482 allocation.[95] These

---

[93] See Asiatic Petroleum Co. v. Commissioner, 79 F.2d 234, 16 AFTR 610 (2d Cir. 1935), cert. denied, 296 U.S. 645 (1935); Hay v. Commissioner, 145 F.2d 1001 (4th Cir. 1944), cert. denied, 324 U.S. 863 (1945); see also *supra*, Sec. 1.05. The "source rules" (*supra* note 90) contain their own allocation principles; see Regs. §1.863-1.

See generally, Plumb and Kapp, Reallocation of Income and Deductions Under Section 482, 41 Taxes 809 (1963).

[94] See 4 Hearings on President's 1961 Tax Recommendations, House Committee on Ways and Means, 87th Cong., 1st sess. (1961) 3534-3551; H.R. Rep. No. 2508, 87th Cong., 2d sess. (1962), reprinted at 1962-3 C.B. 1129, 1146.

[95] Proposed Regs. §1.482-1(d) and §1.482-2, discussed by Jenks, The "Creation of Income" Doctrine: A Comment on the Proposed Section 482 Regulations, 43 Taxes 486 (1965). The procedures applicable to pre-1963 taxable years are set out in Rev. Proc. 64-54, 1964-2 C.B. 1008, and Rev. Proc. 65-31, 1965-51 I.R.B. 42; the exemption for subsidiaries paying 90 percent or more of their earnings to the parent acknowledges that the deferral of U.S. taxes ordinarily obtained by artificial inter-company transactions is wiped out in such cases; note that this result would be achieved by a consolidated return, but that foreign corporations cannot join in such returns (*infra*, Sec. 13.41). The "reimbursement" device is prescribed by Rev. Proc. 65-17, 1965-1 C.B. 833.

For a comprehensive analysis of these issues, see Proposals for Amelioration of Section 482 Allocations Affecting U.S. Taxpayers with Foreign Affiliates, by Committee on International Taxation (P. Miller, chairman), Tax Section, New

administrative procedures recognize that the reallocation of income or deductions after the close of a taxable year has unusually complex ramifications in the domestic-foreign arena, since the foreign corporation's foreign income taxes were computed in accord with the original arrangements between the parties and will not necessarily be refunded merely because the United States determines that the foreign subsidiary received too large a share of the enterprise's world-wide income; moreover, §482 allocations may alter the character of amounts received by the foreign corporation's shareholders and their right to the foreign tax credit.

Before 1962, the statutory pattern of exempting foreign corporations from United States tax on their foreign source income and taxing these earnings to their United States shareholders only on repatriation — the so-called "deferral" privilege — was subject to an exception for "foreign personal holding companies." As already explained (*supra*, Sec. 6.40), the tax avoidance potential of such corporations is nullified by requiring their United States shareholders to report the corporate income as earned, even if it is not distributed to them. In 1962, a similar requirement was enacted for "controlled foreign corporations," under which their United States shareholders must report their pro rata share of certain categories of foreign income, even though it is not distributed to them. Because the 1962 rules embrace foreign corporations engaged in ordinary business operations, however, they are far more important than the foreign personal holding company provisions. In addition to taxing the United States shareholders of a controlled foreign corporation on its undistributed foreign income, the 1962 legislation provides that the shareholder's gain on a sale, exchange, or redemption of the stock of such a corporation or on a liquidating distribution is taxable as ordinary income, rather than as capital gain, in circumstances described *infra*, Sec. 9.06.

Sec. 6.51.   The "controlled foreign corporation"

In examining the 1962 rules applicable to "controlled foreign corporations" [Subpart F (§951-964) of Part III, Subchapter N of the 1954 Code], it should be borne in mind that no change was made in the traditional tax pattern for foreign corporations, under which foreign source income is not taxed to the corporation itself. Whether foreign corporations with American shareholders could be subjected

York State Bar Association (1966), reprinted, 44 Taxes 209 (1966); Kirrane, Observations on Revenue Procedure 64-54, 44 Taxes 168 (1966).

to United States taxation on their foreign income without violating international law or not, there are obvious difficulties in imposing such a tax if the corporation has some foreign shareholders; and Subpart F, like the foreign personal holding company provisions, sidesteps the problem by selecting the corporation's United States shareholders as its target. In an effort to cover every contingency, Subpart F reaches and never leaves a lofty plateau of complexity that the Internal Revenue Code had previously attained only in occasional subsections, though in the end it turns many tasks over to the Treasury to discharge by regulations.[96] The description of Subpart F that follows has been kept within manageable limits only by ruthlessly suppressing many details; in particular, the special rules applicable to income from insuring "United States risks" and to corporations organized in Puerto Rico or United States possessions are not set out. Moreover, the discussion assumes that the income of the foreign corporation in question is attributable entirely to foreign sources, so that no United States tax was payable.

1. Corporations subject to Subpart F. The heart of Subpart F is the *controlled foreign corporation* (hereafter "CFC"), defined by §957(a) as a foreign corporation more than 50 percent of whose total combined voting power is owned by United States shareholders on any day of the taxable year in question. A "United States shareholder" is a "United States person" (defined by §7701(a)(30) to mean a citizen or resident of the U.S., a domestic partnership or corporation, or a non-foreign trust or estate) who owns 10 percent or more of the corporation's total combined voting power. For these

---

[96]See generally McDonald, Controlled Foreign Corporations, 5 Inst. on Private Investments Abroad (Southwest Legal Foundation), p. 5 (1963); O'Connor, United States Taxation of Earnings of American-Controlled Foreign Corporations, 42 Taxes 588 (1964); Harris, Foreign Base Companies Under the 1962 Act; Relief Provisions and Areas for Tax Planning, 1964 So. Calif. Tax Inst. 287; Tillinghast, Problems of the Small or Closely Held Corporation Under the Revenue Act of 1962, 22 N.Y.U. Inst. on Fed. Tax. 697 (1964); Friedman and Silbert, Final Regulations on Controlled Foreign Corporations and Less Developed Country Corporations, *ibid.*, 811; Ross, United States Jurisdiction to Tax Foreign Income, XL1Xb Studies on International Fiscal Law (International Fiscal Association, Hamburg, 1964).

For a classified bibliography on the taxation of foreign income, see 18 Bulletin of A.B.A. Tax Section (Oct., 1964), p. 43.

The enactment of Subpart F, under which the income, earnings and profits, and other financial data for foreign corporations are more important than under pre-1962 law, has brought to the fore a number of difficulties in the computation of such amounts for enterprises whose books and records are often inconsistent with U.S. standards, and which have not had to make the elections (e.g., accounting and depreciation methods) that are usually a prerequisite to the determination of earnings and profits. See articles by Weiss, Hutchison and Stock, and Wilcox, 23 N.Y.U. Inst. on Fed. Tax. 981, 1017, and 1059 (1965); Weiss, Earnings and Profits and the Determination of the Foreign Tax Credit, 43 Taxes 849 (1965).

purposes, and for others, stock owned indirectly and constructively as well as directly is taken into account by §958; in general (but with variations depending on the purpose for which the ownership of stock is relevant), stock held by a foreign corporation, partnership, trust, or estate is imputed to its shareholders, partners, or beneficiaries. The "constructive ownership" rules adopt, with some modifications, the rules of §318(a).[97]

The most important foreign corporations, in size if not in number, that will be classified as CFCs are wholly-owned subsidiaries of domestic corporations, as to whom the elaborate rules of indirect and constructive ownership will either be unnecessary (because all the stock is owned directly by the domestic parent) or readily applied (e.g., to reach a foreign corporation whose stock is held by a foreign subsidiary of the domestic corporation). But for other foreign corporations, there will be difficult issues of statutory construction in working out the web of imputed ownership, as well as problems in ascertaining the facts. These determinations, moreover, must be made not only at year's end, but from day to day, since if a CFC enjoys (if that is the proper word) that status for only part of the year, the amount taxable to its shareholders is appropriately reduced by §951; and if the period is less than 30 consecutive days, none of its income is attributable to them.

It will be noted that a foreign corporation can be wholly owned by U.S. citizens without becoming a CFC (e.g., if its voting stock is equally divided among 11 or more unrelated individuals); the ownership rules require not only that more than 50 percent of the voting power be U.S.-owned, but also that it be concentrated in a limited number of hands.

2. *Attribution of income to U.S. shareholders of CFC.* Every "United States shareholder" of a CFC (i.e., a "United States person" who owns directly, indirectly, or constructively 10 percent or more of the corporation's combined voting power) is required by §951 to report his pro rata share of its "attributable income" (a non-statutory phrase, used here for convenience only; see *infra*, Sec. 6.53). Although stock owned constructively is taken into account in determining whether the shareholder owns the requisite 10 percent, his pro rata share of the CFC's attributable income is computed by reference to the stock owned by him directly or through other foreign corporations or entities in which he is beneficially interested. The attributable income is imputed to those who are shareholders on the last day of the

---

[97] See Alexander, Controlled Foreign Corporations and Constructive Ownership, 18 Tax L. Rev. 531 (1963); on §318, see *infra*, Sec. 7.21.

corporation's taxable year, unless it was a CFC for only part of the year; in this event, the last day when it qualified as a CFC is controlling, and the amount imputed to its shareholders is reduced to reflect that it was a CFC for only part of the year.

Since the purpose of Subpart F is to require the shareholder to report his share of the CFC's *undistributed* income, the amount imputed to him by §951 is so computed as to exclude amounts actually distributed by the corporation. To the extent that undistributed income is taxed to the shareholder, his basis for his stock is increased by §961 (as though the imputed distribution had been reinvested by him); subsequent distributions of these previously taxed amounts are receivable tax-free under §959 (having already paid their way), and the basis of the stock is then reduced. These changes in the basis of the stock are similar to the adjustments prescribed by the Code for foreign personal holding companies and Subchapter S corporations (*supra*, Sec. 6.40, and *infra*, Ch. 14).

If the shareholder to whom income is imputed is a domestic corporation, §960 provides that the attributed income is to be treated like a dividend in computing the "deemed paid" foreign tax credit of §902. A similar provision is applicable to individual shareholders who elect to be taxed at the corporate rate under §962 (*infra*, Sec. 9.54).

Sec. 6.52.   Income attributed to shareholders of CFC

The income that is attributable to the CFC's United States shareholders under §951(a)(1) (*supra*, Sec. 6.51) consists of three components — Subpart F income; withdrawals of Subpart F income previously excluded because invested in less developed countries; and increase in earnings invested in United States property. In more detail, these three components are as follows:

1. Subpart F income. The CFC's "Subpart F income" (defined by §952) consists of its "foreign base company income" (hereafter "FBCI"), plus certain income from insuring U.S. risks.

The term "foreign base company income" is defined in detail by §954, but the label itself implies an effort to restrict the common practice of using a "foreign base company" in international business operations to shelter foreign source income from *foreign* taxes, as well as United States taxes. The device takes many forms, but the shelter at which §954 strikes most directly is the sale of goods manufactured in the United States to a subsidiary incorporated in one foreign country (the "base country"), with the subsidiary in turn selling the goods to an affiliated corporation organized in the country where the goods are to be re-sold to the ultimate consumer (or to unrelated wholesalers). By adroitly fixing the prices at which the goods are sold by the parent to the "base company" and by the "base company" to the affiliate or sub-subsidiary in the country of destination, the lion's share of the spread between the cost of the goods sold and the price paid by the unrelated buyers can be segregated in the "base company"; and if it is organized in a country that imposes no income tax or treats the base company's profit as exempt foreign source income, the taxes paid by the parent to the United States and by the sub-subsidiary to the country of destination are minimized. (The same result may be achieved without a sub-subsidiary if the tax law of the country of destination exempts the foreign base company from local tax, e.g., because it has no local "permanent establishment" or because of a treaty with the base company's country of incorporation.) The device, to be sure, must run the gauntlet of §482; but in practice this statutory weapon is used primarily to insure that an appropriate fraction of the gross profit is reported by the parent, not to allocate income from the foreign base company to the foreign sub-subsidiary in order to prevent the latter from avoiding taxes in its country of incorporation.

Why, however, should the United States be concerned with an avoidance of taxes in the country of destination? The stated purpose of the 1962 provisions was the elimination of "artificial" stimulation to foreign investment, but the legislation strikes primarily, as stated, at tax inducements offered by "base countries"; if the country in which the goods are to be sold or the services performed wishes to reduce its rates, the United States investor may take advantage of *this* stimulus, by operating through a corporation organized in the country of destination.

Returning to the statutory details, FCBI is defined by §954 to consist turn composed of the items described in (a), (b), and (c) below, adjusted as described in (d) and (e).

(a) Foreign personal holding company income. This concept is patterned on the definition of foreign personal holding company income found in §553 (*supra*, Sec. 6.41), and consists of dividends, interest, royalties, and similar categories of passive income, but the definition is relaxed in some respects (primarily to exempt certain amounts derived from the active conduct of a trade or business or received from a related person having a "legitimate" connection with the country in which the CFC is incorporated) and tightened in others.

(b) Foreign base company sales income. This category consists,

roughly speaking, of income derived by the CFC from selling personal property that it purchased from a related person (e.g., a domestic parent engaged in manufacturing) or from buying personal property (e.g., raw materials) for sale to a related person, if the property is both produced and sold for use outside the country in which the CFC is incorporated.[98]

If the CFC is engaged in manufacturing in one foreign country and sells its products in another foreign country, the sales in the second country may generate "foreign base company sales income" under the complex "branch" rule of §954(d)(2). This provision requires the CFC's branch to be treated as a wholly-owned subsidiary in certain circumstances, with the result that the sales component of the CFC's income will constitute "foreign base company sales income" even though there is no formally-organized "related party.[99]

(c) Foreign base company services income. This category consists, again roughly speaking, of income from the performance of technical, managerial, engineering, commercial, and similar services, which are performed outside the country of the CFC's incorporation for a related person.

To illustrate these components of FCBI:

> If P, a United States corporation, owns all the stock of S, a Swiss corporation, FCBI will arise (1) if S buys goods from P and resells them outside Switzerland; (2) if S buys goods outside Switzerland and resells them to P; (3) if P performs services for, or on behalf of, P outside Switzerland; or (4) if S is a holding company receiving dividends, interest, rents, or royalties from a payor which is not a related Swiss business corporation (i.e., a related subsidiary organized and doing business in Switzerland). In category (1), if the goods had been sold in Switzerland (the country of incorporation), no tainted income would result; similarly, in category (2), if the goods had been purchased in Switzerland, there would be no FBCI. In category (3), tainted income could be avoided either by performing the services in the country of incorporation, or by avoiding performance of services for, or on behalf of, a related party. Similarly in categories (1) and (2), no tainted income would result from the purchase and sale of goods by S, if it did not deal with its parent, P.

[98] A "related person" in computing FBCI is defined by §954(d)(3); in general, ownership of more than 50 percent of voting stock is controlling.

"Foreign base company sales income" and "foreign base company services income" are defined by reference to the place where property is manufactured, goods are to be used or consumed, services are performed, etc., and these geographical references create many troublesome questions. See Fimberg, The Foreign Base Company Engaged in Selling Activities: A Reappraisal of the Conduct of Foreign Business, 1965 So. Calif. Tax. Inst. 237, 254-259.

[99] See Fimberg, *supra* note 98, at 259-273.

(d) Adjustments to FBCI. In computing these three components of FBCI, §954(b) excludes income from the use of ships and planes in foreign commerce, as well as any item of income as to which the Treasury is satisfied that a substantial tax reduction did not result from the fact that the corporation was created or organized under the laws of a foreign country. If, after applying these rules, the FBCI is less than 30 percent of the CFC's gross income, none of its income is treated as FBCI; if the FBCI is more than 70 percent of gross income, its entire gross income is treated as FBCI; if the percentage is between 30 and 70, the actual amount is treated as FBCI.

At this point, two more adjustments are made to FBCI (in the amount just determined): each of its three components is reduced by the expenses and other deductions properly attributable to it (so as to convert gross income into net income); and an adjustment is made in respect of any dividends, interest, or gains that the CFC may have derived from its "qualified investments in less developed countries." The latter adjustment requires a separate explanation, which follows.

(e) Qualified investments in less developed countries. The CFC's "qualified investments in less developed countries" is defined by §955-(b) to consist of stock and obligations with a maturity of one year or more of a "less developed country corporation" (provided the CFC owns 10 per cent or more of the LDCC's voting power) and obligations of less developed countries. An LDCC is a corporation engaged in the active conduct of trade or business, which derives 80 percent or more of its gross income from sources within less developed countries and 80 percent of whose assets consist of property used in trade or business and located in less developed countries, bank accounts, stock of other LDCCs, and certain other types of property.[100]

The CFC's "qualified investments in less developed countries" are important because any dividends or interest received from, plus the net gain on sales and exchanges of, such investments are excluded from its FBCI, up to the amount of the increase (if any) in such investments for the year. Thus, if a CFC's sole source of income is dividends from a LDCC, and they are fully reinvested in qualified investments, its FBCI is zero.

2. *Previously excluded subpart F income withdrawn from invest-*

---

[100] Pursuant to §955(b)(3), the President has designated as "less developed countries" all foreign countries in existence after 1962 except Australia, New Zealand, Hong Kong, Japan, South Africa, the countries of Western Europe, and countries within "the Sino-Soviet bloc." Exec. Order 11071, 1963-1 C.B. 137. See Friedman and Silbert, *supra* note 96; Quinn, Tax Advantages of Less Developed Country Corporations, 43 Taxes 556 (1965).

ment in less developed countries. This — the second — component of attributable income is the converse of the item just described; although the shareholders of a CFC are not taxed to the extent that its FBCI is invested in qualified investments in less developed countries, this exclusion is only temporary. A decrease in such investments in a later year constitutes "previously excluded subpart F income withdrawn from investment in less developed countries" under §955(a) and is attributable to the CFC's shareholders in the year of the decrease.

3. *"Increase in earnings invested in United States property."* The CFC's "increase in earnings invested in United States property" — the third component of attributable income — consists of the amount (if any) by which its earnings invested in United States property at year-end exceed the earnings so invested at the beginning of the year. "United States property" means any property (if acquired after Dec. 31, 1962) which is tangible property located in the United States, stock of a domestic corporation, an obligation of a United States person, or a right to use a patent, copyright, invention, secret formula, or similar property in the United States if it was acquired or developed by the CFC for such use — but U.S. bonds, bank deposits, certain debts arising in ordinary course of business from the sale or processing of property, certain property used in transporting persons or property in foreign commerce, and an amount equal to certain pre-1963 earnings and profits are excluded from the term "United States property."

It will be noted that the shareholder of a CFC is taxed on his pro rata share of an increase in its investment in U.S. property without regard to the *source* of the earnings that made the increase possible. This component of "attributable income" thus differs from Subpart F income, which is imputed to the shareholder because of the source from which it is derived; the increase in U.S. investments is imputed to the shareholder on the very different theory that the CFC's earnings have been repatriated pro tanto, even though not distributed by a formal dividend.[101] This "constructive repatriation" provision will reach such methods of indirectly placing the CFC's foreign earnings at the disposal of its parent as making a long-term loan to it, purchasing United States property (e.g., an industrial plant or office building) for lease to it, etc. In appropriate circumstances, some arrangements of this character might have been treated as "constructive distributions" to the parent corporation even under pre-1962 law (*supra*, Sec. 5.05), but §956 provides the government with a more certain remedy. Moreover, although such transactions by the

---

[101] See Stone, *supra* note 92.

CFC with its parent and other related domestic corporations may have provided the impetus for §956, its reach is not limited to dealings by the CFC with related corporations, but includes other United States investments as well, such as the purchase of the marketable securities of unrelated domestic corporations.

Because Subpart F income is defined by reference to the source of earnings, while the CFC's "increase in earnings invested in United States property" is not, the same earnings (if invested in U.S. property) could be counted twice, were it not for §959(a). By virtue of this provision, earnings that enter into the corporation's Subpart F income are excluded in computing its increase in earnings invested in U.S. property.

It may help to put the CFC provisions into perspective if we note that, by and large, they will not affect a foreign corporation if its ownership is widely dispersed, its income is derived from manufacturing,[102] it is incorporated in the country in which its business activities are performed, or its business is not related to a U.S. enterprise controlled by its shareholders. The new rules will be applied primarily to sales and service affiliates of U.S. enterprises (and then only if the country of incorporation is different from the country in which the goods have their origin or destination or the services are performed) and to foreign holding companies. Even when applicable, the new rules will be of limited importance if the foreign subsidiary is subject to high foreign income taxes, since the United States tax on the parent resulting from the attribution of Subpart F income to it may be largely or wholly offset by its "deemed paid" foreign tax credit arising from the subsidiary's foreign tax payments. In such circumstances, of course, the pre-1962 "deferral privilege" enjoyed by the parent was of little value, so it may not be missed.

Sec. 6.53.   Subpart F relief provisions

Several provisions mitigating the full force of Subpart F have already been mentioned: the disregarding of FBCI if it amounts to less than 30 percent of the CFC's gross income; the exclusion from FBCI of certain amounts if tax avoidance is not present; and the 30-consecutive-day rule for determining whether anything is to be attributed to the CFC's shareholders. Three other relief provisions deserve mention:

1. Election by individuals to be taxed at corporate rates. An

[102] For a CFC operating in two countries, however, see the "branch" rule of §954(d)(2), *supra* note 99.

individual shareholder of a CFC may elect under §962 to be taxed at corporate rates (under present law, 22 per cent on the first $25,000, 48 percent on amounts above $25,000) on the income imputed to him by §951(a), in which event he is entitled to employ the derivative foreign tax credit as though he were a domestic corporation. If the election is made, however, later actual distributions are includible in gross income to the extent they exceed the tax previously paid. The election approximates the result that would have been reached if the foreign income had been earned and fully distributed (after corporate tax) by a domestic corporation; it would then have been taxed at the U.S. corporate rate (subject to the foreign tax credit) in the year when the income was earned, and the corporation would have been able to distribute only the balance (i.e., the earnings less taxes) to its shareholders.

2. *Minimum distribution schedule.* If a shareholder of a CFC is a domestic corporation, it may elect under §963 to exclude from income its pro rata share of the CFC's "subpart F income" (but not its share of the other two components of "attributable income") if it received a "minimum distribution" of the CFC's earnings and profits for the taxable year. The amount which must have been distributed is prescribed by statute and is dependent upon the effective foreign tax rate (commencing with 83 percent of earnings and profits if the foreign rate is under 9 percent and declining to zero if the foreign rate is 43 percent or over). In effect, this provision acknowledges that if the foreign taxes paid by the CFC plus the U.S. tax paid by the shareholder on the amounts actually distributed are equal to 90 percent or more of the taxes that would have been paid had the business been operated as a foreign branch of the domestic shareholder, the tax avoidance resulting from the use of a foreign corporation is *de minimis*.[103]

3. *Export trade corporations.* If a CFC constitutes an "export trade corporation," its Subpart F income is reduced by its "export trade income," up to a prescribed amount, to the extent that its export trade income has been included in computing FBCI. A CFC is an export trade corporation under §971 if for a 3-year period (a) 90 percent of its gross income was derived from foreign sources, and (b) 75 percent of its gross income (50 percent in the case of agricultural exports) was "export trade income" (defined as net income from the sale of products manufactured, produced, grown, or extracted

---

[103] See generally Friedman and Silbert, Minimum Distributions Under Section 963 — What Is Left of Subpart F? 23 N.Y.U. Inst. on Fed. Tax. 955 (1965).

in the United States for use, consumption, or disposition outside the United States, from services related to such property, and from similar sources). These sources of income would ordinarily be included in FBCI as foreign base company sales or services income if the export activities were performed for, or related to products acquired from, a related corporation. To the extent that they have been included, FBCI is reduced, but the reduction may not exceed the lesser of three amounts: (1) 1-1/2 times the promotion expenses allocable to the includible export trade income; (2) 10 percent of the gross receipts allocable to the includible export trade income; and (3) the corporation's increase in export trade assets (working capital, inventories, foreign storage and service facilities, and evidences of trade indebtedness).

Evidently the contribution made by exports to a favorable balance of payments was the reason for this special reduction in computing FBCI. The first two of the three restrictions on the amount that may be deducted from FBCI, however, may be based on a suspicion that profits exceeding 10 percent of gross receipts or 150 percent of promotion expenses are more likely to stem from an arbitrary allocation of income to the foreign corporation than from the conduct of the export activities themselves. The third restriction limits the benefits of §970(a) to businesses that are in a formative or expanding period; and it is buttressed by §970(b), providing that if the export trade corporation reduces its investment in export trade assets in a later year, the shareholders must treat the decrease in investment as a "withdrawal of previously excluded subpart F income from qualified investment."[104]

---

[104] See Brudno, Export Trade Corporations, 5 Inst. on Private Investments Abroad (Southwest Legal Foundation), p. 59 (1963).

Chapter Seven

STOCK REDEMPTIONS
AND PARTIAL LIQUIDATIONS

Part A.   The Pre-1954 Background

Sec. 7.01.   Introductory

When a shareholder transfers stock to the issuing corporation in exchange for money or other property, the transaction may resemble an ordinary sale of stock to an outsider in an arm's length bargain or the receipt by the shareholder of a dividend from the corporation. The "sale" analogy is appropriate, for example, when the owner of preferred stock instructs his broker to sell his stock and the broker, by chance, effects a sale to the corporation, which happens to be buying up its preferred stock at the time. The preferred shareholder ought to be able to treat the transaction in the same manner as any other sale, reporting the difference between his adjusted basis and the sales price as capital gain or loss. On the other hand, when the owner of a one man corporation having only common stock outstanding foregoes dividends for a period of years and then "sells" some of his shares to the corporation for cash, the transaction is more like a "dividend" than a "sale." Although the shareholder has surrendered some of his stock, his interest in the corporation's assets and his control of the corporation's fate are undisturbed. If the transaction were not taxed as a "dividend," moreover, the shareholder could enter upon a long-range program of intermittent transfers of stock to his corporation, employing tax-free stock dividends if necessary to replace his shares and to restore the corporation's stated capital for the benefit of nervous creditors. For shareholders who could adopt such a plan of intermittent "sales" of stock, the tax on dividend income would become a dead letter.

It should not be surprising, then, that a "sale" of stock by a shareholder to his corporation is sometimes taxed as a "dividend" instead of as a "sale."[1] The knotty problem that has faced Congress,

[1] Throughout this chapter, the statement that a distribution in redemption of stock is to be treated as a "dividend" is predicated on an assumption that the

the Treasury, and the courts over the years — to which there can never be a universally acceptable solution — is the determination of which transfers of stock are to be classified as "dividends" and which as "sales." For a period of more than 30 years, ending in 1954, the general rule was that such transactions were "sales" unless the transaction was "essentially equivalent to the distribution of a taxable dividend," in which event the entire distribution was taxed under §115(g) of the 1939 Code as a dividend to the extent of current and post-1913 earnings and profits.[2] Although the 1954 Code seeks to provide a more reliable formula, it preserves this ancient and troublesome phrase, and thus there is no escape from a few words of history before we turn to the statutory language of the 1954 Code.

corporation's earnings and profits are sufficient to cover the amount of the distribution. The statement that a redemption is to be treated as a "sale" or an "exchange" means that the distribution is to be treated as payment in exchange for the stock. It is assumed throughout that the redeemed stock is a "capital asset" in the hands of the shareholder; this will ordinarily be true of any taxpayer except a dealer in securities.

For special rules governing the redemption of stock of a collapsible corporation, see *infra*, Sec. 10.03; for redemptions of "section 306 stock" (primarily, preferred stock issued as a tax-free stock dividend), see *infra*, Sec. 8.02.

Ordinarily, of course, the shareholder will prefer the redemption to be treated as a sale of his stock, producing capital gain or loss, rather than as a §301 distribution, taxable to the extent of the corporation's earnings and profits. But if the shareholder is a corporation, entitled to the dividends received deduction of §243 (*supra*, Sec. 2.25), the tax on a §301 distribution may be less painful than the capital gain tax on a sale. For the reversal of roles that may occur in these circumstances, see Pacific Vegetable Oil Corp. v. Commissioner, 251 F.2d 682, 52 AFTR 1104 (9th Cir. 1957), where the taxpayer argued that a redemption was essentially equivalent to a dividend, while the government argued that it was not. A similar reversal of roles may occur if the redeeming corporation has no earnings and profits, since in this event a §301 distribution will be taxable only to the extent it exceeds the shareholder's aggregate basis for all his stock (both the redeemed and the retained shares), see §301(c)(2) and (3); but if the transaction is treated as a sale, the taxpayer will realize gain to the extent the distribution exceeds the basis of the redeemed shares. See the last two sentences of Regs. §1.302-2(a). Note also that pre-1913 appreciation in value is not taxed when distributed under §301 (*supra*, Sec. 5.02), but that it enters into the computation of gain if the redemption is treated as a sale.

[2] The statute was not uniform throughout this period, however; even though the transaction was treated as a sale, the shareholder's gain on partial liquidations was taxable as ordinary income from 1934 to 1936 and as short term capital gain (regardless of the holding period) from 1936 to 1942. For a history of the statutory provisions, see Darrell, Corporate Liquidations and the Federal Income Tax, 89 U. Pa. L. Rev. 907 (1941).

Although §115(g) of the 1939 Code referred only to post-1913 earnings and profits, it was held that if the redemption was essentially equivalent to the distribution of a taxable dividend, it would be taxed as such to the extent of either post-1913 or current earnings and profits, as in the case of any ordinary dividend. W. H. Weaver, 25 T.C. 1067, 1083-4 (1956); see also Vesper Co., Inc. v. Commissioner, 131 F.2d 200, 205, 30 AFTR 245 (8th Cir. 1942); Commissioner v. Bedford's Estate, 325 U.S. 283, 33 AFTR 832 (1945).

Sec. 7.02. Pre-1954 law: §115(g) of the 1939 Code

The "essentially equivalent" language of §115(g), 1939 Code, first appeared in the Revenue Act of 1921, as an aftermath of *Eisner v. Macomber.* On providing in 1921 that stock dividends would not be taxed on receipt (*supra*, Sec. 5.60), Congress recognized the possibility (described *supra*, Sec. 7.01) that stock dividends might be issued and then promptly redeemed as a substitute for ordinary cash dividends. Congress went on, therefore, to provide that the redemption of stock "after the distribution of any such [stock] dividend" could be taxed as a dividend if the transaction was "essentially equivalent to the distribution of a taxable dividend." This provision was defective, however, because it failed to reach a redemption of stock that *preceded* a stock dividend; and this omission was corrected in 1924. Two years later, the provision, which ultimately became §115(g) of the 1939 Code, was amended to apply whenever a corporation cancelled or redeemed its stock "at such time and in such manner as to make the distribution and cancellation or redemption in whole or in part essentially equivalent to the distribution of a taxable dividend," *whether or not such stock was issued as a stock dividend.* Despite this change, the courts at first were reluctant to apply §115(g) unless the redeemed shares had been issued as tax-free stock dividends or in anticipation of a later redemption. Later, however, the courts viewed §115(g) more sympathetically, in that they came increasingly to start with the assumption that any pro rata redemption was equivalent to a taxable dividend, casting on the taxpayer the burden of establishing that it ought to be treated as a sale instead. If the redemption was not pro rata, however, it was ordinarily treated as a sale of stock by the shareholder, on which he would realize capital gain or loss.[3]

---

[3] The "old" Regulations provided: "A cancellation or redemption by a corporation of a portion of its stock pro rata among all the shareholders will generally be considered as effecting a distribution essentially equivalent to a dividend. . . . On the other hand, a cancellation or redemption by a corporation of all of the stock of a particular shareholder, so that the shareholder ceases to be interested in the affairs of the corporation, does not effect a distribution of a taxable dividend." Regs. 118, §39.115(g)-1(a)(2). For an interpretation of this requirement, see Rev. Rul. 54-408, 1954-2 C.B. 165.

Although the pre-1954 Regulations explicitly provided only that a redemption of "all" of the stock of a particular shareholder escaped §115(g), the courts took the position that a redemption of part of the stock of a particular shareholder could be equally efficacious: "It changes, pro tanto, his interest in the corporation in the same way that redemption of all his stock would do." Ferris v. U.S., 135 F. Supp. 286, 288, 48 AFTR 558 (Ct. Cl. 1955). As to redemptions that were superficially non-pro rata, but were pro rata in reality either because the loss of the redeemed shares did not seriously affect the shareholder's relative position or because he was closely related to the remaining shareholders, see J. Natwick, 36 B.T.A. 866, 876 (1937); Pullman, Inc., 8 T.C. 292, 297 (1947) (Acq.); *infra* note 10.

As §115(g) of the 1939 Code came to be the norm by which all pro rata redemptions were tested, rather than the exception, tax-payers found that the most promising escape was a judicial doctrine that a redemption resulting from a "corporation contraction" (or a "legitimate shrinkage") in the corporation's business activities was not essentially equivalent to a dividend. The courts also agreed that a redemption for "legitimate business purposes" was not taxable under §115(g), without, however, agreeing on the meaning of that phrase.[4] Even less helpful was the solemn announcement that the true test was whether the "net effect" of the redemption was the distribution of a dividend. In its infancy, this "test" was an attempt to escape an inquiry into the "motives and plans" of the shareholder and his cor-poration. See Flanagan v. Helvering, 116 F.2d 937, 939-940, 26 AFTR 223, (D.C. Cir. 1940): "But the net effect of the distribution rather than the motives and plans of the taxpayer or his corporation, is the fundamental question in administering §115(g)." But since virtually all pro rata redemptions have the "net effect" of a dividend, the courts finally succeeded in converting this "test" into a restatement of the "essentially equivalent" language of the statute or, sometimes, into a pseudonym for the "business purpose" doctrine which it was created to avoid. See Keefe v. Cote, 213 F.2d 651, 45 AFTR 1620 (1st Cir. 1954): "But the courts generally have not applied the 'net effect' test with strict logic but have broadened its scope to include inquiry into the possible existence of some 'legitimate business purpose' for the redemption, that is to say, a legitimate corporate purpose as dis-tinguished from a purpose to benefit the stockholder by a distribution of accumulated earnings and profits exempt from the imposition of income tax, . . . thus adding a question of motive to the question of ultimate result."

The upshot was that in applying §115(g) of the 1939 Code, there was no escape from an inquiry into all the facts and circumstances of each case, and predictions were hazardous:

> Above all, courts continued to look for a valid business purpose of the corporation, such as (1) enabling the business to operate more efficiently as a sole proprietorship or as a partnership, (2) the conduct of part of its business under separate corporate form, (3) enhancement of its credit rating by calling in stock to cancel stockholder indebtedness, (4) resale of stock to junior executives, (5) provision of a profitable investment for an employees' asso-

---

[4] See Bittker and Redlich, Corporate Liquidations and the Income Tax, 5 Tax L. Rev. 437, 470-3 (1950); Chommie, Section 346 (a)(2): The Contrac-tion Theory, 11 *ibid.* 407, 417-22 (1956).

ciation, (6) adjustment for a legitimate shrinkage of the business following a fire causing a permanent reduction in productive capacity, (7) elimination of unprofitable departments, or (8) contemplation of ultimate liquidation.

Other factors than business purpose entered into the witch's brew. While the pro-rata feature is seldom disregarded and often held controlling, its effect is not always predictable and courts at times find no dividend, though the redemption is pro rata and upon occasion even find that a non pro-rata distribution requires dividend treatment. Other factors of varying degrees of significance have been held to be a poor dividend record, combined with large available earnings or profits; the fact that the initiative for the distribution was taken by the shareholder, rather than by the corporation; and the fact that the consideration paid for the redeemed stock bears no relation to its value, book or otherwise.[5]

Sec. 7.03. The 1954 changes in summary

Before 1954, the statute did not distinguish between "redemptions" and "partial liquidations"; in fact, the term "partial liquidation" was defined as "a distribution by a corporation in complete cancellation or redemption of a part of its stock" by §115(i) of the 1939 Code. This, the draftsmen of the 1954 Code thought, led to confusion:

> Existing law is complicated by the fact that stock redemptions are included within the terms of the partial liquidation provisions. Thus, a redemption of all of the stock of 1 of 2 sole shareholders of a corporation may result in capital-gain treatment to the redeemed shareholder. The result occurs, however, not by reason of the use of any particular assets of the corporation to effect the redemption but because the distribution when viewed at the shareholder level is so disproportionate with respect to the outstanding shareholder interests as not to be substantially equivalent to a dividend.
>
> Your committee, as did the House bill, separates into their significant elements the kind of transactions now incoherently aggregated in the definition of a partial liquidation. Those distributions which may have capital-gain characteristics because they are not made pro rata among the various shareholders would be subjected, at the shareholder level, to the separate tests de-

---

[5] Treusch, Corporate Distributions and Adjustments: Recent Case Reminders of Some Old Problems Under the New Code, 32 Taxes 1023, 1037 (1954) (citations omitted); see also, for pre-1954 law, Bittker and Redlich, *supra* note 4; Chommie, *supra* note 4; Darrell, *supra* note 2; Murphy, Partial Liquidations and the New Look, 5 Tax L. Rev. 73 (1949); Nolan, The Uncertain Tax Treatment of Stock Redemptions: A Legislative Proposal, 65 Harv. L. Rev. 255 (1951); Pedrick, Some Latter Day Developments in the Taxation of Liquidating Distributions, 50 Mich. L. Rev. 529 (1952); Cohen, et al., A Technical Revision of the Federal Income Tax Treatment of Corporate Distributions to Shareholders, 52 Col. L. Rev. 1, 24-38 (1952) (discussing the A.L.I. proposals).

scribed in part I of this subchapter. On the other hand, those distributions characterized by what happens solely at the corporate level by reason of the assets distributed would be included as within the concept of a partial liquidation. (S. Rep. No. 1622, 83d Cong., 2d Sess., 49 (1954)).

The language of the 1954 Code, however, fails in its aim of separating partial liquidations from redemptions. According to §346-(a), a "partial liquidation" (which is to be treated as a sale of the surrendered stock) includes a distribution "in redemption of a part of the stock of the corporation," so long as it is "not essentially equivalent to a dividend." Nothing is said in §346(a) about "distributions characterized by what happens solely at the corporate level by reason of the assets distributed" or about "corporate contractions." Yet §346 is the section that is supposed to provide the exclusive rule for partial liquidations, segregating them from other redemptions. Not only is §346(a) innocent of any reference to "corporate contractions," but its language is virtually identical with parts of §302, the section designed by the draftsmen of the 1954 Code to deal exclusively with those redemptions that are *not* partial liquidations. For §302 provides, among other things, that a redemption shall be treated as a sale of the stock if it "is not essentially equivalent to a dividend." If the draftsmen's goal of separating "into their significant elements the kind of transactions . . . incoherently aggregated [by the 1939 Code] in the definition of a partial liquidation" is achieved, it will be by the painful process of administration and judicial construction of muddy language.[6]

[6] For general discussions of stock redemptions and partial liquidations under the 1954 Code, see Bittker, Stock Redemptions and Partial Liquidations Under the Internal Revenue Code of 1954, 9 Stanford L. Rev. 13 (1956); Moore, Dividend Equivalency — Taxation of Distributions in Redemption of Stock, 19 Tax L. Rev. 249 (1964); Dean, Redemptions: Liquidating and Nonliquidating; Kinds of Distributions, 20 N.Y.U. Inst. on Fed. Tax. 895 (1962); Kamanski, Partial Liquidations — Section 346, 1959 So. Cal. Tax Inst. 137; Greene, Planning for Corporate Stock Redemptions Faces Many Potential Hazards, 19 J. Tax. 2 (1963); Cavitch, Costly "Traps" in Corporate Stock Purchases From Shareholders, 15 West. Res. L. Rev. 338 (1964). Earlier works on the 1954 changes, preceding the promulgation of regulations thereunder, are Chommie, *supra* note 4; Winton and Hoffman, A Case Study of Stock Redemptions Under Sections 302 and 318 of the New Code, 10 Tax L. Rev. 363 (1955); Murphy, Dividend Equivalency — the End of the Beginning? *ibid.* 213; Note, Redemptions and Partial Liquidations under the 1954 Internal Revenue Code: The Dividend Equivalence Test, 103 U. Pa. L. Rev. 936 (1955); Cohen, Redemptions of Stock under the Internal Revenue Code of 1954, *ibid.* 739; Cohen et al., Corporate Liquidations under the Internal Revenue Code of 1954, 55 Col. L. Rev. 37, 51 (1955); Laikin, Stock Redemptions: Sections 302 and 318, 14 N.Y.U. Inst. on Fed. Tax 671 (1956); Owen, Stock Redemptions and Partial Liquidations Under the 1954 Code, 32 Taxes 979 (1954); Windhorst, Stock Redemptions and Constructive Ownership Problems, 33 *ibid.* 917 (1955).

Whatever simplicity is gained by the new statutory framework, moreover, is easily outweighed by the complications introduced by the distinction between "distributions characterized by what happens solely at the corporate level by reason of the assets distributed" (*i.e.*, partial liquidations) and "distributions which may have capital-gain characteristics because they are not made pro rata among the various shareholders" (*i.e.*, certain other redemptions). To determine whether a redemption of stock is to be treated as a sale or as a "dividend" under the 1954 Code, it often will be necessary to examine §302, relating to ordinary redemptions, as well as §331(a)(2) and §346, relating to partial liquidations.[7] The regulations take the position that if a distribution qualifies under §346 as a partial liquidation, §302 is not applicable to it. Regs. §1.346-2 and §1.302-1(a). Ordinarily it will be immaterial to the shareholder which section governs, assuming his distribution qualifies under both; in a few special situations, however, the transaction will be treated differently if it is regarded as controlled by §346 rather than by §302.[8]

In the balance of this chapter, the 1954 Code's treatment of stock redemptions, partial liquidations, and certain related problems will be dealt with in the following order:

1. Stock redemptions (*infra*, Part B);
2. Redemptions of stock by affiliated corporations, under §304 (*infra*, Part C);
3. Redemptions to pay death taxes, under §303 (*infra*, Part D);
4. Partial liquidations (*infra*, Part E);
5. Collateral problems — computation of the shareholder's gain or loss; the "mystery" of the disappearing basis; the shareholder's basis for property received in redemption of stock; recognition of income or loss by the redeeming corporation; and the effect of a redemption on the corporation's earnings and profits (*infra*, Part F).

---

[7] See Regs. §1.302-1(b), as to "excess" distributions in connection with partial liquidations.

In the opinion of the authors, the transfer of stock by a shareholder to his corporation for consideration can qualify as a sale or exchange of a capital asset only if it meets the standards of §302(a), §331(a)(2), or §303. We do not believe, in other words, that such a transaction between the shareholder and his corporation can qualify for capital gain or loss treatment on the independent ground that it is a "sale" of stock, rather than a "redemption," and hence need not run the gauntlet of §302(a), §331(a)(2), and §303. See Bittker, *supra* note 4, at 18n.

[8] E.g., the applicability of §267, disallowing certain losses between a shareholder and a controlled corporation (*infra*, Sec. 7.81); and the collapsible corporation provisions (*infra*, Sec. 10.03, note 5). There are also differences between §346 and §302 transactions so far as the corporation is concerned, if the distribution involves LIFO inventory or property subject to a liability in excess of its basis (*infra*, Sec. 7.81).

Part B.   Stock Redemptions Under §302

Sec. 7.20.   Introductory

Section 302(a), which both in tax planning and in the number of litigated cases has overshadowed in importance the partial liquidation rules of §346, provides that a redemption[9] of stock shall be treated as an "exchange" if it falls into any one of the following four categories: (1) a redemption that is "not essentially equivalent to a dividend" under §302(b)(1); (2) a "substantially disproportionate" redemption under §302(b)(2); (3) a redemption of all the shareholder's stock under §302(b)(3); and (4) a redemption of the stock of certain railroad corporations under §302(b)(4). By virtue of §302(d), a redemption that does not fall within one of these categories is to be treated as a distribution under §301, viz., as a dividend to the extent of current and post-1913 earnings and profits, and a return of capital to the extent of any balance (*supra*, Sec. 5.02). With minor exceptions (*supra* note 1), "exchange" treatment is more advantageous to the shareholder than "distribution" treatment, since the former means that his gain or loss will be capital gain or loss if the stock is a capital asset in his hands.

Of the four categories of redemptions that are treated as exchanges by §302(b), the most important in planning financial transactions are §302(b)(2) ("substantially disportionate" redemptions) and §302(b)(3) (complete termination of shareholder's interest); their rules, if carefully complied with, are safe conduct passes to the promised land. A taxpayer who cannot bring himself within their requirements can try to avail himself of §302(b)(1) by establishing that the redemption was "not essentially equivalent to a dividend" under §302(b)(1) (*infra*, Sec. 7.24), but this is a treacherous route to be employed only as a last resort. The fourth category, §302(b)(4), is a bit of special legislation for certain railroad corporations, devoid of general interest; and it will not be discussed further.

Another important aspect of the 1954 Code's revision of the stock redemption area was the application of elaborate statutory rules of "constructive" stock ownership in determining whether a redemption should be treated as an "exchange" or as a "distribution."[10]

---

[9] The term "redemption" is defined by §317(b) (for purposes of §§301-318) as a corporation's acquisition of its stock from a shareholder in exchange for property, whether or not the stock is cancelled, retired, or held as treasury stock.

[10] The 1939 Code did not explicitly attribute stock owned by one person to another in the application of §115(g). But in 1951, the Treasury Department

These rules, set out in §318, apply to any transaction within the ambit of Subchapter C to which they are "expressly made applicable," and thus are by no means confined to stock redemptions; but they have taken on special importance in this area, and are thus conveniently discussed at this point. As will be seen, these constructive ownership rules are expressly made applicable to §302(b)(2) and §302(b)(3) redemptions by the statute itself; and Regs. §1.302-1(a) provides that they are also applicable to §302(b)(1) redemptions. For this reason, §318 will be examined in some detail before consideration of §302(b).

Sec. 7.21. Constructive ownership of stock: §318

By virtue of §318(a), a taxpayer is "considered as owning" any stock that is: (a) owned by certain members of his family; (b) owned by partnerships, estates, certain trusts, and certain corporations in which he is interested; or (c) subject to an option held by him; and conversely, entities in which he is beneficially interested (partnerships, estates, trusts, and corporations) are treated, subject to certain limitations, as owning stock owned directly by him. The constructive ownership (or "attribution") rules of §318 apply throughout Subchapter C (i.e., §§301-382, covering most but not all of the transactions discussed in this book), but only if "expressly made applicable" by the relevant statutory provision.[11] Although intricately devised, §318 is only one of several sets of constructive ownership rules prescribed by the 1954 Code, which differ from each other in such details as the degree of family relationship warranting the attribution of stock from one person to another and in the way stock owned by a trust is allocated to its beneficiaries. Although appropriate variations in the concept of attribution to suit the transaction under review are

announced a proposal to amend the regulations under §115(g), *supra* note 3, to provide that the redemption of all of the stock of a particular shareholder would "generally" not be subject to §115(g), but that "where such shareholder is closely related to remaining shareholders, that factor will be considered along with all other circumstances of the case in determining whether the distribution is essentially equivalent to a dividend." 16 Fed. Reg. 10,312 (1951). The proposed amendment was withdrawn after the 1954 Code was enacted. 19 Fed. Reg. 7159 (1954). Even without the aid of regulations, however, both the courts and the Internal Revenue Service at times regarded the relationship between a shareholder whose stock was redeemed and the remaining shareholders as significant in applying §115(g). See Rev. Rul. 55-373, 1955-1 C.B. 363; Rev. Rul. 55-547, 1955-2 C.B. 571; William H. Grimditch, 37 B.T.A. 402, 412 (1938); *supra* note 3; but see Lukens' Estate v. Commissioner, 246 F.2d 403, 51 AFTR 877 (3d Cir. 1957).

[11] For some Subchapter C transactions, however, the relevant statutory provision does not adopt §318's rules, but another set, e.g., §341(d) (collapsible corporations) prefers the constructive ownership rules of §544, applicable to personal holding companies.

theoretically conceivable, or even praiseworthy, the differences in the statutory provisions as actually prescribed by the Code are frequently trivial and almost always inexplicable. Not content with these variations, moreover, the draftsmen of the 1954 Code also provided that §318's own rules are to be modified for certain purposes.[12]

The types of attribution prescribed by §318 may be classified into three categories: (a) attribution from one member of a family to another (sometimes called "collateral" attribution); (b) attribution from an entity, such as a trust or corporation, to persons beneficially interested therein, or vice versa ("vertical" attribution; or "direct" attribution when the entity's stock is attributed to its owners or beneficiaries, and "back" attribution when their stock is attributed to the entity); and (c) attribution from an entity to its owners or beneficiaries and from them to members of their family, a combination of (a) and (b) that is sometimes called "chain" or "double" attribution, or "reattribution." Before 1964, a fourth category of attribution was possible, since stock owned by one beneficiary of an entity could be attributed to the entity and thence to another beneficiary; this type of "sidewise" or "double" attribution is now prevented by §318(a)-(5)(C).[13] Stock owned by the entity and attributed to a beneficiary thereof, however, is reattributed to the members of his family; and this form of "sidewise" attribution causes much of the complexity and most of the confusion in the applying §318.

Stated in greater detail, the constructive ownership rules of §318 are as follows:

1. Family attribution. Under §318(a)(1), an individual is deemed to own stock owned by his spouse, children, grandchildren, and parents. (Unlike §267(c)(4) and §544(a)(2), §318(a)(1) does not attribute stock from one brother or sister to another.) Stock attributed from one family member to another under §318(a)(1) is not reattributed from the latter to members of *his* family. Thus, if H, his wife W, their son S, and their grandson G, each owns 25 shares of X Corporation, H, W, and S are each deemed to own 100 shares of X by

---

[12] See generally, Ringel, Surrey, and Warren, Attribution of Stock Ownership in the Internal Revenue Code, 72 Harv. L. Rev. 209 (1958); Reilly, An Approach to the Simplification and Standardization of the Concepts "The Family," "Related Parties," "Control," and "Attribution of Ownership," 15 Tax L. Rev. 253 (1960).

[13] For an example of the type of sidewise attribution eliminated by the 1964 change, see S. Rep. No. 1240, 88th Cong., 2d sess., reprinted in 1964-2 C.B. 701, at 705 (1964). See Sorem v. Commissioner, 334 F.2d 275, 14 AFTR 2d 5131 (10th Cir. 1964), for a narrow escape, via §302(b)(1), from such attribution under pre-1964 law.

virtue of §318(a)(1); G, on the other hand, is deemed to own only 50 shares (25 directly, and 25 constructively from his father, S). If G had a brother, B, no stock would be attributed from G to B through their father S, because of §318(a)(5)(B).

2. *Entity-beneficiary attribution.* Under §318(a)(2), stock owned by a partnership or estate[14] is attributed proportionately to the partners or beneficiaries, stock owned by a trust (other than a §401(a) trust for employees) is attributed to its beneficiaries in proportion to their actuarial interests or, in the case of a trust described in §§671-678, to the person taxable on its income; and stock owned by a corporation is attributed pro rata to those shareholders (if any) who own 50 percent or more of its stock.[15]

Section 318(a)(3) prescribes the rules for attributing stock *to* an entity from its beneficiaries. Stock owned by partners and beneficiaries of an estate is attributed to the partnership or estate; stock owned by a beneficiary of a trust (other than a §401(a) employees' trust) is attributed to the trust unless the beneficiary has only a remote contingent interest (as defined); stock owned by a person taxable on trust income under §§671-678 is attributed to the trust; and stock owned by a shareholder owning 50 percent or more of a corporation's stock is attributed to the corporation. As noted above, however, stock attributed from a beneficiary to an entity is not thereupon reattributed to other beneficiaries of the same entity.

The entity-attribution principles may be illustrated by the following examples, in which it is assumed that the parties are "unrelated" unless otherwise stated:

> (a) A, an individual, owns 50 percent of X Corporation's stock. The other 50 percent is owned by a partnership, in which A has a 20 percent interest. The partnership is considered as owning 100 percent of X, and A is considered as owning 60 percent.
>
> (b) X Corporation's 100 shares of stock are owned as follows: 20 shares each by A, B, and C, who are brothers, and 40 shares by a trust, in which the interests of A, B, and C, computed

---

[14] Regs. §1.318-3(a) provides that stock is "owned" by an estate, for this purpose, if it is subject to administration, notwithstanding that legal title thereto vests immediately on death in the heirs under local law; and also defines the term "beneficiary of an estate." See also Rev. Rul. 60-18, 1960-1 C.B. 145 (residuary legatee of an estate remains a "beneficiary" until the estate is closed).

[15] Regs. §1.318-1(b)(3) provides that stock owned actually and constructively by the shareholder shall be aggregated in applying the 50 percent requirement; see also Regs. §1.318-2(a), Example (4). But attribution to such a 50 percent shareholder is evidently based on his actual, rather than constructive ownership percentage.

actuarially, are 50 percent, 20 percent and 30 percent, respectively. The trust is considered to own all of the stock in X, while A, B, and C, in addition to the 20 shares each owns directly, own 20, 8 and 12 shares constructively, respectively.

If C's interest in the trust was both "remote" (*i.e.*, worth 5% or less) *and* contingent, his stock would not be attributed to the trust, but its stock would be attributed proportionately to him.

(c) A and B own 70 percent and 30 percent of X Corporation's stock respectively. A and X Corporation each own one half of Y Corporation's stock. X is deemed to own 100 percent of Y Corporation, while A is deemed to own 85 percent thereof. Y, on the other hand, is deemed to own 70 percent of X Corporation.

If A and B were "related" family members, B would also be deemed to own 100 percent of Y Corporation (85 percent by attribution from A, and 15 percent in his own right by virtue of his 30 percent direct interest in X). Y would be considered as owning 100 percent of X Corporation (30 percent from B to A, then 100 percent from A to Y). It should be noted that the 1964 changes in §318(a) (5) (C) would have no effect on these facts.

(d) A and B each own 50 percent of X Corporation and Y Corporation. X is considered to own 100 percent of Y and Y to own 100 percent of X.

Before the 1964 changes in §318(a)(5)(C), A and B would each be considered as owning 75 percent of each corporation; but as a result of these changes, the stock that is attributed from A to X and Y is not reattributed to B, nor vice versa. Thus A and B are not considered as owning any of the stock owned by the other.

3. Option attribution. Under §318(a)(4), a person who has an option to acquire stock is deemed to own the optioned stock.[16] If both the option attribution and family attribution rules can apply, the option rules control by virtue of §318(a)(5)(D), thus permitting a reattribution of the optioned stock to another member of the option-holder's family. Thus, if F has an option on the stock owned by his son S, the stock is constructively owned by F's grandfather G; were it not for the option, S's stock would be attributed to F, but not reattributed to G.

Two ambiguities in the language of §318 are clarified by Regs. §1.318-1(b): a corporation is not deemed to own its own stock; and a block of stock is not to be counted more than once (*e.g.*, stock

---

[16] It seems clear that only the optioned stock, and not other stock owned by the optionee is attributed to the option-holder by §318(a)(4). The relation of §318(a)(4) to contingent options (e.g., an option exercisable on a merger or on a shareholder's death) and to options on unissued stock remains to be worked out. See Sorem v. Commissioner, *supra* note 13 (employee stock options on unissued stock are to be taken into account); Regs. §1.302-3(a) (disregarding unissued stock).

owned by a beneficiary of a trust is not attributed to the trust and then back to the beneficiary). In applying the latter principle, however, the stock is to be attributed in such a way as to maximize the taxpayer's ownership; thus, if a 50 percent partner has an option on all of the stock of X Corporation owned by the partnership, he is charged with all rather than only 50 percent of the stock.

Sec. 7.22.   Substantially disproportionate redemptions: §302(b)(2)

An ordinary dividend typically effects a distribution of money or property to the corporation's shareholders without disturbing their relative interests in the assets and earning capacity of the corporation. For this reason, a stock redemption was most likely to be treated as "essentially equivalent to a dividend" under §115(g) of the 1939 Code (*supra*, Sec. 7.02) if it was pro rata among the shareholders. Conversely, a non-pro rata redemption ordinarily escaped the clutches of §115(g). Section 302(b)(2) of the 1954 Code has carried forward this distinction, by providing that a "substantially disproportionate" redemption is to be treated as a sale of the stock rather than as a distribution under §301.

In order to qualify as "substantially disporportionate" under §302(b)(2), the redemption must meet three requirements: (1) immediately after the redemption, the shareholder must own (directly and constructively) less than 50 percent of the total combined voting power of all classes of outstanding stock entitled to vote; (2) his percentage of the total outstanding voting stock immediately after the redemption must be less than 80 percent of his ownership of such stock immediately before the redemption; and (3) his percentage of outstanding common stock (whether or not voting) after the redemption must be less than 80 percent of his ownership before the redemption.[17] These tests are applied shareholder-by-shareholder, so that a redemption may be "substantially disproportionate" as to one but not to others.

The 50 percent restriction in §302(b)(2)(B) presumably is based on the theory that a reduction in the shareholder's proportionate ownership is not significant if he continues to own (directly or constructively) stock representing 50 percent or more of the voting

---

[17] Stock with "contingent voting rights," e.g., preferred stock with a power to vote only if dividends are passed, is generally excluded from the term "voting stock," Regs. §1.302(a). For other problems in defining "common stock," "voting stock," and "stock entitled to vote," and in computing "voting power," see *supra*, Sec. 3.07 and *infra*, Ch. 13.

power. The two 80 percent tests envision a substantial contraction in the redeemed shareholder's equity and voting interest in the corporation. If the corporation redeems only non-voting stock (whether common or preferred), the redemption cannot qualify under §302(b)-(2) because it will not reduce the shareholder's proportionate ownership of voting stock.[18] A redemption of such stock can qualify, however, if it is coupled with a redemption of voting stock that would qualify if it stood alone. Regs. §1.302-3(a). The constructive ownership rules of §318 (*supra*, Sec. 7.21) are applicable in determining whether a redemption is "substantially disproportionate" under §302-(b)(2), and they materially reduce the feasibility of such redemptions by closely-held corporations.

The regulations set out the following example to illustrate the application of §302(b)(2)(C):

> Corporation M has outstanding 400 shares of common stock of which A, B, C and D each own 100 shares or 25 percent. No stock is considered constructively owned by A, B, C or D under section 318. Corporation M redeems 55 shares from A, 25 shares from B, and 20 shares from C. For the redemption to be disproportionate as to any shareholder, such shareholder must own after the redemption less than 20 percent (80 percent of 25 percent) of the 300 shares of stock then outstanding. After the redemptions, A owns 45 shares (15 percent), B owns 75 shares (25 percent), and C owns 80 shares (26⅔ percent). The distribution is disproportionate only with respect to A. (Regs. §1.302-3(b).

This example can be recast in tabular form:

	Shares owned after redemption	Shares owned before redemption	Ratio of percentage owned after redemption to percentage owned before*
A	45 = 15%	100 = 25%	15/25 = 60%
B	75 = 25%	100 = 25%	25/25 = 100%
C	80 = 27%	100 = 25%	27/25 = 108%
D	100 = 33%	100 = 25%	33/25 = 132%
Total	300 = 100%	400 = 100%	

*Must be less than 80% to qualify under §302(b)(2)

In computing the percentage of stock owned by each shareholder after the redemption, care must be taken to reflect the smaller number

---

[18] It is not clear whether the reference in Regs. §1.302-3(a) to a redemption "of voting stock" is intended to embrace a redemption of voting preferred alone; see Bittker, *supra* note 6, at 40, n. 98.

of shares outstanding. In the table above, for example, B owns 25 percent after the redemption (75 shares out of 300), not 18.75 percent (75 out of 400).[19]

To prevent an obvious abuse of §302(b)(2), the statute explicitly provides that it does not apply to any redemption under a plan that contemplates a series of redemptions which, in the aggregate, will not be "substantially disproportionate" with respect to the shareholder. Thus, to return to the illustration above, if the redemption of the stock of A, B, and C was in accordance with a plan by which 75 of D's shares would later be redeemed, the redemption of A's shares would not meet the test of §302(b)(2). For after the second step, A would own 20 percent of the total outstanding shares (45 out of 225), an insufficient reduction in his percentage. The redemption of D's shares, however, would apparently qualify even though it was the occasion for disallowing the redemption of A's shares. It should not be assumed, however, that the explicit reference in §302(b)(2)(D) to a "series of redemptions" is the Commissioner's only weapon against attempts to abuse §302(b)(2). If a redemption viewed in isolation is "substantially disproportionate" as to a shareholder, but the other shareholders have agreed to sell enough stock to him after the redemption to restore the status quo, the redemption will probably not satisfy §302(b)(2).

A final point to be noted is that the Internal Revenue Service will not issue an advance ruling on a redemption if the corporation is to pay for the stock over a long future period or if the stock is held in escrow or as security so that the shareholder may re-acquire it upon the corporation's default.[20] This refusal to rule is a warning that in appropriate cases the Service might argue that the redemption is not "substantially disproportionate" because the shareholder may recapture part or all of the redeemed stock or that the corporation's obligations are so much like stock (*supra*, Sec. 4.02) that the transaction is not a "redemption" within the meaning of §317(b), *viz.*, an acquisition of stock in exchange for "property."[21]

---

[19] A failure to take account of the reduced number of shares outstanding after a redemption produced two erroneous computations in the Senate Finance Committee's report explaining §302; see S. Rep. No. 1622, 83d Cong., 2d sess., at 234-235 and 253 (1954); Bittker, *supra* note 6, at 39, n. 97.

See Freret, A Simplified Computation for Substantially Disproportionate Stock Redemptions, 37 Taxes 767 (1959), for an analysis of minimum percentage formulas under §302(b)(2).

[20] See Rev. Proc. 64-31, Sec. 3.01(5), 1964-2 C.B. 947; but see Rev. Rul. 57-295, 1957-2 C.B. 227 (redemption for cash plus promissory notes payable over a 10-year period).

[21] Once it is decided that the transaction is not a redemption or that the corporation's obligations are not "property," however, the next step is far from

Sec. 7.23.   Termination of shareholder's entire interest: §302(b)(3)

Section 302(b)(3) provides that a redemption shall be treated as a sale if it "is in complete redemption of all of the stock of the corporation owned by the shareholder." If a corporation is owned by A and B, two unrelated persons, a redemption of all the stock of either A or B will qualify under §302(b)(3). A redemption of this type was similarly treated as a sale, rather than a "dividend" distribution, under pre-1954 law.[22] The principal importance of §302(b)(3) lies in its waiver, in certain circumstances, of the family attribution rules of §318; this provides an escape route for closely-held corporations that cannot effect a "substantially disproportionate" redemption because in applying §302(b)(2) the redeemed shareholder is charged with the stock owned by the remaining shareholders. If the redeemed shareholder in such a case is bought out completely,[23] the redemption may qualify as a complete termination under §302(b)(3) even though it is not "substantially disproportionate" under §302(b)(2). Section 302(b)(3) is also of importance in two other situations that cannot be brought within §302(b)(2): a redemption of nonvoting stock alone (*supra*, Sec. 7.22) and a redemption of "section 306 stock" (*infra*, Sec. 8.04).

If all of the stock *actually* owned by a shareholder is redeemed by the corporation, and no stock outstanding thereafter is attributed to him by §318, §302(b)(3) is easily applied and the transaction will be treated as a sale. If such a "clean" redemption is prevented by the family attribution rules, they are waived by §302(c)(2) if the shareholder (a) retains no "interest" in the corporation after the redemption (including an "interest" as officer, director, or employee), other than an interest as a creditor; (b) does not acquire any such interest (other than stock acquired by bequest or inheritance) within 10 years from the date of the distribution; and (c) agrees to notify the Commissioner of the acquisition of any forbidden interest within the 10-year period.[24] The regulations provide that an "interest" in a

---

certain. The transaction might be regarded as a tax-free exchange under §1036 or §368(a)(1)(E), with any down payment in the form of cash being treated as boot. It is also possible that a later payment of the obligations would be regarded as a redemption. See *infra*, Sec. 12.16.

[22] *Supra* note 3.

[23] For a redemption on credit, see *supra* notes 20 and 21.

[24] The agreement is to be filed with a timely tax return for the year of the redemption. The courts have divided on the efficacy of a belated agreement: cf. Georgie S. Cary, 41 T.C. 214 (1963) (Non-Acq.) (consent agreement merely "procedural"), and United States v. G.W. Van Keppel, 321 F.2d 717, 12 AFTR

parent, subsidiary, or successor corporation is equally fatal, Regs. §1.302-4(c). It is important to note that §302(c)(2) waives only the family attribution rules, not the *entity-beneficiary* or *option* attribution rules.[25]

The theory of the family attribution rules and their waiver may be stated in this fashion: a redemption of all the stock of a shareholder is properly treated as a sale because it terminates his interest in the corporation as effectively as a sale to a third person. The sale analogy is not appropriate, however, if stock is owned after the redemption by members of the ex-shareholder's immediate family; it is sufficiently possible that he will thereby continue his interest in the corporation (without the interference from the outside that might have resulted from a sale to a third person) so that an attribution of his relative's shares to him is a reasonable rule of thumb. If he is willing, however, to forego for a 10-year period any "interest" in the corporation (other than an interest retained as a creditor or acquired involuntarily by bequest), it is reasonable to waive the family attribution rules and treat the redemption as a sale. This exception is not made for the entity-beneficiary or option attribution rules, however, because they impute stock on the basis of an economic interest rather than because of a family relationship that does not necessarily bespeak an identity of economic interest.

The principal ambiguity in applying the waiver of §302(c)(2) lies in the uncertain meaning of the term "interest." Although the prohibition on an "interest as officer, director, or employee" might be construed to bar such a relationship only if it was coupled with a profit-sharing or similar financial stake in the corporation, the Service has espoused the stricter view that the performance of services, with

---

2d 5622 (10th Cir. 1963) (accord), with Archbold v. United States, 311 F.2d 228, 11 AFTR 2d 422 (3d Cir. 1963) (contra).

To protect the government, the shareholder is required by §318(c)(2)(A)-(iii) to retain "such records as may be necessary for the application of this paragraph" and the statute of limitations is extended to permit the assessment of a deficiency until one year after he gives notice of his acquisition of a forbidden interest.

[25] *Supra,* Sec. 7.21. Moreover, the Service has ruled that a §302(c)(2) agreement does not prevent stock that is attributed from one member of a family to another from being attributed to an entity of which the latter person is a beneficiary. Rev. Rul. 59-233, 1959-2 C.B. 106 (stock attributed from father to children and thence to a trust of which the children were sole beneficiaries; held, trust cannot qualify for waiver). Had the stock been owned by the children, a redemption from them would have qualified for the waiver; it is hard to justify a different result for the trust's stock, except on the ground that the acquisition of a forbidden interest during the 10-year period by the children, the persons beneficially concerned with the redemption, was not prevented because the agreement required by §302(c)(2)(A)(iii) is to be filed only by the distributee (i.e., the trust).

or without compensation, is fatal.[26] It would be more consonant with the purpose of §302(c)(2) to distinguish between conduct supporting an inference that the ex-shareholder did not effectively terminate his financial interest in the corporation and conduct that is consistent with such a termination, and to waive the family ownership rules if his conduct falls in the latter category. Since §302(c)(2) permits the retention or acquisition of an interest as a "creditor," the shareholder will be able to sell his stock to the corporation on credit, rather than for cash; but the regulations warn that an obligation "in the form of a debt" may, in substance, give the owner a "proprietary interest" in the corporation. The regulations provide that: (a) the ex-shareholder's rights must not be greater than necessary for the enforcement of his claim; (b) the debt must not be subordinate to claims of general creditors; (c) payments of principal must not be contingent on earnings as respects their amount or certainty; and (d) the enforcement of his rights as creditor upon a default by the corporation will not constitute the acquisition of a forbidden "interest" unless stock of the corporation, its parent, or (in certain cases) its subsidiary is thus acquired.[27]

The waiver of the family ownership rules granted by §302(c)(2)-(A) is denied in certain circumstances. Before examining these conditions, which are set out in §302(c)(2)(B), it may be well to see an illustration of their purpose. If A owns all the stock of a corporation and wishes to give his son a gift of cash, he can of course use funds that he received as dividends — but only after they have been reported as income. If he raises the funds by causing the corporation to redeem part of his stock, the redemption will probably be taxed as a dividend.[28] But what if A gives his son some stock in the corporation, and then causes this stock to be redeemed? If the transaction can avoid being classified as a sham,[29] the son could claim the shelter of §302(b)(3), avoiding the family attribution rules of §318 (which

---

[26] Rev. Rul. 56-556, 1956-2 C.B. 177; Rev. Rul. 59-119, 1959-1 C.B. 68; but cf. Rev. Rul. 54-408, 1954-2 CB. 165 (1939 Code). As the Service construes §302(c)(2), the shareholder may be courting trouble if he does no more than serve the corporation as an unpaid consultant or independent contractor.

[27] Regs. §1.302-4(d); see also Mary Duerr, 30 T.C. 944 (1958) (1939 Code); *supra*, Sec. 4.02.

[28] The redemption would not meet the requirements of §302(b)(3), because only part of A's stock was redeemed, nor those of §302(b)(2) (*supra*, Sec. 7.22), because A owns more than 50 percent of the common stock of the corporation after the redemption; and it would not meet the requirements of §302(b)(1) (*supra*, Sec. 7.24), unless other significant facts were present.

[29] A blatant case could be treated as an anticipatory assignment of a dividend, *i.e.*, as though the corporation had redeemed the father's stock and he had made a gift of the proceeds to his son. See Rhodes' Estate v. Commissioner, 131 F.2d 50, 30 AFTR 220 (6th Cir. 1942).

if applicable would take the transaction out of §302(b)(3) by imputing A's unredeemed shares to his son) by foregoing any "interest" in the corporation for a period of 10 years.

To frustrate plans of the type just described, §302(c)(2)(B) provides that the family attribution rules shall *not* be waived:

> 1. If any part of the redeemed stock was acquired, directly or indirectly, within the previous 10 years by the distributee from a related person; or
> 2. If any related person owns stock at the time of the distribution and acquired any stock, directly or indirectly, from the distributee within the previous 10 years, unless the stock so acquired is redeemed in the same transaction.[30]

These limitations on the waiver of the family attribution rules are not applicable if the acquisition (in the case of (1) above) or the disposition (in the case of (2) above) did not have "as one of its principal purposes the avoidance of Federal income tax." The regulations state that a transfer "shall not be deemed" to have as one of its principal purposes the avoidance of Federal income tax "merely" because the transferee is in a lower income tax bracket than the transferor. Reg. §1.302-4(g). It may be, however, that a transfer to such a person *for the purpose* of reducing the total family income tax burden would prevent a waiver of the family attribution rules.[31]

Reviewing the historical progression in the treatment of redemptions that terminate the shareholder's entire interest, we find that the 1954 Code carries forward the administrative and judicial conclusion that such a redemption was not "essentially equivalent to a taxable dividend" under §115(g) of the 1939 Code, but with a series of checks and balances that are as intricate as a minuet. The attribution rules prevent a merely formal termination of the interest of a shareholder who retains an indirect stake in corporate affairs through his family; but this restriction is mitigated by the waiver of the family attribution rules; but the waiver becomes retroactively invalid if an interest is acquired during the 10-year period following the redemption; but this condition is subject to an exception for an interest acquired by bequest (one supposes, voluntarily); however, only those

---

[30] This provision would apply, for example, if a shareholder gave some of his shares to his son and the corporation thereafter redeemed the *retained* shares, unless the shares given to the son were redeemed in the same transaction.

[31] For applications of these principles to particular sets of facts, see Rev. Rul. 56-556, 1956-2 C.B. 177; Rev. Rul. 56-584, *ibid.* 179; Rev. Rul. 57-387, 1957-2 C.B. 225.

can enter the 10-year good behavior period who have not participated during the preceding 10 years in a transfer to or from a related person; but, finally, such a pre-redemption transfer is disregarded if it was not motivated by tax avoidance.

Sec. 7.24.   Redemptions not essentially equivalent to dividends: §302(b)(1)

Section 302(b)(1) provides that a redemption may be treated as a sale of the redeemed stock if it is not "essentially equivalent to a dividend," echoing the language of §115(g) of the 1939 Code. Some commentators have argued that any redemption that could have escaped §115(g) of the 1939 Code will qualify as "not essentially equivalent to a dividend" under §302(b)(1). But the Senate Report on the 1954 Code implies that §302 is concerned solely with "those distributions which may have capital-gain characteristics because they are not made pro rata among the various shareholders." S. Rep. No. 1622, 83d Cong., 2d Sess., 49 (1954). And the legislative history of §302(b)(1) also suggests that it is to play a modest role in the scheme of things. The provision was added by the Senate Finance Committee after the passage by the House of H.R. 8300, which provided for capital gains treatment primarily in circumstances similar to those now set out in §302(b)(2) ("substantially disproportionate" redemptions) and §302(b)(3) (termination of the shareholder's entire stock interest). The addition of §302(b)(1) is explained in the Senate Report on the 1954 Code as follows:

> While the House bill set forth definite conditions under which stock may be redeemed at capital-gain rates, these rules appeared unnecessarily restrictive, particularly in the case of redemptions of preferred stock which might be called by the corporation without the shareholder having any control over when the redemption may take place. Accordingly, your committee follows existing law by reinserting the general language indicating that a redemption shall be treated as a distribution in part or full payment in exchange for stock if the redemption is not essentially equivalent to a dividend. (S. Rep. No. 1622, 83d Cong., 2d Sess., 44-5 (1954).

It is not easy to give §302(b)(1) an expansive construction in view of this indication that its major function was the narrow one of immunizing redemptions of minority holdings of preferred stock.

Against this background, it is not surprising that the Treasury has adopted a narrow construction of the scope and operation of

§302(b)(1). The regulations, Regs. §1.302-2, while stating that dividend equivalence depends upon the "facts and circumstances of each case," provide that the constructive ownership rules must be "considered" in making this determination;[32] in addition, if the redeeming corporation has only one class of stock outstanding, the regulations state that a pro rata redemption "generally" will be treated as a distribution under §301; similarly, if the corporation has more than one class outstanding, redemption of an entire class also generally will fall under §301 if all classes of stock are held in the same proportion. Finally, the only example of a qualified §302(b)(1) redemption given by the regulations is a redemption of one-half of the non-voting preferred stock of a shareholder who owns no shares of any other class of stock.

Because Regs. §1.302-2(b) provides that pro rata redemptions "generally" are to be treated as distributions rather than as sales, it can be argued that some redemptions that are either pro rata or not "substantially" disproportionate under §302(b)(2) may nevertheless qualify for sale treatment. One such possibility is a redemption of part of the stock of a minority shareholder, where the redemption is not "substantially disproportionate" but his remaining stake in the corporation is quite limited; an example, as stated above, is to be found in the regulations themselves.[33] Another area in which this argument may succeed is a redemption that is pro rata only because of the constructive ownership rules of §318, especially if the stock is being attributed from one member of a family to an independent or hostile adult.[34] More dubious is the possibility of applying §302(b)-(1) to a redemption that is pro rata but serves a corporate purpose that might have led to non-dividend treatment under the 1939 Code

---

[32] Regs. §1.302-2(b); this position is weaker than that taken in the regulations as originally proposed, which said flatly that the constructive ownership rules of §318 applied. 19 Fed. Reg. 8240 (1954). Section 318(a) states that its rules are to be applied only where "expressly made applicable"; §302(c)(1) states that these rules shall "apply in determining the ownership of stock for purposes of this section." It has been argued that they are not applicable under §302(b)(1) because it does not expressly refer to the "ownership" of stock. Cohen, *supra* note 6, at 758-759. But the rules of §318(a) are "expressly" made applicable "in determining the ownership of stock" under §302, and consequently it is reasonable to apply them whenever ownership of stock is relevant, whether by statutory direction or otherwise. This is the result reached in the litigated cases; see, for example, Thomas G. Lewis, 35 T.C. 71 (1960).

[33] See also Rev. Rul. 56-183, 1956-1 C.B. 161, holding that a reduction in a group's ownership of stock from 11 percent to 9 percent was not equivalent to a dividend because its minority position justified characterizing the transaction as a "sale"; Rev. Rul. 55-462, 1955-2 C.B. 221 (redemption of preferred stock, to equalize two unrelated shareholders' ownership).

[34] See Estate of Arthur H. Squier, 35 T.C. 950 (1961) (Acq.); Herbert C. Parker, ¶61,176 P-H Memo T.C.

(such as the acquisition by the corporation of shares for resale to junior employees; or the improvement of the corporate balance sheet by a redemption in cancellation of debts owed by the shareholders to the corporation). The 1954 intent to give §346 jurisdiction over redemptions "characterized by what happens solely at the corporate level" (*supra*, Sec. 7.03) suggests that the "business purpose" cases of pre-1954 law are not applicable under §302(b)(1), except to the extent that a business reason for the transaction may add strength to the taxpayer's case when the redemption is not pro rata. The trend of the cases is in this direction, though not unanimously.[35] The result is that pro rata redemptions, especially by closely-held corporations, seldom qualify under §302(b)(1).

Where a corporation has several classes of stock outstanding and redeems all or part of only one class, complexity is compounded, especially if the classes of stock are not held proportionately. In Himmel v. Commissioner, 338 F.2d 815, 14 AFTR 2d 6009 (2d Cir. 1964), one of the few decisions to analyze in detail the considerations involved in such a case, the corporation had three classes of stock outstanding. Of these, the taxpayer owned 100 percent of two classes (non-voting cumulative preferred and voting cumulative preferred), while the common stock was owned one-half by the taxpayer's sons and one-half by an unrelated third person. On a percentage basis, the taxpayer owned 63 percent of the voting power directly (and 82 percent constructively); he owned a similarly dominant percentage of the stock by value. On the redemption of his non-voting preferred stock, the Second Circuit Court of Appeals, reversing the Tax Court, held that the redemption qualified for "sale" treatment under §302-(b)(1). While voting power was unchanged by the redemption, the Court found that the taxpayer's other two "shareholder interests" (*e.g.*, the right to share in corporate earnings and the right to share in net assets on liquidation) were significantly altered by the redemption. Although *Himmel* relied on the "net effect" test (*i.e.*, whether

[35] See Neff v. United States, 305 F.2d 455, 10 AFTR 2d 5157 (Ct. Cl. 1962) (redemption to enable corporation to resell stock to raise additional capital held essentially equivalent to a dividend); Bradbury v. Commissioner, 298 F.2d 111, 9 AFTR 2d 398 (1st Cir. 1962); Kerr v. Commissioner, 326 F.2d 225, 13 AFTR 2d 386 (9th Cir. 1964); Ballenger v. United States, 301 F.2d 192, 9 AFTR 2d 1245 (4th Cir. 1962); and Thomas G. Lewis, 35 T.C. 71 (1960), all finding substantially pro rata redemptions (when viewed in the light of §318) to be equivalent to the distribution of dividends. For taxpayer victories, see United States v. Carey, 289 F.2d 531, 7 AFTR 2d 1301 (8th Cir. 1961); Sorem v. Commissioner, 334 F.2d 275, 14 AFTR 2d 5131 (10th Cir. 1964); Himmel v. Commissioner, 338 F.2d 815, 14 AFTR 2d 6009 (2d Cir. 1964); Robert H. Herzog, ¶63,303 P-H Memo T.C. (redemption of preferred stock issued to common shareholder to eliminate debt owed to him).

For general discussion, see articles cited *supra*, note 6.

the distribution in redemption had the same economic effect as the distribution of a dividend), the opinion went beyond mere analysis of the hypothetical dividend consequences, and considered relative changes with respect to all shareholder interests (*i.e.*, rights to control, earnings, and assets). Though not very helpful in planning transactions because its facts were rather special, *Himmel's* method of analyzing the problem should be useful to taxpayers who are forced for one reason or another to rely on the general non-dividend equivalency test of §302(b)(1).

Sec. 7.25. Redemptions in conjunction with "bootstrap" acquisitions of stock

If the owner of part of the stock of a corporation sells his stock to another investor at a profit, his gain is ordinarily capital; and the same result will attach to a redemption of his stock by virtue of §302(b)(3) if the stock owned by the remaining shareholders is not attributed to him under §318 or if attribution of their stock is waived by §302(c)(2). On such a buy-out, however, the parties often want the corporation to redeem a portion of the stock of the outgoing shareholder while the rest is to be purchased by the incoming shareholder. Similarly, if complete control of the corporation is to be transferred, the business plan often calls for a "bootstrap" acquisition under which a substantial part of the stock owned by the existing shareholders is to be redeemed so that the purchasers need pay for only the balance. Such a combined purchase-redemption is especially appealing if the corporation's cash or liquid assets exceed its probable business needs.[35a]

In a celebrated pre-1954 Code case, involving such a bootstrap acquisition of the stock of a one-man corporation, the Internal Revenue Service asserted that the redemption part of the transaction was a dividend under §115(g) of the 1939 Code, on the ground that the redemption of part of the seller's stock would have been a dividend if it had preceded the sale of the remaining shares, and that the result should be the same where the redemption, by prearrangement, followed the sale. The Sixth Circuit Court of Appeals held to the contrary, Zenz v. Quinlivan, 213 F.2d 914, 45 AFTR 1672 (6th Cir. 1954), stating that the taxpayer intended a complete termination of his stock ownership, so that the redemption did not occur in such a manner as to make the distribution essentially equivalent to a div-

---

[35a] For a discussion of the relation between stock redemptions and §531 (unreasonable accumulations), see *supra*, Sec. 6.07.

idend. The Service acquiesced in *Zenz* with respect to the 1939 Code, and subsequently announced that such a transaction met the requirements of §302(b)(3) of the 1954 Code as well.[36] Although it is usually considered safer to have the sale precede, or occur simultaneously with, the redemption, the government conceded in United States v. Carey, 289 F.2d 531, 7 AFTR 2d 1301 (8th Cir. 1961), that a redemption could not properly be treated as a distribution even if it preceded the sale of the remaining shares, where the two steps were taken to consummate a single plan. The retiring shareholder, therefore, is on safe ground in assuming that the combined sale-redemption, if properly planned, will generate capital gain, rather than dividend income.[37]

Since it takes two to make a contract, however, the mere fact that the selling shareholder is not threatened by a sale-redemption transaction does not by itself settle all doubts in this area. What is the status of the buyer? In answering this question, it should be noted that if he bought *all* of the seller's stock, and at a later date recouped some of his cash outlay by causing the corporation to redeem part of the stock thus acquired, the redemption would clearly fail to meet the standards of §302(b)(3) (complete termination) and §302(b)(2) (substantially disproportionate redemption), and it would almost as clearly fail to qualify under §302(b)(1) (not essentially equivalent to a dividend) because of its pro rata character (*supra*, Sec. 7.24).[38] If the buyer does not pay for the stock at the closing, but acquires it wholly or partly on credit, it is clear that a later payment by the corporation of the buyer's obligation to the seller would be a con-

---

[36] Rev. Rul. 54-458, 1954-2 C.B. 167 (1939 Code); Rev. Rul. 55-745, 1955-2 C.B. 223 (1954 Code). If the selling shareholder retains an "interest" in the corporation, however, the Service might assert that the transaction was not covered by its rulings and seek to reargue *Zenz*, at least for shareholders retaining such an interest. See Bittker, *supra*, note 6, at 35-36.

[37] If the seller is a corporation, however, it may prefer to treat the entire proceeds as a dividend rather than report the excess of the proceeds over its adjusted basis for the stock as capital gain, because of the dividends received deduction of §243 (*supra*, Sec. 2.25). This preference may lead to an effort to cast the redemption in the form of a dividend, *e.g.*, by failing to surrender stock (*infra*, Sec. 7.81) or by separating the distribution from the sale of the stock to the incoming shareholders. See The Steel Improvement & Forge Co. v. Commissioner, 314 F.2d 96, 11 AFTR 2d 953 (6th Cir. 1963); Merrill C. Gilmore, 25 T.C. 1321 (1956); Regs. §1.61-9(c); Grayck, Taxing Income That is Applied Against the Purchase Price, 12 Tax L. Rev. 381 (1957). For the possibility that dividend income resulting from such a transaction may convert the parent corporation into a personal holding company, see McKinley Corp. of Ohio, 36 T.C. 1182 (1961); *supra*, Sec. 6.22.

[38] See Television Industries, Inc. v. Commissioner, 284 F.2d 322, 6 AFTR 2d 5864 (2d Cir. 1960) (redemption of stock owned by 100 percent parent corporation held a dividend, although transaction was used to repay funds borrowed to pay final installment of purchase price of stock).

structive distribution (*supra,* Sec. 5.05) to the buyer, taxable as a dividend to the extent of the corporation's earnings and profits.

A variation on these alternatives was involved in a leading case under the 1939 Code, Wall v. United States, 164 F.2d 462, 36 AFTR 423 (4th Cir. 1947), where the taxpayer contracted to purchase stock of a co-shareholder on the installment plan; subsequently, he caused the corporation to discharge his obligation to the seller by redeeming the stock that he was personally obligated to pay for. The court held that the redemption was equivalent to a payment by the corporation of the taxpayer's personal debt:

> The controlling fact in this situation was that Wall [the buyer] was under an obligation to pay Coleman [the seller] $5,000 in the tax year and that [the corporation] paid this indebtedness for Wall out of its surplus. It cannot be questioned that the payment of a taxpayer's indebtedness by a third party pursuant to an agreement between them is income to the taxpayer. . . . The transaction is regarded as the same as if the money had been paid to the taxpayer and transmitted by him to the creditor; and so if a corporation, instead of paying a dividend to a stockholder pays a debt for him out of its surplus, it is the same for tax purposes as if the corporation pays a dividend to a stockholder, and the stockholder then utilizes it to pay his debt.

The fact that the corporation received shares of its own stock equal in value to the amount paid by it did not, in the court's opinion, require the transaction to be treated as a purchase of stock by the corporation rather than as a distribution; since the taxpayer owned or controlled 100 percent both before and after the redemption, his proportionate interest was unaffected by it.

The principle of the *Wall* case is not applicable, however, if the buyer agrees to purchase part of the seller's stock, and the corporation agrees simultaneously to redeem the rest. The Tax Court has held in Ray Edenfield, 19 T.C. 13 (1952) (Acq.), that a redemption of the seller's stock did not constitute a dividend to the buyer in a case of this type even though he pledged his shares to insure that the corporation would perform its part of the bargain, so long as he had no personal obligation to acquire the shares that were redeemed. If cash is to be paid for the shares at the closing, there is no practical difference to the buyer between a purchase of all the shares, followed by a redemption from him of some, and a purchase of some shares with a simultaneous redemption of the others from the seller. In both cases, the amount received by the seller is the same, and the buyer becomes the sole owner of a corporation whose assets are reduced by the same amount. Under the *Edenfield* case, however, the difference in form would determine whether the buyer received a dividend or not. If some shares are to be paid for at a later date, the *Wall* case finds a dividend if an individual purchaser agrees to buy and then causes the corporation to take over his obligation, while the *Edenfield* case protects the purchaser if only the corporation is liable to the seller. Yet it may be that neither the seller nor the buyer will care, except for tax purposes, whether the buyer's credit or only the corporation's is pledged. The Internal Revenue Service has acquiesced in the *Edenfield* case, however, and it seems to be reasonably well established that the purchase of stock by a corporation is not a taxable distribution to its shareholders, so long as they did not have any personal obligation to buy. And there is authority for the same result even if the shareholders guarantee payment by the corporation.[39]

The outer extremes of the *Wall-Edenfield* conflict thus are clear,[40] but some transactions fall between them. In Holsey v. Commissioner, 258 F.2d 865, 2 AFTR 2d 5660 (3d Cir. 1958), for example, the buyer held an option to purchase another shareholder's stock, but was under no duty to exercise it; when he assigned the option to the corporation, which thereupon redeemed the optioned stock, the govern-

---

[39] E.g., Milton F. Priester, 38 T.C. 316 (1962).

[40] On the *Wall* side of the line are: Schalk Chemical Co. v. Commissioner, 304 F.2d 48, 9 AFTR 2d 1579 (9th Cir. 1962); Ferro v. Commissioner, 242 F.2d 838, 50 AFTR 2084 (3rd Cir. 1957); McGinty v. Commissioner, 325 F.2d 820, 12 AFTR 2d 6139 (2d Cir. 1963); Zipp v. Commissioner, 259 F.2d 119, 1 AFTR 2d 1778 (6th Cir. 1958); and Idol v. Commissioner, 319 F.2d 647, 12 AFTR 2d 5118 (8th Cir. 1963). On the *Edenfield* side are: Holsey v. Commissioner, 258 F.2d 865, 2 AFTR 2d 5660 (3rd Cir. 1958); Niederkrome v. Commissioner, 266 F.2d 238, 2 AFTR 2d 6155 (9th Cir. 1958); Schmitt v. Commissioner, 208 F.2d 819, 45 AFTR 37 (3d Cir. 1954); and Ward v. Rountree, 193 F. Supp. 154, 7 AFTR 2d 1209 (D.C. Tenn. 1961).

On rare occasions, a shareholder who was personally obligated to pay for the shares has successfully established that he was acting as agent for the corporation, with the result that the redemption was treated as a payment by the corporation of its own, rather than the shareholder's, obligation. See Fox v. Harrison, 145 F.2d 521, 33 AFTR 74 (7th Cir. 1944); Commissioner v. Decker, 286 F.2d 427, 7 AFTR 2d 392 (6th Cir. 1960).

One more point: the fact that the redemption is treated as distribution does not automatically lead to its being taxed as a dividend; the taxpayer can still try to make his way under §302(b)(1) (not essentially equivalent to a dividend), but the likelihood of success where the transaction does not alter the percentage of control is *de minimis* (*supra*, Sec. 7.24).

See generally, Polasky, Planning for the Disposition of a Substantial Interest in a Closely Held Business, 46 Iowa L. Rev. 516 (1961); Lange, Bootstrap Financing: The Redemption Technique, 18 Tax L. Rev. 323 (1963); Smith, Recent Developments in the Field of Corporate Business Purchase Agreements, 14 Tax L. Rev. 413 (1959); see also Note, The Use of Life Insurance to Fund Agreements Providing for Disposition of a Business Interest at Death, 71 Harv. L. Rev. 687 (1958); Goldstein, Tax Aspects of Business Use of Life Insurance, 18 Tax L. Rev. 133 (1963).

ment argued that he received an economic benefit from the redemption, viz., complete control of the corporation, justifying a conclusion that the transaction was a constructive distribution to him. The court rejected this argument; and the Service later announced that it would follow *Holsey*, stating that it will not treat the redemption of one shareholder's stock as a distribution to the remaining shareholders "merely because their percentage interests in the corporation are increased," but that "if the stock is in reality purchased by a remaining shareholder and paid for by the corporation, then, regardless of the form of the transaction, the payment will be considered a dividend to the shareholder who made the purchase."[41] The ruling seeks to renounce form as crucial, always a laudable objective; but it cannot obscure the fact that a redemption by the corporation has virtually the same economic consequences whether it relieves the remaining shareholders of an obligation to purchase as individuals or not. Thus, the form of the transaction continues to be controlling despite the Service's acquiescence in *Holsey*.[42]

Another source of trouble is a hasty agreement by the new investors to purchase all the stock, which is called off when a more complete financial or legal analysis suggests the advisability of using corporate assets to pay for part of the stock. If a combined sale-redemption is substituted at the last minute for the original obligation of the investors to buy all the stock, a court properly might find that the transaction was "in reality" a shareholder transaction under principles analogous to Commissioner v. Court Holding Co., 324 U.S. 331, 33 AFTR 593 (1945) (*infra*, Sec. 9.63). The theory would be that the corporation was merely a conduit through which the shareholder obligated himself to acquire the stock.[43] Although this theory has not yet played a significant role in this area, the careful adviser will seek to avoid any occasion for putting it to the test.

[41] Rev. Rul. 58-614, 1958-2 C.B. 920.

[42] See Robert Deutsch, 38 T.C. 118 (1962) (contract "to purchase or cause the corporation to redeem" the selling party's stock; redemption treated as constructive distribution to the buyer, citing *Wall*); but see Rev. Rul. 59-286, 1959-2 C.B. 103 (taxpayer required to purchase stock of deceased shareholder under shareholder agreement or to cause corporation to be liquidated; held, redemption not taxable as distribution to surviving shareholder).

[43] In Milton F. Priester, *supra* note 39, the taxpayer was obligated to buy stock from a co-shareholder, but his arrangement was called off and a third person bought the stock; when the government sought to charge the taxpayer with a constructive distribution because the corporation later redeemed the stock from the third party buyer, the Court held that the latter was a bona fide purchaser, not a straw man for the taxpayer. If the buyer had been the taxpayer's alter ego, however, or if the taxpayer's original agreement had been abandoned in favor of a purchase by the corporation itself, the result might well

Prompted no doubt by fear of the "economic benefit" argument that was advanced (albeit unsuccessfully) by the government in the *Holsey* case, some taxpayers have employed a newly-organized corporate entity in their bootstrap acquisition plans. For example, in Arthur J. Kobacker, 37 T.C. 882 (1962) (Acq.), the investor organized a new corporation to effect the purchase, contributing part of the purchase money thereto and having the corporation borrow the balance by issuing notes. The new corporation then purchased all of the stock of the old corporation; about a year later, the new company was merged into its subsidiary, with the surviving corporation assuming the parent's purchase money debt. The Tax Court refused to treat the surviving corporation's payments on the debt as a dividend to its individual shareholders, stating that no economic benefit was realized by them. In the light of hindsight, it is evident that the same tax result could have been achieved more simply by a combined purchase-redemption on the *Edenfield* model. The same can be said of several other plans in which newly-organized corporations were interposed between the individual investors and the acquired corporation.[44]

This discussion of "bootstrap" acquisitions has focussed on sale-redemption transactions entailing a complete shift of ownership to outsiders, but it is obvious that the same technique may be used to achieve a partial shift of ownership. A minority shareholder, for example, may acquire control by buying some of the majority's stock simultaneously with a redemption of the rest of the majority's interest; if so, the principles just discussed are equally applicable. Such a transfer of stock to an existing shareholder may occur on the death or retirement of another shareholder; although stock retirement agreements often obligate the corporation to acquire the deceased or retiring shareholder's entire interest, circumstances may arise in which a redemption of part of the stock is combined with a purchase by the surviving shareholder of the balance. If the stock retirement

have been different. See also Wolf v. Commissioner, 357 F.2d 483, 17 AFTR 2d 601 (9th Cir. 1966), where the taxpayer was personally obligated to buy stock and sought to have his obligation taken over by a new corporation; the assumption and payment of his liability were treated as a taxable distribution.

For the converse situation, viz., a claim by the shareholder that he was acting as the corporation's agent in acquiring the stock, so that a later corporate payment was for its own account rather than his, see the *Fox* and *Decker* cases, *supra* note 40.

[44] Cromwell Corporation, 43 T.C. 313 (1965); Princess Coals, Inc. v. United States, 239 F. Supp. 401, 15 AFTR 2d 546 (D.W. Va. 1965); but see Wolf v. Commissioner, *supra* note 43; and cf. Jewell v. United States, 330 F.2d 761, 13 AFTR 2d 1258 (9th Cir. 1964), where corporate assumption of the transferor's unpaid purchase money liability for assets transferred in a §351 exchange did not create taxable boot to the transferors under §357(b) (*supra*, Sec. 3.06).

agreement imposes a personal obligation on the surviving shareholder to buy the stock, however, an attempt to substitute a corporate obligation may well run afoul of the *Wall* principle.[44a]

Part C.   Redemptions by Affiliated Corporations: §304

Sec. 7.30.   Introductory

Section 302, which determines when a stock redemption shall be treated as a sale of the stock rather than as a distribution, applies to a "redemption" by a corporation of "its" stock. What if the stock of one corporation is sold to another corporation? If the two corporations are not affiliated in any way, there is no reason why the transaction should not be taken at face value and treated as an ordinary sale of stock, so that the seller will realize capital gain or loss, without regard to §302. But should the same rule apply if the two corporations are affiliated, e.g., if a shareholder sells part of his stock in a parent corporation to its subsidiary? The net effect of such a transaction is about the same as a distribution of assets by the subsidiary to its parent, followed by a redemption by the parent of its own stock; and had the transaction taken the latter form, it would have been taxed as a §301 distribution unless it qualified under §302(b)(1) ("not essentially equivalent to a dividend"), §302(b)(2) ("substantially disproportionate" redemptions), §302(b)(3) ("termination" redemptions), or §303 (redemptions to pay death taxes). An attempt by the Internal Revenue Service to treat such a transaction as essentially equivalent to a taxable dividend under §115(g) of the 1939 Code (*supra*, note 2) was unsuccessful, however, on the ground that it was not a "redemption" by the subsidiary of "its" stock.[45] The 1939 Code was amended in 1950 to require such a transaction to be treated as though the subsidiary had distributed assets to its parent and the parent had redeemed its own stock.

The 1950 legislation did not purport to reach an alternate device, achieving a similar result. If A owns all the stock of two corporations, and sells the stock of one to the other, the economic consequences are the same as though the second corporation had distributed property to him without any surrender of stock, except for the fact (which would often lack any practical consequences) that the second corporation now owns stock of the first corporation. The Internal Rev-

---

[44a] But see Rev. Rul. 59-286, *supra* note 42.

[45] Commissioner v. John Rodman Wanamaker, Trustee, 11 T.C. 365 (1948). aff'd per curiam, 178 F.2d 10, 38 AFTR 1014 (3d Cir. 1949).

enue Service ruled in 1955 that such a "brother-sister" redemption constituted a dividend to the shareholder under the 1939 Code, but revoked this ruling in 1959 after losing several litigated cases.[46]

Sec. 7.31.   Redemptions by affiliated corporations under §304

The 1954 Code carried forward the 1950 legislation on parent-subsidiary redemptions, §304(a)(2), and added new rules to govern "brother-sister" redemptions, § 304(a)(1). The purpose of these provisions is to ensure that a sale of stock by a shareholder to a related corporation will be treated as a redemption under §302, rather than as a sale to an independent third party, as under prior case law. To prevent a "bail-out" of corporate earnings at the capital gain rate, §304 requires the transaction to run the gauntlet of §302, with its attendant safeguards against dividend equivalency.[47]

1. *Acquisition by a brother-sister corporation.* If one or more persons are in control of each of two corporations ("control" for this purpose being defined as 50 percent of either voting power or value, including stock attributed to them by §318[48]), §304(a)(1) treats the transfer of stock in one corporation to the other as a redemption whose status is governed by §302. In applying the standards of §302 to this hypothetical redemption, §304(b)(1) provides that it is to be viewed as though stock of the first (or issuing) corporation had been redeemed; but if it is then found to be a distribution rather than a sale, the second (or acquiring) corporation's earnings and profits control the extent to which the distribution is a taxable dividend. Thus, if A owns all of the stock of X and Y corporations, a sale by A of all or part of his X stock to Y will be treated as a redemption of A's stock in X; this stock is considered to have been transferred by A to Y as a contribution to Y's capital, by virtue of §304(a)(1). In testing the redemption under §302, A will look only to his stock in X, which,

---

[46] Rev. Rul. 55-15, 1955-1 C.B. 361, revoked by Rev. Rul. 59-97, 1959-2 C.B. 684; Westerhaus Co., ¶57,213 P-H Memo T.C.; Emma Cramer, 20 T.C. 679 (1953); Commissioner v. Pope, 239 F.2d 881, 50 AFTR 1240 (1st Cir. 1957); Trianon Hotel Co., 30 T.C. 156 (1958).

[47] See generally, Terry, Section 304 of the Internal Revenue Code of 1954: Redemptions by Related Corporations, 3 Wm. & Mary L. Rev. 457 (1962); Lanahan, Redemptions to Pay Death Taxes: Redemptions Through the Use of Related Corporations (Sections 303, 304), 15 N.Y.U. Inst. on Fed. Tax. 493, 516ff (1957); Diamond, "Brother-Sister Corporations" — Sale of Stock or Other Assets, and Other Problems, 1959 So. Cal. Tax. Inst. 109.

[48] *Supra*, Sec. 7.21, but with the modification provided by §304(c)(2), under which the 50 percent rule for corporation-shareholder attribution of §318(a) is inapplicable. The result is that a corporation is deemed to own all the stock actually owned by *all* of its shareholders, and each of them constructively owns his pro rata share of stock actually owned by it.

on these facts, he is deemed to own in full by virtue of the constructive ownership rules of §318. A's only hope for sale treatment is lack of "dividend equivalence" under §302(b)(1), a result not likely on these facts.[49] If §302(b)(1) is not satisfied, the transaction will be treated as a distribution under §301, and its dividend status will be governed by the earnings and profits of Y. It should be noted, however, that dividend treatment is not automatic merely because the transaction is covered by the provisions of §304. If the hypothetical redemption can meet the tests of §302(b)(1)-(3) or §303 (*infra*, Sec. 7.40), it will be treated as a sale rather than as a distribution. This is far more likely in the case of a non-pro rata transaction than a pro rata one.[50]

2. *Acquisition by a subsidiary corporation.* If a subsidiary corporation acquires the stock of its parent, the transaction falls under §304(a)(2), and will be treated as a redemption by the parent corporation of its stock.[51] If the hypothetical redemption does not qualify as a sale under §302, the proceeds will be taxed as a dividend under §301 to the extent of the parent's earnings and profits, computed as though the amount paid by the subsidiary for the stock had been distributed by it to the parent, and had then been distributed by the parent to the taxpayer.[52]

It has been suggested that every "brother-sister" pair of corporations is also, by reason of the constructive ownership rules of §§304 and 318, a parent-subsidiary group. This suggestion is based on the fact that if a person is in control of two corporations, his stock in each one is attributed to the other, so each corporation is in "control" of the other. The regulations assume to the contrary that "brother-sister" corporations can be distinguished from parent-subsidiary corporations. Regs. §1.304-2(c). This assumption, which must have been shared by the draftsmen of the 1954 Code, finds support in the statement in §304(b)(2)(B) that the acquisition by a subsidiary of its

---

[49] Brother-sister redemptions were found to be the equivalent of dividends in Kerr v. Commissioner, 326 F.2d 225, 13 AFTR 386 (9th Cir. 1964); Radnitz v. United States, 187 F. Supp. 952, 7 AFTR 2d 423 (S.D.N.Y. 1960), aff'd per curiam, 294 F.2d 577, 8 AFTR 2d 5552 (2d Cir. 1961); Charles Swan, 42 T.C. 291 (1964); and United States v. Collins, 300 F.2d 821, 9 AFTR 2d 1119 (1st Cir. 1962); but see Sullivan v. Bookwalter, —— F. Supp. ——, 11 AFTR 2d 565 (W.D. Mo. 1962).

[50] See Rev. Rul. 57-295, 1957-2 C.B. 227; Rev. Rul. 58-79, 1958-1 C.B. 177; Regs. §1.304-2(c), Example (2); Sorem v. Commissioner, 334 F.2d 275, 14 AFTR 2d 5131 (10th Cir. 1964).

[51] A parent's acquisition of its subsidiary's stock is governed by §304(a)(1), rather than by §304(a)(2).

[52] §304(b)(2)(B). This hypothetical distribution to the parent will increase its earnings and profits, see Regs. §1.304-3(a).

parent's stock shall be treated, in computing the parent's earnings and profits, "as if the property were distributed by the acquiring corporation to the issuing corporation and immediately thereafter distributed by the issuing corporation." Since the hypothetical distribution by the acquiring corporation to the issuing corporation could occur only if the latter were an *actual* parent, grandparent, etc. of the acquiring corporation, it is reasonable to limit the parent-subsidiary rule of §304(b)(2)(B) to corporations that could have distributed the property upward in an unbroken chain of actual ownership, relegating the "brother-sister" rule of §304(b)(2)(A) to other related corporations. This may be the theory that underlies the examples in the regulations, §1.302-4(c).

3. Collateral problems involving "cross-ownership" and §304. The above discussion assumes that the stock of a related corporation was acquired for cash or other property. Suppose, however, that a person owning all the stock of two corporations transfers the stock of one to the other in exchange for additional stock of the latter, plus cash or property. This transaction literally falls within §351 (*supra*, Ch. 3) as well as within §304, since the transferor has 80 percent control of the transferee. In Henry McK. Haserot, 41 T.C. 562 (1964), the Tax Court held that §351 takes precedence over §304 in such a case, so as to produce capital gain with respect to the cash under §351(b), rather than a dividend under §§304, 302 and 301. The court relied on the "except as otherwise provided" language in §§301(a) and 302(d) as evidencing a Congressional intent that §351 should take precedence in a case of overlapping jurisdiction. Its conclusion, however, would make a dead letter of §304 in precisely the circumstances where its application is most justified, viz., two corporations under the virtually complete control of a single taxpayer. It is therefore not surprising to find that on appeal the decision was reversed and remanded, with a direction to the Tax Court to determine whether the transaction was "essentially equivalent to a dividend."[53] Presumably the court felt that §302 (and, of necessity, §304) has a definite role to play in this situation, despite the §351 exchange; unfortunately, however, the opinion is cryptically brief on the crucial issue in the case. But it seems reasonably certain that the court intended to overrule the theory of the Tax Court that §351 pre-empted the area.

There is a comparable problem of overlapping jurisdiction be-

---

[53] Haserot v. Commissioner, 355 F.2d 200, 17 AFTR 2d 71 (6th Cir. 1965); *supra*, Sec. 3.13, note 59; Kempf, Section 304 of the Internal Revenue Code: Unmasking Disguised Dividends in Related Corporation Transactions, 33 U. of Chi. L. Rev. 60, 66-75 (1965).

tween §304 and another set of statutory provisions in the complex liquidation-reincorporation area. If A, owning all the stock of X and Y corporations, transfers the stock of X to Y, the consequences to him are governed by §304, whether Y keeps X in existence as a subsidiary or liquidates it.[54] If A should liquidate X first instead of transferring its stock to Y, however, and then transfer part of or all of X's assets to Y, troublesome problems arise; and they are made more difficult if such a liquidation followed by a transfer of assets is viewed as equivalent to a §304 transfer of stock followed by a liquidation. An alternative, posing similar questions, is a sale by X of its assets to Y, followed by a liquidation of X. For discussion of these problems, see *infra*, Sec. 12.22.

Part D.   Redemptions to Pay Death Taxes: §303

Sec. 7.40.   Redemptions under §303

Section 303 provides that a redemption of stock, the value of which has been included in the gross estate of a decedent for Federal estate tax purposes, shall in certain cases be treated as a sale of the stock. If the conditions of §303 are met, the redemption is treated as a sale even though it would, but for §303, be taxed as a dividend under §301. For example, if all the stock of a corporation is held by an estate, a redemption of part of the stock would not qualify for capital gains treatment under §302(b)(2) ("substantially disproportionate" redemptions) or under §302(b)(3) (redemptions in termination of a shareholder's interest); nor, in the absence of other relevant facts, could it qualify under §302(b)(1) (redemptions "not essentially equivalent to a dividend") or §331(a)(2) (partial liquidations). If the conditions of §303 are satisfied, however, such a redemption is treated as a sale.[55] Another example is the redemption of stock from an estate, if the rest of the stock is owned by the decedent's sole beneficiary. Because of the constructive ownership rules, the redemption of part or all of the estate's stock could not qualify under §302(b)(2) or §302(b)(3). The redemption may, however, qualify under §303 for treatment as a sale rather than a dividend.

Section 303 contains the following conditions and limitations:

[54] The basis to Y of X's assets on such a liquidation is debatable. Section 304(a)(1) provides that Y takes a "carryover" basis for the stock of X, since Y is considered to receive it as a capital contribution rather than by purchase. This may mean that Y, on liquidating X, will not obtain a stepped-up basis for its assets under §334(b)(2), for reasons discussed *infra*, Sec. 9.44.

[55] Neither gain nor loss would be realized by the estate, however, if the redemption price was equal to the fair market value of the shares as the date of death, by virtue of §1014(a).

1. The value of the redeemed stock must be included in determining the gross estate of the decedent for Federal estate tax purposes. This requirement is satisfied, of course, if the stock was owned by the decedent at the time of his death. It will also be satisfied if the stock, though not owned by the decedent at death, is included in his gross estate because it was transferred in contemplation of death, because the decedent had a power of appointment over it, because it was held in joint tenancy with the decedent, etc. If stock was included in the gross estate and could have been redeemed under §303, the same privilege is extended by §303(c) to a redemption of "new" stock having a basis determined by reference to the basis of the stock that was actually included, such as stock acquired by the estate as a stock dividend[56] or in a recapitalization or other tax-free exchange.

2. The value of the stock included in the decedent's estate must be either more than 35 percent of the decedent's gross estate or more than 50 percent of his taxable estate. In order to satisfy the 35 or 50 percent requirement, the stock of two or more corporations may sometimes be aggregated. See §303(b)(2)(B); Byrd's Estate, 46 T.C. No. 3 (1966).

3. The total application of §303 cannot exceed the sum of (a) the death taxes imposed because of the decedent's death and (b) the funeral and administration expenses allowable as deductions for Federal estate tax purposes.

4. The benefits of §303 are available only to amounts distributed within a limited period after the death of the decedent.

Section 303 is an expanded version of a provision that was enacted in 1950, whose purpose was then stated by the House Committee on Ways and Means as follows:

> It has been brought to the attention of your committee that the problem of financing the estate tax is acute in the case of estates consisting largely of shares in a family corporation. The market for such shares is usually very limited, and it is frequently difficult, if not impossible, to dispose of a minority interest. If, therefore, the estate tax cannot be financed through the sale of the other assets in the estate, the executors will be forced to dispose of the family business. In many cases the result will be the absorption of a family enterprise by larger competitors, thus tending to accentuate the degree of concentration of industry in this country. . . .
> Your committee is of the opinion that remedial action is desirable in order to prevent the enforced sale of the family

---

[56] This privilege may be exercised even though the stock to be redeemed is "section 306 stock" (*infra*, Sec. 8.02), according to the regulations, §1.303-2(d). Although the statute is not specific on this point, the Senate Report on the 1954 Code takes the same position. S. Rept. No. 1622, 83 Cong., 2d sess., p. 239.

businesses which are so vital and desirable an element in our system of free private enterprise. (H. Rept. No. 2319, 81st Cong., 2d sess., reprinted in 1950-2 C.B. 380, 427-8.)

Despite its stated purpose of protecting against forced sales of family businesses, the danger of which may have been exaggerated and should in any event be allayed by a 1958 amendment to the Internal Revenue Code permitting the federal estate tax to be paid in certain cases in installments over a 10 year period,[57] §303 may be employed whether the estate is liquid or not. Even more surprising, stock may be redeemed from specific legatees of stock, donees of gifts in contemplation of death, trustees of inter vivos trusts, etc., even though they have no obligation to pay any of the death taxes or expenses that give rise to a §303 redemption.[58] The statement in the 1950 House Report that "the circumstances under which . . . relief is available are narrowly defined and will restrict relief to situations in which true hardship exists" (H. Rept. No. 2319, *supra*, 428) is not an accurate description either of the 1950 legislation or of §303 as it exists today.

Part E.   Partial Liquidations Under §346

Sec. 7.60.   Introductory

Section 331(a)(2) provides that amounts distributed in partial liquidation of a corporation shall be treated as part or full payment in exchange for the stock. If the stock is a "capital asset" in the

---

[57] Harriss, Estate Taxes and the Family Owned Business, 38 Cal. L. Rev. 117, 142-44 (1950). Section 6166, added to the Internal Revenue Code in 1958, permits the federal estate tax to be paid in instalments over a 10-year period (with interest at 4 percent) if the estate includes an interest in a closely held business (as defined), provided the value of the interest exceeds either 35 percent of the decedent's gross estate or 50 percent of his taxable estate.

[58] The regulations state that §303 "will most frequently have application in the case where stock is redeemed from the executor or administrator of an estate," and then go on to say that it is also applicable to stock included in the decedent's gross estate and "held at the time of the redemption by any person who acquired the stock by any of the means comprehended by" §§2031-2044 of the Internal Revenue Code (i.e., the provisions defining the gross estate for Federal estate tax purposes). Regs. §1.303-2(f). The regulations deny the benefits of §303 to persons who acquired their stock (a) by gift or purchase from a person "to whom such stock has passed from the decedent," or (b) from the executor in satisfaction of a specific monetary bequest. In thus excluding the transferees of qualified persons, the regulations carry out the purpose of §303, although it contains no such explicit limitation.

Because the benefits of §303 are available to donees in contemplation of death and similar transferees of the decedent, these persons may ally themselves with the Commissioner in an effort to establish that their stock should be included in the gross estate, contrary to the position of the executor. To this incentive is added the stepped-up basis that the stock, whether redeemed or not, will get under §1014(b)(9) if it is included in the gross estate. The benefits

hands of the shareholder, his gain or loss (the difference between the value of the distribution and the adjusted basis of the redeemed stock) will be capital gain or loss. While §331(a)(2) is the operative provision, requiring the distribution in partial liquidation to be treated as the proceeds of a sale of the stock, it is dependent upon §346, which defines the term partial liquidation. Section 346 provides that a distribution "shall be treated as in partial liquidation" of a corporation if it falls into one of three categories:

1. A distribution that is one of a series of distributions in redemption of all the stock (*i.e.*, a complete liquidation) of the corporation. This category of partial liquidations could have been classed with complete liquidations; it does not invoke the "corporate contraction" concept that is ordinarily associated with the term "partial liquidation."

2. A distribution in redemption of part of the stock of a corporation that is "not essentially equivalent to a dividend." This category of partial liquidations is "characterized by what happens solely at the corporate level by reason of the assets distributed." Senate Report on the 1954 Code, quoted *supra*, Sec. 7.03, *i.e.*, it is a statutory adaptation of the "corporate contraction" concept created by the courts under the 1939 Code.

3. A distribution that terminates one of two or more active businesses engaged in by the distributing corporation. This category of partial liquidations was created by the 1954 Code; it is a type of corporate contraction that is *ipso facto* to be treated as a partial liquidation, without reference to the vague criteria of the corporate contraction concept.

These three categories of partial liquidations are discussed hereafter in more detail.[59]

Sec. 7.61.   One of a series of distributions in complete liquidation: §346(a)(1)

Section 346(a)(1) provides that a distribution that is one of a series in redemption of all the stock of the corporation pursuant to

of §303 and §1014(b)(9) may outweigh the estate tax cost of including the stock in the estate, or the shareholder may not care about the estate tax cost because it will have to be paid by someone else (e.g., the residuary legatees in a case where apportionment of the estate tax is not required).

[59] For discussion, see Silverstein, Stockholder Gains and Losses on Partial Liquidations, 14 N.Y.U. Inst. on Fed Tax. 707 (1956); Oberndorfer, Partial Liquidations, 13 *ibid.* 637 (1955); Chommie, Section 346(a)(2); The Contraction Theory, 11 Tax L. Rev. 407 (1956); Kamanski, Partial Liquidation — Section 346, 1959 So. Cal. Tax Inst. 137; Schoettle, Jr., Section 346 of the Internal Revenue Code: A Legislative Enigma, 109 U. Pa. L. Rev. 944 (1961); articles cited *supra*, note 6. See also *infra*, Sec. 9.02, for the problem of determining whether an unlabeled distribution is an ordinary dividend, or a first step in a partial or complete liquidation.

a plan of complete liquidation will be treated as a partial liquidation. If the stock is a capital asset, this means that the shareholder will report capital gain or loss on the transaction. In effect, this category constitutes the interim stages of a "creeping" complete liquidation; as such, its relationship to the complete liquidation rules of 331(a)(1) (*infra*, Ch. 9) is apparent, but unclear.

If a complete liquidation is consumated by a series of periodic distributions unaccompanied by surrender of any stock until the final distribution is made, the courts generally allow a shareholder to apply the distributions against the total adjusted basis of his stock, and recognize gain only after this amount has been fully recovered. An aggregate basis approach is also used in computing loss, a deduction being allowed when the final distribution occurs or at an earlier time if the amount of the loss can be accurately determined then.[60] The regulations, however, require the computation to be made share-by-share (where they were acquired at different times for different prices), at least if a lump sum distribution is received by the shareholder. Regs. §1.331-1(e); see also §1.333-4(a). The difference between the aggregate basis and per-share methods may be illustrated by this example:

> A owns 100 shares in X corporation, 60 of which were purchased in 1950 for $30,000, and 40 in January of 1965 for $50,000. If A receives a lump sum liquidating distribution of $100,000 ($1,000 per share) in June of 1965, his gain, using the aggregate basis approach, would be $20,000 (of which 60 percent apparently would be long term and 40 percent short term). Under the per-share method of the regulations, he would realize a $30,000 long term gain on the 1950 block of X stock, and a $10,000 short term loss on the 1965 block.

If the liquidation just described had occurred in two steps, with A surrendering one-half of his stock in June of 1965 for $50,000 and the other half in January of 1966 for a like amount, there is authority for applying the distributions in chronological sequence against the shareholder's aggregate basis.[61] The 1965 distribution would then be

---

[60] See Letts v. Commissioner, 30 BTA 800 (1943), aff'd other grounds, 84 F.2d 760, 18 AFTR 207 (9th Cir. 1936); Mattison v. United States, 163 F. Supp. 754, 2 AFTR 2d 5107 (D. Idaho 1958), rev'd other grounds (but with approval of the above basic premise), 273 F.2d 13, 4 AFTR 2d 5844 (9th Cir. 1959); McGregor v. United States, —— F. Supp. ——, 5 AFTR 2d 965 (D. Kan. 1960). On the computation of loss, see Palmer, Exec. v. United States, —— F. Supp. ——, 1 AFTR 2d 863 (D. Conn. 1958), and cases there cited.

[61] See Florence M. Quinn, 35 B.T.A. 412 (1937) (Acq.); Karl G. von Platen, ¶53,203 P-H Memo TC (1953).

In practice, shares are ordinarily not surrendered as each interim distribution is made, but are given up when the first or principal distribution occurs, the shareholder receiving a "stub" or receipt as evidence of his right to the

a tax-free recovery of $50,000 of his aggregate basis of $80,000, and the 1966 distribution would be treated as a tax-free recovery of his remaining basis of $30,000 and as capital gain to the extent of $20,000. When §346(a) is read in conjunction with §331(a)(2), however, one might conclude that each distribution should be treated as a separate transaction, the gain or loss being computed by subtracting the basis of the shares actually surrendered on each occasion from the amount of the distribution. On this approach, the result in the foregoing example would depend on whether A surrendered high basis or low basis shares (or a combination thereof) when he received the first distribution. Although this method of computing gain or loss puts a premium on the adroit selection of the shares to be surrendered, it is identical in this respect with the practice employed in computing gain or loss on ordinary sales of securities, where the basis of the specific shares transferred is used whenever identification is feasible.[62]

Sec. 7.62.   Corporate contractions: §346(a)(2)

A distribution is a partial liquidation under §346(a)(2) if it (a) "is not essentially equivalent to a dividend," (b) is in redemption of a part of the stock of the corporation pursuant to a plan, and (c) occurs within the taxable year in which the plan is adopted or within the succeeding taxable year. The first of these requirements invokes the "corporate contraction" doctrine and raises difficult questions of interpretation; the second and third are more formal in nature and ordinarily should be satisfied without difficulty.

1. "Not essentially equivalent to a dividend." This language echoes the phraseology of §115(g) of the 1939 Code and carries forward, to some degree at least, the corporate "contraction" doctrine developed in the pre-1954 law decisions. Thus, the Senate Report on the 1954 Code states (p. 262) that "partial liquidation" in the 1954 revision primarily "involves the concept of 'corporate contraction' as developed under existing law." At another point, the Senate Report states:

> The general language of the proposed draft would include within the definition of a partial liquidation the type of cases involving the contraction of the corporate business. Such as for example,

later distributions. Although there is authority for imputing a surrender of an appropriate number of shares on a partial liquidation (see *infra*, Sec. 7.81), it may be that this approach will not be applied to a partial liquidation that is only a step in a complete liquidation.

[62] See Courtenay D. Allington, 31 B.T.A. 421 (1934); J. Paul McDaniel, 25 T.C. 276 (1955) (Acq.); Meldon v. Commissioner, 225 F.2d 467, 472, 47 AFTR 1895 (3rd Cir. 1955); Regs. §1.1012-1(c).

cases which hold that if the entire floor of a factory is destroyed by fire, the insurance proceeds received may be distributed pro rata to the shareholders without the imposition of a tax at the rates applicable to the distribution of a dividend, if the corporation no longer continues its operations to the same extent maintained by the destroyed facility. Voluntary bona fide contraction of the corporate business may of course also qualify to the same extent as under existing law. (S. Rep. No. 1622, 83d Cong., 2d Sess., p. 49 (1954))

The 1939 Code decisions on corporate contraction embraced not only the well-known "contraction-by-fire" case of Joseph W. Imler, 11 T.C. 836 (1948) (Acq.), but other situations where the reasons for capital gain treatment were at best obscure. Thus, redemptions because a reserve for expansion was no longer required, because a shift in the scale or nature of the corporation's operations had caused a decline in its need for working capital, to shield property from the claims of corporate creditors, or because an unprofitable department had been liquidated, were at times successful in claiming the mantle of corporate contraction, although not without exception.[63]

Notwithstanding the references to "existing law" in the Senate Report, the draftsmen of §346(a)(2) gave at least two indications that the pre-1954 concept of "corporate contraction" was not ratified in every respect: the Report states flatly that "a distribution of a reserve for expansion is not a partial liquidation" (p. 262), thus rejecting at least some pre-1954 cases;[64] and it implies that §346(a)(2) applies only to redemptions that "terminate a part of the business of the corporation," thereby casting doubt on pre-1954 cases holding

---

[63] Reserves for expansion: Commissioner v. Champion, 78 F.2d 513, 16 AFTR 416 (6th Cir. 1935); Samuel A. Upham, 4 T.C. 1120 (1945) (Acq.); contra, McGuire v. Commissioner, 84 F.2d 431, 17 AFTR 1313 (7th Cir. 1936), cert. denied 299 U.S. 591. Decline in working capital needs: Clarence R. O'Brion, ¶51,373 P-H Memo T.C.; Edwin L. Jones, ¶42,555 P-H Memo T.C.; Commissioner v. Quackenbos, 78 F.2d 156, 16 AFTR 330 (2d Cir. 1935); John P. Elton, 47 B.T.A. 111 (1942) (Acq.); contra, Dunton v. Clauson, 67 F. Supp. 839, 35 AFTR 394 (D. Me. 1946). Protection v. creditors: Commissioner v. Sullivan, 210 F.2d 607, 45 AFTR 373 (5th Cir. 1954); see also L. M. Lockhart, 8 T.C. 436 (1947). Liquidation of department: Commissioner v. Babson, 70 F.2d 304, 13 AFTR 972 (7th Cir. 1934), cert. denied, 293 U.S. 571; Scowcroft Heber Inv. Co., ¶45,235 P-H Memo T.C.; but see Chandler's Estate v. Commissioner, 22 T.C. 1158 (1954), aff'd per curiam, 228 F.2d 909, 48 AFTR 842 (6th Cir. 1955).

Because the courts rarely if ever find it necessary to base a decision on a single factor, it cannot be said with assurance that the element of contraction was the sole foundation for any of the foregoing decisions although it appears to have been at least persuasive, if not the turning point, in all. It is entirely possible, however, that some of the earlier cases would not pass the more rigorous judicial examination that has been common recently. See Chommie, *supra.* note 59, at 418.

[64] *Supra*, note 63; see also Regs. §1.346-1(a).

that a distribution of excess working capital could qualify as a partial liquidation. Moreover, the intent to carry forward existing law should not be interpreted as a blanket approval of every judicial decision theretofor rendered, or as preventing further evolutionary developments in what is at best a flexible concept rather than a frozen body of rules. In this respect, the *Imler* case itself, explicitly described and approved by the Senate Report (pp. 49, 262), states:

> The issue here raised presents a question of fact depending on the circumstances of the particular case . . . No sole or universally applicable test can be laid down . . . Though decided cases are not controlling, they are helpful as indicating what elements have been considered important, viz., the presence or absence of a real business purpose, the motives of the corporation at the time of distribution, the size of the corporate surplus, the past dividend policy, and the presence of any special circumstances relating to the distribution. (11 T.C. at 840.)

The difficulty with "corporate contraction" as a standard for determining dividend equivalency stems from the fact that many distributions which contract the size of a corporation possess the major indicia of a dividend distribution: i.e., adequate earnings and profits, pro rata distribution, and continued operation of an active corporate enterprise. The resulting inability of "corporate contraction" to describe a line separating ordinary distributions from others, except possibly in terms of an unexpected reduction of corporate activities, has been frequently noted by commentators, who have argued that the concept be abolished or restricted.[65] Some courts have pointed out the possibility of abuse inherent in the contraction concept, viz., a temporary investment in business assets to be sold when convenient so that a distribution of the proceeds can be plausibly explained as a "contraction" of the business.[66] Recognizing its potential for disguis-

---

[65] See Bittker and Redlich, *supra,* note 4, at 472-473; Cohen, et al., *supra,* note 6, at 37-38; Surrey, Income Tax Problems of Corporations and Shareholders: American Law Institute Tax Project — American Bar Association Committee Study on Legislative Revision, 14 Tax L. Rev. 1, 5 (1958).

[66] See the warning in *Kraus* v. *Commissioner,* 6 T.C. 105, 120-121 (1946) (Acq.), involving a manufacturing company which sold a portfolio of securities and redeemed some of its stock with the proceeds:

The argument is made that an investment business was conducted . . . to support the contention that there was a partial liquidation of the company when the securities were sold. But the liquidation of assets of the character we have here does not necessarily result in a liquidation of a "business," nor does the fact that the $150,000 which was distributed was most of the proceeds from the sale of securities stamp them as liquidating distributions . . . if the securities represented the investment of accumulated profits, as we are compelled to conclude, the sales of the securities in 1940 operated

ing ordinary distributions as partial liquidations is the first step toward consciously policing the concept, but uncertainty in its ambit may be the most effective safeguard against abuse, in view of the ordinary income result that normally attends a failure to qualify for partial liquidation treatment.[67]

2. *Redemption pursuant to a plan.* Section 346(a)(2) requires a "redemption" of stock, and some 1939 Code decisions held that reacquired stock that was held in the treasury had not been "redeemed."[68] Section 317(b) now specifically provides that a redemption occurs whether or not the reacquired stock is cancelled or held as treasury stock, but this definition technically does not apply to §346, though probably by oversight rather than design. If there is no surrender of shares, as in the case of an informal partial liquidation of a closely-held corporation, the transaction may nevertheless qualify as a "redemption," as in Fowler Hosiery Co., Inc. v Commissioner, 301 F.2d 394, 9 AFTR 2d 1252 (7th Cir. 1962), where the court said that a redemption "does not necessarily require the physical surrender or cancellation of the stock." This relaxed approach seems equally applicable to another problem in this area, viz., whether a

to return to the company a fund of accumulated profits.
See also Hyman v. Helvering, 71 F.2d 342, 344, 14 AFTR 270 (D.C. Cir. 1934), cert. denied, 293 U.S. 570:
> And so also if a corporation invests earnings in plant and equipment, which in later years, in a policy of contraction of business activities, it decides to sell and to divide the proceeds among its shareholders, the distribution is none the less a dividend, though the device of canceling some of the outstanding shares be adopted as a method of accomplishing the end sought.
See also Rev. Rul. 60-322, 1960-2 C.B. 118 (distribution of proceeds of investments and excess inventories; held, not a qualified contraction of business).

[67] For cases decided under the 1954 Code, see Cleveland v. Commissioner, 335 F.2d 473, 14 AFTR 2d 5387 (3rd Cir. 1964); Fowler Hosiery Co. Inc., 36 T.C. 201 (1961); Ballenger v. United States, 301 F.2d 192, 9 AFTR 2d 1245 (4th Cir. 1962); and McCarthy v. Conley, Jr., 341 F.2d 948, 15 AFTR 2d 447 (2d Cir. 1965).

See also Rev. Rul. 55-373, 1955-1 C.B. 363 (cancellation of franchise caused "genuine contraction"); Rev. Rul. 56-513, 1956-2 C.B. 191 (termination of one of two separate businesses caused "contraction"); Rev. Rul. 57-333, 1957-2 C.B. 239 (distribution of rental property which generated minor portion of corporate income not a contraction); Rev. Rul. 60-232, 1960-2 C.B. 115 (on a qualified contraction, the distribution may include both the proceeds of selling the unwanted operating assets and the working capital attributable to the terminated business activity; Rev. Rul. 57-333 modified); Rev. Rul. 60-322 (*supra* note 66).

[68] See Kirschenbaum v. Commissioner, 155 F.2d 23, 34 AFTR 1292 (2d Cir. 1946), cert. denied, 329 U.S. 726; Commissioner v. Snite, 177 F.2d 819, 38 AFTR 841 (7th Cir. 1949); contra, Wall v. United States, 164 F.2d 462, 36 AFTR 423 (4th Cir. 1947); Smith v. United States 130 F. Supp. 586, 47 AFTR 1006 (Ct. Cl. 1955). An intermediate position, treating treasury shares as cancelled or redeemed where there was no intention to reissue them, was apparently approved in Boyle v. Commissioner, 187 F.2d 557, 40 AFTR 308 (3d Cir. 1951), cert. denied, 342 U.S. 817.

reduction in the stock's stated or par value accompanied by a distribution constitutes a redemption, although the pre-1954 case law is to
the contrary.[69]

Section 346(a)(2) requires the corporation to redeem its stock
"pursuant to a plan." The term "plan" is not defined in either the
Code or the regulations. Perhaps an informal plan will suffice,[70] as in
other areas where a corporate adjustment must occur under a plan,
but careful counsel will not want to trust to luck.

3. *Distribution in the year the plan is adopted or within the succeeding year.* Since neither the Code nor the regulations defines the
term "plan," it is not surprising that they do not state how the year
of its adoption should be determined. Presumably the time will ordinarily begin to run from the formal action by the shareholders authorizing the redemption, but the Commissioner might be justified on
occasion in determining that the plan was "adopted" by informal action at an earlier date and in disqualifying a distribution as too late
under §346(a)(2).[71]

Sec. 7.63.   Termination of one out of two or more businesses: §346(b)

The shareholders need not concern themselves with the vagaries
of the "corporate contraction" concept if the distribution meets the
requirements of §346(b), relating to a distribution in termination of
an active trade or business by a corporation that is engaged in two
or more active trades or businesses.[72] This provision, which has no
counterpart in the 1939 Code, is summarized by the Senate Report
on the 1954 Code (p. 262) as follows:

---

[69] Sheehan, Exec. v. Dana, 163 F.2d 316, 319, 36 AFTR 48 (8th Cir. 1947);
Beretta v. Commissioner, 141 F.2d 452, 455, 32 AFTR 418 (5th Cir. 1944), cert.
denied, 323 U.S. 720.

The House version of the 1954 Code provided that a reduction of par value
was a redemption, but this provision was omitted by the Senate, which stated
(S. Rep. No. 1622, p. 252) that "no inference is to be drawn by the elimination
of this provision . . . as to the status of existing law in this area." The proposed
regulations under the 1954 Code took the position that a reduction in par value
qualified, Prop. Reg. §1.317-2, 19 Fed. Reg. 8254 (1954), but this provision was
omitted from the final regulations.

[70] Fowler Hosiery Co., Inc. v. Commissioner, *supra*, so held.

See also Rev. Rul. 65-80, 1965-1 C.B. 154, holding that partial liquidation
treatment will not be denied because a corporation fails to file Form 966, the
corporate information return.

[71] For a similar problem in determining when a plan of liquidation was
adopted in applying §337, see *infra*, Sec. 9.64.

See also *infra*, Sec. 9.04, on the problem of determining whether a distribution is an ordinary dividend, or part of a partial or complete liquidation.

[72] See generally, Caplin, The Five-Year Active Business Rule in Separa-

[Section 346(b)] provides a description of one kind of distribution which will be considered as being in partial liquidation. Paragraphs (1) and (2) contemplate that the distributing corporation must be engaged in the active conduct of at least 2 businesses which have been actively conducted (whether or not by it) for the 5-year period ending on the date of the distribution. Neither of such businesses may have been acquired within such period in a transaction in which gain or loss was recognized in whole or in part. Thus, a qualifying business may not have been acquired by purchase or in a corporate reorganization where so-called "boot" was present. If these requirements are met, one of the active businesses may be distributed in kind (or the proceeds of sale of such a business may be distributed) as long as the corporation immediately after the distribution is engaged in the active conduct of a business as described above. The determination of whether the requirements of [Section 346(b)] have been met shall be made without regard to whether the distribution is pro rata among the shareholders of the corporation.

Section 346(b) has much in common with §355, under which a "divisive" reorganization can be effected tax-free. If a corporation is conducting a 5-year old active trade or business and its subsidiary is conducting a second such business, §355 permits the parent to distribute the stock of the subsidiary to its shareholders in a tax-free "spin-off" (subject to conditions discussed *infra*, Ch. 11). Moreover, if both businesses are conducted by a single corporation, one can be transferred to a newly-organized subsidiary as a prelude to a distribution of its stock to the shareholders of the parent. Because §355 provides a tax-free route to such corporate separations, it has overshadowed §346(b). But §346(b) may be the preferable, or even the only feasible, route in some circumstances. For example, if the fair market value of the assets to be transferred is less than the adjusted basis of the shares to be surrendered, a transfer of the business assets themselves under §346(b) will permit the shareholder's capital loss to be recognized. Moreover, §355 permits the business assets to be distributed only if they are held in corporate form; if the shareholder wishes to conduct the distributed business as a sole proprietor or partner, §346(b) is the route to be employed; the shareholder will have to report his capital gain (if any), but this will permit a step-up in the basis of the distributed assets.

To qualify under §346, a distribution must meet the following requirements:

tions and Partial Liquidations, 1961 So. Cal. Tax Inst. 211; Sealy, Jr., The Functions of Spin-Offs and Partial Liquidations, 20 N.Y.U. Inst. on Fed. Tax. 799 (1962); articles cited *supra* note 6.

1. The distribution must be attributable to the corporation's ceasing to conduct, or must consist of the assets of, a trade or business;

2. Immediately after the distribution, the distributing corporation must be actively engaged in a trade or business;

3. Both the retained trade or business and the one that was distributed (or that gave rise to the distribution) must have been actively conducted (though not necessarily by the distributing corporation) throughout the 5 year period preceding the distribution; and

4. Neither trade or business may have been acquired by the distributing corporation within the preceding 5 years in a transaction in which gain or loss was recognized in whole or in part.

This battery of requirements may be understood more easily if their purpose is known. Accepting the "corporate contraction" doctrine as an appropriate test, the draftsmen wanted to create an area in which capital gains treatment would be assured without the necessity of justifying each distribution, case by case, under the vague standards of the courts. They thought that if a corporation with two or more businesses wished to distribute one of them, the distribution should be treated as a partial liquidation. At the same time, they did not want to open a royal road to tax avoidance by allowing a closely-held corporation to accumulate its earnings and profits, invest its surplus cash in assets that the shareholders would like to hold as individuals, and then go through the form of a "corporate contraction" by distributing the newly acquired assets and retaining the business assets. Section 346(b)'s requirement of "actively" conducting a "trade or business" is designed to prevent an evasion of the tax on dividends by a corporate purchase of investment securities or real estate to be distributed in redemption of part of the stock of the corporation. The 5-year rule, coupled with the prohibition on the acquisition of either of the trades or businesses by purchase,[73] is designed to prevent an ac-

---

[73] The prohibition on acquiring the trade or business during the 5-year period "in a transaction in which gain or loss was recognized in whole or in part" was obviously intended to apply to transactions in which the *transferor* recognized gain or loss, even though the *transferee* did not. See the reference to acquisition by "purchase" in the extract from the Senate Report quoted in the text," *supra*. Moreover, acquisition by purchase is probably prohibited even though gain or loss is not recognized by the seller because the price paid happens to be exactly equal to the adjusted basis of the acquired trade or business in his hands. The Senate Report's reference to acquisition by "purchase," as well as the purpose of the section, strongly suggest that the purchase (within the 5-year period) of a trade or business from a corporation that recognizes no gain or loss on the sale under §337 (*infra*, Sec. 9.65) should not qualify; it would seem that gain or loss is recognized in such a "transaction," within the meaning of §346(b), by the shareholders of the selling corporation on its liquidation, since the sale under §337 and the liquidation of the selling corpora-

cumulation of earnings and profits for investment in a business (*e.g.*, a farm, ranch, or similar property) that the shareholders would otherwise have acquired with taxable dividends, with a view to a prompt distribution in "partial liquidation" under §346(b). It will not, however, prevent a similar plan for avoidance of the dividend tax if the shareholders are patient; after the farm or ranch has been held for 5 years (assuming its operation constitutes the "active conduct of a trade or business"), its distribution can qualify under §346(b), with a possible exception for transactions that can be characterized as shams.

The principal problem under §346(b) is the meaning of the phrase "a trade or business which has been actively conducted," since the distribution must either consist of the assets of, or be attributable to the corporation's ceasing to conduct, such a trade or business. The regulations under §346(b) refer to §355, which permits a corporation to make a tax-free distribution of a controlled corporation if the distributing and the controlled corporation are both "engaged in the active conduct of a trade or business." *Infra*, Sec. 11.04. The regulations under §355 state that a trade or business consists of "a specific existing group of activities being carried on for the purpose of earning income or profit from only such group of activities," that the group must include every operation that forms a part of the process of earning income, and that it must ordinarily include the collection of income and the payment of expenses. Among the examples given by the regulations are: an office building owned by a bank which occupies one floor and rents the remaining ten floors; the manufacture and sale of ice cream at a plant in one state by a corporation that manufactures and sells ice cream at another plant in a second state; and a suburban retail store owned by a downtown store, each store being separately managed and having its own warehouse. The regulations go on to state that the term "trade or business" does not comprehend investment

---

tion constitute an integrated transaction. A more sophisticated variation on this theme would be a purchase by the distributing corporation of the stock of a second corporation, followed by a sale by the second corporation of its trade or business to the first corporation, under §337. Here the liquidation of the second corporation would not produce gain or loss to anyone if the liquidating proceeds were equal to the price paid by the distributing corporation for the stock of the second corporation. But the acquisition of the stock of the second corporation would have produced gain or loss to its original shareholders, and this could be regarded as a "transaction in which gain or loss was recognized in whole or in part" within the meaning of §346(b). It should be noted, however, that §346(b) is not as explicit as §355(b)(2), which, in dealing with a similar problem, prohibits not only the acquisition of a trade or business during the 5-year period but also the acquisition of a corporation conducting the trade or business. See Conf. Rep., H.R. No. 2543, 83d Cong., 2d Sess., 37-38 (1954).

property, real estate used in the operation of a trade or business, or a group of business activities that do not independently produce income, giving as examples a research division, a factory building used by a manufacturer, a "captive" coal mine, and an executive dining room.[74]

Although a distribution that does not meet the tests of §346(b) might be able to qualify under §346(a)(2)'s more vague standard of "corporate contraction," there is already a tendency in the rulings to assume the contrary. In many instances, of course, the taxpayer's inability to obtain a favorable ruling under §346 will result in abandoning the proposed distribution, because of the vagaries of litigation and the threat of a dividend tax under §301 if he loses.

Part F. Collateral Problems Arising From Partial Liquidations and Stock Redemptions

Sec. 7.80. Introductory

The foregoing sections of this chapter have been primarily concerned with one question: is the shareholder whose stock has been redeemed to treat the transaction as a sale of his stock, producing capital gain or loss, or as a distribution under §301, producing ordinary income to the extent of the corporation's earnings and profits? The redemption will have collateral consequences for both the shareholder and the corporation, however, and to these we will now turn.

Sec. 7.81. Computation of shareholder's gain or loss

Since a distribution in partial liquidation is to be treated under §331(a)(2) as "payment in exchange for the stock," gain or loss is computed as though the stock had been sold. The same is true of a non-dividend redemption which under §302(a) is to be "treated as a distribution in part or full payment in exchange for the stock" or of a redemption to pay death taxes under §303. If the shareholder owns stock purchased at different times and for different prices, he may select the shares to be surrendered to the corporation for redemption, using shares with a high or low basis and a short or long holding period, as he chooses.[75]

But while the shareholder may be able to control the tax consequences of the transaction by shrewdly selecting the shares to be

---

[74] Regs. §1.346-1(c) and §1.355-1(c) and (d). For more on this subject, see *infra*, Sec. 11.04.

[75] As pointed out *supra*, Sec. 7.61, however, the shareholder may have less freedom to select the shares used in computing gain or loss if the distribution is described by §346(a)(1) (one of a series in complete liquidation).

surrendered, he ought not to be able to manipulate the gain or loss to be recognized by surrendering more shares than would be called for in an arm's length transaction. If the redemption is not pro rata, market value will ordinarily govern the number of shares surrendered. If the transaction is not effected at market value, it may be in part a method of paying compensation or making a gift. Thus, if the shareholder receives more than his shares are worth, the excess may represent compensation or a gift paid to him by the remaining shareholders; conversely, if he receives less than the value of his shares, the difference may represnt compensation or a gift paid by him to them.[76]

If the redemption is pro rata, however, the number of shares to be surrendered will usually be a matter of indifference to the shareholders. Thus, if X Corporation's net worth is $100,000, represented by 100 shares of common stock, owned one-half by A and one-half by B, and it distributes $40,000 in partial liquidation, one would expect A and B to surrender 20 shares each for redemption, but A and B could just as well surrender 25 shares each. Can they minimize their capital gain or create capital losses, by doing so? In Rev. Rul. 56-513, 1956-2 C.B.191, the Internal Revenue Service said of a distribution in partial liquidation that:

> In determining the amount of the gain or loss, regardless of the actual number of shares surrendered for redemption by the stockholders, the total number of shares deemed to have been surrendered is that number which bears the same ratio to the total number of shares outstanding as the [amount] distributed bears to the total fair market value of the net assets of the corporation immediately prior to the distribution.

The ruling does not state how the basis of the shares "deemed to have been surrendered" is to be computed; it would seem reasonable to use an appropriate fraction of the total basis of all shares held by the shareholder in question. Despite this ruling, there have been a number of litigated cases in which stock was redeemed at par value, original cost, book value, or other artificial prices, and the shareholder's gain or loss was apparently computed accordingly, rather than by recasting the transaction as provided by Rev. Rul. 56-513.[77]

---

[76] Rev. Rul. 58-614, 1958-2 C.B. 920.

[77] See Joseph W. Imler, 11 T.C. 836 (1948) (Acq.) (par value and cost); Sam Rosania, Sr. ¶56,116 P-H Memo T.C. (par and cost); Commissioner v. Snite, 177 F.2d 819, 38 AFTR 841 (7th Cir. 1949) (redemption at "somewhat" below market value); Keefe v. Cote, 213 F.2d 651, 45 AFTR 1620 (1st Cir. 1954) (minority shareholder paid substantially more than majority holder); J. Paul McDaniel, 25 T.C. 276 (1955) (varied prices; aggregate proceeds equal to cost); *supra*, Sec. 7.61.

Although Rev. Rul. 56-513 is applicable by its terms whether the shareholder realized gain or loss on the transaction, a caveat should be interposed with respect to gains. If the shareholder surrenders too few shares, so that the amount distributed to him exceeds the value of the shares he gives up, it is not inconceivable that the transaction will be treated as a sale only to the extent of the fair value of the shares, with any excess being subject to §301, taxable as a dividend to the extent of the corporation's earnings and profits. Rev. Rul. 54-408, 1954-2 C.B. 165, holding that a certain redemption constituted a partial liquidation "to the extent that the distribution does not exceed the fair market value of the stock being redeemed," suggests by negative inference that any excess would be a §301 distribution. This approach conflicts with Rev. Rul. 56-513, and the issue cannot be regarded as closed.[78]

Still another problem is the deductibility of a loss, if the shareholder receives less than the adjusted basis of the shares redeemed. Section 267 disallows losses on the sale or exchange of property between an individual and a corporation of which he owns directly or indirectly more than 50 percent of the stock. It goes on, however, to make an exception for "losses in cases of distributions in corporate liquidations." A loss incurred in a partial liquidation would thus come within the exception and would not be disallowed by §267. It has been held that this exemption does not apply to a §302(b)(3) stock redemption, so that a loss incurred thereon cannot be deducted if the shareholder and the corporation are "related persons" under §267(b).[79] Even if the loss is not disallowed by §267, however, it is not necessarily deductible. *Higgins* v. *Smith*, 308 U.S. 473, 23 AFTR 800 (1940), is still to be conjured with, and it might lead to the disallowance of a loss on a partial liquidation of a one-man corporation, especially if the transaction was tax-motivated.[80] Where there are a number of shareholders, however, *Higgins* v. *Smith* should not imperil the deduction if control is dispersed or if the shareholders are affected unequally by the redemption.

[78] See also Rev. Rul. 59-97, 1959-1 C.B. 684; Samuel S. Schahet, ¶59,051 P-H Memo T.C.; Bittker, *supra* note 6, at 51-3; Silverstein, Stockholder Gains and Losses on Partial Liquidations, 14 N.Y.U. Inst. on Fed. Tax. 707, 711 (1956); Oberdorfer, Partial Liquidations, 13 *ibid.* 637, 650 (1955).

[79] McCarthy v. Conley, 341 F.2d. 948, 15 AFTR 2d 447 (2d Cir. 1965); see also Rev. Rul. 57-397, 1957-2 C.B. 225. It is hard to perceive any reason, however, why Congress should have wanted to alter the pre-1954 law in this area, under which the exception for "distributions in corporate liquidations" would seemingly have included all non-dividend redemptions, whether they would now be classified as "partial liquidations" under §331(a)(2) and §346 or as "exchanges" under §302(a).

[80] The cases on this point, collected in Bittker, *supra* note 6, at 54n, are inconclusive.

Sec. 7.82.   The mystery of the disappearing basis

When the redemption of stock is treated as a sale either because the transaction is a partial liquidation or because it is a non-dividend redemption, the taxpayer can offset the basis of his stock against the proceeds of the redemption in computing his gain or loss. But if the redemption is taxed as a dividend, the mystery of the "disappearing" basis presents itself. For example, if A holds all of the stock of Corporation X at a basis of $100,000, and half of the stock is redeemed for $150,000 in a transaction that constitutes a taxable dividend, does the basis of the redeemed shares disappear? If A had received an ordinary dividend of $150,000, without any surrender of shares, his cost basis of $100,000 would remain intact. There is no reason why he should be worse off when the dividend of $150,000 is distributed in redemption of some of his stock. It is said that under the 1939 Code the Internal Revenue Service made appropriate adjustments to preserve the shareholder's basis, but the statutory foundation for such adjustments was flimsy.[81] The 1954 Code is no better, but the Treasury for the first time has stated in the regulations that in such cases "proper adjustment of the basis of the remaining stock will be made with respect to the stock redeemed." In the hypothetical facts set out above, A would hold the remaining stock of the corporation at his original aggregate basis of $100,000. If the corporation has several shareholders, and all the stock of one shareholder is redeemed in a transaction that is taxed as a dividend (e.g., because he constructively owns some of the remaining shares), the "proper adjustment" will be to transfer the basis of the redeemed shares to the shares owned by the related shareholders.[82]

Sec. 7.83.   The basis of distributed property

If the shareholder receives property, rather than money, in redemption of his stock, he must assign a basis to it for computing depreciation, gain or loss on a sale, etc. If the property is received in a distribution in partial liquidation, and if gain or loss is recognized

---

[81] Katcher, The Case of the Forgotten Basis: An Admonition to Victims of Internal Revenue Code Section 115(g), 48 Mich. L. Rev. 465 (1950). On several occasions courts have held that a redemption constituted a sale of the stock rather than a taxable dividend under §115(g) of the 1939 Code partly because they thought that otherwise the shareholder's basis would be forfeited. Commissioner v. Snite, 177 F.2d 819, 38 AFTR 841 (7th Cir. 1949); see Penfield v. Davis, 105 F. Supp. 292, 307-308. 42 AFTR 115 (N.D. Ala. 1952), aff'd, 205 F.2d. 798, 44 AFTR 151 (5th Cir. 1953).

[82] See Regs. §1.302-2(c) Example (2); Regs. §1.304-3(a); Brodsky and Pincus, The Case of the Reappearing Basis, 34 Taxes 675 (1956).

on its receipt, §334 provides expressly that its basis shall be its fair market value at the time of distribution. If the property is received in a non-dividend redemption under §302(a) or §303, the Code does not state explicitly how its basis to the shareholder is to be determined, but probably fair market value is governing here also.[83]

If the redemption is treated as a distribution under §301 rather than as a sale of the stock, however, the shareholder's basis for the property received is determined under §301(d), which distinguishes (see *supra*, Secs. 5.22 and 5.23) between corporate and non-corporate shareholders. For non-corporate shareholders, the basis of the property will be fair market value; for corporate shareholders, the basis will be fair market value or the distributing corporation's adjusted basis, whichever is lower.

Sec. 7.84.   Recognition of corporate gain or loss on distribution in redemption of stock

Does the corporation recognize gain or loss on distributing its appreciated or depreciated property in redemption of its stock? If the redemption is treated not as a sale but as a distribution by the corporation, taxable to the shareholder under §301, the corporation's recognition of gain or loss will be governed by the principles applicable to ordinary distributions of property to shareholders. As stated *supra*, Sec. 5.21, where these principles are discussed in detail, gain or loss is ordinarily not recognized by the corporation, but exceptions are made for a distribution of installment obligations, appreciated LIFO inventory, property subject to a liability in excess of the corporation's basis, depreciable property subject to §1245 or §1250, and "investment credit" property. The same principles apply, according to Regs. §1.311-1(a), for all distributions in redemption of stock, except partial and complete liquidations; and this approach would include a redemption that is treated as a sale of stock under §302(a) rather than as a distribution under §302(d) and §301.[84]

[83] In the absence of some other provision prescribing the basis of property, its "cost" is controlling under §1012. This would be the fair market value of the stock given up. If there is a discrepancy between the value of the stock redeemed and the value of the property received, see Rev. Rul. 56-513, *supra*, Sec. 7.81, on the possibility that the transaction will be recast to bring the values into harmony. See also *infra*, Sec. 9.03.

[84] This part of the regulations is not without its difficulty, since it is at least arguable that a §302(a) transaction is not a distribution "with respect to" stock within the meaning of §311. It should also be noted that the Tax Court has seemingly accepted the theory that a transfer of property by a corporation in exchange for its stock might be treated as a sale of the property by the corporation, although the transaction in question was found to be a partial liquidation. See Farmers Union Corp., ¶60,179 P-H Memo T.C. (1939 Code); Regs. §1.311-1(e)(1), Example (2); see also U.S. v. General Geophysical Co., 296 F.2d

If the redemption constitutes a partial liquidation, a distribution of property is subject to §336, providing that gain or loss is to be recognized only on the distribution of installment obligations.[85] This provision, however, does not overrule the recapture of depreciation by §1245 and §1250, or of the investment credit by §47 in the event of a premature disposal of such property.

Even though the distribution of appreciated property does not itself ordinarily produce taxable income to the corporation, income realized in form by the shareholders following the distribution may be imputed to the corporation under the *Court Holding Co.* case and similar doctrines (*e.g.*, in the case of a prearranged sale of property by the shareholders after a corporate sale was "called off"). These principles (*supra*, Sec. 5.21) apply to a distribution of property in redemption of stock, whether the redemption constitutes a dividend under §302(d), a sale of the stock under §302(a), or a partial liquidation under §331(a)(2) and §346. The courts may be more ready, however, to impute income to the corporation upon the sale of property, especially inventory, if it was distributed in a §302(d) or §302(a) transaction than if it was distributed in partial liquidation of the corporation.[86] An alternative to distributing corporate assets in redemption of stock, when the shareholders intend to sell the distributed assets thereafter, is a sale by them of an appropriate number of shares, in anticipation of a redemption in kind of these shares from the new owner. Since the corporation, original shareholders, and purchasers end up in the same status after such a transaction, it can hardly be regarded as a safe refuge from the *Court Holding Co.* doctrine.[87] It should be noted that §337, providing a statutory escape from that doctrine in certain complete liquidations, does not apply to stock redemptions and partial liquidations (*infra*, Sec. 9.66).

86, 8 AFTR 2d 5602 (5th Cir. 1961) (redemption in kind, followed immediately by repurchase of distributed property to get stepped-up basis, on assumption that no corporate gain would be recognized on the distribution itself, disregarded as sham).

[85] Although §336 is new in the 1954 Code, the same principles were applied under the pre-1954 Regulations. *Infra*, Sec. 9.61; Union Starch and Refining Co., Inc., 31 T.C. 1041 (1959) (Acq.).

[86] See United States v. Lynch, discussed *supra*, Sec. 5.21, for judicial readiness to impute income to the corporation when the inventory of a continuing business is distributed to shareholders for sale by them; McNair Realty Co. v. United States, 188 F. Supp. 451, 6 AFTR 2d 5795 (D.C. Mont. 1960), aff'd per curiam, 298 F.2d 35, 9 AFTR 2d 332 (9th Cir. 1961) (taxpayer distributed 64 percent interest in a building to a shareholder in complete redemption of his stock; following this transaction, the corporation and the shareholder jointly sold the building; held, corporation not taxed on shareholder's portion of income).

[87] Idol v. Commissioner, 319 F. 2d 647, 12 AFTR 2d 5118 (8th Cir. 1963); but see Standard Linen Service, Inc., 33 T.C. 1 (1959).

Sec. 7.85. Effect of redemption on corporation's earnings and profits

The effect of a redemption of stock on the corporation's earnings and profits depends upon whether the redemption is treated as a distribution under §301 or as an exchange of the stock under §302(a) or §331(a)(2). The corporation's earnings and profits account is thus tied to the redemption's impact on its shareholders, even if the corporation is unable to ascertain the identity of its shareholders or whether any of them is the constructive owner of shares registered in another name. Note also that if the shareholder has relied upon §302(c)(2) for relief from the constructive ownership rules, a distribution that appears to come under §302(a) may turn out to be a §301 distribution if the distributee acquires a disqualifying interest in the corporation within the following ten years.

If the redemption is treated as a distribution of property under §301, the corporation's earnings and profits are to be adjusted under §312 in the same way as upon any other dividend, *i.e.*, earnings and profits are reduced by the amount of money, the principal amount of any obligations, and the adjusted basis of any other property distributed, with special adjustments in the case of a distribution of appreciated "inventory assets," LIFO inventory, property subject to liabilities, or depreciable property subject to §1245 or §1250 (*supra*, Sec. 5.24). If the redemption is a partial liquidation or is treated as a sale of the redeemed stock under §302(a) or §303, however, §312(e) provides that the portion of the distribution which is "properly chargeable to capital account" shall not be treated as a distribution of earnings and profits.

In ascertaining the amount of the distribution which is "properly chargeable to capital account" and the amount which is chargeable to earnings and profits, the statute and regulations afford scant if any illumination. The problems in this area are numerous, complex, and as yet unresolved: *e.g.*, (a) how is the "capital account" affected by the fact that stock was issued for property or services rather than money; (b) does "capital account" include the original contributed capital, or do subsequent capital contributions count; (c) is the capital contributed by each shareholder to be traced, and if so, how should intervening sales of stock and disproportionate capital contributions be treated; (d) what is the effect of several classes of stock with different liquidation preferences and other rights; (e) are pro rata partial liquidations treated differently from disproportionate §302 stock redemptions; and (f) is the charge against earnings and profits limited to the redeeming shareholder's "ratable share" of earnings and profits. These issues have for the most part been unexplored by the cases, although there is some authority against a "ratable share" limitation in determining the appropriate charge to earnings and profits.[88]

These problems may be illustrated by the following example: Assume that A and B each contribute $10,000 in cash to X Corporation in exchange for 50 shares of its stock, such shares constituting all of X's outstanding stock. X's original capital account thus would be the $20,000 paid in by A and B, whether their payments are allocated in full to the capital stock account or divided between capital stock and paid-in surplus. After X has earned and accumulated $10,000 after taxes, and when the book value of its stock is $30,000 and its fair market value is $40,000, A's shares are redeemed for $20,000. X's charge to earnings and profits under §312(e), if the *Jarvis* approach is used, would be $10,000, computed as follows: that portion of the capital account ($20,000) which the number of shares redeemed bears to the total number of shares outstanding (50 percent). The balance of the distribution, $10,000, would be the amount chargeable to earnings and profits, thus wiping clean the account even if A was accorded capital gain treatment on the distribution. The *Woodward* formula (*supra*, note 88), on the other hand, would apparently limit the earnings and profits charge to $5,000, the redeemed stock's "ratable share" thereof. It can readily be seen that the *Jarvis* method is favorable to B, the remaining shareholder, since the earnings and profits account is reduced by an amount greater than the redeemed stock's "ratable share" of these earnings, with the result that future distribu-

----

[88] See Helvering v. Jarvis, 123 F. 2d 742, 28 AFTR 404 (4th Cir. 1941); but see Woodward Investment Co., 46 B.T.A. 648 (1942) (Acq.), where a pro rata distribution in partial liquidation was held chargeable to earnings and profits in proportion to the ratio which accumulated earnings bore to the total net worth of the distributing corporation. In G.C.M. 23460, 1942-2 C.B. 190, the Service held that the *Woodward* case was not inconsistent with *Jarvis*, since the *Woodward* distribution was pro rata. The *Woodward* formula, which treats each distribution as consisting in part of capital and in part of earnings (in the proportion which the earnings and profits account bears to the corporation's net worth) seems more equitable than the *Jarvis* formula with its attendant distortions. See the example in the text.

Section 312(1)(3)(A), enacted in 1962 to govern the charge to earnings and profits on a redemption or partial liquidation of stock in a foreign mutual fund (*supra*, Sec. 1.06) prescribes a ratable share approach; whether this was intended to declare, or to change, existing law is not clear.

For an exhaustive analysis of §312(e), see Edelstein and Korbel, The Impact of Redemption and Liquidation Distributions on Earnings and Profits: Tax Accounting Aberrations Under Section 312(e), 20 Tax L. Rev. 479 (1965); see also Albrecht, "Dividends" and "Earnings or Profits," 7 *ibid.* 157, 200-207 (1952).

tions to B are less likely to be taxed as dividends, and future accumulations will be less vulnerable to an attack under §531.

Continuing with the above example, suppose that A's original
capital contribution consisted not of $10,000 of cash, but property
with a tax basis of $2,000 and a value of $10,000. Is X's "capital
account" $12,000 ($2,000 from A and $10,000 from B), or $20,000
(the value of its original assets)? If X's capital account is only
$12,000, is the amount attributable to A's stock interest $2,000, determined by specifically tracing the basis of the property which he contributed, or is it $6,000, his proportionate interest in X's net worth?
In general, it would seem that the corporation's capital account should
reflect the *value* rather than the *basis* of contributed property, in
order to give effect to the economic and corporate law consequences
of the transaction, as well as to reflect the shareholder's proportionate
interest in the corporation's earnings capacity and net worth.[89] This
fair market value approach is equally valid if additional contributions
in property are made by the shareholders at a later time.

---

[89] A short cut method of determining a corporation's "capital account,"
valid in many instances, is to take the book value of its assets (other than
property contributed by shareholders for their stock, which presumably is considered at fair market value), and subtract therefrom liabilities and accumulated earnings of the corporation. This figure should represent the capital
account (which, in turn, may be composed of the capital stock account and
various capital surplus accounts).

Chapter Eight

PREFERRED STOCK BAIL-OUTS

Sec. 8.01. Introductory

One of the most urgent problems before Congress when the 1954 Code was being drafted was the preferred stock "bail-out," an ingenious but simple plan by which shareholders could withdraw corporate earnings and profits as long-term capital gains. A corporation with substantial earnings and profits and liquid assets would distribute a dividend of preferred stock to its shareholders, who would receive the stock tax-free[1] and promptly sell it to an insurance company or other institutional investor. Each shareholder would compute his gain on the sale by subtracting the adjusted basis of the dividend shares (an allocated portion of his basis for the original shares) from the proceeds of sale, and would report the difference as long-term capital gain. The corporation would then redeem the preferred stock from the purchaser at a modest premium, either under a sinking fund or schedule provided in the preferred stock contract or when deemed advisable by the corporation. The net result to both the corporation and its shareholders would be the same as a cash dividend, except for the obligations imposed by the preferred stock contract during the time the shares remained outstanding, but the tax consequences — it was hoped — would be vitally different.

For a period of several years, the Treasury was able to dampen the enthusiasm of most tax advisors for this device by refusing to rule that a dividend of preferred stock was receivable tax-free if an early sale of the dividend shares was intended.[2] Not all advisers were conservative-minded, however, and finally boldness was rewarded. In Chamberlin v. Commissioner, 207 F.2d 462, 44 AFTR 494 (6th Cir. 1953), cert. denied, 347 U.S. 918 (1954), the Court of Appeals

---

[1] Before the enactment of §305 in 1954, the status of a distribution of stock depended upon the case law. A distribution of preferred stock on common, there being no other class outstanding, was held non-taxable in *Strassburger v. Commissioner,* 318 U.S. 604, 30 AFTR 1087 (1943), and §113(a)(19) of the 1939 Code provided for an allocation of basis between the original and the dividend shares. Under §117(h)(3) of the 1939 Code, the holding period of the original shares could be "tacked" in determining the holding period of the dividend shares. *Surpa,* Sec. 5.60.

[2] Darrell, Recent Developments in Nontaxable Reorganizations and Stock Dividends, 61 Harv. L. Rev. 958 (1948); DeWind, Preferred Stock "Bail-Outs" and the Income Tax, 62 *ibid.* 1126 (1949).

for the Sixth Circuit, reversing the Tax Court, held that a dividend
of preferred stock by a corporation having only common outstanding
was not rendered taxable by a pre-arranged plan for its sale, despite
a provision for mandatory retirement of the preferred shares over a
period of seven years. Under the *Chamberlin* case, the painfully
worked-out law of stock redemptions, under which a pro rata redemption was generally taxed as "essentially equivalent to a taxable
dividend" under §115(g) of the 1939 Code (*supra*, Sec. 7.02), could
be circumvented by any prosperous corporation whose shareholders
could sell their preferred stock to a third party; and for many closely-
held corporations, the preferred stock bail-out could have become a
substitute for annual cash dividends. It was, of course, possible that
other courts would limit or reject the *Chamberlin* case once these
possibilities approached fruition;[3] but with Congress already in the
process of drafting a new Code, it was almost inevitable that the decision should elicit a legislative response.

The House version of the 1954 Code met the problem with an
85 percent transfer tax, to be paid by the corporation on the redemption of stock that had been issued within the 10 previous years as a
tax-free stock dividend. The 10-year restriction meant that only a
judicial rejection of the *Chamberlin* case could prevent a bail-out
that was spread over a longer period. There were other objections to
the House provisions, including the fact that the penalty tax would
apply even though all of the common stock of the corporation had
changed hands and the redemption occured under a sinking fund or
other mandatory arrangement. The Senate remedy for the bail-out,
which was adopted as §306 of the 1954 Code, is a more intricate and
fundamentally different measure.

Sec. 8.02.   Bail-outs under the 1954 Code: §306

The 1954 Code meets the challenge of the preferred stock bail-
out by creating a new category of stock — "section 306 stock" —

[3] In view of the sinking fund or redemption commitment typical of these
arrangements, the preferred stock might have been regarded as "debt" rather
than "stock," with the result that the distribution itself would be a taxable dividend to the extent of earnings and profits (*supra*, Sec. 5.40). Since the Service
in most contexts seeks to characterize purported "debt" as "stock" (*supra*, Sec.
4.02), however, this would have required an uncomfortable reversal of its role.
    When the Tax Court faced a post-*Chamberlin* case, it adhered to its origi-
nal position. Estate of Henry A. Rosenberg, 36 T.C. 716 (1961). In *Rosenberg*,
the "bail out" stock was acquired in a non-taxable recapitalization (*infra*, Sec.
12.16) rather than by way of a stock dividend, but the court saw no distinction
between the two cases and treated the transaction as if the corporation had
issued the stock to the new investors for cash and then distributed the cash to
the taxpayers as a dividend.

whose sale or other disposition will usually give rise to ordinary income rather than capital gain. Section 306 consists of (1) a definition of "section 306 stock;" (2) a set of rules providing that the sale or other disposition of "section 306 stock" will produce ordinary income rather than capital gain; and (3) a series of exceptions to these punitive rules.[4] The interpretation and application of §306 can become quite complex in a given case, but one should keep in mind the evil at which the provision was directed; *viz.*, the conversion of potential dividend income into capital gain without dilution of the shareholders' underlying investment in and control of the corporation. In a sense, the provision can be viewed as a Congressional response to an assignment of income problem, a fact to be carefully noted before seeking to confine it to narrow limits by a literal construction of its terms.

Sec. 8.03.   The definition of "section 306 stock"

The definition of "section 306 stock" is aimed primarily at what might be termed the classic arrangement of the *Chamberlin* case: preferred stock held by persons who received it as a tax-free dividend from a corporation with earnings and profits. Because variations on the *Chamberlin* arrangement are possible, however, the statutory definition had to be broad enough to reach a variety of transactions that might be used, either deliberately or incidentally, as a substitute for a preferred stock dividend. The result is a rather elaborate definition embracing three categories of stock:

1. Stock received as a dividend: §306(c)(1)(A). Stock (other than common stock issued with respect to common stock) held by the distributee, if any part of the distribution was not includible in gross income by reason of §305(a).[5] The preferred stock dividend in the

---

[4] See generally Alexander and Landis, Bail-Outs and the Internal Revenue Code of 1954, 65 Yale L.J. 909 (1956); Dean, Rules Governing Preferred Stock Bail-Outs, 14 N.Y.U. Inst. on Fed. Taxation 691 (1956); Young, Preferred Stock Bail-Outs: Statutory Restrictions: Pitfalls and Continuing Opportunities Under the 1954 Code (Section 306), 15 *ibid.* 431 (1957); Harris, The Status of Preferred Stock Bail-Outs, 34 Taxes 403 (1956); and, for a prototype of §306, Cohen, et al., A Technical Revision of the Federal Income Tax Treatment of Corporate Distributions to Shareholders, 52 Col. L. Rev. 1, 17 (1952).

[5] In the case of a distribution of preferred stock by a corporation having only common stock outstanding, it might be argued that the preferred stock is not excluded from gross income "by reason of section 305(a)" but because it is constitutionally immune, *supra*, note 1, and that hence it is not "section 306 stock." This argument, if accepted, would make of §306 a *brutum fulmen*, and should be rejected out of hand.

The language of §306(c)(1)(A) suggests that no matter how small a part of the distribution is tax-free under §305(a), the whole distribution is "section 306 stock." But the regulations take a more lenient view. Regs. §1.306-3(c).

Chamberlin case is the best example of this part of the definition. The exception for common stock issued as a dividend on common recognizes that such stock is ordinarily not a promising instrument for effecting a bail-out, since a sale of the dividend stock would deprive the shareholders of a portion of their voting control and interest in the corporate equity and earning power and hence would be similar to a sale of part of their original common. On the other hand, common stock distributed as a tax-free dividend on preferred stock is not within the exception and hence will be "section 306 stock," although it is not suited to a bail-out.[6]

The term "common stock" is not defined by either the Code or the regulations. If the purpose of §306 is to be achieved, stock that can be used to effect a bail-out should not be treated as "common stock" even though in all other respects it is similar to common stock. In harmony with this reasoning, the Internal Revenue Service has ruled that "non-voting common stock" redeemable at the discretion of the corporation at a price equal to 110 percent of its book value is not to be treated as "common stock" under §306(c)(1)(B), and presumably the same result would follow under §306(c)(1)(A).[7]

By virtue of §306(c)(2), stock distributed by a corporation having no earnings and profits is not "section 306 stock."[8] Since a distribution of money in these circumstances would not have been taxed to the shareholders as dividend income, the stock is not regarded as an appropriate candidate for the punitive rules of §306. Even though the stock is not "section 306 stock," however, its later redemption might be taxed as a dividend under §302, unless the redemption terminates the shareholder's interest, is substantially disproportionate, or is not essentially equivalent to a dividend. *Supra,* Sec. 7.20. As to a sale of such stock under a plan for its immediate redemption from the buyer, see *infra,* Sec. 8.07.

[6] On the disposition of such stock, however, the shareholder would have an appealing claim for relief under §306(b)(4), *infra,* Sec. 8.05.

[7] Rev. Rul. 57-132, 1957-1 C.B. 115. A determination that similar stock is "common stock" as that term is used in §1036, Carnahan v. United States, 188 F. Supp. 461, 6 AFTR 2d 5784 (D.Mont. 1960), may not be applicable to §306, in view of its different function.

See generally Black, Common Stock and the Bail-Out Section, 38 Taxes 395 (1960).

[8] If the corporation has *any* earnings and profits, the *entire* distribution is "section 306 stock." Regs. §1.306-3(a); contrast the less strict view of the phrase "any part" as used in §306(c)(1)(A), *supra,* note 5. See Alexander and Landis, *supra,* note 4, at 940. Relief in some cases might be obtained under §306(b)(4).

The opening afforded by §306(c)(2) when there are no earnings and profits cannot be enlarged by issuing a preferred stock dividend when the corporation has no earnings and profits and changing the conditions and terms of the stock (e.g., increasing its preference or call price) when the corporation becomes prosperous; see §306(g)(3); Regs. §1.306-3(g)(3).

Under §306(c)(1)(A), stock is tainted only while it is held by the person who received it tax-free under §305(a). It is possible for the taint to follow the dividend shares into the hands of another person, such as a donee, but only if the conditions of §306(c)(1)(C), discussed below, are met. Otherwise a transfer of the stock purges it.

2. *Stock received in a corporate reorganization or division: §306(c)(1)(B).* Stock (other than common stock) received in certain wholly or partly tax-free corporate reorganizations and separations, if the effect of the transaction is substantially the same as the receipt of a stock dividend or if the stock is received in exchange for "section 306 stock." This branch of the definition is designed to cope with stock that may be suited for use in a bail-out, if it is distributed in a partially or wholly tax-free transaction (such as a recapitalization) that may serve the same function as a tax-free stock dividend.[9]

3. *Stock with a transferred or substituted basis: §306(c)(1)- (C).* This part of the definition pursues "section 306 stock" into the hands of a transferee if his basis is determined by reference to the basis of the transferor. Thus, "section 306 stock" continues to be tainted in the hands of a donee, unless upon the donor's death the stock is included in his gross estate so that the donee acquires a new basis under §1014(b). Similarly, if "section 306 stock" is exchanged for other stock whose basis is determined by reference to the "section 306 stock," the newly acquired stock becomes "section 306 stock." Thus, if "section 306 stock" is transferred to a controlled corporation under §351, any stock received in exchange (regardless of its class) becomes "section 306 stock." Moreover, although the new stock is tainted, the old stock (now held by the controlled corporation) is not purged, but remains "section 306 stock." A wholly or partly tax-free exchange under §1036 (stock for stock of the same corporation) is likewise within §306(c)(1)(C). If §306(c)(1)(B) — relating to stock received in a corporate reorganization or division — is applicable to the same transaction, however, it takes precedence over §306-(c)(1)(C).

In support of the foregoing tri-partite definition of "section 306 stock," the statute contains provisions to prevent an escape from §306 by the use of stock rights, convertible stock, and changes in the terms and conditions of stock. See §306(d), (e), and (g).

---

[9] See *infra,* Sec. 11.12 (corporate divisions) and Sec. 12.35 (reorganizations).

Sec. 8.04.   Dispositions of "section 306 stock"

The sting of §306 is to be found in §306(a), laying down special rules to govern a redemption, sale or other disposition of "section 306 stock."

If the stock is redeemed, the amount received by the shareholder is to be treated as a §301 distribution, *i.e.*, it is taxable as a dividend to the extent of the corporation's earnings and profits at the time of redemption; the balance, if any, would be a return of capital under §301(c)(2) and (3).[10]

If the stock is sold or otherwise disposed of, the amount realized is ordinary income to the extent of the stock's ratable share of earnings and profits at the time of distribution; the balance, if any, is applicable against the allocated basis of the stock, and any excess is treated as gain from the sale of the stock. No loss is recognizable. Had §306(a)(1), governing sales of "section 306 stock," been in effect when the *Chamberlin* transaction occurred, the shareholders on selling the preferred stock would have realized ordinary income equal to their ratable share of the corporation's earnings and profits, measured as of the time the stock was distributed. The bail-out would then have failed abjectly. In fact, an ordinary dividend in cash may be preferable to a sale of "section 306 stock," since a dividend will reduce the corporation's earnings and profits and will also give rise to a dividends received exclusion under §116. A sale of "section 306 stock," however, is treated simply as a sale of a non-capital asset (to the extent of its ratable share of earnings and profits at the time of distribution), and hence it cannot reduce the corporation's earnings and profits or qualify for the dividends received exclusion.

> To illustrate: A owned 100 shares of X Co.'s common stock, which constituted all of the stock outstanding, with a basis of $6,000. During 1965, when its earnings and profits were $3,500, X issued preferred stock worth $5,000 as a dividend to A; immediately after the distribution, his common stock was worth $10,000. The preferred stock dividend would constitute "section 306 stock," since the issuing corporation had earnings and profits at the time of the distribution. Under §307(a), A's basis for the newly acquired preferred stock would be $2,000, and his basis for the common stock would be $4,000.

[10] It is not clear whether the non-dividend portion of the redemption proceeds, if any, should be applied against the adjusted basis of the "section 306 stock" alone or against the basis of the original stock as well. Ordinarily, a §301 distribution is not taxed as capital gain under §301(c)(2) and (3) until the shareholder has recovered the basis of the stock with respect to which the distribution was received. See Ch. 7, Sec. 7.01, note 1.

In 1967, when X's earnings and profits were $5,000, a sale by A of preferred stock to an outsider for $5,000 would be fragmented into two components, with the following results: (1) Ordinary gain of $3,500 (that portion of the preferred stock dividend which would have been a taxable dividend in 1965 if cash had been distributed instead of stock); (2) a $500 increase in the basis of his common stock to reflect the fact that the remaining sales proceeds of $1,500 were $500 less than the basis of his preferred stock;[11] and (3) no reduction in X's earnings and profits.

If, instead, A's preferred stock had been redeemed by X in 1967 for $5,000, he would have a dividend of $5,000, since X's earnings and profits in 1967 fully covered the amount distributed, and his basis for his common stock would be increased by $2,000 (the basis of the redeemed preferred shares). If X's earnings and profits in 1967 were only $3,500, A's dividend would be limited to $3,500, the balance of $1,500 received by him would be a non-taxable return of capital under §301(c)(2), and the basis of his common stock would be increased by the unrecovered portion ($500) of his basis for the preferred stock.

Section 306(a)(1), treating the proceeds as gain from the sale of a non-capital asset, comes into play if the shareholder "sells or otherwise disposes of section 306 stock" (other than by redemption). The regulations do not define the term "otherwise disposes of," except to say that it may include "among other things" a pledge of the stock, "particularly where the pledgee can look only to the stock itself as its security." Regs. §1.306-1(b)(1); see also S. Rept. No. 1622, 83d Cong., 2d sess., p. 242. Ordinarily, such a pledge does not constitute a disposition of property, so that gain is not recognized even though the amount borrowed exceeds the basis of the pledged property, but a contrary rule for "section 306 stock" is hardly beyond the power of Congress.[12] The regulations do not state whether the "amount realized" on such a pledge of the stock is its fair market value or the amount borrowed; if the latter is controlling, presumably any additional amount realized on selling the stock would also be taxed under §306(a)(1). In Rev. Rul. 57-328, 1957-2 C.B. 229, the Internal Revenue Service ruled that the donation of "section 306

---

[11] Regs. §1.306-1(b)(2), Examples (2) and (3), protect the shareholder against a loss of the preferred stock's basis. See *supra,* Sec. 7.82.

[12] Regs. §1.306-1(b)(1); see also S. Rep. No. 1622, 83d. Cong., 2d sess., p. 242. For comparable problems in the treatment of liabilities in excess of basis, see Woodsam Associates, Inc v. Commissioner, 198 F.2d 357, 42 AFTR 505 (2d Cir. 1952); Lurie, Mortgagor's Gain on Mortgaging Property For More Than Cost Without Personal Liability, 6 Tax L. Rev. 319 (1951); and note the treatment of liability in excess of basis under §357(c) and §311(c), *supra,* Secs. 3.06 and 5.21.

stock" to a tax-exempt charitable foundation did not constitute a
"disposition" by the donor under §306(a)(1), either at the time of
the gift or upon a later sale by the charity, even though the donor
was entitled to deduct the fair market value of the stock as a charitable contribution. The ruling points out that the stock retains its
taint in the hands of the donee, see §306(c)(1)(C), and concluded
from this that the statutory plan was to tax the donee rather than
the donor. Since the donee is tax-exempt, however, it will not be
taxed on a sale or redemption of the stock; moreover, a redemption
will reduce the corporation's earnings and profits. These results are
hard to justify, and it has been suggested that the Code be amended
either to deny the charitable contribution deduction or to treat the
contribution as a disposition of the stock.[13]

Sec. 8.05.   Exceptions to §306(a)

The punitive rules of §306(a), treating the amount realized on
a disposition of "section 306 stock" as a §301 distribution (if the
stock is redeemed) or as gain from the sale of a non-capital asset (if
the stock is sold or otherwise disposed of), are waived by §306(b)
when the disposition of the stock is not suited to the bail-out of
corporate earnings and profits. These exceptions to the rules of §306-
(a) are:

1. *Dispositions that terminate the shareholder's interest in the
corporation: §306(b)(1).* If "section 306 stock" is redeemed, and if
the redemption meets the standards of §302(b)(3) (termination of
shareholder's entire interest), the transaction will be treated as an
ordinary sale of the stock under §302(b)(3), giving rise to capital
gain or loss equal to the difference between the amount received and
the shareholder's basis for the redeemed shares.[14] If the disposition
is not by way of redemption, the punitive rules of §306(a) can be
avoided if the shareholder disposes of his entire stock interest in the
corporation (the constructive ownership rules of §318(a) being applicable) and if the shares are not transferred directly or indirectly
to a person whose stock would be attributed to the shareholder under
§318(a).[15]

---

[13] See *infra*, note 22.

[14] The constructive ownership rules of §318 (*supra*, Sec. 7.21) apply in
determining whether the taxpayer's entire stock interest has been terminated,
but the family attribution rules can be waived on a redemption in certain circumstances (*supra*, Sec. 7.23).

[15] §306(b)(1)(A)(ii) seems to be redundant, since a disposition cannot terminate the shareholder's "entire stock interest" within the meaning of §306(b)-
(1)(A)(iii) if the shares are transferred to a person whose ownership would
be attributed to the transferor.

The justification for these exceptions to §306(a) is that there is no bail-out if the shareholder disposes of his "section 306 stock" either after or simultaneously with a sale of his other stock, since the same result could have been achieved by selling his original shares before the "section 306 stock" was distributed to him.

2. *Liquidations: §306(b)(2).* The rules of §306(a) are not applicable if the "section 306 stock" is redeemed in a partial[16] or complete liquidation. The exemption of complete liquidations from the rules governing dispositions of "section 306 stock" is parallel to the exemption of complete terminations of the shareholder's interest in the corporation: the same result (ordinarily, capital gain or loss on the liquidation) could have been achieved without the intervention of "section 306 stock."[17] As to partial liquidations, the Senate Report on the 1954 Code states that "[a] bona fide contraction of the corporate business is not considered a means of distributing corporate earnings to shareholders at capital gains rates." S. Rept. 1622, 83d Cong., 2d sess., p. 243. The accuracy of this observation will depend upon the care with which the corporate contraction doctrine, which at least in the past has been a slippery concept (*supra*, Sec. 7.62) is applied.

3. *Tax-free exchanges: §306(b)(3).* The rules of §306(a) are not applicable to the extent that gain or loss is not recognized on the disposition of the "section 306 stock." This exception embraces, *e.g.*, dispositions of "section 306 stock" in transactions under §351 and §1036, but the shareholder may get only temporary relief, since the stock received in exchange will become "section 306 stock" by virtue of §306(c)(1)(C). If the transferor of "section 306 stock" receives other property ("boot") in a §351 or §1036 transaction, so that the exchange is only partly tax-free, the fair market value of the "boot" is subject to 306(a).[18]

---

[16] §306(b)(2), granting immunity to a redemption in "partial or complete liquidation," probably does not embrace capital gain or loss redemptions under §302(a). See *supra*, Sec. 7.81, note 79.

[17] Query, whether "section 306 stock" held by the liquidating corporation would qualify for non-recognition treatment under §336 (if distributed in kind) or §337 (if sold after adoption of a plan of liquidation). Section 306(b)(3) would seem to protect the liquidating corporation in such a case, although one may question whether this is the type of non-recognition contemplated by this exception to §306 treatment. Perhaps assignment of income principles could apply to such a case, particularly if the stock had been transferred to the corporation as part of a "plan" for its ultimate disposition. See Lyon and Eustice. Assignment of Income: Fruit and Tree as Irrigated by the P. G. Lake Case, 17 Tax L. Rev. 293, 423 (1962).

[18] Regs. 1.306-3(e); see also §356(e) (receipt of boot in corporate reorganizations in exchange for "section 306 stock").

*4. Transactions not in avoidance of federal income tax :§306(b)-
(4).* This exception is for transactions that, in the opinion of the
Treasury, are not in pursuance of a plan having the avoidance of
Federal income tax as one of its principal purposes. The regulations
refer to "isolated dispositions of section 306 stock by minority shareholders" as an example.[19] The fact that the regulations refer to
"isolated" dispositions is worth noting. If a publicly held corporation
were to adopt a plan of declaring and redeeming preferred stock dividends annually, this exception to §306(a) might not be available
even to minority shareholders. Another area of application for this
exception to §306(a) is a disposition by the shareholder of a fraction
of his "section 306 stock" along with an equal fraction of his original
shares, a transaction that would ordinarily not operate to avoid federal income tax.

Sec. 8.06.   Uses of "section 306 stock"

Despite the penalties of §306(a) on the disposition of "section
306 stock," there is still some room for maneuver in the use of these
securities. Thus, bootstrap sales (*supra*, Sec. 7.25) can be facilitated
by using "section 306 stock" as the "financing paper," since the
shareholder can rely on §306(b)(1) if he disposes of his entire
stock interest in the corporation. The use of "section 306 stock" for
charitable contributions has been noted above. It can also be useful
in making family gifts, if the donee is to retain the stock, since unlike
the common stock of most family corporations, it can usually be easily valued for gift tax purposes. Moreover, since its taint is purged at
death, "section 306 stock" can sometimes be used in estate planning
(e.g., for liquidity at death) without diluting control of the corporation on the death of a shareholder. Alternatively, shareholders may
retain their "section 306 stock" (for fixed dividend income), while
shifting control of the corporation into the hands of the younger
generation or new executives through gifts or sales of the common
stock.[20]

Sec. 8.07.   Is §306 the exclusive remedy for attempted bail-outs?

As stated above, stock issued — either at organization or at a

[19] Regs. §1.306-2(b)(3); for applications, see Rev. Rul. 56-116, 1956-1 C.B.
164; Rev. Rul. 57-103, 1957-1 C.B. 113; Rev. Rul. 57-212, *ibid.* 114; Rev. Rul.
56-223, 1956-1 C.B. 162.

[20] See Wolfberg, Uses of Preferred Stock in Tax Planning for Closely Held
Corporations, 44 Taxes 52 (1966); Schwaighart, Despite 306, Preferred Stock is
Still Very Useful in Corporate Tax Planning, 14 J. of Tax. 348 (1961); on bootstrap acquisitions, see Milton F. Priester, 38 T.C. 316 (1962), and Lange, Bootstrap Financing: The Redemption Technique, 18 Tax L. Rev. 323 (1963).

later time — by a corporation having no earnings and profits cannot be "section 306 stock," by virtue of §306(c)(2). A redemption of such untainted stock, therefore, will not be subject to the punitive rules of §306(a), even if it occurs at a time when the corporation does have earnings and profits. The inapplicability of §306 will not assure the shareholders of capital gain or loss treatment on the redemption, however, since the transaction will be subject to §302 (*supra*, Sec. 7.20); and a pro rata redemption will probably be taxed as a dividend under that provision.

What if the shareholders seek to avoid §302 by selling the untainted stock to a third person, and the corporation thereafter redeems it from the buyer? This question brings us back to the *Chamberlin* case (*supra*, Sec. 8.01), where the court held, on the facts before it, that the transaction was not the equivalent of a taxable dividend. Another court might not view the transaction so leniently, but the government in relitigating the issue would be met by the argument that Congress enacted §306 with the *Chamberlin* case before it and intended §306 to be the exclusive remedy for an attempted bail-out through the medium of a sale and redemption of preferred stock. In answer to this theory, it might be argued that §306 was intended to be an automatic safeguard against bail-outs and that Congress did not want to impose its drastic rules on stock issued when the corporation has no earnings and profits, but that §302 remains unimpaired by the enactment of §306. This view of §306 and §302 would mean that a purchaser of untainted stock might be regarded under §302(d) as a mere conduit through which the original shareholders receive a dividend,[21] if all the surrounding circumstances of the transaction warrant this conclusion. To take an extreme case, if untainted preferred stock is sold under an agreement calling for its redemption within a few days, the government might properly argue that the transaction is in effect a redemption of stock from the original shareholders, rather than from the buyer.[22] If the

---

[21] This of course assumes that the original shareholders participate in the transaction on a pro rata basis, so that none of the escapes provided by §302(b) are applicable. See *supra*, Sec. 7.20.

[22] The same theory might be applied to a gift of stock, whether tainted or not, to a charity or other donee under a plan for its immediate redemption: the transaction might be regarded as the equivalent of a redemption of the stock from the donor, followed by a gift of cash by him to the donee. In Rev. Rul. 57-328, summarized *supra*, Sec. 8.04, the statement of facts specified that "there was no prearrangement for the sale by the [charity] of the preferred stock which it received, or for the redemption by the corporation of any of its preferred stock." Note also the Service's hostile position as to gifts of property if the donee is under an obligation, express or implied, to sell the transferred property. Rev. Rul. 60-370, 1960-2 C.B. 203 ("Pomona plan" charitable gift).

time between the sale and redemption is lengthened, however, the resulting intervention of business and legal risks for all parties makes it increasingly difficult to find that the transferees of the stock are merely conduits for the original shareholders. It may well be, then, that §306 will become the exclusive remedy for all but the most extreme sale-and-redemption cases.

Chapter Nine

COMPLETE LIQUIDATIONS

Part A.   The General Rule of §331 (a) (1)

Sec. 9.01.   Introductory

In the absence of a statutory provision prescribing its tax consequences, the complete liquidation of a corporation might be looked upon as a transfer by each stockholder of his stock in exchange for the liquidating distribution. His profit or loss (*i.e.*, the difference between the adjusted basis of his stock and the value of the liquidating distribution) would then be reported either as capital gain or loss or as ordinary income or loss, depending upon whether the stock was a "capital asset" in his hands and on whether the transaction was regarded as a "sale or exchange" within the meaning of §1222. Another possibility, in the absence of statute, would be to treat the liquidating distribution as a "dividend" (taxable as ordinary income) to the extent of the corporation's earnings and profits; and to treat the balance of the liquidating distribution as a payment in exchange for the stock, with gain or loss to be computed accordingly.

But we are not required to speculate about the possible tax consequences of a corporate liquidation in the absence of a statutory provision. Since 1924, a liquidating distribution has been treated as the proceeds of a sale of the stock by the shareholder. In reporting the bill which became the Revenue Act of 1924, the Senate Finance Committee said:

> The bill treats a liquidating dividend as a sale of the stock, with the result that the gain to the taxpayer is treated not as a [taxable] dividend . . . but as a gain from the sale of property which may be treated as a capital gain. . . . A liquidating dividend is, in effect, a sale by the stockholder of his stock to the corporation; he surrenders his interest in the corporation and receives money in place thereof. Treating such a transaction as a sale and within the capital gain provisions is consistent with the entire theory of the Act and, furthermore, is the only method of treating such distributions which can be easily administered. (S. Rep. No. 398, 68th Cong., 1st Sess., reprinted in 1939-1 (Part 2) C.B. 266, 274.)

The analogy between a complete liquidation and a sale of the stock, however, is not a perfect one. A sale of shares merely substitutes one shareholder for another, leaving the corporation's earnings and profits account intact. The result is that the earnings and profits will be taxed as ordinary income if and when they are distributed to the new shareholder; the outgoing shareholder furnishes the Government with a surrogate, as it were, whose withdrawal of the corporate earnings will be subjected to the graduated individual income tax rate. But on a complete liquidation, no one steps into the shoes of the original shareholder. The earnings and profits account — representing, be it remembered, income which has so far escaped the individual income tax because its distribution has been postponed — is wiped clean. A sale of shares, then, merely puts off the day of reckoning for the accumulated earnings and profits; a complete liquidation guarantees that there will be *no* reckoning, other than a recognition of capital gain or loss.

Liquidation may differ from a sale in another respect. If the assets are not converted into cash but rather are distributed to the shareholder in kind and held by him, the liquidation does not spell an end to the shareholder's interest in the business enterprise. Instead of "selling out," he has only changed the fashion in which he holds title to the assets. Like the shareholder who sells out, he has enjoyed the benefits of operating the enterprise in corporate form. Unlike the vendor of shares, however, he is able to switch the business unit when the corporate form becomes unattractive without losing his investment position. Having used the corporate shell as long as it served his purpose, he discards it at will without paying a personal tax on the accumulated earnings and profits.[1]

Despite the arguments that might be advanced against treating a complete liquidation as a sale, however, the principle adopted by Congress in 1924 has been followed ever since, except for one brief period (1934-36). Before turning to the details of §331(a)(1), which embodies the general rule that a distribution in complete liquidation shall be treated as payment in exchange for the stock, certain exceptions and qualifications should be noted:

---

[1] See generally, Bittker and Redlich, Corporate Liquidations and the Income Tax, 5 Tax L. Rev. 437, 448-51 (1950); Darrell, Corporate Liquidations and the Federal Income Tax, 89 U. of Pa. L. Rev. 907, 930ff (1941); Bromberg, Pitfalls in Corporate Liquidation, 44 Taxes 174 (1966); Subchapter C Advisory Group, Revised Report on Corporate Distributions and Adjustments (and comments thereon), in Hearings before House Committee on Ways and Means, 86th Cong., 1st sess. (Feb. 24-March 4, 1959).

1. Although the ordinary consequence of §331(a)(1) is that the shareholder's gain or loss on a complete liquidation is capital gain or loss, in itself §331(a)(1) merely requires the liquidation to be treated as a sale or exchange of the stock: if the stock is not a "capital asset" in the hands of the shareholder, his gain or loss will be ordinary, rather than capital.

2. Under a judicial doctrine of uncertain scope, §331(a)(1) is not applicable to a liquidation of a corporation whose stock was acquired solely for the purpose of obtaining its assets through liquidation. The two steps (purchase and liquidation) will be telescoped, with the result that the transaction is treated merely as a purchase of the assets themselves, and no gain or loss is recognized on the liquidation. *Infra*, Sec. 9.03.

3. Despite §331(a)(1), the shareholders of a corporation may elect under §333 not to recognize their gain on a complete liquidation. As will be seen *infra*, Sec. 9.21, however, this opportunity to avoid the recognition of gain is of limited usefulness.

4. Despite §331(a)(1), neither gain nor loss is recognized on the complete liquidation of a subsidiary corporation under §332, *infra*, Sec. 9.40.

5. If a "collapsible corporation" is liquidated, the shareholder's gain or loss is computed under §331(a)(1), but any long-term gain is transmuted into ordinary income by §341-(a)(2). *Infra*, Sec. 10.03.

Finally, it should be noted that §331(a)(1) prescribes the effect of a complete liquidation on the shareholders; it is not concerned with the corporation itself. Under principles to be examined *infra*, Sec. 9.60, the corporation ordinarily recognizes neither gain nor loss on the distribution of its assets in complete liquidation (§336); and under a 1954 statutory innovation (§337), the sale of property by the corporation during the 12-month period beginning with the adoption of a plan of complete liquidation will ordinarily produce neither taxable gain nor deductible loss.

Sec. 9.02.   Meaning of "complete liquidation"

The Code does not define the term "complete liquidation," nor do the regulations under §331. The regulations under §332 (*infra*, Sec. 9.41), however, contain this statement, which is probably equally applicable to §331:

A status of liquidation exists when the corporation ceases to be a going concern and its activities are merely for the purpose of winding up its affairs, paying its debts, and distributing any remaining balance to its shareholders. A liquidation may be completed prior to the actual dissolution of the liquidating corporation. However, legal dissolution of the corporation is not required. Nor will the mere retention of a nominal amount of assets for the sole purpose of preserving the corporation's legal existence disqualify the transaction. (Regs. §1.332-2(c).)

The cases support this pragmatic approach to the term "complete liquidation." See, for example, Kennemer v. Commissioner, 96 F.2d 177, 21 AFTR 103 (5th Cir. 1938):

> It is not material that the distribution was not specifically designated as a liquidating dividend or that no formal resolution to liquidate or dissolve the corporation had been adopted when the distribution was made. An intention to liquidate was fairly implied from the sale of all the assets and the act of distributing the cash to the stockholders. Permitting the forfeiture of its right to do business was an additional circumstance which the [Tax Court] properly considered with the other facts in evidence. The determining element was the intention to liquidate the business, coupled with the actual distribution of the cash to the stockholders. (96 F.2d at 178.)

Moreover, although this extract from the *Kennemer* case implies that a sale of the corporate assets is required, it is well established that a distribution in kind is equally efficacious.[2]

While a complete liquidation is ordinarily effected by a dissolution under state law, it is not essential that the corporation dissolve for complete liquidation treatment to apply. Thus, in Rev. Rul. 54-518, 1954-2 C.B. 142, the Service ruled that retention of the corporation's charter to protect the corporate name against appropriation was not inconsistent with a complete liquidation under §333 (*infra*, Sec. 9.20); the ruling seems equally applicable to §331. The prompt reactivation of an allegedly liquidated corporation, however, may retroactively vitiate the tax results of a normal complete liquidation.[3]

Although both the courts and the regulations are willing to give effect to an informal liquidation, it is dangerous to make distributions to the shareholders before the intention to liquidate is evidenced by formal action. In the absence of such formalities, it may take a lawsuit to establish that the earliest distributions in a series were liquidating distributions, subject to §331(a)(1), rather than ordinary distribu-

---

[2] For other examples of informal complete liquidations, see Shore v. Commissioner, 288 F.2d 742, 7 AFTR 2d 653 (5th Cir. 1961); McGregor v. United States, 5 AFTR 2d 965 (D.C. Kan. 1960); Estate of Charles Fearon, 16 T.C. 385 (1951) (distribution in 1942 held to be in liquidation, through process commenced in 1919; delay not unreasonable); *supra*, Sec. 7.61; see also Blawie, Some Tax Aspects of a Corporate Liquidation, 7 Tax L. Rev. 581, 488-96 (1952).

[3] Rev. Rul. 60-50 and 60-51, 1960-1 C.B. 150 and 169; Rev. Rul. 61-191, 1961-2 C.B. 251; see also *infra*, Sec. 9.05, for comparable problems in the liquidation-reincorporation area.

tions, taxable as dividends under §301 to the extent of the corporation's earnings and profits.[4] Similarly, it seems unwise to leave the status of a distribution ambiguous by failing to adopt a "plan" of liquidation, even though §331(a)(1), unlike some other provisions (e.g., §332, §333, and §337), does not insist upon such action,[5] or by neglecting to redeem the stock. The problem of characterization may also be troublesome if the corporation makes a series of distributions, each accompanied by a redemption of part of its stock. As stated *supra*, Sec. 7.61, it is possible that the shareholder's gain or loss will be computed distribution by distribution if there is a series of partial liquidations, but in the aggregate if the transaction is a complete liquidation.

If a business enterprise that has been taxed as a corporation is reclassified as a non-corporate entity as a result of litigation, an election, or otherwise, the change may or may not be treated as a constructive liquidation of the corporate or quasi-corporate entity. Examples are: a professional service enterprise's shift from corporate to partnership or proprietorship tax returns (*supra*, Sec. 2.05); and the termination of an election to report on a corporate basis under §1361 (*supra*, Sec. 2.11).

Sec. 9.03.   Liquidating distributions and shareholder gain or loss

1. General. Section 331(a)(1) provides that amounts distributed in complete liquidation of a corporation shall be treated as full payment in exchange for the shareholder's stock. If the stock is a "capital asset" in the hands of the shareholder, as would normally be the case under §1221 (unless held by a dealer for sale to customers in the ordinary course of business), a complete liquidation will produce capital gain or loss since §331(a)(1) treats the liquidation transaction as an "exchange" of the stock. The amount of the gain or loss, and its character as long or short term capital gain or loss, in turn

---

[4] *Supra*, note 2. The regulations under §332 contain this statement, which seems equally applicable to §331(a)(1): "Where there is more than one distribution, it is essential that a status of liquidation exist at the time the first distribution is made. . . ." Regs. §1.332-2(c).

If the distributee is a corporation, the shoe may be on the other foot, since the tax on a non-liquidating distribution may be less painful by virtue of the dividends received deduction of §243 (*supra*, Sec. 2.25) than the capital gain tax on a complete liquidation. See also Schaefer v. Welch, 252 F.2d 175, 1 AFTR 2d 916 (6th Cir. 1958), holding that pre-1913 appreciation in value is counted in computing the shareholder's capital gain on a complete liquidation even though it could be distributed tax-free in an ordinary distribution; Wallace v. United States, 146 F. Supp. 444, 50 AFTR 942 (Ct. Cl. 1956) (contra).

[5] See Emery, Complete Liquidation of Corporations Under the 1954 Code, 32 Taxes 995 (1954), however, pointing out that §392(a), relating to the effective date of the 1954 Code, asumes that there will be a "plan".

depend upon the shareholder's adjusted basis and holding period for his stock and the value of the liquidating distribution.

The regulations, Regs. §1.331-1(e), require the shareholder's gain or loss on liquidating distributions to be computed on a "per share basis," so that gain or loss is separately calculated for blocks of stock acquired at different prices and dates. For example, if A acquired 100 shares of stock in X corporation for $3,000 in 1950, and 100 shares for $6,000 in January of 1966, a liquidating distribution of $50 per share in June of 1966 would produce $2,000 of long term capital gain on the 1950 block, and $1,000 of short term capital loss on the 1966 block.[6]

2. *Problems of valuation and timing.* A shareholder's gain or loss upon liquidation of the corporation is the difference between the adjusted basis of his stock and the fair market value of the liquidating distribution, §1001(a). Calculating the value of the distributed assets is ordinarily feasible, though appraisals or estimates may be necessary; but disputed claims, contingent contract rights, mineral royalties, business good will,[7] and other rights may be difficult if not impossible to value with reasonable accuracy. If the value of some or all of the assets received by the shareholder cannot be ascertained with reasonable accuracy, the computation with respect to these assets is held "open," under Burnet v. Logan, 283 U.S. 404, 9 AFTR 1453 (1931), until they are sold, collected, or otherwise reduced to property of ascertainable value. Such a delay will affect the year in which gain or loss is recognized by the shareholder, and it may also affect the characterization of the gain or loss. This is because the gain or loss ultimately realized on an "open" liquidation is part of the capital gain or loss generated by the exchange of the stock under §331(a)(1); if the asset in question had been valued when received, however, any gain or loss realized on its later collection, sale, or other disposition (i.e., the difference between the amount ultimately realized and the asset's value at the time of distribution) would be ordinary or capital, depending on whether it was a capital asset in the shareholder's hands or not and on whether it was "sold or exchanged" within the meaning of §1222.

[6] For the computation of gain or loss when the liquidation is effected by a series of distributions over a period of time, see *supra*, Sec. 7.61.

[7] Good will is normally valued by reference to the earnings history and capacity of the business out of which it grows. On the question whether good will is distributed to a shareholder on liquidation if it was his personal efforts as an employee of the corporation that attracted the customers, see Ruth M. Cullen, 14 T.C. 368 (1950).

See generally North American Service Co., Inc., 33 T.C. 677 (1960); Rev. Rul. 66-81, *infra* note 23; Harnack, The Commissioner is Looking for Good Will, 40 Taxes 331 (1962).

To illustrate: A, the sole shareholder of X corporation, receives in complete liquidation of X: cash of $10,000; operating assets with an ascertainable value of $30,000; and a contingent claim against Y in the face amount of $50,000, which may be valueless, depending on later events beyond X's or A's control. A's basis for his stock in X is $50,000. If it is held that X's claim against Y has no readily ascertainable value under *Burnet v. Logan, supra,* the liquidation computation is held open until the claim is finally reduced to money or other property with an ascertainable value. If A subsequently collects $40,000 on the claim, this amount is deemed to have been received in exchange for his stock, and A's gain of $30,000 (agggregate liquidating distribution of $80,000, less $50,000 basis for stock) is taxable as capital gain. If A collected only $7,000 on the claim, his loss of $3,000 ($50,000 basis for stock, less aggregate distribution of $47,000) would be deductible as a capital loss when the claim was settled.

These results may be compared with the consequences of a "closed" liquidation, based on the assumption that the claim against Y was valued at $30,000 when it was distributed to A. His gain on the liquidation would be $20,000 (liquidating distribution of $70,000, less $50,000 basis for stock). On collecting $40,000 on the claim, A would realize gain of $10,000 ($40,000 received, less $30,000 basis for claim under §334(a), *infra,* Sec. 9.04); and this gain would constitute ordinary income for want of a "sale or exchange" of the claim.[8] If he collected only $7,000, he would realize a loss of $23,000 (basis of $30,000, less $7,000 received), which might be an ordinary loss or a capital loss, depending on principles discussed *supra,* Sec. 4.07.

In tabular form, the four examples just described are as follows (dollar amounts in thousands):

	"Open" liquidation		"Closed" liquidation	
	A	B	C	D
1. Amount realized — liquidation				
a. Cash	$10	$10	$10	$10
b. Operating assets	30	30	30	30
c. Claim v. Y	40	7	30	30
d. Total	$80	$47	$70	$70
2. Less: Adjusted basis of stock	50	50	50	50
3. Gain (loss) on liquidation	$30	($ 3)	$20	$20
4. Amount collected on claim v. Y	$40	$ 7	$40	$ 7
5. Less: Adjusted basis of claim v. Y	40	7	30	30
6. Gain (loss) on collection	0	0	$10	($23)

[8] Hale v. Helvering, 85 F.2d 810, 18 AFTR 520 (D.C. Cir. 1936).

It will be noted that the same aggregate gain or loss will be reflected on A's tax returns, whether the liquidation is treated as open or closed when the distribution is made, but the character of his gain or loss and the years of realization will differ. Thus, assuming ultimate collection of $40,000 on the claim, the open liquidation computation produces $30,000 of capital gain in the year the claim is settled; the "closed" computation produces $20,000 of capital gain in the year of liquidation and $10,000 of ordinary income when the claim is settled. The revised assumption, *viz.*, a settlement of the claim for $7,000, is reflected on A's tax return in the year of settlement as a loss of $3,000, assuming an open liquidation; the closed liquidation approach produces capital gain of $20,000 in the year of distribution and a loss of $23,000 when the claim is settled. The way in which the shareholder's economic gain "nets out" as just described can be seen in the above table; the sum of line 3 and line 6 is the same for columns A and C (open and closed liquidations, assuming that $40,000 is collected on the claim), as well as for columns B and D (open and closed liquidations, assuming that $7,000 is collected).

Because of the deferral of tax that results from holding a liquidation open on a plea that the fair market value of assets is not ascertainable, together with the possibility of thus transmuting potential ordinary income into capital gain, the Commissioner has ardently resisted taxpayer arguments that assets were not susceptible of valuation when distributed in liquidation. Thus, Rev. Rul. 58-402, 1958-2 C.B. 15, states that the Service will "continue to require valuation of contracts and claims to receive indefinite amounts of income, such as those acquired with respect to stock in liquidation of a corporation, except in rare and extraordinary cases."[9] The shoe is on the other foot,

---

[9] See also Regs. §1.1001-1(a) (third sentence). If a fair market value can be ascribed to the stock surrendered, United States v. Davis, 370 U.S. 65, 9 AFTR 2d 1625 (1962), supports an assignment of this value to the assets received in exchange, though this would leave a troublesome allocation problem if there is more than one asset of unascertainable value.

The advantage to the shareholder of "open" liquidation treatment would be reduced if it brought §483 (imputed interest on delayed payments for capital assets) into play, since a portion of the gain ultimately realized would then be taxable as ordinary income. Since this possibility is not peculiar to corporate liquidations but would arise in the case of any taxable exchange of a capital asset if the "amount realized" did not have an ascertainable fair market value, an evaluation of it is beyond the scope of this work. It may be noted, however, that §483 was enacted to reach sales of capital assets for a consideration payable at a later time whose value was certain or likely to increase by reason of the delay — the functional equivalent of interest — and "open" liquidations do not necessarily involve such circumstances; nor does an "open" liquidation seem to fit the statutory requirement of §483(c)(1): "any payment . . . under a contract . . . under which *some or all of the payments are due more than a year after the date of such sale or exchange.*" This statutory language might, arguably, be satisfied if the property of uncertain value consists of a right to

however, if the shareholder claims a loss on the liquidation on the ground that assets of this type should be taken into account at a low or nominal value. Here the Service may argue that the difficulty of valuing such assets makes the shareholder's claim premature, and that no loss should be allowed until the claims have been collected or sold.[10]

3. Effect of liabilities on shareholder's gain or loss. If the shareholders assume, or take property subject to, liabilities on a complete liquidation, their gain or loss must be computed with this in mind.

receive property or money at a later date, especially if the corporation itself would have been subject to §483 had it retained the claim, but this would involve only a limited class of "open" liquidations. It is not clear, however, that delayed payments by someone other than the buyer of the capital assets in question can constitute "unstated interest" under §483.

[10] A leading "open" liquidation case is Commissioner v. Carter, 170 F.2d 911, 37 AFTR 573 (2d Cir. 1948), involving oil brokerage commission contracts. Among the myriad other cases in this area, the following are of special interest:

Open liquidations: Westover v. Smith, 173 F.2d 90, 37 AFTR 1001 (9th Cir. 1949) (patent royalty rights); George J. Lentz, 28 T.C. 1157 (1957) (Acq.) (unearned mortgage brokerage commissions); Henry A. Kuckenberg, ¶60,281 P-H Memo TC (partially completed construction contract); Nakatani v. Cullen, 5 AFTR 2d 519 (D.C. Cal. 1959) (breach of contract claim); Commissioner v. Doering, 335 F.2d 738, 14 AFTR 2d 5070 (2d Cir. 1964) (contested movie distribution contract rights).

If assets are incapable of valuation in the year of liquidation but acquire a fair market value in a later year, it would be possible to "close" the liquidation as of that date, even though the assets are not sold or otherwise disposed of until a later time; but there seem to be no reported cases in point.

In Miller v. United States, 235 F.2d 553, 49 AFTR 1754 (6th Cir. 1956), a liquidation in which speculative second mortgage notes were distributed was held to be "open" because a fair market vaule could not be ascribed to them; but on collecting the amounts due, the taxpayer was held to realize ordinary income rather than capital gain because, at the time of the collection, there was not a "sale or exchange' of the notes; the "sale or exchange" character of the liquidation itself did not supply this element. See 262 F.2d 584, 3 AFTR 2d 380 (6th Cir. 1958), citing Osenbach v. Commissioner, *infra,* Sec. 9.22, involving a §333 liquidation; Rev. Rul. 58-402, however, seems to assume that capital gain would be achieved in an open liquidation.

Closed liquidations: Campagna v. United States, 290 F.2d 682, 7 AFTR 2d 1358 (2d Cir. 1961) (second mortgage contracts); Chamberlin v. Commissioner, 286 F.2d 850, 6 AFTR 2d 5967 (7th Cir. 1960) (patent royalty rights); Grill v. United States, 303 F.2d 922, 9 AFTR 2d 1728 (Ct. Cl. 1962) (film distribution contract); Estate of Goldstein, 33 T.C. 1032 (1960) (insurance renewal commission contract rights); Pat O'Brien, 25 T.C. 376 (1955) (movie distribution contract); United Mercantile Agencies, 34 T.C. 808 (1960) (delinquent accounts receivable).

Losses claimed by shareholders: Charles A. Dana, 6 T.C. 177 (1946); Palmer, Exec. v. United States, ——F.Supp——, 1 AFTR 2d 863 (D.C. Conn. 1958); see also Warren v. Commissioner, 193 F.2d 996, 1001, 41 AFTR 668 (1st Cir. 1952).

If the assets distributed to the shareholder (in either an open or a closed liquidation) represent income earned or about to be realized by the corporation, an assignment of income problem may be lurking in the background; see *infra,* Sec. 9.62.

See generally, Farer, Corporate Liquidations: Transmuting Ordinary Income into Capital Gains, 75 Harv. L. Rev. 527 (1962); Eustice, Contract Rights, Capital Gain, and Assignment of Income — The Ferrer Case, 20 Tax L. Rev. 1, 51 ff. (1964).

Thus, if property with a gross value of $100,000, but subject to a liability of $40,000, is distributed in complete liquidation to a shareholder whose stock has a basis of $50,000, his realized gain on the distribution is $10,000, i.e., the "amount realized" under §1001 on the liquidation exchange is the net value of the distribution.[11] If the liability is unknown at the time of distribution, or is so speculative or contingent that it is properly disregarded in computing the shareholder's gain or loss on the liquidation, a later payment of the debt by the shareholder will probably generate a capital loss under the *Arrowsmith* case, rather than a deduction from ordinary income, on the theory that his capital gain on the liquidation was overstated.[12]

4. Judicial exceptions to §331(a)(1). No statute, except a new one, is innocent of judicial exceptions. Suppose a taxpayer acquires all the stock of a corporation for the sole purpose of liquidating the corporation in order to use its assets (e.g., a stock of merchandise that is in short supply) in his own business. If by reason of market fluctuations there is a difference between the cost to him of the shares and the value of the assets at the time he liquidates the corporation, is the gain or loss recognized? On the ground that such a transaction is in substance no more than a purchase of assets, rather than a purchase of stock and a liquidation of the corporation, it was held that no gain is recognizable in H. B. Snively, 19 T.C. 850 (1953).

As to the income produced in the interim by the corporate assets, however, the court held that it should be taxed to the corporation, rather than to the stockholder, despite the plan to liquidate:

> The stock purchase coupled with the intent to dissolve the corporation and the taking of some steps to that end, in our opinion, did not *ipso facto* either destroy the existence of the corporation as a taxable entity or permit the petitioner to appropriate as his own income which would otherwise be taxable to the corporation.[13]

A purchase of stock was similarly treated as the equivalent of a purchase of assets in Ruth M. Cullen, 14 T.C. 368 (1950), where a share-

---

[11] Ford v. United States, 311 F.2d 951, 11 AFTR 2d 433 (Ct. Cl. 1963); see also *infra*, Sec. 9.04, note 15, re the shareholder's basis for the encumbered property.

[12] Arrowsmith v. Commissioner, 344 U.S. 6, 42 AFTR 649 (1952); see Note, Tax Treatment of Stockholder-Transferees' Payments in Satisfaction of Dissolved Corporations' Unpaid Debts, 61 Yale L. J. 1081 (1952). The shareholder's payment of the debt may be treated as a constructive payment by the corporation, entitling it to a deduction if a direct payment by it would have been deductible. Royal Oak Apartments, Inc., 43 T.C. 243 (1964) (Acq.).

[13] 19 T.C. 850, 858; aff'd on appeal, 219 F.2d 266, 46 AFTR 1703 (5th Cir. 1955); see also Western Wine & Liquor Co., 18 T.C. 1090 (1952); United States v. Mattison, 273 F.2d 13, 4 AFTR 2d 5844 (9th Cir. 1959); *infra*, Sec. 9.44 (the "Kimbell-Diamond" doctrine).

holder of a corporation bought out the other shareholders, with the intention of liquidating the corporation and operating its business as a sole proprietorship. Although the price paid for the stock (book value) exceeded the value of the liquidating distribution, the court held that the taxpayer had not sustained a deductible loss, because at the conclusion of the plan he "had neither more nor less than he had paid for."

Strictly speaking, the *Snively* and *Cullen* cases need not be regarded as exceptions to §331(a)(1), since that section neither taxes gain nor allows the deduction of losses. These functions are performed by §61(a) and §165(a); §331(a)(1) merely makes it clear that the stock of a liquidating corporation is to be treated as though it had been sold or exchanged. For the same reason, §331(a)(1) does not preclude application of the *Corn Products* doctrine,[14] with the result that a corporate liquidation that is intimately connected to the shareholder's regular trade or business might, in appropriate circumstances, produce ordinary, rather than capital, gain or loss. The business function of such stock overrides its technical definition as a "capital asset" and requires the gain or loss to be treated as an integral component of the shareholder's regular business income.

Sec. 9.04. Basis of property received in complete liquidation

Section 334(a) provides that the basis of property received in a complete liquidation shall be its fair market value at the time of distribution, if gain or loss was recognized on its receipt.[15] (The same result was reached under the 1939 Code, though without explicit statutory authority.) It will be noted that the basis of the stock given up in the liquidation, plus the gain or minus the loss recognized on the

---

[14] Corn Products Refining Co. v. Commissioner, 350 U.S. 46, 47 AFTR 1789 (1955); see also Commissioner v. Bagley & Sewall Co., 221 F.2d 944, 47 AFTR 790 (2d Cir. 1955); *supra*, Sec. 4.05.

[15] "Recognized" as used in §334(a) probably means "recognizable," so that the failure to recognize gain or loss would not bar an application of the provision, though inconsistency may permit the statute of limitations to be opened up under §1311. But see Commissioner v. Goldstein's Estate, 340 F.2d 24, 15 AFTR 2d 68 (2d Cir. 1965) (refusing to open the (barred) year of liquidation, for want of inconsistency by taxpayer, even though assets were later held susceptible of valuation). See also *supra*, Sec. 3.10, note 43, for an analagous problem when gain should have been, but was not, recognized on the receipt of "boot."

If the shareholders assume, or take property subject to, liabilities, their basis is the unencumbered fair market value of the assets. See Ford v. United States, 311 F.2d 951, 11 AFTR 2d 433 (Ct. Cl. 1963); Crane v. Commissioner, 331 U.S.1, 35 AFTR 776 (1947); but see Columbus & Greenville Railway Co., 42 T.C. 834 (1964) (basis does not include hypothetical liability that is not expected to be paid), aff'd per curiam, 358 F.2d 294, 17 AFTR 2d 643 (5th Cir. 1966).

liquidation, will equal the fair market value of the property received. If no gain or loss is recognized on the liquidation, because the stockholder's basis for the stock he surrenders happens to coincide with the value of the liquidating distribution, the basis of the distributed assets is their "cost," i.e., the value of the stock given up.[16]

By tying the basis of the distributed property to its fair market value on distribution, §334(a) assures that the shareholder's economic profit, measured from the time of his acquisition of the stock to his sale of the liquidating distribution, will be recognized in two steps; the difference between the cost of the stock and the value of the distribution is taxed on liquidation; and the difference between the latter amount and the proceeds of the property on an ultimate sale or other disposition is taxed when the property is sold. For examples, see columns C and D of the table *supra*, Sec. 9.02. As noted in connection with these examples, the gain recognized on the liquidation will almost certainly constitute capital gain under §331(a)(1) and §1221, but the character of the income or loss recognized on the sale or other disposition of the property will depend upon the nature of the assets in the shareholder's hands and on whether the disposition qualifies as a "sale or exchange" under §1222. Assets constituting stock in trade when held by the corporation, for example, may be capital assets when held by the shareholder, or *vice versa*.[17]

It is important to note that the liquidation of a corporation that owns appreciated inventory assets will give the inventory a stepped-up basis at the cost of a capital gains tax, a possibility that may be of great advantage if the shareholders intend to continue the business as partners. This opportunity to acquire a "cheap" stepped-up basis often gives rise to disputes over the valuation of such assets, and is an important incentive to use of the troublesome liquidation-reincorporation device.[18]

Sec. 9.05. Liquidation followed by reincorporation

The concept of complete liquidation normally envisions a termination of the liquidating corporation as an entity, either by a sale

---

[16] §1012. The values of the stock and the liquidating distribution are ordinarily identical; if there is a discrepancy, there is authority for letting the value of the stock control. Avco Mfg. Corp., 27 T.C. 547, 556 (Acq.); Rev. Rul. 56-100, 1956-1 C.B. 624; but cf. Philadelphia Park Amusement Co. v. United States, 126 F. Supp. 184, 46 AFTR 1293 (Ct. Cl. 1954).

[17] Greenspon v. Commissioner, 229 F.2d 947, 48 AFTR 979 (8th Cir. 1956); Acro Mfg. Co. v. Commissioner, 334 F.2d 40, 14 AFTR 2d 5106 (6th Cir. 1964); see also F. W. Drybrough, 45 T.C. No. 40 (1966).

[18] Berg v. United States, 167 F. Supp. 756, 2 AFTR 2d 6061 (W.D. Wisc. 1958); Morton Ollendorff, ¶59,055 P-H Memo TC; *infra*, Sec. 9.05.

of its assets to outsiders and a distribution of the proceeds to the shareholders, or by a distribution of assets to the shareholders so that they may either sell them or operate the business in noncorporate form. (Sometimes these possibilities are combined: some assets are sold by the corporation, others are distributed in kind to the shareholders; and of the latter, some are sold by the shareholders and others are employed by them in a noncorporate business.) On occasion, however, the shareholders intend to conduct the business in corporate form, but hope to obtain the tax advantages of a liquidation, viz., a stepped-up basis for the assets at the capital gain rate (or at no cost, e.g., when the stock was recently inherited and has a basis equal to the value of the assets), plus an elimination of the corporation's accumulated earnings and profits. They may seek to achieve these goals by any of a number of routes, which however complex usually fall into one of two categories: (a) a complete liquidation of the original corporation, followed by a prearranged tax-free transfer of all or part of the operating assets to a second (usually newly organized) corporation under §351 (*supra*, Sec. 3.14); or (b) a transfer by the original corporation of all or part of its operating assets to a second corporation controlled by its shareholders (which may, but need not, have been newly organized by them), for its stock and/or property, followed by a complete liquidation of the transferor corporation.

If these liquidation-reincorporation steps are collapsed and treated as parts of a unitary transaction, the arrangement takes on the character of a "reorganization" coupled with the distribution of a "boot dividend" to the extent of the non-operating or other assets that are not put into the new corporation. The twin factors of continuity of business operation in modified corporate form and continuity of shareholder investment (aside from the bail-out of corporate earnings), lend support to this analysis. Alternatively, it could be argued that the liquidation and reincorporation transactions should be ignored as a "sham," and the net distribution of liquid assets to the shareholders treated as a "dividend" under the general provisions of §301.[18a] Finally, the relationship of the stock redemption rules of §302 and the partial liquidation rules of §346 (*supra*, Ch. 7) to this general area remains to be fully worked out, particularly in regard to the "dividend equivalency" tests of these provisions. (Note, however,

---

[18a] See Gregory v. Helvering, 293 U.S. 465, 14 AFTR 1191 (1935); Bazley v. Commissioner, 331 U.S. 737, 35 AFTR 1191 (1947); Regs. §§1.301-1(1) and 1.331-1(c); and Rev. Rul. 61-156, 1961-2 C.B. 62, for suggestions and analogues

that shareholder sales of stock of one "related corporation" to another "related corporation" have been materially restricted as a "bail out" device by the express provisions of §304(a) (*supra*, Sec. 7.31), although the effectiveness of §304 in this respect seems to contemplate a pre-existing related corporate purchaser which has substantial earnings and profits, §304(b)(2).

Without attempting to be exhaustive on this complex subject, analysis of several decisions will illustrate generally the basic approaches of courts to these questions. In Joseph C. Gallagher, 39 T.C. 144 (1962), the "old" corporation sold its operating assets to a newly created corporation, organized for this purpose, and then liquidated (62 percent of the shareholders in the old corporation who were active in its affairs ended up with 73 percent of the new company's stock, although in different proportions, and the inactive shareholders of the old company were retired; the balance of the stock in the new corporation was issued to employees of the old corporation for cash). A majority of the Tax Court upheld the taxpayer's contention that the transaction amounted to a valid liquidation of the old corporation and hence resulted in capital gain to its shareholders. The Commissioner's various arguments of (a) "dividend equivalency" under §301, and (b) reorganization treatment under §368(a)(1)(E) (recapitalization) or §368(a)(1)(F) (mere change in identity, form or place of organization), with a "boot dividend" under §356(a)(2), were rejected. The majority felt that a Type E reorganization did not occur since the transaction did not take place within the context of a *single*, continuing corporate entity; likewise a Type F reorganization was not effected, since there was a material change in the shareholders' proprietory interests; the Commissioner did not argue for a Type D reorganization, apparently on the grounds that the continuing shareholder group did not have 80 percent control of the new corporation. The dissenters would have found a dividend to the continuing shareholder group on the ground that, as to them, the transaction constituted in substance a "bail out" of corporate earnings under general principles of §301 and *Bazley, supra* note 18a. For a similar decision, see Berghash v. Commissioner, —— F.2d —— (2d Cir. 1966) (in this case the owner of 99 percent of the liquidating corporation's stock ended up with only 50 percent of the newly created corporate transferee's stock, a situation which prevented application of the reorganization approach). It should be noted in this respect that no case has allowed "reorganization" treatment to supplant the ordinary liquidation rules where continuity of shareholder ownership dropped below 80 percent.

Where shareholders of the transferor corporation acquire (or already own) 80 percent or more of the transferee corporation's stock, however, the Commissioner has enjoyed greater success in persuading courts to impose reorganization treatment with a boot dividend distribution to these continuing shareholders. Thus in James Armour, Inc., 43 T.C. 295 (1965), the taxpayers owned 100 percent of two corporations, and, on the sale of all the operating assets of one corporation to the other corporation for cash and an open account debt, followed by a complete liquidation of the "selling" corporation, the court found a reorganization under §368(a)(1)(D), which resulted in "boot dividend" treatment to the shareholders of the liquidating corporation under §356(a)(1) and (2). In order to reach this result, however, the court had to find that the provisions of §354(a) and (b) were satisfied, and this necessitated the following conclusions: (a) an actual "exchange" of stock was unnecessary, since the taxpayers already owned 100 percent of both corporations, thus making a transfer of stock a meaningless gesture; and (b) "substantially all the assets" were transferred within the meaning of §354(b)(1)(A), even though the value of the transferred assets amounted to only 51 percent in value of the total assets, since the assets transferred constituted the basic operating assets of the business, while the assets retained consisted of liquid investment type assets. By focussing primarily on the transfer of operating assets for purposes of the "substantially all" test of §354(b)(1)(A), it would seem that the court adopted a sensibly flexible approach to the concept of a "non-divisive Type D reorganization" in order to prevent what was essentially a capital gain bail-out of corporate earnings.

In David T. Grubbs, 39 T.C. 42 (1962), the court likewise found a "non-divisive Type D reorganization" with boot dividend distributions to the shareholders on similar facts, except that the transferor corporation was not liquidated; instead it redeemed the stock of all but one of its shareholders, and was kept alive as a wholly owned investment company by the unredeemed shareholder. The court held that there had been a "constructive distribution" by the transferor corporation of these undistributed assets to its sole shareholder, and thus the provisions of §354(b)(1)(B) were satisfied. Although the Grubbs decision took some liberties with what would seem to be the "plain meaning" of §354(b)(1)(B), it did so to avoid an essentially absurd result; when coupled with the Armour decision, Grubbs shows judicial readiness to combat the more obvious bail-out schemes in this area.

Finally, if there is no significant change in proportionate shareholder interests, and if substantially the same business is continued by the transferee corporation, reorganization treatment under §368-(a)(1)(F) would seem to be in order, thus eliminating the technical difficulties found in §354(b)(1) and noted above. For example, in Pridemark, Inc., 42 T.C. 510 (1964), the Tax Court found a Type F reorganization and boot dividend treatment where continuity of proprietory interest and substantial continuity of business activity were both present. However, the elasticity of the Type F reorganization definition is doubtful, and the well-informed can probably avoid classification as such with relative ease, see Hyman Berghash, *supra*. This limited applicability of the Type F reorganization provisions is demonstrated by the Fourth Circuit Court of Appeals' reversal of the Tax Court in the *Pridemark* case, 345 F.2d 35, 15 AFTR 2d 853 (4th Cir. 1965), where the court upheld "liquidation" treatment on the ground that the new corporation was not a continuation of the business of the old corporation. Accordingly, the principal attack on "reincorporations" will probably be handled under the Type D reorganization provisions, subject, however, to the technical difficulties noted above (see *Grubbs* and *Armour*) which arose due to the definitional contraction of Type D reorganizations in the 1954 Code; as such, the invocation of reorganization principles may turn out to be of fairly limited scope, being confined to rather special circumstances. Perhaps the *Bazley*-§301 approach might be expanded to cover this situation, if the net effect of the transaction is merely to distribute corporate earnings ratably among the continuing shareholders. For more on the reincorporation problem, see *infra*, Sec. 12.22.

Sec. 9.06.   Liquidation of "controlled foreign corporations"

Under pre-1962 law, the shareholder's gain on a sale of stock in a foreign corporation, on some redemptions of stock, and on a partial or complete liquidation of the corporation constituted, with minor exceptions, capital gain. Rather than repatriate its foreign earnings in the form of dividends taxable as ordinary income, therefore, the shareholders of a foreign corporation might allow the earnings to accumulate and then sell their stock or liquidate the corporation, reporting their profit as long-term capital gain.

To discourage such transactions, §1248 was enacted in 1962 to require the gain realized by certain United States persons on the sale, exchange, or redemption of stock or on the liquidation of a foreign corporation to be treated as a dividend to the extent of the earnings and profits that were accumulated after 1962 and during the period the shareholder held his stock. The new rules apply only if at some time during the 5-year period preceding the transaction, the corporation was a "controlled foreign corporation" (*supra*, Sec. 6.50) and the shareholder owned (directly, indirectly, and constructively) 10 percent or more of its voting power. Although the shareholder's 10 percent ownership must have coincided with the corporation's status as a controlled foreign corporation, §1248 applies even though neither meets these conditions when the gain is realized. In determining the amount of earnings and profits under §1248, amounts that were previously included in the shareholder's gross income under §951 (constructive distributions) are excluded; and there are several other qualifications and limitations on the strict application of §1248. If the shareholder is a corporation, the amount treated as a dividend by §1248 may qualify for the "deemed paid" credit of §902. If the shareholder is an individual, §1248(b) provides a limit on the tax payable (so as to moderate the effect of throwing the accumulated earnings into the shareholder's ordinary income in a single year), which looks to the tax burden that would have been imposed if the controlled foreign corporation had been a domestic corporation.

Section 1248 is best viewed as a backstop to Subpart F (*supra*, Sec. 6.50). Taken together, and disregarding a variety of minor exceptions, these provisions require the principal United States shareholders of a controlled foreign corporation to report their pro rata share of its accumulated earnings as a dividend either (a) under §951, when the earnings are realized by the corporation; or (b) under §1248, when they sell or exchange their stock or the corporation is liquidated.[18b]

Part B.   Non Recognition of Shareholder Gain in Elective One-Month Liquidations Under §333

Sec. 9.20.   Introductory

Section 333 provides that under certain circumstances, a shareholder's gain on the complete liquidation of a corporation may go unrecognized, if he and enough other shareholders so elect. Its principal function is to permit a corporation holding appreciated property, but having no earnings and profits or cash, to be liquidated without the recognition of gain by its shareholders. If the corporation has any

---

[18b] See Irell and Stone, Understanding Section 1248 — The New Tax Law Regarding Sales or Liquidations of Foreign Corporations, 1964 So. Calif. Tax Inst. 321.

earnings and profits or if it distributes either cash or stock or securities acquired by it after December 31, 1953, the shareholder's gain will be recognized in whole or in part, depending upon certain conditions described hereafter. In return for the non-recognition of gain under §333, the Code exacts the usual price of non-recognition: the shareholder's basis for the assets received on the liquidation is the same as his basis for the stock surrendered (adjusted if any gain was recognized), §334(c); with the result that on selling the assets (and assuming no later change in value), the shareholder will recognize the gain that went unrecognized at the time of the liquidation.

Section 333's antecedent, §112(b)(7) of the 1939 Code, was enacted only as a temporary expedient to encourage the liquidation of personal holding companies, but the provision was revived from time to time before 1954, and it now appears to be a permanent part of the Code. Although designed to permit the painless liquidation of personal holding companies, §333 has never been limited to such corporations but is applicable to others as well.[19]

Sec. 9.21.   Non-recognition of gain under §333

The special rules of §333 apply only to the *gain* of a *qualified electing shareholder* on the complete liquidation of a domestic corporation. Section 333 is not applicable to:

1. The loss of a "qualified electing shareholder." Such a shareholder may have a gain on some shares, subject to §333, and a loss on others, unaffected by §333. Regs. §1.333-4(a).
2. The gain or loss of a non-electing shareholder.
3. The gain or loss of an "excluded corporation," defined as a corporation which at any time between January 1, 1954, and the date of the adoption of the plan of liquidation owned stock possessing 50 percent or more of the total combined voting power of all classes of stock entitled to vote on the plan. Such a corporation may not elect to come under §333, and its stock

---

[19] Apparently the provision, enacted in 1938 primarily to permit the liquidation of personal holding companies that had been recently subjected to unexpectedly heavy tax burdens, was made temporary because of a fear that a permanent provision for tax-free corporate liquidations would encourage the organization of corporations to be subsequently liquidated. See Eaton, *infra*, at 12-13. Possibly the later adoption of the collapsible corporation provisions, by limiting the possibility of abuse, led Congress in 1954 to give §333 permanency.

See *infra*, Sec. 9.24, for special §333 liquidation rules dealing with personal holding companies under the Revenue Act of 1964.

See generally Eaton, Liquidation under Section 112(b)(7), 38 Va. L. Rev. 1 (1952); Krekstein, Section 112(b)(7) Liquidations, 55 Dick. L. Rev. 189 (1950); McGaffey, The Deferral of Gain in One-Month Liquidations, 19 Tax L. Rev. 327 (1964); Emanuel, Section 333 Liquidations: The Problems Created by Making Hasty Elections, 21 J. Tax. 340 (1964).

is not counted in determining whether sufficient other share-holders have elected to bring §333 into play for them.

    4. A collapsible corporation, subject to two exceptions.[19a]

When §333 is inapplicable, the recognition of the shareholder's gain or loss will be governed by whatever other provisions of the Code are applicable. Ordinarily, this will result in full recognition under §331-(a)(1) and §1002. If the shareholder is an "excluded corporation," however, its gain or loss will go unrecognized under §332 (*infra*, Sec. 9.41) if the liquidating corporation is an 80 percent subsidiary. See Rev. Rul. 56-212, 1956-1 C.B. 170.

    A "qualified electing shareholder" does not recognize any gain on shares owned by him when the plan of liquidation was adopted if the corporation has no post-1913 earnings and profits, *and* if he receives no money, or stock or securities acquired by the liquidating corporation after December 31, 1953. Otherwise, the "qualified electing shareholder" must recognize his gain, if any, to the extent of the greater of the following:

    1. His ratable share of the post-1913 earnings and profits (computed under accrual principles); or

    2. The sum of the money received by him and the fair market value of any stock or securities so received which were acquired by the liquidating corporation after December 31, 1953.[20]

In the case of a non-corporate shareholder, the gain which must be recognized under the standards just described is taxable as a dividend to the extent of the shareholder's ratable share of the post-1913 earnings and profits,[21] and the reminder, if any, of the gain is taxable as capital gain. In the case of a corporate shareholder, any recognized gain is treated as capital gain in its entirety.

    [19a] The exceptions are: (a) a collapsible corporation that meets the standards of §341(e) (*infra*, Sec. 10.07); and (b) a collapsible corporation to which §341(a) does not apply (e.g., one whose shareholders are exempt from §341(a) because the 3-year waiting period of §341(d)(3) has expired; see Rev. Rul. 57-491, 1957-2 C.B. 232; Rev. Rul. 63-114, 1963-1 C.B. 74; *infra*, Sec. 10.06).

    [20] Cancellation of a debt owed by the shareholder to the corporation has been held to constitute "money" received by him for this purpose, Walker, Exec. v. Tomlinson, —— F. Supp. ——, 10 AFTR 2d 6120 (M.D. Fla. 1962). For the meaning of "acquired," see Rev. Rul. 58-92, 1958-1 C.B. 176; Rev. Rul. 64-257, 1964-2 C.B. 91.

    [21] Although the shareholder's "ratable share of the earnings and profits" might seem to embrace the earnings and profits applicable to stock held by him that is not entitled to the benefits of §333, as well as the portion attributable to his §333 stock, the regulations made it clear that earnings and profits are taken into account only to the extent applicable to the latter. Regs.

These rules may be illustrated by an example:

If the shareholder's stock has an adjusted basis of $12,000 and he receives in liquidation cash in the amount of $1,000, post-1953 stock and securities worth $4,000, and other property worth $20,000, and if his ratable share of post-1913 earnings and profits is $2,500, the gain to be recognized under §333 (e) or (f) would be computed as follows:

1. Amount realized on liquidation:
   a. Cash — $ 1,000
   b. Post-1953 stock and securities — 4,000
   c. Other property — 20,000
   d. Total — $25,000
2. Less: adjusted basis of stock — 12,000
3. Gain realized — $13,000
4. Ratable share of post-1913 earnings and profits — $2,500
5. Sum of money and post-1953 stock and securities — $5,000
6. Gain recognized (line 3, but not in excess of the greater of lines 4 or 5) — $5,000

If the shareholder is an individual, $2,500 of the gain to be recognized would be treated as a dividend under §333(e)(1)[22] and the remaining $2,500 would be treated as short-term or long-term capital gain under §333(e)(2). If the shareholder is a corporation, the entire recognized gain ($5,000) would be taxed as short-term or long-term capital gain by virtue of §331(a)(1) and §1221. For other aspects of the computation of gain, see the examples in Regs. §1.333-4(c)(2).

When the shareholder receives cash in liquidation, §333's requirement that his gain be recognized *pro tanto* is easily understood: since it would not be feasible to give the money a basis less than its face value, the shareholder's gain must be recognized now or never. Thus, if the shareholders' basis for his stock is $10,000, and he receives in liquidation $25,000 in cash, there is no feasible way of postponing the recognition of gain until he spends the money; nor is there any reason to do so, since in an economic sense his gain has been as fully realized as it ever will be. When the shareholder receives other prop-

---

§1.333-4(b)(1). See also Regs. §1.333-4(b)(2), relating to the similarly ambiguous phrases "assets received by him" and "assets received by it" in §333 (e)(2) and (f)(1).

As to the status of current earnings and profits of a deficit corporation, see W. H. Weaver, 25 T.C. 1067, 1084 (1956), where current earnings and profits were treated (under another section of the Code) in the same way as accumulated post-1913 earnings and profits, although the statutory language was restricted to the latter.

[22] §333(e) uses the phrase "treated as a dividend" to insure application of the dividends received exclusion of §116.

erty, however, it is feasible to postpone the recognition of gain by giving the assets a basis equal to the basis of the stock surrendered, and §333 adopts this procedure as its underlying principle. An exception is made, however, for stock and securities acquired by the liquidating corporation after the "cut-off" date (December 31, 1953): these assets are thrown by §333 into the same category as money, requiring the immediate recognition of the shareholder's gain. This is done partly, no doubt, because such assets, at least if listed on the national stock exchanges or traded over the counter, may be the equivalent of money to the shareholder. Another reason is that, absent such a restriction, the corporation could, in advance of liquidation, convert its money into investment securities and thus frustrate §333's requirement that the shareholder's gain be recognized to the extent of any money received. This suspicion of manipulation probably accounts for the cut-off date in §333(e) and (f): an acquisition of stock or securities after December 31, 1953 is more likely than an acquisition before that date to be an anticipatory conversion of cash to avoid the recognition of gain by shareholders. Congress has yet to declare a general amnesty, however, by advancing the critical date.

While it is easy to explain why §333 treats money and post-1953 stock or securities as "boot," requiring the *pro tanto* recognition of gain, it is less easy to explain why post-1913 earnings and profits serve as an alternate measure of taxable gain, nor why the non-corporate shareholder must treat his gain as a taxable dividend to the extent of post-1913 earnings and profits. The difficulty stems from the fact that the shareholders are always free to liquidate under §331(a)(1), in which event the corporation's earnings and profits are ignored, and the shareholders' gain is the difference between the value of the liquidating distribution and the basis of the surrendered stock. Why does not §333 simply provide that if the shareholders so elect, the gain that would otherwise be taxed under §331(a)(1) shall go unrecognized (if they receive no money or post-1953 stock or securities) until they sell the assets? Perhaps it was thought that this would be too much of a good thing, since the recognition of gain on selling the assets is subject to judicious timing by the shareholder and to complete avoidance (by virtue of §1014) if the assets are retained until death; and that nonrecognition of the gain on liquidation under §333 must be limited or denied if the profits created by the assets in question had been subjected only to the corporate tax, without running the gauntlet of the progressive individual rates. On this theory, the full benefit of §333 would be confined to corporations that either had no income or had fully distributed their earnings and profits before liquidation. Another possible explanation lies in the history of §333: it was enacted to encourage the liquidation of personal holding companies (*supra*, note 19), whose shareholders would be required under §333 to report the accumulated earnings and profits as dividend income, and the corporation in return was allowed by §562(b) to deduct this amount in computing its undistributed income for the year of liquidation. Whatever the reason for using earnings and profits as an alternate to money and post-1953 stock or securities as a measure of taxation under §333, or for taxing the non-corporate shareholder on dividend income, the effect of these limitations is that §333 is used primarily by corporations holding appreciated assets, but having little or no money, post-1953 stock or securities, or post-1913 earnings and profits.

There are times, however, when §333 can be advantageously employed even though the corporation is not devoid of these troublesome characteristics. The corporation's cash and post-1953 stock and securities might be used to pay off corporate indebtedness before the liquidation. In many instances such action, even though it reduced the gain to be recognized by the shareholders on the liquidation, would be in accord with normal business practice. If the corporation were to pay off a mortgage under a plan contemplating that the shareholders would borrow against the assets immediately after the liquidation, however, the transaction might be treated as an indirect distribution of cash by the corporation, resulting in taxable gain under §333(e)(2) or (f)(1). (For an analogy, though in reverse, see §357-(b), discussed *supra*, Sec. 3.06.) Another possibility for reducing cash is to cause the corporation to purchase property other than stock or securities. Here again, the transaction might be disregarded for tax purposes (a) if the corporation bought property to be sold by the shareholders immediately after the liquidation, especially if the sale was prearranged, or (b) if the corporation bought property that the shareholders had previously intended or arranged to acquire after the liquidation. Still another possibility is the distribution of cash and post-1953 stock and securities to shareholders with losses or to tax-exempt shareholders, while distributing other property to the shareholders with realized gains. It is not impossible, however, that in the latter instance the Internal Revenue Service would contend that the transaction was in substance a pro rata distribution, followed by a rearrangement by the shareholders of their respective investments, though it can be argued in defense of the transaction that the shareholders seeking to take advantage of §333 will receive neither cash nor post-1953 stock or securities and hence are not frustrating the purpose to be served by §333(e)(2) or (f)(1), especially since their gain will be recognized on a sale of the assets received by them.

While it may be possible, within limits, for the corporation to assist its shareholders by reducing its money and post-1953 stock and securities in anticipation of a liquidation, there is little that can be done about post-1913 earnings and profits. This is because a distribution before the liquidation will be taxed as a dividend; for corporate shareholders this might be preferable to the recognition of gain on the liquidation itself (because the pre-liquidation distribution would give rise to the dividends received deduction of §243), but it would ordinarily not be helpful to non-corporate shareholders, since a pre-liquidation distribution would be taxed as heavily as the dividend portion of a liquidating distribution. Even more important, however, is the possibility that a substantial distribution before the formal liquidation would be treated, despite its label, as a liquidating distribution (*supra*, Sec. 9.02); in this event, the corporation might not have satisfied one of the conditions of §333(a)(2) — viz., "the transfer of all the property under the liquidation . . . within some one calendar month" — and the liquidation would then fall entirely outside the scope of §333.

Sec. 9.22.   Basis of property received

If a shareholder takes advantage of §333, the basis of any property (other than money) received by him is prescribed by §334(c). The underlying principle is that the basis of the shareholder's stock in the liquidating corporation is carried over and becomes the basis of the property received in exchange. More explicitly, §334(c) provides that the basis of the property received is the same as the basis of the stock, less any money received and plus any gain recognized under §333. To use as an example the liquidating distribution described *supra*, Sec. 9.21, the shareholder's basis for the property received would be computed as follows:

1. Adjusted basis of stock	$12,000
2. Less: money received	1,000
3. Remainder	$11,000
4. Plus: gain recognized (*supra*, p. 357, line 6)	5,000
5. Basis of property received	$16,000

The regulations provide that the basis thus determined ($16,000) is to be allocated among the assets received (other than money) in proportion to their fair market values. Since the shareholder received post-1953 stock and securities worth $4,000 and other property worth $20,000, the total basis of $16,000 would be allocated in the proportion 4:20, so that the post-1953 stock and securities would have a basis of $2,667 (4/24ths of $16,000) and the other property a basis of $13,333 (20/24ths of $16,000).[23]

As is ordinarily the case when the basis of property given up in a nontaxable exchange is substituted for the basis of property received, §334(c) has as its purpose the recognition, when the assets are sold or otherwise disposed of, of the gain that went unrecognized at the time of the liquidation. Because a §333 liquidation is a "closed" rather than "open" transaction (*supra*, Sec. 9.03), however, the character of the gain or loss ultimately realized by the shareholder on the distributed assets depends upon whether they are capital or ordinary assets in his hands, and on whether his disposition of them is a "sale or exchange" under §1222. Thus, in Osenbach v. Commissioner, 198 F.2d 235, 42 AFTR 355 (4th Cir. 1952), gain realized by the shareholder on collecting claims that had been distributed to him in a §333 liquidation was taxed as ordinary income, although a substantial portion of it would have been taxed as capital gain at the time the claims were distributed to him had the transaction been a normal §331(a)(1) liquidation.[24]

Under the *Osenbach* principle, §333 may be less advantageous where the shareholders intend to sell or otherwise dispose of the corporation's assets than a normal liquidation under §331(a)(1) followed by sale or collection, even though §333 permits deferral of the shareholder's tax until actual receipt of money or its equivalent, while under §331 the liquidation itself is the taxable event. Thus, if a one-man corporation holds assets valued at $100,000, consisting of inventory worth $75,000 and investment property worth $25,000, and if the shareholder's basis for his stock is $80,000, a §333 liquidation

---

[23] Regs. §1.334-2; Ralph R. Garrow, 43 T.C. 890 (1965). See Rev. Rul. 66-81, 1966-14 I.R.B. p.9 (requiring part of basis to be allocated to good will). Although §334(c) says nothing about liabilities, the regulations contain provisions for adjusting the basis of the property received if the shareholder assumes, or takes property subject to, liabilities. Regs. §1.334-2; see also Rev. Rul. 95, 1953-1 C.B. 162, and, for analogous provisions, §1031(d). Note §1223(1) for "tacking" the holding period of the shareholder's stock to the acquired assets.

[24] *Supra,* Sec. 9.03. See also Ralph R. Garrow, *supra* note 23; Acro Mfg. Co. v. Commissioner, 334 F.2d 40, 14 AFTR 2d 5106 (6th Cir. 1964) (§332 liquidation).

It is arguable that post-liquidation gain in an *Osenbach*-type case might be characterized as capital gain by an extension of Arrowsmith v. Commissioner, 344 U.S. 6, 42 AFTR 649 (1952), although the courts have not as yet applied *Arrowsmith* to closed liquidations. See Campagna v. United States, 290 F.2d 682, 7 AFTR 2d 1358 (2d Cir. 1961); and Grill v. United States, 303 F.2d 922, 9 AFTR 2d 1728 (Ct. Cl. 1962).

(assuming no earnings and profits) will be nontaxable and will result in a basis of $60,000 and $20,000 for the inventory and other
property, respectively. On later sales of these assets, assuming no
change in values, the shareholder will realize $15,000 of ordinary in-
come on the inventory (if it retains its character as such in his hands)
and $5,000 of capital gain on the other property. Had he not elected
§333, however, the liquidation would have produced capital gain of
$20,000, and, under §334(a), a stepped-basis equal to their market
values for the inventory and other property, with no later gain when
these assets were sold.

Sec. 9.23. The election and other conditions of §333

As stated earlier, §333 is applicable only to the gain of a "qualified electing shareholder." We must now turn to the meaning of this
term and to the other conditions that bring §333 into play.

1. "Qualified electing shareholder." Section 333 lays down these
conditions to becoming a "qualified electing shareholder":

a. The shareholder must own stock when the plan of liquidation is adopted and must elect under §333 within 30 days thereafter. The time limit may be troublesome for a publicly-held
corporation, especially since some shareholders may be unwilling
to vote for liquidation unless they can be assured that §333 will
be applicable. Because the election is a consent to have gain
realized on the liquidation treated in the manner prescribed by
§333, the regulations properly provide that the actual owner of
the stock, and not a mere record holder, must make the election.
The election is made on Form 964, which may be executed by
the shareholder's agent or attorney if specifically authorized to
do so.

b. The shareholder must not be an "excluded corporation"
— one which, at any time between January 1, 1954 and the date
the plan of liquidation is adopted, owned stock possessing 50
percent or more of the total combined voting power of all classes
of stock entitled to vote on the adoption of the plan.[25]

c. If the shareholder is not a corporation, he will qualify only
if elections are filed by noncorporate shareholders who own stock,
when the plan is adopted, possessing at least 80 percent of the
total combined voting power of the noncorporate-owned stock
entitled to vote on the adoption of the plan.

[25] Note that §333(b) looks to "stock entitled to vote on the adoption of
such plan [of liquidation]," thus taking in stock that cannot vote for directors
but can, either by charter or under local law, vote on the plan. In point of fact,
the corporation's charter or local law, or both, ordinarily designate the stock
that may vote on *dissolution,* but say nothing about a vote on *liquidation.* See
16 Fletcher on Corporations §7968. In referring to "stock entitled to vote on
the adoption of such plan of liquidation," §333(c)(1) may mean stock entitled
to vote on dissolution, though this is not entirely clear. See also Regs. §1.337-
2(b), which seems similarly to confuse liquidation with dissolution.

d. If the shareholder is a corporation, it will qualify only if elections are filed by corporate shareholders who own stock, when the plan is adopted, possessing at least 80 percent of the total combined voting power of the corporate-owned stock (other than stock owned by an "excluded corporation") entitled to vote on the adoption plan.

As the foregoing indicates, corporate and non-corporate shareholders are taken separately; one group may make use of §333 even though the other group rejects it. Moreover, a shareholder may elect to come under §333 even though his stock cannot vote on the adoption of the plan of liquidation, but his election will be effective only if enough *voting* stock of his group (corporate or non-corporate) makes similar elections. Thus, the right of a shareholder to employ §333 depends upon the willingness of his fellow shareholders to file elections. The history of §333 does not reveal the reason for this application of the democratic process to tax liability, under which shareholders who have a financial stake in §333 may fail to qualify because other shareholders who do not care whether §333 is applicable or not (*e.g.*, non-profit institutions, shareholders who will have a loss on the liquidation, shareholders who intend to sell their stock before the liquidation occurs, etc.) fail to file elections under §333. No doubt the interested shareholder may properly solicit the apathetic ones to elect; query the result if he paid them to do so.

2. *Mechanics and effect of the election.* Rigorous attention to the formalities of an election (e.g., timely filing of the proper forms) is extremely important under §333; although the Commissioner has discretion to waive use of the wrong form, it has been held that he cannot be compelled to do so.[26]

Because noncorporate shareholders must treat gain realized on the liquidation as a dividend to the extent of earnings and profits, a §333 liquidation may be more costly than an ordinary §331 liquidation. Hence an election may be a major blunder if an error is made in computing earnings and profits. In Meyer's Estate v. Commissioner, 200 F.2d 592, 42 AFTR 1005 (5th Cir. 1952), the shareholders were allowed to withdraw their elections upon discovering that the corporation's earnings and profits were not $80,000, as believed when the elections were filed, but $900,000. (The shareholders had made the common mistake of assuming that earned surplus was identical with

---

[26] Lambert v. Commissioner, 338 F.2d 4, 14 AFTR 2d 5862 (2d Cir. 1964); see also Virginia E. Ragen, 33 T.C. 906 (1960). Occasionally a taxpayer has succeeded in getting a private bill enacted to extricate him from a procedural error; see 103 Cong. Rec. 15,912 (1957) (accountant's failure to file form on time).

earnings and profits, *supra*, Sec. 5.03); the discrepancy was caused by earnings and profits "inherited" in a tax-free corporate reorganization in an earlier year, but not reflected in earned surplus.) The regulations, however, provide that the election is irrevocable, and other courts have been less lenient than *Meyer's Estate* in cases involving an improvident election.[27]

3. Plan of liquidation. Section 333(a)(1) requires that the liquidation be pursuant to a plan of liquidation adopted on or after June 22, 1954.[28]

4. Complete cancellation and redemption of stock. Section 333-(a)(2) provides that the distribution must be "in complete cancellation or redemption of all the stock." Despite this requirement, Rev. Rul. 54-518, 1954-2 C.B. 142, permits the retention of the liquidating corporation's charter (to protect the corporate name against appropriation), so long as the corporation distributes all of its assets and goes into a state of quiescence.

5. Transfer of all property in one calendar month. Section 333-(a)(2) provides that the transfer of all the corporation's property under the liquidation must occur "within some one calendar month." No reason comes to mind for this insistence on haste, which is, however, somewhat alleviated by a tolerant attitude in the regulations toward arrangements for paying unascertained and contingent liabilities.[29] Some relief also results from the fact that the month of distribution need not be the month in which the plan of liquidation was adopted, as well as from the fact that dissolution under state law is not necessary. Regs. §1.333-1(b)(1) and (b)(2).

Sec. 9.24. Special rules for liquidation of certain personal holding companies

The Revenue Act of 1964 substantially tightened the personal holding company provisions (*supra*, Sec. 6.20), and special rules were added by §333(g) to permit the liquidation of corporations which become personal holding companies because of these changes (so-called

---

[27] Regs. §1.333-2(b)(1); Raymond v. United States, 269 F.2d 181, 4 AFTR 2d 5992 (6th Cir. 1962); Shull v. Commissioner, 30 T.C. 821 (1958). The *Shull* case was reversed on appeal, 271 F.2d 447, 4 AFTR 2d 5740 (4th Cir. 1959), to permit consideration of a second line of defense (that dissolution of the corporation had occurred prior to a purported adoption of a plan of liquidation, so that the 30-day requirement of §333 was not met), which was rejected by the Tax Court, 34 T.C. 533 (1960), but upheld on a second appeal, 291 F.2d 680, 8 AFTR 2d 5010 (4th Cir. 1961).

[28] For the term "plan of liquidation," see Knox v. Commissioner, 323 F.2d 84, 12 AFTR 2d 5616 (5th Cir. 1964); *infra*, Sec. 9.64.

[29] Regs. §1.333-1(b)(1); Meyer's Estate, 15 T.C. 850, 862-863, reversed on other grounds, *supra;* Rev. Rul. 56-286, 1956-1 C.B. 172.

"would have been" corporations). In general, if such a corporation liquidates under §333 before 1967, securities distributed by it will be taken into account in computing the shareholder's gain only if they were acquired after 1962 (rather than after 1953). Moreover, the shareholder's gain will be taxed as capital gain, even if attributable to corporate earnings and profits, rather than as a dividend. The rules for liquidations of such corporations after 1966 are also liberalized, but not so substantially.[30]

One aspect of the liquidation rules of §333(g) bears special note, the "anti-blunder" provision of §333(g)(4). If a shareholder elects the provisions of §333(g) in the mistaken belief that the corporation was a "would have been" personal holding company, the election will be disregarded if the facts prove otherwise.

Part C.   Non-Recognition of Parent Corporation's Gain or Loss on Liquidating a Subsidiary: §332

Sec. 9.40.   Introductory

As has been seen (*supra*, Sec. 9.01), §331(a)(1) establishes the "general rule" that a complete liquidation of a corporation is to be treated by the shareholder as a sale or exchange of his stock, and §1002 establishes the principle that the entire amount of the gain or loss on the sale or exchange of property is to be recognized "except as otherwise provided in this subtitle." An important exception to the general rule that the shareholder's gain or loss is to be recognized on a complete liquidation is §332, providing that under certain conditions no gain or loss shall be recognized by a parent corporation on the receipt of property distributed in complete liquidation of a subsidiary. This non-recognition provision is coupled with a basis provision, §334(b), which ordinarily requires the parent corporation to take over the distributed assets at the subsidiary's basis.[31]

The prototype of §332 came into the Internal Revenue Code in 1935; Congress hoped that it would encourage the simplification of

---

[30] See *supra*, Sec. 6.26.

[31] See generally, Tobolowsky, Problems in Liquidating Acquired Corporations, 41 Taxes 767 (1963); Wolfram, Tax Consequences of the Liquidation of a Subsidiary, 40 Taxes 1219 (1962); Tobolowsky, Problems in Effecting Complete Liquidation of a Subsidiary, 14 N.Y.U. Inst. on Fed. Tax. 729 (1956); Lewis and Schapiro, Sale of Corporate Business: Stock or Assets? *ibid.* 745; Piper, Combining Parent Subsidiary Corporations, 16 *ibid.* 375 (1958). For discussions of §112(b)(6) of the 1939 Code, the predecessor of §332, see Busterud, The Liquidation of Subsidiaries Under Section 112(b)(6), 58 Yale L.J. 1050 (1949); Colgan and Molloy, Tax-Free Liquidations of Corporate Subsidiaries Under Section 112(b)(6) of the Internal Revenue Code, 4 Tax L. Rev. 306 (1949).

complex corporate financial structures by permitting the liquidation of unnecessary subsidiaries without recognition of gain. Since statutory mergers can be accomplished tax-free, *infra*, Ch. 12, it is not surprising that Congress was willing to extend the same privilege to the "practical" or "upstream" merger that results when a subsidiary corporation is liquidated into its parent. Moreover, since the parent corporation ordinarily "inherits" its liquidated subsidiary's earnings and profits and other tax attributes under §381(a)(1) (*infra*, Ch. 13), the liquidation of a subsidiary is less appropriate as a taxable occasion than the liquidation of other corporations.

Since §334(b) provides that a parent corporation on liquidating a subsidiary under §332 must ordinarily take over the assets at the subsidiary's basis, a later sale of the assets by the parent will (assuming no change in values) require the recognition by it of the gain or loss that would have been recognized by the subsidiary had it made the sale. This result is in accord with §332's underlying assumption that the complete liquidation of a subsidiary works a change of form rather than of substance. But it will be noted that the parent's basis for its stock — representing its investment in the subsidiary — is not taken into account, either when the subsidiary is liquidated or when the assets thus acquired are ultimately sold by the parent. Thus, §332's assumption that the elimination of the corporate veil between parent and subsidiary should have no tax significance, though having much to commend it, necessarily has the effect of obliterating forever the parent's gain or loss on its investment in the subsidiary. This fact is illustrated by the following examples:

	A	B
Parent's basis for stock of subsidiary	$100,000	$100,000
Subsidiary's basis for its assets	40,000	135,000
Fair market value of subsidiary's assets	75,000	125,000

In Example A, the parent has suffered a real loss of $25,000 (basis of stock less value of liquidating distribution), but it will go unrecognized, and on a sale of the assets (assuming no later change in value) the parent will recognize gain of $35,000. In example B, on the other hand, the parent's gain of $25,000 will go unrecognized, and a sale of the assets by the parent will produce a loss of $10,000.[32] Other com-

---

[32] These results under §332 and §334(b)(1) may be somewhat mitigated by the fact that under §381(a)(1) the parent will inherit the tax attributes of the subsidiary. In Example A, there might be a loss carryover from the subsidiary, resulting from its earlier operations in which the investment of $100,000 was pared down to assets with a basis of only $40,000; and in Example B there would probably be earnings and profits resulting from successful operations in the past. But it would be pure accident if these offsetting tax ad-

binations of basis and value are of course possible, but all would have in common a disregard of the parent's gain or loss on its investment in the subsidiary in order to treat the liquidation as a matter of form only. As will be seen, most of the problems under §332 arise from attempts by the parent corporation or the government, as the case may be, to escape from §332 — which at least in form is not an elective provision — in order to recognize the parent's gain or loss on its investment when the subsidiary is liquidated.

Sec. 9.41.   Conditions of §332

Section 332 provides that no gain or loss shall be recognized on the receipt by a corporation of property distributed in complete liquidation of another corporation, provided (1) the corporation receiving the property owns a specified amount of the distributing corporation's stock; (2) there is a complete cancellation or redemption of all of the stock of the distributing corporation; and (3) the transfer of the property occurs within certain time limits. It has been held that the term "property" as used in §332 includes cash, so that a liquidation in which nothing but money is distributed is within §332.[33] Although §334(b)(1), requiring the parent to carry over the subsidiary's basis for the distributed assets, cannot be applied to a distribution of money, the cited cases point out that the subsidiary will have recognized gain or loss on disposing of its assets, so that the function of §334(b)(1) has already been discharged. If an all-cash distribution did not qualify under §332, there would be an unwarranted disparity between a liquidation that followed a sale of assets and one that preceded the sale.

If the parent corporation does not intend to continue the subsidiary's business (*e.g.*, if the subsidiary's assets are sold, by either the subsidiary or the parent, and the parent thereupon devotes the proceeds of sale to a radically different line of business), the cases have divided on the applicability of §332. Judge Hand, in *Fairfield S.S. Corp. v. Commissioner*, said of §112(b)(6) of the 1939 Code

---

vantages and disadvantages counterbalanced the effects of §332 and §334(b)(1) with even the roughest degree of accuracy.

For characterization of the parent's gain or loss on the sale, see Acro Mfg. Co. v. Commissioner, 334 F.2d 40, 14 AFTR 2d 5106 (6th Cir. 1964).

[33] Tri-Lakes S.S. Co. v. Commissioner, 146 F.2d 970, 33 AFTR 456 (6th Cir. 1945); International Investment Corp. v. Commissioner, 11 T.C. 678 (1948) (overruling an earlier Tax Court case to the contrary), aff'd per curiam, 175 F.2d 772, 38 AFTR 124 (3d Cir. 1949); see also Edwards Motor Transit Co., ¶64,317 P-H Memo T.C. (cancellation of parent's debt in merger of parent into subsidiary did not cause gain to parent).

See Friedman, All Cash Distributions Under Section 112(b)(6), 8 Tax L. Rev. 369 (1953).

(the predecessor of §332) that its "underlying purpose was to permit the union in one corporate form of a single business or venture which had theretofore been managed by two corporations" and that "the privilege assumes that the business shall continue and that the liquidation shall not be merely a step in winding it up."[34] In the *International Investment Corp.* case (*supra*, note 33), however, the Tax Court rejected the theory that there must be a "continuation of the precise business of the liquidated subsidiary by the parent," though hinting that §332 might be inapplicable if (as in the *Fairfield S.S. Co.* case) both the subsidiary and the parent were liquidated.

If the subsidiary is insolvent, and its shareholders receive nothing on the liquidation, §332 is inapplicable since there has been no "receipt by a corporation of property distributed in complete liquidation of another corporation." Regs. §1.332-2(b). In this event, the shareholders may deduct their loss on the worthless stock under §165(g). This principle was applied in Commissioner v. Spaulding Bakeries, Inc., 252 F.2d 693, 1 AFTR 2d 986 (2d Cir. 1958), where a parent corporation that owned all the common and non-voting preferred stock of a subsidiary received assets in liquidation with a value less than the liquidating preference of the preferred stock. The court held that §332 was inapplicable, on the theory that nothing was received by the parent in respect to its common stock. An alternative approach would be to disregard the common stock because its equity was zero, cf. Helvering v. Alabama Asphaltic Limestone Co., 315 U.S. 179, 28 AFTR 567 (1942), and to treat the preferred stock as "all [the corporation's] stock" under §332(b)(3), in which event the parent's gain or loss on the preferred stock would go unrecognized under §332.

The effect on the parent of receiving property from its subsidiary in payment of a debt, rather than in liquidation of its stock, is discussed *infra*, Sec. 9.42.

---

[34] 157 F.2d 321, 323, 35 AFTR 117 (2d Cir. 1946), cert. denied, 329 U.S. 774 (1946).

The *Fairfield S.S. Corp.* case erroneously assumed that §332 is applicable to the subsidiary's gain or loss, whereas it is confined to the parent's gain or loss; and an addendum to the opinion fails to clear up the confusion. See Kurz, A Critique of the Fairfield Steamship Case, 25 Taxes 612 (1947); Tax Notes, 32 A.B.A.J. 516 (1946). But the court's view that the provision was enacted to deal with continuations, rather than windings-up, of the subsidiary's business was well-founded, even though the court wrongly thought this was dispositive of the issue before it.

In Acro Mfg. Co. v. Commissioner, *supra* note 32, where the parent corporation immediately sold the assets of its liquidated subsidiary, the court held that the character of those assets did not carry over from the subsidiary to the parent. If the court had applied the *Fairfield S.S. Co.* principle, the

Turning now to the conditions mentioned above for the application of §332:

1. 80 percent stock ownership. Section 332(b)(1) provides that §332 shall apply only if the parent corporation owns (a) stock possessing at least 80 percent of the total combined voting power of all classes of stock entitled to vote, and (b) at least 80 percent of the total number of shares of all other classes of stock (except nonvoting stock which is limited and preferred as to dividends);[35] and that this amount of stock must be owned on the date the plan of liquidation is adopted and at all times thereafter until the receipt of the property. In view of this condition, can §332 be avoided[36] by a sale of stock, either before the plan of liquidation is adopted or between that date and the receipt of the property, so as to reduce the parent's ownership below the 80 percent bench mark? In Commissioner v. Day & Zimmermann, Inc., 151 F. 2d 517, 34 AFTR 343 (3d Cir. 1945), such a sale by the parent for the sole purpose of avoiding §332 was held to be effective. The shares were offered for sale at a public auction after the liquidation had been decided on, and were purchased by the parent corporation's treasurer at "a fair price under all the circumstances" with his own funds and at his own risk and without "being directed by anyone to bid for the shares." Since the subsidiary was about to be liquidated and the amount of the liquidating distribution (to be paid in cash) could be estimated with reasonable accuracy, it is surprising that the transaction was given effect for tax purposes.[37]

If a corporation with 80 percent or more of the stock of another corporation can avoid §332 by reducing its holdings to less than 80

---

liquidation would have been a taxable event, giving the parent a basis for the distributed assets under §334(a) equal to their fair market value.

[35] For problems in identifying the types of stock referred to in §332(b)(1) and in computing voting power, see *infra*, Sec. 13.41.

[36] The parent might wish to avoid §332 in order to take a loss on the liquidation, or it might be willing to recognize gain to get a stepped-up basis for the assets and to forestall inheriting the subsidiary's earnings and profits.

[37] Whatever criticism may be directed against the *Day & Zimmermann, Inc.* case as an interpretation of §112(b)(6) of the 1939 Code, a statutory amendment in 1954 tends to support it as an interpretation of §332 of the 1954 Code. Under §112(b)(6), the parent not only was required to own at least 80 percent of the subsidiary's stock from the date the plan of liquidation was adopted until the property was received by it (as required by §332), but it was also forbidden to dispose of any stock during the intervening period. Because of the latter provision, a disposition by the parent of even an insignificant part of its holdings made §112(b)(6) of the 1939 Code inapplicable to the liquidation. Thus, in Avco Mfg. Corp. 25 T.C. 975, 979 (1956) (N. Acq.), the taxpayer successfully avoided §112(b)(6) by selling 200 shares of its subsidiary's stock for about $1,300, thus reducing its proportionate ownership from 90.88 percent to 90.85 percent and clearing the way for recognizing a loss of about $6.8 million. See also Granite Trust Co. v. United States, 238 F.2d 670, 50 AFTR

percent, does it follow that a corporation with less than 80 percent can bring itself within §332 by increasing its holdings? There is clearly no rule that the requisite 80 percent must have been acquired at one time. But what if some shares are acquired immediately before a liquidation solely to qualify? The requisite 80 percent ownership must exist "on the date of the adoption of the plan of liquidation." Neither §332 nor the regulations thereunder, however, define the term "date of the adoption of the plan." If the shareholders of the subsidiary adopt a resolution authorizing the directors to liquidate, the date of the resolution will probably be controlling in ordinary circumstances, but if the parent corporation has previously decided to liquidate the subsidiary and thereafter acquires additional shares solely in order to meet the 80 percent requirement, it may be held that the plan of liquidation was informally adopted before the additional shares were acquired. If the adoption of the plan is "pre-dated" in this fashion, the acquisition of additional shares, even though it occurs before the formal meeting of the subsidiary's shareholders, will be too late.[38]

2. Complete cancellation or redemption of all the subsidiary's stock in accordance with a plan of liquidation. Section 332 is applicable only if the subsidiary distributes property "in complete cancellation or redemption of all its stock." Ordinarily this requirement is satisfied without any difficulty, since in most cases the corporation distributes all of its assets, calls in and cancels the stock certificates,

763 (1st Cir. 1956), endorsing the same practice; one of the transactions which successfully reduced the parent's stock ownership was a contribution of two shares, worth about $130, to a charitable institution which surrendered them to the subsidiary for a liquidating distribution of cash four days later. The government argued, unsuccessfully. that this transaction was not a gift of stock by the parent, but an anticipatory assignment of cash. When the 1954 Code was enacted, the 80 percent rule was carried forward without change, but the no-reduction-in-ownership condition was dropped "with the view to limiting the elective features of the section." S. Rep. No. 1622, 83d Cong., 2d Sess., p. 255 (1954). A possible negative inference is that §332 is still elective by virtue of the 80 percent rule, i.e., that Congress in effect endorsed the *Day & Zimmermann. Inc.* case for post-1954 liquidations. See *Granite Trust Co. v. United States. supra.* The principal argument to the contrary is that if Congress intended §332 to be elective, it would have provided explicitly for an option in the parent corporation, instead of requiring it to resort to the hocus-pocus of selling some of its stock.

[38] In the *Granite Trust Co.* case, *supra* note 37, the government argued that the plan of liquidation was adopted at least a month before the formal meeting of the shareholders, in the form of a "definitive determination" by the parent corporation to cause the subsidiary's liquidation, but the court did not find it necessary to pass on this contention. See Regs. §1.337-2(b), to the effect that the date of a plan of liquidation is not necessarily the date of the shareholders' meeting, discussed *infra,* Sec. 9.64.

For efforts to achieve nonrecognition of gain on the liquidation of a subsidiary of which the parent owns less than 80 percent of the stock, see *infra.* Ch. 12.

and dissolves under state law. But the regulations provide that a dissolution is not required, and even that the corporation may retain assets in a nominal amount to preserve its legal existence; and it may be that some informality in the liquidating process, though not to be recommended, will be tolerated, as it is under §331(a)(1).[39] As to the requirement of a "plan" of liquidation, §332(b)(2) explicitly provides that a shareholders' resolution authorizing the distribution of all the corporation's assets in complete cancellation or redemption of all the stock "shall be considered an adoption of a plan of liquidation" if the transfer of all the property occurs within the taxable year, even though no time for completing the transfer is specified in the resolution. The term "plan of liquidation" is not necessarily restricted to a shareholders' resolution, however; the statutory requirement should be satisfied by a resolution of the directors if under state law they have the power to liquidate the corporation, and the government has on occasion argued that the term "plan" embraces a determination by the controlling shareholder to liquidate, even though not reduced to writing.[40]

3. *Timing of the distribution.* As already stated, §332(b)(2) provides that the shareholders' resolution authorizing the distribution will be considered an adoption of a plan of liquidation, even though it specifies no time for completing the transfer, if the transfer is in fact completed within the taxable year. Otherwise, the plan of liquidation must provide for the transfer of all the property within 3 years from the close of the taxable year in which the first distribution is made; and the transfer must be completed during this period. If the transfer is not completed within this period, or if the parent corporation does not remain qualified until the transfer is completed, §332 is retroactively inapplicable to all distributions under the plan. Because of this possibility, the Internal Revenue Service may require the taxpayer to post a bond or to waive the statute of limitations on assessment and collection, or both, in order to insure assessment and collection of all income taxes attributable to the distributed property. §332(b), second sentence; Regs. §1.332-4.

The provisions of §332(b)(2) and (3) suggest the possibility of avoiding §332, when the taxpayer so desires, by specifying no limit in the shareholders' resolution, spreading the transfers out over more

[39] Regs. §1.332-2(c); *supra,* Sec. 9.02; see also Rev. Rul. 54-518, 1954-2 C.B. 142, taking a similar position under §333. There appears to be a conflict between Regs. §1.332-2(c) and the requirement of §332(b) of a "complete cancellation or redemption of all the stock."

[40] See Rev. Rul. 58-391, 1958-2 C.B. 139; *supra* note 38.

than one taxable year, and adopting no other formal plan of liquidation. In Burnside Veneer Co. v. Commissioner, 167 F.2d 214, 36 AFTR 929 (6th Cir. 1948), however, it was held that the statute was applicable if the liquidation in fact was completed within the 3-year period, on the ground that the resolutions of the shareholders and directors and the local corporation law contemplated a prompt liquidation. In another case, the Tax Court said: "There is no need for any formal plan of liquidation if one can be discovered from the circumstances surrounding the liquidation."[41] These were cases in which the taxpayer was seeking to avoid §332 on the ground that the arrangements for liquidation did not constitute a sufficiently formal plan of liquidation to meet the statutory requirements. Had the courts acceded to the taxpayers' arguments, §332 would have become an almost entirely optional provision. If it is the Commissioner who objects to the absence of a formal plan of liquidation, however, deficiencies in the paper work may be taken more seriously.

What if the plan provides, in accordance with §332(b)(3), that the liquidation is to be completed within 3 years, but the distributions are deliberately spread out over a longer period? The final clause of §332(b)(3) states that if the transfer is not completed within the 3-year period, none of the distributions will be considered distributions in complete liquidation. While this clause can be used by the government to disqualify a non-conforming transaction, it is not so clear that the taxpayer could avail itself of a deliberate delay that serves no purpose. The parent might be held, in such a case, to have received a "constructive" distribution despite its willingness to wait until after the prescribed 3-year period for an actual distribution.[42]

Sec. 9.42.   Effect of subsidiary indebtedness to its parent

Section 332 provides for nonrecognition of gain or loss when property is distributed to a parent corporation in complete liquidation of its 80 percent subsidiary. If the subsidiary is indebted to the parent at the time of the liquidation, its property may be transferred to satisfy indebtedness, as well as in cancellation of its stock. As noted supra, Sec. 9.41, if the subsidiary is insolvent, so that there is

[41] International Investment Co. v. Commissioner, supra note 33. See also Service Co. v. Commissioner, 165 F.2d 75, 36 AFTR 645 (8th Cir. 1948), holding that the parent corporation could not use its failure to comply with the record-keeping provisions of Regs. §1.332-6 to avoid the application of §332, on the ground that these requirements were "promulgated primarily for the protection of the revenue, not for the advantage of the taxpayer."

[42] Cf. David T. Grubbs, 39 T.C. 42 (1962); for a related problem under §337, see infra, Sec. 9.64, note 78.

no distribution with respect to its stock, the parent's loss is not subject to §332. But even in the case of a solvent subsidiary, a distribution to the parent in its capacity as creditor rather than as shareholder permits recognition of gain or loss thereon by the parent.[43]

Before 1954, the Service took the position that the subsidiary recognized gain or loss on such a transfer, if it satisfied its indebtedness to the parent with appreciated or depreciated property.[44] Because of difficulties in determining which of the subsidiary's assets were used to satisfy its indebtedness and which were distributed in exchange for the stock, however, the Service later ruled that it would not insist upon recognition of gain by the subsidiary if the parent executed a closing agreement agreeing to carry over the subsidiary's basis for all the transferred property. The 1954 Code has adopted this approach by providing in §332(c) that the subsidiary recognizes neither gain nor loss on transfers of property in satisfaction of indebtedness to its parent; and §334(b)(1) provides that the parent's basis for such property shall be the same as the subsidiary's.[45]

Because §332(c) applies only if the subsidiary is indebted to its parent "on the date of the adoption of the plan of liquidation," preplan transfers of appreciated or depreciated property in satisfaction of the subsidiary's debt to its parent will result in recognition of gain or loss to the sudsidiary, and will also confer on the parent a basis

[43] Regs. §1.332-7; Rev. Rul. 59-296, 1959-2 C.B. 87. In its report on §332 of the 1954 Code, the Senate Finance Committee said:
Unlike the provisions of . . . the House bill, [§332(c)] has no application as respects the tax treatment to the parent upon receipt of the asset in satisfaction of the indebtedness. In this connection, your committee intends that present law shall govern in the determining of the tax consquences of such transfer. (S. Rep. No. 1622, 83d Cong., 2d Sess., p. 256 (1954)).
For "present law," see Houston Natural Gas Corp. v. Commissioner, 173 F.2d 461, 37 AFTR 1137 (5th Cir. 1949).
If the subsidiary cannot satisfy its debt to the parent in full, the parent will have a bad debt deduction under §166(a) or a worthless security deduction under §165(g). *Supra,* Sec. 4.07.
Quaere whether the parent, if it wishes to bring the transfer of the subsidiary's assets under §332 (e.g., to inherit a loss carryover), could forgive the debt and thereby lay the foundation for a transfer of the subsidiary's assets in liquidation of the stock. See Stuetzer, Upstream Debts in Section 112(b)(6) Liquidations, 5 Tax L. Rev. 199, 209 (1950). Another possibility, if the subsidiary is indebted to the parent (or to a third party) in an amount exceeding the value of its assets, is that the debt will be treated as the equivalent of stock (on the ground that the creditors would take over the corporation in the event of a bankruptcy reorganization), thus bringing §332 into play for the creditor. But see the *Northern Coal & Dock Co.* case, *infra* note 44.

[44] I.T. 4109, 1952-2 C.B. 138 (gain); Northern Coal & Dock Co., 12 T.C. 42 (1949) (Acq.) (loss).

[45] Section 334(b)(1), carrying over the subsidiary's basis, is inapplicable to *Kimbell-Diamond* liquidations (*infra.* Sec. 9.44); in such cases, the parent's basis for the assets is presumably their fair market value. Section 332(c) itself is inapplicable to property transferred by an insolvent subsidiary, since nothing

for the property equal to its fair market value at the time of the transfer. If the subsidiary's anticipatory payment of its debts is an integral part of the plan of liquidation, however, it may result in a finding that the plan was adopted prior to the date of formal adoption.

Sec. 9.43.   Minority shareholders

Under §332, nonrecognition treatment applies only to the parent corporation's gain or loss on the liquidation. Minority shareholders must determine their gain or loss without regard to §332. Ordinarily such amounts will be recognized under §§1002 and 331(a)(1); but these shareholders may be entitled to elect nonrecognition treatment under §333.[46] It is also possible that minority shareholders may be entitled to nonrecognition treatment by virtue of the reorganization provisions of the Code. For example, if the liquidation of an 80 percent subsidiary takes the form of a statutory merger in which all of its assets are transferred to the parent, and the parent issues its stock to the subsidiary's minority shareholders as consideration for their ratable interest in the subsidiary's property, the transaction may constitute a tax-free reorganization under §368(a)(1)(A). In this event, neither the parent corporation nor the subsidiary's minority shareholders would recognize gain or loss.[47] Where the parent owns less than 80 percent of the subsidiary's outstanding stock, however, tax-free acquisitions of the subsidiary's assets by the parent and nonrecognition treatment for the minority shareholders face greater technical difficulties, with the tax results depending, it would seem, primarily on the form of the transaction. Thus in Rev. Rul. 54-396, 1954-2 C.B. 147, the Service ruled that acquisition of all the assets of a 79 percent owned subsidiary in exchange for the parent's stock, followed by a liquidation of the subsidiary, did not constitute a reorganization under §112(g)(1)(C) of the 1939 Code since the acquiring corporation, in substance, obtained only 21 percent of the subsidiary's assets in exchange for its stock, the balance being acquired as a liquidating distribution in exchange for the parent's 79 percent stock interest. To the same effect is Bausch & Lomb Optical Co. v. Commissioner, 267 F.2d 75, 3 AFTR 2d 1497 (2d Cir. 1959). These problems are discussed further infra, Sec. 12.21.

is distributed with respect to its stock; hence, the authorities cited supra note 44 are probably applicable.

The pre-1954 ruling mentioned in the text is Rev. Rul. 259, 1953-2 C.B. 55.

[46] Supra, Sec. 9.21; Rev. Rul. 56-212, 1956-1 C.B. 170.

[47] See §332(b), last sentence; Regs. §1.332-2(d) and (e).

For the possibility that the reorganization provisions do not apply to a §332 transaction in this situation, see infra, Sec. 12.21.

Sec. 9.44.   Basis of property received by parent corporation: §334(b)

1. In general, §334(b)(1). Upon the liquidation of a subsidiary under §332, the property received by the parent — with an exception to be noted hereafter — carries over the basis that the property had in the hands of the subsidiary under §334(b)(1). As already noted (*supra*, Sec. 9.40), this is one reason why parent corporations sometimes maneuver, ordinarily with little success, to remove a liquidation from the clutches of §332.

If the general rule of §334(b)(1), carrying over the subsidiary's basis, were rigorously applied, it would create an unjustified dichotomy between two otherwise similar methods of acquiring the assets of another corporation: if the purchasing corporation bought the assets from the second, its basis for them would be its cost under §1012; but if it acquired the assets by purchasing the stock of the second corporation and liquidating it, it would have to carry over the second corporation's basis. This inherited basis might, of course, be substantially more or less than the price paid for the stock, since the price reflects the market value of the assets rather than the acquired corporation's basis for them.

For this reason, in a line of pre-1954 cases the courts adopted the position that the purchase by one corporation of the stock of another corporation in order to obtain its assets through a prompt liquidation should be treated as a single transaction, *viz.*, a purchase of the assets, producing a basis equal to their cost rather than a carryover of basis. In the leading case, Kimbell-Diamond Milling Co. v. Commissioner, 14 T.C. 74, aff'd per curiam, 187 F.2d 718, 40 AFTR 328 (5th Cir. 1951), cert. denied, 342 U.S. 827 (1951), the "single transaction" doctrine was applied at the behest of the Commissioner, so as to deny the purchasing corporation the right to carry over a basis in excess of the price paid for the stock; but the *Kimbell-Diamond* principle has been applied to give the acquiring corporation the benefit of its cost, where that exceeded the acquired corporation's basis.[48]

2. The Kimbell-Diamond exception, §334(b)(2). Against this background, in 1954 Congress enacted §334(b)(2) to incorporate

---

[48] See Montana-Dakota Utilities Co., 25 T.C. 408 (1955) (Acq.); Kanawha Gas & Utilities Co. v. Commissioner, 214 F.2d 685, 45 AFTR 1805 (5th Cir. 1954); North American Service Co., Inc., 33 T.C. 677 (1960) (Acq.); Georgia-Pacific Corp. v. United States, 264 F.2d 161, 3 AFTR 2d 778 (5th Cir. 1959); Orr Mills, 30 T.C. 150 (1958); United States v. M.O.J. Corp., 274 F.2d 713, 5 AFTR 2d 535 (5th Cir. 1960); United States v. Mattison, 273 F.2d 13, 4 AFTR 2d 5844 (9th Cir. 1959); Long Island Water Corp., 36 T.C. 377 (1961); E.T.

"rules effectuating principles derived from Kimbell-Diamond Milling Co." S. Rep. No. 1622, 83d Cong., 2d Sess., p. 257 (1954). Section 334(b)(2) provides that the parent corporation's basis for property acquired in a §332 transaction is the cost of the stock (with certain adjustments), rather than the subsidiary's basis for the assets, if at least 80 percent of the stock was acquired by "purchase" (as defined) during a period of not more than 12 months, and if distribution is pursuant to a plan of complete liquidation under §332 adopted not more than two years after the purchase.[49] Of these conditions, the "purchase" requirement will probably cause the most trouble, since §334-(b)(3) defines this term to exclude: (a) transactions in which the basis of the stock carries over from the transferor (*e.g.*, an acquisition by gift, contribution to capital, or tax-free reorganization) or is determined under §1014 (inherited property); (b) acquisitions of stock in exchanges to which §351 applies; and (c) acquisitions from "related persons" within the meaning of §318(a) (*supra*, Sec. 7.21). Thus, the statutory *Kimbell-Diamond* rule applies primarily to stock acquired by the parent corporation from unrelated persons in transactions that, as to them, are taxable events (*i.e.*, in which their gain or loss on the transfer is recognized). In keeping with the theory that a §334(b)(2) transaction is in substance a purchase of the assets by the acquiring corporation, it does not inherit the liquidating corporation's earnings and profits or other tax attributes, as it would in a "normal" liquidation of a subsidiary by its parent. On the other hand, the "purchase of assets" theme is not carried to the point of holding that the liquidating corporation realizes gain or loss on a hypothetical sale of its assets to the acquiring corporation.[50]

Griswold, 45 T.C. 463 (1966); see also Frederick Steel Co., 42 T.C. 13 (1964) (doctrine not applied where both corporations were under common control).

[49] See Regs. §1.334-1(c)(3), stating that the two-year period does not begin to run until after the last purchase in a series of acquisitions which occur within the one-year period.

On §334(b)(2), see generally Lewis and Schapiro, *supra,* note 31, at 750-60; Mansfield, The Kimbell-Diamond Situation: Basis to the Purchaser in Connection with Liquidation, 13 N.Y.U. Inst. on Fed. Tax. 623 (1955); Paulston, How to Plan and Execute the Sale of a Corporate Business Under the Internal Revenue Code of 1954, 1956 So. Calif. Tax Inst. 383; Colborn et al., Buying and Selling a Corporate Business, 10 West. Res. L. Rev. 123 (1959); O'Malley, The Pitfalls of Section 334(b)(2) Liquidations and How To Avoid Them, 24 J. Tax. 138 (1966); Sheppard, Depreciation recapture: some practical problems in working with Section 1245, 24 J. Tax. 194, 196 (1966); Valentine, Some Unexpected Tax Results Where a Business is Acquired by Purchase of Stock, 15 Bus. Lawyer 732 (1960).

[50] See §381(a)(1) (transfer of tax attributes not applicable to §334(b)(2) transactions); Dallas Downtown Development Co., 12 T.C. 114 (1949) (Acq.) (no gain to liquidating corporation); Steubenville Bridge Co., 11 T.C. 789 (1948) (Acq.); Commissioner v. South Lake Farms, Inc., 324 F.2d 837, 12 AFTR 2d

If the conditions of §334(b)(2) are satisfied, the parent corporation's basis for its stock (including any stock that may have been acquired in an unqualified transaction) is to be allocated among the assets received in the liquidating distribution in accordance with the regulations.

To illustrate: assume that the value of X Corporation's assets and its outstanding liabilities on December 31, 1964 are as follows:

Cash	$20,000	
Inventory	50,000	
Receivables	50,000	
Machinery and equipment	80,000	
Land and building	300,000	
Goodwill	20,000	
Total asset values		$520,000
Mortgage on real estate	$100,000	
Unsecured bank loans	10,000	
Total liabilities		110,000
Net worth		$410,000

If P Corporation purchases all of X's stock on January 5, 1965 for $410,000 in cash, and immediately thereafter liquidates X, the transaction would qualify under §334(b)(2) and P would be entitled to allocate the basis of its stock in X among the assets received from X in the liquidating transaction, with appropriate adjustments for the liabilities of P which were assumed by X or to which X's assets are subject. P's basis for its stock in X ($410,000) would be reduced by the $20,000 cash and increased by the unsecured liabilities assumed of $10,000, resulting in a $400,000 figure to be allocated among X's noncash assets. Allocation is then made in proportion to the relative net fair market values, with an adjustment for liabilities that are liens on particular properties, in this case the $100,000 real estate mortage. The net value of X's noncash assets is $400,000 (including the $20,000 of goodwill which would apparently survive liquidation, if P continued to operate X's business as a going concern).[50a] Accordingly, the basis for the acquired assets would be computed as follows: inventory, $50,000 (5/40 × $400,000); receivables, $50,000 (same); machinery, $80,000 (8/40 × $400,000); real

6054 (9th Cir. 1963); but cf. Idol v. Commissioner, 319 F.2d 647, 12 AFTR 2d 5118 (8th Cir. 1963); Blueberry Land Co., Inc., 42 T.C. 1137 (1964). For the relationship between §337 (no gain or loss on certain sales in conjunction with complete liquidation) and §332 liquidations, see *infra*, Sec. 9.66.

[50a] See North American Service Co., Inc., *supra* note 48; Rev. Rul. 66-81, *supra* note 23.

For allocation problems created by the presence of goodwill in a §334(b)-(2) liquidation, see Harnack, The Commissioner is Looking for Goodwill, 40 Taxes 331 (1962).

estate, $300,000 (20/40 $\times$ $400,000, plus $100,000 mortgage liability assumed by P); and goodwill, $20,000 (2/40 $\times$ $400,000).

In this illustration, it was assumed that the liquidation occurred immediately after P acquired X's stock. If the liquidation is de-layed,[51] the process of computing the parent's basis for the assets received may be complicated by a variety of events between the date the stock is acquired and the date of the liquidating distribution. In the interim, for example, the subsidiary may have sold some of the assets, acquired others, made non-liquidating distributions to the parent, etc. The regulations describe and illustrate the adjustments required to take appropriate account of such post-acquisition events.[52]

Unlike the *Kimbell-Diamond* doctrine as judicially formulated, §334(b)(2) is applicable without regard to the acquiring corpora-tion's intent, so that the assets will acquire a new basis if the liquida-tion satisfies the statutory conditions, even though it may not have been contemplated by the acquiring corporation when the stock was purchased. Such an automatic application of §334(b)(2) whenever the statutory conditions are satisfied, however, does not necessarily mean that *Kimbell-Diamond* has no continuing vitality when these statutory conditions are not satisfied. Thus, a deliberate avoidance of the time limits for acquiring the stock or liquidating the acquired corporation might, on a finding of an intent to acquire assets, produce the same result as under pre-1954 law; and even more clearly, the purchase of stock by an individual with an intent to liquidate the corporation in order to obtain its assets — a transaction outside of §334(b)(2) because the purchaser is not a corporation — may be treated as a purchase of assets.[53]

Sec. 9.45.   Liquidation of foreign subsidiary

To avoid the recognition of gain on the liquidation of a foreign subsidiary, a domestic corporation must obtain an advance ruling under §367 (*supra*, Sec. 3.18) by showing that the avoidance of fed-eral income taxes is not one of the principal purposes of the trans-action. If foreign earnings have been accumulated in the subsidiary,

---

[51] The plan of liquidation must be adopted within two years of the last qualifying acquisition of stock, §334(b)(2)(A)(ii), and the liquidation itself may be spread over a three-year period after the plan is adopted, §332(b)(3).

[52] Regs. §1.334-1(c); see also North American Service Co., Inc., *supra* note 48; Rev. Rul. 59-412, 1959-2 C.B. 108 (effect of liabilities assumed by parent).

[53] *Supra,* Sec. 9.03; see also Rev. Rul. 60-262, 1960-2 C.B. 114 (formal steps controlling under §334(b)(2), regardless of "purpose or intent").

In keeping with this emphasis on formality, the Service evidently regards §334(b)(2) as inapplicable when A is acquired by X in order to obtain the

free of United States taxes (*supra*, Sec. 6.50), such a ruling may be conditioned on an agreement to pay these accumulated earnings to the parent as a dividend in advance of the liquidation or to include them in its income when the liquidating distribution is received. As a result, §332 may protect the parent against recognizing gain on the unrealized appreciation in the subsidiary's assets, but not on its accumulated earnings. If the parent refrains from requesting a §367 ruling, or a favorable ruling is denied, its gain on the liquidation will be recognized under §331; and by virtue of §1248 (*supra*, Sec. 9.06), part or all of the gain may be taxed as ordinary income.

Part D.   The Liquidating Corporation's Income and Loss

Sec. 9.60.   Introductory

The preceding sections of this chapter have been concerned with the effect of a complete liquidation on the shareholder. We have seen that §331(a)(1) lays down the general rule that the shareholder is to treat the liquidating distribution as the proceeds of a sale of the stock, which will normally result in captial gain or loss, to be fully recognized by him unless §333 (non-recognition of gain on elective one-month liquidations) or §332 (non-recognition of gain or loss on liquidation of subsidiary corporations) is applicable to the transaction. We now turn to the effect of the liquidation on the liquidating corporation. The principal issues are (1) whether the distribution itself produces gain or loss for the corporation; (2) whether corporate sales, collections, and other transactions in the course of the liquidation are to be recognized for tax purposes; and (3) how the corporation's earnings and profits are affected by the liquidation. A miscellany of collateral issues are also considered in the sections that follow.

Sec. 9.61.   Effect of the distribution itself: §336

Under §336, the corporation recognizes neither gain nor loss on the distribution of its assets in partial or complete liquidation, even though their fair market value exceeds or is less than their adjusted

---

assets of A's subsidiary B, if A is liquidated before B, since then the stock of B is acquired by X from a corporation (A) whose ownership of stock would be attributable to the acquiring corporation under §318. If B is liquidated first, however, this technical objection is eliminated. See XIX ABA Tax Section Bulletin No. 3 (Apr., 1966), p. 84.

A similarly technical point is that a direct or pre-arranged transfer of the assets of an acquired corporation to a subsidiary of the acquiring corporation is regarded by the Service as a reorganization (resulting in a carryover of basis

basis.[54] Section 336 contains an exception for installment obligations, whose distribution in complete liquidation will produce corporate income under §453(d). In this respect, §336 resembles §311, which prescribes the consequences to the corporation of a non-liquidating distribution of property, but §336 does not go on (as does §311, *supra*, Sec. 5.21) to recognize corporate income on a distribution of appreciated LIFO inventory or assets subject to liabilities in excess of basis.

Unlike most nonrecognition provisions, which provide that the transferor or transferee (or both) must carry over the old basis for the transferred property so that the non-recognized gain or loss will be taken into account at a later date, §336 ordinarily results in a permanent nonrecognition of the liquidating corporation's gain or loss. This is because the transferred assets do not preserve their old basis, but acquire a basis equal to their fair market value at the time of the liquidation under §334(a) (*supra*, Sec. 9.04), except in special circumstances when §332 or §333 apply. For this reason, the "recapture" rules of §§1245 and 1250 (depreciable property) and §47(a)(1) (early disposition of "investment credit" property) override §336 by requiring the liquidating corporation to include an appropriate amount in its taxable income or tax liability when property subject to these provisions is transferred.[55] Similarly, since the liquidation itself is often the Service's last clear chance to tax the disappearing corporation on its appreciated assets or other sources of future income, the government frequently seeks to sidestep §336 by asserting a deficiency based on some theory other than the mere distribution of assets in liquidation. We turn now to a discussion of the problems arising in such efforts to tax the liquidating corporation.

Sec. 9.62   Income of the liquidating corporation: "Timely" liquidations and related problems

The adoption of a plan of complete liquidation does not terminate the corporation's existence; under the regulations, death does not occur until the corporation "ceases business and dissolves, retaining

---

for the assets), rather than as a §332 liquidation; on the other hand, if the acquired corporation is liquidated by the acquiring corporation, and its assets are later transferred by the latter to a subsidiary, the Service evidently accepts the view that there is a §332 liquidation followed by a §351 transfer. Ibid., p. 87.

[54] This principle first entered the statute with the enactment of §336 of the 1954 Code, but it was previously applied by Regs. 118, §39.22(a)-20, even while the Internal Revenue Service was urging (unsuccessfully, *supra*, Sec. 5.21) that gain should be recognized by the corporation on a *non-liquidating* distribution of appreciated property.

[55] See generally Gardner, The Impact of Sections 1245 and 1250 on Corporate Liquidations, 17 U. Fla. L. Rev. 58 (1964); Schapiro, Recapture of

no assets."[56] Even though the liquidating process may be quite pro-
tracted, the corporation must continue to file tax returns and pay
the corporate income tax on its sales, collections, commissions, and
other income.[57] If the corporation winds up by selling all of its assets
before making a liquidating distribution and terminating its corporate
existence, it will have paid its debt to society and no further tax problems are likely to arise. Frequently, however, some or all of the assets
are distributed in kind to the shareholders, especially if a going business is to be continued; and such a "mid-stream" liquidation usually
involves the transfer of appreciated assets, accounts receivable, claims
for services rendered, and other sources of future income, some of
which may be associated with expenses that were deducted by the
liquidating corporation in past years. Because the shareholders will
ordinarily take these assets at a basis equal to their fair market value
at the time of distribution under §334(a) (*supra*, Sec. 9.04), so that
accrued appreciation will not be taxed to them when they ultimately
sell or dispose of the assets, the Internal Revenue Service frequently
insists that the liquidating corporation recognize the accrued or potential income inherent in such assets.[58] One or more of the following
theories is ordinarily offered for such an adjustment, which in effect
assumes that §336 is inapplicable to the situation in question:

1. *Anticipatory assignments of income.* The corporation cannot
escape the corporate income tax by an anticipatory assignment of
income to its shareholders, even though the assignment takes the form
of a complete liquidation. This principle is simply an application of a

---

Depreciation and Section 1245 of the Internal Revenue Code, 72 Yale L.J.
1483 (1963); Horvitz, Sections 1250 and 1245: The Puddle and the Lake, 20
Tax L. Rev. 285 (1965).

[56] Regs. §1.6012-2(a)(2); see also *supra,* Secs. 2.08 and 9.02; Rev. Rul.
61-191, 1961-2 C.B. 251 (corporation may be dissolved de facto even though
not dissolved de jure); United States v. Joliet & Chicago R.R. Co., 315 U.S. 44,
28 AFTR 215 (1942) (corporate existence continued after perpetual lease of
property); Hersloff v. United States, 310 F.2d 947, 10 AFTR 2d 6072 (Ct. Cl.
1962) (corporate existence preserved by continuing business activities despite
technical dissolution).

[57] See Estate of Charles Fearon, 16 T.C. 385 (1951) (liquidation spread
over more than 23 years).

[58] See generally, Lyon and Eustice, Assignment of Income: Fruit and Tree
as Irrigated by the P. G. Lake Case, 17 Tax L. Rev. 293, 396 et seq. (1962);
Eustice, Contract Rights, Capital Gain, and Assignment of Income — The
Ferrer Case, 20 Tax L. Rev. 1, 51 et seq. (1964); Weiss, Corporate Contingent
Income: A Case of Tax Planning, 12 Tax L. Rev. 73 (1965).

Similar problems arise when a going business is incorporated under §351,
although in such cases the income would usually be recognized eventually, because of the carryover of basis for the transferred assets; even so, adjustments
are sometimes required to prevent a shifting of tax liability from the transferor
to the transferee corporation by a mid-stream incorporation. See *supra,* Sec.
3.17.

pervasive doctrine of income tax law, under which income is taxed to its source rather than to the person who happens to collect it, a doctrine of such breadth and general application that it falls outside the scope of this work. As an illustration, see J. Ungar, Inc. v. Commissioner, 244 F.2d 90, 51 AFTR 250 (2d Cir. 1957), in which a corporation was taxed on commissions for services performed by it, although the amounts in question were collected by a shareholder after the corporation's assets were distributed to him in complete liquidaion.[59] The anticipatory assignment doctrine is of such uncertain scope that the results in litigated cases are unpredictable; moreover, it may be that the courts will be less willing to apply it if the corporation completely liquidates than if the shareholders receive the property in an ordinary distribution or partial liquidation, for the reason that a complete liquidation usually has more drastic non-tax consequences and is less likely to be employed principally for tax avoidance.

2. *"Clear reflection of income" under §446(b)*. As a general rule, taxable income is computed under the accounting method regularly employed by the taxpayer; but the Commissioner, under §446(b), may compel use of another method if the taxpayer's "does not clearly reflect income." A method of accounting that would clearly be permissible for a continuing business may not properly reflect income where the corporate taxpayer liquidates in mid-stream; and the government has successfully argued, in several cases of this sort, that the taxpayer's method of accounting should be changed in order to prevent distortion of the income stream. Thus, in the well-known *Jud Plumbing* and *Standard Paving* cases, construction companies using the completed contract method of reporting income liquidated before certain construction contracts were fully completed and they were

---

[59] For other cases, see Williamson v. United States, 292 F.2d 524, 8 AFTR 2d 5172 (Ct. Cl. 1961) (cash basis corporation taxed on accounts receivable for previously rendered services); Wood Harmon Corp. v. United States, 311 F.2d 918, 11 AFTR 2d 423 (2d Cir. 1963) (condemnation award, liquidated in amount and paid after distribution to shareholders, taxable to corporation); United States v. Horschel, 205 F.2d 646, 44 AFTR 115 (9th Cir. 1953) (corporation not taxed); Cold Metal Process Co. v. Commissioner, 247 F.2d 864, 52 AFTR 160 (6th Cir. 1957); Telephone Directory Advertising Co. v. United States, 142 F. Supp. 884, 49 AFTR 1888 (Ct. Cl. 1956) (distribution of "unaccrued" future commissions, and termination of existence before item accrued); United Mercantile Agencies, 34 T.C. 808 (1960) (unaccrued commissions contingent on future events); James Poro, Transferee, 39 T.C. 641 (1963) (Acq.) (contingent litigation claims, corporate existence terminated); Pat O'Brien, 25 T.C. 376 (1955) (motion picture distribution contract, corporate existence terminated); see also *supra*, Sec. 5.21.

For the relationship between the date of liquidation and the date the income is paid by the obligor, see Sol C. Siegel Prod., Inc., 46 T.C. No. 2 (1966) (cash basis corporation not taxed in year of distribution, where it did not liquidate until a year later and payments were received before then).

required in effect to shift from the completed contract method (under which income would not be recognized until the work was finished) to the percentage-of-completion method of reporting income.[60] In both cases, the courts relied on the assignment of income doctrine as well as on §446(b); and in *Jud Plumbing*, the court also invoked §482 (permitting income and deductions to be reallocated among related businesses under common control).

3. Contingent or "inchoate" income items and the problem of corporate existence. The above observations must be qualified, where complete liquidations are involved, by considering situations where a liquidating corporation distributes items of potential income too contingent to constitute current income under any ordinary accounting method. In a number of such cases, courts have refused to apply assignment of income doctrines because the corporation either had not "earned" the potential income at the time of distribution, or was not in "existence" at the later time when the uncertain income matured and became definite.[60a] But where corporate "existence" continues, taxability may remain with the liquidating corporation if it is found to have "earned" the income in question.[60b]

[60] Jud Plumbing & Heating Co. v. Commissioner, 153 F.2d 681, 34 AFTR 1025 (5th Cir. 1946); Standard Paving Co. v. Commissioner, 190 F.2d 330, 40 AFTR 1022 (10th Cir. 1951), cert. denied, 342 U.S. 860; see also Kuckenberg v. Commissioner, 35 T.C. 473 (1960), aff'd on this point, 309 F.2d 202, 10 AFTR (9th Cir. 1962) (cash basis construction company required to accrue income on completed contracts); Susan J. Carter, 9 T.C. 364, 373 (1947) (Acq.) (brokerage contracts); Idaho First National Bank v. United States, 265 F.2d 6, 3 AFTR 2d 928 (9th Cir. 1959) (accrued interest taxed to liquidating cash basis bank); Guy M. Shelley, 2 T.C. 62 (1943); Floyd v. Scofield, 193 F.2d 594, 41 AFTR 623 (5th Cir. 1952); Commissioner v. Henry Hess Co., 210 F.2d 553, 45 AFTR 358 (9th Cir. 1954).

Although it is usually thought that the government's use of §446(b) to require adjustments in the year of liquidation does not bring §481 (adjustments required by change of accounting method) into play, the relationship between these provisions in this area remains to be worked out.

[60a] See Cold Metal Process Co. v. Commissioner, *supra* note 59; (income not "earned"); Commissioner v. Henry Hess Co., *supra* note 60 (corporation not in existence when income matured). For other situations where corporations have avoided tax on potential income through a "timely" liquidation, see Telephone Directory Advertising Co. v. United States, *supra* note 59 (distribution of "unaccrued" future commissions, and termination of existence, before item accrued); United Mercantile Agencies, *supra* note 59 (unaccrued commissions contingent on future events); James Poro, Transferee, *supra* note 59 (contingent litigation claims, corporate existence terminated); and Pat O'Brien, *supra* note 59 (motion picture distribution contract, corporate existence terminated).

[60b] See J. Ungar, Inc. v. Commissioner, *supra* (commissions earned, but not yet accruable at date of a liquidation distribution, nevertheless remained taxable to the still "existing" corporation); Wood Harmon Corp. v. United States, *supra* note 59 (liquidating corporation, whose existence continued, held taxable on proceeds of condemnation award, previously distributed to shareholders, although amount of award not fixed until after the distribution); see also Hersloff v. United States, 310 F.2d 947, 10 AFTR 2d 6072 (Ct. Cl. 1962)

On the meaning of corporate existence, the regulations have long provided, substantially as they do now:

> *Existence of Corporation.* A corporation in existence during any portion of a taxable year is required to make a return. If a corporation was not in existence throughout an annual accounting period (either calendar year or fiscal year), the corporation is required to make a return for that fractional part of a year during which it was in existence. A corporation is not in existence after it ceases business and dissolves, retaining no assets, whether or not under State law it may thereafter be treated as continuing as a corporation for certain limited purposes connected with winding up its affairs, such as for the purpose of suing and being sued. If the corporation has valuable claims for which it will bring suit during this period, it has retained assets and therefore continues in existence. A corporation does not go out of existence if it is turned over to receivers or trustees who continue to operate it. Regs. §1.6012-2(a)(2).

See also United States v. Joliet & Chicago R.R. Co., 315 U.S. 44, 28 AFTR 215 (1942), where the corporation had disposed of all its property under a perpetual lease, the lessee agreeing to pay a stated annual dividend to stockholders of the lessor; the court taxed these payments as rental income to the corporate lessor, and noted that "the umbilical cord" between the taxpayer and its shareholders had not been cut. The message thus seems to be that de facto dissolution of the liquidating corporation is necessary to argue "non-existence"; and unless the corporation is a "mere empty shell," it may be deemed to have a life after death, at least for assignment of income purposes where potential income items are involved.

If the liquidation is "timely" (*i.e.*, corporate existence terminates before realization of the inchoate income item), taxation at the corporate level may be avoided; at the same time, this item of potential income is converted into capital gain at the shareholder level, since the distribution, under §331, is treated as a payment in exchange for stock (note also in this latter regard, that the contingencies may prevent valuation of these items under *Burnet* v. *Logan*, thus resulting in "open liquidation" treatment to the distributee shareholders, see *supra*, Sec. 9.03). The tax stakes in this area call to mind the collapsible corporation provisions (*infra*, Ch. 10), designed primarily to discourage this type of ploy; but they are not always fully effective

---

(corporate existence preserved by continued business activities of trustees in dissolution, although technical dissolution occurred many years earlier); Sol C. Siegel Prod., Inc., *supra* note 59.

See also, for the meaning of "complete liquidation," *supra*, Sec. 9.02.

to serve this purpose. Finally, it should be noted that the problems in this area resemble those which arise under §691 on the death of an individual; with the important exception that items of "income in respect of a decedent" retain their "character" in the hands of transferees. Not so on the death of a corporation, with the result that untaxed corporate potential income items may be transformed into shareholder capital gain if the parties plan the timing of the liquidation with due care.

4. Corporate deductions and shareholder income. If a timely liquidating distribution of a potential income item does not run afoul of the foregoing principles, should the corporation at least be required to "give back" any tax benefit it may have obtained by deducting the expenses incurred in creating the transferred item? For example, if a corporation has incurred and deducted the expenses of raising an agricultural crop but liquidates before reaping what it sowed, and if it is not taxed on the harvested crop, should the deductions be retroactively disallowed in order to prevent a distortion of income? (If the crop is sold for more than the cost of its production, such a disallowance of the expenses would be less drastic than taxing the income to the corporation.) Conversely, if the corporation received funds that were not taxed on receipt because of an offsetting liability, should an adjustment be made on liquidation in recognition of the fact that the corporation will not have to incur any expense to discharge the liability? Much can be said for requiring such adjustments in a wide variety of circumstances (*e.g.*, bad debt reserves; business expenses allocable to uncollected claims and rights; capital outlays for tools, subscriptions, and similar assets that by regulation or statute can be deducted; prepaid subscription income; reserves for customer deposits, returnable containers, overcharges; etc.), but the government has pressed the point in only a few areas and has lost the argument as often as it has won.[61] Moreover, the development of stat-

---

[61] See Diamond A Cattle Co. v. Commissioner, 233 F.2d 739, 49 AFTR 1321 (10th Cir. 1956) (operating losses incurred by corporation liquidating in mid-stream allowed); Commissioner v. South Lake Farms, Inc., 324 F.2d 837, 12 AFTR 2d 6054 (9th Cir. 1963) (expenses of raising agricultural crop not restored to income on liquidation); West Seattle National Bank v. Commissioner, 288 F.2d 47, 7 AFTR 2d 790 (9th Cir. 1961) (bad debt reserve taken into income on liquidation after sale of assets); Argus, Inc., 45 T.C. 63 (1965); *infra*, Sec. 9.68.

Schmidt's Estate v. Commissioner, 355 F.2d 11, 17 AFTR 2d 242 (9th Cir. 1966), holding that the bad debt reserve of an unincorporated enterprise was not taxable to the transferor when the business was incorporated under §351 may be inapplicable to liquidations, because of the stepped-up basis acquired by the transferred assets. See Arent, Reallocation of Income and Expenses in Connection with Formation and Liquidation of Corporations, 40 Taxes 995, 1001-1002 (1962); Bonovitz, Restoration to Income of Bad Debt Reserves, 44 Taxes 300 (1966).

utory "recapture" devices (§§1245, 1250, and 47) to deal with analogous problems may stimulate a judicial refusal to police this area on
the ground that Congress can do the job more systematically. Similarly, Fribourg Navigation Co., Inc. v. Commissioner, 383 U.S. 272,
17 AFTR 2d 470 (1966), refusing to disallow depreciation deducted
in the year property was sold for more than its adjusted basis, is not
very sympathetic to judicial or administrative disallowance of an item
that seemed deductible on the facts as known when the expense was
incurred.[62]

Sec. 9.63.   The Court Holding Co. doctrine and its limitations

The purpose of a corporate liquidation is often to set the stage
for a sale of the distributed property by the shareholders. An alternate
route to the same end is a sale of the assets by the corporation itself,
followed by a liquidating distribution of the proceeds of sale to the
shareholders. The enactment of §337, one of the most important 1954
changes in the corporate provisions of the Internal Revenue Code,
greatly alters the tax consequences of such transactions. Before the
1954 change can be explained, however, the development of the law
in this area before 1954 must be described.

An illustration will be helpful. Assume that Jones owns all the
stock of Jones, Inc., with a basis of $50,000, and that the corpora-
tion's sole asset is an apartment house, with an adjusted basis to the
corporation of $40,000 but a fair market value of $100,000. If the
corporation sells the apartment house, it will have a profit of $60,000,
on which the federal income tax would be $15,000 if the profit is
taxable as long-term capital gain under §1231. If the balance of
$85,000 is then distributed in liquidation to Jones, he will have a
profit of $35,000, on which the tax (at the long-term capital gains

---

[62] The force of *Fribourg's* radiations is reduced by its reliance on the legislative and administrative history in the depreciation area, since there is far less
background material of this kind in the liquidation field. On the other hand,
if *Fribourg* had gone the other way, it would probably have stimulated a general
effort to disallow deductions that seemed valid when taken but that became
less convincing in the light of hindsight, e.g., advertising expenses contributing
to the value of good will, if the good will itself was sold or distributed later
in the same taxable year; and this approach might have been extended to
deductions taken under such provisions as §177 (trademark expenditures),
§174 (research and experimental expenditures), etc., if the taxpayer sold or
distributed the assets created by these expenditures in the same taxable year.
Moreover, a logical extension would have been an effort to recapture such
deductions, under the tax benefit doctrine or §446(b), even if they were taken
in prior years. As stated above, the taxpayer victory in *Fribourg* rests on the
special history of §167, and hence does not directly affect these recapture
potentialities, but a government victory on broader grounds would surely have
encouraged the government to explore them with vigor.

rate) will be $8,750. Jones will be left with $76,250. But if Jones liquidates the corporation and *then* sells the apartment house, the after-tax proceeds will be substantially greater. On the liquidation, the corporation would not recognize income (§336, *supra*, Sec. 9.61), but Jones would recognize $50,000 of profit, on which the tax (at the long-term capital gain rate) would be $12,500. But the basis of the apartment house would now be $100,000 (§334(a), *supra*, Sec. 9.04), and there would be no further profit, or tax, on the sale. Jones would be left with $87,500 after taxes.[63]

But while it is easy enough to see the tax difference between a sale by the corporation and a sale by the shareholder, it is much more difficult to know when a transaction falls in one category and when in the other. One of the most famous of all federal income tax cases, Commissioner v. Court Holding Co., 324 U.S. 331, 33 AFTR 593 (1945), was concerned with this distinction. The opinion is brief enough to be quoted almost in its entirety:

> The respondent corporation was organized in 1934 solely to buy and hold the apartment building which was the only property ever owned by it. All of its outstanding stock was owned by Minnie Miller and her husband. Between October 1, 1939 and February 1940, while the corporation still had legal title to the property, negotiations for its sale took place. These negotiations were between the corporation and the lessees of the property, together with a sister and brother-in-law. An oral agreement was reached as to the terms and conditions of sale, and February 22, 1940, the parties met to reduce the agreement to writing. The purchaser was then advised by the corporation's attorney that the sale could not be consummated because it would result in the imposition of a large income tax on the corporation. The next day, the corporation declared a "liquidating dividend," which involved complete liquidation of its assets, and surrender of all outstanding stock. Mrs. Miller and her husband surrendered their stock, and the building was deeded to them. A sale contract was then drawn, naming the Millers individually as vendors, and the lessees' sister as vendee, which embodied substantially the same terms and conditions previously agreed upon. One thousand dollars, which a month and a half earlier had been paid to the corporation by the lessees, was applied in part payment of the

---

[63] A liquidation under §333 (*supra*, Sec. 9.21) would also produce only one tax: the liquidation itself is tax-free, the property's basis in the hands of the shareholder is the basis of the stock given up under §334(c), and the holding period of the property includes the holding period of the stock under §1223(1), so that Jones would recognize long-term capital gain on the sale in the amount of $50,000 and be left with $87,500. But §333 would be less attractive if the corporation had post-1913 earnings and profits, cash, or stock or securities acquired after Dec. 31, 1953.

purchase price. Three days later, the property was conveyed to the lessees' sister.

The Tax Court concluded from these facts that, despite the declaration of a "liquidating dividend" followed by the transfers of legal title, the corporation had not abandoned the sales negotiations; that these were mere formalities designed to "make the transaction appear to be other than what it was," in order to avoid tax liability. The Circuit Court of Appeals, drawing different inferences from the record, held that the corporation had "called off" the sale, and treated the stockholders' sale as unrelated to the prior negotiations.

There was evidence to support the findings of the Tax Court, and its findings must therefore be accepted by the courts. . . . On the basis of these findings, the Tax Court was justified in attributing the gain from the sale to respondent corporation. The incidence of taxation depends upon the substance of a transaction. The tax consequences which arise from gains from a sale of property are not finally to be determined solely by the means employed to transfer legal title. Rather, the transaction must be viewed as a whole, and each step, from the commencement of negotiations to the consummation of the sale, is relevant. A sale by one person cannot be transformed for tax purposes into a sale by another by using the latter as a conduit through which to pass title. To permit the true nature of a transaction to be disguised by mere formalisms, which exist solely to alter tax liabilities, would seriously impair the effective administration of the tax policies of Congress.

It is urged that respondent corporation never executed a written agreement, and that an oral agreement to sell land cannot be enforced in Florida because of the Statute of Frauds, Comp. Gen. Laws of Florida, 1927, vol. 3, §5779. But the fact that respondent corporation itself never executed a written contract is unimportant, since the Tax Court found from the facts of the entire transaction that the executed sale was in substance the sale of the corporation. The decision of the Circuit Court of Appeals is reversed, and that of the Tax Court affirmed.

Since the sale of the property was imputed to the corporation, it was required to report the profit on the sale as corporate income.[64]

Although the moral of the *Court Holding Co.* case — do not arrange for a sale of the corporation's appreciated property before the

---

[64] Unless the corporation happened to retain enough assets to pay the tax liability, the shareholders are liable as transferees under §6901(a)(1)(A). Having computed their capital gains tax on the liquidation on the assumption (now proven erroneous) that the corporation was not liable for a tax on the sale, the shareholders are entitled to a deduction in the year they discharge their liability as transferees. The Supreme Court has held that the appropriate adjustment for the shareholders is a capital loss. Arrowsmith v. Commissioner. 344 U.S. 6, 42 AFTR 649 (1952); see also §1341; Webster, The Claim of Right Doctrine: 1954 Version, 10 Tax L. Rev. 381, 399 (1955).

liquidation has been consummated — was clear enough, it was more easily preached than practiced. For one thing, shareholders persisted in their evil custom of arranging for the sale of their corporation's property before consulting their lawyers. For another, if the corporation was liquidated first, the capital gains tax was payable even if the shareholders were unable to find a buyer for the property,[65] and to the difficulty of finding cash to pay the tax was added the possibility that in the absence of a sale, valuation of the property by the government in computing the shareholder's capital gain might be excessive. A liquidation in advance of a contract of sale could be even more troublesome if the shareholders were numerous and not otherwise associated with each other.

To be sure, the shareholders might eliminate the danger of a taxable liquidation without a buyer by negotiating with possible buyers while the corporation was still alive, but then they must take care to act only in a personal capacity, and not as agents or officers of the corporation. This bit of sophistication was endorsed by the Supreme Court, as a way to avoid corporate tax on the sale, in United States v. Cumberland Public Service Co., 338 U.S. 451, 38 AFTR 978 (1950). There the shareholders first tried to sell the stock of their corporation and, when the buyer refused to buy the stock,[66] they offered to acquire the assets by liquidating the corporation and then to sell the assets. The Court of Claims held that the assets were sold by the shareholders, not by the corporation, and the Supreme Court affirmed, distinguishing the *Court Holding Co.* case on its facts:

> Our *Court Holding Co.* decision rested on findings of fact by the Tax Court that a sale had been made and gains realized by the taxpayer corporation. There the corporation had negotiated

[65] Unless the conditions were ripe for a one-month liquidation under §333, on which gain would not be recognized. See *supra*, note 63.

[66] Although the reasons for the buyer's refusal to purchase the stock are not set out in the opinion, there are many tax and non-tax reasons for a refusal. Among the latter, the possibility of contingent and other liabilities undisclosed on the balance sheet is important; for the use of a guaranteed balance sheet as protection against undisclosed liabilities, see Blustein v. Eugene Sobel Co., 263 F.2d 478, 3 AFTR 2d 537 (D.C. Cir. 1959). Tax reasons for refusing to buy stock are that the corporation may have a low basis for its assets, a large earnings and profits account, an unfavorable accounting method, etc. Buyers may be able to avoid these drawbacks by liquidating the corporation, unless a prompt reincorporation of the assets is necessary, in which case the liquidation might be disregarded. Moreover, before 1954, if the buyer was a corporation, a liquidation of its newly-acquired subsidiary would have resulted in a carry-over of the subsidiary's basis for the assets unless the *Kimbell-Diamond* case (*supra*, Sec. 9.44) was applicable. See Mintz, Recent Developments Under the Court Holding Co. and Cumberland Public Service Co. Case — Sale of Assets or Stock, 11 N.Y.U. Inst. on Fed. Tax. 873, 884-90 (1953); Cary, The Effect of Taxation on Selling Out A Corporation Business for Cash, 45 Ill. L. Rev. 423, 441-51 (1950).

for sale of its assets and had reached an oral agreement of sale. When the tax consequences of the corporate sale were belatedly recognized, the corporation purported to "call off" the sale at the last minute and distributed the physical properties in kind to the stockholders. They promptly conveyed these properties to the same persons who had negotiated with the corporation. The terms of purchase were substantially those of the previous oral agreement. One thousand dollars already paid to the corporation was applied as part payment of the purchase price. The Tax Court found that the corporation never really abandoned its sales negotiations, that it never did dissolve, and that the sole purpose of the so-called liquidation was to disguise a corporate sale through use of mere formalisms in order to avoid tax liability. The Circuit Court of Appeals took a different view of the evidence. In this Court the Government contended that whether a liquidation distribution was genuine or merely a sham was traditionally a question of fact. We agreed with this contention, and reinstated the Tax Court's findings and judgment. Discussing the evidence which supported the findings of fact, we went on to say that "the incidence of taxation depends upon the substance of a transaction" regardless of "mere formalisms," and that taxes on a corporate sale cannot be avoided by using the shareholders as a "conduit through which to pass title."

This language does not mean that a corporation can be taxed even when the sale has been made by its stockholders following a genuine liquidation and dissolution. While the distinction between sales by a corporation as compared with distribution in kind followed by shareholder sales may be particularly shadowy and artificial when the corporation is closely held, Congress has chosen to recognize such a distinction for tax purposes. The corporate tax is thus aimed primarily at the profits of a going concern. This is true despite the fact that gains realized from corporate sales are taxed, perhaps to prevent tax evasions, even where the cash proceeds are at once distributed in liquidation. But Congress has imposed no tax on liquidating distributions in kind or on dissolution, whatever may be the motive for such liquidation. Consequently, a corporation may liquidate without subjecting itself to the corporate gains tax, even though a primary motive is to avoid the burden of corporate taxation.

Here, on the basis of adequate subsidiary findings, the Court of Claims has found that the sale in question was made by the stockholders rather than the corporation. The Government's argument that the shareholders acted as a mere "conduit" for a sale by respondent corporation must fall before this finding. The subsidiary finding that a major motive of the shareholders was to reduce taxes does not bar this conclusion. Whatever the motive and however relevant it may be in determining whether the transaction was real or a sham, sales of physical properties by shareholders following a genuine liquidation distribution cannot be attributed to the corporation for tax purposes.

In an effort to decide the case on something other than "mere formalisms," the Supreme Court contrasted the Tax Court's finding that the Court Holding Co. "never did dissolve" with the Court of Claims' finding that there was a "genuine" liquidation of the Cumberland Public Service Co. In practice, however, this distinction could mean little more than that tax advice came early, rather than late, since the findings of fact in the *Cumberland Public Service Co.* case might not have been so favorable if the shareholders had not been carefully guided during their negotiations. The last words of the Supreme Court in the *Cumberland Public Service Co.* case were:

> It is for the trial court, upon consideration of an entire transaction, to determine the factual category in which a particular transaction belongs. Here as in the *Court Holding Co.* case we accept the ultimate findings of fact of the trial tribunal.

However much they tried to cut their garb to the pattern of the *Cumberland Public Service Co.* case, taxpayers ran the risk of failing to demonstrate that they were negotiating only in anticipation of a liquidation; if they appeared to be acting for the corporation, rather than in a personal capacity, the *Court Holding Co.* case, rather than the *Cumberland Public Service Co.* case, would be controlling.[67]

Because the "result of these two decisions is that undue weight is accorded the formalities of the transaction and they, therefore, represent merely a trap for the unwary" (S. Rep. No. 1622, 83d Cong., 2d Sess., p. 49 (1954)), the Congress in 1954 took action to divorce

[67] For the dangers of advance negotiations, even with advice, see Doyle Hosiery Corp., 17 T.C. 641 (1951) (Acq.). Although the taxpayer won, on the ground that the negotiations that preceded the liquidation were on behalf of the shareholders rather than the corporation, five dissenting judges thought that "the sale was made by petitioner [the corporation] and all that was done by the stockholders in their individual capacities was to indulge in carefully cloaked ritualistic formalities."

A guide to the ritual that was necessary before 1954 to avoid an attribution of a shareholder sale to the corporation (and that is still necessary if §337 is inapplicable) may be found in Mintz, *supra* note 66, at 876-84. Among many other articles on the *Court Holding Co.* and *Cumberland Public Service Co.* cases, see Cary, *supra* note 66, which has a bibliography at 423. The *Cumberland Public Service Co.* case rather clearly rejects the theory, espoused in Wichita Terminal Elevator Co. v. Commissioner, 162 F.2d 513, 35 AFTR 1487 (10th Cir. 1947), and Meurer Steel Barrel Co. v. Commissioner, 144 F.2d 282, 32 AFTR 1189 (3d Cir. 1944), cert. denied, 324 U.S. 860 (1945), that a sale should be imputed to the corporation if there was no business reason for liquidating before the sale rather than selling before liquidation. Nor can *Cumberland Public Service Co.* be reconciled with the ingenious suggestion in the Tax Court's opinion (6 T.C. at 381) in the *Howell Turpentine* case, based on the "corporate opportunity" doctrine of corporate law, that the directors of a corporation have a fiduciary duty to the government, as creditor of the corporation, to make a potential sale in the corporation's name, rather than in their personal capacity as shareholders.

the tax consequences of the liquidation-sale combination from the form of the transaction. The new legislation, §337 of the 1954 Code, adopts as its principle the elimination of the corporate tax, whether the sale is made by the corporation in anticipation of the liquidation or by the shareholders thereafter. By virtue of §337, the tax consequences to the shareholders ordinarily will be identical, whether the corporation sells the assets and then distributes the proceeds in complete liquidation or distributes the assets in kind to the shareholders for sale by them. The *Court Holding Co.* doctrine is not dead, however, since §337 is ordinarily inapplicable to inventory property and installment obligations, nor does it ordinarily apply to liquidations of collapsible corporations, to elective one-month liquidations under §333, or to most liquidations of subsidiary corporations under §332. Moreover, because §337 provides for non-recognition of loss as well as gain, it may have adverse consequences to the shareholders in certain instances.

Sec. 9.64.   §337 — The "anti-Court Holding Co." provision

The "general rule" of §337(a) provides that if a corporation (1) adopts a plan of complete liquidation and (2) distributes all of its assets (less those retained to meet claims) in complete liquidation within the 12-month period beginning on the date of the adoption of the plan, it shall not recognize gain or loss from the sale or exchange of property within the 12-month period.[68] (Although it is commonly said that the plan must be adopted "before" the sales in question, Regs. §1.337-1 provides that sales made on the same day that the plan is adopted are included in §337 even if they precede adoption of the plan.) Section 337 has the effect of changing the result in cases like *Court Holding Co.*, because even if a sale by the shareholders is

---

[68] As will be seen, *infra,* Sec. 9.65, the term "property" is defined by §337(b) to exclude the corporation's inventory property (unless sold in bulk) and some installment obligations, so that sales of its stock in trade in the regular course of business do not qualify for non-recognition under §337(a).

It has been held that gain on property purchased *after* the plan is adopted can qualify for nonrecognition; see Frank W. Verito, 43 T.C. 425 (1965) (gain on marketable securities representing a temporary investment of proceeds of a prior sale under §337).

See generally Note, Tax-Free Sales in Liquidation Under Section 337, 76 Harv. L. Rev. 780 (1963); MacLean, Taxation of Sales of Corporate Assets in the Course of Liquidation, 56 Col. L. Rev. 641 (1956); Boland, A Review of Developments Under Section 337 of the Internal Revenue Code of 1954, 42 Taxes 676 (1964); Paulston, How to Plan and Execute the Sale of a Corporate Business Under the Internal Revenue Code of 1954, 1956 So. Calif. Tax Inst. 383; Lewis and Schapiro, Sale of Corporate Business: Stock or Assets? 14 N.Y.U. Inst. on Fed. Taxation 745 (1956); Silverstein, Section 337 and Liquidation of the Multi-Corporate Enterprise, 16 *ibid.* 429 (1958).

imputed to the corporation on the ground that they acted merely as a "conduit" for a corporate sale, the gain is not recognized by the corporation by virtue of §337(a). So long as the sale is made within the 12-month period following the adoption of the plan of liquidation, there is no difference under §337(a) between a sale by the corporation itself and one that is imputed to the corporation under the *Court Holding Co.* case. This in turn means that in most cases, the corporation itself will negotiate with potential buyers and make the sale; there is no longer any need for the shareholders to liquidate the corporation before looking for a buyer for the assets or to employ the ritual endorsed by the *Cumberland Public Service Co.* case. Moreover, the regulations permit the corporation to negotiate for a sale even before the plan of liquidation is adopted, thus foreclosing a possible government argument that the sale was not made within "the 12-month period beginning on the date of the adoption of such plan" if negotiations began before the plan was adopted. Regs. §1.337-2(a). The regulations go on to state that an executory contract to sell is to be distinguished from a contract of sale, thus implying that the former may precede the adoption of the plan so long as the sale itself occurs within the prescribed period. This suggestion, however, is followed by the ambiguous statement: "Ordinarily, a sale has not occurred when a contract to sell has been entered into but title and possession of the property have not been transferred and the obligation of the seller to sell or the buyer to buy is conditional."

1. The plan — nature and timing. Section 337(a) provides for the nonrecognition of gain *or loss* on sales by the corporation within the prescribed period. Because the section is not elective, it may have the unexpected result of denying a deduction for property sold at a loss in circumstances where the shareholders had no thought of avoiding the *Court Holding Co.* case. For example, a corporation in a declining industry may decide to sell its assets at a loss with the expectation of applying the loss against current profits or carrying it back to earlier years under §172, and then to distribute its assets in complete liquidation. If the sale of the depreciated assets occurs within the 12-month period beginning with the adoption of the plan of liquidation, §337(a) will prevent the recognition of the loss, even though the circumstances that led to its enactment (the possibility of a double tax under the *Court Holding Co.* case) are not present. With advance planning, however, the corporation may be able to avoid the applicability of §337(a), by making the sale before adopting the plan of liquidation. Although the statute does not define the phrase "the date of the adoption of such plan," the regulations provide that it is "ordinarily" the date on which the shareholders adopt a resolution authorizing the distribution of the corporation's assets (other than those retained to meet claims) in redemption of the stock.[69] The regulations go on to provide that if the corporation sells substantially all of its property before the shareholders adopt the resolution, the resolution date will be treated as the date the plan was adopted. The purpose of this part of the regulations is evidently to permit the recognition of loss (or a combination of loss and gain) if the corporation is prepared to sell substantially all of its property outside of §337.

But if the corporation seeks to straddle §337(a) by selling its depreciated property before the shareholders act on the plan of liquidation and its appreciated property thereafter, it may find itself in difficulties. The regulations treat the shareholders' resolution as controlling only if the corporation sells substantially all of its property before that date (thus recognizing both its gains and its losses) or after that date (thus subjecting both gains and losses to nonrecognition under §337). If the corporation splits its sales, the regulations say that "the date of the adoption of the plan of liquidation shall be determined from all the facts and circumstances."[70] In the case of a "straddle," the government might successfully contend that the plan of liquidation was adopted — albeit informally — when the corporation made the first sale of property at a loss, or when it set about doing so. This pre-dating of the plan might make §337(a) applicable to all sales, so that neither gains nor losses would be recognized, or it might make §337(a) totally inapplicable, if more than 12 months elapsed between the "pre-dated" plan and the ultimate distribution of the assets in liquidation. The position of the Internal Revenue Service is evidenced by Rev. Rul. 57-140, 1957-1 C.B. 118, where a corporation sold part of its assets at a loss, then adopted a plan of liquidation by shareholder action, and then sold the rest of the assets. The Service held that the plan was adopted when the shareholders acted, but only on convincing proof that the earlier sale was not in contemplation of liquidation and hence was not connected with the later sale. Had the earlier sale been part of a prearranged plan of liquidation, the ruling would no doubt have been adverse to the taxpayer.

The Service has met with a singular lack of success in its efforts to combat the "straddle" device, however, where taxpayers have been careful to observe the proper formalities. For example, in Virginia

---

[69] Regs. §1.337-2(b); see also §1.337-6(a); *supra* note 25.
[70] Regs. §1.337-2(b).

Ice & Freezing Corp., 30 T.C. 1251 (1958), the government lost in its argument that an "informal" plan of complete liquidation had been adopted at a directors' meeting preceding action by the shareholders, even though one of the directors had in the past regularly received proxies from most of the other shareholders. The formal shareholders' resolution was accepted as the date of adoption of the plan. The stock in this case was dispersed among 26 shareholders, but the corporation in City Bank of Washington, 38 T.C. 713 (1962) (Non-Acq. on this point, 1964-2 C.B. 4), acting with admitted tax motivation, successfully sold its depreciated assets, adopted its plan of liquidation, and sold its appreciated assets under §337 in that order. It is too early to assume that the "straddle" device is wholly reliable, especially if the depreciated and appreciated assets are sold in two installments to the same buyer; but this seems to be a gamble in which the taxpayer has something to win but ordinarily nothing to lose.

In the straddle cases, the taxpayers insisted on formality, arguing that the plan was not adopted before the formal shareholders' resolution. The shoe is often on the other foot, however, since the shareholders of a closely-held corporation may agree informally to liquidate, but sell the assets before taking formal action to adopt a plan of liquidation; indeed, they may distribute the proceeds of sale and close up shop without complying with any of the formalities seemingly required by §337 or by state law. The Internal Revenue Service has ruled that an informal agreement by shareholders owning 75 percent of the stock of a closely-held corporation that the corporation should sell its assets and distribute the proceeds in complete liquidation would be regarded as the adoption of a plan, even though the formal shareholders' meeting and resolution followed the sale, where local law permitted shareholders owning two-thirds of the stock to approve a dissolution of the corporation.[71] In the typical case of an informally-conducted family corporation that sells its assets at a gain, this ruling will be helpful to the taxpayer; but it is not easily reconciled with the "straddle" cases cited in the preceding paragraph. Where no formal resolution was adopted at any time, the courts have come to the taxpayer's rescue on several occasions by holding that a "plan of liquidation" can be "adopted" without a document in writing and that the "plan" can be gleaned from all of the facts of a business transaction.[72] This pattern of behaviour is obviously not to be recommended, however, since

[71] Rev. Rul. 65-235, 1965-2 C.B.——.
[72] See Alameda Realty Corp., 42 T.C. 273 (1964); Mountain Water Co. of La Crescenta, 35 T.C. 418 (1960); supra, Sec. 9.02; but see Whitson v. Rock-

it may take a lawsuit to establish the applicability of §337, and the cases are in conflict. (One can only speculate about the number of fraudulently pre-dated documents that are employed in this area, where the stakes are high and the taxpayer is likely to feel that his failure to adopt a plan in advance was an inconsequential detail.) If a plan *is* adopted (either formally, or by such informal action as qualifies under §337), the Service has ruled that failure to file the information return required by §6043 (Form 966) or the information required by Regs. §1.337-6 will not per se be fatal; here again, however, compliance with the formalities is obviously desirable, since a failure to do so may cause the Service to question whether or when a plan was adopted.[73]

After adopting a plan of liquidation in anticipation of a sale of its assets, the corporation may be unable to consumate the sale; and if a new opportunity to sell the assets arises at a later time, it will be necessary to decide whether the original plan is still pending or a new one should be adopted, so as to insure that a plan is in force before the sale is made and that the proceeds are distributed in complete liquidation before the 12-month period expires. If the original plan was clearly abandoned, a later plan would seem to be necessary and effective; but a corporation that has been engaged in a leisurely process of disposing of all of its assets under a plan that is more than 12 months old can hardly expect to get the benefit of §337 for its final sale by purporting to call off the old plan in favor of an allegedly new one.[74] A corporation that may have to make a quick sale of its assets in circumstances precluding the adoption of a plan on the same day as the sale, but that does not want its plan to be more than 12 months old when the sale is made, may seek to meet the problem by adopting a plan contingent on the sale itself. There is some authority for believing that such a contingent plan is "adopted" when the sale occurs, rather than when the resolution is passed.[75]

2. Complete distribution within 12-month period. Section 337 requires all corporate assets to be distributed in complete liquidation

wood, 190 F. Supp. 478, 7 AFTR 2d 301 (D. N. Dak. 1961), and Intercounty Development Corp., ¶61,217 P-H Memo TC, rejecting claims that an informal plan pre-dated the sale.

See generally, Pustilnik, Liquidation of Closely-Held Corporations Under §337, 16 Tax L. Rev. 255 (1961).

[73] Rev. Rul. 65-80, 1965-1 C.B. 154; Rev. Rul. 65-30, 1965-1 C.B. 155; see Intercounty Development Corp., *supra* note 72 (failure to file Form 966 as evidence that no plan was adopted).

[74] See Malcolm C. Howell, 40 T.C. 940 (1963).

[75] Henry H. Adams, Transferee, 38 T.C. 549 (1962) (loss sales included in §337 period); but see Whitson v. Rockwood, *supra* note 72 (gain sales excluded from §337 period).

within the 12-month period beginning on the date the plan is adopted,[76] except for assets retained to meet claims. Although contingent and unknown, as well as fixed, claims may be provided for, the amount retained must be reasonable and the arrangements for payment must be made in good faith. The regulations state that the term "claims" does not embrace amounts set aside to meet claims of shareholders with respect to their stock. Although the Tax Court may disagree on this point, at least if the claims are insignificant in amount, there is a safer way to provide for payment to shareholders who cannot be located or whose rights are in dispute, viz., a distribution of the net assets to an escrow agent or trustee for the shareholders.[77] The same device may be useful in providing for payment of contingent creditor claims against the corporation; a distribution to a trustee for shareholders, subject to the claims, may avoid the problem of proving that a retention of assets by the corporation itself is reasonable in amount. It will be noted that what is required is a distribution of "all of the assets" (less amounts retained to pay claims) in complete liquidation, not a formal dissolution of the corporation under state law; but here, as elsewhere (*infra*, Sec. 9.67), a prompt or prearranged re-activation of the corporation may be inconsistent with the claim that it was completely liquidated.

Because §337 provides flatly and without exception that the assets must be distributed within a 12-month period beginning when the plan of liquidation was adopted, it penalizes an inadvertent delay in effecting the distribution; and at the same time it invites an effort at avoidance (e.g., to permit a loss on a sale of the assets to be recognized) by stretching out the period of distribution. While it is too early to be sure that the latter maneuver will always be successful, it has been upheld in at least one case.[78] A foresighted taxpayer who

---

[76] Regs. §1.337-2(b) states that §337 cannot apply if the distribution takes more than 12 months from the date the shareholders' resolution is adopted. This outside limit may be shortened, however, if the plan was adopted before the resolution; see *supra*, for this possibility.

[77] See Jeanese, Inc. v. United States, 341 F.2d 502, 15 AFTR 2d 429 (9th Cir. 1965) (inventory assets retained to meet claims); Regs. §1.337-2(b) (retention to pay shareholder claims not allowed; distribution to trustee for shareholders permissible); Mountain Water Co. of La Crescenta, *supra* note 72 (small amounts to meet shareholder claims); Rev. Rul. 63-245, 1963-2 C.B. 144 (distribution of claim that cannot be readily divided to trustee for shareholders for collection and distribution of proceeds; approved); Rev. Rul. 65-257, 1965-2 C.B. —— (distribution to escrow agent for dissenting minority shareholders).

The ubiquitous problem of "stock vs. debt" (*supra*, Sec. 4.02) crops up once more: an amount retained to meet the claims of shareholders-creditors will be fatal to a §337 transaction if their claims turn out to be stock rather than bona fide debt. See John Town, Inc., 46 T.C. No. 9 (1966).

[78] Milwaukee Sanitarium v. United States, 193 F. Supp. 299, 7 AFTR 2d 934 (D.C. Wis. 1961); see also, for inadvertent disqualifications, Harriet Fibel,

wishes to avoid §337 will also refrain from taking any formal action to adopt a plan of liquidation, a refinement which will impose on the Service the formidable burden of (a) proving that a plan was informally adopted, and (b) persuading a court that the deliberate delay in distributing the assets should be disregarded and the distribution treated as complying with §337. The Service's chance of success in these circumstances seems so slight that little would be lost by a formal ruling permitting a taxpayer who wishes to avoid §337 to do so by deliberately stretching out the distribution period.

3. Insolvent corporations. In Rev. Rul. 56-387, 1956-2 C.B. 189, the Service ruled that §337(a) does not apply unless there is a distribution to the shareholders of the corporation, so that an insolvent corporation whose assets will be distributed entirely to its creditors cannot take advantage of §337(a). The theory of the ruling is that §337(a) was designed to obviate double taxation of the corporation and its shareholders, but not to eliminate the tax on gains from sales of corporate assets in conjunction with a liquidation.

Under the ruling, an insignificant distribution to shareholders could eliminate a very large corporate tax. Moreover, whether the shareholders receive a distribution or not, they will not necessarily pay a tax, as the ruling erroneously assumes: the distribution may be less than their basis, they may be tax-exempt institutions, etc. Despite the weakness of the ruling, it was influential in the rejection of a plan of reorganization proposed under Chapter X, on the ground that the hazard of a corporate tax on a sale of the assets of an insolvent corporation was so great that the plan could not be regarded as equitable and feasible.[79]

Sec. 9.65.   §337 — Non-qualifying assets and dispositions

Account must be taken of a number of transactions to which §337 does not apply:

1. Inventory property and installment obligations. Section 337 is inapplicable to sales of the corporation's stock in trade, inventory, and most installment obligations. The reason for excluding these items is that §337 was aimed at winding-up sales, rather than sales

---

44 T.C. 647 (1965); The Covered Wagon, Inc., ¶65,112 P-H Memo TC.

[79] In Re Inland Gas Corp., 241 F.2d 374, 52 AFTR 579 (6th Cir. 1957), cert. denied, 355 U.S. 838. The position adopted in Rev. Rul. 56-387 may have been inspired by the non-applicability of §332 to the liquidation of an insolvent subsidiary (*supra,* Sec. 9.41); but §332 speaks of a "distribution . . . in complete cancellation or redemption of all [the subsidiary's] stock," whereas §337 refers only to a distribution of all of the assets in complete liquidation, less those retained to meet claims.

in the regular course of business even though occurring during the final
months of the corporation's life. In keeping with this spirit, however,
§337(b)(2) makes an exception for a bulk sale of "substantially all"
of the inventory property to one person in one transaction.[80] Although
the statute is silent on the time when the "substantially all" test is
to be applied, Regs. §1.337-3(b) provides that this determination is
to be made at the time of the bulk sale. This means that a corporation can make taxable sales of inventory property in the regular
course of business after adoption of its plan of liquidation, with a tax-
free bulk sale of its remaining stock in trade just before distribution
of its assets in liquidation. Moreover, because §337(b)(2) permits a
bulk sale of stock in trade which is attributable to *a* business of the
corporation, §337(a) will apply to the bulk sale of inventory of one
business, without regard to what the corporation does with the stock
in trade of any *other* business it may be engaged in.[81]

If a corporation holding appreciated inventory property does not
wish to sell it in bulk, it may be possible to avoid a double tax even
though §337(a) does not apply. The property in question might be
distributed in liquidation to the shareholders, and sold by them as
partners in reliance on the *Cumberland Public Service Co.* case (*supra*,
Sec. 9.63). There is some reason to believe, however, that the *Court
Holding Co.* doctrine would be applied even more freely to so-called
shareholder sales of inventory than to their sales of other types of
property, at least if the corporation's business is in effect carried on
by the shareholders at the same place, in the same way, and with the
same customers. In the *Cumberland Public Service Co.* case, the court
said: "The corporate tax is thus aimed primarily at the profits of a
going concern." Sales of the distributed inventory in the ordinary
course of business, even though made in form by the shareholders,
might be regarded as a belated realization of corporate profits.[82]

The treatment of a sale of installment obligations is considerably
more complex, involving as it does an inter-relationship between

---

[80] See The Luff Co., 44 T.C. 532 (1965), holding that a bulk sale of work
in process inventory qualified for §337 nonrecognition treatment (although the
court noted that the failure to transfer raw material inventories might have
vitiated qualification of the transaction as a bulk sale had the Commissioner
so argued); Hollywood Baseball Assoc., 42 T.C. 234 (1964) (inventory includes
certain baseball player contracts), aff'd, 352 F.2d 350, 16 AFTR 2d 5855 (9th
Cir. 1965), remanded (for further consideration in light of Malat v. Riddell.
383 U.S. 569, 17 AFTR 2d 604), 383 U.S. 824, 17 AFTR 2d 645 (1966).

See also Jeanese, Inc. v. United States, *supra* note 77, holding that a bulk
sale of the corporation's stock in trade qualified despite retention of certain
inventory subject to claims based on a purchase contract.

[81] See Regs. §1.337-3(c) and (d); *infra,* Sec. 11.04 ("separate" business
under §355).

[82] See United States v. Lynch (*supra,* Sec. 5.21).

§453(d), §336 and §337(b). In general, §453(d)(1) provides that any "disposition" of an installment obligation by the holder thereof will terminate the deferral privilege with respect to the gain segment of the obligation. However, §453(d)(4)(B) makes an exception for transfers in liquidations if the obligation could have been sold without recognition of gain under §337 (provided it did not arise in a sale of property subject to the recapture of depreciation under §1245 or §1250). Section 337(b) in turn provides generally that installment obligations[83] do not constitute "property" subject to §337(a), unless they arose from the sale of non-inventory property after adoption of the plan of liquidation or from a qualified "bulk sale" of inventory under §337(b)(2). This labyrinthine set of rules may be summarized as follows:

> (a) Installment obligations acquired on a sale of non-inventory property (other than §1245 or §1250 property) or on a bulk sale of inventory after adoption of the plan of liquidation can be sold or exchanged by the corporation under §337(a), or distributed without recognition of gain or loss under §336 and §453-(d)(4)(B).
>
> (b) All other installment obligations will produce gain at the corporate level under §453(d)(1), whether sold under §337 or distributed in kind under §336 (subject to a minor exception, by virtue of §453(d)(4)(A), for §332 liquidations).

It should be noted that whether the corporation recognizes gain on installment obligations distributed to its shareholders or not, their fair market value must be taken into account in computing the shareholders' gain or loss on the liquidating distribution. Thus, when a corporation is arranging for a sale of its assets under §337, its shareholders have nothing to gain from a sale on the installment basis so far as their own tax liability is concerned, although there may of course be a business reason for spreading the payments over a period of time.[84]

2. *The requirement of a sale or exchange.* Nonrecognition treatment is available under §337 only for gain or loss on the "sale or exchange" of property, a term which has generated its own special body of technical minutiae, especially in the capital gain area, where a disposition of property may be a taxable event but not constitute a "sale or exchange" as required by §1222 (definition of captial gain

---

[83] Obligations may be "installment obligations" within the meaning of §337, even though they do not qualify as such under §453. See Family Record Plan, Inc. v. Commissioner, 33 T.C. 305 (1961), aff'd other grounds, 309 F.2d 208, 10 AFTR 5794 (9th Cir. 1962); Sara G. Wimp, ¶61,342 P-H Memo TC.

[84] See Freeman v. Commissioner, 303 F.2d 580, 9 AFTR 2d 1622 (8th Cir. 1962).

and loss).[85] Transactions that have been held to constitute sales in applying §1222 should also be so regarded in applying §337.[86] The status of "artificial" sales — i.e., transactions that are treated as sales in applying §1222 or other provisions, even though they would not otherwise be so characterized — is more problematical. Early in §337's history, the Internal Revenue Service ruled that gain on collecting the proceeds of insurance after a building was destroyed by fire was not realized on "a sale or exchange . . . of property" under §337, although the transaction would be treated as a sale in applying §1231. After several litigation failures, however, the Service held that all gains and losses on the involuntary conversion of property qualify under §337.[87] In some cases, such events would not constitute sales under §1231 or otherwise (e.g., involuntary conversion of assets held for six months or less), and their status under §337 is still debatable, although taxpayers are likely to raise the issue only on incurring a loss. If transactions that enjoy the status of "sales" under §1231 are to qualify for nonrecognition of gain or loss under §337, there seems to be no reason to exclude transactions that are treated as "sales" by other statutory provisions, e.g., losses on worthless securities (§165(g)) and gains and losses on corporate liquidations and redemptions (§331(a)(1) and §302), on the cancellation of leases or distributorship agreements (§1241), and the retirement of bonds (§1232).[88]

It should be noted that a transaction may constitute a "sale" in applying §337 but fail to qualify for non-recognition because it occurred before the plan of liquidation was adopted. Condemnations are especially troublesome in this respect, since under local law title

[85] See Note, The Elements of a Section 117 "Sale or Exchange," 53 Col. L. Rev. 976 (1953); see also Commissioner v. Brown, 380 U.S. 563, 15 AFTR 2d 790 (1965).

[86] In Hollywood Baseball Assoc., *supra* note 80, the Tax Court held that the term should be more liberally construed in applying §337; 4 judges dissented on this issue; see also Comtel Corp., 45 T.C. 294 (1966) (transaction treated as a loan rather than as a sale).

[87] Rev. Rul. 56-372, 1956-2 C.B. 187, revoked by Rev. Rul. 64-100, 1964-2 C.B. 130, citing Towanda Textiles, Inc. v. United States, 180 F. Supp. 373, 5 AFTR 2d 702 (Ct. Cl. 1960); Kent Mfg. Co. v. Commissioner, 288 F.2d 812, 7 AFTR 2d 856 (4th Cir. 1961).

Taxpayers who incur casualty losses may wish to litigate this matter further, on the ground that §1231 overrides Helvering v. William Flaccus Oak Leather Co., 313 U.S. 247, 25 AFTR 1236 (1947) (no "sale" on collection of fire insurance proceeds) only if the gains and losses are *recognized;* and if the corporation's §1231 losses exceed its gains, on the added ground that §1231 creates an "artificial" sale only when gains exceed losses.

[88] See Rev. Rul. 57-243, 1957-1 C.B. 116 (gain on liquidation of 60 percent-owned subsidiary); 84 Woodbine St. Realty Corp. ¶63,262 P-H Memo TC (condemnation; held, "sale" occurred when condemning authority obtained title to property; no §1232 "sale" on collecting award from state).

may pass to the public authority without advance warning to the taxpayer, so that there is no time to adopt a plan of liquidation.[89]

3. Sale of "property" — relation to assignment of income, "clear" reflection of income, and tax benefit principles. As noted earlier (*supra*, Sec. 9.62), a substantial body of case law and rulings has evolved in the complete liquidation area, under which a corporation that distributes its assets in kind may have to recognize the accrued or potential income inherent therein. Whether they invoke assignment of income principles, the requirement of §446(b) that the taxpayer's accounting method must "clearly reflect income," or the tax benefit doctrine, these authorities seem equally applicable to a complete liquidation under §337, so far as assets distributed in kind are concerned. The important question, however, is the extent to which they apply to assets that are sold, rather than distributed, by the liquidating corporation, in view of §337's principle of not recognizing gain or loss on "the sale or exchange [by the corporation] of property."

The function of §337 — to eliminate the distinction between *Court Holding Co.* situations and *Cumberland Public Service Co.* situations — strongly suggests that §337 should be interpreted, whenever possible, in such a way as to minimize the disparities between these situations. If the tax results at the corporate level are to be identical whether the corporation sells the assets itself, or distributes them to its shareholders for sale by them, nonrecognition of gain cannot be accorded to a transaction under §337 if a liquidating distribution in kind of property involved would have generated income under the asignment of income, tax benefit, or §446(b) principles discussed earlier.[90] In keeping with this approach, the cases and rulings exhibit a tendency to limit §337 so as to achieve a parity between sales of assets by the corporation and distributions in kind. In refusing to apply the nonrecognition rule of §337 to gain or income that would have been recognized if there had been a distribution in kind of the assets reflecting the gain, the cases and rulings assert

---

[89] See Wendell v. Commissioner, 326 F.2d 600, 13 AFTR 2d 451 (2d Cir. 1964), and cases there cited.

[90] Sales at a loss (e.g., the sale of a partially-completed construction contract for less than the accumulated costs by a taxpayer using the completed contract method of accounting) are troublesome to fit into this framework: if the loss would go unrecognized on a distribution of the contract rights, a disparity can be avoided only by *applying* the nonrecognition rule of §337. Yet a sale of the same contract at a gain would have to be *excluded* from the nonrecognition rule to avoid a disparity with §336. Of course, the disparity would be avoided if the loss could be recognized on a distribution of the contract in kind; but so far, there have been no §336 cases involving the deductibility of a loss in such cirucumstances.

either that the term "property" in §337(a) does not include so-called "income items"[91] or, more broadly, that the provision taken as a whole was not intended to override the assignment of income, tax benefit, and §446(b) principles that would have applied if the liquidating corporation had distributed its assets in kind. Thus, in Commissioner v. Kuckenberg, 309 F.2d 202, 10 AFTR 2d 5758 (9th Cir. 1962), where a cash basis corporation sold accrued rights to compensation income, the court held the sales proceeds taxable despite §337, by dual reliance on the clear reflection of income language of §446(b) and principles sounding in asignment of income.[92] Similarly, liquidating corporations on selling their accounts receivable have been required to take their bad debt reserves into income, on a tax benefit theory, though recent developments leave this issue somewhat unsettled.[93]

In an effort to confine §337 to its proper role, it is sometimes suggested that it applies only to corporate capital gains, not to ordinary income.[94] While this generalization is roughly correct, it can

[91] See Eustice, *supra* note 58; Lyon and Eustice, *supra* note 58.

[92] See also Rev. Rul. 59-120, 1959-1 C.B. 74 (sale of discount notes with accrued interest by a cash basis taxpayer); Central Bldg. & Loan Ass'n., 34 T.C. 447 (1960) (sales of notes with accrued interest by a cash basis taxpayer); Family Record Plan, Inc. v. Commissioner, 309 F.2d 208, 10 AFTR 2d 5794 (9th Cir. 1962) (sale by a cash basis taxpayer of accounts receivable arising from sales of goods and services); Rev. Rul. 61-214, 1961-2 C.B. 60 (proceeds of sales of supplies, the cost of which had been deducted with tax benefit, not exempt under §337).

[93] West Seattle National Bank v. Commissioner, 288 F.2d 47, 7 AFTR 2d 790 (9th Cir. 1961) (sale at face value); Ira Handelman, 36 T.C. 560 (1961); Citizens Fed. Savings & Loan Ass'n. v. United States, 290 F.2d 932, 7 AFTR 2d 1548 (Ct. Cl. 1961).

If the receivables are sold for less than face, there is authority both for and against taking the bad debt reserve into income; J. E. Hawes Corp., 44 T.C. 705 (1965) (taxable); Mountain States Mixed Feed Co. v. United States, 245 F. Supp. 369, 16 AFTR 2d 5460 (D. Colo. 1965) (contra); see Schmidt's Estate v. Commissioner, *supra* note 61.

In James M. Pierce Corp. v. Commissioner, 326 F.2d 67, 13 AFTR 2d 358 (8th Cir. 1964), the court relied on the *West Seattle Bank* case to require a publisher to take deferred subscription income into account on liquidating, but permitted this to be offset by a deduction on the theory that the taxpayer had paid the buyer to take over the liabilities attributable to the reserve in the form of a reduced sales price for the assets.

[94] The high water mark in assimilating the term "property" in §337 to the term "capital asset" as defined by §1221 is Pridemark, Inc. v. Commissioner, 345 F.2d 35, 15 AFTR 2d 853 (4th Cir. 1965), holding gain on a sale of certain sales contracts taxable despite §337, on the ground that "[t]he incompleted sales contracts not being capital assets, the proceeds received for their assignment are to be taxed as ordinary income." (This language is broader than necessary to the result, however, and it may be treated in later cases as an over-generalization rather than a holding.) See also Calley v. United States, 220 F. Supp. 111, 12 AFTR 2d 5863 (S.D.W.Va. 1963) (applying §337 to insurance agent's "expirations and renewals" on ground that they constituted "capital assets"); Frank W. Verito, *supra* note 68.

be pushed to the point of overkill. Section 337 itself expressly sanctions nonrecognition of gain or loss on a bulk sale of inventory and certain installment obligations, even though such gain or loss if recognized would almost certainly be non-capital. Moreover, it seems quite clear that some other assets qualify for nonrecognition under §337, even though they would yield ordinary gain or loss if sold outside of §337, e.g., *Corn Products* assets; business assets held for six months or less; copyrights or other similar property described by §1221(3); etc.[95] Hence, even though the sales on which Congress focussed in enacting §337 ordinarily involved assets that would generate capital gain or loss under §1221 or §1231, the provision as written is not so narrowly confined. On balance, the "parity" treatment of sales under §337 and distributions in kind under §336, described above, has much to commend it as a solution to the interpretive problems in this area.[96]

4. Recapture of depreciation. The nonrecognition rule of §337 is subordinate to the recapture of "excess" depreciation under §1245 and §1250, as well as to §47(a), providing for a recapture of the investment credit on an "early disposition" of the property on which the credit was based.

5. Effect of nonrecognition of gain on deductions. Section 265(a) forbids the deduction of any amount "which is allocable to one or

[95] See Corn Products Refining Co., 350 U.S. 46, 47 AFTR 1789 (1955) (ordinary income on sale of business-connected futures contracts); Commissioner v. Bagley & Sewall Co., 221 F. 2d 944, 47 AFTR 790 (2d Cir. 1955) (ordinary loss on sale of business-connected government bonds); see also Eustice, *supra* note 58, at 69-70. Although it is impossible to be dogmatic in such a murky area, the limitations on §336 that are discussed *supra,* Sec. 9.61, would have to be pushed beyond their present location to permit recognition of gain or loss on a distribution in kind of assets such as these; but the theory that the nonrecognition rule of §337 does not cover ordinary income or loss would lead to the recognition of gain or loss on a liquidating sale of these assets, and those mentioned in the text. If so, the dichotomy between *Court Holding Co.* and *Cumberland Public Service Co.* would be perpetuated in this area.

It should be noted that the Service has acknowledged that §337 applies to potential ordinary income in at least one ruling: Rev. Rul. 59-308, 1959-2 C.B. 110 (gain on sale of defense facilities embraced by §337, although constituting ordinary income under §1238). Note also that §337 covers short-term capital gain, although it often has the same tax result as ordinary income; Frank W. Verito, *supra* note 68.

[96] See Frank W. Verito, *supra* note 68, at 440:

. . . the purpose of section 337 was to do away with the necessity of deciding who made the sale as long as the corporation is in a state of complete liquidation and the sale (of property) takes place within a certain period of time. Any result which would cause the question of taxation to once again depend upon who made the sale, where the formal requirements of the section have been met, would be a direct violation of the section.

See also Hollywood Baseball Assoc., *supra* note 80, at 269, accepting a judicial duty to harmonize §337 with §336; the disenting judges, however, without discussion of this theory, seem to have rejected it.

more classes of income other than interest . . . wholly exempt from [income] taxes." The Internal Revenue Service ruled in 1960 that gain subject to nonrecognition under §337 was "exempt" for the purpose of applying §265, with the result that expenses and state income taxes attributable thereto were not deductible; after losing a series of cases on this point, however, the Service revoked its 1960 ruling.[97] See also Royal Oak Apartments, Inc. 43 T.C. 243 (1964) (Acq.), holding that a liquidating corporation could deduct state excise taxes imposed on its §337 unrecognized gain, even though actual payment was made by the taxpayer's shareholders, the corporation having retained insufficient assets to discharge the liability. The court found a constructive payment by the corporation, in view of its primary liability. Presumably the shareholders would also be entitled to a capital loss deduction, under Arrowsmith v. Commissioner, 344 U.S. 6, 42 AFTR 649 (1952), if their capital gain or loss on the liquidating distribution was computed and reported without allowance for this liability.

There seems to be little justification for allowing a liquidating corporation to deduct the expenses of selling its assets, in view of the well-established principle that such expenses are an offset against the sales proceeds, reducing the corporation's realized gain or loss. As to sales under §337, however, where the gain or loss goes unrecognized, the cases are in conflict.[98] If the expense of distributing assets in kind can be included in the corporation's deductible liquidation expenses, a denial of a deduction for expenses attributable to assets that are sold will create a disparity between §336 and §337; but ordinarily the cost of arranging an in-kind distribution is slight in comparison to the broker's commissions, legal fees, etc., incurred on a sale of assets.

Sec. 9.66.   §337 — Non-qualified liquidations

Section 337 is made inapplicable to the liquidation of collapsible corporations, as well as to liquidations under §333 and §332 and

---

[97] Rev. Rul. 63-234, 1963-2 C.B. 148, revoking Rev. Rul. 60-236, 1960-2 C.B. 109; Commissioner v. McDonald, Transferee, 320 F.2d 109, 12 AFTR 2d 5162 (5th Cir. 1963).

[98] Pridemark, Inc. v. Commissioner, *supra* note 94 (legal fees incurred in connection with sale of assets allowed as "liquidation expenses"); Otto F. Ruprecht, ¶61,125 P-H Memo TC (contra); see also Towanda Textiles, Inc. v. United States, *supra* note 87 (cost of collecting insurance proceeds required to be "capitalized" as in the nature of selling expenses); Beauchap & Brown Groves Co., 44 T.C. 117 (1965) (§268 requires cost of growing crop to be capitalized, even though gain on sale of land with unharvested crop is unrecognized under §337).

See generally, Note, The Deductibility of Attorney's Fees, 74 Harv. L. Rev. 1409 (1961).

partial liquidations and stock redemptions, for the reasons set out hereafter.

1. Collapsible corporations. If §337 were applicable to "collapsible corporations" (*infra*, Ch. 10), the punitive provisions of §341 would be nullified. For the corporation would then be able to sell its assets, avoiding the recognition of its gain under §337, while the shareholders would escape §341(a), because the corporation would have *realized* (though without recognizing) its gain, and hence would not be a "collapsible corporation" under §341(b). To protect §341, therefore, §337 is made inapplicable to collapsible corporations by §337(c)(1)-(A). The statutory language is below par, because it leaves room for the argument that a corporation that sells its assets has "realized" its gain (even though it is not "recognized") and therefore is not collapsible under §341(b); but the regulations rightly reject this literally possible, but otherwise untenable, construction.[99]

The denial of the benefits of §337(a) to a collapsible corporation, however, does not automatically result in the corporation's recognition of gain on a sale of its property, as is sometimes assumed. The corporation may distribute the assets in liquidation; although the shareholders will be taxed on their gain under §341(a), subject to the limitations of §341(d), they may proceed to sell the assets as individuals, relying on the *Cumberland Public Service Co.* case to avoid an attribution of the sale to the corporation. If the corporation itself makes the sale (or if the sale is attributed to the corporation under the *Court Holding Co.* case), however, it will recognize its gain because §337(a) is inapplicable, but this recognition of gain on the sale will make the punitive provisions of §341 inapplicable to the shareholders by taking the corporation out of the collapsible category.[100]

Under a 1958 amendment (*infra*, Sec. 10.07), a restricted group of otherwise collapsible corporations became eligible for the benefits of §337.

See also §341(f) (*infra*, Sec. 10.08), added in 1964, which provides that sales of "section 341(f) assets" will not qualify for nonrecognition treatment under §337.

2. Elective one-month liquidations under §333. Section 337-

---

[99] Regs. §1.337-1. A second line of defense open to the Commissioner in some circumstances would be to "predate" the adoption of the plan of liquidation to the time the collapsible corporation was organized, in which event the liquidation would probably not be completed within the prescribed 12-month period.

[100] See Rev. Rul. 58-241, 1958-1 C.B. 179; Rev. Rul. 63-125, 1963-2 C.B. 146; Sproul Realty Co., 38 T.C. 844 (1962).

(c)(1)(B) provides that §337 is inapplicable if the corporation is liquidated under §333 (*supra*, Sec. 9.21), providing for nonrecognition of gain by electing shareholders on a one-month liquidation. Although the Senate Report on the 1954 Code does not state why §337 was made inapplicable to such liquidations, presumably this was done so that tax will not be avoided at both the corporate and shareholder levels by a use of §337 and §333 in combination.[101] Since a use of §333 by *any* shareholder bars the use of §337 by the corporation, the shareholders' interests may be very divergent. For example, if the individual shareholders elect to proceed under §333, a sale of assets by the corporation may result in a corporate tax, thus reducing the value of the liquidating distribution for all shareholders. The sale, moreover, will increase the corporation's cash and earnings and profits, thus affecting the computation of gain under §333(e) and (f). These complications may be reduced if the corporation is liquidated under §333 and the property is sold by the shareholders under the shelter of the *Cumberland Public Service Co.* case. If the shareholders fail to bring the transaction within that case, however, and the sale is attributed to the corporation under the *Court Holding Co.* doctrine, there will be a tax at the corporate level, and in addition the shareholders' gain under §333(e) and §333(f) will probably have to be recomputed on the theory that they constructively received the sales proceeds from the corporation, rather than the property itself.

3. *Liquidations of subsidiary corporations under §332.* By virtue of §337(c)(2), sales and exchanges by a subsidiary in conjunction with a §332 liquidation (tax-free liquidation of an 80 percent subsidiary) are not covered by the non-recognition rule of §337(a), except for the limited class of §332 liquidations subject to the statutory *Kimbell-Diamond* provision.[102] Section 337(a) is apparently made inapplicable to the "normal" §332 liquidation because the liquidation itself is not a taxable event, so that if §337(a) were applicable, gain on a sale of appreciated property by the subsidiary would not be recognized by either the subsidiary or the parent. Be-

[101] The corporation, if §337 were applicable, could sell its assets without recognizing gain, invest the proceeds in other property, and distribute the newly acquired property under §333. Unless the transaction were regarded as, in substance, a distribution of money (which does not qualify for non-recognition under §333, *supra*, Sec. 9.21), the shareholders would avoid a tax at the shareholder level except to the extent of the corporation's earnings and profits, which would have been increased by the sale.

[102] *Supra*, Sec. 9.44. For this limited type of §332 liquidation, §337 is applicable, in effect, only to the pre-acquisition appreciation in value; if the subsidiary sells its assets for more than the parent paid for the stock, that part of the gain is taxable. Regs. §1.337-4.

See generally United States Holding Co., 44 T.C. 323 (1965).

cause §337(a) does not apply, however, gain on a sale of the subsidiary's assets will be recognized either by the subsidiary (if it makes the sale or if a sale by the parent is attributed to it under the *Court Holding Co.* case) or by the parent, which must carry over the subsidiary's basis under §334(b)(1) (if the sale is within the *Cumberland Public Service Co.* case). Similarly, losses on the sale of depreciated property will be taken by the subsidiary or by the parent, according to the circumstances of the transaction.[103]

Until 1958, the denial of §337 to liquidations under §332 contained the possibility of unfairness for minority shareholders, who were faced with the prospect of a tax at the corporate level as well as at the shareholder level if the corporation sold the assets. The Technical Amendments Act of 1958, however, added §337(d) to the Code, providing that a minority shareholder shall treat his share of the corporate tax as though it had been (a) distributed to him in liquidation, and (b) paid by him as a tax. The effect of §337(d) is to increase the shareholder's gain (or decrease his loss) on the liquidation by his share of the corporation's tax, and to treat the same amount as a down payment by him on his income tax for the year, with the result that the minority shareholder will be in the same position, in most cases, as though §337 had applied to the liquidation.

4. Non-liquidating distributions, partial liquidations, and stock redemptions. Since §337 applies only if the corporation distributes its assets in complete liquidation, sales in conjunction with non-liquidating distributions, partial liquidations, and stock redemptions are not within the ambit of §337(a). Sales by the shareholders of property received in such distributions will be imputed to the corporation or not according to the non-statutory rules developed under the *Court Holding Co.* and *Cumberland Public Service Co.* cases. "Undue weight" will continue to be accorded "the formalities of the transaction," and these cases will remain "a trap for the unwary," to use the language of the Senate Report on the 1954 Code.[104]

---

[103] Thus it is not possible to avoid completely the risk of *Court Holding Co.* treatment in the case of liquidations qualifying under §332. In this connection, see also the discussion of the *Fairfield SS Co.* case, *supra,* Sec. 9.41, for another possible attack where the parent contemplates an immediate sale of assets acquired on liquidation of its 80 percent subsidiary.

The *United States Holding Co.* case, *supra* note 102, offers an interesting example of the working of §337(c)(2): there, the subsidiary was held entitled to §337(c)(2)(B) nonrecognition with respect to sales of various assets at a *gain,* while losses on sales of other assets were allowed as deductions because of the "general rule" of §337(c)(2)(A).

[104] *Supra,* Sec. 9.64. See McNair Realty Co. v. United States, 188 F. Supp. 451, 6 AFTR 2d 5795 (D. Mont. 1960).

Sec. 9.67.   §337 and reincorporations

Section 337(a) demands a "complete liquidation" of the corporation as a condition to nonrecognition of its gain or loss on the sale of qualified assets. What if a corporation sells its assets to a corporation owned by its shareholders, taking cash or notes in payment; and then distributes the cash or notes to its shareholders in exchange for their stock? The transaction fits within the statutory language of §337, which does not require the assets to be sold to an unrelated buyer; but the net effect of the transaction is substantially identical with a liquidation-reincorporation effected by distributing the assets in kind to the shareholders so that they can transfer them to a new corporation controlled by them (*supra*, Sec. 9.05). As with such a liquidation-reincorporation, the §337 plan just described — if accepted at face value — would give the second corporation a basis for the assets equal to their fair market value and wipe out the earnings and profits account of the original corporation, and the shareholders would get all this in a transaction creating capital gain (or, possibly, loss) equal to the difference between their adjusted basis for their stock of the original corporation and the fair market value of the assets.

The Internal Revenue Service has endeavored to discourage transactions of this type by refusing to issue rulings on the applicability of §337 if assets are sold to a corporation in which the shareholders of the liquidating corporation own more than a "nominal" amount of stock.[105]

The legal status of §337-reincorporations cannot be discussed except in the context of the reorganization provisions, for which see *infra*, Sec. 12.22. It may be suggested here, however, that use of §337 in conjunction with a reincorporation does not seem to justify special treatment: if a reincorporation following a distribution of assets in kind is treated as a "reorganization," a §337 sale to a corporation controlled by the shareholders of the liquidating corporation deserves the same treatment; conversely, if a reincorporation of assets distributed in kind is accepted at face value, there is little reason for a refusal to honor a §337 sale to a related corporation.

Sec. 9.68.   The liquidating corporation's deductions

Just as the process of liquidation creates a number of problems in determining the liquidating corporation's income, so it has ramifi-

---

[105] Rev. Proc. 64-31, 1964-2 C.B. 947. The term "nominal" is not defined; 20 percent or more is probably too much. For an earlier, more relaxed view,

cations in the area of corporate deductions. The principal issues are (a) whether any adjustment is required with respect to expenditures that would ordinarily be deductible, if the corporation liquidates before the economic benefit thereof has been fully reflected in its income stream; (b) conversely, whether expenditures that were not fully deducted in past years because they were expected to have a continuing economic benefit can be deducted when the fact of liquidation terminates their usefulness; and (c) whether the expenses of effecting the liquidation itself can be deducted.

1. Adjustment for expenditures with continuing economic benefit. As noted *supra*, Sec. 9.62, the Internal Revenue Service has endeavored to require a corporation liquidating in mid-stream to report its potential income by invoking assignment of income principles, §446-(b) (accounting method must "clearly reflect income"), and the tax benefit doctrines and — with less success — by disallowing as deductions to the liquidating corporation those expenses which are attributable to its unreported potential income items, on the ground that they are not ordinary and necessary expenses of "carrying on" a trade or business.

A related development is the attempt of the Service to apportion or allocate expenses incurred during the corporation's final tax period, if related to property distributed in kind to its shareholders, between the corporation and the shareholders, under the "clear reflection of income" language of §446(b) and §482. For example, Rev. Rul. 62-45, 1962-1 C.B. 27, holds that real estate taxes for the year of liquidation must be apportioned on a pro rata basis between the liquidating corporation and its distributee shareholders by virtue of §482, a result that is explicitly required by §164(d) if the property is sold. This approach was upheld in Tennessee Life Ins. Co., v. Phinney, 280 F.2d 38, 5 AFTR 2d 1708 (5th Cir. 1960), cert. denied, 364 U.S. 914; but in Simon J. Murphy Co. v. Commissioner, 231 F.2d 639, 49 AFTR 495 (6th Cir. 1956), the liquidating corporation was allowed to deduct such taxes without apportionment. It is difficult to determine the extent to which deductions can be apportioned between the corporation and its shareholders under §482 on a distribution in kind, or limited on a pro rata basis under §446(b) on a sale of the property for whose benefit the expenditure was incurred. It would seem that deductions which accrue ratably over a fixed period of time (such as interest, rent, property taxes, and the like) should be

see Rev. Rul. 56-541, 1956-2 C.B. 189 (sale to corporation owned to the extent of 45 percent by shareholders of the selling corporation; held, §337 applies), revoked by Rev. Rul. 61-156, 1961-2 C.B. 62.

pro-rated to the date when the liquidating corporation's assets are disributed or sold, at least where the corporation is on the accrual method of accounting; this approach is somewhat less appropriate for cash basis taxpayers, who can deduct their expenses when paid, but it might be insisted on even here, especially if the expenditure creates a benefit beyond the year in payment. Pro-ration in these cases would merely reflect the fact that the liquidating corporation has not sustained the entire burden of these expenses, having terminated its operations prior to completion of the period to which they relate.

2. *Unamortized "deferred deductions."* Different considerations may apply, however, when the corporation has previously capitalized long term expenses (such as prepaid rent, insurance premiums, or supplies) and is amortizing these items over the period to which they relate. In practice, these deferred expense items may be reflected on the corporate books as assets, although from a tax viewpoint it is more accurate to view them merely as "deferred deductions." If the unexpired benefits of these expenditures enure to the benefit of the shareholders on a distribution in kind or the purchaser on the sale of a going business, the unamortized cost should not be deductible by the transferor corporation since it has been transferred as part of the assets. If the unused benefits from such expenditures expire with the taxpayer's liquidation (*e.g.*, if the taxpayer's leases or insurance policies are cancelled without refund of the prepaid rent or premiums), however, deductions should be allowed for the unamortized portions of these expenses in the liquidating corporation's final return. In effect, this is the taxpayer's last clear chance to take account of the previous expenditure of funds for these items, which it was required to defer over a ratable period of time, but which nevertheless constituted a cost of doing business. This principle was applied to corporate organizational expenses and similar items by Koppers Co., Inc. v. United States, 278 F.2d 946, 5 AFTR 2d 1597 (Ct. Cl. 1960), on the ground that the corporation on liquidation "lost or abandoned something for which it had paid"; the liquidation antedated the enactment of §248, permitting the corporation to amortize such expenses over a 60-month period (*supra*, Sec. 2.26), but the principle is equally applicable if the corporation elects not to amortize or elects to do so but liquidates before the amortization period expires.[106] On

---

[106] See also Hollywood Baseball Assoc., *supra* note 80 (deduction allowed for "promotional" shares issued for organization services). It may be necessary to decide whether the corporation has been liquidated or merged, since in the latter case a deduction may be disallowed because the expenses inure to the benefit of a successor corporation, and will be deductible only when the latter is liquidated. See Kingsford Corp., 41 T.C. 646 (1964) (Acq.)

the other hand, the liquidating corporation is not allowed to deduct the expenses incurred on issuing its capital stock or stock dividends (e.g., legal fees, printing costs, underwriters' commissions, etc.), although a retirement of its bonds or other debts at the time of liquidation entitles it to deduct any previously unamortized discount or a premium paid on a pre-maturity retirement.[107]

3. *Expenses of effecting liquidation.* The cost of preparing and effectuating a plan of corporate liquidation and dissolution can be deducted as an ordinary and necessary business expense, even though it involves a termination, rather than a "carrying on," of the corporate trade or business. This general rule has been applied to a §332 liquidation, and it seems equally applicable to §333 and §337 transactions as well. A deduction is more debatable in the case of a partial liquidation or stock redemption, but there is some authority for allowing the deduction if there is a contraction of the corporate enterprise.[108]

Sec. 9.69.   The liquidating corporation's indebtedness

The indebtedness of a liquidating corporation must either be paid off before the final distribution of its assets to shareholders or assumed by them or by some other person (e.g., a purchaser of its assets); failing a formal arrangement for a discharge or assumption of the debt, the shareholders will be liable as transferees. Payment of the debt may generate a deduction for unamortized discount or a retirement premium (*supra*, Sec. 9.68); and, if appreciated or depreciated property is used instead of cash, the corporation will realize gain or loss under familiar principles.[109] (The gain or loss may go unrecognized under §337(a), however, if the property is transferred after the plan of liquidation is adopted.) A discharge for less than the face amount of the debt will generate cancellation-of-indebtedness income; although income so arising is not covered by §337 because it is not attributable to a "sale or exchange" by the corporation of "property,"

[107] On bond discount and premium, see Regs. §1.61-12(c)(3); Nassau Lens Co., Inc. v. Commissioner, 308 F.2d 39, 10 AFTR 2d 5581 (2d Cir. 1962); Roberts & Porter Inc., v. Commissioner, 307 F.2d 745, 10 AFTR 2d 5686 (7th Cir. 1962). As to the expense of issuing stock, see Pacific Coast Biscuit Co., 32 B.T.A 39 (1935) (non-deductible).

[108] Pacific Coast Biscuit Co., *supra* note 107 (complete liquidation); Koppers Co., Inc. v. United States, 278 F.2d 946, 5 AFTR 2d 1597 (Ct. Cl. 1960) (§332 liquidation); Pridemark, Inc. v. Commissioner, *supra* note 94 (§337); Gravois Planing Mill Co. v. Commissioner, 299 F.2d 199, 9 AFTR 2d 733 (8th Cir. 1962), and cases there cited (partial liquidation).
   See generally, authorities cited *supra,* Sec. 2.26, note 67.

[109] See generally Eustice, Cancellation of Indebtedness and the Federal Income Tax: A Problem of Creeping Confusion, 14 Tax L. Rev. 225 (1959).

it is possible that an election to exclude it from income under §108
and §1017 would be efficacious, at least if the property whose basis
is reduced under §1018 is to be sold. Unless §337 is applicable, a sale
after such an election would produce a reduced amount of gain or
loss, which is the normal consequence of the election; and if §337
applies, the fact that the reduction of basis would be ineffectual because the gain or loss is not recognized might be regarded as irrelevant.[110] If the property is to be distributed in kind, however, it is
more difficult to justify a reduction in the corporation's basis; and
the same can be said of an attempt to elect under §108 after the
corporate assets have been distributed, so that none remain to absorb
the basis reduction.

If the corporation's debt is assumed by a purchaser of the assets
instead of being paid off, the amount thereof will be taken into account in computing the gain or loss realized by the corporation on
the sale. Unless the sale falls outside §337, however, the gain or loss
will not be reflected in the corporation's tax liability. Although an
assumption of corporate debt by the shareholders on a distribution
of assets to them might have the legal effect of a discharge of the
corporation's liability, and this in turn might be regarded as a transfer
pro tanto by the corporation of appreciated or depreciated property
in payment of its debt, it is highly unlikely that this theory would
be advanced by the Service or entertained by the courts. The transfer of assets by a liquidating corporation to its shareholders, under
an agreement by which they assume its liabilities, is so customary
that it is reasonable to regard it as a "distribution of property in . . .
complete liquidation" within the nonrecognition rule of §336.[111]

Sec. 9.70.   Earnings and profits of the liquidating corporation

In an ordinary complete liquidation, to which the general rule
of §331(a)(1) applies, it is not necessary to determine the effect of

[110] For possible analogies, see Otto F. Ruprecht, *supra* note 98 (reduction
of sales proceeds by selling expenses, despite application of §337) and note 97
(expenses attributable to gain unrecognized under §337 deductible, despite
§265); Leon R. Meyer, 46 T.C. No. 8 (1966) (effect of cancellation of debt
in bankruptcy proceedings on earnings and profits). See also John Town, Inc.,
supra note 77.

A use of appreciated or depreciated property to discharge the corporation's
debt will have the effect described in the text even though the debt is held by
the shareholders; §336 (*supra*, Sec. 9.61) provides for nonrecognition of gain
or loss only if property is distributed "in partial or complete liquidation," and
this seems limited to a distribution in cancellation of *stock*. See §331(a); and
see the discussion of Regs. §1.311-1(e), *supra*, Sec. 5.21.

[111] A contrary result could not be easily reconciled with the fact that the
assumption of debt by shareholders on a non-liquidating distribution in kind

liquidation on the corporation's earnings and profits, because the corporation has no successor and its earnings and profits do not affect the shareholder's tax on the liquidation. In an elective one-month liquidation under §333, however, the corporation's earnings and profits must be determined "as of the close of the month in which the transfer in liquidation occurred," in order to determine what part, if any, of the shareholder's gain shall be recognized under §333(e) (1) or (f)(2). Similarly, when a subsidiary corporation is liquidated under §332, its earnings and profits must be determined because they are inherited by the parent corporation under §381(a)(1) and (c)-(2).[112]

An accurate determination of the liquidating corporation's earnings and profits will also be necessary if it is a "controlled foreign corporation" or a "foreign investment company" since, as pointed out *supra*, Sec. 9.06 and Sec. 1.06, the shareholder's gain on the liquidation of such a corporation may be taxed as ordinary income rather than capital gain to the extent of his ratable share of its post-1962 earnings and profits.

Sec. 9.71.   Bootstrap acquisitions and the liquidating corporation

In many cases, the purchaser of a corporate business is unwilling or unable to acquire all the assets of the selling company. One set of techniques for "slimming" the assets down to fit the size of the buyer's purse, employing stock redemptions, is discussed *supra*, Sec. 7.25. A complete liquidation can sometimes be used for the same purpose, and it may also serve to step up the basis of the operating assets to their fair market value and to eliminate corporate earnings and profits, results that are not achieved by the stock redemption route, since the latter entails (at least in its simplest form) a preservation of the original corporate shell.

Thus, if X Corporation has some properties that are wanted by the buyer and others that he does not want, the "wanted" assets can be sold to him in a transaction qualifying under §337; and the sale proceeds together with the "unwanted" assets can then be distributed to X's shareholders. The buyer will obtain the assets with a basis equal to their fair market value; if he utilizes a corporation to acquire

---

creates income at the corporate level only if the liability exceeds its basis for the property. *Supra*, Sec. 5.21. A contrary result would also perpetuate the *Court Holding Co. — Cumberland Public Service Co.* dichotomy, since the recognition of income could be avoided by selling the assets at the corporate level and distributing the proceeds.

[112] See Nesson, Earnings and Profits Discontinues Under the 1954 Code. 77 Harv. L. Rev. 450 (1964).

them, it will be free of earnings and profits; and X's shareholders will report capital gain (or loss, depending on their basis for their stock) on the liquidation.

At times, however, the parties may have grander aims, as in a transaction recently sanctioned by the Supreme Court, where the transferred business was to be purchased by use of its future earnings.[113] Briefly stated, this arrangement involved the following steps: (a) the sale of corporate stock to a tax-exempt charity; (b) liquidation by the charity of the acquired corporation; (c) a lease of the operating assets by the charity to a newly-created corporation, the rent being dependent on the future profits of the business; and (d) payments by the charity on its purchase money obligations solely out of the rent received by it, it having no personal liability to the seller.

The Commissioner, understandably, was unhappy with these results, and launched his major attack at the capital gain treatment claimed by the seller of the stock. But the *Brown* case upheld the disposition as a bona fide sale, despite the seller's continued economic interest in the profits of the business, stating that this was merely a method of financing the sale. The court rejected the Commissioner's argument that the economic incidents of ownership (*i.e.*, risk of loss and expectation of profits from the business, together with effective control over the operation thereof during the pay-out period of the sale contract) remained with the seller; the majority opinion felt that a true shift of economic ownership, and hence a sale, had been effected so that the taxpayer was entitled to capital gain treatment for the deferred payment proceeds.[114]

---

[113] Brown v. Commissioner, 380 U.S. 563, 15 AFTR 2d 790 (1965).

[114] For discussions of the *Brown* case, see articles by Dauber, Jewell, Hall, Eliasberg, and Kinsey, 23 J. Tax. 2, 42, and 68 (1965); see also Moore and Dohan, Sales, Churches, and Monkeyshines, 11 Tax L. Rev. 87 (1956); Note, The Three-Party Sale and Lease-Back, 61 Mich L. Rev. 1140 (1963).

Note that §483 (the imputed interest provision), added by the Revenue Act of 1964, will dilute the capital gain benefits from this type of deferred payment sale transaction, and that §§1245 and 1250 may require the liquidating corporation on the distribution of its depreciable assets to recognize some ordinary income.

Chapter Ten

COLLAPSIBLE CORPORATIONS

Sec. 10.01.   Introductory

We have seen (*supra*, Sec. 9.01) that §331(a)(1) provides that a complete liquidation of a corporation is to be treated by the shareholder as a sale of his stock, which will ordinarily produce capital gain or loss, and that §334(a) provides that the shareholder's basis for property acquired on the liquidation is its fair market value at the time of distribution. These long-established rules led to the tax avoidance device known as the "collapsible corporation," which in its turn led in 1950 to the enactment of §341, requiring the shareholder's gain on the sale or liquidation of such a corporation to be reported as ordinary income rather than capital gain.

As will be seen, §341 reaches a good many corporations besides those at which it was aimed; and its application is not limited either to "temporary" corporations or to corporate liquidations.[1] Although §341 has thus come to encompass a wide range of corporations and transactions, it can be understood best after the "classic" collapsible corporation is examined.

The collapsible corporation first attracted attention in the motion picture industry. A producer, director, and leading actors would organize a corporation for the production of a single motion picture. They would invest small amounts of cash and agree to work for modest

---

[1] See Burge v. Commissioner, 253 F.2d 765, 767, 1 AFTR 2d 1214 (4th Cir. 1958):

> The word "collapsible" considered apart from its context would be somewhat misleading; but there can be no question, we think, as to what Congress meant by a "collapsible corporation" as used in [§341]. That term was used to describe a corporation which is made use of to give the appearance of a long term investment to what is in reality a mere venture or project in manufacture, production or construction of property, with the view of making the gains from the venture or project taxable, not as ordinary income, as they should be taxed, but as long term capital gains. Because the basic type of transaction which gave rise to the legislation involved the use of temporary corporations which were dissolved and their proceeds distributed after tax avoidance had been accomplished, the term "collapsible corporation" was employed to describe the corporations used for this form of tax avoidance; but the statute was drawn in broad general terms to reach the abuse which had arisen, whatever form it might take.

See also Braunstein v. Commissioner, 374 U.S. 65, 11 AFTR 2d 1606 (1963).

salaries, and the corporation would finance the production with borrowed funds. When the motion picture was completed, but before it was released for public exhibition, the corporation would be liquidated. The stockholders would report the difference between the cost of their stock and the value of their proportionate shares in the completed film (established on the basis of previews) as long-term capital gain under §331(a)(1). For example, if their investment in the stock was $100,000 and the value of the film was $1,100,000, the shareholders' profit would be $1,000,000, on which the capital gains tax would be $250,000. Under §334(a), the basis of the film in the hands of the shareholders would be $1,100,000; and if the net rentals received thereafter equalled that amount, they would have no further gain or loss, since the fair market value of the film could be amortized against the rentals.[2] In effect, the exhibition profit, which would have been taxed as ordinary income to the corporation had it not been liquidated (or to the producers if they had operated in non-corporate form from the outset) was converted into capital gain. Moreover, instead of two taxes (a corporate tax on the exhibition income and an individual tax at the capital gain rate on ultimate sale or liquidation of the corporation), there would be only one.

The collapsible corporation was also used by builders and investors for the construction of homes in residential subdivisions. A corporation would be created to construct the houses, but it would be liquidated before the houses were sold. The stockholders would report as long-term capital gain the difference between the cost of their stock and the value of the completed houses. The houses, which thus acquired a "stepped up" basis under §334(a) equal to their fair market value at the time of distribution, would then be sold, ordinarily with no further gain or loss to be accounted for. Here again, only one tax would be paid instead of two, and that one would be computed at the capital gain rate.

Sec. 10.02.   Non-statutory weapons against the collapsible corporation

Even without specific statutory authority, the Treasury was not entirely helpless in the face of the collapsible corporation. If the

---

[2] If the proceeds exceeded, or fell short of, the estimated fair market value, the shareholders would have additional income or deductible loss. In Pat O'Brien, 25 T.C. 376 (Acq.), it was held that income in excess of the film's basis was taxable as ordinary income. But see Brodsky and King, Tax Savings Through Distributions in Liquidation of Corporate Contracts, 27 Taxes 806 (1949); Farer, Corporate Liquidations: Transmuting Ordinary Income Into Capital Gains, 75 Harv. L. Rev. 517 (1962); *supra*, Sec. 9.04.

promoters receive inadequate salaries, something could be said for treating the stock of the corporation as additional compensation taxable as ordinary income. Another possibility would be to treat the whole transaction as an ineffective anticipatory assignment of income, relying on the principle of Lucas v. Earl, 281 U.S. 111, 8 AFTR 10,287 (1930), that the federal income tax cannot "be escaped by anticipatory arrangements and contracts however skillfully devised." Another argument open to the Treasury was that the collapsible corporation lacks substance and that the arrangement should be taxed as a joint venture of the alleged stockholders.

So far, however, the Treasury has been unsuccessful in two efforts to attack the collapsible corporation with these non-statutory weapons. One of these cases was not an entirely fair test of the cogency of the non-statutory arguments, since the liquidation of the motion picture corporation there involved was not pre-arranged, but resulted from a change in plans after one film had been completed. Herbert v. Riddell, 103 F. Supp. 369, 41 AFTR 961 (S.D. Calif. 1952). But when the Tax Court came to pass on a collapsible corporation whose liquidation was apparently contemplated from its inception, it described Herbert v. Riddell as "almost identical," and similarly held for the taxpayers.[3] While these initial set-backs would not have entirely foreclosed the development of a non-statutory weapon against the collapsible corporation, the Treasury quite naturally shifted in 1950 to its newly enacted statutory weapon, and evidently gave up on pre-1950 transactions after its losses in the *Herbert* and *O'Brien* cases.[4]

Sec. 10.03.   The framework of §341

Although the details of §341 are quite intricate, its basic principle is simple: a shareholder who disposes of his stock in a collapsible corporation in a transaction that would ordinarily produce long-term capital gain must instead report the gain as ordinary income. As applied to the Hollywood collapsible corporation described at the beginning of this chapter, §341(a) would compel the shareholders to report their $1,000,000 gain on the corporation's complete liquidation as ordinary income, a result which may well be more costly than

---

[3] Pat O'Brien, *supra* note 2; see also Gross v. Commissioner, 236 F.2d 612, 618, 50 AFTR 68 (2d Cir. 1956), upholding the Tax Court's refusal to impute a salary to corporate officers who preferred to take their profits on a business venture in the form of capital gain distributions on their stock. For further discussion of possible non-statutory weapons, see Bittker and Redlich, Corporate Liquidations and the Income Tax, 5 Tax L. Rev. 437, 439-448 (1950).

[4] But see Jacobs v. Commissioner, *infra*, Sec. 10.04.

allowing the corporation to remain alive to realize the income from the film with a view to ultimate sale or liquidation of the corporation. If §341(a) were applicable only to complete liquidations, however, the shareholders would be able to escape by means of one of the following devices:

1. A corporate distribution of the property without a surrender of stock, since under §301(c)(3)(A) the excess of the value of the property over the shareholders' basis for their stock would ordinarily be taxed as long-term capital gain if the distribution occurred before the corporation had realized any earnings and profits.
2. A sale or exchange of the stock.[5]
3. A partial liquidation of the corporation, if the criteria of §346 could be satisfied.

In recognition of the fact that the above arrangements might be used as a substitute for a complete liquidation, §341(a) provides that gain realized by a shareholder in any of these ways shall, to the extent that it would otherwise be long-term capital gain, be considered as gain from the sale or exchange of a non-capital asset.[6]

Section 341(a) is applicable only if the shareholder's gain would otherwise be long-term capital gain.[7] The omission of short-term cap-

---

[5] The new shareholders would of course be concerned about the corporation's low basis for its assets, but they could liquidate the corporation without tax cost (since the value of the liquidating distribution would presumably be equal to the price paid for the stock). The property would thereupon take on a new basis equal to its value, either under §334(a), or, if the buyer was a corporation, under §334(b)(2) (the statutory "Kimbell-Diamond" rule), *supra,* Sec. 9.44.

[6] There is a curious omission from this pattern: a distribution in redemption of stock that is treated as long-term capital gain under §302(a). The omission, which probably stems from carrying forward the pre-1954 reference to "partial liquidations" without noting that this term in the 1954 Code no longer includes redemptions (*supra,* Sec. 7.81, note 79), may be neutralized by the fact that most distributions by collapsible corporations will reflect a "corporate contraction" so as to constitute partial liquidations, which are covered by §341(a)(2). (In an effort to bring distributions by collapsible corporations within §341(a)(2), the government may have to construe the term "partial liquidation" expansively, contrary to its usual position.)

It is also possible that a §302(a) redemption could be brought within §341(a)(1), as a "sale or exchange" of stock, though this theory would be open to the objection that the regulations require an "actual" sale or exchange, Regs. §1.341-1; moreover, it would render the inclusion of partial liquidations in §341(a)(2) redundant, since if a §302(a) redemption is covered by §341(a)-(1), so would be a §346 redemption. Note, however, that the term "sale or exchange" is used in §341(c) to include partial and complete liquidations — or at least so the regulations assume. Regs. §1.341-3(a). See also §341(f)(1).

Prior to 1954, the statute did not explicitly reach distributions that were not accompanied by a surrender of stock, but they were held subject to the statute anyway in Pomponio v. Commissioner, 288 F.2d 827, 7 AFTR 2d 1078 (4th Cir. 1961).

[7] Thus, if a corporate distribution of money or property would be treated

ital gain from §341(a) is surprising, since it permits the collapsible corporation to retain its old advantages for the shareholder who has capital losses that can be offset against any short-term capital gain realized on the liquidation or sale. Section 341(a) is also inapplicable to losses. Finally, §341(a) applies to gain that otherwise "would be considered" as long-term capital gain, but it does not of its own force make gain taxable, with the result that it will have no effect upon a tax-free exchange of stock in a collapsible corporation (*e.g.*, under §351 or §1036).

Aside from the basic rules of §341(a), the statute consists of (a) a definition of the term "collapsible corporation"; (b) a statutory presumption in aid of the definition; and (c) three sets of limitations that moderate the rules of §341(a) in certain circumstances. These aspects of §341 will be examined in the remaining sections of this chapter.[8] Two other disadvantages of collapsible corporation status

as dividend income to its shareholders under §301, §341 would not apply. Similarly, if the stock is not a capital asset because the shareholder holds it as "dealer property," ordinary gain would result on its sale without resort to the provisions of §341(a).

The special earnings and profits rule of §312(j) bears special mention in this context. Prior to the enactment of §341 in 1950, a corporation having no earnings and profits could distribute the "excess" mortgage proceeds from government-guaranteed loans and its shareholders would receive return of capital (and hence capital gain) treatment thereon. From 1950-54, however, these transactions were subject to the collapsible corporation provisions of §117(m) of the 1939 code (the predecessor of §341). But for years covered by the 1954 Code, such distributions are taxable as dividend income to the shareholders, since earnings and profits are specifically created for this purpose by §312(j) (*supra*, Sec. 5.03), thus eliminating this type of transaction from the coverage of §341. Note that "conventional" mortgage bail-outs are still subject to §341, however, since §312(j) applies only to federally-insured mortgages.

[8] For an exhaustive examination of §341 (as amended in 1958 but prior to the enactment of §341(f) in 1964), see Axelrad, Collapsible Corporations and Collapsible Partnerships, 1960 So. Calif. Tax Inst. 269.

Other post-1958 discussions are: Seidman, "Collapsible" Corporation — Application to Real Estate Transactions, 15 Tax L. Rev. 121 (1959); Pelletier, Shareholder Intent and Congressional Purpose in the Collapsible Corporation Morass, 20 Tax L. Rev. 699 (1965); Odell, Collapsible Corporations — Some "Softspots" in Section 341, 18 Miami L. Rev. 645 (1964); Donaldson, Collapsible Corporations, 36 Taxes 777 (1958); Anthoine, Federal Tax Legislation of 1958: The Corporate Election and Collapsible Amendment, 58 Col. L. Rev. 1146 (1958).

Earlier discussions are: DeWind and Anthoine, Collapsible Corporations, 56 Col. L. Rev. 475 (1956); Axelrad and Kostas, A Re-Examination of Collapsible Corporations "With a View To" Coexisting with Section 341, 1956 So. Cal. Tax Inst. 549; Weyher and Bolton, Collapsible Corporations as Affected by the 1954 Code — Inventory and Unrealized Receivables, 13 N.Y.U. Inst. on Fed. Tax. 657 (1955); MacLean, Collapsible Corporations — The Statute and Regulations, 67 Harv. L. Rev. 55 (1953); Freeman, Collapsible Corporations, 11 N.Y.U. Inst. on Fed. Tax. 407 (1953); Boland, Practical Problems of the Collapsible Corporation Provisions, 10 *ibid.* 537.

See also Dauber, Use of Reorganization Techniques to Avoid Collapsible Treatment, 49 A.B.A.J. 1214 (1963).

have already been pointed out: (a) Section 337 (non-recognition of corporate gain or loss on certain sales in conjunction with a complete liquidation) is ordinarily inapplicable to collapsible corporations (see *supra*, Sec. 9.66; *infra*, Sec. 10.07); and §333 (non-recognition of shareholder gain on elective one-month liquidations) is also ordinarily inapplicable to collapsible corporations (*supra*, Sec. 9.21; *infra*, Sec. 10.07).

As noted earlier, the penalty of §341 (ordinary gain treatment to shareholders of a collapsible corporation) may be more severe than if the parties had realized the entire gain at the corporate level and then liquidated their corporation at a capital gain. This results from the fact that the top bracket for individuals is 70 per cent (1966 rates), while the total effective rate if the profit is taxed once at the corporate level (as ordinary gain) and then at the shareholder level (as capital gain) would not exceed 61 per cent. (The disparity may be reduced if the shareholder's gain on a sale of the stock of a collapsible corporation is reported on the installment basis under §453, or if the averaging relief of §1301 applies.) It bears noting that there is no doctrine of "partial collapsibility," permitting the shareholder's gain under §341 to be fragmented between capital gain and ordinary income depending on the "mix" of collapsible and non-collapsible assets involved; this all-or-nothing aspect of §341 makes it difficult to settle close cases with the Service.

Sec. 10.04.   The definition of "collapsible corporation"

The term "collapsible corporation" is defined by §341(b) to mean a corporation that is formed or availed of:

> 1. Principally for the "production" of property (or for certain other activities to be discussed below);
> 2. With a view to (a) a sale, liquidation, or distribution before it has realized a substantial part of the taxable income to be derived from the property, and (b) a realization by the shareholders of the gain attributable to the property.[9]

If we take the extreme case of a corporation that is organized solely to produce one motion picture and that, by agreement among the shareholders at the time of its creation, is to be liquidated as soon as the film is completed and before any income is received by the corporation, the applicability of §341(b) is indisputable. Moreover, the

---

[9] In the interest of simplicity, the statutory definition has been paraphrased; some nuances have been sacrificed in order to concentrate on the major issues.

use of an existing corporation for these purposes will not escape §341(b), since it is applicable whether the corporation is "formed" or "availed of" for the specified purpose. Finally, although the collapsible corporation provisions are aimed primarily at attempts to convert untaxed corporate ordinary income into shareholder level capital gain, the Supreme Court has held that there is no implied exception in §341 for profits that would have been taxed as capital gain if the corporate assets had been sold by the shareholders as individuals.[10] Accordingly, the operation of §341 may serve to convert what would otherwise be capital gain into ordinary income solely because of the use of a corporation, a result which was largely responsible for the adoption in 1958 of the "amnesty" of §341(e) (*infra*, Sec. 10.07).

The "collapsible corporation" definition (which should be examined with a lively appreciation of the fact that the term is not confined to such classic collapsible patterns as the use of temporary corporations in the motion picture or construction industries), contains these elements:

1. Formed or availed of. Because §341 reaches corporations that are either "formed" or "availed of" for the proscribed purposes, it is not confined to a corporation that is specially created for the purpose or that is dissolved as soon as the purpose has been achieved.[11] Temporary corporations may be especially vulnerable, but a long life does not insure immunity.

2. Principally for the manufacture, construction or production of property (to any extent). Early debate on this aspect of the definition in §341(b) centered on whether the word "principally" modified the language "manufacture, construction or production," or whether it referred only to the collapsible "view" test; if the latter was the correct interpretation, the statute would have been appreciably narrowed in scope. The regulations adopted the former construction from the outset, and courts soon agreed.[12] The result of these cases is that the corporation need only be formed or availed of principally for the man-

---

[10] Braunstein v. Commissioner, *supra* note 1, rejecting the restrictive theory of Ivey v. United States, 294 F.2d 799, 8 AFTR 5557 (5th Cir. 1961). See also Bailey v. United States, 360 F.2d 113, 17 AFTR 2d 704 (9th Cir. 1966), refusing to find an implied exception in §341 for shareholders whose intent had been to liquidate the corporation in a tax-free liquidation under §333; although the court did not mention it, such a liquidation would not have been permissible in view of the corporation's collapsible character (*supra*, Sec. 9.21).

[11] See Regs. §1.341-2(a); Burge v. Commissioner, 253 F.2d 765, 1 AFTR 2d 1214 (4th Cir. 1958); Glickman v. Commissioner, 256 F.2d 198, 1 AFTR 2d 1883 (2d Cir. 1958).

[12] Regs §1.341-2(a)(2); Weil v. Commissioner, 252 F.2d 805, 1 AFTR 2d 1096 (2d Cir. 1958); Burge v. Commissioner, *supra* note 11; Mintz v. Commissioner, 284 F.2d 554, 6 AFTR 2d 5894 (2d Cir. 1960).

ufacture, etc. of property, a condition present in the case of most if not all ordinary business corporations, and the forbidden "view" need not be the principal reason for formation or use of the corporation.

Similarly, the definition of "manufacture, construction or production" has received an expansive interpretation by courts and the Service. This definition has two distinct elements: (1) whether the questioned activity itself constitutes "production"; and (2) the duration of the activity (since its duration has significance in connection with the "view" requirement, as well as in applying the three year rule discussed *infra*, Sec. 10.06). The earlier opinions and rulings on this question suggested that practically any corporate activity that is materially related to a property-creating transaction would satisfy the statutory test,[13] but the pendulum may be swinging back to a limited extent. Thus, it has been held that the term "construction" does not include: minor alterations and corrections of an existing structure that did not change its character or increase its fair market value; the drilling of dry holes and unsuccessful exploration activities; or various preliminary activities by a real estate construction corporation.[14] If the corporation goes beyond distinctly preliminary activities or mere maintenance of existing assets, however, it may be engaged in "construction"; it should not be forgotten that to do so "to any extent" suffices under §341(b)(2)(A). Although the cases and rulings have not said so explicitly, it may be that the distinction between deductible expenses and capital outlays that has developed under §162 and §263 will afford a useful analogy.

It would seem that any type of property which a corporation is capable of producing will meet the requirements of the statutory definition. Although the vast majority of transactions which run afoul of §341 involve the construction or production of tangible property (buildings, motion pictures, etc.), the creation of such intangibles

---

[13] E.g.: Abbott v. Commissioner, 28 T.C. 795 (1957), aff'd, 258 F.2d 537, 2 AFTR 2d 5479 (3rd Cir. 1958) (corporation owning unimproved land held to have engaged in construction by contracting to install streets, obtaining FHA mortgage commitment, and depositing funds in escrow to insure that improvements would be installed); Ellsworth Sterner, 32 T.C. 1144 (1959) (hiring mortgage broker and architect, application for FHA mortgage insurance, and negotiation of sales contract held construction); Rev. Rul. 56-137, 1956-1 C.B. 178 (rezoning of land from residential to commercial use held construction); Farber v. Commissioner, 312 F.2d 729, 11 AFTR 2d 511 (2d Cir. 1963) (filing of applications for zoning permits and mortgage guarantees, payment of fees, and payments for utility and water connections held construction); Glickman v. Commissioner, *supra* note 11 (construction period extended beyond issuance of final certificate of occupancy, and included landscaping and obtaining of FHA inspector's final approval).

[14] Rev. Rul. 63-114, 1963-1 C.B. 74; Rev. Rul. 64-125, 1964-1 C.B. 131; Morris Cohen, 39 T.C. 886 (1963); V.W. McPherson, ¶62,106 P-H Memo TC.

as good will, secret formulas, industrial know-how, and the like, even by a service business, may also be within the reach of the section, although as yet there seem to be no reported cases in point.

3. *Purchase of "section 341 assets."* Even if the corporation does not engage in the "manufacture, construction, or production of property," it may fall within §341 by engaging in the "purchase" of so-called "section 341 assets," provided this is done with a "view" to a sale, liquidation, or distribution before it has realized a substantial part of the taxable income to be derived from such property. This portion of the definition (which was enacted in 1951 and expanded in 1954) is primarily aimed at the use of collapsible corporations to convert the profit on inventory property and stock in trade into capital gain:

> The procedure used is to transfer a commodity to a new or dormant corporation, the stock of which is then sold to the prospective purchaser of the commodity who thereupon liquidates the corporation. In this manner the accretion in the value of the commodity, which in most of the actual cases has been whiskey, is converted into a gain realized on the sale of stock of a corporation, thus giving rise to the possibility that it might be taxed as a long-term capital gain. (H. Rep. No. 586, 82d Cong., 1st Sess., reprinted in 1951-2 C.B. 357, 375.)

If the transaction described by this committee report was sufficiently blatant, the formation of the corporation and sale of its stock might be treated as a single transaction by which the taxpayer sold the property itself in the ordinary course of business, as in Jacobs v. Commissioner, 224 F.2d 412, 47 AFTR 1445 (9th Cir. 1955); or the repeated use of the device might lead to the conclusion that the corporate stock was held for sale to customers in the ordinary course of business, which would make the capital gain provisions inapplicable.[15] It was evidently thought, however, that a statutory tool would be preferable to the "single transaction" approach of the *Jacobs*

---

[15]For a decision adopting this approach in an extreme case, see Herman Katz, ¶60,200 P-H Memo TC.

For other applications of the *Jacobs* approach, see: Willett v. Commissioner, 277 F.2d 586, 5 AFTR 2d 1223 (6th Cir. 1960); Margolis v. Commissioner, 337 F.2d 1001, 14 AFTR 2d 5667 (9th Cir. 1964); Thomas F. Abbott Jr., ¶64,065 P-H Memo TC.

[16] The language employed by §341(b) to reach the device described in the text is somewhat awkward; it might be argued that the corporation was not formed or availed of for the purchase of stock in trade, inventory property, or property held for sale to customers — as required by §341(b)(3)(A) and (B) — since the whiskey in question was *not* to be sold by the corporation. The regulations, in accord with the obvious legislative intent, state that the status of the property is to be determined without regard to the collapsibility

case.[16] Under §341 as amended, every corporation holding appreciated inventory or stock in trade would be a potential target for §341, and its fate would depend on whether the elusive "view" was present; but the regulations cut down the scope of the statute by conferring immunity on the corporation if its inventory property — more precisely, the property described in §341(b)(3)(A) and (B) — is normal in amount and if it has a substantial prior business history involving the use of such property.[17]

The 1951 amendment reached inventory property, stock in trade, and property held primarily for sale to customers in the ordinary course of trade or business — the categories now found in §341(b)-(3)(A) and (B). In 1954, §341 was expanded, to reach a purchase of "unrealized receivables or fees" and certain property described in §1231(b), by the addition of §341(b)(3)(C) and (D). At the same time, the generic label "section 341 assets" was created for the property reached by both the 1951 and the 1954 legislation.

Although the Senate Report on the 1954 Code does not explain the extension of §341 to cover a purchase of "unrealized receivables or fees,"[18] presumably Congress sought thereby to prevent an individual on the cash basis of accounting from transferring uncollected claims for services or goods to a corporation in order to sell the stock at the capital gain rate, since in the absence of a corporation the taxpayer would have to report the collections as ordinary income.

The 1954 inclusion of §1231(b) property in the category of "section 341 assets" is less clear, since capital gain can ordinarily be realized on the sale of such property without resort to the use of a collapsible corporation. The change may have been intended to

of the corporation, i.e., if the whiskey would be inventory in the hands of a "normal" corporation, it will have the same status in the hands of the collapsible corporation.

For an application of §341(b)(3) to a one-shot purchase and sale of a single parcel of real estate, see Guy A. Van Heusden, 44 T.C. 491 (1965).

On the troublesome question of "dual purpose" property, held for either development or sale, see Malat v. Riddell, 383 U.S. 569, 17 AFTR 2d 604 (1966).

[17] Regs §1.341-5(c)(1); see also Rev. Rul. 56-244, 1956-1 C.B. 176 (inventory, though appreciated in value, was normal in amount for volume of sales and not in excess of average inventory over preceding several years; corporation held not collapsible).

[18] Despite the definition of "unrealized receivables or fees" in §341(b)(4) — or perhaps because of it — the term is most ambiguous, especially as concerns the status of rights under long-term contracts. For some of the difficulties, see DeWind and Anthoine, *supra* note 8, at 496-502. Note also that the "unrealized receivables or fees" must have been "purchased" by the corporation. This implies the acquisition of a chose in action from a third party, but it is essential to the statutory purpose to include untaxed accounts receivable resulting from the corporation's sales of its own merchandise or performance of services.

prevent dealers in apartment houses or other rental property from converting ordinary income into capital gain through the use of a separate corporation for each parcel of property. This device might have been defeated without amending §341, by treating the corporate stock as held for sale to customers in the ordinary course of business and hence, under §1221(1), as a non-capital asset. The remedy that was adopted by Congress, however, was more drastic; the result of treating §1231(b) property as "section 341 assets" is that the typical real estate holding corporation, formed to purchase an apartment house or other rental property, may be collapsible if the requisite view is present, even though the shareholders are investors rather than dealers and would have been entitled to report their profit on the building as capital gain under §1231 in the absence of a corporation. The collapsible corporation provisions have thus come full circle: designed to prevent the transmutation of ordinary income into capital gain, they may now convert capital gain into ordinary income. In recognition of this possibility, Congress in 1958 enacted §341(e) to provide an escape from collapsibility in cases, roughly speaking, where the taxpayers would have enjoyed capital gains had they not used the corporate form. This amendment is discussed *infra*, Sec. 10.07.

Another unexplained 1954 change is that the term "section 341 assets" embraces only property held for a period of less than 3 years. Because of this limitation, if a commodity is held by the corporation for 3 years or more (including the holding period of certain predecessors) after manufacture, construction, production, or purchase has been completed, the shareholders may be able to sell their stock or liquidate the corporation without running afoul of §341(a). This escape is limited, however, by the possibility that a transfer of the property to a corporation for the sole purpose of obtaining capital gain on the sale or liquidation could be attacked as a sham without resort to §341, as in the *Jacobs* case. Or, if the "aging" process enhanced the value of the property, it might constitute the "manufacture, construction, or production" of property, and thus prevent the running of the 3-year period.

4. With a "view" (to "collapse"). Since many, if not most, ordinary business corporations are formed or availed of principally for the production or purchase of property (especially since these terms are broadly defined by §341), the major issue in a §341(b) case is usually the existence of the requisite "view" on the part of the shareholders to effect a sale, liquidation or distribution before the corporation has realized a substantial part of the income to be derived from its property. The classic collapsible corporation was one whose shareholders planned at the very outset to liquidate before it before corporate income was realized. The regulations, however, say that §341(b) is satisfied if a sale, liquidation, or distribution before the corporation has realized a substantial part of the gain from the property "was contemplated, unconditionally, conditionally, or as a recognized possibility." Regs. 1.341-2(a)(2). This seems to imply that the requisite view exists whenever the controlling shareholders can reasonably foresee that they may decide to sell their stock or liquidate the corporation, if the price is "right," before it substantially realizes the income from its collapsible property. If so, the "recognized possibility" test is almost all-embracing, and the courts may be unwilling to go this far, unless the shareholders are experienced professionals in the business at hand.[19]

The regulations go on to state that the persons whose "view" is crucial are those who are in a position to determine the policies of the corporation, whether by reason of majority stock ownership or "otherwise." This approach may be hard on innocent minority shareholders, but without such a rule, §341 could be too easily avoided by keeping one shareholder in the dark. Finally, the regulations provide that the collapsible view must exist at some time during construction, production, or purchase of the collapsible property. Some courts have felt that the regulations are overly generous in this respect, asserting that the view need only be held when the corporation is "availed of" for the collapsible purpose even if production of the property has been completed by then; other decisions, however, have questioned or rejected such a broad interpretation.[20] In any event, determination of the time when the view arose will of necessity be difficult, involving as it does a highly subjective issue of intent, and the chronological breadth of the term "production" makes it difficult to establish that a tainted view, if it existed, did not arise until after production was completed.

It must be concluded, therefore, that the regulations bring within

[19] For a willingness to infer the tainted view in cases involving real estate operators, see August v. Commissioner, 267 F.2d 829, 3 AFTR 2d 1618 (3rd Cir. 1959); Carl B. Rechner, 30 T.C. 186 (1958); Braunstein v. Commissioner, 305 F.2d 949, 10 AFTR 2d 5125 (2d Cir. 1962), affd., *supra* note 10; Payne v. Commissioner, 268 F.2d 617, 4 AFTR 5035 (5th Cir. 1959); Nordberg, "Collapsible" Corporations and the View, 40 Taxes 372 (1962).
[20] Regs. §1.341-2(a)(3). Decisions holding or implying that the regulation is too restrictive: Glickman v. Commissioner, *supra* note 11 (dictum); Sidney v. Commissioner, 273 F.2d 928, 5 AFTR 2d 400 (2d Cir. 1960); Burge v. Commissioner, *supra* note 11; Spangler v. Commissioner, 278 F.2d 665, 5 AFTR 2d 1336 (4th Cir. 1960). For a view more in accord with the regulations, see Jacobson v. Commissioner, 281 F.2d 703, 6 AFTR 2d 5205 (3rd Cir. 1960); Braunstein v. Commissioner, *supra* note 19; Payne v. Commissioner, *supra* note 19; see also Farber v. Commissioner, *supra* note 13.

§341 any corporation that is formed or availed of for the production or purchase of property if the persons in control recognize (before production is completed) the possibility of selling or liquidating the corporation at a profit before it has realized a substantial part of the income from its property. Moreover, the natural tendency of courts and administrators to assume that what actually did happen was intended is evident in this area, so that self-serving declarations about the shareholders' state of mind are likely to be less persuasive than the actual results. This emphasis on objective considerations is evident in Regs. §1.341-5(b), which states that a corporation "ordinarily" will be considered collapsible if (a) gain attributable to property produced or purchased by the corporation is realized by the shareholder on a sale of his stock or non-dividend distribution; (b) the production or purchase of the property was a substantial corporate activity; and (c) the corporation has not realized a substantial part of the taxable income to be derived from such property.

The regulations do mention one avenue of escape: if the decision to sell, liquidate, or distribute is "attributable solely to circumstances which arose after the production or purchase . . . other than circumstances which could reasonably be anticipated at the time of production or purchase." Among the post-production motives that have been held to qualify are: illness of an active shareholder; unexpected changes in the law; dissension among the shareholders, especially if a minority interest is bought out; unexpected changes in the value of the property; and a shareholder's sudden need for funds to enter or expand another business.[21] This exception is less useful than might appear, however, because of the difficulty of proving that the cause of sale could not have been initially anticipated, as well as because the production process may extend well beyond normal concepts of "completion."[22]

    5. Corporate realization of substantial part of taxable income from the property. A corporation can escape the taint of collapsibility

[21] Regs. §1.341-2(a)(3). See Charles J. Riley, 35 T.C. 848 (1961) (illness); Maxwell Temkin, 35 T.C. 906 (1961) (same); Regs. §1.341-5(d), Example (3) (same); Rev. Rul. 57-575, 1957-2 C.B. 23 (sale of property to United States under statute whose enactment was not anticipated); Commissioner v. Lowery, 335 F.2d 680, 14 AFTR 2d 5504 (3d Cir. 1964) (buy-out of minority shareholder who could not make additional investment); see also Goodwin v. United States, 320 F.2d 356, 12 AFTR 2d 5142 (Ct. Cl. 1963); and Commissioner v. Solow, 333 F.2d 76, 13 AFTR 2d 1730 (2d Cir. 1964), for similar decisions; Jacobson v. Commissioner, *supra* note 20 (change in property's value); Southwest Properties, Inc., 38 T.C. 97 (1962) (same); Morris Cohen, *supra* note 14 (same; but see *Braunstein, supra* note 19 (change in value not controlling)); Jack Saltzman, ¶63,080 P-H Memo TC (need for funds).

[22] See Carl Rechner, *supra* note 19; Sproul Realty Co., 38 T.C. 844 (1962).

under §341(b)(1)(A) by realizing a "substantial" part of the taxable income to be derived from each of its produced or purchased properties. Where such property consists of fungible units in an integrated project (e.g., inventory assets of a single business, separate installments of a television or motion picture series, or individual units in a housing project), the determination of substantial realization is to be made by treating the aggregate of these properties as a single unit. Thus, if a corporation constructs two office buildings, the sale of one building will not protect it from collapsible treatment caused by the second building; on the other hand, if it is engaged in constructing a housing project, the entire project would constitute a "single property" for substantial realization purposes.[23]

Apparently the "taxable income to be derived from the property" means the taxable income that would be realized if the property were sold at the time the shareholder's gain arises.[24] This test seems appropriate in the case of property held only for sale (e.g., inventory or residential home units); but where rental property is involved, some courts require an estimate of the projected net rental income to be realized over the economic life of the property, a yardstick which is considerably more difficult to apply.[25] In addition, the fact that the property has produced no net income or is losing money has not precluded a finding of collapsibility where the prohibited view was present.[26] In any event, income which has been realized must be attributable to the collapsible property in order to count towards the substantial realization test.

Once the estimated potential taxable income from the property is determined, the question then arises as to what percentage thereof will be "substantial." Although a determination of this amount would at best represent an ad hoc judgment, the issue is complicated by a question of statutory interpretation: is collapsibility avoided if a "substantial" part of the potential is realized, or must enough be realized so that the unrealized part is *not* substantial? To illustrate: if 30 percent of the total is "substantial," must more than 70 percent be

---

[23] Regs. §1.341-2(a)(4) and §1.341-5(d), Examples (2), (3), and (4); but cf. §341(d)(2), *infra*, Sec. 10.06 (re computation under 70-30 percent rule).

[24] See Levenson v. United States, 157 F. Supp. 244, 1 AFTR 2d 446 (D.C. Ala. 1957); Commissioner v. Kelley, 293 F.2d 904, 8 AFTR 2d 5232 (5th Cir. 1961). See Ryan, What is Substantial Part of the Taxable Income?, 16 J. Tax. 246 (1961).

[25] Sidney v. Commissioner, *supra* note 20; Mintz v. Commissioner, *supra* note 12; Payne v. Commissioner, *supra* note 19. The *Mintz* and *Sidney* cases also held that premiums received from a lender, with which an FHA mortgage was placed, were not part of the net income "to be derived from such property."

[26] Spangler v. Commissioner, *supra* note 20; Short v. Commissioner, 302 F.2d 120, 9 AFTR 2d 1239 (4th Cir. 1962).

realized, or will 30 percent suffice? In the *Kelley* case, the Court of Appeals for the Fifth Circuit held that a realization of about one-third of the potential taxable income was sufficient, a result that seriously impairs the effectiveness of §341 but finds support in the statutory language. The Court of Appeals for the Third Circuit, by contrast, has upheld the Service's insistence that the corporation is collapsible if there is a substantial amount of *unrealized* income.[27]

6. *Realization by shareholders of gain attributable to the property*. This last element of the collapsible definition has generated relatively few problems, since, if the other elements are present, it will be satisfied almost automatically if the collapsible property has appreciated in value at the time of collapse.[28] Problems in determining whether the shareholder's gain is "attributable to such property" are discussed *infra*, Sec. 10.06, in connection with the 70 percent exception of §341(d)(2).

7. *Additional considerations*. To safeguard its statutory purpose, §341 provides that a corporation "shall be deemed to have manufactured, constructed, produced, or purchased property" if any of the following conditions are satisfied:

> 1. If the corporation engages in manufacture, construction, or production of property "to any extent." §341(b)(2)(A). By virtue of this provision, the corporation need not have originated or completed the process of manufacture, construction, or production; any contribution to the process is sufficient.
> 2. If the corporation holds property having a basis deter-

[27] Commissioner v. Kelley, *supra* note 24; Abbott v. Commissioner, *supra* note 13. See also Heft v. Commissioner, 294 F.2d 795, 8 AFTR 2d 5465 (4th Cir. 1961) (17 percent not "substantial"; later distributions in liquidation subjected to §341 even though 51 percent had been realized by then); Commissioner v. Zongker, 334 F.2d 44, 14 AFTR 2d 5242 (10th Cir. 1964) (amount realized, not the amount unrealized, is controlling; Tax Court had intimated that realization of 24 percent of potential would suffice).

The regulations, Regs. §1.341-5(c)(2), are inconclusive on this point, merely stating that a corporation ordinarily will not be deemed collapsible if its unrealized income is not substantial in amount. It is understood that the Service will rule favorably on the status of collapsibility if 85 percent of the income from collapsible property has been realized. See also Rev. Rul. 62-12, 1962-1 C.B. 321 (*Abbott* approach).

In theory, the amount *actually* realized is irrelevant, and the amount which the shareholders *intended* the corporation to realize is controlling. But this would make the corporation collapsible even if all the income had in fact been realized by it, provided the shareholders had earlier entertained the "view" that the income should not be realized by the corporation. The regulations, perhaps treating the events as they occur as the best evidence of what was intended, clearly imply that actual — rather than intended — realization is controlling. Reg. §1.341-2(a)(4) and §1.341-5(c)(2). But see Payne v. Commissioner, *supra* note 19.

[28] See, for example, Payne v. Commissioner, *supra* note 19 (shareholder's view to collapse and realization of gain attributable to collapsible property go hand in hand).

mined by reference to the cost of such property in the hands of a person who manufactured, constructed, produced, or purchased it. §341(b)(2)(B). This provision reaches such devices as the transfer of manufactured property or "section 341 assets" to a corporation by a tax-free exchange under §351, or the use of a second corporation into which a collapsible corporation is merged. The statute does not state whether the successor corporation inherits not only the collapsible property, but also the transferor's "view."

3. If the corporation holds property having a basis determined by reference to the cost of property manufactured, constructed, produced, or purchased by it. §341(b)(2)(C). This provision is designed to prevent an escape from §341 by a plan under which the corporation would manufacture property and transfer it in a tax-free exchange (e.g., under §1031), following which the shareholders would liquidate the corporation or sell their stock before the corporation had realized income from the newly-acquired property.

A further buttress to §341 is the inclusion of holding companies in the term "collapsible corporation." If a corporation is employed to hold the stock of a manufacturing corporation, the parent corporation will be a "collapsible corporation" by virtue of §341(b)(1) if it is formed or availed of with a "view" to a sale, liquidation, or distribution before the manufacturing corporation has realized a substantial part of the taxable income from the property. In Rev. Rul. 56-50, 1956-1 C.B. 174, it was held that the holding company becomes non-collapsible (so as to protect its shareholders) if it sells the stock of the subsidiary and is taxed under §341(a) on its gain, notwithstanding some difficulty in bringing this result within the literal terms of the statute.

Sec. 10.05.   The rebuttable presumption of collapsibility: §341(c)

In 1954, §341 was amended to add a rebuttable presumption of collapsibility if the fair market value of the corporation's "section 341 assets" is (a) 50 percent or more of the fair market value of its total assets and (b) 120 percent or more of the adjusted basis of such "section 341 assets." The theory of the rebuttable presumption is that if the "section 341 assets" are substantial in amount and have risen significantly in value above their basis, it is reasonable to place the burden of disproving collapsibility on the taxpayer.[29] In order to prevent manipulation, §341(c)(2) provides that cash, stock, and cer-

---

[29] Even without the presumption of §314(c), the taxpayer has the burden of overcoming the presumption of correctness that accompanies the Com-

tain securities are to be disregarded in determining the corporation's "total assets"; otherwise, the shareholders of a corporation whose "section 341 assets" have appreciated substantially in value might attempt to avoid the statutory presumption by contributing liquid assets to the corporation's capital to dilute the "section 341 assets" to less than 50 percent of the total assets. Perhaps the "business purpose" doctrine could be used by the Commissioner as an alternative weapon against an attempt to drown the corporation's "section 341 assets" in a sea of other assets by contributions to capital having no non-tax purpose.

In applying the presumption of §341(c), the appreciation in "section 341 assets" is measured against their basis, not against the shareholders' investment. Thus, if the shareholders invest $15,000 in a corporation, and it constructs "section 341 assets" at a cost of $100,000 (represented by $15,000 of equity investment and $85,000 of borrowed funds), the presumption of §341(c) will not be applicable if the assets increase in value to only $115,000 (this being less than 120 percent of their basis), even though the appreciation ($15,000) represents a profit of 100 percent on the shareholders' investment. If the assets increased in value to $120,000, however, §341(c) would become applicable; and this would be true even if the shareholders had financed the entire cost of construction ($100,000) with their own funds and had enjoyed a gain of only 20 percent on their investment.

Since the presumption of §341(c) is rebuttable, it is open to the taxpayer to establish that the corporation is not "collapsible" because it was not formed or availed of principally for the purposes set out in §341(b) or because the requisite "view" did not exist. Section 341(c) also provides that its inapplicability shall not give rise to a presumption that the corporation is *not* a collapsible corporation.

Sec. 10.06.   The statutory limitations of §341(d)

Even though the corporation is "collapsible" under the foregoing principles, §341(d) makes the punitive rules of §341 inapplicable to a particular shareholder[30] if any of the following three conditions is satisfied:

missioner's action in assessing a deficiency. What weight, if any, §341(c) adds to this non-statutory presumption is doubtful. Perhaps it is only "a handkerchief thrown over something covered by a blanket," as Randolph Paul said of an analogous statutory presumption in the federal estate tax law. Paul, Federal Estate and Gift Taxation (1946 Supp.), p. 92.

But note that application of the presumption in §341(c) will probably serve to poison the atmosphere of the taxpayer's case, and, to this extent, it may occupy a significant role. See, *e.g.*, Max Tobias, 40 T.C. 84 (1963).

[30] §341(d) provides relief for the shareholder *only*; the corporation re-

1. Not more than 5 percent of stock. The shareholder is not subject to §341 unless he owns (a) more than 5 percent in value of the outstanding stock, or (b) stock that is attributed to another shareholder who owns more than 5 percent of the stock. The ownership of stock is to be determined under a set of constructive ownership rules,[31] and the specified amount of stock will be fatal if owned when the manufacture, construction, or production of property is begun, when "section 341 assets" are purchased, or at any time thereafter.

2. Not more than 70 percent of gain attributable to collapsible property. Section 341(d)(2) insulates a shareholder's gain on the sale, liquidation, or distribution from collapsible treatment if 70 percent (or less) of that gain is attributable to the collapsible property. Thus, if 30 percent or more of his gain can be traced to non-collapsible property, the entire gain will qualify for capital treatment even though the corporation is collapsible.[32] In computing the gain attributable to the collapsible property for this purpose, Regs. §1.341-4(c)(2) adopts a "but for" approach, i.e., it is the excess of the gain recognized by the shareholder over the gain that he would have recognized if the collapsible property had not been produced or purchased. (In the case of a partial liquidation or non-liquidating distribution, this approach must be refined by taking account of the result that would have been reached on a complete liquidation.) It is important to note that income realized by the corporation in respect of its collapsible property remains attributable to such property under the regulations, and thus counts against the shareholder in applying the 70 percent rule, unless enough of the potential income is realized at the corporate

mains collapsible as respects such provisions as §337(c)(1) (non-applicability of §337), *supra*, Sec. 9.66.

[31] The constructive ownership rules applicable to personal holding companies, §544, are adopted for this purpose, except that the definition of "family" is expanded to include brothers and sisters, and their spouses.

[32] The 70 percent rule of §341(d)(2), which is concerned with the shareholder's gain, should not be confused with the "substantial realization" element of the definition of "collapsible corporation," which is applied solely at the corporate level. A realization of 30 percent of *its* potential collapsible income will free the corporation from collapsibility entirely (under the *Kelley* theory, *supra* note 27), but the shareholder of a corporation that has realized *none* of the income potential from its collapsible property may still escape under §341(d)(2) if 30 percent or more of *his* gain is attributable to non-collapsible property.

Nor should the 70 percent rule be confused with the three-year rule of §341(d)(3). The fact that the collapsible property has been held by the corporation for more than three years after construction is completed immunizes the shareholder's gain under §341(d)(3); but if the shareholder is forced to rely on §341(d)(2), the gain from such a project goes into the collapsible portion of his gain. Rev. Rul. 65-184, 1965-2 C.B. ____.

See generally Goldstein, Section 341(d) and (e) — A Journey Into Never-Never Land, 10 Villanova L. Rev. 215 (1965).

level to make the property non-collapsible. Thus, if the corporation constructs two separate projects, and satisfies the "substantial realization" rule of §341(b)(1) as to one but not the other, all of the shareholder's gain that is attributable to the former project goes into the non-collapsible fraction in applying §341(d)(2), while all of his gain attributable to the latter project (reflecting the corporation's realized as well as its unrealized gain) goes into the collapsible fraction. An unintended side effect of the 70-30 percent rule of §341(d)(2) is to encourage the retention of corporate income derived from non-collapsible property; in the case of the two-project corporation just described, a distribution by the corporation of its profits on the non-collapsible property will make it more difficult for the shareholder to meet the standard of §341(d)(2) on selling his stock or liquidating the corporation.[33]

Under the cases and regulations, gain realized by the shareholder is allocated to the collapsible share even if it is only indirectly attributable to the collapsible property. Thus, in the case of real estate improvements, an increase in the value of the land resulting from a building project is treated as "collapsible" gain, as well as the gain on the improvements themselves; and the same is true of an increase in the value of undeveloped land if attributable to improvements constructed on the developed portion.[34] Similarly, an increase in land value attributable to off-site improvements and a refund from a building contractor have been placed on the collapsible side of the equation.[35]

3. Gain realized after expiration of 3 years. Ordinary gain treatment may be avoided by a shareholder if the gain on his collapsible corporation stock is realized more than three years after completion

---

[33] See Regs. §1.341-5(d), Example (2), where the shareholder would have been saved from collapsible treatment had the corporation accumulated its profits from the realized project rather than distributing them as a dividend.

Another method of diluting the tainted portion of the shareholder's gain would be to make capital contributions of appreciated non-collapsible assets (e.g., securities). Such an attempt to shelter collapsible activities by contributing "pure" assets to the corporation may be vulnerable to the business purpose doctrine, although mere tax avoidance, while often evoking judicial hostility, is not enough per se to vitiate a transaction which otherwise has legal and economic substance. For a useful analogy on this point, see W.H.B. Simpson, 43 T.C. 900 (1965); see also §341(e)(7), discussed *infra*, Sec. 10.07.

[34] Regs. §1.341-4(c)(3); Glickman v. Commissioner, *supra* note 11; Mintz v. Commissioner, *supra* note 12; Payne v. Commissioner, *supra* note 19; August v. Commissioner, *supra* note 19; Short v. Commissioner, 302 F.2d 120, 9 AFTR 2d 1239 (4th Cir. 1962).

[35] Spangler v. Commissioner, *supra* note 20. See generally Farber v. Commissioner, *supra* note 13; Chodorow and De Castro, How to Use the "70-30" Exception to Avoid Collapsible Corporation Treatment, 21 J. Tax. 258 (1964).

by the corporation[36] of production or purchase of collapsible property. (The shareholder's holding period for his *stock* is irrelevant; §341-(d)(3) is concerned only with the corporation's holding period for the property.) Although the statute is not crystal-clear on this point, it is not necessary for all of the corporation's collapsible property to be held for three years to bring §341(d)(3) into play; part of the shareholder's gain may qualify for relief under §341(d)(3) even though the balance is taxable as ordinary income because attributable to collapsible property held for less than three years.[37]

Because the terms "manufacture, construction, and production" have been given such an expansive meaning (*supra*, Sec. 10.04), the 3-year rule of §341(d)(3) is a treacherous exception: the waiting period commences only on "completion" — not partial or substantial completion — of the productive process. Moreover, production of "the" property must be completed; if the corporation is engaged in multi-unit construction activities, it may be difficult to say whether there is only a single project, on which work is continuing, or several projects, one or more of which have been completed.

Hopes have sometimes been built on the fact that §341(d)(3) speaks of gain "realized" after the 3-year period, since this term suggests that a sale of stock on the installment plan or a complete liquidation that is stretched out over a period of time will postpone the date of "realization," at least as to the shareholder's later receipts. The Internal Revenue Service has ruled that gain is realized when stock is sold, rather than when the payments are received, if the shareholder elects under §453 to report on the installment method,[38] but the taxpayer's case would be stronger if he does not rely on such an election (e.g., a cash basis taxpayer's sale of stock on a deferred payment plan if he does not receive negotiable promissory notes or other evidences of indebtedness). If the shareholder's gain or loss on a sale or liquidation cannot be computed because a fair market value cannot be assigned to the property received, his gain is probably not "realized" in applying §341(d)(3) until it can be computed; but, as noted *supra*, Sec. 9.03, such "open" transactions are rarely encountered.

---

[36] In Rev. Rul. 57-491, 1957-2 C.B. 232, it was held that the 3-year period of §341(d)(3) includes the holding period of certain predecessors.

[37] Regs. §1.341-4(d). The balance of the gain might qualify under §341-(d)(2), but in applying the 70-30 percent rule, the gain on the three year property is counted against the shareholder (see *supra* note 32).

[38] Rev. Rul. 60-68, 1960-1 C.B. 151.

Sec. 10.07.   The amnesty of §341(e)

Section 341(e), enacted in 1958, ameliorates the rigors of the collapsible corporation provisions in four respects:

1. Sale or exchange of stock. If certain conditions are satisfied, a shareholder's gain on the sale or exchange of the stock of an otherwise collapsible corporation is exempted from §341(a)-(1), and hence will be taxed as long-term capital gain.

2. Complete liquidation. In certain circumstances, a shareholder's gain on the complete liquidation of an otherwise collapsible corporation is exempted from §341(a)(2), and hence will be taxed as long-term capital gain.

3. Eligibility for §333. Certain otherwise collapsible corporations are made eligible for the benefits of §333 (elective non-recognition of shareholder gain on one-month liquidations, *supra*, Sec. 9.21).

4. Eligibility for §337. Certain otherwise collapsible corporations are made subject to §337 (non-recognition of corporate gain or loss on sales within 12-month period following adoption of plan of complete liquidation, *supra*, Sec. 9.65).

The exemptions described in categories 1 and 2 above are granted shareholder-by-shareholder, so that some shareholders of a corporation may qualify while others do not. The exemptions of categories 3 and 4, however, are granted to the corporation itself. Section 341(e), it will be noted, does not apply to gain realized on a partial liquidation or on a distribution in excess of the basis of stock; these transactions continue subject to the unabated vigor of §341(a)(2) and (3).

Section 341(e) is intended solely as a relief measure: it establishes a zone of safety, and any shareholder who can bring himself within this zone is protected against the collapsible corporation provisions, regardless of the nature of the corporation. Section 341(e)-(11) also provides that the failure to meet its requirements shall not be taken into account in determining whether a corporation is a collapsible corporation under the statutory definition of §341(b), and that this determination shall be made as if §341(e) had not been enacted.

The provisions of §341(e) were thought necessary largely because of the 1954 changes in §341 (*supra*, Sec. 10.04), under which a corporation formed or availed of to purchase rental property (*e.g.*, an apartment house) may be a collapsible corporation by virtue of §341-(b)(3)(D), although the shareholders could in the alternative have acquired the property as individuals and reported their gain on a sale as long-term capital gain unless they were dealers in such property.[39]

---

[39] In Braunstein v. Commissioner, *supra* note 1, the Supreme Court re-

It is perilous to summarize the fearfully intricate conditions of §341-(e), but its underlying theory is that the collapsible corporation provisions should not be applicable if the net unrealized appreciation in the corporation's "subsection (e) assets" (roughly speaking, property held by the corporation which would produce ordinary income if sold by the corporation itself or by its principal shareholders) amounts to less than 15 percent of the corporation's net worth.[40] This theory is applied with important variations to each of the four events listed above.

Before turning to these conditions and variations, we must first examine the term "subsection (e) assets," a new phrase employed throughout §341(e) as the means of determining if there has been a significant appreciation in the value of the corporation's ordinary income assets. This term is defined by §341(e)(5)(A) to include the following categories of property held by the corporation:

> *1. Property not used in the trade or business.* Any such property is a "subsection (e) asset" if the corporation's gain on a sale would be taxed as ordinary income — *i.e.*, if the property is neither a capital asset nor §1231(b) property. Moreover — and this is §341(e)'s unique innovation — property held by the corporation is brought into this category *if in the hands of any shareholder owning (directly or constructively)*[41] *more than 20 percent in value of the corporation's stock* it would not be a capital asset or §1231(b) property. Thus, property held by the corporation constitutes a "subsection (e) asset" if it is stock in trade, inventory property, or property held for sale to customers

fused to provide a judicial escape for property that would have constituted a capital asset in the shareholders' hands, but this decision came after the enactment of §341(e) and relied in part on the existence of this statutory escape.

For a special problem in the determination of "a substantial part of the taxable income to be derived from such property" as it arises in the oil and gas business, which may have contributed to the enactment of §341(e), see Honaker Drlg., Inc. v. Koehler, 190 F.Supp. 287, 7 AFTR 2d 416 (D.C. Kan. 1960); Hambrick, Collapsible Corporations in Oil and Gas: Does the 1958 Act Afford Any Relief? 28 Geo. Wash. L. Rev. 815 (1960).

Section 341 (e) is discussed by Goldstein, *supra* note 32; Boland, Collapsible Corporations Under the 1958 Amendments, 17 Tax L. Rev. 203 (1962).

[40] The terms "net unrealized appreciation" and "net worth" are defined by §341(e)(6) and (7). In computing the corporation's "net worth," §341(e)(7) provides for the exclusion of increases in net worth during the preceding one-year period resulting from transfers for stock or as contributions to capital or paid-in surplus, "if it appears that there was not a bona fide business purpose for the transaction in respect of which such amount was received." Compare the handling of a similar problem under §341(c)(2), *supra*, Sec. 10.05.

[41] Throughout §341(e), constructive ownership rules are applicable. See §341(e)(10) and (8). Note also Regs. §1.341-6(a)(4), stating that dealer status of a more than 20 percent *constructive* shareholder will be attributed to the corporation in determining whether its property constitutes "subsection (e) assets."

in the ordinary course of trade or business in the hands of the corporation, or *if it would have this status were it held by any shareholder owning more than 20 percent of the corporation's stock.* If any more-than-20-percent shareholder is a dealer,[42] in other words, his status taints the corporation's property.

2. *Property used in the trade or business — net unrealized depreciation.* If there is a net unrealized depreciation on assets used in the trade or business, they constitute "subsection (e) assets."[43]

3. *Property used in the trade or business — net unrealized appreciation.* If there is a net unrealized appreciation on such assets, they constitute "subsection (e) assets" if they would be neither capital assets nor §1231(b) assets in the hands of a more-than-20-percent shareholder. This provision is crucial to the purpose of §341(e). If a corporation's sole property is an apartment house or other rental property that has appreciated in value, the property will constitute a "subsection (e) asset" only if a more-than-20-percent shareholder is a dealer in such property.

Although the status of short term trade or business property is not entirely clear, it would seem that it constitutes a "subsection (e) asset"; in the case of trade or business property with a "split" holding period (i.e., property held for more than 6 months with improvements or additions held for six months or less), the property evidently constitutes a "subsection (e) asset" in its entirety, but only the short term gain is taken into account in computing "net unrealized appreciation." See §341(e)(6)(D) and §341(e)(9).

4. *Copyrights and similar property.* A copyright, literary composition, or similar property is a "subsection (e) asset" if it was created in whole or in part by the personal efforts of an individual owning directly or constructively more than 5 percent of the corporation's stock. By virtue of this provision, a motion picture will be a "subsection (e) asset" if created by the personal efforts of a more-than-5-percent shareholder.

---

[42] The term "dealer" is not used in the statute; it is employed here and in the text to denote a person who would treat gain from the sale or exchange of the property as in whole or in part gain from a non-capital and non-§1231(b) asset.

On the status of "dual purpose" property, held for development or sale, see Malat v. Riddell, *supra* note 16.

See Regs. §1.341-6(b)(4), stating that if a corporation holds property *similar* to that held by a more than 20 percent shareholder dealer, such property will constitute dealer property in the hands of the corporation ("segregation" is allowed, however, by Regs. §1.341-6(b)(5) in the case of corporate securities).

[43] The Senate Report on §341(e) (S. Rep. No. 1983, 85th Cong., 2d Sess.) does not state why depreciated property used in the trade or business is included if there is net unrealized depreciation in such assets. Since such assets would ordinarily qualify for the hotch-pot of §1231(b) and give rise to ordinary losses if the net result of the hotch-pot was a loss, it may have been thought appropriate to include them in the §341(e) calculation in order to counterbalance appreciation in inventory and similar property.

The function of the new category of "subsection (e) assets" is to permit a determination of whether there has been a significant increase in the value of the assets which would produce ordinary income upon sale by either the corporation or a more-than-20-percent shareholder,[44] since in the absence of such an increase in the value of the ordinary income assets, there is to be relief from the collapsible corporation restrictions. As stated earlier, however, this test is applied with variations to each of the four situations to which §341(e) is applicable, and we now turn to these variations.

1. Sale or exchange of stock. Section 341(e)(1) makes §341(a)-(1) inapplicable to a sale or exchange of stock if the net unrealized appreciation in the corporation's "subsection (e) assets" does not exceed 15 percent of the corporation's net worth and if the shareholder does not own more than 5 percent of the corporation's stock.[45] If the shareholder owns between 5 and 20 percent of the stock, a similar calculation is made, but it must take into account not only the corporation's "subsection (e) assets" but also any corporate assets which would produce ordinary income if held by the particular shareholder for whom the calculation is made. §341(e)(1)(B). And if the shareholder owns more than 20 percent of the stock, *his* calculation must also take into account any corporate assets which would have produced ordinary income (a) if he owned them and (b) *if he had held in his individual capacity the property of certain other corporations of which he owned more than 20 percent of the stock in the preceeding 3 years.* §341(e)(1)(C).

Thus, the corporate assets will be tainted by the dealer status of any shareholder owning more than 20 percent of the stock of the corporation — and this "taint" will affect all shareholders of the corporation, regardless of the size of their shareholdings. In addition, a shareholder owning more than 5 percent of the stock must take into account any other corporate assets which would be ordinary income assets if he held them in his personal capacity — but this "taint" will affect only him. Finally, as to a more-than-20-percent shareholder, any corporate assets will be tainted by the hypothetical dealer status he would have attained if he had engaged in certain

---

[44] 5 percent in the case of a copyright, literary composition, or similar property.

[45] Such a shareholder might find it simpler to take refuge in §341(d)(1), which makes §341(a) inapplicable to certain not-more-than-5-percent shareholders, but that sanctuary is closed to a shareholder who owned more than 5 percent of the stock *at any time* after manufacturer, etc., commenced, as well as to a shareholder (e.g., an estate or trust) whose shares are attributed to a more-than-5-percent shareholder. Section 341(e)(1) is not quite so exclusive.

transactions as an individual rather than in corporate form, during the preceding 3 years.

The net result of these extraordinary statutory gyrations is that profit on the sale of stock of an otherwise collapsible corporation will qualify as long-term capital gain unless the assets of the corporation reflect a significant amount of unrealized ordinary income — the corporate veil being pierced for the purpose of determining the amount of unrealized ordinary income, in order to take account of assets that might have changed their character by the interposition of a corporation between the shareholders and the assets.

To illustrate the operation of §341(e)(1), assume that a corporation has three stockholders, unrelated to each other, whose holdings by value are as follows:

$$
\begin{array}{ll}
A & \text{5 percent} \\
B & \text{15 percent} \\
C & \text{80 percent}
\end{array}
$$

Assume also that the corporation's assets fall into four categories, as follows:

Class	Net unrealized appreciation	Nature of asset
W	$10,000	Stock in trade in hands of corporation
X	$10,000	Capital asset to corporation; but would be stock in trade if held by C, though not if held by A or B.
Y	$10,000	Capital asset to corporation; but would be stock in trade if held by B, though not if held by A or C.
Z	$20,000	Capital asset to corporation; but would be stock in trade if held by C, but only if sales by certain corporations in which C was interested during preceding 3 years were treated as sales by C or if sales by C of stock in such corporations were treated as sales by him of his share of assets.

Under §341(e)(5)(A), the corporation's "subsection (e) assets" would include Classes W and X. Consequently, on a sale of stock by A the net unrealized appreciation of the corporation would be $20,000, and if this does not exceed 15 percent of the corporation's net worth, the corporation could not be collapsible as to A. On a sale of stock by B, however, the net unrealized appreciation would be $30,000, since §341(e)(1)(A) and (B) require him to take into account not only the corporation's "subsection (e) assets" (Classes W and X), but also any corporate assets which would be "subsection (e) assets" if he held more than 20 percent of the stock (Class Y). *B*, therefore, can take advantage of §314(e)(1) only if $30,000 does not exceed 15 percent of the corporation's net worth. Finally, if *C* invokes §341-(e)(1), he must take into account Classes W, X, and Z (but not Class Y) in determining the net unrealized appreciation. §341-(e)(1)(A) and (C). For him, §341(e)(1) will be applicable only if $40,000 does not exceed 15 percent of the corporation's net worth.

For another example, which is both simpler and more typical of §341(e)'s intended operation, assume a corporation (Smith-Jones, Inc.) owned equally by Smith and Jones (who are unrelated), the sole asset of which is an appreciated apartment house. Assume also that neither Smith nor Jones is a dealer in such property, but that Jones has owned more than 20 percent of the stock of certain other real estate corporations during the preceding 3 years. In these circumstances, Smith-Jones, Inc. owns no "subsection (e) asets," either in its own right or by attribution from Smith or Jones. As to Smith, the net unrealized appreciation under §341(e)(1) is zero, so a sale or exchange of his stock (except to the issuing corporation or to a "related person") is exempt from the operation of §341(a)(1). As to Jones, it is necessary to determine whether more than 70 percent in value of the assets of any of the other corporations are similar or related in use or service to the property held by Smith-Jones, Inc. If so, Jones is to be treated (a) as though any sale or exchange by him of stock in such other corporation (while he owned more than 20 percent of its stock) had been a sale by him of his proportionate share of the corporation's assets, and (b) as though any sale or exchange by such other corporation (while he owned more than 20 percent of its stock) which was subject to §337(a) had been a sale by Jones of his proportionate share of the property. If, taking into account these hypothetical sales or exchanges by Jones, he would have been a dealer in the type of property held by Smith-Jones, Inc.,[46] he

---

[46] When §341(e)(1)(C) is applicable, the shareholder is treated as though he had sold his proportionate share of property held by the other corporations during the preceding 3-year period. The mere fact that these corporations were or were not dealers in the property in question is not relevant; the purpose of imputing sales to the shareholder is to determine *his* status, based on both these hypothetical sales and any actual sales by him of similar properties held in his individual capacity. The number and frequency of sales are usually only two of the factors determining whether the taxpayer is a dealer, however, and it is not clear whether §341(e)(1)(C) attributes to the shareholder not only his proportionate share of the corporations' assets, but also his share of any corporate activity (use of agents, advertising, etc.) that might have resulted in the sales.

can make use of §341(e)(1) only if the net unrealized appreciation in the apartment building owned by Smith-Jones, Inc., does not exceed 15 percent of its net worth.

Section 341(e)(1) cannot be invoked if the stock is sold to the issuing corporation,[47] nor does it apply to a more-than-20-percent shareholder if the stock is sold to a "related person" as defined by §341(e)(8).

2. *Complete liquidations.* A shareholder's gain on a complete liquidation is exempted by §341(e)(2) from §341(a)(2) — and hence can enjoy long-term capital gain treatment — if two conditions are met. The first is that the net unrealized appreciation in the corporation's assets must meet the same test as is imposed by §341(e)(1), *i.e.*, the appreciation in the corporation's "subsection (e) assets" plus, in the case of shareholders owning more than 5 or 20 percent of the stock, the appreciation in certain other assets held by the corporation, may not exceed 15 percent of the corporation's net worth. The second condition is that §337(a) applies to the corporation by reason of §341(e)(4). This condition, as will be seen *infra*, cannot be satisfied unless the corporation sells substantially all of its property before the liquidation; its purpose is to prevent a liquidation in kind of assets subject to depreciation or depletion, which if permitted would give the shareholders a stepped-up basis for such assets (which could thereafter be written off against ordinary income) at the capital gain rate, the classic situation covered by §341.

3. *Elective one-month liquidations under* §333. Ordinarily, the shareholders of a collapsible corporation are excluded from §333 (elective non-recognition of shareholder gain on a complete liquidation within one calendar month), *supra*, Sec. 9.21. Section 341(e)(3) provides that a corporation shall not be considered collapsible for this purpose, however, if the unrealized appreciation in its "subsection (e) assets" does not exceed 15 percent of the corporation's net worth. The term "subsection (e) assets" is modified in applying §341(e)(3), so as to reduce from 20 percent to 5 percent the stock ownership that will impose the shareholder's dealer status on the corporate assets. If the corporation can meet the test of §341(e)(3), all shareholders may take advantage of §333; otherwise, §333(a) remains in full force and no shareholders may do so.

4. *Use of* §337 *by a collapsible corporation.* We have already seen

---

[47] This restriction may reflect an excess of caution, since §341(e)(1) is an exception to §341(a)(1), which embraces sales and exchanges of stock, but not partial or complete liquidations. As to §302(b) redemptions, however, see *supra* note 6.

(*supra*, Sec. 9.66) that §337 (non-recognition of corporate gain or loss on certain sales within the one-year period following the adoption of a plan of complete liquidation) is not applicable to a collapsible corporation. Section 341(e)(4) lifts this barrier to a limited extent, making an otherwise collapsible corporation subject to §337 if:

> 1. At all times following the adoption of the plan of complete liquidation, the net unrealized appreciation in its "subsection (e) assets" does not exceed 15 percent of its net worth;
> 2. It sells substantially all the property owned by it on the date the plan of liquidation was adopted within the 12-month period following that date; and
> 3. Following the adoption of the plan, it does not distribute any depreciable or similar property.

The first of the foregoing conditions (with variations noted above) is common to §341(e)(1), (2), (3), and (4) — relief from the collapsible corporation provisions is granted only to corporations whose ordinary income assets have not appreciated significantly in value. Thus, the shareholders of a corporation holding substantially appreciated assets that in its hands are (or in the hands of any more-than-20-percent shareholder would be) inventory property or stock in trade may not employ §337 to obtain capital gain on a sale by having the corporation sell the property and distribute the proceeds in liquidation. The second and third conditions have a different purpose: even if the corporation's ordinary income assets have not appreciated substantially in value, the corporation is not permitted to distribute some of its assets in kind to its shareholders in order to give them a stepped-up basis at the lenient long-term capital gain rate. Thus, the second condition requires the corporation to sell substantially all of its assets if it wishes to come under §337; it may not sell some, and transfer the rest by a liquidating distribution in kind to its shareholders. The third condition overlaps the second to a considerable degree: it forbids the distribution of corporate property that is depreciable (or subject to amortization or depletion) in the hands of either the corporation or the distributee. Since the second condition requires "substantially all of the properties" held by the corporation when the plan of liquidation is adopted to be sold within the 12-month period thereafter, the third condition would be automatically satisfied as to such properties, but it has the additional effect of preventing the distribution of any depreciable, amortizable, and depletable properties that fall outside the "substantially all" clause or that were not held by the corporation when the plan of liquidation was adopted. If property is distributed before the plan is *formally* adopted in an effort to avoid the impact of these conditions, the plan may be "pre-dated," as suggested *supra*, Sec. 9.64.

A final restriction in §341(e)(4) makes it inapplicable to any sale to a more-than-20-percent shareholder, or to a person related to such a shareholder, if the property so sold is subject to depreciation, depletion, or amortization in the hands of either the corporation or the buyer. By virtue of this restriction, §341(e)(4) and hence §337 may be applicable to some of the corporation's sales but not to others, so that an otherwise collapsible corporation may employ §337 to ward off gain on some sales, while avoiding §337 on sales producing losses (by selling to a more-than-20-percent shareholder), an ironic result in view of the effort to prevent corporations from straddling §337 (*supra*, Sec. 9.64). (The irony will be heightened by the fact that the shareholder, not the government, will be seeking to establish that the corporation is collapsible.) Another problem in this final restriction on §341(e)(4) is whether a "sale" of appreciated corporate property to shareholders pro-rata (*e.g.*, if two 50 percent shareholders each "purchase" a 50 percent interest in depreciable assets) will be treated as a true sale. If so, the corporation will be subject to tax on the sale (probably under §1231(a), at the capital gain rate), but the shareholders will obtain a stepped-up basis for the property; at the same time, the other sales by the corporation will be subject to §337, and the liquidation will produce capital gain for the shareholders by virtue of §341(e)(2). If, on the other hand, the transaction is treated as a distribution in kind of the property, rather than as a "sale" followed by a distribution of the proceeds of sale, §341-(e)(4)(B) and (C) will have been violated, with the result that §337 will not apply to the corporation's sales of other property. This, in turn, will make §341(e)(2) inapplicable at the shareholder level to the liquidation.

Sec. 10.08.   Avoidance of §341 by a §341(f) consent

Not content with the three original escape hatches of §341(d) and the labyrinthine route of §341(e), Congress provided further relief from §341 in 1964 by enacting the consent procedure of §341(f).[48] This provision permits a shareholder to sell his stock on the normal capital gain basis, free of any threat from §341(a), if the corporation

---

[48] See Hall, The Consenting Collapsible Corporation — §341(f) of the Internal Revenue Code of 1954, 12 U.C.L.A. L. Rev. 1365 (1965); Sinrich, New Collapsible Relief Measure is More Useful than Most Tax Men Believe, 22 J. Tax. 148 (1965); S. Rep. No. 1241, 88th Cong., 2d Sess., reprinted in 1964-2 C.B. 684.

consents to recognize gain on its "subsection (f) assets" (primarily, real estate and noncapital assets) when, as and if it disposes of them in a transaction that would otherwise qualify for non-recognition of its gain. Such a consent insures that the gain on the collapsible property will be recognized at the corporate level regardless of the mode employed by the corporation to dispose of the property; just as the shareholder has always been protected against the application of §341(a) if the corporation realizes a substantial part of the collapsible income *before* he disposes of his stock, so §341(f) protects him if the corporation *promises* to recognize the collapsible income *after* he sells his stock. Accordingly, a "consenting corporation" will not be able to avail itself of such non-recognition provisions as §311, §336 or §337 when it ultimately disposes of its "subsection (f) assets." Whether the corporate gain will be taxable at that time as capital gain or as ordinary income, however, will depend on its status and the statutory rules then in force. Similarly, the amount of the gain (if any) will depend on the property's adjusted basis and the amount realized (or, if the disposition is not by sale, exchange, or involuntary conversion, on its fair market value) at the time of disposition. A consent under §341(f) is not conditioned on a showing that the corporation is in fact collapsible; indeed, one of the advantages of §341(f) is that it permits avoidance of such a determination. If the consent is filed, however, it cannot be repudiated at a later time on the ground that it was an empty formality because the shareholder's gain was not within the scope of §341.

1. Requirements and effect of §341(f). Section 341(f) applies only to a "true" *sale* of stock, not to transactions that are assimilated to sales for some purposes (e.g., distributions in redemption of stock, partial or complete liquidations, or non-liquidating distributions). To qualify for §341(f)(1) treatment, the corporation, and any subsidiary (or chain of subsidiaries) connected by stock ownership of 5 percent in value, must file a consent to the special recognition of gain provisions of §341(f)(2). This consent becomes irrevocable as soon as any shareholder has effected a sale of his stock. Section 341(f)(2) then provides for recognition of gain at the corporate level on the ultimate disposition of all "subsection (f) assets," even in a transaction that would otherwise qualify for non-recognition of gain — subject to an exception for tax-free exchanges under §332 (liquidation of subsidiary), §351 (transfer to controlled corporation), §361 (corporate reorganization), §371(a) and §374(a) (bankruptcy reorganizations), if the basis of the assets carries over to the transferee and it files a similar consent to recognize gain when it disposes of them.

For six months after the filing of a consent, any shareholder may safely sell stock of the consenting corporation in one or a number of transactions. When the consent expires, a new one may be filed, which will be similarly effective for a 6-month period, whether the shareholders have made sales under the prior consent or not; and this process may be continued indefinitely. The use of the privilege with respect to *one* corporation, however, precludes the same shareholder, or any person related to him within the meaning of §341(e)-(8)(A), from using it with respect to any other corporation for a 5-year period. There is a "first-in-first-out" quality to this one-shot rule, in that a shareholder cannot disregard a consent applicable to his first sale of stock (either because he had no gain or because he is prepared to prove that the corporation was non-collapsible), in order to get the benefit of a consent filed by another corporation whose stock he sells at a later time.

"Subsection (f) assets" are defined in §341(f)(4) as those non-capital assets which the corporation owns, or has an option to acquire, at the date of any qualified sale of stock by a shareholder. Whether they would otherwise constitute non-capital assets or not, however, land, any interest in real property (except a mortgage or other security interest), and unrealized receivables or fees as defined by §341(b)(4) constitute "subsection (f) assets"; and so do two other categories of property: (a) if any assets of the above categories are being manufactured at the time the stock is sold, the property resulting thereafter from the manufacturing process; and (b) in the case of land or real property, any improvements resulting from construction commencing within two years after the date stock is sold. As already noted, the character and amount of the corporation's gain on disposing of its "subsection (f) assets" depend on their status at the time of disposition, not on their status when the consent is filed or the stock is sold.

2. Uses of §341(f). Section 341(f) was designed to allow the shareholders of a rapidly growing corporation, whose produced or purchased properties have substantially increased in value but have not given rise to a realization of income at the corporate level, to reap the benefit of the company's prospects by selling their stock to a buyer who intends to continue operation of the corporation as a going concern. A sale in such circumstances invites a dispute under §341, and any tincture of "dealership" on the part of the corporation or its shareholders makes it perilous to rely on §341(e). Section 341(f) intervenes at this point to provide a safe harbor for the sellers if the new shareholders are willing to have the potential profit recognized in future years at the corporate level. If the buyers are not willing to continue the corporation as a going concern, however, but intend to liquidate it to acquire the assets, §341(f) gives no practical assistance to the selling shareholders, since the buyers (at least if they are competently advised) will discount the price to reflect the corporate tax liability which will be generated by §341(f)(2) at the time of the liquidation. Moreover, even if they intend to keep the corporation alive, the buyers must take account of its low basis for the assets, since this will be reflected in an increase in corporate gain (or in reduced depreciation deductions) and will adversely affect the value of their shares. Although incoming shareholders can ordinarily remedy an abnormally low basis for corporate assets by liquidating the corporation and getting a stepped-up basis under §334(a) or §334(b)(2), such a liquidation of a consenting corporation is a taxable event.

Sec. 10.09   Peaceful coexistence with §341

While the reach of the collapsible corporation provision is indeed broad, even excessively so, several techniques are available to mitigate or avoid its application. A check-list of these possibilities, some of which are discussed above, would include:

> *1. Selling the assets under §337.* If the corporation is found to be non-collapsible, the corporate gain will go unrecognized; and there will be a tax at the shareholder level only. If, to the contrary, the corporation is collapsible, the realization of income at the corporate level (resulting, usually, in capital gain) will serve to oust §341 of jurisdiction. The tax at the shareholder level will, in such a case, qualify for capital gain treatment.
> *2. Realization at the corporate level.* In jurisdictions following the *Kelley* case (*supra* note 27), realization of one-third (or more) of the potential income at the corporate level will avoid collapsible status for the corporation.
> *3. Election under Subchapter S.* If there is to be a sale of the corporate assets, the shareholders may be able to qualify for a single tax at the capital gain rate by an election under Subchapter S prior to the sale. This possibility, which was drastically curtailed by a statutory change in 1966 under which there may be a tax at the corporate level as well as at the shareholder level, is discussed *infra*, Ch. 14.
> *4. Multiple corporations.* By segregating each potentially collapsible project in a separate corporation, the shareholders may fight the "substantial realization" and "tainted view" issues separately for each corporation — provided they stand up as independent entities. Segregation also has its drawbacks, e.g.,

gain on non-collapsible projects cannot be balanced against the gain on collapsible projects in applying §341(d)(2).

5. *Statutory escape routes.* At the shareholder level, reliance may be placed on the exemptions created by §341(d) for 5-percent shareholders, the 70-30 percent rule, and the 3-year waiting period; or on the special rule applied by §341(e) to "subsection (e) assets." At the corporate level, a consent under §341(f) may be feasible.

6. *Spread-out or splitting of ordinary income.* If ordinary income cannot be avoided, or if the shareholder is forced to rely on an escape route that may prove unavailing, his pain and suffering may be reduced by spreading the gain over a period of years (e.g., by use of the installment method under §453) or among a number of taxpayers (e.g., children, trusts, etc.).

7. *Charitable contributions.* If all else fails, the taxpayer can donate collapsible stock to a charitable institution,[49] thereby avoiding the recognition of gain while deducting the value of the stock under §170.

---

[49] The authors would be happy to introduce persons wishing to employ this suggestion to the treasurers of their respective universities.

Chapter Eleven

CORPORATE DIVISIONS

Sec. 11.01.   Introductory

In this chapter, we will be concerned with the tax consequences of corporate divisions — arrangements by which the shareholders of a single corporation split up their investment among several corporate shells. This has been a troubled area of the tax law, and, although the statutory scheme was extensively revised in 1954, it is impossible to ignore the pre-1954 statutes and judicial doctrines. Before turning to the legal issues, it is important to note that the generic label "corporate division" embraces a broad spectrum of transactions, differing from each other in the following characteristics, among others:

1. Nature of assets. The shareholders of a corporation that is engaged in two or more separate businesses may wish to place the assets of one of the businesses in a separate corporation. At the opposite extreme, the assets to be segregated in a separate corporation may be cash or marketable securities. Between these two extremes, the shareholders of a corporation conducting an integrated business (*e.g.*, manufacturing) may wish to place some of its business assets (*e.g.*, real estate) or business functions (*e.g.*, sales, research and development, or purchasing) in a separate corporation.

2. Purpose. The purpose of the division may be to comply with an anti-trust decree (*e.g.*, by distributing some of the assets of an integrated business or the stock of a competitor or customer); to comply with state or foreign law (*e.g.*, a prohibition on combining several business functions in the same corporation or a requirement that a local enterprise have a stated percentage of local shareholders); to separate a regulated enterprise from an unregulated one; to segregate a risky or speculative enterprise from a more stable one; to reduce federal income taxes (by obtaining an additional surtax exemption — but see §1551 and §269); to prepare for a sale, either prearranged or to be negotiated, of one or both of the corporations; to prepare for a liquidation of one of the corporations so its assets may be held, or sold, by the shareholders as individuals; etc.

3. Ratio of distribution. The distribution may be either pro rata or disproportionate. Thus, two equal shareholders of a corporation who are deadlocked on business policy may wish to divide the assets between two corporations, so that each of them may become the sole owner of one. A corporation may wish to buy out the entire interest of a minority shareholder in exchange for all the stock of a subsidiary (the assets of which may be a separate business, cash or marketable securities, or a combination of such assets). On the other hand, the distribution may be entirely pro rata — and it may either remain so or become disproportionate by reason of sales by some of the shareholders. An intermediate possibility is a distribution under which two equal shareholders in a corporation will wind up, after a divisive distribution, with the stock of two corporations, held in the proportion (e.g.) 60-40 for the first corporation and 40-60 for the second.

4. Form of distribution. When the shareholders of a corporation no longer wish to entrust their eggs to one basket, there are various ways of getting them into several baskets. The corporation may distribute some of its assets to the shareholders pro rata; this will ordinarily constitute a "dividend" if the corporation has post-1913 or current earnings and profits, and the tax cost may be prohibitive. Or, the assets may be distributed to the shareholders in exchange for some of their stock. If the distribution is not pro rata, so that some of the shareholders are bought out entirely or suffer a substantial reduction in proportionate stockholdings, the transaction will produce capital gain or loss for these shareholders under §302(b) (*supra*, Ch. 7.). But if the assets are to be distributed to all shareholders pro rata, each surrendering a proportionate amount of his stock, the redemption may constitute a taxable dividend under §302(d), unless it can qualify as a partial liquidation under §346(a)(2) (corporate contraction) or §346(b) (distribution of an active trade or business), in which event the transaction will produce capital gain or loss (*supra*, Ch. 7).

The methods of dividing the corporate enterprise just described have been discussed in earlier chapters. In this chapter we will consider other methods of accomplishing this result which, upon compliance with an intricate set of statutory conditions, permit the corporation to be divided on a wholly tax-free basis. These methods are known to the tax lawyer as "spin-offs," "split-offs," and "split-ups":

1. Spin-off. A spin-off is a distribution by one corporation of the stock of a subsidiary corporation. Under the 1954 Code, the stock of either an existing subsidiary or a newly created one can qualify for a tax-free spin-off. Before 1954, however, the subsidiary had to be created for the purpose or, if an existing subsidiary was used, the distributing corporation was required to transfer additional assets to it as part of a plan of reorganization.

2. Split-off. The split-off is identical with the spin-off, except that the shareholders of the parent corporation surrender part of their stock in the parent in exchange for the stock of the subsidiary.

3. Split-up. In a split-up, the parent corporation distributes its stock in two or more subsidiaries in complete liquidation. Before 1954, the parent corporation was required either to create the subsidiaries as part of the plan or to transfer additional assets to existing subsidiaries; but neither of these steps is required under the 1954 Code.

Before 1954, the tax consequences of these methods of dividing up a corporate investment were quite divergent, despite the fact that their economic consequences were ordinarily almost identical, and this pre-1954 history was influential in shaping the 1954 statutory provisions. For this reason, as well as for its probable impact on future judical attitudes and administrative practices, a historical note is essential. Thereafter, the 1954 provisions will be discussed.

Sec. 11.02.   Divisive reorganizations before 1954

The Revenue Act of 1924 permitted a spin-off to be accomplished tax-free, by providing (1) that the transfer by a corporation of part or all of its property to a second corporation constituted a "reorganization" if the first corporation or its stockholders (or both) were in control of the second corporation immediately after the transfer; and (2) that no gain was to be recognized by the shareholders of the first corporation if stock of the second corporation was distributed to them as part of the reorganization plan. §203(c), 43 Stat. 256 (1924). This blanket tax exemption for the spin-off held out the possibility of undermining the tax on dividend income on a grand scale since, at least so far as the letter of the statute was concerned, a corporation could transfer its excess funds or liquid assets to a newly organized corporation and distribute the stock of the new corporation to its shareholders, who could thereafter liquidate the new corporation in order to get its assets. By this device, it was hoped, the shareholders would avoid the tax on dividend income; although they would be taxed on liquidating the second corporation (on the difference between the value of the assets received in liquidation and the allocated basis of the stock), this tax would be at the capital gain rate; and not even a capital gain tax would be due if they kept the second corporation alive as a holding company.

But in Gregory v. Helvering, 293 U.S. 465, 14 AFTR 1191 (1935), the Supreme.Court held that full compliance with the letter of the spin-off statute was not enough if the transaction was otherwise indistinguishable from an ordinary dividend. The taxpayer, a Mrs. Gregory, owned all of the stock of United Mortgage Corporation, which held certain assets she wished to sell to a third party. United Mortgage transferred these assets to Averill Corporation, newly organized for the purpose, in consideration for which Averill issued all of its shares to Mrs. Gregory. A few days later, Averill was dissolved, its assets were distributed to Mrs. Gregory, and she was able to sell them to the third party. A deficiency was determined on the theory that the net result of the steps just described was an ordinary dividend distribution of the assets by United Mortgage to Mrs. Gregory, and that the "reorganization" provisions of the 1924 Revenue Act should be confined to transactions having some purpose other than tax avoidance. The Tax Court (then the Board of Tax Appeals) held for the taxpayer:

> As long as corporations are recognized before the law as if they were creatures of substance, there is nothing to distinguish [Averill Corporation] from innumerable others, whether they be devised to achieve a temporary tax reduction or some other legitimate end. Congress has not left it to the Commissioner to say, in the absence of fraud or other compelling circumstances, that the corporate form may be ignored in some cases and recognized in others. Whatever can be said of the wisdom of recognizing the corporate device, the taxing statutes have so plainly accepted it and provided the detailed methods of taxing its transactions, that to disregard it in a case like this would vary the time, method and amount of tax which the statute imposes. . . .
>
> A statute so meticulously drafted must be interpreted as a literal expression of the taxing policy, and leaves only the small interstices for judicial consideration. (Evelyn F. Gregory, 27 B.T.A. 223, 225 (1932).)

The Internal Revenue Service was successful in the Court of Appeals for the Second Circuit, however, where Judge Learned Hand wrote:

> We agree with the Board [of Tax Appeals] and the taxpayer that a transaction, otherwise within an exception of the tax law, does not lose its immunity, because it is actuated by a desire to avoid, or, if one choose, to evade, taxation. Any one may so arrange his affairs that his taxes shall be as low as possible; he is not bound to choose that pattern which will best pay the Treasury; there is not even a patriotic duty to increase one's taxes. . . . Therefore, if what was done here, was what was intended by [the statute], it is of no consequence that it was all an elaborate scheme to get rid of income taxes, as it certainly was. Nevertheless, it does not follow that Congress meant to cover such a transaction, not even though the facts answer the

dictionary definitions of each term used in the articulation of a statutory definition. It is quite true, as the Board has very well said, that as the articulation of a statute increases, the room for interpretation must contract; but the meaning of a sentence may be more than that of the separate words, as a melody is more than the notes, and no degree of particularity can ever obviate recourse to the setting in which all appear, and which all collectively create. The purpose of the section is plain enough; men engaged in enterprises — industrial, commercial, financial, or any other — might wish to consolidate, or divide, to add to, or subtract from, their holdings. Such transactions were not to be considered as "realizing" any profit, because the collective interests still remained in solution. But the underlying presupposition is plain that the readjustment shall be undertaken for reasons germane to the conduct of the venture in hand, not as an ephemeral incident, egregious to its prosecution. To dodge the shareholders' taxes is not one of the transactions contemplated as corporate "reorganization." (Helvering v. Gregory, 69 F.2d 809, 810-11, 13 AFTR 806 (2d Cir. 1934).

The Supreme Court affirmed the judgment of the Court of Appeals, using strikingly similar language:

When [the statute] speaks of a transfer of assets by one corporation to another, it means a transfer made "in pursuance of a plan of reorganization" of corporate business; and not a transfer of assets by one corporation to another in pursuance of a plan having no relation to the business of either, as plainly is the case here. Putting aside, then, the question of motive in respect of taxation altogether, and fixing the character of the proceeding by what actually occurred, what do we find? Simply an operation having no business or corporate purpose — a mere device which put on the form of a corporate reorganization as a disguise for concealing its real character, and the sole object and accomplishment of which was the consummation of a preconceived plan, not to reorganize a business or any part of a business, but to transfer a parcel of corporate shares to the petitioner. No doubt, a new and valid corporation was created. But that corporation was nothing more than a contrivance to the end last described. It was brought into existence for no other purpose; it performed, as it was intended from the beginning it should perform, no other function. When that limited function had been exercised, it immediately was put to death.

In these circumstances, the facts speak for themselves and are susceptible of but one interpretation. The whole undertaking, though conducted according to the terms of [the statute], was in fact an elaborate and devious form of conveyance masquerading as a corporate reorganization, and nothing else. The rule which excludes from consideration the motive of tax avoidance is not pertinent to the situation, because the transaction upon its face lies outside the plain intent of the statute. To hold otherwise would be to exalt artifice above reality and to deprive the statutory provision in question of all serious purpose. (Gregory v. Helvering, 293 U.S. 465, 469-70, 14 AFTR 1191 (1935).)

While the *Gregory* case was moving from the Court of Appeals to the Supreme Court, Congress enacted the Revenue Act of 1934, which eliminated the statutory provision on which Mrs. Gregory had relied. In recommending this change, the House Committee on Ways and Means said that by employing spin-offs, "corporations have found it possible to pay what would otherwise be taxable dividends, without any taxes upon their shareholders" and that "this means of avoidance should be ended." H.R. Rep. No. 704, 73d Cong., 2d Sess., reprinted in 1939-1 C.B. (Part 2) 554, 564. This recommendation was made after the Tax Court had decided the *Gregory* case in favor of the taxpayer; had Congress withheld its legislative hand until after the affirmance of the Court of Appeals by the Supreme Court, it might have decided that the courts could be trusted to distinguish "legitimate" spin-offs from tax avoidance devices. Instead, Congress reduced all spin-offs, whether serving business purposes or not, to the level of ordinary distributions, taxable as dividends to the extent of the corporation's post-1913 and current earnings and profits. Although this legislative action in 1934 robbed the Supreme Court's decision in the *Gregory* case of some of its immediate importance, over the years the decision has so permeated every crevice of the tax law that it must always be in the forefront of the tax lawyer's mind. Moreover, it has had a special impact on the reorganization provisions of the Internal Revenue Code, and the later history of corporate separations has been constantly haunted by the fear that a dividend may be masquerading as a divisive distribution. See also the discussion *infra*, Sec. 12.19.

From time to time after 1934, there were proposals to reinstate the spin-off as a tax-free reorganization, with appropriate restrictions to prevent its use primarily for tax avoidance. These efforts finally bore fruit in 1951, when the Internal Revenue Code of 1939 was amended to provide in §112(b)(11) for the tax-free spin-off of the common stock of a subsidiary under a plan of reorganization, "unless it appears that (A) any corporation which is a party to such reorganization was not intended to continue the active conduct of a trade or business after such reorganization, or (B) the corporation whose stock is distributed was used principally as a device for the distribution of earnings and profits to the shareholders of any corporation a party to the reorganization." Recommending enactment of §112(b)-

(11), the Senate Finance Committee said that "it is economically unsound to impede spin-offs which break-up businesses into a greater number of enterprises, when undertaken for legitimate business purposes."[1]

Condition (A) of §112(b)(11) was designed to prevent a corporation from separating its cash or investment property from its operating assets in order to spin off the stock of a new corporation holding one or the other, since the shareholders would thereby be enabled to liquidate or sell the inactive corporation at the capital gain rate. The *Gregory* case might have been relied upon to prevent this practice, at least if sufficiently blatant, but the statutory language of §112(b)(11) was an additional safeguard. Condition (B) of §112(b)(11) was more vague; it was probably intended to deny tax immunity if the distributing corporation's dividend history suggested that the spin-off was a belated substitute for ordinary dividends, and there was some reason to think that a prompt sale of either corporation, especially if prearranged, would support an inference that the spin-off was a "device" for distributing earnings and profits. As a further safeguard against a bail-out of earnings and profits, §112(b)-(11) permitted only common stock, and not preferred stock or securities, to be distributed tax-free. These provisions of §112(b)(11) did not have an opportunity to acquire a more definite meaning because it was supplanted, only three years after its enactment, by the more elaborate provisions of §355 of the 1954 Code, which will be discussed presently. For this reason, the 1951 legislation is notable mainly for its cautious reinstatement of the tax-free spin-off, with statutory restrictions that are reminiscent of the *Gregory* case and that in turn foreshadow, as will be seen, several limitations in §355 of the 1954 Code.

Turning from the spin-off to the split-up, we find that the transfer of corporate assets to two new corporations, followed by a complete liquidation of the original corporation, was a tax-free re-

---

[1] Sen. Rept. No. 781, 82d Cong., 1st sess., reprinted in 1951-2 C.B. 458, 499. For detailed discussion of §112(b)(11), see Mette, Spin-Off Reorganization and the Revenue Act of 1951, 8 Tax L. Rev. 337 (1953); Note, Tax Treatment of Corporate Divisions, 52 Col. L. Rev. 408 (1952); Wolff, Divisive Reorganizations as Affected by the Revenue Act of 1951, 31 Taxes 716 (1953); Mintz, Divisive Corporate Reorganizations: Split-Ups and Split-Offs, 6 Tax L. Rev. 365 (1951); Paul, *Studies in Federal Taxation* (3d series) 3; Tomasulo, Split-Ups and Related Topics, 12 N.Y.U. Inst. on Fed. Tax. 287 (1954).

For litigation under §112(b)(11) of the 1939 Code, see Bondy v. Commissioner, 269 F.2d 463, 4 AFTR 2d 5362 (4th Cir. 1959); Parshelsky's Estate v. Commissioner, 303 F.2d 14, 9 AFTR 2d 1382 (2d Cir. 1962) (extended historical review and discussion); Wilkins v. United States, 188 F. Supp. 91, 6 AFTR 2d 5927 (S.D. Ill. 1960); Holz v. United States, 176 F. Supp. 330, 4 AFTR 2d 5282 (D. Minn. 1959).

organization as early as 1918. When Congress stripped all spin-offs — good, bad, or indifferent — of their tax immunity in 1934, however, it took no action on the split-up. This is strange, since the tax-free split-up could be employed for the same purpose as the reviled spin-off: a corporation could transfer its business assets to one corporation and its unneeded, liquid assets to another, and distribute the stock of both corporations in a complete liquidation. This would enable the shareholders to carry on the business through the first of the new corporations and to liquidate the second in order to obtain the liquid assets that would otherwise have been distributed to them by the original corporation as a dividend. Perhaps the split-up was left untouched in 1934 on the assumption that the possible loss of franchises or contracts, confusion of customers, etc. that might attend a liquidation of the original corporation would discourage its use as a substitute for ordinary dividends. Whatever the reason for legislative abstinence, the Supreme Court's decision in *Gregory* operated thereafter as a safeguard against sham split-ups.

The 1934 reformers also refrained from action on the split-off, although it too could be pressed into service as a substitute for the spin-off. So far as the language of the pre-1954 statute was concerned, the split-off met the literal requirements of a tax-free reorganization; see §112(g)(1)(D), §112(g)(2), and §112(b)(3) of the 1939 Code. It was arguable, however, that a split-off was no more than a spin-off coupled with a surrender of stock in the original corporation that was a meaningless gesture if pro rata;[2] and that it should be taxed as a spin-off. For a time the Treasury Department accepted the split-off as a tax-free reorganization, however, at least where the *Gregory* case was not applicable, but in 1948 it discontinued the issuance of favorable rulings on the split-off because of a divergence of opinion on whether it should be analogized to the taxable spin-off or to the tax-free split-up.[3] Within a few years thereafter, however, the courts had put their stamp of approval on split-offs serving a business purpose, though the criteria for tax-free status were not entirely clear; and in 1953 the Internal Revenue Service ruled favorably on a pro rata split-off serving a business purpose.[4]

On the eve of the adoption of the 1954 Code, then, the legal status of the divisive reorganization was roughly as follows:

---

[2] Compare §115(g) of the 1939 Code, *supra*, Sec. 7.02.
[3] Wolff, *supra* note 1, at 717.
[4] Chester E. Spangler, 18 T.C. 976 (1952) (Acq.); Riddlesbarger v. Commissioner, 200 F.2d 165, 42 AFTR 930 (7th Cir. 1952); Rev. Rul. 289, 1953-2 C.B. 37.

1. Spin-offs, split-offs, and split-ups were all recognized as tax-free reorganizations in some circumstances, subject to such judicial safeguards as the business purpose doctrine of the *Gregory* case.

2. The spin-off was subject (1951-54) to special statutory regulation by §112(b)(11) of the 1939 Code. In part, this provision may have codified judicial doctrines that were applicable to split-offs and split-ups as well, but it also imposed limitations on the spin-off that were not imposed on these other transactions, despite their functional equivalence to the spin-off.

3. The legal framework for the tax-free status of these transactions was the reorganization provisions of the 1939 Code, under which the distributing corporation was required to make a transfer of part of its assets to a controlled corporation. §112(g)(1)-(D), 1939 Code. This requirement was inconvenient, since the stock of an existing subsidiary could not be distributed unless additional assets were transferred to it by the parent or unless an intervening holding company was created by the parent to hold the stock of the existing subsidiary.

4. The status of non-pro rata split-offs and split-ups (*e.g.*, where a deadlock among shareholders was settled by distributing the stock of a newly organized subsidiary to one shareholder in exchange for all of his stock in the original corporation) was uncertain. See *infra*, Sec. 11.08.

Sec. 11.03.   The 1954 legislation: §355 in outline

The tax status of divisive reorganizations was drastically altered by §355 of the 1954 Code. This provision permits the tax-free distribution[5] by one corporation (the "distributing corporation") of stock or securities in another corporation (the "controlled corporation"), if the following conditions (discussed in more detail subsequently) are satisfied:

1. *Control.* Immediately before the distribution, the distributing corporation must control the corporation whose shares or securities are being distributed. The term "control" is defined by §368(c) (*supra*, Sec. 3.07); the distributing corporation must own (a) stock of the subsidiary possessing at least 80 percent of the total combined voting power, and (b) at least 80 percent of the total number of shares of all other classes of stock.

Special legislation was required to put the spin-off of General Motors stock by DuPont on a tax-free basis (*supra*, Sec. 5.22, note 80), because DuPont owned less than 80 percent of General Motors stock. See also Rev. Rul. 63-260, 1963-2 C.B.

---

[5] Including distributions pursuant to the exercise of rights issued to the shareholders of the distributing corporation; see Oscar E. Baan, 45 T.C. 71 (1965).

147, holding that a contribution of stock to the distributing corporation by its sole shareholder in order to give it "control" of a partially-owned subsidiary should be disregarded in applying §355(a)(1)(A).

2. Post-distribution active conduct of two or more businesses. Immediately after the distribution, both the distributing corporation and the controlled corporation (or corporations) must be engaged in the active conduct of a trade or business; or, if the assets of the distributing corporation consisted solely of stock or securities in two or more controlled corporations, each of the controlled corporations must be so engaged. A corporation is treated as engaged in the active conduct of a trade or business if it is so engaged on its own account or if substantially all of its assets consist of the stock and securities of a controlled corporation which is so engaged.[6]

3. Five-year pre-distribution business rule. The foregoing requirement, relating to the active conduct of a trade or business, is satisfied only if the trade or business (a) was actively conducted throughout the 5-year period ending on the date of distribution; (b) was not acquired within the 5-year period in a taxable transaction; and (c) was not conducted by another corporation the control of which was acquired during the 5-year period in a taxable transaction.

4. Distribution of all stock and securities in controlled corporation. The distributing corporation must either (a) distribute all of its stock and securities in the controlled corporation; or (b) distribute enough stock to constitute "control," as defined by §368(c), *and* establish to the satisfaction of the Treasury that the retention of stock or stock and securities in the controlled corporation is not part of a tax-avoidance plan.

5. Device for distributing earnings and profits. The transaction must not be used principally as a device for the distribution of earnings and profits — but the mere fact that stock or securities of one or more of the corporations are sold after the distribution, unless under a pre-distribution arrangement, is not to be construed to mean that the transaction was used principally as such a device.

These conditions are equally applicable to spin-offs, split-offs, and split-ups. Moreover, the distribution need not be part of a "reorganization," by virtue of §355(a)(2)(C), so that the stock and securities of an existing subsidiary may be distributed tax-free. In

---

[6] Under §112(b)(11) of the 1939 Code, *supra*, Sec. 11.02, a corporation that owned less than 80 percent of a subsidiary corporation could spin it off by transferring it to a newly created corporation for all of the latter's stock and then spinning off the new corporation's stock. (For problems in this area, see Tomasulo, *supra* note 1, at 298-301.) A transaction of this type would not be permitted under §355, however, because the newly created subsidiary would not be engaged in the active conduct of a trade or business, under §355(b)(2)-(A), either in its own right or through "a corporation *controlled* by it."

this respect, §355 departs from pre-1954 law, under which the creation of, or a transfer of assets to, the subsidiary was an essential prerequisite to a tax-free distribution. Section 355 also differs from pre-1954 law in permitting preferred stock as well as common to be distributed tax-free, whereas §112(b)(11) of the 1939 Code prevented a distribution of preferred stock in a spin-off; but under §306(c)(1)-(B) of the 1954 Code, the preferred stock may constitute "section 306 stock" (*supra*, Ch. 8) whose sale or redemption will produce ordinary income rather than capital gain. Finally, a distribution can qualify under §355 whether it is pro rata with respect to the distributing corporation's shareholders or not.

Section 355 embraces the distribution of securities as well as stock. But if the principal amount of the securities received by a distributee exceeds the principal amount of the securities surrendered by him, the fair market value of the excess principal amount is treated as "boot"; and if no securities are surrendered, the entire fair market value of the securities received is so treated.[7] Since only the stock and securities of a controlled corporation can be distributed tax-free under §355(a)(1), any other property that may be distributed in conjunction with a corporate division will be treated as "boot," taxable under §356.

As stated earlier, §355 does not require the distributing corporation to transfer part of its assets to the controlled corporation, as was required by pre-1954 law. If there is such a transfer, however, it will constitute a "reorganization" under §368(a)(1)(D), and this in turn means that the transferor corporation will not recognize gain or loss on the transfer, by virtue of §361(a), and that there will be a carryover of basis from the transferor corporation to the transferee, by virtue of §362(b). See also *infra*, Sec. 11.13.

The foregoing statutory provisions are discussed in more detail hereafter.[8]

[7] *Infra,* Sec. 11.10, n. 56.

[8] See generally Caplin, The Five-Year Active Business Rule in Separations and Partial Liquidations, 1961 So. Calif. Tax Inst. 211; Pennell, New Ideas in Disposing of Part of a Business, 19 N.Y.U. Inst. on Fed. Tax. 529, 541ff (1961); as to the "anti-device" provision of §355, see Cordes, The Device of Divisive Reorganizations, 10 Kansas L. Rev. 21 (1961); Nessen, Earnings and Profits Discontinuities Under the 1954 Code, 77 Harv. L. Rev. 450 (1964).

Earlier discussions: Lyons, Some Problems in Corporate Separations Under the 1954 Code, 12 Tax L. Rev. 15 (1956); Friedman, Divisive Corporate Reorganizations Under the 1954 Code, 10 *ibid.* 487 (1955); Comment, Divisive Reorganizations Under the Internal Revenue Code of 1954, 67 Yale L.J. 38 (1957); Mintz, Corporate Separations, 36 Taxes 882 (1958); Pennell, Divisive Reorganizations and Corporate Contractions, 33 Taxes 924 (1955); Young, Corporate Separations: Some Revenue Rulings Under Section 355, 71 Harv. L. Rev. 843 (1958); Jacobs, Spin-Offs: The Pre-Distribution Two Business Rule — Edmund P. Coady and Beyond, 19 Tax L. Rev. 155 (1964).

Sec. 11.04.   The active business requirement in general: §355(b)

The most important innovation of the 1954 Code in the taxation of corporate divisions, and the most troublesome of §355's requirements, is §355(b)(1). By virtue of this provision, a corporate division cannot qualify under §355 unless:

> 1. Immediately after the distribution, the distributing corporation and the controlled corporation are both engaged in the active conduct of a trade or business; or
> 2. Immediately before the distribution, the distributing corporation had no assets[9] other than stock or securities in the controlled corporations, and each of the controlled corporations is engaged immediately after the distribution in the active conduct of a trade or business.

Section 355(b)(2) goes on to require that such trade or business must have been actively conducted throughout the 5-year period ending on the date of distribution, as well as to disqualify certain methods of acquiring a business (infra, Sec. 11.05).

Although the very heart of §355 is its requirement of two active trades or businesses immediately after the distribution (each having a 5-year history), the crucial term "active conduct of a trade or business" is not defined in the statute.[10] The regulations under §355 provide as follows:

> For purposes of §355, a trade or business consists of a specific existing group of activities being carried on for the purpose of earning income or profit from only such group of activities, and the activities included in such group must include every operation which forms a part of, or a step in, the process of earning income or profit from such group. Such group of activities ordinarily must include the collection of income and the payment of expenses. (Regs. §1.335-1(c).)

The regulations go on to exclude from the concept of "active trade or business" the following activities: (1) The holding of property for investment purposes; (2) the ownership and operation of real estate used in the owner's trade or business (e.g., a factory); and (3) a group of activities that do not independently produce income, even

---

[9] For this purpose, Regs. §1.355-4(a)(2) adopts a de minimis rule.

[10] For the phrase "trade or business" as used elsewhere in the Internal Revenue Code, see Allen and Orechkoff, Toward a More Systematic Drafting and Interpreting of the Internal Revenue Code: Expenses, Losses and Bad Debts, 25 U. of Chi. L. Rev. 1, 42-61 (1957).

We have previously (supra, Sec. 7.63) encountered the similar phrase in §346(b) ("actively engaged in the conduct of a trade or business"), but it too lacks a statutory definition, and the regulations under §346(b) adopt the definition of the §355 regulations. Regs. §1.346-1(c).

though capable of doing so with the addition of other activities or with an expansion in previously incidental activities. Finally, the regulations provide, in Regs. §1.355-1(a), that §355 does "not apply to the division of a single business."

In recent litigation, however, taxpayers have successfuly challenged certain aspects of these regulations, especially their position on the division of a single business; and the likelihood of amendment should be taken into account in reading the discussion that follows.

1. Vertical division of a single business — demise of the pre-distribution two-business rule. One of the basic Treasury approaches to the active business requirement of §355(b) was the so-called pre-distribution two-business rule. Inspiration for this approach stemmed from the fact that §355(b)(1) requires the active conduct of two separate businesses immediately *after* the distribution: since §355-(b)(2) demands a five-year pre-distribution history for "such business," the Service reasoned that *the* business conducted before the distribution had to be the *same* business as that required to be conducted after the distribution. This approach was rejected by the Tax Court (six judges dissenting) in Edmond P. Coady, 33 T.C. 771 (1966), involving a division of a construction company owned by two equal shareholders into two businesses, each owned 100 percent by one of them. The division was effected by a transfer of a major construction contract together with an appropriate amount of cash and equipment to a new corporation, the stock of which was then transferred to one of the shareholders in return for all of his stock in the distributing corporation (i.e., by a split-off); the latter corporation was left with a second major contract, together with the rest of the equipment and cash. In holding that §355 could be used to divide a single, functionally-integrated pre-distribution business into two separate post-distribution businesses, the court invalidated Regs. 1.355-1(a) to the extent that it holds that §355 does not apply to such a transaction. *Coady* was affirmed on appeal and, after it was followed by another appellate court as to a pro rata spin-off involving somewhat similar facts, the Internal Revenue Service agreed to abide by both cases "to the extent that they hold that Regs. 1.355-1(a), providing that §355 does not apply to the division of a single business, is invalid."[11]

---

[11] Coady v. Commissioner, 289 F.2d 490, 7 AFTR 2d 1322 (6th Cir. 1961); United States v. Marett, 325 F.2d 28, 12 AFTR 2d 5900 (5th Cir. 1963) (manufacturing plant producing for a single customer spun-off from two other plants producing for same customer and others); Rev. Rul. 64-147, 1964-1 C.B. 136; see also Patricia W. Burke, 42 T.C. 1021 (1964) (spin-off of branch store);

In *Coady*, there was a "vertical" division of the pre-distribution business, i.e., *each* of the post-distribution businesses carried on all stages or functions of the original business. As will be seen, *Coady* did not settle the status of "horizontal" divisions, in which one post-distribution business takes over one or more functions of the original business (e.g., production, distribution, real estate ownership, management, storage, research, or financing), while the other post-distribution business carries on the remaining functions.

2. *Functional divisions of a single business.* Under Regs. §1.355-1(c), a "business" (as the term is used in §355) must consist of activities that "include every operation which forms a part of, or a step in, the process of earning income or profit," including the collection of income and the payment of expenses;" hence, it does not include a group of activities which, while part of an active business, do not themselves independently produce income — even though such activities would independently produce income with the addition of other activities or with large increases in activities that were previously incidental or insubstantial. Among the examples given by the regulations of activities that do not satisfy this definition of "business," and hence cannot be separated under §355, are a manufacturing company's research department, sales operations, and "captive" coal mine.

Although these functional divisions differ from the vertical all-function division upheld in the *Coady* case, the Tax Court in that decision stated (33 T.C. at 777) that the purpose of the "active business" requirement of §355(b) is "to prevent the tax-free separation of *active* and *inactive* assets into *active* and *inactive* corporate entities," an explanation that would not condemn a functional division of a single business previously operated as an integrated entity. In several later cases that might have been thought to involve functional divisions, however, the Tax Court has carefully avoided the implications of the *Coady* rationale by finding that the separated activities either constituted an independent 5-year-old business[12] or came within the "geographical" concept of the *Coady* case.[13] Pending issuance of new

Jacobs, Spin-Offs: The Pre-Distribution Two Business Rule — Edmond P. Coady and Beyond, 19 Tax L. Rev. 155 (1964).

For a complication arising from *Coady*, in which the forensic roles of taxpayer and government may be reversed, see *infra*, note 16.

[12] Marne S. Wilson, 42 T.C. 914 (1964) (separation of credit and collection assets and activities of retail furniture store), reversed on other grounds (no business purpose), 353 F.2d 184, 16 AFTR 2d 6030 (9th Cir. 1965); H. Grady Lester, Jr., 40 T.C. 947 (1939) (Acq.) (warehouse distribution business separated from business of selling to jobbers); Albert W. Badanes, 39 T.C. 410 (1962).

[13] Patricia W. Burke, *supra* note 11; see also Lockwood's Estate v. Commissioner, 350 F.2d 712, 16 AFTR 2d 5592 (8th Cir. 1965). In the *Burke* case,

regulations,[14] which may clarify the status of functional divisions of a single business, it can be pointed out that an activity with no customers or clients other than the original business itself offers a greater opportunity to siphon off the latter's earnings in the future (by a manipulation of inter-company transactions) than an activity that deals solely or primarily with outsiders. Assuming this possibility (which depends for its success on *future* dealings between the two businesses) to constitute a "bail-out" arrangement, the "device" restriction of §355(a)(1)(B) (*infra*, Sec. 11.06) may be a more persuasive way to cope with it than the assertion that the separated function is not an "active business." Moreover, the Service has other weapons — the assignment of income doctrine, §446(b), and §482 — that can be employed when and if the anticipated manipulation occurs.

There may be an added problem in this area if the separated function was a wholly incidental part of the original business. The regulations contain one example of such an activity — an executive dining room maintained by a manufacturing company — which is disqualified even though it "is managed and operated as a separate unit and the executives are charged for their meals."[15] Assuming that the function is economically viable in the sense that it can operate at a profit if separated from the original business, and that it is not a passive investment, its separation seems no more objectionable than the separation of a more crucial function of the original business. The hostile attitude taken by the regulations seems to reflect the "two business" requirement that was invalidated by *Coady*, rather than an independent requirement that the separated activity have been a major rather than merely minor undertaking.

Would an activity that is disqualified by the regulations (e.g., a research or sales department, captive coal mine, or executive dining room) meet its requirement if it had been segregated in a subsidiary corporation that had dealt with the parent at arm's-length for at least five years? Notwithstanding the absence of any reason of policy for allowing a corporate shell to make a difference under §355, it is pos-

---

the Tax Court came close to extending the *Coady* rationale to a functional division, but there is no explicit discussion of the issue; and in the *Wilson* case, the court quite deliberately refrained from holding that functional divisions are permissible under *Coady*. It should be noted that a division of a business along geographical lines is permitted by several examples in Regs. §1.355-1(d), although *Burke* and *Lockwood's Estate* were thought by the government to fall outside of these examples.

[14] Rev. Rul. 64-147, *supra* note 11, states that a modification of the regulations is under consideration.

[15] Regs. §1.355-(d), Example (16).

sible that a subsidiary whose identity has been honored for tax purposes, including §482, meets the test of a "a group of activities . . . independently producing income" under Regs. §1.355-1(c)(3). One of the shortcomings of these regulations, however, is the deliberate avoidance of a commitment on the question whether a subsidiary corporation (*e.g.*, a purchasing, selling, subcontracting, or management corporation) that deals *only* with its parent is a separate trade or business. Of course, if the regulations are amended or if the *Coady* rationale is judicially extended to include functional divisions, it will not be necessary for the taxpayer to rely on prior separate incorporation to establish the independence of such a business activity.

3. Horizontal integration — "single" versus "separate" business problems. If the corporation to be divided has been actively carrying on two or more distinct and readily identifiable lines of business (*e.g.*, a textile mill and a motion picture theatre), each one will ordinarily constitute a separate income-producing group of activities and hence will be a "business" within the meaning of the regulations that will have to meet the five-year history test in its own right. On the other hand, when a single 5-year-old business is divided under *Coady*, each division automatically shares in the parent's history and thus satisfies the 5-year test. Thus, it is necessary to determine whether the assets and activities which are to be divided constitute one business, or two separate businesses, so as to determine the proper application of the five-year business history rule. If one of the post-distribution activities cannot satisfy the 5-year test in its own right, there will be a reversal of the pre-*Coady* forensic roles: the taxpayer will seek to establish that the separated activities inherited a 5-year history from a *single* pre-distribution business; while the government may assert that there were two businesses — only one of which was properly aged.[16]

In determining the existence of separate businesses, two factors ordinarily are significant: (a) the geographical situs of the particular activities; and (b) the quality or nature of those activities. The reg-

---

[16] Cf. H. Grady Lester, Jr., *supra* note 12, and Patricia W. Burke, *supra* note 11.

The *Coady* rationale, however, would seem to allow an independent, post-distribution business to tack on the period during which it was part of an original business. Thus, if the two businesses that resulted from the separation in *Coady* had been separated 3 years before the distribution (by placing one in a subsidiary corporation, or by separating the personnel, records, etc., into two operating divisions), each one ought to be allowed to include in its history the period of time when they were integrated in the original business. There is no reason, in other words, why *Coady* should be satisfied if the business is divided on the very eve of a distribution, or more than 5 years earlier; but not if it is divided in the intervening years.

ulations rely heavily on the geographical location factor to find separate business status: thus, the manufacture and sale of the same product in different states is treated as a separate business with respect to each state, Examples (8), (9), (13), (14) and (15) of Regs. §1.355-1(d); and Example (10) states that the operation of two retail clothing stores, one in the downtown area and one in the suburban area of the same city, each selling the same products but each having its own manager with control over purchases, constitutes the conduct of separate businesses.[17] Except for the reference in Example (10) to separate control over purchases, it will be noted that the foregoing examples do not, at least explicitly, require that the plants or stores have been separately managed in the past. The mere fact of common ownership will necessarily mean that ultimate responsibility for both businesses has been vested in a single board of directors and a single corporate president; on the other hand, it is evidently assumed by the regulations that each business has its own low echelon employees. But the regulations are inconveniently vague on the question whether each plant or store constitutes "a group of activities . . . independently producing income" if in the past there has been joint, rather than separate, control over hiring and firing, advertising, financial policy, prices, etc.[18] Moreover, although Example (10) specifies separate managers with control over purchases, it is not clear whether this is an essential requirement in view of the omission of such a spécification in Example (8); nor are we told whether separate

---

[17] The regulations also specify that the stores do not have a common warehouse. But such a warehouse is not necessarily fatal. See Regs. §1.337-3(c), providing that a corporation engaged in two or more businesses will not recognize gain or loss on a bulk sale of inventory of any *one* of the businesses if it liquidates under §377. One of the examples is a corporation operating a grocery store at one location and a hardware store at another; although a common warehouse is maintained, the inventory can be separated since the two stores do not handle the same items. Another example is a corporation owning a downtown department store and a suburban department store; there is a common warehouse, but the inventory attributable to each store can be clearly ascertained. These examples are adopted for purposes of §355 by Regs. §1.355-1(e), the implication being that a common warehouse will not prevent a separation under §355 of two stores (or other business activities) if the inventory can be assigned to the proper store. Even if the inventory cannot be so segregated, it may be that a transfer of one store with either an adequate inventory or working capital sufficient to rebuild its inventory would satisfy §355, since it is at least arguable that a separate store constitutes "a group of activities . . . independently producing income" under Regs. 1.355-1(c)(3), even though its inventory cannot be segregated from the inventory of another store under common ownership.

[18] Example (15) of Regs. §1.355-1(d) permits a division of two manufacturing plants whose output had historically been sold through a common sales office. But it does not make clear whether common control over other policies and activities would be fatal, and it may assume that the central sales office was made up of two separate sales forces.

managers, if they are essential, will suffice if their control over purchases is severely limited by budgets or purchasing policies prescribed by the directors, corporate officers, or other high level supervisors.

The regulations do not contain any examples of separate businesses based on the type of business activity conducted, but several rulings indicate that significant variations in the type of products sold or services rendered can establish separate businesses.[19] Several recent decisions have wrestled with the problem of what constitutes a separate business, but have done little to clarify matters in this area. In *H. Grady Lester* (*supra* note 12), separate businesses were found largely on the basis of different customers (one business consisted of activities as a warehouse distributor selling to jobbers; and the other business involved selling the same products to dealers as a jobber), even though both activities were conducted at the same location, with the same employees, without segregation of inventories, and without separate records of income and expenses. In *Marne S. Wilson* (*supra* note 12), the credit department of a retail furniture store was held to constitute a separate business, despite unity of location, personnel, records, management, and advertising.

On the other hand, the Service's emphasis on geographical location as a test for separate business status was rejected in *Lockwood's Estate* (*supra* note 13), the court there finding that the establishment of a new manufacturing and sales branch in a different state was not the creation of a new business, but the continuation of a single nationwide business. To the same effect is *Patricia Burke* (*supra* note 11), holding that a new branch outlet for the corporation's products (consisting of a warehouse and a store), located in a different city in the same state, was merely an extension of a single business.[20]

---

[19] Rev. Rul. 56-655, 1956-2 C.B. 214 (retail appliance branch and retail furniture branch; held, separate businesses); Rev. Rul. 56-451, 1956-2 C.B. 208 (metal industry magazine a separate business from three magazines published to serve the electrical industry — query, whether each electrical industry magazine is also a separate business?); Rev. Rul. 56-554, 1956-2 C.B. 198; Rev. Rul. 56-557, 1956-2 C.B. 199 (bank's management of real estate acquired by foreclosure); Rev. Rul. 57-190, 1957-1 C.B. 121 (sale of different brands of autos at different locations).

It should be noted, however, that the Service requires independent activity before a separate business can be found; thus, a vertically integrated business, even though conducted in different states, was held to constitute a single business in Rev. Rul. 58-54, 1958-1 C.B. 184.

[20] But see Albert W. Badanes, *supra* note 12, suggesting that operation of the same type of business in different cities in the same state was the conduct of separate businesses (the court cited Example (8) of the regulations); United States v. Marett, *supra* note 11, holding that a spin-off of a food processing plant by a corporation owning a second plant in the same city and a third in a different state, constituted the division of a single business. This finding was critical in *Marett* because the spun-off plant was established only a few months prior to the §355 transaction.

4. *Investment property.* The regulations state that holding stock, securities, land, or other property for investment, including "casual sales" thereof, does not constitute the active conduct of a trade or business. As an example, the regulations refer to a manufacturing corporation that owns investment securities which it proposes to place in a new corporation to be spun-off to its shareholders. Regs. §1.355-1(d), Example (1). It is obviously necessary to exclude a transaction of this kind from §355, lest the provision become an open-sesame to avoidance of the tax on dividends. Another illustration of this principle is a ranching corporation that owns land adjacent to property on which oil has been discovered. Before the corporation has engaged in any activity in relation to its mineral rights, it proposes to transfer them to a new corporation to be spun-off to its shareholders. Example (7). Both of these examples might go the other way under different circumstances. A manufacturing corporation could be engaged in the trade or business of buying and selling securities; but this would be a rare combination of business activities, and if the corporation had been reporting its profits on the sale of securities as capital gain, a claim that it was in the securities business in order to permit a tax-free separation under §355 would unquestionably be vigorously resisted by the Internal Revenue Service. It would probably be easier for the ranching corporation to establish that it was engaged in the oil and gas business. The example in the regulations specifies that the corporation had "engaged in no activities in connection with the mineral rights," thus leaving open the possibility that exploration, drilling, production, and sale could in time rise to the dignity of a separate trade or business.[21]

5. *Real property used in the trade or business.* The regulations also exclude from the concept of active "trade or business" under §355 the ownership and operation of land or buildings entirely or substantially used and occupied by the owner in the operation of a trade or business. In illustration of this principle, the regulations give three examples of corporations engaged in a trade or business that wish to employ §355 to separate real estate holdings from their other assets. In one, the real estate is the factory of a manufacturing corporation, and the regulations state that the operation of the factory is not a trade or business separate from the corporation's manufacturing activities. Example (2). Examples (3) and (4) are banks that wish to spin-off the buildings in which their banking operations are carried on. In one case, ten out of eleven floors of an office building

---

[21] See also Example (6) of Regs. §1.355-1(d) (vacant land not an active business); Rev. Rul. 57-492, 1952-2 C.B. 247.

are rented to tenants, the ground floor being occupied by the bank itself, and the bank's real estate department is in charge of the rental, management and maintenance of the building. In the other case, only one-half of the second floor of a two-story building is rented. The regulations state that the first bank's rental activities constitute a trade or business, but that the second bank's rental activity is "only incidental to its banking business." It is not clear whether the first building could be spun-off under §355 if the rental, management, and maintenance had been entrusted to a real estate agent or management corporation, rather than conducted by the bank itself. Example (6) is also concerned with real estate, stating that the ownership of vacant land by a corporation that owns and rents an office building does not constitute a separate trade or business.

On several occasions, the courts have refused to apply the *Coady* rationale to the separation of real estate that was predominantly owner-occupied, on the ground that the activities connected with the "outside" rental income were too insignificant to constitute an active business; by implication, though not directly, the added activity and income attributable to the continued occupancy of the premises by the distributing corporation were regarded as insufficient to create such an active business.[22] To an extent that is not clear, these decisions also rely on the fact that the pre-distribution ownership of the real estate was incidental rather than essential to the income-producing capacity of the existing business. Whatever their rationale, the cases offer little hope of qualifying the ownership of real estate as an "active business" unless there is a 5-year history of dealing on a substantial scale with occupants other than the owner.[23] Although these cases concerned real estate, the same principles will no doubt be applied to a transfer of vehicles or other equipment to a separate corporation, coupled with a lease-back to the distributing corporation.

It was suggested above that the separate incorporation of a sales or research department of a manufacturing business may enhance the taxpayer's claim that it constitutes an "active business." This may also be true of real estate, if the real estate corporation's maintenance or other activities are significant in scale. Where the property is occupied by the parent corporation, however, these activities

---

[22] See Isabel A. Elliott, 32 T.C. 283 (1959); Appleby v. Commissioner, 35 T.C. 755 (1961), aff'd per curiam, 296 F.2d 925, 9 AFTR 2d 372 (3rd Cir. 1962), cert. denied, 370 U.S. 910 (1962); Bonsall v. Commissioner, 317 F.2d 61, 11 AFTR 2d 1447 (2d Cir. 1963).

[23] See Rev. Rul. 56-555, 1956-2 C.B. 210.

are likely to be quite insignificant, so that separate incorporation will probably be of less assistance here than in the case of such functions as sales, purchasing, research, advertising, and the like.[24]

Sec. 11.05.   The 5-year rule: Pre-distribution business history

As has been seen, §355's "active business" requirement is designed to prevent a tax-free separation of liquid assets as a substitute for current dividends. Standing by itself, however, the active business requirement would not prevent a corporation from investing its surplus funds in a new business and spinning it off, in preparation for a sale of the business by the shareholders — a scheme that would have the same economic effect as a distribution of money. Or, if the shareholders desired to invest in a new business as individuals or partners, the corporation might build it up for them and then spin it off, rather than paying ordinary dividends. To prevent such devices, §355-(b)(2)(B) provides that both the distributed business and the retained business (or, in the event of a split-up, both of the distributed businesses) must have been actively conducted throughout the 5-year period ending on the date of the distribution.[25]

The theory underlying the requirement of a 5-year history for each business is prevention of the temporary investment of liquid assets in a new business preparatory to a spin-off or other tax-free corporate division under §355. If the business has been actively conducted for 5 years, it presumably was not created for the purpose of avoiding the tax on dividends. But, even though the business might not have been *created* for this purpose, it might have been *purchased* by the distributing corporation as a temporary investment in anticipation of a distribution. To forestall this possibility, two additional conditions must be met if the business (or the corporation conducting it) has changed hands within the 5-year period ending with the date of the distribution:

> 1. Under §355(b)(2)(C), a trade or business is disqualified if it was acquired within the 5-year period in a transaction in which gain or loss was recognized in whole or in part. As was indicated with respect to the comparable prohibition in §346(b), *supra*, Sec. 7.63, the statutory purpose was to exclude a business that was *purchased* by the distributing or controlled corporation

---

[24] A distribution and lease-back of real estate was held to satisfy the "active business" requirement of §112(b)(11) of the 1939 code in Parshelsky's Estate v. Commissioner, *supra* note 1; but the court pointed out the possibility that the phrase might have a different meaning under §355.

[25] See the comparable requirements of §346(b), designed to serve a similar purpose. *Supra*, Sec. 7.63.

within the preceding 5 years. Since the purchaser would not recognize gain or loss on such an acquisition of an existing business, the phrase "transaction in which gain or loss was recognized in whole or in part" must mean, at least primarily, transactions in which the *seller* recognized gain or loss. (It should also include the acquisition of a business from another corporation which avoided the recognition of gain or loss under §337 (*supra*, Sec. 9.64), but whose shareholders recognized gain or loss on the liquidation.) Moreover, if the seller happens not to recognize gain or loss because it is a tax-exempt institution, or because the sales price of the business is equal to its adjusted basis, the acquisition should be barred by the purpose of §355-(b)(2)(C), although its language is far from satisfactory on this point.

Section 355(b)(2)(C) permits the acquisition of a business in a tax-free transaction, such as the liquidation of a subsidiary under §332, a tax-free merger or consolidation under §368(a)-(1)(A) and §361, or an exchange under §351. But the use of "boot" in an otherwise tax-free exchange will disqualify the transaction, at least if the *transferor* realizes and recognizes gain, since §355(b)(2)(C) forbids the recognition of gain or loss "in whole or in part."[26]

2. Finally, §355(b)(2)(D) strengthens §355(b)(2)(C) by prohibiting — for the 5-year period before distribution — the acquisition of control of a corporation conducting the business, unless the acquisition was a tax-free transaction. This requirement, which was added in conference, forestalls the purchase by one corporation of the stock of another corporation within the 5-year period for the purpose of (a) spinning off the stock of the second corporation, or (b) acquiring its business in a tax-free liquidation in order to spin off the business. See Example, Regs. §1.355-4(b)(2). Section 355(b)(2)(D), however, permits the acquisition of control during the 5-year period by a transaction in which gain or loss was not recognized in whole or in part, or by reason of such transactions coupled with other acquisitions before the 5-year period.

When the distributing or controlled corporation's acquisition of a business (or of a corporation conducting the business) is consistent

---

[26] For discussion, see Oscar E. Baan, *supra* note 5, holding that an acquisition in which the transferor did not recognize gain because it was incurred on an inter-company transfer between members of an affiliated group of corporations filing a consolidated return did not violate the prohibition of §355(b)(2)(C).

If the transferor suffers a loss on the exchange, the transfer of "boot" will not result in the recognition of any part of the loss, because of §356(c), §361(b)(2) and §351(b)(2). Even so, such a transaction ought not to qualify under §355(b)(2)(C), at least if it is the functional equivalent of an ordinary purchase; but the clumsy statutory language may be construed so as to leave an unwarranted opening for such an acquisition. Even less clear is the result where the transferor's boot gain goes unrecognized because it distributes the boot under §361(b)(1)(A) — this problem is similar to the §337 situation noted in the text.

with §355(b)(2)(C) and (D), i.e., in the case of a tax-free acquisition, the predecessor's history is "tacked on" in computing the 5-year period. Thus, if a business that was conducted by a partnership for 3 years was acquired by the distributing corporation in a §351 transaction, and has been conducted by the distributing corporation for 2 more years, it has the requisite 5-year history.[27] A business acquired by purchase, however, must be conducted by the acquiring corporation itself for the full 5-year period to meet the standard of §355(b)-(2)(B).

A problem that is especially troublesome in applying the 5-year rule is to determine whether a group of activities constitutes a separate business which must have its *own* 5-year history, or is a separable part of a larger enterprise that can share in the latter's 5-year history. As pointed out earlier, the taxpayer may find himself on a tightrope here, viz., asserting that the activities are sufficiently distinctive to constitute an active business under the *Coady* rationale after the distribution, but that they were so closely associated with the original business before the distribution as to inherit its 5-year history.[28] The more distinctive and independently viable the activities are, however, the weaker is their claim to an inherited history.

Application of the 5-year rule is further complicated by such problems as: (a) whether the commencement of a business activity is an extension of an old business, or constitutes entry into a new and separate business; (b) whether a change of location constitutes an abandonment of the old business and the start of a new one, or merely a continuation of the old business at a new location; (c) whether a cessation of business activity followed by a resumption of activity constitutes a termination of the old business and the start of a new one, or is a continuation of the old business after a temporary lull; (d) whether expansion constitutes the entry into a new business; and (e) whether the source of funds behind an expansion is significant. The regulations state that changes during the five-year period (e.g., the addition of new products or the dropping of old ones; changes in productive capacity; etc.) shall be disregarded, provided "the changes are not of such a character as to constitute the acquisition of a new business"; and this language has been interpreted by the Service in

---

[27] See Marne S. Wilson, *supra* note 12; see also W. E. Gabriel Fabrication Co., 42 T.C. 545 (1964) (Acq.), holding that the requisite 5-year history was not broken by an unusual "loan" of a business to a shareholder in anticipation of a §355 transaction; Edward H. Russell, 40 T.C. 810 (1963) (date of acquisition and of distribution determined). A fortiori, a transfer of the business from the distributing corporation to the controlled corporation does not break the continuity of its 5-year history.

[28] For discussion, and citation of the relevant cases, see *supra,* Sec. 11.04.

published rulings to permit a change in location or a temporary cessation of business activity by a corporation intending to resume the
business without breaking the 5-year chain.[29] The acquisition by a
dealer holding a franchise for the sale and service of one brand of
automobile tires of a similar franchise for another brand, however,
was held to start a new 5-year period running for the second franchise,
to which the holding period of the first franchise could not be "tacked
on."[30]

   The 5-year rule is also troublesome in the case of a business that
expanded rapidly during the 5-year pre-distribution period. An increase in the size of its productive capacity, labor force, sales, etc., or
a vertical expansion along functional lines, should be treated as a
continuation of the old business, rather than the acquisition of a new
one, even if the "new" assets are substantial in value relative to those
that are over 5 years old.[31] A point may be reached at which the new
assets so completely overshadow the old ones, however, especially if
there has been a horizontal expansion into a new line of activity, that
the latter must be regarded as a new business. In effect, the continuity of business test of §355 requires more than the mere continuation of *a* business; rather, it is *the* business that must be continued
for the five-year period in order to satisfy §355(b)(2)(B). It has
previously been noted (*supra*, Sec. 11.04) that the regulations require
that a group of activities must independently produce income to rise
to the level of a separate trade or business under §355. It may be
difficult to say precisely *when* an activity launched by a corporation
that is expanding horizontally has become a separate business within
the meaning of §355(b)(2)(B), however, and the regulations are
silent on this subject.[32]

   [29] Regs. §1.355-4(b)(3); see also Conference Report on 1954 Code, H.R.
Rep. No. 2543, 83d Cong., 2d Sess. 38 (1954); Rev. Rul. 56-344, 1956-2 C.B.
195 (change of location); Rev. Rul. 57-126, 1957-1 C.B. 123 (temporary cessation of activity in unusual circumstances).
      If independent activities are commenced at a new location without ter-
minating activities at the old location, the Service takes the position that a
new business has been started. See Regs. §1.355-1(d), Example (9); Rev. Rul.
56-227, 1956-2 C.B. 183; but cf. Patricia W. Burke, *supra* note 11; Lockwood's
Estate v. Commissioner, *supra* note 13; and United States v. Marett, *supra*
note 11, to the contrary. See also discussion of "continuity of business enterprise" problems, *infra*, Sec. 12.19.
   [30] Rev. Rul. 57-190, 1957-1 C.B. 121.
   [31] See Lockwood's Estate v. Commissioner, *supra* note 13; Patricia W.
Burke, *supra* note 11. For some rules of thumb that were employed by the
Internal Revenue Service in this area but that may have been abandoned,
see Caplin, Corporate Division Under the 1954 Code: A New Approach to the
Five-Year "Active Business" Rule, 43 Va. L. Rev. 397 (1957).
   [32] See Rev. Rul. 57-492, 1957-2 C.B. 247, involving a spin-off of a subsidiary corporation engaged in exploring for and producing oil by a corporation
engaged in marketing and refining operations, which held that these activities

If two businesses can be identified, but the earnings of one have been employed to finance substantial growth in the other during the 5-year period, the Service may assert that §355 cannot be used to effect a separation. Thus, Rev. Rul. 59-400, 1959-2 C.B. 114, held that §355 did not apply to the spin-off of a rental real estate business where the earnings of a separate hotel business were used to "feed" the growth of the rental business.[33] The precise basis for the ruling is unclear, but its emphasis on the translation of hotel earnings into marketable rental property implies that it was bottomed on §355(a)-(1)(B) (*infra*, Sec. 11.06) — prohibiting a distribution that is "principally a device for the distribution of the earnings and profits of the distributing corporation" — rather than on the theory that the rental activities did not consitute an "active business." The source of the funds used to establish or expand a business may be relevant in applying the "device" rule, but it seems to shed little light on whether corporate activities constitute an "active business" or, if they do, on the "age" of the business. A 1964 ruling on the effect of a substantial capital contribution by a parent corporation to a subsidiary just prior to a distribution of the subsidiary's stock under §355 bears out this theory, though it does not wholly repudiate the notion that the use of earnings generated by one business to expand a second business may weaken the latter's claim to an independent 5-year history.[34]

did not become "the active conduct of a trade or business" until oil was discovered in commercial quantities, on the ground that pre-discovery activities (investigations, negotiations for mineral rights, exploration, and drilling) did not independently produce income or contain all the elements necessary to the production of income.

[33] For a discussion of a contrary ruling on similar facts, see Caplin, *supra* note 31.

[34] Rev. Rul. 64-102, 1964-1 C.B. 136, ruled favorably to the taxpayer where the parent made a large capital contribution to a subsidiary in order to equalize values in preparation for a distribution of the subsidiary's stock to buy out minority shareholders of the parent. In so ruling, the Service distinguished Rev. Rul. 58-68, 1958-1 C.B. 183, where the capital contribution preceded a pro rata spin-off, on the ground that it was a "device" to distribute the parent's earnings and profits to the parent's shareholder; the 1964 transaction, by contrast, was in complete redemption of the minority interest in the parent, could meet the requirements of §302(b)(3) (complete terminations, *supra*, Sec. 7.23), and hence was not a proscribed "device." There is an implicit assumption in the 1964 ruling that the contribution of capital does not affect the subsidiary's business history, and is relevant only to the "device" requirement. This assumption is not crystal-clear, however, since it was stipulated that the 1964 capital contribution "did not cause changes of such a character as to constitute the acquisition of a new or different business." In this connection, it should be noted that a capital contribution (or the use of the earnings of one business to feed another) several years *before* the distribution may have a more substantial impact on the second business than a transfer of funds just before the distribution to a business that is already 5 years old.

See also H. Grady Lester, *supra* note 12 (30 percent of assets transferred by distributing corporation to subsidiary consisted of cash; held, §355 applies).

Sec. 11.06.   The "device" restriction: §355(a)(1)(B)

To be tax-free under §355, a distribution must not be used "principally as a device for the distribution of the earnings and profits of the distributing corporation or the controlled corporation or both." This restriction was taken almost verbatim from the pre-1954 spin-off provision, §112(b)(11) of the 1939 Code, where it seems to have been aimed mainly at prearranged sales of the stock of either corporation, as well as to serve as a statutory "business purpose" rule and to strengthen the "active business" requirement of §112(b)(11).[35]

As enacted by the Senate in 1954, §355(a)(1)(B) contained only the device language quoted in the preceding paragraph. In conference, it was amended to provide that "the mere fact" that stock or securities in either corporation are sold or exchanged (other than pursuant to a pre-distribution arrangement) shall not be construed to mean that the transaction was used principally as a "device." The regulations, giving this clause the narrowest possible meaning, state that a sale of stock or securities that is not prearranged is not "determinative" that the transaction was a "device," but that whether prearranged or not, a sale is "evidence" of that status. Although the regulations refrain from stating explicitly that a prearranged sale is fatal, they refer to the "continuity of interest" doctrine in terms implying that a prearranged sale of a substantial part of the stock of either corporation will make §355 inapplicable.[36] In Rev. Rul. 55-103,

---

[35] Inclusion of the "device" rule in §112(b)(11) was thought to make unnecessary an explicit prohibition on post-distribution sales of stock; see 97 Cong. Rec. 12,215 (1951). Its "business purpose" function is reminescent of the *Gregory* case, *supra*, Sec. 11.02.

The provision was not construed in any cases or rulings prior to the 1954 Code. See Wolff, *supra* note 1, at 721-722, and Mette, *supra* note 1 at 347-351.

[36] Regs. §1.355-2(b)(1); for the "continuity of interest" doctrine as it has developed in the reorganization area, see *infra*, Sec. 12.11.

The statutory language — "pursuant to an arrangement negotiated or agreed upon prior to such distribution" — is construed by Regs. §1.355-2(b)(2).

In Chester E. Spangler, *supra* note 4, holding that a split-off could be accomplished tax-free under the 1939 Code, the Tax Court found as a fact that the distributees sold the stock of both corporations after the distribution, but that before the distribution they did not intend to make such a sale. The Court did not, however, mention these findings in its opinion or indicate whether a pre-distribution intention or plan to sell would have been fatal. Since a divisive reorganization under the pre-1954 law required a transfer by one corporation of part of its assets to a second corporation controlled by it or its shareholders "immediately after the transfer" (§112(g)(1)(D) of the 1939 Code, discussed *infra*, Sec. 12.15), it was arguable under the 1939 Code that a pre-arranged loss of control was fatal. (See the similar problem under §351, discussed *supra*, Sec. 3.09.) Unlike §112(b)(11) of the 1939 Code, §355 does not require a transfer of assets by the distributing corporation. But if there is a transfer, the transferor corporation will ordinarily wish to bring it within either §368(a)(1)(D) or §351, both of which still require control to exist "immediately after" the transfer.

1955-1 C.B. 31, the Service ruled that §355 did not apply to a distribution of stock of a subsidiary corporation that was designed to pave the way for a sale of the stock of the parent to a buyer that did not want to acquire the subsidiary; in this ruling, the Internal Revenue Service treated the "device" provision of §355(a)(1)(B) as though it was a statutory codification of the "continuity of interest" doctrine. See also Rev. Rul. 58-68, 1958-1 C.B. 183, where a disposition of stock in a prearranged merger was cited as evidence that the transaction was a "device," a surprising suggestion on the facts, since the merger was with a corporation owned by the distributee and his wife.

The theory that a post-distribution sale, especially if pre-arranged, is a method of bailing out earnings and profits is frequently advanced, but infrequently examined. The problem reduces itself to a sale of the common stock, since securities will be taxed as "boot" under §355(a)(3) unless securities in an equal or greater principal amount are surrendered, while preferred stock will ordinarily be rendered harmless by §306(c)(1)(B) (*infra*, Sec. 11.12). The central question, then, is whether a sale of the common stock of either the distributing corporation or the controlled corporation is a device for bailing out earnings and profits. Such a sale spells a loss of control of one of the businesses (and a loss of the seller's share in the corporation's earning power and growth potential as well), whereas a bail-out ordinarily means that earnings and profits have been drawn off without impairing the shareholder's interest in the corporation's earning power, growth potential, or voting control. (This is the reason why, except in rare cases, common stock is not brought under the aegis of §306, *supra*, Sec. 8.03) If it were possible under §355 to segregate cash or investment property in a corporation and distribute its stock, the bail-out analogy would be valid, but does the distribution and sale of the stock of a corporation satisfying the 5-year active business requirement of §355(a)(1)(C) produce the effect of a bail-out? Although it is arguable that any distribution by a corporation with current or post-1913 earnings and profits *should* be taxed as a dividend, whether the assets distributed consist of money, marketable securities, or the assets of a separate business (see *supra*, Sec. 7.62), the theory of §355 is, to the contrary, that the distribution of a separate trade or business should be a tax-free transaction. If immunity from taxation is being conferred by §355 only on the assumption that the distributees will continue to operate both businesses after the distribution, it would seem appropriate to require the stock of both corporations to be held for a specified period of time, or to "taint" the stock (as is done under §306). Instead, §355(a)(1)(B) attempts to distinguish between sales that are prearranged and those that are not, a distinction that is difficult to administer and meaningless in any event. In this connection, it should be noted that a partial liquidation is treated as a capital gain (or loss) transaction by §346-(a)(2) ("corporate contractions") and §346(b) (distribution of a separate trade or business), and that the distributees are thereafter free to dispose of either the distributed assets or the original stock.[37] This treatment of partial liquidations cannot be reconciled with the assumption of §355(a)(1)(B) that a prearranged sale demonstrates (or aids in demonstrating) that the distribution is a "device" for the distribution of earnings and profits.

Despite these shortcomings in the theory that a prearranged sale of either the distributing or the controlled corporation is a "device" for distributing earnings and profits, it seems likely that the Internal Revenue Service will ordinarily resist the use of §355 whenever a sale or disposition has been negotiated or agreed upon prior to the distribution.[38] (The fact that the stock of both corporations has been retained by the shareholders does not necessarily mean that the transaction was not a "device," however, although the courts have given some weight to continued ownership in the litigated cases.[39]) Although §355(a)(1)(B) refers to a sale or exchange of stock *or* securities, a disposition of securities may be less objectionable to the Internal Revenue Service than a sale of stock, at least if the distribution of the securities produced dividend income as "boot" under §356(a)(2). Moreover, a prearranged sale by a relatively minor distributee, especially if his plans were not known to the others, would presumably be less important than a prearranged sale by a controlling shareholder.

[37] A "corporate contraction" can qualify under §346(a)(2) only if it is "not essentially equivalent to a dividend." If a prearranged sale of distributed assets is a "device" for distributing earnings and profits, this part of §346(a)-(2) would be violated. But it has ordinarily been assumed that a partial liquidation is not tainted by a subsequent sale of the distributed assets. Moreover, §346(b), relating to the distribution of a separate trade or business, does not even contain the restriction that the transaction must not be essentially equivalent to a dividend.

[38] But see Rev. Rul. 59-197, 1959-1 C.B. 77, stating that a predistribution sale of part of the distributing corporation's stock had the same effect as a binding contract to sell some of the stock after the distribution, but that it was not a "device" for distributing earnings and profits because of the surrounding circumstances, primarily business reasons for selling an interest in the business to a key employee.

[39] H. Grady Lester, *supra* note 12; Mary A. Morris Trust, 42 T.C. 779 (1964); Patricia W. Burke, *supra* note 11; Albert W. Badanes, *supra* note 12; but see Marne S. Wilson, *supra* note 12, where the Tax Court stressed continued ownership in finding that the transaction (a spin-off of a retail furniture store's conditional sales contracts) was not a device, but was reversed on appeal because a business purpose had not been proved.

As applied to prearranged sales of the stock of one of the corporations, the "device" clause serves to insure a continuity of interest on the part of the shareholders; they will be unable to cash in on their investment as part of the divisive transaction. If the stock is transferred by them in a tax-free exchange, however, their pre-distribution proprietary interest will ordinarily continue, and it must then be decided if a §355 transaction can be combined with a tax-free reorganization (or similar transaction) without impairing the tax-free status of either event. An example is a §355 spin-off in anticipation of a tax-free merger of the distributing corporation into an acquiring corporation, the spin-off being used to rid the distributing corporation of a business that the acquiring corporation does not wish to take over. If the spin-off and statutory merger occur back-to-back, has there been a "sale" or "exchange" of the distributing corporation's stock that falls afoul of the "device" restriction of §355?

As an initial matter, such a distribution-acquisition combination does not seem to violate the underlying policies of §355, nor should the "device" clause of §355(a)(1)(B) necessarily be invoked to deny §355 treatment for the anticipatory division of the enterprise. The device clause refers to a *distribution* of earnings and profits and, in this situation, earnings of both the distributing corporation and the controlled corporation remain in corporate solution. Moreover, the shareholders of the corporation whose stock is transferred in the reorganization maintain a continuing interest in the earnings of that corporation by virtue of the stock acquired in exchange for their former stock interest in the transferred corporation. As a result, the forbidden bail-out of earnings and profits envisioned by §355(a)-(1)(B) has not occurred. The Service, however, regards the contemplated disposition of the stock of one of the corporations in a merger as evidence that the §355 transaction was a "device," and the cases on this point are conflicting.[40]

A further aspect of the "device" clause should be noted. If a transaction would — absent §355 — be taxed to the participating shareholders as a sale of their stock, giving rise to capital gain or loss, rather than as a dividend, the Service has ruled that it does not constitute a "device" to distribute earnings and profits.[41] An example is

---

[40] Rev. Rul. 58-68, 1958-1 C.B. 183; Mary A. Morris Trust, *supra* note 39 ("device" prohibition not violated); Curtis v. United States, 336 F.2d 714, 14 AFTR 2d 5685 (6th Cir. 1964) (§355 inapplicable, because corporate existence of distributing corporation was terminated; query result if distributing corporation had survived the merger.)

For further discussion, especially of the corporate reorganization step in such combined transactions, see *infra*, Sec. 12.20.

[41] Rev. Rul. 64-102, *supra* note 34; H. Grady Lester, *supra* note 12.

a split-off in which a shareholder exchanges all his stock in the distributing corporation for all of the stock of the controlled corporation, which would be treated as a capital gain or loss event under §302(b)-(3) (complete termination) if §355 did not apply. This stress on a lack of "dividend equivalency" is likely to be confined to split-offs and split-ups that are non pro-rata in character under §302(b)(2) and (3); pro rata transactions will ordinarily invite closer scrutiny.[42]

Before we leave the "device" restriction of §355(a)(1)(B), it should be noted that the regulations state that in determining whether a transaction was used principally as a "device," consideration should be given "to all of the facts and circumstances of the transaction" and in particular "to the nature, kind and amount of the assets of both corporations (and corporations controlled by them) immediately after the transaction." Regs. §1.355-2(b)(3). This statement is a warning that a distribution may be a "device" for the distribution of earnings and profits even if the distributees do not sell the stock or securities.[43] Thus, if a corporation with substantial earnings and profits owns two qualifying trades or businesses, worth $100,000 each (including working capital), but also holds liquid assets valued at $1,000,000 that are not required in the businesses, the Internal Revenue Service may regard a corporate division as a "device" for the distribution of earnings and profits even though the stock and securities of both corporations are to be retained by the distributees. The last sentence of Regs. 1.355-2(b)(3), moreover, may carry an unfavorable implication for a corporation holding "excess" liquid assets, especially if it has been niggardly in declaring dividends in past years.

Sec. 11.07.   Distribution of all stock and securities in controlled corporation

Section 355(a)(1)(D) requires the distributing corporation to distribute either (a) all of the stock and securities in the controlled corporation held by it immediately before the distribution, or (b) an amount of stock constituting "control" under §368(c); but in the latter event, the Treasury must be satisfied that the retention of stock

---

[42] A "corporate contraction" (*supra*, Sec. 7.62) is not likely to satisfy the two-business rule of §355(b), even though it is not "essentially equivalent to a dividend" under §346(a)(2). As to a §346(b) distribution, it probably passes the "dividend equivalency" test of §346(a)(2) only by statutory fiat; if such a distribution is thought to be not "essentially equivalent to a dividend" in its own right, the "device" restriction of §355 would be satisfied by *every* distribution meeting the two-business requirement of §355(b).

[43] See *supra* note 39.

(or stock and securities) in the controlled corporation was not pursuant to a plan having as one of its principal purposes the avoidance of federal income tax.

The committee reports on the 1954 Code do not explain this limitation on the retention of stock or securities by the distributing corporation, but presumably it was to prevent a parent corporation from making periodic distributions of small amounts of stock and securities in a subsidiary as a substitute for ordinary dividends.[44] It is not clear, however, why periodic distributions of small amounts of the controlled corporation's stock should be treated as a dividend, once the basic policy decision to permit a tax-free distribution of *all* of its stock and securities under §355 was made. The theory that underlies §355, if valid at all, seems as applicable to a partial separation of the controlled corporation as to a complete separation. Perhaps the draftsmen of §355(a)(1)(D) were concerned about a distribution of part of the controlled corporation's stock or securities in anticipation of a sale by the distributees. But the "device" language of §355(a)(1)(B) serves as an independent restriction on sales, at least if they are prearranged (*supra*, Sec. 11.06); and no reason suggests itself for imposing a more severe restriction on sale of all the stock received in a partial separation than on a sale of part of the stock received in a complete separation. As to a distribution of preferred stock as a prelude to a bail-out of earnings and profits, the danger seems no greater in a partial separation than in a complete separation, and §306 was evidently thought to be a sufficient safeguard in the latter instance. (*Infra*, Sec. 11.12). An attempted bail-out with the use of securities (notes, debentures, or bonds) would ordinarily be frustrated by §355(a)(3), under which securities constitute boot if no securities are surrendered or to the extent that their principal amount exceeds the principal amount of any securities surrendered.

Whatever the validity of the reasons for its existence, §355(a)-

---

[44] If this was its purpose, the distribution requirement overlaps and serves as a buttress to the "device" restriction of §355(a)(1)(B), discussed *supra*, Sec. 11.06, which makes §355 inapplicable if the transaction is "used principally as a device for the distribution of the earnings and profits" of either corporation.

The regulations under the pre-1954 spin-off provision (§112(b)(11) of the 1939 Code, *supra* note 1), contained the following statement, upon which §355(a)(1)(D) of the 1954 Code was probably patterned:

Ordinarily, the business reasons (as distinguished from any desire to make a distribution of earnings and profits to the shareholders) which support the reorganization and the distribution of the stock will require the distribution of all of the stock received by the transferor corporation in the reorganization. (Regs. 118, §39.112(b)(11)-2(c).)

(1)(D) must of course be complied with. Although §355(a)(1)(D)-(i) requires the distributing corporation to distribute all of the stock and securities in the controlled corporation held by it immediately before the distribution, it does not explicitly require any stock or securities that may be held by another controlled corporation rather than by the distributing corporation itself to be distributed. Nor does it explicitly preclude a pre-distribution sale or other disposition of such stock or securities, although it is possible that such a transfer might be denied tax effect if made pursuant to the plan of distribution and as a device to defeat §355(a)(1)(D)(i). Aside from such a non-statutory limitation on a pre-distribution transfer, it should be noted that such transfers of stock of the controlled corporation are inhibited to some extent by §355(a)(1)(A), requiring the distributing corporation to have "control" — immediately before the distribution — of the corporation whose stock or securities are to be distributed, so that at best only a limited amount of stock could be disposed of by the distributing corporation.

A degree of flexibility is introduced into the requirement under discussion by §355(a)(1)(D)(ii), providing that stock or securities[45] of the controlled corporation may be retained by the distributing corporation provided (a) it distributes enough stock to constitute "control" under the 80 percent definition of §368(c), and (b) it establishes to the satisfaction of the Treasury that the stock or securities held back are not being retained in pursuance of a plan having as one of its principal purposes the avoidance of Federal income tax. The regulations carry over from the pre-1954 regulations (*supra*, note 44) the statement that "ordinarily" the business reasons for a corporate division — "as distinguished from any desire to make a distribution of earnings and profits" — will require a distribution of all the stock and securities of the controlled corporation. A retention of stock or securities to meet bona fide business commitments (*e.g.*, a stock option plan), not undertaken in anticipation of the §355 division, ought to evoke a favorable ruling from the Internal Revenue Service. The regulations go on to make the curious statement that the fact that the retained stock or securities would constitute taxable boot if distributed does not tend to establish the *absence* of a tax-avoidance plan.[46] This seems obvious; the real problem in this area is whether a retention of such stock or securities tends to establish the *existence*

---

[45] The statute permits a retention of stock or of stock *and* securities, but does not mention a retention of securities alone. But the regulations remedy this oversight. Regs. §1.355-2(d).

[46] Regs. §1.355-2(d). For the circumstances in which the stock of a controlled corporation can constitute "boot," see *infra*, Sec. 11.10.

of such a plan. But there are as yet no published rulings to aid in determining what circumstances will, in the eyes of the Internal Revenue Service, justify a retention of stock or securities.

Sec. 11.08.   Non pro rata distributions

A non pro rata corporate division may be a useful method of settling a dispute among the shareholders of a closely-held corporation. For example, a corporation owned equally by two shareholders who are at loggerheads might transfer part of its assets to a subsidiary and then transfer the stock of the subsidiary to one of the shareholders in exchange for all of his stock in the parent, with the result that the original corporation will be solely owned by one of the shareholders, and the new corporation will be solely owned by the other. Under pre-1954 law, it was held that such a split-off was not a "reorganization" under §112(g)(1)(D) of the 1939 Code, because immediately after the plan was consummated neither the transferor corporation nor its shareholder (nor both together) were in control of the former subsidiary, so that the transaction was a taxable transfer. If, to avoid this problem, the assets of the old corporation were transferred to two new subsidiaries and the old corporation was completely liquidated (a split-up), the transaction might have qualified as a "reorganization" under pre-1954 law, but then it was possible that the continuity of interest doctrine would stand in the way of tax immunity.[47]

Section 355 of the 1954 Code, unlike earlier law, explicitly provides in §355(a)(2)(A) that a corporate division (if otherwise qualified) will be tax-free "whether or not the distribution is pro rata with respect to all of the shareholders of the distributing corporation." This will permit stock of an existing subsidiary to be distributed in a non pro rata division (*e.g.*, transfer of a subsidiary's stock to buy out one of the shareholders of the parent). Moreover, if it is necessary to create a subsidiary (or to transfer additional property to an existing subsidiary) as part of the plan, this can be done tax-free under a 1954 change in the definition of "reorganization." See §368(a)(1)(D), which now provides that a transfer by a corporation of part of its assets to another corporation will constitute a reorganization if immediately after the transfer the transferor, or one or more of its shareshareholders, *including persons who were shareholders immediately before the transfer*, or any combination thereof is in control of the transferee corporation. These statutory provisions will permit share-

---

[47] See Frank W. Williamson, 27 T.C. 647 (1957); Lyons, Realignment of Stockholders' Interests in Reorganizations Under Section 112(g)(1)(D), 9 Tax L. Rev. 237 (1954); *infra*, Sec. 12.11.

holders to go their separate ways on a tax-free basis, whether the stock used to effect the separation is the stock of an existing subsidiary or that of a newly created one.[48]

There will be times, however, when taxpayers will look this gift horse in the mouth with some dissatisfaction, since a shareholder who is "bought out" with the stock of a subsidiary may realize a loss (because his adjusted basis for the surrendered stock exceeds the fair market value of the stock or securities received). Since §355, if applicable, will deny recognition to his loss, the taxpayer may search for a way of avoiding §355, and the government, in its turn, may be in the unusual position of asserting with vigor that the manifold conditions of §355 were clearly satisfied. In this connection, it should be noted that such a shareholder who is bought out with *assets* (rather than with stock) will enjoy a deductible loss under §302(b)(3), at least if §267(a)(1) is inapplicable.

There is one common situation, however, where the tax-free division rules of §355 may be unavailable to the parties: this arises in the case of brother-sister corporations whose stock is held in a "criss-cross" pattern by two groups of shareholders. Thus, if A and B each own 50 percent of corporations X and Y, Regs. §1.355-3(a) apparently prevents the use of §355 to give A complete ownership of X, and B complete ownership of Y. The example in the regulations involves the transfer by A and B of their stock in X and Y to a new corporation Z, which then distributes the X stock to A and the Y stock to B (presumably by way of a split-up). The regulations hold that such a transaction constitutes a taxable exchange between A and B of the stock which they respectively gave up; hence, A's transfer of his 50 percent interest in Y corporation is treated as an exchange for B's 50 percent interest in X corporation.[49]

---

[48] The judiciary's continuity of interest doctrine must bow to the amended definition of "reorganization" in §368(a)(1)(D), at least to a large degree. See the statement of the continuity of interest doctrine in Regs. §1.368-1(b), third sentence, which reflects the statutory change, *infra*, Sec. 12.11.

If the parties are dealing at arm's length, the value of the stock surrendered will be equal to the value of the stock or securities received. If there is a disparity, however, the transaction may be in part a gift or a payment of compensation, taxable despite §355(a)(2)(A), in accordance with its true character. See Rev. Rul. 56-450, 1956-2 C.B. 201, last paragraph; Regs. §1.356-5; Sen. Rept. No. 1622, 83d Cong. 2d Sess., p. 50 ("As in the case of the organization of a corporation [*supra*, Sec. 3.08], a disproportionate distribution which has the effect of a gift or of the payment of compensation will be subject to tax as such.").

[49] But see Albert W. Badanes, *supra* note 12, rejecting the Service's "exchange" argument on similar facts. With the result in *Badanes*, contrast Penn-Warrington Hosiery Mills, Inc., ¶61,211 P-H Memo TC, where the parties achieved a similar economic result by another route, but were held to recognize gain along the way. Using the example in the text to simplify the facts, A

Sec. 11.09.   Judicial limitations on tax-free corporate divisions

Before 1954, spin-offs, split-offs, and split-ups could be effected tax-free only by complying with the "reorganization" provisions of the Code, under which for many years a literal compliance with the statutory language has been insufficient if the transaction did not satisfy the spirit of the law. Thus, the courts have superimposed the "business purpose" doctrine and the requirement of a "continuity of interest" on the more mechanical requirements of the statute.[50] Although it is no longer necessary to have a tax-free "reorganization" as a prelude to a corporate division, the regulations under §355 require spin-offs, split-offs, and split-ups to satisfy the traditional judicial restrictions on the tax-free reorganization:

> The distribution by a corporation of stock or securities of a controlled corporation to its shareholders with respect to its own stock or to its security holders in exchange for its own securities will not qualify under section 355 where carried out for purposes not germane to the business of the corporations. The principal reason for this requirement is to limit the application of section 355 to certain specified distributions or exchanges with respect to the stock or securities of controlled corporations incident to such readjustment of corporate structures as is required by business exigencies and which, in general, effect only a readjustment of continuing interests in property under modified corporate forms. Section 355 contemplates a continuity of the entire business enterprise under modified corporate forms and a continuity of interest in all or part of such business enterprise on the part of those persons who, directly or indirectly, were the owners of the enterprise prior to the distribution or exchange. All the requisites of business and corporate purposes described under §1.368 must be met to exempt a transaction from the recognition of gain or loss under this section. (Regs. §1.355-2(c).)

Although the foregoing portion of the regulations is not based upon cases decided under the 1954 Code, the historic relationship between

transferred his Y stock to X and B transferred his X stock to Y; and X then transferred the Y stock to Y, while Y transferred the X stock to X. At the end of the road, therefore, A had complete ownership of X and B complete ownership of Y. The court's opinion, holding the X-Y exchange to be taxable to the corporations, is obscure, and it may not be the last word on the subject. An alternative approach to the issue would be to treat each corporation's transfer of the stock in the other as a tax-free transaction under §311(a)(2); on this theory, both would be subject to §311(a)(2) on giving up the stock in the other, and neither would be subject to §302 on receiving its own stock in exchange for its stock in the other.

[50] These judicial limitations are discussed elsewhere; for the requirement of a "continuity of interest," see *supra*, Sec. 3.04 and *infra* Sec. 12.11; for the "business purpose" doctrine, see *infra*, Sec. 12.19. See also Regs. §1.368-1(b), summarizing these requirements.

corporate divisions and the reorganization provisions of the Code justifies the assumption that the judicial doctrines worked out for corporation reorganizations will be applied with little modification to distributions under §355, even though effected without a technical "reorganization." Without attempting an exhaustive list of the business purposes that might support a tax-free distribution under §355, the following possibilties come to mind:

     1. Compliance with local law requiring two businesses to be separated.
     2. Compliance with federal anti-trust law.
     3. Segregation of hazardous activities in a separate corporation.
     4. Separation of a business to permit its employees to share in profits or ownership.
     5. Settlement of a shareholder dispute, by giving each group of shareholders control or ownership of one business.

The principal problem under the regulation quoted above is whether a business purpose for the *distribution* must be established, or whether it is sufficient to show a business purpose for carrying on the businesses in separate corporations. Thus, if an employee profit-sharing or stock option plan is to be established for employees in a particular branch of the corporation's activities, it may be necessary to segregate that business in a separate corporation, but the plan would not necessarily require the stock of that corporation to be distributed to the original corporation's shareholders. Similarly, a corporation carrying on both a hazardous business and a stable one could ordinarily protect the assets of the latter business by placing the hazardous business in a subsidiary corporation; if so, it could be argued that no business purpose is served by a distribution of the stock of the subsidiary.

    In a leading case under §112(b)(11) of the 1939 Code, the Court of Appeals for the Second Circuit stated that "in the light of the tax-avoidance possibilities which a spin-off often provides, there must be non-tax reasons not only for the separation of the two businesses but also for direct ownership of both [corporations] by the shareholders."[51] The same approach has been adopted by the Court of Appeals for the Ninth Circuit under §355, in a case reversing the Tax Court's theory that a business reason for the distribution is not necessary if it does not constitute a "device" under §355(a)(1)(B).[52]

---

[51] Parshelsky's Estate v. Commissioner, *supra* note 1; see also Bonsall v. Commissioner, *supra* note 22.
[52] Marne S. Wilson, *supra* note 12.

This judicial demand for a business reason supporting the distribution itself is likely to be most troublesome in spin-offs and other pro rata transactions. If the distribution is non pro rata, its realignment of the shareholders' interests will ordinarily be of sufficient economic significance to pass muster, unless the proportionate change is trivial or the reshuffling is within the family.

As to the requirement of a continuity of interest on the part of those persons who directly or indirectly owned the enterprise prior to the division, this provision stems from a line of cases holding that the tax-free reorganization provisions may not be used to confer tax exemption on a transaction that is, in essence, a sale.[53] Since it is "the owners of the enterprise" who must maintain a continuing interest, the requirement is more applicable to shareholders than to bondholders and other creditors.[54] Moreover, §355(a)(2)(A) expressly validates a distribution that is non-pro rata, so that the continuity of interest requirement is not violated by a transaction that leaves ownership of the distributing corporation in the hands of one shareholder and ownership of the controlled corporation in the hands of another shareholder. It may also be permissible for some of the shareholders to give up their proprietary interest entirely, by exchanging stock for securities or other property, subject to the recognition of "boot"; the reorganization cases tolerate such a loss of interest to some extent, so long as a substantial number of old shareholders retain a proprietary interest.[55] If the shareholders sell or exchange their securities immediately after the distribution, however, the Internal Revenue Service may attack the transaction not only as violating the judicial doctrine of continuity of interest, but also as a "device" for the distribution of earnings and profits under §355(a)(1)(B), as indicated *supra*, Sec. 11.06.

[53] See Pinellas Ice & Cold Storage Co. v. Commissioner, and Le Tulle v. Scofield, *infra*, Sec. 12.11; see also, Rena Farr, 24 T.C. 350 (1955), applying the continuity of interest requirement to a pre-1954 split-off and holding that it was satisfied despite a subsequent sale of stock by the distributee.

[54] The regulations explicitly permit securities of a parent corporation to be exchanged for stock of a controlled corporation, although such a shift from a creditor to a shareholder position is not ordinarily permissible under the reorganization provisions of the Code. Regs. §1.355-2(e)(2). Note also that the regulations state the continuity of interest doctrine in a way that is consistent with such a transaction: "Section 355 contemplates . . . a continuity of interest in all or *part* of such business enterprise on the part of those persons who, directly or indirectly, were the owners of the enterprise prior to the distribution or exchange." Regs. §1.355-2(c), emphasis added.

[55] Southwest Natural Gas Co. v. Commissioner, 189 F.2d 332, 40 AFTR 686 (5th Cir. 1951), cert. denied, 342 U.S. 860; Miller v. Commissioner, 84 F.2d 415, 17 AFTR 1308 (6th Cir. 1936); Reilly Oil Co. v. Commissioner, 189 F.2d 382, 40 AFTR 707 (5th Cir. 1951), discussed *infra*, Sec. 12.11.

Sec. 11.10. "Boot" under §355

When its conditions are satisfied, §355(a)(1) provides that no gain, income or loss shall be recognized on the receipt of "stock or securities" of a controlled corporation. If anything else is distributed, however, it will constitute "boot," the tax treatment of which is prescribed by §356. See §355(a)(4). All of the following categories of property constitute "boot":

1. Money or other property (including stock or securities of a corporation that does not qualify under §355 as a "controlled corporation").

2. Securities of the controlled corporation to the extent that their principal amount exceeds the principal amount of the securities which are surrendered in the distribution; and the full fair market value of such securities if no securities are surrendered.[56]

3. Short term notes and other obligations of the controlled corporation that do not constitute "securities." See the analogous problem under §351(a), discussed *supra*, Sec. 3.03.

4. Stock rights or stock warrants, according to the regulations, §1.355-1(a).[57]

5. Stock of a controlled corporation, if it was acquired within 5 years of the distribution by reason by any transaction in which gain or loss was recognized in whole or in part. §355(a)(3), second sentence. Thus, if the distributing corporation owned 85 percent of the stock of the controlled corporation throughout the five year period, but purchased the remaining 15 percent (directly or through a subsidiary) within the period, the latter portion

---

[56] The drafting of §355(a)(3) is somewhat misleading. §355(a)(3) states flatly that §355(a)(1) — which permits a tax-free distribution of stock or securities — "shall not apply" if the principal amount of securities received exceeds the principal amount of securities surrendered *or* if securities are received and none are surrendered. But §355(a)(4) refers to the boot provision (§356) for the treatment of an excess principal amount, thus implying that the distribution will qualify, but that the fair market value of the excess principal amount will constitute boot. This implication is confirmed by §356(d)(2)(C). There is, however, no reference in §355(a)(4) to the case where securities are received and none are surrendered. This omission, presumably inadvertent. is remedied by the regulations, under which the application of §355 is not defeated by such a distribution, but the fair market value of the securities received is treated as boot. Regs. §1.356-3(a), last sentence, illustrated by Example (1); see also §356(d)(2)(B); S. Rept. No. 1622, 83d Cong. 2d Sess., p. 269.

§355(a)(3) is inadequately drafted in another respect, since it seems to compare the aggregate principal amount of securities received with the aggregate amount surrendered, whereas it is quite clear that this comparison should be made separately for each distributee.

For examples of the treatment of securities constituting boot, see Regs. §1.356-3(b).

[57] But see Oscar E. Baan, *supra* note 5; and note the possibility that rights or warrants could be received tax-free under §305 (*supra*, Sec. 5.63), even though distributed in conjunction with a §355 transaction.

would constitute "other property" on distribution. For an example, see Regs. §1.355-2(f)(2). The purpose of this restriction is to prevent the distributing corporation from investing its excess funds in additional stock of the controlled corporation as a prelude to a tax-free distribution.[58]

If "boot" is received in a §355 *exchange* (split-offs and split-ups), its tax results are prescribed by §356(a), while if "boot" is received in a §355 *distribution* (spin-offs), §356(b) is the operative provision.

For split-offs and split-ups, §356(a)(1) follows the usual principle of recognizing any gain that the recipient may have on the exchange, but in an amount not in excess of the value of the "boot." (If the taxpayer has no gain, because the aggregate value of the stock, securities, and boot received by him is less than the adjusted basis of the stock and securities he surrenders, §356(a) is inoperative; but §356(c) prohibits the recognition of his loss.) Having determined the portion of his gain that is to be recognized under §356(a)(1), the taxpayer turns to §356(a)(2) to ascertain whether it is to be treated as ordinary income or as capital gain. Section 356(a)(2) provides that if the exchange "has the effect of the distribution of a dividend," it must be so treated to the extent of the taxpayer's ratable share of post-1913 earnings and profits.[59] The balance of the recognized gain, if any, is capital gain. For an example, see Regs. §1.356-1(c). There is some authority for the proposition that §356(a)(2) automatically converts any recognized gain into a dividend to the extent of earnings and profits; but a more discriminating approach to the question ought to be adopted. For example, if a minority shareholder receives bonds in exchange for all of his stock in a corporate division, and realizes a profit on the transaction, the exchange (which would give rise to capital gain if effected as a §302(b)(3) redemption) should not be automatically treated as a dividend under §356(a)(2).[60]

If boot is received in exchange for "section 306 stock," a special rule is applicable by virtue of §356(e): regardless of whether the shareholder realizes gain or loss on the exchange, the fair market value of the boot is treated as a distribution of property under §301,

---

[58] Much the same effect, however, could be obtained by transferring the liquid funds to the subsidiary, either as a contribution to its capital or under §351. But such a transaction might be evidence that the later distribution was a "device" for distributing earnings and profits. See Rev. Rul. 58-68, 1958-1 C.B. 183.

For an analogous restriction, see the treatment of post-1953 stock and securities under §333, *supra*, Sec. 9.21.

[59] §356(a)(2) makes no reference to current earnings and profits, nor do the regulations. See *supra*, Sec. 7.01, note 2.

[60] See *infra*, Sec. 12.34.

which means that it will be taxed as a dividend to the extent of his ratable share of the corporation's current and post-1913 earnings and profits. See also Regs. 1.356-4.

As to boot received in connection with a spin-off, since there is no exchange, it is not possible to apply §356(a)(1)'s principle of limiting the recognition of income to the taxpayer's realized gain or to divide the recognized gain between dividend income and capital gain. Instead, §356(b) requires the boot to be treated as an ordinary distribution under §301, so that it will be taxed as a dividend to the extent of current and post-1913 earnings and profits.

Sec. 11.11.   Basis, holding period, and earnings and profits

The basis of property received by the shareholder or security holder in a §355 transaction is prescribed by §358. If no boot is distributed, the aggregate basis of the original stock and securities will be spread over both the distributed and the retained stock and securities, in proportion to their respective market values. If boot is distributed, the basis of the qualified (or "non-recognition") property must be adjusted to reflect the amount of money and the value of any other boot received, as well as any gain or income recognized; and the boot (other than money) takes a basis equal to its fair market value. See §358(b)(2) (split-offs and split-ups); §358(c) (spin-offs); and Regs. §1.358-2.

By virtue of §1223(1), the taxpayer's holding period for any qualified (or "non-recognition") stock or securities received under §355 ordinarily includes the period he held the stock or securities surrendered (if the transaction was a split-off or a split-up) or retained (if it was a spin-off). But see *supra*, Sec. 3.10, note 45. The holding period of boot commences with the distribution, however, since its basis under §358(a)(2) is its fair market value, not an amount determined by reference to the basis of the original stock and securities.

As stated earlier (*supra*, Sec. 11.03), the 1954 Code abandoned the pre-1954 requirement that the distributing corporation make a transfer of some of its assets as a preliminary to the corporate division. If it does engage in such a transfer, however, the transaction will be a "reorganization" under §368(a)(1)(D), and the transferee corporation will carry over the distributing corporation's basis and holding periods under §362(b) and §1223(2).

Section 312(i) provides for "proper allocation" of the earnings and profits of the distributing and controlled corporations, under regulations to be prescribed by the Treasury. In brief, the regulations provide that where the §355 transaction is a Type D reorganization (*infra*, Sec. 12.15), earnings of the distributing corporation are allocated to the newly-created controlled corporation in proportion to the relative values of the assets transferred and retained. The regulations also state, however, that "in a proper case," the allocation should be made in proportion to the net bases (after reduction for liabilities) of the properties transferred and retained; and that other allocation methods may be appropriate in certain cases, although no guidance is given as to when these other methods may be employed. Perhaps a useful analogy and general approach may be found in §482 (and, to some extent, in §446(b) as well), permitting the Commissioner to adjust a taxpayer's accounting practices and methods in order to "clearly reflect income." Where the §355 transaction does not involve a reorganization transfer (e.g., where a pre-existing subsidiary is spun-off), the regulations provide that the distributing corporation's earnings are decreased by the lesser of (a) the amount of the adjustment which would have been required had it transferred the stock of the controlled corporation to a new subsidiary and then distributed the latter pursuant to a Type D reorganization, or (b) the net worth of the controlled corporation; note that the controlled corporation apparently retains its *own* earnings account in such a case. In no event, say the regulations, will a deficit of the distributing corporation be allocated to the controlled corporation.[61]

Sec. 11.12.   Corporate divisions and §306

It will be recalled that the pre-1954 spin-off provision (§112(b)-(11) of the 1939 Code) did not permit the distribution of preferred stock of the controlled corporation. *Supra*, Sec. 11.02. The reason for this restriction was a fear that a tax-free distribution of preferred stock, if permitted, could be used to bail out earnings and profits, since the shareholders could sell the preferred stock (perhaps under an arrangement for its prompt redemption), while retaining the common stock in both corporations. With the enactment of §306 of the 1954 Code as a safeguard against the preferred stock bailout in all of its aspects, it is not surprising that §112(b)(11)'s prohibition on preferred stock was not carried forward into §355 of the 1954 Code.

---

[61] See Regs. §1.312-10; Alexander, Some Earnings and Profits Aspects of the Internal Revenue Code of 1954, 7 Hastings L.J. 285, 302; Nesson, Earnings and Profits Discontinuities Under the 1954 Code, 77 Harv. L. Rev. 450, 474 (1964).

Preferred stock can, therefore, be distributed with impunity under §355, provided that its other conditions are met; but the preferred stock must run the gauntlet of §306.

Section 306(c)(1)(B) provides that stock received by a shareholder under §355 shall be "section 306 stock" in his hands if:

    1. It is not "common stock;
    2. With respect to its receipt, the shareholder's gain or loss went unrecognized to any extent by reason of §355 or §356; and
    3. The effect of the transaction was substantially the same as the receipt of a stock dividend.[62]

Notwithstanding the foregoing, the stock cannot be "section 306 stock" if the corporation had no earnings and profits when it was distributed. §306(c)(2).

If preferred stock is received in a spin-off or in a pro rata split-off or split-up, it would ordinarily seem entirely reasonable to find that "the effect of the transaction was substantially the same as the receipt of a stock dividend." To take a simple example, if a corporation transfers a five-year-old business to a second corporation in exchange for its common and preferred, and spins off all the stock of the second corporation, the effect of the transaction is the same as a transfer of the business for the common stock of the second corporation, followed by a spin-off of the common and a declaration by the second corporation of a dividend of preferred stock. Even if the transaction is not pro rata, it may be similar to a stock dividend. For example, if two shareholders of a corporation are deadlocked, and they compose their differences by a split-off under which one shareholder retains all the stock of the distributing corporation, and the second receives all the common and preferred of a newly created controlled corporation, the transaction has the same effect for the second shareholder as a split-off of the common stock of the controlled corporation, followed by a preferred stock dividend.

On the other hand, some non pro rata divisions do not have the effect of a stock dividend. An example would be a corporation with three unrelated shareholders[63] who arrange a split-up in which each

---

[62] For the meaning of "common stock" as the term is used in §306, see *supra*, Sec. 8.03. Even if the transaction did not have the effect of a stock dividend, the stock received will constitute "section 306 stock" if it was received in exchange for "section 306 stock."

For convenience, the term "preferred stock" is used in the text instead of the more accurate but cumbersome term, "stock which is not common stock."

[63] In determining whether a non pro rata transaction has "substantially" the same effect as a stock dividend, it may be appropriate to consider the relationship of the distributees to each other.

of the first two shareholders receives all of the common stock of a new controlled corporation, while the third shareholder receives preferred stock of either or both controlled corporations. The conclusion that preferred stock in these circumstances would not be "section 306 stock" is buttressed by §306(c)(2), which makes §306 inapplicable if a distribution of cash in lieu of the stock would not have been taxed as a dividend.[64]

Although the "cash substitution" test of §306(c)(2) is a method of determining when preferred stock is *not* "section 306 stock," the regulations have derived from it the inference that preferred stock *is* "section 306 stock" if a distribution of cash in lieu of the stock would have been a dividend. Although not compelled by the statutory language, this inference is not unreasonable in the light of §306's purpose: if a direct distribution of cash would have been taxed as a dividend, it is appropriate to "taint" the stock and compel the shareholder to recognize ordinary income when he disposes of it.[65]

Whatever may ultimately be decided about peripheral cases, however, it is a fair working hypothesis that preferred stock received in a spin-off or in a pro rata split-off or split-up will ordinarily be "section 306 stock" if gain goes unrecognized by virtue of §355 and if the corporation has earnings and profits. A sale or other disposition of such stock, therefore, will be subject to the punitive rules of §306-(a). It will be recalled, however, that these rules are subject to certain exceptions, one of which is §306(b)(1)(A), providing that a sale or other disposition that "terminates the entire stock interest of the shareholder in the corporation" is not subject to §306(a). If the preferred stock was issued by the controlled corporation, however, it is not clear whether "the" corporation under §306(b)(1)(A) is the distributing corporation or the controlled corporation, or both. If a prearranged sale of the common stock of either corporation is a "device" for the distribution of earnings and profits, as is commonly suggested, *supra*, Sec. 11.06, a sale of both the preferred and the common of one of the corporations should be entitled to no better treatment. This line of argument suggests that §306(b)(1)(A) should be available only if the shareholder sells his entire stock interest in both the distributing and the controlled corporation. A similar problem arises under §306(b)(4), which is concerned with a disposition of "section 306 stock" which follows or occurs simultaneously with

---

[64] §306(c)(2) may have intended to grant absolution only in cases where the corporation has no earnings and profits, as is suggested by its catch-line, but its language is much broader.

[65] Regs. §1.306-3(d). For discussion of the "cash substitution" test, see *infra*, Sec. 12.35.

a disposition of "the stock with respect to which the section 306 stock . . . was issued." It is not clear whether "the" stock is the stock of the distributing corporation, the stock of the controlled corporation, or both.

One more point should be noted in this area: the "device" language of §355(a)(1)(B) may apply to a distribution of preferred stock even though the conditions of §306 are not met. Thus, assume a plan for a corporate division under which the shareholder receives preferred and common stock plus enough money or other property so that his gain would be fully recognized under §356(a)(1) or §356-(b). There being no unrecognized gain, §306(c)(1)(B) will not intervene to "taint" the preferred stock. But if the purpose of the transaction is to enable the shareholders to sell their preferred stock under a Chamberlin-type plan calling for its early redemption, the distribution itself may be a "device" for the distribution of earnings and profits.[66] A similar theory might be employed by the government if preferred stock is received in a corporate division by shareholders who have suffered a loss, since here too the preferred stock would not be "tainted."[67] Indeed, a pre-arranged sale or redemption may be a "device" that will take the transaction out of §355 even in cases where §306 would be an alternative weapon for the government.

Sec. 11.13.   The monopoly of §355

In order to prevent the restrictions of §355 from being undermined, it was necessary to prevent divisive reorganizations from finding another route to tax-free status. The principal problem was that the term "reorganization" has long included a transfer by a corporation of all or part of its assets to a controlled corporation, and distributions in the course of a "reorganization" are normally receivable tax-free; indeed, it was only by virtue of these statutory provisions that corporate divisions were tax-free before 1954. The draftsmen of the 1954 Code, therefore, gave §355 a monopoly on divisive reorganizations by providing:

---

[66] This theory might not be acceptable in the Sixth Circuit, which decided in the taxpayer's favor in Chamberlin v. Commissioner, *supra*, Sec. 8.01, unless the redemption was to occur within a much shorter period of time, but other courts might not follow *Chamberlin*.

[67] See §306(c)(2). If the shareholder's basis for the stock he surrenders in a split-off, for example, is $10,000, and he receives common stock of a controlled corporation plus preferred stock, with an aggregate fair market value for both of $8,000, §306(c)(2) apparently insures that the preferred will not be "section 306 stock," since had he received cash in lieu of the preferred stock, he would have had no dividend income.

1. In §368(a)(2)(A), that if a transfer of assets by one corporation to another could qualify as a "reorganization" under both §368(a)(1)(C) and (D), it will be treated as qualifying only under subparagraph (D);

2. In §368(a)(1)(D), that a transfer of assets by one corporation to another will constitute a "reorganization" only if stock or securities of the transferee corporation are distributed in a transaction qualifying under §354, §355, or §356; and

3. In §354(b)(1), that §354(a) will apply to a Type D reorganization only if the transferee corporation acquired substantially all of the transferor corporation's assets and the transferor thereupon distributed all of its assets in pursuance of the plan of reorganization.

By virtue of the foregoing provisions, a divisive reorganization will not be able to qualify under §354, with the result that shareholders who wish to divide up their corporate investment will have to resort to, and satisfy the requirements of, §355. See *infra*, Sec. 12.15.

Sec. 11.14.   Non-qualifying corporate divisions

Section 355 is a non-recognition provision; if its conditions are met, a taxpayer who receives stock or securities in a corporate division does not recognize gain or loss. Section 355 does not, however, lay down any rules for the taxation of distributions that do *not* meet its requirements. Consequently, for the treatment of non-qualifying corporate divisions, we must look to other statutory provisions, as well as to certain doctrines of judicial origin. It will be helpful to consider spin-offs, split-offs, and split-ups separately, since the form of a non-qualifying transaction may be important, even though §355 has endeavored to treat all qualifying transactions alike.

1. Non-qualifying spin-offs. If a spin-off fails to win tax immunity under §355, it seems clear that the distribution of stock or securities to a shareholder of the original corporation will be treated as an ordinary distribution in kind under §301. This means that the distribution will be taxed as a dividend to the extent of the corporation's current and post-1913 accumulated earnings and profits, and as a return of capital if it exceeds them.[68] If the spin-off is preceded by a transfer of part of the distributing corporation's assets to the controlled corporation, the distributing corporation will recognize neither gain nor loss by virtue of §351, and ordinarily none of its earnings and profits will be allocated to the controlled corporation.[69]

---

[68] For further discussion of distributions of property, see *supra*, Sec. 5.22.

[69] Ordinarily, gain or loss on a transfer preparatory to a spin-off goes unrecognized under §361(a). This provision would be inapplicable on the facts

2. Non-qualifying split-ups. The tax consequences of a non-qualifying split-up are less clear. At least *prima facie*, the transaction is a complete liquidation of the distributing corporation, subject to §331(a)(1), so that the shareholders would recognize capital gain or loss, depending upon whether the value of the liquidating distribution exceeds or is less than the adjusted basis of the stock given up. On this theory, any transfer of assets by the distributing corporation to a controlled corporation (*e.g.*, if one or both of the controlled corporations were created as part of the plan) would apparently qualify under §351, so that no gain or loss would be recognized on the transfer.[70] In this respect, the transfer of assets would resemble a transfer in conjunction with a non-qualifying spin-off, as discussed in the preceding paragraph, and there would be no allocation of earnings and profits to either of the controlled corporations.

But while the foregoing consequences seem reasonable enough if the division serves a business purpose and the transaction fails to qualify under §355 only because one of the businesses was conducted for less than five years, what if the division is simply a method of segregating liquid assets in one corporation and business assets in another — possibly preparatory to a liquidation or sale of the liquid asset corporation? Should such a transaction be treated as a complete liquidation, giving rise to capital gain or loss, or as an ordinary distribution of the liquid assets, taxable as a dividend to the extent of earnings and profits?

Before 1954, dividend treatment would probably have resulted in these circumstances, because the transaction would have been a "reorganization" under §112(g)(1)(D) of the 1939 Code, with the stock of the liquid asset corporation constituting "boot" to be taxed as a dividend.[71] Under §368(a)(1)(D) of the 1954 Code (*infra*, Sec. 12.15), however, the transaction is no longer a "D" reorganization. The government has another string to its bow, however, even under the 1954 Code. If a corporation transfers its business assets to one

assumed in the text, however, since the transfer of assets would not constitute a "reorganization" under §368(a)(1)(D) (*infra*, Sec. 12.15). But §351 would apply, as stated in the text, even though §361(a) would not.

On the allocation of earnings and profits, see Regs. §1.312-11(a).

[70] Section 351's "control" requirement is not violated by a distribution of the stock by the transferor corporation, by virtue of §351(c), which seems as applicable to a distribution in complete liquidation as to any other kind of distribution.

[71] Under §112(c)(2) of the 1939 Code, however, the "boot" was taxable as a dividend only to the extent of the *lesser* of (a) the shareholder's gain on the exchange, and (b) his ratable share of the corporation's post-1913 earnings and profits. If the shareholder's basis was high enough, he would have no gain. The same principle (so-called "dividend-within-gain") of taxing boot is to be found in §356(a)(2) of the 1954 Code. See *infra*, Sec. 12.34.

corporation and its liquid assets to a second corporation in preparation for a split-up, the creation of the first corporation might be regarded as a "mere change in identity, form, or place of organization, however effected," in which event the transfer of the business assets would be a reorganization under §368 (a) (1) (F) of the 1954 Code, and the stock of the liquid asset corporation would then constitute "boot" taxable as a dividend.[72] Moreover, the earnings and profits and other tax attributes of the original corporation would be inherited by the business asset corporation under §381 (*infra*, Ch. 13). This theory — that the transaction is an "F" reorganization — can be advanced only if the business asset corporation is created as part of the plan of distribution. It would not be available if the business assets and liquid asset corporations are existing subsidiaries of the liquidating corporation.[73]

An alternate attack on the use of a split-up to segregate liquid assets in a separate corporation is suggested by Regs. §1.301-1(1), providing that §301 is applicable to a distribution "although it takes place at the same time as another transaction if the distribution is in substance a separate transaction whether or not connected in a formal sense." Although the phraseology of the regulations is open to the objection that it requires an integrated transaction to be broken into two elements, it is only a short step from such cases as *Gregory* and *Bazley*[74] to the conclusion that the segregation of liquid assets in a separate corporation coupled with a distribution of its stock is the equivalent of a dividend.

One more point: what if the controlled corporations are both engaged in the active conduct of a five-year-old trade or business, but the distribution fails to qualify under §355 because (by reason of a pre-arranged sale of stock) it is treated as a "device" for distributing earnings and profits? Such a non-qualifying division would seem to be as fair game for dividend treatment as the blatant segregation of liquid assets in a separate corporation; if the distribution is really such a "device," it ought to be taxed for what it is (or is thought by Congress to be[75]): a distribution of earnings and profits.

---

[72] The boot could be taxed as a dividend only to the extent of the shareholder's gain. See *supra*, note 71. If the liquid assets represented the proceeds of selling a separate trade or business or a corporate contraction, however, the distribution might give rise to capital gain or loss under either §346(a)(2) or §346(b).

[73] For more on reincorporations, see *infra*, Sec. 12.22.

[74] *Supra*, Sec. 11.02, and *infra*, Sec. 12.16.

[75] As pointed out *supra*, Sec. 11.06, it is not clear why a prearranged sale *should* mark the transaction as a "device" for the distribution of earnings and profits.

3. Non-qualifying split-offs. If a split-off fails to qualify under §355, it should, at least *prima facie*, be treated as a redemption of the distributing corporation's stock. In this event, the tax consequences of the distribution would be determined by §302 and §346: it would be a dividend (to the extent of available earnings and profits) unless it could meet the tests of §346(a)(2) (corporate contraction), §346-(b) (termination of a business), §302(b)(1) (not essentially equivalent to a dividend), §302(b)(2) (substantially disproportionate redemption), or §302(b)(3) (termination of the shareholder's interest).[76] If the distributing corporation transferred part of its assets to the controlled corporation in preparation for the distribution, the transfer would be tax-free under §351 (§368(a)(1)(D) not being applicable, see *infra*, Sec. 12.15), and a portion of the distributing corporation's earnings and profits might be allocated to the controlled corporation by Regs. §1.312-11(a).

Another — and simpler — approach to the non-qualifying split-off, if it is pro rata among the shareholders, would be to disregard the surrender of stock as having no important business consequences, and to treat the split-off as the equivalent of a spin-off. This approach can be commended for its realism,[77] but it rides rough-shod over the statutory decision to treat a partial liquidation (even though pro rata) as a capital gain or loss transaction rather than as a dividend. Although §346 may be hard to defend as a decision of policy (*supra*, Sec. 7.62), so long as it exists, there is no good reason for excluding from its provisions a distribution of stock of a controlled corporation, if a distribution of the underlying assets would have produced capital gain or loss as a "corporate contraction" or as a "termination of a business" within §346(a)(2) or §346(b).

---

[76]See *supra*, Ch. 7; Rev. Rul. 57-114, 1957-1 C.B. 122, point (2).

[77] This brand of realism did not gain acceptance, however, when invoked by the government in an effort to analogize a pre-1954 split-off to a pre-1954 spin-off in the *Spangler* case, *supra* note 4, at 987-8.

Chapter Twelve

CORPORATE REORGANIZATIONS

Part A. General Considerations

Sec. 12.01. Introductory

The Federal income tax treatment of gains and losses from dispositions of property is controlled by a complex variety of statutory provisions. Section 61(a)(3) provides that the term gross income includes "gains *derived* from dealings in property"; conversely, §165(a) allows, with certain limitations, deductions for losses *sustained*. Hence, a "realizable event" must occur with respect to the taxpayer's property before gain becomes taxable or loss deductible, i.e., mere unrealized appreciation or depreciation in the value of property does not constitute a presently taxable transaction.[1] When a taxable disposition of property occurs,[2] the *amount* of gain or loss arising therefrom is determined under §1001, which provides that the taxpayer's gain or loss is the difference between the "amount realized" for the property and its adjusted basis. Finally, §1002 provides that this realized gain or loss generally must be recognized, unless "otherwise provided" by the statute.

---

[1] There are minor exceptions, *e.g.*, the valuation of inventory at cost or market value, whichever is lower, or, in the case of security dealers who elect to do so, at market value regardless of cost; and reserves for bad debts.

As to whether "realization" is a constitutional requirement or a principle of administrative convenience and economic policy, compare Surrey, The Supreme Court and the Federal Income Tax: Some Implications of the Recent Decisions, 35 Ill. L. Rev. 779 (1941); with Roehner and Roehner, Realization: Administrative Convenience or Constitutional Requirement, 8 Tax L. Rev. 173 (1953).

[2] If the property is disposed of by an "exchange" rather than a sale, account must be taken of Regs. §1.1001-1(a), stating that gain or loss is realized only "from the exchange of property for other property differing materially either in kind or extent." This language apparently reflects certain decisions holding that "refunding exchanges" of substantially identical securities do not give rise to presently taxable gain or deductible loss. See, *e.g.*, Mutual Loan & Savings Co. v. Commissioner, 184 F.2d 161, 39 AFTR 1034 (5th Cir. 1950); Motor Products Corp., 47 B.T.A. 983 (1942); *infra* note 3.

See also the "convertible bond rule," G.C.M. 18436, 1937-1 C.B. 101, by virtue of which the conversion of bonds into stock of the debtor corporation does not cause recognition of gain or loss. See generally Fleischer and Cary, The Taxation of Convertible Bonds and Stock, 74 Harv. L. Rev. 473 (1961).

There are many instances in which the Code does "otherwise provide," and it is one group of such exceptions — the corporate reorganization provisions of §§354-368 — to which this chapter is devoted.

As stated in Regs. §1.1002-1(c), the underlying assumption of the tax-free exchange provisions "is that the acquired property is substantially a continuation of the old investment still unliquidated; and, in the case of reorganizations, that the new enterprise, the new corporate structure, and the new property are substantially continuations of the old still unliquidated." This "continuity of investment" principle lies at the heart of the non-recognition provisions, and is the reason why gain or loss, although realized, is not recognized at the time of exchange. (If along with the qualified "non-recognition property" the taxpayer receives any cash or other "boot," however, his gain must be recognized pro tanto.) In an effort to insure a recognition of the gain or loss at a more appropriate later time, however, the Code provides in general for a carryover of basis, so that the taxpayer's basis for the property received in the exchange will reflect his basis for the property given up. Thus, the gain or loss that went unrecognized at the time of the exchange will be recognized when (and if) he ultimately liquidates his investment. (This deferral theory, which is an underlying assumption of virtually all non-recognition provisions of the Code, is frequently breached in practice; if the taxpayer holds the property received in the exchange until death, it acquires a new basis under §1014 equal to its fair market value at that time, so that the deferred gain or loss is not reflected on either the decedent's income tax return or his heirs'. Moreover, the property that thus acquires a new basis at the taxpayer's death may be the final product of a chain of tax-free exchanges in which he participated during his life.)

In a sense, the corporate reorganization provisions are an analogue or extension of §1031, providing that gain or loss shall not be recognized on the exchange of investment or business property for other property "of a like kind." Although stock and securities are explicitly excluded from §1031,[2a] they may be exchanged tax-free if the transaction is a qualified corporate reorganization. The reorganization rules are considerably more complex than the terms of §1031, but

---

[2a] The exclusion of stock and securities from the scope of §1031 dates from 1923; it was enacted to combat the establishment by brokerage firms of "exchange departments," through which their customers could trade appreciated securities without recognizing gain. (See Seidman's *Legislative History of Federal Income Tax Law (1938-1861)*, p. 798.) Compare the "swap fund" device under §351, *supra,* Sec. 3.01.

both the underlying rationale and the basic statutory approach of these two provisions are similar, i.e., (a) continuity of investment, and (b) deferral of realized gain or loss.

In approaching the taxation of corporate reorganizations, it is essential to grasp at once the simple but often elusive fact that the Internal Revenue Code defines and uses the term "reorganization" in a special way. To the general practitioner, a "reorganization" ordinarily connotes the financial rehabilitation of a bankrupt enterprise. To the tax lawyer, however, the term embraces a much wider variety of corporate readjustments, most of which have the flavor of prosperity rather than depression. As will be seen, "reorganization" is defined for tax purposes by §368(a)(1) to include mergers, consolidations, recapitalizations, acquisitions by one corporation of the stock or assets of another corporation, and changes in form or place of organization. The statutory definition looks primarily to the form rather than the substance of these transactions, since it embraces almost without discrimination one-man enterprises and publicly-held corporations, business corporations and "incorporated pocketbooks," affiliated companies and previously unrelated corporations, big corporations and little ones, successful corporations and bankrupts.[3] The common bond among these mismated transactions is that — subject to the inevitable refinements that will be discussed later — if the readjustment qualifies as a "reorganization," the corporation recognizes neither gain nor loss on the transfer of its property for stock or securities in another corporation that is a party to the reorganization, and the shareholders and creditors may exchange their stock or securities for new instruments without the recognition of gain or loss. Moreover, the tax attributes (loss carryovers, earnings and profits, accounting methods, etc.) of a corporation whose assets are acquired by another corporation in the reorganization are ordinarily inherited by the acquiring corporation (*infra*, Ch. 13).

The statutory definition of reorganization hauls in a most variegated catch but does almost nothing to segregate the transactions according to their economic consequences. Thus, the reincorporation of a corporation in another state, entailing no significant changes in the rights of the corporation's shareholders and creditors, is a "reorganization"; but so is the merger of an independent corner grocery

---

[3] But see Emery v. Commissioner, 166 F.2d 27, 36 AFTR 741 (2d Cir. 1948), holding that the reorganization provisions do not apply to a refunding of the obligations of a municipal corporation. Despite this, the investor does not necessarily recognize gain or loss: if the new obligations are sufficiently similar to the old ones, the transaction may be a mere "extension" rather than an "exchange." See *supra*, note 2; *infra*, note 83.

store into a national food chain, although the local merchant who
has exchanged his stock for the marketable stock of the surviving
corporation may feel, quite rightly, that he has "sold out." A recapitalization in which bondholders get new securities with different
maturities and interest rates is a "reorganization," but so is a recapitalization in which bondholders get common stock with an attendant
shift in the ownership of the corporation. The traditional theory of
the reorganization provisions is that gain or loss should not be recognized on changes of form when the taxpayer's investment remains in
"corporate solution" or when "a formal distribution, directly or
through exchange of securities, represents merely a new form of the
previous participation in an enterprise involving no change of substance in the rights and relations of the interested parties one to another or to the corporate assets."[4] As suggested earlier, however, the
statutory definition of "reorganization" takes in corporate adjustments that go far beyond changes of form only.[5] To some extent, the
treatment of "boot," especially since 1954, is a restraining influence;
and the courts have on occasion intervened to prevent some outright
sales and dividends from disguising themselves as tax-free reorganizations, but the judicial restraints themselves are often matters of form
rather than substance.

The reorganization provisions are extraordinarily complex, even
for the Internal Revenue Code. They endeavor to prescribe, in a few
sentences, the tax treatment of a diversity of transactions that have
little in common when viewed from the standpoint of business, financial, or economic purposes or results. They have been altered by Congress every few years, always *ad hoc*, and the earlier versions continue to govern the basis of assets and stock acquired in ancient reorganizations, as well as to influence the administrative and judicial
construction of today's statute. There is a good deal of interplay, over-

---

[4] Bazley v. Commissioner, *infra*, Sec. 12.16. In point of fact, the transaction before the court in this case, involving a reshuffling of the capital structure
of a family corporation with no change in ownership, met this specification
more clearly than would most mergers and consolidations, although the court
held that it was not a "reorganization." This is not to say that the court failed
to reach the right result, but the quoted language is an accurate description of
very few corporate reorganizations.

[5] There may, of course, be valid economic or other reasons for the non-
recognition of gain or loss, even though Congress has failed to announce them.
Compare Hellerstein, Mergers, Taxes, and Realism, 71 Harv. L. Rev. 254
(1957), and Sandberg, The Income Tax Subsidy to "Reorganizations," 38 Col.
L. Rev. 98 (1938), with Dane, The Case for Nonrecognition of Gain in Reorganization Exchanges, 36 Taxes 244 (1958). See also Surrey, Income Tax Problems
of Corporations and Shareholders: American Law Institute Tax Project —
American Bar Association Committee Study on Legislative Revision, 14 Tax L.
Rev. 1 (1958).

lap, and conflict between the reorganization provisions and such other statutory provisions as §301 (distributions of cash and other property), §302 (redemptions of stock), §305 (stock dividends), §306 (preferred stock bail-outs), §331 (partial and complete liquidations), and §355 (corporate divisions), since any of these events may accompany, be part of, or serve as a substitute for a reorganization. There is a similar conflict of jurisdiction within the reorganization provisions themselves, since — to take but one example — a statutory merger may be indistinguishable in results from an exchange by one corporation of its voting stock for all of the assets of another corporation; but different statutory rules are prescribed for these functionally equivalent reorganizations.

It should be noted that reorganization transactions often involve interdependent tax consequences, since the nonrecognition of gain that is ordinarily desired by transferor corporations and their shareholders carries with it a substituted basis for the property acquired by the transferee and possibly other disadvantages (e.g., an inherited earnings and profits account). This conflict in interest is not unusual in business transactions, of course, and the "tax cost" to each party may be reflected in the business bargain, to the extent that it can be anticipated and assured; but if the tax results are unpredictable, and a binding ruling is not or cannot be obtained from the Internal Revenue Service, the parties may take opposing forensic positions on the tax questions when they arise. This source of conflict among the participants to a corporate exchange may be heightened by differences among the transferors themselves; thus, some shareholders may wish to postpone the recognition of gain on a merger, while their fellow shareholders, who bought their stock at a higher price, may wish to recognize their loss. Finally, the attitude of any one participant in an exchange may depend on whether the tax issue arises at the time of the exchange or when he dispose of the property received (possibly many years later).

Because the stakes are often very high and the sources of conflict among taxpayers and between them and the government are so numerous, almost all reorganization exchanges involving the shareholders of publicly-held corporations, and many private transactions as well, are conditioned on a favorable ruling by the Internal Revenue Service unless the exchange falls in a simple and well-worn pattern. For this reason, the legal form or business bargain is often adjusted to eliminate questions that will be decided adversely by the Service, or — equally important — that it will not answer under its current policy; rarely do the participants deliberately invite a test of strength in the courts, even if they feel a good deal of confidence in the outcome. As a result, the Service can make "law" in this area by a lifted eyebrow. It follows that the practitioner not only must examine with care the statute, regulations, decisions, and published rulings relating to a proposed transaction, but must also determine the informal administrative climate with respect to it. Unfortunately, only a relative handful of the Service's rulings and rules of thumb are published, and practitioners are often forced to glean what they need from informal conferences, trade and financial publications, other lawyers, lecturers at tax institutes, and other sources of fact and fancy.[5a]

Sec. 12.02. The statutory pattern

Turning now to the statute, we find that §368(a)(1) defines "reorganization" to mean:

1. A statutory merger or consolidation ("Type A").

2. The acquisition by one corporation, in exchange solely for all or part of its voting stock (or the voting stock of a parent corporation) of stock of another corporation, if the first corporation has control (as defined) of the second immediately after the acquisition ("Type B").

3. The acquisition by one corporation, in exchange for all or part of its voting stock (or the voting stock of a parent corporation), of substantially all the properties of another corporation ("Type C"). The consideration given by the acquiring corporation must be solely voting stock, except that liabilities of the acquired corporation may be assumed, property may be taken subject to liabilities, and a limited amount of money or other consideration may be paid.

4. A transfer by a corporation of all or part of its assets to another corporation, if immediately after the transfer the transferor, its shareholders (including its former shareholders), or both in combination are in control of the transferee corporation; but only if the stock or securities of the transferee corporation are distributed, under the plan, in a transaction which qualifies under §354, §355, or §356 ("Type D").

5. A recapitalization ("Type E").

6. A mere change in identity, form or place of organization, however effected ("Type F").

In general, Types A and C are methods of combining the assets of two or more corporations (whether previously independent or affil-

---

[5a] An over-the-counter (or under-the-table) clearing house for information about informal rulings is the "Points to Remember" section of the ABA Tax Section Bulletin; see also, for a recent compendium, Freling, What Is New in Subchapter C: The Service's Current Ruling Policy, 23 N.Y.U. Inst. on Fed. Tax. 421 (1965).

iated), Type B is used to acquire a subsidiary, Type D is used either to combine two affiliated corporations or to effect a corporate separation under §355, and Types E and F reflect changes in the structure of a single corporation. But Types A and C may also be used to combine an existing corporation with a newly organized corporate shell, achieving the net result of a Type E or F reorganization. Type B seems to differ from the other types in that the acquired corporation becomes a subsidiary of the acquiring corporation, but the subsidiary may be liquidated as part of the reorganization, with results that often can hardly be distinguished from a Type A or C reorganization. In Type C, the transferor corporation sometimes remains alive as a holding company, but it may be liquidated, so that its shareholders become shareholders of the acquiring corporation, as they would in a Type B reorganization. As will be seen, these examples do not exhaust the areas of overlap between the various types of reorganization. Indeed, the statute itself recognizes that a reorganization may satisfy the requirements of both Type C and Type D.

The problems that arise in applying the statutory definition of the term "reorganization" are examined in Part B of this chapter.

Although §368(a)(1) defines the term "reorganization," it does not of its own force have any operative significance. Its definitions become important only as they are employed in other provisions of the Code, of which the most important are:

> 1. *§354*, providing (with qualifications) that gain or loss shall not be recognized if stock or securities in a corporation that is "a party to a reorganization," a term that is defined by §368(b), are exchanged solely for stock or securities in the same corporation or in another corporation that is a party to the reorganization.
>
> 2. *§361*, under which a corporation that is a party to a reorganization recognizes neither gain nor loss if it exchanges property under the plan of reorganization for stock or securities in another corporation that is a party to the reorganization.
>
> 3. *§356* and *§357*, providing for the treatment of "boot" and liabilities in reorganization exchanges.
>
> 4. *§358* and *§362(b)*, providing substituted basis rules in reorganization exchanges.
>
> 5. *§381*, providing for the transfer of a corporation's net operating loss carryover, earnings and profits, and other tax attributes to a successor corporation in certain reorganizations, subject to the limitations of §382(b) (*infra*, Ch. 13).

These "operative" rules (except for §381) are discussed in Part C of this chapter.

Citations to the vast literature on the corporate reorganization provisions appear at appropriate points hereafter, but discussions of a general or historical character are cited below.[6]

Sec. 12.03.   Judicial limitations — In general

The reorganization provisions of the 1954 Code are the progeny of surprisingly primitive ancestors. For many years, for example, an acquisition by one corporation of substantially all the properties of another corporation was a "reorganization," regardless (so far as the statutory definition was concerned) of the nature of the consideration paid. Faced by such a rudimentary statute, the courts not surprisingly felt called upon to protect the "spirit" of the legislation against its "letter" by segregating "sales" from true reorganizations. The early statute also provided that a transfer by a corporation of part of its assets to a controlled corporation was a reorganization, and that the shareholders of the transferor could receive the stock of the transferee without the recognition of gain. This set of provisions, taken literally, seemed to open the door to the tax-free distribution of dividends, if the distributing corporation went through the ritual of putting the cash or property to be distributed into a newly organized subsidiary and then distributed the subsidiary's stock. Here again, the courts intervened to prevent the reorganization provisions from being used to undermine the statutory scheme for taxing corporate earnings upon distribution to the shareholders. The rudimentary provisions that first evoked the protective instincts of the courts have

---

[6] See generally Darrell, The Use of Reorganization Techniques in Corporate Acquisitions, 70 Harv. L. Rev. 1183 (1957); McDonald and Willard, Tax-Free Acquisitions and Distributions, 14 N.Y.U. Inst. on Fed. Tax. 859 (1956); Fager, Reorganizations: Recapitalizations, Tax-Free Acquisitions, 15 ibid. 413 (1957); de Kosmian, Tax-Free Acquisitions of Assets or Stock, ibid., 677; Merritt, Tax-Free Corporate Acquisitions — The Law and the Proposed Regulations, 53 Mich. L. Rev. 911 (1955); Stinson and Anthoine, Tax-Free Exchanges (P.L.I., 1959) 14-74; Leake, Problems in Corporate Acquisitions, 13 Tax L. Rev. 67 (1957); Cohen et al., The Internal Revenue Code of 1954: Corporate Distributions, Organizations, and Reorganizations, 68 Harv. L. Rev. 393, 414-426 (1955); Darrell, Corporate Organizations and Reorganizations Under the Internal Revenue Code of 1954, 32 Taxes 1007 (1954); Silverman, Debt in Corporate Amalgamations, 44 Va. L. Rev. 873 (1958); Greene, Proposed Definitional Changes in Reorganizations, 14 Tax L. Rev. 155 (1959). For the early history of the reorganization provisions, see Paul, Reorganizations, in Studies in Federal Taxation (3d ser. 1940) 3-165; Miller, Hendricks, and Everett, Reorganizations and Other Exchanges in Federal Income Taxation (1931); Baar and Morris, Hidden Taxes in Corporate Reorganizations (1935).

For more recent discussions, see Johnson, Reorganizations — Minority Stockholders, Including Dissenters, 18 N.Y.U. Inst. on Fed. Tax. 821 (1960); Galvin, Corporate Reorganizations — Some Current Developments, 42 Taxes L. Rev. 421 (1964); Pennell, Developments and Unanswered Questions in Corporate Reorganizations, 42 Taxes 889 (1964).

been revised many times in the intervening years, and in some areas, the amendments have taken over the watchdog function of the courts. But Congress has never ousted the courts of this jurisdiction, so that the sophisticated reorganization provisions of the 1954 Code have not outgrown the judicial restrictions that were imposed in their childhood.

It remains true, therefore, that literal compliance with the reorganization provisions is not enough; a transaction will be governed by the statutory provisions only if it comes within their presuppositions as well as their language. The courts have driven this truth home with a variety of formulations, usually classified as the "business purpose," "step transaction," and "continuity of interest" doctrines. All of them have been encountered at earlier points in this work, and the first two (which often merge into a kind of substance-over-form approach) crop up at so many points in the law of federal taxation as to defy summary, at least in a guidebook. Their relevance at critical points in the reorganization area is discussed hereafter (especially *infra*, Secs. 12.11, 12.19, and 12.20). A convenient summary of their import, which is quoted in almost every government brief in a litigated reorganization case, is to be found in Regs. §1.368-1(b):

> Under the general rule, upon the exchange of property, gain or loss must be accounted for if the new property differs in a material particular, either in kind or extent, from the old property. The purpose of the reorganization provisions of the Internal Revenue Code is to except from the general rule certain specifically described exchanges incident to such readjustments of corporate structures made in one of the particular ways specified in the Code, as are required by business exigencies and which effect only a readjustment of continuing interest in property under modified corporate forms. Requisite to a reorganization under the Code are a continuity of the business enterprise under the modified corporate form. . . . In order to exclude transactions not intended to be included, the specifications of the reorganization provisions of the law are precise. Both the terms of the specifications and their underlying assumptions and purposes must be satisfied in order to entitle the taxpayer to the benefit of the exception from the general rule.[7]

Sec. 12.04.   Background and scope

It should be noted that a tax-free reorganization is merely one method of acquiring stock or business asets; alternatively, they may be purchased in a transaction that is no more complex than the pur-

---

[7] For similar statements, see Regs. §1.368-2(g) and §1.1002-1(c).

chase of an automobile, or acquired by one of the means discussed earlier in connection with stock redemptions (*supra*, Ch. 7) and complete corporate liquidations (*supra*, Ch. 9). If the reorganization route is chosen, the taxpayers must be prepared to prove that the "substance" of the transaction accords with its "form." If the acquisition is found to be a taxable "sale," the fact that the parties label it a tax-free reorganization will not control; conversely, an acquisition formally designated a "sale" may, in substance, constitute a tax-free reorganization.

Assuming a decision to employ a tax-free reorganization for a proposed acquisition, a number of non-tax factors may be relevant in determining the form of the transaction. The principal choice is between acquiring stock or assets; but even within these two basic categories, legal consequences may vary. The most important non-tax matters[8] to be considered in most acquisitions are the following:

1. The possibility of contingent or undisclosed liabilities (or other burdensome obligations) of the acquired corporation, which may make a Type C asset acquisition preferable to a Type B stock acquisition or a Type A merger.

2. Conversely, if preservation of the corporate entity or other non-transferable rights or privileges of the acquired corporation is desired, a Type B stock acquisition may be the only feasible route.

3. A Type A merger usually requires the approval of the shareholders of both corporations, while the shareholders of the acquiring corporation may not have to approve a Type B or C transaction.

4. The percentage of shareholders who must approve an exchange may vary, depending upon the type of reorganization chosen.

5. Appraisal rights for dissenting shareholders of the transferor corporation are more easily avoided by a Type B stock acquisition than a Type A merger or a Type C asset acquisition.

6. SEC, state blue sky, and stock exchange rules and regulations may depend upon the form of the transaction.

Because of their specialized character, reorganizations and exchanges governed by the following provisions are not discussed here:

1. §§371 and 372, relating to reorganizations in Chapter X of the Bankruptcy Act or in receivership, foreclosure, or similar proceedings.[9]

---

[8] See generally Darrell, The Use of Reorganization Techniques in Corporate Acquisitions, *supra* note 6; Woodside, S.E.C. Merger Considerations, 36 Taxes 136 (1958).

[9] See Western Mass. Theatres v. Commissioner, 236 F.2d 186, 49 AFTR

2. §§373 and 374, relating to the reorganization of railroad corporations in a receivership proceeding or under §77 of the Bankruptcy Act.[10]

3. §1071, relating to sales and exchanges of property to effectuate a change in policy or the adoption of a new policy by the Federal Communications Commission with respect to the ownership and control of radio broadcasting stations.

4. §§1081-1083, relating to exchanges and distributions in obedience to orders of the Securities and Exchange Commission under the Public Utility Holding Company Act of 1935.

5. §§1101-1103, relating to distributions under the Bank Holding Company Act of 1956.

Part B. Definitions of Reorganization

Sec. 12.10.   Introductory

As noted earlier, the term "reorganization" has a technical meaning for Federal income tax purposes, and is defined by §368(a)(1) to mean six (and only six) forms of corporate adjustments: statutory mergers and consolidations (Type A); acquisitions by one corporation of the stock or assets of another corporation (Types B and C); transfers to controlled corporations (Type D); recapitalizations (Type E); and changes in the form or place of organization (Type F). In general, these categories can be classified into three functional patterns: (1) "acquisitive" reorganizations, whereby one corporate enterprise absorbs the stock or assets of another corporation (Types A, B, C, and, to some extent, D); (2) "divisive" reorganizations, whereby a single corporate enterprise is divided into two or more separate entities through a process of corporate mitosis (Type D, taken in conjunction with the provisions of §355, *supra*, Ch. 11); and (3) "internal" readjustments in the structure of a single corporate enterprise (Types E and F). In practice, however, these basic patterns may overlap, so that tax consequences may vary depending upon which statutory category of reorganization is deemed controlling. This, in turn, may depend on the form of the transaction, the amount and character of the consideration exchanged, and the change in the parties' legal and economic relationships to the properties involved and among themselves. At times, formal events control the

1986 (1st Cir. 1956); San Antonio Transit Co. v. Commissioner, 30 T.C. 1215 (1958); Nadeau v. United States, 181 F. Supp. 752, 5 AFTR 2d 786 (W.D. Mich. 1960); Atlas Oil and Refining Corp. v. Commissioner, 36 T.C. 675 (1961); Krantz, Loss Carryovers in Chapter X Reorganizations, 16 Tax L. Rev. 359 (1961); Eustice, Cancellation of Indebtedness and the Federal Income Tax: A Problem of Creeping Confusion, 14 Tax L. Rev. 225, 267-270, 277-279 (1959).

[10] See Eustice, *supra* note 9, at 264-267 and 277-279.

tax results; in other instances, form is disregarded, so that a state of tension exists between the words of the statute and the economic or business substance.

In this portion of the chapter, matters relating to the general definition of reorganization will be examined, together with the judicial glosses which the statutory provisions have acquired. Other definitional problems, such as the meaning of "party" to a reorganization and "plan" of reorganization, will also be considered. Because of its fundamental importance to the concept of corporation reorganization, the "continuity of interest" doctrine is considered before discussion of the various categories of reorganization.

Sec. 12.11.   Continuity of proprietary interest

1. In general. Like the business purpose and step transaction doctrines, the requirement that the original owners retain a continuing interest in the reorganized corporation was born of a judicial effort to confine the reorganization provisions to their proper function. The business purpose and step transaction doctrines, however, almost immediately found application throughout the tax law, while the continuity of interest doctrine has seemed relevant primarily in the area that gave it birth and in the related area of transfers of property under §351 (*supra*, Sec. 3.04).

The continuity of interest doctrine, set out in Regs. §1.368-1(b) and (c), can be traced back to Cortland Specialty Co. v. Commissioner, 60 F.2d 937, 11 AFTR 857 (2d Cir. 1932), where substantially all of the properties of one corporation were acquired by another corporation in exchange for cash and short-term promissory notes. Although the transfer came within the literal language of the reorganization provisions, the court held that the term "reorganization" presupposes "a continuance of interest on the part of the transferor in the properties transferred" and that the transaction before the court was too much like a sale to satisfy this criterion. Moreover, the court held that the promissory notes received by the transferor (having serial maturities, of which the longest was fourteen months) were not "securities" within the meaning of what is now §354. The following year, in Pinellas Ice & Cold Storage Co. v. Commissioner, 287 U.S. 462, 11 AFTR 1112 (1933), the Supreme Court held as to a similar transaction that "the seller must acquire an interest in the affairs of the purchasing company more definite than that incident to ownership of its short-term purchase-money notes" if the transaction is to qualify as a reorganization, as well as that the notes (all payable within four months) were not "securities." Two years later the Supreme Court held in Helvering v. Minnesota Tea Co., 296 U.S. 378, 16 AFTR 1258 (1935), that a transfer of substantially all the assets of a corporation for voting trust certificates representing common stock worth about $540,000, plus about $425,000 in cash, was a "reorganization" under the statute applicable to the year in question. Referring to the statement in *Pinellas* that the seller must "acquire an interest in the affairs of the purchasing company," the Court said:

> And we now add that this interest must be definite and material; it must represent a substantial part of the value of the thing transferred. This much is necessary in order that the result accomplished may genuinely partake of the nature of merger or consolidation. . . .
>
> The transaction here was no sale, but partook of the nature of a reorganization, in that the seller acquired a definite and substantial interest in the purchaser.
>
> True it is that the relationship of the taxpayer to the assets conveyed was substantially changed, but this is not inhibited by the statute. Also, a large part of the consideration was cash. This, we think, is permissible so long as the taxpayer received an interest in the affairs of the transferee which represented a material part of the value of the transferred assets. (296 U.S. 378, 385-386 (1935).)

A further development came in LeTulle v. Scofield, 308 U.S. 415, 23 AFTR 789 (1940), in which all the assets of a corporation were transferred for $50,000 in cash and $750,000 in bonds of the acquiring corporation. The Court held that the transaction was not a "reorganization," despite compliance with the language of the statutory definition:

> Where the consideration is wholly in the transferee's bonds, or part cash and part such bonds, we think it cannot be said that the transferor retains any proprietary interest in the enterprise. On the contrary, he becomes a creditor of the transferee; and we do not think that the fact referred to by the Circuit Court of Appeals, that the bonds were secured solely by the assets transferred and that, upon default, the bondholder would retake only the property sold, changes his status from that of a creditor to one having a proprietary stake, within the purview of the statute. (308 U.S. at 420.)

In John A. Nelson Co. v. Helvering, 296 U.S. 374, 16 AFTR 1262 (1935), however, the Court found the requisite continuity of interest where assets were transferred for preferred stock and cash. The preferred stock was non-voting (in the absence of dividend default) and was redeemable at stated intervals, but the Court held that the statute did not require participation by the transferor in the management of the transferee. Finally, in United States v. Hendler, 303 U.S. 564, 20 AFTR 1041 (1938), the Court held that the assumption and payment by the transferee corporation of liabilities of the transferor corporation constituted taxable "boot," although not enough boot was involved to destroy the status of the transfer as a reorganization.

The continuity of interest test has been summarized in Southwest Natural Gas Co. v. Commissioner, 189 F.2d 332, 40 AFTR 686 (5th Cir. 1951), cert. denied, 342 U.S. 860, as follows:

> While no precise formula has been expressed for determining whether there has been retention of the requisite interest, it seems clear that . . . [there must be] a showing: (1) that the transferor corporation or its shareholders retained a substantial proprietary stake in the enterprise represented by a material interest in the affairs of the transferee corporation, and (2) that such retained interest represents a substantial part of the value of the property transferred.

The Court in this case refused to find the requisite continuity where less than one percent in value of the total consideration paid by the transferee consisted of its stock.

Thus, the continuity of interest requirement, as developed in the above decisions, seemed to involve two distinct elements: (1) the qualitative nature of the consideration given by the transferee; and (2) the proportion or quantity thereof which consisted of "continuity-preserving" interests. As to the former, the only type of consideration which carried the requisite continuity "genes" was an equity interest, evidenced by common or preferred stock, whether voting or non-voting. Cash or its equivalent (e.g., short term purchase money notes), long term debt securities, and the assumption of liabilities all failed to meet the test of continuity, since the transferors, by the receipt of such consideration, were either cashing in their investment interest in the property, or switching to a temporary creditor status with respect thereto, rather than retaining a proprietary interest.

As to the relative amounts of equity and non-equity consideration which could be received by the transferors, matters were less clear. The Minnesota Tea case held that it must be a "substantial" or "material" part of the value of the transferred assets, and that a 56 percent equity interest was adequate by this standard; Southwest Natural Gas, on the other hand, held that less than one percent was not.[11]

---

[11] It should be noted that the percentages in question represent the proportion of equity consideration to aggregate consideration received for the trans-

2. *"Remote" continuity — the Groman doctrine.* In Groman v. Commissioner, 302 U.S. 82, 19 AFTR 1214 (1937), the Court held that continuity of interest did not exist to the extent that the transferors received stock of the transferee corporation's parent in exchange for their property. The refusal to find a continuity of interest in such a "triangular" transaction[12] merely because a second corporate shell was interposed between the transferred property and the transferors reflected a surprisingly restrictive and formal view of the continuity doctrine's function. A separable feature of the *Groman* transaction, viz., the receipt by the transferors of stock in both the parent and the subsidiary, however, raised a somewhat different policy consideration, since the transferors thus acquired independent disposable interests in two corporations, and thus could sell one interest while retaining the other. As will be seen (*infra*, Secs. 12.14 and 12.21), the former aspect of the *Groman* case has been modified by subsequent statutory developments; but the decision continues to have vitality where not altered by these amendments.

3. *Continuity of participation by the transferors.* Another aspect of the continuity doctrine relates to the number of former owners who maintain a continuing proprietary interest in the transferred properties. For example, in a merger or consolidation, some shareholders of the transferor corporation may elect to take cash, securities, or other property rather than stock of the acquiring corporation. Is the merger vulnerable because some of the old shareholders have lost their proprietary interest, while others have changed the relative proportions of their proprietary interest? The fact that some shareholders do not agree to the exchange and are paid off in cash was held irrelevant in Miller v. Commissioner, 84 F.2d 415, 17 AFTR

---

ferred assets, not to the relation between the transferor's equity in the transferee and the total equity therein.

[12] In Groman, shareholders of Corporation X transferred their X stock to Corporation Z, a newly-organized subsidiary of Corporation Y, in exchange for cash and non-voting preferred stock of Y and Z; and Z immediately liquidated X. The Court held that the stock of Y received by the old shareholders of X did not give them a continuing interest in X's assets, despite the fact that Y owned all of the stock of Z, which in turn owned the X assets. A companion case, Helvering v. Bashford, 302 U.S. 454, 19 AFTR 1240 (1937), also involved a triangular acquistion, except that the acquired properties were received by the parent itself, and were then transferred by it to a subsidiary as part of a single plan. The Court held that *Groman* was applicable despite these variations in the facts. See also Anheuser-Busch, Inc. v. Helvering, 115 F.2d 662, 25 AFTR 1044 (8th Cir. 1940), cert. den., 312 U.S. 699; Hedden v. Commissioner, 105 F.2d 311, 23 AFTR 169 (3rd Cir. 1939); Mellon v. Commissioner, 12 T.C. 90 (1949), aff'd other issues, 184 F.2d 157, 39 AFTR 1030 (3rd Cir. 1950).

See generally, Lurie, Namorg — or *Groman* Reversed, 10 Tax L. Rev. 119 (1954).

1308 (6th Cir. 1936), stating that it "is an almost universal experience that some nonassenting stock must be acquired otherwise than through the consolidation plan."[13] (Those shareholders who take cash, however, would recognize their gain, if any, under §354(a)(2) and §356.) It cannot be assumed, however, that this tolerant attitude toward the common practice of paying off some shareholders in cash would be displayed toward an exchange in which only a small fraction of the participants received an equity interest in the transferee.[14]

This aspect of the continuity problem also has special features which are peculiar to Type D reorganizations and Type E recapitalizations; these matters are considered *infra*, Sec. 12.15 and 12.16.

Assuming that a sufficent number of stockholders of the transferor corporation acquire a proprietary interest in the transferee corporation, does the continuity of interest doctrine require that their participation arise solely from their status as stockholders of the transferor? Somewhat surprisingly, the courts have held that stock received by shareholder-creditors of the transferor can be counted in applying the continuity of interest doctrine whether it is received in their capacity of creditor or that of shareholder.[15] This conclusion may rest in part on the *Alabama Asphaltic* case, holding that creditors of an insolvent corporation, upon instituting bankruptcy proceedings, "had effective command over the disposition of the property" and that by this action they stepped into the shoes of the old shareholders and succeeded to their former proprietary interest; since this interest was continued in the reorganized corporation, the continuity of interest requirement was satisfied despite elimination of the old stockholders.[16] If the transferor is not insolvent, however, the courts may be less ready to allow stock received in exchange for

---

[13] See also Reilly Oil Co. v. Commissioner, 189 F.2d 382, 40 AFTR 707 (5th Cir. 1951) (69 percent of the stockholders of transferor participated in a creditors' reorganization and secured "control" of the transferee; held, sufficient continuity of interest); Western Mass. Theatres, Inc. v. Commissioner, *supra* note 9 (67 percent participation acceptable, despite a shift in relative proportions); but see Maine Steel, Inc. v. United States, 174 F.Supp. 702, 4 AFTR 2d 5127 (D. Me. 1959) (continuity broken by obligation to dispose of stock); Rev. Rul. 66-23, 1966-1 C.B. — (contra, where stock would not have to be divested for seven years).

[14] See Hyman H. Berghash, 43 T.C. 743 (1965), aff'd, —— F.2d ——, 17 AFTR 2d 1163 (2d Cir. 1966).

[15] Western Mass. Theatres v. Commissioner, *supra* note 9; see also Commissioner v. Huntzinger, 137 F.2d 128, 31 AFTR 355 (10th Cir. 1943); Prairie du Chien-Marquette Bridge Co. v. Commissioner, 142 F.2d 624, 32 AFTR 701 (3rd Cir. 1944).

[16] Helvering v. Alabama Asphaltic Limestone Co., 315 U.S. 179, 28 AFTR 567 (1942). For some of the ramifications of this decision, see Chicago Stadium Corp., 13 T.C. 889 (1949); San Antonio Transit Co., *supra* note 9; Scofield v. San Antonio Transit Co., 219 F.2d 149, 46 AFTR 1659 (5th Cir. 1955), cert. denied, 350 U.S. 823. See generally Atlas Oil & Refining Corp., *supra* note 9;

debt claims to be counted in determining whether the shareholders have established a continuing interest in the transferred property.

4. "Securities" and continuity of interest. As noted earlier, the principal function of the continuity of interest doctrine has been to separate "sales" from "reorganizations"; if the transferors received only debt obligations of the transferee in exchange for their property, continuity would be lacking under the *LeTulle* case, since some form of proprietary interest (represented by common or preferred stock of the transferee) had to be retained by the transferors. If, however, sufficient proprietary continuity was maintained by the transferors so that the transfer qualified as a reorganization, it is then necessary to determine whether any "additional" consideration, such as debt obligations of the transferee, constituted "securities" — which could be received without recognition of gain under prior versions of §§361-(a) and 354(a) — or whether such consideration instead constituted taxable "boot." In Helvering v. Watts, 296 U.S. 387, 16 AFTR 1264 (1935) (involving a transfer of assets for stock and mortgage bonds), the court held that the bonds were "securities" rather than boot; the *Pinellas* case, *supra*, held that short-term notes did not constitute "securities."[17]

In Neville Coke & Chemical Co. v. Commissioner, 148 F.2d 599, 33 AFTR 1131 (3rd Cir. 1945), the court relied on the continuity of interest principle in holding that various creditor claims, exchanged by the taxpayer, did not constitute "securities" (hence, the exchange was ruled taxable even though the consideration received by the taxpayer concededly consisted of "securities"). Pressed to its extreme, the approach of the *Neville Coke* decision could render many recapitalization exchanges and most creditor reorganizations, taxable; and this result cannot be reconciled with the implicit assumption that debt instruments constitute "securities" underlying such central reorganization provisions as §354(a)(2), §356(d), and §361(a). Moreover, the general thrust of the continuity of interest doctrine is to prevent a shift from an "ownership" interest to a less permanent creditor interest; in the *Neville Coke* case, by contrast, the taxpayer was shifting from a less permanent (short term creditor) to a more permanent (long term creditor and shareholder) interest, a result which seems to accord with the underlying policy of the continuity of interest doctrine.[18]

Darrell, Creditors' Reorganizations and the Federal Income Tax, 57 Harv. L. Rev. 1009 (1944); *supra,* Sec. 4.02 (re classification of ambiguous instruments as "stock" or "debt claims").

[17] For the relation of this issue to §351 exchanges, see *supra,* Sec. 3.04.

[18] See generally Griswold, "Securities" and "Continuity of Interest," 58 Harv. L. Rev. 705 (1945).

A final aspect of this problem is the apparent holding in Bazley v. Commissioner, 331 U.S. 737, 35 AFTR 1190 (1947), that long term debt instruments received in a recapitalization exchange did not constitute "securities." As pointed out in the discussion of *Bazley* (*infra*, Sec. 12.16), this dictum cannot be applied generally without serious conflict with the structure and presuppositions of the reorganization provisions, and it has not gained any momentum with the passage of time. Despite *Neville Coke* and *Bazley*, then, it seems clear that debt instruments ordinarily constitute "securities" even though they do not provide the transferor with a continuity of interest in the transferred property.

5. Statutory evolution of the continuity doctrine. Most of the cases in which the continuity of interest doctrine was developed and applied related to transactions attempting to qualify as "reorganizations" under the pre-1934 statutory definition, which said nothing about the nature of the consideration which could be received by transferors. In 1934, however, the definition of "reorganization" was amended so that nothing but voting stock of the acquiring corporation could be used as consideration in an acquisition of the stock or assets of another corporation. (This limitation, somewhat modified since 1934, is to be found in §368(a)(1)(B) and (C) of current law, governing Type B and C reorganizations.) In Helvering v. Southwest Consolidated Corp., 315 U.S. 194, 28 AFTR 573 (1942), the Court drove home this restriction by holding that the transferor's receipt of stock warrants from the transferee prevented the exchange from qualifying as "solely for voting stock," noting that the new statutory test was much stricter than the judicially-created continuity of interest doctrine. Thus, in the case of Type B and C reorganizations, the continuity of interest doctrine is overshadowed by the statutory limits on the consideration that can be received, especially since the courts have served notice that "solely" as used in §368(a)(1) means exactly that.

Later statutory developments have somewhat relaxed the 1934 amendment to take care of several practical problems, but it continues to provide statutory assurance that the transferor will acquire a proprietary interest in Type B and C reorganizations. These post-1934 amendments, which are discussed subsequently, permit:

    1. The assumption of liabilities, or the taking of property subject to liabilities (*infra*, Sec. 12.18);

    2. The use of a limited amount of cash or other property in a Type C reorganization (*infra*, Sec. 12.14); and

3. The use of voting stock of the acquiring corporation's parent in Type B and C reorganizations (*infra*, Secs. 12.13 and 12.14).

Despite these statutory substitutes or buttresses for the judicially-created continuity of interest requirement, it is still important in Type A and E reorganizations, where the statute is silent on the nature of the consideration which can be received by the transferors; in addition, it seems likely that continuity notions will still apply generally to other types of reorganization.[19]

6. Conclusion. Although the continuity of interest doctrine was devised and is applied as a means of denying tax-free status to "sales" that happen to meet the literal requirements of a reorganization, it works more as a blunt instrument than a scapel. Among its shortcomings are these:

1. It assumes that the receipt of stock in exchange for stock necessarily insures a continuing interest, without regard to the economic results of the transaction. In fact, however, the exchange may drastically alter the shareholder's rights and risks. If he gives up the common stock of a closely-held corporation and gets back the stock of a national, publicly-held corporation, the exchange may be substantially the same as a sale of the original stock followed by an investment of the proceeds in a totally different enterprise. Indeed, if the closely-held company is merged into an investment company or other corporation with a broad spectrum of business activities, the exchange may be similar to a sale of the original stock coupled with an investment in a diversified portfolio of investments. Even if the acquiring corporation is not a national colossus, the shareholder's business risks may be fundamentally changed if he exchanges common stock for non-participating preferred, or vice versa.

2. In applying the continuity of interest doctrine, the courts have employed the converse, but almost equally mechanical, assumption that bonds cannot represent a "proprietary" interest in the reorganized corporation.[20] Yet the size or financial status of the obligor may give the "creditor" good reason to worry about the safety of his

---

[19] As to Type D reorganizations, the continuity doctrine raises special problems, discussed *infra*, Sec. 12.15. It should be noted that it is stated as generally applicable to all reorganization transactions by Regs. §1.368-1(b).

Like the 1934 change discussed in the text, the addition of §354(a)(2) in 1954 (*infra*, Sec. 12.34) provides a statutory backstop to the continuity doctrine by making it more difficult for shareholders to up-grade their status to creditors in a reorganization exchange.

[20] An exception presumably could be made for cases of "thin" capitalization, *supra*, Sec. 4.04. See generally W. H. Truschel, 29 T.C. 433 (1957).

investment, and to follow the fate of the transferred assets with acute concern. Thus, the economic fortunes of the bondholders in *LeTulle* v. *Scofield, supra,* may have continued to rest upon the value and income potential of the transferred assets, while the shareholder of a local business who receives stock of a national company in a merger may be virtually independent of fluctuations in the value of the assets in which he was formerly interested.

3. Finally, the exchange of a "proprietary" interest for bonds may not represent much of an economic shift, if the stock given up was non-participating preferred, or common stock of a corporation whose assets were not likely to fluctuate in value or yield. An example is Roebling v. Commissioner, 143 F.2d 810, 32 AFTR 1083 (3d Cir. 1944), where the continuity of interest doctrine was applied to deny tax-free status to an exchange of common stock for bonds, although the exchange did not produce a substantial difference in the investor's financial position.[21]

Sec. 12.12.   Statutory mergers and consolidations (Type A)

Under §368(a)(1)(A), a statutory merger or consolidation is a reorganization.[22] In a merger, one corporation absorbs the corporate enterprise of another corporation, with the result that the acquiring company steps into the shoes of the disappearing corporation as to its assets and liabilities. Consolidations typically involve the combination of two or more corporations into a newly created entity, with the old corporations going out of existence. In both of these transactions, however, shareholders and creditors of the disappearing transferor corporations automatically become shareholders and creditors of the transferee corporations by operation of law. It should be noted that the transferor corporation or corporations in a statutory merger or consolidation disappear as legal entities, with the result that this form of reorganization involves a technical dissolution of the acquired corporation. In a Type C reorganization (*infra*, Sec. 12.14), often called a "practical merger," however, the transferor corporation may be kept alive.

---

[21] See generally Brookes, The Continuity of Interest Test in Reorganizations — A Blessing or a Curse? 34 Cal. L. Rev. 1 (1946); Baker, Continuity of Interest Requirement in Reorganizations Re-examined — The Hickok case, 18 N.Y.U. Inst. on Fed. Tax. 761 (1960).

[22] The statutory requirements of the applicable state law must be satisfied; see Edward H. Russell, 40 T.C. 810, 822 (1963). But an exchange that fails to comply with state law, or that takes place under foreign law, may constitute a Type C or D reorganization, even though it is not a Type A reorganization. See Regs. §1.368-2(b); Rev. Rul. 57-465, 1957-2 C.B. 250.

When two enterprises are to be combined, it is often purely a matter of form whether the parties employ a reorganization of Type A (statutory merger or consolidation), Type B (acquisition by one corporation of the stock of another corporation), or Type C (acquisition by one corporation of substantially all of the properties of another corporation). As will be seen, however, §368(a)(1)(B) permits the use of no consideration other than voting stock in a Type B reorganization and §368(a)(1)(C) affords only slightly more freedom in a Type C reorganization; while §368(a)(1)(A) — quite unaccountably — imposes no restrictions on the type of consideration to be used in a statutory merger or consolidation. Nonvoting stock and securities can be used with impunity, so far as the statutory language is concerned, in a Type A reorganization; and the exchange can qualify as a "reorganization" even if money or other property change hands. The money or other property will constitute "boot," of course, and so will securities in some circumstances, with the consequences discused *infra*, Sec. 12.34; but they will not result in disqualifying the transaction in its entirety, as can occur when money, property or securities are used in a Type B or C reorganization.

The greater flexibility of a Type A reorganization is not without its perils, however; it may lure the taxpayer into an excessive use of securities or other non-proprietary consideration, in violation of the "continuity of interest" doctrine, whereas the more rigid requirements of a Type B or C reorganization help to keep the taxpayer on the straight and narrow tax-free path. Thus, in Roebling v. Commissioner, 143 F.2d 810, 32 AFTR 1083 (3d Cir. 1944), cert. denied 323 U.S. 773, a merger of two corporations was held outside of §368(a)(1)(A) because the shareholders of the absorbed corporation received nothing but bonds of the continuing corporation; although there was a merger under state law, the old shareholders did not retain a continuing proprietary interest in the transferred assets.[23] A statutory merger may fail to qualify even if the shareholders get some stock in the continuing corporation, if the stock represents only a small fraction of the total consideration received by them.[24]

Under §368(a)(2)(C), enacted in 1954, an otherwise qualified Type A reorganization will not lose its tax-free status merely because part or all of the assets acquired in the transaction are transferred to a subsidiary by the acquiring corporation.[25]

---

[23] See also W. H. Truschel, *supra* note 20.
[24] See Southwest Natural Gas Co. v. Commissioner, *supra*, Sec. 12.11.
[25] For the background of this provision, see *supra*, Sec. 12.11. If assets are transferred to a subsidiary under §368(a)(2)(C), the transferor parent is a

Aside from the continuity of interest problem, relating to the proportion of non-proprietary consideration which can be paid by the acquiring corporation, statutory mergers and consolidations ordinarily cause little difficulty. The following special situations, however, require attention:

1. Mergers of affiliated corporations. If the shareholders of brother-sister corporations receive bonds, debentures, or other debt instruments in a merger or consolidation, the net effect of the transaction may be indistinguishable from the payment of a taxable dividend under the *Bazley* doctrine (*infra*, Sec. 12.16). Alternatively, the transaction might be viewed as a redemption of the stock of the merged corporation by its surviving sister corporation, in which event its tax consequences will be governed by §304 (*supra*, Sec. 7.31). Neither of these forbidding possibilities is brought into play, however, by a merger or consolidation of affiliated corporations in which the shareholders do not try to up-grade their status to that of their creditors, but content themselves with an exchange of stock for stock.

The merger of a subsidiary into its parent, or vice versa (so-called up-stream and down-stream mergers, respectively) involves a potential conflict between the rules governing reorganizations and those governing liquidations, discussed *infra*, Sec. 12.21.

If the assets of a party to a statutory merger or consolidation are transferred to a subsidiary of the surviving corporation in a "triangular" acquisition (*supra*, Sec. 12.11), the tax consequences may depend on whether the transaction is treated as a Type A or a Type C reorganization, a question that is discussed *infra*, Sec. 12.21.

2. Merger combined with §355 distributions. In preparation for a merger, one of the corporations may have to rid itself of a separable business that the other corporation does not want to acquire; and it may seek to do so in a tax-free distribution under §355. The possibility of thus combining two tax-free transactions, without an adverse impact on either one, is discussed *infra*, Sec. 12.20.

3. Redemption of minority or dissenting shares. In conjunction with a statutory merger or consolidation, one of the corporations often wishes to redeem some of its shares, either as a convenient way of disposing of assets that the surviving corporation does not wish to acquire, or to eliminate a dissenting group and thereby avoid the assertion of appraisal rights under state law. Does such a transaction

"party" to the reorganization by virtue of §368(b), third sentence, and the subsidiary seems to be a "party" to the reorganization by virtue of §368(b)(2) or, if newly created, §368(b)(1). See Regs. §1.368-2(f), seventh sentence; *infra*, note 45.

endanger the status of the merger by weakening its compliance with the continuity of interest doctrine? As indicated earlier (*supra*, Sec. 12.11), if shareholders representing a "substantial" equity interest in the transferor continue as shareholders of the surviving corporation, the continuity principle will be satisfied, even though the other shareholders are bought out.[25a] At one time, the Service seemed ready to question such transactions, if operating or business assets were used to pay for the redeemed shares, under an amorphous "continuity of business enterprise" doctrine, but its doubts may have been laid to rest (see *infra*, Sec. 12.19).

4. *Mergers that overlap with Type C or D reorganizations.* A statutory merger may also fit the description of a Type C or D reorganization. If it does, must the restrictions imposed on the latter forms be complied with, or can the exchange qualify if it meets the merger rules alone? Section 368(a)(2)(A) arbitrates one such conflict — between Type C and Type D reorganizations — by providing that an exchange described in both definitions shall be treated as a Type D reorganization; but there is no such statutory direction for other instances of overlapping jurisdiction.[26] Legislative history, however, may supply the key: mergers and consolidations have been tax-free transactions since 1918, and it is reasonably clear that the other types of reorganizations defined by §368(a)(1) were added to the law at later times to facilitate business adjustments rather than to resrict the tax-free status of mergers.[27] For this reason, it would be reasonable to resolve cases of overlapping definitions by allowing an exchange to qualify as a Type A transaction whether or not it meets the standards applicable to a Type C or D transaction.

Sec. 12.13. Acquisitions of stock for voting stock (Type B)

A Type B reorganization, as defined by §368(a)(1)(B), is the acquisition of stock of one corporation in exchange solely for part or all of the voting stock of either the acquiring corporation or its parent,[28] provided that the acquiring corporation has "control" of

---

[25a] See Western Mass. Theatres v. Commissioner, *supra* note 9; *supra*, Sec. 12.11; *infra*, Sec. 12.20.

[26] If a transaction is both a reorganization and a §332 liquidation, it is to be treated as a liquidation, at least so far as the parent corporation is concerned, by virtue of §332(b) (last sentence); *infra*, Sec. 12.21; Long Island Water Corp., 36 T.C. 377 (1961) (Acq.).

[27] See Paul, *supra* note 6, at 19-20.

[28] The use of stock of the acquiring corporation's *parent* as consideration in a Type B reorganization was authorized for the first time in 1964; at the same time, §368(a)(2)(C) was amended to permit stock acquired in a Type B

the acquired corporation immediately after the acquisition (whether or not it had such control before the acquisition). Control is defined by §368(c) as the ownership of stock possessing at least 80 percent of total combined voting power, plus at least 80 percent of the total number of shares of all other classes of stock.[29] In a Type B reorganization, the sole consideration that can be used is voting stock[30] of either the acquiring corporation or its parent. Although the voting stock may be either common or preferred, there is no other room to maneuver in a Type B reorganization. The Supreme Court has said that the statutory phrase "solely for voting stock" leaves "no leeway," not even for warrants to purchase additional voting stock of the acquiring corporation; and this strict view has been applied in a number of later cases.[31] Although the statutory requirement as thus interpreted assures that a continuity of interest will exist in a Type B reorganization, it has the effect of disqualifying an exchange if an inconsequential amount of "boot" is used; and, unless a business purpose exception is to be added, it permits taxpayers to

reorganization to be transferred to a subsidiary of the acquiring corporation, and §368(b)(2) was amended to provide that the parent in such a "triangular" acquisition is a "party" to the reorganization. These statutory amendments limit the doctrine of the *Groman* and *Bashford* cases (*supra,* Sec. 12.11). For pre-1964 law, see Rev. Rul. 63-234, 1963-2 C.B.148.

Although the parent's voting stock now qualifies for a Type B acquisition, if used it must be the *sole* consideration; it cannot be combined with stock of the subsidiary.

[29] For discussion of the 80 percent control requirement, see *supra,* Sec. 3.07; on the meaning of "immediately after" the acquisition, see the similar language in §351, *supra,* Sec. 3.09. For the effect on the control requirement of a contemporaneous redemption by the acquired corporation of one class of its outstanding stock (callable preferred), see Rev. Rul. 55-440, 1955-2 C.B. 226 (redeemed stock excluded in computing control).

[30] For the meaning of "voting stock," see Forrest Hotel Corp. v. Fly, 112 F.Supp. 782, 789, 43 AFTR 1073 (S.D. Miss. 1953) (common stock which could not vote at the time of the transaction because of arrearages on the preferred stock, held to be voting stock; preferred stock which was voting because of the arrearages held to be voting stock); see also Firestone Tire & Rubber Co., 2 T.C. 827 (1943) (treasury stock held to be voting stock). See generally *infra,* Sec. 13.41.

[31] Helvering v. Southwest Consolidated Corp., 315 U.S. 194, 28 AFTR 573 (1942); see also Richard M. Mills, 39 T.C. 393 (1962) (no *de minimis* rule applicable to "solely"), reversed on other grounds, 331 F.2d 321, 13 AFTR 2d 1386 (5th Cir. 1964); Commissioner v. Turnbow, 286 F.2d 669, 7 AFTR 2d 357 (9th Cir. 1961), affirmed on other issues, 386 F.2d 337, 8 AFTR 2d 5967 (1961); aff'd, 368 U.S. 337, 8 AFTR 2d 5967 (1961); *infra,* Sec. 12.34, for discussion of related aspects of these decisions. See generally Vernava; The Howard and Turnbow Cases and the "Solely" Requirement of B Reorganizations, 20 Tax L. Rev. 387 (1965); see also Kanter, Cash in a "B" Reorganization: Effect of Cash Purchases on "Creeping" Reorganization, 19 Tax L. Rev. 441 (1964); and, for proposals to amend the definition of a Type B reorganization to permit the use of additional consideration, see Greene, *supra* note 6; Report of the Section of Taxation, American Bar Association, Vol. XVIII, No. 4 (July, 1955).

avoid tax-free status (e.g., so a loss will be recognized) almost at will, viz., by larding an otherwise qualified Type B exchange with a little boot.[32]

Before 1954, the statutory language seemed to require that at least 80 percent of the acquired corporation's stock be acquired in the reorganization exchange itself; hence, it was generally assumed that a corporation which had acquired over 20 percent of another corporation's stock in an unrelated prior transaction could not use a Type B reorganization to increase its ownership to 80 percent or more.[33] A 1954 change in the language of §368(a)(1)(B) makes it clear that "control" need not be obtained in one fell swoop, and that a "creeping" acquisition of control can qualify, as well as an increase in ownership by a corporation that already has "control." For example, if Y Corporation, in four successive and separate transactions, acquired (solely for its voting stock) 40 percent, 30 percent, 20 percent, and finally 10 percent of the stock of X Corporation, the last two acquisitions would qualify as Type B reorganizations under the amended definition.

The 1954 change is not without its difficulties, however, mainly because the term "acquisition" is not defined. Thus, if the acquiring corporation purchases 50 percent of the stock of another corporation in January for cash and exchanges its voting stock for the rest of the stock in July, has it engaged in a "single transaction" that fails to qualify because it was not "solely" for voting stock, or were there two separate acquisitions, one of which was an ordinary purchase and the other a Type B reorganization? The regulations permit a prior cash purchase to be disregarded if it was independent of the stock-for-stock exchange; conversely, stock-for-stock acquisitions in a series are to be aggregated if they occur "over a relatively short period of time such as 12 months."[34]

The principal other problems that arise in Type B reorganizations, stemming mainly from the "solely for voting stock" requirement, are:

1. *Minority or dissenting shares.* Where stock of the acquired corporation is widely held, some of its shareholders may be unwilling

---

[32] With the latter possibility, compare the fact that the receipt of boot in an otherwise tax-free exchange does not ordinarily permit a realized loss to be recognized, e.g., §351(b), §356(c), etc.

[33] See Lutkins v. United States, 312 F.2d 803, 11 AFTR 2d 656 (Ct. Cl. 1963), cert. denied, 375 U.S. 825; Kanter and Vernava, *supra* note 31.

[34] Regs. §1.368-2(c), echoing the language of S. Rep. No. 1622, 83d Cong., 2d Sess., p. 273 (1954); see generally McDonald and Willard, Tax Free Acquisitions and Distributions, *supra* note 6, at 871-876.

to accept the acquiring corporation's stock and will insist on a cash payment for their shares. It is clear that the acquiring corporation cannot, directly or indirectly, make such a payment as part of the plan without destroying Type B reorganization status.[35] But it is apparently permissible for the acquired corporation to redeem the stock of these shareholders for cash or other property, or for persons interested in effectuating the transaction to buy them out, without infecting the Type B reorganization.[36]

2. *Fractional shares.* The exchange ratio in stock-for-stock acquisitions often gives the shareholders of the acquired corporation the right to receive fractional shares of the acquiring corporation. The issuance of fractional shares or of "scrip" evidencing such rights does not violate the "solely for voting stock" requirement.[37] To avoid the distribution of fractional shares, however, the acquiring corporation often makes arrangements with a bank, under which a shareholder can purchase an additional fraction to make up a full share or, alternatively, sell his fractional interest. The Service does not regard such arrangements as constituting additional consideration in violation of the "solely for voting stock" requirement.[38]

3. *Payment or assumption of liabilities.* Unlike §368(a)(1)(C), which explicitly refers to the assumption of the acquired corporation's

---

[35] If the requisite 80 percent control can be obtained in a stock-for-stock transaction, however, it would not be infected by a later purchase of additional shares for cash, if the two transactions are clearly separable. Nor would the reorganization be infected if the dissenters are willing to accept the acquiring corporation's shares but are later redeemed out by the latter, provided the redemption is not part of the original plan of reorganization. See Rev. Rul. 56-345, 1956-2 C.B. 206; Rev. Rul. 57-114, 1957-1 C.B. 122.

As to simultaneous transactions, it has been suggested that an acquisition of 80 percent of the acquired corporation's stock for voting stock and of part or all of the remaining 20 percent for cash would be consistent with §368(a)(1)-(B). This theory is not easily reconciled with the cases cited *supra* note 31; and it becomes even more doubtful when one notes that, if valid, it entails an interpretation of the word "acquisition" that would apparently permit an acquisition of 5 percent of the stock for voting stock to be treated as a Type B reorganization even if the remaining 95 percent was simultaneously purchased for cash.

[36] See Hoboken Land & Improvement Co. v. Commissioner, 138 F.2d 104, 31 AFTR 632 (3rd Cir. 1943); Howard v. Commissioner, 238 F.2d 943, 945-947, 50 AFTR 832 (7th Cir. 1956); see also San Antonio Transit Corp., *supra* note 9; Rev. Rul. 55-440, *supra* note 29; Rev. Rul. 56-184, 1956-1 C.B. 190.

[37] Rev. Rul. 55-59, 1955-1 C.B. 35.

[38] Rubenfeld, Handle expenses, fractional shares, escrows in reorganization with great care, 15 J. Tax. 66 (1961); see also A.B.A. Tax Section Bulletin, Vol. XIX, No. 2 (Jan., 1966), reporting (p. 130) a somewhat restricted Service policy of permitting the acquiring corporation to pay cash in lieu of fractional shares; Mills v. Commissioner, *supra* note 31 (cash in lieu of fractional shares is not additional consideration); Vernava, *supra* note 31, at 397 and 413-415 (1965); Goldman, The C Reorganization, 19 Tax L. Rev. 31, 55, 61, 73 (1963).

liabilities (*infra*, Sec. 12.14), §368(a)(1)(B) makes no mention of liabilities. In most Type B reorganizations, there is no need for any action with regard to the acquired corporation's liabilities, since its creditors simply ride through the reorganization, preserving their claims against the debtor despite the change in ownership of its stock.[39] If the acquiring corporation prefers to assume or refund these obligations, however, the "solely for voting stock" requirement of §368(a)(1)(B) will be violated if the payment or assumption of the liabilities constitutes "boot" under the *Hendler* case.[40] It is arguable that any relations between the acquiring corporation and the acquired corporation's creditors are separable from the stock-for-stock transaction, and that the assumption or payment of such liabilities is not additional consideration for the acquired stock.[41] An assumption or payment of a shareholder's liabilities, on the other hand, would be vulnerable, since such action would ordinarily constitute additional payment for the stock. On the status of stock issued as compensation or a bonus to the exchanging shareholder, see Rev. Rul. 66-112 (*infra* note 43).

4. Expenses. Although it is evidently the Service's practice to rule that stock transfer taxes in a Type B exchange can be paid by the acquiring corporation on the theory that it is jointly liable therefor and hence is not paying any additional consideration to the shareholders of the acquired corporation, rulings often explicitly require the shareholders to pay their own share of the reorganization expenses (e.g., attorneys' fees, accounting expenses, commissions, etc.).[42]

5. Transfer of additional shares. The number of shares to be paid by the acquiring corporation in a Type B exchange is sometimes contingent on future events, e.g., the settlement of a disputed claim against the acquired corporation or the level of its earnings; and shares may be put in escrow pending a determination of the transferor shareholders' right to receive them. The Service evidently concedes that this contingent right to receive additional shares does not violate the "solely for voting stock" requirement (unless evidenced

---

[39] If the acquired corporation is insolvent, however, its creditors may be in effect the sole owners of the proprietary interest therein, so that the acquisition of their claims for voting stock of the acquiring corporation is a Type B reorganization. See Rev. Rul. 59-222, 1959-1 C.B. 80.

[40] See *infra*, Sec. 12.18; §357 does not cover this situation.

[41] The tax treatment of the creditors and the debtor corporation in such a case is obscure; see Rev. Rul. 59-222, *supra* note 39.

[42] See Rubenfeld, *supra* note 38. The A.B.A. Tax Section report cited *supra* note 38, reports that an agreement by the acquiring corporation to pay the costs of SEC registration for the stock issued in a Type B reorganization is not regarded by the Service as disqualifying additional consideration.

by a negotiable instrument),[43] but a portion of the shares, if and when received by the shareholder, may give rise to imputed interest income under §483.

6. *Overlap with Type C reorganization.* If a Type B stock-for-stock acquisition is followed by a prearranged liquidation of the newly acquired subsidiary corporation, these steps have substantially the same effect as a Type A statutory merger or a Type C acquisition of assets for voting stock. Since the stock acquisition is merely an interdependent step in a single plan to obtain the assets of the acquired corporation, it has been held that the transaction constitutes a Type C rather than a Type B reorganization.[44] The principal points at which this difference is felt are: (a) a limited amount of consideration other than voting stock can be used in a Type C reorganization, and there is explicit authority to assume the acquired corporation's liabilities; but (b) "creeping" acquisitions are not permitted (*infra*, Sec. 12.14). The Type B and C definitions also overlap when a holding corporation whose assets consist entirely of stock of a subsidiary transfers the stock to another corporation solely in exchange for the latter's voting stock. The regulations suggest that this would constitute a Type C reorganization,[45] which would have the effects described in the preceding sentence, but there seem to be no rulings or cases in point.

Sec. 12.14.   Acquisitions of property for voting stock (Type C)

A Type C reorganization, defined by §368(a)(1)(C), is an acquisition by one corporation (the "acquiring corporation") of substantially all of the properties of another corporation, in exchange solely for voting stock of the acquiring corporation or its parent or in

---

[43] See Rev. Rul. 66-112, 1966-19 I.R.B., p. 8, acquiescing in the result in James C. Hamrick, *infra* note 65; but warning that the facts "of every delayed stock issuance case . . . will be carefully examined to insure that bona fide business reasons justify not issuing all of the stock immediately, and will also be examined to insure that stock issued as a bonus or compensation to the exchanging shareholders is not treated as received in the exchange."

[44] See Commissioner v. Dana, 103 F.2d 359, 22 AFTR 1071 (3rd Cir. 1939); Goldman, *supra* note 38; see also Regs. §1.382(b)-1(a)(6). This approach is reminiscent of the *Kimbell-Diamond* doctrine (*supra*, Sec. 9.44). As to the acquiring corporation, the liquidation of its newly-acquired subsidiary would be tax-free under §332 (*supra*, Sec. 9.40).

See generally South Bay Corp. v. Commissioner, 345 F.2d 698, 15 AFTR 2d 1059 (2d Cir. 1965); Long Island Water Corp., *supra* note 26.

[45] The suggestion arises by negative inference from Regs. §1.368-2(f), last sentence; if P's stock was S's only asset, S would evidently be treated by the Service as a "party" to the reorganization — but this would be possible under §368(b)(2) only if the exchange is regarded as a Type C reorganization (*i.e.*, "a reorganization resulting from the acquisition by one corporation of stock or properties of another").

exchange for such voting stock and a limited amount of money or other property. Although there are differences in form, a Type C reorganization may have economic consequences substantially the same as Type A (statutory merger or consolidation),[46] but the statute lays down more explicit rules for the Type C reorganization — notably, the fact that the consideration must be voting stock plus, in some instances, a limited amount of money or other property. Type C also has consequences similar to a Type B reorganization (stock for stock) followed by a liquidation of the acquired corporation, but is more flexible in allowing a limited amount of consideration to be used in addition to voting stock.[47] The salient features of §368(a)(1)(C) are:

1. The acquiring corporation must acquire substantially all of the properties of another corporation.

2. The acquisition must be either (a) solely for voting stock of the acquiring corporation or its parent, or (b) solely for such voting stock plus, if certain conditions are met, a limited amount of money or other property.

3. The acquiring corporation may transfer part or all of the acquired assets to a corporation controlled by it.

4. If a transaction meets the requirements of a Type C reorganization but is also described in §368(a)(1)(D) (Type D), it is to be treated as a Type D reorganization.

These requirements are discussed in more detail hereafter.[48]

1. Acquisition of substantially all of the properties of another corporation. The acquiring corporation must, under §368(a)(1)(C), acquire "substantially all of the properties of another corporation." In many instances, the acquiring corporation takes over all of the transferor corporation's assets, without exception, and no problem arises of determining what constitutes "substantially all of the properties." When it becomes necessary to make this determination because the acquiring corporation does not take over all of the assets, it should be remembered that the Type C reorganization was made tax-free to accommodate transactions that had the effect of mergers

---

[46] See George v. Commissioner, 26 T.C. 396 (1956), involving the amalgamation of a Louisiana corporation and a Mississippi corporation into a new Louisiana corporation, which was not a "statutory" consolidation (Type A) because of state law restricting the consolidation of domestic and foreign corporations. The court held, however, that the transaction was a Type C reorganization.

See also Rev. Rul. 56-345, 1956-2 C.B. 206, referring to a §368(a)(1)(C) reorganization as a "practical merger."

[47] On the treatment of transactions that could qualify as either Type B or Type C exchanges, see *supra,* note 44.

[48] See generally Goldman, *supra* note 38.

but could not qualify under §368(a)(1)(A) because for some business reason a statutory merger or consolidation was not feasible. In the light of this history, transactions should not be allowed to qualify as Type C exchanges if they are essentially divisive in character; their proper route is a Type D transaction, which contains restrictions (*infra*, Sec. 12.15) to prevent an end run around §355. Type C transactions, by contrast, should exhibit "merger equivalence."

Although Commissioner v. First Nat'l Bank, 104 F.2d 865, 23 AFTR 119 (3d Cir. 1939), is frequently cited as establishing that 86 percent of total net worth is "substantially all" and Arctic Ice Machine Co. v. Commissioner, 23 B.T.A. 1223 (1931), as establishing that 68 percent is insufficient, a ruling espouses the sounder view that no particular percentage is controlling. Instead, "the nature of the properties retained by the transferor, the purpose of retention, and the amount thereof" are all to be considered. The ruling approved of a retention of cash, accounts receivable, notes, and 3 percent of total inventory, the aggregate value of which was approximately equal to the corporation's liabilities, even though the retained assets amounted (according to the headnote) to 30 percent of the total assets.[49] As a general rule, the percentages of transferred and retained assets are computed by reference to values net of liabilities, rather than gross values.

If the transferor continues in existence after the transfer, as it is entitled to do in a Type C reorganization,[50] and operating assets are retained, either for the purpose of continuing in business or for sale to another purchaser, the "substantially all" requirement may be applied more strictly. Thus, the Service expressly noted in Rev. Rul. 57-518 (*supra*, note 49) that assets could be retained only to pay liabilities, and that any other use (such as sale, investment, or business conduct) might be fatal. The ruling also warned that operating assets could not be retained for the purpose of continuing in business even though such assets were matched by liabilities. The same caveat would be justified if investment assets were retained rather than business assets, in view of the possibility that this would create of achieving a divisive reorganization without running the gauntlet of §368(a)(1)(D) and §355.[51] Moreover, it would also be appropriate

---

[49] Rev. Rul. 57-518, 1957-2 C.B. 253; see also Milton Smith, 34 B.T.A. 702 (1936) (Acq.); Cortland Speciality Co. v. Commissioner, 60 F.2d 937, 11 AFTR 857 (2nd Cir. 1932), cert. denied, 288 U.S. 599 (91 percent of net assets); Schuh Trading Co. v. Commissioner, 95 F.2d 404, 20 AFTR 1114 (7th Cir. 1938) (90-94 percent substantially all).

[50] Helvering v. Minnesota Tea Co., 296 U.S. 378, 16 AFTR 1258 (1935); John A. Nelson Co. v. Helvering, 296 U.S. 374, 16 AFTR 1262 (1935).

[51] A point of similar import is that the transferor's tax attributes ride over

to take account of the *value* of the retained assets, as well as the percentage they represent of the total assets, since a ten million dollar corporation which transfers even 90 percent of its net assets in a putative Type C reorganization still retains a lot of life and should not automatically be deemed to satisfy the "substantially all" requirement of §368(a)(1)(C).

Retention of assets primarily for the purpose of paying off the unassumed liabilities of the transferor, including its reorganization or liquidation expenses, ordinarily is permissible; this transaction is no different in substance from the case where all assets are transferred subject to liabilities and the transferee then pays off the liabilities with part of the acquired assets.[52] Where liabilities are so large, however, that the net assets constitute only a small fraction of the corporation's gross assets, the continuity of interest principle may prevent qualification as a Type C reorganization, on the ground that the shareholders' equity is so thin that the creditors in substance own the proprietary interest in the corporation.[53]

If the transferor corporation is liquidated as part of the reorganization transaction, the courts have been less rigorous in their application of the "substantially all" requirement, especially where the properties retained consist of non-operating assets. See, for example, James Armour, Inc., 43 T.C. 295 (1964), holding that 51 percent of the corporation's assets (consisting of all of its operating assets) was "substantially all" within the meaning of §354(b)(1)(A), where the retained liquid assets were distributed in complete liquidation as part of the plan; and Gross v. Commissioner, 88 F.2d 567, 19 AFTR 158 (5th Cir. 1937), suggesting that the term "properties" is

---

to the transferee in a Type C reorganization by virtue of §381, *infra*, Ch. 13, thus leaving it with a "clean slate" in its earnings and profits account and other tax characteristics as well.

[52] See Rev. Rul. 57-518, *supra* note 49; Rev. Rul. 56-345, *supra* note 35. See also Roosevelt Hotel Co., 13 T.C. 399 (1949) (Acq.); Southland Ice Co., 5 T.C. 842 (1945); Westfir Lumber Co., 7 T.C. 1014 (1946). These cases involved retention of assets to pay claims of dissenting bondholders in a creditor's reorganization; whether they would be equally applicable to claims of dissenting shareholders is unclear. Rev. Rul. 57-518 implies that a distribution to shareholders is not a proper purpose for retention of assets; but where the claims of dissenting shareholders become creditor claims under local law, satisfaction of such obligations may be acceptable. Also, certain private rulings have implicitly sanctioned the retention of assets to pay dissenting shareholder's claims. Compare the problem of retaining assets to pay claims under §337 (*supra*, Sec. 9.64).

Note also Regs. §1.354-1(a), last sentence.

[53] See Rev. Rul. 57-518, *supra* note 49; Civic Center Finance Co. v. Kuhl, 83 F. Supp. 251, 37 AFTR 1273 (E.D. Wis. 1948), aff'd per curiam, 177 F.2d 706, 38 AFTR 835 (7th Cir. 1949); Regs. §1.368-2(d)(1); see also Helvering v. Alabama Asphaltic Limestone Co., *supra* note 16; *infra*, Sec. 12.18.

narrower than "assets" and that it does not include surplus cash that is not needed in the business, could have been paid out as an ordinary cash dividend, and is subsequently distributed as a liquidating dividend pursuant to the reorganization plan.[54]

Whether the acquiring corporation has received "substantially all the properties" of the acquired corporation is ordinarily determined as of the time of the transfer. If the acquiring corporation is not interested in acquiring some of the assets, however, and the unwanted assets are disposed of by the transferor corporation in anticipation of the Type C reorganization transfer, the comparison may be made as of the time the plan was put into action, especially if the anticipatory disposition was tax-free (in which latter case a "divisive" transaction has occurred).[55] For further discussion of this issue, and for the possibility that "stripping" the corporation of unwanted assets may be permissible in Type A and C reorganizations, see *infra*, Sec. 12.20.

These principles may be illustrated by the following examples, in which it is assumed that X Corporation's assets consist of operating assets worth $90 and liquid assets (cash, short term receivables, and investments) worth $30. X Corporation also has $20 of liabilities, so that its net worth is $100.

> (a) If X transfers its operating assets to Y, retaining the liquid assets to discharge its liabilities, the Service probably will rule that the "substantially all" requirement is satisfied, since the assets transferred amount to 90 percent of X's net worth; but the ruling may be conditioned on the liquidation of X.
>
> (b) If X Corporation continues in existence after the transfer, however, the Service may take the view that $30 of retained assets, even though offset by $20 of liabilities, is excessive in view of the divisive effect of the transaction, especially if any operating assets are retained.
>
> (c) If Y assumes X's liabilities in the above examples, the "substantially all" requirement apparently would not be met, since only 70 percent of net assets have been transferred; in general, a transfer of less than 90 percent of the net assets is

[54] See also Commissioner v. First National Bank of Altoona, 104 F.2d 865, 23 AFTR 119 (3rd Cir. 1939), a similar case. But see National Bank of Commerce of Norfolk v. United States, 158 F. Supp. 887, 1 AFTR 2d 894 (E.D. Va. 1958) (retention of 19 percent of operating assets for distribution to shareholders fatal); Rev. Rul. 57-518, *supra* note 49.

[55] See, *e.g.*, Helvering v. Elkhorn Coal Co., 95 F.2d 732, 20 AFTR 1301 (4th Cir. 1937), cert. denied, 305 U.S. 605 (1938), where a prior *tax-free* spin-off of unwanted assets was considered by the court in determining whether the taxpayer had transferred "substantially all of its properties" under the predecessor of §368(a)(1)(C); see also Mellon v. Commissioner, *supra* note 12; Ralph C. Wilson, *infra* note 128.

questionable. But see James Armour, Inc., *supra* (51 percent satisfactory).

(d) If X's liabilities amounted to $100, rather than $20, the transfer of $20 of operating assets, even though constituting 100 percent of X's net worth, arguably would not be considered "substantially all," especially where X continues in existence after the transfer. Either the continuity of interest principle, or the substantial size of the retained assets (which consist of operating properties as well) could, and probably should, defeat Type C reorganization status in this case due to the transaction's lack of "resemblance" to a merger or consolidation.

2. *Consideration paid by the acquiring corporation.* The consideration which can be paid by the acquiring corporation in a Type C reorganization must consist primarily of its own voting stock.[56] There are, however, three exceptions to this rule: (a) since 1954, voting stock of a corporation which is in "control" of the acquiring corporation (*i.e.*, its parent) may be given as alternative consideration for the acquisition; (b) an assumption of the transferor's liabilities by the acquiring corporation (or the acquisition of the properties subject to liabilities) is disregarded in determining whether the acquisition is solely for voting stock; and (c) by virtue of §368(a)(2)-(B) (added in 1954), a limited amount of consideration other than voting stock may be given.

In permitting the use of a parent corporation's voting stock, and in providing in §368(b) that the parent thereby becomes "a party to a reorganization," the intention of the 1954 revisions was to modify the contrary rule of the *Groman* and *Bashford* cases.[57] It should be noted, however, that the regulations provide that voting stock of *either* the acquiring corporation *or* its parent may be used as consideration, but not both.[58] In Rev. Rul. 64-73, 1964-1 C.B. 142, the Service ruled that the assets could be acquired by a wholly-owned sub-subsidiary of the parent corporation whose stock was issued as consideration, on the ground that the 1954 amendments indicated that Congress desired "to remove the [*Groman-Bashford*] continuity-of-interest problem from the section 368(a)(1)(C) reorganization area."

In determining whether the acquisition is "solely" for voting

---

[56] For the meaning of "voting stock," see *supra* note 30.

[57] *Supra*, Sec. 12.11. The parent's status as a "party to a reorganization" becomes important under §354 and §361, *infra*, Secs. 12.32 and 12.34.

[58] Regs. §1.368-2(d)(1). Thus, *Groman* and *Bashford* remain controlling in "split" consideration transactions; but see Rev. Rul. 64-73, *supra*. For more on this problem, see *infra*, Sec. 12.21; Lurie, *supra* note 12; Stinson, Some Subchapter C Trouble Spots — After Two Years, 34 Taxes 890, 894 (1956); Merritt, *supra* note 6, at 915.

stock, §368(a)(1)(C) provides that the assumption of liabilities by the acquiring corporation or the acquisition of properties subject to liabilities shall be disregarded.[59] Note that liabilities are disregarded only in determining whether the exchange is "solely" for stock, and thus in determining whether the transaction constitutes a reorganization; the liabilities may become relevant in the computation of "boot" under §357(b). Moreover, the regulations state that §368(a)-(1)(C) "does not prevent consideration of the effect of an assumption of liabilities on the general character of the transaction" and that an assumption may "so alter the character of the transaction as to place the transaction outside the purposes and assumptions of the reorganization provisions." Regs. §1.368-2(d)(1). This warning may mean that if the net worth of the transferred properties is insignificant, so that the consideration paid is primarily the assumption of indebtedness with only a trivial amount of voting stock to sweeten the bargain, the transaction will fail to qualify as a reorganization for want of a "continuity of interest" on the part of the transferor corporation or its shareholders, as pointed out *supra*, note 53.

In application, the terms "assumption" and "liabilities" as used in §368(a)(1)(C) raise a number of interpretative questions, which are considered *infra*, Sec. 12.18.

Until 1954, voting stock was the sole consideration (aside from assuming liabilities or taking property subject to liabilities) that could be employed by the acquiring corporation in a Type C reorganization; any other consideration would prevent the exchange from qualifying.[60] In 1954, however, §368(a)(2)(B) was enacted to relax this restriction to a very limited degree. Under §368(a)(2)(B), the use of money or other property will not prevent the exchange from qualifying as a Type C reorganization if at least 80 percent of the

---

[59] Although the voting stock of the acquiring corporation's parent may be used in acquiring the properties, apparently the acquiring corporation is the only one that may assume the transferor's liabilities. But if the transferor corporation receives stock of corporation A in exchange for properties that are transferred to Corporation B (a subsidiary of A), is the transaction to be viewed as (a) an acquisition by B in exchange for its parent's stock, so that B is the "acquiring corporation," or (b) an acquisition by A in exchange for its own stock, followed by a transfer of the assets under §368(a)(2)(C) to B, so that A is the "acquiring corporation"? The same problem arises in applying §381 (*infra*, Ch. 13), under which the tax attributes of the transferor corporation are inherited by the "acquiring corporation." See Regs. §1.381(a)-1(b)(2) and (3)(ii).

For the background of this provision, see United States v. Hendler, 303 U.S. 564, 20 AFTR 1041 (1938); Surrey, Assumption of Indebtedness in Tax-Free Exchanges, 50 Yale L.J. 1 (1940); *infra*, Sec. 12.18.

[60] See Helvering v. Southwest Consolidated Corp., *supra* note 31: " 'Solely' leaves no leeway. Voting stock plus some other consideration does not meet the statutory requirement."

fair market value of all of the property of the transferor corporation is acquired for voting stock. Thus, up to 20 percent of the property, by fair market value, may be acquired for money or other property. There are, however, these practical and legal restrictions on the use of §368(a)(2)(B):

a. An error in computing value may be fatal. Thus, if all of the properties of the transferor corporation are thought to be worth $100,000, for which voting stock of the acquiring corporation plus $20,000 of cash is paid, the reorganization will fail to qualify if the properties turn out to be worth less than $100,000.

b. Since at least 80 percent of the fair market value of *all* of the properties of the transferor corporation must be acquired for voting stock, any property that is to be retained by it will reduce the amount of money or other property that may be paid by the acquiring corporation. Thus, assuming properties worth $100,000 of which $15,000 is to be retained, only $5,000 of the transferred assets may be acquired for money or other property.

c. Under the second sentence of §368(a)(2)(B), liabilities assumed by the acquiring corporation (or to which the acquired property is subject) are to be treated as money in determining whether 80 percent of all property is acquired for voting stock. Thus, if the transferor's properties are $100,000 and are subject to liabilities of $17,000, the acquiring corporation could not pay more than $3,000 in money or other property in addition to assuming the liabilities or taking the properties subject to them. In the absence of a ruling to the contrary, contingent liabilities should probably be taken into account for this purpose.

d. Any money or other property used under §368(a)(2)(B) will constitute boot to the transferor corporation, resulting in the recognition of its gain (if any) *pro tanto* under §361(b)(1)(B), unless it is distributed under §361(b)(1)(A), in which event it may produce gain to the transferor's shareholders. But see Regs. §1.361-1, stating that nonvoting stock and securities of the acquiring corporation, used as consideration under §368(a)(2)(B), may be received tax-free.

Because the consideration that may be used by the acquiring corporation in a Type C reorganization is so restricted, even under the 1954 amendment, the acquiring corporation may search out ways to avoid these restrictions. One device would be to acquire only the assets that are essential to its business needs, leaving behind in the transferor corporation cash, marketable securities, accounts receivable, etc. The problem here, as already stated, is that the acquisition might then fail to qualify as a reorganization because less than "substantially all of the properties" would have been acquired. Another possibility is for the transferor corporation to borrow against its properties just before the exchange, and to distribute the borrowed funds; but this too might disqualify the transaction if the distributed funds are treated as part of the transferor's properties in applying the "substantially all" requirement, or if the assumption of such liability is considered a mere substitute for cash boot. Alternatively, the acquiring corporation might buy some of the transferor's assets for cash and then, in an "unrelated" transaction, acquire the balance for voting stock, in the hope that the latter event would be a Type C reorganization. The step transaction doctrine (*infra*, Sec. 12.20) obviously threatens the validity of the allegedly separate "reorganization" in such a case.

Where the acquiring corporation has purchased some of the transferor corporation's *stock* in earlier unrelated transactions (either from those shareholders who desired cash or pro rata from all shareholders), use of §368(a)(1)(C) to acquire the transferor's *properties* may be difficult. If the acquiring corporation has at least 80 percent "control" of the transferor, the latter's assets can be acquired tax-free under §332 (*supra*, Sec. 9.40); but where less than 80 percent control exists, and where the transferor corporation is liquidated, the acquiring corporation may be held to have have acquired part of the transferor's assets in "liquidation," rather than solely for voting stock, so as to render §368(a)(1)(C) inapplicable.[61] If the transferor is kept alive for business reasons, or merged with the acquiring corporation in a Type A statutory merger, this danger may be avoided; another possibility is the interposition of a controlled subsidiary of the acquiring corporation.[62] Finally, if the acquiring corporation owns 20 percent or less of the transferor's stock, its acquisition of the assets may qualify as a Type C reorganization on the ground that the "other property" (i.e., the previously purchased stock) used to acquire its proportionate share of the assets comes within the "boot relaxation" rule of §368-(a)(2)(B).

3. *Transfer of part or all of acquired assets to a subsidiary.* Under §368(a)(2)(C), a transaction that is otherwise a Type C reorganization does not forfeit its status as such because the acquiring cor-

---

[61] See Bausch & Lomb Optical Co. v. Commissioner, 267 F.2d 75, 3 AFTR 2d 1497 (2d Cir. 1959); Grede Foundries, Inc. v. United States, 202 F. Supp. 263, 9 AFTR 2d 1305 (D.C. Wis. 1962).

[62] These possibilities are discussed in more detail *infra*, Sec. 12.21; see also Rev. Rul. 57-278, 1957-1 C.B. 124 (interposition of subsidiary as acquiring corporation); *supra*, Sec. 12.13 (re "creeping acquisitions").

See generally Seplow, Acquisition of Assets of a Subsidiary: Liquidation or Reorganization? 73 Harv. L. Rev. 484 (1960); Fager, The Acquisition of Partly-Held Corporations, 18 N.Y.U. Inst. on Fed. Tax. 799 (1960).

poration transfers part or all of the assets to a corporation controlled by it. This provision was new in 1954, and it is a corollary of the 1954 change (*supra*) under which a parent corporation's stock may be used as the consideration in a Type C reorganization. It is now possible for a corporation to acquire assets in exchange for its parent's stock, for the parent to acquire the assets for its own stock and then transfer them to a subsidiary, or for a corporation to acquire assets for its parent's stock and transfer them to a subsidiary.[63]

4. Overlap of Type C and Type D reorganizations. A reorganization may qualify under both §368(a)(1)(C) and §368(a)(1)(D), *e.g.*, a transfer by one corporation of all of its assets to a second corporation in exchange for all of the second corporation's voting stock, if the first corporation thereafter distributes the second corporation's stock pursuant to the plan of reorganization in a transaction under §354, §355, or §356. Under §368(a)(2)(A), such a reorganization is to be treated as a Type D reorganization. This provision, which is designed to preserve the integrity of §355 and presumably applies even if the transferor fails to make a qualified distribution of the controlled corporation's stock, is discussed *infra*, Sec. 12.15.[64]

Sec. 12.15   Transfers of assets to controlled corporations (Type D)

A Type D reorganization, as defined by §368(a)(1)(D), is a transfer by a corporation of all or part of its assets to a corporation controlled (immediately after the transfer)[65] by the transferor or its shareholders, but only if stock or securities of the controlled corporation are distributed in pursuance of the plan of reorganization by the transferor corporation in a transaction which qualifies under §354-356. As will be seen, the principal transactions that will qualify as Type D reorganizations, as a result of changes in 1954, are:

---

[63] See also Rev. Rul. 58-93, 1958-1 C.B. 188 (§368(a)(2)(C) permits assets to be transferred directly to subsidiary, without passing through hands of parent corporation); §368(b) (third sentence) (acquiring corporation is "a party to a reorganization" even though it transfers the assets to a subsidiary); and discussion *infra*, Sec. 12.21.

See *supra* note 59, on the problem of determining which of several corporations is the "acquiring corporation."

[64] See also Goldman, *supra* note 38, at 39.

[65] For the meaning of the requirement that control exist "immediately after the transfer," see *supra*, Sec. 3.09; Ericsson Screw Machine Prod. Co., 14 T.C. 757 (1950); Maine Steel, Inc. v. United States, *supra* note 13; James Hamrick, 43 T.C. 21 (1964) (Acq.); Burr Oaks Corp., 43 T.C. 635 (1965). Compare Rev. Rul. 59-222, 1959-1 C.B. 80; and Rev. Rul. 59-296, 1959-2 C.B. 87. See also the discussion *supra*, Sec. 12.11. Where creditors are shareholders as well, courts have generally found the requisite control to be present; Darrell, *supra* note 6.

a. A transfer by one corporation of substantially all of its assets to a controlled corporation, followed by a complete liquidation of the transferor corporation.

b. A transfer by one corporation of part of its assets to a controlled corporation, followed by a distribution of the controlled corporation's stock in a spin-off, split-off, or split-up under §355 (*supra*, Ch. 11).

1. Continuity of interest aspects. Section 368(a)(1)(D) permits the acquired assets to be transferred to a corporation controlled by the transferor corporation, by one or more of its shareholders (including persons who were shareholders immediately before the transfer), or by any combination thereof. The parenthetical clause of §368(a)-(1)(D) was added in 1954 (as explained *supra*, Sec. 11.13), to permit the transfer of assets to a corporation as a preliminary to a non-pro rata split-off or split-up, under which the transferee corporation is controlled, after the division, by persons who were, but no longer are, shareholders of the transferor corporation; and Regs. §1.368-1(b) takes note of this provision by implying that Type D reorganizations are not subject to the continuity of interest requirement in the same way as other reorganizations. While the purpose of the 1954 change was to permit corporate divisions under §355 in which the shareholders of the old corporation part company and go their separate ways, it would be a mistake to assume that the continuity of interest requirement has been wholly obliterated in Type D reorganizations. Thus, assume a transfer by Corporation A (owned 99 percent by X and 1 percent by Y) of all of its property to Corporation B (owned 100 percent by Y) in exchange for bonds of B, followed by a complete liquidation of Corporation A. The transaction meets the literal requirements of a Type D reorganization, in that assets were transferred by a corporation (A) to a second corporation (B) which was controlled, immediately after the transfer, by a person (Y) who was previously a shareholder of the transferor (A), and securities of the transferee (B) were distributed by A in a transaction meeting the requirements of §354(b) and §356.[66] Since X, who owned indirectly 99 percent of the assets of Corporation A, receives nothing but bonds of B, the transaction ought to be treated as a sale under *LeTulle* v. *Scofield, supra,* Sec. 12.11, rather than as a tax-free reorganization.

---

[66] A possible infirmity arises under §356 from the fact that A did not distribute any non-recognition property along with the boot (see *infra*, notes 92 and 94); this omission, if relevant, could be corrected if B gave A an insignificant amount of stock along with the bonds as consideration for the assets.

Even though the transferors *in the aggregate* maintain a continuing interest in the transferee, some of them may drop out of the proprietary category. Thus, some shareholders may receive stock in the continuing corporation, but others may receive securities, cash, or other property. Assuming that the old shareholders as a group receive or retain enough stock to satisfy the "control" requirement, is the reorganization vulnerable because some of the shareholders have lost their proprietary interest? As pointed out *supra*, Sec. 12.11, the courts have been rather tolerant of exchanges in which dissenting shareholders are bought out, but a transaction in which only a few of the shareholders retain an interest in the enterprise is more vulnerable than one in which only a few drop out.

When a financially distressed corporation is reorganized, the creditors may become the sole owners of the reorganized corporation; if so, the proprietary interest of the old shareholders is wiped out, not continued. In Helvering v. Alabama Asphaltic Limestone Co. (*supra* note 16), it was held that the creditors, upon instituting bankruptcy proceedings, "had effective command over the disposition of the property" and that this was the equivalent of a proprietary interest; since this interest was continued in the reorganized corporation, the continuity of interest doctrine was satisfied despite the elimination of the shareholders. Whether these creditors obtain the status of "shareholders," so as to satisfy the "control" requirements of §368(a)(1)-(D), however, is unclear.

2. Distribution requirement. The definition of a Type D reorganization was changed in 1954 in another and even more important respect, by the addition of the requirement that stock or securities of the transferee corporation must be "distributed [by the transferor] in a transaction which qualifies under section 354, 355 or 356.[67] If the distribution of stock or securities is to qualify under these provisions, it will have to meet one of the following sets of conditions:

> a. *To qualify under §354* (or under §354 in conjunction with §356), the transaction will have to satisfy the requirements of §354(b), also enacted in 1954, under which the transferee must acquire "substantially all of the assets of the transferor"[68] and

[67] Ordinarily the transferor will have received stock or securities of the transferee in the reorganization itself; but this does not seem essential, since §368(a)(1)(D) is broad enough to reach a contribution to the capital of the controlled corporation. If the reorganization takes this form, the stock or securities to be distributed will be those already owned by the transferor.

[68] The phrase "substantially all of the assets" as used in §354(b) has been, somewhat surprisingly, interpreted more flexibly than the phrase "substantially all of the properties" in §368(a)(1)(C). See James Armour, Inc., 43 T.C. 295 (1964) (51 percent held "substantially all" for this purpose); Ralph C. Wilson, *infra* note 128; and discussion *supra*, Sec. 12.14.

the transferor in turn must distribute all of its properties (the stock, securities, and other property received in the reorganization, as well as its other properties) in pursuance of the plan of reorganization.[69] For the retention of assets by the transferor to pay its debts, see Regs. §1.354-1(a)(2).

Although §354(b) does not explicitly require a complete liquidation of the transferor, the requisite distribution of all of the transferor's properties will have the effect of a complete liquidation (*supra*, Sec. 9.04).[69a] Moreover, since "substantially all of the assets of the transferor" will be held by the transferee corporation, the transaction is similar to a mere reincorporation (a Type F reorganization, *infra*, Sec. 12.17) or, if the capital structure of the transferee is different from that of the transferor, the transaction will have the effect of a recapitalization (Type E, *infra*, Sec. 12.16).

b. *To qualify under §355* (or under §355 in conjunction with §356), the transaction will have to meet the standards of that section, discussed in detail *supra*, Ch. 11.

It will be noted that a Type D reorganization that meets the conditions of §354(b) will not be a vehicle for splitting the corporate assets between two corporations — and hence it cannot be used to circumvent the painfully worked-out rules governing corporate divisions under §355. It is ironic to find that in amending §368 in 1954 in order to protect the integrity of §355, however, Congress materially reduced its effectiveness in combatting the "reincorporation" device, as will be seen in the discussion *infra*, Sec. 12.22.

Section 368(a)(1)(D) speaks of a transfer by a corporation of "all or *a part* of its assets to another corporation." This language must be read in the light of the requirement of a distribution qualifying under §354 or §355, however, with the result that a transfer of "part" of the assets will be a "reorganization" only if there is a §355 division; if the distribution is to qualify under §354 rather than under §355, there must be a transfer of "substantially all of the assets of the transferor."[70]

3. Overlap problems. Before 1954, there was a large area of overlap between §351 (*supra*, Ch. 3) and the Type D reorganization, in that a parent corporation's transfer of part of its property to a newly

---

[69] In a sense, §368(a)(1)(D) and §354(b) are circular, since a transaction is a "reorganization" under §368(a)(1)(D) only if the accompanying distribution qualifies under §354(b), but §354(b) applies only to "an exchange in pursuance of a plan of reorganization within the meaning of §368(a)(1)(D)." The two provisions are not in conflict, however, and a transfer of substantially all the assets of one corporation to a controlled corporation followed by a distribution by the transferor of all of its assets, will satisfy both provisions simultaneously.

[69a] See David T. Grubbs, *infra*, Sec. 12.22.

[70] See Rev. Rul. 57-465, 1957-2 C.B. 250.

organized subsidiary was both a §351 exchange and a Type D reorganization. Now that a Type D reorganization requires a distribution under §354 or §355, however, the overlap has been much reduced; and most transfers to subsidiary corporations will now qualify simply as §351 exchanges.

Mention has already been made of §368(a)(2)(A), providing that a transaction "described" both in §368(a)(1)(C) (Type C reorganizations) and §368(a)(1)(D) (Type D) shall be "treated as described only in" §368(a)(1)(D). The announced purpose of this provision, enacted in 1954, was "to insure that the tax consequences of the distribution of stocks or securities to shareholders or security holders in connection with divisive reorganizations will be governed by the requirements of section 355 relating to [the] distribution of stock of a controlled corporation." S. Rep. No. 1622, 83d Cong., 2d Sess. 274 (1954). The abuse against which §368(a)(2)(A) is aimed seems obscure, however, since a Type C reorganization, in which "substantially all of the properties" of a corporation are placed in another corporation in exchange for voting stock, may not lend itself to a divisive reorganization any more readily than a Type D reorganization that meets the test of §354(b) (transfer of substantially all assets to a transferee corporation followed by a distribution in liquidation by the transferor of all of its property). The effect of §368(a)(2)(A) is equally obscure, since a Type C reorganization that does *not* meet the tests of Type D reorganization may be unaffected by §368(a)(2)-(A), while one that does meet these tests does not seem to be restricted in any way by being treated as exclusively a Type D reorganization.[71] Possibly §368(a)(2)(A) was intended to exclude from Type C any transfer of assets by one corporation to a corporation controlled by the transferor or its shareholders (i.e., any transfer described in the first part of §368(a)(1)(D)), so that such a transaction could qualify as a "reorganization" only if it also satisfied the second part of §368(a)(1)(D); but the language is not well chosen to accomplish this result.

It is worthy of note that, although §368(a)(1)(D) displaces §368(a)(1)(C) where they overlap, §368(a)(1)(D) may in turn be displaced by §368(a)(1)(F) if the reorganization qualifies both as a Type D and a Type F transaction.[72]

---

§[71] 357(c) (taxing the excess of liabilities over adjusted basis as gain) is applicable to Type D reorganizations but not to other types. There is no reason to think that §368(a)(2)(A) was intended to have any bearing on this area; in any event, a reorganization meeting the requirements of both Type C and Type D would probably have been subject to §357(c) even in the absence of §368(a)(2)(A).

[72] See Rev. Rul. 57-276, *infra*, Sec. 12.17.

Sec. 12.16   Recapitalizations (Type E)

Although a "recapitalization" has been a form of "reorganization" since the latter term received its first statutory definition in the Revenue Act of 1921, the scope of "recapitalization" remains cloudy to this day. An early administrative ruling adopted the view of *Cook on Corporations* that a "recapitalization" is "an arrangement whereby the stock and bonds of the corporation are readjusted as to amount, income, or priority, or an agreement of all stockholders and creditors to change and increase or decrease the capitalization or debts of the corporation or both," and the Supreme Court has said, more briefly, that the term connotes "reshuffling of a capital structure within the framework of an existing corporation."[73]

Although these definitions leave many questions unanswered, they seem to confine the term "recapitalization" to the readjustment of the financial structure of a single corporation;[74] and this in turn means that a characterization of the event for tax purposes is ordinarily important only to the persons who have exchanged their stock or securities for other stock or securities. The corporation itself does not ordinarily receive property (other than the surrendered stock or securities) in a recapitalization, and hence is not confronted by any problems of basis; and, since its existence is not terminated, its tax attributes (earnings and profits, loss carryovers, accounting methods, etc.) are not affected by the exchange. This is why §381 (*infra*, Ch. 13) does not refer to a Type E reorganization; since there is no "acquiring corporation" in a recapitalization, there is no need to provide affirmatively for a preservation of tax attributes.[75] A recapitalization can be a method of shifting the ownership of stock in the corporation, however, and it is therefore surprising that the limitations on the net operating loss carryover imposed by §382(a) (change of stock ownership by "purchase" coupled with abandonment of trade or business) and by §382(b) (change of stock ownership in certain reorganizations) are not applicable to recapitalizations.[76]

---

[73] S.M. 3710, IV-1 C.B. 4 (1925), quoted with approval in United Gas Improvement Co. v. Commissioner, 142 F.2d 216, 32 AFTR 564 (3d Cir. 1944), cert. denied, 323 U.S. 739; Helvering v. Southwest Consolidated Corp., *supra* note 31.

[74] An exception might be made for a liquidation followed by a prearranged reincorporation, which might be treated as a recapitalization (*infra*, Sec. 12.22), but even here, the "new" corporation might be regarded not as a second entity, but as a reincarnation of the original corporation.

[75] Since the recapitalized corporation is not dependent upon §381, it retains all of its tax attributes, not merely those listed in §381(c). See Rev. Rul. 54-482, 1954-2 C.B. 148.

[76] *Infra*, Ch. 13; but see §269.

The vague definitions of "recapitalization" that are quoted above have been filled in to some extent by the examples in Regs. §1.368-2-(e), a number of litigated cases, and some rulings. For convenience, the exchanges that may (or may not) be recapitalizations are classified in the discussion which follows by reference to the type of instrument surrendered and the type received. Unless otherwise stated, it is assumed that the transaction serves a business purpose.

1. Exchanges of stock for stock. The regulations provide that the surrender for cancellation of 25 percent of a corporation's preferred stock in exchange for its no par value common is a recapitalization, as well as the converse, a surrender of common in exchange for preferred. Regs. §1.368-2(e)(2) and (3); see also (4).

Since these transactions are recapitalizations under §368(a)-(1)(E), the shareholder on exchanging his preferred stock for common (or vice versa) recognizes neither gain nor loss under §354, provided the exchange is "in pursuance of the plan of reorganization." Ordinarily the requirement of a "plan" will create no difficulty. If preferred stock is issued with a conversion privilege, however, so that the exchange represents no more than an isolated decision by the shareholder to exercise his privilege, it may be that the transaction is not a recapitalization or that, even if it is, the exchange is not "in pursuance of the plan of reorganization." See Rev. Rul. 54-65, 1954-1 C.B. 101. But the Internal Revenue Service has ruled that the exchange of a bond for preferred stock, pursuant to a conversion privilege contained in the bond when it was issued, is not an occasion for recognizing gain or loss. Although the theory of the ruling (no "closed transaction") is not entirely persuasive, it has been recently reaffirmed; and the exchange of preferred stock for common should qualify a *fortiori* for nonrecognition of gain or loss.[77] If preferred is converted into common, the shareholder will hardly care whether the nonrecognition of gain or loss is premised on the reorganization provisions of the Code or on the rulings just cited. If common is exchanged for preferred under a conversion privilege,[78] however, some or all of the preferred received by the shareholder might be section 306 stock (*supra,* Ch. 8) by virtue of §306(c)(1)(B) (stock received "in pursuance of a plan of reorganization," etc.) if the exchange is a recapitalization; if it is not a recapitalization, the preferred would be

[77] G.C.M. 18436, 1937-1 C.B. 101; Rev. Rul. 57-535, 1957-2 C.B. 513; but see Rev. Rul. 54-65, *supra;* Rev. Rul. 56-179, 1956-1 C.B. 187.

See generally Fleischer and Cary, *supra* note 2.

[78] A privilege to convert common into preferred may be possible as a matter of corporate law, though it would be unusual. See §306(e)(2).

section 306 stock only if the exchange could be treated as a stock dividend under §306(c)(1)(A), which would require some stretching of the statutory language.

Although the regulations are concerned mainly with exchanges of preferred for common and vice versa, an exchange of common for common or preferred for preferred could equally well qualify as a recapitalization.[78a] Exchanges of this type may also come within §1036, providing that gain and loss shall go unrecognized if common stock is exchanged for common stock of the same corporation, or preferred for preferred. Although §1036 may have been intended primarily to apply to exchanges among shareholders, the regulations state that it is also applicable to exchanges between shareholders and the corporation, and that it thus overlaps §368(e)(1)(E). Regs. §1.1036-1(a).

Finally, the regulations provide that an exchange of stock for stock may constitute a recapitalization even though the shareholder gives up preferred stock with dividend arrearages and receives stock in discharge of the arrears as well as in exchange for the stock surrendered. Regs. §1.368-2(e)(5). This example is in harmony with a statement in the Senate Report on the 1954 Code, which in turn rests on case law.[79] Since §305(b)(1) provides that a stock dividend discharging preference dividends for the current or preceding taxable year is taxable (*supra*, Sec. 5.62), however, the regulations limit the use of a recapitalization to clear up such arrears. The restriction is that a recapitalization *solely* for the purpose of discharging such arrears shall be treated as a §305(b)(1) distribution *pro tanto*.

2. *Exchanges of bonds for stock.* Turning to exchanges of securities for stock, we find that one of the examples given by the regulations to illustrate the meaning of "recapitalization" is a discharge by a corporation of outstanding bonds with preferred stock instead of cash. Regs. §1.368-2(e)(1). The transaction would presumably qualify just as easily if common were issued for the bonds, or if the instruments given up were debentures, long-term notes, or other securities.[80] Moreover, the recapitalization is tax-free in its entirety even though interest is in arrears on the securities given up and part of the stock received is in discharge of the arrears; the courts so far have

[78a] See Rev. Rul. 54-482, 1954-2 C.B. 148 (common for common); Rev. Rul. 56-586, 1956-2 C.B. 214 (preferred for preferred).
[79] S. Rept. No. 1622, 83d Cong., 2d sess., p. 44; South Atlantic Steamship Line v. Commissioner, 42 B.T.A 705 (1940); Skenandoa Rayon Corp v. Commissioner, 122 F.2d 268, 27 AFTR 837 (2d Cir. 1941).
[80] Although the definitional section, §368(a)(1)(E), does not require the use of securities, so that theoretically a recapitalization could involve short-term notes or open account indebtedness, the operative provision, §354, is more restrictive (*infra*, Sec. 12.34).

refused to divide the exchange into a tax-free recapitalization coupled with a taxable payment of interest, or to treat the instrument surrendered as a "security" (to the extent of the principal amount) and as a separate claim that does not constitute a "security" (to the extent of the interest arrears).[81]

The corporation, on recapitalizing, may be able to pay off its creditors with stock worth less than the principal amount of the securities surrendered by them. At one time, the government argued that the spread represented income on the cancellation of indebtedness, taxable to the corporation under §61(a)(12). The Service has ruled, however, that the "substitution of common stock for debentures and unsecured claims does not effect a cancellation, reduction or discharge of indebtnedness, but rather amounts to a transformation from a fixed indebtedness to a capital stock liability." Although concerned primarily with whether there was a cancellation within the meaning of §270 of the Bankruptcy Act, these rulings seem equally applicable to §61(a)(12).[82]

3. Exchanges of bonds for bonds. For some years, the Internal Revenue Service held the view that an exchange of outstanding bonds (or other "securities") for new securities, if not accompanied by a modification of the corporation's stock structure, was a "refinancing" rather than a "recapitalization." This theory escaped challenge until 1941, perhaps because most such exchanges during the 1930's produced losses which, under the Service's view, could be deducted unless barred by §1091 (wash sales). In 1941, however, the

---

[81] Commissioner v. Carman, 189 F.2d 363, 40 AFTR 703 (2d Cir. 1951), in which the government acquiesced, 1954-2 C.B. 3, after losing Bernstein's Estate, 22 T.C. 1364 (1954), and several other cases on this point; see also Rev. Rul. 59-98, 1959-1 C.B. 76.

[82] Rev. Rul. 59-222, 1959-1 C.B. 80; G.C.M. 25277, 1947-1 C.B. 44; see also Tower Building Corp., 6 T.C. 125 (1946); Commissioner v. Capento Securities Corp., 140 F.2d 382, 32 AFTR 56 (1st Cir. 1944). On the tax consequences to the corporation of a forgiveness of interest in the course of a recapitalization, see Rev. Rul. 58-546, 1958-2 C.B. 143; Eustice, Cancellation of Indebtedness and the Federal Income Tax: A Problem of Creeping Confusion, 14 Tax L. Rev. 225, 238ff (1959).

The corporation would in any event have two other strings to its bow: §354 (though the court in the *Capento* case, *supra,* reserved judgment on whether this provision applies to the reorganized corporation, or only to its shareholders and security holders); and §1032 (whose language might be applied to the transaction described, although it was enacted for quite a different purpose, *supra,* Sec. 3.15). It is also possible that the transaction would come within one of the exceptions to the general principle that income is recognized on the cancellation of indebtedness for less than its face amount. See Eustice, *supra;* see also, as to a discharge of indebtedness in bankruptcy proceedings, Regs. §1.61-12(b).

The "imputed interest" provisions of §483 must also be considered in assessing the tax consequences of a bond-for-stock recapitalization.

Board of Tax Appeals rejected the Service's theory, and its judgment was affirmed by the Court of Appeals for the Second Circuit in Commissioner v. Neustadt's Trust, 131 F.2d 528, 30 AFTR 320 (2d Cir. 1942):

> The Commissioner contends that only a change in authorized or outstanding capital stock of a corporation can properly be denominated a recapitalization or a reshuffling of the capital structure. He describes an exchange of old debentures for new debentures in the same corporation as a mere financing operation. . . . But in common financial parlance the long term funded debt of a corporation is usually regarded as forming part of its capital structure. . . . By changing the interest rate and date of maturity of its old bonds and adding a conversion option to the holders of the new, the corporation could strengthen its financial condition, while the bondholders would not substantially change their original investments by making the exchange. "Recapitalization" seems a most appropriate word to describe that type of reorganization and it is the very kind of transaction where Congress meant the recognition of gain or loss to be held in suspense until a more substantial change in the taxpayer's original investment should occur. (131 F.2d at 529-30.)

After losing several other cases on this point, the Internal Revenue Service acquiesced in *Neustadt's Trust* and revoked its earlier rulings to the contrary.[83]

It should be noted that if in an exchange of securities for new securities, the principal amount of the securities received exceeds the principal amount of those surrendered, the fair market value of the excess is "boot" under §354(a)(2)(A) and §356(d)(2)(B). The taxpayer's gain, if any, would be recognized to the extent of the "boot," and would be taxed as capital gain (if the bonds are capital assets in his hands) under §356(a)(1) and (2), since the transaction does not have "the effect of the distribution of a dividend." Even if the excess principal amount is a method of discharging arrears in interest on the bonds, the bondholder's gain would probably be capital gain rather than ordinary income; although the *Carman* case, *supra* note 81, is not squarely in point, its amalgamation of the bondholder's claim for interest with his claim for principal is not conducive to a separation of the two under §356(a)(1) and (2).[84]

4. *Exchanges of stock for bonds.* The most controversial problem

---

[83] I.T. 4081, 1952-1 C.B. 65.

But see Emery v. Commissioner, *supra* note 3, holding that the bonds of municipal corporations do not come within §368(a)(1)(E), on the ground that Congress could not have intended this result.

[84] See *infra*, Sec. 12.34; and note also §483 in this regard.

in the recapitalization area is the exchange of stock for bonds (or other securities), and the heart of the problem can be quickly illustrated. Assume a prosperous one-man corporation, with only common stock outstanding. If the corporation declares a dividend of its own bonds, debentures, or other securities, the shareholder will realize ordinary income in an amount equal to the fair market value of the bonds, assuming sufficient earnings and profits. Can the same transaction be turned into a "recapitalization" by having the shareholder surrender his stock in exchange for a package consisting of new stock with a different par value (or with other changes) plus bonds? Even if the exchange is a recapitalization, of course, the bonds would constitute boot under §354(a)(2)(B) and §356(d). But if the shareholder realizes no gain on the exchange (because his stock has a higher basis than the value of the stock and bonds received), or if his gain is relatively small,[85] the "recapitalization" — if it can be so characterized — will enable him to bail out earnings and profits at the capital gain rate by selling the bonds or causing the corporation to retire them under §1232(a)(1).[86]

In Bazley v. Commissioner, 331 U.S. 737, 35 AFTR 1190 (1947), the Supreme Court held that an exchange by the shareholders of a family corporation of all of its common stock (1,000 shares, with a total par value of $100,000) for 5,000 shares of new common stock with no par value but an aggregate stated value of $300,000 plus debenture bonds (payable in ten years but callable at any time) of a principal amount of $400,000 was not a "recapitalization," as that term is used in §368(a)(1)(E):

> [Recapitalization] is one of the forms of reorganization which obtains the privileges afforded by [§368(a)]. Therefore, "recapitalization" must be construed with reference to the presuppositions and purpose of [§368(a)]. It was not the purpose of the reorganization provision to exempt from payment of a tax what as a practical matter is realized gain. Normally, a distribution by a corporation, whatever form it takes, is a definite and rather unambiguous event. It furnishes the proper occasion for the determination and taxation of gain. But there are circumstances

[85] Before the enactment in 1954 of §354(a)(2)(B), gain would not have been recognized — *if* the transaction qualified as a reorganization — no matter how low the shareholder's basis for his stock was.

[86] We have previously seen the advantages of using some bonds or other securities in the corporation's original capital structure (*supra*, Ch. 4). The question now is whether a going concern can distribute bonds in a wholly or partly tax-free recapitalization so as to remedy the failure, deliberate or inadvertent, to issue bonds when it was organized. For a parallel, see the *Chamberlin* case, *supra*, Ch. 8 which brought on the enactment of §306 to close off the use of preferred stock dividends for a bailout of earnings and profits.

where a formal distribution, directly or through exchange of securities, represents merely a new form of the previous participation in an enterprise involving no change of substance in the rights and relations of the interested parties one to another or to the corporate assets. As to these, Congress has said that they are not to be deemed significant occasions for determining taxable gain. . . .

No doubt there was a recapitalization of the Bazley corporation in the sense that the symbols that represented its capital were changed, so that the fiscal basis of its operations would appear very differently on its books. But the form of a transaction as reflected by correct corporate accounting opens questions as to the proper application of a taxing statute; it does not close them. Corporate accounting may represent that correspondence between change in the form of capital structure and essential identity in fact which is of the essence of a transaction relieved from taxation as a reorganization. What is controlling is that a new arrangement intrinsically partake of the elements of reorganization which underlie the Congressional exemption and not merely give the appearance of it to accomplish a distribution of earnings. In the case of a corporation which has undistributed earnings, the creation of new corporate obligations which are transferred to stockholders in relation to their former holdings, so as to produce, for all practical purposes, the same result as a distribution of cash earnings of equivalent value, cannot obtain tax immunity because cast in the form of a recapitalization-reorganization. . . .

What have we here? No doubt, if the Bazley corporation had issued the debentures to Bazley and his wife without any recapitalization, it would have made a taxable distribution. Instead, these debentures were issued as part of a family arrangement, the only additional ingredient being an unrelated modification of the capital account. The debentures were found to be worth at least their principal amount, and they were virtually cash because they were callable at the will of the corporation which in this case was the will of the taxpayer. One does not have to pursue the motives behind actions, even in the more ascertainable forms of purpose, to find, as did the Tax Court, that the whole arrangement took this form instead of an outright distribution of cash or debentures, because the latter would undoubtedly have been taxable income whereas what was done could, with a show of reason, claim the shelter of the immunity of a recapitalization-reorganization. (331 U.S. at 740-3.)

Although the result in the *Bazley* case — dividend income in an amount equal to the fair market value of the debentures — is clear enough, the Court gave so many reasons for the result that the case's ambit is quite uncertain. The theory that the debentures produced "for all practical purposes, the same result as a distribution of cash earnings of equivalent value" would seem to condemn any recapitalization in which securities are received pro rata by shareholders, if the securities are marketable or if the corporation's finanical status permits an immediate retirement. The statement that the debentures "were virtually cash because they were callable at the will of the corporation which was in this case the will of the taxpayer"[87] seems to rest on the corporation's liquid asset position, coupled with a unity of interest that might not exist if the stock was widely held or divided evenly among two or more unrelated persons. The theory that the transaction was simply an ordinary distribution of debentures disguised as a recapitalization suggests the possibility that a business reason for the exchange of stock might have helped to validate the distribution of the debentures. This theory also seems applicable only if securities are received by holders of *common* stock, since an exchange of *preferred* for securities could not ordinarily be effected by the dividend route. Finally, the emphasis in *Bazley* on the pro rata character of the transaction suggests that a distribution that is not pro rata would be less vulnerable, at least if the shareholders are not bound together by family ties.[88]

Recapitalizations in which shareholders get securities on a pro rata basis have been on the decline since the *Bazley* case, not only because its rationale is menacingly uncertain, but also because an exchange that slips by *Bazley* must still run the gauntlet of §354(a)-(2)(B) and §356, under which the fair market value of the bonds is "boot" even if the transaction qualifies as a recapitalization.[89] Although "boot" is troublesome only if the taxpayer enjoys a gain on the exchange, see §356(a)(1), this condition is ordinarily present in the case of the closely-held corporation that wishes to engage in this

---

[87] It is not clear whether the Court meant that the debentures were not "securities," a holding that would have important ramifications in such other areas as §351 exchanges (*supra*, Sec. 3.03). It should be noted that there might be a "recapitalization" even though the new claims against the corporation did not constitute "securities" under §354. See L. & E. Stirn, Inc. v. Commissioner, 107 F.2d 390, 23 AFTR 892 (2d Cir. 1939).

[88] See Davis v. Penfield, 205 F.2d 798, 44 AFTR 151 (5th Cir. 1953), involving an exchange of preferred stock for debentures, where *Bazley* was distinguished on various grounds, including the more public character of the corporation and the fact that the debentures were no more marketable than the preferred stock given up. To the same effect is Berner v. United States, 282 F.2d 623, 6 AFTR 2d 5603 (Ct. Cl. 1960).

[89] The *Bazley* opinion suggested, as an alternative basis for decision, that the debentures were "boot" under pre-1954 law. Since §354(a)(2) was not then in force, the Court must have meant that the debentures were the equivalent of cash. Even so, they would have been taxable as a dividend only to the extent that the taxpayer realized a gain on the exchange, by virtue of §112(c) of the 1939 Code, and the Tax Court in *Bazley*, 4 T.C. 897 (1945), did not determine the amount of the taxpayer's gain, if any.

kind of "recapitalization,"[90] and earnings and profits are likely to be large enough to result in dividend treatment under §356(a)(2) for the entire value of the securities. Thus, *Bazley* and the 1954 statutory changes have made the pro rata exchange of common stock for new common stock and bonds an unpopular method of recapitalizing corporations.

There may still be some room, however, for an exchange of stock for securities on a non-pro rata basis. Thus, in Daisy Seide, 18 T.C. 502 (1952), the Tax Court held that *Bazley* did not apply to an exchange of preferred stock for debentures, where the preferred was not held in proportion to the common,[91] and where the debentures were not readily marketable or likely to be retired at an early date because of the corporation's poor earnings record and obsolete plant. See also Wolf Envelope Co., 17 T.C. 471 (1951) (N-A). Such an exchange might be a recapitalization under the 1954 Code, but there are two obstacles to the tax-free treatment it enjoyed under the 1939 Code: (1) Since the shareholders received *only* securities for their stock, §354 would be inapplicable to the exchange;[92] and (2) even if §354 is applicable, the debentures would constitute "boot," with the result that the shareholder's gain (if any) would be recognized to the extent of their fair market value. It should be noted that if a non pro rata exchange fails for any reason to qualify as a recapitalization, the participating shareholders do not necessarily realize dividend income: the transaction is in substance a redemption of their stock, which may produce capital gain or loss if the conditions of §302(b)(1), (2), or (3) are satisfied.[93]

5. *Continuity of interest in recapitalizations.* The consideration that may be used in a Type E reorganization is left unregulated by the statutory definition, but there is authority for the proposition that a

[90] The principal exception would be a corporation whose stock has been inherited recently so that the shareholder has a stepped-up basis under §1014 equal to the stock's fair market value.

[91] All the stock was held by two families; if each family was considered as a unit, the preferred shares (and hence the debentures received in exchange for the preferred) were held pro rata. The court, however, looked to individual ownership only, which was not pro rata. It is entirely possible that family ownership would receive more attention from another court, or even from the Tax Court if the family were small enough, despite the fact that the constructive ownership rules of §318(a) are not expressly made applicable for this purpose. Note the reference in the *Bazley* case to "a family arrangement," and note also that the court referred to "the will of *the* taxpayer" although the stock was divided between husband and wife.

[92] This position is adopted by Regs. §1.354-1(d)(3), Example (3), presumably on the ground that §354 applies only if the taxpayer receives some nonrecognition property. This objection would disappear if the shareholders received some new stock, as well as the securities, in exchange for their old stock.

[93] *Supra*, Sec. 7.20; Rev. Rul. 56-179, 1956-1 C.B. 187.

continuity of interest is not required in the reorganization of a single
corporation. Thus, in Alan O. Hickok, 32 T.C. 80 (1959) (N-A), a
transaction in which a number of shareholders exchanged their stock
for debentures was held to be a tax-free recapitalization, despite their
loss of a proprietary interest in the corporation.[94] It is not clear
whether this principle would be followed in a Type A reorganization
that was the functional equivalent of a recapitalization of a single
corporation (e.g., the merger of a corporation into a newly organized
corporate shell or into a wholly-owned subsidiary) or in a merger of
"brother-sister" corporations.

As to recapitalizations in which some of the shareholders lose
their proprietary interest, in Rev. Rul. 56-179, 1956-1 C.B. 187, the
Internal Revenue Service ruled that a transaction in which some
preferred shareholders exchanged their stock for common stock, while
others received either cash or a combination of bonds and common
stock, constituted a recapitalization. This ruling goes far beyond
Elmer W. Hartzel, 40 B.T.A. 492 (1939) (Acq.), holding that an
exchange in which some of a corporation's common stockholders exchanged their common for preferred stock was a tax-free recapitalization, where the court rejected the government's theory that the
transaction violated the continuity of interest requirement and that
it was the equivalent of a pro rata distribution of the preferred stock
followed by an independent and taxable exchange among the shareholders.[95]

Sec. 12.17.   Changes in identity, form, or place of organization (Type F)

A Type F reorganization is "a mere change in identity, form, or
place of organization, however effected" under §368 (a)(1)(F). This
provision of the statute is not explained further in the regulations and
it has received almost no administrative or judicial attention. In Rev.

---

[94] Under §354(a)(2)(B) of the 1954 Code, however, the shareholders
would have to recognize gain *in full* on such an exchange since the transaction
would be entirely outside the non-recognition provisions of §354 and 356; and
the character of this gain presumably would be tested under §302.

See also Davis v. Penfield, *supra* note 88.

[95] See also Alan O. Hickok. *supra;* Marjorie N. Dean, 10 T.C. 19 (1948)
(Acq.); Friedman and Silbert, The "Continuity of Interest" Test in Bond for
Stock Recapitalizations, 11 N.Y.U. Inst. on Fed. Tax. 361 (1953).

See generally Friedman and Silbert, Recapitalizations — Exchanges of
Stock, Securities and Property of the Same Corporation Under the Internal
Revenue Code of 1954, 13 N.Y.U. Inst. on Fed. Tax 533 (1955); Tarleau, Re-
capitalizations, 11 *ibid.* 371 (1953); Golomb, Recapitalization; The Definitional
Problem, 7 Tax L. Rev. 343 (1952).

Rul. 57-276, 1957-1 C.B. 126, it was applied to the reincorporation of a corporation in another state (effected by creating a new corporation in the other state and then merging into the new corporation), and in Helvering v. Southwest Consolidated Corp., 315 U.S. 194, 28 AFTR 573 (1942), it was held that "a transaction which shifts the ownership of the proprietary interest in a corporation is hardly 'a mere change in identity, form, or place of organization' within the meaning of [§368(a)(1)(F)]." It may be that a reincorporation coupled with a change in the number of shares, par value, voting rights, etc., would be a Type F reorganization, at least if it did not materially change the rights of the shareholders *inter se*,[96] but since this would also probably be a Type E recapitalization, §368(a)(1)(F) seems to add nothing to its status.

In 1940, Randolph Paul said that the Type F reorganization "is so little relied upon by taxpayers that this part of the statute has indeed perished through lack of use" (*Studies in Federal Taxation*, 3d ser., 82), and in 1954 the House proposed its repeal. It was retained in the 1954 Code, however, and may come to play an unexpectedly important role. In Rev. Rul. 57-276, *supra*, the Internal Revenue Service acknowledged that a Type F reorganization will "often" also constitute a Type A, C, or D reorganization. In case of such an overlap, the Service ruled that the transaction should be treated as a Type F reorganization under §381(b), which distinguishes between Types A-D and Type F for purposes of closing the taxable year and carrying back a net operating loss.[97] One of the reasons for Type F's previous obscurity was that other types performing the same functions had the same tax results as a Type F exchange, so that it was not necessary to distinguish between them; under this ruling, however, it may be essential to determine whether a Type A, C, or D reorganization also meets the requirements of Type F.

More important than its role in these areas is Type F's potential

---

[96] See Marr v. United States, 263 U.S. 536, 5 AFTR 5393 (1925), holding such a transaction to be a taxable exchange under the Revenue Act of 1916. See also Ahles Realty Corp. v. Commissioner, 71 F.2d 150, 14 AFTR 259 (2d Cir. 1934) (Type F reorganization, having effect of a recapitalization that would be vulnerable under the subsequently decided *Bazley* case, *supra*, Sec. 12.16).

[97] If the transaction meets the requirements of *both* Type C and D, as well as Type F, however, it is arguable that §368(a)(2)(A) takes hold and requires it to be characterized as a Type D reorganization exclusively.

See also §1244(d)(2), under which a successor corporation in a Type F reorganization is to be treated as the same corporation as its predecessor, which will also require a determination of when a reorganization of another type also meets the standards of Type F.

as a weapon against abuses in the "reincorporation" area. Although the courts have not, as yet, embraced the Type F reorganization as a solution to reincorporation problems, the last word has not been spoken on this subject. For discussion, see *infra*, Sec. 12.22.

Sec. 12.18.   Assumption of liabilities — Effect on reorganization status

1. In general. In United States v. Hendler, 303 U.S. 564, 20 AFTR 1041 (1938), the Supreme Court held that assumption and payment of the transferor corporation's bonded indebtedness by the acquiring corporation constituted boot to the transferor. In view of the 1934 Revenue Act's restrictive changes in the definition of reorganization (limiting the consideration which could be paid in what is now the Type C reorganization to voting stock of the acquiring corporation), the *Hendler* decision was viewed as a practical embargo upon the Type C reorganization under the 1934 provisions, since the assumption of liabilities was essential in the reorganization of most going concerns. In addition, confusion was rampant in the lower courts as to the precise scope of *Hendler*, guaranteeing an abundance of litigation and a long period of uncertainty. Moreover, taxpayers who had relied on the Service's pre-*Hendler* position that liability assumptions did not create boot in a reorganization faced the prospect of deficiency assessments if the statute of limitations had not run on the year of the exchange, while the Service was threatened with refund claims for open years in which taxpayers had sold their stock without increasing their basis to reflect the taxable character (under *Hendler*) of the prior exchange, as well as claims by transferee corporations for an increased basis on assets received in pre-*Hendler* reorganizations. For these reasons, Congress retroactively overturned the *Hendler* decision in 1939 as to all prior years in which the issue was still open. In brief, the *Hendler* legislation provided that:

> a. The assumption of, or taking subject to, liabilities should be disregarded in determining whether an acquisition was solely for voting stock in a Type C reorganization (*supra*, Sec. 12.14).
> b. The assumption of liabilities would not, as a general rule, constitute "boot" to the transferor, unless there was no business purpose for the assumption or it was merely a device to avoid taxes, §357.
> c. The transferor's basis for non-recognition property received in the exchange (*i.e.*, stock or securities) was required to be reduced by the amount of the assumed liability, §358(d) (see *infra*, Sec. 12.32); but the acquiring corporation's basis for its ac-

quired properties was not affected by its assumption or payment of the transferor's liabilities (unless gain was recognized to the transferor, in which case basis could be increased to that extent), H.R. Rep. No. 855, 75th Cong., 1st Sess. 20 (1939).

In 1954, these rules were amplified in two respects: (a) in applying the "boot relaxation" rules of §368(a)(2)(B), liabilities are treated as cash (*supra*, Sec. 12.14); and (b) gain must be recognized to the transferor of property in a Type D reorganization if the liability exceeds its basis.

Despite the intent on the part of Congress to reverse the effects of the *Hendler* case, numerous problems still remain in this area, the most important of which are dealt with in the discussion that follows.

2. *Definition of "liability."* It may be that the term "liability," for purposes of the above provisions, is limited to passive obligations for the payment of money, and does not include such active contractual obligations as the duty to perform services, supply or repair goods, lease or license property, refrain from competition, etc. On the other hand, it does not seem to be necessary that the obligation be fixed or determinable; thus, contingent liabilities should be counted, unless remote or speculative.

As a general matter, the liability assumption rules are not limited to long term capital obligations; current expense obligations (for interest, taxes, compensation, rent, royalties, and the like) should also be treated as liabilities for this purpose, at least if they accrued at or prior to the date of assumption.[98] Unaccrued liabilities for such expense items, on the other hand, may stand on a different footing. It is doubtful, for example, whether a tenant's obligation to pay rent for the balance of the lease term should be treated as a "liability" for this purpose (although there is accounting authority for recognizing such obligations in the liability section of the balance sheet, rather than in a footnote thereto); so also in the case of unaccrued interest on indebtedness, or future liabilities with respect to pension or profit sharing plans.[99] See also §381(c)(16) (*infra*, Sec. 13.12), which seems to provide an *alternative* treatment in certain reorganizations with respect to *unaccrued* liabilities of the transferor which are not "reflected" in the consideration paid by the acquiring corporation for the transferred properties; in this situation, the acquir-

---

[98] See *e.g.*: Stockton Harbor Industrial Co. v. Commissioner, 216 F.2d 638, 46 AFTR 1055 (9th Cir. 1954), cert. denied, 359 U.S. 904; New Jersey Mtge. & Title Co., 3 T.C. 1277 (1944) (Acq.); Roosevelt Hotel Co., 13 T.C. 399 (1949); Alcazar Hotel Co., 1 T.C. 872 (1943); Peabody Hotel Co., 7 T.C. 600 (1946).

[99] If a portion of an assumed liability would constitute imputed interest under §483, there is a possibility that it could be excluded in computing the amount of liabilities assumed.

ing corporation steps into the transferor's shoes with respect to the liabilities and is entitled to a deduction when the obligation matures or is paid, a result not normally obtainable in a case where accrued liabilities are assumed.[100]

The treatment of reorganization expenses bears special mention. In the *Southwest Consolidated Corp.* case, the Supreme Court held that the acquiring corporation could not assume any liability "whose nature and amount were determined and fixed in the reorganization," on the theory that such a liability, though having its origin in a pre-reorganization liability of the transferor, was not a "liability of the other [corporation]" within the meaning of §368(a)(1)(C).[101] This seems to bar the assumption of a liability that is adjusted *in* the reorganization process, and thus to restrict severely the use of §368-(a)(1)(C) in bankruptcy cases. But courts have held that *Southwest Consolidated* does not forbid the acquiring corporation from assuming and paying expenses of the reorganization proceeding itself, a result that seems sensible in view of the fact that assets may be retained by the transferor to discharge its liabilities without violating the "substantially all" requirement of §368(a)(1)(C).[102] Despite this, the Service will apparently not issue favorable rulings on the assumption of liabilities for the reorganization expenses of a solvent transferor.[103]

If a particular liability fails to qualify for treatment as an "assumed liability" under §§357(a) or 368(a)(1)(C), the amount thereof will be treated as the receipt of "boot" by the transferor which could, unless the "boot relaxation" rule of §368(a)(2)(B) applies, disqualify the transaction as a Type C reorganization. In the case of a Type B reorganization, receipt of *any* boot by the transferor apparently will infect the entire reorganization (*supra*, Sec. 12.13); statutory mergers, on the other hand, are tested under general continuity of interest standards (*supra*, Secs. 12.11 and 12.12), which allow more leeway for non-proprietary consideration.

[100] See, *e.g.*, Magruder v. Supplee, 316 U.S. 394, 29 AFTR 196 (1942) (assumed liability treated as part of the acquiring party's "cost" for the property); see also Schuh Trading Co. v. Commissioner, 95 F.2d 404, 20 AFTR 1114 (7th Cir. 1938).

[101] *Supra* note 31. The case involved a judicial insolvency reorganization in which creditors were entitled to the equity interest in the debtor's properties; the debtor borrowed cash to pay off dissenting creditors, and the assumption of this liability by the acquiring corporation was viewed by the Court as an indirect payment of cash in violation of the "solely for voting stock" requirement.

[102] See Roosevelt Hotel Co. and other cases cited *supra* note 98; Southland Ice Co., 5 T.C. 842 (1945) (Acq.); Westfir Lumber Co., 7 T.C. 1014 (1946); Rev. Rul. 56-345, 1956-2 C.B. 206; discussion *supra*, Sec. 12.14.

[103] See Rubenfeld, *supra* note 38.

The ubiquitous "stock vs. debt" issue (*supra*, Sec. 4.02) can arise in the reorganization area: if an alleged debt owed to shareholders is found to be an additional stock investment on their part, a purported "assumption" thereof by the acquiring corporation, evidenced by its own debt securities, would constitute additional consideration. As "boot," this might generate gain to the shareholder, prevent the exchange from qualifying as a Type B or C reorganization, and/or impair the transaction's ability to satisfy the continuity of interest requirement. Conversely, a transaction which is allegedly a taxable purchase, might, if the buyer's deferred payment obligations are held to constitute stock under the "thin capitalization" principle, constitute a reorganization, although this possibility, so far as Type B and C reorganizations are concerned, is made remote by the fact that the consideration must be *voting* stock.[104]

3. Definition of "assumption." In a statutory merger, the surviving corporation assumes the liabilities of the absorbed corporation by operation of law; but in a Type C reorganization, the acquiring corporation will often issue its own debt instruments to replace those of the transferor corporation. In Helvering v. Taylor, 128 F.2d 885, 29 AFTR 741 (2d Cir. 1942), it was held that such an exchange constituted an "assumption" even though the parties failed to use the word "assume." If the terms and conditions of the liability are substantially changed, however, the transaction may go beyond a mere "assumption" and constitute the creation of a new liability, as in Stoddard v. Commissioner, 141 F.2d 76, 32 AFTR 241 (2nd Cir. 1944), where the issuance of mortgage bonds to replace claims of unsecured creditors of the transferor corporation was held to be more than a "mere assumption" of liabilities. (Since the fair market value of the bonds received was less than the taxpayer's basis for the claims surrendered, he was allowed to deduct his loss under §165.) In general, however, courts have been quite liberal in allowing modifications of the terms of an assumed liability, especially if the change merely extends the maturity date or reduces the interest rate.[105]

It is often a close question, however, whether the acquiring corporation (a) has assumed (or taken subject to) liabilities and paid them off, which is permissible; or (b) has paid cash as part of

---

[104] For a case rejecting this argument, see W. H. Truschel, *supra* note 20; but see Reef Corporation, ¶65,072 P-H Memo T.C.

[105] See New Jersey Mtge. & Title Co., 3 T.C. 1277 (1944) (test was whether new bonds were substituted for old, not the extent of modification of interest and maturity terms); Southland Ice Co., *supra* note 102 (issuance of new income mortgage bonds to replace 50 percent of the principal of old mortgage bonds, held an assumption).

the consideration, which is not permissible (except possibly in a Type A reorganization or, within the limits set by §368(a)(2)(B), in a Type C reorganization). See generally Stockton Harbor Industrial Co. v. Commissioner (*supra* note 98) and cases cited therein, holding that prompt payment of assumed liabilities by the acquiring corporation did not affect qualification of the prior transaction as an assumption. If the transferor incurred the liability in contemplation of the reorganization, however, prompt payment by the assuming party may be viewed more hostilely; for a possible line of attack, see the provisions of §357(b), and the discussion *supra*, Sec. 3.06. The test to be applied in such cases is whether the assumption transaction was merely a disguised method for the payment of cash boot, a standard that is easier to state than to apply.

Where the liability is owed by the transferor corporation *to* the acquiring corporation and the latter cancels the debt as part consideration for acquisition of the properties, matters become more difficult. Does the discharge and *satisfaction* of such an indebtedness constitute an "assumption?" Arthur L. Kniffen, 39 T.C. 553 (1962) (Acq.), held that it did in the context of a §351 exchange, so that the transferor debtor was protected from boot treatment by §357(a). The theory of the *Kniffen* case was followed in Edwards Motor Transit Co., ¶64,317 P-H Memo TC, where the debtor merged into its wholly-owned creditor-subsidiary in a §368(a)(1)(A) statutory merger. In both cases, the Tax Court held that the identity of the creditor was irrelevant under §357(a), and that the net result was the same as though the assumed debt had been owed to a third party and had been discharged by the acquiring corporation immediately after its assumption. This approach is difficult to reconcile with the treatment of inter-corporate debt on the liquidation of a debtor-subsidiary by its creditor-parent, where the latter recognizes gain or loss in its capacity as creditor, although the subsidiary is protected from recognition treatment by virtue of §332(c).[106]

4. *Continuity of interest problems.* As noted earlier (*supra*, Sec. 12.14), Regs. §1.368-2(d)(1) warns that an assumption may "so alter the character of the transaction as to place the transaction out-

---

[106] *Supra.* Sec. 9.42. Bausch & Lomb Optical Co. v. Commissioner, 267 F.2d 75, 3 AFTR 2d 1497 (2d Cir. 1959), discussed *infra*, Sec. 12.21, holds that acquisition of a part of the transferor's assets in exchange for its *stock*, already held by the acquiring corporation, did not satisfy the "solely for voting stock" requirement of §368(a)(1)(C). But apparently the acquiring corporation will be permitted to receive at least part of the transferor's assets in its capacity as a creditor because of the special liability assumption rules of §368(a)(1)(C) and §357, although this superior treatment seems difficult to justify.

side the purposes and assumptions of the reorganization provisions."
This statement seems to be concerned primarily with the continuity
of interest principle; hence, if the acquisition is made primarily for
assumption of the transferor's liabilities with only a trivial amount
of voting stock to sweeten the bargain, the transaction more nearly
resembles a foreclosure proceeding than a reorganization. Thus,
reorganization treatment may be denied where the former holders
of the proprietary interest in the property are virtually eliminated
in the transaction.[107] Regs. §1.368-2(d)(3) approves an assumption of
liabilities equal to 50 percent of the value of the transferred properties;
anything over this figure could be vulnerable under general continuity of interest principles.

Although voting stock of the acquiring corporation's parent has
been permissible as the proprietary consideration in a Type C reorganization since 1954, apparently the acquiring corporation is the
only one that may *assume* the transferor's liabilities (although taking
subject to liabilities seems to be more flexible). Thus, in a *Groman*
"triangular acquisition," it may not be permissible for the acquired
assets to pass directly to a subsidiary where the parent assumes the
transferor's liabilities, since the subsidiary would be viewed as "the
acquiring corporation" for this purpose; and the same objection might
be made even if the assets go first to the parent, and then to the
subsidiary. Where the subsidiary assumes the transferor's liabilities,
it may be possible for the parent to guarantee its obligation, however;
this would not appear to constitute an "assumption" by the parent
since it is only secondarily liable on the debt. It is understood that
several favorable rulings have been issued by the Service on such an
arrangement, and a liberal approach to this question seems in order.[108]

Sec. 12.19.   "Business purpose" and "continuity of business enterprise"

1. Business purpose — in general. The regulations under §368
take seriously the "business purpose" requirement, referring at no
less than three points to language culled from that fountainhead of
learning on this subject, the *Gregory* case (*supra*, Sec. 11.02). Thus,
Regs. §1.368-1(b) states that the reorganization provisions are concerned with "readjustments of corporate structures . . . required by
business exigencies"; and Regs. §1.368-1(c) elaborates on this theme

---

[107] See, for example, Civic Center Finance Co. v. Kuhl, *supra* note 53,
where the sole consideration was the assumption of liabilities; *supra*, Sec. 12.11.
[108] See Rev. Rul. 64-73, 1964-1 C.B. 142, for a relaxed view of triangular
transactions.

by providing that a "scheme, which involves an abrupt departure from normal reorganization procedure in connection with a transaction on which the imposition of a tax is imminent, such as a mere device that puts on the form of a corporate reorganization as a disguise for concealing its real character, and the object and accomplishment of which is the consummation of a preconceived plan having no business or corporate purpose," is not a reorganization. For the unconvinced, this message is repeated in Regs. §1.368-2(g), which states that the transactions must be "germane to the continuance of the business of a corporation," and that the statute "contemplates genuine corporate reorganizations which are designed to effect a readjustment of continuing interests under modified corporate forms."

Although *Gregory* may mean all things to all men, its essence is an instinctive judicial attitude that a transaction should not be given effect for tax purposes unless it serves a purpose other than tax avoidance. Thus, a transaction heavily laden with tax avoidance motives may be disregarded as a "sham," or its form may be recast so as to reflect its economic "substance," or interdependent steps in a "single transaction" may be collapsed in order to prevent overreaching taxpayers from doing indirectly what they cannot do directly. As elsewhere in the law of taxation, the lawyer's passion for technical analysis of the statutory language should always be diluted by distrust of a result that is too good to be true. On the other hand, cases like *Cumberland Public Service Co.* (*supra*, Sec. 9.63) bear constant witness to the fact that the deliberate choice of a tax-free route is often given full effect.[109]

Granting that *Gregory* lays down a general principle of tax law that in order to fit within a particular provision of the statute a transaction must comply not only with the letter of the section, but must have a "business purpose," other than a desire to avoid taxes, that falls within its spirit as well, the question then arises as to *whose* business purpose — the corporation's, its shareholder's, or both — is controlling. The regulations, Regs. §1.368-1(b) and (c), seem to focus primarily on corporate business purpose as the critical test. But in Lewis v. Commissioner, 176 F.2d 646, 38 AFTR 377 (1st Cir. 1949), the court refused to distinguish between corporate purpose and shareholder purpose in the case of a closely-held corporation,

---

[109] See generally, Lyon, Federal Income Taxation, 36 N.Y.U.L. Rev. 642, 643 (1961). On the "business purpose" requirement as it relates to corporate reorganizations, see Spear, "Corporate Business Purpose" in Reorganization, 3 Tax L. Rev. 225 (1948); Michaelson, "Business Purpose" and Tax Free Reorganization, 61 Yale L. J. 14 (1952); Bittker, What Is "Business Purpose" in Reorganizations? 8 N.Y.U. Inst. on Fed. Tax. 134 (1950).

rejecting the taxpayer's contention that a transaction did not constitute a "reorganizaion," because it lacked a corporate business purpose. Similarly, in Parshelsky's Estate v. Commissioner, 303 F.2d 14, 9 AFTR 2d 1382 (2d Cir. 1962), the business purpose doctrine was interpreted as requiring an evaluation of all the non-tax-avoidance motives for the transaction, those of the corporation and of its shareholders as well; the court went on to hold that reorganization treatment could not be denied merely because the only purpose therefor was a shareholder, rather than a corporate, purpose. The court did emphasize, however, that the shareholder purpose must be a reason other than avoidance of taxes.

2. *Continuity of business enterprise.* In addition to denouncing shams and disguises, the regulations provide that reorganization requires "a continuity of business enterprise under modified corporate forms," Regs. §1.368-1(b). In several cases where an alleged reorganization was only a step in the winding up of business activity, courts have treated it as part of a taxable liquidation transaction rather than a tax-free reorganization exchange. Thus, in Standard Realization Co., 10 T.C. 708 (1948), the Tax Court held that a transfer of all of a corporation's assets to a second corporation controlled by the shareholders of the transferor was not a "reorganization," although it complied with the literal requirements of a Type D reorganization, because the transferee was to sell the assets under a preconceived plan rather than to continue in a business. Similarly, in Pridemark, Inc. v. Commissioner, 345 F.2d 35, 15 AFTR 2d 835 (4th Cir. 1965), reorganization treatment was denied where a corporation's business assets were sold to an unrelated purchaser and its business activity was suspended for over a year; the court there stated that the old business had been "liquidated," and that the creation of a new corporation to engage in a similar line of business, did not constitute a continuation or "reactivation" of the old business enterprise.[110] Accordingly, where there is a complete termination of corporate business activity, or such an interruption of the business activity that its continuity is broken, the liquidation provisions take precedence over the reorganization provisions.

It should be noted, however, that "liquidation" of one of the corporate parties to a reorganization transaction (as distinguished from a termination of *business* activities) is not inconsistent with the concept of "reorganization" — in fact, many reorganization plans contemplate the liquidation of at least one of the corporations. Thus,

[110] See also George Graham, 37 B.T.A. 623 (1938); on the meaning of "complete liquidation," see *supra*, Sec. 9.02.

in the *Lewis* case, *supra*, it was held that reorganization treatment applied where the corporation sold two of its three lines of business; and, because of a temporary inability to sell the third, placed it in a new corporation pending a sale, and liquidated. The "termination of business" cases did not apply, said the court, merely because the corporation contemplated a sale of its assets at some time in the future, if the business was in fact carried on at the corporate level in the interim.

In addition, the continuity of business enterprise requirement does not demand that the new corporation engage in the same business as its predecessor, or a similar one; all that is required is that there be continuity of business activity. For example, in Becher v. Commissioner, 221 F.2d 252, 47 AFTR 430 (2d Cir. 1955), it was held that a transfer of assets to a corporation controlled by the transferor's shareholders was a "reorganization," even though the transferor's business was terminated, some of its assets were distributed in partial liquidation, and the transferred assets were invested by the transferee in an entirely different business. After flirting with a contrary view for a period of years, the Internal Revenue Service has agreed with *Becher* that continuity of *a* business enterprise, whether it was carried on before the reorganization by a party thereto or not, is sufficient.[111]

Continuity of the pre-organization business may be important in other contexts, however, as in §355 transactions (*supra*, Sec. 11.04), in the reincorporation area (*infra*, Sec. 12.22), and in the carryover of tax attributes (*infra*, Ch. 13).

Sec. 12.20.   Step transactions — Disposition of unwanted assets in connection with a reorganization

1. General. Like the business purpose doctrine, the judicial requirement that all integrated steps in a single transaction must be amalgamated in determining the true nature of a transaction is applied in every nook and cranny of the tax law, not merely in the field of corporate reorganizations. Examples are sprinkled freely through the pages of this book.[112] Here we are concerned with a special aspect

---

[111] Rev. Rul. 63-29, 1963-1 C.B. 77, revoking Rev. Rul. 56-330, 1956-2 C.B. 204, after its approach was rejected in Bentsen v. Phinney, 199 F. Supp. 363, 9 AFTR 2d 685 (S.D. Tex. 1961). See also Morley Cypress Trust, 3 T.C. 84 (1944); Pebble Springs Distilling Co. v. Commissioner, 231 F.2d 288, 49 AFTR 430 (7th Cir. 1956), cert. denied, 352 U.S. 836.

See generally Tarleau, "Continuity of Business Enterprise" in Corporate Reorganization and Other Corporate Readjustments, 60 Col. L. Rev. 792 (1960).

[112] E.g., whether a transferor has control "immediately after the exchange"

of the step transaction problem, viz., if the acquiring corporation is interested in obtaining only part of the assets of the transferor corporation, what tax consequences arise if the unwanted assets are "stripped-off" in anticipation of the pending transfer of the wanted assets? The disposition of unwanted assets in this context can be effected by (a) a sale of these properties to third parties, (b) a distribution in kind to shareholders of the transferor corporation, or (c) a tax-free spin-off under §355 (supra, Ch. 11). The discussion that follows will focus on the way these modes of ridding the transferor corporation of the unwanted assets affect the reorganization status of the simultaneous or subsequent transfer of the wanted assets; but attention must also be given to other statutory provisions that may govern the treatment of the transferor corporation or its shareholders.

To make the discussion more concrete, it will be assumed that X Corporation owns and operates two separate, 5-year old businesses; that the assets of both businesses have appreciated in value substantially, and are about equal in value; that X has a large earnings and profits account; that Y Corporation wishes to acquire one business for voting stock in a tax-free reorganization, but does not want to acquire the other; and that X and its shareholders will receive less than 80 percent of Y's stock and hence will not be in control of Y after the exchange within the meaning of §368(c).

2. *Taxable "strip-off" of unwanted assets.* If X sells the unwanted assets to an unrelated purchaser for cash, transfers the wanted assets to Y for its voting stock, and liquidates, the X-Y exchange will not constitute a Type C reorganization because it is not a transfer of "substantially all" of X's properties under §368(a)(1)(C).[113] As a result, X will have to recognize its gain on both this transfer and on the sale of the other business for cash, unless it meets the requirements of §337 (supra, Sec. 9.64). If the formalities are observed, and if the shareholders of X acquire only a nominal stock interest in Y (e.g., if the transfer is to a large, publicly-held corporation), this should not be difficult, and X's shareholders would then realize capital

---

under §351, supra, Sec. 3.09; whether a purchase of stock coupled with a liquidation is equivalent to a purchase of assets (supra, Sec. 9.44); whether assets of a partially owned corporation can be acquired in a tax-free reorganization (infra, Sec. 12.21); and whether a liquidation, followed or preceded by a reincorporation of all or part of the assets of the liquidating corporation, constitutes a liquidation or a reorganization (supra, Sec. 9.05; infra, Sec. 12.22). For other illustrations, see the works cited supra, Sec. 1.05. See generally West Coast Marketing Corp., 46 T.C. No. 4 (1966).

[113] See supra, Sec. 12.14; Helvering v. Elkhorn Coal Co., supra note 55; see also West Coast Marketing Corp., supra note 112.

gain or loss on its liquidation. If they obtain a larger interest in Y, however, the Service may contest the applicability of §337, but its objections may not be acceptable to the courts.[114]

If instead of selling the unwanted business, X distributed it to its shareholders in exchange for stock, the transaction would constitute a taxable event to the shareholders (either as a dividend under §301, or as capital gain or loss under §302 or §346); a subsequent merger of X into Y (or a transfer of all of X's remaining assets for voting stock of Y in a §368(a)(1)(C) "practical" merger), may qualify as a "reorganization," at least if X is completely liquidated, as would automatically be the case in a true merger. Since the unwanted assets have passed out of X corporation in a *taxable* transaction, reorganization treatment with respect to the subsequent transfer by X to Y of the wanted assets may be permissible under §368(a)(1)(A). There does not seem to be any "substantially all" requirement for statutory mergers, and the shareholders of X presumably retain the necessary continuity of interest in the transferred properties through their receipt of the Y corporation's stock (see *supra*, Sec. 12.11). But Type C reorganization treatment may be more difficult to sustain in this case if the distributed assets must be "considered" for purposes of the "substantially all" test under the *Elkhorn Coal* case (*supra*, note 55). It can be argued that this distribution should not be so considered, however, since, unlike *Elkhorn*, the unwanted assets passed out of corporate solution in a taxable transaction; hence, the transaction was essentially "non-divisive" in character, even when considered in its entirety.[114a] In fact, the Service may argue for a reorganization on these facts so as to assert "boot dividend" treatment to the shareholders of X with respect to their prior receipt of its unwanted assets (for which see *infra*, Sec. 12.34). On the other hand, if the retained unwanted assets are substantial in relation to the transferred wanted assets, as here, the transaction may lack sufficient "resemblance to a merger" under general reorganization theory

[114] Compare Hyman H. Berghash, *supra* note 14 (no reorganization where only 50 percent continuity of control by shareholders of the selling corporation); and James Armour, Inc., 43 T.C. 295 (1964) (held a Type D reorganization where 100 percent continuity of control, even though only 51 percent of selling corporation's assets were transferred, which amount was held to be "substantially all" on the facts); see *infra*, Sec. 12.22.

[114a] See Sec. 12.14; Isabella Sheldon, 6 T.C. 510 (1946) (dividend distribution in connection with Type B reorganization did not affect reorganization status); Rev. Rul. 58-68, 1958-1 C.B. 183 (prior *taxable* spin-off did not affect later statutory merger); Curtis v. United States, 336 F.2d 714, 14 AFTR 2d 5685 (6th Cir. 1964) (similar result); Rev. Rul. 57-114, 1957-1 C.B. 122 (merger not affected by subsequent taxable "split-off" exchange between acquiring corporation and a shareholder of both the acquired and acquiring corporation); Ralph C. Wilson, *infra* note 128.

(which ordinarily contemplates a fusion of the properties of one corporate enterprise with another). In this situation, the shareholders' continuity of proprietary interest (and possibly corporate continuity of business enterprise as well) may be so lacking as to deny reorganization treatment.

3. *Tax-free spin off followed by reorganization.* In the *Elkhorn Coal Co.* case (*supra*, note 55), the transferor, X Corporation, spun-off its unwanted assets by transferring these properties to a newly created corporation and distributing its stock in a transaction which qualified for non-recognition treament under the provisions of §368-(a)(1)(D) and §355; this step was part of a plan in pursuance of which X then transferred the rest of its assets to Y Corporation in what purported to be a Type C reorganization. If these two steps had been unrelated events, this result would clearly have been appropriate, since the wanted assets constituted all of X Corporation's properties after the spin-off. But the Court in *Elkhorn* held that the two steps were part of a single integrated transaction and that the unwanted assets, which were spun off in the earlier step, had to be "considered" in determining whether X Corporation had transferred "substantially all" of its properties under §368(a)(1)(C); since substantially all of the assets did not pass to the acquiring corporation under this approach, Type C reorganization treatment was denied. It should be noted that if the taxpayer had prevailed in *Elkhorn*, the "substantially all" requirement would have been virtually nullified, at least for the well informed. Also, it was significant in *Elkhorn* that the unwanted assets remained in corporate solution, having been separated from the assets to be transferred in a non-taxable transaction; hence, X corporation was attempting to continue operation of the retained business in the newly created corporate vehicle, and at the same time to obtain non-recognition treatment with respect to that part of its assets transferred to the acquiring corporation. This "divisive" feature of the *Elkhorn* transaction perhaps explains the Court's reluctance to treat the two steps as unrelated, since the "substantially all" requirement was then, as it is today, aimed precisely at discouraging this result.

The tax-free character of the prior spin-off transaction in the *Elkhorn* situation is determined by reference to §368(a)(1)(D) (or §351) and §355, which matters are considered in detail *supra*, Ch. 11. See also *supra*, Sec. 12.15. For purposes of this discussion, however, two important aspects of §355 should be noted: (a) the "device clause" of §355(a)(1)(B) denies non-recognition treatment where the transaction is used principally as a device for the distribution of earnings and profits; and (b) the "active trade or business" rules of §355(b) require that both the distributing corporation and the spun-off corporation be engaged in an active business immediately after the distribution and that such business must have been conducted for 5 years prior to the distribution.

The device clause of §355(a)(1)(B) seems concerned primarily with a possible bail out of corporate earnings at capital gain rates, *i.e.*, the type of transaction involved in the *Gregory* case. As such, this provision may not be violated where shareholders of the distributing corporation subsequently exchange their stock in a tax-free transaction. In the case of a *taxable* transfer, however, the shareholders may have converted potential dividend income into capital gain if the prior spin-off distribution qualifies for non-recognition treatment under §355, and this is the result which §355(a)(1)(B) is designed to discourage. Also, continuity of interest principles are inherent in the device clause and any taxable shareholder stock sales could fail to pass muster on this score as well. See *e.g.*, Rev. Rul. 55-103, 1955-1 C.B. 31.

Two recent decisions involve the tax consequences of a spin-off transaction coupled with a statutory merger. In Curtis v. United States, 336 F.2d 714, 14 AFTR 2d 5685 (6th Cir. 1964), unwanted assets were spun-off to shareholders of the transferor corporation, which then transferred the rest of its assets to the acquiring corporation in a statutory merger, with the latter emerging as the surviving corporation. The Court held that the spin-off distribution constituted a taxable dividend because the transaction failed to satisfy the requirement of §355(b)(1)(A) that *the* distributing corporation be engaged in business immediately after the distribution; the distributing corporation no longer "existed," said the court, since it was absorbed by the acquiring corporation in the later statutory merger (which was part of the same transaction). Mary Archer Morris Trust, 42 T.C. 779 (1964), involved virtually identical facts except that the transferor corporation's "existence" continued under the particular consolidation statute there involved; the Court held that the spin-off qualifed for non-recognition treatment under §355. In neither case did the Service attack the "reorganization" status of the subsequent statutory mergers,[115] although, as noted above, if the Type C reorganization route had been used, it could have been attacked under *Elkhorn* and the "substantially all" requirement. *Curtis* would presumably have gone the other way had the transferor corporation been the surviving cor-

---

[115] See also Rev. Rul. 57-114, *supra* note 114a; Rev. Rul. 58-68, 1958-1 C.B. 183 (taxable spin-off did not affect merger reorganization status).

poration in the merger; if so, it turns on a highly technical reading of §355 and on the parties' choice of form. The *Morris* case, on the other hand, seems to reach the proper result, although its force is weakened by the fact that the court did not have to come to grips with the merits of the corporate "existence" issue.

With these observations in mind, the following examples will deal with certain variations on the *Elkhorn* pattern, based on the facts assumed *supra*, page 558:

> a. X spins off the wanted assets by transferring them to Z corporation (a newly created controlled corporation) and distributing the Z stock to its shareholders; Z then transfers all of its assets to Y solely in exchange for the latter's voting stock (in a Type C or Type A reorganization), after which Z liquidates. This transaction is clearly vulnerable under *Gregory*, since Z is a mere conduit for the transfer of X's wanted assets to Y. See also West Coast Marketing Corp., *supra* note 112. As such, its corporate existence should be ignored, and the transaction should be treated as a taxable exchange between X and Y (of the wanted assets for Y stock), followed by a dividend distribution of the Y stock to X's shareholders.

> b. If Z was not liquidated in the above example, its separate corporate existence could not be ignored under *Gregory;* however, the spin-off transaction still would be vulnerable under §355(b)(1)(A) since Z would be a mere holding company after it transfers all of its assets for Y stock. See also Rev. Rul. 58-68, 1958-1 C.B. 183. In addition, *Elkhorn* may deprive the transfer of assets of Type C reorganization status since, if the steps are collapsed, "substantially all" of the assets have not passed to Y.

> c. If, in the above examples, Y acquired all the stock of Z (rather than its assets) in a stock-for-stock exchange, results could be different. The spin-off transaction would not be subject to the *Curtis* attack since both X and Y continue in existence after the distribution (assuming that Y did not, by prearrangement, liquidate Z to obtain its assets, in which case the result would be equivalent to an asset acquisition). As to the "device" clause of §355, however, the spin-off is vulnerable unless the exchange between X's shareholders and Y can be treated as a Type B reorganization; if it is so treated, they have disposed of their Z stock in a non-taxable exchange, and as indicated above, this seems compatible with the "device" provision. Literally, their exchange seems to qualify under §368(a)(1)(B), but there is a ruling to the contrary, asserting that the transaction constitutes in substance a transfer of the wanted assets for the stock of the acquiring corporation.[116] So viewed, it would be

---

[116] Rev. Rul. 54-96, 1954-1 C.B. 111. Unless the transaction is regarded as a transfer of assets, however, it seems to meet the requirement of (368)(a)(1)-(B). See West Coast Marketing Corp., *supra* note 112.

Rev. Rul. 54-96 also held that the initial transfer of assets by X to Z did not

denied reorganization status as involving less than "substantially all" of X's assets. It is by no means clear that this approach would be accepted if the matter were litigated, however, at least if Z is kept alive rather than liquidated by Y.

d. If X spins-off its *unwanted* assets (by transferring them to Z and distributing the Z stock to its shareholders), and X's shareholders then exchange their X stock for Y's voting stock, the plan has the same economic effect as the plan described in the preceding paragraph; but it is possible that its claim to Type B treatment would be stronger. To apply Rev. Rul. 54-96 (*supra*, note 116), it would be necessary to view the acquisition by Y of the stock of an *existing* corporation (X) as the equivalent of an acquisition of assets; by contrast, the ruling itself emphasized that the acquired corporation was newly-created. Unless the courts respond with a new judicial doctrine — possibly similar to the "substantially all of the enterprise" notion of *Elkhorn*, only dealing with stock acquisitions rather than asset acquisitions — Type B reorganization status ought to prevail on these facts.

The Service may attack the tax-free status of the earlier spin-off transaction under the "device" clause of §355(a)(1)(B), however, and a warning to this effect is contained in Rev. Rul. 58-68.[117] It should be noted that the continuity of interest principle is satisfied in this example since the shareholders of X have an interest in both the unwanted assets (through their ownership of Z) and the wanted assets (through the Y stock received in exchange for their X stock); hence, one of the basic ingredients for reorganization treatment is present and perhaps this fact should prevail in determining its status. This is also true in the plan described in (c) above.

Sec. 12.21. Acquisitions by affiliated corporations — Special problems and techniques

Reorganization transactions involving affiliated corporations raise certain special problems, the following of which are considered herein: (a) The treatment of "upstream" and "downstream" mergers (i.e., the merger of a subsidiary into its parent, or of a parent into its sub-

qualify under §351, since "control" was disposed of by prearrangment; on this issue, see *supra*, Sec. 3.09.

An attack based on the theory of Rev. Rul. 54-96 might be avoided if X exchanged the Z stock directly with Y, rather than distributing such stock to its shareholders and having them make the exchange; but in this event, the Y stock could not be distributed tax-free by X to its shareholders since X is not a "party to a reorganization" (*infra*, Sec. 12.32).

117 1958-1 C.B. 183. Regs. §1.355-2(b)(1) speaks of "sales or exchanges" in connection with a §355 distribution; if this language is interpreted to mean *taxable* exchanges, the instant transaction would not be vulnerable under the "device" clause. See Rev. Rul. 55-103, 1955-1 C.B. 31, applying the "device" clause to taxable stock sales and relying on the continuity of interest principle to reach this result.

sidiary); (b) acquisitions of stock or assets of one corporation by another corporation under common control; (c) acquisitions of stock or assets where the acquiring corporation already owns part (but not "control") of the stock of the acquired corporation (the *Bausch & Lomb* problem); and (d) acquisitions of stock or assets by a subsidiary corporation in exchange for stock of its parent (the *Groman-Bashford* problem).

1. Parent-subsidiary mergers. A statutory merger of an 80 percent owned subsidiary into its parent corporation is controlled by the non-recognition provisions of §332 (*supra*, Sec. 9.40), which override the reorganization rules to the extent that the two may conflict. See Regs. §1.332-2(d). This may occur, for example, where the parent has purchased stock of the subsidiary in order to obtain its assets and immediately liquidates (by statutory merger) the newly purchased subsidiary for this purpose. The parent's basis for the assets received from the subsidiary would be determined under §334(b)(2) (*supra*, Sec. 9.44), rather than under the reorganization basis rules of §362(b).[118] Similarly, the carryover of the subsidiary's net operating loss would be governed by §381(a)(1); §382(b)(1), which is applicable to statutory mergers, would be inapplicable (*infra*, Sec. 13.23).

The treatment of minority shareholders of the liquidating subsidiary corporation, who acquire stock of the parent corporation in exchange for their stock of the subsidiary, is less clear. Regs. §1.332-2(d) can be interpreted to permit "reorganization" non-recognition treatment for them, in tandem with "liquidation" non-recognition treatment for the parent under §332. In view of the general preeminence of §332 in the statutory scheme, however, the minority shareholders may have to recognize gain or loss on the "liquidation" of their stock interests in the subsidiary.[119]

If the merger is "downstream," however, reorganization treatment is the order of the day. Thus, in Edwards Motor Transit Co., ¶64,317 P-H Memo TC, a holding company, whose only asset was stock of its 100 percent subsidiary, was merged into the subsidiary in a transaction which qualified as a "reorganization" under §368(a)-

---

[118] This result was reached even before the *Kimbell-Diamond* rule was codified by §334(b)(2). See Georgia-Pacific Corp. v. United States, 264 F.2d 161, 3 AFTR 2d 778 (5th Cir. 1959); Long Island Water Corp., *supra* note 26; South Bay Corp. v. Commissioner, *supra* note 44.

The carryover rules of §§381 and 382 (*infra*, Ch. 13) are applied differently in certain respects, depending upon whether a transaction is a §332 liquidation under §381(a)(1) or a reorganization under §381(a)(2).

[119] See Seplow, Acquisition of Assets of a Subsidiary: Liquidation or Reorganization, 73 Harv. L. Rev. 484, 511 (1960).

(1) (A). In several earlier decisions, the Service had unsuccessfully argued that the merger of a parent holding company into its operating subsidiary was the equivalent of a liquidation of the parent, but the courts disagreed.[120] It is understood that the Service will rule favorably on a statutory merger of an operating parent into its operating subsidiary, but not if the parent owns less than 80 percent of the subsidiary's stock and this is its only asset, where the Service continues to feel that the effect of the "merger" is a mere liquidation of the parent. On the other hand, in Rev. Rul. 57-465, the Service approved "non-divisive" Type D reorganization treatment for the merger of a parent holding company into its wholly-owned subsidiary where the subsidiary's stock constituted over one-half of the parent's assets.[121]

This judicial willingness to see the reorganization provisions take precedence over the liquidation rules in the case of downstream mergers operates as an appropriate inducement to the simplification of corporate structures, a policy similar to that which inspired the enactment of §332. As to upstream mergers, §332 itself provides tax-free treatment. Thus, the elimination of an unnecessary tier of corporations can be accomplished on a tax-free basis whether it is the parent or the subsidiary that is marked for extinction.

2. *Brother-sister acquisitions.* If both the acquired corporation and the acquiring corporation are owned by the same shareholders in the same proportions, it may be difficult to *avoid* reorganization treatment where assets or stock of one such corporation are acquired by the other. It is possible, however, that the transaction could be classified as a "redemption" of stock of a "related corporation" under §304 (e.g., if stock is acquired for stock and bonds of the acquiring corporation), for which see *supra*, Sec. 7.31; or that the net effect of the transaction would be substantially the same as the distribution of a

---

[120] H. Grady Manning Trust, 15 T.C. 930 (1950) (Non-Acq.); Commissioner v. Estate of Gilmore, 130 F.2d 791, 29 AFTR 1183 (3rd Cir. 1942); Commissioner v. Estate of Webster, 131 F.2d 426, 30 AFTR 296 (5th Cir. 1942); see also Isidor Kahn, 36 B.T.A. 954 (1937); Commissioner v. Kann, 130 F.2d 797, 29 AFTR 1189 (3rd Cir. 1942).

See generally Stuetzer and Bergen, Upstairs and Downstairs Mergers, 10 N.Y.U. Inst. on Fed. Tax. 1267 (1952); Cohn, Downstairs Mergers, 7 *ibid.* 1202 (1949); Piper, Combining Parent and Subsidiary Corporations, 16 *ibid.* 375 (1958).

[121] 1957-2 C.B. 250, citing Helvering v. Leary, 93 F.2d 826, 20 AFTR 599 (4th Cir. 1938); and Helvering v. Schoellkopf, 100 F.2d 415, 22 AFTR 121 (2d Cir. 1938), which similarly applied the Type D reorganization provisions to downstream merger patterns.

In approving reorganization treatment, Rev. Rul. 57-465 emphasized the non-divisive character of the transaction, although it appeared to be troubled by the "substantially all" requirement of §354(b) (1) (A) in view of the fact that the parent's principal asset was the subsidiary's stock which was acquired by the latter for cancellation rather than as an "asset".

dividend under *Bazley* (e.g., if assets of one related corporation are acquired for stock and bonds of the other related corporation). These matters are closely related to the "liquidation-reincorporation" area, discussed *infra*, Sec. 12.22.

3. *Acquisition of assets of a partially controlled subsidiary — the Bausch & Lomb case.* In Bausch & Lomb Optical Co. v. Commissioner, 267 F.2d 75, 3 AFTR 2d 1497 (2d Cir. 1959), the taxpayer owned 79 percent of the stock of a subsidiary corporation. In order to acquire its assets, the taxpayer issued its stock in exchange for all the assets; and the subsidiary then liquidated, distributing the parent's stock pro rata to all of its shareholders. The outside shareholders of the subsidiary thus became minority shareholders of the parent. The various steps were held to constitute a single plan having the effect of a taxable liquidation, rather than a tax-free Type C reorganization, on the theory that the assets were acquired by the taxpayer in consideration for its stock of the subsidiary rather than in exchange for its own voting stock, as required by §368(a)(1)(C).[122] The opinion, which is brief and cryptic, may have been bottomed on the continuity of interest principle, in that the parent's former stock investment in its subsidiary was "extinguished" by these transactions. On the other hand, it is difficult to envision how the taxpayer's "interest" in its subsidiary's assets could have risen to a much higher level: it now owned directly that which it formerly owned indirectly through its stock interest in the subsidiary, though, to be sure, this is also the consequence of a complete liquidation. In any event, the *Bausch & Lomb* decision restricts use of a Type C reorganization where the acquiring corporation already owns part of the stock of the corporation whose assets are to be acquired.

There are, however, several possible variations on the *Bausch & Lomb* pattern that should be noted:

> a. If the transferor corporation had remained alive for business reasons, the acquisition of its assets would have been solely in exchange for voting stock of the acquiring corporation, as required by §368(a)(1)(C). Hence, the transferor and the transferee would have obtained non-recognition treatment on the exchange by virtue of §361 and §1032, respectively.
>
> b. If the parent in *Bausch & Lomb* had owned at least 80 percent of the subsidiary, its acquisition of all of the latter's assets in exchange for its own stock would have been tax-free under §332 (as to the assets acquired "in liquidation") and §1032 (as to the assets acquired for its own stock). As to the

---

[122] For a similar result under the 1954 Code, see Grede Foundries, Inc. v. United States, *supra* note 61.

subsidiary, it might be viewed as having sold 20 percent of its assets to the parent for the latter's stock in a taxable transaction, and as having distributed the rest of its assets (to the parent) and the parent's stock (to the outside shareholders) in a distribution that generated neither gain nor loss under §336. The minority shareholders would presumably have to recognize their gain or loss on exchanging their stock in the subsidiary for stock in the parent, unless they are protected by Regs. §1.332-2(d), discussed *supra*.

c. If the acquiring corporation owned 20 percent or less of the acquired corporation's stock, "the boot relaxation" rules of §368(a)(2)(B) would come to the rescue and permit the transaction to qualify as a Type C reorganization, provided the 20 percent limit on the use of boot in such transaction was not exceeded by virtue of an assumption of liabilities. All the parties would then obtain non-recognition treatment on their exchanges, except that the acquiring corporation would recognize gain or loss under §331 on its exchange of its stock in the acquired corporation for the assets attributable thereto.

d. It is understood that the Service will permit the acquiring corporation in a *Bausch & Lomb* situation to "sterilize" its stock in the subsidiary (if such interest is a relatively "minor" one), by transferring it to another subsidiary, in which event the acquiring corporation will obtain all of the acquired corporation's assets in exchange for its voting stock; and on the acquired corporation's liquidation, the parent's stock will go partly to its other subsidiary and partly to the outside shareholders of the acquired corporation.

Granting that the *Bausch & Lomb* decision largely interdicts use of the Type C reorganization to effect a "creeping acquisition" of stock *and* assets of the acquired corporation, it is relatively clear that the stock alone could be acquired in a "creeping Type B reorganization" (see discussion *supra*, Sec. 12.13). Thus, a stock-for-stock exchange between the acquiring corporation and the other shareholders of the acquired corporation could qualify as a Type B reorganization, even though the acquiring corporation already owned part of the stock of the corporation to be acquired. A prompt liquidation of the acquired corporation, however, would render the transaction vulnerable under the *Bausch & Lomb* case. Accordingly, if the Type B reorganization technique is adopted, the newly acquired subsidiary must be kept alive for a decent interval to avoid step transaction arguments.

The Service has also approved statutory merger acquisitions in the *Bausch & Lomb* situation, Rev. Rul. 58-93, 1958-1 C.B. 188, a result implied in the Second Circuit opinion in the *Bausch & Lomb* case. In addition, the Service has ruled that *Bausch & Lomb* does not apply if the acquired assets end up in a controlled subsidiary of the acquiring corporation. In this ruling, the acquiring corporation first transferred its own stock to a newly created subsidiary, which then acquired the assets in exchange for such stock; and the acquired corporation was then liquidated. The theory of the ruling was that the same result could have been accomplished by use of a Type B reorganization and that no difference in tax result should occur where the method adopted had, in substance, the same effect.[123] Thus, the *Bausch & Lomb* case has been limited to those situations where the ultimate transferee of the acquired assets obtains some of them through a liquidation rather than in exchange for its stock.

The *Bausch & Lomb* case, as limited and distinguished in the above situations, now seems to constitute merely a trap for the uninformed, a result which casts doubt on the basic soundness of the original decision. There are so many ways to avoid the *Bausch & Lomb* result, as noted above, that the exceptions, for all practical purposes, have become the general rule in this area.

4. Groman-Bashford acquisitions — special problems. As noted earlier, *supra*, Sec. 12.11, the *Groman* and *Bashford* decisions (which held that stock of the acquiring corporation's parent company did not carry the requisite continuity of interest "genes") have been gradually modified by Congress over the course of the years. The continuing problem with "split consideration" acquisitions (i.e., where stock of *both* the parent *and* the subsidiary is used) has been pointed out earlier (*supra*, Sec. 12.11), however, and attention must also be given to the effect of these cases on the status of acquisitions in which the stock of more remote corporations in a chain are used.

For example, the parent's stock may be used as consideration for a transfer of the assets of the acquired corporation to a sub-subsidiary of the parent or the assets may be acquired by a subsidiary and then transferred to a sub-subsidiary. Such acquisitions of the assets by a second tier subsidiary were approved as valid Type C reorganizations by the Service in Rev. Rul. 64-73, 1964-1 C.B. 142, where both subsidiaries were 100 percent controlled by their respective parents. The ruling stated that its conclusion was influenced by Congress' desire to remove the *Groman* and *Bashford* continuity of interest problem from the Type C reorganization area. Whether this ruling would apply to

---

[123] Rev. Rul. 57-278, 1957-1 C.B. 124. (As to the status of Type B and C "triangular" acquisitions, see *supra,* Secs. 12.13 and 12.14.) The technique approved in the ruling has a result similar to that achieved by example (d) in the text.

See generally Seplow, *supra* note 119; Tillinghast, Acquiring the Remaining Interest in a Partially Owned Corporation, 37 Taxes 713 (1959).

a triangular Type B reorganization under the similar "anti-*Groman*" amendment in 1964 (in which event there would be four tiers of corporations) remains to be seen; and judgment must also be reserved on such acquisitions where the parent owns less than 100 percent of the subsidiary and/or the latter owns less than 100 percent of the sub-subsidiary. There seems little reason to object on continuity of interest grounds to acquisitions by remote subsidiaries if there is 100 percent affiliation with the parent; but if the stock ownership at each level is less than complete, there will be a gradual diminution of interest as additional tiers are added. Perhaps the 80 percent benchmark which is so widely used as a standard in the corporate nonrecognition provisions will prove useful in applying the anti-*Groman* rules to these situations.

Another problem in this area arises from a possible overlap between the Type A and Type C reorganization provisions. Some states permit a subsidiary to consummate a statutory merger with another corporation through use of its parent's stock; if this transaction constitutes a reorganization under §368(a)(1)(A), there is greater leeway in the type of consideration which can be paid by the acquiring corporation than in a Type C transaction (*supra*, Sec. 12.12). It is understood, however, that the Service will test reorganization status for this type of acquisition under the Type C provisions rather than the statutory merger rules of §368(a)(1)(A). The statute is unclear on this point. Section §368(a)(2)(C) permits the acquiring corporation in a Type A reorganization to transfer the acquired assets to a controlled subsidiary, a provision which can be interpreted either to sanction *direct* asset acquisitions by such a subsidiary under §368(a)(1)(A) in exchange for its parent's stock or, on the other hand, to limit merger acquisitions to the corporation whose stock is used in the exchange. On balance, there seems to be no overriding policy reason for denying statutory merger treatment for triangular acquisitions of this sort, although Service hostility may serve to accomplish this result for all but uninformed or strong-nerved taxpayers.

Sec. 12.22. Reincorporations — Liquidation vs. reorganization

1. In general. The liquidation of a corporation followed by a transfer of part or all of the assets to a newly-organized corporation owned by the same shareholders is a device that, if taken at face value, could serve a variety of tax avoidance purposes. Thus, the shareholders of a corporation might liquidate it, and then:

1. Transfer all of the assets to a newly organized corpora-

tion, in order to deduct a loss on the liquidation, if the fair market value of the assets received in the liquidation is less than their adjusted basis for the stock.

2. Transfer all of the assets to a new corporation, in order to give the new corporation a stepped-up basis for the assets under §334(a) and §362(a)(1), or to wipe out the old corporation's earnings and profits or other tax attributes, at the cost of a tax at the capital gain rate on the liquidation.

3. Transfer all of the assets to a new corporation in exchange for common stock plus (a) preferred stock, in the hope that the preferred would not be "section 306 stock" under §306(c)(1)(A) (stock dividends) or §306(c)(1)(B) (distributions in reorganizations); or (b) bonds, in the hope that the reincorporation will be treated as a tax-free exchange under §351 (*supra*, Ch. 3) rather than as a dividend of the bonds under the *Bazley* case (*supra*, Sec. 12.16).

4. Transfer only the operating assets to the new corporation, holding back cash and other liquid assets, in the hope that the retained assets would not be taxed as a dividend or as boot received in a corporate reorganization.

5. Transfer part or all of the assets to a new corporation, after having the old corporation sell its appreciated property, in the hope that the gain on the sale will go unrecognized under §337 (sales within 12-month period after adoption of plan of complete liquidation).

In each of the foregoing cases, it will be noted that the success of the strategem depends upon divorcing the liquidation of the old corporation from the transfer of the assets to the new corporation, and treating each of these as an independent transaction. If they are regarded as successive steps in a single transaction, however, the tax results could be very different. The "liquidation" and "transfer" of assets to the "new" corporation might be disregarded as without substance, so that the "new" corporation would be treated as a continuation of the "old" corporation, with no change in basis, earnings and profits, or other tax attributes. The distribution of bonds or preferred stock (proposal 3) or the retention of assets (proposal 4 and 5) would then be treated as an ordinary distribution by the corporation. Another rationale for the same result, anchored more explicitly in the language of the Code, is that the liquidation and reincorporation constitute, in substance, a Type E or F reorganization as to the exchange of the old stock for the new stock, accompanied either by the distribution of boot or by an unrelated distribution of the bonds or other property.[124]

[124] For other references to the liquidation-reincorporation problem, see *supra*, Sec. 3.14 (reincorporations and §351), Sec. 9.05 (reincorporations and

Reincorporation was a problem before the 1954 Code. In Bard-Parker Co. v. Commissioner, 218 F.2d 52, 46 AFTR 1418 (2d Cir. 1954), cert. denied, 349 U.S. 906, the court insisted on amalgamating a dissolution and reincorporation "since those two transfers were but procedural steps used to complete what, in substance, constituted a single transfer." A different spirit animates United States v. Arcade Co., 203 F.2d 230, 43 AFTR 652 (6th Cir. 1953), refusing to consolidate the steps because the shareholders, on receiving the old corporation's assets in liquidation, "were under no contractual obligations to form a new corporation or to transfer their assets to a new corporation in return for stock therein"; although it may be too early for the last rites, the case does not inspire one with confidence. Even when the liquidation and reincorporation were regarded as successive steps in the consummation of a single plan, however, the pre-1954 cases had to meet the argument of taxpayers that the transaction could not be a "reorganization" because it lacked a business purpose or because it was not undertaken, in the words of Regs. §1.368-2(g), "for reasons germane to the continuance of the business" of the corporation.[125]

In these cases under the 1939 Code, the government had at its disposal the argument (which was successful in several instances, though not uniformly) that the transaction was a reorganization under §112(g)(1)(D) of the 1939 Code. This provision was the predecessor of §368(a)(1)(D) of the 1954 Code, providing for Type D reorganizations, but the 1954 changes in the definition of a Type D reorganization (supra, Sec. 12.15) would preclude application of this provision to many of the transactions described above. This does not mean that the liquidation-reincorporation route to tax avoidance is now wide open, however, since it may be possible to bring these transactions under the aegis of §368(a)(1)(E) or (F), with respect to the exchange of stock in the "old" corporation for stock in the "new" corporation, coupled with a distribution of bonds or other property.[126] The House version of the 1954 Code contained special provi-

§331), Sec. 9.67 (reincorporations and §337), Sec. 11.14 (reincorporations and split-ups), and Sec. 7.31 (reincorporations and §304).

[125] For cases rejecting the *Arcade Co.* approach and treating such transactions as reorganizations under the 1939 Code coupled with the distribution of taxable "boot," see Survaunt v. Commissioner, 162 F.2d 753, 35 AFTR 1557 (8th Cir. 1947); Lewis v. Commissioner, 176 F.2d 646, 38 AFTR 377 (1st Cir. 1949). See also Liddon v. Commissioner, 230 F.2d 304, 49 AFTR 231 (6th Cir. 1956) ("the Tax Court was correct in analyzing what was done in this case from the point of view of its overall net effect, rather than to permit one isolated transaction in a series to determine the tax consequences"); Walter S. Heller, 2 T.C. 371 (1943).

[126] The *Survaunt* and *Lewis* cases (*supra* note 125) relied on the "boot"

sions dealing with the reincorporation device, but this section was dropped in conference with a statement that "It is the belief . . . that, at the present time, the possibility of tax avoidance in this area is not sufficiently serious to require a special statutory provision," and that these questions "can appropriately be disposed of by judicial decision or by regulation within the framework . . . of the bill." H.R. Rep. No. 2543, 83rd Cong., 2d Sess., 41 (1954). The regulations, Regs. §1.331-1(c) and Regs. §1.301-1(1), attempt to provide a framework for attack on the reincorporation problem by stating that a liquidation or other corporate "readjustment" may have the effect of a dividend distribution under §301. The influence of *Bazley* is manifest in these regulations, and the Service has reinforced this approach in Rev. Rul. 61-156, 1961-2 C.B. 62, where it blended *Bazley*, the step-transaction doctrine, and the Type E and F reorganization provisions in response to a proposed reincorporation plan. The efficacy of this line of attack, and of other approaches under the 1954 Code, will be considered in the material that follows.

The concept of "reorganization," as noted by Regs. §1.368-1(b), requires "continuity of business enterprise" under modified corporate forms and "continuity of interest" on the part of those persons who were owners of the enterprise prior to the reorganization. Complete "liquidation," on the other hand, envisions a final termination or winding up of the *corporate* enterprise, either through sales of its assets to outside purchasers, or by elimination of the corporate entity and continued operation of the distributed business enterprise in unincorporated form. The "reincorporation" problem arises when taxpayers seek to combine the benefits of a complete liquidation (*i.e.*, capital gain or loss on the distribution, a new basis for the assets, and elimination of corporate earnings and profits), with the "reorganization" advantages of continued operation of the business in corporate form. Before reorganization treatment can supplant liquidation treatment, however, the twin factors of continuity of business enterprise and continuity of shareholder investment must be present. In addition, the technical requirements of the reorganization sections must be satisfied, although courts have shown a surprising flexibility of interpretation as to some of these provisions in several recent decisions. Finally, the judicial philosophies, approaches, and attitudes of *Bazley*

provisions to find a dividend. so that the dividend-within-gain restriction (*infra*, Sec. 12.34) was applicable. If the distribution of the bonds or other properties is treated as an independent distribution that coincides in time with the reorganization, however, it would be taxable as a dividend under §301. See the *Bazley* case, *supra*, Sec. 12.16.

and *Gregory* (largely codified by Regs. §301-1(1) and 1.331-1(c))
are a hovering omnipresence in this area: while this line of attack has
not, as yet, assumed a major role in reincorporation matters, it may
eventually emerge as the Commissioner's ultimate weapon, at least
in the more egregious cases of abuse.[127]

2. *Reincorporations as Type D reorganizations.* A major government victory in this area is James Armour, Inc., 43 T.C. 295 (1964).
There, the taxpayers owned 100 percent of two corporations; on the
sale of all of the operating assets of one corporation to the other corporation for cash and an open account debt, followed by complete
liquidation of the "selling" corporation, the court found a reorganization under §368(a)(1)(D) which resulted in "boot dividend" treatment to shareholders of the liquidating corporation under §356(a)(1)
and (2). To square this result with the statute, the court had to
decide that: (a) an actual "exchange" of stock was unnecessary on
the facts because the taxpayer shareholders already owned 100 percent of both corporations, so that issuance of additional stock would
have been a meaningless gesture; and (b) "substantially all of the
assets" were transferred within the meaning of §354(b)(1)(A), even
though their value was only 51 percent of total assets.[128] Moffatt v.
Commissioner, —F.2d—, 17 AFTR 2d 1290 (9th Cir. 1966) involved
a variation of the *Armour* pattern, which also was held to constitute a
Type D reorganization coupled with the distribution of a boot dividend. In *Moffatt*, a personal service business carried on by an existing
corporation with a large earnings and profits account was taken over
by a newly organized corporation, employing the same trained staff

[127] For comprehensive discussions of this problem, see Lane, The Reincorporation Game: Have the Ground Rules Really Changed? 77 Harv. L. Rev.
1218 (1964); Nicholson, Recent Developments in the Reincorporation Area, 19
Tax L. Rev. 123 (1964); Morrison, The Line Between Liquidations and Reorganizations, 41 Taxes 785 (1963); Rice, When Is A Liquidation Not A Liquidation for Federal Income Tax Purposes? 8 Stanf. L. Rev. 208 (1956).
    For analysis of the pre-1954 decisions, and of various proposals for change,
see MacLean, Problems of Reincorporation and Related Proposals of the Subchapter C Advisory Group, 13 Tax L. Rev. 407 (1958).
    [128] The court's willingness to overlook the lack of an exchange was inspired
by Commissioner v. Morgan, 288 F.2d 676, 7 AFTR 2d 909 (3rd Cir. 1961),
where the court found a reorganization on the transfer of assets to a controlled
"sister corporation" even though no stock was issued by the acquiring corporation in exchange for such assets. To the same effect on this point are
South Texas Rice Warehouse Co., 43 T.C. 540 (1965); Reef Corporation, *supra*
note 104; and Ralph C. Wilson, 46 T.C. No. 32 (1966).
    On the "substantially all" issue, it should be noted that the transferred
assets constituted the basic operating assets of the business, while the retained assets were of a liquid investment type. See also Retail Properties, Inc.,
¶64,245 P-H Memo TC; and Reef Corporation, *supra*, where the transferred
operating assets similarly were held to constitute "substantially all" for this
purpose. For the term "substantially all" as used in §368(a)(1)(C), see *supra*,
Sec. 12.14.

(whose existence might have been regarded as the equivalent of good will) that was formerly employed by the old corporation; and, pursuant to a plan, the old corporation was liquidated about 14 months later. The court collapsed the intervening steps, stating that they were merely a "devious path" to the shareholders' ultimate goal of substituting their interest in the old corporation for substantially the same interest in the new corporation; and held that the distributions received by the shareholders were taxable dividends to the extent of the old corporation's earnings and profits.[129]

Another facet of the "non-divisive" Type D reorganization provisions is the requirement of §354(b)(1)(B) that the transferor corporation distribute its properties in liquidation pursuant to the plan of reorganization. In David T. Grubbs, 39 T.C. 42 (1962), this provision was at issue; there, the transferor corporation sold its assets to a corporation controlled by the same group of shareholders, but the transferor corporation did not liquidate after this transaction; instead, it redeemed the stock of all but one of its shareholders, and he proceeded to keep the corporation alive as a wholly owned investment company. The court nevertheless found a Type D reorganization and, more precisely, a "constructive distribution" of the retained assets to the unredeemed shareholder so that §354(b)(1)(B) was satisfied. Although the Grubbs decision took liberties with the language of §354(b)(1)(B), it did so to combat what it felt to be a mere bail-out of corporate earnings; as such, the decision illustrates the flexible approach which is possible in the reincorporation area.

In a series of cases in which the shareholders of the original corporation ended up with less than 80 percent of the stock of the acquiring corporation, however, they were successful in avoiding reorganization treatment. (A Type D reorganization is defined by §368(a)(1)(D) as one in which the transferor's shareholders have "control" of the transferee corporation, i.e., 80 percent or more of its stock, immediately after the transfer.) Thus, the Tax Court refused to find a "reorganization" in Joseph C. Gallagher, 39 T.C. 144 (1962), where a group constituting 62 percent of the shareholders of the "sell-

---

[129] Classification as a Type D reorganization also occurred in Reef Corporation, supra note 104, where only 52 percent of the shareholders of the transferor emerged with all the stock of the transferee corporation, the court there holding that §368(a)(1)(D) required only that some of the transferor's shareholders must "control" the transferee (see discussion of this aspect of the continuity of interest test, supra, Sec. 12.11). An added indignity was the court's determination that notes issued by the transferee as part payment for the acquired assets constituted "stock" because it was thinly capitalized. See also South Texas Rice Warehouse Co., supra note 128, holding a similar transaction to be a Type D reorganization; Ralph C. Wilson, supra note 128.

ing" corporation ended up with only 73 percent (in different proportions) of the "purchasing" corporation's stock; and in Hyman H.
Berghash (*supra* note 14), reorganization treatment was denied
where the owner of 99 percent of the selling corporation's stock ended
up with only 50 percent of the newly created corporate transferee's
stock. However, the Service's position on shareholder continuity of
proprietary interest is considerably less rigid than the foregoing decisions. Rev. Rul. 61-156, 1961-2 C.B. 62, held that 45 percent continuity was sufficient for reorganization treatment; and Rev. Rul.
64-31, 1964-2 C.B. 947, states that the Service will not rule on the
liquidation status of a particular transaction where shareholders of
the liquidating transferor corporation obtain "more than a nominal
amount" of stock of the transferee corporation.[130] This position
seems highly optimistic at best; if the *Gallagher* and *Berghash*
decisions are followed, continuity of interest in the neighborhood of 80
percent (at least where the "control" requirement of §368(a)(1)(D)
is involved) may ultimately become the dividing line between "reorganization" and "liquidation" treatment in this area.

If the reincorporation transaction takes the form of a *stock* acquisition rather than an *asset* acquisition, however, the crucial shareholder ownership percentage is only 50 percent by virtue of the
provisions of §304 (*supra*, Sec. 7.31). For example, if a corporation
purchases all the stock of its "brother" corporation, §304 is controlling, and the transaction is treated as a redemption of the purchasing
corporation's stock and tested for "dividend equivalence" under the
rules of §302. In addition, if the acquiring corporation proceeds to
liquidate its newly purchased "subsidiary" in order to obtain its
assets, the stepped-up basis rules of §334(b)(2) (*supra*, Sec. 9.44) will
not apply because of §334(b)(3)(A) (*i.e.*, the transaction does not
constitute a qualified "purchase" of such stock since §304(a)(1)
treats the acquisition as a "contribution to capital"). Thus, the
asset acquisition route is preferable to the stock acquisition route, but
the possibility that a purported asset transaction may be regarded as
the equivalent of a stock transaction, and compelled to run the gauntlet of §304, should not be disregarded.[131]

Another requirement for a "reorganization" is "continuity of
business enterprise," discussed *supra*, Sec. 12.19. Pridemark, Inc. v.

---

[130] According to gossip in the trade, "nominal amount" means 20 percent
or less.
[131] See generally Kempf, Section 304 of the Internal Revenue Code: Unmasking Disguised Dividends in Related Corporation Transactions, 33 U. of
Chi. L. Rev. 60, 83ff (1965); but see West Coast Marketing Corp., *supra* note
112.

Commissioner, 345 F.2d 35, 15 AFTR 2d 853 (4th Cir. 1965), held that the requisite continuity of corporate business had been broken, and thus no "reorganization" occurred, where the bulk of the assets had been sold to an unrelated purchaser and business activity suspended for over a year.[132] Despite later reactivation of the business enterprise in a new corporation (controlled by the same shareholders), the court in *Pridemark* held that business continuity was sufficiently interrupted to prevent reorganization treatment. Although *Pridemark* may be interpreted as requiring continuity of the *same* business in order to constitute a reorganization, the decision most likely turned on the fact that *all* business activity was suspended for a substantial period of time, thus justifying the conclusion that a true "liquidation" had taken place.

3. Reincorporations as Type E and F reorganizations. The Commissioner has attempted, as yet without much success, to classify some reincorporation transactions as Type E or F reorganizations (see *supra*, Secs. 12.16 and 12.17). Rev. Rul. 61-156, *supra*, first articulated this general approach, but the ruling went on to find an ordinary dividend under *Bazley* principles and §301 as well. This aspect of the ruling was rejected by the Tax Court in *Gallagher*, *supra*, but the dissenters there thought the *Bazley* approach had merit. The courts have also been reluctant to use the Type E and F reorganization provisions in this area, where the acquiring corporation has some shareholders who did not have an interest in the original corporation.[133] A Type E reorganization ordinarily is a "reshuffling of a capital structure within the framework of a single corporation," and a Type F transaction involves "a mere change in identity, form, or place of organization"; neither description is applicable to a reincorporation involving a significant change in ownership. This limited applicability of the Type F reorganization definition is evident in the *Pridemark* case, *supra*, where the Fourth Circuit stated that "its application is limited to cases where the corporate enterprise continues uninterrupted, except perhaps for a distribution of some of its liquid assets" and "there is a mere change of corporate vehicles, the transferee being no more than the alter ego of the transferor."[134] At present,

---

[132] See also Book Production Industries, Inc., ¶65,065, P-H Memo T.C.

[133] Joseph C. Gallagher, *supra* (no E or F reorganizations); Hyman H. Berghash, *supra* (no F reorganization); Reef Corporation, *supra* note 104 (not E or F); Book Production Industries, Inc., *supra* note 132 (not F); Pridemark, Inc. v. Commissioner, *supra* (not F).

[134] See also the *Berghash* case, *supra*, where the court similarly viewed the Type F reorganization in a limited manner. The Commissioner's only victory with the Type F reorganization approach was the Tax Court's decision in the *Pridemark* case, 42 T.C. 510 (1964), later reversed on appeal. The court there

the Type E and F provisions seem available in only the most obvious reincorporation cases; accordingly, the principal line of attack in this area will probably be under the Type D rules, subject, however, to the technical difficulties noted *supra*, which arose because §368(a)(1)(D) was contracted by the 1954 Code.

4. Legislative proposals for the reincorporation problem. Various proposals have been advanced to combat the reincorporation device, detailed analysis of which is beyond the scope of this work.[135] One approach would cut back the effect of the 1954 changes in the Type D reorganization, by reducing the control requirement for non-divisive transactions from 80 to 50 percent (thus reaching the transactions in *Gallagher* and *Berghash*), including some indirect asset transfers in the Type D definition, and amending §356 (relating to boot) to include situations in which the shareholders do not receive any stock or securities. Another approach would repeal §354(b) and provide a special boot rule to deal with the non-divisive bail-out pattern in reincorporation cases; one version of this proposal left the 80 percent control rule unchanged, but a revised proposal accepted a reduction to 50 percent. Elimination of the "substantially all" requirement of §354(b)(1)(A) strikes more deeply at the heart of the reincorporation problem; despite the flexible construction of this phrase in *Armour, supra*, it remains a principal stumbling block for the government in attacking reincorporation transactions.

Part C. Treatment of Parties to a Reorganization

Sec. 12.30. Introductory

Section 368(a) defines the term "reorganization" but does not, of its own force, have any operative effect. Its definitions become effective only insofar as they are employed in other provisions of the Code, of which the most important are:

> 1. §354, providing (with qualifications) that gain or loss shall not be recognized if stock or securities in a corporation that is "a party to a reorganization," a term that is defined by §368-(b), are exchanged solely for stock or securities in the same cor-

---

found a total continuity of the business enterprise as well (although this latter aspect of the case was the basis for appellate reversal). The Tax Court in *Pridemark* took a relatively expansive view of §368(a)(1)(F), but its later decisions have retreated materially from the spirit, if not the letter, of the *Pridemark* opinion. See *supra*, note 133.

[135] See MacLean, *supra* note 127; XVIII ABA Tax Section Bull., 32, 40 (July, 1965).

poration or in another corporation that is a party to the reorganization.

2. §361, under which a corporation that is a party to a reorganization recognizes neither gain nor loss if it exchanges property under the plan of reorganization for stock or securities in another corporation that is a party to the reorganization.

3. §356 and §357, providing for the treatment of "boot" and liabilities in reorganization exchanges.

4. §358 and 362(b), providing for substitutions and carryovers of basis in reorganization exchanges.

5. §381, providing for the transfer of a corporation's net operating loss carryover, earnings and profits, and other tax attributes to a successor corporation in certain reorganizations, subject to the limitations of §382(b) (*infra*, Ch. 13).

These operating provisions deal with the tax treatment of various parties to a reorganization: i.e., recognition of gain or loss realized on the respective exchanges; the character of gain required to be recognized, if any; and the basis of property received in the exchanges. All presuppose the existence of a "reorganization" and, in the material that follows, it will be assumed that the underlying transaction satisfies the statutory definition.

Sec. 12.31. Stock or securities — In general

The basic non-recognition provisions relating to reorganization exchanges, §354 and §361, require the receipt of "stock or securities" in order to qualify for non-recognition treatment. The term "stock or securities" (construed by Regs. §1.368-2(h) to mean "stock and/or securities") is not defined in the Code.[136] As an initial matter, it should be noted that this phrase as used in §§354 and 361 is considerably broader than the type of consideration permitted to be received under §368(a)(1)(B) and (C), which latter provisions allow only "voting stock." This distinction is noted in Regs. §1.361-1, stating that non-voting stock or securities can be received tax-free under §361 by the transferor corporation in a qualified Type C reorganization even though only a limited amount of such consideration is permitted in such a reorganization; note that an excess amount would destroy the transaction's status as a reorganization.

1. Definition of "stock." Ordinarily, a share of "stock" embodies the permanent proprietary ownership or equity interest in a corporation which entitles the holder to (a) share proportionately in the profits of the business, (b) vote on matters affecting the corporate enterprise, and (c) share ratably in the assets of the venture (after

---

[136] For the use of the term in §351, see *supra*, Sec. 3.03.

payment of debts) on liquidation. These rights typically are evidenced by a formal certificate registered in the name of the holder on the books of the corporation. However, various "hybrid" instruments may be created which lack one or more of these indicia of stock, and several cases have arisen under the provisions of §1032 (*supra*, Sec. 3.15) as to whether amounts had been received by a corporation in exchange for *stock*.[137]

Another aspect of the definition of "stock" relates to the "thin capitalization" problem (*supra*, Sec. 4.04). If a corporation is thinly capitalized, or if "indebtedness" held pro rata by shareholders is intended by the parties to constitute part of the corporation's permanent capital structure, courts may hold that the debt must be classified as stock under familiar principles that are equally applicable in the reorganization area.[138]

Where contingent rights to acquire stock, rather than stock itself, are issued in connection with a reorganization, recent decisions have rejected the Service's attempts to classify such instruments as "boot." In Carlberg v. United States, 281 F.2d 507, 6 AFTR 2d 5316 (8th Cir. 1960), the court held that "certificates of contingent interest," representing reserved shares of stock held for the account of exchanging shareholders in a merger pending determination of contingent liabilities, constituted "stock" rather than "boot." The *Carlberg* rationale was followed by the Tax Court in James C. Hamrick, *supra* note 65, where the taxpayer acquired a contractual right to receive additional shares of stock of a corporation if a patent which he had transferred to the corporation in a §351 exchange proved profitable. In both *Carlberg* and *Hamrick*, the courts held that the taxpayers' contingent rights to receive additional shares of stock were, in substance, equivalent to the stock itself since the holders of these rights could receive nothing but stock under the agreement.[139]

---

[137] In rare cases, a single instrument may constitute "stock" but also embody rights of a "non-stock" character. To the extent of the value of the latter rights, the transaction may be outside the reorganization provisions. See, for an analogy, Corn Products Refining Co. v. Commissioner, 350 U.S. 46, 47 AFTR 1789 (1955). See also Rev. Rul. 61-18, 1961-1 C.B. 5; *supra*, Sec. 3.15.

[138] See Reef Corporation, *supra* note 104 ("notes" issued by the acquiring corporation in an alleged "purchase" of assets held to constitute stock); but see Book Production Industries, Inc., *supra* note 132; and W. H. Truschel, *supra* note 20, where debt obligations were classified as such, thereby preventing reorganization status, over the Commissioner's assertion that the debt instead constituted an "equity" interest.

[139] See Rev. Rul. 66-112, *supra* note 43, acquiescing in *Hamrick's* result as to a contingent contractual right to additional shares that is not assignable or readily marketable.

Note that §483 could create "imputed interest income" if issuance of the stock is delayed for more than one year from the date of the exchange, although

Interests of the type involved in the *Carlberg* and *Hamrick* cases satisfy the continuity of interest notion (*supra*, Sec. 12.11) underlying non-recognition treatment in this area; since the only interest that can be obtained by these rights is stock, there is no "cashing in" of the taxpayer's investment which would justify present imposition of the tax.

The receipt of rights, warrants, or options to purchase stock may be another matter, however. Regs. §1.354-1(e) states that stock rights or warrants are not included in the term "stock or securities." Inspiration for this treatment may have come from the *Southwest Consolidated Corp.* case (*supra* note 31), holding that warrants did not constitute *voting* stock within the meaning of §368(a)(1)(C), a decision with continuing influence that goes beyond the precise issue there decided.[140]

2. *Definition of "securities."* The question of whether a debt obligation constitutes a "security" has long been shrouded in confusion, much of which stems from the holding in Pinellas Ice & Cold Storage Co. v. Commissioner, 287 U.S. 462, 11 AFTR 1112 (1933), that short term notes received in exchange for property did not constitute "securities" within the intendment of the reorganization provisions. Confusion was compounded when Neville Coke & Chemical Co. v. Commissioner, 148 F.2d 599, 33 AFTR 1131 (3rd Cir. 1945), applied the continuity of interest principle to hold that an exchange of debt instruments for stock did not qualify for non-recognition treatment under §354; and the implication in *Bazley*, that long term debenture bonds received in a recapitalization exchange for stock did not constitute "securities," did little to clarify the situation.[141]

Notwithstanding these difficulties, in determining whether an instrument is a "security" the courts have ordinarily focussed on its maturity date: notes with a five year term or less seem to be unable

---

Regs. §1.483-2(a)(2) states that such interest income will not destroy reorganization status.

[140] See William H. Bateman, 40 T.C. 408 (1963), holding in reliance on the *Southwest* case, that warrants did not constitute stock when received in a merger; but see Estate of Nettie Miller, 43 T.C. 760 (1965) (bearer warrants of a foreign corporation, entitling the holder to vote and to receive dividends, held to be stock).

At the very least, warrants and rights would seem to constitute "securities," as held in E. P. Raymond, 37 B.T.A. 423 (1938); note however, that if only *stock* is surrendered, the receipt of securities becomes taxable under §354(a)-(2)(B), although not under §361(a).

See also Jack I. LeVant, 45 T.C. 185 (1965), holding that the exchange of a non-restricted "compensatory" stock option for stock of the acquiring corporation in a statutory merger did not qualify for non-recognition treatment under §354(a).

[141] See discussion *supra*, Secs. 12.11 and 12.16; Griswold, *supra* note 18.

to qualify as securities, while a term of 10 years or more is apparently sufficient to bring them within the statute. Later decisions, however, seem to have adopted a "continuity of interest" approach, stating that time alone is not decisive and that what is required is an overall evaluation of the nature of the debt, degree of participation and continuing interest in the affairs of the business, the extent of proprietary interest compared with the similarity of the note to a cash payment, and the purpose of the advances.[142]

It should be noted that §483 will apply to securities received in a non-recognition exchange where maturity is more than one year from the date of the exchange, if they do not carry interest or the interest rate is less than 4 percent.

Sec. 12.32   Treatment of corporate transferor: §§361, 357 and 358

1. Non-recognition in general. The transferor corporation, under §361(a), recognizes neither gain nor loss on an exchange of property for stock or securities of a party to the reorganization if the exchange is pursuant to a plan of reorganization.[143]

The non-recognition rules of §361 apply only if the transferor corporation and the corporation whose stock or securities are received are both "parties to a reorganization." This term is defined by §368-(b) to include a corporation resulting from a reorganization and both corporations in the case of an acquisition of stock or properties of another.[144] But a corporation can participate in a reorganization

---

[142] See discussion and cases cited *supra,* Secs. 3.03 and 3.12; Rev. Rul. 59-98, 1959-1 C.B. 76 (secured bonds with an average life of 6 1/2 years constituted securities under §354 when exchanged for stock); Rev. Rul. 59-222, 1959-1 C.B. 80 (exchange of debenture bonds for stock non-taxable, but exchange of unsecured general creditor claims for stock taxable).

Rev. Rul. 59-98 also held that interest arrears formed a part of the debt security and the fact that part of the stock was received in discharge of these arrears did not cause recognition of gain to the exchanging security holder. See discussion *supra,* Sec. 12.16 and note 81; Cutler, Dividend Arrearages, 37 Taxes 309 (1959).

[143] It should be noted that non-voting stock and securities can be received tax-free under §361(a) if issued in a qualified reorganization (i.e., a Type A statutory merger, or in a Type C reorganization under the "boot relaxation" rule), even though they might not constitute permissible consideration in a different type of reorganization (i.e., a Type B exchange). See Regs. §1.361-1.

Unlike §354 (*infra,* Sec. 12.34), §361(a) permits securities to be received tax-free even though none are surrendered or the principal amount of those received exceeds that of those surrendered.

[144] According to Groman v. Commissioner, 302 U.S. 82, 19 AFTR 1214 (1937), the pre-1954 definition was not exclusive, and the 1954 changes, amplifying its scope, do not seem intended to exclude any corporation that would previously have qualified.

See generally, Hays Corp. v. Commissioner, 40 T.C. 436 (1963), aff'd, 331

without being a party thereto under §368(b). Thus, if Corporation P owns all the stock of Corporation S, which it transfers to Corporation Y in exchange for Y's voting stock in a Type B reorganization, S and Y are parties to the reorganization under §368(b)(2), but P is not.[145]

In addition to requiring that the stock or securites received must be those of a "party to a reorganization" and that the transferor of property likewise must be a "party" thereto, §361(a) requires that the exchange be "in pursuance of the plan of reorganization."[146]

Non-recognition of the transferor's gain under §361(a) applies only if the exchange is "solely" for stock or securities, but §361(b) intervenes to moderate this strict rule. Under §361(b), the transferor will not recognize its gain if it distributes all of the boot in pursuance of the plan of reorganization; if it retains part or all of the boot, its gain (if any) must be recognized up to an amount equal to the boot retained. Even if the boot exceeds the corporation's gain (e.g., boot worth $100,000, but gain of only $50,000), it is essential that the entire boot be distributed; §361(b)(1)(B) requires the recognition of gain to the extent that boot is retained. Moreover, the boot must be distributed to shareholders; its application to pay

---

F.2d 422, 13 AFTR 2d 1367 (7th Cir. 1964); Regs. §1.368-2(f), with examples illustrating the definition of §368(b).

[145] Had the transaction been cast in a somewhat different form, however, P would be a "party." See §368(b), second and third sentences, added in 1954. It has been pointed out earlier (*supra*, Secs. 12.12 and 12.14) that §368(a)(2)-(C) permits property to be transferred to a subsidiary of the acquiring corporation in a Type A or C reorganization. This can be done tax-free under §351, so far as the transaction between the acquiring corporation and its subsidiary is concerned. But if the subsidiary's stock or securities are to be used to compensate the original transferor of the assets in a Type A reorganization, they can be received tax-free under §354 only if the subsidiary is a "party to the reorganization." It is curious that when the third sentence of §368(b) was added in 1954 to insure that the acquiring corporation would not lose *its* status as a party to the reorganization by transferring the assets to a subsidiary, nothing was done to make it clear that the subsidiary was also a party. It is possible that the subsidiary is a party by virtue of §368(b)(2) (see note 59 *supra*) or that, if newly created, it may qualify under §368(b)(1); see also *supra*, note 144.

Returning to the example in the text, it should be noted that if the S stock constituted substantially all of the assets of P, the transaction would also be a Type C reorganization; and if P was in control of Y, the transaction would be a Type D reorganization. In either case, P would then be a "party" under §368(b)(2).

[146] On this requirement, see Regs. §1.368-1(g) and Regs. §1.368-3(a); see also Manning. "In Pursuance of the Plan of Reorganization;" The Scope of the Reorganization Provisions of the Internal Revenue Code, 72 Harv. L. Rev. 881 (1959); Silberman, When can an "option to purchase" constitute a "plan of reorganization?" 23 J. Tax. 136 (1965). Note also that the "plan" requirement has been involved in many of the cases arising under the "step transaction" doctrine (especially as applied to the "reincorporation" area), for which see *supra*, Secs. 12.20 and 12.22.

debts of the corporation does not qualify as a distribution under §361(b)(1).[147] The corporation is absolved from the recognition of gain by §361(b)(1) on the theory that it is a "mere conduit" for passing the consideration received in the reorganization to its shareholders, see S. Rep. No. 398, 68th Cong. 1st Sess., reprinted in 1939-1 C.B. (Part 2) 266, 277, but the boot is not necessarily taxable to the shareholder, who may have exchanged his stock in the distributing corporation for a liquidating distribution on which he realized no gain. See *infra*, Sec. 12.34.

Section 361(b)(1) comes into play only if the corporation realizes a gain on the reorganization. If it suffers a loss, §362(b)(2) provides that it cannot be deducted even though boot is received.

2. Assumption of liabilities. For purposes of §361, §357(a) provides generally that the assumption of the transferor's liabilities or the taking of property subject to liabilities (if consistent with the existence of a "reorganization") will not constitute boot under §361-(a). But if tax avoidance motives apply to the assumption of any liability, or if no business purpose can be proved therefor, §357(b) provides that *all* such liabilities must be treated as boot. In view of this penal aspect of §357(b), seemingly concerned with assumptions of liabilities that constitute a disguised payment of boot to the transferor (*supra*, Sec. 3.06), courts have tended to apply it with a merciful hand. If the liabilities assumed or to which the properties are subject exceed their basis, gain must be recognized by the transferor under §357(c) if the transfer occurs in a Type D reorganization.[148]

A transferor corporation which receives property that would constitute boot under §361 if retained can avoid this result by distributing the property under §361(b)(1), but this escape hatch is not available if the boot is created by §357. Although "considered as money" by virtue of §357, an assumption of the transferor's liabilities cannot be "distributed" to its shareholders in any meaningful way.[149]

3. Basis. The applicable basis provision for the corporate transferor of property is §358, which provides, in brief, that non-recognition property (*i.e.*, stock or securities) received by the transferor in exchange for its property takes a substituted basis: its basis for

---

[147] Liquidating Co., 33 B.T.A. 1173 (1936) (N-A). See Minnesota Tea Co. v. Helvering, 302 U.S. 609, 19 AFTR 1258 (1938) (corporation taxable where boot was distributed to shareholders in return for their assumption of corporate debts, since distribution to shareholders "was a meaningless and unnecessary incident in the transmission of the fund to the creditors").

[148] See Cooper, Negative Basis, 75 Harv. L. Rev. 1352 (1962), to the effect that §357(c) should have been made applicable to Type C rather than Type D reorganizations.

[149] See Minnesota Tea v. Helvering, *supra* note 147.

the transferred property, increased by any gain (and decreased by any loss) recognized to the transferor on the exchange, and decreased by any boot received. In addition, §358(d) provides that basis must be reduced by any liabilities assumed (or taken subject to) by the transferee on the exchange.[150] These rules are unimportant to the transferor corporation in a reorganization if, as often occurs, it is liquidated as a part of the reorganization plan. In a Type C reorganization, however, liquidation of the transferor is not necessary (*supra*, Sec. 12.14), so that the basis of stock or securities received in exchange for its property becomes important in this situation.

4. Example. The above rules may be illustrated by the following example: X corporation transfers all of its property, with a basis of $40 and a value of $100, to Y corporation in a Type C reorganization; Y gives voting stock worth $80 and cash of $20 in exchange for X's properties. X will recognize gain of $20 on this exchange, unless it distributes the boot to its shareholders pursuant to the reorganization plan, in which case gain will be recognized only to the extent that boot is retained by it.[151]

If, instead of paying cash, Y assumed X's liabilities in the amount of $20 on the exchange, no gain would be recognized by X unless all or a part of this assumption failed to qualify under §357(a), because of a tax avoidance motive or lack of a "business purpose." In such a case, gain would be recognized by X in the amount of $20 (i.e., to the extent of the liabilities assumed by Y); for this purpose X could not avoid recognition of such gain under §361(b)(1)(A), since boot arising from liability assumptions cannot be "distributed" under §361(b)(1)(A). If the assumed liabilities were $50 instead of $20, and if the assumption was not tainted under §357(b), X would recognize no gain on the exchange; despite the fact that the liabilities exceeded the basis of its properties by $10, §357(c) does not apply to a Type C reorganization. The possibility that X's basis for the stock or securities received from Y would be minus $10 (*supra*, note 150) could be avoided by a distribution to its shareholders, since their basis for these instruments would be determined by reference to their basis for their X stock (*infra*, Sec. 12.34).

---

[150] As to the possibility of a negative basis for stock or securities where assumed liabilities exceed the transferor's basis for its property, see Easson v. Commissioner, 294 F.2d 653, 8 AFTR 2d 5448 (9th Cir. 1961); Cooper, *supra* note 148.

For further discussion of §358 (in the context of §351 exchanges), see *supra*, Sec. 3.10.

[151] Distribution to *creditors* of X in discharge of liabilities is not a protected distribution under §361(b)(1)(A); see Minnesota Tea Co. v. Helvering, *supra* note 147.

Sec. 12.33   Treatment of corporate transferee: §§1032 and 362

1. Non-recognition. A corporation which acquires property in exchange for its stock is protected from recognition of gain or loss thereon by §1032 (*supra*, Sec. 3.15); this is true whether or not the transaction constitutes a "reorganization" under §368. Section 1032 also protects the acquiring corporation from recognition of gain or loss where stock given in the exchange is treasury stock rather than newly issued stock; this provision, enacted in 1954, changed prior law, under which gain or loss could be recognized by a corporation if it dealt with its treasury stock as it would with the shares of another corporation.

Where the transferee corporation issues securities, in addition to stock, as part of the consideration for the acquired property, the authority for non-recognition is less clear; presumably the acquisition is a "purchase" of property by the transferee to this extent and, as such, does not involve recognition of gain or loss. Although this result is not prescribed by an express statutory provision, it is so well established and widely assumed that, no doubt, none was thought necessary by Congress.

Where property is acquired by a subsidiary corporation in exchange for its parent's stock (in a *Groman* "triangular acquisition," *supra*, Sec. 12.11), however, non-recognition treatment to the transferee corporation may not be afforded by §1032. For example, suppose that the parent corporation contributes its own stock to the subsidiary, which then uses this stock as the consideration for the stock or properties acquired from another corporation. Section 1032 applies only to a corporation whose *own* stock is given in exchange for property, and hence would not seem to protect the subsidiary from recognition of gain in such a case of an exchange of its parent's stock for property. In Rev. Rul. 57-278, 1957-1 C.B. 124, however, the Service ruled (without discussion) that no gain or loss was recognized by the subsidiary in such a case.[152]

---

[152] Statutory support for non-recognition treatment of the acquiring subsidiary seems questionable. In the case of an asset for stock acquisition (*i.e.*, a Type C reorganization), §361 would be the only possibility, but that provision has ordinarily been thought to be concerned with the treatment of the property transferor rather than the acquiring party. Moreover, the subsidiary would not retain any "continuity of interest" with respect to the consideration which it gives in the exchange (its parent's stock), so that a fundamental requisite for non-recognition treatment would be lacking as far as the subsidiary is concerned. In the case of a stock for stock acquisition (a Type B reorganization), the literal language of §354(a) seems more hospitable to non-recognition treatment for the acquiring corporation, but even here the transaction may be vulnerable under continuity principles. While the continuity of interest doctrine (*supra*, Sec. 12.11) ordinarily functions as a condition to reorganization status, its scope and radiations may be sufficiently broad to cause the infusion of con-

2. *Basis of acquired property.* Under §362(b), property acquired by a corporation "in connection with a reorganization"[153] ordinarily takes a "carry-over" basis equal to the transferor's basis, increased by any gain recognized to the transferor on such transfer.[154] Since recognition of gain by the transferor is affected by whether it distributed its boot under §361(b)(1), the transferee corporation has a lively interest in the use to which the transferor plans to put any boot paid in the exchange. But §361(b)(1)(A) comes into play only if boot is distributed "in pursuance of the plan of reorganization," so that the transferee corporation should not lose the benefit of an anticipated stepped-up basis merely because the transferor, in an unrelated transaction, chooses to distribute the boot. On the other hand, if the boot is distributed by the transferor pursuant to the plan, the transferee corporation does not obtain a stepped-up basis for any gain recognized to the transferor's *shareholders* because of its boot distributions.[155]

If the acquisition transaction fails to qualify as a reorganization, the transferee corporation is entitled to a "cost" basis for the acquired properties under §1012, presumably equal to the fair market value of the consideration paid by it.[155a] Moreover, the transferee's right to a "cost" basis in this situation is not affected by the fact that no gain or loss was recognized to it on the exchange under §1032.

Although §362(b) prescribes a carry-over basis for property received by the transferee corporation in a reorganization, it does not apply if such property consists of stock or securities in a corporation which is a party to the reorganization, unless they were acquired by the issuance of the transferee's stock or securities as consideration. (See also §358(e), which similarly provides that the substituted basis rules of §358 do not apply to property acquired by the issuance of the transferee's stock or securities as consideration for the transfer.) The general purpose and effect of these provisions is to confine determination of the transferee's basis for its acquired property to the

---

tinuity principles into the non-recognition provisions of §§361 and 354 (and hence to require the acquiring corporation to recognize gain in this situation).

[153] The scope of the phrase "in connection with a reorganization" is unclear. It seems somewhat looser than the usual requirement of an exchange "in pursuance of a plan of reorganization," for which see *supra* note 146.

[154] See *supra*, Sec. 3.11; see also Truck Terminals, Inc. v. Commissioner, 314 F.2d 449, 11 AFTR 2d 901 (9th Cir. 1963) (basis not stepped-up by gain erroneously reported by transferor on exchange).

[155] See Schweitzer & Conrad, Inc., 41 B.T.A. 533, 547-548 (1940); Levin, The Case for a Stepped-Up Basis to the Transferee in Certain Reorganizations, 17 Tax L. Rev. 511 (1962).

[155a] See Moore-McCormack Lines, Inc., 44 T.C. 745 (1965); Nassau Lens Co., Inc. v. Commissioner, 308 F.2d 39, 10 AFTR 2d 5581 (2d Cir. 1962).

rules of §362(b). However, in Firestone Tire & Rubber Co., 2 T.C. 827 (1943) (Acq.), the Tax Court held that the term "issuance" did not reach a transfer of treasury stock (i.e., issuance means "original issue"), so that the transferee corporation in a Type B reorganization was entitled under §358 to use the basis of its treasury stock in determining the basis of stock acquired in the exchange. The court reached this conclusion in large part by reliance on the pre-1954 rule that a corporation could recognize gain or loss on the disposition of its treasury stock; this aspect of the opinion was undermined by the enactment of §1032 in 1954, and *Firestone* is probably inapplicable to post-1954 transactions.

In 1964, the definition of a Type B reorganization was expanded to include acquisitions of stock in exchange for stock of the parent of the acquiring corporation (*supra*, Sec. 12.13). Congress inadvertently neglected to make a corresponding change in the basis rules of §362-(b), however, so that a technical argument can be made that the carry-over basis rules of §362(b) do not apply to the transferee because stock of "*the* transferee" was not used as consideration for the transfer. Since Regs. §1.358-4 provides that §358 does not apply where stock of the transferee's parent is issued as consideration for the transfer, there appears to be a hiatus between §358 and §362(b). If both are inapplicable, the transferee's basis for the stock is presumably its cost under §1012, viz., the fair market value of the parent's stock; and *this* possibility suggests that it might be able to liquidate the acquired corporation in a later unrelated transaction and thereby obtain a stepped-up basis for its assets under §334(b)(2) (*supra*, Sec. 9.44). As a matter of policy, however, such a stepped-up basis for the assets is hard to reconcile with the fact that the stock was acquired in a tax-free transaction; and the Service's position on this issue is unclear.[156]

3. *Carryover of the transferor's tax attributes to transferee.* In addition to inheriting the tax basis of property acquired from the transferor in a reorganization, the transferee corporation steps into the shoes of the transferor with respect to such tax attributes as its earnings and profits, accounting methods, and carryovers for net operating and capital losses. This area is governed by the detailed rules of §381, enacted in 1954, for which see the discussion in Ch. 13.

---

[156] See XIX ABA Tax Section Bull., No. 2, p. 128 (Jan. 1966). For a pre-1954 transaction involving this problem, see Georgia-Pacific Corp. v. United States, *supra* note 118 (stepped-up basis allowed for assets acquired in merger, under *Kimbell-Diamond* principle); see also South Bay Corp. v. Commissioner, *supra* note 44; Long Island Water Corp., *supra* note 26.

Sec. 12.34.   Treatment of stockholders and security holders: §§354, 356, and 358

1. Non-recognition and boot in general. Recognition of gain or loss to exchanging shareholders and security holders in a reorganization is governed generally by the rules of §354(a)(1), which provides:

> No gain or loss shall be recognized if stock or securities in a corporation a party to a reorganization are, in pursuance of the plan of reorganization, exchanged solely for stock or securities in such corporation or in another corporation a party to the reorganization.[157]

If the transaction constitutes a reorganization, and if the exchanges are pursuant to a plan of reorganization and the stock or securities are those of a party to a reorganization, §354(a)(1) takes hold and provides for non-recognition of gain or loss on the respective exchanges of stock or securities.

The non-recognition rule of §354(a)(1) is applicable only if the exchange is "solely" for stock or securities of a corporation that is a party to a reorganization. Moreover, §354(a)(2) (enacted in 1954) provides that the general non-recognition rule of §354(a)(1) shall "not apply" if: (a) the principal amount of securities received exceeds the principal amount of securities surrendered; or (b) securities are received and no securities are surrendered. (For this purpose, the term "securities" means only debt securities.) By virtue of these restrictions, a shareholder whose proprietary interest is up-graded in a reorganization to that of a creditor (or a security holder whose creditor status is enhanced through receipt of obligations in a greater principal amount) will have to recognize his gain *pro tanto*, as though he had received money in the exchange. Accordingly, the taxpayer's realized gain will go wholly tax-free under §354(a)(1) only if (a) stock is surrendered solely for stock, (b) securities are surrendered

---

[157] For the terms used in §354(a)(1), see *supra*, Sec. 12.31 ("stock or securities") and Sec. 12.32 ("plan of reorganization" and "party to a reorganization").

See also §356(f), referring to §2501 and §61(a)(1) for "special rules" if a §354 exchange results in a gift or has the effect of compensation. The warning hardly seems necessary; moreover, to the extent that the exchange has these adventitious effects, it should not be regarded as "a transaction described in section 354."

An exchange in a Type D reorganization is subject to §354(a)(1) only if it meets the additional conditions of §354(b); otherwise, as discussed *supra,* Sec. 12.15, it is subject to §355.

Note also §354(c), making §354(a)(1) applicable to certain railroad reorganizations even though they do not otherwise meet its requirements.

solely for securities in an equal or lesser principal amount, or (c) securities are surrendered for stock and securities in an equal or lesser principal amount.

The purpose of these restrictions is to apply the continuity of interest test (taxpayer-by-taxpayer) to the exchanges in a reorganization. Another purpose of these provisions is to block the "security bail-out" device, whereby debt obligations could be issued pro-rata to shareholders with a view to their subsequent retirement at capital gain rates, thus effecting a distribution of corporate earnings and profits without dividend consequences. The effect of §354(a)(2) is similar to the result in *Bazley*, except that gain is recognized under §354(a)(2) only if gain is realized by the taxpayer on the exchange, whereas *Bazley* treated the securities as a dividend, generating ordinary income to the extent of the corporation's earnings and profits.[158] Thus, if a shareholder exchanged stock with a basis of $100 for stock with a value of $50 and bonds with a value of $75, *Bazley* would require recognition of income to the extent of $75, the fair market value of the bonds; if, however, the transaction qualifies as a reorganization, §354(a)(2) and §356(a)(1) would limit recognition of the shareholder's gain to $25 (the amount of his realized gain).

On its face, §354(a) seems to leave no leeway for the receipt of money or other property in the exchange; however, the cross-reference of §354(a)(3) takes us to §356, governing the receipt of "boot" in an exchange that would "otherwise qualify" under §354. Thus, if the exchange involves the receipt of "other property" or money in addition to property that can be received tax-free, reference must be made to the "boot" rules of §356.

Turning now to §356, we find that it relaxes the stern injunction in §354(a)(1) that the exchange must be "solely" for stock or securities. If the taxpayer receives "boot" as well as non-recognition property, his gain, if any, is to be recognized, but in an amount not in excess of the boot.[159] The receipt of boot does not, however, permit the taxpayer to recognize any loss he may have sustained on the exchange. See §356(c). These principles may be illustrated by the following example:

---

[158] *Supra*, Sec. 12.16; see also Regs. §1.301-1(1).

[159] If securities are the *sole* consideration received in an exchange where no securities are surrendered (*i.e.*, a shareholder exchanges his stock solely for bonds), the transaction appears to be entirely outside the rules of §354 and §356. See Regs. §1.354-1(d), Example (3). In this situation, the exchange resembles a redemption of stock (supra, Ch. 7), as suggested by the cross-reference to §302 in the regulations. If the distribution of bonds is disproportionate rather than pro rata, the result under §302 may be the recognition of capital gain or loss, rather than dividend income; see also *supra*, Sec. 12.16, for the relation of *Bazley* to disproportionate exchanges.

1. Received by taxpayer:
   a. Stock (fair market value) $10,000
   b. Securities (fair market value) 5,000
   c. Money 2,500
                                            $17,500
2. Less: basis of stock surrendered 5,000
3. Gain realized on exchange $12,500
4. Gain recognized under §356(a)(1) (line 3,
   or 1b plus 1c, whichever is lesser) ..... $ 7,500

If the shareholder's basis for the stock surrendered had been $15,000, he would have realized a gain of only $2,500 on the exchange, and only this amount would have been recognized under §356(a). If his basis had been $20,000, he would have realized a loss of $2,500 on the exchange, but it would have gone unrecognized by virtue of §356(c).

The treatment of "securities" as "other property" is determined by §356(d), which states generally that securities will be treated as "boot" except in cases where securities are permitted to be received without recognition of gain under §354 or §355. If the securities do not qualify as non-recognition property, the amount of boot is either the fair market value of the excess of principal amount received over principal amount surrendered or, if no securities are surrendered, the fair market value of the principal amount received. In applying these principles, the regulations treat a portion of the fair market value of *each security received* as boot, based on the ratio which the total "excess" principal amount bears to the total principal amount of all such securities received. For example, if two securities with a total principal amount of $100 are surrendered for two securities with total principal amount of $150 (one of which has a value of $75 and the other $60), one-third of the fair market value of each security received constitutes boot, or $25 and $20 respectively.[160]

The foregoing discussion has been based on the assumption that there was a reorganization as defined by §368(a)(1) and that the "boot" received by the taxpayer, though requiring the partial or complete recognition of his gain, was not inconsistent with the existence of a "reorganization." An example is a statutory merger in which the consideration is partly stock of the surviving corporation and partly money or other property; another is a Type C reorganization in which some money is used, in addition to voting stock, pursuant

[160] See Regs. §1.356-3.

The imputed interest rules of §483, to the extent that they convert "principal" into "interest," will affect the computation of "principal amount" under §356.

to the authorization in §368(a)(2)(B). In these cases, there is a reorganization, so far as the definition in §368(a)(1) is concerned, and the receipt of boot simply requires any taxpayer who realized gain on the exchange to recognize his gain *pro tanto*.

For many years, it had been assumed by tax lawyers that the use of any consideration that is not tolerated by the *definitional* subparagraphs of §368(a)(1) (e.g., the use of money in a stock-for-stock transaction, in violation of the "solely for voting stock" rule of §368-(a)(1)(B), or the use of money beyond the amount permitted by §368(a)(2)(B) in an asset acquisition) would destroy the possibility of a reorganization, making such provisions as §354, §361, and §381(a)(2) totally inapplicable for want of a "reorganization." This basic idea was undermined in 1956 by Howard v. Commissioner, 238 F.2d 943, 50 AFTR 832 (7th Cir. 1956), which held that certain shareholders, who exchanged their stock solely for stock of the acquiring corporation, could take advantage of the non-recognition rules of §354, even though the acquiring corporation paid cash to other transferor shareholders. The court reached this conclusion by reliance on the "but for" language of §356(a)(1); since the transaction would have qualified as an exchange of stock *solely* for voting stock of the acquired corporation if the cash boot was disregarded, the court held that §354 applied, and that no gain was to be recognized by those shareholders who received no cash or other boot. This approach was rejected by the Supreme Court in Turnbow v. Commissioner, 368 U.S. 337, 8 AFTR 2d 5967 (1961), which held that a transaction must constitute a "reorganization" under the definitional rules of §368 before taxpayers can resort to the non-recognition rules of §354 and §356.[161]

2. *Character of recognized gain.* The amount of gain to be recognized having been determined under §356(a)(1), the provisions of §356(a)(2) then determine whether it will be taxed as a dividend or as capital gain. Section 356(a)(2) provides that if the exchange has the "effect of the distribution of a dividend," the taxpayer's recognized gain must be so treated to the extent of his ratable share of post-1913 earnings and profits; the remainder of the recognized gain, if any, is treated as gain from the exchange of property (viz., as capital gain, unless the taxpayer is a dealer in securities). The "dividend-within-gain" approach of §356(a)(2), under which the shareholder reports dividend income only if and to the extent that he realizes gain on the exchange, may be illustrated as follows: if the taxpayer realized a gain of $100 on the exchange, $50 of which

[161] See Vernava, *supra* note 31.

was recognized because of the receipt of boot, the maximum amount of dividend income which could arise under §356(a)(2) would be $50; if the realized gain had only been $20, dividend income would be limited to $20; and if the realized gain had been zero (because the amount realized was equal to the adjusted basis of the stock given up), there would be no dividend income.

Several other features of the "boot dividend" rules of §356(a)(2) should also be noted: (a) this provision refers only to "accumulated" earnings and profits, unlike the ordinary dividend rules of §316(a), which support dividend treatment if either current or accumulated earnings are present;[162] (b) the taxpayer's dividend income is limited to his "ratable share" of earnings under §356(a)(2), a restriction that may not apply under §316 (*supra*, Sec. 5.23); (c) in testing for existence of the requisite earnings and profits, and for "dividend equivalence," §356(a)(2) looks to the effect of a direct distribution by the transferor corporation; and (d) as to corporate distributees, Regs. §1.356-1(d) does not apply the "lower of value or basis" rule of §301(b)(1)(B). As a result, the boot dividend rules of §356(a)(2) seem to constitute an independent dividend test, apart from the "ordinary" dividend rules of §301 and §316.[163] For this reason, the Service evidently regards §356 "dividends" as not qualifying for the intercorporate dividends received deduction of §243 or the dividends received exclusion of §116.

As a result of some imprecise statements in Commissioner v. Bedford's Estate, it was assumed for many years that §356(a)(2) automatically converted any recognized gain into dividend income, to the extent of the distributing corporation's earnings and profits, where the taxpayer continued as a shareholder after the exchange.[164] It is a long step, however, from the facts of the *Bedford* case (which involved cash distributed in a recapitalization to discharge arrearages in preferred dividends) to the "automatic dividend" conclusion; and more recent cases have properly retreated from this view.[165] Rather than an automatic dividend approach (which Congress has explicitly adopted in §356(b) and (e), thus implying a more flexible

---

[162] But see Vesper Co., Inc. v. Commisioner, 131 F.2d 200, 30 AFTR 245 (8th Cir. 1942); *supra*, Ch. 9, note 21; *supra*, Sec. 5.02.

[163] The *Bedford* case, *infra* note 164, however, implies that the definition of §316 is "infused" into §356(a)(2).

[164] 325 U.S. 283, 33 AFTR 832 (1945); Regs. §1.356-1(c), Example (1).

[165] See Idaho Power Co. v. United States, 161 F. Supp. 807, 1 AFTR 2d 1621 (Ct. Cl. 1958); Hawkinson v. Commissioner, 235 F.2d 747, 49 AFTR 1794 (2d Cir. 1956); William H. Bateman, 40 T.C. 408 (1963); Ross v. United States, 173 F. Supp. 793, 3 AFTR 2d 1569 (Ct. Cl. 1959), cert. denied, 361 U.S. 875.

approach elsewhere), the phrase "has the effect of a distribution of a dividend" as used in §356(a)(2) suggests an analysis of the facts similar to that employed under §302(b)(1) (*supra*, Sec. 7.24), §346-(a)(2) (*supra*, Sec. 7.62), and §306(c)(1)(B)(ii) (*infra*, Sec. 12.35). Although there is no explicit statutory coordination between the stock redemption rules of §302 and §346 and the boot distribution rule of §356(a)(2), the principles developed in interpreting §302, and possibly §346, can be helpful in reaching a satisfactory result under §356(a)(2).[166] If boot is received in exchange for "section 306 stock," a special rule is applicable by virtue of §356(e): whether the shareholder realizes gain or loss on the exchange, the fair market value of the boot is treated as an ordinary distribution under §301, which means that it will be taxed as a dividend to the extent of the taxpayer's share of the distributing corporation's current and post-1913 earnings and profits. For priority rules where both section 306 stock and other stock are exchanged by the taxpayer, see Regs. §1.356-4.

3. *Basis.* Exchanging shareholders and security holders determine their basis for property acquired in a §354 exchange under §358(a), which provides that the basis of stock or securities received ("non-recognition property") shall be the same as the basis of the property transferred, (a) decreased by the fair market value of any boot received, and (b) increased by the amount of any gain (and by the amount of any dividend income) recognized on the exchange. Under §358(a)(2), any boot received in the exchange takes a fair market value basis.

If several classes of stock or securities are received in the exchange as non-recognition property, §358(b)(1) requires an allocation of the basis of the property surrendered between the various classes of stock and securities received in the exchange, and Regs. §1.358-2(b) requires the allocation to be made in proportion to their respective market values. For this purpose, stock or securities in different corporations are treated as separate classes of stock or securities, and stock or securities in the same corporation will be so treated if they have differing rights or preferences.

> For example, if the basis of the property surrendered was $8,000, and the taxpayer received in exchange common stock

[166] See generally Darrell, The Scope of Commissioner v. Bedford's Estate, 24 Taxes 266 (1946); Wittenstein, Boot Distributions and Section 112(c)(2): A Re-Examination, 8 Tax L. Rev. 63 (1952); Moore, Taxation of Distributions Made in Connection with a Corporate Reorganization, 17 Tax L. Rev. 129 (1962); and Shoulson, Boot Taxation: The Blunt Toe of the Automatic Rule, 20 Tax L. Rev. 573 (1965).

For proposals to achieve coordination in this area, see XVIII ABA Tax Section Bull., No. 4, 42-45 (July, 1965).

worth $3,000 and preferred stock worth $9,000, the basis of the common stock would be $2,000 and that of the preferred $6,000. Assuming no later fluctuations in value, the taxpayer will realize $1,000 of gain on a subsequent sale of his common stock and $3,000 of gain on a sale of his preferred stock; his total gain of $4,000, it will be noted, is equal to the gain realized but unrecognized on the initial §354 exchange.

If, in addition to the above consideration, the taxpayer received other property with a value of $3,000 on the exchange, gain would be recognized to that extent and the basis of the boot would be its fair market value ($3,000). The basis of the common and preferred stock received in the exchange would be $8,000 (the basis of property given up, $8,000, less boot of $3,000, plus recognized gain of $3,000), to be allocated between the common and preferred stock in proportion to their relative fair market values (one-fourth and three-fourths, respectively).

If a shareholder or security holder owning more than one class of stock or securities receives, with respect thereto, other stock or securities in a non-recognition transaction under §354, Regs. §1.358-2(a)(4) requires a separate basis computation for each class.

For example, if a taxpayer owning stock with a basis of $4,000 and securities with a basis of $6,000 receives in exchange for his stock two classes of stock with respective values of $2,000 and $6,000, and receives with respect to his securities two classes of securities with respective values of $3,000 and $6,000, the basis allocation would be as follows: the $4,000 basis of the stock surrendered would be allocated between the two classes of stock received in proportion to their relative values (*i.e.*, $1,000 and $3,000, respectively); the basis of the securities surrendered likewise would be allocated among the securities received in exchange therefor in proportion to the relative fair market values of the securities received (*i.e.*, $2,000 and $4,000).

If a single class of stock or securities is surrendered in a nontaxable §354 reorganization exchange, consisting of securities acquired by the taxpayer at different dates or for different prices, determination of the substituted basis for the stock or securities received in exchange therefor is ordinarily determined by reference to an "average cost" basis for the stock or securities surrendered, at least if specific shares or securities received cannot be identified with specific items surrendered.[167] The average cost rule is an exception to the

[167] See Commissioner v. Von Gunten, 76 F.2d 670, 15 AFTR 1206 (6th Cir. 1935); Rev. Rul. 55-355, 1955-1 C.B. 418; Commissioner v. Oliver, 78 F.2d 561, 16 AFTR 425 (3d Cir. 1935); Helvering v. Stifel, 75 F.2d 583, 15 AFTR 248 (4th Cir. 1935); Commissioner v. Arrott, 136 F.2d 449, 31 AFTR 180 (3rd Cir. 1942); Commissioner v. Bolender, 82 F.2d 591, 17 AFTR 677 (7th Cir. 1936);

"general rule" of Regs. §1.1012-1(c), that if securities are sold by a taxpayer who purchased or acquired such properties at different dates or at different prices and the lot from which such securities are sold cannot be adequately identified, gain or loss on the sale thereof must be calculated on the "first-in first-out" method.[168] The theory of the "average cost" exception is that the securities surrendered in a reorganization exchange lose their identity in the securities received because the latter are acquired at one time in a single transaction. The average cost rule is limited, however, to acquisitions of stock or securities in a non-taxable reorganization exchange; in addition, it has been held that the rule does not apply where the exchange involves stock or securities of a single corporation received in a recapitalization or Type F reorganization.[169]

While the average cost basis has been sanctioned as a proper method for determining the §358 substituted basis of stock or securities *acquired* in certain non-taxable reorganization exchanges, it should be noted that the exchanging shareholders and security holders must determine their gain or loss separately with respect to each identifiable block of stock or securities *transferred* by them in the exchange. Hence, both gains and losses can be realized by a taxpayer in the same transaction where different blocks of stock or securities are transferred in the exchange. Also, it seems relatively well established that the taxpayer cannot "net" the gains against the losses in this situation, since the transfer of each identifiable block of stock or securities constitutes a separate transaction for gain or loss computation purposes.[170]

Sec. 12.35.   "Section 306 stock" received in corporate reorganizations

In Chapter 8, the use of preferred stock as a method of "bailing out" corporate earnings and profits at the capital gain rate was discussed, along with §306, the statutory remedy enacted in 1954. Since a distribution of preferred stock to the common shareholders in a

---

Crespi v. Commissioner, 126 F.2d 699, 28 AFTR 1499 (5th Cir. 1942).

On the extent to which the average cost rule is merely a principle of administrative convenience, inapplicable if precise identification is feasible, see Bloch v. Commissioner, 148 F.2d 452, 33 AFTR 955 (9th Cir. 1945); 150 F.2d 540, 34 AFTR 59 (9th Cir. 1945).

[168] See Rev. Rul. 61-97, 1961-1 C.B. 394; Curtis v. United States, *supra* note 114a.

[169] See Kraus v. Commissioner, 88 F.2d 616, 19 AFTR 174 (2d Cir. 1937).

[170] See Curtis v. United States, *supra* note 114a; United States Holding Co., 44 T.C. 323 (1965), and cases cited therein; and, for other discussions of §358, *supra*, Sec. 3.10 and 12.32.

corporate recapitalization is an obvious alternative to the declaration of a dividend of preferred stock, it was essential for the statutory remedy to reach recapitalizations as well as stock dividends.[171] Moreover, reorganizations of other types (e.g., a merger of a corporation into a second corporation owned by the same shareholders, under which they receive preferred stock in exchange for their common stock in the absorbed corporation) could also be employed to lay the foundation for a bail-out. The draftsmen of §306, therefore, provided that stock received by a shareholder in pursuance of a plan of reorganization shall be "section 306 stock" in his hands if:

> 1. It is not "common stock" (supra, Sec. 8.03);
> 2. With respect to its receipt, the shareholder's gain or loss went unrecognized to any extent by reason of Part III of Subchapter C (i.e., §354 and §356); and
> 3. The effect of the transaction was substantially the same as the receipt of a stock dividend, or it was received in exchange for "section 306 stock."

If preferred stock is received pro rata by the common shareholders in a Type E reorganization (recapitalization), it will ordinarily have substantially the same effect as the distribution of a stock dividend (see Rev. Rul. 59-84, 1959-1 C.B. 71); and the same would usually be true of preferred stock received in a Type A (merger) or Type C (property for voting stock) reorganization of "brother-sister" corporations. The "cash substitution" test of Regs. §1.306-3(d) (discussed supra, Sec. 11.12), however, is more sweeping, since it is not limited to recapitalizations or reorganizations involving affiliated corporations; and Example (1) thereof states flatly that preferred stock issued in a statutory merger is "section 306 stock" without specifying any facts other than the surrender of common stock for a combination of common and preferred of the acquiring corporation. If the transaction is pro rata, the "cash substitution" test would lead to this result; but if a distribution of cash in lieu of the preferred would not be a dividend under §356(a)(2) because not paid pro rata, "section 306 stock" status is harder to justify.[172] At one time, the Internal

---

[171] Even before the enactment of §306 in 1954, the Service was cautious about the bail-out potential of preferred stock received in a tax-free recapitalization. See Rev. Rul. 54-13, 1954-1 C.B. 109 (last sentence); Estate of Rosenberg, 36 T.C. 716 (1961).

[172] The reach of the "cash substitution" test obviously depends upon the scope of the Bedford case; if it is limited as suggested by the discussion supra, Sec. 12.32 and note 165, a significantly disproportionate distribution of preferred stock would not lead to "section 306 stock" status. See Alexander and Landis, Bail-Outs and the Internal Revenue Code of 1954, 65 Yale L.J. 909, 923-937 (1956).

Revenue Service ordinarily ruled that preferred stock issued in a merger of two publicly-held corporations was "section 306 stock," but simultaneously granted absolution under §306(b)(4) on the ground that the transaction was not in pursuance of a tax avoidance plan. More recently, however, it has sometimes taken the more direct step of ruling that the stock is not "section 306 stock."[173]

The impact of the "cash substitution" test on a shareholder who has no gain on the exchange — and who therefore would not have realized any dividend income under §356 if cash had been distributed to him — is not clear. The rulings cited above (note 173) do not specify that the shareholders realized gain, but see Rev. Rul. 56-586, 1956-2 C.B. 214, under which the stock received is apparently classified as "section 306 stock" only to the extent that the shareholder realized a gain on the exchange.

The statutory scheme of §306(c)(1)(B) seems to leave several gaps in coverage. If a transaction is similar to a reorganization, but fails to qualify (e.g., for want of a business purpose), preferred stock received cannot be "section 306 stock" under §306(c)(1)(B), even though it has bailout potentialities.[174] If the transaction is not only a "reorganization" but also qualifies as an exchange under §1036 (supra, Sec. 12.16), it might be argued that §306(c)(1)(B) is inapplicable on the ground that the shareholder's gain or loss went unrecognized because of §1036, rather than by reason of Part III of Subchapter C. Moreover, the "cash substitution" test presents certain difficulties as applied to stock received in a reorganization, in that the transaction might not have been a "reorganization" if cash had been used in lieu of stock — and hence the hypothetical cash might not have been taxed as a dividend. See also, on this point, §306(c)(2), which might be used as a shield by the taxpayer.

---

[173] Rev. Rul. 56-116, 1956-1 C.B. 164; Rev. Rul. 57-212, 1957-1 C.B. 114 (§306(b)(4) applicable even though stock was to be redeemed under a sinking fund arrangement); Rev. Rul. 56-223, 1956-1 C.B. 162; Rev. Rul. 57-103, 1957-1 C.B. 113.

For current practice, see XIX ABA Tax Section Bull., No. 2, p. 129 (Jan., 1966); see also Rev. Rul. 60-1, 1960-1 C.B. 143 (preferred stock issued in merger to preferred shareholders of surviving corporation, some of whom also owned a small percentage of its common stock, did not constitute "section 306 stock").

See generally: Trimble, The Treatment of Preferred Stock Distributions in Reorganizations Under Section 306 of the Internal Revenue Code of 1954, 19 Tax L. Rev. 345 (1964); Note, Exclusion from Section 306 Treatment in Unifying Reorganizations, 76 Harv. L. Rev. 1627 (1963); Kanter, Voting Preferred Stock Given in "B" Reorganization May be Section 306 Stock, 39 Taxes 88 (1961).

[174] It should be noted that excluding the transaction from §368(a) does not necessarily mean that the shareholder will be taxed on the exchange; his basis for the stock surrendered may be equal to or greater than the value of the stock received. It is possible that preferred stock received in such a transaction could

Sec. 12.36.   Reorganizations of foreign corporations: §367

Section 367 provides that in determining the extent to which *gain* (but not loss) will be recognized in the case of exchanges described in §§354, 355, 356 or 361, a foreign corporation will "not be considered as a corporation" unless, *before* such an exchange, it is established to the satisfaction of the Service that the exchange "is not in pursuance of a plan having as one of its principal purposes the avoidance of Federal income taxes."[175] Since "corporate status" is essential to a tax-free reorganization (by reason of the use of the term "corporation" in §368(a)(1), §354, and §361), a failure to satisfy §367 could result in the recognition of any gain realized by any participant to the reorganization; and some of the gain thus recognized may have to be reported as ordinary income by virtue of such provisions as §§1245, 1249, or 1250. Section 367 may, moreover, be brought into play by a transaction which is found to be a reorganization even though cast in another form; see, for example, Retail Properties, Inc. (*supra* note 128), where the taxpayer "sold" assets to its controlled foreign subsidiary in reliance on §337. On holding that the transaction constituted a Type D reorganization under "reincorporation" principles (*supra*, Sec. 12.22), the court required the transferor to recognize its realized gain because no §367 ruling had been obtained. On the other hand, since §367 aplies only to the recognition of gain, a failure to obtain advance clearance from the Treasury will not exempt any realized loss from non-recognition.[176]

1. Transactions covered by §367. As noted above, §367 applies to every exchange falling under §§354 and 361 where corporate status is essential to non-recognition treatment. Thus, both the transferor and the transferee must be "corporations" in Type A, C, and D reorganizations in order for the non-recognition provisions of §361 to apply. If one or both of such corporations are foreign corporations, gain would be recognized to the transferor on the exchange of its

be classified, in some circumstances, as "section 306 stock" under §306(c)(1)(A) (preferred stock dividend).

[175] Section 367 has been previously discussed in connection with §351 exchanges (*supra*, Sec. 3.18) and the liquidation of foreign subsidiaries (*supra*, Sec. 9.45).

See generally, Ross, The Impact of the Revenue Act of 1962 on Reorganizations and Other Rearrangements Involving Foreign Corporations, 22 N.Y.U. Inst. on Fed. Tax. 761 (1962); McDonald, Section 367 — A Modern Day Janus, 64 Col. L. Rev. 1012 (1964); Lamp, Recent Section 367 Rulings: Their Effect on Reorganization of Foreign Companies, 21 J. Tax. 240 (1964); Rapp, Section 367 Rulings: How The IRS Regards Exchanges With Foreign Corporations, 13 J. Tax. 344 (1960).

[176] As to taxpayers who have both gains and losses, a netting of the latter against the former is probably precluded; see United States Holding Co., *supra* note 170; *supra*, Sec. 3.18, note 81.

property for stock of the transferee. Also, the provisions of §354 and §355 require exchanges thereunder to involve "corporate" stock or securities; hence, a failure to satisfy §367 will render the entire transaction taxable where one of the corporations whose stock is either transferred or received is a foreign corporation. Since §1032 is not among the non-recognition sections to which §367 applies, however, a corporation acquiring property in exchange for its stock will be protected from recognition of gain by §1032 even if other parties to the transaction must recognize gain because of §367. See also Rev. Rul. 64-156, 1964-1 C.B. 139, holding that a §1036 exchange of stock for stock in a foreign corporation did not require a §367 ruling, even though the transaction constituted a "recapitalization" as well.[176a]

The scope of §367 can be illustrated by the following examples:

a. X, a domestic corporation with United States shareholders, transfers all its assets to Y (a foreign corporation with foreign shareholders) in exchange for Y voting stock and then distributes the Y stock to its shareholders in liquidation. In the absence of a §367 ruling, X would be taxable on the transfer of its assets for Y stock, and the shareholders of X likewise would be taxable on the liquidation distributions from X. Y would not be taxable on the acquisition of X's assets by virtue of §1032, and would have a basis for the assets equal to their "cost."

If X were a foreign corporation with foreign shareholders, however, a clearance under §367 is probably not required, since no parties to the exchange would realize gain taxable under §871 or §881; see Rev. Rul. 64-157, 1964-1 C.B. 139, for implications to this effect.

b. If Y is a foreign corporation which owns all of the stock of its foreign subsidiary X, an "upstream merger" (or a §332 liquidation) of X into Y similarly ought not to be subject to §367 for the reason noted above. If recognition of gain to Y on its acquisition of X's assets would cause present tax consequences to any domestic shareholders of Y (e.g., by generating Subpart F income taxable to them under §951), however, the Service takes the position that §367 applies. See Rev. Rul. 64-157, *supra*, which is a departure from a widely-held assumption that the gain referred to in §367 had to be taxable directly to United States taxpayers.

c. If X and Y are domestic subsidiaries of Z, a foreign corporaton, the merger of X into Y does not require clearance under §367, since classification of Z corporation, the foreign parent, as a "corporation" is irrelevant to the tax-free character of the reorganization exchanges between X, Y and Z. See Rev. Rul. 55-45, 1955-1 C.B. 34.

[176a] See also, to the same effect for a Type F reorganization exchange that also qualifies under §1036, Rev. Rul. 66-171, 1966-25 I.R.B. 16.

d. If Y (a foreign corporation with foreign shareholders) acquires all the stock of X (a domestic corporation with U.S. shareholders) in exchange for its voting stock in a Type B reorganization, §367 approval is necessary for non-recognition treatment to the exchanging shareholders of X (but not for Y, which would be protected by §1032). If Y subsequently liquidates X, §332 would not apply to Y's gain or loss on the liquidation unless it obtained a §367 ruling; but if Y is not engaged in business in the U.S., it would probably not be taxed on such gain by virtue of §881. In this respect, the Type B reorganization route is superior to a Type C reorganization; compare the results in example (a) above.

e. If the preceding example is varied by assuming that X acquired all the stock of Y in a Type B reorganization and then liquidated Y without a §367 ruling, Y's shareholders would have been taxable on their exchanges of Y stock for X stock (although such recognized gain may not have been taxed to them under the rules of §§861, 862 and 871); on the other hand, X's recognized gain on the liquidation of Y would have been taxable to it since X is a domestic corporation, and §1248 (*supra*, Sec. 9.45) might be applicable to part or all of the gain.

2. Other aspects of §367. As pointed out previously (*supra*, Sec. 3.18), it is often assumed that a failure to apply under §367 *before* the exchange cannot be excused, and that there is little room for judicial review if the Service refuses to issue a favorable ruling. On the other hand, the Service contends that the §367 clearance procedure was enacted to protect the revenue, and that a taxpayer cannot take advantage of a deliberate failure to obtain a ruling (e.g., to recognize gain in order to achieve a stepped-up basis for assets).[177]

The tax avoidance standard contemplated by §367 ought to be viewed in the context of the rules dealing with the taxation of foreign income. The special gloss of these provisions on the tax avoidance doctrine under §367 is of particular importance in determining whether the transaction will pass muster with the Service. One of the principal efforts of the Service in applying §367 to the reorganization area is to prevent the tax-free repatriation of previously untaxed foreign earnings: if the earnings remain in foreign corporate solution after the reorganization, however, favorable treatment under §367 can usually be expected. Other prohibited transactions which could prevent a favorable §367 ruling include attempts to isolate assets for sale so as to reduce potential U.S. taxes thereon, and ef-

---

[177] Rev. Rul. 64-177, 1964-1 C.B. 14. See Hay v. Commissioner, 145 F.2d 1001, 33 AFTR 150 (4th Cir. 1944), which supplies some support for this view, but on an extreme set of facts.

forts to divert income from possible U.S. taxation.[178] The "business purpose" requirement for a valid reorganization (*supra*, Sec. 12.19) is independent of the tax avoidance standard which must be satisfied under §367; while similar in some respects, it seems clear that the Service views the §367 showing of no tax avoidance as requiring more than mere proof of a "business purpose" for the reorganization.

By its terms §367 is concerned only with "determining the extent to which gain shall be recognized" under the statutory provisions listed therein; but the transactions to which §367 applies, including reorganizations, have many collateral consequences. If a §367 ruling is not obtained, so that gain must be recognized by the participants in a reorganization under §354 and §361, do the other effects of a reorganization (e.g., a carryover or substituted basis for the transferred property; transfer of earnings and profits and other corporate tax attributes) nevertheless apply? A literal reading would suggest that the failure to satisfy §367, and hence failure to qualify the exchanges under §§354 and 361 should also prevent the collateral attributes of reorganization treatment from applying. The basis rules of §358, for example, apply only to "an exchange to which section 351, 354, 355, 356, 361, or 371(b) applies"; §362(b) contemplates the nonrecognition of gain to the transferor; and §381 applies only if the transfer is one to which §361 applies. If, on the other hand, nonrecognition treatment applies with respect to the various exchanges (whether because of a favorable §367 ruling or because such a ruling was not necessary), the Service takes the position that the carry-over rules of §381 and the basis rules of §358 and §362(b) apply, even though the transaction involves only foreign corporations and creates no immediate U.S. tax consequences to the parties.[179]

---

[178] Note that §367 is concerned with the avoidance of United States, not foreign, taxes. For possible analogies, see such other "state of mind" provisions as §§269, 357(b), 482, 531, and 1551.

[179] See Rev. Rul. 64-158, 1964-1 C.B. 140.

Chapter Thirteen

CORPORATE TAX ATTRIBUTES: TRANSFER, SURVIVAL, AND MULTIPLICATION

Part A. Background and Introduction

Sec. 13.01. Corporate tax attributes — In general

As noted earlier, *supra*, Ch. 2, corporations are classified as a special type of taxable entity: they are taxed at special rates (generally non-progressive) and, in addition, are endowed with tax characteristics reflecting this status (e.g., an earnings and profits account, a §11(c) surtax exemption, and a §535(c)(2) minimum accumulated earnings credit). In addition, corporations are subject to most of the substantive provisions of the tax law which are applicable to taxpayers generally (*i.e.*, the provisions dealing with gross income, deductions, tax accounting rules, and capital gains and losses), with the result that, over the course of its operating existence, a corporate taxpayer may build up an extensive "tax history."

The extent to which a corporation's accumulated tax attributes will survive readjustments of its ownership, business operations, and legal or financial structure is the subject of this chapter.

In general, a corporation is treated as an independent taxable entity, unaffected by either the identity of its shareholders or changes in their composition (*supra*, Sec. 1.05). Moreover, changes in the character of its business activity ordinarily do not affect its tax position. The same can also be said of changes in its financial structure, such as refinancing operations, recapitalizations, and the like. However, the combination of a change in business and a change in stock ownership may have unfavorable tax consequences to the corporation despite its continuity as a legal entity. In addition, if the corporation participates in a merger or consolidation, or if all or a part of its assets are acquired by another corporation, a myriad of difficult tax questions arises: does the transferor corporation's taxable year end; does the basis of the transferred properties carry over to the acquiring corporation; does the acquiring corporation inherit the predecessor corporation's earning and profits and net operating loss and capital loss carryovers; must or may new elections be made by the acquiring corporation as to the accounting methods, inventory valuation, depreciation practices, and installment sales of the transferor corporation?

Before enactment of the 1954 Code, there were statutory rules providing for the carryover of basis for property transferred in tax-free reorganization exchanges (*supra*, Sec. 12.33), but the transfer of other corporate tax attributes was not spelled out in the statutes; and some courts relied heavily on form in determining whether the "new" corporation was a continuation of the "old" corporation or not (*infra*, Sec. 13.02). In 1954, Congress set forth specific rules in §381 to provide for the carryover of some corporate tax attributes in certain tax-free acquisitions. But the list of items which carry over to the transferee is not exhaustive and not all tax-free transfers are included in the statutory scheme. Thus, the confusion of prior law is perpetuated as to these "uncodified" matters. Moreover, numerous other statutory provisions and judicial doctrines must be considered in determining the "survivial quotient" of various corporate tax attributes: thus, §382 limits the transfer or survival of a corporation's net operating loss carryovers; §269 prohibits certain acquisitions whose "principal purpose" is the avoidance of taxes; §446(b) empowers the Commissioner to adjust certain tax accounting practices in order to "clearly reflect" income; §482 permits allocation of income and deductions among related taxpayers to prevent avoidance of taxes or to clearly reflect income; §61 has been interpreted to provide that "income must be taxed to the one who earns it"; §1551 denies surtax exemptions and minimum accumulated earnings tax credits to corporations which are created for the "major" purpose of tax avoidance; and finally, the judicial principles and attitudes inspired by Gregory v. Helvering (*supra*, Sec. 12.19) and sounding in tax avoidance, sham, business purpose, form versus substance, and economic reality are a brooding omnipresence in this area.

This combination of a technical and complicated statute, interspersed with vague and uncertainly applied judicial doctrines, makes the task of the tax advisor a formidable one indeed. Moreover, the careful attorney must be able to sense, perhaps instinctively, the outer limits of judicial tolerance with respect to a particular transaction, so that he can adequately advise at what point a court is liable to invent a new judicial doctrine (or revitalize an old one) in order to strike down what is a case of abuse. While this approach does not yield ready answers, it is nevertheless essential to understanding the realities of the tax law in this area.

As an initial matter, the following factors have been emphasized by the courts and Congress in determining whether a corporation's tax attributes will survive business, legal, and financial readjustments of its corporate enterprise: (1) the form of the readjustment (*i.e.*, whether the transaction affects the corporation's "continuity of legal entity"); (2) continuity of the corporation's business activities; (3) continuity of its shareholder ownership; and (4) the element of tax "windfall" or tax avoidance with respect to the transaction (*i.e.*, whether tax motives, as opposed to business or non-tax motives, animated the arrangement). Negotiability of a corporation's tax attributes seems to depend, in the last analysis, on the taxpayer's showing of a favorable balance of these factors: the difficult question, however, is which of these factors is to be considered as controlling in a given case and how much weight is to be given to a particular factor in making this determination. At best the subject is in a state of flux, and Congress' attempts at legislative specificity have not as yet served to resolve many of the conflicts which can develop between taxpayers and the government in this area. It seems safe to say, however, that the judicial climate is hostile to taxpayer efforts to secure corporate tax benefits by merger or other forms of acquisition; some judges and commentators apparently feel that traffic in corporate tax benefits (most notably net operating loss carryovers) is akin to original sin, but not all authorities are so disposed.[1] In any event, the taxpayer must thread his way through a formidable array of statutory provisions and court decisions, most of which are designed to separate bona fide business transactions from those freighted with tax avoidance motives.

Before turning to an analysis of these matters, several observations should be made. Most of the litigation and statutory complexities in this area relate to net operating loss carryover and carryback deductions, so that this tax attribute will receive the major emphasis in the materials that follow. However, numerous other corporate tax attributes may be important in a given case: *e.g.*, earnings and profits or deficits; surtax exemptions and minimum accumulated earnings tax credits; tax accounting methods and elections; and "potential loss" situations (*i.e.*, high basis corporate assets with low current values). In general, the principles applicable to the survival of net operating loss carryovers apply with equal force to these other corporate tax attributes and will be so treated in the ensuing discussion.

---

[1] See Tarleau, The Place of Tax Loss Positions in Corporate Acquisitions, in Joint Committee on the Economic Report, *Federal Tax Policy for Economic Growth and Stability*, 84th Cong., 1st Sess. 610 (1955).

On the special role of "tax motive" in this area, it should be noted that several statutory provisions specifically turn on the presence or absence of tax avoidance motives or purposes with respect to a particular transaction; many of these sections have been noted at other points in this work. On the other hand, the statute also contains many "rule of thumb" provisions, designed to block certain tax advantages by establishing mechanical tests rather than attempting to plumb the taxpayer's state of mind. Moreover, the Code also sanctions certain elections and "choices," even though tax motivation is obviously the determining factor.[2] Finally, if a particular transaction is too heavily laden with tax avoidance motives or if it appears to lack economic reality, courts may ignore it as a "sham," or collapse the interdependent steps in what is essentially a "single transaction"; here one invariably sees a citation to Gregory v. Helvering (*supra*, Sec. 12.19). Thus, some tax motivated transactions are acceptable, others are not, and in still other situations, tax motivation is merely a neutral factor. Determining to which of the above categories a particular transaction belongs is, of course, the difficult question, and, as one would expect, courts are not unanimous in their treatment. At the very least, however, the presence of tax motives with respect to a transaction tends to poison the atmosphere, so that courts will scrutinize the facts with special care to see whether the transaction is in fact what it is in form.

Sec. 13.02.   Acquisition of tax benefits — A chronology of major developments

Before attempting an analysis of the cases and statutory provisions relating to the survival of corporate tax attributes, a brief review of the historical developments in this area may prove helpful. Congress, with an assist from the courts, has constructed a formidable defense against taxpayer efforts to "traffick" in net operating losses

---

[2] State of mind controlling: §269; §1551; the "device" clause of §355(a)(1)-(B) (*supra*, Sec. 11.06); §367 (*supra*, Sec. 12.36); §357(b) (*supra*, Sec. 3.06); §531 (*supra*, Ch. 6); and §341 (*supra*, Ch. 10).

Rules of thumb: §267 (losses on sales between related taxpayers); §541 (personal holding company penalty tax, *supra*, Ch. 6); §§355(b) and 346(b) (five year active business rules for corporate divisions and partial liquidations, *supra*, Ch. 11 and Ch. 7); §382 (limitations on corporate net operating loss carryovers).

Elections: §333 (tax-free liquidations, *supra*, Sec. 9.20); §334(b)(2) (stepped-up basis acquisitions, *supra*, Sec. 9.44); §337 (tax-free liquidation sales, *supra*, Sec. 9.65); §1371 (Subchapter S elections, *infra*, Ch. 14); and §1501 (consolidated return election, *infra*, Sec. 13.42).

See generally Cohen, Taxing The State of Mind, 12 Tax Exec. 200 (1960).

and other corporate tax benefits. As early as the Revenue Act of 1924, when the predecessor of §482 was enacted, the statute has empowered the Commissioner to reallocate income and deductions among "related taxpayers" in order to prevent avoidance of taxes and to clearly reflect income. Moreover, the net operating loss provisions of the 1939 Code restricted the use of net operating losses to "the taxpayer" who sustained the loss (1939 Code, §122).[3] In 1943, the predecessor of §269 was enacted (1939 Code, §129), the terms of which disallowed any deduction, credit, or other allowance in the case of certain acquisitions of stock or property where the "principal purpose" of the acquisition was income tax avoidance. The Revenue Act of 1951 added a more limited provision (the predecessor of current §1551), disallowing multiple surtax exemptions where tax avoidance was the "major purpose" for creation of the corporation, and the 1954 Code broadened this provision to include multiple accumulated earnings tax credits as well. The 1954 Code, in addition to adding the detailed carryover rules of §381, materially restricted the availability of corporate net operating loss carryovers by enactment of §382: §382(a) provides for disallowance of corporate net operating losses where a substantial change in stock ownership is accompanied by a change in business; and §382(b) restricts, in some circumstances, the inheritance of corporate net operating loss carryovers in mergers and other reorganizations. Finally, the Revenue Act of 1964 launched a major assault on the "multiple corporation" problem: (1) the coverage of §1551 was expanded; (2) §1561 limits the "component members" of certain affiliated groups of corporations to one surtax exemption; (3) §1562, however, allows such affiliated groups to elect multiple surtax exemptions at the cost of an additional 6 per cent penalty tax on income subject to normal tax rates (the first $25,000 of taxable income); (4) alternatively, such affiliated groups may elect to file consolidated returns without payment of the former 2 percent penalty tax; and (5) an affiliated group that is willing to give up a claim to multiple surtax exemptions may elect to receive a 100 percent dividends received deduction by virtue of §243(a)(2) and (b), and thereby eliminate tax on any dividends received from corporations within the group.

On the judicial scene, things began badly for taxpayers with the case of Woolford Realty Co. v. Rose, 286 U.S. 319, 11 AFTR 12 (1932), where the Supreme Court held that pre-affiliation net operat-

---

[3] As will be seen (*infra*, Sec. 13.25), this phrase, which became very important under the 1939 Code, was omitted from the corresponding provision (§172) of the 1954 Code.

ing losses of an acquired corporation could not be deducted in computing the post-affiliation consolidated return income of the affiliated group, stating that "the reaction of an impartial mind is little short of instinctive that the deduction is unreasonable and cannot have been intended by the framers of the statute." Several years later, in New Colonial Ice Co., Inc. v. Helvering, 292 U.S. 435, 13 AFTR 1180 (1934), net operating loss carryovers again were denied. There, assets of the loss corporation were absorbed by a newly created corporation, organized for the purpose of taking over the business of the loss corporation, which sought to offset these losses against its current income. The reorganization transaction in *New Colonial* probably constituted a Type F reorganization under present law, but did not qualify as a Type A (statutory merger) reorganization. The Court held that the resulting corporation was not "the same taxpayer" as the corporation which sustained the losses (despite the fact that the creditors, capital structure and businesses of both corporations were substantially identical); accordingly, it was not entitled to carry over the losses of its predecessor as a deduction against current income. In effect, the Court adopted an "entity" theory with regard to the survival of net operating loss carryovers and thereby restricted the deduction for such losses to the same "legal entity" which incurred the loss. The *New Colonial* doctrine dominated the reorganization scene for two decades, and well-advised taxpayers always arranged to have the loss corporation emerge as the surviving corporation in a reorganization transaction so that its loss carryovers (or other beneficial tax attributes) would be preserved; this in turn led to some unwieldly amalgamations, and instances of "minnows swallowing whales" were fairly common during this period.

In Helvering v. Metropolitan Edison Co., 306 U.S. 522, 22 AFTR 307 (1939), however, tax attributes carried over to a successor corporation where the reorganization took the form of a statutory merger; the issue was the successor corporation's right to deduct unamortized bond discount on its predecessor's obligations which were assumed by operation of law in the merger. The Court noted that in a statutory merger, "the corporate personality of the transferor is drowned in that of the transferee." Moreover, courts fairly consistently held that an acquired corporation's accumulated earnings and profits account carried over to the acquiring corporation in a nondivisive corporate fusion transaction. The leading case on this point is Commissioner v. Sansome, 60 F. 2d 931, 11 AFTR 854 (2d Cir. 1932). The *Sansome* doctrine was said to be grounded not on a theory of continuity of corporate enterprise, but rather on the need to prevent avoidance of tax on the absorbed corporation's accumulated earnings;[4] with this as its rationale, the *Sansome* principle played a limited role in determining the extent to which other corporate tax attributes survive a tax-free acquisition.

The *New Colonial* and *Metropolitan Edison* cases occupied center stage in the carryover area until enactment of the 1954 Code. During this period, carryovers generally could be preserved if taxpayers were careful to continue the existence of the loss corporation's legal entity. An extreme example of this approach was Alprosa Watch Corp., 11 T.C. 240 (1948), where the Tax Court allowed various loss deductions despite radical changes in the taxpayer corporation's stock ownership and business activities: all of the taxpayer's stock had been sold to new owners, who then proceeded to discontinue the loss business and embark on a new line of activity — in effect, all that continued was the corporate shell. Similarly, carryovers and carrybacks generally were allowed across the line of "corporate fusion" where the reorganization transaction took the form of a statutory merger. In Stanton Brewery, Inc. v. Commissioner, 176 F.2d 573, 38 AFTR 368 (2d Cir. 1949), for example, operating losses of a wholly-owned subsidiary which merged into its parent holding company were allowed as a carryover to the parent; similarly, Newmarket Manufacturing Co. v. United States, 233 F.2d 493, 49 AFTR 1254 (1st Cir. 1956), cert. denied, 353 U.S. 983 (1957), allowed a carryback of post-acquisition losses after a profitable corporation had reincorporated in another state through a statutory merger into its wholly-owned subsidiary.[5] If the acquisition did not follow the statutory merger route, but took the form of a §332 liquidation or a Type C

---

[4] Compare Commissioner v. Phipps, 336 U.S. 410, 37 AFTR 827 (1949) (deficit of subsidiary liquidated tax-free into its parent did not absorb the parent's accumulated earnings and profits), with *Sansome;* see also Commissioner v. Munter, 331 U.S. 210, 35 AFTR 963 (1947); *infra* note 26.

For discussion of the pre-1954 treatment of earnings and profits and deficits in a reorganization, see Rice, Transfers of Earnings and Deficits in Tax-free Reorganizations; The Sansome-Phipps Rule, 5 Tax L. Rev. 523 (1950); Note, Corporate Reorganizations and Continuity of Earning History; Some Tax Aspects, 65 Harv. L. Rev. 648 (1952).

For the 1954 Code rules, see Halperin, Carryovers of Earnings and Profits, 18 Tax L. Rev. 289 (1963); Nesson, Earnings and Profits Discontinuities Under the 1954 Code, 77 Harv. L. Rev. 450 (1964); Testa, "Earnings and Profits" After Bankrupty Reorganization, 18 Tax L. Rev. 573 (1963).

[5] See also Koppers Co. v. United States, 134 F. Supp. 290, 48 AFTR 112 (Ct. Cl. 1955) (carryback of post-merger excess profits tax credits to pre-merger taxable years of an affiliated group of corporations which had been filing consolidated returns prior to the merger; allowed); E. & J. Gallo Winery v. Commissioner, 227 F. 2d 699, 48 AFTR 485 (9th Cir. 1955) (surviving corporation in a statutory merger allowed to carry over operating loss deductions of the absorbed corporation).

"practical merger," however, carryover of the transferor corporation's tax attributes ordinarily was denied under the principle of *New Colonial Ice.*[6]

Thus, as of the date of the enactment of the 1954 Code, the survival of corporate tax attributes was determined primarily by reference to the form of the particular acquisition transaction: the "entity theory" of *New Colonial Ice* was the dominant theme, permitting favorable corporate tax characteristics to be preserved by having the corporation whose tax attributes were most desirable emerge as the surviving corporation. Alternatively, for those with stronger nerves, the *Metropolitan Edison* "statutory merger" route offered a reasonable chance of success if, under local law, it could be shown that the absorbed corporation's legal identity was submerged by operation of law into that of the acquiring corporation. While subject to the criticisms which formal legal doctrines inevitably inspire, matters were reasonably predictable in this area, at least for the well advised.

However, in Libson Shops v. Koehler, 353 U.S. 382, 51 AFTR 43 (1957), the Supreme Court overturned (or ignored) several well-settled assumptions in this area, propounded a new doctrinal limitation on the carryover of corporate tax attributes, and generally stirred up a hornet's nest of confusion, the outer limits of which are still unresolved. *Libson* involved a statutory merger of 16 "brother-sister" corporations (all owned by the same shareholders in the same proportions, and each of which operated a separate retail store) into another similarly controlled corporation, which then sought to apply the pre-merger net operating losses of three of those corporations against its post-merger income. The loss stores continued to lose money after the merger. The carryover was denied on the ground that the income against which the deduction was claimed was not produced by "substantially the same business which incurred the losses"; the net operating loss deduction was intended to average out the income from a single business, said the Court, not to permit the pre-merger losses of one business to be offset against the post-merger income of another business. *Stanton, Newmarket* and *Koppers* were distinguished as involving essentially a single business enterprise.

---

[6]See *e.g.*, Patten Fine Papers, Inc., v. Commissioner, 27 T.C. 722 (1957), aff'd, 249 F.2d 776, 52 AFTR 918 (7th Cir. 1957) (tax-free §332 liquidation); Dumont-Airplane and Marine Instruments, Inc., 28 T.C. 1308 (1957) (tax-free Type C reorganization). But cf. F. C. Donovan, Inc. v. United States, 261 F.2d 470, 2 AFTR 2d 6221 (1st Cir. 1958) (tax-free liquidation of subsidiary under §332; post-liquidation losses arising from the former subsidiary's business were allowed as carrybacks to pre-liquidation years of the subsidiary).

The "continuity of business enterprise" test thus injected a new requirement into the carryover area and enabled the Court to avoid deciding whether to follow the strict entity theory of *New Colonial* or instead to adopt the "merger of identity by operation of law" approach of *Metropolitan Edison* and *Stanton*. Moreover, the *Libson* opinion seemed concerned with the possibility of a tax "windfall" if the carryovers had been allowed as deductions; absent the merger, operating losses of the three loss corporations could not have been offset against profits of the other corporations since consolidated returns had not been filed prior to the merger.[7]

The precise scope of the *Libson* decision (under both the 1939 Code and the 1954 Code) will be considered *infra*, Sec. 13.25. Suffice it to say that the case has generated an inordinate amount of judicial, administrative, and academic turmoil, which is not likely to be dispelled without further legislation. As will be seen, the relation between *Libson* and the statutory rules of the 1954 Code has been the subject of a steady stream of conflicting judicial and administrative pronouncements.

Sec. 13.03. Statutory and transactional patterns — In general

Statutory provisions relating to the survival of corporate tax attributes can be grouped into three categories, depending upon the particular function which the provision is intended to perform: (1) the carryover rules of §381, which provide, with limitations, that certain enumerated tax attributes will pass from one corporation to another when the transaction constitutes a certain type of tax-free reorganization or liquidation; (2) various restrictions or limitations on the enjoyment of corporate tax attributes (such as §269 and §382), designed to discourage acquisitions of corporations primarily because of their favorable tax characteristics; and (3) an elaborate network of provisions dealing with the "multiple corporation" problem, intended to reduce or eliminate undue tax advantages by operating through multiple corporate entities (*e.g.*, §1551, §1561, §1562, §243(b), and §482). Alternatively, these provisions can be classified on the basis of the various transactional patterns which may invoke their operation, viz.: (1) provisions applicable to acquisitive transactions, whereby one corporation absorbs the stock or assets of another (*e.g.*, §§381, 382, and 269); (2) those which apply to divisive

---

[7] A consolidated return could not have been filed by the 16 corporations unless there had been a re-shuffling of stock ownership to give them a common parent; see *infra*, Sec. 13.41.

transactions, whereby one corporation splits itself into two or more separate entities (*e.g.*, §§1551, 1561, 1562, 243(b), and 269); and (3) those which deal with the effect of various transactions between related members of an affiliated group (*e.g.*, §482, 446(b), and 61). Moreover, the special problems of affiliated corporations which elect to file consolidated returns are part of the statutory tapestry in this area, especially in view of the 1964 Revenue Act's announced policy of encouraging the filing of such returns. Also important to an overall view of this general area are those judicial "tax avoidance" doctrines concerned with matters of sham, form versus substance, business purpose, and economic reality, which principles may be invoked to safeguard the statutory provisions from the erosive effects of transactions excessively laden with tax avoidance motives. Finally, the Treasury Regulations with respect to these various statutory provisions are of more than usual importance, especially in the consolidated returns area, where they are for all practical purposes the subsstantive law.

Before turning to an analysis of these provisions, a brief summary of the possible transactional patterns which can occur, and of the sections potentially applicable thereto, may prove helpful. In the case of acquisitive transactions, the transaction may be either taxable or tax-free and may consist of the transfer of either stock or assets of the acquired corporation. Moreover, the corporation whose favorable tax attributes are to be preserved may, depending upon the form of the acquisition, end up as the surviving corporation or, alternatively, may be absorbed by the other corporation.

For example, assume that L corporation has a history of operating losses and G corporation a history of profits, and that they are owned by unrelated shareholders. If L buys G's profitable business assets for cash, it seems clear that L's loss carryover deductions will not be affected by this transaction; neither §382 nor §269 would apply, and the Service has ruled that a corporation's tax attributes will not be affected (and the principles of the *Libson Shops* case will not be applied) where the corporation merely changes the character of its business.[8] As a policy matter, a loss corporation should be able to overcome its losses by acquiring profitable businesses, so long as there is no substantial change in the ownership of the loss corporation. Similarly, if L buys G's *stock* and either liquidates G under §332 or keeps it alive and files consolidated returns, the Service has

---

[8] See Rev. Rul. 63-40, 1963-1 C.B. 46; Joseph Weidenhoff, Inc., 32 T.C. 1222 (1959) (Acq.); Jackson Oldsmobile, Inc. v. United States, 237 F. Supp. 779, 15 AFTR 2d 35 (M.D. Ga. 1964).

indicated that it will not apply *Libson Shops* or §269 (even though that provision is technically applicable in this situation) to disallow L's loss carryover deductions.[9]

If G purchases L's assets for cash, however, L's tax attributes will not carry over to G since the transaction does not constitute one of the specified types of tax-free acquisitions covered by §381(a). Hence, L's tax attributes remain with it and can only be availed of against future income earned in any new ventures which L might undertake. If G buys L's stock and promptly liquidates L under §332, the carryover of L's loss history would be denied, since the liquidation of L would be subject to the stepped-up basis rule of §334(b)(2) and thus would not constitute a §381 transaction. Alternatively, G may attempt to avail itself of L's operating losses by filing consolidated returns with L (or by merging downstream into L), but here the provisions of §269 and §382(a) would prove to be a major hurdle. Moreover, as will be noted subsequently (*infra*, Sec. 13.25), courts also have applied *Libson* to deny L's net operating loss deductions against the post-acquisition profits from G's business. It is not clear, however, whether *Libson* would be so applied to a 1954 Code taxable year case.[9a]

If the assets of G are absorbed by L in a tax-free reorganization (*e.g.*, by way of a Type A or Type C reorganization), §381 by its terms does not apply with respect to the corporate tax attributes of L; rather, that provision deals only with the tax attributes of the acquired *transferor* corporation, in this case G. Hence, the continuity of business enterprise principle of *Libson Shops* may prevent L's loss carryovers from being used to offset subsequent profits of the acquired business. Moreover, §382(b) may serve to disallow part or all of L's loss carryovers if the shareholders of L do not retain at least a 20 percent continuity of interest in the combined corporate enterprise. Also, §269(a)(2) could apply if the principal purpose of the acquisition was to secure the benefits of a deduction which L would not otherwise enjoy. If L instead acquired the stock of G (in a Type B reorganization), §382(b) would not, by its terms, apply (unless L promptly liquidated G under §332, in which case the steps may be "collapsed" and treated, in substance, as an asset acquisition

---

[9] Rev. Rul. 63-40, *supra* note 8.

[9a] Compare Maxwell Hardware Co. v. Commissioner, 343 F.2d 713, 15 AFTR 2d 692 (9th Cir. 1965) (*Libson* superseded by 1954 Code); and Clarksdale Rubber Co., 45 T.C. 234 (1965) (*Libson* partially displaced by 1954 Code); with J. G. Dudley Co., Inc. v. Commissioner, 298 F.2d 750, 9 AFTR 2d 566 (4th Cir. 1961) (*Libson* survives 1954 Code); and Jackson Oldsmobile, Inc. v. United States, *supra* note 8 (*Libson* applies, but taxpayer satisfied its tests).

subject to §382). However, §269(a)(1) would be applicable, so that if tax avoidance motives inspired the acquisition, this fact could defeat L's attempts to use its loss carryovers against profits of the acquired corporation (*e.g.*, by filing consolidated returns with G). However, if the tax avoidance standard of §269 is satisfied, the consolidated returns regulations apparently permit the loss corporation (L) to file a consolidated return with its newly acquired subsidiary G and to utilize its loss carryovers against the income of the profitable subsidiary (G) in a consolidated return.

If G instead acquires the assets of L in a tax-free Type A or C reorganization, §381 clearly applies to the carryover of L's tax attributes to G. Moreover, the Service has ruled, in Rev. Rul. 58-603, 1958-2 C.B. 147, that *Libson* will not be applied to transactions of this sort since they are specifically covered by §381(a). However, §§382(b) and 269(a)(2) apply in this situation, and the limitations of these provisions must be satisfied before L's loss carryover can be utilized by G.

The above principles can be summarized by the following table:

Transactions	*Applicable rules*
1. L purchases G assets	None
(a) But if substantial change of L stock ownership	§269(a)(1), and maybe *Libson*
2. L purchases G stock and:	
(a) files consolidated returns	§269(a)(1), and maybe *Libson*
(b) liquidates G (§332)	§269(a)(1), and maybe *Libson*
(c) merges "downstream" into G	§§381, 382(b), 269(a)(2)
3. G purchases L assets	None
4. G purchases L stock and:	
(a) files consolidated returns	§§382(a), 269(a)(1), and maybe *Libson*
(b) liquidates L (§332) and:	
(i) §334(b)(2) applies	None
(ii) §334(b)(1) applies	§§381, 382(a), 269(a)(1)
(c) merges "downstream" into L	§§382(b), 269(a)(2), and maybe *Libson*

5. L acquires G assets in Type A or C reorganization	§§382(b), 269(a)(2), and maybe *Libson*
6. L acquires G stock in Type B reorganization and:	
(a) files consolidated returns	§269(a)(1), and maybe *Libson*
(b) liquidates G (§332)	§382(b) (if "step"), 269(a)-(2), and maybe *Libson*
(c) merges "downstream" into G	§§381, 382(b), 269(a)(2)
7. G acquires L assets in Type A or C reorganization	§§381, 382(b), 269(a)(2)
8. G acquires L stock in Type B reorganization and:	
(a) files consolidated returns	§269(a)(1), and maybe *Libson*
(b) liquidates L (§332)	§§381, 382(b) (if "step"), 269(a)(2)
(c) merges "downstream" into L	§§382(b), 269(a)(2), and maybe *Libson*

Corporate separations (or the initial creation of multiple corporate entities) are not covered by the carryover rules of §381 or §382. However, the Commissioner possesses a formidable array of defenses against taxpayer abuses of the multiple corporation device. In addition to the previously noted rules of §269, which have been held applicable to corporate split-ups as well as to amalgamation transactions,[10] consideration also must be given to the complex and inter-related provisions of §§1551, 1561, 1562, 243(b), and 482 (as well as to those general judicial principles involving assignment of income, recognition of the corporate entity, form versus substance, sham transactions, and lack of business purpose). Moreover, if an affiliated group of corporations files consolidated returns, the detailed provisions of the regulations under §1502 must also be consulted, a task of no small proportions at best. These matters are considered in detail, *infra*, Parts D and E of this chapter.

[10] See *e.g.*, James Realty Co. v. United States, 280 F.2d 394, 6 AFTR 2d 5178 (8th Cir. 1960); Coastal Oil Storage Co. v. Commissioner, 242 F.2d 396, 50 AFTR 1999 (4th Cir. 1957).

Part B. Carryovers and §381

Sec. 13.10.   In general

Section 381 was enacted in 1954 to provide a comprehensive set of rules for the preservation of tax attributes, to be "based upon economic realities rather than upon such artificialities as the legal form of the reorganization." S. Rep. No. 1622, 83d Cong., 2d Sess., 52 (1954). The draftsmen hoped to protect taxpayers against the loss of favorable tax attributes, as well as to prevent the avoidance of unfavorable ones by paper reorganizations. The statutory rules are applicable if assets of a corporation are acquired by another corporation:

1. In a liquidation of a subsidiary under §332, unless §334(b)(2) applies (*supra*, Secs. 9.40-9.44); or
2. In a reorganization under §368(a)(1)(A) (statutory merger or consolidation), (C) (acquisition of substantially all of the properties of one corporation for voting stock of another), (D) (transfer of assets to a controlled corporation, but only if §354(b)(1)(A) and (B) apply), or (F) (change in identity, form, or place of organization only).

If the assets are acquired in a transaction fitting within one of the above categories, the acquiring corporation "shall succeed to and take into account" the items specified in §381(c), *viz.*, net operating loss carryovers, earnings and profits, capital loss carryovers, accounting methods, and a number of others. These items are inherited by the acquiring corporation subject to the "operating rules" of §381(b) and to certain limitations imposed by §381(c).[11] Because §381(c) enumerates the items to be carried forward, instead of flatly providing that the acquiring corporation shall step into the shoes of the transferor for all purposes, it might be inferred that unmentioned items do not go over. But the Senate Report on the 1954 Code states that §381 "is not intended to affect the carryover treatment of an item or tax attribute not specified in the section." S. Rep. No. 1622, 83d Cong., 2d Sess., p. 277 (1954). It may be, therefore, that other items (*e.g.*,

---

[11] For a possible restriction on the ostensible scope of §381, see Rev. Rul. 58-603, 1958-2 C.B. 147, hinting that if a loss corporation is acquired in order to carry over its tax attributes to another corporation through the medium of a reorganization within the meaning of §381(a)(2), the absence of a "business purpose" may mean that there is no "reorganization," see Regs. §1.368-1(b), and hence that §381(a)(2) will not come into play to preserve the tax attributes for the successor corporation.

Note also the restrictions on the carryover of net operating losses imposed by §382, *infra*, Secs. 13.22-13.24.

amortizable research and experimental expenditures under §174, organizational expenditures under §248, soil and water conservation expenditures under §175, and foreign tax credit carryovers under §904-(d)), which are hardly distinguishable from a policy standpoint from some of those specified in §381(c), may also be carried forward; but the pre-1954 case law (*supra*, Sec. 13.02) may be relevant to these unenumerated tax attributes.

The Senate Report also states that §381 is not intended to affect "the carryover treatment of items or tax attributes in corporate transactions not described in [§381(a)]." Among the unlisted transactions, in which some items or attributes might be carried over, are transfers of property from one corporation to another in corporate divisions under §355 (*supra*, Ch. 11), insolvency reorganizations under §371, and some transfers of property to subsidiary corporations under §351.[12] These transactions may be governed by the pre-1954 case law, including the continuity of business enterprise theory of *Libson* and perhaps the continuity of entity theory of *New Colonial Ice.*[13]

It should be noted that the acquiring corporation is not dependent upon §381 for the preservation of its *own* tax attributes (since §381 deals only with the tax characteristics of the transferor or distributor corporation); hence, these items will continue unimpaired even though not specified in §381(c), unless some other statutory provision or case law principle applies.[14]

Sec. 13.11.   Section 381(a) transactions

The carryover rules of §381 apply to two categories of tax-free asset acquisitions: liquidations of controlled subsidiaries under §332, if the adjusted basis of the transferred assets carries over to the parent on the liquidation; and various "non-divisive" reorganization asset transfers. If the transaction fails to qualify as a tax-free liquidation or reorganization under the definitional provisions applicable thereto,

[12] As to earnings and profits in such transactions, see §312(i) and Regs. §1.312-10 and -11.

[13] See Regs. §1.381(a)-(1)(b)(3); but see Denver & Rio Grande W. R.R. Co., 38 T.C. 557 (1962), holding that §381 constitutes the exclusive provision in this respect and that a particular carryover item would not be permitted in a transaction not covered by §381(a); *infra*, Sec. 13.13.

[14] But see Stanton Brewery Co., Inc. v. Commissioner, 176 F.2d 573, 38 AFTR 368 (2d Cir. 1949), for the difficulty of determining which, if any, corporation survives in a statutory merger or consolidation. See also the discussion *infra*, Part C, of the statutory and judicial limitations which may prevent a corporation's use of its own or acquired tax attributes (*e.g.*, §§269 and 382, and the continuity of business doctrine of *Libson Shops*).

the transferor's tax attributes will not carry over to the transferee. Thus, initial satisfaction of the definitional rules of §332 (*supra*, Sec. 9.40) or §368(a) (*supra*, Ch. 12) is necessary before consideration can be given to the effects of §381.

1. *Liquidation of controlled subsidiary: §381(a)(1).* Under pre-1954 law, the *New Colonial Ice* continuity of entity doctrine (*supra*, Sec. 13.02) was ordinarily thought to bar a transfer of a subsidiary's tax attributes to its parent on a §332 liquidation.[15] If the liquidation took the form of a statutory merger, however, the Second Circuit held that tax attributes of the transferor corporation carried over to the transferee "by operation of law," Stanton Brewery, Inc., v. Commissioner (*supra*, Sec. 13.02). The 1954 Code altered the reliance on form in this area by permitting the carryover of a subsidiary's tax attributes in a §332 liquidation if the tax basis of the subsidiary's assets carries over to the parent under §334(b)(1).[16]

If the subsidiary is insolvent, however, §332 does not apply to the liquidation (*supra*, Sec. 9.41) and hence the carryover rules of §381 do not come into play. In this situation, the parent is entitled to deduct the loss on its stock or debt investments in the subsidiary (*supra*, Sec. 4.08), and to carry any such losses over to other years under §172 (net operating losses) or §1212(a) (capital losses); but the subsidiary's own tax attributes are extinguished by its liquidation.[17]

2. *Reorganizations: §381(a)(2).* The strict "continuity of legal entity" approach with respect to the survival of corporate tax attributes, inspired by *New Colonial Ice* (and modified to some extent by the "statutory merger" exception of *Metropolitan Edison*), was rejected by the drafters of the 1954 Code. Thus, §381(a)(2) lists four categories of corporate "fusions" (Types A, C, and F reorganizations, and certain non-divisive Type D reorganizations) where tax attributes of the transferor will carry over to the transferee. In each of these situations, the transferor corporation is in effect absorbed by the transferee; but it is no longer necessary, as was the case under pre-1954 law, for taxpayers to go through the ritual of having the loss

[15] See *e.g.*, Patten Fine Papers, Inc. v. Commissioner, *supra* note 6; contra, F. C. Donovan, Inc. v. United States, *supra* note 6.

[16] §381(a)(1) does not apply, however, to a §332 liquidation if the basis of the transferred assets is determined by reference to the cost of the subsidiary's stock under §334(b)(2) (*supra*, Sec. 9.44).

If the liquidation qualifies both under §332 and as a reorganization, it is probably to be treated as a liquidation by virtue of Regs. §1.332-2(d); this may be important in applying §382(b), which covers §381(a)(2), but not §381(a)-(1), transactions.

[17] See Marwais Steel Co., 38 T.C. 633 (1962).

corporation emerge as the surviving legal entity in the acquisition transaction. Section 381 does not apply, however, to corporate divisions, recapitalizations, or insolvency reorganizations, or to some transfers of property to controlled corporations under §351; these transactions remain subject to the pre-1954 rules dealing with the preservation of corporate tax attributes.[18] As a result, the *New Colonial Ice* and *Metropolitan Edison* lines of authority retain a limited viability under the 1954 Code. Moreover, since §381 deals only with the carryover of the transferor corporation's tax attributes, the acquiring corporation must resort to other provisions of the law to determine the preservation of its *own* advantageous tax history (most notably §§382 and 269). Consequently, §381(a)(2) offers only a limited solution to the carryover problem in the corporate readjustment area, albeit a considerably more rational one than that which existed under prior law.

In the case of Type C reorganizations (acquisition of substantially all the assets of one corporation for voting stock of another), some uncertainty exists as to whether the transferor corporation must liquidate after the transfer in order for its attributes to pass over to the transferee under §381. As a general matter, such a liquidation is not necessary in order for the transaction to qualify as a Type C reorganization (*supra*, Sec. 12.14); but if it continues in existence (e.g., as a holding company), and its earnings and profits pass to the transferee, it would be free to distribute its accumulated earnings to its shareholders without dividend consequences. The language of §381 (a)(2) seems to support this conclusion, however, although the Service may refuse to rule favorably on the issue.

Section 381 permits inheritance of the transferor corporation's tax attributes only by *the* acquiring corporation. The regulations state that only a single corporation can constitute the "acquiring corporation," Regs. §1.381(a)-1(b)(2), and that it is the corporation which ultimately acquires, directly or indirectly, all of the assets transferred by the transferor; or, if no one corporation ultimately acquires all of the transferred assets, the corporation which directly acquired them, even though none are retained by it. For example, if all the assets of X corporation are acquired by Y corporation in exchange for its stock and thereafter, pursuant to the plan of reorganization, Y transfers one-half of these assets to its wholly-owned subsidiary, A, and the

---

[18] As to insolvency reorganizations, see generally Krantz, Loss Carryovers in Chapter X Reorganizations, 16 Tax L. Rev. 359 (1961). As to the carryover of earnings and profits in non-§381 transactions, see Regs. §1.312-10; Regs. §1.312-11; articles by Halperin, Nessen, and Testa, *supra* note 4.

other half to a second subsidiary, B, Y will be treated as the acquiring corporation. If, on the other hand, all of X's assets had been acquired by A in exchange for stock of its parent corporation, Y (or, alternatively, if the X assets had been directly acquired by Y and then retransferred by it to A), A, as the ultimate transferee of all of the assets, would be treated as the acquiring corporation and succeed to X's tax attributes.

The limited category of Type D reorganizations covered by §381-(a)(2) is designed to restrict the carryover benefits of §381 to "nondivisive" transactions (*supra*, Sec. 12.15). In effect, this type of reorganization (like that of §368(a)(1)(F), relating to mere changes in identity, form, or place of organization), involves the "reincorporation" of substantially all of the transferor corporation's properties in a new corporate vehicle. The Service has recognized the possible overlap of Type A, C, D, and F reorganizations in this situation, and, where such a transaction satisfies the requirements of §368(a)(1)(F) (*supra*, Sec. 12.17), it will be treated as such for purposes of §381, even if it constitutes a Type A, C, or D reorganization as well.[19]

Sec. 13.12.   Special operating rules: §381(b)

By virtue of §381(b)(1), the taxable year of the transferor corporation ends with the date on which it makes one of the types of transfers specified in §381(a) (except that the acquiring corporation in a Type F reorganization is treated as the transferor corporation would have been, had there been no reorganization). For this purpose, Regs. §1.381(b)-1(b) provides that the "date of the transfer" is the day on which the transfer is finally completed, except that the date on which "substantially all" of the transferor's property was transferred may be used if the transferor corporation ceases all operations (other than liquidating activities) after such date. The regulations permit the retention of a reasonable amount of assets to pay liabilities or to preserve the corporate existence, and go on to state that a corporation is considered to be in a status of liquidation when it ceases to be a going concern and its activities are merely for the purpose of winding up its affairs, paying its debts, and distributing its remaining properties to shareholders (see *supra*, Sec. 9.02 and Sec. 2.08 on the meaning of complete liquidation). A transferor corporation whose taxable year is closed by §381(b)(1) must file a return for the short taxable year period ending on such date; moreover, if it remains in existence, it must file another short taxable year return for the period

---

[19] Rev. Rul. 57-276, 1957-1 C.B. 126; see also Regs. §1.381(b)-1(a)(2).

ending with the date on which its regular taxable year would have ended had there been no §381(a) transfer. In effect, a transferor corporation which continues in existence after a §381 transaction has two short taxable year periods in lieu of its former accounting period. This closing of the transferor's taxable year also has importance in computing the net operating loss deduction which carries over to the transferee under §381(c)(1) (*infra*, Sec. 13.13).

Under another special rule applicable to §381 transactions, the acquiring corporation will not be entitled to carry back a net operating loss sustained in a taxable year ending after the date of the acquisition to a prior taxable year of the transferor corporation.[20] Such a post-acquisition net operating loss, however, can be carried back by the acquiring corporation to its *own* pre-acquisition taxable years under the general rules of §172.[21]

Sec. 13.13. Carryover items and computation mechanics: §381(c)

Section 381(c) enumerates twenty-two tax attributes of the transferor corporation which carry over to the transferee.[22] The most important of these attributes, and the principles governing their application to the transferee, are:

1. Net operating loss carryovers. The rules and limitations respecting inheritance of the transferor corporation's net operating loss carryovers are found in §381(c)(1). These provisions are at points grotesquely complex, and the regulations are even more so. Moreover, as will be subsequently noted, the form of the acquisition transaction can still have a considerable effect in this area despite the 1954 Code's avowed aim of eliminating such distinctions. In effect, tax planning techniques relating to the form and timing of acquisitions have merely shifted to a new and more complex level of analysis; and taxpayers who ignore these considerations can be frustrated in their hopes almost as easily as their like minded predecessors under prior law.

The principal computation rules with respect to the carryover of net operating losses from the transferor corporation to the acquiring corporation are as follows:

a. The acquiring corporation obtains all of the transferor's

[20] This provision overrules the result in F. C. Donovan, Inc. v. Commissioner, *supra* note 6.
[21] Regs. §1.381(c)(1)-1(b); for more on the net operating loss carryover, see *infra*, Sec. 13.13.
[22] On the possibility that other tax attributes may carry over, see the discussion *supra*, Sec. 13.10, and note 13.

unused net operating loss carryovers, even though the acquisition consists of less than 100 percent of the acquired corporation's assets, Regs. §1.381(c)(1)-1(c)(2);

b. Post-acquisition losses of the *acquiring* corporation cannot be carried back to pre-acquisition taxable years of the *transferor* corporation, but such losses can be carried back to prior taxable years of the *acquiring* corporation under the general carryback rules of §172, Regs. §1.381(c)(1)-1(b);

c. If the transferor corporation continues in existence after the transfer, any post-transfer losses which it sustains can be carried back to its *own* pre-transfer taxable years, but cannot be utilized by the acquiring corporation as carrybacks or carryovers, Regs. §1.381(c)(1)-1(b);

d. The transferor corporation's taxable year closes on the effective date of the §381 transfer (§381(b)(1) and (2), *supra*, Sec. 13.12), and this short taxable year period counts as a full year in computing the carryback and carryover time periods of §172(b)(1) with respect to its net operating losses, Regs. §1.381-(c)(1)-1(e)(3);

e. Under §381(c)(1)(A), the first period to which unused loss carryovers of the transferor are to be carried is the taxable year of the acquiring corporation ending after the effective date of the §381 transfer, which period also counts as a full year in applying §172(b)(1);

f. Under §381(c)(1)(B), only a proportionate part of the acquiring corporation's taxable income (computed on a daily basis) for the year during which the two corporations are combined can be offset by a net operating loss *deduction* attributable to loss carryovers of the transferor, Regs. §1.381(c)(1)-1(d); and

g. §381(c)(1)(C) contains elaborate rules for tracing the extent to which, and the sequence in which, the net operating loss carryovers of both the transferor and the acquiring corporations are absorbed under §172(b)(2), in order to implement the tracing mechanics of §172(b)(2) when multiple carryovers or carrybacks are involved, Regs. §1.381(c)(1)-1(e) and (f).

These principles can be illustrated by the following examples, in which both the transferor corporation (X) and the acquiring corporation (Y) use a calendar year accounting period. In addition, the acquisition transactions will be effected on July 1, 1964 (a leap year), which date constitutes the mid-point of the acquiring corporation's taxable year.

a. Y corporation owns 80 percent of X, which has unused loss carryovers. Y liquidates X under §332 and thereby obtains 80 percent of its assets. Y is entitled to all of X's loss carryovers.

b. X merges into Y and Y is the surviving corporate entity; thereafter, Y sustains a net operating loss. Y is not entitled to

carry back this loss to pre-acquisition taxable years of X because of §381(b)(3); however, Y can carry back this loss to its
own pre-acquisition taxable years, Regs. §1.381(c)(1)-1(b).[23]

c. X transfers substantially all of its assets to Y in a Type
C reorganization; X continues in existence after the transfer and
subsequently sustains net operating losses. These losses can
be carried back by X to its own prior taxable years, but cannot
be utilized in any way by Y.

d. At the start of 1964 (the acquisition year), X has an
unused loss carryover from 1961 in the amount of $100; X earns
$20 during the 183-day short period (January 1-July 1, 1964)
preceding the transfer of its assets to Y. The $100 loss carryover
is first applied against X's $20 of income for its short fiscal year
ending July 1, 1964; and the unused portion ($80) is then car-
ried to Y's 1964 taxable year under §381(c)(1)(A); however,
Y's net operating loss deduction with respect to such loss is
limited to 50 percent of its 1964 taxable income by virtue of
§381(c)(1)(B). Thus, if Y earned $60 of income for its 1964
taxable year it would be entitled to claim only $30 of the $80
loss carryover from X as a deduction in its 1964 return. The
unused portion of X's 1961 loss carryover ($50) would then be
carried to Y's 1965 taxable year, but this would be the last
available year of such loss; although its "normal" life would continue until 1966 (viz., the fifth year after 1961, when it arose),
it aged by two years in 1964, by reason of the two short taxable
years into which 1964 was broken.[24]

e. If Y, in the example in (d) above, had a net operating
loss carryover of $40 from 1961, matters become more complex.
Section 381(c)(1)(C) provides generally (first sentence) that
where loss years of the transferor and the acquiring corporations
overlap, priority of consumption is to be given to losses of the
transferor. The second sentence of §381(c)(1)(C) goes on to
provide, however, that in applying the loss carryover tracing
rules of §172(b)(2), Y's 1964 taxable year must be split into
two separate periods, called the pre-acquisition part year and
the post-acquisition part year (since the transfer from X occurred *within* Y's 1964 taxable year) and that loss carryovers
from X will only be absorbed by the post-acquisition part year
taxable income of Y for 1964 (pro rated on a daily basis).
Consequently, Y's 1961 loss carryover would first be applied
against Y's 1964 pre-acquisition part year taxable income of

---

[23] If the acquisition had taken the form of a statutory consolidation of X
and Y into Z, however, Z's post-consolidation losses could not be carried back
to pre-consolidation years of either X or Y, Regs. §1.381(c)(1)-1(b), Example
(2). Thus, if one of the combining corporations is a potential loss candidate,
and if a carryback of the loss is preferable to a carryforward, the parties should
seek to preserve its legal entity.

[24] If Y (the profit company) had merged into X (the loss company) in the
above example, the result would differ in that X, as the surviving company,
would not lose an extra year in the life of its 1961 loss carryover: Y's taxable
year would close on the date of the transfer, but not X's.

$30; the unused $10 portion would then be carried to the post-acquisition part year but, since the $80 loss carryover from X is entitled to priority by virtue of the first sentence of §381(c)(1)-(C), this $10 of Y's unused loss would carryover to Y's 1965 taxable year.[25]

2. *Earnings and profits.* Another major corporate tax attribute which carries over to the acquiring corporation under §381 is the earnings and profits (or deficit) account of the transferor, §381-(c)(2). The applicable rules codify much of the pre-1954 case law on this subject (*supra,* Sec. 13.02). Thus, the *Sansome* rule (earnings and profits of transferor carry over to the corporation that acquires its assets in a tax-free reorganization) and the *Phipps* restriction (deficit in transferor's earnings and profits cannot be applied against transferee's accumulated earnings and profits) are codified by §381(c)(2)-(A) and (B), as is the "hovering deficit" rule of the *Snider* case (deficit inherited from transferor can be applied against transferee's post-acquisition earnings and profits).[26] The regulations elaborate on these general principles by providing: (a) that earnings inherited from the transferor become a part of the acquiring corporation's *accumulated* earnings account (and thus have no effect on computation of its current earnings for the year of acquisition);[27] (b) that current dividend distributions by the acquiring corporation during the year of acquisition come out of its current earnings account before consideration can be given to any deficits inherited from the transferor; (c) that in determining the dividend status of current distributions by the acquiring corporation, deficits inherited from the transferor corporation have no effect on the acquiring corporation's accumulated earnings account; if, on the other hand, there are inherited earnings, they are reduced for this purpose by only a ratable portion of the acquiring corporation's current deficit (computed on a daily basis); and (d) that in determining the amount of the transferor's earnings and profits which are inherited by the acquiring corporation, distributions by the transferor to its shareholders (other than the acquiring

[25] While Y's taxable year is split into two parts for purposes of applying the tracing and consumption rules of §172(b)(2), it counts as one taxable year in applying the carryback and carryover time limits of §172(b)(1) to losses of the acquiring corporation (*i.e.,* in the example, 1964 counts as only one year for Y's 1961 loss carryover). Regs. §1.381(c)(1)-1(f)(2).

[26] *Supra* note 4; United States v. Snider, 224 F.2d 165, 47 AFTR 1368 (1st Cir. 1955).

[27] If the acquiring corporation has an accumulated deficit, the inherited earnings are not offset by it; Regs. §1.381(c)(2)-1(a)(5). This provision is contrary to a dictum in the *Phipps* case, *supra,* stating that pre-acquisition deficits of the acquiring corporation offset accumulated earnings inherited from the transferor; but it is supported by §381 itself.

corporation) pursuant to the plan of reorganization or liquidation reduce such earnings, whether the distribution occurs before or after the effective date of the §381 transfer.[28]

3. Accounting methods. Section 381(c)(4) provides generally that the acquiring corporation must continue to use the accounting method used by the transferor on the date of the §381 transfer if both corporations have been using the same method prior thereto; otherwise, the method to be used is to be determined under regulations adopted by the Commissioner (which, in effect, will be entitled to the force of law in view of the express statutory delegation of authority). As to what constitutes a "method of accounting," §446 and the regulations thereunder provide, in brief, that this term includes not only a taxpayer's "overall" accounting method (*i.e.*, the general method used in computing its taxable income, such as the cash or accrual method), but the accounting treatment of any "material item" of income or deduction (*e.g.*, bad debts; research and experimental expenses; long-term contracts; intangible drilling expense elections; etc). Thus, the accounting method rules of §381(c)(4) are one of the broader categories of carryover items covered by §381, possibly reaching many items not originally thought subject to carryover. It should also be noted that §381(c) deals specifically with various other "item" accounting methods of the transferor (*e.g.*, inventories, §381(c)(5); depreciation method, §381(c)(6); installment rules, §381(c)(7); and assumed "expense liabilities," §381(c)(16)). These specific provisions apply in lieu of the general accounting method rules of §381(c)(4).

If a change of accounting method (either in an overall or an item method) is required because of the §381 transaction, the adjustment rules of §481, designed to prevent doubling up of income or deductions when accounting methods are changed, must be considered; moreover, Regs. §1.381(c)(4)-1(a)(2) warns that §§269 and 482 may be applicable, notwithstanding the fact that §381(c)(4) ordinarily assures carryover treatment. Accordingly, integration of a transferor's accounting methods with those of the acquiring corporation can create problems of no small dimension, the major aspects of which are considered in the following discussion.[29]

---

[28] Such distributions could include "boot" distributions by the transferor to its shareholders pursuant to the reorganization plan; and distributions to minority shareholders on the liquidation of a subsidiary owned less than 100 percent by its parent, Regs. §1.381(c)(2)-1(c).

For illustrations of these principles, see Regs. §1.381(c)(2)-1(a)(7), Examples (1)-(7); see also Halperin and Nessen, *supra* note 4.

[29] See generally Eames, Accounting Method Considerations in Corporate Reorganizations With Special Attention to Section 381 Transactions, 23 N.Y.U. Inst. on Fed. Tax. 853 (1965).

(a) Continuance of transferor's accounting methods. If the transferor corporation and the acquiring corporation have the same accounting methods, then the acquiring corporation will step into the shoes of the transferor with respect to various elections and items of income or deduction of the transferor which, because of its method of accounting, have not been included or deducted in computing its taxable income prior to the date of the §381 transfer; and such items will retain their character in the hands of the acquiring corporation. For example, if X and Y corporations are both on the cash basis method of accounting (or, alternatively, if both are on the accrual method), Y must continue to use X's overall accounting method after it acquires the assets of X in a transaction covered by §381(a); this is true whether Y integrates X's business into its own operations or instead preserves the X business as a separate "division." Hence, if X, as of the date of the transfer, has currently unreportable ordinary income items in the amount of $100 and $20 of currently non-deductible ordinary expense obligations, Y must continue X's treatment with respect to these items and include or deduct them when received, paid, or accrued as the case may be, depending on its accounting method.

If the transferor and acquiring corporations use different methods of accounting, the regulations provide that the acquiring corporation must continue to use the transferor's accounting methods if the acquired business is continued as a separate and distinct enterprise. For example, if X operated a service business and used the cash method of accounting and Y operated a manufacturing business and used the accrual method, Y would have to continue using the cash method of accounting with respect to the acquired service business if it was operated as a separate division after the acquisition.[30]

If the acquiring corporation wishes to adopt a different accounting method from the one required by these principles, it may do so only with the consent of the Commissioner, which may be granted subject to such terms, conditions, and adjustments as are necessary to clearly reflect income, Regs. §1.381(c)(4)-1(d).

(b) Change of accounting method required. If the transferor corporation and the acquiring corporation use different methods of accounting in their businesses and the transferred business is not continued as a separate and distinct enterprise by the acquiring corporation, a change of accounting method is required by the regulations, subject to any adjustments that may be necessary under §481 or

---

[30] Regs. §1.381(c)(4)-1(b)(2) and (3); on the meaning of "separate business," see Regs. §1.446-1(d).

§446(b) in order to give proper effect to the change. Which corporation's overall accounting method is to be used depends upon the "principal accounting method" test: *i.e.*, if the acquiring corporation's accounting method is the "principal" method, then the transferor's accounting method must be converted to this system; if, on the other hand, the transferor's method is the "principal" method, the acquiring corporation's accounting method must be changed. The "principal accounting method" is determined by comparing the adjusted asset bases and gross receipts of the component businesses; if one business predominates on both of these counts, its method is to be employed; otherwise, the Commissioner will determine the method, or combination of methods, to be used. In either event, as stated above, appropriate adjustments may be required to avoid duplicating or omitting items of income and deduction. Moreover, if the Commissioner determines that the principal accounting method will not "clearly reflect income," he may provide for the use of a method which will clearly reflect the income of the acquiring corporation. See generally Regs. §1.381(c)(4)-1(c) and (d).

4. Assumption of liabilities. If, in a transaction to which §381(a) applies, the acquiring corporation assumes (by agreement or operation of law) a liability (not yet taken into account by the transferor) that would, but for the transfer, have been deductible by the transferor when paid or accrued by it, §381(c)(16) permits the acquiring corporation to deduct the liability when, under *its* method of accounting, it is able to claim a deduction therefor (*i.e.*, when paid, if the acquiring corporation is on the cash method, or when accrued, if it is on the accrual method). However, if the transfer is by way of a transaction specified in §381(a)(2) (*i.e.*, certain acquisitive reorganizations), §381(c)(16) does not apply to assumed obligations which are "reflected" in the price paid by the acquiring corporation for the transferred assets.[31] In determining whether a liability was "reflected" in the acquiring corporation's purchase price for the transferred assets, the regulations provide for a presumption in favor of non-reflection, in the absence of facts showing (a) that the parties were aware of a specific liability, and (b) that they reduced the consideration paid for the transferred assets by a specific amount to take account of it.[32]

[31] This restriction does not apply to §332 liquidations of subsidiary corporations, though the carryover rules of §381 ordinarily apply to such transactions by virtue of §381(a)(1).
[32] See Regs. §1.381(c)(16)-1(c), Examples. Note also that §381(c)(16) applies only to liability "assumptions"; merely taking "subject to" the liability will not suffice. For other aspects of the assumption of liabilities in a reorganization, see *supra*, Sec. 12.18.

If §381(a)(16) does not apply to a particular liability assumption, either because the transferor was entitled to take it into account at or before the date of the transfer under its regular accounting method, or because the liability was reflected in the price paid by the acquiring corporation for the transferred assets, the regulations provide that its treatment will be governed by the method of accounting rules of §381(c)(4) *(supra)*.

5. *Other §381(c) items.* Section 381(c) lists numerous other tax attributes of the transferor which qualify for carryover treatment under §381(a):

> a. *Capital loss carryover, §381(c)(3).* The limitations on the carryover of this item are similar to those discussed in connection with net operating loss carryovers *(supra)*.
>
> b. *Inventory methods, §381(c)(5).* These provisions are similar to the carryover rules relating to accounting methods *(supra)*.
>
> c. *Depreciation methods, §381(c)(6).* The acquiring corporation steps into the shoes of the transferor with respect to its accelerated depreciation methods for the transferred assets (but only to the extent that the basis of the acquired depreciable assets is not in excess of their basis in the hands of the transferor).[33]
>
> d. *Installment method, §381(c)(8).* The acquiring corporation steps into the shoes of the transferor with respect to §453 obligations acquired therefrom.
>
> e. *Amortization of bond discount and premium, §381(c)(9).* An acquiring corporation which assumes bonded indebtedness of the transferor must continue to treat issue discount or premium thereon (and, say the regulations, bond issue expenses as well) in the same manner as did the transferor.[34]
>
> f. *Excess contributions to qualified deferred compensation plans, §381(c)(11).* The acquiring corporation succeeds to any unused deductions or excess contributions carryovers which would have been available to the transferor under §404.
>
> g. *Recovery of prior deductions of the transferor, §381(c)-(12).* The acquiring corporation is subject to the "tax benefit"

---

[33] Thus, if the acquiring corporation obtains a stepped-up basis in whole or in part for the acquired depreciable assets (because it paid "boot" to the transferor which was taxable to it under §361(b)(1)(B)), the acquiring corporation is not entitled to use accelerated depreciation methods on this "excess" portion of the assets' adjusted basis. See Regs. §1.381(c)(6)-1(b) and (g).

[34] As to what constitutes an "assumption" for this purpose, see Regs. §1.381(c)(9)-1(d), which provides generally that an exchange or substitution of the acquiring corporation's bonds for those of the transferor in a §381 transaction will be so treated. Note, however, that this provision does not apply if the transferee merely takes "subject to" the liability. For similar problems under §357, see discussion *supra*, Sec. 12.18.

§381(c)(9) partially codifies the holding of Helvering v. Metropolitan Edison Co., 306 U.S. 522, 22 AFTR 307 (1939), which permitted carryover of bond issue discount deductions.

rules of §111 with respect to any post-acquisition recoveries of items previously deducted by the transferor, such recoveries being taxable to it in the same manner as would have occurred had the transferor obtained the recovery.

h. Involuntary conversions under §1033, §381(c)(13). The acquiring corporation is treated in the same manner as the transferor in applying the non-recognition rules of §1033.

i. Investment credit, §381(c)(23). The acquiring corporation presumably steps into the shoes of the transferor with respect to its unused investment credits, at least where the acquired assets are continued in use by the acquiring corporation as "investment credit property."[35]

6. Non-§381(c) items. As noted earlier, §381 does not cover all the possible corporate tax attributes or all the possible forms of tax-free reorganization which can raise a carryover problem. With respect to these unenumerated items and transactions, three interpretations are possible: (a) that no carryover occurs, unless the transaction or item specifically qualifies under §381 (*i.e.*, that §381 is the exclusive provision for carryover treatment); (b) that carryovers of unspecified tax attributes can occur under some residual policy of §381 where the acquisition transaction constitutes a §381(a) type transfer (a theory that is specifically rejected by the regulations); and (c) that carryovers of unspecified items and transactions are controlled by the pre-1954 rules, including the *New Colonial* continuity of entity theory and the continuity of business enterprise requirement of *Libson Shops* (*supra*, Sec. 13.02). In the *Denver & Rio Grand R.R. Co.* case (*supra* note 13), the Tax Court took a long step toward adoption of the first approach, holding that tax attributes of a transferor could carryover to an acquiring corporation *only* if the transaction is mentioned in §381(a). This position seems erroneous in view of the express statements in the Committee Reports that §381 "is not intended to affect the carryover treatment of an item or tax attribute not specified in the section or the carryover treatment of items or tax attributes in transactions not described in §381(a)," S. Rep. No. 1622, 83d Cong., 2d Sess. 277 (1954), and that "no inference is to be drawn from the enactment of this section whether any item or tax attribute may be utilized by a successor or predecessor corporation under existing law." These statements appear to support approach (c) above, and may be the foundation for Regs. §1.312-11, providing for a carryover of earnings and profits in certain circumstances that are not covered by §381.[36]

---

[35] Cf. §47(b)(2), and Prop. Regs. §1.47-3(e).

[36] For general discussions of §381, see Cohen et al., The Internal Revenue

Part C. Limitations on Enjoyment of Corporate Tax Attributes

Sec. 13.20. Introductory

The carryover of tax attributes from one corporation to another (either under the pre-1954 case law or under the 1954 Code rules of §381) can lead to the acquisition of corporations primarily because of their favorable attributes. Although on occasion any of the items that are preserved for the acquiring corporation may be a valuable prize, the most commonly sought attribute is a net operating loss carryover; and for many years advertisements for defunct corporations with such carryovers have been sprinkled through the financial pages of the metropolitan and financial press. As will be seen in the discussion that follows, however, the Service is armed with numerous statutory and judicial weapons to combat such tax motivated transactions:

> 1. §269 (*infra*, Sec. 13.21), which disallows any deduction, credit, or other allowance involved in certain acquisitions of stock or property with the principal purpose of income tax avoidance;
> 2. §382(a) (*infra*, Sec. 13.22), which disallows net operating loss carryovers where a substantial change in the corporation's stock ownership is accompanied by a substantial business discontinuance;
> 3. §382(b) (*infra*, Sec. 13.23), which may partially disallow net operating loss carryovers where the shareholders of the loss corporation fail to retain a minimum continuity of ownership interest in the loss corporation following a reorganization transaction of the type specified in §381(a)(2):
> 4. The *Libson Shops* doctrine (*infra*, Sec. 13.25), which prohibits the carryover in a reorganization of losses against profits of a different business; and
> 5. Various other general principles (*infra*, Sec. 13.26), sounding in "sham," tax avoidance, business purpose, form versus substance, clear reflection of income, step transactions, and assignment of income, and derived in large part from Gregory v. Helvering (*supra*, Sec. 11.02).

Some of these provisions and general principles depend for their applicability on the taxpayer's motives or state of mind (*e.g.*, §269);

Code of 1954: Carryovers and the Accumulated Earnings Tax, 10 Tax L. Rev. 277 (1955); Germain, Carryovers in Corporate Acquisitions, 15 Tax L. Rev. 35 (1959); Reese, Reorganization Transfers and Survival of Tax Attributes, 16 Tax L. Rev. 207 (1961); Comment, Net Operating Loss Carryovers and Corporate Adjustments: Retaining An Advantageous Tax History Under Libson Shops and Sections 269, 381, and 382, 69 Yale L.J. 1201 (1961); Wilson, *infra* note 90.

others adopt mechanical rules of thumb to eliminate probing into tax motivation as such (*e.g.*, §382); others depend on the economic consequences of the transaction (*e.g.*, *Libson Shops*); and some are concerned with whether the form of a particular transaction has independent substance, apart from its tax benefits (*e.g.*, *Gregory*). Litigation has been extensive on all of these points, and, as one would expect, matters unfortunately are not entirely clear. The materials that follow consist of only a sample (and a highly selective one at that) of the many decisions in this area, in the hope that the major trends and points of conflict may be illumined without bogging down in detail. Moreover, the principal focus will be on the survival of net operating loss deductions, although it should be noted that other tax attributes can, and often do, raise similar problems.

Sec. 13.21.   Acquisitions to evade or avoid income tax: §269

1. General scope and operation. Section 269 provides for the disallowance of deductions and other tax benefits when tax avoidance is the principal purpose for the acquisition of control of a corporation or for certain transfers of property from one corporation to another. This statutory restriction was originally enacted in 1943, principally to curb a growing "market" for defunct corporate shells.[37] These hollow entities were in demand because the World War II excess profits tax exempted a corporation's "normal" profits, based on its historic earnings or invested capital; and some owners of booming war businesses hoped to shield themselves against taxable "excess" profits by carrying on their activities through a corporation that in the past had enjoyed substantial earnings or invested capital. Other negotiable tax benefits were loss carryovers and potential deductions to be created by selling high basis assets (usually §1231 property) with low current values. Although the Treasury was not wholly devoid of weapons against acquisitions that were motivated solely by the hope of avoiding taxes (see Rudick, *supra* note 37, at 216-222), §269 was enacted in 1943 on the Treasury's recommendation to provide a more specific statutory sanction for an attack on these devices. Except for the presumption of §269(c), enacted in 1954, there have been virtually no changes in the statute in the intervening years.

---

[37] Thus, a seller advertised in the *New York Times* in 1943: "For sale. Stock of corporation having 1943 tax loss deduction $120,000. Sole assets are $80,000 in cash and equivalent." A buyer advertised in the *Wall Street Journal* that he wanted "To acquire all the outstanding stock of a corporation with original invested capital of several hundred thousand dollars with present assets at nominal values." Rudick, Acquisitions to Avoid Income or Excess Profits Tax: Section 129 of the Internal Revenue Code, 58 Harv. L. Rev. 196 (1944).

Section 269 is applicable if:

1. Any person or persons (including, by virtue of §7701-
(a)(1), a corporation) acquire control of a corporation, directly
or indirectly; or
2. Any corporation acquires, directly or indirectly, property
of another corporation if the latter corporation was not controlled, directly or indirectly, immediately before the acquisition
by the acquiring corporation or its shareholders and if the acquiring corporation's basis for the property is determined by reference to the transferor corporation's basis; and
3. The principal purpose of the acquisition (which must have
occurred on or after October 8, 1940[38]) is evasion or avoidance
of Federal income tax by securing the benefit of a deduction,
credit, or other allowance which such person or corporation would
not otherwise enjoy.

"Control" is defined by §269(a) to mean the ownership of stock possessing at least 50 percent of the total combined voting power of all
classes of stock entitled to vote or at least 50 percent of the total value
of all classes of stock. Under §269(c), enacted in 1954 and applicable
only to acquisitions after March 1, 1954, the payment of a purchase
price that is "disproportionate" to the tax basis of the acquired corporation or property and the tax benefits resulting from the acquisition is "prima facie evidence of the principal purpose of evasion or
avoidance of Federal income tax."

Because discussions of §269 frequently focus on the purchase of
"loss" corporations to serve as a shell for the conduct of a successful
business whose profits are to be offset by a carryover of the losses of
prior years, it is important to note that §269 is not confined to such
transactions, and that it may embrace devices in which the acquired
corporation is not even kept alive. The pre-1954 regulations illustrated
the potential range of §269 by referring to (a) the acquisition of a
corporation with *current, past, or prospective* credits, deductions, net
operating losses, etc., in order to bring these allowances "into conjunction" with the income of a profitable enterprise; (b) the transfer
of business assets producing a high level of profits to a subsidiary in
order to permit the parent, by selling its retained depreciated assets at
a loss, to obtain a refund of taxes by operation of the net operating
loss carryback,[39] and (c) the acquisition by a corporation of property

---

[38] October 8, 1940, is the date on which the Excess Profits Tax of 1940 was
enacted. As stated in the text, §129 stemmed in large part from the acquisition
of loss corporations as a means of avoiding this tax.

[39] By this device, the subsidiary would be paying current taxes so the
parent could get a refund of past taxes; this would be advantageous if the rates
in earlier years were higher (*e.g.,* excess profits tax years).

having a substituted basis materially in excess of fair market value (*e.g.*, by acquiring another corporation with such assets and liquidating it under §332, *supra*, Sec. 9.40), in order to generate tax-reducing losses, presumably by selling the property or taking depreciation deductions with respect to it.[40]

When §269 is applicable, the taxpayer's purpose of securing the benefit of a deduction, credit, or other allowance that he would not otherwise enjoy is frustrated by the simple device of denying "such deduction, credit, or other allowances." The Treasury is vested with authority by §269(b), however, to mitigate this result by allowing the deduction, credit, or allowance in question in part, by allocating gross income and the disallowed deductions, etc., among the corporations or properties, or by allowing the items in part and allocating in part, provided it determines that such action will not result in the tax avoidance that motivated the acquisition.

Although §269 has most frequently been applied to deny the carryover of net operating losses to a period following a change in control of the corporation (or the acquisition of the loss-generating assets in a tax-free transaction), its reach is considerably broader than this particular tax benefit. Thus, in Army Times Sales Co., 35 T.C. 688 (1961), §269 was applied to disallow corporate deductions for interest paid on the corporation's bonds, and to convert a sole shareholder's claim for capital gain treatment on the redemption thereof into ordinary income.[41] Other examples of deductions, credits, or allowances which may be denied under §269 include: excess profits tax credits; foreign tax credits; investment credits; depreciation deductions; rental deductions; capital, ordinary, or §1231 losses; earnings and profits deficits; surtax exemptions under §11(c); minimum accumulated earnings tax credits under §535(c)(2); the privilege of filing consolidated returns; the special deduction for Western Hemisphere Trade Corporations of §922; and losses from the sale of assets acquired with a "built-in" loss at the date of the acquistion (*i.e.*, property having a high basis and a low value).[42]

---

[40] Regs. 118, §39.129-3(b) and (c); the regulations under the 1954 Code are even broader in scope, Regs. §1.269-3.

[41] See also, Brown Dyna-Lube Co. v. Commissioner, 297 F.2d 915, 9 AFTR 2d 547 (4th Cir. 1962); J. T. Slocomb Co. v. Commissioner, 38 T.C. 752 (1963), aff'd, 334 F.2d 269, 14 AFTR 2d 5086 (2d Cir. 1964); but cf. The Humacid Co., 42 T.C. 894 (1964).

[42] But see John F. Nutt, 39 T.C. 231 (1962) (Acq.), holding that §269 did not empower the Commissioner to disregard the corporate entity and tax the corporation's income directly to its shareholders; and cf. Pauline W. Ach, 42 T.C. 114 (1964), aff'd, 358 F.2d 342, 17 AFTR 2d 700 (9th Cir. 1966), approving a reallocation of the bulk of a corporation's income to its controlling shareholder under §482.

The treatment of losses sustained *after* the date of the §269 acquisition (either post-acquisition net operating losses or losses resulting from post-acquisition declines in value) is less clear, however. In R. P. Collins & Co., Inc. v. United States, 303 F.2d 142, 9 AFTR 2d. 1485 (1st Cir. 1962), the court applied §269 to deny a deduction for post-acquisition net operating losses on the ground that such losses were tainted by the taxpayer's prohibited tax avoidance purpose with respect to other built-in losses of the acquired corporation.[43] On the other hand, the taxpayer was successful in resisting the application of §269 to post-acquisition operating losses (and to losses from the sale of assets which had declined in value after the date of the acquisition transaction) in Zanesville Investment Co. v. Commissioner, 335 F.2d 507, 14 AFTR 2d 5453 (6th Cir. 1964).[44]

If the forbidden tax avoidance purpose exists with respect to the acquisition of one tax benefit, does that motive also infect all other favorable tax attributes which might be available by virtue of the acquisition? The Tax Court has held that it does. Thus, in Zanesville Investment Co., 38 T.C. 406 (1962), the court stated that "[w]e do not believe that the statute requires at the time of acquisition a precise awareness of every deduction, credit, or other allowance that such acquisition will bring to the taxpayer. It is enough if at the time of acquisition the principal purpose was to obtain a tax benefit."[45]

For several years, the Tax Court adhered to the position that §269 did not apply to the *acquired* corporation, an interpretation which served to deprive that section of much of its vitality for those who had the presence of mind, or careful tax advice, to retain the legal entity of the corporation whose favorable tax attributes were desired. This theory was first enunciated in Alprosa Watch Corp., 11 T.C. 240 (1948), where a virtually defunct corporation was acquired

---

[43] See also Elko Realty Co. v. Commissioner, 29 T.C. 1012 (1958), aff'd, 260 F.2d 949, 2 AFTR 2d 6121 (3rd Cir. 1958); Temple Square Mfg. Co., 36 T.C. 88 (1961); American Pipe & Steel Corp. v. Commissioner, 243 F.2d 125, 50 AFTR 2121 (9th Cir. 1957), cert. denied, 355 U.S. 906; and J. D. & A. B. Spreckels Co., 41 B.T.A. 370 (1940). These decisions generally denied the use of post-acquisition losses which were built-in or "accrued" at the time of the §269 acquisition. For similar provisions under the consolidated returns regulations with respect to sales of capital and §1231 assets, see Regs. §1.1502-31A (b)(9) and Prop. Regs. §1.1502-15. But in Brick Milling Co., ¶63,305 P-H Memo T.C., the court flatly held, citing *Collins*, that §269 applies to disallow post-acquisition operating losses.

[44] See also F. C. Publication Liquidating Corp. v. Commissioner, 304 F.2d 779, 10 AFTR 2d 5057 (2d Cir. 1962); Hawaiian Trust Co. Ltd. v. United States, 291 F.2d 761, 7 AFTR 2d 1553 (9th Cir. 1961). See generally, Adlman, Recent Cases Increasingly Extend Section 269 to Disallow Post-Acquisition Operating Losses, 17 J. Tax. 282 (1962).

[45] See also Temple Square Mfg. Co., *supra* note 43; R. P. Collins & Co., Inc. v. United States, 303 F.2d 142, 9 AFTR 2d 1485 (1st Cir. 1962).

by a partnership, which then poured a promising business venture into the corporate shell and applied the corporation's pre-acquisition losses against its post-acquisition profits. When the Service disallowed the offset, the Tax Court said that §269 "would seem to prohibit the use of a deduction, credit, or allowance only by the acquiring person or corporation and not their use by the corporation whose control was acquired." This theory, though dictum in the *Alprosa* case itself, was applied in later decisions, thus preserving the market in "loss" corporations when a profitable business could be added by the new owner, and also stimulating the enactment of §382(a) (*infra*, Sec. 13.22) as an alternative attack on such carryovers. The *Alprosa* construction was rejected, however, in Commissioner v. Coastal Oil Storage Co. (*supra* note 10), and other courts, including the Tax Court, gradually fell into line with the *Coastal Oil* view.[46] Thus, in the *British Motor Car* case (*supra* note 46), the Ninth Circuit stated that: "We would be closing our eyes to the realities of the situation were we to refuse to recognize that the persons who have acquired the corporation did so to secure *for themselves* a very real tax benefit to be realized *through* the acquired corporation and which they could not otherwise have realized."

This widespread, and seemingly conclusive, rejection of the notion that §269 does not apply to the acquired corporation shifts the focus of analysis to the merits: *i.e.*, whether the principal purpose of the acquisition was the avoidance of income taxes. As will be seen, the Service's frustrations during the "*Alprosa* years" seem to have inspired a skeptical attitude toward any acquisition of an unprofitable company.[47]

[46] Commissioner v. British Motor Car Distributors, Ltd., 278 F.2d 392, 5 AFTR 2d 1277 (9th Cir. 1960); James Realty Co. v. United States, *supra* note 10; Mill Ridge Coal Co. v. Patterson, 264 F.2d 713, 3 AFTR 2d 919 (5th Cir. 1959); Thomas E. Snyder & Sons Co. v. Commissioner, 34 T.C. 400 (1960), affd, 288 F.2d 36, 7 AFTR 2d 875 (7th Cir. 1961); Frank Spingolo Warehouse Co., 37 T.C. 1 (1961); Urban Redevelopment Corp. v. Commissioner, 294 F.2d 328, 8 AFTR 2d 5503 (4th Cir. 1961); Temple Square Mfg. Co., *supra* note 43; F. C. Publication Liquidating Corp. v. Commissioner, *supra* note 44; J. T. Slocomb Co. v. Commissioner, *supra* note 41; Pauline W. Ach, *supra* note 42; H. F. Ramsey Co., Inc., 43 T.C. 500 (1965).

Moreover, other courts began applying the "continuity of business enterprise" approach of *Libson Shops* (*infra*, Sec. 13.25) to disallow losses in these situations, even where the taxpayer was able to prove absence of tax avoidance motives and thereby escape the clutches of §269, *e.g.*: Mill Ridge Coal Co. v. Patterson, *supra*; J. G. Dudley Co., Inc. v. Commissioner, *supra* note 9a; Norden-Ketay Corp. v. Commissioner, 319 F.2d 902, 12 AFTR 2d 5093 (2d Cir. 1963); Frederick Steel Co., 42 T.C. 13 (1964); Commissioner v. Virginia Metal Products, Inc., 290 F.2d 675, 7 AFTR 2d 1395 (3rd Cir. 1961), cert. denied, 368 U.S. 889 (1961).

[47] For general discussions of §269, see Kirkpatrick, Section 269 of the 1954 Code — Its Present and Prospective Function in the Commissioner's Arsenal,

2. Section 269 transactions. As noted above, §269 embraces two principal types of transactions: (a) acquisitions of control, *i.e.*, stock of a corporation, §269(a)(1); and (b) tax-free acquisitions of one corporation's assets by a previously unrelated corporation, §269-(a)(2). If such a transaction is effected for the prohibited tax avoidance purpose, the hoped-for tax benefits will be denied. Acquisition of "control" within the meaning of §269(a)(1) includes not only a direct purchase of stock sufficient to bring the acquiring party's ownership up to the requisite 50 percent level, but various tax-free acquisitions and indirect methods of acquiring "control" of a corporation as well (*i.e.*, the redemption of the stock of other shareholders, the use of "chains" of controlled corporations, and possibly even the use of convertible debentures or options to acquire additional stock, although matters are less clear in these latter situations). Although §269(a)(1) is not clear on this point, presumably all persons whose acquisitions of stock were motivated by the forbidden tax avoidance purpose are to be aggregated in computing "control"; but it would seem reasonable for a shareholder's tax avoidance purpose to infect not only the stock owned by him directly and indirectly (e.g., through a dummy, trust, or other entity), but also, in some circumstances, stock owned by his spouse, minor children, and possibly other intimates. Section 269 does not adopt the constructive ownership rules of §318, as does §382(a), however, so such an attribution ought to be selective rather than automatic.[48]

The regulations give three non-exclusive examples of transactions that may constitute a "control acquistion" under §269(a)(1): (a) the acquisition of a corporation having current, past, or prospective tax benefits, in order to bring these items into conjunction with the income of a profitable enterprise (including, for this purpose, *Alprosa*-type transactions); (b) the creation of two or more corporations instead of a single corporation in order to obtain multiple corporation benefits (*infra*, note 50, and the discussion *infra*, Part D of this chapter); and (c) the separation of profitable assets from assets producing net operating losses by transferring the income-producing

15 Tax L. Rev. 137 (1960); Peterson, Corporate Acquisitions for Tax Avoidance Purposes: The Ever-Tightening "Loophole," 19 J. Tax. 322 (1963); Peterson, the "Principal Purpose" Test Under Section 269: How It's Being Applied in the Courts, 20 J. Tax. 16 (1964); Feder, The Application of Section 269 to Corporations Having Net Operating Loss Carryovers and Potential Losses, 21 N.Y.U. Inst. on Fed. Tax. 1277 (1963).

[48] The attribution issue may arise in other contexts under §269, *e.g.*, in a taxpayer effort to establish that he had "control" before 1940. For a comparable claim, where the court refused to apply the constructive ownership rules of §267(c), see Thomas Snyder & Sons Co. v. Commissioner, *supra* note 46; see also Brick Milling Co., *supra* note 43, and Pauline W. Ach, *supra* note 42.

assets to a controlled corporation and thereafter using losses generated by the retained assets to produce loss carryback refunds. Regs. §1.269-3(b). Another likely candidate for application of §269(a)(1) is a transaction of the type involved in Diamond A Cattle Co. v. Commissioner, 233 F.2d 739, 49 AFTR 1321 (10th Cir. 1956), where an individual acquired control of a corporation engaged in a cyclical business and liquidated the enterprise in midstream (*i.e.*, after incurring expenses but before realization of the related income therefrom), thereby generating large net operating loss carryback refunds.[49] The deduction was allowed in the *Diamond A* case under the general net operating loss provisions of §172; but the Commissioner did not specifically assert §269, an oversight that is not likely to be repeated.

The second category of transactions covered by §269 involves an acquisition of the *assets* of one corporation *by another corporation* if (a) the basis for such assets carries over to the transferee and (b) the corporations were not under common control immediately prior to the acquisition. The major focus of this provision is on tax-free reorganizations, since these transactions generally activate the carryover rules of §381 (*supra*, Sec. 13.11). But the regulations state, and recent decisions generally agree, that §269(a)(2) has a considerably broader reach. Thus, in the *Coastal Oil Storage Co.* case (*supra* note 10), §269(a)(2) was applied to disallow a newly created subsidiary corporation's surtax exemption on the ground that the subsidiary "could not have enjoyed the benefit of the surtax exemption . . . but for the acquisition of the property producing the income from or against which the exemption [was] claimed."[50] This aspect of the *Coastal Oil* decision creates a considerable area of overlap between §269 and §1551 (*infra*, Sec. 13.31). Moreover, its rejection of the *Alprosa* doctrine has much enlarged the scope of §269(a)(2), as well as that of §269(a)(1). The *Coastal Oil* case is also notable for its rejection of the notion that §269(a)(2) comes into play only if the tax benefit in question is dependent on a carryover basis for the transferred assets, and Reg. §1.269-3(c) similarly rejects this idea. But the legislative history of §269, with its emphasis on "trafficking"

---

[49] For general discussion of the midstream liquidation problem, see *supra*, Sec. 9.62.

[50] For the use of §269(a)(1) to disallow surtax exemptions of multiple corporations created by individual shareholder transferors, see James Realty Co. v. United States, *supra* note 10; Bonneville Locks Towing Co., Inc. v. United States, 343 F.2d 790, 15 AFTR 2d 673 (9th Cir. 1965); Joe Dillier, 41 T.C. 762 (1964), aff'd, 357 F.2d 647, 17 AFTR 2d 466 (9th Cir. 1966); Kessmar Construction Co. v. Commissioner, 336 F.2d 865, 14 AFTR 2d 5597 (9th Cir. 1965); Samuel Napsky, ¶65,284 P-H Memo T.C.

in corporate shells, suggests the contrary;[51] moreover, it seems evident that Congress, in enacting §269, was concerned with acquisitions of stock or assets from "outside interests," rather than with a reshuffling of property within the same economic group. Hence, *Coastal Oil* probably represents the high water mark of the Commissioner's efforts under §269; as such, it is a decision of major importance.

There are, however, many types of asset acquisitions which are not covered by §269(a)(2): (a) acquisitions from non-corporate transferors (but cf. §269(a)(1), which could apply to this situation if the transferors obtain 50 percent control of the transferee); (b) purchases or other taxable transactions where the transferee obtains a "cost" basis for the acquired properties under §1012; (c) like kind exchanges under §1031, which result in a substituted, as opposed to a carryover, basis to the transferee; (d) acquisitions of cash, since the basis of this type of property presumably does not carryover from the payor; and (e) acquisitions from a corporation which is controlled (under the 50 percent test of §269) by the acquiring corporation or its shareholders.[52]

While §269(a)(2) does not apply to asset transfers between commonly controlled corporations, there is no such common control exception for §269(a)(1);[53] but the existence of such control may prove helpful to taxpayers on the primary issue of tax avoidance, at least in situations where the facts are unclear as to the principal purpose for the transaction or are susceptible of varying interpretations. Moreover, in situations where true common control exists, §269(a)(1) ought to be applied with restraint in view of the fact that the transaction can, in most instances, just as easily be arranged as an asset acquisition of the §269(a)(2) variety, in which case it would clearly be outside the reach of §269. On the other hand, courts which have

[51] The conference report on the Revenue Act of 1943 is also susceptible to this interpretation. H. Rept. No. 1079, 78th Cong., 2d sess., reprinted in 1944 C.B. 1059, 1069-70.

[52] This "common control" exception to the applicability of §269(a)(2) relates to transfers between "brother-sister" corporations and to transfers pursuant to the liquidation of a controlled subsidiary under §332. However, *Coastal Oil* ignored this exception where the assets were transferred *by* the parent corporation *to* a newly created subsidiary in a §351 transaction (a result which may likewise apply to "downstream mergers" of the parent into its subsidiary and to contributions to the subsidiary's capital by its parent). Moreover, transitory common control immediately prior to the relevant asset acquisition presumably would be ignored in applying this exception, as has been the case with similar provisions. For possible analogies, see discussion *supra*, Sec. 3.09; Regs. §1.382(a)-1(e)(2) and §1.382(b)-1(a)(6).

[53] See Zanesville Investment Co., 38 T.C. 406 (1962); Brick Milling Co., *supra* note 43; Southland Corp. v. Campbell, 358 F.2d 333, 17 AFTR 2d 673 (5th Cir. 1966).

been faced with this argument have so far refused to show much leniency, despite the admittedly harsh results accruing because of the particular form which the taxpayer elected to follow.

3. *The forbidden tax-avoidance purpose.* The crux of §269 is the forbidden state of mind which motivates the particular transaction; *i.e.*, "the principal purpose"[54] of evasion or avoidance of Federal income tax. Like most statutory provisions turning on the taxpayer's motive or intent, considerable difficulty in application is to be expected, and §269 has proved to be no exception to this rule. The question is, of course, one of fact, and, in view of the presumption of correctness attaching to the assertion of a deficiency, the early litigation under §269 produced surprisingly few government victories. The courts seemed willing to accept almost any reasonable business excuse as justification for the challenged transaction.[55] More recently, however, the judicial climate has decidedly changed, possibly because cases have been selected by the Service with greater care. The *Coastal Oil* case, *supra*, is a striking illustration of this skeptical attitude on the part of courts as to why the taxpayer chose one tax route over all others or why it selected a particular "loss" corporation for acquisition.[56] While this critical judicial attitude does not go so far as to com-

---

[54] As passed by the House in 1943, §269 was applicable if tax avoidance was "one of the principal purposes" of the acquisition. The language was changed by the Senate, on the recommendation of the Senate Finance Committee that "the section should be operative only if the evasion or avoidance purpose outranks, or exceeds in importance, any other one purpose." S. Rept. No. 627, 78th Cong., 1st Sess., reprinted in 1944 C.B. 973, 1017. See Malat v. Riddell, 383 U.S. 569, 17 AFTR 2d 604 (1966) (construing "primarily" as used in §1221).

[55] Thus, in a number of cases involving the transfer of property by a corporation to newly created subsidiaries, it was found as a fact that the creation of additional corporate entities served various business purposes (*e.g.*, limiting liability, avoiding exclusive franchises and loan restrictions, creating the reputation of local control, etc.) and was not for the principal purpose of tax avoidance. Commissioner v. Chelsea Products, Inc., 197 F.2d 620, 42 AFTR 212 (3d Cir. 1952); Berlands, Inc., 16 T.C. 182 (1951); Alcorn Wholesale Co., *ibid.* 75. See also WAGE, Inc., 19 T.C. 249 (1952); Commodores Point Terminal Corp., 11 T.C. 411 (1948), finding that other transactions, alleged by the government to violate §269, served business purposes.

[56] See *e.g.*: James Realty Co. v. United States, *supra* note 10 (creation of multiple real estate development corporations); American Pipe & Steel Corp. v. Commissioner, *supra* note 43 (purchase of stock of corporation having large potential losses due to high basis low value assets and an attempt to use these subsequently realized losses in consolidated return); Mill Ridge Coal Co. v. Patterson, *supra* note 46 (*Alprosa*-type acquisition); Elko Realty Co. v. Commissioner, *supra* note 43 (§269 applied to deny right to file consolidated return with subsidiary whose stock was purchased presumably in anticipation of using future excess of depreciation allowances over income as an offset to consolidated income). See generally H. F. Ramsey Co., *supra* note 46 (loss carryover not disallowed by §382(a), because "same business" continued; but taxpayer failed to prove lack of tax avoidance so that §269(a)(1) denied the deduction).

pel the taxpayer to adopt the least favorable tax route out of several possible alternatives, it does seem to require that he be able to show that the choice of the most favorable tax route was motivated by substantial business reasons in addition to, and overbalancing, the opportunity to obtain the particular tax benefits inherent in the method selected. But where taxpayers have been able to prove substantial business, as opposed to tax avoidance, reasons for their acquisitions, they have escaped the toils of §269.[57]

The regulations (which were not finally promulgated until 1962) have this to say on the principal purpose standard of §269:

> Characteristic of such circumstances [*i.e.*, disallowance under §269] are those in which the effect of the deduction, credit, or other allowance would be to distort the liability of the particular taxpayer when the essential nature of the transaction or situation is examined in the light of the basic purpose or plan which the deduction, credit, or other allowance was designed by the Congress to effectuate. The distortion may be evidenced, for example, by the fact that the transaction was not undertaken for reasons germane to the conduct of the business of the taxpayer, by the unreal nature of the transaction such as its sham character, or by the unreal or unreasonable relation which the deduction, credit, or other allowance bears to the transaction. The principle of law making an amount unavailable as a deduction, credit, or other allowance in cases in which the effect of making an amount so available would be to distort the liability of the taxpayer, has been judicially recognized and applied in several cases. Included in these cases are Gregory v. Helvering . . .; Griffiths v. Helvering . . .; Higgins v. Smith . . .; and J. D. & A. B. Spreckels Co. v. Commissioner . . . In order to give effect to such principle, but not in limitation thereof, several provisions of the Code, for example, section 267 and section 270, specify with some particularity instances in which disallowance of the deduction, credit, or other allowance is required. Section 269 is also included in such provisions of the Code. The principle of law and the particular sections of the Code are not mutually exclusive and in appropriate circumstances they may operate together or they may operate separately. See, for example, §1.269-6.

[57] See John B. Stetson Co., ¶64,146 P-H Memo TC; Hawaiian Trust Co., Ltd. v. United States, *supra* note 44 (no tax avoidance purpose at time stock acquired); Baton Rouge Supply Co., 36 T.C. 1 (1961) (Acq.) (purchase of stock to obtain necessary assets owned by old shareholder who would only sell in a "package"); Superior Garment Co., ¶65,283 P-H Memo T.C. (purchase of stock to acquire source of supply and to make an investment in related line of business); see also, Virginia Metal Products, Inc. v. Commissioner, 38 T.C. 788 (1960), rev'd on *Libson Shops* ground, *supra* note 46 (expansion into related lines of business).

See generally, Peterson, *supra* note 47.

The regulations continue with this statement:

> In either instance [of a §269 acquisition] the principal purpose for which the acquisition was made must have been the evasion or avoidance of Federal income tax by securing the benefit of a deduction, credit, or other allowance which such other person, or persons, or corporation, would not otherwise enjoy. If this requirement is satisfied, it is immaterial by what method or by what conjunction of events the benefit was sought. Thus, an acquiring person or corporation can secure the benefit of a deduction, credit, or other allowance within the meaning of section 269 even though it is the acquired corporation that is entitled to such deduction, credit, or other allowance in the determination of its tax. If the purpose to evade or avoid Federal income tax exceeds in importance any other purpose, it is the principal purpose. This does not mean that only those acquisitions fall within the provisions of section 269 which would not have been made if the evasion or avoidance purpose was not present. The determination of the purpose for which an acquisition was made requires a scrutiny of the entire circumstances in which the transaction or course of conduct occurred, in connection with the tax result claimed to arise therefrom.[58]

It is evident from this language that the Service views §269 in an expansive manner, and further examples contained therein reinforce this conclusion. The regulations' specific reference to the *Gregory, Griffiths,* and *Smith* cases is also of particular note, since these decisions are often cited for the proposition, apparently infused into the general framework of §269, that transactions heavily freighted with tax avoidance motives can be disregarded by the courts, or recast so as to give effect to their underlying economic reality. As a result, the reach of §269 is indeed a broad one; while courts will no doubt resist excessive applications of the section, its *in terrorem* radiations are perhaps even more significant, as a practical matter, than the litigation box score. In any event, it will be the rare corporate acquisition which will not have to at least consider the potential application of §269.

Some of the criteria which have been considered in determining whether an acquisition satisfies the business purpose standard of §269 are: (a) whether the acquiring parties were aware of the challenged tax benefits at the time of the acquisition, and, if so, whether they took them into consideration;[59] (b) whether the acquired cor-

---

[58] Regs. §1.269-2(a) and -3(a).

[59] See generally John B. Stetson Co., *supra* note 57. Suppose that the acquiring person's advisers offer no hope for survival of the acquired corpora-

poration has a going business which will continue to be operated on a substantial scale after the acquisition (the acquisition of a corporation that is virtually a shell, or whose assets are suitable only for liquidation, is not likely to survive an attack under §269); (c) whether the acquisition of control or assets is necessary or useful to the acquiring person's business or investment activities (*i.e.*, whether the acquiring party was expanding or diversifying its business activities via the acquisition route rather than by internal growth, or made the acquisition to protect its competitive position);[60] (d) the relative value of the acquired tax benefit as compared to the economic profit inherent in the enterprise;[61] (e) whether the challenged benefit could have been utilized by the taxpayer absent the particular acquisition transaction (*i.e.*, whether enjoyment of the tax benefit flows directly or proximately from the acquisition transaction); (f) if the acquisition is by a purchase of stock rather than assets, whether this route was the more feasible method of acquiring the business or assets of the acquired corporation;[62] and (g) if assets are acquired in a nontaxable reorganization, whether such method was more feasible than a cash purchase thereof. Of course, no one of these factors is controlling, and the ultimate issue in every case is the acquiring person's intent or state of mind with respect to the challenged transaction. This, in turn, places a premium on the development of contemporaneous records showing business (as opposed to tax) reasons for a particular transaction, with the attendant artificialities (and, at times, ethical problems) which this may entail.

Several aspects of the principal purpose requirement of §269 bear special note. Prompt discontinuance of the acquired corporation's business after the acquisition tends to poison the atmosphere;

---

tion's tax benefits because of §269: will evidence of this advice be relevant (or persuasive) on the issue of tax avoidance if the transaction is consumated in any event? It would seem so, subject of course to reasonable limits of credibility.

See also Hawaiian Trust Co., Ltd. v. United States, *supra* note 44, holding that post-acquisition tax motives did not retroactively infect the transaction under §269.

[60] This factor seems related to the "reasonable needs of the business" test of §533(a) applied with respect to the accumulated earnings tax. See generally, Superior Garment Co., *supra* note 57 (source of supply); John B. Stetson Co., *supra* note 57 (distribution outlet).

[61] See R. P. Collins & Co., Inc. v. United States, *supra* note 45.

[62] In Baton Rouge Supply Co., *supra* note 57, taxpayers were able to purchase various properties which they desired only if they agreed, in addition, to buy the stock of the loss company (of whose tax benefits they were unaware at the time of purchase). This factor seems tangentially related to the principles of the *Kimbell-Diamond* case, *supra*, Sec. 9.44, which held that an acquisition of stock in order to acquire assets will be treated, in substance, as a direct asset acquisition.

continuance of the business as a substantial going concern, on the other hand, creates a favorable inference that the acquisition was not motivated by tax avoidance.[63]

On the question of *when* the prohibited purpose must be held, the crucial date presumably is the time when the transaction which activates §269 is effected (*i.e., post*-acquisition tax motives do not retroactively invoke the provisions of §269), and courts generally seem to agree.[64] However, it is clear that all integrated steps in what is essentially a single acquisition transaction will be considered as a unitary plan for this purpose.[65]

4. *Limitations on operation of §269 and special problems.* Before §269 can be applied to disallow a particular tax benefit or allowance, three conditions must be satisfied: (a) one of the two types of acquisitions specified in §269(a) must occur; (b) the acquisition must be made for the principal purpose of avoiding income taxes; and (c) the taxpayer must thereby secure the benefit of a deduction, credit or allowance that it would not otherwise enjoy. On the third point, the recent case of Cromwell Corp., 43 T.C. 313 (1964), is instructive. There, the taxpayer corporation was formed for the purpose of effecting a "bootstrap acquisition" (*supra*, Sec. 7.25), pursuant to which it borrowed a substantial portion of the purchase price to be paid for the stock of the acquired corporation, purchased the stock with these funds plus additional sums contributed by its shareholders, filed a consolidated return with its newly acquired subsidiary, and then had the subsidiary distribute a dividend which the taxpayer used to discharge its purchase money indebtedness. The Service attacked this transaction under §269, alleging that the taxpayer was not entitled to file a consolidated return with the subsidiary or, if it was, that it was not entitled to eliminate the intercompany dividend (as is normal on consolidated returns, *infra*, Sec. 13.43); and that if a consolidated return was not proper, the dividend did not qualify for the 85 percent dividend received deduction of §243. The Tax Court rejected

---

[63] See *e.g.*, J. T. Slocomb Co. v. Commissioner, *supra* note 41, holding that such fact, while not determinative on the principal purpose issue, was nevertheless entitled to considerable weight (although the court there refused to reverse a Tax Court finding of tax avoidance as clearly erroneous). See also Virginia Metal Products, Inc. v. Commissioner, *supra* note 46; but cf. H. F. Ramsey Co., Inc., *supra* note 46, where continuance of the business did not save the taxpayer from disallowance of its loss carryovers under §269.

[64] Hawaiian Trust Co., Ltd. v. United States, *supra* note 44; Zanesville Investment Co. v. Commissioner, 335 F.2d 507, 14 AFTR 2d 5453 (6th Cir. 1964); Challenger, Inc., ¶64,338 P-H Memo T.C.; but cf. R. P. Collins & Co., Inc. v. United States, *supra* note 45.

[65] J. T. Slocomb Co. v. Commissioner, *supra* note 41; Temple Square Mfg. Co., *supra* note 43; see generally, *supra*, Sec. 12.20; see also Southland Corp. v. Campbell, *supra* note 53.

all of these assertions, stating that irrespective of the taxpayer's purpose in affecting the transaction in this manner, it did not thereby obtain a tax benefit which it would not "otherwise have enjoyed." The court noted that other methods could have been used in making the acquisition (*supra*, Sec. 7.25), all of which would have produced the same net effect for tax purposes as the method chosen by the parties, *i.e.*, the acquisition of another corporation with a limited equity investment. The purpose of §269, said the court, is to prevent a "distortion" of the taxpayer's net income, as "where a taxpayer is attempting to secure the benefit of built-in tax advantages, typically a net operating loss carryover, by combining two corporations via an acquisition;" here, the purchasers merely obtained, through their use of an intervening holding company to effect the acquisition, control of the desired enterprise with a limited out-of-pocket investment, a result which did not contravene the limitations of §269.

The *Cromwell* decision thus represents a judicial retreat from the more sweeping implications of the *Coastal Oil* case, which seemed to suggest that if the tax benefit in question was generated by virtue of the particular transaction, then §269 may be invoked to deny effective use of the benefit. The approach adopted in *Cromwell* was to ask whether the form employed in effecting the business transaction was the only feasible device by which enjoyment of the tax benefit can be obtained. If the latter is true, then §269 may be relevant, although even here it must still be established that the taxpayer's principal purpose for obtaining the enjoyment of that benefit was avoidance of taxes. The availability of other routes to the same end in *Cromwell*, however, led to the conclusion that §269 was inapplicable.

Another significant limitation on the potential application of §269 was noted by the Service in Rev. Rul. 63-40, 1963-1 C.B. 46, in which it was conceded that a change in the taxpayer's business activities, without more, was not sufficient to invoke the application of §269. The ruling involved a loss corporation which purchased the assets of a profitable business (or, alternatively, bought stock of the profitable corporation in order to acquire its assets and immediately liquidated that corporation in a transaction covered by §334(b)(2)), discontinued its own loss business, and then attempted to apply its loss carryovers against the profits of the acquired business. The ruling approved this practice if there was no more than a "minor change" in the loss corporation's stock ownership and if the purchase price was not payable over a substantial period of time or in excess of fair market value.[66] The theory of the ruling, that a loss corpora-

[66] But cf. Kolker Bros., Inc., 35 T.C. 299 (1960)(NA), where there was a

tion should be free to rehabilitate its financial affairs by acquiring profitable activities, is scarcely open to serious question. The fact that it thereby obtains the "enjoyment" of its previously generated loss carryovers is of no consequence, since the benefit of the deductions inures to the shareholders who owned the corporation, and therefore indirectly suffered the losses, when the unprofitable business activities occurred; the corporation's tax benefits from the loss carryover deductions have not been "negotiated" to outside interests. In other words, the fact that tax benefits accrue from a particular transaction or course of conduct is not enough *per se* to invoke the application of §269. Hence, the mere fact of filing a consolidated return, electing the benefits of Subchapter S (*infra*, Ch. 14), or organizing a corporation to carry on the taxpayer's business operations ought not to inspire the application of §269, even though tax considerations were involved in making the decision to adopt that particular choice, as would perhaps necessarily be the case in almost any well-advised commercial venture.[67]

Thus, there are some "tax motives" which are not considered reprehensible for purposes of §269; see, for example, I.T. 3757, 1945 C.B. 200, holding that the organization of a Western Hemisphere Trade Corporation subsidiary for the purpose of obtaining the special tax advantages granted to such corporations (*supra*, Sec. 1.06) did not violate the tax avoidance principles of §269. The difficult question, of course, is determining when a tax-motivated transaction crosses the line of proper "business planning" and enters the area of tax "windfall" or unjust enrichment patrolled by §269.

5. *Presumption.* In 1954, because "[t]he effectiveness [of §269] has been impaired by the difficulty of establishing whether or not tax avoidance was the principal purpose of the acquisition," S. Rep. No. 1622, 83d Cong., 2d Sess., p. 39, Congress enacted the presumption of §269(c). It provides that if the consideration paid on an acquisition is "substantially disproportionate" to the aggregate of (1) the adjusted basis of the acquired corporation's property, in cases under §269(a)(1), or of the acquired property, in cases under §269(a)(2), and (2) the tax benefits (to the extent not reflected in the adjusted basis of the property) not available to the acquiring person otherwise than as a result of the acquisition, this fact shall be prima facie evi-

---

change of 46 percent of the loss corporation's stock ownership; see also T.I.R. 773, October 13, 1965, presumably modifying this portion of Rev. Rul. 63-40 by permitting changes of stock ownership of less than 50 percent, apparently by reference to similar percentage tests in §269 and §382(a). The applicability of §269 to these transactions was specifically reserved, however.

[67] See John B. Stetson Co., *supra* note 57.

dence of the principal purpose of tax avoidance.[68] "Substantially dis-proportionate" can, of course, mean a payment that is unreasonably large as well as one that is unreasonably small; the draftsmen presumably meant only the latter. See S. Rep., *supra*, at p. 228. There is a paradox in §269(c), arising from the fact that a person wishing to acquire a corporation who has no interest in its tax attributes would ordinarily pay a price equal to the fair market value of its assets. If he does so, however, and if the corporation's assets are held at a high basis (or if it has an operating loss carryover or other favorable tax attributes), his acquisition may run afoul of §269(c) because the consideration will be disproportionate to the sum of adjusted basis and tax benefits. If, however, the purchaser wishes to take advantage of the corporation's tax attributes, he would be willing to pay a higher price, thus making the consideration less disproportionate and §269(c) less easily applied!

Sec. 13.22.   Disallowance of net operating loss carryovers because of change of ownership and abandonment of business: §382(a)

1. In general. On the ground that §269 (*supra*, Sec. 13.21) had proved to be "ineffectual" as a weapon against the traffic in loss corporations "because of the necessity of proving that tax avoidance was the primary purpose of the transaction," Congress in 1954 enacted two new restrictions on the net operating loss carryover. The first is §382(a), applicable to changes of ownership through the purchase of stock, which provides for the complete disallowance of the carryover if, roughly speaking, 50 percent of the corporation's stock changes hands in a two-year period and if the corporation's old trade or business is abandoned. The second restriction (discussed in more detail *infra*, Sec. 13.23) is §382(b), applicable only to changes of ownership through a tax-free reorganization, under which the carryover is reduced proportionately if the old owners receive less than 20 percent of the stock of the reorganized corporation and is eliminated if they receive none. Neither restriction is dependent upon a showing of tax avoidance purpose; the function of both branches of §382 is to reduce or eliminate the carryover in appropriate cases even though

---

[68] For §269(c) to apply, the acquisition must be "described" in §269(a). Taken literally, this would mean that the acquisition must be motivated by tax avoidance, as shown by the facts, before the presumption would apply. This *gaffe* is only one of the drafting infelicities in §269, however, as will be seen in the text.

For more on the presumption of §269(c), see Cohen et al., *supra* note 36; H. F. Ramsey Co., *supra* note 46; Baton Rouge Supply Co., *supra* note 57.

they cannot be brought within §269. But §269 is not repealed, and Regs. §1.269-6 explicitly states that it will be applied whether the transaction is also covered by §382 or not.

Section 382(a), which is one of the few statutory provisions under which a change in stock ownership impinges on the corporation's tax attributes (*supra*, Sec. 1.05), provides that net operating losses may not be carried forward if:

> 1. At the end of the corporation's taxable year, its ten principal shareholders own a percentage of the corporation's outstanding stock (taken at total fair market value) that is 50 percentage points or more greater than they owned at the beginning of the same taxable year or at the beginning of the prior taxable year;[69]
> 2. The increase results from a purchase of stock from an unrelated person or from a decrease in the amount of stock outstanding; and
> 3. The corporation has not continued to carry on a trade or business substantially the same as that conducted before any change in stock ownership.

These conditions are refined by the statute in some detail. Thus, ownership of stock is determined by reference to the constructive ownership rules of §318 (*supra*, Sec. 7.21); related persons are treated as a single person in determining the 10 principal stockholders; the purchase of stock in a holding company or of an interest in a trust or partnership may be treated as a purchase of stock in the loss corporation itself; and "stock" means all shares except nonvoting stock that is limited and preferred as to dividends.

2. Change of ownership. Conditions 1 and 2 are of course satisfied in the blatant case of an outright purchase of all of the stock of a loss corporation by outside interests; but they can also be satisfied by less drastic changes in ownership, such as the purchase by outside interests of one-third of the stock coupled with a redemption (except under §303 (*supra*, Sec. 7.40) of another one-third from the original shareholders.[70] Moreover, nothing in §382(a) requires a showing that

---

[69] An increase in "percentage points" is not identical with an increase in "percentage." Thus, if A owns 80 percent of the stock and B 20 percent, and B purchases 10 percent from A, so that the stock is held 70 percent by A and 30 percent by B, B's interest has increased by 50 percent but by only 10 "percentage points." His ownership would have to rise to 70 percent before §382(a) could become applicable.

[70] §382(a)(1)(B) does not expressly state that a combination of purchase and redemption is reached by the statute, but the provision would be crippled if the change in ownership had to be attributable to one or the other, but not both. The regulations specifically provide that a combination is covered, Regs. §1.382(a)-1(b)(2).

the purchase and redemption were part of a single plan to shift ownership, and such a requirement seems to conflict with the desire of the 1954 draftsmen to lay down relatively mechanical rules to avoid the probing into purpose required by §269. Thus, it may be that §382(a) would be invoked even if the redemption occurred a year after the acquisition of stock as a result of an unanticipated disagreement among the shareholders. Similarly, the independent acquisition of stock by ten unrelated investors may bring §382(a) into play.[71]

Section 382(a) is applicable only if the requisite change in ownership is accomplished by "purchase" (or by a decrease in the outstanding stock), and hence it does not reach changes that result from gifts, bequests, or exchanges that are tax-free in whole or in part. Moreover, since the term "purchase" is defined by §382(a)(4) to exclude a transaction between related persons, as defined by §382(a)-(3), §382(a) does not destroy the carryover if the corporation is transferred within the same economic group.[72] The language of §382-(a)(1)(B) suggests that the statutory increase must be attributable to the purchase or redemption transactions, rather than to general "market rises," but the regulations are silent on this point.

3. Change of business. Although the rules with respect to changes in stock ownership are quite precise and ordinarily cause little difficulty, the same cannot be said of the change of business limitations of §382(a)(1)(C), which require that the corporation continue (until the close of the two-year period) to carry on a business substantially the same as that conducted before the first increase in stock ownership.[73] Of course, a blatant discontinuance of the old business, coupled

---

[71] For detailed discussion and examples with respect to this aspect of §382(a), see Regs. §1.382(a)-1(c), (d), (f), and (g). See aiso Maxwell Hardware Co. v. Commissioner, *supra* note 9a, for a well-tailored acquisition plan which avoided §382(a).

[72] Note, however, that Regs. §1.382(a)-1(e)(2) attempts to disregard the effect of purchases which are made to *create* an attribution and thereby avoid the application of §382(a) under the "related persons" exception. This approach is questionable at best, and could probably be successfully attacked if the taxpayer could prove that such a purchase had, in fact, been made, even though its purpose was to avoid application of §382(a). Cases such as *Day & Zimmermann, Granite Trust,* and *Avco Mfg. Co., supra,* Sec. 9.41, are relevant on this point.

[73] §382(a)(1)(C), relating to the continuation of the old business, does not contain a time limit. In conjunction with §382(a)(1)(A) and (B), however, it seems to mean that if all the stock of a calendar year corporation changes hands on Jan. 1, 1968, the carryover will be entirely lost if the old business is abandoned during 1968, that it will be lost for 1969 and later years if the business is abandoned during 1969, and that it will not be affected (at least not by §382(a)) if the business is continued until 1970. See Regs. §1.382(a)-1(h)(1), stating that the critical time period for change of business starts with the first increase in ownership which is counted for the 50 percent test. But a change in business made "in contemplation" of a change in stock ownership will be pushed forward to such date. Regs. 1.382(a)-1(h)(3).

with an entry into a totally unrelated activity (like the transactions involved in the *Alprosa* case, *supra*), would clearly fall within §382-(a)(1)(C), but such a radical change would often be sufficient proof that tax avoidance motivated the acquisition of the corporation's stock so as to make §269 applicable to the transaction and §382(a) unnecessary.

Confusion rapidly accelerates, however, when the new owners are sufficiently astute (and the tax stakes are sufficiently alluring) to continue the old business to some extent. Must it be continued on the same scale; or can it be contracted and, if so, to what extent? Can a new line of business be added, or the old business be expanded; if so, are there any limits to such growth? Are changes to be viewed more sympathetically if they arise from post-acquisition economic or business conditions? What is "the same business enterprise" for purposes of the §382(a)(1)(C) continuity rules? What is the effect of a suspension or cessation of business activities, either temporary or total and either voluntary or involuntary? Does subsequent reactivation of a suspended business preserve continuity and, if so, how long can suspension last? Is it sufficient if one out of several separate businesses previously conducted by the corporation is continued; if so, can manufacturing activities be continued and sales activities dropped (or vice versa), or are both of these functions merely a part of a single integrated business?[74] If the corporation has abandoned its business *before* the shift in ownership of its stock, is §382(a)(1)(C) automatically violated on the ground that no business has been *conducted* prior to the change in ownership? What is a "business," as opposed to mere "investment" activity, for purposes of these rules? What relationship, if any, does §381(a)(1)(C) bear to the "continuity of business enterprise" doctrine of the *Libson Shops* case (*infra*, Sec. 13.25)? Finally, what if the old shareholders of the corporation abandon the loss business, shift to a different business, and *then* sell their stock to new owners who intend to continue that business?[75] These and other questions are dealt with at length in Regs. §1.382(a)-1(h), and in several recent decisions interpreting the effect of §382(a)-(1)(C).

The regulations provide generally that: (a) holding or trading, for investment purposes, of securities or similar property (presumably

---

[74] For analogous problems under the five year active business rules of §355(b), see discussion *supra*, ch. 11.

[75] See Regs. §1.382(a)-1(h)(1) and (3), discussed *supra*, note 73, which provide generally that the critical date for the change of business test begins with the time of the first change in stock ownership (unless the business is changed "in contemplation" thereof).

commodity contracts and rental real estate) does not constitute a "business" for purposes of §382(a), unless such activities historically have constituted the corporation's primary function, Regs. §1.382(a)-1(h)(4); (b) whether there has been a change of business is basically a question of fact, and among the relevant factors to be considered are changes in the corporation's employees, plant, equipment, product, location, customers, and other "significant items," Regs. §1.382(a)-1(h)(5); (c) a corporation which is inactive or dormant at the time of the stock ownership change automatically fails to satisfy §382(a)-(1)(C) even though it is subsequently reactivated in the same line of business (but a temporary suspension of business due to involuntary abnormal circumstances, such as a fire or other casualty, will not per se break the chain of continuity), Regs. §1.382(a)-1(h)(6); (d) discontinuance of "more than a minor portion" of a corporation's business may constitute a change of business, Regs. §1.382(a)-1(h)(7); (e) addition of a new business does not work a change of business if conduct of the old enterprise continues substantially undiminished, Regs. §1.382(a)-1(h)(8);[76] (f) change of location of a major portion of the corporation's activities may, in certain instances, violate §382(a)(1)(C), if the location change works a substantial alteration in the character of the corporation's business, Regs. §1.382-(a)-1(h)(9); and (g) in the case of a personal service business, identity of the persons who perform the services is the major determining factor for business continuity, Regs. §1.382(a)-1(h)(10).[77]

It should be noted that these regulations are, in many instances, heavily influenced by the *Libson Shops* decision (*infra*, Sec. 13.25); the extent to which *Libson's* "continuity of business enterprise" notions have been (or can be) infused into the business continuity rules of §382(a) is unclear, but the attempt to do so on the part of the Service in its regulations under §382(a) is unmistakable.[78]

---

[76] The regulations contain a pointed reference to §269, and, in this respect, see Rev. Rul. 63-40, 1963-1 C.B. 46, discussed *supra*, Sec. 13.21 and *infra*, Sec. 13.25.

[77] For discussion of these provisions, see Blake, Carryovers and Limitations on Carryovers of Net Operating Losses in Corporate Acquisitions, 21 N.Y.U. Inst. on Fed. Tax. 1247 (1963).

[78] See The Humacid Co., *supra* note 41, stating (42 T.C. at 907) that "continuity of business enterprise" means "something different from identity or similarity of economic endeavors," and that what the Supreme Court had in mind in the *Libson* decision "was something more in the nature of an economic concept prohibiting separate business *units* from combining so that profits from one separate *enterprise* might be offset against losses of another." Compare Clarksdale Rubber Co., *supra* note 9a, holding that *Libson* has been preempted by the specific provisions of §382(a); with TIR-773 (Oct. 13, 1965), apparently equating the continuity of business test of §382(a)(1)(C) with the *Libson* doctrine. This problem is considered in detail, *infra*, Sec. 13.25.

Judicial constructions of the continuity of business provisions of §382(a)(1)(C) have, in general, been surprisingly liberal. Thus, in Commissioner v. Goodwyn Crockery Co. (*infra* note 84), the taxpayer was held to have substantially continued its business as a general wholesale merchandising concern despite the addition of a new line of merchandise, the opening of a retail outlet, and two relocations of its headquarters. The court felt that the basic character of the taxpayer's business continued unchanged notwithstanding these alterations and additions. The number and degree of changes in the character of the taxpayer's business in *Goodwyn* probably place the decision at the outer limits of judicial tolerance in this area; the appellate court noted the closeness of the case, but was reluctant to overrule the Tax Court's finding as clearly erroneous. Moreover, the fact that the trial of the case antedated the regulations under §382 (which did not become final until Nov. 22, 1962), may have been significant to the outcome (this fact was noted by the reviewing court, which refused to give retroactive effect to the regulations). In any event, the *Goodwyn* decision, as the first decided case under §382(a), represented a substantial taxpayer victory, not only as to its specific holding, but in respect to the court's general attitude toward that provision as well. The taxpayer in *Goodwyn* also won on the question of whether the more general provisions of §269 applied to the transaction, it having been found that the acquisition was motivated by genuine business reasons rather than for tax avoidance (*supra*, Sec. 13.21).

In other decisions under §382(a), courts have similarly responded with sympathy to taxpayers' continuity of business arguments. Thus, in H. F. Ramsey Co., Inc. (*supra* note 46), §382(a) was held inapplicable to a case where the taxpayer loss corporation temporarily suspended virtually all of its business activities for about one year in order to regain its financial health (most of its operating assets were liquidated during this period to pay claims); the taxpayer was reactivated after the sale of its stock to new owners and reentered the same type of business activity as before the suspension. (The loss carryovers were disallowed, however, under §269(a)(1), the court holding that the new owners acquired the taxpayer's stock for the principal purpose of taking advantage of its loss history.) Similarly, in Clarksdale Rubber Co. (*supra* note 9a), a "temporary suspension" of business activity for a two-year period *following* the purchase of the taxpayer's stock did not constitute a "change of business" within the meaning of §382(a)(1)(C): the taxpayer's assets were leased to a "sister" corporation during this period of inactivity and it was thereby able to work out its financial difficulties; following this event, the taxpayer reacquired its business assets and returned to the conduct of its former line of activity (with certain incidental alterations which were not deemed sufficient to effect a change of business).[79]

On the other hand, in Fawn Fashions, Inc. (*infra* note 83), a change of business occurred under §382(a)(1)(C) where the taxpayer loss corporation had been placed in receivership, during which its assets were sold and, for over a year before the purchase of its stock by new owners, was kept alive merely as a corporate shell. After the stock purchase, the corporation was put through a bankruptcy proceeding by its new owners and then reactivated in the same line of business. The court (in addition to disallowing the taxpayer's loss carryovers under §269 because of tax motives for the acquisition), held that the corporation had not been carrying on any *active* business at the time of the acquisition of its stock and therefore was subject to the automatic disallowance rules of §382(a) as well; the opinion specifically approved the validity of Regs. §1.382-1(h)(6) that §382(a) automatically applies to corporations which are inactive at the date of the increase in stock ownership.[80] See also, in this respect, Euclid-Tennessee, Inc. v. Commissioner, 41 T.C. 752 (1964), aff'd, 352 F.2d 991, 16 AFTR 2d 6003 (6th Cir. 1965), where suspension of business activities for three years prior to change in stock ownership, which was followed by the addition of a new line of business, failed to satisfy the business continuity requirements of §382(a)(1)(C). During the three-year suspension period, the taxpayer rented out various unliquidated real estate which it was unable to dispose of when it abandoned its former business. The court held that these rental activities did not themselves constitute an *active* business for purposes of §382(a) and, in any event, the addition of the new business was so overwhelming as to change the basic character of the taxpayer's old business (even assuming that the rental activities constituted a business for this purpose). Thus, the *Euclid* case clearly warns that an expansion of the taxpayer's business can work a "change of business" for purposes of

---

[79] To the same effect is Barclay Jewelry, Inc., ¶65,265 P-H Memo TC, where the temporary suspension of business likewise occurred *after* the purchase of the taxpayer's stock. On the change of business issue generally, see The Wallace Corp., ¶64,010 P-H Memo TC, where substantial business continuity was found despite various changes in "the ways and means" by which that business was operated.

The court in *Clarksdale* also held that the *Libson Shops* doctrine did not apply; see discussion of this aspect of the opinion, *infra*, Sec. 13.25.

[80] To the same effect is Glover Packing Co. v. United States, 328 F.2d 342, 13 AFTR 2d 632 (Ct. Cl. 1964); see also United States v. Fenix & Scisson, Inc., 360 F.2d 260, 17 AFTR 2d 996 (10th Cir. 1966).

§382(a)(1)(C) if the expansion is of such magnitude or diversity that the basic character of the old business is substantially altered thereby.

These principles may be illustrated by the following examples, in which L corporation is assumed to be engaged in the manufacture and sale of electronics products (wherein it has sustained net operating losses) and the requisite change of stock ownership has occurred so as to bring a §382(a) into play:

>   a. L expands the sales volume of its existing product lines and thereby begins to earn profits — this clearly would not constitute a change of business under §382(a)(1)(C);
>   b. L begins manufacturing and selling a new line of products, in addition to its existing operations, which venture produces profits — same;
>   c. L acquires the assets and personnel of a retail sales outlet for the purpose of marketing its products in a new location (and this results in substantial profits) — same;
>   d. L acquires a research and consulting service business, which it operates at a profit as a separate division from its electronics manufacturing business — the mere addition of a new business does not, *per se*, constitute a change of business according to Regs. §1.382(a)-1(h)(8).[81]

For purposes of the following examples, assume that L corporation has, in addition to its electronics business, a separate research and consulting service business, which, measured by capital invested, gross expenditures, employee payrolls, gross receipts, and the like, is one-third the size of the electronics business:

>   a. L's electronics business is profitable; but its research business incurs losses and, because of this fact, is discontinued (after the requisite change of stock ownership). This fact would not appear to violate the literal terms of §382(a)(1)(C), which merely requires continuance of *a* business, rather than *the* business. The regulations, however, specifically state that abandonment of "more than a minor portion of its business" can be fatal, Regs. §1.382(a)-1(h)(7).
>   Moreover, these same provisions specifically adopt a *Libson Shops* test for this purpose: *i.e.*, that in determining whether the discontinuance was "minor," consideration must be given to whether the effect of the transaction is to allow offset of losses created by one business against profits of another unrelated business. The statutory support for this approach is obscure, and the case of *Clarksdale Rubber Co.* (*supra* note 9a) seems essentially contrary thereto.

[81] But see *supra* note 76; and note that the Euclid-Tennessee case *supra*, indicates that expansion can be so extensive as to work a change in the basic character of the taxpayer's business under §382.

b. If, in the above example, the discontinued research business had been the profitable business, however, and the losses had been incurred in the electronics business, the regulations imply that abandonment of the "minor business" would not constitute a change of business, Regs. §1.382(a)-1(h)(7), Ex. (2).

c. If the electronics business is temporarily suspended prior to the change of stock ownership, and then reactivated, the regulations provide that this inactivity will break the chain of continuity unless the suspension is due to abnormal circumstances (*e.g.*, a fire or other casualty) and is merely "temporary." Regs. §1.382(a)-1(h)(6), Ex. (1) and (2).[82]

As to the effect of a change of location on the business continuity requirement of §382(a)(1)(C), Regs. §1.382(a)-1(h)(9) provides generally that a change of location can, in certain instances, result in a change of business character. For example:

a. A change of business occurred where a manufacturing enterprise moved to a new state, disposed of its old plant and equipment, and laid off the majority of its old employees, notwithstanding the fact that the taxpayer continued to produce the same product for substantially the same group of customers. Example(1). The *Goodwyn Crockery* case, *supra*, seems essentially contrary to this example, however.

b. Continuity was present, on the other hand, where a retail department store moved from the downtown area of a city to a suburb thereof, retaining most of its former employees, product lines, and customers, but disposing of its city building and equipment. Example (2).

c. Business continuity was broken, however, where a retail liquor store moved to a nearby town, changed half of its employees, most of its customers, and was obliged to obtain a new liquor license and franchise; this was true notwithstanding the corporation's retention of its inventory and one half of its employees. Example (3). Again the *Goodwyn Crockery* case, *supra*, seems contrary; see also Kolker Bros., Inc. (*supra* note 66), where a retail grocery business shifted from selling food and liquor to the public to the business of selling meat to hotels, restaurants, and institutions; the court there found that while there had been a change in the character of the taxpayer's business, the essential nature thereof continued (i.e., retail sales of food).

The treatment of personal service businesses depends primarily

[82] On "suspension of activities" as a change in business, see the *Ramsey, Clarksdale, Barclay Jewelry, Fawn Fashions, Euclid-Tennessee,* and *Glover Packing* cases (*supra*); see also Jackson Oldsmobile, Inc. v. United States, *supra* note 8.

on the identity of the individuals who perform the service: if the "principal talent" of a service business changes, the regulations hold that this fact will cause a change of business; on the other hand, if the services of the discontinued employee or employees are not unique or substantial, then business continuity will be present. Regs. §1.382-(a)-1(h)(10), Ex. (1) and (2).

It is clear from these cases and regulations that the change of business issue is, and will continue to be, difficult to resolve in practice: the essentially factual nature of this determination, and the immense variety of business and economic considerations which can arise in a particular case practically ensure a high level of uncertainty. Moreover, these problems are distressingly similar to those encountered under the five-year active business rules of §355(b) (*supra*, Secs. 11.04 and 11.05), an area which has also been productive of a high level of confusion. See also the discussion of "business continuity" requirements with respect to tax-free reorganization status generally, *supra*, Sec. 12.19.

4. Relation of §382 to §269. As noted earlier, §382 was added by the draftsmen of the 1954 Code to remedy certain presumed weaknesses in the operation of §269. As such, it was designed to supplement §269 and, in addition, to provide for mechanical rule of thumb tests (*i.e.*, change of ownership coupled with a change of business) so as to avoid the difficulties inherent in applying the subjective "state of mind" standard of §269. But, as noted *supra*, Sec. 13.21, the courts have infused §269 with new vitality in recent decisions; so much so, it would seem, that §269 is in danger of swallowing whole the provisions of §382. Many of these decisions have involved the asserted application of both §§269 and 382 by the Commissioner: in some, taxpayers were successful in avoiding the reach of §382, only to be caught by §269; in others, both provisions have been applied to disallow loss carryovers; while in still others, taxpayers have been snared by §382 even though the forbidden tax avoidance motive of §269 was absent.[83] On the other hand, taxpayers have, on several occasions, successfully steered the treacherous course between these two provisions.[84]

While the transactional patterns covered by these two provisions

---

[83] See H. F. Ramsey Co., *supra* note 46 (§269 but not §382); Fawn Fashions, Inc., 41 T.C. 205 (1963) (§269 plus §382); Glover Packing Co., *supra* note 80 (§382 but not §269).

[84] The most notable in this respect is Clarksdale Rubber Co., *supra* note 9a; but see also Commissioner v. Goodwyn Crockery Co., 37 T.C. 355 (1961), aff'd, 315 F.2d 110, 11 AFTR 2d 1149 (6th Cir. 1963); The Wallace Corp., *supra* note 79.

are quite similar, several differences should be noted:

> a. §269(a)(1) relates to the acquisition of stock giving at least 50 percent control, to be measured by voting power or value; §382(a), on the other hand, requires a change of 50 percentage points in stock ownership measured by *value*, which must occur by virtue of a purchase or redemption of stock and not involve an acquisition of stock from related persons.
>
> b. §269(a)(2) applies to any acquisition of property in which the basis carries over to the transferee, while §382(b) covers only the categories of tax-free reorganizations specified in §381(a)(2), and then only if shareholders of the loss corporation fail to retain at least a 20 percent continuity of interest after the transaction.

Moreover, §269 applies to a wide variety of tax benefits, while §382 is concerned solely with net operating loss carryovers. In addition, §382(a) comes into play only if the taxpayer corporation "changes its business," a condition not necessary for application of §269. The most important distinction between the two provisions, however, is the tax avoidance motivation required by §269, a factor not necessary for invocation of §382. On the other hand, the Commissioner is empowered, by virtue of §269(b), to grant a partial amnesty in applying the disallowance rules thereof; not so with §382, where disallowance (or reduction) of loss carryovers is automatic.

With these factors in mind, it is surprising to note that the Senate Report on the 1954 Code contains a statement that if §382 applies to a particular transaction, §269 shall not also apply thereto, S. Rep. No. 1622, 83d Cong., 2d Sess. 284 (1954). This comment may have some semblance of meaning (although the result is preposterous) when applied to §382(b) (*infra*, Sec. 13.23), but as applied to §382(a) it is about as helpful as a provision that a man who is being executed for murder shall not also be executed for rape.[85] More to the point, however, is that part of the Senate Report (p. 284) which states that §382's inapplicability "shall have no effect upon whether §269 applies." Thus, if a corporation is acquired for the principal purpose of tax avoidance through use of its loss carryovers, §269 will take hold even though the change of ownership is not drastic enough for §382(a) (because applicable only to common stock value and not total value), or fast enough (because spread over more than two years); and even though the old business was continued[86] or the stock was

---

[85] It is possible, though not likely, that the purpose of this statement is to prevent a partial amnesty under §269(b) if §382(a) is applicable.

[86] A continuation of the old business may be helpful to the taxpayer, though not controlling, on the tax avoidance issue under §269.

purchased from related persons or acquired by gift. The position of the Service on the overlap between §269 and §382(a) is clear, however: Regs. §1.269-6 provides that §269 applies, if its conditions are satisfied, *regardless* of whether or not §382 is applicable.

Sec. 13.23.   Restriction of net operating loss carryovers because of change of ownership resulting from reorganization: §382(b)

In addition to disallowing the net operating loss carryover where (roughly speaking) 50 percent of the corporation's stock changes hands and the old business is abandoned, the draftsmen of the 1954 Code imposed a limitation, embodied in §382(b), on the carryover where the corporation goes through one of the tax-free reorganizations listed in §381(a)(2) (*supra*, Sec. 13.11). The limitation comes into play if the shareholders of the loss corporation receive, in exchange for their stock, less than 20 percent of the stock (taken at fair market value) of the acquiring corporation.[87] The limitation operates in mathematical stages — *i.e.*, if the original shareholders receive only 15 percent of the reorganized corporation, 25 percent of the carryover is disallowed; if they receive 10 percent, 50 percent is disallowed; if they receive 5 percent, 75 percent is disallowed — and it applies, unlike §382(a), even though the original business is continued. An example of the operation of §382(b) is the merger of a loss corporation into a profitable corporation: if the shareholders of the loss corporation receive less than 20 percent of the stock of the merged corporation,[88] the net operating loss carryover will be reduced as provided by §382(b)(2). (For a general discussion of continuity of interest principles, see *supra*, Sec. 12.11). The percentage limitation

---

[87] Although §382(b) is inapplicable if the shareholders of the loss corporation receive 20 percent or more of the reorganized corporation's stock, the carryover may be disallowed under §269. See Senate Report, p. 284 (". . . the fact that a limitation under [§382] does not apply shall have no effect upon whether section 269 applies"), in the light of which the statement in the same report that "if the shareholders of the old corporation have 20 percent of the stock of the new corporation the loss carryover is available to the new corporation without diminution" must be regarded as loose language: the carryover in such an instance will be available without diminution by §382(b), but it must nevertheless run the gauntlet of §269. See Regs. §1.269-6. Moreover, the statement just quoted must also be modified in another respect: the test under §382(b) is not whether the loss corporation's shareholders *have* 20 percent of the reorganized corporation's stock, but whether they *receive* that much stock in exchange for their old stock. Stock in the reorganized corporation that is acquired by them in other ways does not count, except to the limited extent provided by §382(b)(3).

[88] Like §382(a), §382(b) measures ownership of stock in terms of fair market value (excluding nonvoting stock that is limited and preferred as to dividends).

is not applicable, however, if both corporations are owned by substantially the same persons in the same proportion; thus, the carryover is not reduced by §382(b) even though less than 20 percent of the reorganized corporation's stock is issued in exchange for the stock of the loss corporation, if in effect there is merely a merger of two corporations owned in the same proportion by the same interests. In the same vein, §382(b)(5) and (6) take account of certain other instances of interlocking ownership of both corporations.[89]

Sec. 13.24. The relation of §382(a) and §382(b) to each other and to §269

There are many ambiguities, conflicts, and omissions in the statutory scheme of §382, especially when examined in conjunction with §269, and it is not feasible to discuss them comprehensively in a guidebook.[90] The following points should be at least noted, however:

1. If the original shareholders of a loss corporation cause it to purchase additional assets, producing a new source of income, neither §382 nor §269 restricts the carryover of the losses.[91]

2. §382 is applicable only to net operating loss carryovers; it does not operate as a limit on other tax advantages, such as operating losses incurred during the early part of the taxable year (see *Alprosa Watch Corp., supra*, Sec. 13.21), capital loss carryovers, potential losses which can be realized by selling depreciated assets, deficits in earnings and profits, etc. But §269 may be applicable.

3. The inapplicability of §382(a) and (b) is of no assistance to a corporation that, for other reasons, cannot avail itself of a predecessor corporation's tax attributes. An example is the reorganization of an insolvent corporation which, though tax-free under §371, fails to qualify as a "reorganization" as that term is defined by §368(a)(1)(A), (C), (E), or (F). If the existence of the original corporation is terminated, its loss carryover will be lost, since its tax attributes will not pass to the acquiring corporation.

---

[89] See generally Regs. §1.382(b)-1; Blake, *supra* note 77.

[90] See *supra,* Sec. 13.22; see also articles cited *supra* note 36; Wilson, Survival of Net Operating Loss and Carryovers, 1966 So. Calif. Tax Inst. 231; articles by Sanden, Blake, Feder, and Harris, 21 N.Y.U. Inst. on Fed. Tax. 1227-1307 (1963); Rice, Changes in the Net Operating Loss Carry-Back, Carry-Forward, and Acquisition of Loss Corporations, 1955 So. Calif. Tax Inst. 433; Tarleau, *supra* note 1; Advisory Group on Subchapter C, House Committee on Ways and Means, *Revised Report on Corporate Distributions and Adjustments* (1958) pp. 89-95; Arent, Current Developments Affecting Loss Corporations, 35 Taxes 956 (1957).

[91] In *Libson Shops (infra,* Sec. 13.25), the Supreme Court reserved judgment on this technique for utilizing the losses of prior years (353 U.S. at 390n); see discussion of Rev. Rul. 63-40, *infra,* Sec. 13.25.

4. The Senate Report on the 1954 Code (p. 284) states that §269 is inapplicable if §382 limits the carryover. This suggests the curious result that a 5 percent limitation on the carryover under §382(b) would protect the remaining 95 percent against disallowance under §269, even where control of the corporation was acquired for the principal purpose of tax avoidance.

5. The percentage limitation of §382(b) comes into play only in case of a reorganization specified in §381(a)(2). Other tax-free exchanges, even though they result in a substantial shift in ownership, are not reached by §382(b). An example is the tax-free exchange under §351 (*supra*, Ch. 3) by new interests of appreciated or depreciated property in exchange for 80 percent or more of the loss corporation's stock. Moreover, §382(a) is also inapplicable, even if the old business is abandoned, since the acquisition is not a "purchase." But §269 may apply.

6. Similarly, §382(b)'s failure to reach reorganizations under §368(a)(1)(B) may lead to avoidance of both §382(b) and §382(a). This is because a profitable corporation may issue an insignificant amount of its voting stock for all the stock of a loss corporation in a tax-free reorganization under §368(a)(1)-(B), hold the stock for a period of time, and then liquidate the loss corporation under §332 (*supra*, Sec. 9.40). The tax attributes of the liquidated subsidiary would be inherited under §381(a), and, unless the step transaction doctrine is applied, §382(b) would be inapplicable. The potential application of this doctrine is noted by Regs. §1.382(b)-1(a)(6), however, and *Libson Shops* as well as §269(a)(1) may also have an impact on such a transaction.

Sec. 13.25.   The Libson Shops doctrine and its radiations

1. Background. In the now famous case of Libson Shops, Inc. v. Koehler, 353 U.S. 382, 51 AFTR 43 (1957), the Supreme Court announced a new and controversial limitation on the survival of net operating loss carryovers after a statutory merger, the "continuity of business enterprise" theory. The taxpayer was a corporation into which 16 other corporations (each operating a separate retail store), owned by the same shareholders in the same proportions, were merged; the surviving corporation sought to apply the pre-merger net operating losses of 3 of these absorbed corporations to the post-merger income of the total enterprise. The stores formerly operated by the loss corporations continued to produce losses, and the Court held that the net operating loss deduction was intended to average out the income from a single business, not to permit pre-merger losses of one business to be offset against post-merger income of another business. The decision in *Libson* thus required that there be a continuity of business enterprise before loss carryovers or carrybacks would be permitted across the line of corporate fusion: in other words, a taxpayer would be entitled to offset prior year's losses against current year's income only to the extent that such income was derived from the operation of "substantially the same business" which incurred the losses. (For a discussion of the historical developments leading up to the *Libson* decision, see *supra*, Sec. 13.02.) This decision, not surprisingly, injected a further element of confusion into an area already noted for its obscurity.

The questions raised by *Libson* were almost as numerous and difficult of solution as those which had plagued the tax law in this area for over two decades. For example: (a) did *Libson* apply where the loss corporation was the surviving legal entity after merger with a profitable enterprise; (b) where a loss corporation was merged into a profitable corporation, did *Libson* permit pre-merger or post-merger losses of the absorbed corporation to be carried over or carried back against identifiable income of that business; (c) what constituted "substantially the same business" for this purpose and, assuming that the identity of a particular business could be adequately traced, to what extent would the taxpayer be required to maintain separate accounting records with respect to such business; (d) did *Libson* modify or displace the "continuity of entity" limitations of *New Colonial Ice* (so that carryovers would be permitted, subject to the *Libson* restriction, in any tax-free corporate acquisition, regardless of its form), or did the acquisition still have to go through the ritual of preserving the "legal identity" of the corporation whose attributes were sought to be carried over; and finally (e) did *Libson* have any continuing impact on years covered by the 1954 Code, despite the extensive revisions of the carryover area effected by §§381 and 382? As would be expected, these matters generated (and are still generating) substantial litigation, the final outcome of which is still in doubt on certain points.

2. Some post-Libson developments under the 1939 Code. In Rev. Rul. 59-395, 1959-2 C.B. 475, the Service set forth its position as to the effect of *Libson* on transactions subject to the 1939 Code. First, carryovers and carrybacks would be allowed only where the acquisition transaction constituted a transfer "by operation of law" in a statutory merger or consolidation (*i.e.*, the *New Colonial Ice* doctrine remained intact as an initial barrier to the carryover or carryback). Second, carryovers and carrybacks would be permitted across the line of "corporate fusion" in three situations: (a) where the pre-merger and post-merger enterprise constituted basically "a single business";

(b) where the combined corporations had been filing consolidated returns prior to their merger or consolidation; or (c) where "substantially the same business" as generated the favorable tax attributes also produced the income against which the benefits were to be offset.[92] Thus, as viewed by the Service, carryover possibilities in the light of *Libson* were remote at best, and, as will be noted subsequently, the courts generally accepted this restrictive view.

At least one court held that *Libson* superseded the "continuity of legal entity" test of *New Colonial Ice*, noting that "we think it is no longer satisfactory to distinguish [*New Colonial Ice*] on the basis of the distinction between a statutory merger and other forms of corporate reorganization," and the "continuity of business enterprise" approach of *Libson* is the exclusive test to be applied in this area; but other courts disagreed with this view.[93]

In general, taxpayer efforts to avoid application of *Libson* have been unrewarding, at least with respect to years governed by the 1939 Code.[94] Moreover, the "continuity of business enterprise" notions of that decision have been extended to include various situations which could arguably be distinguished from the strict holding in *Libson*. Thus, in Mill Ridge Coal Co. v. Patterson (*supra*, note 46), loss carryovers of a corporate shell were disallowed, following a complete change in stock ownership coupled with a change in the type of business, under *Libson*. Other decisions reaching a similar result quickly followed: in some, the loss carryovers were disallowed by resort to both *Libson* and §269;[95] while in others, the courts relied exclusively on

---

[92] On point (a), the ruling cited, as examples of a "single business," the decisions in Stanton Brewery, Inc. v. Commissioner, *supra* note 14, and Newmarket Mfg. Co. v. United States, discussed *supra*, Sec. 13.02. The *Stanton* case involved a merger of an operating subsidiary into its parent holding company, while in *Newmarket*, a corporation merely "reincorporated" its operations in a different state.

On point (b), the ruling cited the decision in Koppers Co. v. United States, *supra* note 5; see also Joseph Weidenhoff, Inc., *supra* note 8.

To qualify under (c), the taxpayer was required to segregate the income and deductions of the businesses by sufficiently precise accounting records, a condition that could be exceedingly difficult to satisfy in practice.

[93] F. C. Donovan, Inc. v. United States, *supra* note 6; contra, Patten Fine Papers, Inc. v. Commissioner, *supra* note 6. But see J. G. Dudley Co., Inc. v. Commissioner, *supra* note 9a, and Federal Cement Tile Co. v. Commissioner, 338 F.2d 691, 14 AFTR 2d 5803 (7th Cir. 1964), stating that continuity of business, rather than continuity of corporate structure, was the critical test.

This problem is, of course, gradually diminishing in importance by virtue of the 1954 Code provisions of §381, which clearly rejects the *New Colonial Ice* doctrine.

[94] See generally Bookwalter v. Hutchens Metal Products, Inc., 281 F.2d 174, 6 AFTR 2d 5068 (8th Cir. 1960); Fawick Corp. v. Commissioner, 342 F.2d 823, 15 AFTR 2d 617 (6th Cir. 1965), and cases cited therein.

[95] See *e.g.*: J.G. Dudley Co., Inc. v. Commissioner, *supra* note 9a.

Libson.[96] What is most significant about these decisions, however, is their application of the principles of *Libson* (and §269) to the *same legal entity* (albeit a corporate "shell") which sustained the losses in question, thus confirming the fears of many that continuity of corporate structure would not necessarily guarantee preservation of that entity's favorable tax attributes. In effect, these decisions interpreted the *Libson* doctrine as requiring the ultimate beneficiaries of a loss carryover or other tax benefit to be substantially the same persons who suffered the loss or incurred the tax benefit involved. Accordingly, it now appears relatively well established that substantial changes in a corporation's stock ownership, coupled with a radical change in its business operations, can result in the destruction of its favorable tax attributes under the *Libson* doctrine, despite the preservation of its technical corporate identity (in addition, it should be noted that §269 can be, and has been, applied to disallow these "tax benefits," as would the provisions of §382 for years governed by the 1954 Code). Moreover, in the *Willingham* case (*supra* note 96), continuity of business enterprise was broken merely by changes in the loss corporation's stock ownership and capital structure, notwithstanding reactivation of the same corporate business following its reorganization in bankruptcy. In effect, this decision applied *Libson* to a case where the only significant corporate change was in ownership and capital.

Some courts appear to draw the line, however, where substantial continuity of shareholder ownership can be shown. For example, in Norden-Ketay Corp. v. Commissioner (*supra* note 46), the court suggested that substantial continuity of shareholder ownership of the corporation that suffered the losses might justify allowing the carryover even though there had been a complete change in the character of the corporate activity, since the purpose of the statute is ultimately directed toward granting a legitimate tax advantage to the shareholders behind the corporate entity. The opinion stated that "it may well be that shareholders who sustain a loss and then are wise enough to liquidate an uneconomic enterprise and embark on a different and profitable field of endeavor through the same corporation are equally entitled to offset the earlier losses as those who see an unprofitable corporation through the lean years into the good ones in

---

[96] See *e.g.*: Virginia Metal Products, Inc. v. Commissioner, *supra* note 46; Norden-Ketay Corp. v. Commissioner, *supra* note 46; Huyler's v. Commissioner, 327 F.2d 767, 13 AFTR 2d 625 (7th Cir. 1964); Frederick Steel Co., *supra* note 46; The Humacid Co., *supra* note 41.

See also Willingham v. United States, 289 F.2d 283, 7 AFTR 2d 1220 (5th Cir. 1961), where various changes in the corporation's stock ownership and capital structure alone were held to terminate continuity of its business enterprise.

the same activity."[97] To the same effect is Rev. Rul. 63-40, 1963-1 C.B. 46, where the Service announced that it would not apply *Libson* to a case where the same taxpayer merely changed the character of its business, so long as there was no more than a "minor change" in its stock ownership. More recently, the Service relented even further on the continuity of ownership requirement by holding, in TIR-773 (Oct. 13, 1965), that *Libson* would be applied (to 1954 Code years) only "where there has been *both* a 50 percent or more shift in the 'benefits' of a loss carryover (whether direct or indirect and including transactions having the effect of shifting the benefit of the loss by shifting assets, stock, profit interests, or other valuable rights) *and* a change in business as defined in §382(a)."[98]

On the other hand, several courts have refused to consider shareholder continuity of ownership as a controlling factor for application of the *Libson* doctrine (noting, with special emphasis, the fact that in the *Libson* case itself the corporations had been owned by the same shareholders in the same proportions). Most notable in this respect was the decision in Julius Garfinkel & Co., Inc. v. Commissioner (*infra* note 101); there, a profitable corporation was merged into a loss corporation and both businesses were continued after the merger. Despite substantial continuity of stock ownership (the 58 percent parent of the loss corporation subsidiary caused it to acquire the wholly owned profit corporation subsidiary, with a consequent increase in the parent corporation's ownership of the surviving loss corporation to 95 percent), and despite the fact that the loss corporation was the surviving legal entity, carryovers were denied on the authority of *Libson*. The court held, although not without difficulty, that the surviving corporation's pre-merger losses could not be deducted from post-merger profits of the combined enterprise because those profits were produced by a different business, that of the ac-

---

[97] In Kolker Bros., Inc., *supra* note 66, the Tax Court refused to apply *Libson* to a case where the shift of ownership amounted to 46 percent and where, although the character of the taxpayer corporation's business changed, its essential nature was held to have continued (*i.e.*, the taxpayer continued to sell food at retail although it changed from a general retail grocery business to one of supplying a limited type of food to a particular group of customers). See also Meridan Corp. v. United States, 253 F. Supp. 636, 17 AFTR 2d 646 (S.D.N.Y. 1966) (shift of 49 percent of stock; *Libson* applied); Jackson Oldsmobile, Inc. v. United States, *supra* note 8, where, despite changes in the character of the taxpayer's business (*i.e.*, its name, location, employees, product line, and capital structure), the court allowed the loss carryovers on the grounds that its majority stock ownership remained unchanged and that "essentially the same business" continued.

[98] This pronouncement was in response to the decision in Maxwell Hardware Co. v. Commissioner, *supra* note 9a, holding that *Libson Shops* had no vitality under the 1954 Code.

quired corporation. In a subsequent decision, Allied Central Stores, Inc. v. Commissioner, 339 F.2d 503, 14 AFTR 2d 6112 (2d Cir. 1964), *Libson* was again invoked to deny a deduction for loss carryovers where various wholly owned subsidiary corporations were merged into a single corporate entity (the loss corporation constituted the surviving entity in this transaction, as in the *Garfinkel* case). The court held that even complete continuity of ownership did not rescue the taxpayer from disallowance of its carryovers under *Libson;* rather, the rationale of that decision demanded that the same business *unit* which produced the losses must also generate the income against which those losses were to be applied, and, since the taxpayer was not able to prove such fact from its records, the losses were denied.[98a]

Several aspects of *Libson's* "continuity of business enterprise" requirement bear special note. In the *Humacid Co.* case (*supra* note 41), the Tax Court pointed out that continuity of business enterprise means something different from identity or similarity of economic endeavors; what the Supreme Court had in mind in *Libson*, said the court, "was something more in the nature of an economic concept prohibiting separate business *units* from combining so the profits from one separate enterprise might be offset against the losses of another." This "separate business" aspect of the *Libson* doctrine should be compared not only to the somewhat similar considerations involved in §355(b) (*supra*, Secs. 11.04 and 11.05), but also with the "change of business" rules of §382(a)(1)(C) (*supra*, Sec. 13.22). The "change of business" standard in §382(a), as noted earlier, relates to a change in the *nature* or *character* of the corporation's business activities, unlike *Libson* where continuity of identifiable business units is the test. This distinction was further emphasized in the *Clarksdale Rubber Co.* case (*supra*, note 9a), where the court held that the phrase "same business" as used in *Libson* does not mean the same as it does under §382(a) (as such, the court refused to apply *Libson* to a transaction covered by the 1954 Code rules of §382(a), even though the taxpayer was successful in avoiding disallowance of its loss carryovers under those provisions).

Other ramifications of *Libson* include a suggestion in the *Humacid* case, *supra*, that losses could be disallowed if attributable to a decline in value prior to a substantial change in stock ownership. Such a disallowance of "built-in losses" under *Libson* may parallel similar developments under §269 (*supra*, Sec. 13.21). Although the bulk of cases applying *Libson* have involved attempts to carry forward

---

[98a] To the same effect is Frank Ix & Sons Vir. Corp., 45 T.C. No. 52 (1966).

operating or capital losses realized before the change in ownership, at least one holds that the corporation may not take advantage of a built-in loss that was realized after ownership changed.[99] Unless confined to built-in losses that the new owners expect to realize promptly (e.g., because some old activities are about to be terminated), however, this application of *Libson* would require an appraisal of all assets when ownership changes, and a segregation of those that have depreciated (or, if "netting" is to be allowed, of all assets on hand, whether depreciated or appreciated) so that they can be separately accounted for as losses are realized thereon.

3. *Libson Shops and the 1954 Code.* To what extent, if any, does the continuity of business enterprise test of *Libson* apply to transactions governed by the 1954 Code? The extensive revisions in the carryover rules effected by §§381 and 382 (and the elimination of the language in §172 referring to "the taxpayer") suggest that *Libson* should have no application thereunder,[100] but the Service and some courts disagree. As an initial matter, Rev. Rul. 58-603, 1958-2 C.B. 147, held that *Libson* would "not be relied on . . . as to a merger or any other transaction described in §381(a) of the 1959 Code." Presumably this meant that where particular tax attributes passed from one corporation to another by virtue of §381 (*supra*, Sec. 13.11), *Libson* would not be invoked as a limitation on the transferability of such items; but it left unsettled the applicability of *Libson* to acquisitions that are not specified in §381(a), to items that are not enumerated in §381(c), and to survival of the acquiring corporation's own tax attributes; nor did the ruling say whether the Service regarded *Libson* as applying to attributes other than a net operating loss carryover. In Rev. Rul. 63-40, 1963-1 C.B. 46, the Service ruled that it would apply *Libson* to 1954 Code transactions where a single corporation discontinued a loss business and purchased a profitable business if, at about the same time, a significant change in stock ownership occurred. This ruling was favorably commented on in several 1939

[99] Meridan Corp. v. United States, *supra* note 97. The issue before the court was a carryover to 1954 of a built-in operating loss sustained in 1953, the change in ownership (by merger) having occurred in 1951. If a single corporation had been involved, and its stock had changed hands in the middle of its taxable year, the logic of the decision would evidently prevent an offset of built-in losses realized during the latter part of the year against income realized during the same period. In the case of a merger of a loss corporation into a profitable one, this is the result that would be produced by a closing of the loss corporation's taxable year (*supra*, Sec. 13.13); but if the loss corporation survives the merger, the result is less clear.

See also Frank Ix & Sons Vir. Corp., *supra* note 98a.

[100] For a persuasive arugment to this effect, see Sinrich, Libson Shops — An Argument Against Its Application Under the 1954 Code, 13 Tax L. Rev. 167 (1958).

Code decisions, and other courts have similarly indicated that *Libson* principles may have continuing vitality under the 1954 Code.[101]

On the other hand, the Service's rigorous continuity of ownership standard in Rev. Rul. 63-40 may be too severe, and the Tax Court has so held in Kolker Bros., Inc. (*supra* note 66), where the carryover was allowed despite a 46 percent shift of ownership. This aspect of Rev. Rul. 63-40 was modified by TIR-773 (Oct. 13. 1965), where the Service's position on the applicability of *Libson* to 1954 Code years was stated as follows:

> Accordingly, the Service will apply *Libson Shops* in any loss carryover case under the 1954 Code, not contemplated by the announcement in Rev. Rul. 58-603 . . ., where there has been both a 50 percent or more shift in the benefits of a loss carryover (whether direct or indirect and including transactions having the effect of shifting the benefit of the loss by shifting assets, stock, profit interests or other valuable rights) and a change in business as defined in §382(a) and the regulations thereunder.

This approach seems designed to infuse the *Libson* doctrine into the structure of §382(a) (*supra*, Sec. 13.22) and may be of doubtful validity in view of the Tax Court's position that "continuity of business," as that term is used in §382(a)(1)(C), is different from what is meant by such term in the *Libson* context.[102] But in Euclid-Tennessee, Inc. v. Commissioner (*supra* note 101) the court stated that, "We cannot and do not read *Libson* into the 1954 Code, but its broad principles may be *relevant* except as the 1954 Code, under limited conditions, permits what the 1939 Code, construed by *Libson*, forbade." In short, the extent of *Libson's* applicability under the 1954 Code (either as an independent limitation, or merely as an overriding influence on the interpretation of the explicit statutory sections) is unclear. In two recent decisions, however, the issue has been squarely raised, and taxpayers were victorious in both in obtaining judicial rejection of *Libson*.

The first of these cases, Maxwell Hardware Co. v. Commissioner (*supra* note 9a), involved a carefully tailored arrangement whereby

---

[101] See *e.g.*, Huyler's v. Commissioner, *supra* note 96 (1939 Code); Julius Garfinkel & Co., Inc. v. Commissioner, 335 F.2d 744, 14 AFTR 2d 5206 (2d Cir. 1964) (1939 Code); J. G. Dudley Co., Inc. v. Commissioner, *supra* note 9a; Jackson Oldsmobile, Inc. v. United States, *supra* note 8; the Wallace Corp., *supra* note 79; Euclid-Tennessee, Inc. v. Commissioner, 352 F.2d 991, 16 AFTR 2d 6003 (6th Cir. 1965).

[102] See The Humacid Co., *supra* note 41; Clarksdale Rubber Co., *supra* note 9a; but cf. The Wallace Corp., *supra* note 79, where the court assumed, without discussion, that these two problems involved "similar considerations."

the parties successfully avoided the literal terms of both §269 and §382(a). The corporate taxpayer therein had accumulated substantial net operating loss carryovers from its hardware business; the corporation entered into an agreement with two real estate developers whereby a separate real estate department was established to develop a subdivision, the funds therefor being contributed by these developers in exchange for non-voting preferred stock of the taxpayer (worth about 30 percent of the corporation's net worth). The agreement provided that the real estate department would be accounted for independently; that it would be continued for at least 6 years; that the preferred stock could not be sold during this period; and that the preferred stock could be redeemed on a discontinuance of the real estate held by the department. In addition, a voting trust restricted control of the common stock, without, however, shifting control of the voting stock to the new investors. The hardware business was then discontinued and the real estate business operated at a profit; and net operating losses generated by the hardware business were claimed as deductions against profits of the real estate business. The Tax Court (*sub. nom.*, Arthur T. Beckett, 41 T.C. 386) held that neither §269 nor §382(a) applied to this situation: §269 did not apply, despite a finding of tax avoidance motivation, because the new investors did not obtain at least 50 percent of the total voting power or value of the taxpayer's stock, nor did the voting trust arrangement change this result since the effect thereof was merely to shift voting control from the common stockholders to an independent agent, not to the new investors who harbored the forbidden purpose; also §382(a) did not apply because the change in stock ownership resulted in an increase in value of only 30 percentage points and, as an additional ground, §382(c) specifically exempts non-voting preferred. Moreover, the court rejected the Commissioner's argument that these transactions constituted merely a "sham" arrangement and that profits from the real estate venture could be taxed directly to the new preferred stockholders. This left only *Libson* as a basis for disallowing the taxpayer's loss carryovers and the Tax Court held that it could be applied: it felt that Congress did not intend in the 1954 Code to reject the continuity of business enterprise principle and thereby invite well-advised and technically skillful taxpayers to "traffic" in loss carryovers.[103]

The Ninth Circuit, however, reversed, holding that *Libson* had

---

[103] The "trafficking" problem referred to by the Tax Court in the *Beckett* case involved the situation where the shareholders who benefit from a particular corporate tax attribute are not the same persons as those who were shareholders when the attribute was created.

no application to years governed by the 1954 Code. This court concluded, contrary to the view of the Tax Court, that Congress had indeed intended to permit "trafficking" in net operating loss carryovers except as specifically restricted by the terms of §§269 or 382: in other words, the Ninth Circuit felt that Congress, in enacting the 1954 Code, intended that the explicit statutory provisions of §§172, 381, 382, and 269 should be the exclusive limitations on the negotiability or survival of various corporate tax attributes. The appellate court noted, however, that the Commissioner was not helpless in this situation, referring pointedly to the income and deduction allocation rules of §482 (where dealings between "related taxpayers" may be recast so as to clearly reflect income); that provision, had it been asserted by the Service, could have afforded an adequate remedy to check any egregious abuses, said the court (§482 was not argued at the Tax Court trial, however, for reasons not likely to be repeated in subsequent litigation). The *Maxwell Hardware* case thus represents a major taxpayer victory in the *Libson Shops* saga (and a triumph of careful tax planning as well), although the cautious advisor would do well to avoid premature celebrations over *Libson's* demise, especially since the Service announced, in TIR-773 (Oct. 13, 1965), that it would not follow the decision in *Maxwell Hardware*.

The other notable decision involving the application of *Libson Shops* to 1954 Code transactions is *Clarksdale Rubber Co.* (*supra* note 9a), where the Tax Court refused to apply *Libson* principles to a situation specifically covered by §382(a). There, the requisite change of ownership had occurred, but the Tax Court held that the corporation had thereafter continued to carry on "substantially the same business" within the meaning of §382(a)(1)(C), and that the taxpayer was not required to satisfy the business continuity standard of *Libson*. The court stated its conclusions on this issue as follows: "Consequently, we hold that where the requisite change-in-ownership conditions of §382(a)(1)(A) and (B) are met, the provisions of §382(a)(1)(C) exclusively govern the issue as to whether 'the same business' is thereafter carried on." The opinion further noted that the "continuity of business enterprise" test of *Libson* related to an economic concept prohibiting separate business *units* from combining so that profits from one separate enterprise might be offset against losses of another, while the business continuity required by §382(a)-(1)(C) deals with the identity or substantial similarity of the corporation's economic endeavors. Hence, the *Libson* case was held irrelevant in determining whether the taxpayer had satisfied the limitations of §382(a)(1)(C).

Consequently, it would seem that the *Libson* doctrine is destined for a fairly limited role under the 1954 Code, the Service's views to the contrary notwithstanding. Perhaps the most that can be said for its applicability to 1954 Code taxable years is that its attitudes and radiations may be relevant in applying the specific statutory provisions of §§381 and 382 (this tendency is already evident in the regulations under §382(a), discussed *supra*, Sec. 13.22). The Service's announcement in TIR-773 also appears to be moving in this general direction: *i.e.*, infusing *Libson's* general principles into the statutory framework of §§382 and 269. On the other hand, it is still too early to say that *Libson* has been wholly preempted by the 1954 legislation: the *Maxwell* case is the only decision to go this far, and *Clarksdale* limited its rejection of *Libson* to transactions falling within the specific confines of §382(a). It may be that *Libson* could still exert considerable force with respect to items not specified in §381(c), or with respect to the survival of the acquiring corporation's own tax attributes, or, finally, with respect to tax-free acquisitions not covered by the terms of §381(a).[104]

Sec. 13.26 Other limitations on survival of corporate tax attributes

While the foregoing limitations on survival of corporate tax attributes constitute a formidable array of statutory and judicial defenses, the Commissioner has yet another series of more general weapons at his disposal which may be invoked in egregious cases of tax manipulation and abuse. Several have been noted at other points in this work and the following is more of a check list than a full discussion:

> *1. "Business purpose" and "economic reality."* If a transaction fails to qualify as a "reorganization" because it lacks a "business purpose" (*supra*, Sec. 12.19), §381(a) will not come into play to preserve the tax attributes of the transferor corporation for the successor corporation.

> *2. Recognition of the corporate entity.* If the corporate enterprise is of such an evanescent or dormant character as to lack "economic reality," the separate entity status thereof may be disregarded. For a general discussion of this subject, which is derived in large part from *Gregory*, see *supra*, Sec. 1.05 and Sec.

---

[104] See generally, Harris, *Libson Shops* and Related Cases, 21 N.Y.U. Inst. on Fed. Tax. 1307 (1963); Cowan, Libson Shops: A Question of Survival, 34 U. of Cinc. L. Rev. 462 (1965); Levine and Petta, *Libson Shops:* A Study in Semantics, 36 Taxes 445 (1958); Levine and Petta, *Libson Shops* Applied to the Single Corporate Taxpayer, ibid. 562.

2.09. Courts on the whole, however, seem reluctant to ignore the separate entity status of a corporation,[105] and this particular line of attack has been reserved for extreme cases only.

3. *Assignment of income principles.* In a sense, the *Libson Shops* doctrine and its subsequent judicial extensions can be viewed as an offshoot of the general principle that income must be taxed to "the one who earns it" or to the "owner of the property which produces it."[106] While *Libson* forbade the assignment of tax benefits by one "business enterprise" to another, the thrust of that decision is reminiscent of the classic assignment of income approach. At least where there is a change of ownership, to allow the post-change income to be offset by losses or other benefits whose economic cost fell on the old shareholders is to allow the new owners to avoid the tax burden of "their" income; and even if ownership does not change, a transfer of tax benefits from one taxable entity to another raises assignment of income problems. On the other hand, the carryover rules of §381 (and the limitations of §§269 and 382) probably restrict assignment of income principles to a limited role in this area, and this conclusion seems borne out by the paucity of decided cases resorting to this approach.

4. *De facto dissolution.* A corporation in the process of liquidation may eventually reach such a point of dormancy that its corporate "existence" will be held to have terminated (see *supra*, Sec. 9.02); consequently, operating losses or other tax benefits generated after this event cannot be carried back to prior years of viability. See generally in this respect, Rev. Rul. 61-191, 1961-2 C.B. 251, where the Service ruled that post-liquidation net operating losses and excess profits tax credits could not be carried back to pre-liquidation years of a corporation which had been dissolved *de facto*. See also Willingham v. United States (*supra* note 96), for an application of this approach, although with overtones of *Libson Shops*, to a corporation which had passed through a major insolvency reorganization. On the whole, however, courts have been reluctant to apply the *de facto* dissolution theory to disallow net operating loss carrybacks generated during the process of liquidation.[107]

5. *Reallocation of income or deductions under §482.* The Commissioner has broad discretionary power under §482 to reallocate income, deductions, credits, or other allowances between or among related taxpayers in order to "clearly reflect income." For an application of §482, see Pauline W. Ach (*supra* note 42);

---

[105] See *e.g.*: Arthur T. Beckett, 41 T.C. 386 (1963); Pauline W. Ach, *supra* note 42; John F. Nutt, *supra* note 42.

[106] See generally Lyon and Eustice, Assignment of Income: Fruit and Tree as Irrigated by the P.G. Lake Case, 17 Tax L. Rev. 293 (1962).

[107] See *e.g.*: Jackson Oldsmobile, Inc. v. United States, *supra* note 8; Joseph Weidenhoff, Inc., *supra* note 8 (Acq.). For problems raised by corporations which liquidate in mid-stream, see *supra*, Sec. 9.62; see also *supra*, Sec. 2.08, for the tax treatment of corporations in the process of winding up.

and for an invitation to the Service to use §482 where the parties sucessfully avoid the clutches of §§382 and 269, see Maxwell Hardware Co. v. Commissioner (*supra* note 9a). It should be noted, however, that §482 authorizes only the reallocation of income or deductions; it does not permit disallowance of deductions, and hence cannot be used in the same manner as §§269 and 382, which provide for total disallowance of various beneficial tax allowances.

Before leaving this area, a word of caution seems in order. The preceding materials may have created the impression that corporate tax attributes will survive adjustments and changes in a corporation's stock ownership, financial structure, legal entity, or business enterprise only in rare and unusual cases. In point of fact, however, the scope of corporate carryovers is a broad one (especially since the 1954 Code), and denial of these benefits may well be the exception rather than the rule. Although the Service's position in litigated cases may suggest implacable opposition to any and all transfers of tax attributes, most corporate reorganizations and other adjustments pass smoothly through the audit or tax ruling process with their carryovers intact. The reader, therefore, should not focus so exclusively on the barriers to a transfer of attributes as to overlook the possibility of their preservation.

Part D. Multiple Corporations

Sec. 13.30. Introductory

The tax advantages that may be achieved by operating a business through multiple corporations have at times encouraged taxpayers to proliferate excessively the number of corporations used to conduct what is basically a single economic enterprise. These tax advantages can take several forms:

1. Multiple surtax exemptions. The potential dollar savings resulting from multiple surtax exemptions under §11(c) can be considerable. For example, if a business with taxable income of $1,000,000 can effectively spread its income among 21 corporations, rather than operating as a single corporation, the 20 additional surtax exemptions can reduce aggregate tax liability by $130,000 at 1965 rates (26 percent of $25,000 or $6,500 per exemption). If the income can be spread among an even greater number of "alphabet corporations," tax savings increase apace.

2. Accumulated earning credits. Another tax saving created by multiple corporations is the reduction in exposure to the unreasonable accumulations tax of §531 (*supra*, Ch. 6), resulting from proliferation of the $100,000 minimum accumulated earnings credits allowed by §535(c)(2).[108]

3. Separate elections, accounting methods, and other similar "timing" benefits. Another advantage of operating through multiple corporations is the opportunity for various segments of the business to adopt the accounting methods, periods, and elections (*e.g.*, depreciation, inventory valuation, bad debt, installment sale, and foreign tax credit elections) that are most suitable to their needs.

4. Facilitating future sales of parts of the business. Initial establishment of multiple corporate entities may provide greater flexibility at a later date to divide up and sell off parts of the business without running the gauntlet of such provisions as §355 (corporate divisions, *supra*, Ch. 11), §346 (partial liquidations, *supra*, Ch. 7), and §341 (collapsible corporations, *supra*, Ch. 10). Tax planning looking toward the realization of accumulated corporate earnings at capital gain rates can be greatly facilitated through the multiple corporation device.

5. Miscellaneous benefits. Multiple corporations can facilitate the securing of numerous other tax benefits: qualification of segments of the business for the Western Hemisphere Trade Corporation or Possessions Corporation benefits of §§921 and 931; avoidance of the anti-discrimination limitations for pension and profit plan coverage; or selective participation of various key employees in stock purchase plans without excessively diluting control of the overall business.

While this is not an exhaustive list of the tax benefits accruing to multiple corporations, these items represent the major tax stakes typically involved in this area. On the other hand, multiple corporations may be less advantageous in some circumstances (*e.g.*, if one corporation suffers losses while others are profitable, and consolidated returns (*infra*, Part E) are not permissable).

As is to be expected, however, the Commissioner is not without legal weapons for limiting the use or abuse of multiple corporations. Among the major avenues of attack on this problem, some general and others specifically directed thereto, are the following:

1. *Sections 1551 and 269 (infra, Sec. 13.31).* Where tax avoidance motivates the establishment of multiple corporations, the principal benefits thereof may be disallowed in whole or in part under provisions of §1551 (recently strengthened by the 1964 Revenue Act) and §269 (recently applied with a broader brush by the courts, *supra*, Sec. 13.21).

---

[108] Other limitations may also be multiplied: for example, investment credit allowances under §48(c); additional first-year depreciation allowances under §179(b) (but cf. §179(d)(6), which restricts this advantage).

2. Disregard of the corporate entity (infra, Sec. 13.32). If the multiple corporate entities fail to engage in significant business activity, other than avoiding taxation, their separate existence may be ignored (*supra*, Sec. 1.05), and the income and deductions allocated either to a dominant member of the group or directly to their shareholders.

3. Assignment of income (infra, Sec. 13.32). Income is taxable, under §61, to the one who "earns" it and several recent decisions have applied this doctrine to the multiple corporation area by allocating the income of the several corporations to the dominant member of the group which is held to have "earned" it.

4. Section 482 reallocation (infra, Sec. 13.32). Where multiple corporations are controlled, directly or indirectly, by the same interests, the Commissioner may reallocate income, deductions, credits or other allowances between or among the corporations so as to "clearly reflect income"; the practical effect of a §482 reallocation in this context may be a "compulsory" consolidated return for the affiliated group of corporations.

5. Treatment as an "association" under §7701(a)(3) (infra, Sec. 13.32). This approach, although always a threat, has not thus far been accepted by the courts, for reasons that will be examined.

6. Multiple corporation legislation, §§1561 and 1562 (infra, Sec. 13.33). The multiple corporation area acquired yet another dimension of complexity by virtue of statutory provisions enacted by the Revenue Act of 1964 designed to restrict the benefits of this device.

The potency of these weapons, applied either singly or in combination, depends upon a variety of factors, not the least of which is the Service's ability to detect on audit the appropriate cases for attack, and the willingness of judges to support its application of a particular weapon. Moreover, whichever method of attack is adopted by the Commissioner, the inherently factual nature of these problems further ensures the perpetuation of a high degree of uncertainty. Also, in many multiple corporation situations, taxpayers have little to lose by attempting the multiple corporation ploy: *i.e.*, the additional taxes assessed as a deficiency if the multiple set-up fails are likely to be the same as those that would have been imposed had a single corporate entity been used at the outset.[109] This atmosphere is not conducive to the reduction of litigation; taxpayers who get caught in a multiple corporation scheme may feel that they have merely "played

---

[109] There are, of course, situations where reallocation or disallowance of various tax benefits can result in personal holding company problems; accumulated earnings tax problems; deficiency, interest and, in extreme cases, fraud penalties; and the like, all or some of which items may not have arisen in the absence of multiple corporations.

the game and lost," and that the next go-around may bring more
fortunate results. A system of legal rules which fosters, or even
tolerates, such an attitude seems destined for eventual judicial or legislative reappraisal.[110]

Sec. 13.31.   Disallowance of surtax exemption, accumulated earnings credit, and other multiple benefits: §1551 and §269

1. In general. Section 1551, while closely associated with §269
(*supra*, Sec. 13.21), is narrower in its ramifications since it disallows
only the $25,000 surtax exemption of §11(c) and the $100,000 minimum accumulated earnings credit of §535(c)(2) where certain "controlled" corporations (primarily subsidiaries, although, since 1964,
certain brother-sister corporations are included as well) are created
by the transfer of property from their shareholders and such corporations are unable to establish "by the clear preponderance of the
evidence that the securing of such exemption or credit was not a
major purpose of such transfer." Except for technical changes in 1954
and 1964, §1551 is substantially similar to §15(c) of the 1939 Code,
enacted in 1951 as a compromise after the House had passed a bill
providing that a group of "related" corporations (as defined) could
have but one surtax exemption, regardless of the purpose that animated the multiplication of the corporate entities.[111] There is a considerable degree of overlap between the provisions of §1551 and the
more general rules of §269, a situation that has already been noted
(*supra*, Sec. 13.21) and that resulted in large part from the broaden-
ing of §269's scope by the *Coastal Oil Storage* case. As a result,
§§1551 and 269 (either jointly or severally) constitute two of the
most important statutory weapons available to the Service in attacking the multiple corporation device. The discussion that follows, however, will focus primarily on the provisions of §1551, in view of the
extensive treatment afforded §269 at an earlier point in this chapter.

2. Section 1551. Section 1551 is brought into play if the following
conditions are satisfied:

---

[110] See generally Ferguson and Ross, 1964 Ann. Survey of Am. L. 201, 250
(1965); Sharp, Multiple Tax Benefits Through Multiple Incorporation: Some
Thoughts on the Law As It Is, and As It Ought To Be, 40 Bost. U. L. Rev. 375
(1960); Note, Multiple Incorporation To Obtain Additional Accumulated Earnings Credits and Surtax Exemptions, 44 Minn. L. Rev. 485 (1960); Emmanuel
and Lipoff, Commissioner v. Corporate Complex: An Expanding Attack, 15 U.
Fla. L. Rev. 352 (1963).

[111] For a discussion of this proposal, see H.R. Rep. No. 586, 82d Cong., 1st
Sess., reprinted in 1951-2 C.B. 357, 374; S. Rep. No. 781, *ibid.* at 458, 506-7.

a. A corporation, or five or fewer individuals who are in control of a corporation, transfer property (other than money), directly or indirectly, to a transferee corporation;[111a]

b. The transferee corporation was created for the purpose of acquiring the property, or was not actively engaged in business at the time of the acquisition; and

c. The transferor corporation or its shareholders, or the five or fewer individual transferors, are in control of the transferee during some part of its taxable year. "Control" is defined in §1551(b) as ownership of at least 80 percent of voting power or value, "ownership" being determined under the constructive ownership rules of §1563(e). In the case of transfers to sister corporations by five or fewer individuals, the "control" must be essentially pro rata as well.

If these conditions are met, the surtax exemption and accumulated earnings tax credit of the transferee corporation will be disallowed unless it establishes, by the clear preponderance of the evidence, that securing the benefit of these allowances was not "a major purpose" of the transfer. It should be noted that §1551(c) recognizes the possibility of overlap with §269 by providing that the exemption or credit may be allowed in part by the Service under the authority of §269(b), thus permitting partial allowance of these items if tax avoidance will not result.[112]

The scope of §1551 was expanded by the Revenue Act of 1964. Prior thereto, only direct transfers of property by one corporation to another "controlled" corporation were presumably subject to §1551. Hence, "indirect" transfers could at least arguably be made between controlled corporations without fear of attack under §1551 and, perhaps even more important, groups of individual incorporators could, at the start of their corporate venture, divide up a single tract of real

---

[111a] As stated in the text, the phrase "directly or indirectly" applies only to transfers after June 12, 1963; and transfers by individual transferors are similarly embraced only if made after that date. Transfers by corporations, however, are within §1551 if made on or after January 1, 1951.

[112] The regulations give, as an example of the dispensing power under §269(b), the case of a parent that transfers all of its property to two new subsidiaries and then dissolves. Assuming §1551's applicability, the Internal Revenue Service might exercise its power under §269(b) by allowing one exemption and one credit, to be allocated between the two surviving corporations. Regs. §1.1551-1(b)(2).

For an important decision upholding the Commissioner's disallowance of such items under both §1551 and §269, see Coastal Oil Storage Co. v. Commissioner, *supra* note 10; see also James Realty Co. v. United States, *supra* note 10; Kessmar Construction Co. v. Commissioner, *supra* note 50; Joe Dillier, *supra* note 50; Samuel Napsky, *supra* note 50. See also Regs. §1.1551-1(b), stating that §1551 must not be interpreted as delimiting other general principles, such as those of §269 and §482, and that these provisions are not mutually exclusive but may operate together or separately in appropriate cases.

estate and transfer separate parcels to a number of corporations, or split up the functions of a manufacturing or mercantile business among numerous "brother-sister" corporations. The 1964 amendments, however, provided for two additional categories of §1551 transfers to combat these practices: (a) transfers made "indirectly" to a controlled corporation; and (b) transfers by five or fewer individuals to a "sister" corporation controlled in essentially the same proportions by the same shareholders. On the meaning of "indirect" transfers, the House Committee report, H.R. Rep. No. 749, 88th Cong., 2d Sess. A211 (1963), listed the following examples:

> a. A transfer of money by one corporation to a newly created subsidiary, which was then used by the subsidiary to purchase stock in trade from its parent.[112a]
> b. The shareholders of one corporation acquire property therefrom and, as a part of the "same transaction," transfer the property to a controlled sister corporation.[113]

The limited inclusion of pro rata brother-sister incorporations within the scope of §1551 transactions, while a significant extension of that section, may not have much practical importance in view of the apparent willingness of courts to apply §269 to this situation,[114] except to the extent that the tax motivation standard under §1551 is more rigorous than that of §269. If the number of individual transferors exceeds 5 or if the shareholders' common control of the brother-sister corporations is essentially non-pro rata, however, §1551 will not apply and the Commissioner will perforce have to rely on the more general provisions of §§269 and 482.

Once a business has been committed to a single corporation, §1551 stands as a formidable barrier to any efforts to multiply the corporate entities which conduct the enterprise. While "indirect" transfers are now explicitly covered by §1551 since the Revenue Act of 1964, problems still can arise over what constitutes a "transfer of

---

[112a] The somewhat ambiguous statement in Regs. §1.1551-1(d) to the effect that "the transfer of cash for the purpose of expanding the business of the transferor corporation through the formation of a new corporation is not a transfer within the scope of §1551 irrespective of whether the new corporation uses the cash to purchase from the transferor corporation stock in trade or similar property," seems to have been explicitly overruled by this amendment.

[113] This example seems to overrule the decision in Airlene Gas Co. v. United States, 2 AFTR 2d 5880 (W.D. Ky. 1958), which held that such a transaction was not covered by §1551. However, the force of the opinion on this issue is reduced by the fact that the transfer to the shareholders (prior to the retransfer to the sister corporation) preceded the enactment of §1551.

[114] See e.g., Joe Dillier, supra note 50; Samuel Napsky, supra note 50; Bonneville Locks Towing Co., Inc. v. United States, supra note 50.

property" for purposes of this section. For example, does a lease, license, loan, or sale of property constitute a "transfer" for purposes of §1551, or must the transaction constitute a tax-free exchange or contribution to capital (under §§351, 361, 118, or 1032) to be so considered? Does "property" include goodwill, franchises, territorial marketing rights, trade names, "know-how," or other intangible benefits? What about a transfer of employees or other personnel to the newly created corporation? Courts have generally agreed that a "sale of assets" constitutes a property transfer for purposes of §1551, thus neutralizing, to a substantial extent, the pre-1964 failure to refer to cash transfers where the money was subsequently used by the transferee to purchase assets from the transferor.[115] Moreover, it has been held that the leasing of assets constitutes a transfer for purposes of §1551.[116] At least one court has indicated, however, that it might reach a different conclusion on the §1551 "transfer" issue where the rights are created by the alleged transfer transaction itself, as in the case of a franchise to distribute goods manufactured by an affiliated corporation, rather than transferred from the pre-existing business enterprise to the new corporation.[117]

In the latter respect, the courts, and to some extent the Service, seem to distinguish between inter-corporation transfers that divide up an existing business (and which must run the gauntlet of §1551), and those that are for the purpose of expanding or diversifying the corporation's business activities. See, for example, Hiawatha Home Builders, Inc. (*supra* note 115), and Regs. §1.1551-1(d). This distinction between "expansions" and "divisions" may be traceable to a statement in the staff summary of the Revenue Act of 1951, noted in the *Hiawatha* case; the distinction, however, is easier to state than to apply.

It should be noted that §1551 is applicable to transfers of property only if the transferee corporation is created "for the purpose of acquiring such property" or was not actively engaged in business at the time of the acquisition.[118] Thus, inter-corporate transfers after the new or previously inactive corporation has gotten under way are not inhibited by §1551. On the other hand, if a transfer is em-

---

[115] Hiawatha Home Builders, Inc. 36 T.C. 491 (1961); Challenger, Inc., *supra* note 64; New England Foundry Corp., 44 T.C. 150 (1965). But cf. The Esrenco Truck Co., ¶63,072 P-H Memo TC.

[116] Rev. Rul. 57-202, 1957-1 C.B. 297; Theatre Concessions, Inc., 29 T.C. 754 (1958); Perfection Foods, Inc., ¶65,015 P-H Memo TC.

[117] Bush Hog Mfg. Co., Inc., 42 T.C. 713 (1964).

[118] The inclusion of inactive corporations prevents avoidance of §1551 by the purchase of a corporate shell. For the meaning of "not actively engaged in business," see Regs. §1.1551-1(b)(3).

braced by §1551, the surtax exemption and accumulated earnings credit are disallowed not only for the taxable year in which the transfer occurs, but also for any later taxable year during which the transferee corporation is controlled by the transferor, its shareholders, or both. Moreover, a transfer of property that is beyond the reach of §1551 only because the requisite control did not exist when the transfer occurred will become subject to §1551 if and when control is acquired. An example is the "creeping control" case set out in Regs. §1.1551-1(c), in which the transferor corporation owns only 60 percent of the transferee's stock when the transfer of property occurs, but acquires an additional 20 percent in a later taxable year.

By requiring the taxpayer to prove by "a clear preponderance of the evidence" that securing the surtax exemption or accumulated earnings credit was not "a major purpose" of the transfer of property, §1551 seeks to impose a more severe burden than §269, which comes into play only if tax avoidance is "the principal purpose" and which does not alter the usual rules governing burden of proof. On the meaning of "a major purpose," see Regs. §1.1551-1(e). It is doubtful that the "clear preponderance of the evidence" requirement adds very much to the usual presumption of correctness that is attendent upon a deficiency assertion or to the customary judicial rule that the taxpayer has the burden of proof in both deficiency and refund cases.

The crucial question under §1551 is not whether the transferee corporation was created or revived in order to get the exemption or credit, but whether the *transfer of the property* was so motivated. The transfer of property that does not and is not likely to produce income could hardly have as a major purpose the securing of an exemption or credit. The same might be said of a transfer of income-producing property to a corporation which has acquired, from other sources, property that produces enough income to exhaust the exemption and credit. Moreover, if a corporation transfers *all* of its property to a second corporation and then dissolves, the transfer does not secure an *additional* exemption or credit, and hence should not be reached by §1551. The reference in §1551 to a transfer of "all" of a corporation's property should be confined to cases where the original corporation remains alive, or the property is divided among two or more transferees, so that a proliferation of exemptions and credits is possible.

Courts, on the whole, have been surprisingly receptive to taxpayers' explanations of "business reasons" for the creation of multiple corporations, despite the seemingly more rigorous anti-tax motivation standards of §1551 and the inherent evidentiary problems of proving a "negative."[119] This has been especially true in the case of manufacturing or mercantile businesses that can demonstrate that segregation of certain elements or functions of their business into separate corporations serves genuine business needs: *e.g.*, limitation of liabilities and other business or investment risks; expansion of credit or other financing opportunities; resolution of labor or management problems; expansion or diversification of product lines and marketing or distribution coverage; increased operating efficiencies, and the like.[120] On the other hand, where the alleged business goals could be just as easily effected by use of a separate branch or division, rather than by creation of a new subsidiary corporation, courts have been more skeptical of the lack of tax motives for such transactions. The *Coastal Oil* case (*supra* note 10) is a striking example of this approach. Moreover, where the activities or fuctions of the multiple corporations substantially overlap, proof of genuine business needs for the use of separate corporations is more difficult. Such duplications of effort, functions, or activities tend to show that tax rather than business reasons animated the creation of additional corporations and that the parties merely intended to fragment what was basically a single integrated business enterprise. "Alphabet" real estate corporations have been especially vulnerable to this argument.[121] The "business purpose" limitations of §1551 should be compared with the somewhat similar considerations applicable to the tax-free division rules of §355 (*supra*, Sec. 11.09); however, courts generally have been more receptive to the business reasons which would justify separation of assets at the *corporate* level than to attempts to attain split ownership at the *shareholder* level under §355.[122] This may help to explain why the initial use of multiple corporations has been so popular; later tax-free divisions must satisfy the stringent requirements of §355, as well as those of §1551.[123]

---

[119] Bush Hog Mfg. Co., Inc., *supra* note 117; Sno-Frost, Inc., 31 T.C. 1058 (1959) (Acq.); Truck Terminals, Inc., 33 T.C. 876 (1960); Hiawatha Home Builders, Inc., *supra* note 115; Constroms Mfg., Inc., 36 T.C. 500 (1961); The Esrenco Truck Co., *supra* note 115; New England Foundry Corp., *supra* note 115.

[120] See V. H. Monette & Co., Inc., 45 T.C. 15 (1965).

[121] See Samuel Napsky, *supra* note 50; Kessmar Construction Co. v. Commissioner, *supra* note 50; James Realty Co. v. United States, *supra* note 10; see also Joe Dillier, *supra* note 50.

[122] See Parshelsky's Estate v. Commissioner, 303 F.2d 14, 9 AFTR 2d 1382 (2d Cir. 1962).

[123] See generally, Weiss, How to Plan Multi-Corporate Activities to Avoid the Impact of Section 1551, 23 J. Tax. 84 (1965); Slade, Cash, Property, and Stock Transfers Among Affiliated and Related Corporations: The Effect of Section 1551, 23 N.Y.U. Inst. on Fed. Tax. 299 (1965). For discussions of §1551 prior to the 1964 amendments, see Emmanuel, Section 15(c): New Teeth for

3. Section 269. The provisions of §269 have already been discussed in detail, *supra*, Sec. 13.21. However, it may be useful to compare its operation in the multiple corporation area with the rules of its more limited statutory companion, §1551:

    a. Consequences. Section 269 can be invoked to disallow a broader range of tax "allowances" than §1551; the latter is limited to surtax exemptions and minimum accumulated earnings tax credits, while the former can result in the disallowance of other items or benefits such as deductions, credits, elections, capital gain treatment, etc.

    b. Included transactions. Section 269 covers a wider range of transactions than §1551: thus, it applies where only a 50 percent stock interest is acquired (while §1551 requires at least 80 percent control); it covers incorporation transfers by individuals as well as the creation of new subsidiary corporations by transfers from a parent (while §1551 is confined, in large part, to inter-corporate transfers and, since 1964, some brother-sister incorporation transfers); and §269 applies to transfers of property to existing active subsidiaries or active brother-sister corporations, while §1551 does not.

    On the other hand, §1551 has been applied to inter-corporate sales and to transactions where the transferor already had the requisite control: in neither of these situations would §269 apply. See Challenger, Inc. (*supra* note 115).

    c. Requisite motivation or intent. In this respect, §269 seems somewhat narrower in scope than §1551, since it requires tax avoidance to be "the principal purpose" and provides that the taxpayer must clearly establish the absence of the taint. Thus, the taxpayer's formal burden is more onerous under §1551, although in practice this disparity may have little importance.

The breadth of §269, as compared with §1551, may result in the gradual absorption of the latter by the former. Evidence of this tendency is already discernable in recent multiple corporation litigation: in these cases, the Service has been relying on a multiplicity of statutory theories (*e.g.*, §§269, 1551, 61(a), 482, etc.), some of which are cumulative, while others are alternative, lines of attack; several courts have responded to this shotgun approach by treating the §269 and §1551 aspects more or less interchangeably.[124] Whatever may have been the intent of Congress, §1551 is at present decidedly overshadowed by §269.

the Reluctant Dragon? 8 Tax L. Rev. 457 (1953); Cohen, Exemptions and Credits of Multiple Corporations: Sections 15(c) and 129, 1953 So. Calif. Tax Inst. 1, 15-36.

    [124] See The Esrenco Truck Co., *supra* note 115; V. H. Monette & Co., Inc., *supra* note 120; Bush Hog Mfg. Co., Inc., *supra* note 117; Kessmar Construction Co., *supra* note 50; Samuel Napsky, *supra* note 50.

Sec. 13.32.   Other weapons against multiple corporations

1. Disregard of corporate entity. Under long-standing judicial principles (*supra*, Sec. 1.05), the separate existence of a corporation may be disregarded if the facts demonstrate that the alleged corporate enterprise was merely a "sham" or lacked economic reality. This approach, though generally applied with restraint, has nevertheless been invoked with occasional success by the Commissioner in the multiple corporation area.[125] These decisions held that to be afforded recognition for tax purposes, the corporation must be a viable business entity, formed or availed of to engage in substantial business activity other than avoiding taxation, and clothed with a sufficient business purpose to give economic substance to the corporate enterprise. Moreover, the Tax Court in the *Aldon* case (*supra* note 125) held that a corporate taxpayer's activity must be substantially productive of the income sought to be attributed to it; thus, the court stated that the various alphabet corporations involved therein "carried on no separate independent income-producing activities and served no function except as corporate devices to split the income . . . and reduce taxes," and that "they were mere corporate shells acting as conduits" for the dominant taxpayer corporation (Aldon), and that "every material step in the production of the income was taken by Aldon or those who controlled it." In the *Aldon* case, the parties did not themselves treat the various alphabet corporations as independent entities; and this lack of arm's length dealing further evidenced their economic unreality.

While the facts in *Aldon* and *Shaw* (*supra* note 125) were extreme, justifying the courts' disregard of the separate corporate entities in view of their almost complete lack of capital, employees, income-producing assets, or business functions, later decisions have been reluctant to adopt such a "blunt instrument" approach.[126] However, these decisions clearly indicate that judicial tolerance of egregious tax avoidance schemes is quite low, and that the courts will not hesitate to strike down such arrangements as shams or transparent devices. The effect of disregarding the corporate entities in

[125] See especially Aldon Homes, Inc., 33 T.C. 582 (1959); Shaw Construction Co. v. Commissioner, 35 T.C. 1102 (1961), aff'd, 323 F.2d 316, 12 AFTR 2d 5625 (9th Cir. 1963); see generally, Watts, Tax Problems of Regard for the Corporate Entity, 20 N.Y.U. Inst. on Fed. Tax. 867 (1962).

[126] Bush Hog Mfg. Co., Inc., *supra* note 117; V. H. Monette & Co., Inc., *supra* note 120; Columbian Rope Co., 42 T.C. 800 (1964) (identity of foreign subsidiary upheld); Sanford H. Hartman, 43 T.C. 105 (1964) (separate business entities upheld against Commissioner's argument of sham); Royle Co., ¶63,157 P-H Memo TC (separate entities given effect); Pauline W. Ach, *supra* note 42.

this situation is to tax their income directly to the shareholders (or possibly to the dominant corporation in the multiple group, as in the *Shaw* and *Aldon* cases).

2. *Assignment of income: §61.* Closely related to recognition of the corporate entity principles is the long-standing judicial doctrine that income will be taxed to the one who earns it and that anticipatory attempts to deflect it to another entity will be disregarded.[127] This doctrine (which as applied to the multiple corporation area resembles the government's approach to family partnerships), has been invoked with some success by the Service, most notably in the *Aldon* and *Shaw* cases (*supra* note 125). On the whole, however, assignment of income principles, like those which result in disregard of the corporate entity, have been sparingly applied by the courts. See generally *Sanford H. Hartman* (*supra* note 126), where separate business entities (a corporation and a partnership) were recognized as viable business units, and where one of those entities withstood further attack under the family partnership rules of §704(e).

As a general rule, it would seem that if a corporate entity has substantial assets or engages in sufficient business activities so as to withstand an attack on its separate "existence," these factors will go a long way toward resisting the application of §61 principles to reattribute its earnings. If, however, the corporate taxpayer is so inert that it is held, in substance, not to have been the true "earner" of the income in question, then §61 can be invoked to attribute such income to the person whose efforts actually produced it. The practical effects of applying the assignment of income doctrine are often indistinguishable from those which occur when the corporate entity is disregarded: see *e.g.*, the *Aldon* and *Shaw* cases, *supra*, where these approaches were applied in tandem.

3. *Section 482 reallocation.* Where multiple corporations are controlled directly or indirectly by the same interests, the Commissioner has broad discretionary powers under §482 to allocate between or among such corporations their respective gross incomes, deductions, credits, or allowances where he determines that such reallocation is necessary to prevent avoidance of taxes or to clearly reflect income. This provision is premised, in the first instance, on recognition of the separate identity of commonly-controlled corporate entities; but it allows the Commissioner to prevent artificial distortions of the "true net income" of such a group, which may arise by means of inter-cor-

[127] See generally, Lyon and Eustice, *supra* note 106; Eustice, Contract Rights, Capital Gain, and Assignment of Income — The Ferrer Case, 20 Tax L. Rev. 1 (1965).

porate transactions effected at less than arm's length and which result in a shifting of income between the members of the group.[128]

However, courts generally have not permitted the use of §482 to redistribute the operating results of a business which is conducted by a group of related corporations where sound business reasons can be shown for the existence of separate corporations. Moreover, the mere power or opportunity of the related group to shift or distort their income is not enough to invoke §482; it is the actual exercise of that power in a less than arm's length manner which is necessary before the Commissioner can make a reallocation under this provision.[129] Also, §482 does not empower the Commissioner to *disallow* a particular deduction, credit, or allowance; he may only allocate or redistribute the item to another member of the group.[130] Thus, the scope of §482 is not as broad as that of §269 in this respect (whereunder the Service may disallow in whole or in part a particular tax benefit, *supra*, Sec. 13.21). It should be noted, however, that the Commissioner has considerable discretion in applying §482, and that his determinations thereunder will be sustained unless a court finds that he has abused such discretion.

While §482 ordinarily may not be used to effect what is essentially a "compulsory consolidated return" for affiliated corporations, the section has, on occasion, been precisely so applied. Thus, in Hamburgers York Road, Inc., 41 T.C. 821 (1964), the entire taxable income of one corporation was allocated under §482 to its affiliate owned in the same proportions by the same shareholders. One of these corporations operated a downtown retail store while its sister corporation conducted the same type of business at a suburban location. The Tax Court held that "the two stores (which in form were operated by two separate corporations) were in substance and in fact, actually parts of a single, integrated retail men's clothing business with the downtown store . . . serving as the headquarters, and with the suburban . . . store serving merely as a branch or division." By holding that the business operations of these two related corporations constituted in substance a unitary enterprise, the court, in effect, consolidated their income and deductions in a single tax-

---

[128] For applications of §482, see Pauline W. Ach, *supra* note 42; Nat Harrison Associates, Inc., 42 T.C. 601 (1964); Challenger, Inc., *supra* note 64; see also Miller, Proposals for Amelioration of Section 482 Allocations Affecting U.S. Taxpayers with Foreign Affiliates, 44 Taxes 209 (1966).

[129] See Bush Hog Mfg. Co., Inc. *supra* note 117; V. H. Monette & Co., Inc., *supra* note 120; The Esrenco Truck Co., *supra* note 115.

[130] Challenger, Inc., *supra* note 64; see also South Lake Farms, Inc., 36 T.C. 1027 (1961).

able entity.[130a] Compare the decision in Joe Dillier (*supra* note 50), where an integrated business enterprise was divided along functional lines (*e.g.*, production, sales, transportation, etc.) between four corporations: the court upheld the Commissioner's disallowance of surtax exemptions to three of these corporations under §269, but no attempt was made to reallocate their income and deductions under §482. Although the tax results in *Hamburgers* and *Diller* were roughly comparable (because corporations are taxed at a flat rate at income levels above the surtax exemption), §482 is normally invoked to effect only a partial allocation among members of the affiliated group.

The reallocation rules of §482 seem to be strongly infused with assignment of income notions. While not identical in scope or outlook, these two approaches nevertheless often involve parallel considerations. Thus, a major issue in many §482 cases is whether a particular taxpayer has in substance "earned" the income in question. This in turn often depends upon whether such taxpayer is a viable business entity; hence, a multiple corporation case may involve extended discussion and analysis of all three of these general theories, either singly or together, even though the underlying issue is substantially identical with respect to each.

4. Association status. The Service has argued in some multiple corporation cases that the affiliated corporations carried on a common venture for profit as a group in a manner characteristic of a single corporation and, as such, should be treated as an "association" under the principles discussed *supra*, Sec. 2.01ff. Courts thus far have not accepted this argument, and, in one reported decision, the Commissioner expressly abandoned this approach at the trial: Stater Bros., Inc., ¶62,147 P-H Memo TC. The reason for this hesitation may be that the operation of a group of multiple corporations is unlike that involved in the traditional "association" line of cases where a group of individuals is seeking partnership or trust status although their relationship to the venture exhibits some indicia of corporate status. Moreover, the consequences of applying the association doctrine in the multiple corporation context could be quite drastic if it led to three levels of taxation: the association (taxed on the business profits); the corporations (taxed as "associates," on hypothetical distributions of the association's profits); and the individual shareholders (taxed on distributions from the corporations). In addition to this triple tax potential, the "association" theory could have a

[130a] See also J. R. Land Co. v. United States, — F.2d —, 17 AFTR 2d 988 (4th Cir. 1966), involving a similar allocation under §482.

bewildering variety of peripheral consequences: personal holding company tax or accumulated earnings tax penalties at the second level; loss of Subchapter S status at the second level; etc. There is no reason to believe that the Service cannot police the multiple corporation area with the weapons discussed above (§§61, 269, 482, 1551, etc.), without resorting to the "excessive force" inherent in an "association" approach; but taxpayers who crowd their luck with extreme devices invite extreme responses.

Sec. 13.33. Multiple corporation legislation of 1964: §§1561, 1562, and 243(b)

1. In general. The Revenue Act of 1964 dealt specifically with the multiple corporation problem, although in a fairly limited fashion, by providing, in general, that: certain "controlled groups" of corporations (affiliated either as parent-subsidiary or as brother-sister corporations) will be entitled to only one surtax exemption (§1561), unless the group elects under §1562 to claim multiple surtax exemptions, in which event each member of the group must pay an additional tax of 6 percent on its income subject to normal tax (taxable income not in excess of $25,000). (Thus, the members of an electing controlled group will be taxed (1966 rates) at the rate of 28 percent, rather than 22 percent, on taxable income up to $25,000; the 48 percent rate above $25,000 is unchanged.) For a "controlled group" that is also an "affiliated group" within the meaning of §1504, another choice is available: it may elect to file consolidated returns (*infra*, Part E of this chapter); while such a group that permits itself to be taxed under §1561(a) (denial of multiple surtax exemptions) may elect to receive a 100 percent dividends received deduction under §243(b), which election, however, carries with it the loss of various multiple corporation tax benefits (such as the accumulated earnings tax credit, etc.). The elections inherent in these provisions, and their complexity, practically ensure a high degree of "blunder potential." Moreover, these provisions contain a number of wide delegations of authority to the regulations, requiring that even more than the usual attention be given thereto. Also, it must be emphasized that these provisions do not displace the weapons (*supra*, Sec. 13.31 and 13.32) which the Service may invoke to attack multiple corporation arrangements. Finally, the formation of new or enlarged multiple corporation groups was made more difficult by the 1964 amendments to §1551 (*supra*, Sec. 13.31), which strengthened that section in several respects.

The major aspects of §§1561, 1562, and 243(b) will be examined herein,[131] while consolidated returns matters are considered *infra*, Part E of this chapter.

2. *Surtax exemption elections: §§1561 and 1562.* In general, a "controlled group" of corporations (as specially defined) is limited by §1561(a) to one surtax exemption, which may either be allocated equally among the component members of the group, or apportioned under a "plan" to which each member of the group consents; however, such a controlled group may affirmatively elect, under §1562, to retain multiple surtax exemptions for the members of the group at the price of an extra 6 percent tax on the first $25,000 of taxable income of each corporation.[132] Hence, the maximum value of a surtax exemption for each of the affiliated corporations in the group which is subject to these provisions is reduced from $6,500 to $5,000 at 1965 rates (*i.e.*, only 20 percent of the 26 percent surtax is avoided on taxable incomes below $25,000). The election under §1562 to retain multiple surtax exemptions and to pay the additional 6 percent tax will generally be desirable where the group has a combined taxable income of about $32,500 or more; below this figure, careful allocation of a single $25,000 surtax exemption under §1561(a) generally will produce a lower tax burden. Note also that the additional 6 percent tax imposed by §1562(b)(1) is treated as a tax imposed by §11, so that it will not apply to various long-term capital gains where the corporation uses the "alternative tax" computations of §1201(a) with respect thereto. The net effect of these provisions is to dilute, but not eliminate, one of the principal tax benefits of the multiple corporation device.

Detailed procedural rules with respect to the various elections and consents required by §1562 are spelled out in the recently adopted regulations thereunder. Among the more important features of the §1562 election are the following:

a. The initial election under §1562 relates to taxable years of the members of the controlled group which include a particular

---

[131] See generally, Maier, Use of Multiple Corporations Under the 1964 Revenue Act, 42 Taxes 565 (1964); Cromartie, Affiliated Organizations and Multiple Corporations, 43 Taxes 51 (1965); articles by Dunn, Jones, et al., 23 N.Y.U. Inst. on Fed. Tax. 255-359 (1965); Horwich, A Comparative Study of Consolidated Returns and Other Approaches to the Multiple Corporations Problem, 20 Tax L. Rev. 529 (1965); Hannam, Planning for Controlled Corporations Under the Revenue Act of 1964, 1965 So. Calif. Tax Inst. 85.

[132] Note, however, that §1562(b)(1) provides that the additional 6 percent tax will not apply if (a) such corporation is the only member of the group which has taxable income, or (b) its surtax exemption is disallowed under some other provision of the statute (*e.g.*, §1551 or §269).

December 31 for which such selection is made, and the election continues thereafter until terminated, §1562(a)(2).

b. Considerable leeway is allowed so as to permit retroactive elections and terminations of such elections (*i.e.*, an initial election may be made within three years following the due date of the first return of a component member which includes the particular December 31 for which such election is made, and a prior election may be terminated within three years of the December 31 for which such termination is made), §1562(e).

c. Consents to a §1562 election must be filed by each corporation which is a component member of the group on the December 31 for which the election is made or on any *succeeding* December 31 before the day on which such election is filed, §1562(a)(1).

d. The §1562 election may be terminated by the unanimous consent of the members, by the refusal of a new member to consent to the election, by the filing of a consolidated return, or by the termination of "controlled group" status, §1562(c).

e. After an election has been terminated for any reason, a new election cannot be made by the same group[133] for five years, §1562(d).

f. By virtue of §1562(g), the statute of limitations with respect to deficiencies or refunds caused by an election or termination of an election is extended for one year after the date on which such election or termination is made.

While these rules permit considerable flexibility in making or terminating an election under §1562, numerous practical problems may nevertheless arise. The improvident or mistaken election, which the Service considers to be binding, Regs. §1.1562-1(a)(1)(ii), is one example; others include the necessity of obtaining consents for a retroactive election or termination from members of the group who are no longer under its "control," a matter which may have to be handled by contract between the parties.

Much of the new statute is taken up with elaborate definitions of the key terms used in the §1561-1562 complex, *i.e.*, "controlled group" and "component member." The term "controlled group" is defined by §1563(a) to include three principal categories of affiliation:

> *a. Parent-subsidiary controlled group:* One or more chains of corporations connected with a common parent corporation through 80 percent or more in stock ownership (determined by voting power or value).

---

[133] Whether or not the "same group" (or a "successor group") exists is to be determined by regulations and, for this purpose, the presence of a "successor group" is to be based on a "predominant equitable ownership" test. §1562(f)(1); see Regs. §1.1562-5.

  b. Brother-sister controlled group: Two or more corporations each of whose stock is owned 80 percent or more (by vote or value) by one individual, estate, or trust.

  c. Combined group: Three or more corporations, each of which is a member of a parent-subsidiary group or a brother-sister group, and one of which is a common parent corporation.

  The "component members" of a controlled group are determined on a December 31 which falls on or within its taxable year, §1563(a)-(1). However, certain corporations with a special status are excluded from the group by §1563(b)(2): corporations exempt from tax under §501; non-resident foreign corporations; certain "franchised corporations," specially defined in §1563(f)(4); and corporations which have been a member of the group for less than one-half the number of days in their taxable year which precede the December 31 membership determination date. Other special rules in §1563(b)(3) may add, as an additional member, a corporation that was a member for at least one-half the number of days in its taxable year preceding the applicable December 31 date, even though it was not so related on that date. Finally, if a corporation is a member of more than one group, §1563(b)(4) provides that it may belong to only one such group and, in determining to which group it is to be assigned, the regulations will control.[134]

  Special rules are also provided in §1563(c), (d), and (e) for determining stock "ownership." For this purpose, certain stock is to be excluded from consideration while other stock may be attributed from one person to another under elaborate constructive ownership rules. "Excluded" stock consists generally of non-voting preferred stock and treasury stock, §1563(c)(1); with respect to other kinds of stock, excludability depends upon whether a parent-subsidiary or a brother-sister group is involved. As to the former, if the parent owns (directly or constructively) 50 percent or more (by vote or value) of a subsidiary's stock, stock of the subsidiary will be excluded if it is held by certain deferred compensation trusts, by officers or 5 percent or more shareholders of the parent, or by employees of the subsidiary if such stock is held under certain restricted rights of disposition, §1563(c)(2)(A). In the case of brother-sister groups, if the potential common owner (*i.e.*, the individual, trust, or estate which must own at least 80 percent of two or more corporations' stock) owns (directly or constructively) 50 percent or more (by vote or value) of

---

[134] See Regs. §1.1563-1(c), which assigns such a corporation to the group of which it is a member by virtue of owning 80 percent in *value* of another corporation's stock.

the stock in one of such corporations, there is excluded such corporation's stock held by a §401(a) trust for its employees, or by its employees under certain arrangements which restrict their disposition of such stock, §1563(c)(2)(B). The net effect of these "exclusions" is to increase the likelihood that two or more corporations will constitute a "controlled group" subject to §1561 and 1562. Their purpose is to frustrate efforts to avoid these provisions by "decontrol" tactics that reduce effective dominion over the stock in form only.

In determining stock ownership for purposes of these provisions, broad constructive ownership rules provide for attribution of stock, depending upon whether a parent-subsidiary or a brother-sister group is involved, §1563(d) and (e):

> a. *Parent-subsidiary group.* Constructive ownership for this purpose is limited to stock which is subject to an option, §1563(d)(1)(B).
>
> b. *Brother-sister group.* Attribution is considerably more extensive in this case, since §1563(d)(2)(B) incorporates all of the constructive ownership rules of §1563(e). These provide, in brief, that stock will be attributed from one person to another person in the following situations: (i) stock which is subject to an option will be attributed to the holder thereof; (ii) stock held by a partnership, to the 5 percent partners in proportion to their interest; (iii) stock held by a trust or estate, to any 5 percent beneficiary in proportion to his maximum actuarial interest; (iv) stock held by a corporation, to its more than 5 percent (by value) shareholders in proportion to such interest; and (v) stock held by various family members, to other related members thereof, subject to certain conditions and limitations.

Moreover, various special rules found in §1563(f)(2) and (3) provide that: "double" or "chain" attribution of stock will be possible (except between family members); the option attribution rule will take precedence over all others; ownership will be attributed, in event of alternatives, in such manner as to create a controlled group; and constructive ownership will take precedence over the stock "exclusion" rules if this will create a controlled group.[135]

3. Inter-corporate dividend elections — §243(b). The dividends received deduction rules of §243 (*supra*, Sec. 2.25) were also amended as part of the 1964 Revenue Act's multiple corporation package. These amendments permit certain affiliated groups of corporations (defined generally in §243(b)(5) as a parent-subsidiary controlled

---

[135] For examples, see Regs. §1.1563-3. For the comparable, but less rigorous, attribution rules of §318, see *supra,* Sec. 7.21.

group that is eligible to file a consolidated return) to elect a 100 percent dividends received deduction for dividends received by the parent corporation out of post-1963 earnings and profits of its "controlled" subsidiary corporation if: (a) the subsidiary both earned and distributed these profits during a taxable year in which it was "affiliated" with the parent; and (b) no multiple surtax exemption election under §1562 was in effect for either corporation during that period. In other words, if a parent and its controlled subsidiary choose to forego the multiple surtax exemption benefits of §1562, they may obtain one of the principal benefits of filing consolidated returns (elimination of tax on inter-company dividends) without the disadvantages and complexities of filing such returns (e.g., the need for consistency of accounting methods and periods). Moreover, the §243(b) election is, in effect, an annual election since it may be terminated at will by the affiliated group, §243(b)(4).

On the other hand, an election under §243(b) carries with it certain disadvantages, viz., (a) multiple surtax exemptions cannot be elected for the same taxable year, so that the affiliated group is limited to one such exemption (to be allocated among the members pursuant to §1561); (b) the group is to be treated as "one taxpayer" for purposes of foreign tax credit elections; and (c) the group is limited to one $100,000 minimum accumulated earnings tax credit, and is subject to certain other restrictions set out in §243(b)(3)(C). The benefit gained by electing under §243(g) (the right to deduct 100, rather than 85, percent of dividends received) will not offset these disadvantages (amounting to a "partial consolidation" of the group), unless a very large amount of qualifying intercorporate dividends are received.[136]

Part E. Consolidated Returns

Sec. 13.40.   Introductory

Section 1501 provides that an "affiliated group of corporations" may elect to file a consolidated return in lieu of separate returns. The basic principle of the consolidated return is that the group is taxed upon its consolidated taxable income, representing principally the results of its dealings with the outside world after the elimination of inter-company profit and loss. The tax is computed at the usual rates, except that only one surtax exemption is allowed regardless of the

---

[136] See Cohen, Election of Tax-Free Intercorporate Dividends Under the Revenue Act of 1964, 42 Taxes 791 (1964).

number of includible corporations.[137] (An additional tax of 2 percent of consolidated taxable income, imposed for many years on the privilege of filing consolidated returns, was repealed in 1964.) With certain exceptions, an affiliated group that elects to file a consolidated return must continue to do so in later years, unless the law is changed to make the filing of such returns substantially less advantageous. The statutory provisions governing consolidated returns (§§1501-1504) are quite brief, mainly because §1502 provides that the Secretary of the Treasury:

> shall prescribe such regulations as he may deem necessary in order that the tax liability of any affiliated group of corporations making a consolidated return and of each corporation in the group, both during and after the period of affiliation, may be returned, determined, computed, assessed, collected, and adjusted, in such manner as clearly to reflect the income tax liability, and in order to prevent avoidance of such tax liability.

Pursuant to this authority, the Treasury has promulgated a lengthy and intricate set of regulations, which for practical purposes constitute the "law" of consolidated returns.[138]

Consolidated returns date from the excess profits tax of 1917, when the Treasury required their use by affiliated corporations in order to prevent the arbitrary shifting of income within the group. With the repeal of the World War I excess profits tax, and the enactment of the antecedent of §482 (permitting a reallocation of income among two or more businesses under common control, in order to reflect income more accurately, *supra*, Sec. 13.32), Congress made the filing of consolidated returns optional, and they remained so for the period 1921-33. From 1934-41, however, the privilege of filing consolidated returns was abolished except for railroad corporations and a few others. With the adoption of the World War II excess profits

---

[137] Upon the filing of a consolidated return election, the accumulated earnings tax of §531 (*supra*, Ch. 6) and the personal holding company tax of §541 (*supra*, Ch. 6) are also computed on a consolidated basis. See Regs. §1.1502-30A(a) and (b)(4); and Prop. Regs. 1.1502-2.

[138] Regs. §§1.1501-1.1504. A comprehensive revision of the regulations was promulgated, in proposed form, in 1965; as of this writing (June, 1966), the final form of the revision has not been announced. See articles by Cohn, Dale, and Peel, in 18 Tax Exec., No. 2 (Jan. 1966); Cohen, The new consolidated regulations: A bird's-eye view of the extensive changes, 24 J. Tax. 82 (1966).

Under the proposed regulations, the old regulations continue applicable to taxable years beginning before Jan. 1, 1966, and are designated by the addition of the latter "A" (*e.g.*, Regs. §1.1502-1 would become Regs. §1.1502-1A, etc.). Although not yet in force, this designation has been incorporated herein, and relevant changes in the proposed regulations have been set out. The proposed regulations use Jan. 1, 1966 as their effective date, but it is possible that the date will be advanced if and when they are promulgated in final form.

tax, however, the consolidated return election was reinstated, subject to an additional tax of 2 percent of consolidated taxable income. The principal statutory changes since then were the reduction, in 1954, of the intercorporate stock ownership requirement from 95 percent to 80 percent, and the repeal, in 1964, of the additional 2 percent tax.[139]

Sec. 13.41.   Eligibility to file consolidated returns

A consolidated return may be filed by an "affiliated group" of corporations, a term that is defined by §1504 to mean certain "includible corporations" connected in a specified way through stock ownership.

An "includible corporation" is any corporation except:

    1. Corporations exempt from taxation under §501 (*supra*, Sec. 1.06).
    2. Insurance companies subject to taxation under §§802 or 821, unless made eligible by §1504(c).
    3. Foreign corporations, unless within the limited exception of §1504(d) (100 percent subsidiary formed to comply with foreign law).
    4. Corporations subject to §931 ("Possessions Corporations" *supra*, Sec. 1.06).
    5. China Trade Act corporations (*supra*, Sec. 1.06).
    6. Regulated investment companies subject to tax under Subchapter M (*supra*, Sec. 1.06).
    7. Unincorporated business enterprises electing to be taxed as corporations under §1361 (*supra*, Sec. 2.11).
    8. Small business corporations electing to be taxed under Subchapter S (*infra*, Ch. 14).

The stock ownership rule of §1504(a) requires that the "affiliated group" consist of one or more chains of includible corporations connected through stock ownership with a common parent corporation (which must also be an includible corporation) in the following manner:

    1. Stock with at least 80 percent of the voting power of all

---

[139] A detailed examination of the formidible corpus of rules embodied in the consolidated returns regulations (*supra,* note 138) is beyond the scope of this treatise. The standard work is Peel, *Consolidated Tax Returns* (1959). See also Salem, Advantages and Disadvantages of Filing Consolidated Returns: A Fresh Look, 18 Tax Exec. 166 (1966); Salem, The Consolidated Return Regulation Revision: Its Genesis and Objectives, 17 Tax Exec. 163 (1965); Note, The Affiliated Group as a Tax Entity: A Proposed Revision of the Consolidated Returns Regulations, 78 Harv. L. Rev. 1415 (1965); Cuddihy, Consolidated Returns, 16 N.Y.U. Inst. on Fed. Taxation 351 (1958); Swift, The Consolidated Return, 36 Taxes 583 (1958); Hellerstein, Consolidated Federal Income Tax Returns, 5 Amer. Univ. Tax Inst. 415 (1953); Blitman, Consolidated Returns in the Federal Tax System, 8 Nat'l Tax J. 260 (1955); *infra* note 151.

classes of stock and at least 80 percent of each class of the non-
voting stock of each of the includible corporations (other than
the common parent) must be owned directly by one or more of
the other includible corporations; and

2. The common parent must own directly stock with at least
80 percent of the voting power of all classes of stock and 80 percent of each class of the nonvoting stock of at least one of the
other includible corporations.

The prescribed amount of stock must, under §1504(a), be
owned "directly" by members of the affiliated group, so that two corporations whose stock is owned by an individual or group of individuals,[140] or by a non-includible corporation do not constitute "an
affiliated group or corporations."[141]

The 80 percent stock ownership requirement of §1504 is a relaxation, enacted in 1954, of prior law, which set the test of affiliation at 95
percent.[142] This change will magnify the private law problems created
by an election to file a consolidated return, which may be beneficial
to the group as a whole at the expense of the minority shareholders
of one of the included corporations.[143] In this connection, it should
be noted that every includible corporation must participate in the
consolidated return, Regs. §1.1502-2A(b)(1); it is not possible to exclude a particular corporation because of possible objections by its
minority shareholders.

Under §1504(a), it is necessary to determine whether at least
80 percent of the "total voting power" of all classes of stock of each
includible corporation (other than the parent) is owned by another
member of the group. The term has come to mean the power to elect
the directors to the exclusion of the power to vote on such extraordinary events as merger, sale of assets, etc.[144]

---

[140] The suggestion of Libson Shops, Inc. v. Koehler, 353 U.S. 382, 51 AFTR
43 (1957), that the corporations there involved, owned by the same individuals
in the same proportion, could have filed a consolidated return is erroneous.

[141] See West Boylston Mfg. Co. v. Commissioner, 120 F.2d 622, 27 AFTR
491 (5th Cir. 1941); Regs. §1.1502-2A(b). But ownership of record is not required; beneficial ownership will suffice. Rev. Rul. 55-458, 1955-2 C.B. 579
(stock in escrow qualifies); G.C.M. 7331, VIII-2 C.B. 135 (1929) (stock held by
nominee).

[142] The continued use of the 95 percent benchmark in §165(g)(3), relating
to worthless stock and securities of subsidiary corporations, is an anomaly, as
pointed out supra, Sec. 4.07.

[143] Up to now, minority shareholders seem to have been either ignorant or
complacent, unless they have been lying in ambush. But see Western Pacific
R.R. Corp. v. Western Pacific R.R. Co., 345 U.S. 247, 43 AFTR 367 (1953),
206 F.2d 495, 44 AFTR 291 (9th Cir. 1953), 216 F.2d 513, 46 AFTR 1017 (9th
Cir. 1954); Johnson, Minority Stockholders in Affiliated and Related Corporations, 23 N.Y.U. Inst. on Fed. Tax. 321 (1965).

[144] See I.T. 3896, 1948-1 C.B. 72 (discussing method of computing "total
voting power" where one class of stock could elect one director and another

In applying the stock ownership rule of §1504(a), the term "stock" does not include nonvoting stock which is limited and preferred as to dividends. Such stock may be owned by persons outside the affiliated group, and for this reason is sometimes used by one or more members of the affiliated group to raise equity capital.[145]

If a corporation is acquired by another corporation solely in order to make use of its tax attributes on a consolidated return, the requisite affiliation may be found lacking, despite compliance with the literal terms of the statute. See Elko Realty Co. v. Commissioner (*supra* note 43), involving the acquisition by a successful corporation of all the stock of two other corporations, which had been operating and continued to operate at a loss. The Court of Appeals affirmed the Tax Court, which, in denying the parent the right to use these losses on a consolidated return to offset its post-affiliation profits, acted not only under §269 (*supra*, Sec. 13.21), but also on the theory that "the two corporations were in any event not affiliates of the taxpayer privileged to join in a consolidated return under section 141 of the Internal Revenue Code of 1939 [§§1501-1504, 1954 Code] since the taxpayer's acquisition of them served no business purpose, as distinguished from a tax-reducing purpose."[146] For some purposes, it would be immaterial whether the acquisition was found to violate §269 or the requisite affiliation was found to be lacking; but for other purposes, the latter ground is more drastic, since it would require separate returns, perhaps for all time, whereas §269 might dis-

---

class the remaining six directors); Anderson-Clayton Securities Corp., 35 B.T.A. 795 (1937) (prior law).

If a class of stock can vote on routine matters that are ordinarily entrusted to the directors, it might be regarded as having "voting power" even though it could not elect directors. Query also the effect of stockholders' voting agreements on the computation of "total voting power."

[145] As to the meaning of "nonvoting stock," see Erie Lighting Co. v. Commissioner, 93 F.2d 883, 20 AFTR 609 (1st Cir. 1937) (stock that cannot vote for directors is "nonvoting stock" despite power to vote on increase of capital stock or indebtedness, number of directors, time of stockholders' meetings, etc.); Vermont Hydro-Electric Corp., 29 B.T.A. 1006 (1934) (preferred stock with right to vote for directors only on default in dividends is "nonvoting stock" until contingency occurs); Rudolph Wurlitzer Co. v. Commissioner, 81 F.2d 971, 17 AFTR 452 (6th Cir. 1936), cert. denied, 298 U.S. 676 (1936) (stock with power to vote for directors under Illinois law is not "nonvoting stock" despite attempt to eliminate such power in articles of incorporation); I.T. 3896, 1948-1 C.B. 72; Tannenbaum, Nonvoting Stock for the Consolidated Return, 29 Taxes 679 (1951). As to the meaning of "limited and preferred as to dividends," see Pioneer Parachute Co. v. Commissioner, 162 F.2d 249, 35 AFTR 1443 (2d Cir. 1947) (participating preferred is not "limited" as to dividends, even in a year in which nothing is paid beyond the preference); Erie Lighting Co. v. Commissioner, *supra* (*contra*).

[146] See also, to the same effect, American Pipe & Steel Corp. v. Commissioner, *supra* note 43 (consolidation denied under §269); J. D. & A. B. Spreckels Co., *supra* note 43 (consolidation denied under *Gregory*).

allow only the use on the consolidated return of the deduction, credit, etc. that motivated the acquisition. As will be seen (*infra*, Sec. 13.43), the consolidated returns regulations themselves impose certain automatic restrictions (regardless of purpose) on the use of the pre-affiliation net operating losses and some post-affiliation losses as well, when membership in the affiliated group changes; but they do not go so far as to deny that the new member is part of the affiliated group. The approach of *Elko Realty Co.*, which appears to deny affiliation for all purposes, is more far-reaching; but there are other decisions taking a more lenient attitude.[147]

Sec. 13.42.   The election to file a consolidated return

A consolidated return may be made only if all corporations which at any time during the taxable year have been members of the affiliated group consent to the consolidated return regulations prescribed under §1502.[148] Under Regs. §1.1502-11A(a), the affiliated group must continue to file on a consolidated basis in subsequent taxable years unless one of the following events occurs:

> 1. A corporation, other than one created or organized directly or indirectly by a member of the group, becomes a member of the group in a subsequent taxable year. Although the regulations do not say so explicitly, presumably the acquisition of the new member must serve a function other than escape from the consolidated return; and see Rev. Rul. 56-271, 1956-1 C.B. 440; §269 (*supra*, Sec. 13.21).
> 2. Subtitle A of the Code (income taxes) or the regulations under §1502 have been amended so as to make the continued filing of consolidated returns "substantially less advantageous to affiliated groups as a class."[149]

---

[147] See Zanesville Investment Co. v. Commissioner, *supra* note 64, and cases discussed therein; discussion *infra*, Sec. 13.43; see also Hawaiian Trust Co. v. United States, *supra* note 44 (consolidation privilege and losses both allowed, despite attack under §269 and *Spreckels* theories). But in R. P. Collins & Co., Inc. v. United States, *supra* note 61, the Commissioner successfully invoked §269 to deny loss deductions on the consolidated return; see discussion of these cases *supra*, Sec. 13.21.

[148] The taxpayer's "consent" to the regulations does not preclude an attack upon the Treasury's authority to issue a particular provision. See Corner Broadway-Maiden Lane, Inc. v. Commission, 76 F.2d 106, 15 AFTR 398 (2d Cir. 1935).

[149] The Internal Revenue Service ordinarily announces whether, in its opinion, such an amendment has occurred. See, *e.g.*, Rev. Rul. 58-471, 1958-2 C.B. 429 (3-year carryback of net operating losses, in lieu of former 2-year carryback, warrants new election); Rev. Rul. 56-681, 1956-2 C.B. 597 (extension of 30 percent normal tax rate on corporations does not permit new election). Under Prop. Regs. §1.1502-75(c), this automatic right to shift back to separate returns when consolidated taxpayers are adversely affected *as a group* would be eliminated; and the right would be dependent upon the Commis-

　　3. The Commissioner of Internal Revenue, for "good cause," grants permission to change. See Rev. Rul. 57-3, 1957-1 C.B. 290.

　　The regulations also make each member of the affiliated group severally liable for the entire tax (including any deficiency), with qualifications for corporations in bankruptcy or receivership and subsidiaries that are sold before the tax is assessed. Regs. §1.1502-15A. This liability cannot be reduced by intercompany agreements, but presumably an agreement will be effective as between the parties. Under §1552, enacted in 1954, a method is provided for allocating the tax liability in computing each corporation's earnings and profits.

　　The parent corporation is, by Regs. §1.1502-16A, made the agent of all includible corporations to receive deficiency notices, to file refund claims, to execute waivers of the statute of limitations, etc.[150]

Sec. 13.43.　Computation of consolidated taxable income and of tax liability

　　1. In general. The tax liability of an affiliated group filing a consolidated return is computed on its "consolidated taxable income." The starting point is the taxable income of each includible corporation, computed in accordance with the rules applicable to separate corporations, but with the elimination of unrealized profits and losses in transactions between members of the affiliated group and of dividend distributions within the group, and the segregation of the group's capital gains and losses, charitable contributions, transactions under §1231, net operating losses and certain other items. After these adjustments, the separate taxable incomes are combined, and capital gains and losses, charitable contributions, §1231 transactions, net operating losses, etc. are computed on a consolidated basis and taken into account. There are many vexing accounting adjustments in this process of converting the taxable incomes of the separate corporations into the affiliated group's "consolidated taxable income," but they are beyond the scope of this work.[151]

　　Whether an affiliated group should elect to file a consolidated

---

sioner's determination of "good cause," including a determination that "the net result of all amendments" to the Code or regulations has a "substantial adverse effect" on the consolidated liability of the *particular* group applying for a change.

　　[150] The regulations also state that the parent is the agent of the other members of the group for conducting proceedings in the Tax Court. Regs. §1.1502-16A. But see *Community Water Service Co.,* 32 B.T.A. 164 (1935) (NA), stating that the court's rules of procedure take precedence.

　　[151] See Peel, *supra* note 139; Paton, *Accountants' Handbook* (4th ed. 1960), Section 23; Childs, *Consolidated Financial Statements* (1949).

return depends upon a variety of complex and competing factors. Among the principal advantages of consolidation are: losses of an affiliate may be offset against profits of other members of the group; certain inter-corporate distributions may be received tax-free from other members of the group, see Prop. Regs. §1.1502-14; and gain or loss on certain inter-company transactions is "deferred," under elaborate rules found in Prop. Regs. §1.-1502-13, until realized outside the group or by virtue of certain other events. These opportunities became relatively more attractive in 1964, when the additional 2 percent tax on consolidated taxable income was eliminated and the advantages of filing separate returns (e.g., the multiplication of surtax exemptions) were restricted vis-a-vis affiliated groups (*supra*, Sec. 13.33). On the other hand, filing a consolidated return carries with it certain disadvantages, including: the requirement of consistent accounting methods, elections, and periods within the group (but see Prop. Regs. §1.1502-17(a), permitting separate accounting methods for separate businesses under the general rules of §446); the rule that to the extent losses of one affiliate are used to reduce consolidated taxable income, the basis of stock or obligations of the loss corporation must be correspondingly reduced (see also Prop. Regs. §1.1502-19, for recapture of certain "excess losses" of a subsidiary); the general limitation that the members of a consolidated group must share a single surtax exemption, accumulated earnings tax credit, and any other special exemption or credit; under the proposed regulations, various inter-company transactions now must be taken into account currently, Prop. Regs. §1.1502-13; the fact that the consolidated returns regulations themselves (even the proposed edition) are so complicated, in many instances, inordinately so; and finally, the fact that the election is a binding one (absent the above-mentioned instances where a new election is permitted). In addition, the balancing of these pros and cons can itself be one of the tax adviser's more difficult assignments: the practical response to a consolidated return issue is often to request an extension of time for more "thorough deliberation," and the longer the better.

2. *Outline of proposed consolidated return regulations.* The proposed consolidated return regulations completely revise both the substance and format of the old regulations; these new provisions are applicable to taxable years beginning after 1965. It may be helpful to briefly outline the major features of these regulations as they relate to the computation of consolidated tax liability. (In this discussion, the regulations will be cited by section number, but it should be noted that they presently are only in proposed form; moreover, the old reg-

ulations are retained for pre-1966 taxable years with the same numbering except for addition of the letter "A" thereto.) In general, the proposed regulations consist of four major subject headings: (a) computation of "consolidated tax liability" (§§1.1502-2 through 1.1502-6); (b) computation of "consolidated taxable income" (which, in turn, is divided into three principal subheadings — computation of "separate taxable incomes" of the various affiliates, §§1.1502-12 through 1.1502-19; computation of various "consolidated items," §§1.1502-21 through 1.1502-27; and special rules pertaining to basis, stock ownership, and earnings and profits, §§1.1502-31 through 1.1502-34); (c) provisions dealing with special taxes and taxpayers (*e.g.*, alternative capital gains tax, accumulated earnings tax, and personal holding company tax); and (d) administrative and procedural rules (§§1.1502-75 through 1.1502-80).

The computation of an electing group's consolidated tax liability involves the following steps: (1) the "separate taxable income" (or loss) of each member of the affiliated group is determined as if a separate return had been filed (subject to certain special rules and "adjustments" for such items as inter-company transactions, inter-company distributions, accounting methods, inventories, etc.), Regs. §1.1502-12; (2) these separate taxable incomes are then combined to arrive at consolidated taxable income; in addition, various other separately computed "consolidated items" (*e.g.*, consolidated net operating loss deduction, capital gain, §1231 gain or loss, charitable contributions, etc.) are then taken into account, Regs. §1.1502-11; (3) gross consolidated tax liability is then computed by adding up the various taxes imposed by §§11, 541, 531, 1201, etc. on the consolidated taxable income of the group as determined above; and (4) from this figure, the consolidated investment credit and the consolidated foreign tax credit are subtracted, Regs. §1.1502-2. The basic concept underlying these provisions is that the consolidated group constitutes, in substance, a single taxable enterprise, despite the existence of technically distinct entities; as such, its tax liability ought to be based on its dealings with "outsiders," rather than on intra-group transactions. This "single taxpayer" concept lies at the heart of the treatment, both past and present, of inter-company transactions which, in general, are eliminated in computing the group's consolidated taxable income.

The most important features of the computation procedure described above are its treatment of inter-company transactions and distributions, accounting methods, inventories, and net operating loss deductions. These matters will be considered in the discussion that follows.

3. Inter-company transactions and distributions. The treatment of inter-company transactions and distributions has been significantly revised by the proposed regulations; these changes are perhaps the most significant feature of the new provisions, especially their treatment of inter-company transactions.

a. Inter-company transactions. For this purpose, a distinction is made between two types of inter-company transactions: (1) so-called "deferred inter-company transactions," which are subject to the new deferred accounting rules and which consist of sales or exchanges of property, the performance of services where the expense thereof is capitalized, and any other capitalized expenditures between members of the group; and (2) all other inter-company dealings, such as the payment of currently deductible interest, rent, royalties, or compensation by one member of the group to another, which are not subject to the new deferred accounting treatment. With respect to these latter items, the approach of the proposed regulations is to require the payor and the payee to deduct and to include such amounts *currently*, depending on their respective accounting methods; however, the item of income and the correlative deduction therefor ordinarily must be reflected in the same taxable year. The net effect of this treatment is, of course, a "wash" so far as the group's consolidated taxable income is concerned. See Prop. Regs. §1.1502-13(b).

The treatment of "deferred inter-company transactions," on the other hand, is more complicated and represents a major change from prior law. For these items, the proposed regulations adopt a "deferral" or "suspense" account approach whereunder inter-company profits and losses are deferred by recording them in a "suspense account" until the later happening of certain specified events; these events will trigger the reporting of both the amount and character of such items by the member of the group that originally "earned" the profit or "sustained" the loss. In general, this treatment follows the traditional accounting practice of attributing gain or loss from an inter-company transaction to the member that actually earned or incurred it. Under the prior regulations, however, such profits or losses were, in effect, shifted to another member of the group: this occurred as a result of certain rules which provided for "elimination" of such gains or losses from the "selling" member's return with a corresponding carryover of the basis of such property to the "purchasing" member, who then reported gain or loss thereon when the property was sold to an "outsider." See Regs. §1.1502-31A(b)(1)(i). The proposed regulations, on the other hand, while similarly deferring the gain or loss from such transactions until the property is sold to an outsider (or until certain other specified events occur), assign the ultimate profit or loss from such transactions to the particular member that produced it.

> For example: suppose that P sold property, having a basis of $80 and a value of $100, to its wholly-owned subsidiary S during a period when P and S were filing consolidated returns; in a later year, S sold the property to A, an outsider, for $110. Under the old regulations, the inter-company profit of $20 would be eliminated from the computation of consolidated taxable income and S would carry over P's $80 basis for the property. On selling the property to A for $110, S would report the entire $30 of gain, even though $20 thereof reflected appreciation in value during P's ownership of the property. The proposed regulations, however, would tax $20 of the profit to P — but only in the taxable year of the sale to A — and would give S a cost basis of $100 (rather than a carryover basis of $80) for the property, so that the remaining $10 would be taxed to it. Thus, each member of the group would be taxed on the portion of the gain which it "earned." Moreover, the *character* of P's gain (capital or ordinary) is the same as it would have been had P made the sale directly, rather than by means of an inter-company transaction through S. See generally, Prop. Regs. §§1.1502-13(b)-(h) and 1.1502-31(a).

The purpose of this change in the treatment of inter-company sales is to prevent the result sanctioned in several litigated cases, which permitted consolidated groups to avoid completely the tax on inter-company sales (*e.g.*, where P sold the *stock* of S after transferring property to it and the new buyer liquidated S under §334(b)(2) (*supra*, Sec. 9.44) and thereby obtained a stepped-up basis for S's assets).[152] This ploy would not be possible under the proposed regulations, since P's deferred inter-company profit must be recognized if either the buying member or the selling member leaves the affiliated group before the property has been sold to an outsider. Prop. Regs. §1.1502-13(f)(1)(iii). Other events which will trigger recognition of deferred gain or loss include:

> 1. Depreciation or amortization deductions on the property by the "purchasing" member; here, only a partial restoration of

---

[152] Henry Beck Builders, Inc., 41 T.C. 616 (1964) (inter-company profit of parent which was properly eliminated from consolidated taxable income held not taxable when parent sold its subsidiary's stock). Accord: Commissioner v. United Contractors, Inc., 344 F.2d 123, 15 AFTR 2d 714 (4th Cir. 1965). The Service has agreed to follow the *Beck* case for tax years ending before 1965, T.I.R. 764 (Sept. 28, 1965); and this acquiescence is embodied in Prop. Regs. §1.1502-13(h), Example (17).

the deferred gain or loss occurs, the amount thereof being reported at the same rate at which the asset is depreciated.[153]

2. The filing of separate returns by members of the group
triggers a restoration of all deferred inventory profits and, if consolidated returns were filed for less than three consecutive years
preceding the filing of separate returns, all other deferred gains.

3. The worthlessness, collection, or redemption of debt
obligations or stock that were the subject of a deferred inter-
company transaction will trigger recognition of such deferred
gain or loss.

4. If the acquired property is sold by the purchasing member on the installment method (under §453), deferred gain is
reported ratably by the selling member as collections thereon are
made.

The proposed treatment of inter-company transactions has been
criticized as violating the "single corporate taxpayer" concept of the
consolidated returns provisions;[154] but the likelihood of successfully
contesting the regulations on this point seems remote, in view of the
broad delegation of regulatory authority effected by §1502. Although
profits and losses from some types of inter-company transactions will
be currently taxable (and deductible) under the new rules, while
others are handled under the "deferred accounting" treatment discussed above, the major thrust of the new provisions is concerned
with the *identification of the proper taxpayer* to report such items,
rather than with the question of recognition or non-recognition of
profits. As such, the regulations seem clearly to be a valid exercise of
the Commissioner's discretion, and perhaps even a desirable one as
well. Moreover, although the consolidated return is based on the
theory that inter-company transactions should in general be disregarded, it also assumes that the group's gains from transactions with
outsiders will be fully recognized at the proper time; seen in this light,
the proposed changes are justified, and the cases which allowed some

---

[153] See Prop. Regs. §1.1502-13(d), providing that the amount of recapture
is that percentage of the deferred gain or loss which the amount of the annual
depreciation deduction bears to the asset's depreciable basis (*i.e.*, cost less salvage value). For example, if the asset in the text example was depreciable, was
held by S for use (rather than sold to A), and had a useful life of 10 years and
a salvage value of $20, and if S used straight line depreciation, P would report
10% of its $20 of deferred profit, or $2, annually (*i.e.*, $8 of annual depreciation
over $80 depreciable basis, or annual depreciation rate (10 percent) times the
deferred profit of $20). Moreover, the profit must be reported as ordinary income
by P in this situation, regardless of the character of the asset in its hands when
sold to S. In effect, these provisions treat the depreciation of the asset by S
as a "gradual sale" or consumption thereof by S.

[154] See Dale, Consolidated Return Regs Introduce New Concepts for Taxing Inter-Company Profits, 24 J. Tax. 6 (1966).

gains to escape taxation (*supra* note 152) rested on defects in the old regulations rather than on any concept inherent in the consolidated return itself.

b. Inter-company distributions. In general, dividend distributions between members of a consolidated group are eliminated from the computation of consolidated taxable income. Prop. Regs. §1.1502-14(a)(1). This treatment is consistent with the theory that the group is, in effect, a single taxable enterprise. Note, however, that the "basis adjustment" rules of Prop. Regs. §1.1502-32 may require the basis of stock (or obligations) of a member of the group to be reduced on account of distributions made from its pre-affiliation earnings and profits, except to the extent that the member has undistributed earnings and profits accumulated during affiliation years. This means that a distribution from pre-affiliation earnings, which is not taxed to the member of the group receiving it, will be taken into account (or applied to reduce loss) if and when the distributing corporation's stock or securities are sold; no such adjustment is required for distributions from post-affiliation earnings, since such accumulations are not reflected in the basis of the distributing corporation's stock or securities.

The treatment of non-dividend inter-company distributions (*i.e.*, those which either constitute a return of capital to the distributee under §301(c)(2), or which are treated as being received in exchange for stock under §302 and 331) is more complex. In this situation, taxable gain will result (assuming that the distribution transaction does not fall within the non-recognition provisions of §332) to the extent that the distribution consists of cash in excess of the distributee corporation's basis for its stock or obligations of the distributing corporation. Distributions in kind, on the other hand, do not result in taxable gain to the distributee, but the basis of the distributed property takes account of the non-taxable character of the distribution; in general, Prop. Regs. §1.1502-31 requires the distributee to use the basis of its stock and obligations of the distributing corporation as its basis for the distributed property.

Gains and losses with respect to inter-company obligations are, in general, handled under principles similar to the deferred inter-company transaction rules discussed above: *i.e.*, gains or losses realized by one member of the group from the inter-company sale, retirement, or worthlessness of an obligation of another member of the group are generally deferred until certain later events, such as a disposition to an outsider, Prop. Regs. §1.1502-14(d), in keeping with the theory that the consolidated group is a single taxable enterprise and that only its dealings with outsiders have genuine significance.

4. Accounting methods and inventory. A major change in the proposed regulations permits each member of the consolidated group to determine its method of accounting under §446 as if it were filing a separate return. Prop. Regs. §1.1502-17. Under the old regulations, on the other hand, the members were required to adopt consistent accounting methods unless the Commissioner consented to the use of different methods. The adoption of consistent accounting *periods* by the affiliates is still necessary, however, such period being determined by reference to that of the common parent. Prop. Regs. §1.1502-76. Moreover, where the requisite affiliation is established during the common parent's taxable year, all of its income for the year must be included in the consolidated return; income of the other affiliates, however, is included in the consolidated return for only that part of the parent's taxable period during which they were members of the affiliated group.

> For example, if P acquired all the stock of S on June 30, 1965 and elected to file a consolidated return for 1965, all of P's 1965 income would be included in such return while S's income would be included only for the period July 1, 1965 through December 31, 1965. S would file a separate return with respect to its pre-affiliation income.

The treatment of inter-company inventory transactions is governed by the provisions of Prop. Regs. §1.1502-18, which, in general, adopts the deferral technique described above; the thrust of these rules is to tax the profit from inter-company sales of inventory items to the member of the group which "earned" it, but only when the property is sold to an outsider. Moreover, special adjustments to inventories are required when an affiliated group filing separate returns switches to a consolidated return. These adjustments are necessary in order to "normalize" the group's income for the year of change to consolidated reporting and to prevent the tax windfall that might occur if inventories were not adjusted to take account of pre-consolidation inter-company inventory transactions.

5. Treatment of net operating losses and related problems. One of the most commonly cited advantages of filing a consolidated return is the rule that current operating losses of one affiliate can be offset against profits of another affiliate in computing consolidated income (or loss) of the group. If losses of some members of the group exceed profits of other members of the group, a consolidated net operating loss results, and the rules relating to the computation of the consolidated net operating loss deduction are found in Prop. Regs.

§1.1502-21. But see Prop. Regs. §1.1502-32(a)(2), requiring the basis of the loss affiliate's stock and obligations held by other members of the group to be reduced to the extent that its losses are "availed of" by the group (either currently or as carryback or carryover deductions) in computing consolidated taxable income. Moreover, to the extent that losses of a subsidiary are availed of by the group in an amount which exceeds its basis for the subsidiary's stock and obligations, the "excess" amount will be recaptured, as ordinary income, when the loss subsidiary is disposed of by the group.[155] This aspect of the proposed regulations is a significant change from prior law, which made no such "negative basis" adjustment.

For example, P and its wholly owned subsidiary have been filing consolidated returns, P's basis for its investment in S is $100,000, and S suffers net operating losses of $100,000 in 1966 and $50,000 in 1967. Assume also that these losses are fully absorbed as current offsets or as carryover or carryback deductions in the determination of the group's consolidated taxable income. In 1968, P sells all of S's stock for $70,000. Under the old regulations, P's $100,000 basis for its stock in S would be adjusted down to (but not below) zero by the 1966-67 losses which were "availed of" in the consolidated return. As a result, P would recognize $70,000 of capital gain on selling its S stock, although the consolidated return would have reflected $150,000 of deductions in respect of a net investment outlay of only $30,000 (viz., $100,000 paid by P for S stock, less $70,000 received on its sale). By contrast, the proposed regulation would require P to report as ordinary income $50,000 of its $70,000 gain on selling the stock of S, this amount being the excess of the deductions taken ($150,000) over its investment in the stock ($100,000).[156] Thus the tax returns, reporting $150,000 of deductions and $120,000 of gain, will correspond to the economic results to P of its investment in S ($100,00 paid for stock, less $70,000 received on sale).

The consolidated return regulations contain their own protective

---

[155] A "disposition," for this purpose, includes not only a sale of the subsidiary's stock, but also the worthlessness of such stock and the discharge of an indebtedness of the loss affiliate under certain circumstances. Prop. Regs. §1.1502-19.

[156] In requiring the "excess" deductions to be reported as ordinary income, the proposed regulations are roughly analogous to the recapture of excess depreciation under §1245, but they are less far-reaching. In the example, note that only $50,000 of P's aggregate gain of $120,000 is ordinary income.

See also the somewhat comparable treatment of losses sustained by partnerships or Subchapter S corporations, where the amount that can be deducted by the partners or the shareholders is limited to the adjusted bases for their interests in the partnership or Subchapter S corporation. See §§704(d) and 1374(d)(2).

measures against the acquisition of a loss corporation in order to apply its net operating loss deductions against the income of the more prosperous members of the group. In general, pre-affiliation losses can be utilized in computing post-affiliation consolidated taxable income only to the extent that the new member of the group contributes to the consolidated income; and similar limitations are imposed with respect to such other tax attributes as capital loss, investment credit, and foreign tax credit carryovers.[157] (This limitation is reminiscent of the "continuity of business enterprise" doctrine of the *Libson Shops* case (*supra*, Sec. 13.25), which denied the use of pre-merger losses against post-merger profits produced by different business "units" from those which incurred the losses.) It should be noted, however, that corporate tax attribute carryovers in the consolidated return context are treated less favorably in this respect than carryovers based on the acquisition of assets, which are subject to the rules of §381 and §382 (*supra*, Part B of this chapter). While numerous limitations apply to tax-free asset acquisitions (*supra*, Part C), it is relatively clear that the "continuity of business enterprise" approach of *Libson Shops* is not one of them. This lack of parallelism between stock acquisitions (followed by the filing of consolidated returns) on the one hand, and asset acquisitions on the other, is difficult to justify as a policy matter.

The proposed consolidated return regulations permit net operating losses attributable to a separate return year to be carried forward to a consolidated return year, without regard to the loss corporation's income in the later year, however, provided that the loss corporation was a member of the affiliated group on each day of the loss year and provided that the loss corporation did not elect multiple surtax exemptions under §1562 (*supra*, Sec. 13.33) during the loss year. Prop. Regs. §§1.1502-1(f), and 1.1502-21(c). This provision substantially incorporates a 1965 amendment to the old consolidated return regulations (T.D. 6813), which permitted similar benefits with respect to consolidated returns filed in 1964 and thereafter.

It should be noted that while the consolidated return regulations (and various other limitation provisions, such as §269, *supra*, Sec. 13.21) generally discourage profitable affiliated groups from ac-

---

[157] Prop. Regs. §1.1502-21(c) (net operating losses); Prop. Regs. §1.1502-3(c) (investment credit carryovers); Prop. Regs. §1.1502-4(f) (foreign tax credit carryovers); Prop. Regs. §1.1502-22(c) (capital loss carryovers).

See also Woolford Realty Co. v. Rose, 286 U.S. 319, 11 AFTR 12 (1932), where the Supreme Court similarly disallowed a carryover for pre-affiliation losses against post-affiliation consolidated taxable income before the regulations contained an explicit limitation.

quiring loss corporations to take advantage of their loss carryover deductions, the converse of this rule does not necessarily hold true; *i.e.*, a loss group presumably is free to acquire a profitable subsidiary (where there has been no material change in stock ownership of the acquiring group's common parent corporation) and apply its unused net operating loss carryover deductions against income generated by the newly acquired corporation. In this latter respect, however, the proposed regulations have added a new concept, "consolidated return change of ownership." This term is defined as a 50 percent change of ownership in the common parent corporation which occurs during a 2 year period, resulting from a purchase, a redemption, a reorganization, or a combination thereof. If such a change of ownership occurs, the group's consolidated operating losses sustained before such a change in ownership can be carried over to consolidated return years ending after the change only to the extent that those corporations which were members of the group before the change generate income in these later years.[158] This limitation is aimed at the acquisition of a loss group by the owners of a profitable corporation, who then seek to apply the former's loss carryovers against the latter's income on a consolidated return. This rule, in effect, merely extends to an acquired group the general principle that the losses of an acquired subsidiary can be carried over only against its own income. Prop. Regs. §1.1502-21(e) also incorporates the limitations of §382 as an additional limitation on the use of net operating loss carryovers by the group.

The rules governing the carryover or carryback of consolidated net operating losses *from* a consolidated return year *to* a separate return year of the members of the group are found in Prop. Regs. §1.1502-79(a). In brief, these provide that:

> a. That portion of a consolidated net operating loss which is attributable to an affiliate who was a member of the group during the year the loss was sustained may be carried back or carried forward to a separate return year of such member; the portion of the loss attributable to each member of the group is determined on the basis of the relative amounts of separate net operating losses of each member of the group which sustained losses during the year.
>
> b. That portion of a consolidated net operating loss which is attributable to a member of the group which was not in exist-

---

[158] Prop. Regs. §1.1502-21(d). For a possible analogy to this approach, see §382(a) (*supra*, Sec. 13.22).

Moreover, similar limitations apply to other favorable tax attributes of the group as well (*e.g.*, investment credits, foreign tax credits, and capital losses).

ence in a potential carryback year, will be carried back to prior consolidated return years of the group (or to the equivalent separate return year of the common parent), provided such member became a member of the group immediately after its organization. (To the same effect under prior law, see Rev. Rul. 64-93, 1964-1 C.B. 325.)

    c. Losses attributable to a member whose stock becomes worthless during or subsequent to the consolidated net operating loss year will be attributed solely to such member. These losses ordinarily will be "wasted," since they cannot be carried forward to later consolidated return years of the continuing members of the group.[159]

These principles set out in (a) and (b) above can be illustrated by the following example:

Assume that P was organized on January 1, 1966 and filed a separate return for the calendar year 1966. P formed S, a subsidiary, on June 30, 1967 and P and S thereafter filed a consolidated return for 1967. On January 1, 1968, P purchased all the stock of T, which had been filing separate returns for prior years. P, S, and T join in filing a consolidated return for 1968, during which period the group sustains a consolidated net operating loss of $100, $10 of which is attributable to P, $30 to S, and $60 to T. Only $40 of the 1968 consolidated net operating loss (that portion which is attributable to P and S), can be carried back to P's 1966 separate return year; any unconsumed portion of this amount is then carried to P and S's 1967 consolidated return year to the extent of their income for such period. The portion of the 1968 consolidated loss which is attributable to T ($60) is carried back to T's separate return years; the unconsumed portion, if any, is carried forward as part of the group's consolidated net operating loss carryover deduction to post-1968 years if P, S, and T continue to file consolidated returns.

The consolidated return regulations also inhibit the acquisition of a corporation with "built-in" losses or other deductions (such as depreciated stock in trade, plant, equipment, or capital assets and debts that are about to become worthless) for the purpose of utilizing these losses to offset post-affiliation consolidated taxable income attributable to other members of the group. Prop. Regs. §1.1502-15. In

---

[159] But see United States v. Northern Railroad, 334 F.2d 936, 14 AFTR 2d 5332 (1st Cir. 1964), reaching a contrary result; there, the court permitted carryover of a consolidated net operating loss generated by the sale of assets of two subsidiaries (which thereafter became dormant) to later separate return years of the parent. To the same effect: Joseph Weidenhoff, Inc., *supra* note 8; Hawaiian Trust Co., Ltd. v. United States, *supra* note 44; see also F. C. Donovan, Inc. v. United States, *supra* note 6.

general, "built-in" deductions are defined by the regulations as those which are "economically accrued" by the subsidiary prior to its acquisition but which are technically realized (by sale, write-off, worthlessness, abandonment, etc.) after such acquisition, as well as depreciation deductions attributable to the built-in loss element of an asset; but the term does not include operating deductions or losses which are incurred both economically *and* for tax recognition purposes *after* affiliation (including, for this purpose, those incurred in rehabilitating the acquired corporation). These deductions are not entirely disallowed by the regulations, however. Rather, they are treated as though sustained by the acquired corporation prior to its acquisition and hence are subject to the limitations on the carryover of pre-acquisition losses discussed above, viz., they can be deducted only from the post-affiliation income generated by the new member. Hence, the acquired corporation's assets which reflect such built-in deductions must be segregated, so that the subsequently realized losses therefrom will be taken only against the income of that corporation. This sanction does not apply, however, if the corporation was acquired more than 10 years before the taxable year in question or if the aggregate basis of its assets (other than cash or goodwill) did not exceed the value of those assets by more than 15 percent. Moreover, the limitations apparently do not apply to the acquiring group's *own* built-in deductions, though it is possible (but not certain) that a "consolidated return change in ownership" of the common parent's stock would bring the limitations of Prop. Regs. §1.1502-21(d) (*supra*, note 158), into play so as to restrict such deductions to income of the old members of the group.

6. *Other limitations on survival of corporate tax attributes applicable to affiliated groups.* The consolidated return regulations specifically warn that the Code, or other general principles of law, continue to apply to affiliated groups to the extent not excluded thereby; of special note in this respect, is the express reference to §§269 and 482 by these regulations. Prop. Regs. §1.1502-80. Hence, inter-company (or extra-group) transactions may result in a reallocation of the group's income and/or deductions under §482 in order to "clearly reflect" its income (*supra*, Sec. 13.26), in a disallowance of net operating loss carryovers of a newly acquired affiliate under §382(a) (*supra*, Sec. 13.22), or in a disallowance of benefits for tax-motivated acquisitions under §269 (*supra*, Sec. 13.21).[160]

---

160 See R. P. Collins & Co., Inc. v. United States, *supra* note 45, where §269 was invoked to deny not only "built-in" losses of a newly acquired affiliate, but post-affiliation operating losses generated thereby as well, which the court held to be "tarred with the same brush." Prop. Regs. §1.1502-15 may be contrary to the *Collins* decision on the latter point. Compare Zanesville Investment Co. v.

As to the relationship of the *Libson Shops* doctrine (*supra*, Sec. 13.25) to the consolidated returns area, see F. C. Donovan, Inc. v. United States (*supra* note 6); and note also that the consolidated return regulations themselves (*supra*) incorporate limitation principles similar to *Libson's* "continuity of business enterprise" approach where pre-affiliation tax attributes are sought to be carried into a consolidated return. On the other hand, where affiliated corporations filed consolidated returns during the period when a particular member's tax attributes were generated, it is generally assumed that *Libson* would not apply to restrict the transfer of these attributes to other members of the affiliated group (*supra*, Sec. 13.25), since the fact of filing consolidated returns causes the group to be treated as a "single business enterprise."

Commissioner, *supra* note 64, where the court refused to apply §269 to disallow deductions for post-affiliation losses incurred by a recently acquired corporation which filed a consolidated return with the profitable affiliate; see discussion *supra*, Sec. 13.21, and Adlman, Recent Cases Increasingly Extend Section 269 to Disallow Post-Acquisition Operating Losses, 17 J. Tax. 282 (1962).

See also discussion of the *Spreckels* and *Elko Realty* decisions, *supra*, Sec. 13.41, where the provisions of §269 (or general "business purpose" principles) were invoked to deny inclusion of the acquired corporation as a member of the affiliated group, a more drastic approach than disallowing the use of its tax attributes in the group's consolidated return.

Chapter Fourteen

CORPORATE ELECTIONS UNDER SUBCHAPTER S

Sec. 14.01. Introductory

Over the years, there have been many suggestions that the Internal Revenue Code be amended to permit (or require) the shareholders of closely-held corporations to be taxed as though they were carrying on their activities as partners, *i.e.*, relieving the corporation from taxation on condition that each stockholder report his share of the corporation's income, whether distributed to him or not, on his individual income tax return. Such a proposal was passed by the Senate in 1954 to permit "small corporations which are essentially partnerships to enjoy the advantages of the corporate form of organization without being made subject to possible tax disadvantages of the corporation" and to "eliminate the influence of the Federal income tax in the selection of the form of business organization which may be most desirable under the circumstances." The 1954 proposal was eliminated by the conference committee; but the idea was revived in 1958 and enacted into law as Subchapter S of the Internal Revenue Code (§§1371-77), for the announced purposes of allowing businesses to select their legal forms free of undue tax influence, aiding small business by taxing the corporation's income to shareholders who may be in lower brackets than their corporations, and permitting the shareholders of corporations that are suffering losses to offset the losses against individual income from other sources.[1]

The principal features of Subchapter S, which will be discussed in detail hereafter, are these:

1. Eligibility. Subchapter S is applicable only to a "small business corporation," defined by §1371(a) as a domestic corporation which does not have more than 10 shareholders (all of whom must be either individuals or estates) or more than one class of stock. The corpora-

---

[1] For the 1954 proposal, see S. Rep. No. 1622, 83d Cong., 2d Sess., p. 119 (1954); for the 1958 version, as enacted, see S. Rep. No. 1983, 85th Cong., 2d Sess., p. 87 (1958).

Although the 1954 proposal for permitting corporations to elect non-corporate treatment was not enacted, a companion provision allowing certain unincorporated businesses to elect to be taxed as corporations found favor in legislative eyes; but after a period of trial, it was found wanting, or unnecessary, and it was repealed in 1966. See *supra*, Sec. 2.11.

tion may not be a member of an affiliated group (as defined in §1504, relating to the privilege of filing consolidated returns, *supra*, Sec. 13.41), and it may not have a nonresident alien as a shareholder.

2. *Election.* A "small business corporation" becomes an "electing small business corporation," so as to bring Subchapter S into play, by filing an election, which is valid only if all shareholders consent. Once made, the election is effective for the taxable year for which it is made and for all succeeding taxable years, unless it is terminated (a) by the failure of a new shareholder to consent to the election, (b) by revocation, with the consent of all shareholders, (c) by disqualification (*e.g.*, acquisition of stock by a trust, corporation, or other ineligible shareholder, issuance of a second class of stock, etc.), (d) by the corporation's deriving more than 80 percent of its gross receipts from sources outside the United States, or (e) by the corporation's deriving more than 20 percent of its gross receipts from "passive investment income."

Once an election has been terminated or revoked, the corporation (and any successor corporation) is ineligible to make another election under Subchapter S for five years, unless the Treasury consents.

3. *Undistributed corporate income.* While the election is in effect, the corporation is not subject to the corporate income tax, the accumulated earnings tax, or the personal holding company tax; and the corporate income, whether distributed or not, is taxed to the shareholders. Not having been subjected to a tax at the corporate level, however, the income is not eligible for the dividend received exclusion (*supra*, Sec. 5.06) in the hands of the shareholder. In the interest of simplicity, the income must be treated as ordinary income by the shareholder, without regard to any special characteristics it may have had at the corporate level, except that the excess of long-term capital gain over short-term capital loss is passed through to the shareholder. Since he is taxed on the corporation's undistributed income, provision is made for a later non-dividend distribution to him of this previously taxed income.

4. *Corporate losses.* If a corporation suffers a net operating loss for a year during which the Subchapter S election is in effect, it is passed through to the shareholders, each of whom may use his share of the loss (up to the aggregate basis of his investment in the corporation, in the form of stock or indebtedness) to offset his income from other sources. The excess of net operating loss over income from other sources, if any, may be carried back to prior years and forward to later years as though the loss had been incurred in his individual business. If the shareholder's pro rata share of the corporation's net

operating loss exceeds his basis in the corporation's stock and indebtedness owed him, the excess is not allowable as a deduction for any taxable year.

5. *Adjustments to basis.* The shareholder's basis for his stock is increased to reflect the fact that he was taxed on his share of the corporation's undistributed income, and is decreased if this previously taxed income is distributed to him. If the corporation suffers a net operating loss, the shareholder must reduce the basis of his stock (and, if necessary, of any corporate obligations he may hold) to reflect the fact that such loss has been passed through to him for use on his individual tax return.

This rough summary of Subchapter S will be amplified in later pages, but it should be noted at the outset that the term "small business corporation" is misleading. The size of the corporation's income, assets, net worth, or other financial characteristics plays no part in determining its eligibility under Subchapter S; the only restriction of this type is that it may not have more than 10 shareholders.[2] More imporant than labels, however, is the fact that an electing corporation remains a corporation — not only as a matter of state law, but also for many federal income tax purposes.[3] This point cannot be over-emphasized, because it is often erroneously said that Subchapter S permits corporations to be treated as partnerships. In point of fact, there are many differences between a partnership and an "electing small business corporation." Even while the election is in effect, corporate redemptions, liquidations, reorganizations, and many other transactions are governed by the tax law applicable to corporations, rather than by the law of partnerships,[4] and if the election is terminated, the corporate income tax will once again become fully applicable. Recognizing these facts, some commentators have sought to sum them up in a label — "pseudo-corporation," "conduit-corporation," and "hybrid corporation," to say nothing of more barbarous coinages like "corpnership" and "pseudo-type corporation."

---

[2] Cf. §1244 (*supra,* Sec. 4.09), which defines a "small business corporation" in terms of its equity capital and the amounts received by it for stock, as contributions to capital, and as paid in surplus. This definition does not apply to Subchapter S.

[3] Regs. §1.1372-1(c), and see *infra,* Sec. 14.09.

In certain respects, the Subchapter S corporation is treated as a "conduit" and, therefore, it bears comparison with a number of other business and investment arrangements which are treated, to a greater or lesser degree, as conduits by other provisions of the Code: *e.g.,* Subchapter K (partnerships); Subchapter J (trusts); §551-558 (foreign personal holding companies); §§851-855 (mutual funds); §856-858 (real estate investment trusts); and §§951-964 (controlled foreign corporations).

[4] See *infra,* Sec. 14.09.

The authors prefer the more neutral terms "electing corporation" or "Subchapter S corporation," however, because they serve as a constant reminder that the corporation does not cease to be a corporation by electing to come under Subchapter S.[5]

Sec. 14.02.   Eligibility to elect under Subchapter S

To make an election under Subchapter S, a corporation must be a "small business corporation," defined by §1371(a) as a domestic corporation[6] meeting the following conditions:

1. Not more than 10 shareholders. The corporation may not have more than 10 shareholders. The regulations provide that "ordinarily" the persons who would have to include the corporation's dividends in gross income are to be considered as shareholders, so that each joint tenant, etc. is "generally" to be considered as one shareholder.[7] In 1959, §1371(c) was added to provide that stock held by a husband and wife as joint tenants, tenants by the entirety, tenants in common, or community property is to be treated as owned by only one shareholder.[8] This statutory change, dealing with a specific class of co-tenants, seems to buttress the regulation's position (which, in proposed form, was promulgated before the statutory change) that each joint tenant and tenant in common is ordinarily a separate shareholder where they are not related as husband and wife. The regulations also provide that if stock is held by a nominee, agent, guardian, or cus-

---

[5] For discussions of Subchapter S, see Nagel, The Tax-Option Corporation, 44 Taxes 364 (1966); Lourie, Subchapter S after six years of operation: an analysis of its advantages and defects, 22 J. Tax. 166 (1965); Lourie, Subchapter S After Three Years of Operation, 18 Tax L. Rev. 99 (1962); Hrusoff, Election, Operation and Termination of a Subchapter S Corporation, 11 Villanova L. Rev. 1 (1965); Caplin, Subchapter S v. Partnership: A Proposed Legislative Program, 46 Va. L. Rev. 61 (1960); Stein, Optional Taxation of Closely Held Corporations Under the Technical Amendments Act of 1958, 72 Harv. L. Rev. 710 (1959), which is continued in 3 Tax Counselor's Quarterly, No. 2, 63 (1959); Anthoine, Federal Tax Legislation of 1958: The Corporate Election and Collapsible Amendment, 58 Col. L. Rev. 1146, 1149-75 (1958); Roberts and Alpert, Subchapter S: Semantic and Procedural Traps in its Use; Analysis of Dangers, 10 J. Tax. 2 (1959); Moore and Sorlien, Adventures in Subchapter S and Section 1244, 14 Tax L. Rev. 453 (1959); Goodson, Election to Tax Corporate Income to Shareholders, 1959 So. Calif. Tax Inst. 75; Horwich, The Small Business Corporation, 37 Taxes 20 (1959); Hoffman, Let's Go Slow With Tax Option Corporations, *ibid* 21; Meyer, Subchapter S Corporations, 36 Taxes 919 (1958).

[6] Regs. §1.1371-1(b) refers to §7701(a)(3), thus including an "association" within the meaning of "corporation." See *supra,* Sec. 2.01.

See J. W. Frentz, 44 T.C. 485 (1965) (no election until *de facto* corporate "existence" began).

[7] Regs. §1.1371-1(d)(1).

[8] This provision was made retroactive to 1958 and 1959, if the shareholders and corporation so elect, by §23 of the Revenue Act of 1962.

todian, the beneficial owner is "generally" to be treated as the shareholder; and that if stock is held by a partnership, the partnership and not its partners will be considered the shareholder.

2. *Individual shareholders (or estates) only.* All of the stock must be owned by individuals or estates; a corporation is ineligible to file an election under Subchapter S if any of its stock is owned by a trust, a partnership, or another corporation.[9]

3. *One class of stock.* The corporation may not have more than one class of stock. The regulations state that a class of stock is to be counted for this purpose only if it is issued and outstanding, so that treasury stock or authorized but unissued stock of a second class will not disqualify the corporation. The term "class of stock" is not defined by the statute; the regulations state that if the outstanding shares "are not identical with respect to the rights and interest which they convey in the control, profits, and assets of the corporation," the corporation is considered to have more than one class. Despite this, two or more "groups" of stock will be considered one "class" if they are identical in all respects except that each "group" has the right to elect members of the board of directors in a number proportionate to the number of shares in the group.[10] The Service has ruled that a contractual agreement among the shareholders, requiring inactive shareholders to grant irrevocable voting proxies to the active shareholders, creates rights in the latter that are not identical with the rights of the inactive shareholders; and hence results in two classes

---

[9] If the grantor of a trust is "treated as the owner" of the corpus under §§671-677 because he has a power to revoke, etc., it is arguable that he rather than the trust is the shareholder for purposes of eligibility under Subchapter S; but Regs. §1.1371-1(e) and §1.1371-1(d)(1) explicitly reject this theory. These regulations also treat voting trusts on a par with other trusts, in spite of the fact that holders of voting trust certificates are considered the equitable owners of stock, and are thus deemed shareholders for tax purposes. See, *e.g.,* Federal Grain Corp., 18 B.T.A. 242 (1929); Commissioner v. National Bellas Hess, Inc., 220 F.2d 415, rehearing denied, 225 F.2d 340, 47 AFTR 341 and 1870 (8th Cir. 1955); see also, Catalina Homes, Inc., ¶64,225 P-H Memo TC.

As to stock held by a custodian under the Uniform Gifts to Minors Act, the Internal Revenue Service has ruled that the stock is owned by the minor, not by a trust. TIR-113 (Nov. 26, 1958).

Although estates are eligible shareholders, see generally Old Virginia Brick Co., 44 T.C. 724 (1965), where an election was invalidated when the existence of an estate was terminated (because of unreasonably prolonged administration) and its stock passed to a trust.

For the disqualification of partnership-owned stock, see Rev. Rul. 59-235, 1959-2 C.B. 192.

[10] Regs. §1.1371-1(g). Cf. TIR-113 (Nov. 26, 1958), which states that one class exists where both Class A and Class B are outstanding and identical in all respects except that each class can elect one half of the board of directors. The regulations seem to take a narrower view in such a case, inasmuch as they require that the right to elect members of the board be limited to a number of board members proportionate to the number of shares in each group.

of stock within the meaning of the above-quoted portion of the regulations.[11] This position has been criticized on the ground that the one-class-of-stock rule was enacted to avoid difficulties in allocating corporate income and loss among the shareholders, a problem that does not arise if the only differences among them relate to their relative voting power; and was intended to apply to differences created by corporate action only, not to differences created by shareholder agreements.

The regulations state that the term "stock" includes "stock which is improperly designated as a debt obligation." "Disguised" stock of this type (*supra*, Sec. 4.02) would seem to disqualify the corporation, since it confers rights on the holders different from those created by their common stock, unless it can be totally disregarded under state law or viewed as evidence of a contribution to capital, rather than as a separate class of stock. In W. C. Gamman, 46 T.C. 1 (1966), the Tax Court held that the regulation would be beyond the Treasury's authority if construed to require *all* "instruments which purport to be debt obligations but which in fact represent equity capital" to be treated as a second class of stock. It is necessary, the court held, to determine in each case whether the rights conferred on the "creditors" justify treating the obligations as a second class of stock; looking to "the realities of the situation," including the fact that the notes in question were held pro rata by the shareholders and that their formal terms were waived or ignored, the court held that the advances for which the notes were given "were simply contributions of additional capital which were in reality reflected in the value of the common stock already held by [the shareholders]." Although the decision curbs the scope of the regulation to some extent (sufficiently to cause 5 judges, who thought it was not "plainly inconsistent" with §1371(a)(4), to dissent), the ultimately factual nature of the court's analysis means that shareholder-held debt will continue to cloud the status of electing corporations.[12]

[11] Rev. Rul. 63-226, 1963-2 C.B. 341. In addition to its holding on the facts, the ruling provided:

> In the event that the outstanding stock of a corporation is subject to any other type of voting control device or arrangement, such as a pooling or voting agreement or a charter provision granting certain shares a veto power or the like, which has the effect of modifying the voting rights of part of the stock so that particular shares possess disproportionate voting power as compared to the dividend rights or liquidation rights of those shares and as compared to the voting, dividend and liquidation rights of the other shares of stock of the corporation outstanding, the corporation will be deemed to have more than one class of stock.

For criticism, see Note, Shareholder Agreements and Subchapter S Corporations, 19 Tax L. Rev. 391 (1964); see also Catalina Homes, Inc., *supra* note 9.

[12] In Catalina Homes, Inc., *supra* note 9, it was held that shareholder open

4. No nonresident alien shareholders. The corporation may not have any nonresident alien shareholders. This restriction reflects the fact that the corporate income is exempt from tax under Subchapter S on the assumption that it will be subjected to the graduated individual income tax rates, whereas some nonresident aliens are taxed under §871(a)(1) at the flat rate of 30 percent.

5. Not a member of an "affiliated group" under §1504. The corporation may not elect under Subchapter S if it is a member of an "affiliated group" defined by §1504, relating to consolidated returns.[13] The highly restrictive exception of §1371(d) (enacted in 1964) for a subsidiary that has not engaged in business and has no taxable income for a specified period, is designed to permit a Subchapter S election by a corporation that has subsidiaries in other states solely to protect its corporate name against appropriation.

6. The election. Rules governing the time and method of making the election and its effective date are prescribed by §1372, which is amplified by Regs. §1.1372-2 and -3. The election is made by the corporation, but all of the shareholders must consent. The regulations state that the consent of a minor shall be made by the minor himself, his legal guardian, or his natural guardian if no legal guardian has been appointed, and the Internal Revenue Service has ruled that this requirement is applicable even if the stock is held by a custodian.[14] Failure to follow these mechanics with precision may vitiate an otherwise valid attempt to use Subchapter S; this hazard adds to the

account advances to the corporation were preferred over no-par common stock and thus constituted a second class of stock, which disqualified the corporation from Subchapter S status. Regs. §1.1371-1(g) speaks of an "instrument purporting to be a debt obligation," but the court seemed to attach no significance to the fact that the obligation was an open account debt. This possibility of transmuting debt into a second class of stock should be kept in mind when contemplating modes of avoiding the restrictions on distribution of previously taxed income, discussed *infra*, Sec. 14.08. See also Henderson v. United States, 245 F. Supp. 782, 16 AFTR 2d 5512 (M.D. Ala. 1965).

Catalina Homes was distinguished in *Gamman* on the ground that it assumed, rather than examined, the validity of the regulation.

See also Burr Oaks Corp., 43 T.C. 635, 649 (1965), where the court treated promissory notes held by shareholders of the obligor corporation as preferred stock in applying §351 because the holders occupied a preferred position vis-a-vis the holders of the common stock. The notes were held pro rata with the common by families, but not if shareholders were viewed individually.

[13] See *supra*, Sec. 13.41. When Subchapter S was enacted, the consolidated return provisions were amended to provide that an electing corporation was not an "includible corporation," with the result that a corporation that properly elected did not become disqualified by acquiring a subsidiary, even though such a subsidiary would have barred an election in the first place. This provision, §1504(b)(8), was repealed by Public Law 86-376, enacted Sept. 23, 1959. Hereafter an election under Subchapter S will terminate if the corporation becomes a member of an affiliated group under §1504.

[14] Regs. §1.1372-3(a); TIR-113, *supra* note 9.

already large number of minor blunders that can generate substantial adverse tax consequences. See, for example, William Pestcoe, 40 T.C. 195 (1963), where late filing of the requisite forms, although perhaps excusable, prevented a valid election.

The regulations also state that a shareholder's consent may not be withdrawn once a valid election is made by the corporation, Regs. §1.1372-3(a), a reasonable provision in view of the fact that §1372-(e)(2) permits a revocation of the election only if all of the shareholders consent.

Concern about the "one-shot" use of Subchapter S, especially in connection with corporate sales of assets (infra, Sec. 14.06), led to a statement in the proposed regulations, for which explicit statutory support is lacking, that a corporation may not make a Subchapter S election if it is in the process of complete or partial liquidation, has adopted a plan for such liquidation, or "contemplates" such action "in the near future." Proposed Regs. §1.1372-1(a)(2). The final regulations, however, abandoned this position; and in Hauptman v. Director of Internal Revenue, 309 F.2d 62, 10 AFTR 2d 5829 (2d Cir. 1962), cert. denied, 372 U.S. 909 (1963), the Second Circuit treated this omission as a concession by the government that an election is not barred where bankruptcy is imminent. The court also found an implication to this effect in the fact that the statute allows a pass through of net operating losses and that such losses often lead to corporate liquidation. It held that "the likelihood that an otherwise qualifying corporation may be liquidated is not a factor that should be considered in order to justify a judicial restriction" on the right to elect Subchapter S.

Sec. 14.03. Termination of the election

Once made, an election under Subchapter S is effective for the taxable year of the corporation for which it is made and for all succeeding taxable years, unless it is terminated under §1372(e) in one of the following ways:

1. *Non-consenting new shareholders.* New shareholders must consent to the election within the time prescribed by the Treasury under §1372(e)(1). Under the regulations, the consent must be filed within the 30-day period beginning on the day the person becomes a shareholder, with a limited extension of time for estates to permit the appointment of an executor or administrator.[15] It is too early to

---

[15] Regs. §1.1372-3(b). The statute provides that a termination shall be effective for the taxable year of the corporation in which such a person becomes a

say whether a sale or other transfer of an insignificant amount of stock for the sole purpose of introducing a non-consenting new shareholder will be effective.[16] If it is, every shareholder carries in his knapsack a formidable baton for use if he should wish to terminate the election. This in turn suggests an expansion of the typical shareholder buy-sell agreement to impose restraints on transfers of stock to non-consenting shareholders or to such unqualified shareholders as trusts and corporations.

2. *Revocation.* After the election has been effective for one taxable year, it can be terminated by a revocation under §1372(e)(2). The revocation must be filed by the corporation, but all shareholders must consent.

The power to terminate the election by a revocation under §1372-(e)(2) is fundamental to tax planning in this area. It permits the shareholders to use Subchapter S to deduct a net operating loss incurred in the early years of a new venture or in a poor year for an older company, without permanently committing themselves to these provisions.[17] Revocations also play a role in the use of Subchapter S by corporations realizing substantial capital gains (e.g., on the sale of an industrial plant or other real estate) that are to be passed on to shareholders; although such arrangements were inhibited in some cir-

shareholder. The Service has ruled that the executor or administrator of a deceased shareholder, rather than his legatee or heir at law, is a "new shareholder" within the meaning of §1372(e)(1) (relating to elections by "new shareholders"), if the stock is subject to his possession for purposes of administration, notwithstanding the fact that title to the stock passes directly to the legatees or heirs at law under applicable state law. Rev. Rul. 62-116, 1962-2 C.B. 207. See Old Virginia Brick Co., *supra* note 9, on the possibility that an election will terminate if the administration of an estate is unduly prolonged.

[16] For an analogy, see *Commissioner* v. *Day & Zimmerman, Inc., supra,* Sec. 9.41, note 37. The regulations state with respect to the determination of shareholders in applying §1373 (relating to "constructive dividends"), that a donee or purchaser "is not considered a shareholder unless such stock is acquired in a bona fide transaction and the donee or purchaser is the real owner of such stock." Regs. §1.1373-1(a)(2). But the regulations do foresee transfers late in the year, because just prior to the above-quoted portion they provide, "If stock is transferred on the last day of the taxable year of the corporation, the transferee (and not the transferor) will be considered the shareholder of such stock for the purposes of section 1373." The courts may look upon a transfer of this type with a jaundiced eye, in view of the fact that termination by revocation is available only if made during the first month of a taxable year and the consent of all shareholders is needed for a revocation of the election. Thus, they might hold that the non-consenting new shareholder is an agent of the old shareholder, imported to effect the termination; and treat the ploy as an invalid revocation. See *infra,* note 25.

[17] Since §1372(e)(2) provides that a revocation is valid for the taxable year in which made only if made before the close of the first month of such taxable year, only an omniscient taxpayer can be sure that he is doing the right thing. The same is true of the election itself, since §1372(c) requires it to be made in (or before) the first month of the taxable year for which it is to be effective.

cumstances by the enactment of §1378 in 1966 (*infra*, Sec. 14.06).

3. Disqualification. The election is terminated under §1372(e)(3) if the corporation ceases to be a "small business corporation" as defined by §1371(a) — *i.e.*, by the acquisition of more than 10 shareholders, a non-resident alien shareholder, or a shareholder who is not an individual or estate, or by the issuance of a second class of stock.[18] On its face at least, §1372(e)(3) terminates the election if a single shareholder transfers a single share of stock to an unqualified shareholder, even though the transferee be a corporation that is wholly owned by the transferor or, if Regs. §1.1371-1(e) is valid, a paper-thin revocable trust. A decent respect for the legislative pattern, however, requires some restraint on such attempts to terminate the election by a meaningless gesture; otherwise, the requirement of unanimous consent for a voluntary revocation under §1372(e)(2) is nullified.

4. Foreign income. The election is terminated under §1372(e)(4) if in any taxable year the corporation derives more than 80 percent of its gross receipts from sources outside the United States. The term "gross receipts" is not defined by the Internal Revenue Code itself; but Regs. §1.1372-4(b)(4) and (5)(ii) attempt a definition, with illustrations, and refer to §§861-864 of the Code for the meaning of the term "sources outside the United States."

5. Passive investment income. The election terminates under §1372(e)(5) if in any taxable year more than 20 percent of the corporation's gross receipts constitute "passive investment income," defined to include gross receipts from royalties, rents, dividends, interest and annuities, and gains from the sale or exchange of stock or securities — *i.e.*, sources that are similar to, though not identical with, those that constitute personal holding company income under §543(a) (*supra*, Sec. 6.22). The purpose of this limitation is to restrict the use of Subchapter S to corporations having substantial amounts of "operating," as opposed to investment, income. Under an amendment enacted in 1966, however, the restriction is not applied to an electing corporation for the first or second taxable year of active con-

---

[18] In Rev. Rul. 64-94, 1964-1 C.B. 317, the Service ruled that a statutory merger of a Subchapter S corporation into a non-electing corporation does not terminate the former's election under §1372(e)(3) with respect to its final taxable year ending on the date of the merger. The ruling is based on the theory that §1372(e)(3) applies to a corporation which ceases to be a Subchapter S corporation by virtue of an event which does not terminate its taxable year; if the disqualifying event also terminates the Subchapter S corporation's taxable year, it remains a Subchapter S corporation throughout the taxable year so terminated. In Rev. Rul. 64-250, 1964-2 C.B. 333, the Service ruled that a reorganization under §368(a)(1)(F) did not cause a termination of a Subchapter S corporation's election.

duct of a trade or business if its passive investment income is less than $3,000; this relaxation of §1372(e)(5) protects the election for a corporation in its initial years if, for example, its principal source of gross receipts is interest on bank accounts because normal operations have not gotten under way. This new rule can be applied retroactively to years beginning after 1962 if the shareholders so elect.

It should be noted that §1372(e)(5) looks to the corporation's "gross receipts," rather than its "gross income," apparently to facilitate use of Subchapter S by corporations operating at a loss, which might be disqualified by the 20 percent requirement if gross income were the relevant standard (*e.g.*, where sales of inventory produce no gross income because the proceeds are less than the cost). "Gross receipts" is defined by Regs. §1.1372-4(b)(5)(ii) as the total amount received or accrued, depending on the corporation's method of tax accounting, from sales, services or investments. These amounts are not reduced by items of cost, returns and allowances, or other allowable deductions. However, the term does not include amounts received from non-taxable sales or exchanges (other than those to which §337 applies), nor borrowed funds, repayments of a loan, or contributions to capital. In addition, the corporation's method of accounting controls the time when gross receipts are includible (*e.g.*, if the installment method of reporting gain is elected under §453, payments actually received in a given year will constitute gross receipts for that year).

Although the term "passive investment income" as used in §1372(e)(5) is similar to "personal holding company income" (indeed, before 1966, the latter term rather than the former was used), there are important differences in coverage. Thus, rents and royalties are includible in full in "passive investment income"[19] even if they are excluded from "personal holding company income" as defined by §543; conversely, income from personal services is excluded from §1372(e)(5) even if included under §543; and the use of the "gross receipts" standard by §1372(e)(5) creates additional distinctions (*e.g.*, tax-exempt interest is "passive investment income" though it is not "personal holding company income").[20] The inclusion of gross

---

[19] See United States v. 525 Co., 342 F.2d 759, 15 AFTR 2d 592 (5th Cir. 1965), holding that receipts from a reserved oil payment were not included in §1372(e)(5), although incudible in "personal holding company income" under Regs. §1.543-1(b)(11).

[20] The treatment of life insurance proceeds, excludible by virtue of §101, is less clear. The only example in Regs. §1.1372-4(b)(5)(vii) relates to inclusion of amounts "received as an annuity," a statement which suggests that life insurance proceeds received at death would not constitute forbidden gross receipts under §1372(e)(5). This issue will be important for electing corporations with shareholder-retirement agreements funded by life insurance.

receipts from "rents" in §1372(e)(5) bears special mention: Regs. §1.1372-4(b)(5)(iv) distinguishes between passive rental income, and receipts from an active business where "significant services" are rendered to the lessee, which latter category is not considered "rent." Thus amounts received from operating a hotel or motel, a warehouse storage business, or a parking lot do not constitute "rent" if significant services are rendered; on the other hand, where rental of space is the principal activity (*e.g.*, leasing of apartments, or offices in an office building), rental income would result.[21] This "business versus investment" distinction in the case of rental income has numerous analogues in other provisions of the Code.[22] Finally, it should be noted that statutory provisions creating "constructive" interest or dividend income in certain circumstances (e.g., §483, relating to imputed interest on the sale of capital assets, and §78, providing for a gross up of dividends from some foreign corporations) may cause the unexpected loss of Subchapter S status for the unwary.

Sec. 14.04. Election after termination

If an election is terminated or revoked under §1372(e), the corporation may not make a new election for any year before the fifth taxable year beginning after the first year for which the termination or revocation was effective. This period of disqualification, which is equally applicable to any "successor corporation" of the electing corporation, may be shortened by the Internal Revenue Service under §1372(f). The Code lays downs no standards for the exercise of judgment under §1372(f), but the regulations state (a) that the corporation has the burden of persuasion, (b) that a transfer of more than 50 percent of the stock to outsiders will "tend to establish that consent should be granted," and (c) that otherwise consent will ordinarily be denied unless the termination was involuntary so far as the corporation and its major shareholders were concerned. Regs. §1.1372-5(a). A termination that might evoke favorable action by the gov-

---

[21] For recent rulings holding that various receipts did not constitute "rents" in this context, see: Rev. Rul. 61-112, 1961-1 C.B. 399 (crop-share agreement where "material participation" in crop production was present); Rev. Rul. 64-232, 1964-2 C.B. 334 (equipment rental business where significant services were performed); Rev. Rul. 65-91, 1965-1 C.B. 431 (warehousing, storage, and parking lot businesses involving performance of significant services); Rev. Rul. 65-83, 1965-1 C.B. 430 (payments for the use of various types of personal property did not constitute "rents" because significant services were rendered by the corporation).

[22] *E.g.*: §1402(a)(1) (net earnings from self employment); §911(b) (earned income); §37 (retirement income); and §954(c) (foreign personal holding company income of a controlled foreign corporation).

ernment under §1372(f) would be a transfer to a nonconsenting or ineligible shareholder by a minority shareholder in an effort to compel the others to buy him out.

The Internal Revenue Service is given no authority to mitigate the impact of §1372(c)(1), which provides that an election must be made during the first month of the taxable year for which it is to be effective, or during the preceding month. This means that a termination, unless it occurs during the first month of a taxable year, will make Subchapter S inapplicable for at least one year,[23] no matter how generously the Internal Revenue Service may wish to exercise its discretion to shorten the 5-year waiting period of §1372(f).

The 5-year waiting period of §1372(f) is applicable not only to the corporation whose election was terminated, but also to any "successor corporation," defined by the regulations as a corporation that acquires a substantial part of the electing corporation's assets or whose assets were in substantial part owned by the electing corporation, provided 50 percent or more of its stock is owned directly or indirectly by persons who owned 50 percent or more of the stock of the electing corporation when the termination became effective. Regs. §1.1372-5(b). Since §1372(f) forbids only a *new* election by the successor corporation, the assets of a corporation whose election has terminated may evidently be transferred to another corporation that has *previously* made a valid election, even though it is controlled by the same or substantially the same shareholders, without necessarily terminating the second corporation's election. This suggests that the shareholders of an electing corporation who forsee a termination of its election because of some transitory condition (*e.g.*, excessive foreign gross receipts, temporary non-consent by a new shareholder, etc.) may organize a new corporation before the disqualifying event occurs, cause it to elect under Subchapter S, and then transfer the assets of the disqualified corporation to the awaiting vehicle immediately after the first corporation's election terminates, hoping thereby to avoid the 5-year waiting period of §1372(f). If the attempt to circumvent §1372(f) is too blatant, the election by the second corporation might be regarded as a new election by a "successor corporation" under the statute even though it was made before the first corporation's election was terminated and its assets transferred.

---

[23] This will not only revive the corporate income tax for the year of disqualification, but also irrevocably break the period during which previously taxed income may be distributed under §1375. Regs. §1.1375-4(d) (last sentence); *infra*, Sec. 14.08.

Sec. 14.05. Taxation of corporate income to shareholder

While an election under Subchapter S is in effect, the corporation is not subject to the corporate income tax,[24] and its income is taxed directly to its shareholders. Since amounts *actually* distributed to the shareholders are taxed to them in any event, the major concern of Subchapter S is with the corporation's *undistributed* taxable income. Section 1373(b) provides that each person who is a shareholder of an electing corporation on the last day of the corporation's taxable year shall include in gross income "the amount he would have received as a dividend, if on such last day there had been distributed pro rata to its shareholders by such corporation an amount equal to the corporation's undistributed taxable income for the corporation's taxable year." Since the shareholder's status is determined as of the last day of the taxable year, it will be possible to transfer stock to a member of the family for income splitting purposes at the last minute, subject to general assignment of income and similar principles.[25]

There are three steps in the computation of the "constructive dividend[26] that is taxed to the shareholders under §1373(b):

> 1. The corporation's "taxable income" is determined in the usual fashion, except that certain deductions are not allowed.

---

[24] §1372(b)(1) provides for exemption from "the taxes imposed by this chapter," which include not only the corporate income tax of §11, but also the accumulated earnings tax of §531 and the personal holding company tax of §541. In theory, an electing corporation is also relieved of the more exotic taxes imposed by §802 (insurance companies), §852 (regulated investment companies), §594 (certain mutual savings banks), and §881(a) (certain foreign corporations), but the first two classes could rarely, and the second two never, qualify as electing corporations under Subchapter S.

Although tax-exempt, the electing corporation is required by §6037 to file an annual information return.

[25] *Supra*, Sec. 5.07.

In Henry D. Duarte, 44 T.C. 193 (1965), it was held that purported transfers of a Subchapter S corporation's stock by the taxpayer to his two minor children lacked economic reality and were not bona fide; accordingly, the taxable income allocable to the children's shares was taxable to the taxpayer. See Regs. §1.1373-1(a)(2); *supra* note 16; and cf. the family allocation rules of §1375(c).

In Rev. Rul. 64-308, 1964-2 C.B. 176 the Service held that where a shareholder of a Subchapter S corporation died 15 days before the end of the corporation's taxable year and the executor of his estate filed a timely election, no part of the corporation's undistributed taxable income is income in respect of a decedent under §691 and no deduction for estate tax purposes is allowable under §691(c). Since only shareholders on the last day of the corporation's taxable year are required to include "constructive dividends" in their gross income, no part of the corporation's undistributed taxable income for the taxable year in which the shareholder died was includible in his gross income.

[26] This phrase is used herein as a brief label for the amount includible in gross income under §1373(b). The Code uses the phrases "amount treated as a dividend under section 1373(b)" and "amount required to be included in the gross income of such shareholder under section 1373(b)." §§1375(b) and

These are (a) the deduction for net operating losses incurred in other years[27] and (b) the special deductions allowed only to corporations by §242 (partially tax-exempt interest) and §§243-6 (dividends received from other corporations).

2. From the corporation's taxable income, as thus adjusted, there is deducted any money distributed as dividends during the taxable year, to the extent that the distribution was out of current earnings and profits.[28] The remainder is the corporation's "undistributed taxable income."

3. The amount that would have been a dividend to the shareholders based on a hypothetical distribution of the corporation's undistributed taxable income on the last day of its taxable year, is computed. Since a distribution of the corporation's undistributed taxable income would be a dividend only to the extent of the corporation's earnings and profits,[28a] the "constructive dividend" may be less than the shareholder's pro rata share of the undistributed taxable income.

As an illustration of these steps:

1. Assume that the taxable income of a Subchapter S corporation is $60,000 and its current earnings and profits $90,000, the difference between taxable income and current earnings and profits being attributable to the receipt of tax-exempt interest. It has no accumulated earnings and profits. The corporation distributes $70,000 in cash to its shareholders during the taxable year. The $70,000 would be treated as a regular dividend to the shareholders since distributed "out of earnings and profits." But there is no amount to be included as "a constructive dividend" under §1373(b) since the corporation has no undistributed taxable income for the taxable year; the actual cash distribution is in excess of taxable income.

2. Assume that the corporation's taxable income and cur-

1376(a). The phrase "dividend resulting from constructive distribution of undistributed taxable income" is used in Regs. §1.1373-1(e).

The Internal Revenue Service has ruled that a minority shareholder of a Subchapter S corporation is subject to the penalty imposed by §6654(d) (substantial underpayment of estimated tax) resulting from his lack of information about the corporation's undistributed taxable income, despite the fact that he endeavored but was unable to get the information from the officers of the corporation. Rev. Rul. 62-202, 1962-2 C.B. 344.

[27] If such losses were incurred by the corporation in a year for which the Subchapter S election was in effect, they would have been passed through to the shareholders (infra, Sec. 14.07), and a duplication of deductions would occur if they were allowed again in another year. If the losses occurred in a non-election year, they may be used by the corporation itself in other non-election years (infra, note 40).

[28] Distributions of property, stock, or corporate obligations are not deducted, nor are distributions of any type that are attributable to earnings and profits accumulated in earlier years.

[28a] See §1377(b) for a special rule in computing current earnings and profits, insuring that shareholders will be taxed on a "floor" of corporate taxable income as if the business had been conducted as a proprietorship or partnership.

rent earnings and profits for the year are both $90,000. It has no accumulated earnings and profits. It distributes $30,000 as a cash dividend to its shareholders, which amount is includible as such in their gross income. The undistributed taxable income of the corporation is $60,000 — $90,000 of taxable income, minus the $30,000 cash dividend. This amount, since fully covered by earnings and profits, constitutes a "constructive dividend" to the shareholders on the last day of the corporation's taxable year.

3. Assume the same facts as example 2, except that the corporation also distributes property with a basis of $15,000 and a fair market value of $30,000. The undistributed taxable income of the corporation for the year is $60,000 — $90,000, minus the cash dividend of $30,000 — since the property distribution does not reduce taxable income for the purpose of computing undistributed taxable income. Although a property distribution does not reduce undistributed taxable income, some of the current earnings and profits must be allocated to it. The regulations provide that the excess of earnings and profits over distributions of money should be allocated ratably between the constructive distribution of undistributed taxable income and the actual distribution of non-cash property (taken into account at fair market value).[29] In this case, $40,000 of earnings and profits would be allocated to the undistributed taxable income, and $20,000 to the property distribution. Therefore, although the undistributed taxable income is $60,000, only $40,000 of it would be treated as a dividend if distributed as such, and that is the amount the shareholders must include in gross income pursuant to §1373(b). The distribution of property is a dividend only to the extent of its allocable share of the earnings and profits, $20,000. If the corporation has accumulated earnings and profits, the regulations state that they too would be allocated between the constructive dividend and the actual distribution of property. For further illustrations, see Regs. §1.1373-1(g).

Because the "constructive dividend" of §1373(b) is includible in gross income, the shareholder is allowed by §1376(a) to increase the basis of his stock *pro tanto*. In effect, the "constructive dividend" is treated as though it had been distributed to him and then reinvested in the form of a contribution to capital.[30] As will be seen

---

[29] Regs. §1.1373-1(e) sets up three levels for the allocation of current earnings and profits: (1) they are first allocated to current distributions of money; (2) any excess is allocated ratably between the constructive distribution of undistributed taxable income and actual distributions of property (other than money) which are not in exchange for stock; and (3) the remainder (if any) is available to be allocated to distributions in exchange for the stock of the corporation, such as distributions under §302 or §331.

[30] For analogies, see the "consent dividend" procedure applicable to the accumulated earnings tax and personal holding company tax, and the treat-

(*infra*, Sec. 14.08), the shareholder will not be taxed on a later distribution of the amount previously taxed as a "constructive dividend," provided certain conditions are satisfied; and the basis of his stock will be appropriately reduced to reflect such later tax-free receipts.

Because the current income of an electing corporation is taxed directly to the shareholders, rather than to the corporation, special rules for the treatment of dividends (both actual and constructive) at the shareholder's level are prescribed by §1375(b) and (c). They are as follows:

1. Dividends received exclusion disallowed. In recognition of the fact that there is no "double taxation" of the income of an electing corporation, §1375(b) denies the dividends received exclusion of §116 as to certain dividends paid by an electing corporation.[31] The retirement income credit of §37 is also made inapplicable to such dividends, presumably because individual proprietors and partners may not treat their business income as "retirement income."

2. Reallocation of dividends within family. To curb the use of Subchapter S as a detour around the family partnership rules of §704(e),[32] §1375(c) provides that dividends (both actual and constructive) received by a shareholder may be apportioned or allocated among members of his family if they are shareholders and the Internal Revenue Service finds this action necessary to reflect the value of services rendered to the corporation by them. The definition of "family" that is applicable to family partnerships, §704(e)(3), is adopted for this purpose. Unlike §704(e), however, §1375(c) permits an allocation or apportionment to reflect the value of a shareholder's services not only if the other members of his family acquired

ment of undistributed income taxed to the United States shareholders of a foreign personal holding company (*supra*, Ch. 6).

[31] Prior to its amendment by the Revenue Act of 1964, §1375(b) also disallowed the §34 dividends received credit. With the repeal of this credit by the Revenue Act of 1964, the language of §1375(b) was amended to omit reference to the credit.

In any given year, the shareholder's dividends from an electing corporation may be attributable to current earnings and profits, to accumulated earnings and profits, or both. The special rule of §1375(b) is applicable only to distributions out of current earnings and profits. For the method of allocating current and accumulated earnings and profts to particular distributions, see Regs. §1.1373-1(d)-(g); see also *infra*, Sec. 14.08.

[32] Under §704(e), a detailed consideration of which is beyond the scope of this work, a partner reports his distributive share of the partnership income, but if he acquired his partnership interest by gift, appropriate allowance must be made for reasonable compensation for services rendered to the partnership by the donor. See Comment, Family Partnerships and the Revenue Act of 1951, 61 Yale L.J. 541 (1962); Beck, Use of the Family Partnership as an Operating Device — The New Regulations, 12 N.Y.U. Inst. on Fed. Tax. 603 (1954). See also *supra*, note 25.

their stock from him, but also where their stock was acquired from outsiders in an arm's-length transaction. In another respect, however, §1375(c) is narrower than §704(e); the latter permits a reallocation as between donor and donee regardless of their relationship, but §1375(c) permits allocation or apportionment only within a family.

Except for the pass-through of net long-term capital gains under §1375(a), *infra*, Sec. 14.06, Subchapter S contemplates that the shareholder will report his dividends (both actual and constructive) from an electing corporation as ordinary income, regardless of the character of the income at the corporate level.

Sec. 14.06.   Pass-through of long-term capital gain

Subchapter S adopts a true "conduit" approach for only one class of corporate income, viz., long-term capital gain. Under §1375-(a), if an electing corporation has an excess of net long-term capital gain over net short-term capital loss for its taxable year, each shareholder is entitled to treat a pro-rata portion of his "dividend income" (both actual and constructive) as long term capital gain. This capital gain pass-through is applicable only to distributions out of *current* earnings and profits, however; and it cannot exceed the corporation's taxable income for the year, computed under §1373(d).

> For example, if a corporation with three equal shareholders has taxable income and current earnings of $90,000 (including a long-term capital gain of $15,000), but makes no actual distributions during the year, each shareholder will include $30,000 in gross income as a constructive dividend under §1373(b), of which $5,000 will constitute long-term capital gain by virtue of §1375(a). If instead, the corporation had made actual distributions of $90,000 during the year, the results would be the same. But if either the corporation's taxable income or its current earnings and profits had been less than the amount of its capital gain, the capital gain pass-through could not exceed the lower of these two figures, regardless of the shareholder's "dividend" income.[33]

[33] If the taxable year of the corporation includes portions of two taxable years of a particular shareholder (because one is on a fiscal year and the other on a calendar year), the regulations require further allocation of his capital gain pass-through in proportion to the amount of his dividend income for each of those years. Regs. §1.1375-1(c) and (e), Example (3). Thus, if one shareholder in the example in the text was on a June 30 fiscal year, and received $12,000 of his total $30,000 dividend distribution in March and $18,000 in September, $2,000 of the March distribution would constitute long-term capital gain (40 percent of $5,000) as would $3,000 of the September distribution (60 percent of $5,000).

The character of gain from the sale of property by an electing corporation is, according to Regs. §1.1375-1(d), ordinarily to be determined at the corporate level. If the gain is attributable to the sale of "trade or business property" (which is treated as long-term capital gain by virtue of §1231), however, its character as "section 1231 gain" does not pass-through to the shareholders; they merely report their allocable share of this item as long-term capital gain in accordance with the rules of §1375(a). Lest the pass-through of long-term capital gain be employed by "dealers" in property as a means of converting ordinary income into capital gain by the device of transferring property to an electing corporation (or a series of such corporations), the regulations provide that the character which the property would have had in the hands of a "substantial" shareholder may influence the determination of whether the corporation realized capital gain or ordinary income on the sale.[34]

Until 1966, the pass-through of long term capital gains under §1375(a) encouraged "one-shot" elections under Subchapter S by corporations that were about to realize a substantial capital gain on the sale of real estate or other assets and that wished to pass some or all of the gain on to shareholders. Absent a Subchapter S election, the corporation would realize capital gain on the sale, and the distribution to shareholders would be a taxable dividend to the extent of earnings and profits, unless it could qualify for "sale" treatment under §302 or §346. Subchapter S, on the other hand, offered the advantage of a single capital gain tax to the shareholders, with no additional tax on the distribution of the sales proceeds up to the amount of the passed-through gain.[35] (An abortive effort to prevent Subchapter S

[34] Regs. §1.1375-1(d). For an analogy which may have inspired this effort to cure a defect in the statutory drafting scheme, see §341(e), *supra*, Sec. 10.07, which at several points requires the corporation to treat property as it would be treated in the hands of shareholders.

The validity of the regulation, except in instances of egregious abuse, is debatable: the contemporaneous enactment of §341(e) and Subchapter S may imply that the inclusion of elaborate shareholder-level characterization rules in the former excludes similar principles from the latter; on the other hand, there is no reason to think that the enactment of Subchapter S was intended to undermine the effectiveness of §341.

[35] This possibility was facilitated by the enactment in 1964 of a provision permitting an electing corporation and its shareholders to treat distributions of proceeds from the sale of capital or §1231(b) assets, made in the first 75 days of the corporation's year following the year of sale, as if made in the year of sale. The purpose of this amendment was to prevent such capital gains from becoming "locked-in" at the corporate level, a problem considered in greater detail, *infra*, Sec. 14.08. The provision was repealed in 1966, and replaced by a 75-day grace period of much broader scope. See *infra*, Sec. 14.08.

In Rev. Rul. 65-292, 1965-49 I.R.B., p. 9, the Service ruled that if the corporation elected to report capital gain on the installment method under §453, the deferred capital gain can be passed through ratably to the shareholders under §1375(a).

elections by corporations contemplating a partial liquidation is described *supra*, Sec. 14.02.) After the pass-through and distribution, the corporation's Subchapter S election would be revoked and it would assume its prior status. This possibility of exploiting Subchapter S for a brief interlude was limited by the enactment of §1378 in 1966, providing for a tax at the corporate level (coupled with a pass-through under §1375(a)(3) of the capital gain, less the corporate tax thereon, for taxation at the shareholder level), if three conditions are met: (1) the excess of net long-term capital gain over short-term capital loss exceeds $25,000 and also exceeds 50 percent of the corporation's taxable income; (2) the corporate taxable income exceeds $25,000; and (3) the corporation was not subject to Subchapter S in the 3 immediately preceding taxable years (subject to an exception for new corporations that have been subject to Subchapter S since inception). (A special rule, to prevent manipulative transfers of appreciated property to an "aged" Subchapter S corporation, applies if it holds property, acquired during the three year period preceding the sale, with a substituted basis determined by reference to the basis of a non-electing corporation.) Although the enactment of §1378 reduces the incentive to elect Subchapter S for a single year, it does not wholly eliminate the advantage of doing so; the maximum burden under the new provision will be somewhat less than two taxes at the capital gain rate,[36] whereas the sale-redemption route described earlier may generate ordinary income at the shareholder level in addition to capital gain at the corporate level.

Another way of exploiting the capital gain pass-through of §1375-(a) — changing the taxable year of an electing corporation in order to segregate a long-term capital gain in a "short" taxable year, so that the election can be used to pass the capital gain through to shareholders, isolated from ordinary income — is prohibited by Regs. §1.442-1(b)(1). See also, *infra*, Sec. 14.09, for use of Subchapter S as a means for undercutting the elaborate rules governing collapsible corporations.

---

[36] Under §1378(b), the tax at the corporate level is the lesser of (a) 25 percent of the corporation's net capital gain in excess of $25,000, and (b) the tax that would have been imposed if the corporation had not elected under Subchapter S. This means that the first $25,000 of capital gain per year is passed through as it was before 1966, unscathed by the new tax; and since the computation is made year-by-year, rather than transaction-by-transaction, the $25,000 exemption can be multiplied by a corporate election to report a larger capital gain on the installment basis method under §453 (see Rev. Rul. 65-292, *supra* note 35).

Sec. 14.07.   Pass-through of corporate net operating loss

One of the announced functions of Subchapter S is to permit "small corporations realizing losses for a period of years where there is no way of offsetting these losses against taxable income at the corporate level" — presumably for lack of corporate income during the 8-year carryover period allowed by §172 (deduction of net operating losses) — to pass these losses through to the shareholders for use as an offset against personal income from other sources. S. Rep. No. 1983, 85th Cong., 2d Sess., p. 87. Except for Subchapter S, corporate losses are reflected on the shareholder's individual income tax return only when, as, and if his investment in the corporation becomes worthless, at which time the loss is almost always a capital loss rather than a deduction from ordinary income.[37] For this reason, taxpayers who anticipate a series of losses in the formative years of a new business enterprise sometimes conduct their affairs as a partnership at the outset, and incorporate only if and when the enterprise commences to be profitable. The pass-through of current net operating losses of a Subchapter S corporation, provided by §1374, offers an alternative method of achieving this result. Moreover, the shareholders of an old, well-established corporation that anticipates a heavy non-recurring loss may file an election under Subchapter S in order to offset the loss against their individual income for that year, and then revoke the election for later years.

Under §1374, each shareholder of an electing corporation carries his share of the corporation's net operating loss over to his individual return (where it is treated, by virtue of §1374(d)(1), as a deduction attributable to a trade or business), to be applied against his other income. Any unused excess is carried back 3 years and forward 5 years by the shareholder in the usual manner provided by §172.[38] There is, however, an important limitation on this pass-through of the corporation's net operating loss: under §1374(c)(2), it may not

---

[37] The shareholder's loss on worthless stock or securities is usually a capital loss under §165(g), except for the limited ordinary loss deduction on §1244 stock ($25,000 in any one year for individuals, $50,000 for husband and wife filing a joint return), and an individual shareholder's loss on loans not evidenced by "securities" is ordinarily a capital loss under §166(d). See *supra*, Secs. 4.08-4.10.

[38] The corporation's net operating loss is computed in the usual fashion under §172, except that the special corporate deductions of §§242-6 are disallowed, as in computing the electing corporation's undistributed taxable income under §1373(d) (*supra*, Sec. 14.05).

§1374(d)(2) provides an interim rule for taxable years beginning prior to the effective date of Subchapter S, under which the shareholder cannot carry an electing corporation's loss back to such years but instead employs it in later years.

exceed the adjusted basis of the shareholder's investment in the corporation (including indebtedness as well as stock).[39] This restriction is similar to the partnership rule of §704(d), under which a partner may deduct his distributive share of partnership losses only to the extent of the adjusted basis of his interest in the partnership. The shareholder may be able to circumvent the limitation of §1374(c)(2) by increasing his investment in the corporation, but if the corporation is on its last legs, this may be throwing good money after bad. If this stratagem is not adopted, however, any unused portion of the corporation's net operating loss will be lost forever, since the enactment of Subchapter S was accompanied by an amendment to the net operating deduction provision, §172(h), under which a net operating loss for any year in which the corporation is an electing corporation under Subchapter S may not be carried over by it to a non-electing year. For election years, in other words, the net operating loss belongs exclusively to the shareholders, but they may use it only to the extent of the basis of their investment in the corporation.[40]

We have already seen (*supra*, Sec. 14.01) that the shareholder's basis for his stock in an electing corporation is increased to reflect any "constructive dividends" taxed to him by §1373(b). Conversely, if a net operating loss is passed-through to him, it must be applied in reduction of the basis of his stock under §1376(b); once the basis of the stock is reduced to zero, any excess is applied to reduce (but not below zero) the basis of any corporate indebtedness held by him. These adjustments to basis survive the election, see §1016(a)(18), and will therefore affect his computation of gain or loss on a sale or other disposition of the stock or indebtedness in later years.

Unlike §1373(b), which allocates the corporation's undistributed taxable income to those persons who are shareholders on the last day of the corporation's taxable year, §1374(b) and (c)(1) provide that

---

[39] The adjusted basis of the shareholder's investment is determined as of the close of the corporation's taxable year, unless he disposed of some or all of his stock during the year. See §1374(c)(2)(A) and (B).

In the case of stock or debt received by gift, the shareholder's basis for determining gain may be different from his basis for determining loss, see §1015(a), but §1374(c)(2) does not state which basis is to be employed. The shareholder's basis for computing loss should probably be controlling.

See generally Byrne v. Commissioner, —— F.2d ——, 17 AFTR 2d 1272 (7th Cir. 1966).

[40] Conversely, a net operating loss incurred by the corporation in a non-election year may not be employed by the shareholders in an election year, by virtue of §1373(d)(1), but it may be carried forward or backward by the corporation to other non-election years. Intervening election years are counted in determining the 3-year carryback and 5-year carryover periods, but the corporate income of such years is not applied in reduction of the carryback or carryover, according to Regs. §1.1374-1(a), third and fourth sentences.

the corporation's net operating loss shall be allocated among all persons who owned stock at any time during the taxable year. This method of allocating the operating loss, presumably adopted to curb the market in "loss" corporations, requires a computation of the corporation's "daily net operating loss" (the net operating loss divided by the number of days in the taxable year), which is then assigned pro rata to the persons owning shares on that day. Unless there have been many transfers of stock, however, the allocation is simpler than the language of §1374(c)(1) suggests.[41]

The pass-through of corporate losses under Subchapter S is restricted to the net *operating* loss. A *capital* loss incurred by an electing corporation will be applicable against its capital gains, and any excess can be carried forward under §1212 to be applied against the corporation's capital gains for the succeeding 5 taxable years. The unused balance, if any, is lost.

It seems clear that a Subchapter S corporation may not be used as a device for obtaining loss deductions from activities which would not create allowable deductions if carried on directly by a shareholder. The general tenor of Subchapter S itself requires conduct of a "business" by the electing corporation; and the language of §1374(c)(1) specifically states that the net operating loss subject to pass-through treatment is computed in accordance with the terms of §172(c), which in turn provides that a net operating loss is the excess of *allowable* deductions over gross income. Thus, if an electing corporation is engaged primarily in the conduct of a "hobby," sport, or recreation for the benefit of its shareholders, rather than a profit-motivated activity, losses resulting from such operations should not be available to the shareholders despite their use of a Subchapter S corporation.[42]

Sec. 14.08. Distributions of previously taxed income

Since the shareholders of an electing corporation must include the corporation's undistributed taxable income in their gross income (to the extent provided by §1373, *supra*, Sec. 14.05), a mechanism is provided so that the actual distribution of these constructive dividends

[41] For illustrations, see Regs. §1.1374-4. For the effect of corporate capital gains on the computation of the net operating loss pass-through, see John E. Byrne, *supra* note 39.

[42] In DuPont v. United States, 234 F. Supp. 681, 14 AFTR 2d 5293 (D. Del., 1964), the court stated that "hobby loss" corporations could not effectively pass-through losses by the election of Subchapter S, but found on the facts that the taxpayer's corporation was engaged in a trade or business so as to qualify for the loss pass-through treatment of §1374. See also Regs. §1.1374-2, stating that the shareholders' deduction may be of the type which is subject to the "hobby loss" limitations of §270.

in a later year will not produce a second round of dividend income. Under §1375(d), the shareholder's "net share of the corporation's undistributed taxable income" is computed, consisting of:

> 1. The sum of the amounts included in his gross income as "constructive dividends" under §1373(b) for prior taxable years, less:
> 2. The sum of (1) the amounts allowable as deductions under §1374(b) (pass-through of net operating losses) for prior years, and (2) the amounts previously distributed under §1375-(d) itself.

Under Regs. §1.1375-4, any distribution of money by an electing corporation — if it would otherwise be a dividend out of accumulated earnings and profits[43] — is to be considered a distribution of such previously taxed income. This means that the distribution will not be treated as a dividend; it will instead be applied against the shareholder's basis for his stock under §301(c)(2), with any excess over basis being taxed as capital gain under §301(c)(3).

The right to receive a non-dividend distribution of previously taxed income is subject to these qualifications:

> 1. Under Regs §1.1375-4(b), the distribution must be of money; a distribution of property will not qualify.
> 2. The right is not transferable, so that a transferee of stock in an electing corporation does not acquire any part of his transferor's share of the previously taxed income. (Thus an estate, being a new shareholder, does not inherit the decendent's previously taxed income amount.) This rule should serve to restrain transfers of stock to members of the family as a means of splitting income under the year-end rule of §1373(b) (*supra*, note 16). On the other hand, a shareholder who disposes of part of his stock does not suffer any reduction in his share of the previously taxed income, so that the dividends received by him thereafter on his remaining stock are evidently eligible for the non-dividend treatment of §1375(d) to the full extent of his original share of the previously taxed income. Regs. §1.1375-4(e). For the possibility of a shareholder's reacquiring a "lost" account, see *ibid*.
> 3. The corporation, with the consent of its shareholders, may forego the right to make a non-dividend distribution under Regs. §1.1375-4(c).

Although the purpose of §1375(d) is to permit a non-dividend

---

[43] To the extent of *current* earnings and profits, any money distributed must be treated as a dividend under Regs. §1.1373-1(d)-(e). Hence, the corporation must make an actual distribution of money in excess of its current earnings and profits before §1375(d) comes into force.

distribution of amounts previously taxed to the shareholders as "constructive dividends" under §1373, it does not follow that there is no difference between current distributions by a Subchapter S corporation and later distributions under §1375(d). For one thing, if the corporation accumulates its taxable income and then suffers a net operating loss, the shareholder's net share of previously taxed income must be reduced under §1375(d)(2)(B)(i) because the loss was passed through to him under §1374(b). A distribution after the loss may, therefore, be taxed as a dividend even though the same amount would have enjoyed the protection of §1375(d) had it been distributed earlier. Moreover, a tax-free distribution under §1375(d) can be made only after the corporation's current earnings and profits have been distributed (*supra* note 43). Finally, the right to make a non-dividend distribution of previously taxed income under §1375(d) lasts only as long as the Subchapter S election remains in force, and evaporates if the election is terminated.[44] A post-termination distribution will be governed by the usual rules of §301, under which all current and accumulated earnings and profits must be distributed as dividends before the corporation can make a non-dividend distribution. Thus, a distribution that would have been shielded by §1375(d) if the Subchapter S election had remained in effect, may constitute a dividend if made after the election is terminated. Of course, this will be true only if the corporation has current or accumulated earnings and profits when the distribution is made. In this connection, it should be noted that the corporation might have earnings and profits because (1) it had an accumulation of earnings and profits when it made the Subchapter S election, which were not distributed while the election was in force; (2) it accumulated some earnings and profits during the Subchapter S period;[45] or (3) its operations after the election was terminated produced earnings and profits.

Because a delay in making distributions may alter their character, some commentators have suggested that a Subchapter S cor-

[44] Regs. §1.1375-4(a) (last sentence), which is based upon the parenthetical qualification in §1375(d)(2)(A). The same statutory provision supports Regs. §1.1375-4(d) (last sentence), providing that a new election does not revive the right to make a non-dividend distribution of income accumulated in years before the new election.

For an analysis of this area, see Note, "Locked-In Earnings" — How Serious A Problem Under Subchapter S? 49 Va. L. Rev. 1516 (1963).

[45] The possibility of accumulating earnings and profits while the Subchapter S election is in force is somewhat limited, since the corporation's undistributed taxable income is taxed to the shareholders under §1373(b), with a consequent reduction in earnings and profits under §1377(a). But differences in computing earnings and profits and taxable income (*supra*, Sec. 5.03) may result in an accumulation during the Subchapter S period despite the taxability of the "constructive dividends" under §1373(b).

poration should make an *actual* distribution each year of the amount that would otherwise constitute a "constructive dividend" under §1373(b). Such a program of distributions would be feasible only if the corporation can finance its operations without retaining its earnings, since to accomplish their purpose the distributions must be in money rather than in property or obligations.[46] If the corporation distributes money and the shareholders, by prearrangement, turn the funds back to the corporation as a loan, the transaction might well be treated as the distribution of a corporate obligation rather than money. Moreover, it is not inconceivable that, in some circumstances, the "obligation" would be regarded as a second class of stock (*supra*, Sec. 14.02), resulting in a termination of the election under §1372-(e)(3) and §1371(a)(4).

Until 1966, however, a corporation that wished to distribute its earnings currently in order to avoid a "lock-in" in later years faced an annoying problem of timing: the precise amount to be distributed to the shareholders can rarely be determined by midnight of the last day of the corporation's taxable year, so that some gap between the amount distributed and the amount that should have been distributed is almost inevitable. A limited corrective was enacted in 1964 (*supra*, note 35), permitting an election under which a distribution of money in the first 75 days of the taxable year following a sale of capital assets would be treated as a distribution during the year of sale. This provision was repealed in 1966, and it was replaced by §1375(f), a non-elective rule under which all distributions of money during such a 75-day period to persons who were shareholders on the last day of the preceding year are to be treated (subject to certain conditions) as distributions of the corporation's undistributed taxable income for the preceding year.[47] This gives the corporation that wants to keep its cash distributions to shareholders in perfect balance with the "undistributed taxable income" previously taxed to them a grace period, during which its accounts for the prior taxable year can be closed and reviewed. Moreover, a cash distribution in the 75-day period will be attributed to the prior year even if the corporation's Subchapter S status for the current year is lost by revocation or otherwise during the grace period.

---

[46] Distributions of property do not serve to reduce the corporation's undistributed taxable income, §1373(c), and the regulations state that distributions of property do not qualify as distributions of "previously taxed income" under §1375(d). Regs. §1.1375-4(b).

[47] §1375(f) applies to all distributions after its enactment (Apr. 14, 1966); and it can be applied retroactively if the corporation and its shareholders so elect, subject to adjustment rules of great complexity.

Sec. 14.09. Relation of other corporate provisions to Subchapter S

As noted earlier, a Subchapter S corporation remains a "corporation" for numerous purposes under the tax law; i.e., the provisions of Subchapter C dealing with stock redemptions, liquidations and reorganizations remain applicable to an electing corporation and its shareholders, to the extent "not inconsistent" with the rules of Subchapter S, Regs. §1.1372-1(c). Thus, a stock redemption or distribution in partial liquidation by a Subchapter S corporation must satisfy the requirements of §§302, 303, 304, or 346 in order to generate capital gain or loss at the shareholder level. Similarly, the computation of an electing corporation's earnings and profits is made in the same manner as if there had been no election (except for the special adjustments provided by §§1375(d)(1) and 1377). Likewise, the tax consequences of a distribution in kind to the distributing corporation and to its shareholders are controlled by the provisions of §§311 and 301 even though made by an electing corporation. Despite this overlap between Subchapter C and Subchapter S, however, several situations exist where use of Subchapter S offers an alternative course of action which is superior to the more general corporate provisions.

1. Subchapter S and §341. There is a curious lack of correlation between the provisions of §341 and Subchapter S. This stems from the fact that the capital gain pass-through of an electing corporation does not constitute a "collapsible transaction" within the meaning of §341(a) (*i.e.*, sale of stock, capital distribution, or liquidation distribution). As a result, a collapsible corporation that contemplates the sale of an appreciated capital or §1231 asset may consider employing a Subchapter S election to pass the gain thereon through to its shareholders; if it had distributed the property to permit the sale to be made by the shareholders, they would have realized ordinary income on the distribution under §341(a), unless §341(e) (*supra,* Sec. 10.07) applied. In many situations, of course, §341(e) would provide a safe refuge, so that a Subchapter S election would offer no special advantage. If the property (though a capital or §1231 asset in the hands of the corporation) would not qualify under §341(e) because it would have been "dealer property" if held directly by the shareholders, however, the capital gain pass-through of §1375(a) seems to afford a safer route to the realization of capital gain at the shareholder level. The regulations seek to restrict this possibility by providing that the shareholders' other business activities may "infect" otherwise pure capital gains in applying §1375; but, as already pointed out (*supra* note 34), the validity of this provision is open to argument.

The importance of this issue was reduced somewhat by the 1966 restrictions on "one-shot" elections (*supra*, Sec. 14.06), under which both the corporation and the shareholders will be taxed if there is a last minute effort to make use of Subchapter S to pass through a substantial capital gain.

2. Use of Subchapter S by liquidating corporations. In view of the Service's apparent concession that Subchapter S may be used by corporations in the process of, or contemplating, complete liquidation (*supra*, Sec. 14.02), it must be added to the list of statutory techniques for effecting liquidation sales of corporate assets with only a single capital gain tax at the shareholder level.[48] The relationship of Subchapter S to the special liquidation rules of Subchapter C can, however, become quite complex. For example, Subchapter S may yield results superior to the non-recognition rule of §337 (*supra*, Sec. 9.64), where the parties desire the benefits of installment sale treatment under §453 with respect to asset liquidation sales, since such gains of an electing corporation can be passed-through to the shareholders when collected under Subchapter S (*supra* note 35), a technique not available where the §337 route is used. In addition, §337 cannot be used by a collapsible corporation, §337(c)(1)(A); but §341, as noted above, may not be applicable to asset sales by Subchapter S corporations. Similarly, liquidations under §337 must follow a rigid statutory timetable (*viz.*, adoption of complete liquidation plan, sale of assets, then distribution within 12 months of the "plan" date), a restriction not present when the sales are made by an electing Subchapter S corporation.

In some cases, however, a Subchapter S election may be worse than reliance on §337: thus, if the corporate assets would produce ordinary gain when sold (*e.g.*, "dealer" property, short term capital or "business" assets, and "artistic" property), §337 is superior to Subchapter S in that corporate non-recognition can be obtained with respect to sales thereof under §337, while use of Subchapter S would result in a pass-through of ordinary income to shareholders. Also, if the shareholders' stock basis is greater than the corporation's basis for its assets, use of Subchapter S to effect the sale of assets can result in distortions of the liquidation transaction considered as a whole,

---

[48] The discussion assumes that the Subchapter S election has been in effect for the 3-year period required by §1378; otherwise, the two-tax principle enacted in 1966 (*supra*, Sec. 14.06) will apply.

especially if the sale and liquidation occur in different years. For example, assume that A, the sole shareholder of X corporation, has a basis of $200 for his stock, while the corporate assets have a basis of $100 and a value of $400 in the hands of X. Sale of the assets under Subchapter S would result in a pass-through of $300 of gain to A, whose stock basis would be stepped up to $500 by virtue of §1376. Upon the subsequent liquidation of X, which would distribute $400 to A, he would realize a capital loss of $100. If transaction had come within §337, however, A would have realized $200 of gain on the liquidation of X, the difference between his basis for the X stock and the fair market value of the liquidation distribution.

Where the corporation incurs a net operating loss during the year it proposes to sell all or part of its assets at a gain, the decision to use Subchapter S or §337 depends upon the following considerations: (1) whether the parties wish to preserve the net operating loss as a carryback deduction at the corporate level, in which case a sale of assets tax-free under §337 would be preferable; or (2) whether it is more desirable to pass-through the corporation's net operating loss to the shareholders, in which case Subchapter S should be elected. If Subchapter S is elected, however, recognized gain from the sale of corporate assets must be set off against the corporation's operating losses in determining the amount of income (or loss) which will be passed-through to shareholders. But this dilution of the Subchapter S net operating loss pass-through could be avoided, it would seem, by causing the electing corporation to sell its assets under the provisions of §337; in this case, the gain would not be recognized, and thus would not enter into the net operating loss computation. This simultaneous use of §337 and the Subchapter S election is not expressly prohibited by the statute, although it does appear somewhat too good to be true. The Commissioner therefore, may seek to deny either (a) the Subchapter S loss pass-through, or (b) non-recognition of gain on the corporate sale of its assets, by arguing that Congress did not intend to confer such a double tax benefit in this situation. Whether a court would, or should, accept such an argument is still an open question.

Sec. 14.10. Advantages of Subchapter S election

Probably the principal tax advantage flowing from an election under Subchapter S is elimination of the corporate tax, thereby avoiding the "double taxation" of corporate earnings, while at the same time preserving the traditional legal advantages of operating in corporate form. Certainly the underlying purpose of Subchapter S was to promote "tax neutrality" in the choice of the form of doing business: to the extent that the corporate tax influenced this choice, it often served to distort normal business practices. Election of Subchapter S treatment will, of course, be most favorable where the shareholders are in lower tax brackets than their corporation, a situation that became more common after the 1964 reduction in individual tax rates than it was when Subchapter S was enacted in 1958. Also, it should be noted that Subchapter S is only one of several devices for avoiding the effects of corporate "double taxation"; others include (a) "thin capitalization (*supra*, Ch. 4); (b) payment of "salaries" to shareholder-employees; and (c) having shareholders lease property to the corporation. As such, Subchapter S may have merely added another "tax factor" to be considered in selecting the form of business entity.

While elimination of the corporate tax is the main concern of Subchapter S, several other important uses of the election have been noted: (a) the pass-through of current corporate net operating losses, especially in the early years of a new business (*supra*, Sec. 14.07); (b) "one-shot" elections for the purpose of passing through non-recurring capital gains from the sale of corporate property (*supra*, Sec. 14.06); (c) avoiding the collapsible corporation provisions (*supra*, Sec. 14.09); and (d) obtaining the benefits of §453 deferral where corporate assets are sold on the installment method (*supra*, Sec. 14.09). In addition, the following collateral tax advantages of a Subchapter S election should also be noted:

1. Different taxable years for corporation and shareholders. Since the undistributed taxable income of an electing corporation is includible in shareholder gross income in their taxable years in which or with which the corporation's taxable year ends, §1372(b)(2), adoption of a corporate fiscal year (typically in the case of a newly organized electing corporation) will serve to defer reporting of the first year's income from the business for one year. For an illustration of this technique, see R. E. Hughes, Jr., 42 T.C. 1005 (1964); but note that the Commissioner's approval is required for change of an existing corporation's tax period, §442.

2. Partial liquidation sales. Where a corporation wishes to sell part, but not all, of its assets (at the price of a single capital gain tax to its shareholders), §337 non-recognition of gain treatment is available only if the corporation is willing to completely liquidate. Although a partial liquidation distribution in kind of these assets under §346, followed by a sale thereof at the shareholder-level, might be effective to avoid corporate tax on the gain, possible application of the *Court Holding Company* doctrine (*supra*, Sec. 9.63) may render this method unattractive. An electing corporation can sell the assets without liquidating, and the gain will be taxed to the shareholders; but, as pointed out *supra*, Sec. 14.06, there may also be a gain at the corporate level if the election is a "one-shot" affair, as a result of the enactment of §1378 in 1966.

  3. Neutralizing problems of "thin capitalization" and "unreasonable compensation." Subchapter S, as noted above, affords a "cleaner" and less litigious method of avoiding double taxation of corporate earnings than resort to shareholder "loans" and payment of "excessive" compensation to shareholder-employees. As such, it offers a relatively safe harbor for those who are weary of wrangling with the Service over questions of shareholder-held debt and salary.

  4. Availability of corporate "fringe benefits" for shareholder-employees. One of the attractions of a Subchapter S corporation, as opposed to the partnership form of doing business, is that shareholders, as "employees," may participate in the deferred compensation benefits of pension and profit-sharing plans, which are closed to individual proprietors and partners (*supra*, Sec. 2.05), as well as in other tax benefits that require "employee status": *e.g.*, §101(b) (employee death benefits); §§104-106 (accident and health compensation); §119 (meals and lodging for the convenience of the employer); §79 (group-term life insurance premiums); §§421-424 (stock options); and §217 (employee moving expenses).

TABLE OF CASES

TABLE OF REGULATIONS AND RULINGS

INDEX